Shffa / 2 /

saidi
351-2463

355-

KENT SERIES IN ACCOUNTING

AlHashim and Arpan, *International Dimensions of Accounting*, 2/e
Austin, *Big Game Company: A Computerized Auditing Practice Set*
Bainbridge, *Drillmaster: A Computerized Tutorial T/A Principles of Accounting*
Bayes and Nash, *Cases in Accounting Information Systems*
Bazley, Nikolai, Grove, *Financial Accounting: Concepts and Uses*, 2/e
Bierman, Dyckman, Hilton, *Cost Accounting: Concepts and Managerial Applications*
Bryan, *Principles of Accounting Problems Using Lotus 1-2-3*
Bryan, *Intermediate Accounting Problems Using Lotus 1-2-3*
Diamond, Flamholtz, Flamholtz, *Financial Accounting*, 2/e
Dominiak and Louderback, *Managerial Accounting*, 6/e
Flamholtz, Flamholtz, Diamond, *Principles of Accounting*
Evans, Taylor, Holzmann, *International Accounting and Reporting*
Flesher, Kreiser, Flesher, *Introduction to Financial Accounting*
Gelinas, Oram, Wiggins, *Accounting Information Systems*
Gibson, *Financial Statement Analysis: Using Financial Accounting Information*, 4/e
Gibson and Frishkoff, *Cases in Financial Reporting*, 2/e
Hansen, *Management Accounting*
Henke, *Accounting for Nonprofit Organizations*, 5/e
Henke, *Introduction to Nonprofit Organization Accounting*, 3/e
Henke and Spoede, *Cost Accounting and Managerial Use of Accounting Data*
Hirsch, *Advanced Management Accounting*
Hirsch and Louderback, *Cost Accounting: Accumulation, Analysis & Use*, 2/e
Hudson, *Cost Accounting Problems Using Lotus 1-2-3*
Kent/Bentley Journal of Accounting and Computers, Volume VI
Marshall, Misiewicz, Parker, *Programmed Guide to Tax Research*, 4/e
Nash, *Accounting Information Systems*, 2/e
Nikolai and Bazley, *Financial Accounting*, 3/e
Nikolai and Bazley, *Intermediate Accounting*, 5/e
Nikolai, Bazley, Stallman, *Principles of Accounting*, 3/e
Ochi and Hughes, *Accounting with Lotus 1-2-3*
Pearson and Stiner, *A Review of the Accounting Cycle for the IBM-PC*
Porter and Perry, *EDP: Controls and Auditing*, 5/e
Stiner and Pearson, *Managerial Accounting Problems for the IBM-PC*
Thomas, Ward, Henke, *Auditing: Theory and Practice*, 3/e
Thompson and Brady, *Essential CPA Law Review*, 7/e
Ulmer, *Lotus 1-2-3 Applications for Management Accounting*
Vaccaro, *Accountants' General Ledger*
Verreault and Verreault, *Cost Accounting Applications and Extensions Using Lotus 1-2-3*
Verreault and Verreault, *Managerial Accounting Applications and Extension Using Lotus 1-2-3*, 2/e
Wallace, *Auditing*, 2/e
Weiss and Raun, *McGEE: A Computerized Accounting Information System*
Wolk, Francis, Tearney, *Accounting Theory: A Conceptual and Institutional Approach*, 2/e
Wolk, Gerber, Porter, *Management Accounting: Planning and Control*

SECOND EDITION

FINANCIAL ACCOUNTING

Concepts and Uses

■ **John D. Bazley**

Professor, School of Accountancy
University of Denver

■ **Loren A. Nikolai**

Ernst & Young Professor, School of Accountancy
University of Missouri—Columbia

■ **Hugh D. Grove**

Professor, School of Accountancy
University of Denver

PWS-KENT PUBLISHING COMPANY
Boston

PWS–KENT
Publishing Company

Sponsoring Editor: Al Bruckner
Assistant Editor: Susan Gay
Editorial Assistant: Kelle Karshick
Production Editor: Chris Crochetière
Production Service: Hockett Editorial Service
Manufacturing Coordinator: Marcia A. Locke
Interior Designer: Julie Gecha
Cover Designer: Lindgren Design Associates
Typesetter: Graphic Typesetting Service, Inc.
Printer/Binder: Arcata/Halliday

PWS-KENT Publishing Company is a division of Wadsworth, Inc.

Material from *Accounting Research Bulletins* and *Accounting Principles Board Opinions* is reprinted with the permission of the American Institute of Certified Public Accountants, Inc., copyright © 1970, 1972, and 1973.

Material from Uniform CPA Examinations and Answers, copyright © 1965, 1966, 1969, 1971, 1973, 1975, 1977, and 1979 by the American Institute of Certified Public Accountants, Inc., is reprinted (or adapted) with permission.

Material from the FASB, copyright © by Financial Accounting Standards Board, High Ridge Park, Stamford, Connecticut 06905, U.S.A. Reprinted with permission. Copies of the complete documents are available from the FASB.

Material from the 1989 General Motors Annual Report is reprinted with permission.

Material from the 1989 Nike, Inc., Annual Report is reprinted with permission.

Material from the 1989 CSX Corporation Annual Report is reprinted with permission.

Printed in the United States of America

1 2 3 4 5 6 7 8 9 — 95 94 93 92 91

Library of Congress Cataloging-in-Publication Data

Bazley, John D.
   Financial accounting: concepts and uses / John D. Bazley, Loren
A. Nikolai, Hugh D. Grove. — 2nd ed.
     p.   cm.
   ISBN 0-534-92366-6
   1. Accounting.   I. Nikolai, Loren A. II. Grove, Hugh D.
III. Title.
HF5635.B35   1991
657'.3—dc20   90-22769
                                CIP

■ CONTENTS

14 ADDITIONAL ASPECTS OF FINANCIAL REPORTING AND FINANCIAL ANALYSIS   892

■ ABOUT THE AUTHORS

JOHN D. BAZLEY

John D. Bazley, Ph.D., CPA, is Professor of Accounting in the School of Accountancy at the University of Denver, where he has received the University's 1990 Distinguished Teaching Award, the Alumni Award for Faculty Excellence, and the Jerome Kesselman Endowment Award for Excellence in Research. Dr. Bazley earned a B.A. from the University of Bristol in England and an M.S. and Ph.D. from the University of Minnesota. He has also taught at the University of North Carolina at Chapel Hill and holds a CPA certificate in the state of Colorado. He has taught national professional development classes for a major CPA firm and was a consultant for another CPA firm. Dr. Bazley is coauthor of *Intermediate Accounting* (fifth edition), *Principles of Accounting* (third edition), and *Financial Accounting* (third edition) (PWS-KENT Publishing Company). Dr. Bazley has published articles in professional journals, including *The Accounting Review, Management Accounting, Accounting Horizons, Oil and Gas Tax Quarterly, Petroleum Accounting and Financial Management Journal, Practical Accountant,* and the *Academy of Management Journal,* and is a member of the Editorial Boards of *Issues in Accounting Education* and the *Journal of Managerial Issues.* He is also a coauthor of a monograph on Environmental Accounting published by the National Association of Accountants. He is a member of the American Institute of Certified Public Accountants, the Colorado Society of Certified Public Accountants, and the American Accounting Association.

LOREN A. NIKOLAI

Loren A. Nikolai, Ph.D., CPA, is the Ernst & Young Professor in the School of Accountancy at the University of Missouri—Columbia. He received his M.B.A. from St. Cloud State University and his Ph.D. degree from the University of Minnesota. Professor Nikolai has taught at the University of Wisconsin at Platteville and at the University of North Carolina at Chapel Hill. He has received awards for outstanding teaching at both the University of Wisconsin at Platteville and the University of Missouri and was the recipient of the Federation of Schools of Accountancy 1989 Faculty Award of Merit. Professor Nikolai was also the recipient of the 1990 Distinguished Alumni Award from St. Cloud State University. He holds a CPA certificate in the state of Missouri and previously worked for the 3M Company. Professor Nikolai is the lead author of *Intermediate Accounting* (fifth edition), *Principles of Accounting* (third edition), and *Financial Accounting* (third edition) (PWS-KENT Publishing Company). He has published numerous articles in *The Accounting Review, Journal of Accounting Research, The CPA Journal, Management Accounting, Policy Analysis, Academy of Management Journal, Journal of Business Research,* and other professional journals. He was also lead author of a monograph published by the National Association of Accountants. He is a member of the American Accounting Association, the American Institute of Certified Public Accountants, and the Missouri Society of CPAs. He has chaired or served on several American Accounting Association committees, and was Director of Education from 1985–87.

HUGH D. GROVE

Hugh D. Grove, D.B.A., CPA, is Professor of Accounting in the School of Accountancy at the University of Denver. Dr. Grove earned a B.B.A. and an M.B.A. from the University of Michigan and a D.B.A. from the University of Southern California. He has also taught at California State Polytechnic University—Pomona and holds a CPA certificate in the state of Michigan. Dr. Grove has published articles in *The Accounting Review, Journal of Accounting Research, Accounting, Organizations and Society, Advances in Accounting, Petroleum Accounting and Financial Management Journal, Oil and Gas Tax Quarterly,* and other journals. He is the coauthor of *Measurement, Accounting and Organizational Information* and *Contemporary Issues in Cost and Managerial Accounting.* He has contributed chapters to *Handbook of Accounting for Natural Resources, Evaluation of Human Service Programs, Sage Criminal Justice System Annuals* and other books. Dr. Grove was also the corecipient of a Peat, Marwick, Mitchell Foundation Research in Auditing Grant and is a member of the American Accounting Association, the American Institute of Certified Public Accountants, the Institute of Management Science, and the Petroleum Accountants Society.

■ PREFACE

PURPOSE

Financial accounting is a growing and dynamic discipline. Similarly, the financial statements prepared by companies are becoming more complex as the business environment and transactions become more complex and disclosure requirements increase. The subject matter can be made more relevant and understandable by a book that contains (1) clear, direct discussion that anticipates the student's learning process, (2) up-to-date treatment of accounting principles, (3) the frequent use of examples, (4) illustrations taken from financial statements of real companies, and (5) plentiful and varied assignment materials. We feel that we have incorporated these teaching and learning tools into this book.

Our goal is to provide students with a comprehensive yet readable text, one that will enable the reader to develop a sound understanding of the principles underlying the accounting information included in financial statements and the uses to which that information is put. The book is intended for students who wish to develop a thorough understanding of the meaning of accounting information, whether they are undergraduate or graduate students, accounting majors or not. We believe that an understanding of the content of, and principles underlying, financial statements is valuable for the students' future careers as accountants, bankers, managers, investors, or owners of their own businesses.

GENERAL OVERVIEW

Financial Accounting: Concepts and Uses, second edition, has been developed for an introductory course, or courses, in financial accounting. It is written with the same care and thought as our textbooks *Intermediate Accounting* (fifth edition by Nikolai and Bazley), *Principles of Accounting* (third edition by Nikolai, Bazley, and Stallman), and *Financial Accounting* (third edition by Nikolai and Bazley), all published by PWS-KENT Publishing Company. Our goal is to include the most educationally effective blend to facilitate an understanding of accounting principles, the concepts underlying those principles, and the practical implementation of those principles in the financial statements. The book is organized in a fairly traditional manner because we do not believe that rearranging the order of coverage, just for the sake of being different, is sound pedagogy. On the other hand, we have chosen to expand the coverage of some topics (e.g., pensions, earnings per share, and consolidations) that are important to an understanding of the financial statements, and to reduce that of other topics (e.g., discounts, exchanges, and retail inventory) that are unlikely to affect the financial statements materially. We believe that this blend of topics will provide a more relevant introduction to accounting and financial statements.

PEDAGOGY

Although the first exposure to accounting principles is sometimes difficult for students, we believe that these principles can be made more understandable and interesting by using a clear, direct, building block discussion that anticipates a student's learning process and that is written at the student's reading level. Numerous real-world examples are used to provide an understanding of the way in which the principles are actually implemented. Each chapter begins with a set of learning objectives—what the student should understand after reading the chapter—and an introduction that presents the topics to be covered. Each topic is then discussed in a logical order. Generally, each topic is introduced by a brief practical and conceptual overview, followed by a discussion of the related accounting principles and their implementation in the financial statements. This discussion often includes the use of visuals: diagrams, sets of steps designed to facilitate the student's understanding, and real-world examples. At the appropriate place in the discussion, an example is presented to reinforce the student's learning process. Each example is straightforward, is fully explained, and avoids quantum leaps that might confuse the student. Illustrations of the effects on the accounting equation and the financial statements as well as the notes and supporting schedules are abundant and meaningful. Any issues regarding the interpretation of those principles in the financial statements are discussed. Only after the current principles and practices have been thoroughly explained is the appropriateness of those principles discussed, and any alternative principles explained and evaluated.

Within each chapter, headings separate the material into logically ordered, understandable portions for the student. Key definitions are **boldfaced**; *italics* are used for emphasis. Excerpts from the 1989 annual report of Nike, Inc., are used throughout the book; the remaining portions of that annual report are included in Appendix A at the end of the book. Also included in Appendix A is the entire financial section of the 1989 annual report of General Motors.

COVERAGE

The book consists of 14 chapters divided into three parts: The Fundamentals of Accounting and Financial Statements; Accounting for Assets, Liabilities, and Stockholders' Equity; and Additional Aspects of Financial Reporting. Because of the complexity of accounting principles and the economic transactions that occur in today's business environment, the book may include more topics than an instructor wishes to cover in a single class. The book is written so that the instructor may select topics without detracting from the ability of the student to understand those topics. For example, pensions, primary and fully diluted earning per share, and alternative methods of revenue recognition are self-contained topics that may be omitted. The overall analysis of financial statements is included in a separate chapter, and accounting for changing prices and international operations, while included in the same chapter, may be discussed separately. *Our philosophy is not to exclude items that are relevant to an understanding of a company's published financial statements, but to allow the instructor to select the appropriate coverage. Therefore, the book will also be a valuable resource to the student after the class when topics omitted from the class are encountered, whether in another academic class or in a working environment.* Suggestions regarding the selection of topics are included in the *Instructor's Manual*.

SPECIFIC FEATURES

In our combined 50 years of teaching experience we have identified many aspects of sound pedagogy; these have been incorporated into the book. Some of the major features are summarized:

1. *Nontechnical GAAP.* The book introduces and explains generally accepted accounting principles (GAAP) in understandable nontechnical language without repeatedly quoting formal pronouncements.

2. *Revenues and expenses.* Discussion of revenues and expenses is deferred until Chapter 2, after a clear discussion of assets, liabilities, and stockholders' equity in Chapter 1, causing less confusion for the students.

3. *Corporations.* The book focuses on the corporate form of entity because that is the most likely entity that the student will encounter. Other types of entities are briefly discussed.

4. *Mechanics of accounting.* The book reduces the emphasis on debits and credits by focusing on the accounting equation when transactions are being analyzed. Also T-accounts are used to support the analysis so that the student will understand the "balancing" aspect of accounting.

5. *Characteristics of accounting information and audit reports.* Chapter 4 contains an extensive discussion of the characteristics of accounting information, such as relevance and reliability, as well as the purpose and types of audit reports. The purpose of this discussion is to give the student a perspective for understanding the realities of financial reporting. Instructors may prefer to assign some of this material earlier, for example, as the first chapter.

6. *Real-world understanding.* Frequently, once a topic has been explained, the impact on the financial statements is discussed. Examples include the impacts of LIFO, LIFO liquidation, conversion from LIFO to FIFO, the recognition or nonrecognition of contingencies, the appropriateness of the 40-year period for amortizing intangibles, and the selection of purchase or pooling.

7. *Receivables and liabilities.* Accounts receivable are discussed in Chapter 5, while liabilities are discussed in Chapters 8 and 9. This arrangement lessens the confusion often found in many texts that discuss the accounting for receivables and payables in the same chapter.

8. *Income tax issues integrated.* Rather than devoting an entire chapter to the specifics of income taxes, the discussion of income taxes is integrated in each chapter where it applies to specific topics (e.g., inventory, depreciation, deferred income taxes, and operating loss carrybacks and carryforwards). This organization allows the student to understand the general relationship of accounting principles and income taxes while leaving the detailed discussion of specifics to a separate tax course.

9. *Effective interest method.* The discussion of bonds focuses on the effective interest method because that method is also applied to mortgages, notes, and leases. The straight-line method is also explained.

10. *Consolidated financial statements.* Because of the importance of acquisitions in the business world, the basic characteristics of purchase and pooling are discussed, as well as the preparation of a balance sheet on the date of acquisition. More complex topics, including minority interest and preparation of year-end balance sheets, are discussed in two appendices.

11. *International accounting.* Because of the increasing importance of international transactions and subsidiaries, both topics are discussed. The conversion of foreign financial statements, when a foreign currency is the functional currency and when the U.S. dollar is the functional currency, is discussed.

12. *An abundance of end-of-chapter assignment materials is included.* A boldfaced note preceding each assignment indicates the subject at issue, *without* providing a hint as to the appropriate solution. The assignment materials are divided into three separate classifications, questions, problems and cases, and annual report problems. The first group includes questions that address key concepts and terms and may be most useful for class discussion or for the student to review the key items in the chapter. The second group includes problems and cases that typically require numerical solutions or narrative answers; generally they are organized in order of difficulty and follow the order of the topics in the chapter. The third group includes assignments that focus on financial statements and financial reporting issues involving real-world companies. These assignments require the student to apply the concepts developed in the chapter to the financial statements of actual companies. Therefore, they may require an ability by the student to understand the use of different terminology, to apply the principles to alternative situations, and to integrate topics from different chapters. (If the assignment requires knowledge of a topic not yet discussed in the sequential order of the chapters, a note is included in the *Instructor's Manual.*)

MAJOR CHANGES

To improve the pedagogy and to reflect significant changes in accounting principles, numerous changes have been made in this second edition. The major changes are summarized as follows:

1. *Clarification of discussion.* The discussion and examples of procedures have been thoroughly reviewed and modified as necessary to clarify the explanations.

2. *Rearrangement of topical coverage.* The topics in Chapter 1 have been moved to Chapter 4. However, the discussion of external and internal users has been kept at the beginning of Chaper 1.

3. *Modification and expansion of visual aids.* Many visual aids have been added or modified to help in the student's learning process. For instance, the additions include a diagram for computer software costs, physical and functional causes of depreciation, disposals of assets, costs of intangibles, the items included in, and excluded from, research and development (all in Chapter 7), the procedures for operating loss carrybacks and carryforwards (Chapter 9), a typical organization chart, stock conversion, stock splits, stock dividends (all in Chapter 10), consolidated financial statements, the computation of interest on a bond investment, the principles of consolidation (all in Chapter 11), types of information used in external decision-making, and the relationship of consolidated financial statements to segment reports (both in Chapter 14). Modifications have been made to clarify the visual aids relating, for instance, to accounting information and its use in decision making, interrelationships among financial statements (both in Chapter 1), cost as an asset or expense (Chapter 2), and summary of major activities affecting financial reporting (Chapter 4).

4. *Addition of real-world problems and cases.* To enhance the real-world orientation of the book, 42 problems and cases that are based on the financial statements of companies have been added.

5. *Usefulness of financial statements.* To provide early reinforcement of the usefulness of financial statement information, the gross profit percentage, profit margin, and return on total assets have been added to Chapter 2.

6. *Expanded use of appendices.* Coverage of several topics has been moved to a chapter appendix. For instance, appendices are included for purchases discounts (Chapter 6); LIFO perpetual (Chapter 6); exchanges of property, plant, and equipment (Chapter 7); and supplementary disclosures of the effects of changing prices (Chapter 13).

7. *Expanded discussion of capital markets.* So that students better understand the relationships between corporate capital transactions and financial reporting, a discussion of primary and secondary capital markets has been added to Chapter 1, and the discussion of efficient capital markets has been expanded in Chapter 14.

8. *Additional excerpts from annual reports.* To bridge the gap between the classroom and practice, additional excerpts from annual reports have been added. These additional excerpts include disclosures of inventory, plant assets, and long-term debt (all in Chapter 1), related party disclosures (Chapter 2), and discontinued operations and extraordinary items (Chapter 10).

9. *Relationships among the three financial statements.* To emphasize the relationships among the three financial statements, two exhibits have been added to Chapter 2, one exhibit has been added to Chapter 3, and two exhibits have been added in Chapter 12. Also an exhibit has been added in Chapter 2 to distinguish among transactions, transactions affecting income, and transactions affecting cash.

10. *Expansion of cash flow discussions.* The discussion of the statement of cash flows in Chapter 3 has been expanded to include an explanation of the types

of investing and financing cash flows as well as the indirect and direct methods of computing net cash flow from operating activities. A statement of cash flows has been added to the summary example in Chapter 3. In Chapter 12, two new exhibits have been added that emphasize the interrelationships among the three financial statements. Additional explanations of the cash flows relating to the operating cycle and the effects of foreign exchange have also been added.

11. *Auditor's report updated.* The discussion and illustrations of the auditor's report have been updated to reflect the new formats of the report.

12. *Expansion of discussion of sociopolitical environment.* The section in Chapter 4 on the sociopolitical environment has been expanded to include a general discussion of the impact of lobbying and compromise on the standard-setting process.

13. *Management's selection of an inventory cost flow assumption.* A section has been added in which management's selection of an inventory cost flow assumption is discussed.

14. *Property, plant, and equipment.* A discussion of the use of alternative depreciation methods has been added, an exhibit giving MACRS percentages has been added, and a method of approximating the effects of accelerated depreciation compared with straight-line depreciation has been added. A discussion of the impairment of noncurrent assets has also been added.

15. *Additional discussion of current liability issues.* The discussion of current liabilities in Chapter 8 has been expanded to include executory contracts and illustrations of contingency disclosures.

16. *Discussion of present value.* An analysis of present value principles used in financial reporting has been added in Chapter 8.

17. *Troubled-debt restructuring.* In Chapter 8, financial reporting of troubled debt restructurings by the creditor, and an evaluation of accounting for troubled debt restructurings, have been added.

18. *Leases.* A section on sale-leasebacks has been added and the discussion of the lessor's asset from a capital lease has been simplified by showing only the net amount in the transaction.

19. *Revision of accounting for income taxes.* In Chapter 9, the text has been modified to be consistent with *FASB Statement No. 96.* An explanation of the effects of foreign tax credits has been added.

20. *Addition of OPEB discussion.* A discussion of postemployment benefits other than pensions (OPEBs) has been added as an appendix to Chapter 9. This material is consistent with *FASB Statement No. 106.* Related homework has also been added.

21. *Exit values.* A discussion and example of exit values has been added to Chapter 13. The discussion of the supplementary disclosures of the effects of changing prices has been moved to an appendix.

22. *Marketable securities.* The coverage of noncurrent marketable securities has been reorganized to provide better continuity from the discussion of current marketable securities.

23. *Expanded coverage of financial reporting topics.* Chapter 14 has been expanded to include discussions of the uses of segment information, uses of interim financial statements, management's discussion and analysis (MD&A), payables turnover, and cash flow ratios.

24. *Revision of homework assignments.* In addition to the new problems and cases, the numbers and solutions have been changed in over 70% of the previous homework.

25. *Addition of parentheses for clarity.* In response to user's suggestions, parentheses have been added to schedules and financial statements to clarify subtractions and negative numbers.

SUPPLEMENTARY MATERIALS

In addition to the textbook, an *Instructor's Manual* is available. It includes a suggested solution for each assignment and helpful notes to the instructor. Also included at the beginning of each chapter are teaching notes for the instructor. The financial statements of CSX Corporation are included and may be reproduced as transparencies or copied for distribution to the students. Finally, *Check Figures* are available in quantity at no charge to adopters.

ACKNOWLEDGMENTS

The authors wish to express their appreciation to the individuals who served as reviewers and who provided insightful comments and valuable suggestions in the development of the manuscript.

Phillip Buchanan	George Mason University
Thomas Buchman	University of Colorado at Boulder
Bill Cummings	Northern Illinois University
Janet Daniels	University of Hartford
David Drinkwater	Babson College
Wayne Ingalls	University of Maine
David Koeppen	Boise State University
Kris Raman	University of Texas at Arlington
Richard Sapp	Portland State University
Nancy Tang	Portland State University

We wish to thank Mary-Margaret Fleming, Ross Snyer, Kit Herrmann, Joyce Frakes, and Patsy Lee for their invaluable technical assistance in the preparation of the book and supporting materials. Appreciation is also extended to our editorial and production staffs including Al Bruckner, Susan Gay, Kelle Karshick, and Chris Crochetière at PWS-KENT, and Rachel Hockett at Hockett Editorial Service. We are grateful to our respective schools of accountancy for their support and to the American Institute of Certified Public Accountants, the Financial Accounting Standards Board, Nike Inc., General Motors, and CSX Corp. for permission to quote from their respective pronouncements and financial statements. We are also grateful to our families and friends for their moral support and understanding during the entire manuscript production process.

John D. Bazley
Loren A. Nikolai
Hugh D. Grove

The Fundamentals of Accounting and Financial Statements

Understanding the Balance Sheet

After reading this chapter, you should understand

- Decisions made by external users of financial statements
- Purposes of the balance sheet
- Elements of the balance sheet
- Measurement of the elements
- Current assets and current liabilities
- Noncurrent assets and noncurrent liabilities
- Stockholders' equity
- Analysis of transactions affecting the balance sheet
- Scope of the book

Accounting has been described as the process of identifying, measuring, recording, and communicating economic information to permit informed judgments and decisions by users of information. In the U.S. economy most published accounting information is about business enterprises. As discussed in Chapter 4, most business enterprises are corporations, but we typically use the more general term *company*. Because users have a limited ability to absorb large amounts of data, a goal of the accounting function is to establish a processing and communication system that summarizes large amounts of information about companies into understandable segments. In this sense accounting can be viewed as the link between a company's economic activities and decision makers, as summarized in Exhibit 1–1.

■ USERS OF ACCOUNTING INFORMATION AND THEIR DECISIONS

The U.S. economy is a free-market economy where buyers and sellers influence the demand for and supply of products and services offered by companies. In order to compete, companies need large amounts of capital for their activities. They obtain this capital by issuing capital stocks or bonds, borrowing from lending institutions, or from resources generated by their activities. The exchange

EXHIBIT 1–1   Acccounting information: economic activities and decision making

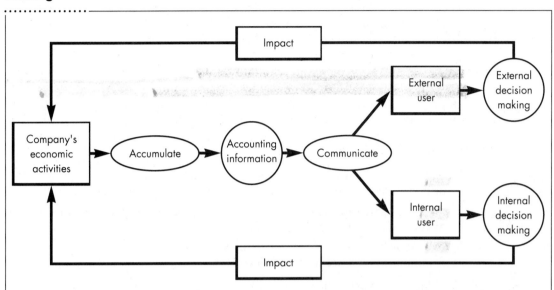

of capital by investors for the stocks or bonds of companies occurs in **capital markets**.

Companies may initially issue capital stocks or bonds through public offerings or private placements. **Public offerings** involve the advertising and sale to the general public. **Private placements** involve the advertising and sale to a few private institutions such as insurance companies and pension funds. These capital markets are sometimes called **primary markets** because the exchange is directly between the company and the investors.

Once the capital stocks or bonds have been sold by a company, they may be traded on formalized, and regulated, capital markets such as the New York Stock Exchange and the American Stock Exchange. These markets are sometimes referred to as **secondary markets** because the exchanges are between the investors themselves; the company initially issuing the capital stocks or bonds is *not* a party to the exchange.

An investor in capital stocks is interested in earning dividends and an increase in the market price of the stocks. Investors in bonds are interested in receiving interest and the return of their resources (and for publicly traded bonds an increase in their market price). These investors are interested in the efficient allocation of their scarce resources to achieve these objectives. Accounting information is useful in the decision making for this allocation process. It is also useful for other purposes.

External and Internal Users

The decision makers, or users of accounting information, can be divided into two major categories: external users and internal users, as shown in Exhibit 1–1. These two user groups have somewhat dissimilar information needs because of their different relationships to the company providing the economic information. **External users are actual or potential investors (stockholders and bondholders), creditors such as suppliers and lending institutions, and other users** such as employees, financial analysts, advisers, brokers, underwriters, stock exchanges, taxing and regulatory authorities, labor unions, and the general public.[1] Investors have the most direct relationship to the company, and their capital market information needs revolve around three basic decisions:

1. *Buy.* A potential investor decides to purchase a particular security (e.g., stock or bond) on the basis of communicated accounting information.
2. *Hold.* An actual investor decides to retain a particular security on the basis of communicated accounting information.
3. *Sell.* An actual investor decides to dispose of a particular security on the basis of communicated accounting information.

Creditors such as suppliers and lending institutions do not purchase securities, although they make similar decisions requiring accounting information. The decisions in this case are to extend credit, not to extend credit, or to maintain the credit relationship. Other users employ accounting information in their decision making. For example, stock exchanges use accounting information for listings, cancellations, and rule-making decisions. Labor unions use accounting information in negotiating wage agreements. Financial analysts use accounting information for making buy-hold-sell decisions.

Buy-hold-sell decisions are continuously reevaluated. A timely communication of information to external decision makers is imperative if their needs are to be satisfied. The publication of financial statements is a primary method by which relevant information is communicated. However, studies have shown that decision makers also use other reporting sources to satisfy their information needs. For example, in addition to the use of published financial statements, accounting information may also be communicated to external users by reports filed with the Securities and Exchange Commission, news releases, and management's forecasts. This area of study, known as *efficient capital markets* research, is discussed briefly in Chapter 14. The content of financial statements and the related schedules and notes are the topics included in this textbook.

Internal users are the company's managers who are responsible for the planning and control of operations on a day-by-day and long-term basis. In

· · · · · · · · · · · · · · · · · · ·

[1] In a recent survey, security analysts were rated as of "high importance" as users of financial statements by 58% of the respondents, present institutional investors by 57%, present individual investors by 18%, and potential individual investors by 14%. See *Financial Accounting Series No. 005* (Stamford, Conn.: FASB, September 16, 1985).

EXHIBIT 1–2   Relationship between financial and managerial accounting

	Financial Accounting	Managerial Accounting
1. Source of authority	Generally accepted accounting principles (GAAP)	Internal needs
2. Time frame of reported information	Primarily historical	Present and future
3. Scope	Mainly total company	Individual departments, divisions, and total company
4. Type of information	Primarily quantitative	Qualitative as well as quantitative
5. Statement format	Prescribed by GAAP, oriented toward investment and credit decisions	Decision oriented, focused upon specific decisions being made
6. Decision focus	External	Internal

contrast to external users, who mainly use financial statement information in their decision processes, internal users may request any type of information that they need, and that the accounting system is capable of providing, to make decisions on internal operations. For example, internal users may request information relating specifically to the purchase of new facilities, the addition of a new product, or reports on the performance of a division.

Two major branches of accounting have evolved to meet the specialized needs of external and internal users. **Financial accounting is the information accumulation, processing, and communication system designed to satisfy the investment and credit decision-making information needs of external users.** Financial accounting information is communicated through published financial statements and is constrained by the pronouncements of several policy-making groups. **Managerial accounting is the information accumulation, processing, and communication system designed to meet the decision-making information needs of internal users.** Managerial accounting information is communicated via internal company reports and is not subject to the policy standards applying to externally transmitted information. It is constrained by the usefulness of the information provided for a specific decision and the cost of providing that information. Financial and managerial accounting thus have somewhat different objectives, as they provide information with which to make different decisions. Some of their more important differences are summarized in Exhibit 1–2. Both types of information are produced from the company's accounting system. Therefore, the information comes from the same data base, and the differences lie in the selection and presentation of the communicated information. Because the management of a company is often evaluated on performance criteria (e.g., net income and rate of return), the financial accounting reports may influence the managerial accounting system, or vice versa. That is, the amounts reported or methods used for the financial statements may influence management decisions or management may use the managerial accounting system in its own interest to influence the financial reports.

The focus of this book is the communication of financial information and its use in the efficient allocation of resources in capital markets. The primary method of such communication is through the issuance of *financial statements*. Both the New York Stock Exchange and the American Stock Exchange, as well as the Securities and Exchange Commission, require certain companies to issue an annual report. **An annual report is a report published by a company once a year that contains its audited financial statements.** In addition, banks may require a company to provide its financial statements when applying for a loan. Other types of economic entities, such as universities and charitable organizations, also issue financial statements.

■ THE THREE FINANCIAL STATEMENTS

The major financial statements included in a company's annual report are (1) the income statement, which summarizes the results of the company's income-producing (operating) activities for the accounting period, (2) the balance sheet, which summarizes the company's financial position at one point in time in the accounting period, and (3) the statement of cash flows, which summarizes the cash inflows and outflows of the company during the accounting period. At a minimum, the annual report should include two balance sheets, one for the end of the previous period (e.g., December 31, 1992) which is usually referred to as the beginning balance sheet, and one for the end of the current period (December 31, 1993), and two income statements and statements of cash flows (1993 and 1992). Several supporting schedules and explanatory notes are included as a supplement to these financial statements.

The interrelationship of the information contained in the major financial statements is illustrated in Exhibit 1–3. The solid lines indicate the major flow of interrelated financial accounting information among the financial statements as a result of transactions and events during the period. For instance, assets (economic resources) from the beginning balance sheet may be consumed in an income-producing activity or may be sold as a source of cash. The related financial accounting information will affect the income statement and the statement of cash flows, respectively. The information relating to the income-producing activities in the income statement and information pertaining to the cash inflows and outflows reported in the statement of cash flows will both affect the accounting information reported in the ending balance sheet. The dashed line indicates a secondary flow of the interrelated information; that is, the income-producing activities reported on the income statement also affect the source of cash from operating activities. The relationship between these financial statements is further explored in the remaining sections of this chapter and in the subsequent chapters of this book.

EXHIBIT 1–3 Interrelationship of financial statements

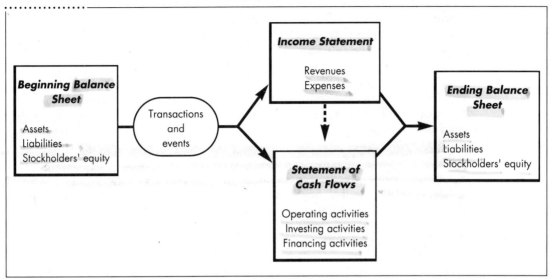

The focus of this chapter is on the balance sheet, its supporting schedules, and the accompanying notes. The balance sheet is the first financial statement discussed because the components of income are defined in terms of changes in assets and liabilities. Thus, an understanding of the nature and measurement of assets and liabilities is needed to understand net income and its components. Furthermore, the chapters of this book follow basically a balance sheet framework. Consequently a reasonably complete, albeit elementary, understanding of its purpose, content, format, and preparation is helpful in understanding the more complex issues discussed later. When certain issues are introduced in this chapter, reference is made to subsequent chapters in which more extensive discussions are presented. The income statement and statement of cash flows are discussed in Chapter 2.

■ PURPOSES OF THE BALANCE SHEET

One objective of financial reporting for a company, as discussed further in Chapter 4, is to help investors, creditors, and others in assessing the amounts, timing, and uncertainty of the prospective net cash inflows of the company. To meet this objective, it was suggested that certain types of accounting information should be provided in a company's financial statements. One specific objective of those statements is to provide information about a company's economic resources, obligations, and stockholders' equity. This information is reported on a balance sheet. **A balance sheet summarizes the** *financial position* **of a company at a particular date.** A balance sheet may also be called a **statement of financial position.** The financial position of a company includes its economic resources (assets), economic obligations (liabilities), stockholders' equity, and their relationships to each other on a particular date. The statement reports a company's *resource structure* (major classes and amounts of assets) and its *financial structure* (major classes and amounts of liabilities and equity). Its name evolved because the balance sheet is a detailed summary of the basic accounting equation (which must always remain in balance):

$$\text{Assets} = \text{Liabilities} + \text{Stockholders' Equity}$$

Together with other financial statements and other information, the balance sheet of a company should provide information that is useful to external users who desire to make their own estimates of the company's value. More specifically, the balance sheet of a company is intended to help external users (1) to assess the company's liquidity, financial flexibility, and operating capability and (2) to evaluate information about the company's income-producing performance during the period. The balance sheet, however, is not intended to show directly the value of the company.

Liquidity, Financial Flexibility, and Operating Capability

One purpose of the balance sheet is to provide information about a company's liquidity, financial flexibility, and operating capability. **The term liquidity is used to describe the amount of time until an asset is converted into cash or a liability is paid.** That is, liquidity refers to the "nearness to cash" of a company's economic resources and obligations. Information about liquidity is important in evaluating the *timing* of cash flows in the near future. Information about short-term cash inflows is useful because these cash inflows are part of long-term cash inflows. Furthermore, short-term cash inflows are necessary for a company to take advantage of new investment opportunities and to meet short-term obligations. Liquidity is one aspect of a company's financial strengths and weaknesses, or its financial flexibility.

Financial flexibility refers to the ability of a company to use its financial resources to adapt to change. Adaptation may be thought of as being "offensive" or "defensive." Offensive adaptation is necessary for a company to take advantage of an unexpected new investment opportunity, while defensive adaptation is required to survive a problem caused by a change in operating activities. Financial flexibility comes from a quick access to the cash generated from a company's more "liquid" economic resources. But liquidity is only part of financial flexibility. Financial flexibility stems from a company's ability to generate sufficient net cash inflows from operating activities, from additional capital contributed by investors or long-term creditors, or from liquidation of long-term economic resources without disrupting continuing operations. Information about a company's financial flexibility is important to external users in assessing the uncertainty of its future cash flows.

Operating capability refers to the ability of a company to maintain a given physical level of operations. This level may be indicated by the quantity of goods or services produced in a given period (e.g., inventory) or by the physical capacity of the operating assets (i.e., property, plant, and equipment) used to produce the goods or services. Information about a company's operating capability may be helpful to external users in understanding its performance and predicting future changes in its volume of activity and related cash flows.

Capital and Capital Maintenance

A second purpose of the balance sheet is to provide a basis for evaluating a company's income-producing performance during a period. In this regard, a company's capital is important. **The capital of a company is the economic resources (assets) less economic obligations (liabilities).** The assets less the liabilities are also known as the **net assets.** For a corporation, the stockholders' equity is the capital. This capital is used by the management of the corporation in fulfilling its responsibilities to the corporate stockholders. When a stockholder invests in a corporation, the stockholder is interested in a return *of* investment as well as a return *on* investment (i.e., dividends). To provide for a return of investment, the stockholders' equity (capital) of the corporation must be maintained; this is referred to as **capital maintenance.** Once this capital is maintained, any income of the corporation is an increase in stockholders' equity and is the basis for providing a return on capital (dividends) to stockholders. Thus, information about a corporation's capital is important in assessing the adequacy of a corporation's profits and its ability to provide a return on investment.

Another way of looking at Exhibit 1–3 is to think in terms of capital and capital maintenance. In a sense, the beginning balance sheet can be thought of as presenting the capital of the company at the beginning of the accounting period. The income statement in combination with the statement of cash flows discloses the results of management's activities to use, maintain, and increase the capital during the accounting period. The ending balance sheet reports the capital at the end of the accounting period. But before it can be determined whether capital is maintained or a company has earned income, the beginning and ending capital must be determined.

■ RECOGNITION IN THE BALANCE SHEET

An item of information related to the balance sheet can be disclosed in the balance sheet, in a supporting schedule, or as part of the notes accompanying the financial statements. **Recognition is the process of formally recording and reporting an element in the financial statements.** It includes depiction of an element in both words and numbers, with the amount included in the totals. Generally, the most useful (i.e., the best combination of relevance and reliability) information about assets, liabilities, and stockholders' equity should be recognized and included in the main body of the balance sheet. The concepts of usefulness, relevance, and reliability (among others) are discussed in Chapter 4. To be recognized, an item (and information about it) must: (1) meet the definition of an element, (2) be measurable, (3) be relevant, and (4) be reliable.[2] Thus, to

....

[2]"Recognition and Measurement in Financial Statements of Business Enterprises," *FASB Statement of Financial Accounting Concepts No. 5* (Stamford, Conn.: FASB, 1984), par. 58–64.

meet the objectives of a company's balance sheet—to provide relevant and reliable information to assess the company's liquidity, financial flexibility, and operating capability and to evaluate its income-producing performance during the period—the company must determine what are elements, and how and where to disclose them in the balance sheet. That is, the company must complete a three-stage process:

1. Identification of what items meet the definitions of the elements.
2. Measurement (valuation) of the elements.
3. Reporting (classification) of the elements.

Each of these stages is discussed in the following sections.

■ ELEMENTS OF THE BALANCE SHEET

For an item of information to be reported in a balance sheet, it must meet the definition of an element. **The elements of the balance sheet are the broad classes of items comprising it.** They are the "building blocks" with which the balance sheet is prepared. Each of the elements of a company's balance sheet—assets, liabilities, and stockholders' equity—is defined and discussed in the following sections.[3]

Assets

Assets are probable future economic benefits obtained or controlled by a company as a result of past transactions or events. Assets are the economic resources used to carry out a company's economic activities of consumption, production, and exchange. The primary attribute of all assets is *service potential,* the capacity to provide services or benefits to the company that uses them. An economic resource of a company must have three characteristics to be considered an asset.

1. The resource must singly, or in combination with other resources, have the capacity to contribute directly or indirectly to the company's future net cash inflows. This service potential may exist because the asset is expected to be exchanged for something else of value to the company, to be used in producing goods or services or otherwise increase the values of other assets, or to be used to settle its liabilities.

2. The company must be able to obtain the future benefit and control others' access to it. Control means that the company generally can deny or regulate the ability of others to use the asset.

3. The transaction or event giving rise to the company's right to or control over the benefit must have already occurred. That is, a company has no asset for a particular future benefit if the transaction or event giving it access to or

. . . .

[3]"Elements of Financial Statements," *FASB Statement of Financial Accounting Concepts No. 6* (Stamford, Conn.: FASB, 1985).

control over the benefit has yet to occur. As a corollary, once an asset is acquired by a company it continues to be an asset until it is exchanged or used up or until some other event destroys the future benefit or removes the company's ability to obtain or control it.

Assets also may have other characteristics. They may be natural or man-made, tangible or intangible, and either exchangeable or useful only in the company's activities. Furthermore, they may be acquired by purchase, production, stockholder investments, discovery, or other nonreciprocal (one-way) transfers.

Liabilities

Liabilities are probable future sacrifices of economic benefits arising from present obligations of a company to transfer assets or provide services to other entities in the future as a result of past transactions or events. An obligation of a company must have three characteristics to be considered a liability.

1. The obligation must entail a responsibility to another entity or entities that will be settled by a sacrifice involving the transfer of assets, provision of services, or other use of assets at a specified or determinable date, on occurrence of a specified event, or on demand. The specific identity of the "creditor" need not be known with certainty for a liability to exist as long as a future transfer or use of assets to settle the liability is probable.

2. The responsibility must obligate the company in such a way that it has little or no discretion to avoid the future sacrifice. Although most liabilities involve legal rights and duties, some are the result of equitable (ethical or moral) obligations or constructive (inferred from the facts) obligations. Thus, the company must be bound by a legal, equitable, or constructive responsibility to transfer assets or provide services to one or more other entities.

3. The transaction or other event obligating the company must already have occurred. Once a liability has been incurred by a company, it continues to be a liability until the company settles it or another event discharges it or removes it from the company's responsibility.

Liabilities arise primarily from deferring payment for goods or services received and from borrowing funds. Other liabilities result from collecting economic resources in advance of providing goods or services to customers. Liabilities also arise from selling products subject to warranties, from regulations imposed by governmental units, and from nonreciprocal transfers to owners or other entities.

Stockholders' Equity

Equity is the residual interest in the assets of a company that remains after deducting its liabilities. The equity of a company is equal to the company's *net* assets (assets minus liabilities). Equity stems from ownership rights and therefore it is the ownership interest. Since a company is generally not obligated to transfer assets to its owners, owners' equity ranks after liabilities as a claim to or interest in the assets and therefore is a residual interest. For a corporation, stockholders' equity records the interest of the stockholders who bear the ultimate risks and uncertainties involved in the company's operations and activities and who obtain the resulting rewards. It is created by stockholders' investments of economic resources and is subsequently modified by additional investments, dividends, and net income.

■ MEASUREMENT OF THE ELEMENTS OF THE BALANCE SHEET

For an element to be reported on the balance sheet of a company, it must be reliably measured (valued) in monetary terms. Five alternative valuation methods are shown in Exhibit 1–4. Stockholders' equity is not included in the exhibit because it does not exist apart from assets or liabilities. That is, the measurement of assets and liabilities (i.e., net assets) will determine the dollar amount of stockholders' equity. To conserve space, the discussion is in terms of the measurement of assets, but the comments generally are equally applicable to liabilities.

Historical Cost

The historical cost of an asset is the exchange price in the transaction in which the asset was acquired. The historical exchange price is measured by the cash paid for the asset. In the case of a noncash exchange, the historical cost is measured by the estimated cash equivalent of the noncash asset or liability exchanged. After acquisition, the historical cost of an asset may be reduced due to the recognition of depreciation (discussed in Chapter 2). In a company's financial statements, historical cost is the most commonly used measurement method.

Current Cost

The current cost of an asset is the amount of cash (or equivalent) that would be required on the date of the balance sheet to obtain the same asset. The "same asset" may be an identical asset or one with equivalent productive capacity. Alternative methods for obtaining the current cost of an asset include quoted market prices for the acquisition of a similar item, the use of specific price indexes, and appraisals (these are discussed more fully in Chapter 13).

Current Exit Value

The current exit value of an asset is the amount of cash (or equivalent) that could be obtained on the date of the balance sheet by selling the asset, in its present condition, in an orderly liquidation. An orderly liquidation means the

EXHIBIT 1–4 Measurement of assets and liabilities

Alternative	Assets	Liabilities
1. Historical cost/historical proceeds	Initially, the amount of cash (or its equivalent) paid to acquire an asset (historical cost); subsequent to acquisition, the historical amount may be adjusted for depreciation.	Initially, the amount of cash (or its equivalent) received when an obligation was incurred (historical proceeds); subsequent to incurrence, the historical amount may be adjusted for amortization.
2. Current cost/current proceeds	Amount of cash (or its equivalent) that would have to be paid if the same asset were acquired currently.	Amount of cash (or its equivalent) that would be obtained if the same obligation were incurred currently.
3. Current exit value	Amount of cash (or its equivalent) that could be obtained currently by selling the asset in orderly liquidation.	Cash outlay (or its equivalent) that would be required currently to eliminate the liability.
4. Net realizable value	Amount of cash (or its equivalent) into which the asset is expected to be converted in due course of business less direct costs necessary to make that conversion.	Amount of cash (or its equivalent) expected to be paid to eliminate the liability in due course of business including direct costs necessary to make those payments (nondiscounted amount of expected cash outlays).
5. Present value	Present value of future cash inflows into which the asset is expected to be converted in due course of business less present value of cash outflows necessary to obtain those inflows.	Present value of future cash outflows to eliminate the liability in due course of business including cash outflows necessary to make those payments.

[handwritten note: What can we sale for today.]

SOURCE: "Conceptual Framework for Financial Accounting and Reporting: Elements of Financial Statements and Their Measurement," *FASB Discussion Memorandum* (Stamford, Conn.: FASB, 1976), p. 193.

asset is disposed of in a systematic and organized fashion. A current exit value would be determined by obtaining a quoted market price for the sale of an asset of similar kind and condition.

Net Realizable Value

The net realizable value of an asset is the amount of cash (or equivalent) into which the asset is expected to be converted in the ordinary operations of the company, less any expected conversion costs (e.g., completion, disposal, or collection costs). Net realizable value differs from current exit value by being based on expected *future* sales proceeds of the asset (perhaps in a different form) rather than upon the *current* disposal value of an asset in its existing form. Net realizable value is sometimes referred to as *expected exit value.*

Present Value

The present value of an asset is the net amount of discounted expected cash inflows less the discounted expected cash outflows relating to the asset (discounting and the computation of present value are discussed in Chapter 8). The expected cash flows used to determine present value are the same as those used to determine net realizable value; the difference between the two alternatives is that under the present value approach, consideration is given to the time value of money (i.e., interest).

Valuation on Today's Balance Sheet

As indicated earlier, the valuation method primarily used in the balance sheets of companies is historical cost. In general, each asset and liability of a company is recorded at the exchange price of the transaction in which the asset is obtained or the liability is incurred. Usually this exchange price is then reported in the company's balance sheet until another exchange has taken place. Certain assets, such as property, plant, and equipment, are measured at their historical cost adjusted for depreciation. Historical cost is used extensively as a valuation method because it is based on transactions and provides information that has a high degree of *reliability.* It has been criticized, however, because some users of financial statements argue that historical cost is not as *relevant* as the amounts reported under some alternative valuation methods (relevance and reliability are discussed in Chapter 4).

In some situations, relevance can be increased without significantly reducing reliability. Thus, in certain circumstances the alternative valuation methods of current cost, current market value, net realizable value, and present value are used for selected elements of the balance sheet. The valuation method used for each type of asset and liability is identified in the next section and discussed more fully in later chapters. As increased emphasis is placed on reporting information concerning a company's liquidity, financial flexibility, and operating capability, valuation methods other than historical cost may be increasingly used on the balance sheet (or related notes) of companies. The extent of the use of other valuation methods will depend, among other considerations, on the tradeoff between relevance and reliability.

■ CONTENT OF THE BALANCE SHEET

The arrangement of each company's balance sheet items and subtotals should be designed in a manner to be useful to its various external user groups in their decision-making processes. Flexibility in classifications is necessary to ensure such usefulness, due to differences in companies, industries, and economic conditions. Nonetheless, a general classification scheme may be presented that captures the majority of items disclosed by most companies.

The balance sheet is usually divided into three parts, with a separate section containing (1) assets, (2) liabilities, and (3) stockholders' equity. The items reported within each of these three sections are usually grouped in some informative manner. The following is a representative classification for a corporation:

1. Assets

    a. Current assets
    b. Property, plant, and equipment
    c. Intangible assets
    d. Long-term investments
    e. Other assets

2. Liabilities

    a. Current liabilities
    b. Long-term liabilities
    c. Other liabilities

3. Stockholders' equity

    a. Contributed capital
       (1) Capital stock
       (2) Additional paid-in capital
    b. Retained earnings

Each of these groupings is discussed in the following sections and in more detail in later chapters. A comprehensive illustration of a balance sheet at December 31, 1993, for the Caron Manufacturing Company is shown in Exhibit 1–6. For selected items, illustrations of disclosures of actual companies are shown in related exhibits. The balance sheets of General Motors and Nike are included in Appendix A.

Current Assets

Current assets are cash and other assets that are expected to be converted into cash, sold, or consumed within one year or the normal operating cycle, which-ever is longer. An operating cycle is the average time taken by a company to

EXHIBIT 1–5   Operating cycle of a company

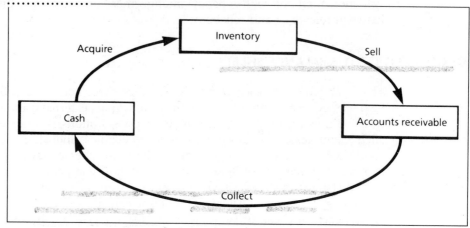

pay cash for inventory, process and sell the inventory, and collect the cash from the customer. Most companies have operating cycles of a year or less. A few, such as lumber, distillery, and tobacco companies, have operating cycles longer than one year. In that case the longer time period should be used to determine the current assets. A pictorial description of an operating cycle is shown in Exhibit 1–5. The elements of the exhibit are expressed in terms of current assets. Many current liabilities, primarily accounts payable, wages payable, and notes payable, are also incurred in the process.

Current assets may include five items: (1) cash, (2) temporary investments in marketable securities, (3) receivables, (4) inventories, and (5) prepaid items. These items are usually presented in the current asset section in the order of their liquidity, as shown in Exhibit 1–6.

Cash includes cash on hand and readily available in checking and savings accounts. It is listed at its monetary value. Cash equivalents, highly liquid investments, are often included with cash on the balance sheet. Cash and cash equivalents are discussed in Chapter 5. **Temporary investments in marketable securities** are items such as stocks and bonds that are held as short-term investments, are readily marketable, and that management intends to convert into cash within one year or the normal operating cycle, whichever is longer. They are discussed in Chapter 11. Alternative captions are *current marketable securities* and *short-term investments*. They are listed at their cost or market value (current exit value), whichever is *lower* (although if the market value is higher, this value is usually disclosed parenthetically. **Receivables** include accounts receivable which are listed at their estimated collectible amounts (net realizable values) by subtracting the allowance for uncollectible accounts from the receivables. Receivables also include notes receivable with maturity dates of less than one year or the operating cycle, whichever is longer. Receivables are discussed in Chapter 5. **Inventories** include goods held for resale in the normal course of business plus, in the case of a manufacturing company, raw materials (items to be converted into finished goods) and goods in process (partially completed goods) inventories. They are listed at their cost or market value (current cost), whichever is lower. The inventory costing method (LIFO, FIFO, average cost) is disclosed parenthetically or in the related notes. To reduce the detail on its balance sheet, a company might show a total inventory amount in current assets and then include a breakdown in the notes to the financial statements. This procedure is used by Apple Computer as shown in Exhibit 1–7. Inventories are discussed in Chapter 6. **Prepaid items** such as insurance, rent, and office supplies will not be converted into cash but will be consumed. Prepaid items are listed at historical cost and are discussed in Chapter 3.

Property, Plant, and Equipment

The property, plant, and equipment section of the balance sheet includes all the tangible assets used in the operations of the company. Often these are referred to as the *fixed assets,* or *operating assets,* because of their relative permanence in the company's operations and their use in the company's operating activities. In this category those assets are listed that have a physical existence, such as **land, buildings, equipment, machinery, furniture,** and **natural resources.** Except for land, all the fixed assets are depreciable or depletable (in the case of natural resources). Land is listed at its historical cost, while the remaining fixed assets are listed at their **book values** (historical cost less accumulated depreciation or depletion, as discussed in Chapter 3). Accumulated depreciation, a **contra-asset,** is usually used to reduce the fixed assets (except natural resources) to their book values while the historical cost is still disclosed. The method(s) of depreciating the property, plant, and equipment is disclosed in the notes to the financial statements. Some companies show a total amount of property, plant, and equipment on their balance sheets and a breakdown in the related notes. This procedure is used by Campbell Soup for its plant assets, as shown in Exhibit 1–8. Property, plant, and equipment is discussed in Chapter 7.

Certain **long-term lease contracts** relating to leased property, plant, and equipment are also included in this section. Long-term leases of assets have become a popular way by which a lessee may acquire the rights to the use of the assets without the immediate payment of the purchase price. In the case of a *capital lease,* one that contains many of the characteristics of a purchase, both the assets and the liabilities sections of the lessee's balance sheet are affected. Since the lease allows the lessee company relatively unrestricted rights to the use of the asset for an extended period, the rights represent economic resources to the company, even though the asset is not legally owned. A capital lease is initially recorded by the lessee as an asset—Leased Equipment Under Capital Lease—at the present value of the future lease payments and is amortized in a manner similar to other legally owned assets of the company. The book value of the leased asset is disclosed in the property, plant, and equipment section. Similarly, since the capital lease payments are usually noncancelable over an extended number of years, these payments represent a long-term liability of the

EXHIBIT 1–6

. . . .

CARON MANUFACTURING COMPANY
Balance Sheet
December 31, 1993

ASSETS

Current assets			
Cash		$ 14,300	
Temporary investments in marketable securities			
(market value $20,600)		19,700	
Accounts receivable	$ 68,200		
Less: Allowance for uncollectible accounts	(3,200)	65,000	
Inventories (at lower of average cost or market):			
Raw materials	$ 32,000		
Goods in process	49,500		
Finished goods	66,100	147,600	
Prepaid items:			
Insurance	$ 4,800		
Office supplies	2,200	7,000	
Total current assets			$253,600
Property, plant, and equipment			
Cost		$656,000	
Less: accumulated depreciation		(270,700)	
Net property, plant, and equipment			385,300
Intangible assets			
Trademarks (net)		$ 12,600	
Patents (net)		16,900	
Total intangible assets			29,500
Long-term investments			
Investment in Bounce Company bonds (at cost)		$ 17,000	
Fund to retire long-term bonds payable		17,400	
Total long-term investments			34,400
Total assets			$702,800

lessee company. The obligation for a capital lease is also initially recorded at the present value of the future lease payments and subsequently reduced by the amount of each lease payment (after adjustment for interest). As discussed later, the capital lease liability is disclosed in the long-term liabilities section of the balance sheet. Accounting for leases is a complex issue and is discussed in Chapter 9.

Intangible Assets

Intangible assets are those economic resources that are used in the operations of the company but have no physical existence. They generally derive their value from the rights held by the company for their use. They include **patents,**

EXHIBIT 1–6 *(continued)*
....

LIABILITIES

Current liabilities		
Accounts payable	$ 87,100	
Salaries payable	3,300	
Income taxes payable	27,400	
Advances from customers	19,600	
Current portion of mortgage payable	8,400	
Total current liabilities		$145,800
Long-term liabilities		
Bonds payable (10%, due 2006)	$90,000	
Less: unamortized bond discount	(8,200)	$ 81,800
Mortgage payable (12%, due 1998)		87,300
Total long-term liabilities		169,100
Other liabilities		
Deferred income taxes		14,300
Total liabilities		$329,200

STOCKHOLDERS' EQUITY

Contributed capital (see Exhibit 1–10)		
Common stock, $5 par (20,000 shares authorized,		
14,300 shares issued and outstanding)	$ 71,500	
Additional paid-in capital on common stock	173,900	
Total contributed capital		$245,400
Retained earnings (see Exhibit 1–10)		128,200
Total stockholders' equity		$373,600
Total liabilities and stockholders' equity		$702,800

copyrights, franchises, computer software costs, trademarks, goodwill, and **organization costs.** Intangibles are initially recorded at the historical cost incurred in an external transaction and are listed on the balance sheet at their book values (historical cost less accumulated amortization), although the contra-asset is sometimes reported. The method of amortizing the intangibles is disclosed in the notes to the financial statements. Intangible assets are discussed in Chapter 7.

Long-Term Investments

Companies make investments for a variety of reasons. They may be interested in appreciation of the investment, in income in the form of interest or dividends, in exercising control over certain companies as in the case of a subsidiary or a

EXHIBIT 1–7   Inventory disclosures: Apple Computer, Inc.
   (in thousands of dollars)

	September 29, 1989	September 30, 1988
Current assets (in part):		
Inventories	$475,377	$461,470

NOTES TO CONSOLIDATED FINANCIAL STATEMENTS (in part):

Inventories

Inventories consist of the following:

	1989	1988
Purchased parts	$116,664	$160,599
Work in process	77,088	56,639
Finished goods	281,625	244,232
	$475,377	$461,470

EXHIBIT 1–8   Plant assets: Campbell Soup Company
   (in millions of dollars)

	July 30, 1989	July 31, 1988
Assets (in part):		
Plant assets, net of depreciation	$1,540.6	$1,508.9

NOTES TO CONSOLIDATED FINANCIAL STATEMENTS (in part):

Plant Assets (in part):

	1989	1988
Land	$ 55.8	$ 53.2
Buildings	705.8	735.5
Machinery and equipment	1,619.2	1,624.4
Projects in progress	162.2	126.6
	2,543.0	2,539.7
Accumulated depreciation	(1,002.4)	(1,030.8)
	$1,540.6	$1,508.9

major supplier, and in the use of the investment for specific future purposes such as plant expansion. Whether or not the investment is readily marketable, **if management expects to hold the item for more than one year or the normal operating cycle, whichever is longer, it is properly classified as a long-term (noncurrent) investment.**

Long-term investments include holdings of equity securities such as capital stock of other companies, other securities such as bonds and notes receivable of unaffiliated companies, as well as securities of and long-term advances to unconsolidated affiliated companies. **Investments in property and equipment** being held for use in future operations, such as land being held for a future building site, are also included. **Special funds** established to retire bonds payable or redeemable preferred stock (often called sinking funds), or to acquire future facilities are included as long-term investments. Finally, **miscellaneous investments,** including the cash surrender value of life insurance policies, should be listed in this section of the balance sheet. Investments are listed at their historical cost, book value, present value, or lower of cost or market value, depending on the type of investment. The method of valuation for each long-term investment should be disclosed either parenthetically or in the notes to the financial statements. Long-term investments are discussed in Chapter 11.

Other Assets

Finally an "other assets" section is occasionally used to report miscellaneous assets that may not be readily classified within one of the previous sections. This section is sometimes referred to as *deferred charges*. Examples of items that have been classified in this section include long-term prepayments (such as for rent, insurance), deferred income taxes, bond issue costs, organization costs, idle fixed assets, cash from security deposits of customers on returnable containers, assets leased to others, and assets temporarily restricted by foreign countries. Classification within this section should be made judiciously. Many items that have been listed in this section should be correctly classified in one of the previous sections.

Current Liabilities

Current liabilities are those obligations whose liquidation is expected to require the use of current assets, or the creation of other current liabilities within one year or the normal operating cycle, whichever is longer. Several types of liabilities may be included as current liabilities: (1) obligations for items (goods or services) that have entered the operating cycle, such as **accounts payable, salaries payable,** and **income taxes payable;** (2) advance collections for the future delivery of goods or performance of service, such as **unearned rent** and **unearned ticket sales** (these are sometimes referred to as short-term deferred revenues); and (3) other obligations that will be paid within one year of the operating cycle, such as **short-term notes payable, dividends payable,** the estimated liability for short-term product **warranties,** and the portions of long-term liabilities that **mature during the next year.** These obligations are listed on the balance sheet at the amount owed (historical proceeds) or estimated to be owed, and are discussed in Chapters 3 and 8.

Working Capital

The working capital of a company relates primarily to the financial resources utilized in its operating cycle. **Working capital is the excess of current assets over current liabilities.** It is an indicator of the short-run liquidity of the company and is often used by creditors and others for such an evaluation. Often a slightly different computation, the **current ratio** (current assets divided by current liabilities), is used for the same purpose. Neither working capital nor the current ratio is usually disclosed explicitly, but each may be easily calculated. Care must be taken in the use of working capital information because the liquidity *composition* of the working capital components (particularly current assets) is of critical importance. For example, the *liquid* asset of temporary investments in marketable securities is immediately convertible into cash. Receivables and inventories must be *separated* from the company to be converted into cash, but there will be some time lag and conversion costs. Prepaid items usually cannot be converted into cash, but will be used up in the operations of the company.

Long-Term Liabilities

Long-term (noncurrent) liabilities are those obligations that are *not* expected to require the use of current assets or creation of current liabilities within one year or the normal operating cycle, whichever is longer. Included in this category are such items as **long-term notes payable, bonds payable, obligations under capital lease contracts, mortgages payable,** and **estimated liabilities from long-term warranties.**

As a means of financing its activities, a company may issue long-term bonds. A bond entails a written promise to repay a specific amount (its *face value*) at some future maturity date. Nearly all bonds also pay a specified interest rate (usually semiannually) which varies from company to company. Many bonds sell in a bond market similar to that of a stock market. Frequently, a company may issue a bond at more or less than its face value. This occurs when the bond pays a stated interest rate less or greater than the yield investors can earn elsewhere on a similar security, consequently making it more or less valuable.

When a bond is issued for more than its face value, it is said to have been sold at a *premium;* when it is issued for less, it is sold at a *discount*. At the time of sale the Bonds Payable are recorded at the face value of the bond and an amount called Premium on Bonds Payable (or Discount on Bonds Payable) is recorded for the amount by which the selling price is greater than (less than) the face value. Subsequently, this premium (or discount) is amortized as an adjustment to periodic interest expense (generally by use of a present value approach), and at the maturity date only the bonds payable face value remains. Whenever a balance sheet is prepared, the remaining premium is added to (or the discount is subtracted from) the face value of the bonds payable to determine the book value. Other long-term liabilities are usually listed at the present values of the amounts owed. Any applicable interest rates, maturity values, and other provisions are disclosed parenthetically on the balance sheet or in the notes to the financial statements. Some companies show a total amount of long-term liabilities on their balance sheets and a breakdown in the related notes. This procedure is used by Martin Marietta for its long-term debt, as shown in Exhibit 1–9. Long-term liabilities are discussed in Chapters 8 and 9.

EXHIBIT 1–9 Long-term debt: Martin Marietta Corporation
(in thousands of dollars)

Liabilities and Shareowners' Equity (in part):	December 31, 1989	December 31, 1988
Long-term debt	$477,504	$483,784

NOTES TO FINANCIAL STATEMENTS (IN PART):

	1989	1988
9½% notes due 1995	$125,000	$125,000
9¼% notes due 1997	125,000	125,000
7% debentures due 2011	97,888	97,234
Adjustable rate notes	68,465	68,465
8⅝% real estate mortgage due 2012	18,644	18,902
Industrial development revenue bonds	17,800	18,800
Adjustable rate real estate mortgage due 1991	12,000	12,000
Other notes and capital lease obligations	16,886	21,617
Total	481,683	487,018
Less current maturities	4,179	3,234
Long-term debt	$477,504	$483,784

The 9½% Notes were sold at 99.85% of their principal amount in a public offering in May, 1988. The notes are not redeemable in whole or in part at any time prior to maturity.

The 9¼% Notes were sold at par in a public offering in June, 1987. The notes are callable at par in 1992.

The 7% Debentures were sold at 53.835% of their principal amount of $175,000,000 in 1981. These debentures are carried net of original issue debt discount, which is being amortized by the interest method over the life of the issue. The effective interest rate is 13.25%. The debentures are redeemable in whole or in part at the Corporation's option at any time at 100% of their principal amount.

Other Liabilities

A final section is sometimes used to disclose miscellaneous liabilities not meeting the definition of either a current or a long-term liability. This section might include such items as deferred income taxes and long-term advances from customers. As in the case of other assets, this category should be used judiciously.

Transactions and Events Not Recorded as Assets and Liabilities

Some items are *not* included as assets and liabilities. For example, suppose a company signs a multiyear employment contract with the chief executive, or a contract to purchase natural gas for the next five years. Such contracts are not recorded as an asset or liability because the "transaction or event" has not occurred. The signing of a legal contract is not considered a transaction or event for accounting purposes. It becomes a transaction or event when the employee provides services to the company, the company uses the natural gas, or cash is paid.

Conceptual Guidelines for Reporting Assets and Liabilities

The previous sections discussed the typical classifications of assets and liabilities in a company's balance sheet. A company should classify its assets and liabilities in the most useful manner for external users. Therefore, the user should be aware of alternative classes of assets and liabilities that may be relevant.

1. Classifying assets according to their type or expected function in the central operations or other activities of the company. For example, assets held for resale (inventory) should be reported separately from assets held for use in production (property, plant, and equipment).
2. Classifying, as separate items, assets and liabilities with different implications for the financial flexibility of the company, for example, assets used in operations, assets held for investment, and assets subject to restrictions (such as leased equipment).
3. Classifying assets and liabilities according to the measurement method used to value the items—for example, assets and liabilities measured at net realizable value versus those measured at current cost.

These alternative classifications might help users to assess the nature, amounts, and liquidity of available resources, including the intentions of management regarding their functional use and the amounts and timing of obligations that require liquid resources for settlement.

Stockholders' Equity

Stockholders' equity is the residual interest of the ownership group in the assets of the company; that is, the equity of the owners is the company's assets less the liabilities. Stockholders' equity consists of two components: (1) contributed capital and (2) retained earnings.[4]

••••••••••••••••••••••

[4] Companies may have other items in stockholders' equity. For example, a company may receive donated assets or it may discover previously unrecorded assets. In either case recognition of the asset's fair market value is accompanied by an increase in stockholders' equity. In other instances: (1) certain unrealized losses on long-term investments in equity securities (discussed in Chapter 11), (2) any excess of additional minimum pension liability over unrecognized prior service cost (discussed in Chapter 9) must be listed as *negative* components of stockholders' equity. Also, some effects of the translation of a foreign subsidiary's financial statements into U.S. dollars (discussed in Chapter 13) are included in stockholders' equity.

Contributed Capital

Ownership in a corporation is evidenced by holding shares of stock. A stockholder may acquire shares directly from the corporation or by purchase on the stock market. In the first instance the acquisition affects the corporation's balance sheet, whereas the second has no affect. States have established various ways of protecting the interests of stockholders and creditors (discussed in Chapter 10). However, most of the laws entail the establishment of a certain amount of legal capital. **Legal capital is the minimum amount that the corporation may not pay out in dividends.** This legal capital is one element of the total amount of contributed capital. The accounting for contributed capital relates as much to the satisfaction of these legal requirements as it does to the provision of significant financial information. Contributed capital is usually separated into two components, capital stock (relating to the legal capital) and additional paid-in capital.

Capital Stock and Additional Paid-In Capital

Corporations may issue two types of capital stock, preferred stock and common stock. **Preferred stock** is usually nonvoting and often has slightly different ownership features (which some investors consider more attractive), including preference to a fixed dividend, should one be paid. **Common stock,** while not specifying a dividend, carries the right to vote at the annual stockholders' meeting and to share in residual profits. The number of shares that a corporation is legally authorized to issue as well as the types and characteristics of its capital stock are included in the corporate charter issued by the state. Common stock is the most prevalent type of capital stock. Each of these types of stock typically sells on a stock market which establishes its *market value* per share. The stock of a "nonpublic" corporation does not sell on a stock market.

Based on state laws, a corporation may issue (1) par value, (2) stated value, or (3) no-par (no stated value) capital stock. Capital stock may legally be required to carry a par value or a stated value. Par value or stated value refers to a specific dollar amount per share that is printed on the stock certificate.[5] Often this par value is a very nominal amount, say $1 or $5 per share, because states generally do not allow the issuance of stock at less than par. The par value of a share of stock has no direct relationship to the share's market value. Nonetheless, the legal (par) value must be separately disclosed.

When a corporation issues par value capital stock (common or preferred), the proceeds (market price) must be allocated between the capital stock for the par value and the difference between the par and the market value. This latter

. . . .

[5]There are certain legal differences between par value and stated value. These are discussed in Chapter 10. Since the accounting for stated value stock is virtually identical to that for par value stock, the remaining discussion focuses on par value stock.

Stock holder equity

*— addition
paid in
Capital*

amount is entitled in various ways such as Additional Paid-in Capital, Paid-in Capital in Excess of Par, or Premium on Common (or Preferred) Stock. For instance, if a corporation sold 100 shares of its $5 par common stock for $30 per share, the company would report Common Stock of $500 (100 × $5) and Additional Paid-in Capital of $2,500 [(100 × $30) − $500].

Many states also allow corporations to issue no-par capital stock. When no-par capital stock is issued, the total proceeds from the sale usually constitute the legal capital, and the entire amount is reported as common (or preferred) stock.

A corporation will sometimes repurchase its own capital stock. This reacquisition reduces the number of shares outstanding. The *cost* of the reacquisition is usually reported as Treasury Stock and is deducted from the total of contributed capital and retained earnings to determine total stockholders' equity.

Regardless of whether the corporation issues par or no-par stock, the amounts of the Preferred Stock, Common Stock, and Additional Paid-in Capital are listed separately on the balance sheet and summed to determine the total amount of contributed capital. The par value or stated value per share as well as the number of shares authorized, issued, and outstanding should be disclosed either parenthetically in the contributed capital section or in the notes to the financial statements.

Retained Earnings

Retained earnings is the total amount of corporate earnings that has not been distributed to stockholders in the form of dividends. A corporation may retain the assets generated from these earnings for use in its daily operations, to maintain its productive facilities, or for growth. In any event the existence of a retained earnings balance has no relationship to the funds that are available for cash dividends. The resources generated by earnings are invested in all assets. The Retained Earnings balance is added to the contributed capital to determine the total stockholders' equity. A negative retained earnings balance (due to cumulative losses and dividends exceeding cumulative earnings), properly entitled a *deficit*, would be subtracted from contributed capital.

■ SCHEDULE OF CHANGES IN STOCKHOLDERS' EQUITY

When financial statements are issued, a disclosure of the changes in the separate stockholders' equity amounts is required. This disclosure may be in the form of a supporting schedule or in a note accompanying the financial statements. The intent is to help report on the changes in a company's financial structure to aid in assessing its financial flexibility. Many companies will combine the retained earnings changes normally contained in a retained earnings statement with the other changes in capital in a single schedule entitled Schedule of Changes in Stockholders' Equity. This is illustrated in Exhibit 1–10. Note that the totals of the columns in the exhibit are the same as those shown in the stockholders'

EXHIBIT 1–10

	Common Stock, $5 par	Additional Paid-in Capital	Retained Earnings	Total
SCHEDULE A				
CARON MANUFACTURING COMPANY				
Schedule of Changes in Stockholders' Equity				
For Year Ended December 31, 1993				
Balance, January 1, 1993	$65,000	$154,400	$ 88,300	$307,700
Net income			68,500	68,500
Cash dividends paid			(28,600)	(28,600)
Common stock issued	6,500	19,500		26,000
Balance, December 31, 1993	$71,500	$173,900	$128,200	$373,600

EXHIBIT 1–11

CARON MANUFACTURING COMPANY
Statement of Retained Earnings
For Year Ended December 31, 1993

Retained earnings, January 1, 1993	$ 88,300
Add: net income for 1993	68,500
	156,800
Less: dividends for 1993	(28,600)
Retained earnings, December 31, 1993	$128,200

equity section of Exhibit 1–6. Alternatively, if the only changes in stockholders' equity are those that affect retained earnings, a Statement of Retained Earnings may be reported for simplicity. This alternative is illustrated in Exhibit 1–11.

■ ANALYSIS OF TRANSACTIONS AFFECTING THE BALANCE SHEET

The process of identifying, measuring, and reporting the elements of the balance sheet is discussed in this section. Assume that the Wells Company was formed on January 2, 1993, and was involved in six transactions during January. Each transaction is discussed in the following paragraphs and is summarized in Exhibit 1–12.

On January 2 the company issued 10,000 shares of common stock. Based on state laws, a corporation may issue par value, stated value, or no-par capital

EXHIBIT 1–12

WELLS COMPANY
Analysis of Transactions
For Month Ended, January 31, 1993

ASSETS

	Cash	Land	Building	Office Supplies	Office Equipment	Accounts Receivable
1/2/1993	+$300,000					
1/3/1993	− 180,000	+$30,000	+$150,000			
1/5/1993				+$7,000		
1/12/1993	− 10,000				+$30,000	
1/15/1993	− 3,500					
1/28/1993					− 4,000	+$4,000
Balances 1/31/1993	$106,500 +	$30,000 +	$150,000 +	$7,000 +	$26,000 +	$4,000

---

stock, as discussed in Chapter 10. We will assume that the Wells Company issued par value stock. If the Wells Company common stock has a par value of $1 per share and was sold for $30 per share, the total proceeds of $300,000 (10,000 × $30) are allocated between the par value of $10,000 (10,000 × $1) and the additional paid-in capital of $290,000 (10,000 × $29).

The company established a simple accounting system (Exhibit 1–12) by listing the accounting equation of assets, liabilities, and stockholders' equity as separate column headings with subheadings for specific elements within each category. Each transaction is recorded by entering the amounts in the appropriate columns to preserve the equality of the accounting equation. As a result of the sale of the 10,000 shares, the company has an asset, Cash, of $300,000 and stockholders' equity of $300,000, allocated between Common Stock of $10,000 and Additional Paid-in Capital of $290,000. Note that three entries were made to record this transaction and that the accounting equation is in balance because both sides of the equation were increased by the same amount.

It is important to recognize the difference between the transaction just described and the transfer of stock between two stockholders. In the latter situation, two individuals exchange the ownership of a certain number of shares at an agreed price. Because the company does not participate in this transaction, its balance sheet is unaffected.

To conduct its operations, the Wells Company purchased land for $30,000 and an office building for $150,000 on January 3, 1993, paying $180,000 cash. The land and building are expected to provide future economic benefits to the company by providing facilities to conduct its business. As a result, the land and building are both assets and are recorded as increases in the two asset categories—Land and Building—for $30,000 and $150,000, respectively. Because cash was paid out, the asset—Cash—must be decreased by the total amount paid, $180,000. After recording the transaction, the accounting equation remains

EXHIBIT 1–12 (continued)
....

=	LIABILITIES		+	STOCKHOLDERS' EQUITY	
	Accounts Payable	Notes Payable		Common Stock	Additional Paid-in Capital
				+$10,000	+$290,000
	+$7,000	+$20,000			
	− 3,500				
=	$3,500	+ $20,000	+	$10,000	+ $290,000

in balance because two assets were increased by a total of $180,000 and another asset was decreased by $180,000.

On January 5, 1993, the Wells Company purchased $7,000 of office supplies from City Supply Company, agreeing to pay for half of the supplies on January 15 and the remainder on February 15. Because the office supplies are expected to provide future economic benefits to the company, they are recorded as an asset—Office Supplies—for $7,000. Since Wells has agreed to pay for the supplies in the future, it has incurred a liability—Accounts Payable—for $7,000. Note that the increase in the company's assets was financed by a creditor, City Supply Company, not the stockholders. The accounting equation remains in balance because the increase in assets is accompanied by an equal increase in liabilities.

On January 12, 1993, the Wells Company purchased office equipment from Ace Equipment Company at a cost of $30,000. It paid $10,000 down and signed a note, agreeing to pay the remaining $20,000 at the end of one year. The office equipment is expected to provide future economic benefits to the company and is recorded as an asset—Office Equipment—for its cost of $30,000. The asset—Cash—is decreased by the amount paid, $10,000. Since the company has an obligation to pay $20,000 in one year, a liability—Notes Payable—is also recorded for that amount. The effect of this transaction is to increase assets by $20,000 and liabilities by the same amount, so the accounting equation still remains in balance.

On January 15, 1993, the Wells Company paid the City Supply Company half the amount owed for the supplies purchased on January 5 by issuing a check for $3,500. Because the debt owed to City Supply Company is reduced, the liability—Accounts Payable—is decreased by $3,500. The company made a cash outlay so the asset—Cash—is also decreased by $3,500. Again, the accounting equation remains in balance.

Finally, on January 28, 1993, the Wells Company decided that it did not need

EXHIBIT 1–13

....

WELLS COMPANY
Balance Sheet
January 31, 1993

ASSETS

Current assets		
Cash	$106,500	
Accounts receivable	4,000	
Office supplies	7,000	
Total current assets		$117,500
Property, plant, and equipment		
Land	$ 30,000	
Building	150,000	
Office equipment	26,000	
Total property, plant, and equipment		206,000
Total assets		$323,500

LIABILITIES

Current liabilities		
Accounts payable	$ 3,500	
Notes payable	20,000	
Total current liabilities		$ 23,500

STOCKHOLDERS' EQUITY

Common stock	$ 10,000	
Additional paid-in capital	290,000	
Total stockholders' equity		300,000
Total liabilities and stockholders' equity		$323,500

---

some of the office equipment it had purchased on January 12 for $4,000. There-fore, it sold the equipment to Kathy Baker, an insurance agent, for use in her office. The agreed selling price was $4,000, to be paid on February 7. Because the company disposed of one of its economic resources, the asset—Office Equip-ment—is decreased by its cost of $4,000. Since the amount to be received in February is a different economic resource, the Wells Company records an asset—Accounts Receivable—for $4,000, again preserving the equality of the accounting equation.

We have now recorded six typical transactions for the Wells Company. In each case we identified, measured, and recorded the monetary information from the transactions. Our accounting system now contains all the information relating to the company's financial position at the end of January. We can now summarize and communicate this information in a balance sheet. The January 31, 1993, balance sheet of the Wells Company is shown in Exhibit 1–13.

The balance sheet lists the ending amounts for each item of assets, liabilities, and stockholders' equity. The assets are classified as current assets and property, plant, and equipment, and the current assets are listed in the order of their liquidity, as discussed earlier. Note that the assets of $323,500 equal the liabilities of $23,500 plus the stockholders' equity of $300,000.

In this example, for simplicity we assumed that the company did not engage in any earnings activities. In addition, we included only basic balance sheet transactions. Earnings activities are introduced in Chapter 2, and more complex transactions are introduced in Chapter 3 and the rest of the book.

■ SCOPE OF THE BOOK

Two general approaches are used in teaching, and learning, accounting. They are usually described as the "preparer" and "user" approaches. The *preparer approach* teaches students what they need to know in order to become professional accountants. It must place great emphasis, therefore, on the details of accounting principles and the practices and procedures companies use to prepare their financial statements. In contrast, the *user approach* is concerned with teaching students to understand the content of financial statements for use in their decision making. The user approach is also relevant to students who become executives in companies and need to understand the impacts of management decisions on financial statements. This book adopts the user approach.

One of the most difficult judgments that all authors must make is what to include in and exclude from a book. There are many accounting principles and practices that are important to the operations of companies but are unlikely to have a material impact on the financial statements. There are also many accounting principles that are specific to particular industries. The authors have resolved these issues by deciding to include in this book only topics that can be expected to have a material impact on the financial statements of a typical company and the related notes, or be relevant to an understanding of those statements. Therefore, the student should be aware that as a user of financial statements, there may be situations in which an unusual, or industry-specific, event occurs that will require additional investigation.

A second issue that must be addressed by authors of accounting textbooks is whether to include the mechanics of accounting or to use what is often referred to (disparagingly) as the debit/credit approach. Because debits and credits do not appear in financial statements, it can be argued that their existence is irrelevant to the student following the user approach. However, two arguments can be made to support their inclusion. One is that an understanding of the basic mechanics that underlie the accounting system can help the student organize and interrelate the information. The second is that because accountants, managers, and financial analysts use a certain language in their oral and written communication, students who wish to be perceived as qualified users of financial statements are at a disadvantage if they do not understand that language. In this book the mechanics of accounting are used to support the understanding of accounting information. However, the authors do not, and students should not, assume that an understanding of the mechanics is sufficient. The emphasis must always be on "why" and "why not."

In summary, the purpose of this book is to enable the reader to understand the content and meaning of financial statement information and the impact of transactions and events on the financial statements. This emphasis is appropriate because financial statements are used to transmit information to external decision makers such as investors and creditors and these financial statements are the mechanism by which the financial impacts of managers' decisions are reported to the outside world.

To reinforce the learning obtained from the textual material, the assignments are of three general types. First are questions that need a narrative answer and can be used to reinforce an understanding of the basic concepts developed in the chapter. Second, problems are given that involve using the information presented to answer certain questions. These problems are intended to enable students to obtain reassurance that they have a basic understanding of the material in the chapter and can manipulate accounting information in a fairly straightforward way. Generally, these problems give some facts and ask for the impact on the financial statements. The third type of assignment presents financial statement information that requires the student to perform some kind of analysis or interpretation. These assignments test the understanding needed by the user of financial statements and many are based on financial statements of actual companies.

Finally, the reader should not be misled by the inevitable simplifications that must be included in a book of this nature. For example, many examples use a month instead of the year to reduce the volume of repetitive situations that must be discussed. Amounts are often kept small for similar reasons. However, the reader can be assured that none of these simplifications detracts from the concepts involved or from an understanding of the information contained in financial statements.

QUESTIONS

1. Distinguish between the categories of users of financial statements. Why might their decision-making needs be different?

2. Compare and contrast financial and managerial accounting.

3. What is the purpose of a company's balance sheet?

4. Define liquidity, financial flexibility, and operating capability.

5. Define an asset. What are the three characteristics of an asset?

6. Define a liability. What are the three characteristics of a liability?

7. What is stockholders' equity?

8. Identify the five alternatives for measuring (valuing) assets. Which is the valuation method primarily used in a company's balance sheet?

9. List the major sections (and the components of each section) of a balance sheet.

10. a. How are current assets defined and what are the major items that may be included in current assets?

b. How are current liabilities defined? Give three examples of such liabilities.

✓ **11. a.** Define a company's operating cycle.

b. How does cash flow relate to this cycle?

12. What items are properly classified as (a) long-term investments, (b) property, plant, and equipment, and (c) intangible assets?

13. What items are properly classified as (a) long-term liabilities and (b) other liabilities?

14. Define (a) capital stock, (b) additional paid-in capital in excess of par, (c) retained earnings, (d) treasury stock, and (e) deficit.

PROBLEMS AND CASES

15. Accounting Equation. Each of the following cases is independent of the others:

Case	Assets	Liabilities	Stockholders' Equity
1	A	$20,000	$42,000
2	$65,000	B	31,000
3	28,000	13,000	C

Required Determine the amounts of A, B, and C.

16. Change in Accounting Equation. At the beginning of the year the Ellis Company had total assets of $59,000 and total liabilities of $20,000. During the year total assets increased by $10,000. At the end of the year stockholders' equity totaled $55,000.

Required Determine (1) the stockholders' equity at the beginning of the year and (2) the total liabilities at the end of the year.

17. Manipulate Accounting Equation. At the end of the year a company's total assets are $71,000 and its total stockholders' equity is $43,000. During the year the company's liabilities decreased by $11,000 while its assets increased by $4,000.

Required Determine the company's (1) ending total liabilities, (2) beginning total assets, and (3) beginning stockholders' equity.

18. Valuation and Assets and Stock. A friend of yours has come to you for advice. He states that he owns several shares of stock in a corporation. He has examined the most recent balance sheet of the corporation and has found that the common stock issued and outstanding totals 40,000 shares, and the market price per share is $25 on the balance sheet date. He is sure that the balance sheet must be in error because in his words "the total assets are $800,000 and this current value should be the same as the $1,000,000 total value of the outstanding common stock."

Required Explain to your friend how the "values" of the various assets of the corporation typically are measured and reported on its balance sheet, and how the "value" of the $800,000 total assets is determined. Continue the discussion by explaining to your friend why the "values" of the assets and the stock are not the same.

19. Current Assets. Listed below are certain items and amounts of the Jenkins Company at the end of 1993:

Land	$12,000
Prepaid insurance	1,530
Cash on hand	840
Notes receivable (due 1996)	4,300
Cash in bank	5,600
Marketable securities (short-term)	3,380
Accumulated depreciation	8,700
Accounts receivable	15,200
Office supplies	970
Buildings	27,200
Inventory	17,800

Required Prepare the current asset section of the balance sheet.

20. Stockholders' Equity. Below are several items and amounts of the Graf Corporation at the end of 1993.

Common stock, $10 par	$ 48,500
Bonds payable (due 1997)	126,000
Additional paid-in capital on preferred stock	19,800
Retained earnings (unrestricted)	154,000
Premium on bonds payable	12,300
Unearned rent	4,800
Preferred stock, $50 par	32,700
Additional paid-in capital on common stock	53,900
Mortgage payable	18,400
Treasury stock (cost)	7,600
Retained earnings restricted due to bond contract	63,000
Donated capital from land	8,200

Required Prepare the stockholders' equity section of the 1993 ending balance sheet.

21. Classifications on Balance Sheet. A balance sheet may contain the following major sections:

A. Current assets
B. Property, plant, and equipment
C. Intangible assets
D. Long-term investments
E. Other assets

F. Current liabilities
G. Long-term liabilities
H. Other liabilities
I. Contributed capital
J. Retained earnings

Below is a list of fourteen financial statement items. Using the letters A through J, indicate in which section of the balance sheet each item would be classified. If an item cannot be classified in any of the above sections, explain why.

1. Temporary investments in marketable securities
2. Premium on bonds payable (bonds due in five years)
3. Additional paid-in capital on common stock
4. Accounts receivable
5. Notes payable (due in five years)
6. Patents (net)
7. Preferred stock
8. Unearned rent (to be earned within next six months)
9. Mortgage payable
10. Trademarks (net)
11. Deficit
12. Salaries payable
13. Land
14. Investment in Ace Company preferred stock

22. Classifications on Balance Sheet. The balance sheet contains the following major sections:

A. Current assets
B. Property, plant, and equipment
C. Intangible assets
D. Long-term investments
E. Other assets

F. Current liabilities
G. Long-term liabilities
H. Other liabilities
I. Contributed capital
J. Retained earnings

Below is a list of several financial statement items. Using the letters A through J, indicate in which section of the balance sheet each item would be classified. If an item cannot be classified in any of the above sections, explain why.

1. Cash
2. Bonds payable (due 2002)
3. Machinery
4. Deficit
5. Unexpired insurance
6. Franchise (net)
7. Fund to retire preferred stock
8. Current portion of mortgage payable
9. Accumulated depreciation
10. Copyrights (net)
11. Investment in X Company bonds
12. Notes payable (due in six months)
13. Notes receivable (due in three years)
14. Property taxes payable
15. Deferred income taxes payable
16. Premium on preferred stock
17. Premium on bonds payable (due 2002)
18. Goods in process
19. Common stock, $1 par
20. Land
21. Treasury stock (at cost)

23. Classifications on Balance Sheet. The December 31, 1993, balance sheet of Day Company contains the following major sections:

A. Current assets
B. Property, plant, and equipment
C. Intangible assets
D. Long-term investments
E. Other assets

F. Current liabilities
G. Long-term liabilities
H. Other liabilities
I. Contributed capital
J. Retained earnings

The following is a list of 34 financial statement items. Using the letters A through J, indicate in which section each item would be classified. If an item cannot be classified in any of the above sections, explain why.

1. Notes receivable (due in five months)
2. Income taxes payable
3. Organization costs
4. Unearned rent (for ten months)
5. Discount on bonds payable (long-term bonds)
6. Data processing center
7. Furniture
8. Land held for future expansion
9. Timberland (net)
10. Treasury stock, at cost
11. Advances to sales personnel
12. Idle machinery
13. Deferred income taxes
14. Raw materials
15. Computers
16. Pollution control facilities
17. Cash from security deposits of customers on returnable containers
18. Trademarks (net)
19. Finished goods
20. Cash dividends payable
21. Bond sinking fund
22. Temporary investments
23. Retained earnings
24. Advances to affiliated company (long-term)
25. Cash surrender value of life insurance
26. Leased equipment under capital lease
27. Additional paid-in capital on preferred stock
28. Interest receivable (due in five months)
29. Office supplies
30. Obligation under capital lease contract
31. Investment in two-year certificates of deposit
32. Unearned ticket sales
33. Estimated warranty (six-month) obligations
34. Cash

24. **Balance Sheet.** The balance sheet items and amounts of the Baggett Company as of December 31, 1993, are shown in random order as follows:

A=L+E

L-C Income taxes payable	$ 3,800	*A-C* Allowance for uncollectible	
A-C Prepaid items	1,800	accounts	-$ 1,200
E-CC Premium on common stock	9,300	*L-L* Bonds payable (due 2003)	23,000
A-prop Land	12,200	*A-PP* Buildings	58,000
L-Long Notes payable (due 1996)	6,000	*A* Sinking fund to retire	
A-long Notes receivable (due 1995)	15,500	bonds payable	5,000
A-C Accounts receivable	12,600	Advances from customers	
L-L Premium on bonds payable	1,400	(long-term)	2,100
L-C Accounts payable	11,300	*A-C* Cash	3,000
A-C Inventory	7,400	Accumulated depreciation:	
A Accumulated depreciation:– buildings	21,000	equipment	9,700
A-Intro Patents (net)		*E* Retained earnings	18,500
A-PP Equipment	4,000	*E-CC* Preferred stock, $50 par	18,600
E-CC Premium on preferred stock	28,700	*L-C* Wages payable	1,400
	7,900	*E-CC* Common stock, $10 par	13,000

add to Bond payable →

(A) Building's Fund ←

Required Prepare a December 31, 1993, balance sheet for the Baggett Company.

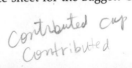

25. Balance Sheet. The December 31, 1993, balance sheet items and amounts of the Hitt Company are shown below in alphabetical order:

Accounts payable	$ 24,200	Cash	$ 5,100
Accounts receivable	21,500	Common stock, $10 par	30,000
Accumulated depreciation:		Current taxes payable	10,400
buildings	53,000	Discount on bonds payable	6,900
Accumulated depreciation:		Equipment	72,400
equipment	35,100	Inventory	37,200
Additional paid-in capital on		Land	30,000
common stock	24,000	Marketable securities	
Additional paid-in capital on		(short-term)	5,900
preferred stock	4,500	Patents (net)	9,500
Allowance for uncollectible		Preferred stock, $100 par	21,000
accounts	800	Retained earnings	54,500
Bonds payable (due 2007)	77,000	Salaries payable	2,000
Buildings	144,000	Trademarks (net)	4,000

Required Prepare the December 31, 1993, balance sheet of the Hitt Company.

26. Balance Sheet. Below is an alphabetical list of the December 31, 1993, balance sheet items and amounts for the Green Manufacturing Company:

Accounts payable	$18,700	Income taxes payable	$ 8,900
Accounts receivable	15,300	Interest payable	1,400
Accumulated depreciation:		Investment in stocks	15,100
buildings	30,800	Land	17,000
Accumulated depreciation:		Machinery and equipment	57,800
machinery and equipment	30,000	Marketable securities	
Allowance for uncollectible		(short-term)	8,400
accounts	1,040	Notes payable (short-term)	6,000
Bond sinking fund	7,700	Mortgage payable	13,900
Bonds payable (due 2007)	28,000	Premium on common stock	17,800
Buildings	92,500	Premium on preferred stock	7,000
Cash	7,100	Patents (net)	9,000
Common stock, $10 par	44,500	Preferred stock, $100 par	30,000
Deferred income taxes	2,800	Prepaid insurance	2,600
Discount on bonds payable	2,500	Raw materials	9,300
Dividends payable	5,600	Retained earnings	28,660
Finished goods	23,800	Unearned rent	5,000
Goods in process	14,700	Wages payable	2,700

Required Prepare a properly classified balance sheet for the Green Manufacturing Company on December 31, 1993. List the additional parenthetical or note disclosures (if any) that should be made for each item.

27. Balance Sheet. Below is a list (in random order) of the December 31, 1993, balance sheet items and amounts of the Midwest Company:

Additional paid-in capital on preferred stock	$ 1,000	Accounts payable	$16,100
Accounts receivable	13,800	Prepaid insurance	900
Dividends payable	1,800	Discount on bonds payable	2,000
Buildings	50,000	Common stock, $10 par	15,000
Bonds payable (due 2000)	29,000	Equipment	29,000
Retained earnings	24,700	Allowance for uncollectible accounts	700
Office supplies	1,600	Preferred stock, $50 par	10,000
Current income taxes payable	4,200	Accumulated depreciation: buildings	12,400
Accumulated depreciation: equipment	8,300	Current interest payable	2,100
Organization costs	2,200	Investment in stock (long-term)	10,000
Notes payable (due January 1, 1996)	13,000	Cash	5,000
Inventory	22,400	Treasury stock (at cost)	1,500
Additional paid-in capital on common stock	7,700	Accrued wages	3,900
Sinking fund for bond retirement	4,000	Land	7,500

Required Prepare a properly classified balance sheet for the Midwest Company on December 31, 1993.

28. Correction of Balance Sheet. On December 31, 1993, the Stevens Company bookkeeper prepared the following erroneously classified balance sheet:

STEVENS COMPANY
Balance Sheet For Year Ended December 31, 1993

Current assets		Current liabilities	
Inventory	$ 6,000	Accounts payable	$ 7,400
Accounts receivable	5,900	Allowance for uncollectible accounts	800
Cash	1,800	Salaries payable	1,500
Treasury stock (at cost)	3,400	Taxes payable	2,500
Long-term investments		Long-term liabilities	
Temporary investments in marketable securities	1,300	Bonds payable (due 2000)	12,000
Investment in X Company stock	10,300	Unearned rent (for three months)	900
Plant and equipment			
Land	10,100		
Office supplies	600		

		Owners equity	
Buildings and equipment	35,600		
Intangibles		Retained earnings	26,200
Patents (net)	4,700	Accumulated depreciation on	
Prepaid insurance (for six		buildings and equipment	9,200
months)	1,200	Premium on common stock	10,400
Discount on bonds payable	1,000	Common stock, $10 par	11,000
Total assets	$81,900	Total credits	$81,900

Required You determine that the amounts listed on the balance sheet are correct but, in certain cases, the items are incorrectly classified. Prepare a properly classified balance sheet as of December 31, 1993.

29. Corrections to Balance Sheet. The Cable Company prepared this balance sheet:

CABLE COMPANY
Balance Sheet For Year Ended December 31, 1993

Working capital	$ 28,200	Noncurrent liabilities	$ 65,000
Other assets	154,300	Stockholders' equity	117,500
Total	$182,500	Total	$182,500

Your analysis of the above items and amounts reveals the following information:

1. Working capital includes:

Land	$20,000
Accounts due from customers	18,000
Accounts due to suppliers	(24,000)
Inventories, including office supplies of $2,500	34,500
Income taxes owed to government	(16,400)
Wages owed to employees	(2,900)
Note owed to bank (due December 31, 1995)	(17,000)
Securities held as a temporary investment	16,000
	$28,200

(handwritten annotations: A–pro Land; A–rec Accounts due from customers; L–payable Accounts due to suppliers; A–C Inventories; L–Tax pay Income taxes; L–wage Wages; L–NO Note owed to bank; A–cur Securities; 16600)

2. Other assets include:

Cash	$ 14,000
Prepaid insurance	2,400
Buildings and equipment	100,000
Discount on bonds payable	3,000
Investment in Buy Company stocks	30,000
Treasury stock (at cost)	4,900
	$154,300

(handwritten annotations: Cash A–C; Prepaid insurance A–C; Buildings and equipment A–p; Discount on bonds payable L–Bond payable – dis Bond payable; Investment in Buy Company stocks – Asset – longterm; Treasury stock (at cost) – is subtract from SE CC to get Total Equity.)

3. Noncurrent liabilities include:

Bonds payable (due 2003)	$35,000
Allowance for uncollectible accounts	1,400
Premium on preferred stock	3,600
Common stock, $5 par	25,000
	$65,000

4. Stockholders' equity includes:

Accumulated depreciation: buildings and equipment	$ 40,000
Preferred stock, $100 par	14,000
Premium on common stock	15,600
Retained earnings	40,700
Mortgage payable	7,200
	$117,500

Required Based on your analysis, prepare a properly classified December 31, 1993, balance sheet for the Cable Company.

30. Change in Stockholders' Equity. On January 1, 1993, the Powder Company listed the following stockholders' equity section of its balance sheet:

Contributed capital	
Preferred stock, $100 par	$ 92,800
Common stock, $5 par	37,400
Additional paid-in capital on preferred stock	21,500
Additional paid-in capital on common stock	58,700
Total contributed capital	$210,400
Retained earnings	186,700
Total stockholders' equity	$397,100

During 1993 the following transactions and events occurred and were properly recorded:

1. The company issued 1,700 shares of common stock at $14 per share.

2. The company issued 320 shares of preferred stock at $130 per share.

3. The company earned net income of $39,750.

4. The company paid a $6 per share dividend on the preferred stock and a $1 per share dividend on the common stock outstanding at the end of 1993.

Required Prepare a schedule of changes in stockholders' equity for 1993.

31. Change in Stockholders' Equity. On January 1, 1993, the Knox Company showed the following alphabetical list of stockholders' equity balances:

Additional paid-in capital on common stock	$130,000
Additional paid-in capital on preferred stock	18,000
Common stock, $10 par	100,000
Preferred stock, $100 par	50,000
Retained earnings	200,000

During 1993 the following events occurred and were properly recorded by the company.

1. The company issued 2,000 shares of common stock for $24 per share.

2. The company issued 100 shares of preferred stock for $120 per share.

3. The company reacquired 400 shares of its common stock as treasury stock at a cost of $26 per share.

4. The company earned net income of $57,000.

5. The company paid a $7 per share dividend on the preferred stock and a $1.25 per share dividend on the common stock outstanding at the end of 1993 (treasury stock is not entitled to dividends).

Required Prepare a schedule of changes in stockholders' equity for 1993.

32. Impact of Transactions on Accounting Equation. The following transactions are taken from the records of the Lee Company:

1. Shareholders purchased no-par shares for $20,000 cash.
2. Paid $4,000 cash to acquire land and a small building for the business.
3. Received $650 cash from A. B. Jacobs, as payment for office equipment that Jacobs purchased from the company on credit last month.
4. Issued a $1,200 check in payment of a note issued last month.

Required Determine the overall effect of each transaction on the assets, liabilities, and stockholders' equity of the Lee Company.

33. Recording Transactions. The Wilman Company entered into the following transactions during the month of June:

6/1	Shareholders purchased no-par shares for $15,000 cash
6/10	Purchased $650 of office supplies from Timmer Supplies, agreeing to pay for half the supplies by June 30 and the remaining balance by July 15.
6/15	Purchased a 3-year fire insurance policy on a building owned by the company, paying $300 cash.
6/30	Paid Timmer Supplies half the amount owed for supplies purchased on June 10.

Required Record the above transactions using the accounting equation.

34. **Recording Transactions.** The Parsons Company was established on June 1, 1993. The following transactions occurred during the month of June:

   1. Shareholders purchased no-par shares for $30,000 cash.

   2. Office equipment was purchased. The cash price of $2,600 was paid by writing a check to the supplier.

   3. Land and an office building were acquired at a cost of $3,000 and $16,000, respectively. The company paid $4,000 down and signed a note for the remaining balance of $15,000. The note is due in 6 months.

   4. Office supplies totaling $250 were purchased on credit. The amount is due in 30 days.

   5. One piece of office equipment was sold for $600 cash to a real estate agent. The equipment had been purchased earlier this month at a cost of $600.

   6. Purchased a one-year fire insurance policy for $1,000.

   Required Record the effects of the above transactions on the accounting equation.

35. **Recording Transactions.** The Johnson Company was established on October 1, 1993. The following transactions occurred during the month of October:

   1. Shareholders purchased shares for $50,000 cash.

   2. Land and an office building were acquired at a cost of $3,200 and $20,000, respectively. A down payment of $8,000 was made and a note for $15,200 was signed. The note is due in one year.

   3. Several pieces of office equipment were purchased for a cash price of $4,600. The amount was paid immediately.

   4. Office supplies totaling $850 were purchased on credit. The amount is due in early December.

   5. Two pieces of office equipment that had been acquired earlier in the month at a cost of $1,300 were sold to the Jackson Company. The selling price of $1,300 was received in cash.

   6. Purchased a one-year fire insurance policy for $200.

   Required Record the effects of the transactions on the accounting equation.

36. **Recording Transactions and Preparing Balance Sheet (Sole Proprietorship).** L. Snider, a young CPA, started an accounting practice on September 1, 1993. During the month of September, the following transactions took place:

   1. L. Snider invested $50,000 cash to start the new business.

   2. Land and building were purchased for the business at a cost of $3,000 and $24,000, respectively. The company made a down payment of $5,000 and signed a note for the remaining balance of $22,000. The note is due in one year.

   3. Office equipment totaling $3,500 was purchased for cash.

   4. One piece of office equipment was sold to D. Popper. The selling price, $570, was

the same as the cost at which the office equipment was originally purchased. Popper agreed to pay the $570 at the end of October.

5. Office supplies were purchased for a total price of $1,700. The amount was paid by writing a check to the supplier.

Required 1. Record the effects of the transactions on the accounting equation.

2. Prepare a September 30, 1993, balance sheet for the company, L. Snider, CPA.

37. Recording Transactions and Preparing a Balance Sheet (Sole Proprietorship). F. Ryan, a young attorney, decided to start a law firm on December 1, 1993. During the month of December the following transactions took place:

1. F. Ryan invested $45,000 cash to start the new business.

2. Land and an office building were purchased for $2,000 and $16,000, respectively. Out of the total purchase price of $18,000, $4,000 was paid in cash and a note for the remaining balance of $14,000 was signed and given to the seller. The note is due in three months.

3. Office equipment was purchased for a cash price of $5,600.

4. Office supplies were purchased on credit from a local supplier. The purchase price of $660 is due next month.

5. One piece of office equipment that had been purchased earlier was sold at its original cost of $470. A check in the amount of $470 was received.

Required 1. Record the effects of the transactions on the accounting equation.

2. Prepare a December 31, 1993, balance sheet for the company, F. Ryan, Attorney.

38. Recording Transactions and Preparing Balance Sheets. The Envoy Investment Company was recently established by the owner, G. Envoy. The following transactions took place during April 1993:

1. On April 1 G. Envoy set up the business by purchasing no-par shares issued by the company for $45,000 cash.

2. On April 3 land and a building were acquired to be used as the office. A note for the entire purchase price of $24,000 (land, $2,500; building, $21,500) was signed and given to the seller. The note is due in one year.

3. On April 6 several pieces of office equipment were purchased for a price of $4,200. A check for that amount was written and given to the seller.

4. On April 15 office supplies totaling $740 were purchased on credit. The amount is due at the end of May.

5. On April 23 one piece of office equipment was sold at a selling price equal to its original cost of $830. The amount was collected in cash.

Required 1. Record the effects of the transactions on the accounting equation.

2. Prepare a balance sheet after each transaction has taken place (a total of five balance sheets is required).

39. Recording Transactions and Preparing Balance Sheets. The Lawrence Travel Agency was established by the owner, K. Lawrence. The following transactions took place during July 1993:

1. On July 1 K. Lawrence set up the business by purchasing shares issued by the company for $45,000 cash.

2. On July 7 land and a building were acquired for a price of $3,000 and $26,000, respectively. A down payment of $7,000 was made and a note in the amount of $22,000 was signed. The note is due in 6 months.

3. On July 13 office equipment was purchased for a total price of $5,500. A cash payment of $1,500 was made and the remaining balance of $4,000 is due in 30 days.

4. On July 24 office supplies totaling $880 were purchased on credit. The amount is due at the end of August.

5. On July 31 one piece of office equipment was sold at its original cost of $2,040. The amount was collected in cash.

Required 1. Record the effects of the transactions on the accounting equation.

2. Prepare a balance sheet after each transaction has taken place (a total of five balance sheets is required).

40. Analyzing Cash Transactions. All the transactions that took place during the month of February for the Van Tassel Company are as follows:

1. On February 1 the company was formed by selling shares for $56,000.

2. Land and an office building were purchased for $23,000. A down payment of $8,000 was paid by check; a note was signed for the remaining $15,000. The note is due in 3 months.

3. A $4,340 check was written to pay for the entire purchase price of office equipment.

4. A check in the amount of $620 was written to acquire office supplies.

5. One piece of office equipment was sold to D. Clark at its original purchase price, and the cash collected was deposited in the company's checking account.

Required Assuming all the transactions of the Van Tassel Company in the month of February were properly recorded and the balance of the checking account at the end of February was found to be $43,810, compute the selling price of the piece of equipment sold in item 5 above. Show your calculations.

41. Analyzing Cash Transactions. All the transactions that took place during the month of November for the Patrick Company are as follows:

1. On November 1 the company was formed by selling shares for $50,000.

2. An office building and land were purchased for the new business. A check in the amount of $4,500 was written to pay for the down payment and a 3-month note for the remaining $18,500 was signed.

3. A check in the amount of $7,700 was written to pay for the entire purchase price of office equipment.

4. One piece of equipment that had been purchased earlier was sold to J. Collins at its original cost of $1,200. The $1,200 was collected and deposited in the company's checking account.

5. Office supplies were purchased, and a check was written for the purchase price.

Required Assuming all the transactions of the Patrick Company in the month of November were properly recorded and the balance of the checking account at the end of November was found to be $37,300, compute the purchase price of the office supplies in item 5 above. Show your calculations.

42. **Recording Transactions.** Cato Company was formed on January 1 of the current year, and the company engaged in the following transactions during the month of January:

Date	Transaction
Jan. 2	Shareholders purchased no-par shares for $10,000 cash.
2	Purchased land and building at a cost of $3,000 and $20,000, respectively, paying 15% down and signing a 10-year mortgage for the balance.
3	Purchased office equipment costing $2,000 by paying $500 cash and signing a 90-day note for $1,500.
4	Purchased $540 of office supplies on account.
6	Purchased a 3-year insurance policy for $450 cash.
10	Purchased office furniture at a cost of $800, paying 25% down with the balance due at the end of the month.
15	Paid the amount due for office supplies purchased on January 4.
30	Paid balance due on office furniture purchased on January 10.

Required Record the effects of the transactions on the accounting equation.

43. **Identifying Transactions from Successive Balance Sheets.** The bookkeeper of the Smith Company prepares a balance sheet immediately after each transaction is recorded. During March, the first month of operations, the following five balance sheets were prepared:

1.

SMITH COMPANY
Balance Sheet
March 1, 1993

ASSETS		LIABILITIES AND STOCKHOLDERS' EQUITY	
Cash	$80,000	Common stock, no par	$80,000
		Total liabilities and	
Total assets	$80,000	stockholders' equity	$80,000

2.

SMITH COMPANY
Balance Sheet
March 3, 1993

ASSETS		LIABILITIES AND STOCKHOLDERS' EQUITY	
Cash	$75,000	Notes payable	$15,000
Land	3,000	Common stock, no par	80,000
Building	17,000	Total liabilities and	
Total assets	$95,000	stockholders' equity	$95,000

3.

SMITH COMPANY
Balance Sheet
March 7, 1993

ASSETS		LIABILITIES AND STOCKHOLDERS' EQUITY	
Cash	$75,000	Accounts payable	$ 1,300
Office supplies	1,300	Notes payable	15,000
Land	3,000	Total liabilities	$16,300
Building	17,000	Common stock, no par	80,000
		Total liabilities and	
Total assets	$96,300	stockholders' equity	$96,300

4.

SMITH COMPANY
Balance Sheet
March 8, 1993

ASSETS		LIABILITIES AND STOCKHOLDERS' EQUITY	
Cash	$71,500	Accounts payable	$ 1,300
Office supplies	1,300	Notes payable	15,000
Land	3,000	Total liabilities	$16,300
Building	17,000	Common stock, no par	80,000
Office equipment	3,500	Total liabilities and	
Total assets	$96,300	stockholders' equity	$96,300

5.

SMITH COMPANY
Balance Sheet
March 29, 1993

ASSETS		LIABILITIES AND STOCKHOLDERS' EQUITY	
Cash	$71,920	Accounts payable	$ 1,300
Office supplies	1,300	Notes payable	15,000
Land	3,000	Total liabilities	$16,300
Building	17,000	Common stock, no par	80,000
Office equipment	3,080	Total liabilities and	
Total assets	$96,300	stockholders' equity	$96,300

Required Describe the nature of the five transactions that took place during the month of March.

44. **Identifying Transactions from Successive Balance Sheets.** Lisa Wallace, owner of the Wallace Company, believes that current information is necessary for successful business operations. Accordingly, she requires that a balance sheet be prepared and submitted to her immediately after each transaction takes place. During the month of August, the following five balance sheets were prepared and submitted to her by the company's bookkeeper:

1.

WALLACE COMPANY
Balance Sheet
August 1, 1993

ASSETS		LIABILITIES AND STOCKHOLDERS' EQUITY	
Cash	$65,000	Common stock, no par	$65,000
		Total liabilities and	
Total assets	$65,000	stockholders' equity	$65,000

2.

WALLACE COMPANY
Balance Sheet
August 2, 1993

ASSETS		LIABILITIES AND STOCKHOLDERS' EQUITY	
Cash	$59,000	Notes payable	$15,000
Land	5,000	Common stock, no par	65,000
Building	16,000	Total liabilities and	
Total assets	$80,000	stockholders' equity	$80,000

3.

WALLACE COMPANY
Balance Sheet
August 4, 1993

ASSETS		LIABILITIES AND STOCKHOLDERS' EQUITY	
Cash	$59,000	Accounts payable	$ 1,400
Office supplies	1,400	Notes payable	15,000
Land	5,000	Total liabilities	$16,400
Building	16,000	Common stock, no par	65,000
		Total liabilities and	
Total assets	$81,400	stockholders' equity	$81,400

4.

WALLACE COMPANY
Balance Sheet
August 9, 1993

ASSETS		LIABILITIES AND STOCKHOLDERS' EQUITY	
Cash	$56,000	Accounts payable	$ 1,400
Office supplies	1,400	Notes payable	25,000
Land	5,000	Total liabilities	$26,400
Building	16,000	Common stock, no par	65,000
Office equipment	13,000	Total liabilities and	
Total assets	$91,400	stockholders' equity	$91,400

5.

WALLACE COMPANY
Balance Sheet
August 24, 1993

ASSETS		LIABILITIES AND STOCKHOLDERS' EQUITY	
Cash	$52,800	Accounts payable	$ 1,400
Office supplies	4,600	Notes payable	25,000
Land	5,000	Total liabilities	$26,400
Building	16,000	Common stock, no par	65,000
Office equipment	13,000	Total liabilities and	
Total assets	$91,400	stockholders' equity	$91,400

Required Describe the nature of the five transactions that the bookkeeper recorded during the month of August.

45. Identifying Transactions. The five transactions that occurred during June, the first month of operations for the Brown Company, were recorded as follows:

		ASSETS							
Trans.	Date	Cash	+	Office Supplies	+	Land	+	Building	+
1.	6/01/1993	+$75,000							
2.	6/05/1993	− 8,000				+$5,000		+$23,000	
3.	6/08/1993	− 270		+$270					
4.	6/17/1993	− 4,000							
5.	6/26/1993			+ 480					
Balances	6/30/1993	$62,730	+	$750	+	$5,000	+	$23,000	+

Office Equipment	=	Accts. Payable	+	Notes Payable	+	Common Stock	+	Additional Paid-in Capital
						STOCKHOLDERS' EQUITY		
	=	**LIABILITIES**	+					
						+$50,000		+$25,000
				+$20,000				
+$12,000				+ 8,000				
		+$480						
$12,000	=	$480	+	$28,000	+	$50,000	+	$25,000

Required 1. Describe the nature of the five transactions that took place during the month of June.

2. Prepare a balance sheet at June 30, 1993.

46. **Identifying Transactions.** The following transactions were recorded by the Sutton Company for the month of May, its first month of operations:

Trans.	Date	Cash	+	Office Supplies	+	Land	+	Building	+
				ASSETS					
1.	5/01/1993	+$55,000							
2.	5/02/1993	− 8,000				+$6,000		+$18,000	
3.	5/07/1993	− 2,500							
4.	5/10/1993			+$1,100					
5.	5/22/1993	+ 300							
Balances	5/31/1993	$44,800	+	$1,100	+	$6,000	+	$18,000	+

Office Equipment	=	Accts. Payable	+	Notes Payable	+	Common Stock	+	Additional Paid-in Capital
						STOCKHOLDERS' EQUITY		
	=	**LIABILITIES**	+					
						+$30,000		+$25,000
				+$16,000				
+$6,500				+ 4,000				
		+$1,100						
− 300								
$6,200	=	$1,100	+	$20,000	+	$30,000	+	$25,000

Required 1. Describe the nature of the five transactions that were recorded during the month of May.

2. Prepare a balance sheet at June 30, 1993.

47. **Stolen Checkbook.** On March 9, 1993, Peter Bailey started his own company by purchasing no-par shares issued by the Bailey Company for $10,000 cash. On March 13, 1993, the Bailey Company checkbook was stolen. During that period of time the Bailey Company had entered into several transactions, but unfortunately it had not established an accounting system for recording the transactions. Bailey did save numerous documents, however, which had been put into an old shoebox.

In the shoebox is a fire insurance policy dated March 11, 1993, on a building owned by the Bailey Company. Listed on the policy was an amount of $300 for one year of insurance. "Paid in Full" had been stamped on the policy by the insurance agent. Also included in the box was a deed for land and a building at 800 East Main. The deed was dated March 10, 1993, and showed an amount of $40,000 (of which $8,000 was for the land). The deed indicated that a down payment had been made by the Bailey Company and that a mortgage was signed by the company for the balance owed.

The shoebox also contained an invoice dated March 11, 1993, from the Ace Office Equipment Company for $600 of office equipment sold to the Bailey Company. The invoice indicates that the amount is to be paid at the end of the month. A $35,000 mortgage, dated March 10, 1993, and signed by the Bailey Company, for the purchase of land and a building is also included in the shoebox. Finally, a 30-day, $4,000 note receivable is included in the shoebox. It is dated March 13, 1993, and is issued to the Bailey Company by the Ret Company for "one-half of the land located at 800 East Main."

The Bailey Company has asked for your help in preparing a balance sheet as of March 13, 1993. Peter Bailey indicates that company checks have been issued for all cash payments. Bailey has called its bank. The bank's records indicate that the Bailey Company's checking account balance is $9,500, consisting of a $10,000 deposit, a $200 canceled check made out to the Finley Office Supply Company, and a $300 canceled check made out to the Patz Insurance Agency.

You notice that the Bailey Company has numerous office supplies on hand. Peter Bailey indicates that a company check was issued on March 9, 1993, to purchase the supplies, but none of the supplies had been used.

Required Based on the above information prepare a balance sheet for the Bailey Company on March 13, 1993. Be prepared to support each amount shown.

48. **Asset Concepts.** The concept of an asset for balance sheet presentation was developed in the chapter.

Required Which of the following items would be shown as an asset in the balance sheet and in which category?

1. A manufacturing plant lease that has been prepaid for next year.

2. The key sales and production personnel of the firm.

3. Inventory used as collateral for a loan.

4. Equipment purchased with a loan from a bank that has retained title to the equipment until the loan is repaid.

5. Accounts receivable sold at a discount to a financing company in order to raise cash.

6. The favorable attitudes of customers toward the company.

7. Sales orders received but not yet filled due to production constraints.

8. Land in a commercial park given to the company by the city.

49. Liability Concepts. The concept of a liability for balance sheet presentation is developed in the chapter.

Required Which of the following items would be shown as a liability in the balance sheet and in which category?

1. A promise to perform services for a customer who has not yet deposited any cash with the company.

2. The purchase and receipt of inventory from a supplier who has not yet sent an invoice.

3. Employment contracts with senior executives for next year.

4. Customer deposits for services yet to be performed.

5. A line of credit established at a local bank.

6. Use of one-half of the line of credit.

7. Payroll taxes calculated for last week's payroll.

8. A new labor union contract.

ANNUAL REPORT PROBLEMS
· ·

50. General Motors. Review the financial statements and related notes of General Motors in Appendix A.

Required Answer the following questions and indicate on what page of the financial report you located the answer. (*Note:* All answers may be found in the annual report, and no calculations are necessary).

1. What was the amount of total assets on December 31, 1989?

2. What was the amount of cash and marketable securities on December 31, 1989?

3. What is the par value of the company's common stock? How many shares had been issued at the end of 1989?

4. What was the total amount of inventories on December 31, 1989? What were the major classes of inventory and related amounts on this date?

5. What was the amount of notes and loans payable on December 31, 1989? Of this total, how much was for 8.7% notes due in 1994?

6. What was the amount of interest payable on December 31, 1989?

7. What was the amount of accounts payable on December 31, 1989?

8. What inventory costing (valuation) method was used for substantially all domestic inventories?

9. What was the amount of retained earnings on December 31, 1989?

10. What was the total amount of real estate, plants, and equipment before and after accumulated depreciation on December 31, 1989?

11. What was the amount of the total liabilities on December 31, 1989?

51. **Balance Sheet and Ratios.** Listed below in random order are the titles and amounts included in Kellogg Company's December 31, 1988, balance sheet (in millions of dollars):

Cash and temporary investments	$ 185
Common stock	39
Accounts payable	365
Accounts receivable (net)	405
Prepaid expenses	110
Accrued liabilities	300
Long-term debt	631
Intangible assets	103
Accumulated depreciation	785
Taxes payable	78
Inventory	363
Additional paid-in capital	65
Property, plant, and equipment	?
Total liabilities and shareholders' equity	3,298
Retained earnings	?
Debt due within one year	440

Required 1. Prepare a December 31, 1988, balance sheet in good form for Kellogg Company.

2. Prepare a preliminary estimate of the company's liquidity and stability using the following ratios (refer to Chapter 14 for more details on these ratios):
   a. Liquidity: Current ratio equals current assets divided by current liabilities (a 2:1 ratio is an approximate guideline for an adequate liquidity position).
   b. Stability: Debt ratio equals total liabilities divided by total assets (a 1:2 ratio is an approximate guideline for an adequate solvency position).

52. **Balance Sheet and Ratios.** Bell Atlantic Corporation is the eastern regional company of the seven Bell companies created by the divestiture of the Bell system. Listed below in random order are the titles and amounts included in its December 31, 1988, balance sheet (in millions of dollars):

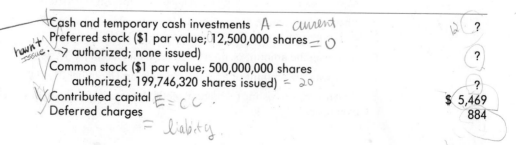

Cash and temporary cash investments	?
Preferred stock ($1 par value; 12,500,000 shares authorized; none issued)	?
Common stock ($1 par value; 500,000,000 shares authorized; 199,746,320 shares issued)	?
Contributed capital	$ 5,469
Deferred charges	884

Accounts receivable (net)	2,122
Accounts payable	1,622
Inventories	317
Accrued liabilities	853
Dividend payable	201
Prepaid expenses	466
Total assets	24,730
Long-term debt	?
Debt maturing within one year	1,589
Deferred income taxes and credits	4,730
Plant, property and equipment	27,570
Notes receivable (long term)	2,465
Reinvested earnings	3,509
Accumulated depreciation	9,396
Total current assets	3,207

Required 1. Prepare a December 31, 1988, balance sheet in good form for Bell Atlantic.

2. Prepare a preliminary estimate of the company's liquidity and stability using the following ratios (refer to Chapter 14 for more details on ratios):

   a. Liquidity: Current ratio equals current assets divided by current liabilities (a 2:1 ratio is an approximate guideline for an adequate liquidity position).

   b. Stability: Debt ratio equals total liabilities divided by total assets (a 1:2 ratio is an approximate guideline for an adequate solvency position).

53. Analysis of Transactions. Mobil Oil is one of the ten largest companies in the *Fortune* 500 list of U.S. companies. Its December 31, 1988, condensed balance sheet is as follows (in millions of dollars):

MOBIL OIL
Balance Sheet
December 31, 1988

ASSETS		LIABILITIES AND STOCKHOLDERS' EQUITY	
Cash	$ 191	Current notes payable	$ 810
Marketable securities	846	Accounts payable	6,043
Accounts receivable	5,113	Taxes payable	3,402
Inventories	4,481	Long-term debt	12,879
Prepaid expenses	547	Contributed capital	835
Properties, plants, and equipment	47,287	Retained earnings	14,851
Less: accumulated depreciation	(19,645)		
Total	$ 38,820	Total	$38,820

Assume the following transactions (in millions of dollars) occurred during January 1989:

1. Mobil sold marketable securities for $100. These securities had originally cost $100.

2. Mobil then used the cash proceeds from the marketable securities sale to purchase $200 of oil properties and financed the rest of the purchase with long-term debt.

3. Accounts receivable of $50 were collected.

4. Income taxes of $80 were paid.

5. Accounts payable of $50 were paid.

6. Common stock was issued for $30.

7. Inventories of $20 were purchased from OPEC on account.

8. Long-term debt of $40 was retired in exchange for some Mobil oil properties that had cost $40.

9. OPEC notified Mobil that no more oil could be purchased because of political conflicts.

10. Long-term notes payable of $10 are now due.

Required Analyze the impact on the balance sheet of the transactions. Prepare a balance sheet for January 31, 1989.

54. Analysis of Transactions. International Business Machines Corporation (IBM) is the world's largest computer company. Its December 31, 1988, condensed balance sheet is as follows (in millions of dollars):

INTERNATIONAL BUSINESS MACHINES CORPORATION
Balance Sheet
December 31, 1988

ASSETS		LIABILITIES AND STOCKHOLDERS' EQUITY	
Cash	$ 4,175	Taxes payable	$ 2,225
Marketable securities	1,948	Short-term loans payable	4,862
Accounts receivable	18,100	Accounts payable	2,702
Inventories	9,565	Accrued expenses	7,598
Prepaid expenses	1,555	Long-term debt	16,141
Plant, property, and		Contributed capital	8,323
equipment	44,882	Retained earnings	31,186
Less: accumulated			
depreciation	(21,456)		
Long-term investments	14,268		
Total	$ 73,037	Total	$73,037

Assume the following transactions (in millions of dollars) occurred during January 1989:

1. Purchased $10 of inventory on account.

2. Collected $20 of accounts receivable.

3. Sold for $30 a plant that had cost $30. Received $10 in cash and the balance as a note due in two years.

4. Purchased $10 of marketable securities.

5. Purchased $20 of insurance coverage which starts February 1, 1989.

   6. Sold marketable securities that had cost $500 for $500.

   7. Repaid $400 of long-term debt with proceeds from item 6.

   8. Used the rest of the proceeds from item 6 to retire common stock.

   9. Paid accrued expenses of $10.

   10. Decided to bring a new computer to the market in February 1989.

Required Analyze the impact on the balance sheet of the transactions. Prepare a balance sheet for January 31, 1989.

Understanding the Income Statement and the Statement of Cash Flows

After reading this chapter, you should understand

- Purposes of the income statement
- Elements of the income statement
- Recognition of the elements
- Income statement content
- Statement of cash flows
- Other disclosure issues
- Reporting techniques
- Analysis of transactions affecting the income statement

The income statement summarizes the results of a company's operations for the accounting period. This statement is alternatively referred to as a *statement of income, statement of earnings,* or *statement of operations.* It is often considered to be the most important financial statement in the annual report. The operations of a company may encompass routine ongoing activities as well as activities that are infrequent or unusual. Each of the routine ongoing activities that are included in the computation of net income is included in this chapter. The discussion of activities that are infrequent or unusual is included in Chapter 10.

■ PURPOSES OF THE INCOME STATEMENT

The purposes of the income statement include providing useful information relating to return on investment, risk, financial flexibility, and operating capability. **Return on investment is a measure of overall company performance.** Stockholders (investors) invest capital to obtain a return *on* capital. Before a company can provide a return on investment, its capital must be maintained.

Risk is the uncertainty or unpredictability of the future results of a company. The greater the range and time frame within which future results are likely to fall, the greater the risk associated with an investment in or extension of credit to the company. Generally, the greater the risk, the higher the rate of return expected. **Financial flexibility is the ability of a company to adapt to unexpected needs and opportunities.** Financial flexibility stems from, among other qualities, the ability of a company to adapt operations to increase net operating cash flows and the ability to sell assets without disrupting operations. **Operating capability refers to a company's ability to maintain a given physical level of operations.** This level of operations may be indicated by the quantity of goods or services (e.g., inventory) produced in a given period or by the physical capacity of the fixed assets (e.g., property, plant, and equipment).

The contribution of the income statement to the preceding purposes of financial reporting can be improved by providing the following:

1. Information about a company's operating performance separately from other aspects of its performance
2. The results of particular activities or events that are significant for predicting the amounts, timing, and uncertainty of future income and cash flows
3. Information useful for assessing the return on investment in the company
4. Feedback to users to assess their previous predictions of income and its components
5. Information to help assess the cost of maintaining the operating capability of the company
6. Information about how effectively management has discharged its stewardship responsibility regarding the company resources[1]

More specific guidelines have been provided to aid in decisions concerning the reporting of revenues, expenses, gains, and losses. These guidelines are summarized as follows.

1. Those items that are judged to be unusual in amount based on past experience should be reported separately.
2. Revenues, expenses, gains, and losses that are affected in different ways by changes in economic conditions should be distinguished from one another. For instance, changes in revenues are the joint result of changes in sales volume and selling prices. Information about both types of changes is helpful in assessing future operating results.
3. Sufficient detail should be given to aid in understanding the primary relationships among revenues, expenses, gains, and losses. In particular, it is helpful to report separately: (a) expenses that vary with volume of activity

....
[1]"Reporting Income, Cash Flows, and Financial Position of Business Enterprises," *FASB Proposed Statement of Financial Accounting Concepts* (Stamford, Conn.: FASB, 1981), par. 7–34.

or with various components of income, (b) expenses that are discretionary, and (c) expenses that are stable over time or depend on other factors, such as the level of interest rates or the rate of taxation.

4. When the measurements of revenues, expenses, gains, or losses are subject to different levels of *reliability*, they should be reported separately.

5. Items whose amounts must be known for the calculation of summary indicators (e.g., rate of return) should be reported separately.

These guidelines are intended to provide assistance for decisions concerning the grouping of items to show the components of net income and what elements should be reported separately. Unfortunately, many companies do not follow these guidelines. Also, the benefits of any additional information should, of course, be weighed against the costs of providing the information.

■ ELEMENTS OF THE INCOME STATEMENT

In order for an item of information to be included in the income statement, it must meet the definition of an element. The elements of the income statement are the broad classes of items comprising the statement. They are the "building blocks" with which the income statement is prepared. Each of the four elements—revenues, expenses, gains, and losses—and related issues are discussed next.[2]

Revenues

Revenues are increases in the assets of a company or decreases in its liabilities (or a combination of both) during a period from delivering goods, rendering services, or other activities that constitute the company's ongoing major or central operations. Revenues represent increases in net assets (assets minus liabilities) that have occurred as a result of the company's ongoing primary operating activities. The primary operating activities are the main business activities through which a company expects to make a profit. These activities are principally under the control of management. Revenues are a measurement of the accomplishments of the operating activities of a company during the accounting period. It is very important to understand that revenues are a component of stockholders' equity. For example, a sale of an item for cash results in an increase in an asset—cash—and in stockholders' equity—revenue.

Information on earnings and its components is one of the specific objectives of financial reporting, as discussed in Chapter 4. Because of the importance of the revenue information to users of financial statements, revenue is reported as

....
[2]"Elements of Financial Statements," *FASB Statement of Financial Accounting Concepts No. 6* (Stamford, Conn.: FASB, 1985).

a separate item in the income statement. Therefore, users obtain information about the earnings activities of the company rather than just receiving information about the stockholders' equity in the balance sheet.

Revenue Recognition.   Recognition is the process of formally recording and reporting an item in the financial statements. Most revenues are the joint result of many operating activities of a company and are "earned" gradually and continually as a result of this entire set of activities. These activities may be described as the **earning process** and include purchasing, producing, selling, delivering, administrating, and cash collecting. However, **revenues are generally recognized when two criteria have been met: (1) realization has taken place and (2) the revenues have been earned.** These criteria provide an acceptable level of assurance (i.e., reliability) of the existence and amounts of revenues.

The first criterion, *realization*, is the process of converting noncash resources into cash or rights to cash. The second criterion is met when revenues have been earned and the earning process is complete or virtually complete. This earning process occurs when the company has accomplished what it must do in order to be entitled to the benefits (e.g., assets) represented by the revenues.

Revenue recognition usually takes place at the time goods are sold or services are rendered. Generally at this point, realization has occurred and the earning process is complete or virtually complete. Exceptions to this general rule arise, however, and revenue may be recognized in a period before or after the sale to reflect more accurately the nature of a company's operations (i.e., to increase the predictive value and representational faithfulness of the accounting information). These *exceptional* cases arise in the following situations:

1. The economic substance of the event takes precedence over the legal form of the transaction so as not to distort economic reality (i.e., the earning process is complete before the legal title has passed).

2. There is great uncertainty about the collectibility of the receivable involved in a sale (i.e., realization has not occurred).

3. The risks and benefits of ownership are not transferred at the time of sale (i.e., the earning process is not complete even though legal title has passed).

The alternative methods by which revenue is recognized in a period other than the period of sale are discussed in Chapter 10.

Expenses

Expenses are decreases in assets or increases in liabilities (or a combination of both) during a period from delivering goods, rendering services, or carrying out other activities that constitute the company's ongoing major or central operations. Expenses represent decreases in net assets (assets minus liabilities) that have occurred as a result of the company's primary operating activities during the period. Expenses are a measurement of the efforts or sacrifices made in the operating activities.

As with revenues, it is very important to understand that expenses are components (decreases) of stockholders' equity. For example, the payment of wages results in a decrease in an asset—cash—and a decrease in stockholders' equity—wage expense. The expenses are reported in the income statement because it is important for users of financial statements to be able to focus on the earning activities of the company.

Expense Recognition.   To determine the earnings related to the company's primary operations during the accounting period, the expenses (efforts) are matched against the revenues (benefits). **Matching is the principle of recognizing the expenses involved in obtaining the revenues of the period in the same accounting period in which those revenues are recognized.** Three pervasive expense recognition principles are used to properly match expenses against revenues:

1. *Association of Cause and Effect.* Certain costs should be recognized as expenses on the basis of a presumed direct association with specific revenues. In most companies, some transactions result simultaneously in both a revenue and an expense. The revenue and expense are directly related to each other, so that the expense should be recognized at the same time as the revenue. Examples include costs of products sold, transportation costs for delivery of goods to customers, and sales commissions.

2. *Systematic and Rational Allocation.* Some costs should be recognized as expenses in a particular accounting period on the basis of a systematic and rational allocation among the periods in which benefits are provided. Many assets provide benefits to a company for several periods. In the absence of a direct cause-and-effect relationship, a portion of the cost of each of these assets should be rationally expensed each period. The allocation system should be based upon the pattern of benefits anticipated and should appear reasonable to an unbiased observer. Examples include depreciation of fixed assets, amortization of intangible assets, and the allocation of prepaid insurance costs.

3. *Immediate Recognition.* Some costs are recognized as expenses in the current accounting period because (a) the costs incurred during the period provide no discernible future benefits, or (b) the allocation of costs among accounting periods or due to cause-and-effect relationships is not considered to serve a useful purpose. Examples of costs immediately recognized as expenses in the current period include items such as officers' salaries and most selling and administrative costs.

To distinguish among the terms—cost, asset, and expense—the diagram in Exhibit 2–1 is helpful. *Cost* refers to the amount at which a transaction is recorded. A cost is an *asset* when a company acquires an economic resource that is expected to provide future benefits to the company. A cost is an *expense* if it occurs from selling goods or providing services to customers in an accounting period and is not expected to provide future benefits. An asset is recognized as an expense as its benefits are used up.

EXHIBIT 2–1   Cost: asset or expense

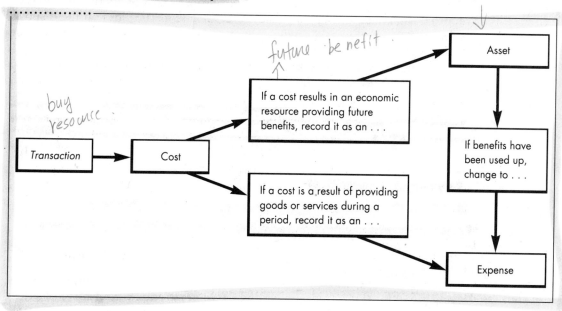

Gains and Losses

Gains are increases in net assets from peripheral or incidental transactions of a company and from all other transactions and other events and circumstances affecting the company during a period except those that result from revenues or investments by owners.

Losses are decreases in net assets from peripheral or incidental transactions of a company and from all other transactions and other events and circumstances affecting the company during a period except those that result from expenses or distributions to owners.

Revenues and gains are similar, and expenses and losses are similar, but two differences are important in communicating information about a company's performance. First, while revenues and expenses are associated with a company's major operating activities, **gains and losses are identified with peripheral activities** or with the effects of other events and circumstances, many of which are beyond the company's control. All four elements, however, are components of stockholders' equity. Second, revenues and expenses are reported at "gross" amounts, which are matched against each other to determine earnings, whereas **gains and losses are reported "net"**—either because two or more measures are offset against each other or because they involve only a single increase or decrease in an asset or liability without an offsetting or related decrease or increase in some other asset or liability. For example, sales and cost of goods sold are each reported separately on the income statement. The gain or loss on the disposal of an asset is reported as a single amount and the proceeds and the book value are *not* reported separately.

Although the definitions of revenues, expenses, gains, and losses give broad guidance, they do not distinguish precisely between revenues and gains and between expenses and losses. The distinction depends to a significant degree upon the nature of the company, its operations, and its other activities. Items that are revenues (expenses) for one company may be gains (losses) for another. In general, gains and losses may be classified in three categories as being derived from:

1. Exchange transactions *used equipment*
2. The holding of resources or obligations while their values change
3. Nonreciprocal ("one-way") transfers between a company and nonowners

② unrealized gain/loss
③ lawsuit

An item falling in the first category, such as a gain or loss on the sale of used equipment, is the net result of comparing the proceeds to the sacrifice involved in the exchange transaction. Examples of gains or losses resulting from value changes include those from the writing down of inventory from cost to market, from the change in the market price of temporary investments in marketable securities, and from the change in a foreign exchange rate. Finally, gains or losses from nonreciprocal transfers include those due to lawsuits, assessments of fines or damages by a court, or natural catastrophes such as an earthquake or fire.

Revenues, expenses, gains, and losses are classified and measured in accordance with accounting principles. The results of the major operating activities as well as peripheral activities are reported on the income statement. Companies select their disclosure methods, however. For example, a company may include a category, "other revenues and expense," which includes interest revenue and expense as well as gains and losses. This type of disclosure is appropriate if the individual items are not material.

■ RELATIONSHIP BETWEEN THE INCOME STATEMENT AND THE BALANCE SHEET

The preceding discussion emphasized that revenues, expenses, gains, and losses affect assets and liabilities and are components of stockholders equity. Therefore, the net amount of these four items, the net income, must be added to stockholders' equity in the balance sheet and is equal to the net increase in assets minus liabilities. The net income is added to retained earnings. **Retained earnings is a measure of the lifetime amount of the corporation's earnings retained in the corporation and not distributed to stockholders.** Dividends paid to stockholders are *not* an expense but are amounts distributed to stockholders as a return *on* their investment and are a reduction of retained earnings. These relationships are illustrated in Exhibit 2–2.

EXHIBIT 2–2 Transactions affecting the balance sheet

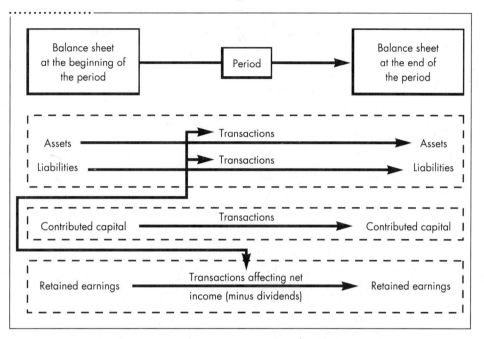

As discussed in Chapter 1, the assets are the economic resources of the corporation. There are two sources from which these resources may be obtained: (1) borrowing from creditors (liabilities) and (2) stockholders. Stockholders' equity has two components: (1) capital contributed through the purchase of shares and (2) earnings that the stockholders have allowed to be retained by the corporation. Whenever a corporation has a net income, net assets (assets minus liabilities) are also increased. As we saw in Chapter 1, many transactions affect assets, liabilities, and stockholders' equity without affecting income. The transactions that do affect income (revenues, expenses, gains, and losses) are considered to be so important to users of financial statements that they are reported not just as net changes in balance sheet amounts but also in a separate financial statement (the income statement).

To illustrate some of these relationships, consider the following simple example. A retail corporation purchases an item for $20 on credit and later sells it for $50 cash. First, the purchase for $20 is the acquisition of an asset—inventory—and an increase in a liability—accounts payable. Therefore, there is no change in *net* assets. Second, the sale of the item results in a revenue of $50 and an asset—cash—of $50. Third, the cost of the item is an expense—cost of goods sold—of $20 and a decrease in an asset—inventory—of $20. In summary, the transaction with the customer has increased the net assets by $30 (cash of $50 less inventory of $20). The net assets have been increased by a particular cause: the selling of goods to customers for a profit. Therefore, income of $30 is recognized (revenue of $50 less cost of goods sold of $20). Note that the transaction

EXHIBIT 2–3 Relationship between the income statement and balance sheet

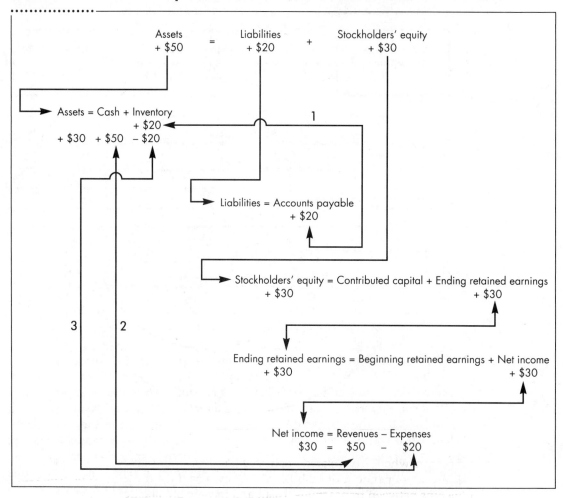

caused a revenue rather than a gain because the sale of the item is part of the company's primary, rather than peripheral, operations. These transactions may be summarized as shown in Exhibit 2–3.

In this example, the revenue transaction involves the receipt of cash while the expense transaction does not involve a payment. Note that the definitions of revenue and expense, discussed earlier, made *no* mention of cash. Rather, revenue and expense are defined in terms of changes in net assets (assets minus liabilities). Thus, cash may be received coincidentally at the same time as revenue is recognized. But in today's credit-based society, it is much more likely that revenue is recognized at a different time than when any related cash is received. Similarly, a cash outflow may occur coincidentally at the same time as an expense is recognized. Again, it is just as likely that the expense is recognized at a different

EXHIBIT 2–4 Relationships between transactions, cash, and income

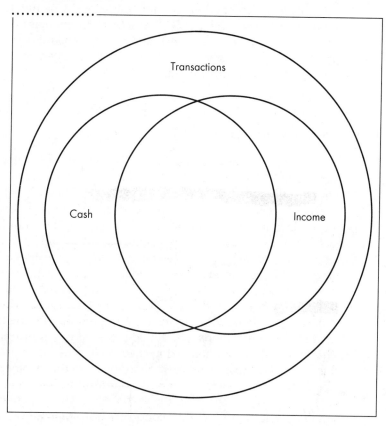

time than when any related cash is paid. This recognition of revenues and expenses independent of cash flows is known as the **accrual** concept. The relationships between transactions, cash, and income are illustrated in Exhibit 2–4.

■ CONTENT OF THE INCOME STATEMENT

Although the *form* of the income statement may differ from company to company, its *content* has become relatively standard. Outlined below are the major items included in the income statement.

1. Income statement
   a. Sales revenue (net)
   b. Cost of goods sold
   c. Operating expenses
   d. Other revenues and expenses
   e. Gains and losses
   f. Income tax expense
   g. Net income
2. Earnings per share

Not every income statement will include all these items, nor will they necessarily be listed in the sequence shown. Each is discussed in the following sections of this chapter. A comprehensive illustration of the Banner Company income statement is shown in Exhibit 2–5. The income statement is prepared under a multiple step approach (discussed later). Supporting schedules for this income statement are illustrated in related exhibits. The income statements of General Motors and Nike are included in Appendix A.

All-Inclusive Versus Current Operating

For years there have been debates over which items should be included in net income to make the income statement most informative. Some people advocated the **current operating performance** concept. They argued that only the normal, ordinary, recurring results of operations for the current period should be included in net income. Any unusual and nonrecurring items of income or loss should be recorded directly to retained earnings and should be disclosed in the statement of retained earnings. The reasoning was that investors are interested primarily in continuing operating income and that the disclosure of additional information would unnecessarily "clutter" the income statement. Others advocated the **all-inclusive** concept. Under this viewpoint all transactions increasing or decreasing stockholders' equity during the current period, with the exception of dividends and capital transactions, should be included in net income. Here it was argued that unusual and nonrecurring income or loss items are part of the earnings history of a company and their omission from the income statement might cause them to be overlooked. Several accounting pronouncements have been issued over many years regarding these concepts. The net effect of these pronouncements is that the all-inclusive concept is now generally accepted. However, there are a few exceptions to the all-inclusive income statement and these are discussed in later chapters.

Condensed Income Statements

In the interest of full disclosure the financial statements should disclose all information of sufficient importance to influence the judgment of informed external users. However, disclosures may be made in a variety of ways. With respect to the income statement, it is argued that all items related to the profit-making activities of the company should be reported on the face of the statement, but a counterargument is that *too much* detail detracts from the readability of the statement. Most companies take a compromise position and present a condensed income statement. Here only the major items of significance are disclosed directly on the income statement, frequently in an aggregated form, while supporting schedules and disclosures in the notes supplement this information. In the

EXHIBIT 2–5 Multiple step income statement

BANNER COMPANY
Income Statement
For Year Ended December 31, 1993

Sales revenue		$150,000
Less: Sales returns and allowances	$ 4,000	
Sales discounts	2,300	(6,300)
Net sales		$143,700
Cost of goods sold (Exhibit 2–6)		(86,000)
Gross profit		$ 57,700
Operating expenses		
Selling expenses (Exhibit 2–8)	$10,200	
General and administrative expenses		
(Exhibit 2–8)	16,000	
Depreciation expense (Exhibit 2–8)	7,800	
Total operating expenses		(34,000)
Operating income		$ 23,700
Other revenues and expenses		
Interest revenue	$ 1,800	
Dividend revenue	600	
Interest expense	(2,100)	
Total other revenues and expenses		300
Gains and Losses		
Loss on sale of equipment		(4,000)
Income before income taxes		$ 20,000
Income tax expense		(6,000)
Net income		$ 14,000
		Earnings per share
		(5,000 shares)
Net income		$2.80

following discussion, we identify those items that are likely to be aggregated on the income statement and give illustrations of the related supporting schedules.

Net Income

Net income includes sales revenue, the various expenses related to these sales, other revenues and expenses, gains and losses, and income tax expense.

Sales Revenue (Net).   Sales revenue includes the gross charges to customers for the goods and services provided during the period. To determine the *net* sales revenue (or simply "net sales"), any sales returns or allowances given to customers (or reasonably estimated) and any sales discounts taken by credit

EXHIBIT 2–6   **Cost of goods sold: merchandising company**

BANNER COMPANY Schedule 1: Cost of Goods Sold For Year Ended December 31, 1993	
Inventory, January 1, 1993	$ 41,000
Purchases (net)	83,000
Cost of goods available for sale	$124,000
Less: inventory, December 31, 1993	(38,000)
Cost of goods sold	$ 86,000

customers (or reasonably estimated) are deducted from sales revenue. In order to increase the predictive value of the sales revenue information, sales volume and sales price information would be useful. To date, very few companies present this information.

Cost of Goods Sold. The cost of goods sold is the cost of the inventory items sold to customers during the period. Usually the computation of the cost of goods sold is not shown on the face of the income statement, but instead in a supporting schedule. The form of the schedule will depend on whether the company is a merchandising concern or a manufacturing concern. In the case of a merchandising company, **cost of goods available for sale** is the beginning inventory plus the net purchases.[3] The ending inventory is deducted from the cost of goods available for sale to determine the **cost of goods sold.** The cost of goods sold schedule for the Banner Company is shown in Exhibit 2–6.

In the case of a company that manufactures instead of purchasing its inventory, a **cost of goods manufactured** amount replaces the (net) purchases. To determine the cost of goods manufactured, initially the current factory cost is computed by summing (1) the cost of **raw materials** used in the production process, (2) the cost of **direct labor** used to convert raw materials into partially or fully completed inventory, and (3) the cost of the other factory items (referred to as **factory overhead**), such as factory utilities and depreciation, supervision, maintenance, and supplies. This total current factory cost is added to the beginning goods in process inventory (partially completed inventory from the previous period), from which the ending goods in process inventory is deducted to determine the cost of goods manufactured. The cost of goods sold is computed by adding the cost of goods manufactured to the beginning finished goods inventory and subtracting the ending finished goods inventory. The cost of goods

[3]Net purchases include gross purchases plus freight costs less any purchases returns, allowances, and discounts. Theoretically such costs as receiving, storing, and insurance during transport should also be included in purchases. However, as a practical matter these latter costs are usually treated as expenses of the period (immediate recognition).

EXHIBIT 2-7   Cost of goods sold: manufacturing company

BANNER MANUFACTURING COMPANY		
Schedule 1: Cost of Goods Sold		
For Year Ended December 31, 1993		
Raw materials used		$ 35,000
Direct labor		29,000
Factory overhead:		
Depreciation of factory items	$5,100	
Heat, light, and power	4,000	
Indirect factory labor	7,300	
Repairs and maintenance	3,400	
Miscellaneous factory expense	1,200	21,000
Current manufacturing costs		$ 85,000
Add: goods in process inventory, January 1, 1993		27,000
Less: goods in process inventory, December 31, 1993		(29,000)
Cost of goods manufactured		$ 83,000
Add: finished goods inventory, January 1, 1993		41,000
Cost of goods available for sale		$124,000
Less: finished goods inventory, December 31, 1993		(38,000)
Cost of goods sold		$ 86,000

sold schedule, assuming that the Banner Company is a manufacturing concern, is shown in Exhibit 2-7.

Gross profit is the sales revenue minus the cost of goods sold. The **gross profit percentage** is calculated by dividing the gross profit by the gross sales. In the case of the Banner Company, the gross profit percentage is 38.5% ($57,700 ÷ $150,000). The managers of a company, and the users of financial statements, should keep a close watch on the gross profit percentage. A small change may have a great impact on the percentage change in income before income taxes. For example, a $1,000 increase in cost of goods sold for the Banner Company would decrease the gross profit percentage by 1.7% ($1,000 ÷ $57,700), causing income before income taxes to decrease by 5% ($1,000 ÷ $20,000).

Operating Expenses.   Operating expenses are those primary recurring costs (other than cost of goods sold) incurred in order to generate sales revenues. These expenses are typically classified according to *functional categories*. A common classification scheme is to separate **selling expenses** from **general and administrative expenses.** Because of its significance, depreciation expense (excluding the depreciation included in cost of goods manufactured) is often shown as a separate classification. In the case of manufacturing companies, research and development expense may also be shown as a separate classification. Frequently, single aggregate amounts are listed on the income statement for the selling, general and administrative, and depreciation expense classifications. When this occurs, a supporting schedule may be included that identifies

EXHIBIT 2–8

BANNER COMPANY Schedule 2: Operating Expenses For Year Ended December 31, 1993	
Selling expenses	
Delivery expense	$ 1,800
Advertising expense	3,300
Sales salaries expense	4,100
Sales supplies expense	700
Miscellaneous selling expenses	300
Total selling expenses	$10,200
General and administrative expenses	
Administrative salaries	$ 6,900
Office salaries	3,700
Taxes and insurance expenses	2,200
Bad debts expense	1,500
Office supplies expense	700
Miscellaneous expenses	1,000
Total general and administrative expenses	$16,000
Depreciation expense	
Office equipment	$ 3,300
Store equipment	4,500
Total depreciation expense	$ 7,800

the amounts of the individual expenses contained in each major classification. This supporting schedule for the Banner Company is shown in Exhibit 2–8.

Other Revenues and Expenses. Included here are those significant recurring items of revenue and expense that are not directly related to the primary operations of the company. Examples include dividend revenue, interest revenue and expense, and items such as rent, storage, and service revenues (for a manufacturing or merchandising company).

Gains and Losses. Included in this section are those material but "nonextraordinary" gains and losses that result from events that are *either* unusual in nature *or* infrequent in occurrence, such as the write-down of obsolete inventories or the disposal of property (these terms and items are discussed in Chapter 10). As shown in Exhibit 2–5, a loss on the sale of equipment is included in this section of the Banner Company income statement because the sale is considered to be an infrequent but not unusual event and is classified as a loss because it is the result of an incidental or peripheral activity.

Income Tax Expense. In Exhibit 2–5 the Banner Company has computed income before income taxes from which the income tax expense has been deducted. The net amount is the net income for the period.

Single-Step and Multiple-Step Formats. The *form* in which the net income is disclosed may vary from company to company. Many variations of two basic forms, the *single-step* and the *multiple-step* formats, are found in actual practice. **Under the pure single-step format, items are classified into two groups, revenues (and gains) and expenses (and losses).** All operating revenues and other revenues and gains are itemized and their amounts summed to determine total revenues (and gains). The cost of goods sold, operating expenses, other expenses and losses, and income tax expense are itemized and summed to determine total expenses (and losses). Net income is computed in a single step as the difference between the totals of the two groups, hence the term single-step format. A variation in this format involves the income tax expense. Because of the magnitude of the income tax expense, this amount frequently is listed as a separate item of net income. In this case a subtotal entitled "income before income taxes" is computed, from which the associated income tax expense is deducted to determine net income. The single-step format has been advocated because of its simplicity and flexibility and because the limited number of subclassifications does not impart more importance to certain items of revenue and expense than may be warranted. Although it is still a fairly common form of income statement, the number of companies using it is decreasing. Currently about 40% of surveyed companies use some variation of the single-step format.[4] This format is illustrated in Exhibit 2–9.

Some accountants argue that the simplicity of the single-step format detracts from the usefulness of the income statement to investors, creditors, and other users. They suggest that **additional subclassifications make the income statement more informative and advocate a multiple-step format.** This format has a number of variations, but typically at least three subtotals are derived. Initially the cost of goods sold amount is deducted from net sales to determine the **gross profit** or **gross margin on sales.** The operating expenses are then deducted from (i.e., matched against) gross profit to derive **operating income.** The other revenues and expenses, including gains and losses, those important but nonoperating items that do not relate to the primary activities of the firm, are then summarized in a subsequent section often entitled "other revenues and expenses." The net total of this section is added to (or deducted from) operating income to derive income before income taxes, which is reduced by the related income tax expense to determine **net income.**

Two criticisms may be raised against the multiple-step format. First, this format may give the misleading inference that there is a priority in the recovery of expenses. However, *all* expenses must be recovered in order to earn income.

....
[4]*Accounting Trends and Techniques* (New York: AICPA, 1989), p. 231.

EXHIBIT 2–9   Single step income statement

····················

BANNER COMPANY
Income Statement
For Year Ended December 31, 1993

Revenues		
Sales revenue (net of $2,300 discounts and $4,000 returns and allowances)	$143,700	
Interest revenue	1,800	
Dividend revenue	600	
Total revenues		$146,100
Expenses		
Cost of goods sold (Exhibit 2–6)	$ 86,000	
Selling expenses (Exhibit 2–8)	10,200	
General and administrative expenses (Exhibit 2–8)	16,000	
Depreciation expense (Exhibit 2–8)	7,800	
Loss on sale of equipment	4,000	
Interest expense	2,100	
Income tax expense	6,000	
Total expenses		(132,100)
Net income		$ 14,000
		Earnings Per Share
		(5,000 shares)
Net income		$2.80

Second, disagreement, particularly across different industries, as to what items of revenues and expenses should be classified as operating (or primary) and nonoperating can lead to different classification schemes and result in noncomparable income statement formats. Nonetheless the multiple-step format is becoming more popular and is currently being used by about 57% of surveyed companies. The multiple-step format is the one used in Exhibit 2–5.

Evaluation of Profitability

A company's profit margin, return on total assets, and earnings per share may all be used to evaluate the profitability of a company.

Profit Margin.   **Profit margin** is calculated by dividing net income by net sales. A company with a higher profit margin than previous years or other companies is doing a good job of controlling its expenses in relation to its sales or of selling its products at higher prices. The profit margin of the Banner Company is 9.7% ($14,000 ÷ $143,700).

Return on Total Assets.   **Return on total assets** is calculated by dividing net income by total assets. The return on total assets measures how well a company is using its economic resources to achieve a profit, and can be compared to the results of previous years or other companies. If we assume that the total assets of the Banner Company are $280,000, the return on total assets is 5% ($14,000 ÷ $280,000). Each of these ratios is discussed more fully in Chapter 14.

Earnings per Share. Net income is often referred to as the "bottom line" on the income statement because it is the result of combining all the revenues, expenses, gains, and losses. Actually the term *bottom line* is a misnomer because **earnings-per-share information must be disclosed on the face of the income statement, and this disclosure usually is shown directly below the net income figure.**[5]

Earnings per share is a ratio of considerable importance in financial analysis. It is often used in predicting future earnings and in comparison to the market price at which a stock is currently selling to determine the attractiveness of that stock. **In its simplest form earnings per share is computed by dividing the net income by the number of common shares outstanding throughout the entire year.** However, many companies have preferred stock outstanding that has first priority to dividends, and they also have shares of common stock outstanding for only a portion of the year. Other companies have complex capital structures that include securities such as convertible preferred stock, convertible bonds, and stock options that may be converted into shares of common stock. The conversion of these securities to common stock would have an impact on the denominator (and in certain cases the numerator) of the earnings per share ratio. To improve the comparability of the earnings per share amounts listed by different companies, a complicated set of rules is used to measure earnings per share in such situations, as discussed in Chapter 10.

■ STATEMENT OF CASH FLOWS

Traditionally, every company prepared an income statement and a balance sheet at the end of its accounting period. The income statement reported the results of its income-producing activities, and the balance sheet reported its ending financial position. Certain external users asked questions about a company's cash flows: How was cash from operations generated? How was expansion financed? How was debt retired? What happened to the proceeds from the issuance of capital stock? These questions could not always be answered directly from the income statement and balance sheet. Therefore, a statement of cash flows is a useful complement to the balance sheet and income statement.

A company must present a statement of cash flows for the accounting period along with its income statement and balance sheet. There are two purposes for the statement of cash flows. **The primary purpose is to provide information about a company's cash receipts and cash payments during an accounting period.**

balance   Change   over the period

....

[5]This disclosure requirement does *not* apply to companies that are not required to file with the Securities and Exchange Commission.

A secondary purpose of a statement of cash flows is to provide information about a company's operating, investing, and financing activities during an accounting period. A complete discussion of the statement of cash flows is given in Chapter 12. Because this statement is interrelated to the other financial statements and is an integral part of a company's annual report, it is now briefly discussed.

Conceptual Overview and Uses of the Statement

One of the specific objectives of financial reporting is to provide information about a company's cash flows, as discussed in Chapter 4. The statement of cash flows is useful in meeting this objective. Furthermore, in Chapter 1 we observed that external users are interested in information with which to assess a company's *liquidity* (the nearness to cash of its assets and liabilities), *financial flexibility* (the ability to take effective actions to alter the amount and timing of future cash flows so the company can respond to unexpected needs and opportunities), and *operating capability* (the ability to maintain a given physical level of operations). The statement of cash flows is useful in meeting these information needs. It should help external users to assess:

1. A company's ability to generate positive future cash flows
2. A company's ability to meet its obligations and pay dividends
3. A company's need for external financing
4. The reasons for differences between a company's net income and associated cash receipts and payments
5. Both the cash and noncash aspects of a company's investing and financing transactions during the accounting period

Reporting Guidelines and Practices

To aid users in making the preceding assessments, a statement of cash flows must report on a company's cash inflows, cash outflows, and net change in cash from its operating, investing, and financing activities during the accounting period, so that the net change in cash reconciles to the cash balances in the beginning and ending balance sheets. The statement of cash flows includes three sections: (1) net cash flow from operating activities, (2) cash flows from investing activities, and (3) cash flows from financing activities.

The **net cash flow from operating activities** section reports on the cash flows from the operating activities of the company. *Operating activities* include all transactions and other events that are not investing and financing activities. These include, for instance, transactions that involve acquiring, producing, selling, and delivering goods for sale, and providing services. The most common way of preparing this section is called the *indirect method*. Under the indirect method, net income is listed first and then adjustments (additions or subtractions) are made to net income (1) to eliminate certain amounts (such as depreciation expense) that were included in net income but did not involve a cash inflow or cash outflow for operations, and (2) to include any changes in the current assets (other than cash) and current liabilities involved in the company's operating cycle that affected cash flows differently than net income. The intent is to convert net income to the net cash flow provided from (or used in) operations. The alternative way of preparing this section is called the *direct method.* Under the direct method, the cash inflow and cash outflows are listed directly with titles such as "collections from customers," "payments to suppliers and employees," "payments of interest" and "payments of income taxes." Most companies use the indirect method.

Essentially, the **net cash flow from operating activities** section reports on the cash flows associated with the operations of the company whereas the income statement reports on the income flows. For example, in the income statement a company reports its revenue and cost of goods sold, whereas in the cash flow statement a company reports the cash received from customers and the cash paid to acquire inventory.

The **cash flows from investing activities** section includes all cash inflows and cash outflows involved in the investing activities transactions of the company. *Investing activities* include transactions that involve lending money and receiving repayment, acquiring and selling property, and equipment, and acquiring and selling long-term investments. The most common cash inflows from and cash outflows for investing activities are:

1. Receipts from selling property, plant, and equipment
2. Receipts from selling investments in stocks and debt securities (e.g., bonds)
3. Payments for purchases of property, plant, and equipment
4. Payments for investments in stocks and debt securities

The **cash flows from financing activities** section includes all cash inflows and cash outflows involved in the financing activities transactions of the company. *Financing activities* include transactions involving obtaining resources from stockholders and paying them dividends, as well as obtaining resources from creditors and repaying the amounts borrowed. The most common cash inflows from and cash outflows for financing activities are:

1. Receipts from the issuance of debt securities (e.g., bonds, mortgages, and notes)
2. Receipts from the issuance of stocks
3. Payments of dividends
4. Payments to retire debt securities
5. Payments to acquire or retire stock (e.g., treasury stock or redeemable preferred stock)

The statement of cash flows of the Martin Company for 1993 is shown in Exhibit 2–10, using the *indirect* method for the computation of net cash flow from operating activities. The net increase in cash of $10,300 is reconciled to the cash in the balance sheets at the beginning and end of 1993.

EXHIBIT 2–10

MARTIN COMPANY
Statement of Cash Flows
For Year Ended December 31, 1993

Cash flows from operating activities		
Net income	$68,500	
Adjustments for differences between income flows and cash flows from operating activities:		
Add: Depreciation expense	13,600	
Amortization expense	2,000	
Bond discount amortization	1,100	
Decrease in prepaid items	400	
Increase in salaries payable	700	
Increase in income taxes payable	2,200	
Increase in deferred income taxes	900	
Less: Increase in accounts receivable (net)	(1,800)	
Increase in inventories	(7,300)	
Decrease in accounts payable	(2,600)	
Decrease in advances from customers	(1,300)	
Net cash flow from operating activities		$76,400
Cash flows from investing activities		
Purchase of building	$(73,900)	
Purchase of investment in bonds	(5,000)	
Proceeds from sale of land, at cost	9,000	
Net cash used by investing activities		(69,900)
Cash flows from financing activities		
Payment of dividends	$(14,200)	
Payment of mortgage payable	(8,000)	
Proceeds from issuance of common stock	26,000	
Net cash provided by financing activities		3,800
Net increase in cash		$10,300
Plus: cash balance, January 1, 1993		8,000
Cash balance, December 31, 1993		$18,300

The alternative way of reporting cash flows from operating activities is the *direct method*. This method has the advantage of separately reporting the operating cash inflows from the operating cash outflows, which may be useful in estimating future cash flows. The most common cash inflows from and cash outflows for operating activites are:

Operating Cash Inflows

1. Collections from customers
2. Interest and dividends collected

Operating Cash Outflows

1. Payments to suppliers and employees

2. Payments of interest

3. Payments of income taxes

If the Martin Company had used the direct method *instead* of the indirect method, the operating cash flows section of Exhibit 2–10 would have been as follows:

Cash inflows		
Collections from customers	$254,100	
Interest and dividends collected	3,800	
Cash inflows from operating activities		$257,900
Cash outflows		
Payments to suppliers and employees	$140,600	
Payments of interest	17,200	
Payments of income taxes	23,700	
Cash outflows for operating activities		(181,500)
Net cash provided by operating activities		$76,400

Note that the $76,400 reported as the net cash provided by operating activities is the same under the direct and indirect methods; only the approach to determining the amount is different. The remainder of the statement of cash flows is the same under either method. The direct and indirect methods are fully explained in Chapter 12.

◼ RELATIONSHIPS AMONG THE THREE FINANCIAL STATEMENTS

The relationships among the three financial statements are illustrated in Exhibit 2–11. In Chapter 1, assets, liabilities, and stockholders' equity that constitute the balance sheet were discussed. The other two statements, discussed in this chapter, are links between two of the categories included in the balance sheet. The income statement, less the dividends paid, is the link between the beginning and ending retained earnings for the period. The cash flow statement is the link between the beginning and ending cash for the period. Obviously there are links between all the beginning and ending balances in the balance sheet, but these two are supported by separate statements because of their perceived importance to users.

All transactions affect the balance sheet. However, some transactions affect the income statement as well as the balance sheet (e.g., a credit sale), some affect the cash flow statement as well as the balance sheet (e.g., the collection of cash from a credit sale), and some affect all three statements (e.g., a cash sale). An understanding of which transactions affect which financial statements is, of course, essential to the user of those statements.

◼ OTHER DISCLOSURE ISSUES

All the relevant financial information pertaining to a company's activities cannot be disclosed directly in the body of the financial statements because certain items do not meet the recognition criteria discussed earlier. As indicated throughout

EXHIBIT 2–11   Relationships among the three financial statements

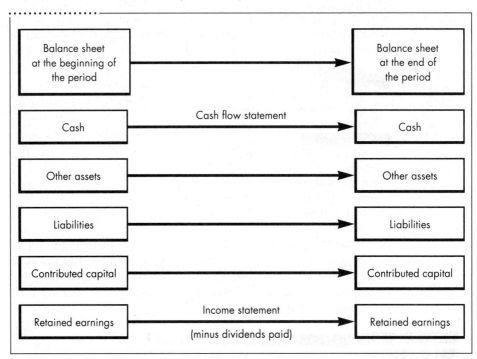

the discussions of the financial statements, many disclosures may be made in the notes accompanying the financial statements. Other significant disclosure issues are discussed next.

Summary of Accounting Policies

A knowledge of the accounting practices and methods used by a company is necessary to understand the content of the financial statements. For this reason generally accepted accounting principles require the disclosure of certain information in the annual report presented to external users.

When financial statements are presented, "a description of all significant accounting policies of the reporting entity should be included as an integral part of the financial statements."[6] The disclosure should encompass principles relating to revenue and expense recognition, particularly when these principles and methods involve (1) a selection from existing acceptable alternatives, (2) principles and methods peculiar to the industry in which the company operates, and (3) unusual or innovative applications of generally accepted accounting principles. Examples cited include, among others, those policies related to the basis for consolidation, depreciation methods, amortization of intangibles, inventory

. . . .

[6]"Disclosure of Accounting Policies," *APB Opinion No. 22* (New York: AICPA, 1972), par 8.

pricing, recognition of profits on long-term contracts, and revenue recognition from franchise and leasing operations. Although allowing for flexibility, it is suggested that the disclosure is particularly useful when made in a separate *Summary of Significant Accounting Policies* preceding the notes to the financial statements or as the initial note. This summary is included in the financial statements of General Motors and Nike in Appendix A.

Interim Reports

Corporations whose stock is publicly traded are required by the Securities and Exchange Commission as well as by the stock exchange on which their stock is traded to issue quarterly financial statements (Form 10-Q). These statements rarely are as comprehensive as those contained in the annual report (Form 10-K). In fact, in many instances only a condensed income statement is presented. The generally accepted accounting principles for interim reports focus primarily on the resolution of problems arising from revenue and expense recognition *within* the annual accounting period and upon the minimum necessary disclosures for a fair presentation of the firm's activities.[7] The requirements are discussed in greater detail in Chapter 14.

Segment Reporting

Companies that do business in more than one industry are now required to report on revenue, income, and asset data about each significant industry segment. Companies are also required to report on their foreign operations, major customers, and export sales.[8] Information on a segment must be reported if the segment contributes 10% or more of a company's total revenue, operating profit or loss, or identifiable assets. The required disclosures for each significant segment include such items as (1) **revenues** (*excluding* general corporate revenues such as interest revenue), (2) **pretax operating profit or loss,** which is defined as revenues less all direct and allocable operating expenses (*excluding* general corporate expenses such as interest expense and income taxes), and (3) **identifiable assets** (excluding general corporate assets). The revenues, pretax operating profits, and identifiable assets are combined and reported, respectively, for any insignificant industry segments. These segment totals must be *reconciled* to the total revenues, income before income taxes, and assets of the entire company.

Although the segment information may be reported directly on the face of the financial statements, most companies make the disclosure in the notes or in separate schedules. General Motors, whose financial statements are presented in Appendix A, discloses its segment information in a separate schedule. Segment reporting is discussed more fully in Chapter 14, along with the disclosures of Nike.

....

[7] "Interim Financial Reporting," *APB Opinion No. 28* (New York: AICPA, 1973).
[8] "Financial Reporting for Segments of a Business Enterprise," *FASB Statement of Financial Accounting Standards No. 14* (Stamford, Conn.: FASB, 1976), par. 3.

EXHIBIT 2–12   Related party disclosure

....

CONSOLIDATED PRODUCTS, INC.
Notes to Consolidated Financial Statements (in part)
Related Party Transactions

Kelley & Partners, Ltd. owns 538,810 shares or 14% of the Company at September 27, 1989. Additionally, certain partners, who also serve as officers and/or directors of the Company, individually control 990,560 shares or 26% of the Company's outstanding stock at September 27, 1989.

Kelley & Partners, Ltd. leases three restaurant properties to Consolidated Specialty Restaurants, Inc. The lease agreements expire in June 2000 with annual rental amounts aggregating approximately $271,000. The discounted values of that portion of the lease obligations related to the buildings are being accounted for as capital leases (the capital leases and related obligations approximate $868,000 and $1,068,000, respectively, at September 27, 1989).

The Company purchased certain products aggregating $454,000 in 1989, $397,000 in 1988 and $381,000 in 1987 from a supplier whose majority shareholder and another officer are directors and officers of the Company, as well as managing general partners of Kelley & Partners, Ltd. These products were purchased at prices and terms no less favorable to the Company than would have been available in the absence of the relationship described.

Related Party Transactions

Transactions between related parties frequently occur in the normal course of business. Related parties of a company include its management, its principal owners or immediate families, affiliated companies such as subsidiaries, and trusts for the benefit of employees. Relationships between related parties may enable one of the parties to exercise influence over the other so that it is given preferential treatment. To provide sufficient information for external users to understand a company's financial statements, certain disclosures by the company are required. For each related party these include (1) the nature of the relationship involved, (2) a description of the transactions, (3) the dollar amounts of the transactions, and (4) any amounts due to or from the related party on the balance sheet date.[9] An example of such a disclosure is shown in Exhibit 2–12.

Comparative Financial Statements

The illustrations in Exhibits 1–6, 2–5, and 2–10, presented the ending balance sheet, the income statement, and the statement of cash flows for a single year. Many external users are interested in comparing the current financial statements

....

[9]"Related Party Disclosures," *FASB Statement of Financial Accounting Standards No. 57* (Stamford, Conn.: FASB, 1982), par. 2.

with those of the previous year. Many times *trend* information will reveal useful insights as to a company's past performance and future success. For this reason nearly all companies present comparative financial statements for the current and preceding accounting periods. Furthermore, the Securities and Exchange Commission (SEC) requires comparative balance sheets for *two* years and comparative income statements and statements of cash flows for *three* years. In a supplemental schedule most companies will present a summary of important accounting information for, say, the past 10 years. General Motors presents comparative financial statements as well as a supplemental schedule, as may be seen in Appendix A. The SEC also requires *specific* disclosures for a *five-year period*. These include net sales or operating revenues, net income and related earnings per share, total assets, long-term obligations and redeemable stock, and cash dividends declared per share. The SEC encourages the inclusion of other information that will help users understand and highlight trends.

Management's Discussion

Management must include a discussion and analysis of the company's financial condition, changes in financial condition, and results of operations. The discussion is intended to provide information that does not clearly appear in the financial statements but is useful in evaluating cash flows from operations and from outside sources. The major features should include specific information about liquidity and capital resources, a narrative discussion of the impact of inflation on sales and on income from continuing operations, explanations of material changes in financial statement items between years, and known events and uncertainties expected to affect future operations. Other kinds of "forward-looking" information (e.g., forecasts or plans) are encouraged but not required. These items are discussed in Chapter 14.

Common Stock Market Prices and Dividends

The principal trading markets for the company's common stock, the high and low market prices for each quarter in the last two years, the approximate number of stockholders, the dividends paid in the last two years, and any dividend restrictions must all be disclosed.

Miscellaneous Disclosures

In addition to the disclosures discussed throughout this chapter, numerous other disclosures are necessary to provide adequate information concerning a company's activities. These include information about such items as the company's stock option, pension, and insurance plans, long-term lease and purchase commitments, long-term debt, bond indenture provisions, and notes receivable and payable provisions. Specific disclosure requirements are discussed as we address each topic in the remaining chapters.

■ REPORTING TECHNIQUES

Numerous reporting techniques are used in the presentation of the annual report. The major ones relating to the financial statement presentations are discussed in this section.

Statement Format

The formats of the financial statements for a particular company depend on its size, the industry in which it operates, certain regulatory requirements, and tradition. Users of financial statements should not expect that each company will use an identical or even similar format. The user should be able to understand the content of financial statements without being confused by alternative formats.

Two alternative formats for the income statement were discussed earlier in the chapter. Three basic formats are generally used for the balance sheet: (1) the report form, (2) the account form, and (3) the financial position form. The **report form** is used by most companies. Here the balance sheet takes a vertical format. The assets are listed first and the liabilities and stockholders' equity items are listed in sequential order directly below the assets. In contrast, the **account form** of the balance sheet is organized in a horizontal fashion, with the assets listed on the left-hand side and liabilities and stockholders' equity items listed on the right-hand side. This is the format used in Exhibit 1–6. In the seldom used **financial position form,** current assets and current liabilities are vertically listed first to derive the working capital. The remaining assets are added and the remaining liabilities deducted to derive the residual stockholders' equity. Of 600 companies surveyed, the account form, report form, and financial position form are used by 392, 205, and 3 companies, respectively.[10]

Combined Amounts

To reduce the size of the financial statements, certain related amounts are often combined, as illustrated earlier and in Chapter 1. It is *not* proper, however, to offset asset and liability accounts (except in a few special circumstances), even though they may be related. For instance, the amount in a special sinking fund to retire long-term bonds would not be offset against the bonds payable balance.

Rounding

Rounding is usually undertaken to increase readability and to reduce the likelihood that users will attach more precision to the numbers than is warranted. In fact, many major companies round to the nearest thousand or million dollars. In the General Motors and Nike financial statements, the amounts have been rounded as indicated.

· · · · · · · · · · · · · · · · · · · ·

[10] *Accounting Trends and Techniques, op cit.,* p. 101.

Notes, Supporting Schedules, and Parenthetical Notations

Additional information not included in the accounts on the financial statements is disclosed by means of a note, supporting schedule, or parenthetical notation.

The **notes** (or *footnotes*) accompanying the financial statements are extremely useful ways of presenting additional information. Notes usually contain narrative discussion, additional monetary amounts, and sometimes supplemental schedules.

Supporting schedules may be freestanding or part of the notes. A supporting schedule may complement an entire financial statement (such as the schedule of changes in stockholders' equity) or may explain a summary amount on a specific financial statement (such as an itemization of inventories). Supporting schedules are discussed and illustrated throughout the text.

Parenthetical notations following specific accounts are used to explain such items as the method of valuation (for example, cost, lower of cost or market), the cost flow assumption (for example, average cost), or to cross-reference certain related asset and liability accounts (for example, bond sinking fund and bonds payable).

■ ILLUSTRATIVE STATEMENTS

The actual financial statements and accompanying notes of General Motors for the year ended December 31, 1989, are shown in Appendix A. In addition, many excerpts from the annual report of Nike, Inc., are included throughout this book. The company's financial statements and certain other items are also included in Appendix A. Although a complete understanding may be currently beyond the scope of the reader, particular attention should be paid to each statement's format and content, the notes accompanying the reports, and the audit report (discussed in Chapter 4).

■ ANALYSIS OF TRANSACTIONS AFFECTING THE INCOME STATEMENT

To illustrate the accounting for revenue and expense transactions (and related items), we continue with the Wells Company example introduced in Chapter 1. A review of Exhibit 1–12 may be helpful; a dividend payment is also included in this example.

During February 1993, the Wells Company entered into eight transactions, each of which is recorded in Exhibit 2–13. Since this exhibit covers the month of February, it begins with the ending amounts that resulted from the transactions recorded in January in Exhibit 1–12.

On February 1, the company purchased 1,000 units of product X for resale to customers. Each unit cost $50 for a total of $50,000, and the company agreed to pay the full amount in 30 days. Because the units are expected to provide future economic benefits to the company, an asset — Inventory — is recorded. Since Wells agreed to pay for the inventory in the future, it also has a liability

EXHIBIT 2–13

WELLS COMPANY
Analysis of Transactions

	Cash		Land		Building		Office Supplies		Office Equipment		Accounts Receivable		Inventory	=	Accounts Payable
		+		+		+		+		+		+		=	LIABILITIES
Balances 1/31/93	$106,500	+	$30,000	+	$150,000	+	$7,000	+	$26,000	+	$4,000			=	$ 3,500
2/1/93	+12,000												+$50,000		+50,000
2/3/93															
2/7/93	+4,000										− 4,000		− 5,000		
2/10/93											+ 24,000				
2/15/93	− 3,500												− 10,000		− 3,500
2/20/93	+ 8,000		−5,000												
2/28/93	− 7,200														
2/28/93	− 1,000														
2/28/93															+ 1,700
2/28/93	−10,000														
Balances 2/28/93	$108,800	+	$25,000	+	$150,000	+	$7,000	+	$26,000	+	$24,000	+	$35,000	=	$51,700

(continued)

EXHIBIT 2–13 *(continued)*

		Contributed Capital		(Revenues and Gains)		(Expenses and Losses)				Dividends
						STOCKHOLDERS' EQUITY				
Notes Payable	+	Common Stock	Additional Paid-in Capital	+ Sales	Gain on Sale of Land	− Cost of Goods Sold	Salaries Expense	Telephone Expense	Utilities Expense	− Dividends Paid
+$20,000	+	$10,000	+ $290,000							
				+$12,000		−$ 5,000				
				+ 24,000		− 10,000				
					+$3,000					
							−$7,200			
								−$1,000		
									−$1,700	
										−$10,000
+$20,000	+	$10,000	+ $290,000	+ $36,000	+ $3,000	− $15,000	− $7,200	− $1,000	− $1,700	− $10,000

Note: Increases in expenses and dividends paid are reductions of stockholders' equity.

— Accounts Payable — for $50,000. For each transaction discussed, note that the accounting equation remains in balance.

On February 3, the Wells Company sold 100 units of inventory for $120 each for a total of $12,000. The customer paid cash. The asset — Cash — is increased by the amount received, $12,000. Since the company has an inflow of assets from delivering goods to a customer, it also recognizes a revenue — Sales — of $12,000. Stockholders' equity is increased by $12,000 because, as discussed earlier, revenue is a component of stockholders' equity. In other words, the assets of the company have increased by $12,000 and the increase has benefited the owners of the company.

As part of the sale the company has given up ownership of the 100 units of inventory that it sold and therefore has to reduce its inventory by the cost of those units. Each unit was purchased for $50, and therefore the asset — Inventory — must be reduced by $5,000 (100 × $50). Since the company has an outflow of assets from delivering goods to its customers, it also recognizes an expense — Cost of Goods Sold — of $5,000. Shareholders' equity is reduced by $5,000 because, as discussed earlier, an expense is a component of stockholders' equity. In other words, the assets of the company have decreased by $5,000 and the decrease has to be absorbed by the owners of the company. However, if we look at the net effect of the sale, the assets and stockholders' equity have both increased by $7,000 ($12,000 − $5,000). It is important not to become confused about the recording of the cost of goods sold in Exhibit 2–13. We have shown the $5,000 as a *reduction* in stockholders' equity because there is an *increase* in Cost of Goods Sold (i.e., all expenses are reductions in stockholders' equity). Therefore, a "minus" for an expense component of stockholders' equity is an increase in an expense.

On February 7, the Wells Company received a check for $4,000 from James Baker for the office equipment he had purchased on January 28. The asset — Cash — is increased by $4,000, and the asset recorded in January — Accounts Receivable — is decreased by $4,000. Note that there was no revenue recognized in January because the company is not in the business of selling office equipment. Also, no gain or loss was recognized because the equipment was sold for the same amount as it had cost the company.

On February 10 the Wells Company sold 200 units of inventory for $120 each to customers who agreed to pay in 30 days. The company has an economic resource that is expected to provide future cash inflows when the customers pay. Therefore, the asset — Accounts Receivable — is increased by $24,000 (200 × $120). Because the company has an inflow of assets from delivering goods to customers, it also recognizes a revenue — Sales — of $24,000. Once again, remember that the revenue is a component of, and an addition to, stockholders' equity.

As before, the company has to record the reduction of $10,000 (200 × $50) in the asset — Inventory — because the company no longer owns the 200 units sold. The company also recognizes an expense — Cost of Goods Sold — of $10,000 because the outflow of the inventory resulted from delivering goods to customers. Again, remember that a minus recorded in cost of goods sold is a reduction in stockholders' equity but an increase in an expense. The accounting equation therefore remains in balance because assets and stockholders' equity have both been reduced.

At this point, it is desirable to review three of the transactions we have discussed. On February 3 and 7 the company received cash. However, only one receipt was recognized as a revenue because it resulted from a delivery of goods to a customer while the other was an exchange for another asset — Accounts Receivable. On February 3 and 10 the company recognized revenue. However, in only one transaction was cash received, the other being a credit sale with Accounts Receivable being recorded. Thus, it may be seen that revenue recognition *may or may not* accompany the receipt of cash. As discussed earlier in the chapter, revenue is defined as the inflow of assets or the decrease in liabilities from providing goods and services to customers. That definition does not mention cash.

To continue with the Wells Company transactions, on February 15 the company issued a check for $3,500 to City Supply Company to complete payment for the supplies purchased in January. The asset — Cash — is decreased, and the liability — Accounts Payable — is decreased by $3,500.

On February 20 the Wells Company sold a portion of the land it owned. The cost of the portion sold was $5,000 and the agreed selling price was $8,000 cash. The asset — Cash — is increased by $8,000, and the asset — Land — is decreased by $5,000. The increase in the net assets of $3,000 ($8,000 − $5,000) is from a peripheral or incidental transaction (the company is not in the business of buying and selling land) and is therefore recognized as a gain. The accounting equation remains in balance because both net assets and stockholders' equity have increased by $3,000. In contrast, if the company were in the business of buying and selling land, it would have recognized a revenue of $8,000 and an expense of $5,000 instead of the net gain of $3,000. Alternatively, if the company had sold the land for $4,000, it would have recognized a loss (and therefore a decrease in income and stockholders' equity) of $1,000 ($5,000 − $4,000).

On February 28, the Wells Company issued paychecks of $1,200 to each of its six employees for their monthly salaries. The asset — Cash — is decreased by $7,200 (6 × $1,200). Since the outflow of assets results from the activities of the company in providing goods and services to its customers, an expense — Salaries Expense — is recorded as a reduction in stockholders' equity of $7,200. Again, remember that the reduction in stockholders' equity is an increase in an expense.

Also on February 28, the company paid a bill from the phone company for $1,000. The asset — Cash — is decreased by $1,000. Again the outflow of cash resulted from the activities of the company in providing goods and services to its customers, and therefore an expense — Telephone Expense — is recorded as a reduction of stockholders' equity for $1,000.

On February 28, the company also received a utility bill of $1,700 for February. The bill will be paid in March. The company increases a liability — Accounts Payable — for $1,700 because it has an obligation to pay that amount. It also records an expense — Utilities Expense — for $1,700 as a reduction in stockholders' equity because a liability has been incurred in providing goods and services to its customers.

At this point, it is again desirable to review several of the transactions we have discussed. On February 15 and 28, the company paid cash. However, only the payments on February 28 were recorded as expenses because they resulted from the outflow of assets in the providing of goods and services to customers. The payment on February 15 was to reduce a liability — Accounts Payable. On February 3, 10, and 28 the company recognized expenses. However, for only two of the expenses recognized on February 28 was there a cash outflow. For the expenses recognized on February 3 and 10, there was a decrease in an asset — Inventory — while a liability was increased when the Utilities Expense was recognized on February 28. Thus it may be seen that expense recognition *may or may not* accompany the payment of cash. As discussed earlier in the chapter, an expense is defined as the outflow of assets or the increase in liabilities from providing goods and services to customers. That definition does not mention cash.

Finally on February 28, the Wells Company paid a dividend of $1 per share on each of the 10,000 shares issued in January. The asset — Cash — is decreased by $10,000. The payment of a dividend is *not* an expense because it does *not* have anything to do with providing goods and services to its customers. Instead, it is a voluntary distribution to the owners of the company and therefore is a reduction in stockholders' equity — Dividends Paid. Both expenses and dividends are reductions in stockholders' equity, but only expenses are included in the computation of net income.

■ PREPARATION OF THE FINANCIAL STATEMENTS

After recording the transactions, the financial statements are prepared. The income statement is prepared first because the amount of net income (or loss) increases (or decreases) the stockholders' equity on the balance sheet. Next, the schedule of changes in stockholders' equity is prepared as a supporting schedule to the balance sheet. Finally the balance sheet is prepared.

Income Statement

The income statement summarizes the earnings activities of a company for the accounting period. The Wells Company income statement for the month of February is shown in Exhibit 2–14. The company has only one category of revenue, which totals $36,000. The cost of goods sold of $15,000 is subtracted to compute the gross profit of $21,000. It has three categories of operating expenses, totaling $9,900. In addition, the company has a gain of $3,000 (and no losses). The net income for February of $14,100 is the revenue less the total expenses plus the gain. Note that dividends are *not* included in the income statement

EXHIBIT 2–14

WELLS COMPANY

Income Statement
For Month Ended February 28, 1993

Sales		$36,000
Cost of goods sold		(15,000)
Gross profit		$21,000
Operating expenses		
Salaries expense	$7,200	
Telephone expense	1,000	
Utilities expense	1,700	
Total operating expenses		(9,900)
Operating income		$11,100
Other revenues and expenses		
Gain on sale of land		3,000
Net income		$14,100

EXHIBIT 2–15

WELLS COMPANY
Schedule of Changes in Stockholders' Equity
For Month Ended February 28, 1993

	Common Stock $1 par	Additional Paid-in Cap- ital	Retained Earnings	Total
Balance, 1/31/93	$10,000	$290,000		$300,000
Net income			$14,100	14,100
Cash dividends paid			(10,000)	(10,000)
Balance, 2/28/93	$10,000	$290,000	$ 4,100	$304,100

because they are not related to providing goods and services to customers. Instead, they are transactions with stockholders.

Schedule of Changes in Stockholders' Equity

There are only two items that affect the stockholders' equity of the Wells Company during February, as shown in Exhibit 2–15. The net income of $14,100 increases the balance in Retained Earnings, and the Dividends Paid reduces the balance by $10,000. The ending balances of stockholders' equity are carried to the balance sheet. Alternatively, a Statement of Retained Earnings could have been prepared, as discussed in Chapter 1.

EXHIBIT 2–16

···················

WELLS COMPANY
Balance Sheet
February 28, 1993

ASSETS			LIABILITIES		
Current assets			Current liabilities		
Cash	$108,800		Accounts payable	$ 51,700	
Accounts receivable	24,000		Notes payable	20,000	
Office supplies	7,000		Total current		
Inventory	35,000		liabilities		$ 71,700
Total current assets		$174,800			
Property, plant, and equipment					
Land	$ 25,000		**STOCKHOLDERS' EQUITY**		
Building	150,000		Common stock	$ 10,000	
Office equipment	26,000		Additional paid-in		
Total property, plant and equipment		201,000	capital	290,000	
			Retained earnings	4,100	
			Total stockholders' equity		304,100
			Total liabilities and		
Total assets		$375,800	stockholders' equity		$375,800

Balance Sheet

The balance sheet for the Wells Company on February 28 is shown in Exhibit 2–16. There is one additional current asset — Inventory — and total assets are $375,800. The liabilities total $71,700, and the total stockholders' equity is $304,100 from the Schedule of Changes in Stockholders' Equity.

Summary of the Financial Statements

After preparing the financial statements, it is often helpful to describe the results. Such a description may help remove some of the mystery from all the accounting concepts we have developed so far. For example, a description of the Wells Company's financial statements might be as follows. In February 1993, the Wells Company sold goods to its customers for $36,000. The cost of the items sold was $15,000, resulting in a gross profit of $21,000. Other costs of the period of $9,900 were incurred to generate those sales and therefore were also recognized as expenses. Thus, the company had an operating income of $11,100. The company also sold land for $3,000 more than it cost and therefore had a gain of $3,000. The company earned a net income of $14,100 from these transactions.

Of this amount, it paid dividends of $10,000 to its shareholders, thereby leaving $4,100 of the profit retained in the company. At the end of February, the company had four assets with a total cost of $174,800, which it expected to dispose of or use up within one year or the normal operating cycle, whichever is longer. It also had three items of property, plant, and equipment with a total cost of $201,000. The total assets of $375,800 have been financed in two ways. The company borrowed $71,700, and the stockholders financed the remainder by investing $300,000 in the company and allowing income of $4,100 to be retained in the company.

The alert reader will have noticed that the Wells Company example is incomplete. There is a need to recognize depreciation on the building and office equipment, the use of office supplies, interest on the note, and the income tax expense for the period. Each of these adjustments is discussed in the next chapter, along with an explanation of a basic accounting system used to generate these financial statements.

QUESTIONS

1. Discuss (a) return on investment, (b) risk, (c) financial flexibility, and (d) operating capability.

2. List the specific conceptual guidelines for reporting (displaying) revenues, expenses, gains, and losses.

3. Define revenues. What operating activities are likely to result in revenues?

4. What is realization? What is recognition?

5. What two criteria must ordinarily be met before revenues are recognized? When is revenue usually recognized?

6. Why might revenue be recognized at a time other than the sale?

7. Define expenses. Of what are expenses a measurement?

8. What are three principles for recognizing the expenses to be matched against revenues? Give examples of expenses that would be recognized under each principle.

9. List the reasons why external users use information about a company's (a) income and its components, and (b) cash flows.

10. What is cost? When is a cost an asset and when is it an expense?

11. Define gains and losses. Give examples of three different types of gains and losses.

12. Why do companies prepare condensed income statements? What items are likely to be aggregated on the income statement?

13. What items are included in the cost of goods manufactured, and how is the cost of goods manufactured computed?

14. What items would be listed as other revenues and expenses?

15. Where is earnings per share disclosed in the financial statements?

16. What is a statement of cash flows? What information should the statement provide in regard to a company's liquidity, financial flexibility, and operating capability?

17. What items of information must be disclosed in the financial statements for each significant industry segment of a business?

18. What are the major financial statements and what information does each summarize?

19. What accounting policies should be disclosed in the notes accompanying the financial statements? Why is this disclosure important?

20. Why are comparative financial statements important?

PROBLEMS AND CASES

. . . .

21. Financial Statement Interrelationship. Draw a diagram which shows the interrelationship between the beginning balance sheet, income statement, retained earnings statement, and ending balance sheet.

22. Income Statement. On June 30, 1993, the Robinskon Consulting Company showed the following revenue and expense amounts for June:

Consulting service revenues	$2,500
Salaries expense	1,100
Telephone expense	125
Office supplies expense	25
Utilities expense	90
Rent expense	350
Depreciation expense: office equipment	15

Required Prepare the June 1993 income statement for the Robinskon Consulting Company.

23. Income Statement. The Benzer Company has the following items and amounts on February 28, 1993 (the end of its monthly accounting period):

Cash	$13,744
Supplies	5,000
Land	2,000
Building	11,500
Accumulated depreciation: building	530
Equipment	10,000
Accumulated depreciation: equipment	320
Accounts payable	1,560
Common stock	39,000
Dividends paid	1,000
Service revenues	9,000
Salaries expense	4,000
Supplies expense	1,250
Telephone expense	45
Utilities expense	785
Depreciation expense: building	54
Depreciation expense: equipment	32

Required Prepare the February 1993 income statement for the Benzer Company.

24. Stockholders' Equity Account. Four independent cases related to the stockholders' equity of the Cox Company are as follows:

Case	Stockholders' Equity May 1, 1993	Net Income May 1993	Dividends Paid in May	Stockholders' Equity May 31, 1993
1	$ A	$2,700	$1,500	$27,700
2	37,000	B	1,720	40,750
3	28,200	900	C	24,800
4	34,000	1,820	1,500	D

Required Determine the amounts of A, B, C, and D.

25. Assets and Expenses. During the month of October the Wilson Company incurred the following costs:

1. Paid $400 to an insurance company for a two-year comprehensive insurance policy on the company's building.
2. Purchased office supplies costing $770 on account from Bailey's Office Supplies.
3. Paid the telephone company $110 for telephone service during the month of October.
4. Paid the $770 owed to Bailey's Office Supplies.
5. Paid $1,200 in dividends.
6. Found that of the $770 of office supplies purchased in item 2 above, only $700 remained at October 31.

Required Which of the above transactions would be recorded as expenses by the Wilson Company for the month of October? Explain.

26. Revenues. Gertz Rent-A-Car is in the business of providing customers with quality rental automobiles at low rates. The following transactions were engaged in by the company during the month of March.

1. J. Gertz purchased for $1,600 additional shares issued by the company.
2. Collected $1,050 in car rental fees for the month of March.
3. Borrowed $6,000 from the 1st National Bank to be repaid in one year.
4. Completed arrangements to provide fleet service to a local company at a price of $18,000 per year; this amount was collected in advance.

Required Which of the above transactions would be recorded as revenues by Gertz Rent-A-Car for the month of March? Explain.

27. Financial Statements. On September 30, 1993, the bookkeeper of Kerrel Lawn Service Company prepared the following amounts (the income statement amounts reflect only September transactions):

Cash	$ 1,240
Supplies	852
Prepaid rent	1,375
Land	13,000
Trucks	28,900
Accumulated depreciation: trucks	105
Lawn equipment	7,920
Accumulated depreciation: lawn equipment	82
Accounts payable	1,300
Notes payable	6,400
Common stock	20,000
Retained earnings	23,200
Dividends paid	1,250
Lawn service revenues	5,364
Salaries expense	715
Gas and oil expense	300
Supplies expense	100
Telephone expense	67
Utilities expense	270
Rent expense	275
Depreciation expense: trucks	105
Depreciation expense: lawn equipment	82

Required 1. Prepare an income statement for the month ended September 30, 1993.

2. Prepare a statement of retained earnings for the month ended September 30, 1993.

3. Prepare a September 30, 1993, balance sheet.

28. Cost, Expense, and Loss. During a meeting of the Board of Directors of Sebal Manufacturing Corporation, one director asked, "What are the precise meanings of the terms *cost, expense,* and *loss*? These terms seem sometimes to identify similar items and other times dissimilar items."

Required 1. Explain the meanings of the terms (a) *cost*, (b) *expense*, and (c) *loss* as used for financial reporting in conformity with generally accepted accounting principles. In your explanation, discuss the distinguishing characteristics of the terms and their similarities and interrelationships.

2. Classify each of the following items as a cost, expense, loss, or other category, and explain how the classification of each item may change:

   a. Cost of goods sold
   b. Bad debts expense
   c. Depreciation expense for plant machinery
   d. Organization costs
   e. Spoiled goods
   (AICPA adapted)

29. Cost and Expense Recognition. A user of accounting information must be familiar with the concepts involved in determining earnings of a company. The amount of earnings reported for a company is dependent on the proper recognition, in general, of revenue and expense for a given time period. In some situations costs are recognized as expenses at the time of product sale; in other situations guidelines have been developed for recognizing costs as expenses or losses by other criteria.

Required 1. Explain the rationale for recognizing costs as expenses at the time of product sale.

2. What is the rationale underlying the appropriateness of treating costs as expenses of a period instead of assigning the costs to an asset? Explain.

3. Some expenses are assigned to specific accounting periods on the basis of systematic and rational allocation of asset cost. Explain the underlying rationale for recognizing expenses on this basis. *(AICPA adapted)*

30. Accrual Accounting. Generally accepted accounting principles require the use of accruals and deferrals in the determination of income.

Required How does accrual accounting affect the determination of income? Include in your discussion what constitutes an accrual and a deferral, and give appropriate examples of each. *(AICPA adapted)*

31. Capital Maintenance. At the beginning of 1981 the Hill family organized the Hill Corporation and issued 8,000 shares of stock to family members for $20 per share. During 1984 it issued an additional 1,600 shares of stock for $25 per share to family members. The 9,600 shares were held by the family until the liquidation of the corporation at the end of 1993. At that time the corporate assets were sold for $600,000, and the $50,000 of corporate liabilities were paid off. The remainder was returned to stockholders. During the 13 years of operation the corporation had a volatile operating life. It started out slowly but then increased its activities in later years. It had operated in several industry segments, being quite successful in some, not so successful in others. It had survived a major earthquake, but not without incurring significant losses. The corporation paid out dividends of $100,000 during its lifetime.

You are a member of the Hill family who has just inherited a sizable fortune from one of your relatives. Although you were quite young during the operating life of the Hill Corporation, you are considering establishing and investing in a new corporation operating in some of the same lines of business, providing the corporation would be profitable. You have just received your undergraduate accounting degree and find on investigation that, with the exception of the above information, all the corporate accounting records were destroyed in a recent fire. You have been told that these records were sketchy at best, but that a capital maintenance approach to income measurement might yield some useful information.

Required Compute the lifetime income of the Hill Corporation and comment on what additional information you would desire before making your investment decision.

32. Framework of Income Statement. The following is an alphabetical list of financial statement items for the Mack Company:

Accounts payable
Accounts receivable
Accumulated depreciation: buildings
 and office equipment
Accumulated depreciation: store and
 delivery equipment
Administrative salaries
Advertising expense
Allowance for doubtful accounts
Bad debts expense
Bonds payable
Buildings
Cash
Cash dividends declared
Common stock, $10 par
Delivery expense
Depreciation expense: buildings and
 office equipment
Depreciation expense: store and
 delivery equipment
Dividend revenue
Dividends payable
Fund to retire long-term bonds
Gain on sale of equipment
Income tax expense
Insurance expense
Interest expense
Interest payable
Interest revenue

Inventory, December 31, 1993
Inventory, January 1, 1993
Investment in securities (long-term)
Loss on sale of office equipment
Miscellaneous office expenses
Miscellaneous sales expenses
Mortgage payable
Office salaries
Office supplies used
Paid-in capital on common stock
Prepaid office supplies
Property tax expense
Purchases
Rent revenue
Retained earnings, January 1, 1993
Salaries payable
Sales
Sales commissions
Sales discounts
Sales returns and allowances
Sales salaries
Service revenues
Unearned rent
Unexpired insurance
Utilities expense

Required Select the appropriate accounts and prepare (ignore amounts):

1. A multiple-step income statement with proper subheadings.

2. A retained earnings statement.

33. **Classifications.** Given the following code letters and components of financial statements, indicate where each item would be reported in the financial statements by using the corresponding code letters.

Code Letter	Component
A	Sales revenues (net)
B	Cost of goods sold
C	Selling expenses
D	General and administrative expenses
E	Other revenues and expenses
F	Additions to retained earnings
G	Deductions from retained earnings
H	Notes to financial statements
I	Ending balance sheet

B 1. Purchases
E 2. Loss on sale of equipment
D 3. Utilities expense
G 4. Cash dividends declared on common stock ✓
d 5. Bad debts expense
C 6. Sales salaries
A 7. Sales discounts
F 8. Net income ✓
IV G 9. Premium on bonds payable
E 10. Gain on sale of land
E 11. Interest expense
C 12. Delivery expense
E 13. Expenses incurred as a result of a strike

H v 14. Summary of accounting policies
E 15. Interest revenue
IV E 16. Additional paid-in capital on common stock
E 17. Loss from write-down of obsolete inventory
d 18. Administrative salaries
A 19. Sales returns
D 20. Depreciation expense for office equipment
C 21. Sales commissions
C 22. Promotion expense
B 23. Merchandise inventory add (beginning)

34. Simple Income Statement. Listed below are selected items and amounts of the Albertson Company as of December 31, 1993:

Purchases (net)	$ 63,000
Inventory, January 1, 1993	20,000
Gain on sale of equipment	5,000
Sales (net)	120,000
Operating expenses	22,000

The inventory on December 31, 1993, is $31,000. Ten thousand shares of common stock have been outstanding the entire year.

Required Assuming a 30% income tax rate, prepare an income statement using (1) a multiple-step format and (2) a single-step format.

35. Simple Income Statement, Manufacturing. Below are selected items and amounts of the Dibb Manufacturing Company on December 31, 1993:

Finished goods inventory, January 1, 1993	$ 75,000
Loss on sale of land	5,000
Cost of goods manufactured	120,000
Sales (net)	213,000
Operating expenses	47,000

The finished goods inventory on December 31, 1993, is $60,000. Twelve thousand shares of common stock were outstanding the entire year.

Required Assuming a 30% income tax rate, prepare an income statement using (1) a multiple-step format and (2) a single-step format.

36. Classifications. Where would each of the following ten items be reported in the financial statements?

1. Sales discounts

2. Depreciation expense on sales equipment

3. Earnings per share

4. Gain on sale of land

5. Administrative salaries

6. Cash dividends on common stock

7. Advertising expense

8. Merchandise inventory (ending)

9. Loss from write-off of obsolete inventory

10. Net income

37. Classifications. Where would each of the following nine items be reported in the financial statements?

1. Loss on sale of equipment

2. Office supplies used

3. Raw materials used

4. Delivery expense

5. Dividend revenue

6. Summary of accounting policies

7. Sales returns and allowances

8. Income tax expense

9. Goods in process inventory (ending)

38. Income Statement and Retained Earnings. The Senger Company presents the following partial list of items and amounts at December 31, 1993:

Retained earnings, January 1, 1993	$ 97,800
Sales (net)	123,000
Interest expense	3,700
Purchases (net)	67,000
Operating expenses	31,900
Inventory, January 1, 1993	18,400
Common stock, $5 par	22,500

The following information is also available for 1993 and is not reflected in the above amounts:

1. The ending inventory is $19,600.

2. The common stock has been outstanding all year. A cash dividend of $1.28 per share was declared and paid.

3. Land was sold at a gain of $7,800.

4. The income tax rate is 30%.

Required 1. Prepare a 1993 multiple-step income statement.

2. Prepare a retained earnings statement.

39. Income Statement and Retained Earnings. The Cobler Manufacturing Company presents the following partial list of items and amounts at December 31, 1993:

Operating expenses	$ 34,800
Dividend revenue	1,000
Retained earnings, January 1, 1993	74,200
Sales (net)	142,600
Common stock, $15 par	45,000
Finished goods inventory, January 1, 1993	26,000
Cost of goods manufactured	79,200

The following information is also available for 1993 and is not reflected in the above amounts:

1. The common stock has been outstanding the entire year. A cash dividend of 84¢ per share was declared and paid.

2. The income tax rate is 30%.

3. The ending finished goods inventory is $27,900.

4. Obsolete raw materials were written off at a loss of $6,600.

Required 1. Prepare a cost of goods sold schedule.

2. Prepare a 1993 single-step income statement.

3. Prepare a retained earnings statement.

40. Partial Income Statement. The following are selected items and amounts of the Rule Company:

Cash	$3,900
Sales returns and allowances	600
Inventory, January 1, 1993	5,200
Sales salaries expense	1,200
Sales revenue	15,800
Accounts payable	6,000
Inventory, December 31, 1993	3,500
Purchases	9,500
Delivery expense	800
Sales discounts	200

Required Prepare a partial income statement through gross profit on sales.

41. Income Statement Calculations. Below is partial information from the Ferdon Company income statements for 1993 and 1994:

	1993	1994
Beginning inventory	$_____ (2)	$_____ (4)
Sales	220,000	_____ (6)
Purchases	118,000	140,000
Ending inventory	48,000	68,000
Sales returns	2,000	3,000
Gross profit	_____ (1)	77,000
Cost of goods sold	108,000	_____ (5)
Expenses	65,000	48,000
Net income	_____ (3)	29,000

Required Fill in the blanks numbered 1 through 6. (*Hint:* It is probably easiest to work through the blanks according to the sequential numbers.)

42. Financial Statements. The following are the items and amounts of the Turtle Company for the year ended December 31, 1993:

Cash	$ 1,200
Accounts receivable (net)	2,400
Inventory, January 1, 1993	1,900
Equipment	5,400
Accumulated depreciation	1,700
Accounts payable	2,400
Salaries payable	300
Income taxes payable	200
Common stock (400 shares)	3,200
Retained earnings	2,700
Dividends distributed	300
Sales revenue	8,000
Purchases	4,700
Selling expenses	1,800
Administrative expenses	600
Income tax expense	200

Required The Turtle Company has determined that its ending inventory on December 31, 1993, is $1,800. Prepare for 1993 in proper form:

1. An income statement

2. A retained earnings statement

3. An ending balance sheet

43. Financial Statements. The following are the items and amounts of the Stern Company on December 31, 1993:

Cash	$ 1,500
Accounts receivable	2,700
Allowance for doubtful accounts	200
Inventory, January 1, 1993	5,100
Prepaid insurance	800
Land	4,240
Buildings and equipment	31,000
Accumulated depreciation	15,000
Accounts payable	3,150
Salaries payable	420
Unearned rent	360
Income taxes payable	2,300
Note payable (due July 1, 1997)	5,000
Interest payable (due July 1, 1997)	750
Common stock (1,500 shares)	9,000
Retained earnings, January 1, 1993	6,870
Dividends distributed	1,200
Sales revenue	35,000
Sales returns	2,200
Rent revenue	1,440
Purchases	18,900
Selling expenses	5,300
Administrative expenses	3,500
Interest expense	750
Income tax expense	2,300

In addition, the company took its annual physical inventory on December 31, 1993. It determined that its ending inventory is $6,500.

Required Prepare the proper form for 1993:

1. The income statement

2. The retained earnings statement

3. The ending balance sheet

44. **Financial Statements.** The following are the items and amounts of the Action Company on December 31, 1993:

Accounts payable	$ 6,500
Accounts receivable	5,400
Accumulated depreciation: buildings	19,000
Accumulated depreciation: equipment	11,000
Additional paid-in capital	14,000
Administrative expenses	6,300
Allowance for doubtful accounts	600
Buildings	40,000
Common stock, $1 par (4,000 shares)	4,000
Cash	3,000

Current income taxes payable	3,800
Dividends distributed	2,400
Equipment	22,000
Income tax expense	3,800
Interest expense	500
Interest payable (due July 1, 1994)	500
Inventory, January 1, 1993	10,200
Land	6,400
Notes payable (due July 1, 1997)	10,000
Purchases	31,000
Rent revenue	2,800
Retained earnings, January 1, 1993	13,800
Sales revenue	59,000
Sales discounts	1,200
Sales returns and allowances	3,000
Selling expenses	9,700
Unearned rent	700
Unexpired insurance	1,600
Wages payable	800

Additional data: The December 31, 1993, ending inventory is $11,200.

Required Prepare the following three items in proper form for 1993:

1. The income statement

2. The retained earnings statement

3. The ending balance sheet

45. **Misclassifications.** The Rox Corporation multiple-step income statement and retained earnings statement for the year ended December 31, 1993, as developed by its bookkeeper, are shown below:

ROX CORPORATION
Revenue Statement
December 31, 1993

Sales (net)		$195,000
Less: dividends declared ($1.50 per common share)		(7,500)
Net revenues		$187,500
Less: selling expenses		(20,800)
Gross profit		$166,700
Less: operating expenses		
Interest expense	$ 4,100	
Cost of goods sold	113,700	
Income tax expense	11,960	
Total operating expenses		(129,760)
Operating income		$ 36,940

Miscellaneous items		
Dividend revenue	$ 1,800	
General and administrative expenses	(24,300)	(22,500)
Net income		$ 14,440

ROX CORPORATION
Retained Earnings Statement
December 31, 1993

Beginning retained earnings	$58,000
Add: net income	14,440
Adjusted retained earnings	$72,440
Less: loss on sale of land	(4,000)
Ending retained earnings	$68,440

You determine that the amounts listed in the statements are correct but, in certain cases, the items are incorrectly classified. No shares of common stock were issued or retired during 1993.

Required 1. Review both statements and indicate where each incorrectly classified item should be classified.

2. Prepare a correct multiple-step income statement.

3. Prepare a correct retained earnings statement.

46. **Misclassifications.** The bookkeeper for the Olson Company prepared the following income statement and retained earnings statement for the year ended December 31, 1993:

OLSON COMPANY
December 31, 1993
Expense and Profits Statement

Sales (net)		$220,000
Less: selling expenses		(19,000)
Net sales		201,000
Add: interest revenue		2,300
Add: gain on sale of equipment		3,200
Gross sales revenues		$206,500
Less: costs of operations		
Costs of goods sold	$125,100	
Dividend costs ($0.50 per share for 8,300 common shares)	4,150	
		(129,250)
Taxable revenues		$ 77,250
Less: income tax expense		(19,280)
Net income		$ 57,970
Miscellaneous deductions:		
administrative expenses		(29,800)
Net revenues		$ 28,170

OLSON COMPANY
Retained Revenues Statement
For Year Ended December 31, 1993

Beginning retained earnings	$69,000
Add: Net revenues	28,170
	$97,170
	(3,400)
Less: Interest expense	
Ending retained earnings	$93,770

The amounts are correct but, in certain instances, the items are incorrectly classified.

Required Prepare a corrected multiple-step income statement and a retained earnings statement.

47. Effects on Accounting Equation. The Both Plumbing Company entered into the following transactions during the month of May:

May 4	Installed plumbing in new house under construction; contractor agreed to pay contract price of $1,600 in 30 days.
15	Made plumbing repairs for customer and collected $45 for services performed.
28	Paid $79 for May telephone bill.
31	Paid $800 to employees for May salaries.
31	Received $100 utility bill, to be paid in early June.

Required Record the effects of each transaction on the accounting equation.

48. Effects on Accounting Equation. The Aline Taxi Service entered into the following transactions during the month of September.

Sept. 1	Paid $300 rent on garage for the month of September.
15	Cash receipts for taxi fares for the first half of the month totaled $1,540.
23	Paid $980 for September fuel bill from Wildcat Oil Company.
29	Paid dividends of $400.
30	Paid salaries amounting to $1,200 to employees.
30	Cash receipts for taxi fares for the second half of the month totaled $1,340.

Required Record the effects of each transaction on the accounting equation.

49. Effects on Accounting Equation. The Riles Landscaping Company entered into the following transactions during the month of March:

Mar. 1	Paid three months' rent in advance at $200 per month.
2	Provided landscaping service for customer, collecting $475 cash.
5	Purchased $50 of repair parts on account from LT's, a small engine service company, to be used immediately in repairing one of the company's mowers.
6–10	Provided landscaping service for customer; customer agreed to pay the contract price of $2,350 in 15 days.
15	Paid $50 due to LT's for repair parts purchased on March 5.
25	Collected $2,350 from customer for service provided on March 6–10.
31	Paid $40 for March utilities bill.
31	Paid $1,800 to employees for March salaries.
31	Received $82 March telephone bill, to be paid in early April.

Required Record the effects of each transaction on the accounting equation.

50. **Effects on Accounting Equation.** The Stevel Storage Company entered into the following transactions during the month of April:

Apr. 1	Purchased a three-year insurance policy on the company's building for $360 cash.
6	Purchased office supplies on account at a cost of $64.
14	Paid $30 on account for supplies purchased on April 6.
15	Collected storage fees totaling $720 for the first half of the month.
30	Paid April telephone bill of $82.
30	Collected storage fees totaling $750 for the last half of the month.
30	Paid $600 to employee for April salary.
30	Received $98 April utility bill, to be paid in early May.

Required Record the effects of each transaction on the accounting equation.

51. **Effects on Accounting Equation.** The Jardine Consulting Company was established on January 2, 1993. The company engaged in the following transactions during January:

Jan. 2	The company sold no-par shares for $30,000 cash.
3	Acquired land and a building at a cost of $3,000 and $21,000, respectively. A $4,000 down payment was made and a mortgage was signed for the remaining balance.
5	Purchased office equipment costing $8,000 by signing a note due in one year.
10	Office supplies costing $735 were purchased for cash.
21	Performed consulting services for customer and collected $3,020.
31	Paid $1,450 for employee's salary.
31	Paid utilities bill for January of $188.
31	Paid dividends of $650.

Required Record the effects of each transaction on the accounting equation.

52. Effects on Accounting Equation. The Salanar Service Company was established on March 1, 1993. The company entered into the following transactions during March:

Mar.	1	The company sold no-par shares for $25,000 cash.
	4	Acquired land and a building at a cost of $4,000 and $25,000, respectively. A $3,000 down payment was made and a mortgage was signed for the remaining balance.
	7	Purchased office equipment costing $5,000 by signing a note due in one year.
	8	Office supplies costing $330 were purchased for cash.
	20	Collected $2,764 from customers for services performed.
	31	Paid $845 for employee's salary.
	31	Paid $82 for March utilities bill.
	31	Paid dividends of $900.

Required Record the effects of each transaction on the accounting equation.

53. Erroneous Financial Statements. The bookkeeper for the Powell Company was confused when he prepared the following financial statements:

POWELL COMPANY
Profit and Expense Statement
December 31, 1993

Expenses:		
Salaries expense	$21,000	
Utilities expense	3,400	
Accounts receivable	2,600	
Dividends paid	20,000	
Office supplies	1,500	
Total expenses		$48,500
Revenues:		
Service revenues	$52,000	
Accounts payable	1,100	
Accumulated depreciation: office equipment	1,800	
Total revenues		54,900
Net revenues		$ 6,400

POWELL COMPANY
Balancing Statement
For Year Ended December 31, 1993

LIABILITIES		ASSETS	
Mortgage payable	$22,000	Building	$44,000
Accumulated depreciation:		Depreciation expense:	
building	6,400	building	1,600
Total liabilities	$28,400	Office equipment	9,700
		Depreciation expense:	
Common stock, no par	20,000	office equipment	900
Retained earnings	12,000ª	Cash	4,200
Total liabilities and			
stockholders' equity	$60,400	Total assets	$60,400

ª$5,600 beginning balance + $6,400 net revenues.

C. Powell has asked you to examine the financial statements and related accounting records. You find that, with the exception of office supplies, each amount is correct even though the item might be incorrectly listed in the financial statements. You determine that the office supplies used during the year amount to $800 and the office supplies on hand at the end of the year amount to $700.

Required 1. Review each financial statement and indicate any errors you find.

2. Prepare a corrected 1993 income statement, statement of retained earnings, and ending balance sheet.

54. Revenue Recognition. The concept of revenue recognition is very important to an understanding of financial statements.

Required Which of the following items should be recognized as revenue under the accrual basis of accounting?

1. A company receives a deposit from a customer for services to be performed.

2. A company performs services for a customer who has not yet paid the company.

3. A bank loans money to a customer for a car loan.

4. A wholesale company receives an order from a retailer.

5. Cash is collected from customers to whom sales have been made on credit.

6. Common stock is issued by a company.

7. Goods are produced by a manufacturing company.

8. "Much of Nucorp's profit stemmed from the accounting practice of prebilling where revenues were booked from sales that hadn't yet occurred. Prebilling was defended as a proper way to bill customers by officials of Nucorp." (*Wall Street Journal*, July 5, 1983)

55. Expense Recognition. The concept of expense recognition and the matching concept are very important to an understanding of financial statements.

Required Which of the following items should be recognized as an expense under the matching concept?

1. An insurance policy is prepaid for next year.

2. Inventory is ordered.

3. Inventory is received.

4. Inventory is sold.

5. An insurance policy's coverage has expired.

6. Utility bills are received.

7. A sale is made on a commission basis.

8. Sales tax is charged on a sale.

56. Statements with Unsound Reasoning. The following statements about financial accounting may contain some unsound reasoning:

1. One function of financial accounting is to measure a company's net income for a given period of time.

2. An income statement measures a company's true net income if it is prepared in accordance with generally accepted accounting principles.

3. Other financial statements are basically unrelated to the income statement.

4. Net income is measured as the difference between revenues and expenses.

5. Revenues are an inflow of cash to the enterprise and are realized when recognized.

6. Income measurement may be accomplished by recognizing revenues as sales are made or during the production activity.

Required Identify and correct each example of unsound reasoning.

ANNUAL REPORT PROBLEMS
....

57. General Motors. Review the financial statements and related notes of General Motors in Appendix A.

Required Answer the following questions and indicate on what page of the financial report you located the answer. (*Note:* All answers may be found in the annual report, and no calculations are necessary.)

1. What was the net income for 1989? What was the earnings per share related to $1\frac{2}{3}$ par value common stock?

2. Does the company use a multiple-step or single-step format on its income statement? Explain.

3. What was the amount of interest expense incurred in 1989?

4. What depreciation method was used in 1989?

5. What was the amount of the income tax expense in 1989?

6. What was the amount of the research and development expense in 1989?

7. What was the amount of cash dividends paid per share and in total on the $1⅔ par value common stock?

8. How are the patents and related technology recorded in the acquisition of Hughes being amortized?

9. What was the amount of the net sales and revenues and the net income for the fourth quarter of 1989?

10. What were the principal lines of business of the company in 1989?

11. What was the amount of the total net sales and operating revenues in Europe in 1989?

58. **Preparation of Statements and Profitability.** Listed below in random order are the titles and amounts included in Kellogg Company's 1988 consolidated statements of earnings and retained earnings (in millions of dollars):

Net sales	$4,368
Dividends to shareholders	?
Retained earnings balances:	
Beginning of year	1,718
End of year	2,011
Selling, administrative, and other expenses	1,360
Cost of goods sold	2,233
Income taxes	294
Per common share:	
Net earnings	?
Dividends	?
Average common shares outstanding (in millions):	123

Required 1. Prepare 1988 statements of earnings and retained earnings in good form for Kellogg Company.

2. Prepare a preliminary estimate of the company's profitability using the following ratios (refer to Chapter 14 for more details on these ratios and 5% to 10% is an approximate guideline for adequate returns for both ratios):

a. Profit margin equals net income divided by net sales.

b. Return on total assets equals net income divided by average total assets (average total assets are $3,298).

59. **Preparation of Statements and Profitability.** Bell Atlantic is the eastern regional company of the seven regional companies created by the Bell System divestiture. Listed below in random order are the titles and amounts included in its consolidated statements of income and reinvested earnings for 1988 (in millions of dollars):

Operating revenues:	
Local service	$?
Network access	2,650
Toll service	1,492
Directory advertising and other	1,404
Other communications and financial services	1,150
Provision for uncollectibles	95
Provision for income taxes	530
Other expenses	398
Dividends on common stock	807
Reinvested earnings:	
Beginning balance	3,179
Ending balance	3,688
Other operating expenses	2,940
Employee costs	3,342
Depreciation and amortization	2,354
Earnings per common share (average number of common shares outstanding: 200,000,000)	?

Required 1. Prepare the 1988 Bell Atlantic statements of income and reinvested earnings in good form.

2. Prepare a preliminary estimate of the company's profitability using the following ratios (refer to Chapter 14 for more details on these ratios and 5% to 10% is an approximate guideline for adequate returns for both ratios).

   a. Profit margin equals net income divided by net sales.
   b. Return on total assets equals net income divided by average total assets (average total assets are $24,730).

60. **Analysis of Transactions.** Mobil Oil is one of the ten largest U.S. corporations according to the *Fortune* 500 rankings. Its December 31, 1988, balance sheet was summarized in Problem 53 of Chapter 1. That problem updated Mobil's balance sheet to January 31, 1989, as shown below, with a series of hypothetical balance sheet transactions (in millions of dollars):

MOBIL OIL
Hypothetical Balance Sheet
January 31, 1989

ASSETS		LIABILITIES AND STOCKHOLDERS' EQUITY	
Cash	$ 141	Current loans payable	$ 820
Marketable securities	746	Accounts payable	6,013
Accounts receivable	5,063	Taxes payable	3,322
Inventories	4,501	Long-term debt	12,929
Prepaid expenses	547	Contributed capital	865
Properties	47,447	Retained earnings	14,851
Less: accumulated depreciation	(19,645)		
Total	$38,800	Total	$38,800

The following transactions (in millions of dollars) occurred during February 1989:

1. Sold inventory costing $100 for $125 on account.

2. Collected $50 of the sale in item 1.

3. Purchased $80 inventory on account.

4. Paid $10 for February insurance coverage.

5. Prepaid rent expenses of $20 expired in February.

6. Sold marketable securities costing $200 for $250.

7. Paid $50 of the accounts payable.

8. Selling personnel were paid $5.

9. Paid $5 dividend.

10. Ignore income taxes.

Required Analyze the above transactions and prepare an income statement for February 1989 and a balance sheet for February 28, 1989.

61. **Analysis of Transactions.** IBM is the world's largest computer company. Its December 31, 1988, balance sheet was summarized in Problem 54 of Chapter 1. That problem updated IBM's balance sheet to January 31, 1989, as shown below, with a series of hypothetical balance sheet transactions (in millions of dollars):

IBM
Hypothetical Balance Sheet
January 31, 1989

ASSETS		LIABILITIES AND STOCKHOLDERS' EQUITY	
Cash	$ 4,165	Taxes payable	$ 2,225
Marketable securities	1,458	Short-term loan payable	4,862
Accounts receivable	18,080	Accounts payable	2,712
Inventories	9,575	Accrued liabilities	7,588
Prepaid expenses	1,575	Long-term debt	15,741
Long-term investment	14,288	Contributed capital	8,223
Plant, property and equipment	44,852	Retained earnings	31,186
Less: accumulated			
depreciation	(21,456)		
Total	$72,537	Total	$72,537

The following transactions (in millions of dollars) occurred during February 1989:

1. Received invoices of $5 for various utility expenses.

2. Purchased $20 of inventory on account.

3. Sold computers costing $100 for $200 on account.

4. Sales personnel salaries earned but not yet paid were $20.

5. Plant and equipment depreciation was $10.

6. Paid the salaries owed in item 4.

7. Paid $10 of amount owed in item 2.

8. Collected $100 of the amount due in item 3.

9. Purchased $50 equipment with a two-year note.

10. Ignore income taxes.

Required Analyze the above transactions and prepare an income statement for February 1989 and a balance sheet for February 28, 1989.

Adjustments at the End of the Period and the Accounting System

After reading this chapter, you should understand

- The need for adjustments
- Recognition of an expense and the elimination of (part of) an asset
- Recognition of a revenue and the elimination of (part of) a liability
- Recognition of a previously unrecorded expense and liability
- Recognition of a previously unrecorded revenue and asset
- The accounting system, including accounts, debit and credit rules, and the general journal

In the first two chapters we discussed the three financial statements and some of the transactions that affect those statements. In this chapter we look at additional transactions and events that lead to adjustments at the end of the period. We also introduce the basic characteristics of the financial accounting system that is used by companies, including accounts, debit and credit rules, and the general journal. The chapter ends with a summary example.

■ ADJUSTMENTS AT THE END OF THE PERIOD

Most companies use, and accounting principles require, the *accrual* basis of accounting, in which revenues are recorded in the accounting period when products are sold and services are performed for customers and not necessarily when cash is collected. All the related expenses are then matched against these revenues, regardless of the outflow of cash. Many of the revenue and expense balances will not show the correct dollar amounts for the period simply as a result of the transactions that were recorded. Certain amounts must be *adjusted* to report the appropriate net income on the income statement and the correct ending financial position on the balance sheet.

These adjustments affect both a balance sheet and an income statement amount. Adjustments may be grouped into four categories:

1. Recognition of an expense and the elimination of (part of) an asset
2. Recognition of a revenue and the elimination of (part of) a liability
3. Recognition of a previously unrecorded expense and liability
4. Recognition of a previously unrecorded revenue and asset

A discussion and illustration of the adjustments for each category are presented in the following sections.

■ RECOGNITION OF AN EXPENSE AND THE ELIMINATION OF (PART OF) AN ASSET

In Chapter 2 (see Exhibit 2–1) we discussed the differences between the terms *cost, asset,* and *expense.* The cost refers to the amount at which a transaction is recorded. This cost may be recorded as an asset (unexpired cost) when a company acquires an economic resource that is expected to provide future economic benefits. The cost may be recorded as an expense (expired cost) if it relates to, or is matched with, goods sold or services provided to customers in an accounting period. If a cost is recorded as an asset, part or all of the related cost must be changed from an asset (unexpired cost) to an expense (expired cost). This procedure is necessary because most assets eventually lose their potential for providing future benefits. Another way of stating this concept is to say that the cost must be *apportioned* (allocated) between the assets (portion remaining) at the end of an accounting period and the expenses incurred (portion used up) during the period. Companies experience many examples of this situation in which expenses need to be matched against the revenues. The two most common examples are discussed here: the apportionment of depreciable assets and the apportionment of prepaid items.

Apportionment of Depreciable Assets

Companies frequently acquire physical economic resources that they expect to use for many years in their operating activities. These resources are recorded as assets at their acquisition cost. Examples of these assets are land, buildings, office equipment, trucks, machinery, and automobiles. All of these assets, except land, are depreciable. Land, although it is a physical asset, is not depreciable because it is not considered to have a limited useful life or to decline in value. **A depreciable asset is a long-term physical asset whose expected economic benefits expire over its service life.** The cost of a depreciable asset must be apportioned as an expense in the accounting period during which it is used. **Depreciation expense is the part of the cost of a long-term physical asset allocated as an expense to each accounting period in the asset's useful life.**

Calculation of Depreciation Expense. There are several methods for computing depreciation expense, and these methods are fully discussed in Chapter 7. One method of depreciation is referred to as the straight-line method. This method records an equal portion of the cost of the asset as depreciation expense in each accounting period over the expected service life of the asset. The following equation is used to compute *annual* straight-line depreciation:

$$\text{Annual Depreciation Expense} = \frac{\text{Cost} - \text{Estimated Residual Value}}{\text{Estimated Service Life in Years}}$$

The cost is the amount at which the physical asset was recorded. **The estimated residual value is the expected amount to be received from the disposal of the asset at the end of its service life.** Because of difficulties in making this estimate accurately, companies often assign an arbitrary value, such as 10% or zero to the residual value. **The estimated service life is the number of years that management expects the asset to be used before its disposal.** This estimate is also difficult to make, but management has the responsibility for developing the best possible estimate.

To illustrate the calculation of depreciation, the related adjustments, and the resulting book values, the 1993 depreciation for two physical assets of the Stalley Company are discussed:

1. *Store Equipment.* On January 2, 1993, the company purchased store equipment at a cost of $12,000. The estimated service life is ten years on that date, and the estimated residual value is zero.

2. *Building.* On January 2, 1985, the company purchased a building for $60,000. The estimated service life is 25 years at that date, and the estimated residual value is $10,000. Accumulated depreciation of $16,000 on January 1, 1993, resulted in a book value of $44,000 ($60,000 − $16,000) on that date.

The company computes its 1993 depreciation expense as follows:

Store Equipment:

$$\text{Annual Depreciation Expense} = \frac{\$12,000 - \$0}{10 \text{ years}}$$

$$= \$1,200$$

Building:

$$\text{Annual Depreciation Expense} = \frac{\$60,000 - \$10,000}{25 \text{ years}}$$

$$= \$2,000$$

Many companies prepare financial statements for accounting periods shorter than a year (e.g., quarterly reports to stockholders). These companies would compute the depreciation expense for the shorter period based on a fraction of the year.

Recording Depreciation. The adjustment to the financial statements to record the depreciation involves an increase to the expenses (thereby reducing net income and stockholders' equity) and a decrease to the asset. This *decrease* in the asset, however, is achieved by *increasing* accumulated depreciation. Because accumulated depreciation is always subtracted from the cost of the asset, an increase in that amount will always decrease the net (book) value of the asset.

Cost of asset
— accumulated deprec(t)

To illustrate this procedure consider the recording of the depreciation of the store equipment and building for the Stalley Company. Although the two accumulated depreciation amounts are listed on the asset side of the accounting equation, they have a negative effect on the assets. After the depreciation for the equipment has been recorded, the Accumulated Depreciation: Store Equipment is $1,200 (since this is the first year that the store equipment was used). The resulting book value of the store equipment reported on the company's December 31, 1993, balance sheet is as follows:

Store equipment	$12,000	
Less: Accumulated depreciation	(1,200)	$10,800

The effects of the acquisition of the asset and the depreciation in 1993 are as follows:

		Assets		= Liabilities +	Stockholders' Equity
	Cash	Store Equipment	Accumulated Depreciation: Store Equipment		Depreciation Expense: Store Equipment
(1)	−$12,000	+$12,000			
(2)			−$1,200		−$1,200

After the depreciation for the building has been recorded, the Accumulated Depreciation: Building is $18,000. This amount results from having depreciated the building for 8 years (1985 through 1992) at $2,000 per year ($16,000) and adding $2,000 depreciation for 1993. The resulting book value of the building reported on the company's December 31, 1993, balance sheet is as follows:

Building	$60,000	
Less: Accumulated depreciation	(18,000)	$42,000

The book value of the building has decreased from $44,000 ($66,000−$16,000) on December 31, 1992, to $42,000 on December 31, 1993, because the Accumulated Depreciation was increased by $2,000 in 1993. The $42,000 book value will be reduced to a book value of $10,000 after $2,000 annual depreciation has been recorded in each of the remaining 16 years of service life. The effects of the depreciation in 1993 are as follows:

Assets	= Liabilities +	Stockholders' Equity
Accumulated Depreciation: Building		Depreciation Expense: Building
−$2,000		−$2,000

[handwritten: book value = unexpired cost —]

Instead of reducing the asset directly, the accumulated depreciation is recorded separately as a contra-asset. Therefore, the balance sheet includes the cost of the asset, the remaining unexpired cost (the book value), and the total expired cost (the accumulated depreciation). By examining these amounts, the user of the financial statements can gain insights into the age of the assets. This information is useful in evaluating the need for the company to replace its physical assets and the likely timing of this replacement.

Apportionment of Prepaid Items

A prepaid item is an economic resource that is expected to be used in one year or the normal operating cycle, whichever is longer. Prepaid items (often called prepaid expenses) are similar in several ways to depreciable assets; that is, they are economic resources that a company has acquired and expects to use in its current and future operating activities. Prepaid items differ from depreciable assets because they may or may not be physical in nature and are expected to provide economic benefits for only a short period of time. Examples of prepaid items include prepaid insurance, prepaid rent, office supplies, and store supplies.

When goods or services involving a prepaid item are acquired, the cost is recorded as an asset. At the end of the accounting period, a part of the goods or services has been used in order to earn revenues. The expired cost must be matched, as an expense, against the revenues of the period, while the unexpired cost remains as an asset on the ending balance sheet. The apportionment (allocation) of the cost of each prepaid item between an expense and an asset is recorded in an adjustment at the end of the accounting period. Conceptually, therefore, the apportionment of a prepaid item is the same as the apportionment of a depreciable asset.

Recording the Adjustment to Prepaid Items. When a prepaid item initially has been recorded as an asset, the adjustment at the end of the period involves an increase to an expense (thereby reducing net income and stockholders' equity) and a decrease to the asset. Unlike a depreciable asset, the amount subtracted is not separately recorded for each prepaid item because of the relatively short expected life of the asset.

The calculation of the amount of the adjustment depends on the type of prepaid item. In the case of prepaid insurance, for example, the total cost of the insurance coverage is apportioned on a *straight-line* basis over the life of the policy. A similar procedure would be followed for prepaid rent. For office supplies and store supplies, however, a physical count is made of the supplies on hand at the end of the accounting period and the related costs are determined. The difference between the cost of the supplies on hand at the end of the accounting period and the cost of the supplies available for use during the period is the supplies expense for the period.

To illustrate the accounting for prepaid items, assume that the Stalley Company acquires two prepaid items during 1993, summarized as follows:

1. *Office Supplies.* On December 31, 1992, the company had $240 of office supplies on hand. On May 8, 1993, the company acquired an additional $80 of

office supplies. A physical count on December 31, 1993, determines that $170 of office supplies are on hand on that date.

2. *Prepaid Insurance.* On November 1, 1993, the company paid $540 for a one-year comprehensive insurance policy.

The year-end adjustments based on this information for office supplies and prepaid insurance are explained next.

Office Supplies. The office supplies purchased on May 8, 1993, were an economic resource to the company and were recorded as an asset by increasing Office Supplies by $80 and decreasing Cash by $80. Office Supplies then had a balance of $320 ($240 + $80), the office supplies available for use. On December 31, 1993, office supplies with a cost of $170 were still on hand. Since $320 of office supplies were available for use and $170 were left, $150 ($320 − $170) were used during the year. The $150 is recorded as an expense — Office Supplies Expense — on the 1993 income statement (thereby reducing net income and stockholders' equity). The $150 decrease to Office Supplies, after it is deducted from the previous $320 balance, will result in a $170 ending balance, which is listed as an asset on the December 31, 1993 balance sheet. The effects of these events are as follows:

Assets   = Liabilities + Stockholders' Equity

	Cash	Office Supplies		Office Supplies Expense
(1)	−$80	+$ 80		
(2)		− 150		−$150

Prepaid Insurance. On November 1, 1993, when the company paid $540 for the one-year insurance policy, the right to the insurance protection was an economic resource of the company. At that time the transaction was recorded by increasing the asset — Prepaid Insurance — by $540 and decreasing Cash by the same amount. At the end of the year, two months of insurance protection (for November and December) or $90 [($540 ÷ 12) × 2 months] has expired and 10 months of insurance protection or [$450 ($540 ÷ 12) × 10] remains in force (unexpired). The $90 expired insurance is included as an expense — Insurance Expense — on the 1993 income statement. The $90 decrease to Prepaid Insurance, when it is deducted from the $540 balance, results in a $450 ending balance that is listed as an asset on the December 31, 1993, balance sheet. The effects of these events are as follows:

Assets   = Liabilities + Stockholders' Equity

	Cash	Prepaid Insurance		Insurance Expense
(1)	−$540	+$540		
(2)		− 90		−$90

■ RECOGNITION OF A REVENUE AND THE ELIMINATION OF (PART OF) A LIABILITY

In Chapter 2 we defined revenues as increases in assets (or decreases in liabilities) during a period from delivering or producing goods or rendering services to customers. We also noted that the inflow of cash and the recording of revenues are not always directly related.

In some cases customers may make an advance payment to a company for goods or services to be provided in the future. Even though an asset — Cash — has increased at the time of the transaction, the company has not earned revenue because the goods or services have not been provided. Instead the company has incurred a liability because it has an obligation to provide the future goods or services (or return the cash). **An unearned item is an advance receipt for goods or services to be provided in the future, and it is recorded as a liability** (often called unearned revenue). At the end of each accounting period, an adjustment must be made to reduce the liability and increase the revenues of the period for the value of the goods and services actually provided during the period. As a result, the income statement properly shows all the revenues in the period in which they are earned and the ending balance sheet reports the remaining liabilities of the company.

Example of Adjustment of Unearned Revenue

To illustrate, assume the building that the Stalley Company owns is too large for its current operations and that the company therefore rents a portion of the building to another company. On December 1, 1993, the other company pays $720 in advance for six months rent ($120 per month). Upon receipt of the money, the Stalley Company incurred an economic obligation (liability) to provide the use of the rented space to the other company for six months. No revenue should be recorded at this point because no service has been provided. Thus, the Stalley Company recorded this transaction as an increase to Cash of $720 and an increase to a liability — Unearned Rent — of $720. At the end of the period, one month of rent revenue, or $120 ($720 ÷ 6), has been earned and five months rent, or $600 ($120 × 5), is still unearned. Therefore, an adjustment is required. The liability — Unearned Rent — is reduced by $120, and Rent Revenue of $120 is recognized. The $120 rent revenue is included on the 1993 income statement (thereby increasing net income and stockholders' equity). The $120 decrease to Unearned Rent, when it is deducted from the $720 balance, results in a $600 ending balance that is listed as a liability on the December 31, 1993, balance sheet. The effects of these events are as follows:

	Assets	= Liabilities +	Stockholders' Equity
	Cash	**Unearned Revenue**	**Rent Revenue**
(1)	+$720	+$720	
(2)		− 120	+$120

This form of adjustment will arise whenever a company collects cash in advance of providing the goods or services. Other examples are the collection of premiums by an insurance company, the collection of subscriptions by a magazine publishing company, and the collection of advance payments for air fares by an airline.

■ RECOGNITION OF A PREVIOUSLY UNRECORDED EXPENSE AND LIABILITY

Many of a company's expenses are recorded when payment is made. At the end of an accounting period some expenses of the company usually have not been recorded, although they have been incurred. **An accrued expense is an expense that has been incurred during the period but has been neither paid nor recorded.** An adjustment must be made for each accrued expense at the end of the period in order to match correctly the expenses against the revenues of the period. The adjustment involves an increase to an expense and the recognition of a liability in the balance sheet. Three of these expenses — salaries, interest, and income taxes — are discussed further.

Recognition of Salaries Expense and Salaries Payable

Companies have different policies for payment of their employees' wages and salaries. Employees are seldom paid in advance but usually after the completion of their duties in the pay period. Some employees of a company may be paid weekly, some twice a month, and others monthly. Seldom does an accounting period end on the same day as the payment date for all employees. Nevertheless, the wages and salaries earned by the employees from the date of the last salary payment through the end of the accounting period are an *expense* of the period even though they will be *paid* in the next accounting period. An adjustment must be made at the end of the period to record the expense and liability.

To illustrate, assume that the Stalley Company has six employees, each earning $300 per week for a five-day workweek (Monday through Friday). The employees are paid every Wednesday at the end of the day. December 31, 1993, is a Friday. The employees' salaries totaling $720 ($300 × 6 × 2/5) for the Thursday and Friday of the last week of December are an expense of 1993 even though they will not be paid until 1994. The adjustment is made to include an expense — Salaries Expense — of $720 on the income statement for 1993 and a liability of $720 — Salaries Payable — on the December 31, 1993 balance sheet. The effects of these events are as follows:

$$\text{Assets} = \text{Liabilities} + \text{Stockholders' Equity}$$

	Salaries Payable	Salaries Expense
	+$720	-$720

At the time of the first salary payment of $1,800 in 1994, part of the payment will eliminate the liability of $720, and the $1,080 balance of the payment is recognized as an expense for 1994, as follows:

Assets = Liabilities + Stockholders' Equity

Cash	Salaries Payable	Salaries Expense
− $1,800	− $720	− $1,080

Recognition of Interest Expense and Interest Payable

Many companies enter into transactions involving the issuance or receipt of a note. **A note is a written legal document in which one party (the *issuer*, or *maker*) agrees to pay another party a certain amount of money (the *principal*) on an agreed future date (the *maturity date*).** Notes may be exchanged for cash or for goods or services. Most notes are interest bearing. An *interest-bearing note* is a note for which the issuer is charged interest on the principal. The *annual* interest rate is included on the note. In the case of an interest-bearing note, the issuer may pay both the principal and the interest on the maturity date. Between the date that the note is issued and the maturity date, interest accumulates (accrues) daily on an interest-bearing note. These relationships are as follows:

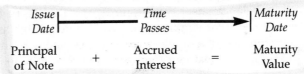

If a company signs an interest-bearing note, the interest is an expense of doing business. Even though the interest accrues daily, interest expense is normally recorded when the note is paid on the maturity date. When a company has issued a note in the current accounting period but the maturity date is not until the next accounting period, part of the interest expense applies to the current period and part to the next period. An adjustment must be made at the end of the current period to record the interest expense and the liability. The amount of interest that has accrued on the note at any time is computed by multiplying the principal times the *annual* interest rate for the length of time the note has been issued.

To illustrate, assume that on November 1, 1993, the Stalley Company borrowed $12,000 from a local bank. The company signed and issued a $12,000, three-month, 10% note requiring it to repay the principal plus $300 interest ($12,000 × 10% × 3/12) on February 1, 1994. At the date of issuance the company recorded the transaction by increasing Cash by $12,000 and increasing the liability — Notes Payable — by $12,000. At the end of the period two of the three months life of the note have passed, and therefore an expense — Interest Expense — of $200 ($12,000 × 10% × 2/12) is included on the income statement for 1993 (thereby reducing net income and stockholders' equity). A liability — Interest Payable — of $200 is included on the December 31, 1993, balance sheet. The effects of these events are as follows:

$$\text{Assets} = \text{Liabilities} + \text{Stockholders' Equity}$$

	Interest Payable		Interest Expense
	+$200		−$200

Again, when payment of the total interest occurs in 1994, $200 of the payment represents the elimination of the liability and the remaining $100 is an expense for 1994.

Recognition of Income Tax Expense and Income Taxes Payable

Corporations are assessed income taxes. These income taxes are an expense of doing business and are computed as a percentage of income before income taxes. Therefore, in accordance with the matching concept, income tax expense is deducted on the income statement in the computation of net income. Since a corporation pays its taxes in an accounting period subsequent to the one in which it recognizes the expense, the corporation would also recognize a liability on its balance sheet. In the next period when payment occurs, the liability is eliminated. (For simplicity, we will often assume as we have here that the corporation makes a single income tax payment in the next year, although many corporations must pay their income taxes on a quarterly basis.) An illustration of the computation of income taxes is included in the summary example later in the chapter. A more detailed discussion of the impacts of income taxes on financial statements is included in Chapter 9.

■ RECOGNITION OF A PREVIOUSLY UNRECORDED REVENUE AND ASSET

Most revenues of a company are recorded at the time goods or services are provided to a customer. At the end of an accounting period, some revenues of a company may not yet have been recorded. These revenues are often called accrued revenues. **An accrued revenue is a revenue that has been earned during the accounting period but has been neither collected nor recorded.** An adjustment must be made for each accrued revenue at the end of the period in order to record correctly the revenues in the period in which they were earned and to record the correct ending assets of the period. The adjustment involves an increase to an asset and an increase to a revenue. Examples of previously unrecorded revenues are relatively infrequent; examples are the recognition of revenue on a note received by a company, interest earned but not received by banks, and services provided but not billed by utilities. Another example of a previously unrecorded revenue is a service organization, such as a consulting company or a law firm, that has not billed for activities it has performed for a client.

Previously Unrecorded Interest Revenue

Assume that on May 1, 1993, the Stalley Company sold some land to the Trage Company for $9,000. The land had originally cost $9,000 and was recorded by the Stalley Company as an asset at the time it was purchased. The Trage Company paid $1,000 down and signed a one-year, 12% note for the $8,000 balance. At that time the Stalley Company recorded the transaction by increasing Cash for $1,000, increasing the asset — Notes Receivable — for $8,000, and decreasing the asset — Land — for $9,000. By the end of the year the note has been outstanding for eight months (May through December). Therefore, the company recognizes interest revenue of $640 ($8,000 × 12% × 8/12) on the 1993 income statement. The company also recognizes an asset — Interest Receivable — on the December 31, 1993, balance sheet. The effects of these events are as follows:

$$\text{Assets} \quad = \quad \text{Liabilities} + \text{Stockholders' Equity}$$

Interest Receivable	Interest Revenue
+ $640	+ $640

The discussion of adjustments has focused on the routine adjustments that are necessary for the financial statements to reflect the proper amount of assets, liabilities, revenues, and expenses. There are other types of adjustments that may result from unusual events such as the restructuring of operations. Often these unusual events affect the same items as the routine adjustments. These are discussed in the appropriate chapters of the book.

■ THE ACCOUNTING SYSTEM

In this section, we discuss the major characteristics of the accounting system. These mechanics, however, are not essential to an understanding of the rest of the book. This discussion is most useful for readers who expect to be involved in using an accounting system in their careers or who expect to have extensive communications with accountants. However, an understanding of the account (or T-account) is often helpful in organizing complex information. Readers who skip this section may find the summary example at the end of the chapter (without all the mechanics) useful as a review of many of the concepts that have been introduced so far.

We have used a simple columnar accounting system based on the accounting equation to record transactions and to prepare a balance sheet. Although this system was helpful for explaining the accounting process, it is not very practical in today's business world. Within the period of a year most companies have thousands or millions of transactions involving many assets, liabilities, and stockholders' equity items. These transactions not only affect the balance sheet but also the other financial statements. Setting up a column for recording transactions affecting all the assets, liabilities, and stockholders' equity items of most companies would result in a very large accounting record, which would be impractical for an actual business.

A better system for processing accounting information is needed. This system would include a set of accounting procedures and documents for recording, retaining, and reporting all the information about each transaction. The accounting system shown here is used for either manual or computer information processing. For ease of learning, the discussion in this book involves manual processing.

Accounts

In the previous chapters we used a single column to record and retain the increases and decreases in each asset, liability, and stockholders' equity category. In the business world, an account is used to record this information. **An account is used to record and retain the monetary information from business transactions.** Separate accounts are used for each asset, liability, and stockholders' equity item. For example, a company may have accounts for Cash, Accounts Receivable, Notes Receivable, Office Supplies, Prepaid Insurance, Equipment, Land, Buildings, Accounts Payable, Notes Payable, Common Stock, Additional Paid-in Capital, Retained Earnings, Sales, Cost of Goods Sold, Salaries Expense, and Depreciation Expense, to name only a few. The number, types, and names of the accounts for each company depend on the particular company's operations, the types of assets it has, the types of liabilities it has incurred, and the types of revenues earned and expenses incurred. **A general ledger is the entire set of accounts for a company.** For this reason, sometimes accounts are referred to as *general ledger accounts*.

An account can take several physical forms. It might be a location on a computer disk or tape, or a standardized business paper in the case of a manual system. The general ledger might be a computer disk or tape, or a loose-leaf binder containing all the accounts of a manual system. Regardless of the physical form, all accounts are used for recording and retaining accounting information.

Components of an Account

No matter what physical form is used, the same logical format is used throughout for recording and retaining accounting information in the accounts. This format is easiest to understand for a manual system. A simple format for the accounts in a manual system is called a *T-account* because it looks like the capital letter *T*. As shown in the following example, each T-account has three basic parts: (1) a place at the top for the *title* of the particular asset, liability, or stockholders' equity category, (2) a *left* side, called the *debit* side, and (3) a *right* side, called the *credit* side. The left (debit) and the right (credit) sides of each account are used for recording and retaining the monetary information from business transactions. **A debit entry is a monetary amount recorded (debited) in the left side of an account. A credit entry is a monetary amount recorded (credited) in the right side of an account.**

Title of Account	
Left (debit) side	Right (credit) side

Debit and Credit Rules

Each account accumulates information about both increases and decreases from various business transactions. There are two rules for recording these increases and decreases in the accounts. The first rule is that **for each account all increases are recorded in one side of the account and all decreases are recorded in the other side of the account.** This rule makes it easy to determine the total increases and decreases for a particular account. It does not indicate, however, whether the increases or decreases should be recorded in the debit (left) or credit (right) side of the account.

A second rule is *the debit and credit rule.* This rule relates to the basic accounting equation: **Asset accounts (accounts on the left side of the accounting equation) are increased by debit entries (i.e., recorded amounts on the left side) and decreased by credit entries. Liability and stockholders' equity accounts (accounts on the right side of the equation) are increased by credit entries (i.e., recorded amounts on the right side) and decreased by debit entries.**

This rule and its relationship to the accounting equation are illustrated as follows:

Assets	=	Liabilities	+	Stockholders' Equity

Asset Accounts		Liability Accounts		Stockholders' Equity Accounts	
(debit)	(credit)	(debit)	(credit)	(debit)	(credit)
Increase	Decrease	Decrease	Increase	Decrease	Increase
+	−	−	+	−	+

The debit and credit rule is essential for understanding how to record business transactions. It may be separated into parts as follows:

1. **Assets**

   a. An increase in an asset is recorded in the left (debit) side of the asset account, by a debit entry.
   b. A decrease in an asset is recorded in the right (credit) side of the asset account, by a credit entry.

2. **Liabilities**

    a. An increase in a liability is recorded in the right (credit) side of the liability account, by a credit entry.

    b. A decrease in a liability is recorded in the left (debit) side of the liability account, by a debit entry.

3. **Stockholders' Equity**

    a. An increase in stockholders' equity (e.g., common stock, additional paid-in capital, retained earnings, and revenue) is recorded in the right (credit) side of the stockholders' equity account, by a credit entry.

    b. A decrease in stockholders' equity (e.g., expenses and dividends paid) is recorded in the left (debit) side of the stockholders' equity account, by a debit entry.

Remember that a revenue is an increase in stockholders' equity and the rule for recording a revenue is therefore as a right (credit) entry. Also remember that an expense and a dividend paid are both decreases in stockholders' equity and each is therefore recorded by a left (debit) entry.

Contra Accounts and Book Values

Earlier in the chapter, we explained that accumulated depreciation is subtracted from the related asset amount. The Accumulated Depreciation account is a contra (negative) account to its related account. **A contra account is an account whose balance is subtracted from another related account in order to determine a resulting amount.** A contra account always has a balance opposite of the account to which it is related. The debit and credit rule that applies to a contra account is also the opposite of the rule that applies to the related account. Thus each Accumulated Depreciation account is increased by credit entries (and decreased by debit entries) and has a credit balance. The credit balance of each Accumulated Depreciation account is subtracted from the debit balance of its related long-term physical asset account on the ending balance sheet for the accounting period to determine the remaining *unexpired* cost. This unexpired cost is referred to as the book value of the asset. **The book value (or carrying value) is the cost of a depreciable asset less its related accumulated depreciation.** Each year, after the depreciation expense has been recorded for a physical asset, the related Accumulated Depreciation account balance increases and the book value decreases. The accounting equation remains in balance, however, because the decrease in the book value of the asset is accompanied by a decrease in stockholders' equity due to recording the depreciation expense. Eventually, at the end of the asset's life, the Accumulated Depreciation account credit balance will be equal to the related asset account debit balance (assuming no residual value), and therefore the asset will have a zero book value.

Balance of an Account

The balance of an account is the difference between the total increases and decreases recorded in the account. Usually, the balance of each account is computed when the accounting information is to be communicated in a financial statement. Each asset account and some stockholders' equity accounts (e.g., expenses, losses, and dividends paid) normally have a debit balance because the total increases (debits) exceed the total decreases (credits) in that account. Each liability and some stockholders' equity accounts (e.g., common stock, additional paid-in capital, retained earnings, revenues, and gains) normally have a credit balance because the total credits (increases) exceed the total debits (decreases) in each account.

To illustrate, look at the following Cash account:

	Cash		
6/1/93 Balance	2,000	6/2/93	900
6/4/93	5,000	6/10/93	3,000
		6/26/93	700
-------		-------	
6/30/93 Balance	2,400		

Note that on June 1, 1993, the account had a $2,000 debit balance (this was the ending balance for May, the difference between the total debits and credits in the account to that date). On June 4 a transaction occurred that increased (debited) the Cash account by $5,000, while on June 2, 10, and 26 the Cash account was decreased (credited) by $900, $3,000, and $700, respectively. The debit balance of the Cash account is $2,400 on June 30, 1993, because the total debits ($7,000) exceed the total credits ($4,600). Debit and credit entries in accounts are illustrated later in the chapter.

Double Entry Rule

The double entry rule states that when recording each transaction, the total amount of the debit entries must be equal to the total amount of the credit entries for that transaction. Thus, for each recorded transaction there must be at least one debit entry and one credit entry (although there could be more entries of each type), and the total amounts must be equal. For example, suppose a company purchased land for cash at a cost of $2,000. To record this transaction, an asset account — Land — would be increased by a debit entry of $2,000 and another asset account — Cash — would be decreased by a credit entry of $2,000. Thus the total debits equal the total credits in this transaction.

It is important to understand the consistent relationship between the accounting equation, the debit and credit rule, and the double entry rule. Recall that the accounting equation must always be in balance. Recall also that when recording a transaction, it is not necessary to affect both sides of the equation or even two components of the equation. It is possible to record a transaction as affecting only the left side, the right side, or both sides of the equation provided that the equation remains in balance. If the debit and credit rule and the double entry rule are followed, the accounting equation will *always* remain in balance. For instance, in the land example just given, the debit entry *increased* the Land account while the credit entry *decreased* the Cash account. The total debits equaled the total credits, and thus the double entry rule was followed. Only the left side of the accounting equation (the asset component) was affected, but the equation remained in balance because there was no change in *total* assets. The left side of the equation therefore remained equal to the right side of the equation. Additional examples are presented later in the chapter.

Checklist of Important Rules

Up to this point we have stated several important rules that must be followed in an actual accounting system. These rules are summarized as follows to help you remember them and their relationship:

1. **The accounting equation (assets equal liabilities plus stockholders' equity) must always remain in balance.**
2. **All increases in an account are recorded on one side of the account; all decreases are recorded on the other side of the account.**
3. **The debit and credit rule states that:**
   a. **Asset accounts are increased by debit entries and decreased by credit entries.**
   b. **Liability and stockholders' equity accounts are increased by credit entries and decreased by debit entries.**
4. **Asset accounts normally have debit balances. Liability and stockholders' equity accounts normally have credit balances, except for expenses, losses, and dividends.**
5. **The double entry rule states that for all recorded transactions, the total amount of the debit entries must be equal to the total amount of the credit entries.**

General Journal and Journalizing

Our examples of recording transactions have included relatively few situations. Remember that in reality a company may engage in thousands or millions of transactions and have hundreds or thousands of accounts. Recording such a large number of transactions directly in the accounts could result in errors because of the numerous accounts in the general ledger. In addition, if the accountant reviews a debit entry in an account, it would be very difficult, if not impossible, to find the related credit entry. Finally, no written description of the transactions would exist if the transactions were recorded directly in the accounts. For these reasons, transactions are *not* initially recorded directly in a company's accounts.

General Journal

The business transactions of a company are first recorded in a journal, after which the information is transferred to the accounts. **A general journal is used** to record the date of the transaction, the accounts to be debited and credited, the amounts of the debit and credit entries, and an explanation of each transaction. In a manual accounting system the general journal is a book of columnar pages. A journal is often referred to as the *document of original entry* because each transaction is first, or originally, entered in the journal.

A journal entry is the recorded information for each transaction. A general journal can be used to record all types of transactions. Many companies also have a number of *special journals,* each designed for recording a particular type of business transaction. For instance, one special journal is the Cash Receipts Journal used to record all receipts of cash. Although special journals are not discussed further, the following discussion applies to all types of journals.

There are many advantages to using a journal for initially recording a company's transactions. First, use of a journal helps to prevent errors. Since the accounts and the debit and credit amounts for each transaction are initially recorded on a single journal page rather than directly in the many accounts, this method makes it easier to prove that the debits and credits are equal. Second, all the information about the transactions (including the explanation) is recorded in one place, thereby providing a complete "picture" of the transaction. This aspect proves very useful during the auditing process or if an error is discovered later in the accounting process. An accountant can look in the journal to see all of the accounts involved and find an explanation for the transaction. Finally, since the transactions are recorded chronologically (day by day), the journal also provides a chronological "history" of the company's financial transactions.

Listed below are the procedures for recording a journal entry.

1. The title(s) of the account(s) to be debited is (are) entered first. The amount of the debit is entered in the debit column.

2. The title(s) of the account(s) to be credited is (are) entered on the next line(s). The title(s) of the account(s) is (are) indented to the right. The amount of the credit is entered in the credit column.

3. A brief explanation is entered on the line below the last credit entry of each transaction.

Journals used by companies may contain more information (e.g., the date of the transaction), but such items are unnecessary for our understanding of the basics of an accounting system.

To illustrate the format of a journal entry, suppose a company purchases inventory on account for $10,000. As we have discussed, this entry requires a debit (increase) in an asset and a credit (increase) in a liability. The format of the journal is as follows:

Inventory	10,000	
Accounts payable		10,000
To record the purchase of inventory on account		

To summarize, the general ledger is designed to facilitate the preparation of the financial statements by collecting all the information about each asset, liability, and stockholders' equity account in one place. The general journal is designed to facilitate the operation and control of a company by collecting all the information about each transaction and event in one place. Each supports and complements the other, and in total each contains the same information.

Accounts and Posting

In the journalizing process each transaction is initially entered in one record, the journal, to (1) minimize errors, (2) have all the debit and credit information for each transaction in one place, and (3) have a chronological list of all the company's financial transactions. However, the accounting information from each transaction is not yet recorded in the accounts, the so-called "storage units" for the company's accounting information. To do so, we must post the accounts from the journal to the ledger accounts. **Posting is the process of transferring the debit and credit information for each journal entry to the proper accounts in the general ledger.** Thus, the debit entries are recorded on the left sides of the appropriate accounts, and the credit entries are recorded on the right sides of the appropriate accounts.

Trial Balance

In discussing the journalizing and posting process, we have set up procedures so that the double entry rule is followed: The total amount of the debit entries is equal to the total amount of the credit entries. By following these procedures the accounting equation remains in balance and errors are minimized.

People can make mistakes, however, and therefore it is desirable to reduce the chance that a journalizing or posting error may be included in the financial statements used to communicate the accounting information. If we follow the double entry rule in journalizing and posting each transaction, the total of the debit balances in all the accounts should be equal to the total of the credit balances in all the accounts. Before preparing the financial statements, it is useful to perform an additional procedure to check for errors. This procedure involves proving the equality of the debit and credit account balances by preparing a trial balance.

A trial balance is a schedule that lists the titles of all the accounts in the general ledger, the debit or credit balance of each account, and the totals of the debit and credit balances. To prepare a trial balance the balance of each account in the general ledger is computed if this has not already been done. Next the accounts and debit or credit balances are listed on the trial balance according to the order in which the accounts are listed in the general ledger. Finally, the debit and credit columns are totaled to determine their equality. A trial balance is illustrated later in the chapter.

The trial balance is an accounting working paper used to prove the equality of the debit and credit account balances in the accounts. It is *not* a formal accounting statement. After it is prepared, it is kept in the accounting records for future reference if necessary.

Summary of Accounting System

The key procedures in a simple accounting system are as follows:

1. Record all the transactions in the general journal.
2. Record all the adjustments at the end of the period.
3. Periodically post the information from the general journal to the general ledger.
4. Prepare a trial balance.
5. Prepare the income statement.
6. Prepare the schedule of changes in stockholders' equity or a statement of retained earnings.
7. Prepare the balance sheet.
8. Prepare the statement of cash flows (discussed in more detail in Chapter 12).

■ SUMMARY EXAMPLE

We have now covered the basic concepts of assets, liabilities, stockholders' equity, revenues, expenses, gains and losses, the financial statements, and the components of an accounting system. We will now present a summary example. To be realistic, this example covers an annual period but only uses a small number of transactions by eliminating many routine or repetitive transactions. The example also is for a continuing rather than a new company.

The balance sheet of the Ross Company on December 31, 1992, is shown in Exhibit 3–1. The transactions and events occurring during 1993 are listed in Exhibit 3–2. Note that dates are not given for transactions that are summary amounts for the year but only for those items for which the date is necessary. The journal entries are listed in Exhibit 3–3; for simplicity the descriptions of the transactions are omitted. The ledger (or T) accounts are shown in Exhibit 3–4. Note that the balances from the beginning balance sheet are included as the opening balances of the ledger accounts for this ongoing company. The trial balance is shown in Exhibit 3–5. The income statement for 1993 is shown in Exhibit 3–6, the schedule of changes in stockholders' equity in Exhibit 3–7, and the balance sheet at December 31, 1993, in Exhibit 3–8. Although only briefly discussed in Chapter 2 (and extensively in Chapter 12), the statement of cash flows is shown in Exhibit 3–9. The statement is shown with the cash flows from operating activities under the direct method, with the alternative indirect method also shown. Finally, the amounts affecting the three financial statements are combined in Exhibit 3–10 so that a better understanding of the relationships among the statements may be obtained.

EXHIBIT 3-1

ROSS COMPANY
Balance Sheet
December 31, 1992

ASSETS

Current assets			
Cash		$30,000	
Accounts receivable		20,000	
Inventory		15,000	
Total current assets			$ 65,000
Property, plant, and equipment			
Land		$30,000	
Building	$60,000		
Less: accumulated depreciation	(20,000)	40,000	
Office equipment	$50,000		
Less: accumulated depreciation	(15,000)	35,000	
Total property, plant, and equipment			105,000
Total assets			$170,000

LIABILITIES

Current liabilities	
Accounts payable	$ 15,000
Noncurrent liabilities	
Notes payable	40,000
Total liabilities	$ 55,000

STOCKHOLDERS' EQUITY

Common stock, $5 par	$35,000	
Additional paid-in capital	50,000	
Retained earnings	30,000	
Total stockholders' equity		115,000
Total liabilities and stockholders' equity		$170,000

EXHIBIT 3–2

·················

ROSS COMPANY
Transactions and Events for 1993

1. Purchases of inventory for the year were $80,000. All were on account.

2. Sales for the year were $200,000. All were on account.

3. Cost of goods sold for the year was $70,000.

4. On July 1, a one-year insurance policy was purchased for $2,400 cash.

5. Cash collections during the year from sales to customers on account were $185,000.

6. Cash payments during the year for purchases of inventory on account were $72,000.

7. The building is being depreciated by the straight-line method over 30 years to a zero residual value.

8. The equipment is being depreciated by the straight-line method over ten years to a zero residual value.

9. The employees were paid salaries of $50,000 during the year and are owed an additional $600 at the end of the year.

10. The interest rate on the notes payable is 15%, but no interest was paid during the year.

11. On September 1, a portion of the building was rented to the Hadad Company for six months at $900 per month, for which a check for $5,400 was received.

12. Dividends of $5,000 were paid.

13. Additional office equipment is purchased for $12,000 cash on December 31. No depreciation is recorded in the current year.

14. Notes payable of $4,000 were repaid on December 31. Interest expense computed above is not affected.

15. Half of the insurance has expired.

16. Four months of rent has been earned.

17. The income tax rate is 30%, and the income taxes will be paid next year.

EXHIBIT 3–3

·········

ROSS COMPANY
Journal Entries for 1993

1. Inventory	80,000	
Accounts payable		80,000
2. Accounts receivable	200,000	
Sales		200,000
3. Cost of goods sold	70,000	
Inventory		70,000
4. Prepaid insurance	2,400	
Cash		2,400
5. Cash	185,000	
Accounts receivable		185,000
6. Accounts payable	72,000	
Cash		72,000
7. Depreciation expense: building	2,000[a]	
Accumulated depreciation: building		2,000
[a]$60,000 ÷ 30		
8. Depreciation expense: office equipment	5,000[b]	
Accumulated depreciation: office equipment		5,000
[b]$50,000 ÷ 10		
9. Salaries expense	50,600	
Cash		50,000
Salaries payable		600
10. Interest expense	6,000[c]	
Interest payable		6,000
[c]$40,000 × 15%		
11. Cash	5,400[d]	
Unearned rent		5,400
[d]$900 × 6		
12. Dividends paid	5,000	
Cash		5,000
13. Office equipment	12,000	
Cash		12,000
14. Notes payable	4,000	
Cash		4,000
15. Insurance expense	1,200	
Prepaid insurance		1,200
16. Unearned rent	3,600	
Rent revenue		3,600
17. Income tax expense	20,640[e]	
Income taxes payable		20,640

      [e]*Note:* This journal entry can be prepared only
      after the income before income taxes is computed
      ($68,800 × 30%).

EXHIBIT 3–4

ROSS COMPANY
General Ledger for 1993
Asset Accounts

Cash					Accounts Receivable			
12/31/92	30,000	(4)	2,400	12/31/92	20,000	(5)		185,000
(5)	185,000	(6)	72,000	(2)	200,000			
(11)	5,400	(9)	50,000					
		(12)	5,000					
		(13)	12,000					
		(14)	4,000					
12/31/93	75,000			12/31/93	35,000			

Inventory				Land		
12/31/92	15,000	(3)	70,000	12/31/92	30,000	
(1)	80,000					
12/31/93	25,000			12/31/93	30,000	

Prepaid Insurance			
(4)	2,400	(15)	1,200
12/31/93	1,200		

Building				Accumulated Depreciation: Building			
12/31/92	60,000					12/31/92	20,000
						(7)	2,000
12/31/93	60,000					12/31/93	22,000

Office Equipment				Accumulated Depreciation: Office Equipment			
12/31/92	50,000					12/31/92	15,000
(13)	12,000					(8)	5,000
12/31/93	62,000					12/31/93	20,000

EXHIBIT 3–4 *(continued)*

Liability Accounts

Accounts Payable					Salaries Payable		
(6)	72,000	12/31/92	15,000				
		(1)	80,000			(9)	600
		12/31/93	23,000			12/31/93	600

Interest Payable				Unearned Rent			
		(10)	6,000	(16)	3,600	(11)	5,400
		12/31/93	6,000			12/31/93	1,800

Income Taxes Payable				Notes Payable			
						12/31/92	40,000
		(17)	20,640	(14)	4,000		
		12/31/93	20,640			12/31/93	36,000

EXHIBIT 3–4 *(continued)*

Stockholders' Equity Accounts

Common Stock				Additional Paid-in Capital	
	12/31/92	35,000		12/31/92	50,000
	12/31/93	35,000		12/31/93	50,000

Retained Earnings		
	12/31/92	30,000

Sales			Rent Revenue		
	(2)	200,000		(16)	3,600

Cost of Goods Sold			Depreciation Expense: Building		
(3)	70,000		(7)	2,000	

Depreciation Expense: Office Equipment			Salaries Expense		
(8)	5,000		(9)	50,600	

Interest Expense			Insurance Expense		
(10)	6,000		(15)	1,200	

Income Tax Expense			Dividends Paid		
(17)	20,640		(12)	5,000	

EXHIBIT 3–5

ROSS COMPANY
Trial Balance
For Year Ended December 31, 1993

	Debits	Credits
Cash	$ 75,000	
Accounts receivable	35,000	
Inventory	25,000	
Prepaid insurance	1,200	
Land	30,000	
Building	60,000	
Accumulated depreciation: building		$ 22,000
Office equipment	62,000	
Accumulated depreciation: office equipment		20,000
Accounts payable		23,000
Salaries payable		600
Unearned rent		1,800
Interest payable		6,000
Income taxes payable		20,640
Notes payable		36,000
Common stock		35,000
Additional paid-in capital		50,000
Retained earnings		30,000
Sales		200,000
Rent revenue		3,600
Cost of goods sold	70,000	
Depreciation expense: building	2,000	
Depreciation expense: office equipment	5,000	
Salaries expense	50,600	
Interest expense	6,000	
Insurance expense	1,200	
Income tax expense	20,640	
Dividends paid	5,000	
Totals	$448,640	$448,640

EXHIBIT 3–6

····················

ROSS COMPANY
Income Statement
For Year Ended December 31, 1993

Revenues		
Sales revenues		$200,000
Cost of goods sold		(70,000)
Gross profit		$130,000
Operating expenses		
Depreciation expense: building	$ 2,000	
Depreciation expense: office equipment	5,000	
Salaries expense	50,600	
Insurance expense	1,200	
Total operating expenses		(58,800)
Operating income		$ 71,200
Other revenues and expenses		
Rent revenues	3,600	
Interest expense	(6,000)	
Nonoperating income (expense)		(2,400)
Income before income taxes		$ 68,800
Income tax expense		(20,640)
Net income		$ 48,160

EXHIBIT 3–7

····················

ROSS COMPANY
Schedule of Changes in Stockholders' Equity
For Year Ended December 31, 1993

	Common Stock $5 par	Additional Paid-in Capital	Retained Earnings	Total
Balances, 12/31/1992	$35,000	$50,000	$30,000	$115,000
Net income			48,160	48,160
Cash dividends paid			(5,000)	(5,000)
Balances, 12/31/1993	$35,000	$50,000	$73,160	$158,160

EXHIBIT 3–8

··················

ROSS COMPANY
Balance Sheet
December 31, 1993

ASSETS

Current assets			
Cash		$75,000	
Accounts receivable		35,000	
Inventory		25,000	
Prepaid insurance		1,200	
Total current assets			$136,200
Property, plant, and equipment			
Land		$30,000	
Building	$60,000		
Less: accumulated depreciation	(22,000)	38,000	
Office equipment	$62,000		
Less: accumulated depreciation	(20,000)	42,000	
Total property, plant, and equipment			110,000
Total assets			$246,200

LIABILITIES

Current liabilities			
Accounts payable		$23,000	
Salaries payable		600	
Unearned rent		1,800	
Interest payable		6,000	
Income taxes payable		20,640	
Total current liabilities			$52,040
Noncurrent liabilities			
Notes payable			36,000
Total liabilities			$88,040

STOCKHOLDERS' EQUITY

Common stock, $5 par		$35,000	
Additional paid-in capital		50,000	
Retained earnings		73,160	
Total stockholders' equity			158,160
Total liabilities and stockholders' equity			$246,200

EXHIBIT 3–9

ROSS COMPANY
Statement of Cash Flows
For Year Ended December 31, 1993

Cash flows from operating activities (direct method)		
Cash inflows:		
Collections from customers	$185,000	
Collections of rent	5,400	
Cash inflows from operating activities		$190,400
Cash outflows:		
Payments to suppliers	$ 72,000	
Payments to employees	50,000	
Payments for insurance	2,400	
Cash outflows for operating activities		(124,400)
Net cash provided by operating activities		$ 66,000
Cash flows from investing activities		
Payment for office equipment	(12,000)	
Net cash used for investing activities		(12,000)
Cash flows from financing activities		
Payment of notes payable	(4,000)	
Payment of dividends	(5,000)	
Net cash used for financing activities		(9,000)
Net increase in cash		$45,000
Plus: cash balance, January 1, 1993		30,000
Cash balance, December 31, 1993		$ 75,000
Cash flows from operating activities (indirect method)		
Net income	$48,160	
Adjustments for differences between income flows and cash flows from operating activities		
Depreciation expense: building	2,000	
Depreciation expense: office equipment	5,000	
Increase in accounts receivable	(15,000)	
Increase in inventory	(10,000)	
Increase in prepaid insurance	(1,200)	
Increase in accounts payable	8,000	
Increase in salaries payable	600	
Increase in unearned rent	1,800	
Increase in interest payable	6,000	
Increase in income taxes payable	20,640	
Net cash flow from operating activities		$ 66,000

EXHIBIT 3–10

················

ROSS COMPANY
Relationships Among the Three Financial Statements

Beginning Balance Sheet		Income Statement	
Accounts receivable	$20,000	Revenue	$200,000
Inventory	15,000	Cost of goods sold	(70,000)
Prepaid insurance	0	Insurance expense	(1,200)
Land	30,000		
Building (net)	40,000	Depreciation expense	(2,000)
Office equipment (net)	35,000	Depreciation expense	(5,000)
Accounts payable	15,000		
Salaries payable	0	Salaries expense	(50,600)
Unearned rent	0	Rent revenue	3,600
Interest payable	0	Interest expense	(6,000)
Income taxes payable	0	Income tax expense	(20,640)
Notes payable	40,000		
Common stock	35,000		
Additional paid-in cap.	50,000		
Retained earnings	30,000	Net income	$ 48,160
Cash	30,000		

*Purchases = Cost of goods sold + Increase (– Decrease) in Inventory
 Payments = Purchases – Increase (+ Decrease) in Accounts payable
 $72,000 = $70,000 + ($25,000 – $15,000) – ($23,000 – $15,000)
Note: The parentheses indicate subtractions in the vertical columns (i.e., they indicate neither debits and credits, nor subtractions in the horizontal rows).

EXHIBIT 3–10 *(continued)*

	Cash Flow Statement				
	Operating Activities	**Investing Activities**	**Financing Activities**	**Ending Balance Sheet**	
Collections from customers	$185,000			Accounts receivable	$35,000
Payments for purchases	(72,000)*			Inventory	25,000
Payments for insurance	(2,400)			Prepaid insurance	1,200
				Land	30,000
				Building (net)	38,000
Payment for office equipment		$(12,000)		Office equipment (net)	42,000
	*			Accounts payable	23,000
Payments to employees	(50,000)			Salaries payable	600
Collections of rent	5,400			Unearned rent	1,800
				Interest payable	6,000
				Income taxes payable	20,640
Payment of notes payable			$(4,000)	Notes payable	36,000
				Common stock	35,000
				Additional paid-in cap.	50,000
Dividends paid			(5,000)	Retained earnings	73,160
	$ 66,000	$(12,000)	$(9,000)		
				Cash	75,000

QUESTIONS

1. Why are adjustments necessary?

2. What are prepaid expenses and unearned revenues? Give an example of an adjustment to update each of these items at year-end.

3. What are accrued expenses and accrued revenues? Give an example of an adjustment to record each of these items at year-end.

4. Give an example of an adjustment to record depreciation.

5. Discuss the relationship between the accounting equation and the double entry system of recording transactions.

6. Define the following:

   a. Account.
   b. Contra account.
   c. Ledger.
   d. Journal.
   e. Posting.

7. Why is it advantageous to initially record each transaction in a journal?

8. Give examples of transactions that

   a. Increase an asset and a liability.
   b. Increase an asset and a stockholders' equity account.
   c. Increase an asset and decrease an asset.
   d. Decrease an asset and a liability.
   e. Decrease an asset and a stockholders' equity account.

9. Give examples of transactions that

   a. Increase a revenue and decrease a liability.
   b. Increase an expense and a liability.
   c. Increase an expense and decrease an asset.
   d. Increase a revenue and an asset.

10. What are the key procedures in the accounting system? Briefly discuss each procedure.

11. What is a contra account? What is a book value? Show how the book value of a building costing $14,000 and having accumulated depreciation of $5,000 would be listed in a balance sheet.

PROBLEMS AND CASES

12. Depreciation. On January 1, 1993, the McCartney Company purchased store equipment for $6,300 cash. The equipment has an estimated useful life of nine years and a residual value of zero. The company uses the straight-line depreciation method.

Required 1. Record the effects on the accounting equation of:

   a. The purchase of the store equipment on January 1, 1993.
   b. The necessary adjustment at the end of 1993.

2. If the adjustment had *not* been made in Requirement 1b, discuss what effect this error would have had on the accounts and totals listed in the income statement and balance sheet.

13. Prepaid Items. On October 1, 1993, the Bourdon Company paid $600 for a one-year comprehensive insurance policy on the company's building.

Required Record the effects on the accounting equation of the purchase of this insurance policy and the adjustment at the end of 1993.

14. Unearned Revenue. On October 1, 1993, the Sagir Company received $1,800 in advance for six months rent of office space to the Land-Ho Real Estate Agency.

Required 1. Record the effects on the accounting equation of:

      a. The receipt of the payment.
      b. The adjustment for rent revenue at the end of 1993.

    2. If the adjustment had *not* been made in Requirement 1b, discuss what effect this error would have had on the accounts and totals listed in the income statement and balance sheet.

15. Accrued Expense. The Clinkscales Company employs five employees, each earning $250 per week for a five-day workweek (Monday through Friday). The employees are paid every Friday; November 30, 1993, the end of the company's fiscal year, falls on Tuesday.

Required Record the effects on the accounting equation on:

    1. November 30, 1993.

    2. December 2, 1993.

16. Accrued Interest Expense and Revenue. On October 1, 1993, the Scotch Company purchased two acres of land from the Irist Company at a cost of $20,000. The Scotch Company signed (issued) a one-year, 10% note requiring it to repay the $20,000 principal plus $2,000 interest on October 1, 1994, to the Irist Company. The Irist Company had originally purchased the land for $20,000.

Required Record the effects on the accounting equation of the transaction on October 1 and the adjustment at the end of 1993 for:

    1. The Scotch Company.

    2. The Irist Company.

17. Adjustments. The following partial list of accounts and account balances has been taken before and after the adjustments of the Mane Company:

| | BEFORE ADJUSTMENT | | AFTER ADJUSTMENT | |
Account Titles	Debit	Credit	Debit	Credit
Accumulated depreciation		$5,000		$6,600
Interest payable		0		218
Prepaid insurance	$350		$250	
Salaries payable		0		550

Required Prepare the adjustment in journal entry form that caused the change in each account balance.

18. Adjustments. At the end of the current year the Rulem Company provides you with the following information:

1. Depreciation expense on equipment totals $1,670 for the current year.

2. Accrued interest on a note payable issued on October 1 amounts to $850 at year-end.

3. Unearned revenue in the amount of $1,000 has become earned.

4. Supplies used during the year total $310.

Required Record the effects of the adjustments on the accounting equation at the end of the current year based on the above information.

19. **Adjustments.** The following information for the December 31, 1993, year-end adjustments of the Sullivan Company is available:

1. Salaries at year-end that have accumulated but have not been paid total $1,350.

2. Annual straight-line depreciation for the company's equipment is based on a cost of $30,000, an estimated life of eight years, and an estimated residual value of $2,000.

3. Prepaid insurance in the amount of $800 has expired.

4. Interest that has been earned but not collected totals $500.

5. Unearned rent in the amount of $1,000 has become earned.

6. Interest on a note payable that has accumulated but has not been paid totals $600.

7. The income tax rate is 30% on current income and is payable in the first quarter of 1994. The pretax income before the above adjustments is $6,800.

Required Record the effects of each adjustment on the accounting equation.

20. **Adjustments.** Provided below are several transactions of the Pruitt Company that occurred during 1993 and were recorded in balance sheet accounts:

Date	Transaction
April 1	Purchased a delivery van for $5,000, paying $1,000 down, and issuing a one-year, 12% note payable for the $4,000 balance. It was estimated that the van would have a four-year life and a $600 residual value; the company uses straight-line depreciation. The interest on the note will be paid on the maturity date.
May 15	Purchased $850 of office supplies.
June 2	Purchased a two-year comprehensive insurance policy for $960.
Aug. 1	Received six months rent in advance at $300 per month.
Sept. 15	Advanced $600 to sales personnel to cover their future travel costs.
Nov. 1	Accepted an $8,000, six-month, 12% (annual rate) note receivable from a customer, the interest to be collected when the note is collected.

The following information also is available:

1. On January 1, 1993, the Office Supplies account had a $250 balance. On December 31, 1993, an inventory count showed $190 of office supplies on hand.

2. The weekly (five-day) payroll of Pruitt Company amounts to $2,000. All employees are paid at the close of business each Tuesday. December 31, 1993, falls on a Friday.

3. Sales personnel travel cost reports indicate that $490 of advances had been used to pay travel expenses.

4. The income tax rate is 30% and is payable in the first quarter of 1994. The pretax income before the adjusting entries is $8,655.

Required Record the effects of each adjustment on the accounting equation.

21. Adjustments. The following partial list of accounts and account balances of the Barker Company has been taken before and after adjustments:

Account Titles	BEFORE ADJUSTMENT Debit	BEFORE ADJUSTMENT Credit	AFTER ADJUSTMENT Debit	AFTER ADJUSTMENT Credit
Accumulated depreciation		$5,500		$6,900
Income taxes payable		0		2,000
Interest payable		0		380
Prepaid insurance	$340		$110	
Salaries payable		0		720
Unearned rent		1,000		400

Required Record the effects of each adjustment on the accounting equation.

22. Transactions. The Mead Company engaged in the following transactions during the month of May:

Date	Transaction
May 1	Made cash sales of $6,100.
5	Purchased $2,400 of inventory on account.
9	Made credit sales of $3,300.
13	Paid sales salaries of $900 and office salaries of $600.
14	Paid for the May 5 purchases.
18	Purchased sales equipment costing $8,000; made a down payment of $1,500 and agreed to pay the balance in 60 days.
21	Purchased $600 of inventory for cash.
27	Sold land that had originally cost $2,100 for $2,600.
31	Cost of goods sold for the month was $1,400.

Required Record the effects of each transaction on the accounting equation.

23. Transactions. The following are selected accounts and account balances of the Sawyer Company on May 31, 1993:

	Debit (Credit)
Cash	$12,576
Accounts receivable	8,052
Inventory	21,705
Office equipment	35,860
Accumulated depreciation	(10,540)
Notes payable	(13,245)
Accounts payable	(7,500)
Sales revenue	(47,872)
Cost of goods sold	20,000
Gain on sale of office equipment	(400)
Utility expense	1,124

The Sawyer Company entered into the following transactions during June:

Date	Transaction
June 3	Sold for $600 office equipment that had cost $2,000 and has associated accumulated depreciation of $1,500.
7	Made sales of $3,500 on account.
10	Purchased $1,000 of merchandise for cash.
15	Purchased new office equipment costing $4,000, paying $1,500 and signing a 90-day note for the balance.
16	Received $3,500 check for June 7 credit.
17	Made cash sales of $4,200.
20	Purchased $2,200 of merchandise on account.
29	Paid for the June 20 purchase.
30	Paid the monthly utility bill, $210.
30	Cost of goods sold for the month was $3,000.

Required Record the effects of each adjustment on the accounting equation.

24. Adjustments. The following 1993 information is available concerning the Drake Company:

1. Salaries accrued but unpaid total $1,980 on December 31, 1993.

2. The $247 December utility bill arrived on December 31, 1993, and has not been paid or recorded.

3. Buildings with a cost of $78,000, 30-year life, and a $6,000 residual value are to be depreciated; equipment with a cost of $47,000, 12-year life, and a $2,000 residual value is also to be depreciated. The straight-line method is to be used.

4. A count of supplies indicates that the Store Supplies account should be reduced by $128 and the Office Supplies account reduced by $412 for supplies used during the year.

5. The company holds a $3,000, 12% (annual rate), six-month note receivable dated September 1, 1993, from a customer. The interest is to be collected on the maturity date.

6. An analysis of the company insurance policies indicates that the Prepaid Insurance account is to be reduced for the $548 of expired insurance.

7. A review of travel expense reports indicates that $310 advanced to sales personnel had been used by these personnel.

8. The income tax rate is 20% and will be paid in the first quarter of 1994. The pretax income of the company before adjustments is $12,180.

Required Record the effects of each adjustment on the accounting equation.

25. **Effects of Errors.** During the current accounting period the Page Company makes the following errors:

Error	Net Income	Total Assets	Total Liabilities	Total Stockholders' Equity
Example: Failed to record a cash sale.	U	U	N	U
1. The purchase of equipment for cash is recorded as a debit to Equipment and a credit to Accounts Payable.	N	N	N	N
2. Failed to record the purchase of inventory on account.	O	O	U	O
3. Cash received from a customer as payment of its account is recorded as if the receipt were for a current period sale.				
4. Failed to record a credit sale.	N	U	N	N
5. At the end of the year the receipt of money from a 60-day, 12% bank loan is recorded as a debit to Cash and a credit to Sales Revenue.				
6. Failed to record the depreciation at the end of the current period.	O	O	N	O

Required Indicate the effect of the errors on the net income, total assets, total liabilities, and total stockholders' equity at the end of the accounting period by using the following code: O = overstated, U = understated, N = no effect. Disregard income taxes.

26. **Adjusting Entries.** The trial balance of the Halsey Company on December 31, 1993 (the end of its annual accounting period), included the following account balances before adjustments:

Note receivable	$14,000	debit
Prepaid insurance	7,200	debit
Equipment	15,000	debit
Building	92,000	debit
Unearned rent	6,240	credit
Note payable	10,000	credit
Supplies	1,600	debit

In reviewing the company's recorded transactions and accounting records for 1993, you find the following data pertaining to the December 31, 1993, adjustments:

1. On July 1, 1993, the company had accepted a $14,000, one-year, 10% note receivable from a customer. The interest is to be collected when the note is collected.

2. On October 1, 1993, the company had paid $7,200 for a three-year insurance policy.

3. The building was acquired on January 1, 1982, and is being depreciated using the straight-line method over a 20-year life with no residual value.

4. The equipment was purchased on April 1, 1993. It is to be depreciated using the straight-line method over a 15-year life with no residual value.

5. On July 1, 1993, the company had received two years rent in advance for a portion of its building rented to the Shields Company.

6. On November 1, 1993, the company had issued a $10,000, three-month, 9% note payable to a supplier. The $225 total interest is to be paid when the note is paid.

7. On January 1, 1993, the company had $200 of supplies on hand. During 1993 the company purchased $1,400 of supplies. A physical count on December 31, 1993, revealed that there are $90 of supplies still on hand.

Required Prepare the adjusting entries that are necessary to bring the Halsey accounts up to date on December 31, 1993. Each journal entry explanation should summarize your calculations.

27. **Adjusting Entries.** The trial balance of the Cronell Company on December 31, 1993 (the end of its annual accounting period) included these account balances before adjustments:

Note receivable	$ 6,000	debit
Prepaid rent	4,320	debit
Supplies	2,000	debit
Equipment	10,000	debit
Unearned service revenues	1,025	credit
Note payable	5,000	credit

Reviewing the company's accounting records, you find the following data pertaining to the December 31, 1993, adjustments:

1. On October 1, 1993, the company had accepted a $6,000, six-month, 12% note receivable from a customer. The $360 total interest is to be collected when the note is collected.

2. On January 2, 1993, the company paid for one year of rent in advance at $360 per month.

3. On January 1, 1993, $400 of supplies were on hand. During 1993 the company purchased $1,600 of supplies. A physical count on December 31, 1993, revealed that there are $330 of supplies on hand.

4. The equipment was purchased on July 1, 1993. It is to be depreciated using the straight-line method over a five-year life with no residual value.

5. On October 1, 1993, the company received $1,025 in advance for services to be rendered. On December 31, 1993, $225 remained unearned.

6. On April 1, 1993, the company had issued a $5,000, one-year, 10% note payable to a supplier. Interest is to be paid when the note is paid.

Required Prepare the adjusting entries necessary to bring the Cronell Company accounts up to date on December 31, 1993. Each journal entry explanation should summarize your calculations.

28. **Adjusting Entries.** Several transactions of the Paribus Company that occurred during 1993 and were recorded in balance sheet accounts are as follows:

Date	Transaction
Mar. 1	Purchased equipment for $12,000, paying $3,000 down, and issuing a one-year, 12% note payable for the $9,000 balance. The equipment has an estimated life of 10 years and a zero residual value. The interest on the note will be paid on the maturity date.
May 24	Purchased $320 of office supplies. The office supplies on hand at the beginning of the year totaled $145.
June 2	Purchased a two-year comprehensive insurance policy for $960.
Sept. 1	Received six months rent in advance at $350 per month and recorded the $2,100 receipt as unearned rent revenue.
Oct. 1	Accepted a $3,000, 6-month, 10% note receivable from a customer. The $150 total interest is to be collected when the note is collected.

Additional Information:

1. On December 31, 1993, the office supplies on hand totaled $47.

2. All employees work Monday through Friday. The weekly payroll of the Paribus Company amounts to $5,000. All employees are paid at the close of business each Wednesday for the previous five working days (including Wednesday). December 31, 1993, falls on a Friday.

Required On the basis of the above information prepare journal entries to record whatever adjustments are necessary on December 31, 1993. Each journal entry explanation should show any related computations.

29. Adjusting Entries. Several transactions of the Marlin Company that occurred during 1993 and were recorded in balance sheet accounts are as follows:

Date	Transaction
Apr. 2	Purchased equipment for $18,000, paying $3,000 down and issuing a one-year, 10% note payable for the $15,000 balance. The equipment has an estimated life of 15 years and a zero residual value. The interest on the note will be paid on the maturity date.
June 14	Purchased $750 of office supplies. The office supplies on hand at the beginning of 1993 totaled $250.
July 1	Received six months rent in advance at $300 per month and recorded the $1,800 receipt as unearned rent revenue.
Nov. 1	Accepted a $4,000, six-month, 12% note receivable from a customer. The $240 total interest is to be collected when the note is collected.

Additional Information:

1. On December 31, 1993, the office supplies on hand totaled $210.

2. All employees work Monday through Friday. The weekly payroll of the company amounts to $6,000. All employees are paid at the close of business each Tuesday for the previous five working days (including Tuesday). December 31, 1993, falls on a Friday.

Required On the basis of the above information, prepare journal entries to record whatever adjustments are necessary on December 31, 1993.

30. Adjusting Entries. A partial list of accounts and account balances of the Rowland Company taken before and after the adjustments is as follows:

Account Titles	BEFORE ADJUSTMENT Debit	BEFORE ADJUSTMENT Credit	AFTER ADJUSTMENT Debit	AFTER ADJUSTMENT Credit
Supplies	$1,200		$282	
Prepaid insurance	500		150	
Accumulated depreciation: building		$5,000		$6,500
Accumulated depreciation: equipment		800		1,100
Interest payable		0		94
Salaries payable		0		573
Unearned rent		2,250		750

Required Prepare the adjusting entry that caused the change in each account balance.

31. Adjusting Entries. A partial list of accounts and account balances of the Triton Company taken before and after the adjustments is as follows:

Account Titles	BEFORE ADJUSTMENT Debit	BEFORE ADJUSTMENT Credit	AFTER ADJUSTMENT Debit	AFTER ADJUSTMENT Credit
Office supplies	$ 675		$136	
Prepaid rent	3,300		550	
Accumulated depreciation		$1,000		$1,600
Interest receivable	0		112	
Salaries payable		0		355
Unearned revenue		1,275		275

Required Prepare the adjusting entry that caused the change in each account balance.

32. **Adjusting Entries.** Selected accounts and account balances of the Ritter Company taken before and after the adjustments at the end of 1993 are shown below:

Account Titles	BEFORE ADJUSTMENT Debit	BEFORE ADJUSTMENT Credit	AFTER ADJUSTMENT Debit	AFTER ADJUSTMENT Credit
Depreciation expense	$ 0		$4,400	
Interest payable (due May 15, 1995)		$ 0		$ 650
Utilities expense	1,370		1,682	
Rental revenue		1,650		2,300
Income tax expense	0		2,740	
Prepaid insurance	1,684		1,380	
Office salaries payable		0		540
Rent expense	0		1,200	
Accumulated depreciation		14,820		19,320
Interest receivable (due March 1, 1994)	0		320	
Prepaid rent	1,600		400	
Office salaries expense	5,600		6,140	
Income taxes payable		0		2,740
Insurance expense	300		604	
Interest expense	0		650	
Unearned rent		500		0
Utilities payable		0		312
Interest revenue		620		940
Sales salaries expense	7,300		7,650	
Office supplies	1,150		700	
Rent receivable	0		150	
Advances to salespersons	570		220	
Office supplies expense	0		450	

Required Determine the adjusting entries that were made on December 31, 1993. Prepare your answers in general journal form.

33. Adjusting Entries. The Trishia Company on December 31, 1993 (the end of its annual accounting period) had the following account balances before adjustments:

Notes receivable	$ 8,000	debit
Prepaid insurance	4,200	debit
Delivery equipment	14,000	debit
Building	75,000	debit
Unearned rent	4,320	credit
Notes payable	7,200	credit
Office supplies	1,000	debit

Reviewing the company's recorded transactions and accounting records for 1993, you find the following data pertaining to the December 31, 1993, adjustments:

1. On July 1, 1993, the company had accepted an $8,000, nine-month, 10% (annual rate) note receivable from a customer. The interest is to be collected when the note is collected.

2. On August 1, 1993, the company had paid $4,200 for a one-year insurance policy.

3. The building was acquired in 1987 and is being depreciated using the straight-line method over a 25-year life. It has an estimated residual value of $5,000.

4. The delivery equipment was purchased on April 1, 1993. It is to be depreciated using the straight-line method over a five-year life with an estimated residual value of $4,000.

5. On September 1, 1993, the company had received two years rent in advance ($4,320) for a portion of a building it is renting to Oscar Company.

6. On December 1, 1993, the company had issued a $7,200, three-month, 12% (annual rate) note payable to a supplier. The interest is to be paid when the note is paid.

7. On January 2, 1993, the company purchased $1,000 of office supplies. A physical count on December 31, 1993, revealed that there are $125 of office supplies still on hand. No supplies were on hand at the beginning of the year.

Required Prepare the adjusting entries necessary to bring the Trishia Company accounts up to date on December 31, 1993. Each journal entry explanation should summarize your calculations.

34. Adjusting Entries. The Franklin Retail Company entered into the following transactions during 1993. The transactions were properly recorded in balance sheet accounts.

Date	Transaction
Jan. 25	Purchased $480 of office supplies.
Feb. 1	Rented a warehouse from Tropple Company, paying one year's rent of $3,600 in advance.
March 1	Borrowed $10,000 from the bank, signing a one-year note at an annual interest rate of 12%.

Date	Transaction
May 1	Purchased office equipment for $13,000, paying $3,000 down and signing a two-year, 10% (annual rate) note payable for the balance. The office equipment is expected to have a useful life of ten years and a residual value of $1,000. Straight-line depreciation is appropriate.
May 31	Purchased a three-year comprehensive insurance policy for $720.
Aug. 1	Sold land for $9,000. The purchaser made a $2,000 down payment and signed a one-year, 10% note for the balance. The interest and principal will be collected on the maturity date.
Oct. 1	Rented a portion of the retail floor space to a florist for $120 per month, collecting six months rent in advance.
Nov. 12	Issued checks to sales personnel totaling $900. The checks are advances for expected travel costs during the remainder of the year.

On December 31, 1993, the following additional information is available:

1. Property taxes for 1993 are due to be paid by April 1, 1994. The company has not paid or recorded its $2,300 property taxes for 1993.

2. The $312 December utility bill has not been recorded or paid.

3. Salaries accrued but not paid total $927.

4. Travel cost reports indicate that $787 of travel advances have been used to pay travel expenses.

5. The Office Supplies account had a balance of $137 on January 1, 1993. A physical count on December 31, 1993, showed $174 of office supplies on hand.

6. On January 1, 1993, the Buildings account and the Store Equipment account had balances of $100,000 and $65,000, respectively. The buildings are expected to have a $10,000 residual value, while the store equipment is expected to have a $2,000 residual value at the end of their respective lives. They are being depreciated using the straight-line method over 20- and 10-year lives, respectively.

7. The income tax rate is 20% and is payable in the first quarter of 1994. The pretax income of the company before adjustments is $27,829.

Required On the basis of the above information prepare journal entries to adjust the company's books as of December 31, 1993. Each entry explanation should include supporting computations. (Round to the nearest dollar.)

35. Journal Entries, Posting, and Trial Balance. The trial balance of the Antel Company on November 1, 1993, is shown:

	Debit	Credit
Cash	$ 7,800	
Accounts receivable	12,530	
Notes receivable	6,000	
Inventory, November 1, 1993	25,670	

	Debit	Credit
Prepaid insurance	840	
Office supplies	465	
Land	74,350	
Buildings	66,580	
Accumulated depreciation: buildings		$ 21,400
Equipment	37,620	
Accumulated depreciation: equipment		11,480
Patents	25,000	
Accounts payable		38,750
Notes payable		2,400
Common stock, no par		165,000
Retained earnings, November 1, 1993		24,680
Sales revenue		38,400
Cost of goods sold	32,000	
Sales salaries expense	6,200	
Office salaries expense	4,300	
Advertising expense	1,250	
Utility expense	1,845	
Interest revenue		550
Interest expense	210	
	$302,660	$302,660

During the month of November the following transactions took place:

Date	Transaction
Nov. 2	Made cash sales of $2,400.
4	Purchased $800 of merchandise for cash.
6	Sold an unused 1/2 acre of land for $4,000; the land had originally cost $3,750.
7	Purchased a two-year comprehensive insurance policy for $572.
10	Leased an unused portion of its building to Charles Company, collecting six months rent in advance at $220 per month.
13	Made $2,200 of sales on account to Grant Company.
15	Collected the $200 monthly payment plus $30 interest on a customer's note receivable.
16	Purchased $1,500 of merchandise on account from Mason Company.
21	Purchased land for a future building site. Made a $2,000 down payment and signed a 12%, 90-day, $6,000 note payable for the balance.
23	Collected the Grant Company account for the November 13 sale.
25	Paid for the November 16 purchase of merchandise.
27	Paid the city newspaper $470 for advertising that had appeared during November.
29	Paid $520 of sales salaries and $390 of office salaries.
30	Cost of goods sold for the month was $3,050.

Required 1. Prepare general journal entries to record the above transactions.

2. Post to the general ledger accounts.

3. Prepare a trial balance on November 30, 1993.

36. **Faulty Financial Statements.** Ray Young is the principal stockholder of a repair service called Ray's Rapid Repairs Company. It is the end of the year and his bookkeeper has recently resigned to move to a warmer climate. Knowing only a little about accounting, Ray prepared the following financial statements, based on the ending balances in the company's accounts on December 31, 1993:

RAY'S RAPID REPAIRS COMPANY
Income Statement
For Year Ended December 31, 1993

Repair service revenues		$29,000
Operating expenses		
Rent expense	$ 3,800	
Salaries expense	9,900	
Utilities expense	1,100	
Dividends paid	16,000	
Total operating expenses		(30,800)
Net loss		$(1,800)

Balance Sheet
December 31, 1993

ASSETS		LIABILITIES AND STOCKHOLDERS' EQUITY	
Cash	$ 1,600	Accounts payable	$ 2,600
Repair supplies	2,300	Note payable (due 1/1/1995)	10,000
Repair equipment	15,000	Total liabilities	$12,600
		Common stock, no par	2,000
		Retained earnings[a]	4,300
		Total liabilities and	
Total assets	$18,900	stockholders' equity	$18,900

[a]Beginning retained earnings—net loss.

Ray is upset and says to you, "I don't know how I could have a net loss in 1993. Maybe I did something wrong when I made out these financial statements. Could you help me? My business has been good in 1993. In these times of rising prices, people have been getting their appliances and other items repaired by me instead of buying new ones. I used to have to rent my repair equipment, but business was so good that I purchased $15,000 of repair equipment at the beginning of the year. I know this equipment will last ten years even though it won't be worth anything at the end of that time. I did have to sign a note for $10,000 of the purchase price, but the amount (plus 12% annual interest) will not be due until the beginning of 1995. I still have to rent my repair shop, but I paid $3,800 for two years of rent in advance at the beginning of 1993, so I am OK there. And besides, I just counted my repair supplies and I have $1,300 of supplies left from 1993, which I can use in 1994."

He continues, "I'm not too worried about my cash balance. I know that customers owe me $700 for repair work I just completed in 1993. These are good customers and always pay, but I never tell my bookkeeper about this until I collect the cash. I am sure I will collect in 1994, and that will also make 1994 revenues look good. In fact, it will just about offset the $800 I collected in advance (and recorded as a revenue) from a customer for repair work I said I would do in 1994. I still have to write a check to pay my bookkeeper for his last month's salary, but he was my only employee in 1993. In 1994 I am only going to hire someone on a part-time basis to keep my accounting records. You can have the job if you can determine whether the net loss is correct, and if not, what it should be and what I am doing wrong."

Required 1. Prepare any adjustments you think are appropriate for 1993. Show any calculations in your explanations.

2. Prepare a corrected 1993 income statement, a statement of changes in stockholders' equity, and an ending balance sheet.

3. Write a brief report to Ray Young summarizing your suggestions for improving his accounting practices.

37. Effects of Adjusting Entry Errors. During the current accounting period the bookkeeper for the Nallen Company made the following errors in the year-end adjusting entries:

		EFFECT OF ERROR ON:					
Error		Revenues	Expenses	Net Income	Assets	Liabilities	Stockholders' Equity
Example: Failed to record $200 of accrued salaries		N	U $200	O $200	N	U $200	O $200
1. Failed to adjust prepaid insurance for $400 of expired insurance.		N	U 400	O 400	N	O 400	O 400
2. Failed to record $500 of interest expense that had accrued during the period.		N	U 500	O 500	N	O 500	O 500
3. Inadvertently recorded $300 of annual depreciation twice for the same equipment.							
4. Failed to record $100 of interest revenue that had accrued during the period.		U 100	N	U 100	U 100	N	U 100
5. Failed to reduce unearned revenues for $600 of revenues that were earned during the period.							

Required Assuming that the errors are not discovered, indicate the effect of each error on revenues, expenses, net income, assets, liabilities, and stockholders' equity at the end of the accounting period. Use the following code: O = Overstated, U = Understated, and N = No effect. Include dollar amounts.

38. Financial Statements from Incomplete Records. On January 1, 1993, Paula Randolph opened a boutique called P.R.'s Boutique. At that time she invested $30,000 cash by purchasing shares (no par) in the business. With this cash the business immediately purchased $8,000 of inventory and $16,000 of store equipment, and paid two years rent in advance for store space. Paula estimated the store equipment would last for eight years and after that it would be worthless.

During the year the boutique appeared to operate successfully. Paula did not know anything about accounting, although she did keep an accurate checkbook. Her checkbook showed the following summarized items on December 31, 1993:

Payments of two years rent for store space	$ 2,400
Receipts from cash sales	38,000
Payments for purchases of merchandise	15,000
Payments for operating expenses	12,000
Withdrawals of cash for personal use	11,000

Paula has asked for your assistance. She says, "The ending cash balance in the company checkbook is $3,600. Since the beginning cash balance was $30,000, the company seems to have had a net loss of $26,400. Something must be wrong. I am sure the company did better than that. Please find out what the company's earnings were for 1993 and its financial position at the end of 1993."

You agree to help Paula. She has just finished "taking inventory" and indicates the cost of the ending inventory is $9,000. She has kept copies of invoices made out to customers who purchased merchandise on account. These uncollected invoices total $13,000. Paula also has a file of unpaid invoices of suppliers. These unpaid invoices add up to $8,000. Just as you begin your calculations, Paula says, "Oh yes, I also owe my employees $750 of salaries that they have earned this week."

Required Prepare a 1993 income statement and a December 31, 1993, balance sheet for P.R.'s Boutique. Include explanations for all amounts shown.

39. Corrections to Balance Sheet. The bookkeeper of the Washet Company prepared the following balance sheet as of December 31, 1993:

WASHET COMPANY
Balance Sheet
For Year Ended December 31, 1993

Working capital	$ 27,100	Noncurrent liabilities	$ 25,400
Other assets	118,900	Stockholders' equity	120,600
Total	$146,000	Total	$146,000

Your analysis of these items reveals the following information (the amounts in parentheses indicate deductions from each item):

1. Working capital consists of:

Equipment	$ 30,000
Land	10,000
Accounts due to suppliers	(28,000)
Inventory, including office supplies of $3,700	34,700
Salaries owed to employees	(2,600)
Note owed to bank (due December 31, 1995)	(17,000)
	$ 27,100

2. Other assets include:

Cash	$ 7,000
Prepaid insurance	1,900
Buildings	70,000
Long-term investment in government bonds	29,000
Dividends paid	11,000
	$118,900

3. Noncurrent liabilities consist of:

Mortgage payable	$ 33,000
Accumulated depreciation: equipment	16,000
Accounts due from customers	(16,600)
Notes receivable (due December 31, 1996)	(7,000)
	$ 25,400

4. Stockholders' equity includes:

A. Common stock, no par	$ 80,000
Retained earnings	24,900
Accumulated depreciation: buildings	24,000
Securities held as a temporary investment	(10,000)
Interest payable (due July 1, 1994)	1,700
	$120,600

Required Based on your analysis prepare a properly classified December 31, 1993, balance sheet for the Washet Company.

40. Accounting Scams. The following excerpts are from the *Wall Street Journal*, "Accounting Scams on the Rise," July 9, 1982:

1. JWT Group, the parent of the J. Walter Thompson advertising agency, disclosed it would have to charge $30 million to pretax earnings for 1978 through 1981 because it had discovered phony revenue.

2. McCormick, a spice maker, informed the Securities and Exchange Commission and its stockholders that it had restated earnings from 1977 through most of last year because employees had improperly deferred expenses and otherwise juggled the books. [Assume a $10 million amount was involved.]

3. Saxon Industries, which is operating under the protection of federal bankruptcy laws, said that inventories at one of its divisions had been overstated by at least $24 million.

Required Assume these scams all occurred in just one year. Make the original (incorrect) journal entry that summarizes each accounting scam and then make the adjusting journal entry to correct each scam (ignore income taxes).

41. Analysis of Transactions. The account balances after each of the first six transactions relating to the creation and first-year operation of a boat marina are as follows:

Cash	Prepaid Insurance (one-year life, purchased in first month)	Docks and Equipment (10-year life, purchased in first month)	Note Payable (10% interest, $1,000 principal and interest due at end of each year)	Paid-in Capital	Retained Earnings
1. $2,220				$2,220	
2. 2,100	$120			2,220	
3. 100	120	$10,000	$8,000	2,220	
4. 3,100	120	10,000	8,000	2,220	$3,000
5. 2,100	120	10,000	8,000	2,220	2,000
6. 1,100	120	10,000	7,000	2,220	2,000

Required 1. Recreate the journal entries for each transaction and briefly describe the nature of each transaction.

2. Create any necessary adjusting journal entries for the first year of operation and briefly describe the nature of each adjustment. Assume that the income tax rate is 30%.

3. Prepare the income statement for the year. Was the first year of operation profitable? Compute the profit margin (net income divided by net sales).

4. Prepare the balance sheet at the end of the first year. Is the company solvent? Compute the current ratio (current assets divided by current liabilities).

42. Calculations of Unknown Amounts. Four independent situations are given:

	A	B	C	D
Assets				
Beginning	$20	G	$30	$10
Ending	25	$40	M	30
Liabilities				
Beginning	10	H	10	S
Ending	A	I	N	T
Stockholders' equity				
Beginning	B	20	O	10
Ending	15	30	P	U
Revenues	C	30	40	50
Expenses	D	J	Q	V
Net income (loss)	E	K	R	W
Dividends	0	5	0	10
Profit margin (net income divided by net sales)	0.167	L	0.25	0.20
Return on assets (net income divided by average assets)	F	0.2	0.25	X
Additional equity investments	0	5	0	15

Required Solve for the unknown amounts in each situation.

ANNUAL REPORT PROBLEMS

43. **Preparation of Financial Statements.** The following are the February 28, 1989, balance sheet and the February income statement (before adjustments) for Mobil Oil from Problem 60 of Chapter 2 (in millions of dollars):

MOBIL OIL
Hypothetical Balance Sheet
February 28, 1989

ASSETS		LIABILITIES AND STOCKHOLDERS' EQUITY	
Cash	$ 371	Current loan payable	$ 820
Marketable securities	546	Accounts payable	6,043
Accounts receivable	5,138	Taxes payable	3,322
Inventories	4,481	Long-term debt	12,929
Prepaid expenses	527	Contributed capital	865
Properties	47,447	Retained earnings	14,886
Less: accumulated depreciation	(19,645)		
Total	$38,865	Total	$38,865

Hypothetical Income Statement
February 1989

Revenues	$125
Cost of oil sold	100
Insurance expense	10
Rent expense	20
Selling expense	5
Gain on sale of marketable securities	50
Income before income taxes	$ 40

Assume the following information is available for the adjustments to the February 1989 income statement and the balance sheet on February 28, 1989 (in millions of dollars):

1. Depreciation for the month is $294.

2. Prepaid insurance of $6 expired in February.

3. February oil sales of $1,000 on account have not been recorded. Gross profit averages 50% on these sales.

4. Prepaid rent of $5 expired in February.

5. Selling salaries earned in February but not yet paid are $10.

6. A customer receives a $2 reduction of its account receivable from a February oil sale.

7. Interest on long-term debt averages 1% per month or $153 for February and will be paid March 31, 1989.

Required Prepare a revised balance sheet and income statement for Mobil Oil. For convenience, use a T-account to summarize the adjustments to the stockholders' equity in the balance sheet.

44. **Preparation of Financial Statements.** The following are the February 28, 1989, balance sheet and the February income statement (before adjustments) for IBM from Problem 61 of Chapter 2 (in millions of dollars):

IBM
Hypothetical Balance Sheet
February 28, 1989

ASSETS		LIABILITIES AND STOCKHOLDERS' EQUITY	
Cash	$ 4,235	Taxes payable	$ 2,225
Marketable securities	1,458	Short-term loan payable	4,862
Accounts receivable	18,180	Accounts payable	2,722
Inventories	9,495	Accrued liabilities	7,593
Prepaid expenses	1,575	Long-term debt	15,791
Plant, property, and equipment	44,902	Contributed capital	8,223
Less: accumulated depreciation	(21,466)	Retained earnings	31,251
Long-term investments	14,288		
Total	$72,667	Total	$72,667

Hypothetical Income Statement
February 1989

Revenues	$200
Cost of goods sold	(100)
Utilities expense	(5)
Administrative expenses	(20)
Depreciation expense	(10)
Income before income taxes	$ 65

The following information is available for the adjustments to the February 1989 income statement and the balance sheet on February 28, 1989 (in millions of dollars):

1. Included in the accrued liabilities are $2,000 of customer deposits for computers that were just delivered to these customers in February 1989. Assume a gross profit margin of 60% on these computers.

2. Interest on marketable securities for February is $50, which has not been recorded.

3. Prepaid utility expenses of $9 have expired.

4. Interest on long-term debt for February is $90, which has not been recorded.

5. Prepaid rent expenses of $20 have expired in February.

6. Additional unrecorded depreciation is $200 for February.

7. Salaries earned in February but not yet paid are $236.

8. The effective income tax rate is 30%.

Required Prepare a revised income statement and balance sheet for IBM. For convenience, use a T-account to summarize the adjustments to the stockholders' equity in the balance sheet.

45. Review of Accounting Cycle. Exxon's condensed balance sheet for December 31, 1988, is as follows (in millions of dollars):

EXXON
Balance Sheet
December 31, 1988

ASSETS		LIABILITIES AND STOCKHOLDERS' EQUITY	
Cash	$ 2,333	Accounts payable	$ 9,535
Marketable securities	176	Taxes payable	2,995
Accounts receivable	6,094	Accrued expenses	4,949
Inventories	5,151	Long-term debt	25,047
Prepaid expenses	1,092	Stockholders' equity	31,767
Properties, plants and equipment	95,111		
Less: accumulated depreciation	(35,664)		
Total	$74,293	Total	$74,293

The following information is available for the January 1989 income statement and the balance sheet on January 31, 1989 (in millions of dollars)

1. Exxon sold inventory costing $3,000 for $8,000 on account.

2. Exxon purchased inventory costing $400 on account.

3. Accounts receivable of $600 were collected.

4. Accounts payable of $1,000 were paid.

5. Exxon sold marketable securities for $76. These securities had originally cost $176.

6. Exxon purchased $500 of oil properties and financed the entire purchase with long-term debt.

7. Common stock was issued for $100.

8. Exxon paid out $400 in cash as follows: $200 to reduce long-term debt principal and another $200 for interest expense on long-term debt.

9. Exxon paid dividends of $200.

10. Prepaid insurance expense of $100 expired in January.

11. Depreciation for January is $400.

12. Salaries earned in January but not yet paid were $300.

13. Revenues earned in January but not yet recognized or collected were $100.

14. Assume that the Exxon tanker oil spill in Alaska occurred on January 23, 1989. Exxon's oil cleanup plan is estimated to cost $500 and related lawsuit damages are estimated to cost another $500. No cash has been paid by Exxon as of January 31, 1989. The total cost is recognized and will be tax deductible.

15. Exxon's effective income tax rate is 30%.

Required 1. Show how the accounting equation was affected by the above transactions and information.

2. Prepare an income statement in good form for January, 1989.

3. Prepare a balance sheet in good form as of January 31, 1989.

46. Error Analysis. An Internal Evaluation Committee (IEC), established by the Board of Directors of MiniScribe, indicated that the company's assets and net income for 1987 were intentionally overstated as a result of fraudulent schemes developed and executed by the company's senior management. The following items were cited by the IEC for 1987 in the Securities Exchange Commission Form 8K filed by MiniScribe in September, 1989:

1. MiniScribe's allowance for doubtful accounts averaged 1% of its accounts receivable balance of $50 million at 1987 year end. The comparable industry average was 5%.

2. To cover a shortfall in actual inventory, MiniScribe included $9 million of obsolete parts and scrap in 1987 year-end inventory. It also included an additional $4 million of bricks in the 1987 year-end inventory of computer disk drives.

3. About $2 million in profits relating to $10 million of inventory costs may have been improperly recognized in 1987. Late in 1987, MiniScribe established three of its own "just-in-time" (JIT) warehouses near three major independent distributors (or customers) of MiniScribe products. This arrangement enabled the distributors to obtain delivery of MiniScribe products within hours of a request. Under the agreements, terms for payment did not begin until after the products were shipped from these MiniScribe JIT warehouses to the distributors. However, MiniScribe recognized this $2 million profit on the $10 million inventory as it was shipped from MiniScribe's manufacturing plant to its JIT warehouses.

4. One million dollars for internally built equipment was inappropriately recorded as an asset.

5. Scrap and obsolete parts of $2 million were recorded as customer service parts and included as "other long-term assets."

Required 1. Use the accounting equation to analyze the impact of the errors or irregularities upon MiniScribe's financial statements. Be sure to identify specific assets affected. Ignore income taxes.

2. In its 1987 income statement, MiniScribe reported net income of $31 million. Based upon your above adjustments, what would you report as 1987 net income for MiniScribe? Use MiniScribe's effective income tax rate of 10% for 1987. Show all calculations and list each income statement item affected.

3. In its public disclosures concerning 1988 operations, MiniScribe reported net income of $26 million. The IEC learned that in late 1988, MiniScribe's management had apparently made decisions to eliminate certain product lines. However, once the financial impact of these decisions became apparent, the company decided not to record any such adjustment for 1988. Information distributed to the Board of Directors reflected potential end-of-life inventory adjustments for such obsolete products of $22 million. How would MiniScribe's 1988 reported net income of $26 million be adjusted by the above information? Use MiniScribe's 10% effective income tax rate in your calculations.

Financial Reporting:
The Environment

After reading this chapter, you should understand

- The environment and development of accounting standards
- Objectives of financial reporting
- Qualitative characteristics of accounting information
- Accounting assumptions and conventions

- Management's responsibility for the financial statements and the auditor's report
- The accountancy profession

In previous chapters, the three financial statements, and transactions and events affecting them, were introduced. The environment of financial reporting is explained in this chapter. The source of the accounting standards used to report the various transactions and events in the financial statements are also discussed, as well as the objectives of financial reporting and the qualitative characteristics and accounting assumptions and conventions underlying the accounting standards. The responsibility of management and the role of the auditor are explained, along with a discussion of the accountancy profession. More complex transactions and events are discussed in later chapters.

■ THE ENVIRONMENT AND DEVELOPMENT OF ACCOUNTING STANDARDS

The information communicated to external users in financial statements is based on accounting standards that establish generally accepted accounting principles. **Generally accepted accounting principles (GAAP)** incorporate the consensus among accountants at a particular time concerning the economic resources and obligations of a company that should be recorded as assets and liabilities (discussed in Chapter 1), which changes in them should be recorded, which changes represent revenues and expenses (discussed in Chapter 2), when the changes should be recorded, how the recorded assets and liabilities and changes in them should be measured, what information should be reported and how and when it should be disclosed, and which financial statements should be prepared.

In the absence of a particular type of modified audit opinion (discussed later in the chapter), the user of the financial statements can accept that GAAP have been followed in the preparation of the statements. Therefore, the user of financial statements needs to understand the generally accepted accounting principles that are discussed throughout this book and the sources of these principles, as illustrated in Exhibit 4–1.

Even though accounting records dating back thousands of years have been discovered in various parts of the world, there was little organized effort to develop accounting standards in the United States prior to the 1930s. One of the most important initial attempts to develop standards began shortly after the onset of the Great Depression in 1929 with a series of meetings between representatives of the New York Stock Exchange and the American Institute of Accountants which was later to become the American Institute of Certified Public Accountants (AICPA). The goal was to discuss accounting and reporting problems involving the interests of investors, the New York Stock Exchange, and accountants. Since these meetings several groups have been influential in the establishment of generally accepted accounting principles in the private sector of the United States.

Committee on Accounting Procedure (CAP)

In 1938, the AICPA formed the **Committee on Accounting Procedure (CAP).** This group was given the authority to issue pronouncements on accounting procedures and practice, and its deliberations were published as *Accounting Research Bulletins.* However, the CAP was not given the authority to enforce its pronouncements. From its inception until 1953 the CAP issued 42 *Accounting Research Bulletins,* and in 1953 these pronouncements were reviewed and codified into *Accounting Research Bulletin No. 43.* The CAP subsequently issued eight more *Accounting Research Bulletins,* ending with No. 51 and it was replaced by the Accounting Principles Board in 1959. All *Accounting Research Bulletins* still constitute generally accepted accounting principles unless specifically amended or rescinded by other authoritative bodies.

Accounting Principles Board (APB)

In the 1950s the processes of formulating accounting principles were increasingly criticized, and wider representation in rule making was sought. In 1959 the **Accounting Principles Board (APB)** was formed by the AICPA as an attempt to (1) alleviate this criticism and (2) create a policy-making body whose rules would be binding rather than optional. The APB was comprised of 17 to 21 members, selected primarily from the accounting profession. Representatives from industry, the government, and academia also served on the Board. The pronouncements of the APB were termed *Opinions of the Accounting Principles Board,* and 31 of these Opinions were issued. All *APB Opinions* also still constitute generally

EXHIBIT 4–1 Sources of generally accepted accounting principles

1. Pronouncements of the Financial Accounting Standards Board (FASB) and its predecessors, the Accounting Principles Board (APB) and the Committee on Accounting Procedure. Included are FASB *Statements of Financial Accounting Standards* and *Interpretations*, APB *Opinions*, and American Institute of Certified Public Accountants (AICPA) *Accounting Research Bulletins* (as well as Securities and Exchange Commission *Regulation S–X* and *Financial Reporting Releases*).

2. FASB *Technical Bulletins* and AICPA *Industry Audit Guides, Industry Accounting Guides*, and *Statements of Position*. The AICPA has established auditing and accounting guidelines for several industries because of the special nature of the industries.

3. General practice. Principles used by others for similar transactions (for example, reference may be made to the AICPA *Interpretations* and *Accounting Trends and Techniques*).

4. Other accounting literature. This includes, for example, APB *Statements*, AICPA *Issue Papers*, FASB *Statements of Concepts*, FASB Emerging Issues Task Force *Consensus Positions* and accounting texts and articles.

accepted accounting principles unless specifically amended or rescinded. Many of these Opinions were based upon *Accounting Research Studies*. These studies were commissioned by the APB from a specific individual or individuals as a method of obtaining information about a topic. However, the conclusions drawn in these studies were solely the opinion of their author(s), and in several cases the APB either did not act on the recommendations or came to different conclusions.

The members of the APB were volunteers whose employers allowed them time to perform whatever duties that service on the Board required. But by the late 1960s criticism again arose concerning the development of accounting principles. This criticism centered on three factors:

1. *Independence.* The members of the APB were part-time volunteers whose major responsibilities were to the business, governmental, or academic organizations employing them.

2. *Representation.* The public accounting firms and the AICPA were too closely associated with the development of accounting standards.

3. *Response Time.* Emerging problems were not solved quickly enough by the part-time members of the APB.

The AICPA reacted to those criticisms by appointing a committee to evaluate the method of formulating accounting principles. This committee, termed the Wheat Committee after its chairman Francis Wheat, recommended that the APB be abolished and that a new full-time body be established with even wider representation.

Financial Accounting Standards Board (FASB)

The AICPA adopted the recommendations of the Wheat Committee. The APB was phased out and replaced in 1973 by a new body, the **Financial Accounting Standards Board (FASB)**.

Organization. The FASB is organized as follows. A panel of "electors" from several organizations interested in the formulation of accounting principles appoints the board of trustees that governs the Financial Accounting Foundation (FAF). The FAF, in turn, appoints the Financial Accounting Standards Advisory Council (FASAC), which is responsible for advising the FASB about major policy issues, the agenda of topics, the selection of task forces, and other matters. The FAF also is responsible for appointing the seven members of the FASB and raising the funds necessary to operate the FASB. Appointees to the FASB are full-time, fully paid members with no other organizational ties and are selected to represent a wide cross section of interests. Each Board member is required to have a knowledge of accounting, finance, and business and a concern for the public interest regarding financial reporting. Currently, the FASB includes (1) three members who are Certified Public Accountants (CPAs) and who have been in public practice and (2) four members from other areas related to accounting (e.g., academia, government, and industry).

The FASB issues four types of pronouncements:

1. *Statements of Financial Accounting Concepts.* These Statements do *not* create generally accepted accounting principles. Instead, they establish a theoretical foundation upon which to base financial accounting and reporting standards. These Statements are the output of the FASB's "conceptual framework" project, which is the basis for much of the conceptual discussion in the first two chapters and in this chapter.

2. *Statements of Financial Accounting Standards.* These Statements establish generally accepted accounting principles. They are releases indicating the methods and procedures required on specific accounting issues.

3. *Interpretations.* These pronouncements provide clarification of conflicting or unclear issues relating to previously issued *FASB Statements of Standards, APB Opinions,* or *Accounting Research Bulletins.* Interpretations also establish or clarify generally accepted accounting principles.

4. *Technical Bulletins.* These bulletins are issued by the staff of the FASB to provide guidance on accounting and reporting problems related to *Statements of Standards* or *Interpretations.* The guidance may clarify, explain, or elaborate upon an underlying standard.

Operating Procedures. Before issuing a statement of concepts or standards, the FASB generally completes a multistage process, as outlined in Exhibit 4–2. Initially, a topic or project is identified and placed on the FASB's agenda. This topic may be the result of suggestions from the FASAC, the accounting profes-

EXHIBIT 4–2 FASB operating procedures

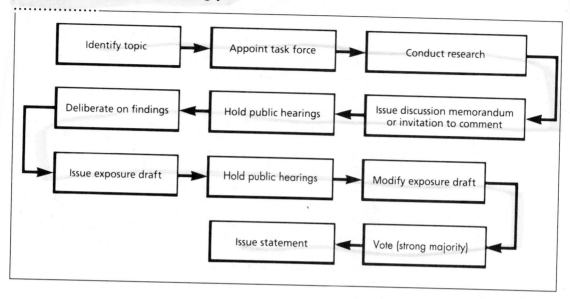

sion, industry, or other interested parties. On major issues a Task Force may be appointed to advise and consult with the FASB on such matters as the scope of the project and the nature and extent of additional research. The Research and Technical Staff then conducts any research specifically related to the project.

A Discussion Memorandum or Invitation to Comment, which outlines the research related to the issues, is often published. Public hearings, similar to those held by Congress, are usually held. The intent is to obtain information from and views of interested individuals and organizations on the issues. Many parties submit written comments or make oral presentations. These parties include representatives of public accounting firms and interested corporations, security analysts, members of professional accounting associations, and academicians, to name a few. After deliberating on the views expressed and information collected, the FASB issues an Exposure Draft of the proposed statement. Interested parties have a specified period to provide written comments of reaction and another public hearing is often held. A modified draft is then prepared, if necessary, and brought to the FASB for a final vote. After a *strong majority* (i.e., at least 5 to 2) vote is attained, the Statement is issued.

Sociopolitical Environment.   As can be seen from Exhibit 4–2 and the related discussion, the operating procedures of the FASB are designed so that accounting standards are developed in an efficient manner, with due process, and in a public forum. The intent is to consider all related research on a particular topic as well as the views of all interested parties before coming to a logical conclusion concerning the appropriate accounting standard for the topic. A naive viewer of the FASB operating procedures might think that accounting standards are always "ideal" because they are the result of "rational policy making," where there are clearly defined objectives, an integrated body of theory, and known consequences of the actions. Yet this may not always be the case because accounting is part of a broader social system. Often, objectives are not clear, research results are conflicting, and only "best guesses" can be made of the future consequences of current standards. It may be argued that ". . . in no instance involving complex social [e.g., accounting] issues has anyone demonstrated . . . that a particular [accounting] policy decision was 'right' in the sense of coming closer than another decision to specified objectives."[1]

Furthermore, a former member of the Accounting Principles Board argues that "the setting of accounting standards is as much a product of political action as of flawless logic. . . ."[2] Since accounting standard setting is a social decision that places restrictions on behavior, these decisions must be accepted by the affected parties. To achieve "acceptable decisions," it is only natural for the affected parties to attempt to influence the decisions. Since the FASB holds public hearings and open meetings, it is relatively easy for various external user groups (e.g., investors and creditors) and other interested groups (e.g., affected companies and public accounting firms), often with conflicting views, to attempt to influence the FASB to develop new standards or change old standards in their own best interests. Because the FASB has such a wide constituency and focuses on general purpose financial reporting (discussed later), it must often establish accounting standards that are the result of *compromise*.

When a compromise is necessary, negotiations within the FASB must occur so that a majority vote on the topic can be obtained. Often the compromise makes some of the FASB's constituency unhappy because they perceive the new accounting principle to be "unfair." This dissatisfaction is especially true when only the minimum "strong" majority (5 to 2 vote) is attained. Many of the constituency then find fault with the FASB, criticizing it for failing to listen to them, for moving too quickly, for not giving sufficient consideration to cost/benefit issues, for creating logically inconsistent rules, and for establishing complex rules that are too difficult to implement. The FAF and the FASB attempt to be sensitive to such criticisms. Compromise, however, is not necessarily bad; in fact, it can be beneficial. In a democratic society, ". . . only politically responsible institutions have the right to command others to obey their rules."[3] Accounting standards are not immutable. The FASB fulfills its responsibility by (1) establishing standards that are the most rational, given the various affected constituencies, and (2) continually monitoring the consequences of its actions so that revised standards can be issued where appropriate.

---

[1]D. L. Gerboth, "'Muddling Through' with the APB," *Journal of Accountancy* (May, 1972), p. 43.
[2]C. T. Horngren, "The Marketing of Accounting Standards," *Journal of Accountancy* (October, 1973), p. 61.
[3]D. L. Gerboth, "Research, Intuition, and Politics in Accounting Inquiry," *The Accounting Review*, (July, 1973), p. 481.

Other Organizations Influencing Generally Accepted Accounting Principles

In addition to the policy-making bodies discussed in the previous section, several other organizations have had an impact on the development of generally accepted accounting principles during the past several decades.

Securities and Exchange Commission (SEC). The SEC was created to administer various securities acts under powers provided by Congress in the Securities Act of 1933 and the Securities Exchange Act of 1934. Under these Acts, **the SEC has the legal authority to prescribe accounting principles and reporting practices for all companies issuing publicly traded securities.** While this authority has seldom been used, from time to time the SEC has exerted pressure on the CAP, the APB, and the FASB. It has been especially interested in narrowing areas of difference in financial reporting.

The 1933 Act requires companies offering securities for public sale on the open market to file a registration statement and to provide each potential investor with a proxy statement. The 1934 Act established extensive reporting requirements to aid in full disclosure. Among the most commonly required reports are:

- *Form 10.* A registration statement.
- *Form 10-K.* An annual report.
- *Form 10-Q.* A quarterly report of operations.
- *Form 8-K.* A report used to describe any significant events that may affect the company.
- *Form S-1.* Registration for public offering of securities.
- *Proxy Statement.* A report used when management requests the right to vote through proxies for shareholders at stockholders' meetings.

The SEC establishes accounting principles with respect to the information contained within the above reports and issues reporting guidelines in the form of its *Regulation S-X* and its *Financial Reporting Releases*. In some instances the SEC has required the disclosure of information not typically found in published financial reports, as discussed in Chapter 14.

Generally speaking, the impact of the SEC has been felt through its informal approval of *APB Opinions* and *FASB Statements* before their issuance. While the SEC has the authority to decide what constitutes "generally accepted accounting principles," in many cases this authority has been exercised in the form of persuasion rather than edict. Evidence of the SEC's position can be found where it endorsed the concept of "substantial authoritative support" by asserting that "principles, standards, and practices promulgated by the FASB in its *Statements* and *Interpretations* will be considered by the Commission as having substantial authoritative support, and those contrary to such FASB promulgations will be considered to have no such support."[4] **This position has allowed accounting**

....

[4]"Codification of Financial Reporting Policies," *SEC Accounting Rules* (Chicago: Commerce Clearing House, August, 1988), sec. 101.

principles to be formulated in the private sector rather than by the government. However, the SEC has been criticized for abrogating its responsibility, and there is no assurance that the position will remain in effect. In 1977 the Senate Sub-committee on Reports, Accounting, and Management, known as the Metcalf Committee after its chairman Senator Lee Metcalf, which had been charged with investigating the current methods of formulating accounting principles, consid-ered the suggestion that the FASB might be replaced by a governmental board. Although this suggestion was not implemented, the possibility of additional governmental involvement in the formulation of accounting principles should not be discounted. For example, at the time of writing this book, a committee of the House of Representatives chaired by John Dingell was examining many aspects of the accounting profession, including the role of the FASB, the SEC's oversight of the accounting profession, and the functions of the auditor. (In fact, during 1978 the SEC refused to support *FASB Statement No. 19* requiring the use of the successful-efforts method in the oil and gas industry, and the FASB reacted by suspending the effective date of this release until it was incorporated into the SEC regulations.)

American Institute of Certified Public Accountants (AICPA). The AICPA, dat-ing back to 1887, is the national professional organization for certified public accountants in the United States. To be a member of the AICPA an individual must pass the Uniform CPA Examination, possess a CPA certificate, agree to abide by its bylaws and Code of Professional Ethics, and after the year 2000 have the equivalent of a Master's degree. The primary purpose of the AICPA is to assure that CPAs serve the public interest in performing quality professional services. The AICPA has published many documents that may be considered as sources of generally accepted accounting principles. Among these are *Industry Audit Guides, Industry Accounting Guides, Statements of Position*, and *Accounting Trends and Techniques.*

FASB Emerging Issues Task Force (EITF). The EITF was established in 1984 in response to criticisms that the FASB did not provide timely guidance on new accounting issues. The EITF includes technical experts from all major CPA firms and representatives from industry, including the Chief Accountant of the SEC. The EITF identifies significant emerging issues and develops *consensus* positions on the implementation issues involving the application of standards. These con-sensus positions are viewed as the best available guidance on generally accepted accounting principles, particularly as they relate to new accounting issues.

Cost Accounting Standards Board (CASB). The CASB was established in 1970 as an agency of the Congress of the United States. It ceased to exist in 1980 when Congress failed to vote funds for its continuation, but was reinstated in 1988. The CASB is charged with the responsibility of promulgating cost account-ing standards designed to achieve uniformity and consistency in the cost accounting principles followed by defense contractors and subcontractors under negotiated federal contracts. The CASB was created after hearings before the Senate Banking Committee in 1968, where it was asserted that the government could save $2 billion on negotiated procurements if there were better accounting procedures. Prior to 1968, cost accounting for government contracts was based on the *Armed Services Procurement Regulations (ASPR)*, which were dependent, in part, on generally accepted accounting principles. In the hearings it was stated that generally accepted accounting principles were not sufficiently definitive in many areas to protect the government. The CASB is responsible only for negotiated defense contracts and has issued several *Cost Accounting Standards* in this regard. Since the basis for external financial statements in many cases is the internal cost accounting procedures employed, these cost accounting standards occasionally influence external reporting.

Internal Revenue Service (IRS).   The IRS administers the provisions of the Internal Revenue Code enacted by Congress. Federal income tax laws have had a significant impact upon financial reporting practices since they were first enacted in 1913. Although the Internal Revenue Code does *not* directly affect financial accounting practice, companies have attempted to lessen its impact upon their accounting systems. The result in many cases has been the adoption of those accounting methods and procedures that result in the lowest taxable income, without regard for what is proper from the standpoint of financial accounting theory and practice.

It should be understood that accounting for income tax purposes and for financial reporting purposes *is* and *should be* different. The goal of financial accounting is to provide information to financial statement users so that they can make decisions. The goal of income tax accounting is to legally minimize or postpone the payment of income taxes. Frequently, the goals of financial reporting and income tax reporting come in conflict. For this reason in this text we are concerned with determining the proper *financial* accounting recording and reporting procedures. What is, or should be, proper under the Internal Revenue Code is an entirely different question, which in general is not discussed. (The impact of the Internal Revenue Code on financial accounting is discussed in Chapter 9.)

American Accounting Association (AAA).   The AAA is an organization comprised primarily of academicians and practicing accountants. The goals of this organization are to (1) advance accounting knowledge, (2) encourage accounting research, (3) improve accounting practice, and (4) promote the development of accounting standards. These goals are primarily implemented in various meetings, publication of journals, and the work of various committees such as the AAA Committee on Financial Accounting Standards (FAS), which responds to the FASB's exposure drafts relating to proposed statements of concepts and standards. The AAA has no official stature in the development of financial accounting practice, so its impact is through education and persuasion rather than through formal pronouncements.

Governmental Accounting Standards Board (GASB).   The GASB was established in 1984 and operates under the auspices of the Financial Accounting Foundation (and therefore is very different from the CASB). The GASB operates in a manner similar to the FASB. It consists of a full-time chairperson and four other members, with a supporting staff. The GASB's responsibility is to establish accounting standards for certain state and local governmental entities. Its impact on accounting principles for the private sector is minimal, but its pronouncements are the primary source of GAAP for governmental accounting.

■ OBJECTIVES OF FINANCIAL REPORTING

The FASB's first pronouncement in its conceptual framework developed the objectives of financial reporting by companies.[5] In introducing this first "concepts" statement, the FASB observed that the objectives are those of *general purpose* external reporting by companies. That is, the objectives related to a *variety of external* users (as opposed to specific internal users, such as management) who do not have the authority to prescribe the financial information they desire from a particular company and therefore must use the information that the management of the company communicates to them.

The FASB identified several objectives of financial reporting. These objectives proceeded from the more general to the more specific. They are shown in Exhibit 4–3 and are discussed in the following sections.

Information Useful in Decision Making

The most general objective is shown at the top of Exhibit 4–3. This objective states that **financial reporting should provide useful information for present and potential investors, creditors, and other external users in making their investment, credit, and similar decisions.** Investors include both equity security holders (stockholders) and debt security holders (bondholders), while creditors include suppliers, customers and employees with claims, individual lenders, and lending institutions. Other external users include brokers, lawyers, security analysts, regulatory agencies, and the like.

Information Useful in Assessing External Users' Cash Receipts

The second objective shown in Exhibit 4–3 relates to external users' needs. It states that **financial reporting should provide information that is useful to external users in assessing the amounts, timing, and uncertainty of prospective cash receipts.** This objective is important because individuals and institutions make cash outflows by investing and lending activities primarily to increase their cash inflows. Whether they are successful depends on the extent to which they receive a return of cash, goods, or services greater than their investment or loan. That is, they must receive not only a return *of* investment, but also a return *on*

....

[5]"Objectives of Financial Reporting by Business Enterprises," *FASB Statement of Financial Accounting Concepts No. 1* (Stamford, Conn.: FASB, 1978).

EXHIBIT 4–3 Objectives of financial reporting

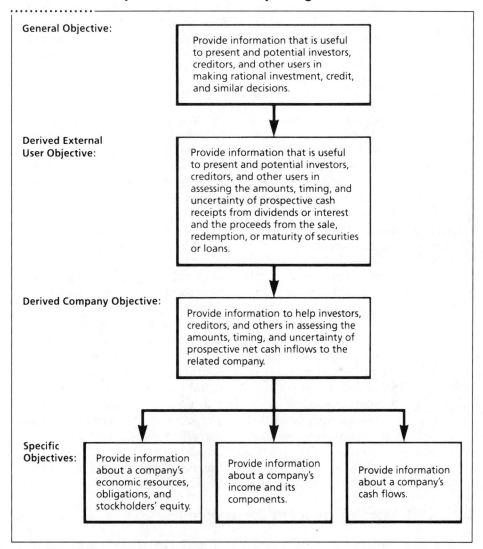

General Objective:

> Provide information that is useful to present and potential investors, creditors, and other users in making rational investment, credit, and similar decisions.

Derived External User Objective:

> Provide information that is useful to present and potential investors, creditors, and other users in assessing the amounts, timing, and uncertainty of prospective cash receipts from dividends or interest and the proceeds from the sale, redemption, or maturity of securities or loans.

Derived Company Objective:

> Provide information to help investors, creditors, and others in assessing the amounts, timing, and uncertainty of prospective net cash inflows to the related company.

Specific Objectives:

> Provide information about a company's economic resources, obligations, and stockholders' equity.

> Provide information about a company's income and its components.

> Provide information about a company's cash flows.

investment commensurate with the risk involved. Investment and credit decisions involve choices between present and prospective future cash flows. Financial information is needed to help establish expectations about the timing and amount of prospective cash receipts (e.g., dividends, interest, proceeds from resale or repayment) and to assess the risk involved.

Information Useful in Assessing Company Cash Flows

Because investors invest in and creditors lend to a particular company, their current and prospective cash receipts are affected by the cash flows of the company. Thus, a third objective shown in Exhibit 4–3 is that **financial reporting should provide information to help external users in assessing the amounts, timing, and uncertainty of the prospective net cash inflows to the related company.** This objective logically flows from the second objective because companies also invest cash in noncash resources to earn more cash and receive a return *on* their investment in addition to a return *of* their investment.

A company's activities regarding its investments are more complex, however, than those of external users. The company completes an "operating cycle" or cycles where goods or services are acquired, their value is increased, the goods or services are sold, and the selling price is collected. Within this operating cycle numerous cash receipts and payments are collected and paid, in no precise order. The company's ability to generate net cash inflows affects both its ability to pay dividends and interest and the market prices of its securities, which, in turn, affect investors' and creditors' cash flows.

Information About Economic Resources and Claims to These Resources

The bottom tier of objectives in Exhibit 4–3 is the most specific. These objectives indicate the types of information about a company that should be provided in financial reports. **A specific objective of financial reporting is to provide information about a company's economic resources, obligations, and stockholders' equity.** This information is useful to external users for four reasons: (1) to identify a company's financial strengths and weaknesses and to assess its liquidity, (2) to provide a basis to evaluate information about a company's performance during a period, (3) to provide direct indications of the cash flow potentials of some resources and the cash needed to satisfy obligations, and (4) to indicate the potential cash flows that are the joint result of combining various resources in the company's operations. Information about a company's economic resources, obligations, and stockholders' equity is presented in the company's balance sheet (as discussed in Chapter 1), although the FASB does not advocate any particular type, form, or content of financial statements.

Information About Income and Its Components

Another specific **objective of financial reporting is to provide information about a company's financial performance during a period** in order to help external users form expectations about its future performance. **The *primary* focus of financial reporting about a company's performance is information concerning a company's *income* and its components.** Information about a company's income is useful to external users in (1) evaluating management's performance, (2) estimating the "earning power" or other amounts perceived as representative of its long-term income-producing ability, (3) predicting future income, and (4) assessing the risk of investing or lending to the company.

To reflect a company's financial performance during a period, the measurement of income should relate (match) the costs (expenses) of operations against the benefits (revenues) from those operations. This measurement should also include the benefits and costs of other nonoperating transactions, events, and circumstances. This objective is accomplished through the use of **accrual accounting,** where the financial effects of transactions and events are related to the period in which they occur rather than when the cash receipt or payment takes place. Information about a company's income and its components is reported in the company's income statement (as discussed in Chapter 2).

Information About Cash Flows

Although information about income is a significant concern of external users, **another specific objective of financial reporting is to provide information about a company's cash flows.** This information includes how the company obtains and spends cash, how it borrows and repays and in what amounts, its capital transactions, including cash dividends and other distributions of company resources to owners, and other factors that may affect the company's liquidity. External users use cash flow information about a company (1) to help understand its operations, (2) to evaluate its financing and investing activities, (3) to assess its liquidity, and (4) to interpret the income information provided. Information about a company's cash flows is reported in the company's statement of cash flows (as discussed briefly in Chapter 2 and more extensively in Chapter 12).

Other Issues

The FASB raised two other important issues in its first *Statement of Concepts.* First, **financial reporting should provide information about how the management of a company has discharged its stewardship responsibility to owners (stockholders) for use of the company resources entrusted to it.** The management is responsible to the owners for the custody and safekeeping of company resources, their efficient and profitable use, and their protection against unfavorable economic impacts, technological developments, and social changes.

Second, **financial statements and other means of financial reporting should include explanations and interpretations by management to help external users understand the financial information provided.** This approach is often referred to as **full disclosure.** Since management knows more about a company's activities than do "outsiders," the usefulness of financial information can be enhanced by, for instance, (1) explanations of certain transactions, events, and circumstances, (2) interpretations of the effects on the financial results of dividing continuous operations into accounting periods, and (3) explanations of underlying assumptions or methods used and any related significant uncertainties. This information is usually presented in notes and supplementary schedules, which are an integral part of the financial statements.

The establishment of the objectives of financial reporting was the FASB's first step in developing its conceptual framework for financial accounting and reporting. The FASB intends the objectives within this framework to act as guidelines for providing financial information for investment and credit decisions, thus facilitating the efficient operation of the capital markets and promoting the efficient allocation of scarce resources.

■ QUALITATIVE CHARACTERISTICS OF ACCOUNTING INFORMATION

As we have seen, the general objective of financial reporting is to provide accounting information that is useful in investment and credit decision making. The qualitative characteristics or "ingredients" that accounting information should possess in order to be most useful were specified in the FASB's second pronouncement in the conceptual framework.[6] These characteristics should be considered when choosing among accounting alternatives, because these qualities distinguish more useful from less useful information.

Each accounting alternative, however, may possess more of one quality and less of another. Although considerable agreement exists about the qualitative characteristics that "good" accounting information should possess, no mathematical "model" or "equation" has been developed to determine precisely which information has the "best" combination of qualitative characteristics for decision-making purposes. Furthermore, the FASB strives to meet the needs of all users through *general purpose* financial statements. This diversity does not reduce the importance of using the qualitative characteristics to establish common accounting standards. The qualitative criteria are helpful to the FASB in establishing "minimum" and "maximum" limits of useful accounting information so that it can develop logical accounting standards consistent with these "limits."

Hierarchy of Qualitative Characteristics

A hierarchy of the qualitative characteristics of accounting information is shown in Exhibit 4–4. This section presents an overview of the hierarchy, after which each component is defined and discussed. The hierarchy is bounded by two constraints: (1) in order to justify providing the accounting information, *the benefits must be greater than the costs* and (2) *the dollar amount of the information must be material* (i.e., large enough to make a difference in decision making).

Understandability serves as a "link" between the decision makers and the accounting information. *Decision usefulness* is the overall quality by which to judge accounting information. The primary qualities that make accounting information useful are relevance and reliability. If either of these is lacking, the information will not be useful. To be *relevant*, accounting information must be timely and must possess either predictive value or feedback value, or both. Information is *reliable* when it has representational faithfulness and is verifiable and neutral.

....

[6]"Qualitative Characteristics of Accounting Information," *FASB Statement of Financial Accounting Concepts No. 2* (Stamford, Conn.: FASB, 1980).

EXHIBIT 4—4   A hierarchy of qualitative characteristics of accounting information[a]

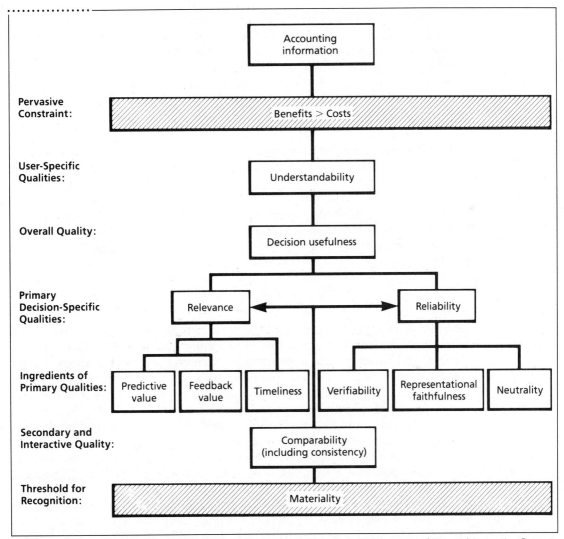

[a]Adapted from Figure 1 in "Qualitative Characteristics of Accounting Information," *FASB Statement of Financial Accounting Concepts No. 2* (Stamford, Conn.: FASB, 1980), p. 15.

Comparability (including *consistency*) is a secondary quality, interacting with both relevance and reliability to contribute to information usefulness.

The hierarchy is not designed to assign priorities among the qualitative characteristics in all circumstances. To be useful, accounting information must have each of the qualitative characteristics to a minimum degree. However, different situations may require trade-offs whereby the level of one quality is sacrificed for an increase in another quality.

Understandability

Accounting information should be understandable to users who have a reasonable knowledge of business and economic activities and who are willing to study the information with reasonable diligence. Since the FASB establishes standards for general purpose financial statements, it is concerned with the understandability of accounting information to *broad classes* of decision makers.

Decision Usefulness

Decision usefulness is the *overall* qualitative characteristic to be used in judging the quality of accounting information. Whether information is useful depends on the decision to be made, the way in which it is made, the information already available, and the decision maker's ability to process the information. Since the FASB establishes standards for broad classes of users, however, it must consider the quality of decision usefulness in a broad context. For purposes of evaluation, this overall quality can be separated into the primary qualities of relevance and reliability.

Relevance

Relevant accounting information is information that can make a difference in a decision by helping users to form predictions about the outcomes of past, present, and future events or to confirm or correct prior expectations. In this context, "event" is a happening that is significant to a company (e.g., receipt of a sales order), while "outcome" is the effect or result of an event or series of events (e.g., the income of last year). To be relevant, accounting information need not be expressed as a prediction. Information about the current status of a company's resources or obligations or about its past performance is commonly useful as a basis for expectations. To be relevant, accounting information should have either predictive or feedback value, or both. In addition, it should be timely.

Predictive Value and Feedback Value. Accounting information has **predictive value** when it helps decision makers to forecast the outcome of past or present events. Accounting information has **feedback value** when it enables decision makers to confirm or correct prior expectations. Often, information has both predictive value and feedback value because knowledge about the previous actions of a company (i.e., feedback) will generally improve the decision makers' abilities to predict the results of similar future actions. An example is an interim income statement that provides feedback about past income to date and serves as a basis for forecasting the annual income.

Timeliness. Timeliness is having information available to decision makers before it loses its capacity to influence decisions and is an ingredient of relevance. If information is not available when it is needed, it lacks relevance and is of little or no use. Timeliness alone cannot make information relevant, but a lack of timeliness reduces its potential relevance. However, a gain in relevance resulting from increased timeliness may involve a sacrifice of other desirable qualitative characteristics (e.g., reliability). Currently, timeliness for an annual report is defined by the SEC, which requires that each company that comes under its jurisdiction must file a Form 10-K annual report within 90 days of its fiscal year-end. Similarly, a Form 10-Q quarterly report must be filed within 45 days of the end of the quarter.

Reliability

To be useful, accounting information must be reliable as well as relevant. **Reliable information is reasonably free from error and bias and faithfully represents what it is intended to represent.** That is, to be reliable, information must be verifiable, possess representational faithfulness, and be neutral. While reliable information is dependable, it is not necessarily precise. For instance, estimates may be reliable. Reliability has different degrees, and what is an acceptable degree of reliability will depend on the circumstances.

Verifiability. To be reliable, accounting information must have the qualitative characteristic of verifiability. **Verifiability** (sometimes called **objectivity**) is the ability of measurers (accountants) to form a consensus (agree) that the selected method has been used without error or bias—that is, that the measurement results can be duplicated. Verification is useful in reducing *measurer bias,* because by repeated measurements using the same method both unintentional and intentional errors are reduced. Verification does not, however, ensure the appropriateness of the accounting methods used. That quality of accounting information is representational faithfulness.

Representational Faithfulness. Reliable accounting information must have representational faithfulness. **Representational faithfulness** (validity) is the degree of correspondence between the reported accounting measurements or descriptions and the economic resources, obligations, and transactions and events causing changes in these items. For instance, a company may record an item leased from another firm on a long-term basis as an economic resource even though it does not own the item. This recording increases the representational faithfulness of the reported economic resources available to the company. Having a high degree of representational faithfulness is useful in reducing *measurement bias.* Having representational faithfulness in one decision-making context, however, does not mean that accounting information will have validity for other decisions. For instance, the current cost would be important for an economic resource that a company expected to replace in the near future, but it might not be valid if there were no intention of replacing it.

Neutrality. Accounting information is **neutral** when there is an absence of bias intended to attain a predetermined result or to influence behavior in a *particular* direction. Neutrality does not mean that accounting information has no purpose or does not influence human behavior. The purpose of providing accounting information is to serve a variety of different users with diverse interests. Furthermore, accounting information is intended to be useful in decision making, thereby influencing the decision makers' behavior but not in a predetermined direction. Neutrality also implies a *completeness* of information. An omission of information can lead to bias if it is intended to induce or inhibit (i.e., influence) a particular behavior.

Comparability and Consistency

A secondary qualitative characteristic of accounting information is comparability (including consistency). Information about a company is more useful if it can be compared with similar information from other companies (this is referred to as *intercompany* comparison) or with similar information from past periods within the company (*intracompany* comparison). Comparability is an *interactive quality* of the relationship between two or more pieces of information. **Comparability of accounting information enables users to identify and explain similarities and differences between two (or more) sets of economic phenomena.**

Closely linked to comparability is consistency. **Consistency means conformity from period to period, with accounting policies and procedures remaining unchanged.** Consistency, like comparability, is a quality of the relationship between numbers rather than a quality of the numbers themselves. Consistency is an important condition to enhance comparability across periods. Without consistency, it would be difficult to determine whether differences in results were caused by economic differences or simply by differences in accounting methods. On the other hand, a change in accounting method is sometimes desirable. Economic situations may change, or new, more preferable accounting methods may evolve. Some sacrifice in consistency must be made at certain times in order to improve the usefulness of accounting information.

Constraints to the Hierarchy

Two constraints to the hierarchy of qualitative characteristics help to further identify what accounting information should be disclosed in financial reports. The first is a benefit/cost constraint; the second is a threshold-for-recognition, or materiality, constraint.

Benefits Greater Than Costs.   Accounting information is a commodity. Unless the benefits expected to be received from a commodity exceed its costs, the commodity will not be wanted. The costs of providing financial information fall initially on the company and then are passed on to consumers. These costs include the cost of collecting, processing, auditing, and communicating the information as well as those associated with losing a competitive advantage by disclosing the information. The benefits are received by a diverse group of investors and creditors, by consumers (they are assured a steady supply of goods and services), and by the company (for use in internal decision making). To be reported, accounting information must not only be relevant and reliable but it must also satisfy the benefit/cost constraint. That is, before a decision is made to implement a standard requiring certain accounting information to be reported, the FASB must have reasonable assurance that the benefits of implementation will exceed the costs.

Materiality. The second constraint, that of materiality, is really a *quantitative* "threshold" constraint very closely linked to the qualitative characteristic of relevance. **Materiality refers to the magnitude of an omission or misstatement of accounting information that, considering the circumstances, makes it likely that the judgment of a reasonable person relying on the information would have been influenced by the omission or misstatement.** Materiality and relevance are both defined in terms of the influences that affect a decision maker, but the two terms can be distinguished. A decision to disclose certain information may be made because users have a need for that information (it is relevant) *and* because the amount is large enough to make a difference (it is material). Alternatively, a decision not to disclose certain information may be made because the user has no need for the information (it is not relevant) *or* because the amount is too small to make a difference (it is not material).

The FASB did not set overall quantitative guidelines for materiality in its second *Statement of Concepts*. It felt that materiality is a judgment factor and that no general standards could be set that took into account all the elements of sound human judgment. Materiality judgments should be concerned with thresholds of recognition. Is an item large enough to pass over the threshold that separates material from immaterial items? To answer that question, the FASB suggested that consideration should be given to (1) the *nature* of the item (e.g., items considered too small to be significant when they result from routine transactions might be material if they arose from abnormal circumstances) and (2) the *relative size* rather than absolute size of an item (e.g., a $10,000 error in inventory of a large firm may be insignificant, whereas a similar $10,000 error by a small firm may be material). The FASB observed that quantitative guidelines have been and will continue to be set for specific accounting issues where appropriate.

■ ACCOUNTING ASSUMPTIONS AND CONVENTIONS

To this point we have identified the objectives of financial reporting and the qualitative characteristics of useful accounting information. Consideration of the objectives and the qualitative characteristics is necessary for the establishment of generally accepted accounting principles. In addition, certain accounting assumptions and conventions have had an important impact upon the development of generally accepted accounting principles. Exhibit 4–5 is useful in understanding the relationship among the objectives, qualitative characteristics, accounting assumptions and conventions, and generally accepted accounting principles. The accounting assumptions and conventions listed in Exhibit 4–5 are discussed in this section. Others will be discussed later in the text as they apply to specific generally accepted accounting principles.

EXHIBIT 4–5   Framework of financial accounting theory and practice

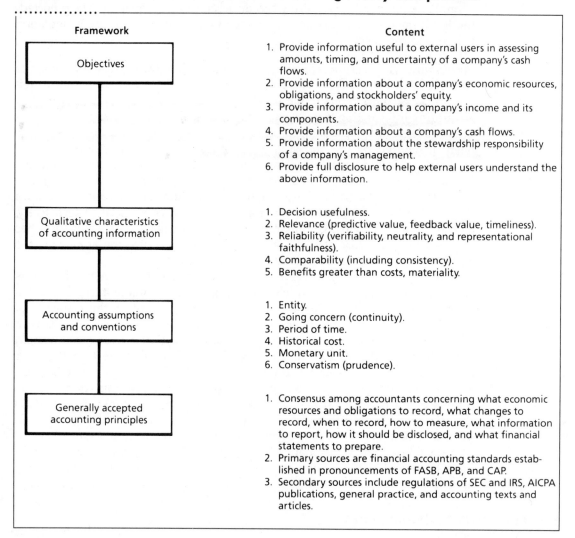

Framework	Content
Objectives	1. Provide information useful to external users in assessing amounts, timing, and uncertainty of a company's cash flows. 2. Provide information about a company's economic resources, obligations, and stockholders' equity. 3. Provide information about a company's income and its components. 4. Provide information about a company's cash flows. 5. Provide information about the stewardship responsibility of a company's management. 6. Provide full disclosure to help external users understand the above information.
Qualitative characteristics of accounting information	1. Decision usefulness. 2. Relevance (predictive value, feedback value, timeliness). 3. Reliability (verifiability, neutrality, and representational faithfulness). 4. Comparability (including consistency). 5. Benefits greater than costs, materiality.
Accounting assumptions and conventions	1. Entity. 2. Going concern (continuity). 3. Period of time. 4. Historical cost. 5. Monetary unit. 6. Conservatism (prudence).
Generally accepted accounting principles	1. Consensus among accountants concerning what economic resources and obligations to record, what changes to record, when to record, how to measure, what information to report, how it should be disclosed, and what financial statements to prepare. 2. Primary sources are financial accounting standards established in pronouncements of FASB, APB, and CAP. 3. Secondary sources include regulations of SEC and IRS, AICPA publications, general practice, and accounting texts and articles.

Entity

The majority of economic activity in the United States can be directly or indirectly attributed to business entities, of which there are three basic types. A **sole proprietorship** is a business owned by one individual who is usually also the manager of the business. Therefore, a sole proprietorship is usually a small organization such as a retail store, service firm, or professional business.

A **partnership** is a business owned by two or more individuals. The responsibilities, obligations, and benefits of the partners usually are described in a contract called a *partnership agreement*. Public accounting firms and law firms are examples of partnerships. Although partnerships are usually small, they may become very large; for example, each of the largest international accounting firms has more than one thousand partners.

A **corporation** is a business incorporated as a separate legal entity according to the laws of the state in which it is registered. Shares of *capital stock* are issued to owners, the *stockholders*, as evidence of the ownership rights in the corporation. A corporation may be owned by one stockholder or, in the case of a large corporation, by many thousands of stockholders.

The title *company* may be applied to each of these entities and is used frequently in this book because generally accepted accounting principles may be applied to any type of business entity. The focus of the book, however, is on corporations, and this title is used when it is most appropriate. Although sole proprietorships and partnerships outnumber corporations, corporations produce and sell far more goods and services. For example, according to recent government statistics, corporations comprised only 19% of the number of U.S. companies, but provided 90% of the total revenues of all companies.

Financial accounting is concerned with recording and reporting the economic activity of each of these entities, regardless of its size. In certain instances the financial records of related but separate legal entities may be *consolidated* (combined) to more realistically report the resources, obligations, and operating results of the overall economic entity (as discussed in Chapter 11).

The entity assumption distinguishes each organization from its owners, and it is the individual business unit that is considered to own the resources committed to its purpose and to operate to achieve its objectives. Consequently, financial records and reports are prepared for each separate entity, and the personal transactions of the owners are kept separate from those of the company.

Going Concern

The **going-concern assumption** is also known as the **continuity assumption.** This assumption is that the company will continue to operate in the near future unless substantial evidence to the contrary exists. Obviously, not all companies are successful, and failures do occur. However, the continuity assumption is valid in the majority of cases and is necessary for many of the accounting principles used. For example, if the company is not regarded as a going concern, fixed assets should not be depreciated over their expected useful lives or inventory should not be recorded at its cost, because the receipt of future economic benefits from these items is uncertain.

Nevertheless, the continuity assumption does not imply permanence. It simply indicates that the company will operate long enough to carry out its existing commitments. In the event the company appears to be on the verge of going bankrupt, the continuity assumption must be discarded and the company should be reported on a liquidation basis, with all assets and liabilities valued at the amounts estimated to be collected or paid when they are sold or liquidated.

Period of Time

The profit or loss earned by a company cannot be determined *accurately* unless it ceases to function. At that time the total lifetime profit or loss for the company may be determined by comparing the cash on hand after liquidating the business plus any cash distributions to the owners during the period of operations with the amount invested by the owners during the company's lifetime. Obviously financial statement users need more current information to evaluate a company's profitability, and the year has been adopted as the primary reporting period. In accordance with the **period-of-time assumption,** financial statements are prepared at the end of each fiscal year and disclosed in a company's annual report. Furthermore the annual reporting period is used for reports issued to government regulators such as the IRS and the SEC.

The period-of-time assumption is the basis for the adjustment process in accounting (as discussed in Chapter 3), because if financial statements were not prepared on a yearly (or shorter time) basis, there would be no reason to determine the time frame affected by particular business transactions. Historically, the calendar year was adopted as the reporting period for most companies. However, many companies are now choosing a fiscal year that more closely approximates the company's annual *business cycle*. (The yearly period from lowest sales through highest sales and back to lowest sales is known as a business cycle.) For example, consider Exhibit 4–6. This exhibit illustrates the annual sales pattern for Company G. Notice that peak sales occur each year in January, while the lowest sales volume occurs in June. Such a sales pattern might be representative of a company that sells snow tires. If Company G were to report on a

EXHIBIT 4–6 Company G annual business cycle

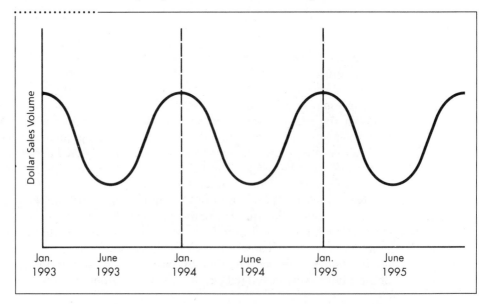

calendar-year basis, the financial reports would be prepared at about the time of peak yearly sales (i.e., the midpoint of the business cycle). Alternatively, a fiscal year that ended on June 30 would incorporate a single complete annual business cycle. Fiscal-year reports incorporating an annual business cycle contain information that is more easily comparable to past and future periods because annual sales patterns are not broken by the reporting period. Furthermore, fiscal-year reporting enables the management of a company to prepare the financial report when operations do not require its full attention.

In addition to annual reports, publicly traded companies issue financial statements for interim periods. These interim reports are considered integral parts of the annual periods, but they essentially disclose summary information to provide investors with more timely information and are not audited.

Historical Cost

The economic activities and resources of a company are initially measured by the exchange price of a transaction at the time the transaction occurs. Usually the exchange price (the **historical cost**) is retained in the accounting records as the value of an item until the item is consumed, sold, or liquidated and removed from the records. That is, recognition in the financial statements of gains and losses resulting from value changes of assets (or liabilities) generally is delayed until another exchange has taken place. The rationale behind the use of historical cost (as opposed to other valuation methods such as current market value or appraisal value) is that it is *reliable* and that source documents are usually available to verify the recorded amount. Historical cost also provides evidence that an independent buyer and seller were in agreement on the value of an exchanged good or service at the time of the transaction and thus has the qualities of representational faithfulness, neutrality, and verifiability.

One of the most frequently heard criticisms of financial reporting comes from those who would prefer alternative valuation methods that purportedly would disclose information more *relevant* for user decisions. Historical cost information may not always be completely relevant for all decisions, but it does have a significant degree of reliability. In certain situations, valuation methods other than historical cost are used in the financial statements when there is consensus that these methods provide more relevant information that possesses an acceptable degree of reliability. Generally, however, it is accepted that the measurement problems inherent in alternative valuation methods are greater than those of historical cost. That is, reliability often takes precedence over relevance. The FASB, however, has recognized the significance of this relevance/reliability trade off by encouraging companies to disclose *supplemental* current value information in their annual reports. This topic is discussed in Chapter 13.

Monetary Unit

Since the time when gold and other precious metals were accepted in exchange for goods and services, thereby replacing the barter system, there has been a unit of exchange. This unit of exchange is different for almost every nation, but

EXHIBIT 4–7   Statement of management responsibilities

Management of NIKE, Inc. is responsible for the information and representations contained in this report. The financial statements have been prepared in conformity with the generally accepted accounting principles we considered appropriate in the circumstances and include some amounts based on our best estimates and judgments. Other financial information in this report is consistent with these financial statements.

The Company's accounting systems include controls designed to reasonably assure that assets are safeguarded from unauthorized use or disposition and which provide for the preparation of financial statements in conformity with generally accepted accounting principles. These systems are supplemented by the selection and training of qualified financial personnel and an organizational structure providing for appropriate segregation of duties.

An Internal Audit Department reviews the results of its work with the Audit Committee of the Board of Directors, presently consisting of three directors of the Company. The Audit Committee is responsible for recommending to the Board of Directors the appointment of the independent accountants and reviews with the independent accountants, management and the internal audit staff, the scope and the results of the annual examination, the effectiveness of the accounting control system and other matters relating to the financial affairs of the Company as they deem appropriate. The independent accountants and the internal auditors have full access to the Committee, with and without the presence of management, to discuss any appropriate matters.

companies and accountants generally have adopted the national currency of the reporting company as the unit of measure in preparing financial reports.

In using the dollar or any other currency as the unit of measure, accountants have traditionally assumed that it is a stable measuring unit. Prior to the FASB, accounting policy-making bodies had taken the position that fluctuations in the value of the dollar were not a serious enough problem to have an adverse effect upon the comparability of accounting information and thus did not warrant any adjustment in the monetary unit assumption.

In today's world the assumption that the dollar or any other national currency is a stable measure over time is not necessarily valid. Consider the building you are now in. Real estate prices have changed during the past several years and will undoubtedly continue to vary, thereby reflecting changing monetary measures of value even though the historical cost to a particular owner remains the same.

There are two primary reasons for the changes in reported values over time:

1. The real value of the item in question may change in relation to the real value of all other goods and services in the economy.

2. The purchasing power of the measuring unit (in this case the dollar) may change.

Although currently the dollar is considered to be a stable monetary unit for the preparation of a company's financial statements, as mentioned earlier, to enhance comparability, the FASB encourages companies to make supplemental disclosures relating to the impacts of changing prices.

Conservatism

The convention of **conservatism** states, in effect, that when alternative accounting valuations are equally possible, the accountant should select the one that is least likely to overstate assets and income. Over the years conservatism gained prominence because of the optimism of management and the tendency to overstate assets and net income on financial statements that characterized the first three decades of the twentieth century.

The FASB has attempted to modify the convention of conservatism so that it is more synonymous with **prudence**. That is, conservatism should be a prudent reaction to uncertainty so as to ensure, to the extent possible, that the uncertainties and risks inherent in business situations are adequately considered. These uncertainties and risks should be reflected in accounting information so as to improve its predictive value and neutrality. Prudent reporting based on a healthy skepticism promotes integrity and best serves the various users of financial reports. Several accounting principles that are discussed later in the book are based on the principle of conservatism.

■ MANAGEMENT'S RESPONSIBILITY FOR THE FINANCIAL STATEMENTS AND THE AUDITOR'S REPORT

Clearly, an important element in the communication of accounting information is the annual report, which includes a company's financial statements. The financial statements are prepared by the management of the company and are audited by a public accounting firm (accounting firms and certified public accountants are discussed later in the chapter).

Management's Responsibility for the Financial Statements

A company's Board of Directors represents the interests of the stockholders. The Board usually includes representatives of management as well as qualified nonemployee outsiders such as senior management of other corporations. While most of the practical responsibilities for running the company belong to management, the legal responsibilities clearly lie with the Board. For convenience, we will use the term *management* in a general sense to include the Board of Directors.

An example of a statement expressing management's responsibilities for the financial statements is shown in Exhibit 4–7 (excerpts from the financial statements of Nike are included throughout the book and in Appendix A). Several aspects of the statement are important. First, management is responsible for preparing the financial statements. A common misconception is that the financial statements are prepared by the auditor, but that is clearly not the case. Second, management is responsible for maintaining a system of internal controls. In 1977, Congress passed the Foreign Corrupt Practices Act, which requires (in addition to prohibiting bribery and other corrupt practices) that a company registered with the SEC keep accurate and reasonably detailed records of transactions and maintain a system of internal controls.

Third, the independent auditor is hired to examine the financial statements and to issue a report on them. Finally, the Audit Committee of the Board of Directors is responsible for maintaining a liaison with the auditor. To ensure open communication between the auditor and the Board, the Audit Committee should not include employees of the company. This channel of communication, established outside the control of management, is intended to help the auditor fulfill its responsibility to the stockholders and maintain independence. The auditor is legally responsible to the stockholders for the performance of the audit as are the Board of Directors for the operation of the company. Not all companies have audit committees, although the New York Stock Exchange does require companies whose shares are traded on the Exchange to have such a committee. The SEC has encouraged, but not yet required, companies to have audit committees.

Auditor's Report

Many major financial decisions by investors, bankers, other creditors, and other users are based on the financial information presented within the financial statements. In order to help ensure a fair presentation of a company's financial resources, obligations, and activities, most financial statements and accompanying notes presented to external users are audited by an independent certified public accountant (CPA). Companies that file with the SEC and are listed on stock exchanges must obtain an audit. Also, many banks require audited financial statements as a condition for granting loans. Other companies, however, may not obtain an audit of their financial statements and also may not follow generally accepted accounting principles. In an audit the independent auditor is responsible for making an examination of the accounting system, records, and reports *in accordance with generally accepted auditing standards* and, based on this examination, expressing an *opinion* as to the fairness *in accordance with generally accepted accounting principles* of the financial statements and accompanying notes. Although this opinion is *not* itself part of the financial statements, it is an extremely important item of information, upon which external users place much significance.

One of the most important characteristics of an auditor is **independence**, meaning that the auditor, although paid by the company, is unrelated to the company and is therefore objective. The user of the financial statements can rely on the auditor's fairness and impartiality.

The auditor's report may take several forms, depending on the results of the audit examination. The most favorable and most common report includes **an unqualified opinion,** also known as a "clean" opinion. The suggested standard report for an unqualified opinion is shown in Exhibit 4–8. The first paragraph, known as the *introductory* paragraph, lists the financial statements that

EXHIBIT 4−8 Auditor's report: unqualified opinion

To the Board of Directors and Shareholders of Xerox Corporation

We have audited the consolidated balance sheets of Xerox Corporation and consolidated subsidiaries as of December 31, 1989 and 1988 and the related consolidated statements of income and cash flows for each of the years in the three-year period ended December 31, 1989. These consolidated financial statements are the responsibility of the Company's management. Our responsibility is to express an opinion on these consolidated financial statements based on our audits.

We conducted our audits in accordance with generally accepted auditing standards. Those standards require that we plan and perform the audit to obtain reasonable assurance about whether the consolidated financial statements are free of material misstatement. An audit includes examining, on a test basis, evidence supporting the amounts and disclosures in the consolidated financial statements. An audit also includes assessing the accounting principles used and significant estimates made by management, as well as evaluating the overall consolidated financial statement presentation. We believe that our audits provide a reasonable basis for our opinion.

In our opinion, the consolidated financial statements appearing on pages 34, 35, 37, 43, 45, 46 and 48−65 present fairly, in all material respects, the financial position of Xerox Corporation and consolidated subsidiaries at December 31, 1989 and 1988 and the results of their operations and their cash flows for each of the years in the three-year period ended December 31, 1989, in conformity with generally accepted accounting principles.

Stamford, Connecticut   KPMG Peat Marwick
January 30, 1990,
except as to Subsequent Events
in Note 7 on Page 54, which is
as of February 13, 1990.

were audited, states that management is responsible for those statements and that the auditor is responsible for expressing an opinion on them.

The second paragraph, known as the *scope* paragraph, describes what the auditor has done. Specifically, it states that the auditor has examined the financial statements in accordance with generally accepted auditing standards and has performed appropriate tests. The auditor does *not* examine all of the information used to generate the financial statements, but performs tests to evaluate the reasonableness of the information. The auditor exercises skill and judgment in deciding what evidence to examine, when to examine it, and how much to examine. Because financial statements include estimates made by management, an auditor also designs tests to evaluate the reasonableness of the assumptions and other factors used in those estimates. The auditor also assesses the reasonableness of these estimates, but does not guarantee their accuracy.

The third paragraph, known as the *opinion* paragraph, gives the auditor's opinion. This opinion is based on professional judgment, not absolute certainty. When the opinion is unqualified, the auditor states that the financial statements present *fairly* in accordance with *generally accepted accounting principles* (GAAP). Thus the emphasis is not on presenting "fairly" in the general meaning of the word, but on presenting in accordance with GAAP. In other words, GAAP is defined as being fair. The user of the financial statements, therefore, must understand GAAP to be able to understand and interpret the statements. (In exceptional cases, the management of the company and the auditor may agree that a method other than GAAP provides more useful and "fairer" information about a transaction or event. In such a case, the other method would be fully disclosed.) The auditor's opinion also emphasizes that the statements comply with GAAP in all material respects, thereby indicating reasonable, rather than absolute accuracy. In summary, the unqualified audit opinion provides an economical and reasonable level of assurance that the financial statements are free of material misstatements. An audit enhances the confidence of users because the auditor is an objective, independent expert who is knowledgeable about the company's business and financial reporting requirements.

There are three things, however, that the audit report does *not* say. First, an unqualified opinion is not a "clean bill of health." The report does not, for example, endorse a company's policy decisions, its use of resources, or even the adequacy of its internal control. Second, an unqualified opinion provides no assurance of the future success or survival of the company. Generally accepted auditing standards include procedures used to examine the financial viability of the company. However, a company may suffer financial difficulty, or even failure, within a relatively short time of receiving an unqualified opinion, but such a failure does not indicate that the audit was negligent. In other words, there is a difference between a business failure and an audit failure. Third, an audit report does not guarantee that fraud has not been committed by a member, or members, of the company. An audit is planned and performed with professional skepticism. The auditor assesses the risk of material misstatement and designs the audit to provide reasonable assurance of detection of significant errors or fraud. However, fraud that is concealed through forgery and collusion among the personnel of the company, especially management, may escape detection by the auditor. For large companies, such fraud would have to involve millions of dollars to be material.

The user of financial statements should be alert to those situations in which an auditor has provided a modified report or has given an alternative opinion from an unqualified opinion. The **modified report** includes a fourth explanatory paragraph. The two common types of modified reports are caused by material uncertainties and changes in accounting principles. Examples of each type of modified report are illustrated in Exhibits 4–9 and 4–10.

The material uncertainty is usually related to either litigation or the going-concern assumption. For example, if the company is being sued for a *material* amount and if the auditor, after consultation with the lawyers, perceives a sufficient likelihood of the company losing the lawsuit, a modified report is issued. Similarly, if the auditor believes that there is a sufficient likelihood that the company will be unable to continue as a going concern for the next year, an additional paragraph is added.

EXHIBIT 4–9   Auditor's modified report: change in accounting principle

·················

To the Shareholders of The Quaker Oats Company:

We have audited the accompanying consolidated balance sheets of The Quaker Oats Company (a New Jersey corporation) and Subsidiaries as of June 30, 1989, 1988 and 1987, and the related consolidated statements of income, common shareholders' equity and cash flows for the years then ended. These financial statements are the responsibility of the Company's management. Our responsibility is to express an opinion on these financial statements based on our audits.

We conducted our audits in accordance with generally accepted auditing standards. Those standards require that we plan and perform the audit to obtain reasonable assurance about whether the financial statements are free of material misstatement. An audit includes examining, on a test basis, evidence supporting the amounts and disclosures in the financial statements. An audit also includes assessing the accounting principles used and significant estimates made by management, as well as evaluating the overall financial statement presentation. We believe that our audits provide a reasonable basis for our opinion.

In our opinion, the financial statements referred to above present fairly, in all material respects, the financial position of The Quaker Oats Company and Subsidiaries as of June 30, 1989, 1988 and 1987, and the results of their operations and their cash flows for the years then ended in conformity with generally accepted accounting principles.

As discussed in Note 1 to the financial statements, effective July 1, 1988, the Company adopted the Last-In, First-Out, method of determining cost for the majority of its U.S. Grocery Products inventories.

Arthur Andersen & Co.

Chicago, Illinois,
August 7, 1989.

A fourth paragraph is also added when a change in accounting principle occurs because the FASB adopts a new standard or when a company adopts a preferable method from among existing alternatives. In each of these cases, the additional paragraph gives a brief explanation of the items causing the modified report. A reference is also made to the note to the financial statements where the reason for the modified report is discussed.

The **alternative opinions** are a qualified ("except for") opinion, a disclaimer of opinion, or an adverse opinion. The *except for* opinion indicates that there is a material restriction on the scope of the auditor's work, or a material departure from GAAP. A *disclaimer* indicates that scope restrictions are so pervasive that the auditor cannot form an opinion. An *adverse* opinion indicates that there are pervasive departures from GAAP. These three opinions are rare because they

EXHIBIT 4–10   Auditor's modified report: material uncertainty

. . . .

Stockholders and Board of Directors
E-Systems, Inc.
Dallas, Texas

We have audited the consolidated balance sheets of E-Systems, Inc. and subsidiaries as of December 31, 1989 and 1988, and the related consolidated statements of income, stockholders' equity and cash flows for each of the three years in the period ended December 31, 1989. These financial statements are the responsibility of the Company's management. Our responsibility is to express an opinion on these financial statements based on our audits.

We conducted our audits in accordance with generally accepted auditing standards. Those standards require that we plan and perform the audit to obtain reasonable assurance about whether the financial statements are free of material misstatement. An audit includes examining, on a test basis, evidence supporting the amounts and disclosures in the financial statements. An audit also includes assessing the accounting principles used and significant estimates made by management, as well as evaluating the overall financial statement presentation. We believe that our audits provide a reasonable basis for our opinion.

In our opinion, the financial statements referred to above present fairly, in all material respects, the consolidated financial position of E-Systems, Inc. and subsidiaries at December 31, 1989 and 1988, and the consolidated results of their operations and their cash flows for each of the three years in the period ended December 31, 1989, in conformity with generally accepted accounting principles.

As discussed in Note J to the consolidated financial statements, the Company is the subject of a criminal investigation by the U.S. Government to determine if the Company violated procurement regulations. The ultimate outcome of the Government's investigation and any impact on the consolidated financial statements related to the findings of the investigation cannot be reasonably determined.

Ernst and Young

Dallas, Texas
January 31, 1990

---

are not acceptable to the SEC or stock exchanges. A company may also hire a CPA to "review" or "compile" financial statements. In these situations the CPA attaches a report that makes it clear that the financial statements were *not* audited.

As we have seen, the audit opinion states that the financial statements are presented in accordance with GAAP. Since GAAP cannot specifically address all the novel and complex business transactions possible, companies and their auditors should determine the appropriate accounting for such transactions based on some pervasive fundamental accounting principle, or on an accounting convention such as conservatism, or by comparing them to transactions with a similar economic substance. The SEC staff does encourage companies and their auditors to discuss such situations with them. Also, if material, the details of such unusual transactions should be fully disclosed.

■ THE ACCOUNTANCY PROFESSION

Accountancy has emerged as a profession, alongside the professions of medicine and law. The study and practice of accountancy require a broad understanding of concepts in such areas as economics, sociology, psychology, and business and public administration as well as in-depth knowledge of specialized accounting areas. The three main fields of accountancy include (1) public accounting, (2) managerial accounting, and (3) governmental and quasi-governmental accounting, each of which has several accounting specialty areas. Standardized national examinations are given at regular intervals for people who desire to work in some of these areas. Each of these fields is discussed next and summarized in Exhibit 4–11.

Public Accounting

A *certified public accountant* (CPA) is an independent professional who provides accounting services to clients for a fee. In order to practice accountancy, each CPA must hold a license issued by the state in which the CPA works. Licensing is designed to help to ensure that high-quality, professional service is provided by accountants. Although the licensing requirements vary from state to state, all CPAs must pass the Uniform CPA Examination, a national examination given twice a year across the United States. The examination is administered by the American Institute of Certified Public Accountants (AICPA) and includes the topics of accounting practice and theory, auditing, and business law. In addition, states have minimum educational and practical experience requirements such as requiring the equivalent of a Master's degree and two years of relevant experience. Several specialty areas of public accounting are discussed next.

Auditing. **Auditing involves examining the accounting records of a company and the resulting financial statements to attest to the fairness of the accounting information in the statements.** Auditing is necessary because financial statements are prepared by the management of the company issuing the statements. Because of the potential bias of management, external users of the financial statements need assurance that the statements present fairly the accounting information about the company. Consequently, these financial statements must be audited by an *independent* CPA because a CPA is the only person licensed to do so.

Auditing is the primary professional service offered by a CPA, who is an independent and unbiased observer. Based on the evidence gathered in the auditing process, the CPA expresses a professional opinion as to the fairness of the financial statements (discussed earlier in the chapter). Because many external users rely on the CPA's opinion, auditing plays an important role in society.

EXHIBIT 4–11 The accountancy profession

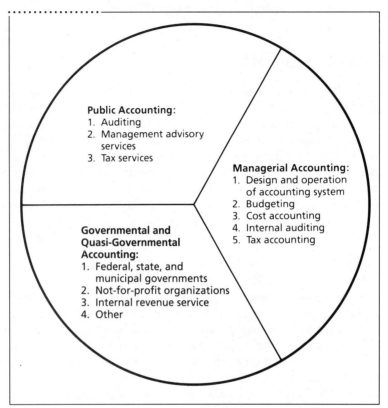

Most CPAs work in CPA firms, and auditing is done by many local and regional CPA firms. In addition, the large size of many businesses, some of which span the United States as well as the world in their activities, has led to the growth of large CPA firms with offices in most major U.S. and international cities. The six largest CPA firms, known as the "big 6," are Arthur Andersen, Coopers & Lybrand, Deloitte & Touche, Ernst & Young, KPMG Peat Marwick, and Price Waterhouse.

Management Advisory Services. The accounting records kept by the company are part of its *management information system*. CPA firms develop a strong understanding of the strengths and weaknesses of the operating activities and information systems of companies. Therefore, in addition to auditing departments, CPA firms have established separate management advisory services departments to offer organizations constructive criticism about how to improve their internal operations and to conduct special studies to aid management in its various activities.

Management advisory services in CPA firms include the design or improvement of the financial accounting system for identifying, measuring, recording, retaining, and reporting accounting information. These services also may include assistance in developing cost control systems, planning manufacturing facilities, and installing computer operations. Providing these services requires CPA firms to hire people with specialties other than accounting, for example, lawyers, industrial engineers, and systems analysts.

Tax Services. The federal government as well as most state governments require the filing of income tax returns and the payment of taxes. The various federal and state tax regulations are designed to collect taxes in a fair manner and to stimulate (or discourage) certain activities and investments. Because of the high tax rates, complex tax regulations, and special tax incentives today, most companies (and individuals) can benefit from carefully planning their activities to minimize or postpone their tax payments.

Most CPA firms have established tax services departments to provide both tax planning and tax return preparation (compliance) services for their clients. The firms employ tax professionals who are experts in the various federal and state tax regulations to assist these companies and individuals in tax planning. Similarly, company or individual income tax returns, reflecting the results of these tax planning activities, are frequently prepared by the tax services department of the CPA firms.

Managerial Accounting

A managerial accountant is employed by a company to perform its internal (managerial) accounting activities. A senior manager usually coordinates these activities. This manager frequently reports directly to the top management of the organization, such as the vice-president of finance or the controller, an indication of how important the accounting functions are to the organization's operations.

Another indication of the importance of managerial accounting is the Certificate in Management Accounting (CMA). The CMA is granted to persons who meet specific educational and professional standards and who pass a uniform CMA examination, administered twice yearly by the Institute of Certified Management Accountants. The examination covers several topics, including economics and business finance, organizations and behavior, public reporting standards, internal reporting and analysis, and decision analysis. Although the CMA is not required as a license to practice, accountants holding the CMA are recognized as professional experts in the area of managerial accounting.

Managerial accounting activities encompass several areas: (1) design and operation of accounting systems, (2) budgeting, (3) cost accounting, (4) internal auditing, and (5) tax accounting.

Design and Operation of Accounting Systems. An accounting system is a means by which accounting information about a company's activities is identified, measured, recorded, and retained so that it can be reported. As is shown in this book, certain general principles (rules) apply to the operation of an efficient accounting system for all companies. Within these principles, however, each company can design and operate its accounting system in the way that best meets its needs. The accounting system should be able to provide the information needed by management as well as that needed for the preparation of financial statements. One duty of the managerial accountant is to design and operate the company's accounting system. This function is sometimes referred to as *general accounting* because of the wide variety of activities involved. These activities include, among others, determining the computer applications for the accounting system, integrating the accounting activities for different departments, designing accounting forms and reports, and establishing standard operating and recording procedures. The accounting system aggregates data for use in the financial statements and disaggregates the data for use by management.

Budgeting. The management of a company includes two functions, planning and controlling. **Planning** means developing a plan of action for the short-, mid-, and long-term future of the organization. Planning enables the company to develop strategies to meet its goals and to provide the resources required to implement these strategies. A company establishes strategies by identifying the quantities and types of products sold, determining how to produce these products, and setting the selling price. Providing the required resources means having the necessary personnel, facilities, supplies, and finances. **Budgeting is the process of quantifying the plans of management to show their impact on the company's operating activities.** The quantification of a plan is known as a *budget* (or *forecast*). Frequently included in a budget are forecasted (or projected) financial statements.

Controlling is the process of monitoring whether the actual operations of the various parts of the company achieve the established plans. As an aid in the control function, another aspect of budgeting is the frequent comparison of actual quantified results to the budget so that differences between actual and planned results may be seen and corrective action may be taken when necessary. Budgeting, as part of both the planning and control functions of management, is an important aspect of managerial accounting.

Cost Accounting. **Cost accounting is the process of determining and accumulating the costs of certain activities within a company.** For a company, cost accounting is primarily concerned with product costs—that is, determining the cost of producing a unit of a product. Cost accounting, however, may also involve calculating the cost of operating a particular department, a manufacturing process, or a marketing technique. Cost accounting cannot be separated from budgeting because the accounting information used to determine, for example, the unit cost of a product is the same information used in the controlling (comparing actual to planned costs) aspect of budgeting. The difference is that in cost accounting actual costs are computed for other purposes as well, such as establishing selling prices and determining operating profits. Cost accounting is an interesting area of managerial accounting because many costs apply to different products, processes, and departments.

Internal Auditing.   Earlier we discussed the design and operation of an accounting system. One part of the design is establishing good internal control. **Internal control involves the procedures to safeguard the company's economic resources and to promote the efficient and effective operation of its accounting system.** Internal auditing is a part of the internal control procedures and reviews operations to ensure that these procedures are being followed throughout the company. Internal auditing is becoming increasingly important because the procedures for the external audit and the size of the audit fee depend, to a great degree, on the quality of the internal control. As evidence of professionalism in internal auditing, an accountant may become a certified internal auditor (CIA). The CIA certificate is awarded by the Institute of Internal Auditors, Inc.. Although it is not a license to practice, the certificate states that the holder has met strict educational and practical experience requirements and has passed a uniform CIA examination of four parts covering the topics of theory and practice of internal auditing, quantitative methods, information systems, accounting, finance, and economics.

Tax Accounting.   Although companies often assign their tax work to the tax services department of a CPA firm, many still maintain their own tax departments. This department is staffed by accountants with expertise in the tax laws relating to the business. These accountants handle income tax planning and the preparation of state and federal income tax returns. They also work on sales and excise taxes, real estate taxes, personal property taxes such as taxes on inventories, and other taxes.

Governmental and Quasi-Governmental Accounting

Certain governmental and quasi-governmental agencies employ accountants. These agencies include (1) federal, state, and municipal governments, (2) not-for-profit organizations, (3) the Internal Revenue Service, and (4) other quasi-governmental organizations.

Federal, State, and Municipal Governments.   Officials of federal, state, and municipal governments are responsible for the imposition, collection, and control of tax revenues and tax expenditures. They are also involved in the management of the various departments and programs of the government entities.

Not-For-Profit Organizations.   Administrators of federal, state, municipal, and other not-for-profit organizations such as colleges and universities, hospitals, and mental health agencies are responsible for their efficient and effective operations. The accounting information needed by these organizations is the same in many respects as that needed by companies. But because they are not-for-profit organizations financed in part by public funds, they are required to use somewhat different accounting procedures (called *fund* accounting).

EXHIBIT 4–12 Summary of major activities affecting financial reporting

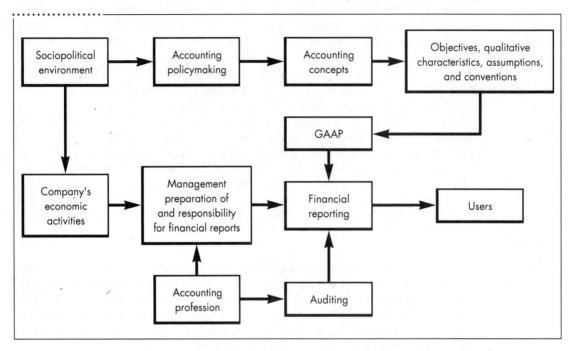

Internal Revenue Service. The Internal Revenue Service (IRS) is responsible for administering the collection of federal income taxes. This role includes the processing of individual and corporate tax returns, payments, and refunds, as well as the investigation (auditing) of selected tax returns. The IRS also issues various regulations, based on research and other activities, designed to explain the Internal Revenue Code. State revenue agencies also perform similar functions.

Other Governmental Organizations. Several other governmental organizations are involved in accounting activities. The Securities and Exchange Commission (SEC) has the responsibility of overseeing the financial statements of certain companies and has the legal authority to establish accounting regulations for them. It identifies appropriate accounting procedures and verifies that existing regulations are being followed. The General Accounting Office (GAO) has the responsibility of cooperating with various agencies of the federal government in the development and operation of their accounting systems to improve the management of these agencies. Other federal and state agencies also prepare and use accounting information, such as the Interstate Commerce Commission, the Environmental Protection Agency, and the Federal Communications Commission.

■ SUMMARY OF MAJOR ACTIVITIES AFFECTING FINANCIAL REPORTING

The major items discussed in this chapter, and some of their major relationships are summarized in Exhibit 4–12. There are numerous additional interactions other than those shown. For example, the accounting profession has a significant impact on GAAP.

QUESTIONS

1. What are generally accepted accounting principles? List the sources of generally accepted accounting principles.

2. What are (were) the CAP, APB, and FASB? What documents that constitute generally accepted accounting principles have been issued by each of these organizations?

3. Briefly discuss the types of pronouncements issued by the FASB.

4. Why do external users use information about an enterprise's (a) economic resources and claims to these resources, (b) earnings and its components, and (c) cash flows?

5. What is relevant accounting information? Identify and define the ingredients of relevant accounting information.

6. What is reliable accounting information? Identify and define the ingredients of reliable accounting information.

7. What is materiality and how does it relate to relevance?

8. Discuss the relationship between historical cost and reliability.

9. What is conservatism and how might it conflict with neutrality?

10. What is the going concern (continuity) assumption and why is it necessary?

11. What is an audit, and why is the auditor's report an important item of information?

12. Describe the responsibilities of management and of the Board of Directors that relate to the financial statements. How are these responsibilities different from those of the auditor?

13. What are the differences among unqualified opinions, modified reports, disclaimers, and adverse opinions?

14. Describe the two types of modified reports. Give an example of the circumstances that might cause each to be used.

PROBLEMS AND CASES

15. **Qualitative Characteristics.** Several qualitative characteristics of useful accounting information were identified in the chapter. Below is a list of these qualities as well as a list of statements describing the qualities.

A. Comparability
B. Decision usefulness
C. Relevance
D. Reliability
E. Predictive value
F. Feedback value

G. Timeliness
H. Verifiability
I. Neutrality
J. Representational faithfulness
K. Consistency
L. Materiality

1. Ability of measurers to form a consensus that the selected accounting method has been used without error or bias.

2. Having information available to decision makers before it loses its capacity to influence decisions.

3. Capacity to make a difference in a decision.

4. Overall qualitative characteristic.

5. Absence of bias intended to influence behavior in a particular direction.

6. Reasonably free from error and bias.

7. Helps decision makers to correctly forecast.

8. Validity.

9. Interactive quality; helps identify and explain similarities and differences.

10. Quantitative "threshold" constraint.

11. Conformity from period to period.

12. Helps decision makers to confirm or correct prior expectations.

Required Use the appropriate letter to identify each quality with the statement describing the quality.

16. **Accounting Assumptions and Conventions.** Certain accounting assumptions and conventions have had an important impact on the development of generally accepted accounting principles. Below is a list of these assumptions and conventions as well as a list of statements describing certain accounting practices.

A. Entity	D. Historical cost
B. Continuity	E. Monetary unit
C. Period of time	F. Conservatism

1. The business rather than its owners is the reporting unit.

2. Accounting measurements are reported in dollars.

3. The year is the normal reporting unit.

4. In the absence of evidence to the contrary, the business will operate long enough to carry out its existing commitments.

5. Exchange price is retained in the accounting records.

6. An accounting alternative is selected that is least likely to overstate assets and income.

Required Use the appropriate letter to select the accounting assumption or convention that justifies each accounting practice.

17. **Accounting Principles.** At the completion of the Darby Department Store audit, the president asks about the meaning of the phrase "in conformity with generally accepted accounting principles" that appears in the audit report on the company's financial statements. He observes that the meaning of the phrase must include more than what he thinks of as "principles."

Required 1. Explain the meaning of the term "accounting principles" as used in the audit report. (Do not discuss in this part the significance of "generally accepted.")

2. The president wants to know how you determine whether or not an accounting principle is generally accepted. Discuss the sources of evidence for determining whether an accounting principle has substantial authoritative support. Do not merely list the titles of publications. (*AICPA adapted*)

18. **Inconsistent Statements on Accounting Principles.** The following two statements have been taken directly or with some modification from the accounting literature. Each is either taken out of context, involves circular reasoning, and/or contains one or more fallacies, half-truths, erroneous comments, conclusions, or inconsistencies (internally or with generally accepted principles or practices).

Statement 1	*Statement 2*
Accounting is a service activity. Its function is to provide quantitative financial information that is intended to be useful in making economic decisions about and for economic entities. Thus the accounting function might be viewed primarily as being a tool or device for providing quantitative financial information to management to facilitate decision making.	Financial statements that were developed in accordance with generally accepted accounting principles, which apply the conservatism convention, can be free from bias (or can give a presentation that is fair with respect to continuing and prospective stockholders as well as to retiring stockholders).

Required Evaluate each of the above statements as follows:

1. List the fallacies, half-truths, circular reasoning, erroneous comments or conclusions, and/or inconsistencies.

2. Explain by what authority and/or on what basis each item listed in (1) can be considered to be fallacious, circular, inconsistent, a half-truth, or an erroneous comment or conclusion. If the statement or a portion of it is merely out of context, indicate the context(s) in which the statement would be correct. (*AICPA adapted*)

19. **Accounting Standard Setting.** Critics of the Financial Accounting Standards Board accuse it of moving too slowly and of producing little of substance when it finally does act. Some business people say that accounting rules are unnecessary, complex, and costly. Replacing the FASB with a government body has been discussed.

Required Discuss arguments for and against the FASB setting accounting standards.

20. **Financial Statements.** The major financial statements in an annual report are illustrated in Appendix A.

Required How do the major financial statements in an annual report relate to the specific objectives of financial reporting in "Objectives of Financial Reporting by Business Enterprises"?

21. **Qualitative Characteristics.** "Qualitative Characteristics of Accounting Information" discusses the qualitative characteristics of accounting information.

Required Discuss the two primary decision-specific qualities of accounting information and their relationship.

22. **Accounting Assumptions and Conventions.** Six accounting assumptions and conventions were discussed in this chapter: entity, continuity, period of time, historical cost, monetary unit, and conservatism.

Required For each of the following cases, identify the assumption(s) or convention(s) that has (have) been violated:

1. The treasurer of Wino Corp. wishes to prepare financial statements only during downturns in wine production, which occur periodically when the grape crop fails. In no event would more than 24 months pass without statements being prepared.

2. The Yoohoo Telephone Co. has a large amount of property, plant, and equipment that was purchased over a long time period. The company has decided to issue only current cost financial statements since the price level has changed significantly over this time period.

3. When President Milhouse was in office, he had the government pay for numerous improvements to his personal residence at San Clemency, which he later sold for a substantial personal profit.

4. P/L Co. cannot afford to pay the interest on its current debt and is attempting to renegotiate the debt with the bank by having the unpaid interest added to the principal, which will be repaid over a much longer time period.

5. Wish Co. has just sued its major competitor and will file the lawsuit papers with the judge in the near future. Wish Co. now shows a lawsuit receivable asset and corresponding profit on its financial statements.

23. **Auditor's Report.** The auditor's report was introduced in this chapter.

Required Discuss the relevance and reliability of an auditor's report.

ANNUAL REPORT PROBLEM

24. **Auditors' Report.** General Electric's goal is to run businesses that are number one or two in their global markets or, in the case of services that have a substantial position, are of a scale and potential appropriate to a $50 billion enterprise. The following independent auditors' report is from its 1988 financial statements:

To Share Owners and Board of Directors of General Electric Company:

We have audited the accompanying statements of financial position of General Electric Company and consolidated affiliates as of December 31, 1988 and 1987 and the related statements of earnings and cash flows for each of the years in the three-year period ended December 31, 1988. These consolidated financial statements are the responsibility of the Company's management. Our responsibility is to express an opinion on these consolidated financial statements based on our audits.

We conducted our audits in accordance with generally accepted auditing standards. Those standards require that we plan and perform the audit to obtain reasonable assurance about whether the financial statements are free of material misstatement. An audit includes examining, on a test basis, evidence supporting the amounts and disclosures in the financial statements. An audit also includes assessing the accounting principles used and significant estimates made by management, as well as evaluating the overall financial statement presentation. We believe that our audits provide a reasonable basis for our opinion.

In our opinion, the aforementioned financial statements appearing on pages 24–29 and 44–70 present fairly, in all material respects, the financial position of General Electric Company and consolidated affiliates at December 31, 1988 and 1987, and the results of their operations and their cash flows for each of the years in the three-year period ended December 31, 1988, in conformity with generally accepted accounting principles.

As discussed in note 1 to the consolidated financial statements, in 1988 the Company changed its method of inclusion of previously unconsolidated affiliates; and in 1987 the Company changed its methods of accounting for income taxes and overhead recorded in inventory. We concur with these accounting changes.

Peat Marwick Main & Co.
Stamford, Connecticut
February 10, 1989

Required Discuss the relevance of each paragraph in the above independent auditors' report for the user of GE's financial statements. (The information in note 1 is explored in Problem 11–73 of this book.)

Accounting for Assets, Liabilities, and Stockholders' Equity

Cash and Accounts Receivable

After reading this chapter, you should understand

- Accounting for cash
- Cash management
- Accounts receivable
- Uncollectible accounts receivable
- Measurement of bad debt expense
- Sales returns and allowances, sales discounts, and sales when a right of return exists.

Financial statement users focus on a variety of information in making credit and investment decisions. Investors, long-term creditors, and short-term creditors are interested in a company's **financial flexibility:** the ability to use its financial resources to adapt to change. As part of the company's financial flexibility, these external users are concerned about its **liquidity.** That is, they are concerned about the availability of liquid assets (cash or assets that may be converted quickly into cash) to pay dividends and interest and to repay short-term debts. Two common types of liquid assets are cash and accounts receivable. In this chapter we discuss the measurement and valuation procedures associated with these items, including uncollectible amounts, sales returns and allowances, sales discounts, and sales when a right of return exists.

■ CASH

The accurate measurement of cash is important to users of financial statements because cash represents the amount of resources on hand to meet planned expenditures and emergency situations. **Any amount reported as cash in the current assets section on the balance sheet must be available to pay current obligations.** It should not be subject to any contractual restrictions that prevent these monies from being used to satisfy current debts. For example, many corporations establish sinking funds into which they deposit cash over an extended period. At the end of the period, the cash (plus accumulated interest) is to be used for a specific purpose (e.g., to retire long-term bonds). Amounts appropriated to sinking funds should not be classified under the cash heading on the balance sheet; sinking funds normally are reported on the balance sheet in the long-term investments category because the funds are not available to pay current obligations.

The measurement of cash classified as a current asset includes **coins, currency, unrestricted funds on deposit with a bank or other financial institution, negotiable checks, money orders, and bank drafts.** On the other hand, some items may be confused with cash but normally are categorized under other balance sheet captions according to generally accepted accounting principles. Among these items are certificates of deposit, bank overdrafts, postdated checks, IOUs, and travel advances.

1. *Certificates of deposit (CDs)* are short-term investments normally issued by banks that allow a company to invest idle cash for short periods of time. Although CDs may be sold by investors at any time, an interest penalty may result unless they are held until the stated maturity date. Consequently, certificates of deposit are normally classified as temporary investments.

2. *Bank overdrafts* are overdrawn checking accounts. They should be disclosed as current liabilities and should not be offset against positive balances in other bank accounts.

3. *Postdated checks* are checks bearing future dates that may be deposited only on a date subsequent to the issue date. Postdated checks should be included as receivables until the date they become negotiable.

4. *IOUs* are acknowledgments of debts, but they are not negotiable and usually may not be used by the holder to satisfy other obligations. IOUs should be classified as receivables until collected or written off as uncollectible.

5. *Travel advances* are funds or checks given to company employees to cover out-of-pocket expenses while traveling on company business. Since travel advances normally are satisfied when the employee submits receipts for business expenses, they are not included as a component of cash. Travel advances generally are classified as prepaid items.

In summary, to be classified under the current asset caption — Cash — on the balance sheet, amounts must be immediately available to pay current debts and may not be bound by any contractual or legal restrictions. Items that do not meet these criteria must be reported elsewhere within the assets (or liabilities) section on the balance sheet.

Cash and Cash Equivalents

Cash equivalents are investments that are short-term, highly liquid, and involve very little risk. Securities such as commercial paper, treasury bills, and money market funds are examples of cash equivalents. An increasing number (approximately 27%) of companies report *cash and cash equivalents* as a single amount on the balance sheet.[1]

....

[1] *Accounting Trends and Techniques* (New York: AICPA, 1989), p. 102.

Compensating Balances

In recent years it has become commonplace for banks to require a portion of any amount loaned to remain on deposit in the bank for the duration of the loan period. These required deposits are termed **compensating balances.** For example, a bank loaning a company $100,000 may require that the company maintain a $10,000 deposit with the bank until the loan is repaid. Such arrangements have two main effects. First, they reduce the amount of cash available to the borrower, and, second, they increase the effective interest rate the borrower pays for the use of the funds. For example, if the stated interest rate for the $100,000 loan is 12%, the effective rate for the actual funds used for a year is 13.33% ($12,000 ÷ $90,000), assuming the $10,000 compensating balance does not earn any interest.

Compensating balances against short-term borrowings are separately stated in the current assets section of the balance sheet, whereas compensating balances for long-term borrowings are separately stated as noncurrent assets (as either investments or other assets). Compensating balance agreements that do not legally restrict the amount of funds shown on the balance sheet should be described in the notes to the financial statements.

Cash Management

The efficient management of cash is of primary importance to every company. Care must be taken to ensure that adequate cash resources are available to meet current obligations. However, the fact that idle cash is a nonproductive resource must also be recognized.

For a few years after the Great Depression many companies wished to protect themselves against business failure. Consequently, companies amassed large amounts of cash in order to keep themselves liquid. Business managers soon realized that such monies were simply idle resources and that company prospects and performance could be improved by investing them. For example, at the time this book was written, placing idle cash balances in savings accounts that pay interest resulted in a return of up to 7%, and certificates of deposit, money market securities, or other relatively risk-free investments provided returns of as much as 9%. Proper cash management requires the investment of idle funds. However, it is necessary to determine the estimated timing of cash inflows and outflows and to ensure the availability of cash to meet the company's needs prior to embarking on a short-term investment program.

The management of cash can be subdivided into its cash planning and cash control aspects. **Cash planning** systems consist of those methods and procedures adopted to ensure that adequate cash is available to meet maturing obligations and that any unused or excess cash is invested. **Cash control** systems are the methods and procedures adopted to ensure the safeguarding of the organization's funds.

The major component of a cash planning system is the cash budget. **The cash budget is a plan of cash activity that forecasts cash inflows and outflows**

and identifies the timing of potential cash surpluses and shortages. The cash budget is primarily a managerial accounting technique and as such is outside the scope of this book.

Cash control systems are effected through adequate internal control measures. **Internal control** has been defined as:

> The plan of organization and all of the coordinate methods and measures adopted within a business to safeguard its assets, check the accuracy and reliability of its accounting data, promote operational efficiency, and encourage adherence to prescribed managerial policies.[2]

Internal control measures are designed to reduce the possibility of errors or omissions throughout the organization. Since cash cannot be traced easily, internal control over cash is enhanced by routine reviews of the accuracy of the recording of cash transactions and by the separation of employee duties. These procedures will help to ensure that theft can occur only if there is collusion among employees. However, care must be exercised in the adoption of internal control measures to ensure that the cost associated with the use of the measures does not exceed the value of the derived benefits. Any measure that costs more than its derived benefits will ultimately result in lower profits for the company.

Cash control systems can be subdivided into two main functions: (1) control over receipts and (2) control over disbursements. The control procedures adopted for receipts should be designed to safeguard all cash inflows from the time they arrive at the company until they are deposited in the company's bank account. Among the key elements in a cash receipts internal control system are (1) an immediate counting of receipts by the person opening the mail or the salesperson using the cash register, (2) a daily recording of all cash receipts in the accounting records, and (3) the daily deposit of all receipts intact in the company's bank account.

The control procedures for disbursements should ensure that only authorized payments for actual company expenditures are approved and forwarded. The key elements in a cash disbursements internal control system include (1) making all disbursements by check so that a record exists for every company expenditure, (2) authorizing and signing checks only after an expenditure is verified and approved, preferably signed by two officers of the company, and (3) periodic reconciliations of bank statement cash balances. More specific procedures used for internal control are beyond the scope of this book.

One of the most important sources of cash for a company is from accounts receivable. After the initial credit sale, the amount collected is a function of the uncollectible amounts due to bad debts. Other issues in the recording of sales and any related receivables are sales returns, sales allowances, sales discounts, and sales when a right of return exists. Each of these topics is discussed in the following sections.

. . . .
[2]*Codification of Statements on Auditing Standards* (New York: AICPA, 1990), sec. 320.08.

■ RECEIVABLES

The sales of goods and services are usually made on "open accounts" that result in short-term extensions of credit by the seller. The recognition of revenue from credit sales is based on the revenue recognition criteria discussed in Chapter 2. That is, revenue is recognized when *realization occurs* (i.e., a noncash resource is exchanged for cash or rights to cash) and the *revenue is earned* (i.e., the earning process is complete or virtually complete). Typically, the sale of goods and services on credit results in the creation of an asset termed *a receivable* and the recognition of revenue at the time of sale. Receivables also may arise from other types of transactions.

Receivables consist of a variety of claims against customers and other parties arising from the operations of the company. Most receivables are satisfied through the receipt of cash, although others may be canceled through the receipt of either other assets or services. Receivables are reported on the balance sheet as either **current** or **noncurrent** items. **Those receivables expected to be collected or satisfied within one year or the normal operating cycle, whichever is longer, are classified as current assets; the remainder are classified as noncurrent.** Customers sometimes overpay their accounts in anticipation of future purchases, or in error. Such balances should be reported as liabilities because the company is obligated to the customers for those amounts. In other words, they should not be deducted from the accounts receivable of other customers. Furthermore, receivables are often grouped within classified balance sheets as trade receivables and nontrade receivables.

Trade receivables arise from the sale of the company's products or services to customers and generally comprise the majority of the total receivables balance. Trade receivables may be subclassified into **accounts receivable** (nonwritten promises by customers to pay for goods or services) and **notes receivable** (unconditional written agreements to receive a certain sum of money on a specific date).

Nontrade receivables arise from transactions that are not directly related to the sale of goods and services. Nontrade receivables should be disclosed on the balance sheet in individual groups as current or noncurrent assets, depending on the length of their collection period. Examples of nontrade receivables include deposits with utilities, advances to subsidiary companies, deposits made to guarantee performance, declared dividends, and interest on investments.

Deposits with utility companies are often required to guarantee utility expense payments. Normally, these deposits are classified as noncurrent receivables because the timing of repayment by the utility company is indeterminate. Advances to subsidiaries are also typically classified as long-term because repayment may be postponed indefinitely. Deposits made to guarantee contract performance are classified as either current or noncurrent, depending on the expected completion date of the project guaranteed. Declared dividends and interest on investments are disclosed as current assets.

In this chapter we focus on the valuation problems associated with current accounts (trade) receivable, because it is the major receivable recorded on the balance sheet of a typical company.

ACCOUNTS RECEIVABLE

Accounts receivable result from credit sales. Many credit sales are made on unsecured 30-day accounts, and the dollar amount of each sale is recorded as an account receivable. Companies make sales on credit for two primary reasons. The first is that it may be more convenient to sell on credit than for cash (as discussed earlier, checks received at the time of a sale are considered to be cash). For example, when a company is selling a product that has to be shipped, it is a common business practice for the purchaser to pay for the goods after receiving them. Between the time that the purchaser acquires title to the goods and the time payment is received by the seller, credit has been extended by the seller to the purchaser. The second reason why credit sales are made is that management may believe that offering credit will encourage a purchaser to acquire an item that would not otherwise be purchased. This is particularly common in retail sales when the purchaser may not have sufficient cash available to make the purchase. The seller, or retail store, offers credit terms so that the purchaser will agree to the sale.

The disadvantage of credit sales is that they may require a significant management effort because the company must make credit investigations, prepare and mail bills, and ensure collection from the customers. All of these activities involve a cost to the company in money and employee time. Also, credit sales result in a certain amount of bad debt losses due to nonpayment by customers. When a company is considering whether to sell on credit, it must consider the tradeoff between the additional gross profit received from the expected credit sales and the additional expenses and losses incurred due to these credit sales. Some companies have decided that this tradeoff is negative. These companies apparently feel that they can lower costs and increase profits by selling exclusively for cash.

If a company decides to sell on credit and establishes a credit department, it must install an effective internal control system for processing sales on account and cash collections. The internal control procedures used to ensure the integrity of the collection procedures were discussed earlier, but it is also necessary to establish internal control procedures for the accounts receivable processing function. These control features include (1) prenumbered sales invoices so that all invoices are accounted for and (2) the separation of the sales function from the cash collection responsibilities so that collusion is required for theft to take place.

Once management is satisfied that a reasonable tradeoff exists between the incremental revenues and expenses associated with credit sales, and an adequate system of internal control for credit sales has been established, a variety of other issues may arise in recording accounts receivable. These issues are discussed in the following sections.

Valuation of Accounts Receivable

As discussed in Chapter 1, one purpose of reporting current assets is to disclose the liquidity of a company, that is, the "nearness to cash" of its economic resources. In this regard, the major accounting issues associated with the valuation of current accounts receivable are (1) the initial recording of the receivables based on the expected future cash flows and (2) the estimation of the probability of collection. Generally, accounts receivable are recorded at their net realizable values, which is the amount of cash into which the receivable is expected to be converted in due course of business. This procedure is used because the collection period for most accounts receivable is fairly short (e.g., 60 days or less). The uncertainty of collection also affects the value of receivables. Whenever credit is extended, the likelihood exists that some receivables will not be collected, and this factor should be recognized in the valuation of receivables on the balance sheet.

■ UNCOLLECTIBLE ACCOUNTS RECEIVABLE

Uncollectible accounts receivable are the accounts receivable that a company will not collect. At the time of the credit sales, the company does not know which customers will not pay. Although a company agrees to sell on credit based on a customer's credit references, the references indicate only the past record of the customer's payments and do not guarantee that the customer will pay in the future. Thus, a period of time, perhaps several months or even years, may pass before the company decides that it will not collect a particular account. When this decision is made, the account is **written off,** which means that continuing attempts are not made to collect the account even though hope for eventual collection may continue.

Whether credit sales are made for convenience or to attract customers, the costs associated with making these sales is an expense. **Bad debt expense is the expense for the accounting period because of the eventual noncollection of accounts receivable.** Recording these costs as bad debt expense is consistent with the treatment of other costs associated with the sale that are also treated as expenses. Although there is no rule that specifies how a company must classify the expense in the income statement, it is more common to include the amount as an operating expense in the category of general and administrative expenses. Since the decision to grant credit is normally made by the credit department rather than by the selling department, it is appropriate to classify bad debt expense as an administrative expense rather than a selling expense.

Accounting for bad debt expense and uncollectible accounts receivable raises two basic questions. The first relates to the period in which the expense should be recognized. The second is the amount of the expense that should be recognized and the value that should be shown for accounts receivable on the balance sheet at the end of the accounting period. Each of these questions, as well as the effects of recognizing a bad debt expense, is discussed in the following sections.

When Should the Uncollectibility Be Recognized?

As mentioned, a period of time elapses between recording the sale and the write-off of a particular receivable. Sometimes these two events occur in the same accounting period, in which case there is no issue. More often, however, the sale is recorded in one accounting period and the write-off of the related account occurs in a later period. This suggests two alternatives for the time period in which the bad debt expense could be recognized. The expense could be recognized in either the time period in which the sale is made or the period of the write-off. The alternatives are shown in the following diagram:

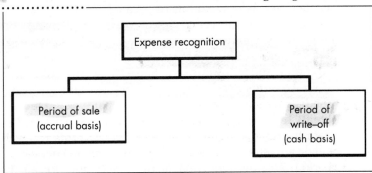

The accrual basis is discussed now and the cash basis is discussed later in the chapter. To illustrate the logic of the accrual basis, suppose that the Marlin Company sells a product in August 1993 to John Jones for $150. John Jones later encounters financial difficulty and declares bankruptcy in July 1995 before he has paid Marlin. Should Marlin recognize this expense in 1993 or 1995?

A review of the matching principle, which was first discussed in Chapter 2, should make it very clear which answer is correct. **The matching principle requires that the cost of generating sales revenue be matched against the revenue in the period in which the revenue is recognized.** We have clearly seen this principle being applied when the cost of the product sold (the cost of goods sold) is matched against the sales revenue in the period of the sale even though the purchase may have been made in an earlier period and the cash payment made in an earlier or later period. The cost of goods sold is *not* recognized in, for example, the period of the purchase or the cash payment, but rather the period in which the product is sold. Similarly, the bad debt expense that is associated with the sales of a period should be matched against the sales of that period.

In order to adhere to the matching concept the allowance method of accounting for uncollectible accounts receivable is used. **The allowance method requires the recognition of the bad debt expense in the period of the sale and *not* in the period of the actual write-off.** Referring to the example in the previous paragraph, the Marlin Company has a bad debt expense in 1993 and *not* in 1995. Since the uncollectibility will not be known until 1995, however, the bad debt expense for 1993 must be *estimated* (this estimate is discussed in the next section). Once again the recognition of accounting expenses is being separated from the related cash flow, or in this case the lack of a cash flow.

Recognition of Bad Debt Expense

Before explaining in the next section the problem of estimating the amount of the bad debt expense (before the write-off occurs) under the allowance method, let us review how the financial statements are affected by the recognition of a bad debt expense in the period of sale.

if the bad debt doesn't recognized in beginning then value of the asset would be over stated

When the bad debt expense is recognized, the company is accepting the fact that a portion of the accounts receivable will not be collected. Therefore, the value of the accounts receivable should also be reduced because otherwise the value of the asset would be overstated. An allowance for uncollectible accounts is used for this purpose. **Allowance for Uncollectible Accounts is a contra-asset account in which a company records its estimate of the amount of accounts receivable that it will not collect.** Alternative titles are Allowance for Doubtful Accounts and Allowance for Bad Debts. The Allowance account is subtracted from Accounts Receivable to give net accounts receivable, which is reported in the balance sheet. In the Marlin Company example we discussed the uncollectibility in terms of a single account; in actual practice, however, companies evaluate the uncollectibility of their entire accounts receivable at one time. Thus a single adjustment is used to recognize the bad debt expense (for the accounting period) and the reduction of the asset value for all the company's estimated uncollectible accounts (using assumed amounts):

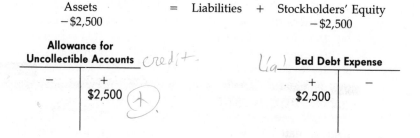

Assets	=	Liabilities	+	Stockholders' Equity
− $2,500				− $2,500

Allowance for Uncollectible Accounts	credit		Bad Debt Expense	
−	+		+	−
	$2,500		$2,500	

In this chapter, we indicate the increases and decreases in the account with a "+" and a "−". Note, however, that with a contra-account, such as Allowance for Uncollectible Accounts and Bad Debt Expense, an increase in the account is a decrease in the related asset, liability, or stockholders' equity item. Therefore, the increase (credit) to the Allowance account has the same effect as a decrease (credit) to the Accounts Receivable account would have; that is, the Allowance account is a contra-asset account and an increase in the account decreases net accounts receivable. The advantage of using the Allowance account is that the Accounts Receivable account still includes the total amount that the company is legally entitled to receive. The net accounts receivable — the balance of the Accounts Receivable less the balance of the Allowance for Uncollectible Accounts — indicates the company's *estimate* of the amount of cash it will actually receive and is disclosed in the current asset section on the ending balance sheet as follows (using assumed amounts):

Accounts receivable	$95,000
Less: Allowance for uncollectible accounts	(3,200)
Net accounts receivable	$91,800

No direct effect

Write-Off of an Uncollectible Account

Eventually certain specific customer accounts will be judged to be uncollectible. When a company writes off an account receivable, it is recognizing the noncollection of an amount that was included in its previous estimation of uncollectible accounts. Therefore, **the write-off does *not* affect the total assets or expenses of the company.** The expense and the reduction in the asset were both recorded at the time of the estimate by means of the adjustment. The write-off of a specific uncollectible account receivable of $200 is recorded as follows:

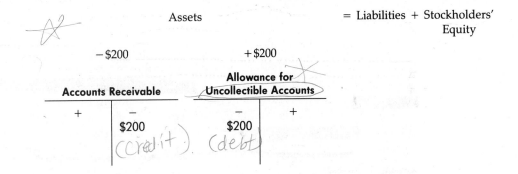

Assets   = Liabilities + Stockholders' Equity

−$200   +$200

Accounts Receivable   Allowance for Uncollectible Accounts

$200 (credit) $200 (debit)

Note that the effect of this entry is to reduce (debit) a contra asset — Allowance for Uncollectible Accounts — and reduce (credit) an asset — Accounts Receivable. The net effect on the assets of the company therefore is zero, as illustrated by the following balance sheet amounts:

Why

	Before the Write-off	After the Write-off
Accounts receivable	$95,000	$94,800
Less: allowance for uncollectible accounts	(3,200)	(3,000)
Net accounts receivable	$91,800	$91,800

Recovery of Accounts Written Off

After a company has written off an account receivable, the receivable may later be collected. This recovery of a previously written-off account receivable is usually completed with a two-step process. First, the original write-off of the account is reversed by an increase (debit) to Accounts Receivable and an increase (credit) to Allowance for Uncollectible Accounts (thereby having no effect on net accounts receivable). Second, the collection of cash on the reinstated account receivable is recognized. Therefore, the recovery of a $200 account previously written off is recorded as follows:

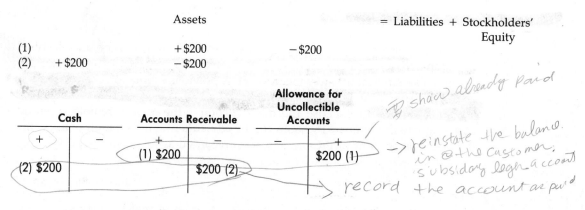

Since the net effect of the two entries is to increase Cash and decrease net Accounts Receivable, it is important to recognize why two entries are made instead of a single combined entry (increasing Cash and reducing Accounts Receivable). When an (debit or credit) entry is made in the Accounts Receivable account, an entry is also made in the accounts receivable subsidiary ledger. The details of subsidiary ledgers are beyond the scope of this book, but, as the name implies, they are used to record detailed information in addition to that in the general ledger. Thus, an accounts receivable subsidiary ledger contains information about every individual customer account, including amounts billed and the dates, amounts received and the dates, amounts overdue and so on. In contrast, the general ledger contains summary information about total amounts billed and total amounts received. The first entry is necessary to reinstate the balance in the customer's subsidiary ledger account, and the second entry is necessary to record the account as paid. This two-entry process provides a complete record of the customer's account that may be useful in determining whether to offer credit to this customer in the future. For control purposes, furthermore, the total of all the subsidiary accounts must agree with the balance in the general ledger account.

■ MEASUREMENT OF BAD DEBT EXPENSE

An obvious issue arises when the bad debt expense is recognized in the period of the sale and not in the period that the account is written off. How is the amount that is eventually to be written off known in the period the sale is made? The amount is not known for certain, but the company can *estimate* how much it will not collect in the future. Two methods of estimation are used.[3] The percent of sales method uses an estimate that is based on the sales of the current period. The aging method uses an estimate that is based on the balance in accounts receivable.

. . . .

[3]When a company has a relatively small number of large receivables (e.g., a bank), it may be appropriate to analyze each account and estimate the amount expected to be collected. This procedure is more costly but may be desirable for certain types of companies.

[handwritten marginalia top:] Credit sale − Sale discount − Sale return and allowance = Net credit sale X % estimated to be uncollectible

[handwritten:] base on past experience of company

① Percent of Sales Method of Estimating Bad Debt Expense

[handwritten arrows:] ← I/S approach

A company can estimate its bad debt expense by using the percent of sales method. **The percent of sales method requires the company to estimate the bad debt expense by multiplying the net credit sales of the period by the percent estimated to be uncollectible.** Net credit sales are credit sales less sales discounts and sales returns and allowances. The estimated percentage can be based on the past experience of the company or on other information, such as the experiences of other companies published in a trade journal, and adjusted for changes in economic conditions. For example, suppose that a company has net credit sales of $200,000 in 1993 and its past experience indicates that 1.5% of its net credit sales are never collected. Therefore in order to match expenses against revenues the company must recognize a bad debt expense of $3,000 (1.5% × $200,000) in 1993. The effect is to reduce income for 1993 and reduce the value of accounts receivable. Note that this procedure does not give any consideration to the balance in the Allowance account because the bad debt expense is based solely upon net credit sales for the period.

[handwritten left margin:] you may over or under estimate and lead to incorrect valuation of account

While the percent of sales method matches the bad debt expense against the sales revenue in the current period, a major disadvantage is that there is no verification of the reasonableness of the balance of the Allowance for Uncollectible Accounts. Recall that the account is increased (credited) when the estimate is made and reduced (debited) when the write-off occurs. Therefore, if the company overestimates the bad debts (the estimated amount exceeds the write-offs), the allowance account will have a positive (credit) balance that exceeds the value of the accounts that will be written off in the future. If this overestimation is not offset by an equal underestimation in subsequent periods, the balance will never be removed. Such a *permanent* balance leads to an incorrect valuation of the accounts receivable and indicates that the bad debt expense of previous periods has been estimated incorrectly. While it is possible for the company to eliminate periodically any balance that has accumulated in the Allowance account, the aging method of estimating the bad debt expense prevents such an incorrect balance from being created in the account.

[handwritten left margin T-accounts:] Bad Debt Exp — D 3750 | Allow — 3750 / 2000 | Acct Rec — 2000

② Aging Method of Estimating Bad Debt Expense

[handwritten:] (Balance Sheet approach)

[handwritten right:] base the estimate of the balance in allowance for uncollectible account on age of individual account

Instead of basing the estimate of bad debt expense on net credit sales, the aging method bases the estimate of the balance in the Allowance for Uncollectible Accounts on the age of the individual accounts included in the ending balance of Accounts Receivable. The rationale for this method is that the bad debts result from the accounts receivable that are outstanding rather than from the sales themselves. Therefore, an excessive balance cannot build up in the Allowance for Uncollectible Accounts because each period's estimate of the amounts uncollectible is based on the particular accounts receivable balance at the end of that period. The aging method is also generally considered to be more accurate for valuing the net accounts receivable that are collectible at the end of the period because the estimate is based on the age of the specific customer's accounts receivable outstanding. As the length of time a customer's account has been outstanding increases, the likelihood of the account not being collected is increased. For example, a company is much more likely to collect an account that is 30 days old than an account that is 360 days old. As the proportion of old accounts increases, therefore, the balance in the Allowance for Uncollectible Accounts should also increase in proportion to the larger expected write-offs.

The aging method requires that a company categorize each individual account into age groups based on the length of time it has been outstanding. The total amount in each age group is then multiplied by a historically based estimated percent uncollectible to give the estimate of the amount uncollectible in each age group. The amounts in each age group are summed to determine the required ending balance in the Allowance for Uncollectible Accounts. As with the percent of sales method these estimates would be based on the past experience of the company or on other information, and adjusted for changes in economic conditions. To illustrate the application of the aging method, suppose that the Joyce Company makes credit sales during 1993 and has a balance in accounts receivable of $100,000 at the end of 1993. This total balance is made up of amounts within each age group and percents expected to be uncollectible as follows:

Age Group	Amount	Estimated Percentage Uncollectible	Estimated Amount Uncollectible
Not yet due	$ 40,000	0.5%	$ 200
1 – 30 days past due	25,000	1	250
31 – 60 days past due	20,000	2	400
61 – 120 days past due	10,000	5	500
More than 120 days past due	5,000	20	1,000
Total	$100,000		$2,350

Since the Joyce Company has accounts receivable of $40,000 that are not yet due, and the company's experience shows that 0.5% of these accounts will become uncollectible, the expected amount uncollectible is $200 (0.5% × $40,000). Applying this analysis to each age group provides a total estimated amount uncollectible of $2,350. Therefore the expected collectible amount is $97,650 ($100,000 − $2,350) and is shown as a current asset in the balance sheet as follows:

Accounts receivable	$100,000
Less: Allowance for uncollectible accounts	(2,350)
Net accounts receivable	$ 97,650

The $2,350 is the required *balance* of the Allowance for Uncollectible Accounts and *not* the amount of the Bad Debt Expense. The Bad Debt Expense is instead the amount that is needed to increase the existing balance of the Allowance for Uncollectible Accounts up to the required ending balance of $2,350. Therefore, if it is assumed that the Joyce Company had a positive (credit) balance of $400 in the account before it performed the aging analysis, the bad debt expense for the year is $1,950 ($2,350 − $400).[4]

It is important to understand why there is a $400 positive (credit) balance in the Allowance for Uncollectible Accounts before the year-end adjustment. The balance results from the estimates of uncollectible accounts from previous years less the amounts written off to date. It exists because the company may wait more than one year before writing off certain accounts or because actual experience has not been equal to the percentages estimated to be uncollectible. The addition of $1,950 to the positive (credit) balance in the Allowance account of $400 results in the correct ending balance of $2,350. Thus, the ending accounts receivable is properly valued at the expected amount collectible of $97,650. The analysis of the balance in the Allowance for Uncollectible Accounts may be summarized as follows:

Allowance for Uncollectible Accounts

−	+
Actual amounts written off during the year.	Beginning balance reflects the estimated amount of the related Accounts Receivable that will not be collected in the current and future periods.
If a negative (debit) balance results, the actual amount written off to date exceeded the estimated amount. The debit balance is added to the desired ending credit balance to calculate the expense for the period.	If a positive (credit) balance results, the estimated amount exceeded the actual amount written off to date. The credit balance is subtracted from the desired ending credit balance to calculate the expense for the period.

Also note that use of the aging method does *not* consider the sales for the period. Consequently, the use of the aging method avoids the possibility of creating an incorrect ending balance in the Allowance for Uncollectible Accounts as is possible with the percent of sales method.

While the aging method is a more accurate method for valuing accounts receivable than the percent of sales method, it requires more information for its application. This added knowledge of the estimated percent of uncollectibles by age groups, however, is useful information that management should know for

· · · · · · · · · · · · · · · · · · · ·

[4]If the Allowance account has a negative (debit) balance because the actual amounts written-off during the year were greater than the estimate at the end of the previous year, the balance in the account would be *added* to the required balance to compute the bad debt expense. For example, if the Joyce Company had a negative (debit) balance of $500 in the Allowance account, the bad debt expense would be $2,850 ($2,350 + $500).

effective control of its credit operations. As individual accounts move to older age groups, the credit department should make increasing efforts to collect the accounts.

amount of the year .

— end of the year -

Summary of Percent of Sales and Aging Methods

In summary, it can be said that the percent of sales method is an income statement approach that properly matches expenses against revenues, although it tends to ignore the valuation of the accounts receivable in the ending balance sheet. In contrast, the aging method focuses on the valuation of the account receivable in the balance sheet, although it puts less emphasis on the expense in the income statement. In other words, the percent of sales method computes the amount of the year's net credit sales that will not be collected, whereas the aging method computes the amount of the accounts receivable at the end of the year that will not be collected. Whichever method is used, the amounts that are recorded in the two accounts, Accounts Receivable and the Allowance for Uncollectible Accounts, can be summarized as follows:

Accounts Receivable		**Allowance for Uncollectible Accounts**	
Beginning balance Credit sales	Cash received		Beginning balance
	Accounts written off	Accounts written off	Amount recorded as bad debt expense
Amounts recovered from write-offs			Amounts recovered from write-offs
Ending balance			Ending balance

■ DIRECT WRITE-OFF METHOD

Although the allowance method is required by generally accepted accounting principles, some companies use the direct write-off method. **The direct write-off method recognizes the bad debt expense in the period when the account is written off because it is uncollectible.** Therefore, no estimate of bad debt expense is made in the period of sale. The direct write-off method is *not* a generally accepted accounting principle for several reasons.

1. It violates the matching principle and causes income to be overstated in the period of sale and understated in the period of the write-off.
2. The accounts receivable are recorded in the balance sheet at an amount greater than the cash that is expected to be collected.

acct receivas are over-state at end of period

3. The method provides an opportunity for management to manipulate income as it selects the period of write-off.

The method may be used, however, in three circumstances. First, it may be used if the effect on the financial statements is not materially different from using the allowance method (materiality was discussed in Chapter 4). Thus, if the effect of using the direct write-off method instead of the allowance method does not result in a materially different measure of income or assets, its use is acceptable. Second, many companies are not required to follow generally accepted accounting principles in the preparation of their financial statements and therefore may use the direct write-off method. For example, companies whose stock is not publicly traded are not *required* to follow generally accepted accounting principles. It may be a shortsighted policy, however, not to follow generally accepted accounting principles. Whenever the company comes into contact with third parties such as banks and various regulatory authorities, the absence of generally accepted accounting principles may cause considerable difficulties. In addition, the eventual conversion to generally accepted accounting principles may be expensive and time-consuming. Third, the direct write-off method is required for federal income tax reporting.

Accounting for the direct write-off method is simpler than for the allowance method. No estimate of bad debt expense is made, and no allowance account is used. When an account receivable is judged to be uncollectible, the bad debt expense is recognized (debited) and the account receivable written off (credited). Although the direct write-off method may be simpler for a smaller company that is not required to follow generally accepted accounting principles, management should be careful to keep track of accounts receivable to avoid incurring unnecessary losses.

■ SALES RETURNS, ALLOWANCES, AND DISCOUNTS

A company may sell goods to its customers either for cash or on account, as we discussed in Chapter 2. Occasionally, these goods are returned by customers or are found to be damaged, which requires an adjustment either for the return of the goods by the customer or for the offer of an allowance to the customer against future purchases. When the likelihood of returns is significant, questions arise as to whether revenue should even be recognized at the time of the sale. Also, when goods are sold on credit, many companies offer an incentive for prompt payment. These items, affecting the amount of the net sales reported in the income statement and the cash collected, are discussed next.

Sales Returns and Allowances

When goods are sold to a customer in either a wholesale or retail transaction, it is assumed by both the company and the customer that the goods are not damaged and are acceptable to the customer. Occasionally, upon checking the goods after purchase, the customer may find that they are damaged, of inferior quality, or simply the wrong size or color. Most companies have a *satisfaction guaranteed* policy and allow the customer to return the goods or make an adjustment in the sales price. **A sales return is the return of previously purchased goods by a customer.** The effect of a sales return is to cancel the sale. **A sales allowance occurs when the customer agrees to keep the goods, and an adjustment (reduction) is made in the original sales price.** In most industries, sales returns and allowances are not material. In some industries, however, such as book publishing, the right of return is common and the amounts may have a material impact on the financial statements.

When the goods were originally sold, the revenue account Sales was increased (credited) by the amount of the sale. For a sales return or allowance, the Sales account could be decreased (debited) by the amount of the return. Both transactions are reductions of sales recorded earlier. Most companies do *not* reduce Sales directly, however. A Sales Returns and Allowances account is used to record the total sales returns and allowances. This account is a contra account to the Sales account (and thus has a debit balance and is increased by debit entries and decreased by credit entries). The Sales Returns and Allowances account provides useful information to the managers of a company and to other users about customer satisfaction with the company's goods. Accompanying the recording of the Sales Returns and Allowances, either Cash or Accounts Receivable is reduced (credited) depending on whether the customer has, or has not yet, paid for the item.

The recording of sales returns and allowances, as discussed, is consistent with the definition of revenues. Revenues include the prices charged to a company's customers for goods sold during an accounting period. When sales returns or allowances are recorded in the Sales Returns and Allowances account, since this account is a contra account to Sales, net revenues are reduced because part (or all) of the price charged to customers is returned to them.

The preceding discussion assumed the sales returns and allowances are recorded in the same period as the sales. In some situations, however, the return or allowance may occur in a later period than the sale. In such situations, the future sales returns and allowances should be estimated so that they can be subtracted from the sales of the period. In addition, the company would recognize a contra account to Accounts Receivable.

Sales Discounts

When goods are sold on account, the terms of payment are normally listed on the sales invoice. These terms vary from company to company, although most competing companies tend to have similar credit terms. Many companies offer a cash discount as an incentive for early payment of accounts by customers. **A cash discount is a percentage reduction of the invoice price for payment of the invoice within a specified time period.**

The payment terms for an invoice are usually expressed in a standard format. For instance, a common payment term is n/10/EOM. This term means that the total amount (n) of the invoice is due 10 days after the end of the month (EOM) in which the sale occurred. Thus, if a credit sale is made on July 7, 1993, payment of the invoice is due by the 10th of August.

In this example no cash discount was allowed for early payment. Cash discount terms might read 2/10, n/30. The first number is the percentage discount (2%) and the second number (10) is the number of days in the discount period. **The discount period is the period of time from the date of the invoice within which the customer must pay the invoice to receive the cash discount.** The term n/30 means that full payment of the invoice is due within 30 days of the invoice date. Thus 2/10, n/30 is read as "a 2% discount is allowed if the invoice is paid within 10 days and the total amount of the invoice is due within 30 days." If a $500 sale on account is made with terms of 2/10, n/30 and the customer pays the invoice within 10 days, $490 would be collected [$500 − (0.02 × $500)].

When a sale is made on account and the terms of payment include a cash discount, Accounts Receivable is increased (debited) and Sales is increased (credited) for the full invoice price because the merchandising company does not know whether the customer will pay within the discount period. If the customer pays the invoice (less the discount) within the discount period, the cash collected from the sale is less than the accounts receivable initially recorded. The sales revenue initially recorded at the time of the sale was essentially overstated. Sales Discounts, which is a contra account to Sales, is used to record the amount of cash discounts taken by customers in the accounting period. This account is used instead of reducing the Sales account directly. Sales Discounts is a contra account to Sales (and therefore it has a debit balance).

To illustrate this procedure assume that on March 16, 1993, a customer purchased $1,000 of goods on account, with terms of 3/10, n/30. The customer remitted a check for $970 [$1,000 − (.03 × $1,000)] on March 25, 1993. The sale and the cash collection are recorded as follows:

	Assets	= Liabilities +	Stockholders' Equity
(1)	+$1,000		+$1,000
(2)	+$970 −$1,000		−$30

Cash		Accounts Receivable		Sales		Sales Discounts	
+	−	+	−	−	+	+	−
(2) $970		(1) $1,000	$1,000 (2)		$1,000 (1)	(2) $30	

Two additional points are important for sales discounts. First, if a sales return or allowance is granted on an invoice, the cash discount terms apply to the amount owed on the invoice *after* deducting the return or allowance. This is because the cash discount is allowed only on the amount of the goods actually purchased by the customer. Second, if a customer pays an invoice after the discount period has expired, the collection of the total invoice price is recorded in the usual manner by an increase (debit) to Cash and a decrease (credit) to Accounts Receivable.

Net Sales

Because contra accounts for sales returns and allowances and sales discounts are used to reduce the total amount of sales revenues, the revenues section of a company's income statement must be expanded to include these items. On the income statement both the Sales Returns and Allowances account and the Sales Discounts account are deducted from the Sales account to determine Net Sales. The Sales account is frequently entitled *Gross Sales* on the income statement to show that it is not the same as the Net Sales. Exhibit 5–1 illustrates the revenues section of a typical company. Many companies, however, simply report net sales because the returns, allowances, and discounts are immaterial.

Recording Sales When a Right of Return Exists

Earlier we discussed the return of a product by a customer who intends to use the product. In other situations, the likelihood of returns is more significant. For example, companies often "sell" products to retailers under terms that allow the retailer to return unsold items. The following criteria must be met for a sale to be recorded:

1. The price has been agreed.
2. The buyer's payment is not contingent on resale of the product.
3. The buyer's obligation would not be changed by destruction or damage of the product.
4. The buyer has economic substance separate from the seller.
5. The seller does not have significant obligations for future performance to bring about resale of the product by the buyer.
6. The amount of the future returns can be reasonably estimated.[5]

The purpose of these rules is to ensure that a "real" sale has occurred and that the transfer of ownership to the buyer will not be reversed except for a relatively small number of items that may be returned. The estimation of future returns is especially difficult when a new product is being sold to consumers. For example, home video games were very popular for a short period, but then sales suddenly slowed dramatically. When companies were shipping those games, revenue was recorded because the only returns that were expected were defective units. When sales slowed, however, many of the unsold units were returned to the manufacturers. Thus, revenues that had already been recorded and reported in the published financial statements had to be canceled. Even when the agreed expiration date for returns has passed, a company may still accept the return of unsold units to maintain good relations with the retailers. Thus, a revenue recorded and reported in good faith may have to be reversed in a future period. This situation emphasizes that it is important for the financial statement user to

....

[5] "Revenue Recognition When Right of Return Exists," *FASB Statement of Financial Accounting Standards No. 48* (Stamford, Conn.: FASB, 1981).

EXHIBIT 5–1

···············

HINES DEPARTMENT STORE

HINES DEPARTMENT STORE
Partial Income Statement
For Year Ended December 31, 1993

Revenues:

Gross sales		$89,200
Less: Sales returns and allowances	$2,900	
Sales discounts	3,600	(6,500)
Net sales		$82,700

understand the nature of the industry in which a company operates as well as understand accounting principles for revenue recognition.

Some companies have recorded sales when units have been shipped to sales employees who had not yet received orders for those units or have prebilled prior customers who had not yet reordered. Unlike the preceding situation, however, these transactions are not sales, never should have been recorded as revenue, and are a clear violation of revenue recognition rules. The establishment, and effective operation, of an internal control system should prevent such abuses if top management wishes to do so. Internal auditors also can be effective in the discovery of such manipulations but external auditors would be expected to discover them only if they are material.

■ INTERPRETING THE FINANCIAL STATEMENTS

The user of financial statements often can utilize available information to determine amounts that are not directly provided. For example, many users are interested in the relationships between income flows and cash flows, such as that between sales (an income flow) and cash collections from those sales (a cash flow). It is unlikely that the cash collections from sales would be reported in the financial statements (as discussed in Chapter 12), and therefore it is necessary to calculate the amount indirectly. Since sales revenue and the beginning and ending balances of accounts receivable normally are reported, the cash collections can easily be computed. If accounts receivable have increased during the period, cash collections must have been less than credit sales by the amount of the increase in the receivables. Therefore, cash collections can be calculated by *subtracting* the *increase* in the accounts receivable from the sales of the period. Similarly, a *decrease* in accounts receivable would be *added* to sales to compute cash collections for the period. Even if some of the total sales were cash sales, the computations provide the correct amount of the *total* cash collections. Also, as the summary accounts earlier in the chapter show, the above analysis ignores the amount of any accounts written off and the amounts recovered from write-offs.

The use of ratios, discussed in Chapter 14, can be helpful to users. For example, the accounts receivable turnover ratio is often used to determine the efficiency with which a company collects receivables. This ratio is calculated as follows:

$$\frac{\text{Accounts Receivable}}{\text{Turnover}} = \frac{\text{Net Credit Sales}}{\text{Average Net Accounts Receivable}}$$

In the example in Chapter 14, the ratio is calculated as 11.2 times per year, or an average collection period of 33 days (based on a 365-day business year). When this ratio is calculated from information available in financial statements, however, it is unlikely that net credit sales will be known. Instead, total sales will be reported, and therefore the comparison must use that amount. A user making a comparison for one company over time must assume that the proportion of sales made on credit each year remains constant. Alternatively, a user comparing different companies must assume that each company makes the same proportion of its sales as credit sales.

The discussion shows that many of these types of calculations rely on certain assumptions that the user of the financial statements may not be able to confirm with certainty. However, if the user chooses the types of analyses and the assumptions with care, the likelihood of a material error arising in the analysis can be made very low. In addition, it is unlikely that any information considered material by the user has been omitted, because any such information considered by the management of the company or the auditors to be material would have been disclosed.

QUESTIONS

1. What are the components of cash? What items may be confused with cash, but normally are categorized under other balance sheet captions?

2. Define the two main aspects of cash management.

3. What is internal control?

4. What effect do seasonal fluctuations in sales have on cash flows?

5. For what two reasons might a company choose to make credit sales? If a company does not collect some of its accounts receivable, does it mean that the company's policy of making credit sales is wrong?

6. Why are bad debts recognized in the period of the sale?

7. How can the use of the direct write-off method be justified?

8. What accounting principle supports the use of an estimate of bad debt expense? Explain.

9. Why is it desirable to keep the amount of a company's uncollectible accounts in the Allowance for Uncollectible Accounts?

10. Explain how the financial statements are affected by recording the estimated accounts receivable that will not be collected. How are the financial statements affected by recording the eventual write-off of an account receivable? By the recovery of a receivable previously written off?

11. How is bad debt expense estimated when the percent of sales method is used? When the aging method is used?

12. Which method of estimating bad debt expense is considered to be an income statement approach? Which is considered to be a balance sheet approach? Why?

PROBLEMS AND CASES
••

13. Items Included in Cash. The accountant of the Sherman Company is considering whether the following items should be included in the company's cash balance at December 31, 1993:

1. The Sherman Company bid on a contract on December 14, 1993. It included a "good faith" check of $5,000 dated January 14, 1994, with the bid. The bid was rejected on January 10, 1994, and the check was returned.

2. Two checks of $125 were received in December from a customer for payment of its $125 account balance. One of the checks was returned in January.

3. A check was received and deposited for $175 in December. The check was returned by the bank in January marked "Not Sufficient Funds."

4. A check from a customer for $87 was received and deposited in December. In January it was discovered that it was in payment of an invoice in the amount of $78. A check for $9 was issued and mailed by the Sherman Company to the customer.

Required For each of the items indicate how much, if any, should have been included in the cash balance on the balance sheet at December 31, 1993.

14. Computing the Cash Balance. Indicate whether each of the following items should be included in the cash balance presented on the balance sheet. Also indicate the normal balance sheet treatment for those items not included as cash.

Item	Include in Cash Balance	Classification of Items Excluded
1. Savings account		
2. Postdated checks		
3. IOUs		
4. Cash on hand		
5. Cash in sinking fund		
6. Travel advance		
7. Bank draft		
8. Traveler's checks		

15. Reporting Cash on the Balance Sheet. The Watt Corporation discovers the following information:

1. Balance in First National Bank checking account	$2,360.75
2. Balance in City National Bank checking account	(40.20)
3. Balance in First Federal savings account	28,750.00
4. Certificate of deposit	30,000.00
5. Employee's IOU	125.00
6. Employees' travel advances	1,640.00
7. Cash on hand (undeposited sales receipts)	3,169.40
8. Traveler's checks	600.00
9. Customer's postdated check	290.40

Required 1. What amount should be reported as cash on Watt's balance sheet?

2. Describe the balance sheet treatment of the items not included in the cash balance.

16. Internal Control. The following independent situations exist in a company:

1. The mail is delivered to the bookkeeper, who distributes it unopened to various employees around the company, including the cash receipts clerk.

2. Cash is often received in the mail without an accompanying invoice for credit purchases made by customers. The bookkeeper opens this mail.

3. A manager prepares the invoices and signs the checks for items purchased.

4. The cash in the cash register is not counted before each employee's work period.

5. The company does not reconcile its cash account to the bank statement because it trusts that the bank will not make a mistake.

Required For each of the situations explain the weakness in the internal control and suggest how it could be overcome.

17. Percent of Sales Method. The Redford Company uses the percent of sales method for estimating its bad debt expense. In 1993 the company made credit sales of $300,000 and had sales returns and allowances for credit of $20,000. In past years approximately 2% of net credit sales have been uncollectible. At the end of the year, before the bad debt expense is recorded, the accounts receivable balance was $45,000 and the credit balance in the allowance for uncollectible accounts was $300.

Required 1. Compute the bad debt expense for 1993 using the percent of sales method.

2. Show how the net accounts receivable would be reported in the balance sheet at the end of 1993.

18. Aging Method. Use the facts for the Redford Company in Problem 17. In addition, the company has found that 2% of accounts receivable that are not overdue at the end of any particular year are never collected and 6% of accounts receivable that are overdue at year-end are never collected. Of the accounts receivable balance at the end of 1993, 40% are not overdue.

Required 1. Compute the bad debt expense for 1993, using the aging method.

2. Show how the net accounts receivable would be reported in the balance sheet at the end of 1993.

19. Aging Method. At the end of the year the accounts receivable of the Andrews Company were categorized as follows:

Age Group	Amount	Estimated Percentage Uncollectible
Not yet due	$ 80,000	0.5%
1 – 30 days past due	30,000	1
31 – 60 days past due	20,000	2
61 – 90 days past due	15,000	4
More than 90 days past due	8,000	7
	$153,000	

Before recording the bad debt expense, the positive (credit) balance in the Allowance for Uncollectible Accounts was $800.

Required 1. Compute the bad debt expense for 1993, using the aging method.

2. Show how the net accounts receivable would be reported in the balance sheet at the end of the year.

20. **Direct Write-Off Method.** The Newman Company made credit sales of $100,000 during the year. In addition, the company wrote off $3,500 of uncollectible accounts receivable in 1993 and uncollectible accounts receivable have averaged 4% of the ending balance of accounts receivable in recent years. The ending balance of accounts receivable is $30,000.

Required 1. Compute the bad debt expense for 1993, using the direct write-off method.

2. Show how the net accounts receivable would be reported in the balance sheet at the end of 1993.

21. **Write-Off and Recovery of Uncollectible Accounts.** During 1993 the Ross Company wrote off uncollectible accounts of $600 and recovered accounts of $300 that had been written off in 1992. In addition, the following information is available:

	December 31, 1992	December 31, 1993
Accounts receivable	$30,000	$40,000
Allowance for uncollectible accounts (positive)	1,000	1,600

Required 1. Record the effects on the accounting equation of the write-off and recovery of the uncollectible accounts in 1993.

2. How much bad debt expense was recorded in 1993?

22. **Direct Write-off vs. Estimation of Bad Debts.** The Blunt Company sells products for $21,000 during the month of February 1993. During 1993 collections are received on February sales of $20,400, accounts representing $600 of these sales are written off as uncollectible, and a $150 account previously written off is collected.

Required Record the effects on the accounting equation of the above information if:

1. The bad debts are recorded as they actually occur.

2. Bad debts are estimated as 3% of sales at the time of sale.

23. **Estimating Bad Debts from Receivable Balances.** The following information is extracted from the accounting records of the Shelton Corporation at the beginning of 1993.

Accounts receivable	$67,000
Allowance for doubtful accounts	2,100 (positive)

During 1993, sales on account amounted to $575,000, $559,700 was collected on outstanding receivables, and $3,400 of receivables were written off as uncollectible.

On December 31, 1993, Shelton estimates its bad debts to be 3% of the outstanding gross accounts receivable balance.

Required **1.** Record the effects on the accounting equation of Shelton's estimate of bad debt expense for 1993.

2. Prepare the accounts receivable section of Shelton's December 31, 1993, balance sheet.

24. Aging Analysis of Accounts Receivable. Cowen's, a large department store located in a metropolitan area, has been experiencing difficulty in estimating its bad debts. The company has decided to prepare an aging schedule for its outstanding accounts receivable and estimate bad debts by the due dates of its receivables. This analysis discloses the following information:

Balance	Age of Receivable	Estimated Percentage Uncollectible
$198,000	Under 30 days	0.8%
114,000	30 – 60 days	2.0
73,000	61 – 120 days	5.0
39,000	121 – 240 days	20.0
25,000	241 – 360 days	35.0
20,000	Over 360 days	50.0
$469,000		

Required **1.** Use the above analysis to compute the estimated amount of uncollectible receivables.

2. Record the effects on the accounting equation of Cowen's estimated uncollectibles, assuming the balance in the Allowance for Doubtful Accounts prior to adjustment is:

a. 0
b. $14,600 negative (debit)
c. $5,700 positive (credit)

25. Comparison of Bad Debt Estimation Methods. The following information (prior to adjustment) is available from the accounting records of the Bradford Company on December 31, 1993.

Cash sales	$ 92,600	
Net credit sales	272,900	
Total sales (net)		$365,500
Accounts receivable		126,300
Allowance for doubtful accounts		(3,150) (positive)

Required Record the effects on the accounting equation of the estimate of Bradford's bad debt expense for 1993, assuming:

1. Bad debts are estimated to be 1.5% of total sales (net).

2. Bad debts are estimated to be 3% of net credit sales.

3. Bad debts are estimated to be 6% of gross accounts receivable.

26. Receivables — Bad Debts. At January 1, 1993, the credit balance in the allowance for doubtful accounts of the Master Company was $400,000. For 1993, the provision for doubtful accounts is based on a percentage of net sales. Net sales for 1993 were $50,000,000. Based on the latest available facts, the 1993 provision for doubtful accounts is estimated to be 0.7% of net sales. During 1993, uncollectible receivables amounting to $420,000 were written off against the allowance for doubtful accounts.

Required Prepare a schedule computing the balance in Master's allowance for doubtful accounts at December 31, 1993. Show supporting computations in good form. (*AICPA adapted*)

27. Accounts Receivable and the Aging Method. The Newman Company operates a retail store in which most of its sales are made on credit. In 1993 the company had credit sales of $575,000, sales returns and allowances on credit sales of $12,000, and gave sales discounts of $560 on collections of accounts receivable of $28,000. Additional collections of accounts receivable were made with no sales discounts. During 1993 the company has written off accounts amounting to $1,200 and recovered accounts of $300 that had been written off in 1992. In addition, the following information is available:

	December 31, 1992	December 31, 1993
Accounts receivable	$80,000	$98,000
Allowance for uncollectible accounts	(500)(positive)	?

The accounts receivable at the end of 1993 were classified as follows:

Age Group	Balance	Estimated Percentage Uncollectible
Not yet due	$50,000	0.5%
1 – 30 days past due	22,000	1
31 – 60 days past due	9,000	2
61 – 120 days past due	5,000	5
More than 120 days past due	12,000	25

Required 1. Record the effects of these events on the accounting equation, including the bad debt expense.

2. Show how the net accounts receivable would be reported on the December 31, 1993, balance sheet.

3. Is the aging method or the percent of sales method more desirable to use in the financial statements?

28. Accounts Receivable and the Aging Method. The Gere Company operates a wholesale outlet that makes most of its sales on credit. In 1993 the company had credit sales of $950,000, sales returns and allowances on credit sales of $21,000, and gave sales discounts of $400 on collections of accounts receivable of $40,000. Additional collections of accounts receivable were made with no sales discounts. During 1993 the company has written off accounts totaling $35,000 and recovered accounts of $12,000 that had been written off in 1992. In addition, the following information is available:

	December 31, 1992	December 31, 1993
Accounts receivable	$190,000	$325,000
Allowance for uncollectible accounts	(5,000) (positive)	?

The accounts receivable at the end of 1993 were classified as follows:

Age Group	Balance	Estimated Percentage Uncollectible
Not yet due	$130,000	3%
1 – 30 days past due	75,000	5
31 – 60 days past due	50,000	9
61 – 120 days past due	30,000	15
More than 120 days past due	40,000	30

Required **1.** Record the effects of these events on the accounting equation, including the 1993 bad debt expense.

2. Show how the net accounts receivable would be reported on the December 31, 1993, balance sheet.

3. Do you think that the Gere Company's credit policy is adequate? What, if any, changes would you suggest? Explain.

29. Analyzing Bad Debt Expense. In 1993, three years after it began operations, the Pearce Corporation decided to change from the direct write-off method of recording bad debts to estimating bad debts. The following information is available to you:

	YEAR			
	1990	1991	1992	1993
Sales	$125,000	$180,000	$250,000	$280,000
Credit sales	90,000	158,000	210,000	235,000
Collections on accounts receivable				
1990 sales	78,000	8,500	200	0
1991 sales		134,000	14,200	300
1992 sales			178,800	19,500
1993 sales				200,000
Accounts receivable written off				
1990 accounts	2,500	500	300	0
1991 accounts		4,600	700	400
1992 accounts			6,200	1,000

Required **1.** Prepare an analysis to determine Pearce's estimated bad debt expense percentage based on the average relationship of actual bad debts to (a) credit sales and (b) outstanding year-end accounts receivable.

    2. What amount should Pearce record as bad debts expense for 1993 if:

      a. Bad debts are estimated as a percentage of credit sales?
      b. Bad debts are estimated as a percentage of outstanding accounts receivable?

30. Aging Accounts Receivable. On September 30, 1992 (the end of its fiscal year), the Lufkin Corporation reported accounts receivable of $331,800 and an allowance for doubtful accounts of $16,700. During fiscal 1993 the following transactions occurred:

Credit sales	$992,000
Collections on accounts receivable	956,000
Accounts receivable written off	16,200

On September 30, 1993, an aging of the accounts receivable balance indicated the following:

Age	Amount	Estimated Percentage Uncollectible
Under 30 days	$143,400	0.8%
30 – 90 days	100,100	1.6
91 – 180 days	55,900	5.0
181 – 360 days	38,200	15.0
Over 360 days	14,000	40.0
	$351,600	

Required **1.** Record the effects on the accounting equation of the credit sales, collections on account, write-off of accounts receivable, and the bad debts expense for Lufkin for fiscal 1993.

    2. What are Lufkin's September 30, 1993, balances in accounts receivable and allowance for doubtful accounts and how will they be disclosed on the September 30, 1993, balance sheet?

31. Estimating Bad Debts. An examination of the accounting records of the Keegan Corporation disclosed the following information for 1993:

Cash sales	$680,000
Net credit sales	528,000
Accounts receivable (12/31/93)	190,000
Allowance for doubtful accounts (12/31/93, prior to adjustment)	1,500 (negative)

Keegan wishes to examine the effect of various alternative bad debt estimation policies.

Required **1.** Record the effects on the accounting equation of the adjustment that would be required under each of the following methods:

   a. Bad debts are estimated at 1% of total sales (net).
   b. Bad debts are estimated at 3% of net credit sales.
   c. Bad debts are estimated at 7.5% of gross accounts receivable.
   d. An aging of accounts receivable indicates that half of the outstanding accounts will incur a 3% loss, a quarter will incur a 6% loss, the remaining quarter will incur a 20% loss.

   2. Discuss the difference between the income statement and balance sheet approaches to estimating bad debts.

32. Accounts Receivable. The Midler Boutique has expanded its sales significantly in recent years by offering a liberal credit policy. As a result bad debt losses have also increased. The following summarized income statements have been prepared.

	1990	1991	1992	1993
Sales on credit	$31,000	$50,000	$70,000	$90,000
Cost of goods sold	(12,000)	(19,000)	(26,000)	(33,000)
Bad debt expense	(1,302)	(2,200)	(3,220)	(4,320)
Other expenses	(10,000)	(12,000)	(14,000)	(16,000)
Net income	$ 7,698	$16,800	$26,780	$36,680
Accounts written off	$ 200	$ 1,000	$ 1,600	$ 2,100

The company uses the percent of sales method to calculate its bad debt expense. The accounts written off each year relate to credit sales made in the previous period.

Required Prepare a report for Ms. Midler that explains the trend in bad debts as compared to other items in the income statement. Does it appear that the liberal credit policy is successful? What do you think the bad debt expense for 1994 should be if credit sales were $120,000 that year?

33. Accounting for Bad Debts. Your friend has been operating a business for two years and has been making many sales on credit. His accountant has told your friend that an estimate of amounts that will be uncollectible in the future must be included in this year's financial statements. Your friend is upset because he does not want "guesses" appearing in the financial statements and he knows that accounting information should be reliable. Since he knows that you are currently studying accounting, he buys you dinner and before picking up the check asks you for your opinion.

Required How would you answer your friend? Explain in detail why the accountant is suggesting that an estimate of uncollectible accounts be included in this year's financial statements and why your friend's concerns are not critical.

34. Sales Transactions. During 1993 the Hopkins Company made credit sales of $80,000 and gave sales returns and allowances on credit of $5,000. In addition, sales discounts taken by credit customers were $200, which was 2% of the accounts collected. At the end of the year the company estimated that 3% of net credit sales would be uncollectible. The Hopkins Company uses the percent of sales method for estimating bad debts.

Required Indicate the effects of these events on the financial statements.

35. Returns and Allowances. Towbin Products sells merchandise on credit for $6,000 on December 1, 1993. The company estimates that returns and allowances will amount to 5% of sales. On December 23, 1993, a customer returns for credit merchandise originally sold on December 1 for $200.

Required **1.** Record the effects on the accounting equation of the above sale and the return of merchandise if returns are recorded as they occur.

2. Record the effects on the accounting equation of the above sale, the estimation of returns and allowances, and the actual return of goods if returns and allowances are estimated at the end of the period of sale.

3. How would the above information be reflected on Towbin's December 31, 1993, financial statements if:

a. Returns are recorded as they occur.
b. Returns are estimated in the period of sale.

ANNUAL REPORT PROBLEMS

36. Cash. Excerpts from the 1988 annual report of General Electric (GE) relating to cash and marketable securities are as follows (in millions of dollars):

	1988	1987
Cash (note 12)	$2,187	$2,543
Marketable securities (note 13)	5,779	5,353

Note 12:
Deposits restricted as to usage and withdrawal or used as partial compensation for short-term borrowing arrangements were not material.

Note 13:
Carrying value of marketable securities for GE was substantially the same as market value at year-ends 1988 and 1987.

Management's Discussion of Financial Resources and Liquidity (in part):
Cash and equivalents (cash and marketable securities) aggregated $8,000 at the end of 1988. Marketable securities for GE are cash equivalents and are part of GE's near-term cash management.

Required **1.** What is the purpose of note 12 in GE's annual report?

2. Do you agree that cash and marketable securities should be discussed together?

37. Cash and Accounts Receivable. Rockwell International Corporation is a leading aerospace company with sales under U.S. government contracts averaging just over 50% of total sales for the years 1988 and 1987. The following excerpts relate to its cash and accounts receivable from its 1988 balance sheet and related notes (in millions of dollars):

	1988	1987
Cash (including time deposits and certificates of deposit: 1988, $783.7; 1987, $990.9)	$ 899.7	$1,103.4
Accounts and notes receivable Commercial, less allowance for doubtful accounts (1988, $24.1; 1987, $29.9)	1,150.2	1,012.0
U.S. government	268.9	146.7

Required **1.** Why are the amounts of time deposits and certificates of deposit disclosed separately within the current cash amount?

2. Cash decreased by 18% in the last year. On what financial statement would you look to determine why cash decreased (or increased)?

3. How could you determine the reasonableness of the 1988 allowance for doubtful accounts? Why is the U.S. government account receivable shown separately with no allowance for doubtful accounts?

38. Accounts Receivable. The following excerpts are from Eastman Kodak's 1988 annual report relating to accounts receivable (in millions of dollars):

	1988	1987
Receivables	$4,071	$3,144

Major Accounting Policies Note (in part):

Current receivables are shown after deducting an allowance of $111 (1987 — $68).

Required **1.** How could you determine if the 1988 allowance for doubtful accounts is reasonable? (Sales were $17,034 in 1988 and $13,305 in 1987 in millions of dollars.) Which method is the company using to estimate its bad debts?

2. Assume that all sales are made on account and that the provision for bad debts was $60 million in 1988. Also, assume that sales returns before any cash was collected from these customers were $10 million in 1988 and that in 1988 there were no recoveries of accounts receivable previously written off. Using the T-account approach, analyze just the transactions that affected the accounts receivable and allowance for doubtful accounts in 1988. What were the amounts of cash collected (from accounts receivable) and accounts receivable written off in 1988?

39. Accounts Receivable. The following excerpts are from the 1988 balance sheet of General Electric (GE) relating to accounts receivable (in millions of dollars):

	1988	1987
Current receivables (note 15)	$7,110	$6,782

Note 15:
December 31
Receivable from

	1988	1987
Customers	$5,289	$5,463
Associated companies	160	155
Others (advances to suppliers)	1,857	1,374
	7,306	6,992 29937
Less: allowance for losses	(196) 28953	(210) 29937
	$7,110 28953	$6,782
	2.8%	3.1

Management's Discussion of Financial Resources and Liquidity (in part):
    Receivables "turned over" 7.01 times in 1988 compared with 6.8 times in 1987. ("Turnover" relates receivables to sales and is a measurement of collection efficiency. Higher turnover indicates faster collections.) GE's trend in this area has been improving since 1985, as a result of vigorous management attention to credit and collections. The overall condition of customer receivables remained excellent at the end of 1988.

Required **1.** In assessing the overall condition of customer receivables, determine if the allowance for losses at the end of 1988 was reasonable. Sales were $28,953 million in 1988 and $29,937 million in 1987. Should the allowance cover all accounts receivable or just the customer accounts?

2. Assume all sales were on account. Also, assume that cash collected on accounts receivable was $27,800 million and that sales returns on account were $100 million. Using the T-account approach for customer accounts receivable and allowance for losses accounts, find the amounts of the account receivables written off and the provision for bad debt expense in 1988.

3. Compute the accounts receivable turnover ratio (sales divided by average net receivable from customers). Compare your answer with the calculation made by G.E.

40. Uncollectible Accounts Receivable. Bell Atlantic Corporation is a leading provider of voice and data communications, mobile telephone services, computer maintenance, and a full range of equipment leasing and financing products. It was created in 1984 by bringing together seven former Bell System telephone companies primarily serving the East coast region.

Management's Discussion and Analysis (in part):
    The Company achieved increases in revenues, net income, and earnings per share in 1988, marking the fourth consecutive year of solid growth since it began operations in 1984. These results reflect the continued expansion of market demand for communications and related services in the mid-Atlantic region. The increase in the provision for uncollectibles in 1988 was related to revenue growth; the 1987 increase

was due primarily to revised credit policies and collection procedures required by state regulators for one of the telephone subsidiaries.

The following are excerpts from the financial statements (in millions of dollars):

	1988	1987	1986
Operating revenues	$10,880	$10,747	$10,054
Provision for uncollectibles	(95)	(92)	(47)
Net earnings	1,317	1,240	1,167
Accounts receivable	$ 1,844	$ 1,783	$ 1,859
Less: allowance for doubtful accounts	(96)	(82)	(60)
Net receivables	$ 1,748	$ 1,701	$ 1,799

Required 1. Are the 1988 provision for uncollectibles and allowance for doubtful accounts reasonable? Include the accounts receivable turnover ratio in your calculations and use the ending (not average) receivables balance in your calculations.

2. Are doubtful accounts material to Bell Atlantic's financial statements? Include calculations in your answer.

41. Accounts Receivable and Sales. Unisys Corporation is one of the largest computer manufacturers in the world. The following excerpts are from its 1988 balance sheet (in millions of dollars):

Current Assets:	1988	1987
Accounts and notes receivable (note 7)	$2,784.6	$2,915.0
Note 7. Current and Long-Term Receivables		
Accounts receivable, net	$2,606.3	$2,628.9
Sales-type leases, net	969.1	897.9
Installment accounts, net	73.3	159.3
Total, net	3,648.7	3,686.1
Less: current receivables, net	2,784.6	2,915.0
Long-term receivables, net	$ 864.1	$ 771.1

Note 1. Summary of Significant Accounting Policies (in part):
E. Revenue Recognition. Revenue from sale contracts is generally recorded upon shipment of product in the case of sales contracts and upon installation in the case of sales-type leases. Revenue from service and rental agreements is recorded as earned over the lives of the respective contracts.

Required 1. Explain each line item in note 7 and use the information in note 1 where appropriate.

2. Comment on the clarity of these disclosures.

42. Accounts Receivable and Revenue Recognition. Listed below are excerpts from Boeing's 1988 annual report relating to its accounts receivable (in millions of dollars):

	1988	1987
Accounts receivable	$1,559	$1,546

Note 1. Summary of Significant Accounting Policies (in part):
Revenue Recognition. Sales under commercial programs and U.S. government and foreign military fixed-price type contracts are generally recorded as deliveries are made. For certain fixed-price type contracts that require substantial performance over a long time period before deliveries begin, sales are recorded based upon attainment of scheduled performance milestones. Sales under cost-reimbursement contracts are recorded as costs are incurred and fees are earned.

Note 2: Accounts Receivable:
Accounts receivable at December 31 consisted of:

	1988	1987
Amounts receivable under U.S. government contracts	$1,199	$1,109
Accounts receivable from commercial and foreign military customers	360	437
	$1,559	$1,546

Accounts receivable at December 31, 1988, included unbillable amounts of $395, principally relating to sales values recorded upon attainment of scheduled performance milestones, which differ from contractual billing milestones. No significant amounts in accounts receivable represent retainages under contracts.

Required **1.** Why isn't there an allowance for doubtful accounts disclosed separately in these financial statements?

2. Assume that the allowance for doubtful accounts should be increased by 1% of the commercial and foreign military accounts receivable at year-end 1988. What would be the impact on the 1988 financial statements?

3. Explain how the recognition of revenues affects the accounts receivable for Boeing Company. Is Boeing's approach reasonable?

4. Would there be a material impact on accounts receivable and net income if Boeing used contractual billing milestones, instead of scheduled performance milestones, to recognize revenues? Boeing's net income for 1988 was $614 million. Use the 34% statutory income tax rate.

43. Cash and Receivables. United Telecom provides local and long-distance communication services with complimentary ventures in directory publishing, equipment distribution, "900" and operator services. The following excerpts are from its 1988 financial statements (in millions of dollars):

Consolidated Balance Sheet (in part):	**1988**	**1987**
Cash and temporary cash investments	$617.1	$ 74.4

Accounts receivable:

Long-distance communications services, net of allowance for doubtful accounts of $118.7	382.7	—
Other, net of allowance for doubtful accounts of $13.8 ($11.9 in 1987)	467.6	450.4

Note 1. Accounting Policies (in part):
Basis of Consolidation

As a result of United's assumption of management control of U.S. Sprint Communications Company in 1988 with a 50% ownership interest, the 1988 consolidated financial statements also include the accounts of U.S. Sprint.

Classification of Operations

United's long distance communications services consist of communications revenues and related operating expenses associated with carrying voice and data communications across certain specified geographical boundaries and are not rate-regulated. For 1988, such operations consist of those of U.S. Sprint. Revenues for long-distance communications services are recorded based on communication services rendered after deducting an estimate of the services which will either not be billed or collected.

Local communications services consist principally of the revenues and operating expenses of United's rate-regulated telephone operations. These operations provide local exchange services, access to United's local exchange facilities to telephone customers and other carriers, and toll services within specified geographical areas.

Cash and Temporary Cash Investments

Temporary cash investments generally include highly liquid investments with original maturities of three months or less and are stated at cost, which approximates market value. At December 31, 1988 and 1987, outstanding checks in excess of cash balances of $160.6 and $63.9, respectively, are included in accounts payable.

Required 1. Comment on the presentation of cash and temporary cash investments in United's balance sheet.

2. Why did the accounts receivable for long-distance services first appear in 1988?

3. Why is the allowance for doubtful accounts proportionately so much higher for long-distance services than for other, including local, services?

44. Recording Sales With Right of Return. MiniScribe Company manufactures and sells disk drives for various types of computers. In early 1989, a three person Independent Evaluation Committee (IEC) was appointed from newly elected members of the company's Board of Directors to investigate MiniScribe's accounting and management practices over the previous three years. The IEC made the following findings concerning the issue of recording sales when the right of return may exist:

The IEC believed that about $1.8 million of profit relating to shipments to MiniScribe's just-in-time (JIT) warehouses may have been improperly recognized in 1987. Late in 1987, the company established three JIT warehouses near the warehouses of three major distributors of MiniScribe products. This arrangement enabled the distributors to obtain delivery within hours of a request of MiniScribe products. Under the agreements, terms for payment did not begin until after the product was removed from the JIT warehouse. The largest one was in Los Angeles where an owner of the major electronics-parts distributor said his company wasn't invoiced until it received a shipment from this JIT warehouse. MiniScribe, however, was recognizing shipments into the warehouse as sales. Because the JIT operation was not under the distributor's complete control, the number of disk drives shipped into the JIT warehouse was at MiniScribe's discretion.

During 1988, shipments to the JIT warehouses increased dramatically. The company used these increased shipments to artificially increase reported revenue by $56.4 million and gross profits by $5.4 million. These particular shipments remained in the JIT warehouses at year end. The IEC's view is that none of those sales should have been recorded in 1988 because the risks of ownership of the product did not pass to the distributors until the product was released from the JIT warehouses.

Source: Form 8-K filed with the Securities and Exchange Commission. The form is used to describe significant events that have affected a publicly held company.

Required Do you agree with the IEC's conclusion that "none of these sales should have been recorded"?

Inventories and Cost of Goods Sold

After reading this chapter, you should understand

- Inventory classifications
- Periodic and perpetual inventory systems
- Determination of inventory quantities and costs
- Alternative cost flow assumptions

- Evaluation of alternative cost flow assumptions
- Lower of cost or market method
- Gross profit method
- Purchase discounts (Appendix 1)
- LIFO perpetual (Appendix 2)

Inventories are the assets of a company that are (1) held for sale in the ordinary course of business, (2) in the process of production for sale, or (3) held for use in the production of goods or services to be made available for sale. The category of inventory specifically excludes any assets that are not sold in the normal course of business, such as marketable securities or property, plant, and equipment the company intends to sell.

Accounting for inventories is especially significant because of the importance of the acquisition, manufacture, and sale of products to the profitability of companies. The cost of the inventory usually has a material impact on the balance sheet. It also affects the cost of goods sold and therefore the net income on the income statement. In addition, various accounting practices, such as alternative cost flow assumptions and valuation principles, are in widespread use and may have a significant impact on asset valuation and income determination.

■ THE IMPORTANCE OF INVENTORY

Inventory is a very important asset for most companies and is of particular interest to users of the company's financial statements. Inventory is typically the largest current asset (except for a service company) and represents a source of revenue in the near future through sales of the goods.

The cost of goods available for sale is the sum of the beginning inventory for the period and the costs of the net purchases made during the period. The cost of the ending inventory is subtracted from the cost of goods available for sale to compute the cost of the goods sold. The cost of goods sold is then subtracted from net sales to determine the gross profit. These relationships may be stated in the following three equations:

$$\text{Cost of Goods Available for Sale} = \text{Beginning Inventory} + \text{Purchases (Net)}$$

$$\text{Cost of Goods Sold} = \text{Cost of Goods Available for Sale} - \text{Ending Inventory}$$

$$\text{Gross Profit} = \text{Sales (Net)} - \text{Cost of Goods Sold}$$

The term "purchases" used in the above discussion is appropriate for retail companies that buy goods from suppliers and resell them. In a manufacturing company, the equivalent amount is cost of goods manufactured and the related inventory is finished goods inventory. In this chapter, for convenience, we will use the term purchases, but cost of goods manufactured may be substituted in each case.

Once the cost of goods available for sale has been found, any change in the costs assigned to the ending inventory will change the cost of goods sold, and vice versa (how the cost of the inventory is determined is discussed later in the chapter). Any change in the cost of goods sold, in turn, will have a corresponding effect on gross profit. In addition, since the ending inventory of one accounting period is the beginning inventory of the next period, the cost assigned to the ending inventory will also affect the cost of goods available for sale, the cost of goods sold, and the gross profit of the next period. Thus, we can see that the determination of the cost of the ending inventory has a major impact on current and future balance sheets and income statements of the company and therefore may affect the perceptions that the users of the financial statements have of the company. In summary, if ending inventory is overstated (understated) income for the period is overstated (understated).

For example, suppose that a company has the partial income statement shown in Alternative 1 of Exhibit 6–1. Now suppose that ending inventory was computed instead as $1,200, which is an increase of $200 or 20%. As can be seen from Alternative 2, gross profit is increased by $200, which is an increase of 40% ($700 ÷ $500 = 1.40). In this case a percentage change in the recorded amount of the ending inventory has had a *proportionately* much larger percentage impact on the gross profit.

In addition to the accounting considerations, proper management of inventory is important for effective management of the company. For example, it is important to have appropriate amounts of inventory on hand to fill customer orders and prevent inadequate or excessive inventory.

EXHIBIT 6–1   Effect of the cost of ending inventory on the gross profit

	Alternative 1		Alternative 2	
Sales (net)		$10,000		$10,000
Beginning inventory	$ 800		$ 800	
Purchases (net)	9,700		9,700	
Cost of goods available for sale	$10,500		$10,500	
Less: ending inventory	(1,000)		(1,200)	
Cost of goods sold		(9,500)		(9,300)
Gross profit		$ 500		$ 700

■ CLASSIFICATIONS OF INVENTORY

Inventory may be classified in several alternative accounts, depending on the type of business. A merchandising company, whether wholesale or retail, acquires goods for resale and does not alter their physical form. Consequently, it needs only one type of inventory account, usually entitled **merchandise inventory**. A manufacturing company *does* change the physical form of the goods and uses three inventory accounts, usually called **raw materials inventory**, **goods in process inventory**, and **finished goods inventory**. The flow of inventory costs through these two types of entities is diagramed in Exhibit 6–2. The three categories of inventory accounts used by a manufacturing company are discussed in the following sections.

Raw Materials Inventory

Raw materials inventory includes the tangible goods acquired for direct use in the production process. This inventory includes materials acquired from natural sources, such as the iron ore used by a steel mill. Raw materials may also include some products purchased from other companies, such as the steel or subassemblies used in the manufacture of appliances. Raw materials should be contrasted with **parts inventory**, which is the term often used for the inventory of replacement parts.

Materials not directly incorporated in the manufacturing process but necessary for its successful operation are sometimes included in raw materials inventory. However, they are more normally isolated in a separate account called **factory supplies**, **manufacturing supplies**, or **indirect materials**. Examples of materials in this category include lubricating oil and cleaning supplies.

Goods in Process Inventory

Goods in process (sometimes called **work in process**) **inventory includes the products that have been started in the manufacturing process but have not yet been completed.** This partially completed inventory includes three cost components: (1) raw materials; (2) direct labor, which is the cost of the labor used

EXHIBIT 6–2

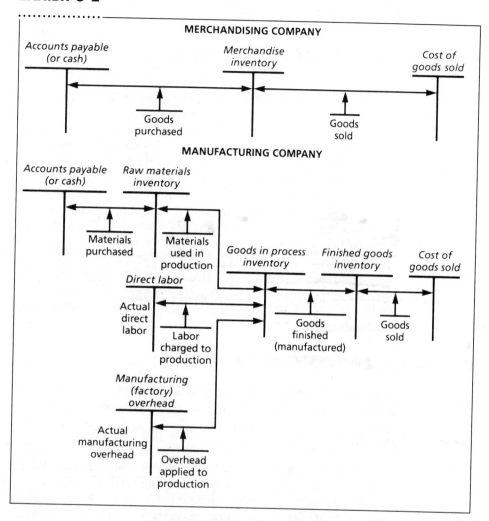

directly in the manufacture of the product; and (3) manufacturing (or factory) overhead, which is the costs other than raw materials and direct labor that are associated with the manufacturing process. These latter costs include **variable manufacturing overhead**, such as supplies and some indirect labor that vary with the level of production, and **fixed manufacturing overhead**, such as insurance, property taxes, and depreciation on the assets used in the production activities that do not vary with the level of production.

Finished Goods Inventory

Finished goods inventory includes the completed manufactured products awaiting sale. The inventory includes the same three cost components as the goods in process inventory, but all the costs are combined into a single cost per unit for all the completed units.

REPORTING INVENTORIES ON THE BALANCE SHEET

The reporting of inventories on the balance sheet can follow many different formats. Two examples of the commonly used methods are shown in Exhibit 6–3. Johnson & Johnson and Champion International report a single inventory figure in the balance sheet and show the breakdown in the notes to the financial statements. Johnson and Johnson categorizes its inventory by the traditional breakdown of raw materials, goods in process, and finished goods while Champion International categorizes its inventory by type of product.

The inventory costs shown in the balance sheets are the final amounts resulting from a series of steps. First, the company must identify and count the physical inventory quantities and therefore has to decide what items to properly include in the inventory. Then the costs of the units purchased or produced during the accounting period must be determined. A cost flow assumption is then used to allocate these costs, plus those of the beginning inventory, between ending inventory and cost of goods sold. Each of these steps is discussed in the following sections.

ALTERNATIVE INVENTORY SYSTEMS

Inventory quantities and costs may be accounted for using either the **periodic system** or the **perpetual system**, as selected by management.

Periodic Inventory System

A company using the periodic system does *not* maintain a continuous record of the quantities (or costs) of inventory on hand. The number of units in inventory is counted periodically, which must be at least once a year. This is the only time(s) when quantities on hand, and therefore the quantities used or sold during the period, are known accurately. The cost of the ending inventory is found by attaching costs to the quantities on hand, based on the cost flow assumption used. Then the cost of goods sold is calculated by subtracting the ending inventory from the cost of goods available for sale, which is the sum of the beginning inventory and the net purchases. This system is adequate for relatively low value inventory items, particularly when the costs of a perpetual inventory system are likely to outweigh its benefits.

In the periodic system acquisitions of inventory are not added directly to an inventory account. Such a procedure would lead to an overstatement of the permanent Inventory account because the account is not reduced during the period for the cost of the inventory sold. Therefore in a periodic system the costs of acquisitions of inventory are usually added to a temporary account,

EXHIBIT 6–3

JOHNSON & JOHNSON AND SUBSIDIARIES (in millions)		
	December 31	
Assets (in part):	1989	1988
Inventories (Notes 1 and 3)	$1,353	$1,273
Note 3. Inventories (in part):	December 31	
	1989	1988
Raw materials and supplies	$ 435	$ 388
Goods in process	259	238
Finished goods	659	647
	$1,353	$1,273

CHAMPION INTERNATIONAL CORPORATION (in thousands)		
	December 31	
Assets (in part):	1989	1988
Inventories (Note 2)	$465,622	$411,892
Note 2. Inventories	December 31	
	1989	1988
Paper, pulp, and packaging products	$151,846	$132,752
Wood products	40,009	50,933
Logs	85,181	71,580
Pulpwood	19,040	13,465
Raw materials, parts, and supplies	169,546	143,162
	$465,622	$411,892

At December 31, 1989 and 1988, inventories stated using the last-in, first-out (LIFO) method, representing approximately 20% of total inventories, were $93,330 and $80,883, respectively. If the lower of average cost or market method (which approximates current cost) had been utilized for inventories carried at LIFO, inventory balances would have been increased by $67,474 and $64,090 at December 31, 1989 and 1988, respectively.

Purchases, while the beginning inventory cost remains in the Inventory account. Purchases returns and allowances, purchases discounts, and freight-in are usually recorded in separate accounts. Each of these amounts is used in the computation of net purchases as follows:

$$\text{Net Purchases} = \text{Purchases} + \text{Freight-in} - \frac{\text{Purchases Returns}}{\text{and Allowances}} - \frac{\text{Purchases}}{\text{Discounts}}$$

Perpetual Inventory System

A company using the perpetual system maintains a continuous record of the physical quantities (and costs) in its inventory. The purchase, or production, and use of each item of inventory are recorded, although often only in units without including costs. Such a perpetual physical system is virtually essential if adequate management planning and control over inventory are to be maintained and stockouts avoided. Many perpetual systems also include costs so that the preparation of periodic financial statements is facilitated. Such systems are becoming much more common with the increased sophistication and lower cost of computer-based accounting systems. For example, most retail stores use "point of sale" cash register systems in which each product has a unique code that is entered into the system as each unit is sold. This system enables the retailer to immediately update its Inventory and Cost of Goods Sold accounts as each sale is made, thereby making it possible for both amounts to be continually known. As in the periodic system, purchases returns and allowances, purchases discounts, and freight-in affect the cost of the inventory.

When the perpetual system is used, the number of units in inventory must be counted at least once a year to confirm the balance in the inventory account. Variation between the quantities counted and the account balance results from errors in recording, shrinkage, waste, breakage, theft, and other causes, and the cost of the difference in the two quantities is entered into the records to bring the perpetual records into agreement with the count. In addition, the size of the difference is useful information for management control purposes and therefore represents another advantage of the perpetual system.

In summary, the difference between the periodic and the perpetual inventory systems can be illustrated by the following equations:

Periodic Inventory System:
    Beginning Inventory + Purchases (net) − Ending Inventory = Goods Sold

Perpetual Inventory System:
    Beginning Inventory + Purchases (net) − Goods Sold = Ending Inventory

Note that each equation can be thought of in terms of *units* or *costs*. Also, for a manufacturing company, the (cost of) goods manufactured is substituted for purchases. The advantages of the periodic system are:

1. It is less expensive and simpler to operate.
2. It is most appropriate for relatively low-cost inventory items, because in these cases it is not as important for management to know continually the physical inventory for control and reordering purposes.

The advantages of the perpetual system are:

1. It allows management to exercise better control over the operations of the company, because the cost of goods sold and inventory are continually known and can be used for inventory control and in evaluating the performance of the company whenever management chooses to do so.

2. The difference between the ending inventory according to the balance in the inventory account and the ending inventory determined when the physical inventory is taken provides a measure of the amount of theft, breakage, and spoilage that has occurred during the period. Management may consider this information to be useful because it helps in the control of the company's activities.

■ DETERMINATION OF INVENTORY QUANTITIES AND COSTS

Determining the correct number of units in the inventory and the correct costs to assign to those units is essential for providing financial statements useful to external users.

Inventory Quantities

The basic criterion for including items in inventory is *economic control* rather than physical possession. However, for inventory, economic control is usually consistent with legal ownership. Thus, when control transfers to a company, the item should be included in its inventory, even though the company may not have physical possession. Normally, goods are recorded in inventory when received by the purchaser and recorded as sold by the seller when shipped. When financial statements are prepared, however, all goods under economic control should be included in inventory whether or not the company has physical possession (or legal ownership). Before transfer of control, the item should be included in the inventory of the seller, even though the seller may not have physical possession. Likewise, when control passes to a customer because of a sale, the item should be excluded from the seller's inventory, even though the company may still have physical possession. Similarly, the buyer should include that item in inventory if control has passed, even though it may not have physical possession.

Inventory Count

As we have seen, counting the numbers of units in inventory is essential under either the perpetual or periodic inventory system. The purpose of the inventory count (often referred to as "taking a physical inventory") varies according to the system used. When the periodic system is used, the inventory count is necessary to determine the ending inventory and the cost of goods sold. When the perpetual system is used, the inventory count acts as a check on the accuracy of the ending inventory included in the perpetual records and indicates the extent of losses from theft, breakage, or spoilage. At a minimum, the inventory count occurs at the end of each fiscal year. In many businesses an inventory count is taken more frequently, perhaps as often as each month, although this count may be for only part of the inventory. Management must evaluate the tradeoff between the cost of taking the inventory and the information that results.

It is usual to count the inventory outside of regular business hours so that the procedure is not affected by goods being sold or received while the count is in progress. The inventory count may indicate that an adjustment to the financial statements is necessary. For example, if the perpetual inventory system indicated that there was an inventory of $100,000 and the physical inventory indicated only $90,000, the $90,000 would be recorded in the balance sheet and cost of goods sold would be increased by $10,000 ($100,000 − $90,000). This adjustment is included in cost of goods sold because the cost is considered to be an inevitable part of the process of selling products.

Inventory Costs

There are two aspects in the determination of inventory costs. The costs attached to each unit *available for sale* are discussed in this section. The costs attached to the *ending inventory* and *cost of goods sold* (the inventory cost flow assumption) are discussed later in this chapter.

Inventory is recorded at cost, which is the price paid or consideration given to acquire the asset.[1] **Inventory cost therefore includes applicable expenditures and charges directly or indirectly incurred in bringing an item to its existing condition and location** (which includes maintaining it until it is sold). For an item of inventory, a decision must be made on each cost as to whether it meets this definition and is thus included in the cost of the inventory or whether it does not and is therefore a period cost, which is expensed directly. The cost of inventory should include the purchase price (net of purchase discounts, as discussed in Appendix 1 of the chapter) and payments directly associated with the inventory, such as freight, receiving, unpacking, inspecting, storage, insurance, personal property, sales and other applicable taxes, and similar costs.

Some costs which by the above criteria logically should be attached to inventory are normally excluded on the grounds of materiality. For example, the costs of the purchasing department are necessary to bring the item to its existing condition and location, but the allocation of such costs to the separate items in inventory is unlikely to have a material effect on the cost of the ending inventory on the balance sheet or the measurement of cost of goods sold and other expenses on the income statement.

Two common issues in the determination of inventory costs are manufacturing overhead costs and purchases discounts.

Manufacturing Overhead Costs

The question arises as to which overhead costs should be considered as being "directly or indirectly incurred." Accounting principles require that inventory

---

[1] "Restatement and Revision of Accounting Research Bulletins," *Accounting Research and Terminology Bulletins, Final Edition, No. 43* (New York: AICPA, 1961), ch. 4, par. 4.

costs include acquisition and production costs (including manufacturing overhead), whereas general and administrative expenses are included as expenses of the period, except for the portion of such expenses that is clearly related to production and thus included as part of inventory costs. Selling expenses are *not* included as part of inventory costs. The (exclusion) of all overhead from inventory costs is not an accepted accounting principle.[2]

Manufacturing costs directly related to the production of inventory and included in the cost of that inventory may be either variable or fixed manufacturing overhead. The inclusion of variable overhead costs (costs that change as activity levels change) in the cost of inventory raises no particular accounting issues, but it should be recognized that the allocation of fixed overhead costs (costs that do *not* change as activity levels change) is a difficult issue and that the final allocation of costs usually involves somewhat arbitrary procedures. A discussion of these issues is beyond the scope of this book but may be found in a managerial accounting textbook. An interpretation of "directly related" also presents some practical problems; one way in which this criterion can be applied is to ask whether the economic benefit to be derived from the asset in the future (i.e., sales revenue) has been directly increased by the expenditure in question. In other words, **the relationship between the costs incurred and the benefits produced has to be traceable**.

For example, the expenditure on a supervisor's salary directly increases the economic benefit associated with the asset because without the supervisor the item might not have been produced with the same quality. That is, there is a traceable relationship. Therefore a portion of the supervisor's salary should be included in the cost of the inventory. In contrast, the company president's salary does not lead directly to an increase in the economic benefits to be derived from a particular unit of inventory. In this case, there is not a traceable relationship and therefore the salary should be a period expense. Similarly, the cost of normal spoilage is considered an inventory cost because some spoilage is an inevitable part of the production process. However, the cost of abnormal spoilage is an expense of the period because it has not increased the economic benefits to be derived from the inventory.

In addition to traceability, **materiality is relevant to the decision to include overhead costs in the cost of inventory**. If the inclusion or exclusion of the cost will not have a material effect on the financial statements, for simplicity the costs typically will be expensed in the period incurred.

Some costs should never be considered for inclusion in the cost of inventory, because they are not associated with bringing the item to its existing condition and location. For example, selling costs are properly considered to be a cost of the period and not an inventory cost because they apply to the units sold during the period and not to the units held in inventory.

· · · · · · · · · · · · · · · · · · · ·

[2] *Ibid.*

EXHIBIT 6–4   Illustration of unit and cost flow relationships

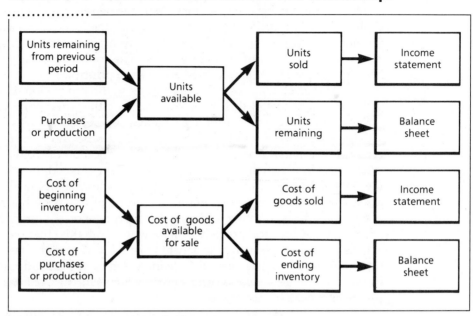

■ COST FLOW ASSUMPTIONS

A company typically starts an accounting period with some units in the beginning inventory and then purchases or produces additional units during the
period. Together these constitute the *goods available for sale*, which then either
are sold or remain in the ending inventory.

For financial statement purposes *costs* must be attached to these units. The
cost of the beginning inventory is the cost of the ending inventory of the preceding period. This amount is the beginning balance in the Inventory account.
The costs attached to the purchases or production during the period have already
been discussed. The beginning balance in Inventory and the cost of purchases
or production constitute the *cost of the goods available for sale*. This total cost is
allocated between the cost of goods sold and ending inventory by means of a
cost flow assumption. The major cost flow assumptions currently used are specific identification; first-in, first-out (FIFO); average cost; and last-in, first-out
(LIFO). Both the unit relationship and the cost flow relationship are illustrated
in Exhibit 6–4.

Cost flow assumptions are important for two reasons. First, a company
continues to hold inventories. If there were no ending inventory, then all the
cost of goods available for sale would be transferred to cost of goods sold. Second,
the costs of purchases and production change. If costs did not change, all units
would have the same cost and therefore alternative cost flow assumptions would
not affect either the cost of goods sold or the ending inventory. Thus, the effects

EXHIBIT 6–5

DAVIS COMPANY
Inventory Information

Beginning inventory, January 1	100 units @ $5.00 per unit	$ 500
January 10, purchase	50 units @ $5.50 per unit	275
January 22, purchase	90 units @ $6.00 per unit	540
Cost of goods available for sale	240 units	$1,315
Sales during January	(130) units	
Ending inventory, January 31	110 units	

Notes: 1. The units are sold for $13 per unit.
2. The Davis Company uses the periodic inventory system. For computational simplicity, it is assumed that the physical inventory is taken monthly.

on the financial statements of using different cost flow assumptions are caused by changes in the costs of the inventory manufactured or purchased.

Note the use of the word *cost* in the phrase *cost flow assumptions*. **The physical flow of the items in the inventory is *irrelevant* for the purposes of reporting cost of goods sold and inventory.** Of course, management of the physical inventory flows is important for the efficient operation of a company, but for the preparation of the financial statements we are concerned only with the allocation of costs between the cost of goods sold and ending inventory. For example, it is likely that most companies will use a FIFO physical inventory management system to reduce the risk of obsolescence while accounting for the inventory costs on a LIFO basis.

Each cost flow assumption is discussed in the following sections using the information for the Davis Company given in Exhibit 6–5. For simplicity, it is assumed that the company is a merchandising company, although the cost flow assumptions are applied to manufacturing companies by following the same principles. Also a month is used for convenience. The calculations (except for a LIFO example in Appendix 2 of this chapter) assume the use of the periodic inventory system because the calculations are simpler and it is very unlikely that the selection would have a material impact on the financial statements. As we will see, however, the choice of the cost flow assumption may have a very material impact on the statements. The cost flow assumption that a company is using is disclosed in the notes to the financial statements. However, a company may use more than one method because it applies one cost flow assumption to one segment of its inventory and an alternative method to another segment.

The Davis Company has a beginning inventory of $500 and has made two purchases during January with a total cost of $815 ($275 + $540). Therefore, the cost of goods available for sale is $1,315 ($500 + $815), which must be divided between the 130 units sold (the cost of goods sold) and the ending inventory of 110 units.

Each of the four inventory cost flow assumptions produces different amounts for the cost of goods sold and ending inventory. Note that each of the methods is based on actual costs incurred and is an acceptable interpretation of the historical cost principle. Although a company is able to select one of the four cost flow assumptions to account for its inventory, it is expected that once the selection is made the method will be consistently applied from period to period. If a change is made, the effects of the change must be fully disclosed in the financial statements. The computations to determine the cost of goods sold and ending inventory under each method are discussed in the following sections.

Specific Identification

Specific identification is a method of assigning costs to cost of goods sold and ending inventory by identifying a specific cost incurred with each unit sold and each unit in ending inventory. If a unit has been sold, the related cost is included in cost of goods sold; if a unit remains in inventory, the related cost is included in the cost of the ending inventory. For example, when the Davis Company sells a unit at the end of January, the following three alternatives are possible:

	Sell a Unit from the Beginning Inventory	Sell a Unit from the January 10 Purchase	Sell a Unit from the January 22 Purchase
Sales	$13.00	$13.00	$13.00
Cost of goods sold	(5.00)	(5.50)	(6.00)
Gross profit	$ 8.00	$ 7.50	$ 7.00

Depending on the unit selected, the gross profit can vary from a low of $7 to a high of $8, which is a difference of 14.3% ($8 ÷ $7 = 1.143). Although the specific identification method is often referred to as a cost flow assumption, it may be more accurate to state that it is an actual cost flow rather than a cost flow assumption. The method is particularly appropriate for a company with a small volume of separately identifiable units in inventory, such as an automobile dealership. When a company has an inventory consisting of large quantities of similar items, however, the method may be inefficient, time-consuming, and perhaps impossible to use. For example, the specific identification method would not be suitable for the inventory of frozen foods in a large grocery store. When identical units are carried in inventory, the specific identification method is very arbitrary and perhaps may be manipulated by management to change gross profits as particular units with different costs are selected for sale. Although the specific identification method could be used with the periodic inventory system, it is more compatible with the perpetual system, in which the cost of each unit is identified as it is sold.

EXHIBIT 6–6

DAVIS COMPANY
First-In, First-Out Cost Flow Assumption
(Periodic Inventory System)

Ending inventory (110 units)

90 units @ $6.00 per unit (from January 22 purchase)		$540
20 units @ $5.50 per unit (from January 10 purchase)		110
110		$650

Cost of Goods Sold = Beginning Inventory + Purchases − Ending Inventory
$665   = $500   + $815   − $650

or

Cost of Goods Sold (130 units)

100 units @ $5.00 per unit (from beginning inventory)		$500
30 units @ $5.50 per unit (from January 10 purchase)		165
130		$665

First-In, First-Out

The first-in, first-out (FIFO) cost flow assumption includes the earliest costs incurred in the cost of goods sold, and the latest costs are included in the ending inventory. That is, the first costs incurred are assumed to be the first costs of units sold. Under this method the Davis Company computes the ending inventory to be $650 and the cost of goods sold to be $665, as shown in Exhibit 6–6.

The Davis Company has an ending inventory of 110 units, and the costs of these units are assumed in the FIFO method to be the latest costs incurred, which include the cost of the 90 units from the purchase on January 22 ($540) and the cost of the 20 units remaining from the purchase on January 10 ($110). Consequently, the cost of goods sold ($665) includes the earliest costs—that is, the cost of the 100 units from the beginning inventory—and the cost of the 30 units from the purchase made on January 10.

Average Cost

The average cost flow assumption allocates the average cost for the period to both the ending inventory and the cost of goods sold. That is, the costs of all the units available for sale are commingled, and the resulting average cost is used for both the ending inventory and the cost of goods sold. As shown in

EXHIBIT 6-7

DAVIS COMPANY
Average Cost Flow Assumption
(Periodic Inventory System)

Average Cost per Unit = Cost of Goods Available ÷ Number of Units Available
for Sale   for Sale
= $1,315 ÷ 240
= $5.48 per unit (rounded)

Ending Inventory   = Number of Units × Average Cost per Unit
= 110 × $5.48
= $603 (rounded to the nearest dollar)

Cost of Goods Sold   = Beginning Inventory + Purchases − Ending Inventory
__$712__   = $500   + $815   − $603

or

Cost of Goods Sold   = Number of Units × Average Cost per Unit
= 130 × $5.48
= $712 (rounded)

Exhibit 6–7, the average cost per unit of $5.48 for the Davis Company is calculated by dividing the total cost of goods available for sale ($1,315) by the number of units available for sale (240, which includes the 100 units in the beginning inventory plus the 140 units purchased).

The ending inventory is computed as $603 for the 110 units on hand at the average cost of $5.48 per unit and the cost of goods sold as $712, which includes the 130 units sold at the average cost of $5.48 per unit.

Last-In, First-Out (Periodic)

The last-in, first-out (LIFO) cost flow assumption includes the latest costs incurred in the cost of goods sold, and the earliest costs (part or all of which are costs incurred in previous periods) are included in the ending inventory. That is, the last costs incurred are assumed to be the first costs of units sold. The Davis Company computes the ending inventory to be $555 and the cost of goods sold to be $760, as shown in Exhibit 6–8. The company has an ending inventory of 110 units, and the costs of these units are assumed in the LIFO method to be the earliest costs incurred, which include the cost of the entire beginning inventory and the cost of the 10 units remaining from the January 10 purchase. Consequently, the cost of goods sold includes the latest costs—that is, the cost of the goods from the January 22 purchase ($540)—and the cost of 40 units from the January 10 purchase ($220).

EXHIBIT 6–8

....

DAVIS COMPANY
Last-In, First-Out Cost Flow Assumption
(Periodic Inventory System)

Ending inventory (110 units)

100 units @ $5.00 per unit (from beginning inventory)	$500
10 units @ $5.50 per unit (from January 10 purchase)	55
110	$555

Cost of Goods Sold = Beginning Inventory + Purchases − Ending Inventory
$760 = $500 + $815 − $555

or

Cost of Goods Sold (130 units)

90 units @ $6.00 per unit (from January 22 purchase)	$540
40 units @ $5.50 per unit (from January 10 purchase)	220
130	$760

Additional Periodic Illustration

To further illustrate the differences among FIFO, average cost, and LIFO, we continue the Davis Company example through February. The inventory information for the Davis Company for February is shown in Exhibit 6–9. The cost of the ending inventory on February 28 and the cost of goods sold for February are shown for the FIFO, average, and LIFO cost flow assumptions. It is important to note that the beginning inventory for February is the ending inventory for January, and therefore the amount is different for each cost flow assumption. The calculations otherwise follow the same procedures as for January.

■ EVALUATION OF THE THREE ALTERNATIVES

The advantages and disadvantages of the FIFO, average, and LIFO cost flow assumptions are discussed in this section (the advantages and disadvantages of the specific identification method were discussed earlier). Although the terminology is rarely used, some prefer to think of FIFO as LISH (last-in, still here) and LIFO as FISH (first-in, still here). That is, the focus is on ending inventory rather than on cost of goods sold.

Effects on the Financial Statements

The choice made by management to adopt any one of the three cost flow assumptions has an impact on both the income statement and the balance sheet. Using

EXHIBIT 6—9

················· ——————————————————————————————————————

DAVIS COMPANY
Ending Inventory and Cost of Goods Sold for February
(Periodic Inventory System)

ADDITIONAL INFORMATION

Beginning inventory, February 1	110 units	
February 5, purchase	40 units @ $6.20 per unit	$248
February 20, purchase	80 units @ $6.40 per unit	$512
	230 units	
Sales during February	(100) units	
Ending inventory, February 28	130 units	

FIRST-IN, FIRST-OUT

Beginning Inventory = 20 units @ $5.50 per unit + 90 units @ $6.00 per unit
(from Exhibit 6—6)
= $650

Ending Inventory = 80 units @ $6.40 per unit
+40 units @ $6.20 per unit
+10 units @ $6.00 per unit
= $820

Cost of Goods Sold = Beginning Inventory + Purchases − Ending Inventory
= $650 + $760 (i.e., $248 + $512) − $820
= $590

or

Cost of Goods Sold (100 units)

20 units @ $5.50 per unit (from January 10 purchase)	$110
80 units @ $6.00 per unit (from January 22 purchase)	480
100	$590

AVERAGE COST

Average Cost per Unit = Cost of Goods Available ÷ Number of Units Available
for Sale   for Sale
= [$603 (from Exhibit 6—7) + $760] ÷ [110 + 120]
= $5.93 per unit (rounded)

Ending Inventory = Number of Units × Average Cost per Unit
= 130 × $5.93
= $771 (rounded to the nearest dollar)

Cost of Goods Sold = Beginning Inventory + Purchases − Ending Inventory
= $603 + $760 − $771
= $592 (or 100 units × $5.93 with a $1 rounding error)

EXHIBIT 6–9   (continued)

··················

or

Cost of Goods Sold   = Number of Units × Average Cost per Unit
                                  = 100 × $5.93
                                  = $593 ($1 rounding error)

LAST-IN, FIRST-OUT

Beginning Inventory   = 100 units @ $5 per unit + 10 units @ $5.50 per unit
                                   = $555 (from Exhibit 6–8)

Ending Inventory   = 100 units @ $5 per unit
                                       + 10 units @ $5.50 per unit
                                       + 20 units @ $6.20 per unit
                                   = $679

Cost of Goods Sold   = Beginning Inventory + Purchases − Ending Inventory
                                   = $555 + $760 − $679
                                   = $636

or

Cost of Goods Sold (100 units)
  80 units @ $6.40 per unit (from February 20 purchase) $512
  20 units @ $6.20 per unit (from February 5 purchase)   124
  100 $636

the Davis Company example, the following comparative gross profit figures result from selling 130 units for $1,690 in *January* (assuming a selling price of $13 per unit):

	FIFO		Average Cost		LIFO	
Sales		$1,690		$1,690		$1,690
Cost of goods available for sale	$1,315		$1,315		$1,315	
Ending inventory	(650)		(603)		(555)	
Cost of goods sold		(665)		(712)		(760)
Gross profit		$1,025		$ 978		$ 930

In this example costs rose throughout the period, and as a result the FIFO method produces the lowest cost of goods sold because it includes the oldest, and lowest, costs. Since the cost of goods sold is lowest, the income is highest. Correspondingly, the ending inventory using FIFO has the highest cost because it includes the latest, and highest, costs. In contrast, the LIFO method produces the highest cost of goods sold (and the lowest income) because it includes the latest, and highest, costs. The LIFO ending inventory is lowest because it includes the earliest, and lowest, costs. The average cost figures are between the FIFO and LIFO extremes because the ending inventory and the cost of goods sold include an average of both the lower and higher costs of the period.

The Davis Company was experiencing rising costs, but if costs were falling consistently, the opposite relationships would develop. The use of LIFO would produce a higher ending inventory and a lower cost of goods sold (and a higher net income) than FIFO. When costs fluctuate, no general relationships can be described.

It should be noted that there is a simplifying assumption included in the Davis Company example for January that has made the differences less than they might otherwise be. It was assumed that the beginning inventory consisted of 100 units at $5 under all three alternatives. Recall, however, that the beginning inventory of the period is the ending inventory of the previous period. Therefore, if each method had been used in the previous period and costs had changed during that period, the beginning inventory would be different under each of the alternatives, just as the ending inventory for January is different under each method. This relationship can be seen clearly in the calculations for February in which the beginning inventory is different in all three situations. This factor can become very significant when the LIFO cost flow assumption is used. If the number of units in the inventory increases during each period, the costs included in the beginning inventory are carried over for each period. As years pass, however, these costs may become very outdated. For example, many companies adopted LIFO in the late 1930s and others during the period of high inflation in the middle of the 1970s. Therefore, the inventories disclosed in today's balance sheets may include elements of costs from many years ago.

In summary, it is often said that FIFO takes a balance sheet approach by recording the inventory at a cost close to the current cost to replace the inventory (and therefore understates cost of goods sold). In contrast, LIFO takes an income statement approach by matching current costs against revenues (and therefore understates ending inventory).

Liquidation of LIFO Layers

Earlier it was stated that during periods of rising costs, use of LIFO will result in a lower income figure than FIFO or average cost. The one exception to this general rule is caused by the building up of "layers" of inventory under LIFO. To illustrate the concept of layers, consider the $679 February ending inventory for the Davis Company under LIFO, as illustrated in Exhibit 6–9. The inventory consists of 130 units comprised of three layers: the "base," or beginning, inventory of 100 units, which cost $5 per unit; a layer of 10 units added in January at a cost of $5.50 per unit; and a layer of 20 units added in February at a cost of $6.20 per unit. (Remember that we are only accounting for costs and are not suggesting that physical units purchased at those particular times remain in the

liquidation of
LIFU layer→ unit sale > unit purchase
#$ when→

inventory.) **A liquidation of LIFO layers occurs when a company using LIFO decreases the number of units in inventory over a period.** This occurs when unit sales exceed unit purchases during the period. As a result, costs assigned to the beginning inventory are included in cost of goods sold for the period. Following LIFO principles, the first costs included in cost of goods sold will be the last costs added to the inventory in a previous period. Therefore, the greater the decline in inventory, the older the costs that will be included in the cost of goods sold. In times of rising costs, these older costs will be lower and therefore income will be higher. **Liquidation profit is the additional profit that arises when a liquidation of LIFO layers occurs.**

To illustrate the concept of a liquidation profit when there is a liquidation of LIFO layers, suppose that the Davis Company has the following transactions in March:

> Purchased 100 units @ $7 per unit
> Sold 122 units

Since the number of units sold (122) exceeds the number purchased (100), there has been a liquidation of LIFO layers (22 units). The March ending inventory is 108 units (130 + 100 − 122) and has a cost as follows:

> 100 units @ $5 per unit = $500
> 8 units @ $5.50 per unit =   44
> March Ending Inventory $544

Therefore the March cost of goods sold is $835 ($679 + $700 − $544). Note that this cost of goods sold includes the following:

> 100 units @ $7 per unit = $700 (purchased in March)
> 20 units @ $6.20 per unit =   124 (purchased in February)
> 2 units @ $5.50 per unit =   11 (purchased in January)
> March Cost of Goods Sold $835

We can see that the March cost of goods sold includes costs incurred in February and January, thereby causing a LIFO liquidation profit. This profit is calculated, as follows, as the difference between the LIFO cost and the cost of purchasing units during the current period (i.e., March):

> Units purchased in February: 20 units × ($7 − $6.20) = $16
> Units purchased in January: 2 units × ($7 − $5.50)   =   3
> Total LIFO liquidation profit $19

Note that the company's income is higher because cost of goods sold includes older, and lower, costs, even though there may be no **economic substance to the higher income and the company would pay additional income taxes** (because of the higher taxable income reported under the LIFO conformity rule, discussed later in the chapter).

When LIFO is used for large inventories over a long period of time during which costs rise substantially, the effect of a LIFO liquidation may become very significant. The decision to liquidate, or not to liquidate, LIFO layers can be used as a strategy by management to manipulate income, as discussed later. However, there may be a valid reason for the liquidation. For example, the company may be unable to acquire inventory because of a strike by a supplier or the unavailability of raw materials. Also, many companies are adopting a "just-in-time" inventory system, which leads to a reduction in the desired quantities of inventory.

Income Measurement

For financial reporting, the basic criterion to be used for the choice of a cost flow assumption is to achieve a proper measurement of income through the process of matching appropriate costs against the revenues. Remember that there is no requirement that the assumed flow of costs be related to the actual physical flow of goods. Most companies would be expected to use a FIFO method for the physical management of inventory, reducing the likelihood of obsolescence. Such companies may use any of the alternative cost flow assumptions in their financial statements.

But what are "appropriate" costs? Unfortunately, there is no simple answer as to whether income is better measured by matching the *latest* costs incurred with revenue (LIFO) or by matching the *earliest* costs with revenue (FIFO). Both methods do match actual costs incurred against revenues, but **the major argument in favor of LIFO is that it matches the most recent costs as expenses against revenue.** The most recent costs are closer to replacement costs (cost to replace inventory in the current market) and therefore LIFO excludes from net income some (but not all) of the holding gain, so that net income reflects the earnings after capital has been maintained. **The holding gain (or inventory profit) is the difference between the historical cost and the replacement cost of the units sold.** It is an illusory profit that results from recording cost of goods sold at lower historical costs than the replacement cost of the units sold.

To illustrate this point, consider the Davis Company in *January*. If the company uses the FIFO method, it would be selling units and recording a cost of $5 per unit and a gross profit of $8 per unit during January (the $13 selling price less the $5 cost). The company has to replace the inventory during the month by paying $5.50 or $6 per unit, however. Therefore, $.50 or $1 of the profit must be used to buy the replacement units of inventory, and only $7.50 or $7 represents the real profit of the Davis Company. The holding gain is $.50 or $1 per unit sold. Since the holding gain cannot be distributed to the owners as dividends without reducing the ability of the company to replace the units of inventory sold, many users argue that the holding gain should be excluded from income. A more complete discussion of the problems of accounting under conditions of changing prices is included in Chapter 13.

Another factor to consider is that bonuses are often paid to management on the basis of reported income. This tends to discourage management from using LIFO in periods of rising costs because the lower reported income produces lower bonuses. In addition, a higher income results in higher earnings per share and a higher rate of return, factors that many users of financial statements consider important (as discussed in Chapters 10 and 14).

Income Manipulation

As we have seen, the liquidation of inventory under LIFO, whether intentional or not, results in higher income (assuming rising costs). Such a liquidation may be caused by economic factors beyond the control of the company, such as a strike or a scarcity of raw materials, or as a result of a management decision, such as the adoption of a "just-in-time" inventory system, which results in a permanent reduction in the size of the inventory. Also a liquidation may be deliberately created by delaying purchases. Intentional liquidation to increase income artificially is a significant concern. If a company is facing a period of lower profits, it can intentionally increase profits by liquidating inventory. This can be achieved by delaying purchases until after the end of the fiscal year.

Another form of manipulation is possible under LIFO. A company may influence its income by increasing its purchases. To illustrate, refer back to the Davis Company LIFO example for January in Exhibits 6–5 and 6–8 and assume that the company purchased an additional 40 units on January 29 at $7 per unit. Total purchases would then be $1,095 ($815 + $280). The ending inventory would then consist of 150 units (110 + 40) and have a cost of $775 (100 units at $5 each from the beginning inventory + 50 units at $5.50 each from the January 10 purchase). The cost of goods sold would be computed as follows:

Beginning Inventory + Purchases − Ending Inventory = Cost of Goods Sold
$500   + $1,095   − $775   = $820

Thus, purchasing additional units has increased cost of goods sold by $60 ($820 − $760) even though unit sales remain unchanged. **It is inconsistent with the revenue recognition principles for income to be affected by the purchasing activities of a company,** but it is an inevitable result of the LIFO method. The FIFO and average cost methods do not produce unusual results when inventory liquidation occurs, nor are they as susceptible to profit manipulation by management.

Income Tax Effects

As has been seen, LIFO produces the lowest *accounting* income under conditions of rising costs. Although it might be thought that management would consider it undesirable to report low income, it must be remembered that lower *taxable* income results in payment of lower income taxes. For example, according to their recent annual reports three long-time LIFO users—Amoco, General Electric, and U.S. Steel—have together saved more than $3 billion in taxes compared to what they would have paid using FIFO.

The use of LIFO for the computation of federal income taxes presents a special situation. **The Internal Revenue Code permits the use of LIFO for income**

[handwritten margin note: only can use LiFo for Tax purpose if you also use lifo for financial Statement]

tax purposes only if it is also used in the company's financial statements. This requirement is known as the **LIFO conformity rule.** Management might prefer to report the highest income for financial reporting when costs are rising by using FIFO even though, as discussed earlier, the income is overstated because holding gains are included. The LIFO conformity rule prevents management having "the best of both worlds" by using FIFO in the financial statements and LIFO for income taxes, in contrast to many situations in which different methods can be used (for example, when straight-line depreciation is used for financial statements and accelerated depreciation for income tax reporting). Management must decide whether it is willing to report a lower accounting income in order to achieve the advantages of the real economic benefits of reduced cash payments for income taxes.

This tax saving is a very strong, practical argument in favor of LIFO when costs are rising because companies avoid cash payments for income taxes and therefore have more cash available than they otherwise would for such items as dividends, paying employees, investing in property, plant, and equipment, or reducing liabilities. As would be expected, LIFO is used least in those industries that typically experience declining costs, such as the electronics industry.

The Tax Reform Act of 1986 established "uniform capitalization rules" that require companies to include in inventory certain costs that previously had been expensed as incurred. These costs include such items as purchasing, warehousing, and distribution costs, including related officer salaries and administrative costs. Because a cost must be capitalized for income tax purposes does not mean that capitalizing it for financial reporting is preferable, or even appropriate. Each situation should be analyzed based on the particular circumstances. In many situations the likely result is that inventory cost will be different between financial reporting and income tax reporting.

Inventory Valuation

The LIFO method produces a lower ending inventory value on the balance sheet (again assuming rising costs) because the oldest costs remain in this inventory. The balance sheet value of this inventory often bears little or no relationship to the costs of the current period or the costs that will be incurred to replace the inventory. This low valuation affects the computation and evaluation of current assets, working capital, and any financial ratios (discussed in Chapter 14) that include inventory, thereby reducing comparability between companies using LIFO and those using FIFO. Furthermore, comparability between two or more companies using LIFO is impaired because the inventory valuation depends on the year in which LIFO was adopted by each company. For example, if companies in the same industry adopted LIFO in different years, the beginning inventory in the year LIFO was adopted will include costs of different years. (The year of adoption is *not* a required disclosure.) In addition, if the companies increase their inventories by different amounts in later years, the additional LIFO layers will have been added at different costs.

The FIFO method produces a higher ending inventory value on the balance sheet (assuming rising costs) because it includes the latest costs. This value tends to approximate the costs that will be incurred to replace the inventory, but how closely depends on when the purchases included in the ending inventory were made and how fast costs are rising.

Additional Costs

The use of the LIFO method is more costly than the FIFO method because of the additional costs of record keeping and financial statement preparation. These costs result from the need to keep track of the LIFO layers for each type of inventory and from requirements imposed by the Internal Revenue Service. The dollar-value LIFO method alleviates some of these problems and is widely used. It is beyond the scope of the text, however. For a small company, these additional costs may be greater than the income tax savings that would result from the adoption of LIFO. For larger companies, however, the income tax savings are likely to exceed the additional costs (assuming rising costs), as is evidenced by the increase in the number of companies that use LIFO since 1973 (see Exhibit 6–12).

■ MANAGEMENT'S SELECTION OF AN INVENTORY COST FLOW ASSUMPTION

There are many factors involved in the selection of an inventory cost flow assumption. In most cases, however, the decision should focus on the expectation of future cost changes.

If the management of a company expects that costs will *rise* for several years, LIFO should be selected because it is a better measure of income. The LIFO conformity rule will allow the use of LIFO for income tax reporting and will save income taxes for the company (net cash will increase assuming that the tax savings exceed the additional costs of operating the LIFO system). Therefore, the financial reporting rules and the income tax rules are consistent.

If the expectation is that costs will *fall* for several years, the decision is not as simple. For financial reporting purposes, it can be argued that LIFO is still preferable because the latest (and lowest) costs should be included in cost of goods sold because the inventory can be replaced at those lower costs. For income tax purposes, however, the use of FIFO is preferable because the company pays less income taxes. Although a company could use LIFO internally and FIFO for income taxes, it is unlikely to do so because of the additional record-keeping costs it would incur. Therefore, if falling costs are expected, FIFO will be used. Unfortunately, this means that income tax considerations are determining the accounting principle used for financial reporting.

Arguments are sometimes made that LIFO should not be adopted even when costs are expected to rise because of the lower income that will result. The possible perception that the company is less successful might cause lower stock prices. However, efficient capital markets research, discussed in Chapter 14, has indicated that stock market prices are *not* affected by the selection of an inventory cost flow assumption.

Although our discussion has focused on FIFO and LIFO, many manufacturing companies that expect falling costs use the average cost flow assumption in their financial statements. This method is used because (1) the company operates a standard cost system (discussed in a managerial accounting book) for its budgeting and control and (2) it is unlikely to result in significantly more income taxes than FIFO.

■ CONVERSION OF FINANCIAL STATEMENTS FROM LIFO TO FIFO

As we have seen, in a time of rising costs companies may be expected to use LIFO because of the tax savings that can be realized. Many companies, however, continue to use a non-LIFO method, perhaps because they expect to experience declining costs for their inventories; for example, many high-technology companies have experienced declining costs for their inventory items over many years. Therefore, it is advantageous for the financial statement user who is interested in making comparisons among companies to be able to convert the financial statements of a company from LIFO to a non-LIFO method. Alternatively, it may be useful to determine the tax savings that have occurred because LIFO is used. Typically, it is possible only to convert a LIFO company to a non-LIFO method, and not a non-LIFO company to LIFO.

The conversion is made possible by the way in which companies disclose their inventory costs. Frequently, a company uses LIFO for income tax purposes but uses another method for *internal* accounting and reporting. The tax law, however, permits the use of LIFO for tax purposes only if it is also used in the company's published financial statements. Therefore, an adjustment must be made by the company to convert the internally reported inventory amounts to LIFO for external financial reporting. The inventory account, however, is usually not adjusted directly. Instead, a valuation adjustment is used. This adjustment has a variety of names but probably the most frequently used is "LIFO reserve." This term is inappropriate because there is no "reserve" established. A more descriptive term is "Valuation Allowance." For convenience, we will use the term *LIFO reserve* in this discussion. However titled, the amount must be disclosed in reports filed with the SEC.

The *total* amount of the LIFO reserve in the balance sheet (or disclosed in the notes) is the total difference on that date between the non-LIFO inventory cost and the same inventory at LIFO cost. That is, the inventory at LIFO is equal to the non-LIFO inventory less the LIFO reserve. The *change* in the LIFO reserve during the year is the difference between the non-LIFO cost of goods sold and the cost of goods sold under LIFO. That is, **the cost of goods sold under the non-LIFO method is equal to the cost of goods sold under LIFO minus (plus) the increase (decrease) in the LIFO reserve during the period.** Thus, the non-LIFO income is higher (lower) if the LIFO reserve increases (decreases).

To illustrate this process consider the alternative financial statements in Exhibit 6–10. The Stall Company could present a partial income statement for

EXHIBIT 6–10

STALL COMPANY
Gross Profit for 1993 Computed Under FIFO and LIFO

	FIFO		LIFO	
Sales		$15,000		$15,000
Cost of goods sold				
Beginning inventory	$ 2,000 *2100*		$ 1,000	
Purchases	10,000		10,000	
Cost of goods available for sale	$12,000		$11,000	
Less: ending inventory	(4,000) *4100*		(2,500)	
		(8,000)		(8,500)
Gross profit		$ 7,000		$ 6,500

Alternative Calculation:

FIFO Beginning Inventory − LIFO Beginning Inventory = $2,000 − $1,000
$\qquad\qquad$ = $1,000

FIFO Ending Inventory − LIFO Ending Inventory $\quad$ = $4,000 − $2,500
$\qquad\qquad$ = $1,500

LIFO Cost of Goods Sold − FIFO Cost of Goods Sold = Difference in the Ending Inventory −
$\qquad\qquad\qquad\qquad\qquad\qquad\qquad\qquad\qquad$ Difference in the Beginning Inventory
$\qquad\qquad\qquad\qquad\qquad\qquad\qquad\qquad\qquad$ = $1,500 − $1,000
$\qquad\qquad\qquad\qquad\qquad\qquad\qquad\qquad\qquad$ = $500[a]

Therefore:

FIFO Cost of Goods Sold = LIFO Cost of Goods Sold − $500
$\qquad\qquad\qquad\qquad$ = $8,500 − $500
$\qquad\qquad\qquad\qquad$ = $8,000

Using different terminology, the relationship may be expressed as follows:

LIFO Cost of Goods Sold = FIFO Cost of Goods Sold + (Ending LIFO Reserve − Beginning
$\qquad\qquad\qquad\qquad\qquad$ LIFO Reserve)

[a]The relationships can be derived in equation form as follows:

FIFO: $BI_F + P - EI_F = CGS_F$
LIFO: $BI_L + P - EI_L = CGS_L$
Subtracting: $CGS_F - CGS_L = (BI_F - BI_L) - (EI_F - EI_L)$
$\qquad\qquad\qquad\qquad$ = Beginning LIFO Reserve − Ending LIFO Reserve
$\qquad$ or $CGS_F = CGS_L$ − Increase in LIFO Reserve
$\qquad$ or $CGS_F = CGS_L$ + Decrease in LIFO Reserve

1993 under FIFO or LIFO, as shown. The sales and purchases are, of course, unaffected by the use of FIFO or LIFO. It is assumed that the company has experienced rising costs, and the LIFO inventories are lower than the FIFO inventories as shown. The LIFO cost of goods sold is greater than the FIFO cost of goods sold by $500.

To illustrate how calculations can be made by using only information available from published financial statements, suppose that the Stall Company used FIFO internally and LIFO for financial reporting and taxes and that it reported the following information in its financial statements:

BALANCE SHEETS

	12/31/93	12/31/92
Inventory at FIFO	$4,000	$2,000
Less: LIFO reserve	(1,500)	(1,000)
Inventory at LIFO	$2,500	$1,000

INCOME STATEMENT, 1993

Sales	$15,000
Cost of goods sold	(8,500)
Gross profit	$ 6,500

The purchases (or cost of goods manufactured) can be computed from this published information as follows:

LIFO:

$$\begin{array}{ccccc} \text{Beginning} & + \text{Purchases} & - & \text{Ending} & = \text{Cost of Goods} \\ \text{Inventory} & & & \text{Inventory} & \text{Sold} \end{array}$$

$$\$1,000 \quad + \text{Purchases} \quad - \quad \$2,500 \quad = \quad \$8,500$$

Therefore,

$$\begin{aligned} \text{Purchases} &= \$8,500 + \$2,500 - \$1,000 \\ &= \$10,000 \end{aligned}$$

Then for FIFO:

$$\begin{array}{ccccc} \text{Beginning} & + \text{Purchases} & - & \text{Ending} & = \text{Cost of Goods} \\ \text{Inventory} & & & \text{Inventory} & \text{Sold} \end{array}$$

$$\begin{array}{ccccc} \$2,000 & + & \$10,000 & - & \$4,000 & = \text{Cost of Goods} \\ & & & & & \text{Sold} \end{array}$$

Therefore,

$$\text{Cost of Goods Sold} = \$8,000$$

Instead of developing the information for two separate income statements, it is possible to compute the difference more directly as described earlier and as shown in the lower part of Exhibit 6–10. The difference between the two amounts for cost of goods sold is equal to the change in the differences between the beginning and ending inventory values under FIFO and LIFO. That is, the difference is equal to the change in the LIFO reserve for the period. The LIFO reserve increased by $500 ($1,500 − $1,000), and therefore FIFO cost of goods sold is lower by the amount of the increase and in total is $8,000 ($8,500 − $500).

Unfortunately, companies that use a non-LIFO method rarely, if ever, disclose the comparative LIFO values, so the possibility of converting non-LIFO values to LIFO amounts is rare. As discussed, LIFO companies usually disclose sufficient information to enable their financial statements to be converted to a non-LIFO method. If the company does not report the LIFO reserve directly, it may instead give the non-LIFO values of the inventory. Another reporting technique is to give the "replacement" or "current" cost of the inventory in the notes to the statements. Although these amounts would not be exactly the same as the FIFO inventory values, they may be used as approximate substitutes. For example, the Stall Company might disclose the current costs of its inventories as $4,100 on December 31, 1993, and $2,100 on December 31, 1992. In that case, the LIFO reserve has increased from $1,100 ($2,100 − $1,000) to $1,600 ($4,100 − $2,500) and the increase of $500 is again the difference in cost of goods sold.

Remember that the difference in the cost of goods sold also affects other items on the income statement. To continue the Stall Company example, LIFO cost of goods sold is $500 more than the FIFO amount. Therefore, the gross profit under LIFO is $500 lower and income before income taxes is $500 lower. Assuming an income tax rate of 30%, the income tax expense is $150 (30% × $500) lower and the net income is $350 ($500 − $150) lower.

The difference between the FIFO and LIFO inventory values (the total LIFO reserve) at any point in time is the total difference between FIFO and LIFO cost of goods sold since LIFO was adopted. Therefore, multiplying that amount by the average tax rate experienced by the company gives the total tax savings since LIFO was adopted. Also, the effect on total income (and retained earnings) can be computed by subtracting the tax savings from the LIFO reserve. For example, consider Mead Corporation's disclosures illustrated in Exhibit 6–13. The "inventory valued at replacement cost" (LIFO reserve) at December 31, 1989, was $217.3 million higher than LIFO. Therefore, since LIFO was adopted the cumulative LIFO cost of goods sold has been $217.3 million higher than FIFO cost of goods sold would have been. Also, income before income taxes has been lower by the same amount. Assuming a 40% average tax rate, the company has saved $86.92 million ($217.3 million × 0.40) of taxes since it adopted LIFO. Its cumulative net income and retained earnings are $130.38 million ($217.3 million − $86.92 million) lower because of the use of LIFO.

■ INCOME FLOWS AND CASH FLOWS

The discussion has focused on the impact of inventory values on income flows, but an understanding of the relationships between income flows and cash flows is also important. For example, a company may be profitable, but it may be suffering cash shortages from purchasing or producing extra inventory, or deteriorating liquidity from an increase in accounts payable.

Since the cost of goods sold and the beginning and ending balances of inventory normally are reported, the purchases (or production) of inventory can easily be calculated. If inventory has increased during the period, purchases (or production) of inventory must have been greater than the amount sold. Therefore, purchases (or production) can be calculated by *adding* the *increase* in inventory to the cost of goods sold. Similarly, a *decrease* in inventory would be *subtracted* from the cost of goods sold. Because the beginning and ending balances of accounts payable normally are reported, the cash payments can be calculated (assuming that accounts payable relates only to the acquisition of inventory). If accounts payable have increased during the period, cash payments must have been less than the costs of purchasing or producing the inventory. Therefore, cash payments can be calculated by *subtracting* the *increase* in the accounts payable from the purchases (or production). Similarly, a *decrease* in accounts payable would be *added* to purchases to compute cash payments for the period. Even if some of the purchases were paid in cash, these calculations provide the correct amount of the *total* cash payments.

The use of ratios, discussed in Chapter 14, can be helpful to users of financial statements. For example, the inventory turnover ratio is often used to determine the efficiency with which a company manages its inventory. This ratio is calculated as follows:

$$\text{Inventory Turnover} = \frac{\text{Cost of Goods Sold}}{\text{Average Inventory}}$$

In the example in Chapter 14, the ratio is calculated as 7.8 times per year, or an average holding period of 47 days (based on a 365-day business year). Of course, this ratio is affected by the particular cost flow assumption used by the company and, if using LIFO, by any liquidation of LIFO layers.

■ LOWER OF COST OR MARKET RULE

The requirement that inventory be recorded at its historical cost is modified in one situation. When the market value of the inventory falls below the cost, the inventory should be written down to its market value and the corresponding loss should be included in the income statement.[3] That is, **the inventory is recorded at the lower of its cost or market value.** The cost is the amount determined under the company's cost flow assumption. The use of the term *market value* may lead to confusion. It should be clearly understood that it refers to the cost of replacing the item and *not* the selling price.

The cost of replacing the item is known as the replacement cost. **The replacement cost is the cost that would have to be paid at the present time to purchase an item of inventory in normal quantities from the usual suppliers, including any transportation costs ordinarily incurred.** A decline in the replacement cost of the inventory may result from physical deterioration, obsolescence, or perhaps a declining price level.

For example, suppose that the Barnhill Company has 100 units of inventory for which it paid $50 per unit. If the replacement cost declines to $40 per unit, the inventory should be included in the balance sheet at $40 per unit because the $50 cost is an overstatement of the value of the inventory. Similarly, the

....

[3]There are upper and lower limits to the market value that can be used. See Nikolai and Bazley, *Intermediate Accounting*, 5th ed. (Boston: PWS-KENT Publishing Co., 1991), chap. 8.

tendency to keep things as they are. [handwritten]

EXHIBIT 6–11   Effect of conservatism on the income statement

Beginning Inventory + Purchases − Ending Inventory = Cost of Goods Sold

COST BASIS
Year 1: $1,000 + $10,000 − $2,000 = $ 9,000
Year 2: $2,000 + $12,000 − $3,000 = $11,000

decrease in MV [handwritten]

LOWER OF COST OR MARKET
Year 1: $1,000 + $10,000 − $1,500 = $ 9,500
Year 2: $1,500 + $12,000 − $3,000 = $10,500

company has lost $10 per unit by owning the inventory while its cost declined. If it had delayed the purchase, it could have acquired the inventory for only $40 per unit. The lower of cost or market method is an example of the application of the conservatism principle (briefly discussed in Chapter 4).

The conservatism principle holds that accounting principles should be developed so that there is little likelihood that assets or income is overstated. Therefore, losses are recognized when there is evidence to support their existence whereas gains are recognized when an actual transaction occurs. This principle does *not* state that assets or income should be understated, but when there is a doubt about the likely effect of an accounting method, the bias should be toward the conservative method. The rationale for the conservatism principle is that the users of financial statements are least likely to be misled if the least favorable alternative valuation is used; conservatism also tends to offset the optimistic view of management. Many users disagree with the conservatism principle, however, because they believe that accounting should strive to obtain the best valuation with a bias neither toward nor against conservatism.

It is also possible that conservatism may be unfair to present stockholders and biased in favor of prospective stockholders because of the lower valuation. Furthermore, since the long-term income of the company is the same whether or not conservatism is applied, reducing income or asset values in the current period will inevitably result in higher income in the future than would otherwise have been reported. To illustrate this situation, consider the relationships shown in Exhibit 6–11. If the *cost* basis is used, cost of goods sold is $9,000 and $11,000 in each of the two years. When the *lower of cost or market* method is used, it is assumed that the ending inventory of the first year is valued at the market of $1,500 instead of the cost of $2,000. This *lower* ending inventory value causes cost of goods sold to be *higher* by $500 and income before income taxes to be *lower* by $500. That is, the loss due to the decline in the value of the inventory is included in the income statement of the period. In the second year it is assumed that the market value of the ending inventory is *not* lower than the cost. Therefore, the lower beginning inventory value of $500 for the second year lowers the cost of goods sold for the period by $500 because the lower value of the *ending* inventory of the *first* year is also the lower value of the *beginning* inventory of the *second* year. Note that the total cost of goods sold for the two years is the same. The effect of the conservatism is to increase cost of goods sold in one period and reduce it in the second period.

Despite the arguments against the conservatism principle, it has affected several accounting practices, including the lower of cost or market method. The use of the lower of cost or market method is also consistent with the matching concept. The loss associated with the decline in value is recorded in the period of the decline, not in the period in which the inventory is ultimately sold.

Another argument in favor of the lower of cost or market method is based on the assumption that the relationship between cost and selling price remains fairly constant. That is, a common practice is to set the selling price at a certain percentage (called the *markup*) above the cost of the inventory. For example, if the Barnhill Company normally sells for $100 the units that cost $50, it is receiving a markup of 100% of cost. If the replacement cost of the inventory drops to $40, it might be expected that the selling price will drop to $80, thus maintaining the 100% markup on cost. Continuing to value the inventory at $50 per unit would reduce the markup to 60% ($80 ÷ $50 = 1.60). Use of the lower of cost or market method thus separates the loss on holding the inventory ($10) from the gross profit that results from selling the inventory ($80 − $40).

The lower of cost or market method is often used when inventory becomes obsolete. However, there are two practical problems that arise in such situations. First, it is often difficult to decide when an item of inventory has become obsolete. Second, the appropriate market value may be difficult to determine. Obviously such decisions require considerable judgment, often resulting in disagreements between the management and the company's auditor. Management, often reluctant to admit that obsolescence has occurred, is perhaps interested in selecting the period of the write-down in order to manage its income. For example, a company might prefer to write off inventory in a successful period in order to "conceal" its effect, or to write it off in an unsuccessful period so that the write-off is "ignored" in comparison to the other events.

The lower of cost or market method is normally applied separately to each item in inventory as indicated in the following example:

	Quantity	Unit Cost	Unit Market	Total Cost	Total Market	Lower of Cost or Market
Item A	100	$20	$18	$ 2,000	$ 1,800	$ 1,800
Item B	200	30	31	6,000	6,200	6,000
Item C	200	25	20	5,000	4,000	4,000
Item D	100	40	43	4,000	4,300	4,000
				$17,000	$16,300	$15,800

The value of the inventory under the lower of cost or market method applied to individual items is $15,800. In this case a loss of $1,200 ($17,000 − $15,800) reduces the asset value and income as follows:

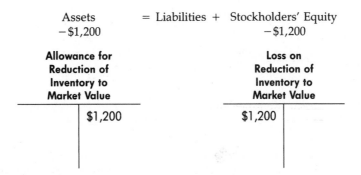

	Assets	= Liabilities +	Stockholders' Equity
	−$1,200		−$1,200

Allowance for Reduction of Inventory to Market Value		Loss on Reduction of Inventory to Market Value	
	$1,200		$1,200

The inventory is included in the current asset section of the balance sheet at its cost less the allowance as follows:

Inventory, at cost	$17,000
Less: allowance for reduction to market value	(1,200)
	$15,800

A less conservative method of application is to record the lower of cost or market of the inventory as a whole (this method is not allowed for income tax purposes). The inventory would be valued at $16,300 and a loss of $700 recorded under this alternative. In either case the loss would be included in either Cost of Goods Sold or in the Other Revenues and Expenses section of the income statement.

■ ESTIMATING INVENTORY COSTS

It is sometimes necessary to estimate the cost of inventory. If a company is using the periodic inventory system, the management may need to estimate the cost of the inventory during the year for the preparation of interim financial statements without going to the expense of taking a physical inventory. If a company experiences a loss of inventory in a fire or theft, or if the accounting records are destroyed, it may also need to estimate the remaining inventory (and corresponding loss) without taking a physical inventory. The gross profit method is often used in such situations.

Gross Profit Method

The gross profit method is used to estimate the cost of inventory by applying a gross profit rate (gross profit ÷ net sales) based on the income statements of previous periods to the net sales of the current period. The resulting estimated gross profit is deducted from the net sales to determine the estimated cost of goods sold. The estimate of the cost of goods sold is then subtracted from the cost of goods available for sale to provide the estimate of the ending inventory.

For example, suppose that the beginning inventory of a company for the current period is $12,000, net purchases are $28,000, and net sales are $50,000. If the gross profit rate based on the company's income statements of previous periods is 40%, the ending inventory of the current period is computed by four steps as follows:

Step 1: Gross Profit = Gross Profit Rate × Net Sales
$$= 40\% \times \$50,000$$
$$= \$20,000$$

Step 2: Cost of Goods Sold = Net Sales − Gross Profit
$$= \$50,000 - \$20,000$$
$$= \$30,000$$

Step 3: Cost of Goods Available for Sale = Beginning Inventory + Net Purchases
$$= \$12,000 + \$28,000$$
$$= \$40,000$$

Step 4: Ending Inventory = Cost of Goods Available for Sale − Cost of Goods Sold
$$= \$40,000 - \$30,000$$
$$= \$10,000$$

These relationships can be illustrated in income statement format as follows (steps 1–4 are listed in parentheses):

Net sales		$50,000 (100%)
Cost of goods sold:		
Beginning inventory	$12,000	
Net purchases	28,000	
Cost of goods available for sale (actual)	(3) $40,000	
Less: ending inventory (estimated)	(4) (10,000)	
Cost of goods sold (estimated)		(2) (30,000) (60%)
Gross profit (estimated)		(1) $20,000 (40%)

The validity of the gross profit method depends on the reasonableness of the estimate of the gross profit rate. Since the rate is based on the gross profit and net sales relationships of past periods, it is a valid indicator of the gross profit rate of the current period only if the gross profit relationships are largely unchanged. If it is known that conditions have changed, the gross profit rate should be adjusted so that the estimate of the cost of the ending inventory will be more accurate.

If the company is using the gross profit method to estimate a casualty loss, the amount of the loss would be calculated by subtracting the cost of any salvaged inventory from the estimated cost of the ending inventory.

■ DISCLOSURE OF INVENTORY VALUES AND METHODS

It has been seen that there are many alternative inventory valuation methods. The relative use of the different methods by 600 surveyed companies and the proportion of the inventory cost determined by LIFO are shown in Exhibit 6–12. The trend toward the increasing use of LIFO is clearly indicated, especially the numerous changes that occurred as a result of the high inflation from the mid

EXHIBIT 6–12 Inventory cost determination

	NUMBER OF COMPANIES					
	1988	1985	1982	1979	1976	1973
Methods						
First-in, first-out (FIFO)	396	381	373	390	389	394
Last-in, first-out (LIFO)	379	402	407	374	331	150
Average cost	213	223	238	241	232	235
Other	50	48	53	56	107	146
	1,038	1,054	1,071	1,061	1,059	925
Use of LIFO						
All inventories	20	26	28	20	9	8
50% or more of inventories	207	231	206	194	167	49
Less than 50% of inventories	90	83	88	94	84	78
Not determinable	62	62	85	66	71	25
Not used	221	198	193	226	269	440
	600	600	600	600	600	600

Source: Accounting Trends and Techniques (New York: AICPA, 1976, 1981, 1986, and 1989).

1970s to the early 1980s. There were more than 600 responses to the methods used, since many companies apply more than one method, as indicated by the categories listed in the second section.

Examples of the way in which three companies disclose the methods used for inventory are shown in Exhibit 6–13. Companies are required to disclose the inventory method, or methods, used, but they are not required to disclose the dollar impact of using one particular cost flow assumption as opposed to another unless LIFO is used. Nike, Reynolds Metals, and Mead are examples of companies using LIFO and disclose the use of lower of cost or market. Reynolds Metals also uses average cost or FIFO for a substantial portion of its inventory, and discloses the effect of a LIFO liquidation in 1989. Nike reports the effect of LIFO liquidation and the resulting change in income, as required by the SEC.

■ APPENDIX 1: PURCHASES DISCOUNTS

In this section, two methods of accounting for purchases discounts are discussed.

The Gross Method

Purchases discounts, which are offered by sellers to encourage prompt payment of amounts owed, should be deducted from the cost of purchases. One method of accounting for discounts is the gross method. **The gross method requires the**

EXHIBIT 6–13   Examples of disclosure of inventory values and methods

· · · · · · · · · · · · · · · · ·

NIKE, INC.

Note 2. Inventories:
Inventories by major classification are as follows:

	May 31,	
	1989	**1988**
	(in thousands)	
Finished goods	$216,033	$194,263
Work-in-process	4,708	2,523
Raw materials	2,183	1,684
	$222,924	$198,470

The excess of replacement cost over LIFO cost approximated $19,264,000 at May 31, 1989 and $14,792,000 at May 31, 1988. During 1989, 1988 and 1987, certain inventory quantities were reduced resulting in liquidations of LIFO inventory quantities carried at different costs prevailing in prior years as compared with the cost of 1989, 1988 and 1987 purchases. For the years ended May 31, 1989, 1988 and 1987 the liquidation of LIFO inventory quantities resulted in an increase (decrease) to cost of sales of approximately ($359,000), ($769,000) and $1,432,000 and to earnings per share of $.01, $.01 and ($.02) respectively.

REYNOLDS METALS COMPANY
NOTES TO CONSOLIDATED FINANCIAL STATEMENTS (in part):

Note A
Significant Accounting Policies (in part)

Inventories.   Inventories are stated at the lower of cost or market. Cost of inventories of approximately $267 million in 1989, $283 million in 1988 and $321 million in 1987 is determined by the last-in, first-out method (LIFO). Remaining inventories of approximately $504 million in 1989, $422 million in 1988 and $385 million in 1987 are determined by the average or first-in, first-out (FIFO) methods. If the FIFO method was applied to LIFO inventories, the amount for inventories would increase by approximately $546 million at December 31, 1989, $576 million at December 31, 1988 and $498 million at December 31, 1987. As a result of LIFO, costs increased by $9 million in 1989, $78 million in 1988 and $29 million in 1987. Costs decreased $39 million in 1989 resulting from liquidation of certain LIFO inventories carried at lower costs prevailing in prior years as compared with current costs.
    Since certain inventories of the Company may be sold at various stages of processing no practical distinction can be made between finished products, in-process products and other materials, and therefore inventories are presented as a single classification.

EXHIBIT 6–13 *(continued)*

....

MEAD CORPORATION

NOTES TO FINANCIAL STATEMENTS (in part):

A. Accounting Policies (in part):

Inventories. The inventories of finished and semifinished products and raw materials are stated at the lower of cost or market, determined on the last-in, first-out (LIFO) basis. Stores and supplies are stated at cost determined on the first-in, first-out (FIFO) basis.

B. Inventories

	December 31	
	1989	1988
(in millions)		
Finished and semifinished products	$235.3	$224.2
Raw materials	97.6	82.7
Stores and supplies	51.7	48.7
	$384.6	$355.6

For purposes of comparison to non-LIFO companies, inventories valued at current replacement cost would have been $217.3 million and $190.7 million higher than reported at December 31, 1989 and 1988, respectively.

---

inventory and accounts payable to be recorded at their gross amounts and the **purchases discount to be recorded when the discount is taken at the time of cash payment.** For example, suppose that the Wembley Company purchases merchandise for $1,000 and the seller offers a 2% discount if payment is made within 10 days. If the discount is not taken, full payment is required within 30 days. These terms are usually abbreviated as 2/10, n/30. The purchase and payment within 10 days are recorded as follows:

	Assets	=	Liabilities	+ Stockholders' Equity
	+$1,000		+$1,000	

Inventory (or Purchases)		Accounts Payable	
$1,000			$1,000

Assets		=	Liabilities	+ Stockholders' Equity
−$980	−$20		−$1,000	

Cash	Purchases Discounts Taken	Accounts Payable
$980	$20	$1,000

If purchases returns and allowances occur before payment is made, they are recorded at the gross amount before computing the discount. The Purchases Discounts Taken account is a contra account to Inventory (and therefore has a credit balance). It represents a reduction in the cost of the inventory. The discounts taken are normally recorded in a separate account so that management will know the total amount of the discounts taken. For example, if the discounts taken decrease over time as a proportion of purchases, it may indicate that the company is being less efficient in its payments and is losing discounts that it should have taken. If payment was not made within ten days, it is recorded as follows:

Assets	=	Liabilities	+ Stockholders' Equity
−$1,000		−$1,000	

Cash	Accounts Payable
$1,000	$1,000

The Net Method

An alternative method of accounting for purchases discounts is the net method. **The net method requires the purchases discount available to be deducted at the time of the purchase and the purchases and accounts payable to be recorded at their net amounts.** The net amount is the gross amount less the purchases discounts available. For example, the Wembley Company records the purchase of merchandise for $1,000 on terms of 2/10, n/30 at the net amount of $980 [$1,000 − (2% × $1,000)] as follows:

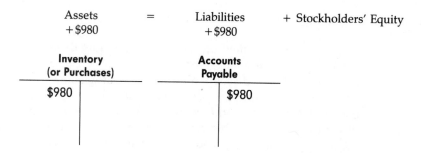

Assets	=	Liabilities	+ Stockholders' Equity
+$980		+$980	

Inventory (or Purchases)		Accounts Payable	
$980			$980

If payment is made within the discount period of 10 days, the payment is recorded as follows:

Assets	=	Liabilities	+ Stockholders' Equity
−$980		−$980	

Cash		Accounts Payable	
	$980	$980	

If payment is not made within the discount period, the cash paid is greater than the balance in the Accounts Payable account and the difference is recorded as Purchases Discounts Lost as follows:

Assets	=	Liabilities	+ Stockholders' Equity
−$1,000		−$980	−$20

Cash		Accounts Payable		Purchases Discounts Lost	
	$1,000	$980		$20	

If purchases returns and allowances occur before payment is made, they are recorded at the *net* amount in the usual manner. The Purchases Discounts Lost is included in the Other Revenues and Expenses section of the income statement as a financing expense (similar to interest expense).

Implications for Management

Although the gross method is used more frequently, the net method has definite advantages for the management of a company. The decision not to take advantage of a purchases discount may be very costly. Consider the Wembley Company example. If the company does not take advantage of the discount, it delays payment by 20 days (the 30 days allowed as a maximum minus the 10-day discount period). For this privilege it pays 2% extra. Therefore, the company is incurring a cost of 2% to delay payment by 20 days. This is an approximate annual cost of 36% (2% × 360 ÷ 20). It would be less expensive for the company to borrow money from a bank to pay for the purchases within the discount period.

Given the high cost of not taking a discount, management should be very interested in knowing if any discounts have *not* been taken. The net method indicates this fact directly because any discounts not taken are included in the Purchases Discounts Lost account. In contrast, the gross method includes in the Purchases Discounts Taken account only the discounts that were available and were taken. It does not indicate the discounts that were available but *not* taken.

■ APPENDIX 2: LAST-IN, FIRST-OUT, PERPETUAL

The illustrations of inventory cost flow assumptions in the chapter assumed the use of the *periodic* inventory system. In that system, cost of goods sold is determined by subtracting the ending inventory from cost of goods available for sale. When a company uses the *perpetual* inventory system, cost of goods sold is determined each time units are sold, and the ending inventory is calculated by subtracting cost of goods sold from cost of goods available for sale, as shown earlier. When FIFO is used, cost of goods sold and ending inventory are the same amounts under both the periodic and perpetual inventory systems. When the average cost method is used, an average cost is computed after each purchase and that cost is used to compute the cost of goods sold for each unit sold until the next purchase is made and a new average cost is computed. Therefore, differences will arise in the cost of goods sold and ending inventory between the periodic and perpetual inventory systems. The calculation of these differences is beyond the scope of this book. Under LIFO, more significant differences may be obtained depending on the inventory system being used.

The application of LIFO under a perpetual inventory system is illustrated in Exhibit 6–14. This illustration uses the same information as Exhibit 6–5 except that the 130 units were sold as follows: 40 units on January 6, 60 units on January 18, and 30 units on January 25. Note that the cost of goods sold and the ending inventory are different under the LIFO perpetual method ($705 and $610, as shown in Exhibit 6–14) and the LIFO periodic method ($760 and $555, as shown in Exhibit 6–8). The differences result from the difference in the assumptions about the timing of the sales. Under the periodic system the whole accounting

EXHIBIT 6–14

. . . .

DAVIS COMPANY

LIFO with a Perpetual Inventory System

INVENTORY INFORMATION

Beginning inventory, January 1	100 units @ $5.00 per unit	$ 500
January 6, sale	40 units	
January 10, purchase	50 units @ $5.50 per unit	275
January 18, sale	60 units	
January 22, purchase	90 units @ $6.00 per unit	540
January 25, sale	30 units	
		$1,315

CALCULATIONS

Cost of Goods Sold (130 units):

January 6	40 units @ $5.00 per unit	$ 200
January 18	60 units: 50 units @ $5.50	275
	10 units @ $5.00	50
January 25	30 units @ $6.00 per unit	180
		$ 705

Ending Inventory (110 units):

Ending Inventory = Beginning Inventory + Purchases − Cost of Goods Sold

$610 = $500 + $815 − $705

or

50 units @ $5.00 per unit (from beginning inventory)	$250
60 units @ $6.00 per unit (from January 22 purchase)	360
110	$610

period (a month in this example) is treated as a single unit, and the sales are assumed to occur after all the units have been purchased during the period. Therefore, the cost of goods sold includes the costs of the *latest purchases of the period*. Under the perpetual system the cost of goods sold is calculated when each sale is made and therefore includes the costs of the *most recent purchase(s) at that time*. For example, the first sale occurs on January 6, and under the perpetual system we assume that the cost of those units is taken from the beginning inventory of $5.00 per unit. Under the periodic system, however, since the number of units purchased by the company exceeds the number of units sold for the month, none of the cost of the beginning inventory is included in the cost of goods sold. Instead, the cost of the 130 units sold is taken from the cost of the purchases during the period.

QUESTIONS

1. Distinguish between the types of inventory accounts used for merchandising and manufacturing companies.

2. What are the cost components of each of the three inventory accounts of a manufacturing company?

3. Explain the differences between the perpetual and periodic inventory systems in terms of inventory quantity and cost. Does the use of the perpetual system eliminate the need for an inventory count?

4. What is the purpose of an inventory count? How often should an inventory be counted?

5. In which of the following types of businesses would a perpetual inventory system be practical: (a) an automobile dealer, (b) an auto parts store, (c) a bookstore, and (d) a restaurant?

6. What is the general rule used to determine if an item should be included in the inventory?

7. What criteria should be used to decide between alternative inventory cost flow assumptions?

8. How is the cost of the ending inventory determined under the FIFO cost flow assumption? Average cost? LIFO? Does the use of a particular method affect the quantities included in the ending inventory?

9. If costs are rising, which cost flow assumption will give the lowest net income in the current accounting period? The highest net income? The lowest ending inventory cost? The highest ending inventory cost? An ending inventory cost closest to the current replacement cost?

10. What are the advantages and disadvantages of the specific identification method?

11. What is the liquidation of a LIFO layer? What is a liquidation profit? How does a liquidation profit affect net income?

12. What is a holding gain? Why do some accountants believe holding gains should be excluded from net income?

13. Why might the management of a company choose the LIFO cost flow assumption even though its use causes the company's net income to be lower?

14. If the ending inventory for 1993 is valued at market under the lower of cost or market rule, what is the effect on the financial statements for 1993? 1994? What is the meaning of the term *market*?

15. Indicate the effect of each of the following errors on the balance sheet and income statement of the current and succeeding years:

    a. The ending inventory is overstated.

    b. Merchandise received was not recorded in the purchases account until the succeeding year although the item was included in inventory of the current year.

    c. Merchandise purchases were not recorded in either the purchases account or the ending inventory.

16. When a company changes from FIFO to LIFO, what effect does the change have on net income and working capital of the current year?

17. Appendix 1: Describe the difference between the gross method and the net method of accounting for purchases discounts. Which method provides more useful information to management? Explain.

18. Appendix 2: Discuss the cost flow assumptions of the LIFO inventory method. Under what conditions would the ending inventory differ under a perpetual and a periodic LIFO system?

PROBLEMS AND CASES
· ·

19. **Inventory Accounts for a Manufacturing Company.** The Fujita Company produces a single product. Costs accumulated at the end of the period are as follows:

not included

Raw material purchases	$ 54,000
Depreciation on manufacturing equipment	3,000
Sales commissions	20,000
Factory labor	36,000
Property tax on manufacturing equipment	3,500
Production supervisor's salary	20,000
Shipping costs on units sold	43,500
Materials used in production	81,400
Goods completed	115,000
Costs of units sold	150,000

Assume the beginning raw material inventory to be $77,500, the beginning finished goods inventory to be $128,500, and no beginning goods in process inventory.

Required Compute the closing account balances of each of the three inventory accounts: Raw Materials, Goods in Process, and Finished Goods.

20. **Cost of Goods Sold.** The following information for the Clark Company is available:

Beginning inventory	$10,000
Sales	62,000
Purchases	33,000
Ending inventory	12,200

Required Compute the cost of goods available for sale, the cost of goods sold, and the gross profit.

21. **Cost of Goods Sold.** The Redman Company uses the FIFO cost flow assumption, and the following summary information was available at the end of the year:

Beginning inventory	$20,000
Purchases	60,000
Sales	92,000
Sales discounts	3,000
Sales returns and allowances	2,000
Ordering costs	500
Ending inventory	22,000

The company followed a policy of expensing the ordering costs rather than allocating them to the units of inventory.

Required **1.** Prepare an income statement through to the calculation of gross profit.

2. The management of the company is considering changing from the FIFO method. It estimates that the ending inventory under average cost and LIFO would have been $20,000 and $14,500, respectively. What would the percentage increase or decrease in the gross profit be from changing to each alternative?

22. Cost of Goods Sold. The Perth Company uses the LIFO cost flow assumption and the periodic inventory system. The following summary information was available at the end of the year:

Beginning inventory	$15,000
Purchases	70,000
Sales	97,000
Sales discounts	1,000
Sales returns and allowances	5,000
Ordering costs	500
Ending inventory	28,000

The company followed a policy of expensing its ordering costs rather than allocating them to the units of inventory.

Required **1.** Prepare an income statement through to the calculation of gross profit.

2. The management at Perth is considering changing from the LIFO method. It estimates that the ending inventory would have been $33,000 under FIFO and $30,000 under average cost. What would be the percentage increase or decrease in the gross profit from changing to each alternative?

23. Beginning Inventory. The following information of the Mears Company is available:

Sales	$80,000
Purchases	30,000
Sales returns and allowances	900
Ending inventory	20,000
Cost of goods sold	38,000

Required Compute the beginning inventory and the gross profit.

24. Alternative Cost Flow Assumptions. The Foyt Company uses the periodic inventory system and makes the following purchases and sales during September.

Sept. 1	Inventory	200 units @ $27 = $5,400
Sept. 10	Purchases	100 units @ $31 = 3,100
Sept. 15	Sales	150 units
Sept. 22	Purchases	80 units @ $33 = 2,640
Sept. 28	Sales	50 units

Required Compute the ending inventory and the cost of goods sold if the company uses:

1. The FIFO cost flow assumption.

2. The average cost flow assumption.

3. The LIFO cost flow assumption.

25. **Alternative Cost Flow Assumptions.** The Nevens Company uses a periodic inventory system. During November the following transactions occurred:

Date	Transaction	Units	Cost/Unit
November 1	Balance	400	$3
November 8	Sale	300	
November 13	Purchase	200	4
November 21	Purchase	400	6
November 28	Sale	200	

Required Compute the cost of goods sold for November and the inventory at the end of November for each of the following cost flow assumptions:

1. FIFO

2. LIFO

3. Average cost

26. **Alternative Cost Flow Assumptions.** The Ginther Company made the following purchases and sales during January and February and uses the periodic inventory system:

Jan. 1	Inventory	100 units
Jan. 10	Purchases	50 units for $100 each
Jan. 20	Purchases	40 units for $102 each
Feb. 5	Purchases	20 units for $104 each
Feb. 18	Purchases	60 units for $108 each

Sales during January and February were 80 units and 100 units, respectively. The FIFO, average, and LIFO cost of each unit in the beginning inventory was $95, $93, and $62, respectively.

Required 1. Compute the ending inventory and the cost of goods sold for each month if the company uses:

    a. The FIFO cost flow assumption.
    b. The average cost flow assumption.
    c. The LIFO cost flow assumption.

  2. Which cost flow assumption provides the more realistic balance sheet valuation? Which provides the more realistic measure of income? Why?

27. Alternative Cost Flow Assumptions. The Johnson Company made the following purchases and sales during July and August and uses the periodic inventory system:

July 1	Inventory	250 units
July 8	Purchases	40 units for $20 each
July 27	Purchases	90 units for $21 each
Aug. 18	Purchases	50 units for $22 each
Aug. 24	Purchases	60 units for $23 each

Sales during July and August were 200 units and 150 units, respectively. The FIFO, average, and LIFO inventory cost of each unit in the beginning inventory was $20, $18, and $13, respectively.

Required **1.** Compute the ending inventory and the cost of goods sold for each month if the company uses:

    a. The FIFO cost flow assumption.
    b. The average cost flow assumption.
    c. The LIFO cost flow assumption.

    2. Which cost flow assumption provides the more realistic balance sheet valuation? Which provides the more realistic measure of income? Why?

28. Alternative Cost Flow Assumptions. The Habicht Company was formed in 1991 to produce a single product. The production and sales for the next four years were as follows:

	PRODUCTION		SALES		
	Units	**Total Costs**	**Units**	**Sales Revenue**	**Units in Ending Inventory**
1991	100,000	$200,000	80,000	$410,000	20,000
1992	120,000	234,000	110,000	550,000	30,000
1993	130,000	247,000	150,000	750,000	10,000
1994	130,000	240,500	120,000	600,000	20,000

Required Determine the gross profit for each year under each of the following periodic inventory methods:

1. FIFO.

2. LIFO.

3. Average cost (round unit costs to 3 decimal places).

29. LIFO Liquidation Profit. The Hammond Company adopted LIFO when it was formed on January 1, 1991. Since then, the company has had the following purchases and sales of its single inventory item:

Year	Units Purchased	Cost per Unit	Units Sold	Price per Unit
1991	10,000	$5	8,000	$12
1992	12,000	6	9,000	13
1993	15,000	8	14,000	16

In December 1994, the controller realized that because of an unexpected increase in demand the company had sold 22,000 units, but had only purchased 18,000 units during the year. In 1994 each unit had been sold for $19, and each unit purchased had cost $10. The income tax rate is 40%.

Required 1. If the company makes no additional purchases in 1994, how much will be the LIFO liquidation profit that it has to report?

2. If the company purchases an additional 7,000 units in December, 1994, how much income tax will the company save?

3. If the company purchases the additional 7,000 units, how much income tax has the company saved over the four-year period by using LIFO instead of the FIFO cost flow assumption?

30. FIFO Used Internally, LIFO Used Externally. The Grimstad Company uses FIFO for internal reporting purposes and LIFO for financial reporting and income tax purposes. At the end of 1993 the following information was obtained from the inventory records:

	1992	1993
Ending inventory, FIFO	$100,000	$140,000
Ending inventory, LIFO	80,000	115,000

Required 1. Record the effects of the adjustment on the accounting equation, assuming that the accounts are converted to LIFO at the end of 1993.

2. Indicate how the inventory value would be disclosed on the comparative balance sheets prepared at the end of 1993.

31. Conversion from LIFO to FIFO. The Rye Company disclosed the following information in its financial statements and accompanying notes:

	12/31/94	12/30/93
Inventory at FIFO cost	$160,000	$120,000
Less: LIFO reserve	(60,000)	(40,000)
Inventory at LIFO	$100,000	$ 80,000

Cost of goods sold in 1994 and 1993 was $400,000 and $375,000, respectively. Net income in 1994 and 1993 was $500,000 and $460,000, respectively. The income tax rate was 30% in each year.

Required **1.** Compute the amount that the cost of goods sold would have been in 1994 if the company had used FIFO.

2. Compute the amount that the net income would have been in 1994 if the company had used FIFO.

3. Compute the amount of income taxes that the company saved by using LIFO in 1994.

4. Assume that the company's tax rate has always been 30%; compute the amount of income taxes that the company has saved since it adopted LIFO.

32. Conversion from LIFO to FIFO. The Wembley Company disclosed the following information in its financial statements and accompanying notes:

	12/31/94	12/31/93	12/31/92
Inventory	$790,000	$680,000	$720,000

The company uses the LIFO inventory method. The current replacement costs of the inventory at 12/31/94, 12/31/93, and 12/31/92 were $180,000, $140,000, and $150,000 higher than the LIFO amounts, respectively. Cost of goods sold in 1994 and 1993 was $2,500,000 and $1,900,000, respectively. Net income in 1994 and 1993 was $2,000,000 and $1,700,000 respectively. The income tax rate was 30% in each year.

Required **1.** Compute the amount that the cost of goods sold would have been in 1994 and 1993 if the company had used a method other than LIFO. Which cost flow assumption is most consistent with your answer?

2. Compute the amount that the net income would have been in 1994 and 1993 if the company had used a method other than LIFO.

3. Compute the amount of the income taxes that the company saved by using LIFO in 1994 and 1993.

4. Assume that the company's tax rate has always been 30%; compute the amount of the income taxes that the company has saved since it adopted LIFO.

5. Explain the possible causes of any unusual amounts that you found in your analysis.

33. Errors. The Lerner Company uses a periodic inventory system and the following errors are discovered in the current year.

1. Merchandise with a cost of $17,500 was properly included in the final inventory, but the purchase was not recorded until the following year.

2. Merchandise purchases in transit have been excluded from the inventory, but the purchase was recorded in the current year on the receipt of the invoice of $4,300.

3. Merchandise purchases in transit have been omitted from the purchases account and the ending inventory. The purchases were recorded in the following year.

Required For each error indicate the effect on the ending inventory and the net income for the current year and on the net income for the following year.

34. Errors. The following errors are made by a company that uses the periodic inventory system.

1. A purchase on account is omitted from the purchases account and the ending inventory.

2. A purchase on account is omitted from the purchases account, but the ending inventory is correct.

3. The ending inventory is overstated, but purchases are correct.

Required Indicate the effect of the preceding errors on the income statement and the balance sheet of the current and succeeding years.

35. Errors. The accounting records of the Hill Company, which uses the periodic inventory system, showed the following information at the end of the year:

Beginning inventory	$ 21,500
Purchases	42,000
Sales	102,000
Sales returns	2,700
Ending inventory	22,000

Required 1. Using an income statement format, compute the cost of goods sold and the gross profit.

2. Suppose a mistake was made in taking the physical inventory and the ending inventory should be $18,000. Using an income statement format, compute the resulting cost of goods sold and the gross profit.

3. A purchase of $2,500 was erroneously recorded at $5,200. What is the effect of the error on the financial statements of the current year? (The answer to Requirement 3 is independent of the answer to Requirement 2.)

36. Errors. The accounting records of the Kirkpatrick Company, which uses the periodic inventory system, showed the following information at the end of the year:

Beginning inventory	$ 35,000
Purchases	90,000
Sales	160,000
Sales returns	2,000
Ending inventory	46,000

Required 1. Using an income statement format, compute the cost of goods sold and the gross profit.

2. Suppose a mistake was made in taking the physical inventory and the ending inventory has a cost of $40,000. Using an income statement format, compute the resulting cost of goods sold and the gross profit.

3. A purchase of $6,200 was erroneously recorded as $2,600. What is the effect of the error on the cost of goods sold, gross profit, and ending inventory? (The answer to Requirement 3 is independent of the answer to Requirement 2.)

37. Errors. The financial records of Burnett Co. for the year ended December 31, 1993, indicate the following:

Inventory at January 1, 1993, was understated by $4,000.

Inventory at December 31, 1993, was overstated by $3,000.

During 1993 the company received a $1,000 cash advance from a customer for merchandise to be manufactured and shipped during 1994. The $1,000 had been recorded as sales revenue. The company's gross profit on sales is 50%.

Net income reported on the 1993 income statement (before reflecting any adjustments for the above items) is $20,000.

Required What is the correct net income for 1993? (*AICPA adapted*)

38. Lower of Cost or Market. The Brabham Company had the following costs and replacement cost of units in inventory:

Item	Number of Units	Unit Cost	Unit Replacement Cost
804	100	$10	$ 8
603	150	12	13
331	320	8	5
928	70	20	22

Required **1.** Compute the value of the ending inventory under the lower of cost or market method, applied to the individual items.

2. How will the financial statements be affected by the application of the lower of cost or market method?

3. Show how the ending inventory would be reported on the balance sheet.

39. Lower of Cost or Market. The following information is taken from the records of the Aden Company:

Product	Group	Units	Cost/Unit	Market/Unit
A	1	300	$ 1.00	$ 0.80
B	1	250	1.50	1.55
C	2	100	5.05	5.25
D	2	200	6.50	6.40
E	3	80	25.00	24.60

Required What is the correct inventory value if the lower of cost or market is applied to each of the following?

1. Individual items.

2. Groups of items.

3. The inventory as a whole.

40. Lower of Cost or Market. The Seaman Company's ending inventory included the following items:

Item	Number of Units	Unit Cost	Unit Replacement Cost
A12B	50	$100	$90
L15C	100	76	83
P27X	200	50	55
W08S	400	10	9

Required 1. Compute the value of the ending inventory under the lower of cost or market rule applied to individual items.

2. Record the effects on the accounting equation of the reduction of the inventory to its market value.

3. Show how the ending inventory would be reported on the balance sheet.

4. If the lower of cost or market method is applied to the inventory as a whole, how would your answer to Requirement 1 change?

5. If at the end of the next year none of the items in inventory has a market value below cost, how will the financial statements for the second year be affected by the application of the lower of cost or market method in the first year?

41. Lower of Cost or Market. The Thodes Company's ending inventory included the following items:

Item	Number of Units	Unit Cost	Unit Replacement Cost
SP5	20	$500	$400
CX3	300	62	70
TL9	95	220	180
FN6	250	80	90

Required 1. Compute the value of the ending inventory under the lower of cost or market rule applied to the inventory as a whole.

2. Record the effects on the accounting equation of the reduction of the inventory to its market value.

3. Show how the ending inventory would be reported on the balance sheet.

4. If the lower of cost or market rule is applied to the inventory on an individual item basis, how would your answer to Requirement 1 change?

5. If at the end of the next year none of the items in the inventory has a market value below cost, how will the financial statements for the second year be affected by the application of the lower of cost or market method in the first year?

42. Gross Profit Method. On March 31, 1993, the Ireland Company needed to estimate its ending inventory for preparation of its first quarter's financial statements. The following information is available:

Inventory, January 1, 1993	$30,000
Purchases (net)	35,000
Sales (net)	85,000

An examination of past income statements indicates that a gross profit rate of 30% of net sales is appropriate.

Required Compute the cost of goods sold and the ending inventory.

43. Gross Profit Method. The Williams Company estimates its ending inventory for its quarterly financial statements by using the gross profit method. The following information is available:

	First Quarter	Second Quarter	Third Quarter
Inventory, January 1	$20,000		
Purchases	50,000	$55,000	$ 64,000
Purchases returns	1,000	2,000	1,000
Sales	98,000	93,000	102,000
Sales returns	2,000	1,000	3,000

The company used a gross profit rate of 40% of net sales in the first two quarters, but in the third quarter the company's estimated gross profit rate decreased 10%. The company did not increase its prices, however.

Required Compute the cost of goods sold and the ending inventory for each quarter.

44. Estimate of Inventory Lost in Theft. When Janet Guthrie arrived at her dress shop on the morning of June 15, 1994, she found that thieves had broken in overnight and stolen much of her merchandise. The agent of the Alright Insurance Company agreed to visit in the afternoon and promised he would write a check for the amount of the loss if she could verify it. Since it would be very time-consuming to take a physical inventory, Ms. Guthrie needed to make an estimate of the loss so that she could collect the insurance money and buy new merchandise. She asked for your help, and you agreed to look at her accounting records. She told you that the store had been in business since January 1, 1993. You obtain the following information:

Inventory, January 1, 1993	$ 5,000
Purchases (net), 1993	40,000
Purchases (net), 1994	30,000
Sales (net), 1993	80,000
Sales (net), 1994	45,000
Delivery charges on purchases, 1993	2,000
Delivery charges on purchases, 1994	1,500
Inventory, January 1, 1994	15,000

Required How much would you recommend that Ms. Guthrie settle for with the insurance company? What is the major assumption underlying your answer?

45. Inventory and Holding Gains. The Birkin Company uses the FIFO inventory cost flow assumption. The following amounts are included in the company's financial statements:

Inventory, January 1	$100,000
Purchases	300,000
Cost of goods sold	250,000
Inventory, December 31	150,000

The company sells only one product, and purchases and sales are made evenly throughout the year. The replacement cost of the inventory at January 1 and December 31 is $130,000 and $195,000, respectively. The cost of the company's purchases was 20% higher at the end of the year than at the beginning.

Required The owner of the Birkin Company asks you to analyze the above information and tell her the following:

1. How much would the cost of goods sold be if it were computed on the basis of the average replacement cost for the period?

2. What is the holding gain (inventory profit) included in the income computed on a FIFO basis?

3. Did the number of units in inventory increase or decrease during the year?

46. Appendix 1: Purchases Discounts. The Collins Company made purchases of $57,000 during the year on terms of 2/10, n/30. The company took advantage of the discount on 60% of the purchases. It paid for the remainder after the discount period had expired. The company uses the periodic inventory system.

Required 1. Record the effects on the accounting equation of the purchases and both payments under (a) the gross method and (b) the net method.

2. If half the purchases are still in the inventory at the end of the year, what is the cost of the ending inventory under both methods?

47. Appendix 1: Purchases Discounts. The Gurney Company purchased inventory for $24,000 on terms of 2/10, n/30. The company paid for half the purchase within 10 days and paid for the remainder after the discount period had expired. The company uses the periodic inventory system.

Required 1. Record the effects on the accounting equation of the above events using (a) the gross method and (b) the net method of accounting for purchases discounts.

2. If the company sold half the inventory for $31,000, how much would its gross profit be under each method?

3. How much would the gross profit be if the company deducted all the discounts available from the cost of the inventory under each method?

48. Appendix 2: Alternative Cost Flow Assumptions. The Moss Company uses the perpetual inventory system and makes the following purchases and sales during March:

Mar. 1	Inventory	100 units @ $ 8 = $ 800
Mar. 5	Purchases	50 units @ $10 = 500
Mar. 12	Sales	40 units
Mar. 23	Purchases	80 units @ $13 = 1,040
Mar. 26	Sales	70 units

Required Compute the cost of goods sold and ending inventory if the company uses:

1. The FIFO cost flow assumption.
2. The LIFO cost flow assumption.

49. Appendix 2: Periodic and Perpetual Inventory Systems and FIFO and LIFO. The Schukter Company makes the following purchases and sales during May:

May 1	Inventory	300 units @ $10 = $3,000
May 5	Purchases	120 units @ $11 = 1,320
May 12	Sales	160 units
May 22	Purchases	150 units @ $12 = 1,800
May 25	Sales	80 units

Required Compute the ending inventory and the cost of goods sold if the company uses:

1. The periodic inventory system and the FIFO cost flow assumption.
2. The periodic inventory system and the LIFO cost flow assumption.
3. The perpetual inventory system and the FIFO cost flow assumption.
4. The perpetual inventory system and the LIFO cost flow assumption.

50. Appendix 2: LIFO, Perpetual and Periodic. The inventory records of the Riedel Company showed the following transactions for the fiscal period ended June 30:

	Units	Cost/Unit
June 1 Inventory	700	$6.20
June 3 Purchases	400	6.40
June 15 Sales @ $12.00	300	
June 22 Sales @ $12.50	600	
June 30 Purchases	600	6.70

Required Compute the ending inventory and the cost of goods sold under the LIFO cost flow assumption, assuming both a perpetual and a periodic inventory system. Explain any difference in the final inventory valuations.

51. Appendix 2: Alternative Cost Flow Assumptions. The Garrett Company has the following transactions during the months of April and May:

Date		Transaction	Units	Cost/Unit
April	1	Balance	400	
	17	Purchase	200	$5.50
	25	Sale	150	
	28	Purchase	100	5.75
May	5	Purchase	250	5.50
	18	Sale	300	
	22	Sale	100	

The cost of the inventory on April 1 is $5, $4, and $2 per unit, respectively, under the FIFO, average, and LIFO cost flow assumptions.

Required 1. Compute the costs of goods sold for each month and the inventories at the end of each month for the following alternatives:

   a. FIFO periodic.
   b. FIFO perpetual.
   c. LIFO periodic.
   d. LIFO perpetual.
   e. Average cost (round unit costs to 2 decimal places).

2. Reconcile the difference between the LIFO periodic and the LIFO perpetual results.

52. **Appendix 2: Alternative Cost Flow Assumptions.** The Totman Company has the following transactions during the months of January and February:

Date		Transaction	Units	Cost/Unit
January	1	Balance	100	
	10	Purchase	50	$25
	22	Sale	40	
	28	Purchase	60	27
February	4	Purchase	30	28
	14	Sale	40	
	23	Sale	20	

The cost of the inventory at January 1 is $24, $23, and $15 per unit, respectively, under the FIFO, average, and LIFO cost flow assumptions.

Required 1. Compute the cost of goods sold for each month and the inventories at the end of each month for the following alternatives:

   a. FIFO periodic.
   b. FIFO perpetual.
   c. LIFO periodic.
   d. LIFO perpetual.
   e. Average cost (round unit costs to 2 decimal places).

2. Reconcile the difference between the LIFO periodic and the LIFO perpetual results.

3. If the company had purchased an additional 25 units for $30 each on February 27, compute the cost of goods sold for February under FIFO periodic and LIFO periodic.

ANNUAL REPORT PROBLEMS

53. LIFO. The 1976 financial statements of the Ford Motor Company included the following note:

Note 1 (in part): Inventory valuation. Inventories are stated at the lower of cost or market. In 1976 the company changed its method of accounting from first-in, first-out (FIFO) to last-in, first-out (LIFO) for most of its U.S. inventories.

    The change to LIFO reduced net income in 1976 by $81 million or $0.86 a share. There is no effect on prior years' earnings resulting from the change to LIFO in 1976 and, accordingly, prior years' earnings have not been restated. If the FIFO method of inventory accounting had been used by the company, inventories on December 31, 1976, would have been $166 million higher than reported.

Required 1. What arguments must have been used in favor of LIFO for the management of Ford to accept a reduction in net income of $81 million?

2. What disadvantages are likely to result from the adoption of LIFO?

3. Why is the effect on earnings $81 million when the effect on the inventory valuation is $166 million?

4. Would your answers to Requirements 1 and 2 change if you were discussing a change to LIFO for a Ford dealer?

54. FIFO and LIFO. Safeway Stores is the nation's largest grocery chain. The following excerpts are from its 1988 annual report relating to inventories (in thousands of dollars):

	1988	1987
Merchandise inventories		
FIFO cost	$1,136,044	$1,054,740
Less LIFO reserves	26,537	9,465
	$1,109,507	$1,045,275

Note A. Summary of Significant Accounting Policies (in part):
Merchandise Inventories: Approximately 55 and 51 percent of consolidated merchandise inventories are valued on a last-in, first-out (LIFO) basis at year-end 1988 and 1987, respectively. Inventories not valued on a LIFO basis are valued at the lower of cost on a first-in, first-out (FIFO) basis or replacement market. Inventories on a FIFO basis include meat and produce in the U.S. and all inventories of foreign subsidiaries. Application of the LIFO method resulted in increases in cost of goods sold of $17,100 in 1988 and $9,800 in 1987.

Required 1. Why is a LIFO reserve account used? Use inventory and retained earnings T-accounts to explain the financial statement impact from using the LIFO method in each year. Use the 34% statutory income tax rate.

2. Compute the following ratios for both the LIFO and FIFO methods with this

information excerpted from Safeway's 1988 financial statements (in thousands of dollars). Are the differences significant in each year?

a. Profit margin equals net income divided by net sales.
b. Return on assets equals net income divided by average total assets.

Use the following data in computing these ratios (in thousands of dollars):

	1988	1987
Net income	$ 31,195	$ (487,676)
Sales	13,612,393	18,301,265
Average total assets	4,371,686	4,917,479

3. Why are only meats and produce on a FIFO basis in U.S. stores?

55. **FIFO and LIFO.** The following excerpts are from Amoco Corporation's 1988 annual report relating to inventories (in millions of dollars).

Note 1. Accounting Policies (in part):
Inventories: Inventories are carried at the lower of current market value or cost. Cost is determined under the last-in, first-out (LIFO) method for the majority of inventories of crude oil, petroleum products, and chemical products. The costs of remaining inventories are determined on the first-in, first-out (FIFO) or average cost methods.

Note 4. Inventories:
Inventories at December 31, 1988 and 1987, are shown in the following table:

	1988	1987
Crude oil and petroleum products	$ 385	$310
Chemical products	364	289
Other products and merchandise	39	31
Minerals and supplies	277	269
	$1,065	$899

Inventories carried under the LIFO method represented approximately 52 percent of total year-end inventory carrying values in both 1988 and 1987. It is estimated that inventories would have been approximately $1,100 higher than reported on December 31, 1988, and approximately $1,500 higher on December 31, 1987, if the quantities valued on the LIFO basis were instead valued on the FIFO basis.

Required 1. Why does Amoco use both LIFO and FIFO methods of inventory? Is this permissible under generally accepted accounting principles?

2. Assume FIFO was used in all past periods instead of LIFO. Use T-accounts to show the impact on the balance sheet for 1988 if FIFO, rather than LIFO, were used. Compute the impact on net income and earnings per share ($2,063 million and $4.00, respectively, in 1988). Assume a 34% income tax rate. Would such a conversion be material to net income?

3. How much did Amoco save in income taxes by using LIFO in 1988? How much has Amoco saved in income taxes since it adopted LIFO?

56. FIFO and LIFO. The following excerpts are from Eastman Kodak's 1988 annual report relating to inventories (in millions of dollars):

Major Accounting Policies (in part):
Inventories: Inventories are valued at cost, which is not in excess of market. The cost of most U.S. inventories is determined by the last-in, first-out (LIFO) method. The cost of other inventories is determined by the first-in, first-out (FIFO), or average cost method.

Inventories: Inventories at year-end consisted of the following:

	1988	1987
At average cost		
Finished goods	$1,729	$1,371
Work in process	1,261	935
Raw material and supplies	1,011	806
	4,001	3,112
LIFO reserve	(976)	(934)
	$3,025	$2,178

Required 1. Why does Kodak use a LIFO reserve account?

2. Assuming no changes in the physical amounts of U.S. inventories in 1988, how much inflation or deflation occurred in Kodak's inventories in 1988?

3. Use T-accounts to analyze the impact on the balance sheet for 1988 if FIFO, rather than LIFO, was used in all past periods. Assume that the income tax rate is 34%. Would such a conversion be material to the net income of $1,397 in 1988?

57. FIFO and LIFO. General Signal Corp. is a leader in instrumentation and control technology for semiconductor production, telecommunications, industrial automation, energy management, and rail transportation. The following are excerpts from its annual reports (in thousands of dollars):

	1988	1987	1986
Net sales	$1,760,209	$1,603,026	$1,583,368
Cost of sales	1,266,701	1,151,503	1,114,564
Net earnings	25,198	69,378	74,622
Inventories (note 2)	$ 372,823	$ 343,064	$ 360,382
Total assets	1,396,600	1,397,397	1,458,106
Note 2. Inventories:			
Finished goods	$ 97,275	$ 92,633	$ 103,405
Work in progress	142,223	133,827	126,667
Raw materials	177,838	157,212	167,972
Total FIFO cost	$ 417,336	$ 383,672	$ 398,044

Excess of FIFO cost			
over LIFO inventory	(44,513)	(40,608)	(37,662)
Net carrying value	$ 372,823	$ 343,064	$ 360,382

Inventories are stated at the lower of cost or market. Certain domestic inventories are valued using the last-in, first-out (LIFO) method. Remaining inventories are valued using the first-in, first-out (FIFO) method. The effect on net earnings of converting inventories from FIFO to LIFO was not significant in 1987. Of the net carrying value of inventories, those valued on a LIFO basis were approximately $161,715, $151,149, and $165,396 at December 31, 1988, 1987, and 1986, respectively.

Required 1. Do you agree with management's note that the conversion of inventories from FIFO to LIFO was not significant in 1987? Include LIFO and FIFO ratios for profit margin and return on total assets in your answer. Ignore income taxes.

2. Assuming insignificant changes in inventory quantities in 1988, was there an inventory cost inflation problem for General Signal in 1988? Include the inventory turnover ratio in your calculations.

3. How much cash has General Signal saved by using LIFO for federal income tax purposes as of the end of 1988? Use the statutory federal income tax rate of 34%.

4. Is there a material effect if General Signal is converted back to FIFO in 1988? Include LIFO and FIFO ratios for profit margin and return on total assets in your answer. Ignore income taxes.

58. **Inventory Methods and Comparability.** You are attempting to compare the company profitability of Sara Lee and Quaker Oats in 1988. The following inventory disclosures are included in the respective annual reports (in millions of dollars):

Sara Lee Inventories

	1988	1987
Finished goods	$ 674	$ 641
Work in process	109	86
Materials and supplies	344	285
Total	$1,127	$1,012

Inventories are valued at the lower of cost (approximately 37% at last-in, first-out and the remainder at first-in, first-out in 1988) or market. Inventories recorded at LIFO are $33 at year end 1988, and $24 at year end 1987, lower than their respective FIFO valuation. Components of inventory include materials, labor, and manufacturing costs.

Quaker Oats Inventories

	1988	1987
Finished goods	$396	$359
Grain and raw materials	154	144
Packaging materials and supplies	39	37
Total	$589	$540

Inventories are stated at the lower of cost or market, using various cost methods, and include the cost of raw materials, labor and overhead. The percentage of 1988 year-end inventories valued using each of the methods is as follows: average method – 21%; LIFO – 65%; and FIFO – 14%. If the LIFO method of valuing certain inventories were not used, total inventories would have been $60 and $24 higher than reported at year-end 1988 and 1987, respectively.

Additional 1988 Data Extracted from Both Annual Reports:

	Sara Lee	Quaker Oats
Net income	$ 325	$ 203
Sales	10,424	5,724
Total assets	5,012	3,222

Required 1. Compute the 1988 company profitability ratios of profit margin and return on total assets for both Sara Lee and Quaker Oats. First, compute these ratios with the amounts in the annual reports. Then, recompute the ratios after converting both companies to an estimated FIFO inventory method. Use a 30% income tax rate and round to the nearest million dollars. Were these conversions material?

2. Which company had the best profitability performance? Why?

59. Classification of Inventories. United States Tobacco Company is one of the largest tobacco companies in the world. The following excerpts are from its 1988 annual report relating to inventories (in thousands of dollars):

Inventories

	1988	1987
Leaf tobacco	$ 85,934	$ 76,208
Products in process and finished goods	72,225	70,764
Other materials and supplies	16,663	15,275
	$174,822	$162,247

At December 31, 1988 and 1987, $83,100 and $73,600 of inventories were valued using the LIFO method. The current costs of these inventories were greater than the amounts at which these inventories are carried in the Consolidated Statement of Financial Position by $24,000 and $15,800, respectively.

Summary of Significant Accounting Policies (in part):

Inventories: Inventories are stated at lower of cost or market. The major portion of leaf tobacco and briar inventory costs is determined by the last-in, first-out (LIFO) method. The cost of the remaining inventories is determined by the first-in, first-out (FIFO) and average cost methods. Leaf tobacco and wine inventories are included in current assets as a standard industry practice notwithstanding the fact that such inventories are carried for several years for the purpose of curing and aging.

Required 1. Is the treatment of leaf tobacco and wine as current assets in accordance with generally accepted accounting principles?

2. Would the alternative treatment of leaf tobacco as a long-term asset significantly affect the current ratio? (Current assets are $291,006,000, current liabilities are $69,935,000 at the end of 1988, and the current ratio is current assets divided by current liabilities.) Would your answer change if FIFO was used for leaf tobacco inventories? Which alternative would you choose if the company had a bank loan with a clause or covenant that specified that the company had to maintain a 4.5 current ratio or the loan could be immediately due?

60. **Change to FIFO and LIFO Liquidation.** The following excerpts are from Dow Chemical's 1985 and 1988 financial statements concerning inventories and the related auditor's report (in millions of dollars, except earnings per share amounts).

1985
Opinion of Independent Public Accountants (in part):
In our opinion, such financial statements present fairly the financial position of The Dow Chemical Company . . . and the results of their operations and the changes in their financial position . . . in conformity with generally accepted accounting principles applied on a consistent basis, after restatement for the change, with which we concur, in the method of accounting for foreign inventories as described in Note A to the consolidated financial statements.

Note A. Accounting Change:
As a result of continued high inflation rates in many foreign countries and the devaluation of their currencies against the U.S. dollar, Dow's worldwide use of the last-in, first-out (LIFO) inventory accounting method no longer yields the best matching of costs and revenue. Effective January 1, 1985, management has decided to change its method of accounting for most of the foreign inventories from LIFO and adopt the first-in, first-out (FIFO) or average cost methods to provide a better matching of costs and revenue, consistent with conservative accounting practices.

   Inventories in the United States and Dow's foreign hydrocarbon inventories remained on LIFO. On a restated basis, net income was reduced $25 or $.13 per share and $6 or $.03 per share in 1984 and 1983, respectively, and $78 or $.41 per share and $34 or $.18 per share in 1982 and 1981, respectively.

1988
Inventories
Inventories are stated at the lower of cost or market. The cost of substantially all domestic and foreign hydrocarbon inventories were determined by the last-in, first-out method. The cost of the Company's operating supplies and nonhydrocarbon foreign inventories were determined by the first-in, first-out or average cost method.

   The amount of reserve required to reduce inventories from the first-in, first-out basis to the last-in, first-out basis at December 31, 1988 and 1987 was $101 and $97, respectively.

   At December 31, 1988 and 1987, 45% of the total inventories were valued on a LIFO basis.

Required 1. Do you concur with Dow and its auditor in the change to FIFO for nonhydrocarbon inventories? How can the use of FIFO "provide a better matching of costs and revenue, consistent with conservative accounting practices"? If so, why didn't Dow use FIFO for all its inventories?

2. Was there a material impact on Dow's 1988 net income of $2,398 million from not

using LIFO for nonhydrocarbon foreign inventories and operating supplies? Ignore income taxes.

61. LIFO. The following excerpts are from K Mart's 1989 annual report relating to inventories (in millions of dollars).

Merchandise Inventories:
A summary of inventories by method of pricing and the excess of current cost over stated LIFO value follows:

	January 25, 1989	1988
Last-in, first-out cost (not in excess of market)	$5,090	$5,104
Lower of cost (first-in, first-out) or market	581	467
Total	$5,671	$5,571
Excess of current cost over stated LIFO value	$ 898	$ 738

Required **1.** Why does K Mart use the end of January, rather than December, for its fiscal year?

2. Is there a material difference between using the LIFO and FIFO methods of inventory for K Mart? Why or why not? (Cost of merchandise sold was $19,914 million and $18,564 million in 1989 and 1988, respectively and net income was $803 million and $692 million in 1989 and 1988, respectively.)

3. For another perspective concerning the difference between LIFO and FIFO in periods of changing prices, calculate the following ratio: Inventory turnover equals cost of goods sold divided by average inventory. Use ending, rather than average, inventory in the turnover calculations since no 1987 inventory amount was given.

62. Capitalization of Inventory Costs and Pricing for Inflation. The following excerpts are from General Electric's (GE) 1988 annual report (in millions of dollars):

Note 1. Summary of Significant Accounting Policies (in part):
Inventories. The values of most inventories are determined on a last-in first-out, or LIFO, basis and do not exceed realizable values. Effective January 1, 1987, GE changed its accounting procedures to include in inventory certain manufacturing overhead costs previously charged directly to expense. Among the more significant types of manufacturing overhead included in inventory as a result of the change are (1) depreciation of plant and equipment; (2) pension and other benefits of manufacturing employees; and (3) certain product-related engineering expenses. GE believes this change was preferable because it provides a better matching of production costs with related revenues in reporting operating results. In accordance with generally accepted accounting principles, the cumulative effect of this change for periods prior to January 1, 1987 ($281 after providing for taxes of $215) is shown separately in 1987 in the Statement of Earnings. There was virtually no effect from this change on 1987 results after recording the cumulative effect, and the pro forma effect on prior-years results was immaterial.

Note 16. GE Inventories

	1988	1987
Raw materials and work in process	$5,603	$5,515
Finished goods	2,863	2,546
Unbilled shipments	246	280
	8,712	8,341
Less revaluation to LIFO	(2,226)	(2,076)
LIFO value of inventories	$6,486	$6,265

LIFO revaluations increased $150 in 1988 primarily because of price increases. LIFO revaluations increased $324 in 1987, mostly related to the accounting change described in note 1, but decreased in total by $104. Included in these changes were decreases of $23, $22, and $51 (1988, 1987, and 1986, respectively) because of lower inventory levels. In 1988 and 1987, there was a net current-year price increase but in 1986 there was a price decrease. About 86% of total inventories is valued using the LIFO method of inventory accounting.

Management's Discussion of Earnings (in part):

The Consolidated Statement of Earnings shows that revenues were $50,100 in 1988 compared with $48,200 in 1987 and $42,000 in 1986. GE sales for 1988 were $38,800, 1% less than the year before. Total volume of shipments in 1988 was down about 2%, but the effect was partly offset by higher prices in some markets.

Required 1. Do you agree with GE that the capitalization of the additional costs to inventories "provides a better matching of production costs with related revenues in reporting operating results"? Do you agree with GE that "there was virtually no effect from this change on 1987 results after recording the cumulative effect"? Net earnings were $3,386 million in 1988, $2,915 million in 1987, and $2,492 million in 1986.

2. GE mentioned that lower sales volume in 1988 was partly offset by higher sales prices. If GE wanted to completely offset the effect of inflation or the higher prices it paid for its inventory, by what percent would GE have had to raise its own sales prices in 1988? Repeat the analysis for 1987.

Property, Plant, and Equipment; Intangibles; and Natural Resources

After reading this chapter, you should understand

- Characteristics of property, plant, and equipment
- Acquisition cost of property, plant, and equipment
- Concept of depreciation
- Calculation of the amount of depreciation under the straight-line, sum-of-the-years'-digits, double-declining-balance, and activity methods
- Depreciation for income tax purposes
- Accounting for expenditures incurred after the acquisition of property, plant, and equipment

- Characteristics of intangible assets
- Nature of research and development costs
- Patents, trademarks and tradenames, franchises, computer software costs, organization costs, and goodwill
- Natural resource assets
- Difference between cost depletion and percentage depletion
- Disposal by sale or exchange of property, plant, and equipment (Appendix)

Property, plant, and equipment are very important components of a company's operating activities. In physical terms, they include assets that are necessary for a company to conduct its business, such as land, office buildings, factories, machinery, equipment, retail stores, office equipment, warehouses, and delivery vehicles. In financial terms, property, plant, and equipment are usually a major portion of the total assets of a company, and therefore an understanding of the accounting principles used is essential to an understanding of financial statements. Intangible and natural resource assets are discussed later in the chapter.

SECTION A Property, Plant, and Equipment

 ■ **CHARACTERISTICS**

Property, plant, and equipment are the long-term physical assets acquired for use in the operations of a company. An asset classified as property, plant, and equipment must have the following three characteristics:

1. *The Asset Must Be Used in the Operating Activities of the Company.* To be included in property, plant, and equipment an asset does not have to be used continuously. For example, machinery owned for standby purposes in case of breakdowns would be included in the category. Also note that a particular kind of item will be categorized differently depending on the type of company. For example, an automobile owned by a car dealer that is intended for resale is included in inventory, whereas the same type of car owned by a company for use by employees would be included in property, plant, and equipment. Similarly, land owned by a real estate company that is intended for resale is included in inventory, whereas similar land on which a company builds a warehouse is categorized as property, plant, and equipment. Land held for speculative purposes or for future use as a building site would be classified as an investment.

2. *The Asset Must Have a Life of More Than One Year.* The asset represents a bundle of future services that will be received by the company over the life of the asset. To be included in property, plant, and equipment, the benefits must extend for more than one year, and therefore the asset is distinguished from other assets, such as supplies or inventory, that are expected to be consumed within one year or the operating cycle, whichever is longer. For example, a truck may have an expected life of 100,000 miles and the company will receive the benefits from operating the truck over more than a year. In addition, a company owning a building can expect to receive benefits from that building for more than a year.

3. *The Asset Must Be Tangible in Nature.* The asset must have a physical substance that can be seen and touched. Intangible assets, in contrast, do not have a physical substance.

 ■ **ACQUISITION COST OF PROPERTY, PLANT, AND EQUIPMENT**

The acquisition cost of an asset includes all the expenditures that are necessary and reasonable to acquire the asset and prepare it for its intended use. For an asset included in property, plant, and equipment these costs include the following:

1. The contract price less any discounts available

2. Transportation costs

3. Sales tax

4. Installation and testing costs

5. Other related necessary and reasonable costs

The contract (invoice) price is used rather than the list price because it represents the actual cost paid for the asset. The list price may only be an advertised price that is used as a basis for negotiating the contract price. Cash discounts, whether taken or not, *should* be subtracted from the contract price. If they are not taken, they should be treated as an interest (or financing) expense because management decided to forego early payment. The added cost should not be included in the cost of the asset because it was not a necessary cost of the acquisition. If the amount is not material, some companies do not deduct discounts that are not taken from the acquisition cost.

Transportation costs incurred by the company are included in the cost of the asset. Installation and testing costs include the costs of salaries and materials directly associated with these activities. Thus these costs are included in the cost of the asset and not in salaries expense or cost of goods sold. Costs that are unnecessary and unreasonable, such as damage during transportation, are excluded from the cost of the asset and are recorded as an expense of the period (unless reimbursed by the transportation company or the supplier).

A company often purchases many low cost items that benefit future periods such as typewriters and filing cabinets. These items should be included as property, plant, and equipment and then depreciated over their useful lives (as discussed later). Many companies, however, expense such items in the period of acquisition because the cost is not *material* and the *benefits do not exceed the costs* involved in the accounting procedures. Companies typically develop a policy that defines a minimum dollar amount for an acquisition to be recorded as an asset.

Types of Property, Plant, and Equipment

There are several types of property, plant, and equipment, including land, buildings, machinery and equipment, leased assets, and leasehold improvements.

Land. The acquisition cost of land includes (1) the contract price; (2) the cost of closing the transaction and obtaining title, including real estate commissions, legal fees for examining the correct ownership of the property, and past-due taxes; (3) the costs of surveys; and (4) the costs of preparing the land for its particular use, such as clearing, grading, and razing old buildings (net of the proceeds for any salvaged items), when such improvements have an indefinite life. The costs of improvements with a limited economic life, such as landscaping, streets, sidewalks, and sewers, should be recorded as Land Improvements.

Buildings. The acquisition cost of buildings includes (1) the contract price, (2) the costs of excavation for the specific building (if not included in the contract price), (3) architectural costs and the cost of building permits, and (4) legal fees associated with the acquisition. If a used building is purchased, the costs of remodeling and reconditioning necessary to prepare the building for its intended use are included in the acquisition cost.

Machinery and Equipment.   The acquisition cost of machinery and equipment includes (1) the contract price and (2) installation and testing costs that are necessary to prepare the machinery and equipment for its intended use.

Leased Assets.   Many companies lease property, plant, and equipment rather than purchase these assets. Although these leases do not transfer legal ownership of the asset, they do enable the company to obtain the use of the asset for an extended period of time. Consequently, many leases result in the recording of an asset that is included in property, plant, and equipment on the balance sheet. Leases are discussed in Chapter 9.

Leasehold Improvements.   When leased assets are improved by the lessee, the expenditures should be recorded as a separate asset, Leasehold Improvements, and depreciated over the life of the lease or the life of the improvements, whichever is shorter. This procedure is necessary because the company no longer has the use of the leasehold improvements after the end of the life of the lease, and therefore it does not receive any more benefits.

Illustration of Accounting for Acquisition Cost

To illustrate the acquisition of an asset, suppose that the Gentry Company purchases a machine with a contract price of $10,000 on terms of 2/10, n/30. Sales tax is 5% of the price, or $500 (5% × $10,000). The company incurs transportation costs of $1,500 and installation and testing costs of $1,000. The discount of $200 (2% × $10,000) is deducted, and the net invoice price is $9,800 ($10,000 − $200). Remember that the discount should be deducted whether or not it is taken. (Note that this procedure is different from the gross method that is often used for discounts on purchases of inventory.) In this example it is assumed that the discount is taken, and therefore the cash payment is $9,800. During the transportation of the machine, uninsured damages of $100 were incurred in an accident, and they were paid by the company.

The cost of the machine is calculated as follows:

Contract price	$10,000
Sales tax	500
Transportation costs	1,500
Installation and testing	1,000
Less: cash discount	(200)
	$12,800

The sales tax, transportation, installation, and testing costs are included in the cost of the asset because they are necessary for the asset to be able to produce the benefits for which it was purchased. The cost of repairing the damages is excluded from the cost of the asset and therefore recorded as an expense because it was not necessary to incur these costs to receive the benefits associated with the machine. If the discount of $200 had not been taken, the cash payment would have increased by $200 and interest expense of $200 would have been recorded. As mentioned earlier, some companies would include the extra $200 in the cost of the asset because the amount is not material.

Acquisition Cost in a Lump-Sum Purchase

Frequently, land and buildings are purchased in a single package. In this case it is necessary to separate the cost of the land from the cost of the buildings because the buildings have a limited economic life and are depreciated, whereas land is considered to have an indefinite life and is not depreciated. The cost of each component is determined by its relative fair market value, which may be implicit in the purchase contract or may have to be determined by an appraisal. For example, suppose that land and a building are purchased for $200,000 and an independent appraisal shows that the land would be worth $100,000 and the building $140,000 if they were acquired separately. The cost at which to record each asset is determined as follows:

	Appraisal Value	Relative Fair Market Value	×	Total Cost	=	Allocated Cost
Land	$100,000	$100,000 ÷ $240,000	×	$200,000	=	$ 83,333
Building	140,000	140,000 ÷ 240,000	×	200,000	=	116,667
	$240,000					$200,000

Note that the sum of the costs recorded for the land and the building is $200,000, which is the total acquisition cost and *not* the total appraisal value of $240,000.

In the above situation it was assumed that the company intended to use the building. However, if a company purchases land and a building with the intent to demolish the building and erect a new one, the total cost is assigned to Land because the existence of the building was incidental to the acquisition of the land. In addition, the costs of demolishing the old building, net of any salvageable materials, are also added to the cost of the land.

Acquisition by Self-Construction

Many companies construct assets for their own use. For example, utilities often construct their own generating plants over a period of several years or a manufacturing company may make a special purpose machine for its own use. When an asset is self-constructed, all the costs directly related to the construction should be included in the cost of the asset. These costs include those related to materials, labor, and architect and engineering fees. Two special accounting issues arise in an acquisition by self-construction.

Interest During Construction. During construction a company often borrows money to finance the costs incurred. The question arises whether these interest costs should be expensed as they are incurred or included in the cost of the asset. **Accounting principles require that any interest costs actually incurred during the construction period on amounts borrowed and invested in the asset should be included in the cost of the asset.** Thus, interest costs are treated as an acquisition cost in the same way as the labor and material costs incurred during construction. If a loan is negotiated specifically to finance the construction, the interest on the amount borrowed and invested is included in the cost of the asset (capitalized).[1] Alternatively, if a company does not acquire a special loan but has debt outstanding such as long-term notes payable, the average interest rate on the debt is used to compute the interest to be added to the cost of the asset. The reason for using outstanding debt if a special loan was not obtained is that some companies do not borrow for specific projects. Instead, they plan their overall level of operations, and then decide the amount of money that needs to be borrowed to support that level of operations. The average interest cost to be included in the cost of the asset for the year is computed as follows:

$$
\begin{matrix}
\text{Interest cost} \\
\text{to be included} \\
\text{in the cost} \\
\text{of the asset}
\end{matrix}
=
\begin{matrix}
\text{Average cumulative} \\
\text{cost incurred} \\
\text{for construction} \\
\text{during the year}
\end{matrix}
\times
\begin{matrix}
\text{Average} \\
\text{interest rate} \\
\text{on debt}
\end{matrix}
$$

where:

$$
\begin{matrix}
\text{Average cumulative} \\
\text{cost incurred} \\
\text{for construction} \\
\text{during the year}
\end{matrix}
=
\left(
\begin{matrix}
\text{Cumulative construction} \\
\text{costs incurred at} \\
\text{the beginning} \\
\text{of the year}
\end{matrix}
+
\begin{matrix}
\text{Cumulative construction} \\
\text{costs incurred} \\
\text{by the end of} \\
\text{the year}
\end{matrix}
\right)
\div 2
$$

For simplicity, we will assume that a company does not acquire special loans for each specific project. Therefore, the interest cost to be included in the asset cost for the construction period is calculated by multiplying the average interest rate by the average amount of the total costs invested in the construction activity during the period. For example, suppose that a construction company starts a construction activity on January 1, 1993, as follows:

Annual expenditures on the project:
    1993 $1 million
    1994 $3 million
Weighted average interest rate on the company's borrowings: 12%

The average amounts of the total costs invested in the construction activity are computed as follows:

. . . .

[1]"Capitalization of Interest Cost," *FASB Statement of Financial Accounting Standards No. 34* (Stamford, Conn.: FASB, 1979).

average costs

1993	$500,000	[($0 + $1,000,000) ÷ 2]
1994	$2,500,000	[$1,000,000 + $4,000,000) ÷ 2]

Note that the average *total* costs are used because the interest costs are incurred each period on the amounts invested in the construction. The amount of interest to be capitalized in each of the two years is calculated as follows:

$$\text{Capitalized Interest, 1993} = \text{Average Cost} \times \text{Interest Rate}$$
$$= \$500,000 \times 12\%$$
$$= \$60,000$$

$$\text{Capitalized Interest, 1994} = \text{Average Cost} \times \text{Interest Rate}$$
$$= \$2,500,000 \times 12\%$$
$$= \$300,000$$

The effects on the financial statements of capitalizing the interest costs for the above example are as follows:

1. The cost of the asset is higher by $60,000 at December 31, 1993, and higher by $360,000 ($60,000 + $300,000) at December 31, 1994 (assuming that no depreciation has been recorded).

2. Income before income taxes is higher by $60,000 in 1993 and $300,000 in 1994 because interest costs are capitalized rather than expensed.

3. If it is assumed that the income tax rate is 30%, the income tax expense is higher by $18,000 ($60,000 × 30%) in 1993 and higher by $90,000 ($300,000 × 30%) in 1994.

4. Net income is higher by $42,000 ($60,000 − $18,000) in 1993 and higher by $210,000 ($300,000 − $90,000) in 1994.

5. If it is assumed that income taxes payable are equal to the income tax expense, income taxes payable are higher by $18,000 at December 31, 1993, and higher by $90,000 at December 31, 1994.

6. Retained earnings is higher by $42,000 at December 31, 1993, and higher by $252,000 ($42,000 + $210,000) at December 31, 1994.

If the construction company subsequently used the asset in its own operations, depreciation expense in each year of use would be higher because of the higher cost, and therefore income before income taxes would be lower. Alternatively, if the company sold the asset, the gross profit on the sale would be lower because the cost of goods sold would be higher, and income before income taxes would again be lower. In either case, the profit from the beginning of the construction to the eventual disposal of the asset would be the same total amount because the higher profit during construction is offset by the lower profit in subsequent periods.

Note that if a company has not borrowed any money, it cannot impute an interest cost and include that amount in the cost of an asset. Therefore, other things being equal, if two companies build identical assets and one has outstanding debt and the other has no liabilities on which it is paying interest, the cost of the assets will be different.

Profit on Self-Construction.   If a company builds an asset for less than it would have cost to purchase the same asset, should it recognize a profit of the difference between the two costs? **Accounting principles allow the recognition of profit only when sales are made and not for the acquisition of an asset.** Further support for recording the asset at cost is provided by the conservatism principle and because of the lack of a reliable valuation of the purchase price. In addition, accounting is based on actions taken, not on what might have occurred. The savings obtained by building rather than purchasing the asset are *not* recognized as profit, but they will be reflected by a lower depreciation expense each year over the life of the asset, since depreciation is based on the lower recorded cost of the asset. If construction costs are materially greater than the fair market value of the asset, the asset should only be recorded at the fair market value and a loss should be recognized.

■ DEPRECIATION

As we have already discussed, assets included in property, plant, and equipment provide benefits to the company owning (or leasing) the items for more than one year. The *matching* principle, which was discussed in Chapter 2, requires that the costs of generating revenue be matched against the revenue in the accounting period when the revenue is earned. As we saw in Chapter 6, the cost of inventory (cost of goods sold) is matched against the sales revenue in each accounting period, and therefore the amount of the income provides a relevant measurement of the success of the company. Similarly, the cost of using the property, plant, and equipment (except land) acquired by a company must be matched in each accounting period against the revenue that these assets help to produce. This cost is the depreciation expense. **The depreciation expense is the portion of the cost of a long-term physical asset allocated as an expense to each accounting period in the asset's service (useful) life.** For a typical company, buildings, machinery and equipment, and vehicles are all examples of items of property, plant, and equipment that are necessary for making sales, and therefore their depreciable (defined later) cost should be matched against the sales revenue they help to produce over their productive lives.

It may be helpful to consider a property, plant, and equipment asset as a "bundle of services" which are to be used up over the life of the asset. These services are used to provide benefits which are recognized as revenue. When the asset is purchased, the company is paying in advance for those services to be received over several years. Therefore, the asset is conceptually the same as other assets, such as prepaid rent or inventory because each provides benefits in the future. The differences are that the property, plant, and equipment asset will provide the benefits over a much longer time period and in a less well-defined manner. For example, a factory building may be expected to provide a bundle of services for 30 years. However the benefits may arise in future years from products that have not even been invented yet. Depreciation is the process of matching the cost of the bundle of services against the benefits produced by those services.

To illustrate depreciation expense, first we review a simple and commonly used method for computing depreciation expense, the straight-line method, which was introduced in Chapter 3, and then we discuss several principles that affect our understanding of depreciation. We then explain the other methods of computing depreciation that are used in practice.

Straight-Line Depreciation

The straight-line depreciation method is a method of depreciating an asset in which the cost of an asset less its estimated residual value is allocated equally to each period of the asset's service (useful) life. It is the simplest and most commonly used way of calculating the amount of depreciation. There are three factors involved in the calculation of the amount of depreciation: **(1) the cost of the asset; (2) the estimated service life of the asset, which is the life over which the asset is expected to be useful; and (3) the estimated residual value of the asset, which is the estimated proceeds from the sale or disposal of an asset at the end of its estimated service life.** The service life is often referred to as the **economic life,** and the residual value as the **salvage value.** The cost of the asset is determined according to the principles discussed earlier. The service life and the residual value must be estimated by management when the asset is acquired. The factors affecting these estimates are discussed later, but it should be recognized that these estimates may be difficult to make in practice and they may involve some fairly arbitrary assumptions. The amount of the straight-line depreciation is computed as follows:

$$\text{Depreciation per Year} = \frac{\text{Cost} - \text{Estimated Residual Value}}{\text{Estimated Service Life}}$$

The numerator of this depreciation equation is known as the **depreciable cost.** It is the estimated total portion of the acquisition cost that will be allocated to depreciation over the service life.

For example, suppose that the Marbal Company buys a copying machine for $12,000 on January 1, 1993, and estimates that it will be sold for $1,000 (the residual value) after being used for five years (the service life). The depreciable cost of the copying machine to the company is the acquisition cost of $12,000 less the $1,000 it expects to obtain when the asset is sold after five years. This $11,000 is allocated equally to each year of the asset's life, or at the rate of $2,200 per year. The straight-line depreciation expense is computed as follows:

$$\text{Depreciation per Year} = \frac{\$12,000 - \$1,000}{5 \text{ years}} = \$2,200$$

Each year the recording of the depreciation expense and the accumulated depreciation reduces the income of the company and the book value of the asset. **Accumulated depreciation is the total depreciation recorded on an asset to date. The book value of an asset is the cost of the asset less the accumulated depreciation.** A summary of the straight-line depreciation over the life of the asset is as follows:

STRAIGHT-LINE DEPRECIATION SCHEDULE

Year	Depreciation Expense	Accumulated Depreciation	Book Value at the End of the Year
1993	$2,200	$ 2,200	$9,800
1994	2,200	4,400	7,600
1995	2,200	6,600	5,400
1996	2,200	8,800	3,200
1997	2,200	11,000	1,000

The amount of straight-line depreciation expense may also be expressed as a percentage of the cost of the asset. In this example, it would be 18.33% ($2,200 ÷ $12,000).

Effects of Depreciation on the Financial Statements

Recording depreciation has two effects on the financial statements. The cost that is matched against the revenues in a particular accounting period is included as depreciation expense in the income statement or added to the cost of the inventory (goods in process) if the asset is used in manufacturing activities. This expired cost also represents a reduction in the book value of the asset (acquisition cost minus accumulated depreciation). Rather than reduce (credit) the asset account directly, the normal procedure is to increase (credit) a contra-asset account, Accumulated Depreciation (contra-asset accounts were discussed in Chapter 3). Either procedure has the same effect of reducing the book value of the asset, but the use of the contra-asset account is preferable because it aids in preparing the financial statements, in which both the acquisition cost and the sum of the accumulated depreciation to date have to be disclosed in the balance sheet (or in the notes). For example, the Marbal Company would disclose the following information in its balance sheet for December 31, 1993 and 1994 (note that in most comparative financial statements, the most recent year is listed first):

	1994	1993
Machinery, cost	$12,000	$12,000
Less: accumulated depreciation	(4,400)	(2,200)
	$ 7,600	$ 9,800

Recording the cost and the accumulated depreciation in separate accounts makes the information more readily available.

Each year the balance in the Accumulated Depreciation account grows until the asset is fully depreciated. Therefore, at the end of the estimated service life, the book value of the asset is equal to its expected residual value. For example, in the straight-line depreciation situation the book value at the end of 1997 is $1,000, the same as the estimated residual value.

To summarize, Depreciation Expense is included as an expense that is matched against sales revenue in the income statement, or is recorded as part of the cost of the inventory manufactured and is included in the expense, Cost of Goods Sold, when the inventory is sold. The addition to Accumulated Depreciation reduces the book value of the asset in the balance sheet. The depreciation expense and accumulated depreciation should be reported for each class of asset.

Causes of Depreciation

The service life of an asset, which is the period over which the asset is expected to provide benefits, may be limited by several factors, which can be divided into the categories of physical causes and functional causes, as follows:

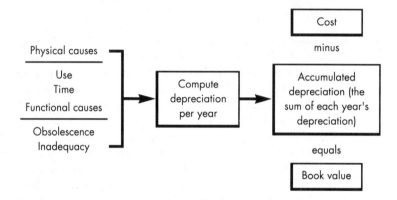

Physical Causes. Physical causes include wear and tear due to operational *use*, deterioration and decay caused by the passage of *time*, and damage and destruction.

Functional Causes. Functional causes limit the life of the asset, even though the physical life is not exhausted. *Obsolescence* is a common occurrence in a technologically advanced economy when an asset is made obsolete by the introduction of new technology. *Inadequacy* occurs when an asset is no longer suitable for the company's operations even though it may still be physically sound.

The lives of most assets are not limited by a single factor operating alone. In most cases a primary cause can be identified, however. For example, the life of a delivery truck is primarily limited by physical causes, in which wear and tear, deterioration and decay, and damage and destruction may all be expected to contribute. In contrast, the useful life of a computer is likely to be limited by a functional cause, whether it be obsolescence resulting from the availability of newer, more efficient computers, or inadequacy resulting from the needs of the company outgrowing the capacity of the computer.

The straight-line method of depreciation discussed earlier is appropriate when the usefulness of the asset is expected to be equal each period. If the benefits are equal each period, the total *remaining* benefits decline equally each period. This pattern of depreciation occurs when physical deterioration and decay occur at a steady rate over the life of the asset or when the usefulness is reduced by a functional cause. Then it is reasonable to record an equal amount of depreciation expense each period by using the straight-line method.

Service Life and Residual Value

The estimated service life of an asset is affected by the perceptions of management of the various physical and functional causes. This estimated service life also directly affects the estimate of the residual value. In some cases it may be management's intention to keep the asset until its physical life is exhausted. In this case the estimated residual value will be close to zero (or it may even be negative if disposal costs are significant and exceed the value of any salvaged material, such as for a nuclear power plant). Alternatively, management may dispose of the asset well before its physical life is exhausted, in which case the estimated residual value may be very large. For example, airlines often sell their planes long before the end of their physical lives. In practice, it may be difficult to estimate the service life and residual value of an asset, but management must make realistic estimates using the best information available.

Allocation of Cost Not Valuation

As we discussed earlier, the process of depreciation involves the matching of the acquisition cost of the asset as an expense against the revenue. **Depreciation is *not* an attempt to provide an estimate of the value of the asset at any given time.** As we saw with the straight-line method, the purpose of depreciation is to allocate the cost of an asset as an expense over its service life and in so doing reduce the book value of the asset to its estimated residual value (which is an estimate of the market value of the asset at the *end* of its life). Depreciating an asset, however, is *not* an attempt to estimate the market value of an asset *during* its life. Therefore, it is only at the time of acquisition and at the end of the life of an asset (if the original estimate of the residual value is accurate) that the book value can be expected to equal the asset's market value. During the life of the asset, the book value is the cost of the remaining "bundle of services" that the company expects to obtain from the asset, and *not* the value of those services. However, certain supplemental disclosures of the values of property, plant, and equipment are encouraged in the annual reports of companies, as discussed in Chapter 13.

Systematic and Rational Allocation of Costs

Since depreciation is not an attempt to measure the value of an asset, it is reasonable to ask, "What is the purpose?" Remember the discussion of matching expenses with revenues with which we introduced the subject of depreciation. The cost of the asset should be matched as an expense against the revenues (benefits) it helps to produce. Since it is usually impossible to measure precisely the benefits that a particular asset provides, the underlying principle is that costs should be matched in a "systematic and rational"[2] manner against revenues. **The term systematic is used to indicate that the calculation should follow a formula and not be determined in an arbitrary manner.** The straight-line method and the alternative methods discussed below are all considered systematic. **The term rational is used to indicate that the amount of the depreciation should relate to the benefits that the asset produces in any period.** Thus, the straight-line method should be used when it may be reasonably assumed that the asset produces equal benefits each period over its life. Then an equal cost each period is matched as an expense against an equal benefit (revenues) each period. An accelerated method should be used when it is considered that the benefits generated by an asset are highest early in the life of the asset and decline in each succeeding period. **An accelerated depreciation method is a method of depreciation in which most depreciation is recognized in the first year of the asset's life and lesser amounts are recognized in each subsequent year.**

It is sometimes suggested that the management of a company has a free hand in the selection of a depreciation method. The above discussion should have made it clear that the selection of a particular method is based on specific criteria that management should follow.

Accelerated Depreciation Methods

Two accelerated depreciation methods, the double-declining-balance and the sum-of-the-years'-digits methods, are often used. These methods are also known as *declining charge* methods because the amount of depreciation declines in each succeeding period. The early recognition of higher depreciation, however, is offset by recognizing less depreciation later in the life of the asset, and therefore the *total* depreciation recognized over the life of the asset is always the same (the total depreciation equals the depreciable cost, which is the cost less the estimated residual value). Each of these accelerated methods is discussed below.

Double-Declining-Balance Method.   **The double-declining-balance method is an accelerated depreciation method in which the depreciation expense is computed by multiplying the book value of the asset at the beginning of the period by twice the straight-line rate.** Note that the method uses twice the *rate* that is used for the straight-line method (*not* twice the amount) and that the residual value is *not* considered in the calculation of the depreciation expense. The asset, however, should never be depreciated below the estimated residual value, as discussed later. The depreciation on an asset in any year is computed as follows:

$$\text{Depreciation per Year} = 2 \times \text{Straight-Line Rate} \times \begin{matrix} \text{Book Value at the} \\ \text{Beginning of the Year} \end{matrix}$$

$$= 2 \times \frac{1}{\text{Life}} \times \begin{matrix} \text{Book Value at the} \\ \text{Beginning of the Year} \end{matrix}$$

....
[2]*Accounting Terminology Bulletin No. 1* (New York: AICPA, 1953), par. 56.

For example, consider the Marbal Company example introduced when straight-line depreciation was discussed. The copying machine was purchased at the beginning of 1993 and had the following characteristics:

Cost	$12,000
Estimated residual value	1,000
Estimated service life	5 years

Since the asset has a life of five years, the straight-line depreciation rate is 20% per year (one-fifth of the depreciable cost is depreciated each year). Therefore the double-declining-balance depreciation rate is 40% per year, and the depreciation expense each year and the book value of the asset at the end of each year are calculated as follows:

DOUBLE-DECLINING-BALANCE DEPRECIATION SCHEDULE

Year	Book Value at the Beginning of the Year	Depreciation Calculation	Depreciation Expense	Accumulated Depreciation	Book Value at the End of the Year
1993	$12,000	40% × $12,000	$4,800	$ 4,800	$7,200
1994	7,200	40% × 7,200	2,880	7,680	4,320
1995	4,320	40% × 4,320	1,728	9,408	2,592
1996	2,592	40% × 2,592	1,037	10,445	1,555
1997	1,555		555[a]	11,000	1,000

[a]40% × $1,555 = $622, but depreciation expense is limited to $555. See discussion below.

Note that the calculation of the depreciation in the first year was based on the total acquisition cost of $12,000 and *not* on the acquisition cost less the estimated residual value. In 1997 a modification has to be made to the usual calculations because the asset should not be depreciated below its estimated residual value. Therefore, in 1997 the depreciation expense should be only $555 (instead of 40% × $1,555, or $622), which reduces the book value to $1,000 at the end of the year so that it is equal to the estimated residual value.

To avoid the unusually small (or large) amount of depreciation in the last year(s), companies often adopt a policy of changing to the straight-line method at the mid-point of the asset's life. Another alternative is to change to the straight-line method in the year in which straight-line depreciation results in a larger depreciation amount than the double-declining-balance method. Either alternative is acceptable if it is applied consistently.

The double-declining-balance method is the most accelerated method of depreciation that is allowed under generally accepted accounting principles. Another accelerated method that is sometimes used is the 150% declining-balance method. This method is applied in exactly the same way as the double-declining method, except that, as the name implies, the rate that is used is 1½ times the straight-line rate. If the Marbal Company used this method, it would depreciate the book value of the copying machine at the rate of 30% per year ($1\frac{1}{2} \times 20\%$), and the depreciation expense in 1993 would be $3,600 (30% × $12,000).

Sum-of-the-Years'-Digits Method.   The sum-of-the-years'-digits method is an accelerated depreciation method in which the depreciation is computed by multiplying the depreciable cost by a fraction that declines each year. Thus, the depreciation expense on an asset in any year is computed as follows:

$$\text{Depreciation per Year} = (\text{Cost} - \text{Residual Value}) \times \text{Fraction}$$

The fraction each year is calculated as follows:

$$\text{Fraction} = \frac{\text{Number of Years Remaining in the Asset's Life at the Beginning of the Year}}{\text{Sum of the Years' Digits}}$$

The sum of the years' digits for an asset with a 5-year life is $5 + 4 + 3 + 2 + 1 = 15$.[3] The annual depreciation expense and the book value at the end of each year for the Marbal Company's copying machine with a depreciable cost of $11,000 ($12,000 − $1,000) is computed as follows:

SUM-OF-THE-YEARS'-DIGITS DEPRECIATION SCHEDULE

Year	Depreciation Calculation	Depreciation Expense	Book Value at the End of the Year
1993	$11,000 × 5/15	$3,667	$8,333
1994	11,000 × 4/15	2,933	5,400
1995	11,000 × 3/15	2,200	3,200
1996	11,000 × 2/15	1,467	1,733
1997	11,000 × 1/15	733	1,000

Note that the book value at the end of the last year of the asset's life equals $1,000, which is the estimated residual value of the asset. This value results because the sum of the fractions used in the calculation of the depreciation totals 15/15, and the amount being depreciated is the cost less the estimated residual value.

The effect of the straight-line and the two accelerated depreciation methods on depreciation expense and book value for the Marbal Company's machine is illustrated by the diagrams in Exhibit 7–1.

The depreciation methods discussed so far—the straight-line, double-declining-balance, and the sum-of-the-years'-digits methods—are all based on the life of the asset measured in years. It may be more reasonable, however, to measure the life of the asset in terms of its expected physical activity, and therefore to base the depreciation on that activity.

· · · · · · · · · · · · · · · · · · · ·
[3]The general formula to compute the sum of the years' digits is $n(n + 1) \div 2$. Thus, for an asset with a 20-year life, the sum is $(20 \times 21) \div 2 = 210$.

EXHIBIT 7–1 Depreciation expense and book value for alternative depreciation methods

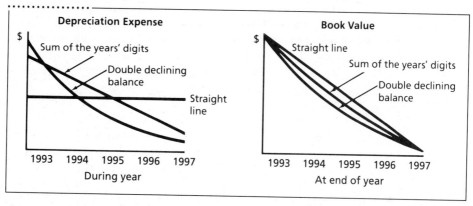

Activity Depreciation Methods

An activity method is a depreciation method in which the depreciation expense is based on the level of physical activity of the asset. The activity (or use) of an asset may be measured in terms of the number of units the asset is expected to produce, or perhaps the number of hours it is expected to operate. For example, the Marbal Company might estimate that its copying machine would be expected to produce 500,000 copies or operate for 10,000 hours during its useful life. The depreciation *rate* could be computed on the basis of the number of copies or the hours as follows:

$$\text{Depreciation Rate} = \frac{\text{Cost} - \text{Estimated Residual Value}}{\text{Total Lifetime Activity Level}}$$

$$= \frac{\$12,000 - \$1,000}{500,000 \text{ copies}} = \$0.022 \text{ per copy}$$

or

$$\text{Depreciation Rate} = \frac{\$12,000 - \$1,000}{10,000 \text{ hours}} = \$1.10 \text{ per hour}$$

When the depreciation is based on the activity level of the asset, it is sometimes referred to as the *units-of-production* method. **The depreciation expense for the year is computed by multiplying the depreciation rate times the activity level for the year.** For example, if the Marbal Company makes 110,000 copies and operates the machine for 1,900 hours in 1993, the depreciation expense would be computed under the two alternatives, as follows:

$$\begin{aligned}
\text{Depreciation Expense} &= \text{Rate per Copy} \times \text{Number of Copies} \\
&= \$0.022 \times 110,000 \text{ copies} \\
&= \$2,420
\end{aligned}$$

or

$$\begin{aligned}
\text{Depreciation Expense} &= \text{Rate per Hour} \times \text{Number of Hours} \\
&= \$1.10 \times 1,900 \text{ hours} \\
&= \$2,090
\end{aligned}$$

Although in this example we illustrate depreciation based on both activity levels, it should be noted that the company has to select one measure of the activity level and use that measure consistently for its computation of depreciation. The effect of these activity methods on the financial statements should be compared to the straight-line method. The activity methods produce a constant depreciation rate per *unit* (hour or copy in this example), but the total depreciation expense will vary per *year* as the activity level varies. In contrast, the straight-line method produces a constant depreciation expense per *year*, but the amount will vary per *unit* as the activity level varies.

To illustrate these differences, consider the following situation in which a company produces 10,000 units and sells them at $4 per unit and has a depreciation expense of $10,000. In the next period, it is assumed that the company produces and sells 20,000 units. If the company is using the straight-line method, the depreciation expense does not change even though the level of activity has doubled. Therefore, the amount of *gross* profit more than doubles (net income will not double because of the many other income items included in the income statement). Alternatively, if the company is using an activity method, the depreciation expense doubles to match the doubling of the number of units produced and sold. The amount of the gross profit also doubles.

| | 10,000 UNITS | 20,000 UNITS | |
		Straight Line	Activity
Sales	$40,000	$80,000	$80,000
Depreciation expense	(10,000)	(10,000)	(20,000)
Gross profit	$30,000	$70,000	$60,000

It can be seen from this comparison that an activity method is more appropriate when the service life of the asset is limited by physical reasons (especially wear and tear) and the level of activity varies from period to period. For example, using a truck twice as much in one period as compared to the previous period should cause the depreciation expense to double because twice as much of the asset would have been used up. The straight-line method is most appropriate when the service life of the asset is limited by functional causes (inadequacy and obsolescence). For example, a computer has a certain capacity to perform tasks and, given adequate maintenance, does not wear out; therefore, straight-line depreciation is appropriate. If a company increases its use of the computer from 12 to 24 hours per day, it is appropriate that depreciation expense should remain the same because the estimated service life should not be affected by the greater utilization.

Use of Alternative Depreciation Methods

The use of alternative depreciation methods for 600 surveyed companies is shown in Exhibit 7–2. There are more than 600 responses because many companies

EXHIBIT 7–2 Use of alternative depreciation methods

| | NUMBER OF COMPANIES | | |
	1988	1982	1976
Straight line	563	562	567
Declining balance	44	57	66
Sum of the years' digits	11	20	37
Accelerated method, not specified	70	69	71
Units of production	53	62	41

Source: Accounting Trends and Techniques (New York: AICPA, 1977, 1983, and 1989).

use more than one method of depreciation. Clearly the straight-line method is by far the most widely used method because the assets of most companies are assumed to provide equal benefits each period.

■ ADDITIONAL DEPRECIATION CONSIDERATIONS

Several additional considerations are discussed in this section. The recognition of depreciation expense when an asset is acquired or disposed of during a period; the effect of depreciation on income taxes; a revision of the estimate of residual value or service life; and an evaluation of the alternative depreciation methods, including the relationship between depreciation and cash flows are all discussed.

Depreciation and Fractional Periods

In the discussion of depreciation so far, we have implicitly assumed that the asset was acquired at the beginning of the year and therefore a full year's depreciation expense was recorded in the year of acquisition. Assets are usually purchased throughout the year, however, and rules have to be developed for determining the amount of depreciation to record for each period in such situations. Three of the commonly used alternatives are as follows:

1. *Compute Depreciation Expense to the Nearest Whole Month.* An asset purchased on or before the 15th of the month is depreciated for the whole month, and an asset purchased after the 15th of the month is not depreciated in the month of acquisition. For example, if an asset is purchased on May 20, depreciation is recorded in the first year for June through December, or 7 months.

2. *Compute Depreciation Expense to the Nearest Whole Year.* A full year's depreciation is recorded in the year of acquisition if the asset is acquired in the first half of the fiscal year. No depreciation is recorded in the year of acquisition if the asset is acquired in the second half of the fiscal year. A full year's depreciation is recorded in the year of disposal if the asset is disposed of in the second

half of the fiscal year. No depreciation is recorded in the year of disposal if the asset is disposed of in the first half of the fiscal year.

3. *Record One-Half Year's Depreciation Expense on All Assets Purchased or Sold During the Year.* No matter when the asset is acquired or disposed of during the fiscal year, one-half year's depreciation is recorded in both the year of acquisition and the year of disposal.

Depreciation and Income Taxes

Although depreciation is an expense that is deducted in the income statement, it is also deducted by a company in reporting its taxable income under the provisions of the Internal Revenue Code. Because the depreciation rules are different for income tax purposes than for accounting purposes, **the amounts of depreciation expense in any year for financial reporting and for income tax reporting are different** (as discussed below). It should not be surprising that the amounts are different because the objectives of financial reporting and the Internal Revenue Code are quite different. An objective of the generally accepted accounting principles used in financial reporting is to prepare income statements that fairly present the income-producing activities of the company and are useful to decision makers. In contrast, the objectives of the Internal Revenue Code, among others, are to obtain revenue for the operation of the federal government and to provide certain kinds of investment incentives for business activity.

Management has a responsibility to minimize the income taxes paid by the corporation without violating the law. Therefore it is desirable for a corporation to record, for income tax purposes, as much depreciation as possible early in the life of an asset. Higher depreciation reduces the corporation's taxable income, thereby reducing the income taxes paid. In 1981 the Accelerated Cost Recovery System (ACRS) was introduced by Congress as the method to be used for depreciating assets for income tax purposes; in 1984 minor revisions were made, and in 1986 more extensive changes were made.[4] The method is now known as the Modified Accelerated Cost Recovery System (MACRS). There are three ways in which the depreciation deducted for income tax purposes under MACRS is different than depreciation deducted in the financial statements:

1. *Different Life.* All assets are depreciated over a tax life which is defined for each type of asset by the Internal Revenue Code. These lives are used no matter what the service life is estimated to be for the computation of depreciation for financial reporting purposes. Typically, the tax life is shorter than the service life.

2. *No Residual Value.* The residual value is ignored, and the asset is depreciated to a zero residual value, thereby making the total depreciation over an asset's life equal to its cost.

· · · · · · · · · · · · · · · · · · · ·

[4]Assets acquired in years prior to 1981 are depreciated for income tax purposes by different rules that may use the accelerated depreciation methods discussed earlier. Assets acquired in years prior to 1987 are depreciated for income tax purposes by the ACRS method, but the lives and methods used are different.

EXHIBIT 7–3 MACRS depreciation as a percentage of the cost of the asset

Year of Life	TAX LIFE OF ASSET IN YEARS					
	3	5	7	10	15	20
1 ...	33.33%	20.00%	14.29%	10.00%	5.00%	3.750%
2 ...	44.45	32.00	24.49	18.00	9.50	7.219
3 ...	14.81	19.20	17.49	14.40	8.55	6.677
4 ...	7.41	11.52	12.49	11.52	7.70	6.177
5 ...		11.52	8.93	9.22	6.93	5.713
6 ...		5.76	8.92	7.37	6.23	5.285
7 ...			8.93	6.55	5.90	4.888
8 ...			4.46	6.55	5.90	4.522
9 ...				6.56	5.91	4.462
10 ...				6.55	5.90	4.461
11 ...				3.28	5.91	4.462
12 ...					5.90	4.461
13 ...					5.91	4.462
14 ...					5.90	4.461
15 ...					5.91	4.461
16 ...					2.95	4.461
17 ...						4.462
18 ...						4.461
19 ...						4.462
20 ...						4.461
21 ...						2.231

3. *Specified Method.* MACRS requires the use of the double-declining-balance method for assets with a tax life of 3, 5, 7, or 10 years. The 150%-declining-balance method is used for assets with a 15- or 20-year tax life. Buildings are depreciated by the straight-line method over 27½ years (residential) or 31½ years (nonresidential). The use of the accelerated method will usually result in depreciation under MACRS being greater than for financial reporting. Alternatively, a company may select the use of the straight-line method for any asset (over the tax life).

All the MACRS depreciation calculations for tax purposes are based on the half-year convention; that is, depreciation for half a year is recorded in the year of acquisition and in the final year of depreciation for tax purposes. Also when an accelerated method is used, a change is made to the straight-line method in the period in which the straight-line depreciation exceeds the amount calculated under the accelerated method. Most companies use the straight-line method for financial reporting purposes, as shown in Exhibit 7–2, and the MACRS method for income tax reporting. To simplify the calculation of MACRS depreciation, tables have been prepared by the IRS, as illustrated in Exhibit 7–3.

To illustrate the differences in the two methods, assume that the Arc Company purchased an asset on January 1, 1993. Information about the asset is given

EXHIBIT 7–4 Computation of income tax depreciation

ARC COMPANY
Computation of Depreciation
for Income Tax Reporting

Cost of asset:	$13,500
Purchased:	January 1, 1991
MACRS life:	3 years
Residual value:	Zero

MACRS Depreciation Amounts[a]
1991 $4,500 ($13,500 × 33.33%)
1992 $6,000 ($13,500 × 44.45%)
1993 $2,000 ($13,500 × 14.81%)
1994 $1,000 ($13,500 × 7.41%)
1995 $0

Computation of Depreciation
for Financial Statements

Cost of asset:	$13,500
Purchased:	January 1, 1991
Service life:	5 years
Residual value:	$1,000
Method:	Straight line

Financial Statement Depreciation Amounts
1991 $2,500 {($13,500 − $1,000) ÷ 5 years}
1992 $2,500
1993 $2,500
1994 $2,500
1995 $2,500

[a]Percentages from Exhibit 7–3. Amounts are rounded.

---

in Exhibit 7–4 along with the calculation of the depreciation for income tax purposes. The calculation of the depreciation for financial statements is also shown for comparison. Thus, it can be seen that the depreciation each year on the financial statements is very different from that reported on the income tax return. However, note that the total depreciation for income tax purposes is $13,500 over the three-year tax life, whereas in the financial statements the total depreciation expense is $12,500 over the five-year service life of the machine. If the machine is sold for $1,000 (the estimated residual value) at the end of 1995, a gain of $1,000 is recognized for income tax purposes, whereas no gain would be recognized in the financial statements because the asset was sold for an amount equal to its book value at the time (gains and losses on disposals of assets are discussed later). Therefore, after the sale of the asset the total deductions recorded to date on the company's income statements ($12,500 total depreciation expense) are equal to the total net deductions reported for income tax purposes ($13,500 total depreciation expense less the $1,000 gain on the sale).

The use of the MACRS procedures, however, accelerates the deductions taken for income tax purposes, thereby delaying the payment of income taxes until later in the life of the asset. The effect of the differences between the income tax expense and the income taxes paid is discussed in Chapter 9.

Computation of Effects of Accelerated Depreciation

Most companies use the straight-line depreciation method in their financial statements, but since some use accelerated methods it is helpful to evaluate the effects that accelerated depreciation would have on the financial statements of those companies using the straight-line method. An approximation of the effects of accelerated depreciation may be obtained from the disclosure of deferred income taxes, which is discussed in Chapter 9. In the disclosure, the amount by which the tax obligation has been lowered by the use of accelerated depreciation (the Modified Accelerated Cost Recovery System) is reported; that is, the amount reported is the effect on income taxes of the difference in depreciation methods. When the corporate income tax rate is 34%, this after tax difference may be multiplied by 3 to indicate the approximate amount of the difference between straight-line and accelerated depreciation.[5] The difference may be multiplied by 2 to indicate the approximate effect on net income.[6] For example, if a company is using straight-line depreciation in its financial statements and reports the effect on income taxes of the difference in depreciation as $1,000, the depreciation expense under the accelerated method would be approximately $3,000 higher. Also, the net income would be approximately $2,000 lower if accelerated depreciation had been used.

Impairment of Noncurrent Assets

Under generally accepted accounting principles, an asset is initially recorded at its acquisition cost and then depreciated over its life to its expected residual value by use of a systematic and rational method. There is no provision for use of the

....

[5]Pretax difference $\times$ Tax rate = After tax difference

or

$$\text{Pretax difference} = \frac{\text{After tax difference}}{\text{Tax rate}}$$

$$= \frac{\text{After tax difference}}{0.34}$$

= After tax difference $\times$ 2.94, or approximately 3

[6]After tax effect on net income = Pretax difference $\times$ (1 − Tax rate)

$$= \frac{\text{After tax difference}}{\text{Tax rate}} \times (1 - \text{Tax rate})$$

$$= \text{After tax difference} \times \frac{(1 - 0.34)}{0.34}$$

$$= \text{After tax difference} \times \frac{0.66}{0.34}$$

= After tax difference $\times$ 1.94, or approximately 2

lower of cost or market method, in contrast to accounting for inventories (discussed in Chapter 6) and marketable equity securities (discussed in Chapter 11) where the method must be used. In recent years, however, many companies have written down the carrying value of their noncurrent assets such as property, plant, and equipment, even though they have no intention of disposing of them. In effect, the companies are applying the lower of cost or market method. Usually this write-down occurs at the time of a major restructuring of the operating activities and/or the financial structure of a company.

Since the criteria used in these situations are uncertain, it is often suggested that the asset be written down to its net realizable value if the book value of the asset cannot be recovered through use (or sale). A wide variety of recognition criteria, measurement methods, terminology, and disclosure have been used, resulting in a lack of *comparability*. Among the issues that need to be resolved are:

1. Which types of assets should be written down?
2. When should the impairment be recognized?
3. Does the write-down have to be part of a general restructuring?
4. How should the impairment be measured? Should present values (discussed in Chapter 8) or net realizable value be used?
5. Should individual assets, or groups of assets, be revalued?

Revision of Estimates

As we have seen, the calculation of depreciation depends on making estimates of the service life and the residual value of an asset. Sometimes these estimates have to be revised because new knowledge is acquired or operating conditions change. **When estimates are changed, depreciation is computed on the basis of the revised amounts, and therefore the remaining undepreciated cost is depreciated over the remaining service life.** For example, suppose that a building has the following characteristics at the time of acquisition:

Acquisition cost	$90,000
Date of purchase	January 1, 1989
Estimated residual value	$10,000
Estimated service life	40 years
Annual depreciation expense (straight line)	$2,000　[($90,000 − $10,000) ÷ 40]

At December 31, 1993, the accumulated depreciation and book value are:

Accumulated depreciation	$10,000	(5 × $2,000)
Book value	$80,000	($90,000 − $10,000)

At the beginning of 1994 (after five years), the following revised estimates are made:

Estimated residual value	$20,000
Estimated remaining service life	20 years (for a total life of 25 years)

The depreciation per year is computed, using the remaining book value and the revised estimates, as follows:

$$\text{Depreciation per Year} = \frac{\text{Book Value} - \text{Estimated Residual Value}}{\text{Estimated Remaining Service Life}}$$

$$= \frac{\$80,000 - \$20,000}{20}$$

$$= \$3,000 \text{ per year}$$

This revised amount of depreciation expense would be recorded each year for the remainder of the asset's life. Note that the amounts recorded in previous periods are not changed. The effects of the change are disclosed in the notes to the financial statements.

To illustrate the impact on the financial statements that may arise when a company revises its estimate of the service life of an asset, in 1990 Tyson Foods extended the useful life of its poultry processing equipment from 6 to 10 years. This change increased net income by 18%, but without the change net income would have decreased 10%. It should be emphasized that the decision regarding the appropriate life of an asset is made by management and is reviewed for reasonableness by the auditor. While management is supposed to make an unbiased decision based on its intentions and expectations as best it can judge them, it is clear that the selection of the life can be made with an intent to influence the amount of the company's net income.

Evaluation of Depreciation Methods

The use of any one of the previously discussed depreciation methods is acceptable, provided the method relates the allocation of the depreciable cost of the asset to the expected pattern of benefits to be derived from the asset. The choice of a particular method can have a significant impact on income and assets, as may be seen by comparing the various depreciation amounts and the book value of the asset computed for the Marbal Company. These differences were illustrated in Exhibit 7–1. Use of an inappropriate method has an adverse impact on the measurement of income each year, although total income over the life of the asset is unaffected because the same total depreciable cost is expensed. For example, if an asset produces equal benefits each year, but an accelerated depreciation method is used, income will increase each year of the asset's life (if other factors remain the same each period), even though there has been no change in the physical activity each period. The rising income may be misleading to users of the financial statements.

The selection of the depreciation method should be considered together with the expected repair and maintenance costs, so that it is the matching of the *total* costs associated with the asset and the benefits derived from the asset which is

EXHIBIT 7–5 Selection of depreciation method according to expected maintenance costs to obtain constant total cost

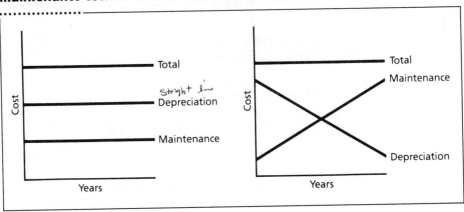

evaluated. For example, if similar repair and maintenance costs are expected and it is also expected that the total economic benefits of the asset remain similar each period, a similar total cost each period can be achieved through straight-line depreciation and the similar repair and maintenance costs. Alternatively, if increasing repair and maintenance costs are expected, accelerated depreciation and the increasing repair and maintenance costs each period may also produce similar total costs each period, as illustrated in Exhibit 7–5. Alternatively, if it is expected that benefits will decline each year for the life of the asset and that maintenance costs will be constant each period or not rise as fast as the depreciation is declining, a declining total cost will be achieved by using accelerated depreciation along with the expected repair and maintenance costs.

It should also be recognized that inflation is likely to have a significant effect on the measurement of the benefits, or revenue, over the life of the asset. In selecting a depreciation method, consideration should be given to whether benefits are to be measured in terms of constant dollars or dollars realized in future periods. For example, selling prices in some high technology industries decline each period. Therefore, if the physical output of a machine is constant and its benefits are measured in terms of sales revenues generated, the sales revenue will decline each period. In such cases, accelerated depreciation would be appropriate because the declining amounts of depreciation would be matched against the declining revenue. Also, in the current environment of technological change, an asset is more likely to become obsolete before the end of its originally estimated useful life. Therefore, there is greater risk associated with the estimated operating cash flows near the end of the life of the asset than for those at the beginning. Use of accelerated depreciation may be appropriate in such situations since lower depreciation recorded late in the life of the asset reduces the amount of revenues that have to be earned for the asset to be profitable.

It is also possible that a depreciation method, service life, and residual value are selected by management solely because of their impact on income over the

EXHIBIT 7–6 Effect of depreciation on rate of return

| | | MARBAL COMPANY | |
Year	Net Income	Book Value of Asset at Beginning of Year	Rate of Return
1993	$1,000	$12,000	8.33%
1994	1,000	9,800	10.20
1995	1,000	7,600	13.16
1996	1,000	5,400	18.52
1997	1,000	3,200	31.25

life of the asset. The selection, however, would be inappropriate not only because it violates accounting principles but because it also distorts income and asset values. Because of the estimates involved, however, such actions would be difficult for an auditor to detect.

A ratio commonly used in financial analysis is the rate of return on total assets, which may be defined simply as the net income divided by the assets. An unfortunate impact of recording depreciation is that the rate of return on assets increases over time. Refer back to the Marbal Company example using straight-line depreciation earlier in the chapter. Suppose, in addition, that net income after depreciation and income taxes is $1,000 per year and that the company only owns this one asset. The rate of return earned by the company increases each year as shown in Exhibit 7–6. The calculation of the rate of return could also be based on the average of the beginning and ending book values of the asset. The increase in the rate of return over the life of the asset would be even more dramatic if an accelerated depreciation method were used. As a result of this relationship, caution should always be exercised when the rate of return is calculated during financial statement analysis. Comparison between two companies can be distorted if one company has a newer asset base and hence a lower rate of return. Alternatively, if one company is analyzed over time, its rate of return will increase as its asset base gets older, other things being equal.

It should also be recognized that there are some things that depreciation is not attempting to do. As discussed earlier, it is *not* an attempt to measure the *value* of the asset, but only to allocate the cost in a systematic and rational manner. Also, depreciation is not charged in an attempt to provide funds for the replacement of the asset. Over the life of the asset the total depreciation expense is equal to the depreciable cost. Since depreciation is a tax-deductible expense, there is an income tax savings over the life of the asset, but it is equal only to the tax rate multiplied by the total amount of tax depreciation. Therefore, there can be no expectation that there will be sufficient cash saved over the life of the asset. Also the purchase of an asset requires that cash be available at the time of the purchase, or that the company be able to obtain the necessary funds by borrowing or selling stock. However, the cash saved in income taxes may have been used to finance the operations of the company and be unavailable for asset acquisitions. Furthermore, in times of rising prices the cost of replacing the asset will be higher than the original cost, so that additional funds will be required for the replacement. Depreciation based on the current value of assets is discussed in Chapter 13.

Depreciation and Cash Flows

One of the most misunderstood relationships in accounting is that between depreciation and cash flows. For example, a recent article stated that an airline would finance its acquisition of new planes "with existing cash plus money generated internally from earnings and depreciation." At this point, such a statement should make little sense. In fact, it is a logically incorrect statement. We will see why this kind of statement is widespread when we discuss the Statement of Cash Flows in Chapter 12. As we have seen in this chapter the recording of depreciation in the financial statements has no *direct* effect on cash. To record depreciation expense and increase accumulated depreciation has no effect on the cash balance.

As we have also seen, the depreciation used for income tax reporting is different than that used for the financial statements. Since income tax rules determine the amount of taxes *paid*, the cash flow is determined by those rules and not by the amount of depreciation recorded in the financial statements. As we will see in Chapter 9, the difference between the income tax expense and income taxes paid affects deferred income taxes. It is only when depreciation expense and the change in deferred income taxes are considered together that any logically correct statement can be made that ties together depreciation and cash flows.

■ SUBSEQUENT EXPENDITURES

After an asset has been acquired, further expenditures on the asset are often made during its economic life. These expenditures and their appropriate accounting treatment can be categorized as follows:

1. **Capital Expenditures. Capital expenditures are expenditures that increase the benefits to be obtained from an asset and should be capitalized. Capitalization is the recording of the cost as an increase in the book value of the asset.** An increase in the book value of an asset may be accomplished by an increase (debit) in the asset account or a decrease (debit) in the related accumulated depreciation account. If the expenditure increases the usefulness of the asset, it should be added (debited) to the asset account; and if it extends the life of the asset, it should be subtracted from (debited to) the accumulated depreciation account.

2. **Operating Expenditures. Operating expenditures are expenditures that only maintain the benefits that were originally expected to be obtained from the asset and should be expensed in the period incurred.** These operating expenditures are often referred to as *revenue* expenditures.

Capital Expenditures

Examples of capital expenditures are additions, improvements, replacements, and extraordinary repairs such as adding a new wing to a building, installing additional insulation, replacing the roof of a building so that the life of the building is longer than originally expected, or repairing a boiler in such an extensive way that its life is extended. All costs associated with these items, which are often called "renewals and betterments," should be capitalized.

Ideally, capital expenditures should be accounted for by removing from the accounts (in the manner discussed later) the cost and accumulated depreciation that relate to the part of the old asset being replaced or improved. Then the expenditure would be added (debited) to the appropriate asset account. Since the cost and accumulated depreciation on the part of the asset being replaced or improved are often impossible to determine, however, the common practice is to add the cost to the asset account if the expenditure is being made to increase the usefulness of the asset. Alternatively, the cost is subtracted from the Accumulated Depreciation account if the expenditure is being made to extend the life of the asset. The effect of this latter entry is to *decrease* the Accumulated Depreciation account, thereby *increasing* the book value of the asset by the amount of the expenditure. For example, a capital expenditure of $20,000 to replace a roof on a warehouse, thereby extending the life of the warehouse, is recorded as follows:

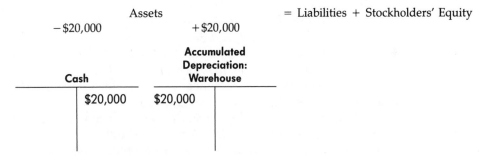

Alternatively, if an expenditure of $20,000 to enlarge a warehouse increases the usefulness of the warehouse, the cost is added to the asset account as follows:

It should be noted that the net effect of both entries is to increase the book value of the asset by $20,000. One entry decreases the accumulated depreciation, and the other entry increases the cost of the asset.

Operating Expenditures

Expenditures that maintain the benefits that were originally expected from the asset should be expensed when incurred. These expenditures are known as operating (or revenue) expenditures. The major item in this category is routine repair and maintenance costs. For example, if a company buys an automobile that it expects to use for 60,000 miles, it knows that it will have to perform repairs and maintenance during that time. Consequently, each routine repair merely maintains the ability of the car to last for 60,000 miles and does not extend its life beyond the 60,000 miles and is recorded as an expense when the costs are incurred.

Some items that should be considered capital expenditures are often accounted for as operating expenditures because the dollar amounts are so small as to be considered immaterial. For example, the company owning the car mentioned above might decide to buy a new engine for the car at 50,000 miles so that the car can be used for another 30,000 miles. This is a capital expenditure because it extends the life of the car beyond the original 60,000 miles, although it is often accounted for as an operating expenditure (i.e., it is recorded as an expense) because it is not material.

■ DISPOSALS OF PROPERTY, PLANT, AND EQUIPMENT

When the asset is disposed of at the end of its useful life to the company, the disposal must be properly recorded. Three alternative situations may arise: The asset may be sold for an amount equal to the book value or for an amount greater or less than the book value, in which case a gain or loss is recognized. Also, an asset may be exchanged for a similar asset, in which case a loss but no gain may be recognized, as discussed in the Appendix.

All disposals have some characteristics in common. Depreciation for the fraction of the year up to the date of disposal should be recorded. In the following discussion it is assumed that the necessary depreciation has already been recorded. At the time of the disposal, the balances in the asset account and its related accumulated depreciation account must be removed. This is accomplished by reducing (crediting) the Asset account by an amount equal to its recorded acquisition cost and reducing (debiting) the Accumulated Depreciation account by an amount equal to the current (credit) balance in the account. Both the Asset and the Accumulated Depreciation accounts will then have a zero balance because the respective (debit and credit) amounts recorded at the disposal exactly offset the balance being carried in each account before disposal. Disposals range from the very simple, where there is no cash involved and the book value is zero, to more complex transactions in which gains or losses on the disposal must be recognized, because the actual selling price is not equal to the book value.

In addition, it should be noted that an entry to record the disposal is recorded only when an asset is sold, *not* when it is fully depreciated to its estimated residual value. An asset that is fully depreciated but is still being used is kept in the accounting records at a book value equal to the estimated residual value (the asset minus the accumulated depreciation equals the estimated residual value). This provides evidence of the continued existence of the asset and is necessary for the operation of the internal control function, which ensures that assets listed in the accounting records are in the physical control of the company, and for the reporting of property taxes.

Disposal of a Fully Depreciated Asset with No Cash Proceeds

In the simplest situation an asset that is fully depreciated to a zero residual value is discarded. That is, it is disposed of and no cash is received. For example, suppose that a machine that originally cost $10,000 and is fully depreciated to a zero residual value is discarded and no cash is received. The asset and the related accumulated depreciation are removed as follows:

Assets		= Liabilities + Stockholders' Equity
− $10,000	+ $10,000	

Machine			Accumulated Depreciation: Machine	
Bal. $10,000				Bal. $10,000
	$10,000	$10,000		
Bal. $0				Bal. $0

Note that this entry has no effect on the total assets in the balance sheet. The entry simply reduces (credits) an asset account and reduces (debits) a contra-asset account for the same amount.

Sale at an Amount Equal to the Residual Value

Suppose that the machine in the previous example had an estimated residual value of $1,000, is fully depreciated to that amount, and is sold for $1,000 cash. In this case, the following entry is made to record the sale:

	Assets		= Liabs. + S. Eq.
+ $1,000	− $10,000	+ $9,000	

Cash		Machine			Accumulated Depreciation: Machine	
		Bal. $10,000				Bal. $9,000
$1,000			$10,000	$9,000		
		Bal. $0				Bal. $0

In this situation, an asset with a book value of $1,000 ($10,000 − $9,000) that is included in property, plant, and equipment is removed and another asset, cash, is increased by $1,000. Thus, a noncurrent asset has been replaced by a current asset of equal value.

Sale Above Book Value (Gain)

In most practical situations, assets are not sold for an amount equal to the book value. Therefore, suppose that the same machine as discussed above which had an estimated residual value of $1,000 is sold for $1,500. A diagram of the relationships between the various dollar amounts is shown below:

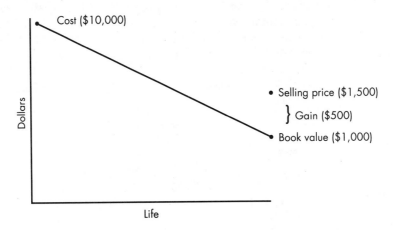

Based on the information in the diagram, the following entry is required to record the sale:

	Assets		= Liabs. +	S. Eq.
+$1,500	−$10,000	+$9,000		+ $500

Cash		Machine		Accumulated Depreciation: Machine		Gain on Sale of Machine
$1,500		Bal. $10,000	$10,000	$9,000	Bal. $9,000	$500
		Bal. $0			Bal. $0	

In this situation, a machine with a book value of $1,000 is sold for $1,500 and a gain of $500 is recognized on the sale; the gain is computed by comparing the cash received ($1,500) to the book value ($1,000). The gain arises because the original estimate of the residual value, made at the time the asset was acquired, was incorrect. This is not surprising given the difficulty of making such estimates, but it does mean that the amount of depreciation recorded in previous years is technically incorrect. Changing the amount of depreciation recorded in the financial statements of previous years, however, would be very confusing to the users of the statements. Therefore, the gain is considered to be an increase in income for the period of the sale. The total amount included in the income statements over the life of the asset by recording depreciation each period and the gain on the sale in the period of the sale is the difference between the acquisition cost and the actual disposal value. The gain is recorded as an increase to an account, Gain on Sale of Machine. When the financial statements are prepared, the gain is included in the income statement in the Other Revenues and Expenses section. It should *not* be included as sales revenue because it is not part of the sale of goods or services in the normal course of business.

Sale Below Book Value (Loss)

If the same machine just discussed is sold for $700, the company incurs a loss of $300 ($1,000 book value – $700 proceeds) on the sale, as shown in the following diagram:

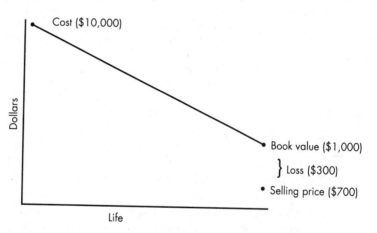

Based on the information in the diagram, the sale is recorded as follows:

+$700	Assets − $10,000	+$9,000	= Liabs. +	S. Eq. − $300

Cash	Machine		Accumulated Depreciation: Machine		Loss on Sale of Machine
$700	Bal. $10,000	$10,000 $9,000		Bal. $9,000	$300
	Bal. $0			Bal. $0	

The loss is included in the income statement as a negative component of Other Revenues and Expenses.

Sale Before the End of the Estimated Service Life

It was assumed in the previous examples that the asset had been depreciated to its estimated residual value before disposal. Therefore, the book value at the time of disposal was equal to the estimated residual value. However, a company may decide to sell an asset earlier than originally anticipated before it has been fully depreciated. In this case, the book value is not equal to the estimated residual value. The principles underlying the recording of the disposal are not changed. The depreciation must be brought up to date using one of the fractional period methods discussed earlier in the chapter. The Asset account and the Accumulated Depreciation account must be reduced (credited and debited, respectively) to remove the balances in these accounts. The gain or loss on the sale is still the difference between the book value of the asset and the cash received. For example, suppose that a company sells a machine with the following characteristics:

Original cost	$20,000
Date of purchase	Jan. 1, 1988
Estimated life	10 years
Estimated residual value	Zero
Depreciation method	Straight line
Cash proceeds from sale	$10,000
Date of disposal	July 1, 1993

At this point, the Machine account has a balance of $20,000. Since the machine now has had 5½ years depreciation (1988 through half of 1993) recorded on it, the Accumulated Depreciation account has a balance of $11,000 ($2,000 per year for the 5½ years) and the asset has a book value of $9,000 ($20,000 − $11,000). When the machine is sold for $10,000 a gain of $1,000 ($10,000 proceeds − $9,000 book value) is recognized. A diagram of the relationships between the various dollar amounts is shown below. Note that this diagram is similar to the one shown earlier except that here the gain is computed by comparing the selling price to the book value instead of the estimated residual value because the asset is sold before the end of its estimated service life.

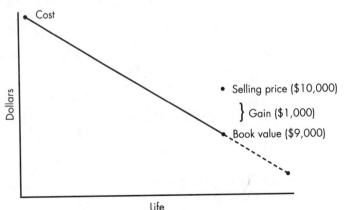

Based on the information in the diagram, the sale is recorded as follows:

+ $10,000	Assets − $20,000	+ $11,000	= Liabs. +	S. Eq. + $1,000

Cash	Machine		Accumulated Depreciation: Machine		Gain on Sale of Machine
$10,000	Bal. $20,000	$20,000	$11,000	Bal. $11,000	$1,000
	Bal. $0			Bal. $0	

If the disposal occurs because the asset has been stolen or destroyed by an accident or fire, the procedures are the same as those described above except that the gain or loss would have an appropriate title, such as Loss Due to Fire, or Gain Due to Accident. Note that this latter title does not indicate that the company has "gained" from the accident, but only that the recovery value of the asset, the cash received from the insurance company, is greater than its book value at the time of the accident. Although the insurance company pays the fair value of the used asset, the company may not have gained anything. The company will almost certainly have suffered an economic loss because of other incidental costs related to the accident, such as a disruption of its normal activities. In addition, the company may have to replace the used asset with a new asset that is likely to require a greater cash outlay than the amount received from the insurance company.

To illustrate, in 1988 a fire destroyed a factory owned by R. G. Barry Corporation. The company reported a gain of $800,000 because the proceeds from the insurance exceeded the book value of the assets destroyed. The company's net income was only $23,000. In this situation, it is difficult to argue that the gain reported by the company is an indication that it, or the shareholders, are better off. It is also important to note that the size of the gain is a function of the book value, which has been determined on the basis of the depreciation method used and the estimated life and residual value. It may be argued that the company is worse off because of the disruption to its activities.

SECTION B Intangibles, Natural Resources, and Disclosure

■ INTANGIBLE ASSETS

In addition to property, plant, and equipment, many companies have another category of noncurrent assets called intangible assets. **Intangible assets are non-current assets that do not have a physical substance.** Their value to the company typically results from the use of the *legal rights* associated with the intangible asset rather than from physical use. Examples of intangibles are patents, copyrights, trademarks and tradenames, franchises, computer software costs, organization costs, leases and leasehold improvements, and goodwill. It should be noted that the recording of intangibles does not change the accounting principles discussed earlier in this book. For example, advertising costs are expensed in the period incurred and are not considered to be an intangible asset because, presumably, they do not provide benefits that can be *reliably* measured beyond the period of the expenditure. Also, of course, they provide no legal rights to the company. Even though accounts receivable and prepaid items do not have a physical substance they are not recorded as intangible assets because they are not long term. If a company had a long-term receivable, it could be argued that the receivable should be classified as an intangible asset because it meets the appropriate criteria. It would not be classified as such, however, because the nature of the asset is very different from the other intangibles.

Intangible assets are similar in many ways to tangible assets such as property, plant, and equipment because (1) they are used in activities related to the production process and they are not held for investment, (2) they have an expected life of more than one year, (3) they derive their value from their ability to generate revenue for their owners, and (4) they should be expensed in the periods in which their benefits are received.

Intangible assets generally have five characteristics that distinguish them from tangible assets:

1. Intangible assets do not have a physical substance but more often, though not exclusively, result from legal rights.
2. There is generally a higher degree of uncertainty regarding the future benefits that can be expected to be derived from them.
3. Their value is subject to wider fluctuations because it may depend to a considerable extent on competitive conditions.
4. They may have value only to a particular company.
5. They may have expected lives that are very difficult to determine.

The cost of an intangible asset is expensed over its life in a similar manner to property, plant, and equipment. However, this expense is called amortization expense rather than depreciation expense, as discussed later. Before each kind of intangible asset is explained, accounting for research and development is discussed because it may affect the dollar amounts included as intangible assets.

Research and Development Costs

Many companies engage in research and development (R&D) to improve their products. Expenditures on R&D by technologically oriented companies may represent a significant part of their total expenditures each period. For example, in 1989 General Motors and IBM together spent over $12 billion on R&D.

Research is a planned search or critical investigation aimed at discovery of new knowledge; development is the translation of research findings into a plan

EXHIBIT 7–7 Examples of activities included in and excluded from R&D

INCLUDED IN R&D	EXCLUDED FROM R&D
(a) Laboratory research aimed at discovery of new knowledge.	(a) Engineering follow-through in an early phase of commercial production.
(b) Searching for applications of new research findings or other knowledge.	(b) Quality control during commercial production including routine testing of products.
(c) Conceptual formulation and design of possible product or process alternatives.	(c) Trouble-shooting in connection with breakdowns during commercial production.
(d) Testing in search for or evaluation of product or process alternatives.	(d) Routine, ongoing efforts to refine, enrich, or otherwise improve upon the qualities of an existing product.
(e) Modification of the formulation or design of a product or process.	(e) Adaptation of an existing capability to a particular requirement or customer's need as part of a continuing commercial activity.
(f) Design, construction, and testing of preproduction prototypes and models.	(f) Seasonal or other periodic design changes to existing products.
(g) Design of tools, jigs, molds, and dies involving new technology.	(g) Routine design of tools, jigs, molds, and dies.
(h) Design, construction, and operation of a pilot plant that is not of a scale economically feasible to the enterprise for commercial production.	(h) Activity, including design and construction engineering, related to the construction, relocation, rearrangement, or start-up of facilities or equipment other than (1) pilot plants and (2) facilities or equipment whose sole use is for a particular research and development project.
(i) Engineering activity required to advance the design of a product to the point that it meets specific functional and economic requirements and is ready for manufacture.	(i) Legal work in connection with patent applications or litigation, and the sale or licensing of patents.

Source: *FASB Statement of Financial Accounting Standards* No. 2 (Stamford, Conn.: FASB, 1974), par. 9 and 10.

or design for a new product or process.[7] Examples of items included in and excluded from R&D are shown in Exhibit 7–7. The costs included in R&D are those for such items as materials, equipment, and facilities used in R&D projects, the salaries of R&D employees, and a reasonable allocation of general and administrative costs. **Costs incurred for research and development are required to be**

....

[7]"Accounting for Research and Development Costs," *FASB Statement of Financial Accounting Standards No. 2* (Stamford, Conn.: FASB, 1974), par. 8.

expensed as incurred, and the amount must be disclosed directly in the financial statements or in the notes.

Each year many companies spend large amounts of money on R&D because they expect to receive total future benefits that exceed the costs incurred. While total future benefits are expected to exceed the total costs incurred, not all R&D projects are successful. Some projects will be unsuccessful (costs exceed benefits), and others will be successful (benefits exceed costs) so that, overall, the benefits are expected to exceed the costs. If benefits are expected to exist for many periods in the future, it could be argued that the cost of acquiring these benefits should be recorded as an asset. The decision to require the expensing of all R&D costs was made to avoid the complexity of capitalizing (recording as an asset) any such costs expected to provide future benefits. For example, if accounting principles required the capitalization of R&D projects that were expected to be successful and the expensing of unsuccessful projects, many difficult problems would arise. How reliable would such decisions be on the expected success of projects? Who would make the decisions? How would the accountant verify the decisions? What is the expected life of the benefits? What is the pattern of the expected benefits? It was because of the difficulty of answering these kinds of questions that the FASB required the expensing of all R&D costs. This requirement has the advantage of providing uniformity among all companies even though it may not be the most conceptually sound alternative when future benefits are expected. In other words, the FASB chose a *reliable* method. The creation of uniformity should enhance *comparability* between companies and therefore help users of financial statements.

To illustrate the accounting for R&D suppose that a company incurs the following costs for R&D activities:

Materials used from inventory	$ 50,000
Wages and salaries	120,000
Allocation of general and administrative costs	20,000
Depreciation on building housing R&D activities	25,000

All these costs are included in R&D expenses and therefore are recorded as follows:

	Assets		= Liabs. +	S. Eq.
−$140,000	−$50,000	−$25,000		−$215,000

Cash (or Payables)	Inventory	Accumulated Depreciation: Building	Research and Development Expenses
$140,000	$50,000	$25,000	$215,000

Note that the depreciation is included in R&D expense rather than listed as depreciation expense.

Patents

A patent is an exclusive right granted by the federal government giving its owner the control of the manufacture, sale, or other use of an invention for 17 years. Patents cannot be renewed, but their effective life is often extended by obtaining new patents on modifications and improvements to the original invention. The costs of obtaining a patent are capitalized as an intangible asset. Since all the research and development costs associated with the internal development of an invention are expensed, however, the costs that are capitalized primarily consist of the costs of acquiring the patent, such as the costs of processing the patent application and any legal costs incurred. Alternatively, if a patent is purchased from another company, the entire acquisition cost is capitalized. If a company incurs a cost for the successful defense of a patent against infringement by another company, the cost is added (debited) to the Patent account. Of course, if the patent defense is unsuccessful, the costs would have to be expensed and the remaining balance in the Patent account would have to be removed (credited) and a loss recognized (debited) because the patent would no longer provide benefits.

Copyrights

A copyright is an exclusive right granted by the federal government covering the right to publish, sell, or otherwise control literary or artistic products for the life of the author plus an additional 50 years. Copyrights cover such items as books, music, and films. As with patents, the costs of obtaining the copyright are capitalized. The cost of producing the item under copyright would be accounted for separately. For example, the costs of producing a film are accounted for separately from the copyright on the film and therefore are recorded as an asset entitled, say, Film Production. This asset would be depreciated over its revenue-producing life.

Trademarks and Tradenames

A trademark or tradename is registered with the U.S. Patent Office and establishes a right to the exclusive use of a name, symbol, or other device used for product identification. Pepsi and Kleenex, for example, are tradenames. The right lasts for 20 years and is renewable indefinitely as long as the trademark or tradename is used continuously. Again, only the costs directly associated with obtaining the trademark or tradename are capitalized. The costs of promoting the name and producing the product are accounted for separately as advertising expense and inventory, respectively.

Franchises

A franchise is an agreement entered into by two parties in which, for a fee, one party (the franchisor) gives the other party (the franchisee) rights to perform certain functions or sell certain products or services. In addition, the franchisor may agree to provide certain services to the franchisee. For example, many McDonald's restaurants are locally owned and operated under a franchise agreement with the McDonald's Company. As with other intangibles, the cost incurred by the franchisee to acquire the franchise is capitalized as an intangible asset.

Computer Software Costs

Until the early 1980s, most companies expensed the cost of software development. At that time many companies started to adopt a policy of capitalizing software costs. In 1985, the FASB adopted accounting principles that clarified the accounting for computer software costs. For accounting purposes, there are three categories of costs associated with software that is to be sold, leased, or otherwise marketed directly or indirectly as part of a product, process, or service.[8] First, there are **software production costs** such as design, coding, testing, documentation, and preparation of training materials. These costs are recorded as research and development expenses until technological feasibility of the product is established. Since companies use different development methods, **technological feasibility** is established either on the date of the completion of a detail program design or, in its absence, on completion of a working model of the product. After this date, all software production costs are capitalized until the product is available for sale to customers. Any software production costs incurred after the product is ready for sale are expensed. The accounting for software production costs may be summarized as follows:

The capitalized software production costs are amortized over the expected life of the product which will typically be a relatively short period, such as 5 years. The amount of the amortization expense is the greater of either (1) the ratio of current gross revenues to the total amount of current and anticipated future gross revenues or (2) the straight-line method. If the market value of the software product becomes lower than the asset's book value, the asset is written down

....

[8]"Accounting for the Costs of Computer Software to Be Sold, Leased, or Otherwise Marketed," *FASB Statement of Financial Accounting Standards No. 86* (Stamford, Conn.: FASB, 1985).

to this value and a loss recognized. The lower value is then recognized as the new cost and the write-down may not be recovered.

The second category of costs is the **unit cost** of producing the software, such as costs of the disks and duplication of the software, packaging, documentation, and training materials. These unit costs are recorded as inventory and expensed as cost of goods sold when the related revenue is recognized. The third category of costs is the **maintenance and customer support costs** incurred after the software is released. These costs are expensed as incurred.

Note that these rules do *not* apply to the costs of software that is developed for internal use. If such an activity is considered to be research and development, the costs are expensed until it can be concluded that the software project no longer is research or development. Also, the costs of developing or improving software used in a company's selling or administrative activities, such as an airline's computer reservation system or a company's management information system, are not included as research and development.[9] Therefore, such costs may be capitalized or expensed, although most companies do follow the practice of expensing them.

Organization Costs

Organization costs are the costs associated with the formation of a corporation. When a corporation is formed (incorporated) certain costs are incurred, such as legal fees, stock certificate costs, accounting fees, and fees associated with promoting the sale of the stock. These organization costs are also capitalized as an intangible asset entitled Organization Costs. While it may be argued that this asset has an expected life equal to the life of the company, Organization Costs must be amortized over a period not to exceed 40 years, as discussed below. In practice, however, most corporations amortize organization costs over 60 months because this is the shortest time period allowed by the Internal Revenue Service for federal income tax purposes.

Leases and Leasehold Improvements

A lease is an agreement conveying the right to use property, plant, or equipment without transferring legal ownership of the item. A **lessee** is the company that acquires the right to use the property, plant, and equipment; a **lessor** is the company giving up the right. Therefore, a lease is an intangible asset to the lessee because a right to use property is held by the lessee while the property is still legally owned by the lessor. A lease may be accounted for as a capital

....

[9]"Applicability of FASB Statement No. 2 to Computer Software," *FASB Interpretation No. 6* (Stamford, Conn.: FASB, 1975).

lease or an operating lease by the lessee, as discussed in Chapter 9. Capital leases are typically included on the balance sheet of the lessee within property, plant, and equipment rather than under intangible assets. **A leasehold improvement is an improvement made to the leased property, plant, or equipment by the lessee.** An example is an improvement to the interior design of a leased retail store. Leasehold improvements are also typically classified on the balance sheet of the lessee within property, plant, and equipment. Since the improvement would become the property of the lessor at the end of the lease, a leasehold improvement is amortized over its economic life or the life of the lease, whichever is shorter.

Goodwill

Goodwill is another intangible asset that might appear on the balance sheet. Goodwill is recorded when a company purchases another company or a significant portion of another company. Goodwill is often called "excess of cost over net assets of acquired companies." **Goodwill is the difference between the price paid to buy a company and the fair market value of the identifiable net assets (assets minus liabilities) acquired.** The reason why a purchaser may be willing to pay more than the market value of the identifiable net assets is that there are some "assets" that are not recorded under generally accepted accounting principles, and therefore the purchaser can expect to obtain higher than normal earnings. For example, a company may have established a reputation for high-quality products and service on those products, or it may have valuable patents or R&D in progress, or it may have recruited and trained employees who are above average. Such characteristics make the company more valuable than the sum of the recorded net assets, and so the purchaser of the company should be willing to pay more than the fair market value of the net assets that are included on the balance sheet. The following steps should be completed to determine the goodwill involved in the acquisition of another company:

1. Identify any assets and liabilities that are not included on the financial statements of the company being acquired, but which should be recorded (under generally accepted accounting principles).

2. Determine the fair market value of the assets and liabilities recorded on the financial statements of the company being acquired, as well as the fair market value of the assets and liabilities identified in step 1.

3. Compute the value of goodwill as the difference between the purchase price of the company and the total of the amounts determined from step 2.

For example, suppose that the balance sheet of the Windsor Company includes assets of $200,000 and liabilities of $75,000. Thus, the book value of the recorded net assets (assets minus liabilities) is $125,000. Furthermore, assume that the fair market value of these net assets is $185,000 and that the company has unrecorded intangible assets with a fair market value of $25,000. If the Castle Company decides to purchase the Windsor Company for $240,000, the goodwill is computed as follows:

Purchase price		$240,000
Book value of the recorded net assets	$125,000	
Excess of fair market value over book value of recorded net assets ($185,000 − $125,000)	60,000	
Fair market value of unrecorded identifiable intangible assets	25,000	
Less: value of identifiable net assets		(210,000)
Value of goodwill purchased		$ 30,000

The identifiable tangible and intangible net assets are individually recorded at their respective fair market values totaling $210,000, and the purchased goodwill is separately recorded as an intangible asset at its purchase price of $30,000. It is then amortized over its expected life (not to exceed 40 years). Amortization of goodwill is not an expense that can be deducted when computing corporate federal income taxes. The acquisition of one company by another is discussed further in Chapter 11.

Amortization of Intangibles

Recall that R&D costs are expensed as incurred. On the other hand, since the costs of the intangible assets discussed above are capitalized, they must be expensed over the expected life of the benefits they produce. **Amortization expense is the allocation of a portion of the acquisition cost of an intangible asset as an expense.** Therefore, it is exactly the same concept as depreciation expense, with only a change in the title. Below is a diagram that illustrates the differences between the expensing of R&D costs and other intangible assets:

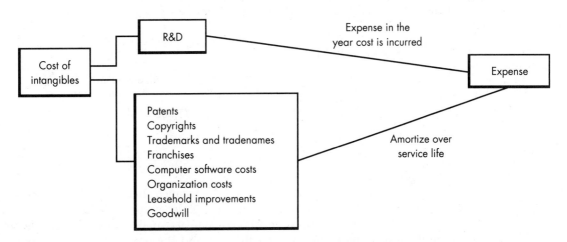

Note that the cost of an intangible is amortized over its expected *service* life and not necessarily over its legal life. For example, although a patent has a maximum legal life of 17 years, its expected service life may be less than 17 years. The patent would be expensed over the lesser of the two periods, its actual service life or its legal life of 17 years. As we have seen, some intangibles have very long lives, and in the case of trademarks and tradenames a potentially indefinite life. Because of the difficulty of determining the likelihood of benefits so far into the future, however, an arbitrary maximum economic life of 40 years has been imposed. **The general rule for amortization of intangibles, therefore, is that the expected life of the intangible is the lesser of the service life or the legal life, up to a maximum of 40 years.** In addition, the *straight-line* amortization method should be used unless there is convincing evidence that an alternative method provides a better matching of expenses against revenues. Since it is unlikely that an intangible asset will have a residual value, none will be used in this chapter.

To illustrate, suppose that a company acquires a patent on a new type of production process at the beginning of the year for $10,000. The production process is expected to be useful for 10 years, after which newer technology will replace it. For this reason, the patent is amortized over the 10-year expected service life rather than the 17-year legal life. The acquisition of the patent is recorded as follows:

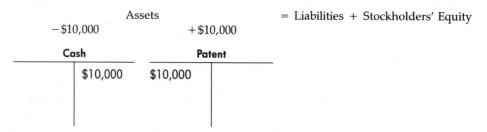

At the end of the year, the amortization is recorded as follows:

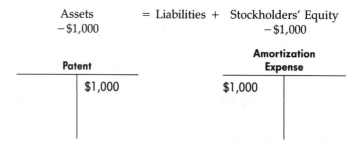

Intangible assets are usually listed on the balance sheet in a separate section below Property, Plant, and Equipment. Intangible assets are valued at cost less the accumulated amortization. This book value is usually shown as a single net amount because disclosure of both the cost and the accumulated amortization is not required. That is why the (credit) entry can be made directly to the asset account as shown in the preceding example. Two examples of the disclosure of intangible assets are shown in Exhibit 7–8. It should be recognized that the market value of intangibles is often much greater than their book value disclosed on the balance sheet.

EXHIBIT 7–8 Examples of disclosure of intangibles

....

MONSANTO

Assets (in part):

	At December 31	
	1989	1988

(in millions)
Intangible Assets, net of accumulated amortization of $1,029
in 1989 and $798 in 1988 ... $1,682 ... $1,790

NOTES TO FINANCIAL STATEMENTS (in part):

Significant Accounting Policies (in part):

Intangible assets are recorded at cost less accumulated amortization. The components of intangible assets, and their estimated remaining useful lives, were as follows:

	Estimated Remaining Life*	1989	1988
Patents	4	$ 679	$ 864
Goodwill	34	737	653
Other intangible assets	21	266	273
Total		$1,682	$1,790

*Weighted average, in years, at December 31, 1989.

Patents obtained in a business acquistion are recorded at the present value of estimated future cash flows resulting from patent ownership. The cost of patents is amortized over their legal lives. Goodwill is the cost of acquired businesses in excess of the fair value of their identifiable net assets and is amortized over the estimated periods of benefit (5 to 40 years). The cost of other intangible assets (principally product rights and trademarks) is amortized over their estimated useful lives.

INTERNATIONAL MULTIFOODS

Notes (in part)
Intangibles primarily represent costs in excess of net tangible asset values of businesses acquired. Excess costs arising prior to November 1, 1970, are being carried until such time as there may be evidence of diminution of value or the term of existence of such value becomes limited. Excess costs arising since October 31, 1970, are being amortized over not more than a 40 year period. Other intangibles are being amortized over 5 to 10 year periods on a straight-line basis.

Although an intangible asset is amortized on the basis of its expected service life at the time of acquisition, this life should be reviewed periodically to ensure that it is reasonable. For example, before the trucking industry was deregulated in 1980, many trucking companies included in their balance sheets an intangible asset relating to the franchises they owned allowing them to engage in interstate trucking. When the industry was deregulated these franchises became worthless, and therefore the asset had to be eliminated and a loss recognized.

Exception to the General Rule for Amortization

The accounting principle that mandated the amortization of intangible assets over their economic lives, not to exceed 40 years, was adopted in 1970. Intangible assets acquired before November 1, 1970, do not have to be amortized if there is no evidence of a limited life or a decline in value. Therefore, many companies are currently not amortizing such intangible assets, particularly goodwill. As discussed below, many users disagree with this practice. It should also be noted that this situation of two different principles being applied depending on the date of the original transaction is not typical. Normally, any new accounting principle is applied to *all* previous transactions.

The Income Tax Rules for Amortization of Intangibles

The income tax rules allow the amortization of most intangible assets. For those assets that have an indefinite life, or for which there is no evidence of a decline in value, however, amortization is not allowed. For example, the cost of a National Football League franchise cannot be amortized for tax purposes because there is no evidence of a limited life or a decline in value at this time. The cost of the franchise would have to be amortized for financial statements prepared under generally accepted accounting principles (unless it was acquired before November 1, 1970). Also, the amortization of goodwill is not deductible for computation of taxable income unless there is evidence of a limited life or a decline in value.

■ EVALUATION OF ACCOUNTING FOR INTANGIBLES

For some companies, intangibles are perhaps their most important "asset." For example, Coca-Cola Company's strength might be said to rely heavily on the secret formula for its syrup, its tradename, and its image among consumers, which is developed and maintained through advertising and promotion. Similarly, IBM's strength might be said to rely heavily on its technological ability and its marketing and customer service skills. None of these items appears as an asset on the balance sheet of Coca-Cola or IBM, because either the accounting rules require that the costs be expensed (e.g., advertising, R&D, and employee training), or the intangible was internally developed so long ago that it would be fully amortized (e.g., a tradename), or the intangible was internally developed at an immaterial cost (e.g., a patent). Of course, these accounting values bear little or no relationship to a market value.

As discussed earlier, the maximum life of 40 years over which intangibles may be amortized is arbitrary. However, many users would argue that many, or perhaps most, intangibles should be amortized over a much shorter period.

Who is able to predict with a reasonable degree of confidence that an asset will provide benefits for the next 40 years, say to the year 2030? For example, suppose that a company purchased the Coca-Cola Company for more than the fair value of the identifiable net assets and therefore recorded goodwill on the acquisition. The maintenance of Coca-Cola's market share depends heavily on the advertising and promotion of the company. If it stopped incurring such costs, how long would Coca-Cola survive? Will people even be drinking cola in 40 years? Certainly, all the employees with significant managerial skills will no longer be with the company. All these arguments suggest that the amortization period should be much shorter than 40 years.

In contrast to this situation, it can be argued that certain intangible assets should not be amortized, because there is no evidence of a limited life, just as land is not depreciated. For example, the NFL franchise mentioned earlier does not appear to have a limited life or a decline in value at this time and therefore perhaps should not be amortized. However, remember that accounting principles require that *all* intangible assets, unless acquired before November 1, 1970, must be amortized for financial statement purposes.

It is important to distinguish the *purchased* goodwill discussed above from what is often referred to as "internally developed goodwill." For example, many companies develop reputations for exceptionally reliable products, good customer service, high quality research and development, and good management. None of these components of internally developed goodwill are recognized as assets; instead the costs associated with these items are expensed in the period that they are incurred. No asset is recognized because there has been no transaction with another entity to establish the value of the asset as there has been when purchased goodwill is recorded.

Since the appropriate life for an intangible is so difficult to determine, the user of financial statements should be aware of the impact of the choice of a certain life on the financial statements. The longer the life that is used, the lower the amortization expense will be, and the higher the income will be. This is one of the reasons that companies typically use the longest life that is allowed under generally accepted accounting principles. For example, 67% of the companies that were amortizing goodwill in 1988 used a life of 40 years or "a life not exceeding 40 years." It is also interesting to note that 14% of the companies reporting goodwill were not amortizing it, and that goodwill is the most frequently occurring intangible, representing 70% of those intangibles reported.[10]

To illustrate the importance of goodwill, Phillip Morris acquired Kraft in 1988 for $12.9 billion and recorded goodwill of $11.6 billion. Phillip Morris then had total goodwill of $15 billion, which is nearly triple the net worth of the company. Similarly, Time acquired Warner Communications for $14 billion, of which goodwill was nearly $11 billion. The amortization of this goodwill over 40 years will result in an expense of nearly $300 million per year.[11]

· · · · · · · · · · · · · · · · · · ·

[10] *Accounting Trends and Techniques* (New York: AICPA, 1989), p. 151.
[11] *Business Week*, July 31, 1989.

■ NATURAL RESOURCE ASSETS

In addition to property, plant, and equipment and intangible assets, many companies have natural resource assets. **A natural resource asset is a productive asset that is used up as it is converted into inventory.** Examples of natural resource assets are oil, coal, gravel, and timber. Natural resource assets are usually disclosed in a separate section of the balance sheet. They may appear above or below property, plant, and equipment, depending on the relative importance of the two categories of assets to the particular company. These assets are accounted for in the same manner as the other categories of productive assets. That is, their acquisition costs are capitalized and expensed over their expected service lives. **Depletion expense is the allocation of a portion of the acquisition cost (less the estimated residual value) of a natural resource asset as an expense.** Thus we see that one concept has three different titles—depreciation for property, plant, and equipment, amortization for intangible assets, and depletion for natural resource assets. Three special aspects of natural resource assets require further consideration.

Method of Computing Depletion Expense

Depletion expense is computed using the units-of-production method discussed earlier. That is, the depletable cost (cost minus estimated residual value) is expensed according to the estimate of the production to be obtained from the asset. This method is usually considered appropriate because it results in equal depletion for every unit produced. For example, suppose that a coal mine is purchased for $100,000, the mine is expected to produce 10,000 tons of coal, and the estimated residual value is zero. The depletion per ton of coal mined would be computed as follows:

$$\text{Depletion per Unit} = \frac{\text{Cost} - \text{Estimated Residual Value}}{\text{Units of Production}}$$

$$= \frac{\$100,000 - \$0}{10,000 \text{ tons}}$$

$$= \$10 \text{ per ton}$$

If the company produces and sells 1,200 tons in the first year, the following would be recorded:

Assets	= Liabilities +	Stockholders' Equity
−$12,000		−$12,000

Coal Mine		Depletion Expense	
$12,000		$12,000	

Note that the reduction in the book value of the asset (credit) can be made directly to the asset account, Coal Mine, because separate disclosure in the financial statements of the accumulated depletion is not required. Also, if some of the coal is not sold at year-end, the depletion expense is based on the number of tons sold, with the remaining depletion included in the cost of the inventory.

Often a company purchases or builds tangible assets that have a life that is dependent on the life of the natural resource asset. Such assets should be depreciated over the life of the natural resource. For example, if a company builds housing that has a life of 20 years at a mine that has a life of 10 years, the housing should be depreciated over the expected life of the mine, or 10 years, because the housing will have no use after the mine is exhausted. The depreciation expense on the housing may also be calculated by using the units-of-production method since the usefulness of the housing expires as the coal is mined rather than through the passage of time.

Revised Estimates of Productive Capacity

Because it is often difficult to measure the expected lifetime productive capacity of a natural resource asset, revisions in the estimates are frequently required. Continuing the above example, suppose that at the beginning of the second year the company discovers that by spending an additional $14,600 it can increase the capacity of the mine by 2,000 tons. Assuming this additional cost is incurred, the new depletion rate is computed as follows:

$$\text{Depletion per Unit} = \frac{\text{Book Value} + \text{Additional Costs} - \text{Estimated Residual Value}}{\text{Remaining Units of Production (including additional units)}}$$

$$= \frac{(\$100,000 - \$12,000) + \$14,600 - \$0}{(10,000 - 1,200) + 2,000 \text{ tons}}$$

$$= \frac{\$102,600}{10,800 \text{ tons}}$$

$$= \$9.50 \text{ per ton}$$

If the company produces and sells 1,300 tons in the second year, the depletion expense will be $12,350 ($9.50 × 1,300).

Cost Depletion and Percentage Depletion

For financial statement purposes, depletion expense is based on the cost of the asset, and over the life of the asset the total depletion expense is limited to the cost less the expected residual value. It is known as *cost* depletion and is related to the expected pattern of benefits produced by the asset. This is the method discussed above.

For corporate federal income tax purposes, depletion expense involves a different concept. **Percentage (or statutory) depletion is computed by multiplying a corporation's "gross income" from a natural resources asset by a statutory percentage.** Gross income is essentially the selling price of the natural resource;

the statutory percentage varies, depending on the type of natural resource, from a minimum of 5% to a maximum of 22% (complexities in the computation of the percentage depletion expense, such as the ceiling limitations, are beyond the scope of this book). Since the percentage depletion expense is based on the stated percentage and gross income, the total percentage depletion expense over the life of the asset for federal income tax purposes is *not* limited by the depreciable cost of the asset.

The special income tax laws for depletion are intended to encourage exploration and development of natural resources, whereas depletion expense for financial statement purposes is intended to match the costs against the benefits derived from the asset. There has been much discussion about whether or not percentage depletion encourages exploration and development, with the natural resource companies supporting the method and many consumer groups objecting to it. Although there does not appear to be any definitive evidence of its success, the percentage depletion method is still allowed for income tax purposes. Therefore, most corporations compute a different amount of depletion expense for income tax purposes than for financial statements. The difference between cost depletion and percentage depletion is required to be disclosed in the notes to the financial statements.

■ DISCLOSURE IN THE FINANCIAL STATEMENTS

We have used the title Property, Plant, and Equipment in this chapter because it is the most frequently used caption in the balance sheet. Variations of this title are sometimes used, however, such as Plant and Machinery, Land and Buildings, or for a merchandising company, Property and Equipment. Companies are required to disclose the following items in the financial statements or in the notes accompanying these statements:

1. Depreciation expense for the period.
2. Balances of major classes of depreciable assets by nature (such as land, buildings, equipment) or function (such as petroleum exploration, chemical, construction) at the balance sheet date.
3. Accumulated depreciation, either by major classes of assets or in total, at the balance sheet date.
4. A general description of the method or methods used in computing depreciation with respect to the major classes of depreciable assets.[12]

Two examples of disclosure are illustrated in Exhibit 7–9. It should be noted that a company may use different depreciation methods for different types of assets, because of differences in the pattern of benefits generated by each group.

....
[12]"Omnibus Opinion–1967," *APB Opinion No. 12* (New York: AICPA, 1971), par. 5.

EXHIBIT 7–9 Examples of disclosure of property, plant, and equipment

---

NIKE, INC.

Note 5–Property, plant and equipment:
Property, plant, and equipment includes the following:

	May 31,	
	1989	**1988**
	(in thousands)	
Land	$10,829	$ 9,245
Buildings	19,272	13,412
Machinery and equipment	90,752	79,258
Leasehold improvements	10,275	8,836
Construction in process	23,186	1,271
	154,314	112,022
Less accumulated depreciation	64,332	54,319
	$ 89,982	$ 57,703

ATLANTIC RICHFIELD COMPANY

(in millions of dollars)
7. Fixed Assets
Property, plant and equipment, including capitalized leases and related accumulated depreciation, depletion and amortization at December 31, 1989 and 1988, were as follows:

	1989	1988
Owned Assets, at Cost		
Resources:		
Oil and gas	$19,432	$19,018
Coal	789	666
Products:		
Refining and marketing	2,591	2,314
Transportation	3,311	3,249
Intermediate chemicals and specialty products	1,851	1,565
Integrated petrochemical and petroleum processing	—	2,025
Other operations	457	442
	28,431	29,279
Accumulated depreciation, depletion and amortization	12,774	13,348
Net owned	$15,657	$15,931

Expenses for maintenance and repairs for 1989, 1988 and 1987 were $518, $469, and $369, respectively.

■ APPENDIX: EXCHANGE OF PROPERTY, PLANT, AND EQUIPMENT

When a company decides to dispose of an asset, it may choose to trade in the asset for a new asset. For example, a used delivery van is often exchanged for a new van. The trade-in allowance (assumed to be equal to the fair market value of the asset) is deducted from the cost of the new delivery van, and the balance owed is paid according to the terms of the agreement. **Boot is the cash paid in the exchange of assets.** Thus, the company acquires a new asset by giving up an old asset and paying boot.

Exchange of Dissimilar Productive Assets.   **Productive assets are assets such as inventory, property, and equipment that are used in the production of goods and services.**[13] Productive assets may be classified as similar or dissimilar. The accounting for the exchange of dissimilar productive assets is discussed first because it is less complex. **Dissimilar productive assets are assets that are not of the same general type, do not perform the same function, or are not employed in the same line of business.** When dissimilar productive assets are exchanged (e.g., trading in a delivery van toward the acquisition of a building), the exchange is considered as two separate transactions. The disposal of the old asset is recorded as discussed earlier (with the proceeds being the fair market value of the old asset rather than the cash paid), and the acquisition of the new asset is recorded at the acquisition cost, although both the disposal and acquisition are recorded at one time. For example, suppose that a delivery van is traded in for a building (a dissimilar productive asset) and the transaction has the following characteristics:

Original cost of van	$10,000
Accumulated depreciation to date of exchange	6,000
Cost of building	40,000
Cash paid (boot)	37,000

Since the van and cash of $37,000 are exchanged for the building, which costs $40,000, the van must be worth $3,000. The van has a book value of $4,000 (the cost of $10,000 less the accumulated depreciation of $6,000), and therefore there is a loss of $1,000 on the disposal of the van ($4,000 book value − $3,000 fair market value). The exchange is recorded as follows:

		Assets		= Liabs. +	S. Eq.
− $37,000	+ $40,000	− $10,000	+ $6,000		− $1,000

Cash	Building	Delivery Van	Accumulated Depreciation: Delivery Van	Loss on Disposal of Delivery Van
$37,000	$40,000	Bal. $10,000 $10,000 $6,000 Bal. $0	Bal. $6,000 Bal. $0	$1,000

[13]"Accounting for Nonmonetary Transactions," *APB Opinion No. 29* (New York: AICPA, 1973), par. 3.

Gains on exchanges of *dissimilar* productive assets are recorded in the same way as losses. In other words, they are recognized in full in the period in which they occur.

Exchange of Similar Productive Assets. **Similar productive assets are assets of the same general type, that perform the same function, or that are employed in the same line of business.** When similar productive assets are exchanged, special accounting practices are used. For example, the trade of player contracts by professional sports organizations or the trade of a used delivery truck for a new delivery truck would be considered exchanges of similar productive assets.

The special accounting procedure for an exchange of similar productive assets is that a gain on the trade-in of the old asset is *not* recognized. This is justified by the argument that the earning process on the old asset has not been completed. For example, suppose that a company buys a warehouse that has an expected life of 20 years. The expectation is that the company will get 20 years of benefits. Suppose that the company exchanges the warehouse for another warehouse after five years. Since the 20-year productive life of the original warehouse will be completed by the new warehouse, any "gain" on the trade is ignored.

To illustrate the accounting for similar productive asset exchanges, suppose that the following facts relate to the exchange of two delivery trucks by a company:

Original cost of old truck	$20,000
Accumulated depreciation on old truck	4,500
Book value of old truck	15,500
Contract price for new truck	22,000
Cash paid (boot)	4,000

Since the new delivery truck has a contract price of $22,000 but only $4,000 is paid, the trade-in allowance on the old truck is $18,000. Therefore, the seller has an implied gain of $2,500 (trade-in of $18,000 − book value of $15,500) on the old truck, but *this gain is ignored*, and the new truck is recorded as follows:

$$\text{Book Value of New Asset} = \text{Book Value of Old Asset} + \text{Cash Paid}$$
$$= \$15,500 + \$4,000$$
$$= \$19,500$$

The exchange is recorded as follows:

Assets				= Liabs. + S. Eq.
− $4,000	+ $19,500	+ $4,500	− $20,000	
Cash	**Truck (new)**	**Accumulated Depreciation: Truck (old)**	**Truck (old)**	
			Bal. $4,500 Bal. $20,000	
$4,000	$19,500	$4,500	$20,000	
		Bal. $0 Bal. $0		

The effect of ignoring the gain at the time of the exchange is to reduce the cost of the new asset and therefore the amount of depreciation to be recorded over the life of the newly acquired asset. Thus the "gain" is spread out over the life of the new asset because the lower recorded cost results in lower depreciation expense and higher income before income taxes over that life.

Many users of financial statements disagree with this procedure because they argue that the substance of the transaction (the gain) is ignored. If similar productive assets are exchanged in the future and no loss is ever incurred, a virtually permanent nonrecognition of subsequent gains may be possible. It must be emphasized that this special procedure applies only when there is an implicit gain on the exchange. A *loss* is recognized by the same procedure discussed earlier for the exchange of dissimilar productive assets. The recognition of a loss is justified by the conservatism principle, which was discussed in Chapter 4.

Federal Income Tax and the Exchange of Similar Productive Assets

For corporate income tax purposes, the Internal Revenue Code requires that either a a gain or a loss be recognized when dissimilar productive assets are exchanged. On the other hand, the Code requires that either a loss or a gain be *ignored* when similar productive assets are exchanged and cash is *paid* by the company acquiring the asset. (Special procedures, which are beyond the scope of this book, apply when cash is *received* by the company that has a gain. These special procedures also apply to financial reporting.) These similarities and differences are summarized below:

	Dissimilar Productive Assets		Similar Productive Assets	
	Accounting	**Tax**	**Accounting**	**Tax**
Gain	Recognized	Recognized	Not recognized*	Not recognized*
Loss	Recognized	Recognized	Recognized	Not recognized

*Special rules exist when cash is received (beyond the scope of the text).

Thus it can be seen that there is a difference between financial reporting and income tax reporting for the exchange of similar productive assets. This difference occurs because a loss is not recognized for income tax purposes, whereas, as we have seen, it is recognized for financial reporting purposes. This difference would be disclosed in the notes to the financial statements.

QUESTIONS

1. What characteristics are necessary for an asset to be included in the category of property, plant, and equipment?

2. What is the general criterion used to decide whether an expenditure should be included in

the cost of property, plant, and equipment rather than being expensed?

3. What is the relationship between the book value and the market value of an asset during the life of the asset?

4. When several assets are purchased for a single lump sum, what is the principle used for cost apportionment? Why is it necessary to apportion the cost?

5. Explain how the amount of interest to be capitalized is determined when a company constructs an asset.

6. A company borrows some money which it uses to acquire a parcel of land for a real estate development project. Before construction begins, a period of time elapses while the company obtains the necessary planning permission. May the company capitalize interest during this period? If so, should the interest be capitalized to the land or the building?

7. May profit be recognized during self-construction of an asset under generally accepted accounting principles? May a loss be recognized?

8. Distinguish among the use of the terms depreciation, depletion, and amortization.

9. Briefly explain the meaning of the three factors that are involved in the computation of the periodic charge for depreciation.

10. What is the objective of accounting for depreciation?

11. Explain how charging depreciation affects (a) the income statement and (b) the balance sheet.

12. Does the straight-line method produce a constant or variable depreciation amount per unit? Is your answer different for the units-of-production method?

13. "We will be able to buy the new machine that costs $80,000 because we have over $100,000 of accumulated depreciation." Do you agree?

14. Why may depreciation on the financial statements be different from depreciation charged for income tax purposes?

15. What are the primary causes of depreciation? For each cause indicate which depreciation method may be most appropriate. Would it be desirable to require all companies to use the same method?

16. Under what circumstances are accelerated methods of depreciation most appropriate?

17. If a company uses accelerated depreciation for a building rather than the straight-line method, what effect does that choice have on the financial statements in the year of acquisition?

18. Under what circumstances would the depreciation charged on an asset not be included in total in the current income statement?

19. In a year in which the cost of replacing an asset rises, should depreciation be charged on that asset? Why?

20. An accelerated depreciation method should be used because of the large decline in the value of an asset early in its life. Evaluate this statement.

21. The manager of a utility stated that since its transmission lines are kept in good condition by regular repairs and maintenance and their efficiency remains constant, the lines do not depreciate. Do you agree with this statement?

22. What is the distinction between a capital and an operating (revenue) expenditure? Give two examples of each.

23. Are gains and losses from disposals of assets reported in the income statement in the same way as depreciation expense? If not, how are they reported?

24. What characteristics distinguish intangible assets from tangible assets? What characteristics are similar?

25. Are all intangible assets amortized? If not, which ones are not? Why?

26. Which amortization method is required for intangibles? Are there any exceptions?

27. What is meant by the terms *research* and *development*?

28. How would a patent worth $100,000 be recorded if: (a) It had just been purchased for $90,000? (b) It had been developed by the company?

29. What is the maximum life over which the following intangible assets should be amortized: (a) patent; (b) copyright; (c) franchise; and (d) goodwill?

30. What is meant by the term *goodwill*? Describe two factors that might cause a purchaser to pay more than the fair market value of the net assets of a company.

31. What is a natural resource asset? How is it accounted for?

32. Describe how depletion expense is calculated under the cost depletion method. How does the calculation differ under percentage depletion?

PROBLEMS AND CASES

33. Assets Included in Property, Plant, and Equipment. The Young Company owned the following assets at the end of its accounting period:

1. Land on which a warehouse had been built.
2. Land on which it is planning to build a new store two years from now.
3. A retail store.
4. Shelving in the store used for the display of products.
5. Old cash registers that had been replaced by point-of-sale systems and will be sold next year.
6. Goods held in a warehouse for later sale.

Required Which of the assets should be considered as property, plant, or equipment? Explain your reasoning.

34. Inclusion in Property, Plant, and Equipment. Which of the following would be included in property, plant, and equipment on the balance sheet?

1. Idle equipment awaiting sale.
2. Land held for future use as a plant site.
3. Land held for investment.
4. Deposits on machinery not yet received.
5. Progress payments on building being constructed by a contractor.
6. Fully depreciated assets still being used.
7. Leasehold improvements.
8. Assets leased to others.

35. Lump Sum Purchase. The Gibson Company purchased a building and some machinery on January 1, 1993, by paying $140,000 cash. The building was appraised for $90,000 and the machinery for $60,000. The estimated lives of the building and machinery were 20 years and 7 years, respectively, and the estimated residual values were zero. The straight-line depreciation method is used.

Required **1.** Record the effects of the purchase on the accounting equation.

2. Compute the depreciation expense for 1993.

36. Acquisition of Land and Building. On February 1, 1993, Edwards Corporation purchased a parcel of land as a factory site for $50,000. An old building on the property was demolished, and construction began on a new building, which was completed on November 1, 1993. Costs incurred during this period are:

Demolition of building	$ 4,000
Architect's fees	20,000
Legal fees for title investigation and purchase contract	2,000
Construction costs	500,000

Required At what amount should Edwards record the cost of the land and the new building, respectively? *(AICPA adapted)*

37. Interest During Construction. On January 1, 1993, the Bromley Company started the construction of a building for its own use. By the end of the year, the company had incurred construction costs of $160,000. The company borrowed money at 10% to finance the construction.

Required 1. Compute the amount of interest cost that the company should include in the cost of the building.

2. Describe the effects on the financial statements of including interest in the cost of the building rather than recording it as interest expense.

38. Interest During Construction. The Alta Company is constructing a production complex which qualifies for interest capitalization. The following information is available:

Capitalization period: January 1, 1992, to June 30, 1994.
Expenditures on project (incurred evenly during each period):
    1992 $2 million
    1993 $4 million
    1994 $6 million
Amounts borrowed and outstanding:
    $6 million borrowed on July 1, 1989, at 14%
    $14 million borrowed on January 1, 1986, at 8%

Required 1. Compute the amount of interest costs capitalized each year.

2. If it is assumed that the production complex has an estimated life of 20 years and a residual value of zero, compute the straight-line depreciation in 1995.

39. Depreciation Methods. The Sorter Company purchased equipment for $200,000 on January 1, 1993. The equipment has an estimated service life of eight years and an estimated residual value of $15,000.

Required Compute the depreciation charge for 1993 under each of the following methods:

1. Straight line.

2. Sum of the years' digits.

3. Double declining balance.

40. Depreciation Methods. The Desmond Company purchased a machine on January 1, 1993, for $75,000. The estimated life and residual value are ten years and $10,000, respectively. It is expected that the machine will operate for 20,000 hours and produce 100,000 units.

During 1993 the machine was operated for 2,200 hours and produced 10,500 units. During 1994 there was a strike and the machine operated for only 1,600 hours and produced only 7,500 units.

Required **1.** Compute the depreciation expense for 1993 and 1994 under each of the following methods:

    a. Activity level: units produced.
    b. Activity level: hours used.
    c. Straight line.
    d. Sum of the years' digits.
    e. Double declining balance.

    2. Show how the asset would be disclosed in the balance sheet at December 31, 1993, under each method.

    3. Should the strike affect the application of any of the listed depreciation methods? Explain.

41. Depreciation Methods. The Prentiss Company purchased a machine on January 1, 1993, for $20,000. The estimated life and residual value are four years and $2,000, respectively. The machine is expected to operate for 30,000 hours and produce 200,000 units. During 1993 the machine was operated for 6,500 hours and produced 50,000 units. During 1994 there was a strike and the machine operated for only 3,200 hours and produced only 24,000 units.

Required **1.** Compute the depreciation expense for 1993 and 1994 under each of the following methods:

    a. Activity level: units produced.
    b. Activity level: hours used.
    c. Straight line.
    d. Sum of the years' digits.
    e. Double declining balance.

    2. Should the strike affect the application of any of the listed depreciation methods? Explain.

42. Depreciation Methods. The Nickle Company purchased an asset for $25,000 on January 1, 1993. The asset has an expected residual value of $1,000. The depreciation expense for 1993 and 1994 are shown below for three alternative depreciation methods:

Year	Method A	Method B	Method C
1993	$6,000	$9,600	$9,375
1994	6,000	7,200	5,859

Required **1.** Which depreciation method is being used in each example?

    2. Compute the depreciation expense for 1995 and 1996 under each method.

43. Depreciation and Rate of Return. The Burrell Company purchased a machine for $20,000 on January 1, 1993. The machine has an estimated service life of five years and a zero estimated residual value. The asset earns income before depreciation and income taxes of $10,000 each year. The tax rate is 35%.

Required Compute the rate of return earned (on the average net asset value) by the company each year of the asset's life under the straight-line and the double-declining-balance depreciation methods. Assume that the machine is the company's only asset.

44. Depreciation and Income Taxes. The Paul Company purchased an asset on January 1, 1993, for $50,000. The asset has an expected life of five years, a residual value of zero, and a life of three years under the Modified Accelerated Cost Recovery System.

Required Compute the depreciation expense recorded (1) on the company's financial statements and (2) on its income tax returns for each year of the asset's economic life.

45. Depreciation for Financial Statements and Income Tax Purposes. The Dinkle Company purchased equipment for $50,000. It has an estimated residual value of $5,000 and an expected useful life of ten years. The company uses straight-line depreciation for its financial statements.

Required What is the difference between the company's income before income taxes reported on its financial statements and the taxable income reported on its tax return in each of the first two years of the asset's life if the asset was purchased on January 1, 1993, and the company uses the MACRS method over five years for income tax purposes?

46. Depreciation for Financial Statements and Income Tax Purposes. The Hunter Company purchased a light truck on January 1, 1993, for $18,000. The truck, which will be used for deliveries, has the following characteristics:

Estimated life: six years

Estimated residual value: $3,000

Depreciation for financial statements: straight line

Depreciation for income tax purposes: MACRS (five-year life)

From 1993 through 1998, each year the company had sales of $100,000, cost of goods sold of $60,000, and operating expenses (excluding depreciation) of $15,000. The truck was disposed of on December 31, 1998, for $2,000.

Required 1. Prepare an income statement for financial reporting through income before income taxes for each of the six years, 1993 through 1998.

2. Prepare, instead, an income statement for income tax purposes through taxable income for each of the six years, 1993 through 1998.

3. Compare the total income for all six years under requirement 1 and requirement 2.

47. Revision of Estimates. The Peterson Company purchased a computer on January 1, 1993, for $40,000. The economic life and the residual value are estimated to be ten years and $6,000, respectively. The straight-line depreciation method is used. In

January 1994, because of advances in technology, the company adjusts its estimates to a six-year total life and a residual value of $500.

Required Compute the depreciation expense for 1994.

48. Depreciation and Cash Flows. In 1992, the Expansion Company had the following income statement:

Cash revenue	$800,000
Cash expenses	(400,000)
Depreciation expense	(200,000)
Income before income taxes	$200,000
Income tax expense (30%)	(60,000)
Net income	$140,000

At the beginning of 1993, the company purchases additional assets at a cost of $1 million. Each year these assets provide additional cash revenues of $400,000 and incur cash expenses of $200,000. The assets have a ten-year life, and the company uses the straight-line depreciation method for all assets. The existing assets produce the same cash revenues and incur the same cash expenses as in 1992. Assume that income taxes are paid on December 31 each year.

Required **1.** Prepare an income statement for 1993.

2. Compute the net cash inflow from the company's operations in 1993 if it is assumed that the company paid income taxes equal to the income tax expense.

3. Compute the net cash inflow from the company's operations in 1993 if it is assumed that the company's MACRS depreciation was twice the straight-line amount.

49. Capital and Operating Expenditures. The following events occurred in a company during the year:

1. Installed a solar energy collector in a warehouse.

2. Installed a hydraulic lift door in a delivery truck.

3. Put a new roof on a warehouse.

4. Painted a new advertising logo on the fleet of the company trucks.

5. Redecorated offices.

6. Repaired a company car involved in an accident; the car was not covered by insurance.

Required Classify these items as capital or operating expenditures. Explain your reasoning.

50. Capital and Operating Expenditures. Which of the following ten items would be recorded as a capital expenditure and which as an operating expenditure?

1. Cost of installing machinery.

2. Cost of moving machinery.

3. Repairs as a result of an accident.

4. Cost of major overhaul.

5. Installation of safety device as a result of an OSHA inspection.

6. Property taxes on land and buildings.

7. Property taxes on land and buildings held for investment.

8. Cost of rearranging offices.

9. Cost of repainting offices.

10. Ordinary repairs.

51. Disposal of an Asset. The Snowdon Company purchased a machine for $70,000 on January 1, 1990. It is being depreciated on a straight-line basis over five years to a zero residual value. On December 31, 1993, the machine is sold.

Required Record the effects on the accounting equation of the depreciation expense for 1993 and the disposal of the machine if it is sold for:

1. $14,000.

2. $8,000.

3. $17,000.

52. Research and Development Activities. Which of the following activities are considered R&D? Justify your reasons for each answer.

1. Building an oil shale plant to test the feasibility of large-scale exploitation.

2. Testing a new type of machine to evaluate its potential usefulness in production.

3. Modifying a machine to make it suitable for filling a customer's order.

4. Designing a new plant to produce the same products more efficiently.

5. Testing in an attempt to find a more efficient production method.

53. Research and Development Costs. Which of the following should be included in R&D costs of the current period? Justify each answer.

1. Current-period depreciation on the building housing the R&D activities.

2. Cost of a market research study.

3. Current-period depreciation on a machine used in R&D activities.

4. Salary of the director of R&D.

5. Salary of the vice-president who spends one-third of her time overseeing the R&D activities.

6. Pension costs for the salaries in items 4 and 5.

54. R&D Costs. The controller of the Halpern Company prepared the following financial statements at the end of the first year of the company's existence:

INCOME STATEMENT

Sales revenue	$40,000
Cost of sales	(20,000)
Operating expenses	(8,000)
Net income	$12,000

BALANCE SHEET

Cash	$ 33,000	Accounts payable	$ 5,000
Inventory	24,000	Notes payable	40,000
R&D costs	30,000	Common stock	51,000
Property, plant, and equipment (net)	21,000	Retained earnings	12,000
	$108,000		$108,000

Investigation shows that R&D costs include, among others, half the year's operating costs because "the company is not yet operating at capacity." In addition R&D costs include $5,000 of materials that were wasted during early production because "our employees made some stupid mistakes."

Required Prepare the financial statements according to generally accepted accounting principles.

55. Intangible Assets. The Noyce Company was involved in the following transactions:

1. Purchased a patent from another company.

2. Developed a design for a new type of machine for use in its production process.

3. Purchased a franchise for exclusive regional sale of a product.

4. Developed an advertising campaign for a new product.

5. Purchased another company for more than the fair market value of its identifiable net assets.

Required Explain whether each of these items requires the company to record an intangible asset. If not, how would each item be recorded?

56. Cost of a Patent. The Befort Company received a patent on a new type of machine. The legal and patent application costs totaled $12,000. R&D costs incurred to create the machine were $75,000. In the year in which the company received the patent, $27,000 was spent in the successful defense of a patent infringement suit.

Required 1. At what amount should the patent be capitalized?

2. How would you determine the economic life of the patent?

57. Cost of a Patent. On January 5, 1993, the Franc Company purchased for $27,000 a patent which had been granted five years earlier. The patent covered a manufacturing process that the company planned to use for 15 years. On January 1, 1994, the company paid its lawyers $10,000 for successfully defending the patent in a lawsuit.

Required Record the effects on the accounting equation of all the events associated with the patent in 1993 and 1994.

58. Cost of a Tradename. On January 10, 1993, the Hughes Company applied for a tradename. Legal costs associated with the application were $20,000. In January, 1994, the company incurred $8,500 of legal fees in a successful defense of its tradename.

Required Compute the amortization and ending book value of the tradename for 1993 and 1994 if the company amortizes the tradename over the maximum allowable life.

59. Intangible Assets. The Shipton Company was involved in the following transactions during the current year:

1. Developed a design for a new production process at a cost of $82,000. Legal costs to apply for a patent were $7,000.

2. Paid $20,000 to employees who worked on the development of the design for the new production process.

3. Paid $10,000 legal costs to successfully defend a copyright against infringement by another company. The original copyright was purchased four years ago at a cost of $30,000 and was being amortized over a ten-year life.

4. Agreed to pay $70,000 to a racing driver to have the company name prominently displayed on his car for the year.

5. Acquired the copyright to a novel for $30,000.

Required 1. Record the effects on the accounting equation of the above transactions.

2. Record the effects on the accounting equation of the first year's amortization of intangible assets. Use the maximum life allowable unless a shorter life is indicated.

60. Natural Resources. The Skiddaw Company purchased land for $12 million. The company expected to be able to mine one million tons of molybdenum from this land over the next 20 years, at which time the residual value would be zero. During the first two years of the mine's operation 30,000 tons were mined each year and sold for $80 per ton. The estimate of the total lifetime capacity of the mine was raised to 1.2 million tons at the beginning of the third year and the residual value was estimated to be $1 million. During the third year, 50,000 tons were mined and sold for $85 per ton.

Required Compute the depletion expense for each of the three years and prepare the journal entry to record the depletion expense in each year.

61. Natural Resource Assets. On January 1, 1993, the Newton Company purchased a developed mine for $6 million. The expected capacity of the mine was 500,000 tons. The cost of restoring the land after the mine would be exhausted was estimated to be $100,000. In addition, the company built housing for the miners for $60,000 that had a life of 20 years but which would have no value after the capacity of the mine has been exhausted. In 1993 the company incurred labor costs of $100,000 to mine 60,000 tons, which it sold at $17 per ton. The company also incurred administrative costs of $140,000.

In January 1994 additional costs of $70,000 were incurred, which resulted in the capacity of the mine being increased to 100,000 tons greater than originally expected. In 1994 the company mined 100,000 tons, which it sold at $20 per ton, and incurred related labor costs of $200,000 and administrative costs of $300,000.

The labor costs are expensed each period. Ignore income taxes.

Required Prepare income statements for 1993 and 1994.

62. Natural Resource Assets. On January 1, 1993, the Eiger Company purchased a developed mine for $12 million. The expected capacity of the mine was one million tons. The cost of restoring the land at the end of the life of the mine was estimated to be $2 million. In addition, the company built housing for the miners for $150,000 that had a life of 20 years but which would have no value after the capacity of the mine has been exhausted. In 1993 the company incurred labor costs of $500,000 to mine 100,000 tons, which it sold at $28 per ton. The company also incurred administrative costs of $350,000.

In January 1994 additional costs of $250,000 were incurred, which resulted in the capacity of the mine being increased to 100,000 tons greater than originally expected. In 1994 the company mined 150,000 tons, which it sold at $31 per ton, and incurred related labor costs of $700,000 and administrative costs of $400,000.

The labor costs are expensed each period. Ignore income taxes.

Required Prepare income statements for 1993 and 1994.

63. Cost and Percentage Depletion. In a given year a mine owned by the Eskdale Corporation that had a cost of $960,000 and had an expected residual value of $160,000 produced 40,000 tons of ore out of its lifetime expected capacity of 320,000 tons. The ore was sold for $26 per ton. The percentage depletion rate is 15%.

Required 1. Compute the cost depletion expense and the percentage depletion expense for the year.

2. If the selling price and costs remain constant, is it advantageous for the corporation to use percentage depletion for federal income tax purposes over the life of the mine?

64. Goodwill. The Caraway Company acquired the Forester Company for $120,000. The balance sheet of the Forester Company showed assets of $90,000 and liabilities of $30,000. The fair market value of the assets was $25,000 higher than the book value. In addition, an intangible asset that was not included on the balance sheet had a fair market value of $6,000.

Required 1. How much goodwill would the Caraway Company record in regard to the purchase of the Forester Company?

2. Where would the goodwill appear in the financial statements of the Caraway Company?

3. Over what life should the goodwill be amortized?

65. Goodwill. The Floyd Company acquired the Palmer Company for $330,000. The balance sheet of the Palmer Company showed assets of $400,000 and liabilities of

$200,000. The fair market value of the assets was $40,000 higher than the book value. In addition, an intangible asset that was not included on the balance sheet had a fair market value of $20,000.

Required 1. How much goodwill would the Floyd Company record in regard to the purchase of the Palmer Company?

2. Where would the goodwill appear in the financial statements of the Floyd Company?

3. Over what life should the goodwill be amortized?

66. Depreciation Concepts. Evaluate each of the following statements separately:

1. "Since our plant was shut down all year, we will not charge depreciation on it. Although the plant is useful, depreciating it would increase our costs and overstate the inventory."

2. "I think we should use an increasing-charge depreciation method because it will increase the funds recovered near the end of the asset's life when maintenance costs are high and we will need to replace the asset. Also I think tax rates will be higher toward the end of the asset's life, so we will be better off to have larger depreciation then."

67. Choice of Depreciation Method. Coltrane Corporation is a newly formed company and has purchased a building, office equipment, a machine to be used in production, and three company cars. The company is considering which depreciation method to select for each asset for financial reporting.

The president wants to report the highest possible net income and pay the lowest possible income taxes. He also argues that the building is unlikely to go down in value in the next five years, so there is no need to depreciate for that time. He wants to "save the depreciation" until later in the life of the building when the value will go down. The chief accountant agrees that it is possible to minimize the payment of income taxes, but argues that it is incorrect to select a depreciation method in order to maximize net income or to relate to the value of an asset.

Required 1. Evaluate the correctness of each argument.

2. Which depreciation method is it likely that the chief accountant would suggest for each asset? Explain.

68. Depreciation and Replacement of Assets. Ten years ago, the Davis Corporation purchased some equipment for $150,000. The equipment has been depreciated on a straight-line basis and is now about to be replaced. The income tax rate has been 40%. The president is shocked to find out that the company does not have enough cash available to replace the equipment because the selling price has doubled. The president lends the company enough money to buy the new equipment, but says that "now we will record twice as much depreciation as before so that we don't have this problem again."

Required 1. Considering only the above facts, by how much will the cash balance of the company have changed over the life of the equipment?

2. Can the company implement the president's proposed depreciation policy? Do you agree that it would be desirable?

69. Effect of Depreciation on Financial Statements. Charles Parker is considering purchasing either the Gordon Company or the Rollins Company. Both companies started business five years ago, and at that time each company purchased property, plant, and equipment for $137,500 that are being depreciated over ten years with no residual value. The Gordon Company is using straight-line depreciation and the Rollins Company is using sum-of-the-years'-digits depreciation. The two companies have very similar products and reputations, and their total assets (other than property, plant, and equipment) and total liabilities on the balance sheet are also very similar.

Required 1. Compute the book value of the property, plant, and equipment for each company at the end of five years.

2. Which company represents the more desirable purchase? Explain your reasoning. Ignore income taxes.

70. Acquisition Cost. The Morgan Company was planning to expand its production facilities. Therefore it acquired one-year options to purchase two alternative sites. Each option cost $5,000 and could not be applied against the contract. One of the sites was bought for $100,000. The company was unsure whether to capitalize the land at $100,000, or $105,000, or $110,000.

Required Present arguments in favor of each alternative.

71. Intangible Assets. The Internal Revenue Service has the following rules regarding the amortization of intangibles for federal income tax purposes:

Patents:	17 years maximum
Copyrights:	40 years maximum
Franchises:	Length of franchise
Research and development:	Write-off in period incurred

Intangible assets that have indefinite lives may not be amortized (including goodwill).

Required 1. Explain clearly how these rules differ from the rules for the preparation of financial statements.

2. In each case in which there is a difference, explain how net income and income computed for federal income tax purposes by a corporation would differ.

3. In each case in which there is a difference which alternative do you think is best for financial reporting?

72. Goodwill. The Fastgro Company has increased its profits to five times the level of six years ago. The board of directors is meeting to discuss the sale of the company to a larger competitor. The following comments are made during the meeting:

"We should add some goodwill on the balance sheet, and then we can sell the company at a price equal to the net assets" (assets minus liabilities).

"We can't add goodwill to the balance sheet because that would violate generally accepted accounting principles. However, the company that buys us will record goodwill. I don't see why they can and we can't."

"It doesn't matter whether we add goodwill or not, because the price paid to buy this company will not be affected by the goodwill being on the balance sheet or not."

"You mentioned that the buyer will record goodwill on its balance sheet. I was wondering how they will decide how much the goodwill is, how they will decide whether or not to amortize it, and over what life?"

Required Explain how you would respond to each of the comments.

73. **Appendix: Exchange of Productive Assets.** The Whillans Company owns a machine that had an original cost of $45,000 and accumulated depreciation of $30,000. The company trades in the machine on a new model, which has an invoice price of $26,000 and pays cash of $8,000.

Required **1.** What is the acquisition cost of the new machine?

2. If instead the company traded in the old machine and paid $17,000 in the exchange, what is the acquisition cost of the new machine?

74. **Appendix: Exchange of Productive Assets.** The Scafell Company owns a machine that had an original cost of $65,000 and accumulated depreciation of $12,000. The company trades in the machine on a piece of land and pays $6,000. The machine has a fair market value of $46,000.

Required **1.** What is the acquisition cost of the land?

2. If the company paid $11,000 on the exchange, what is the acquisition cost of the land?

ANNUAL REPORT PROBLEMS

75. **Gain on Destruction of Asset.** In 1985 Cyclops Corporation disclosed that it suffered significant property damage to one of its steel manufacturing facilities. As a result of the insurance settlement, the company reported a gain of $1,776,000 after deducting taxes of $1,262,000. The insurance proceeds were expected to be sufficient to replace the facility.

Assume that the cost of the steel facility was $10 million and its book value was $8 million.

Required **1.** Record the effects of the following events on the accounting equation:

  a. The occurrence of the damage.
  b. The collection of the insurance proceeds.
  c. The replacement of the facility.

2. Evaluate the relationship between the financial reporting and the impact of the events on the company.

76. **Property, Plant, and Equipment and Intangibles.** The following excerpts are from Safeway Stores' 1988 annual report relating to property, plant, and equipment (in thousands of dollars):

	1988	1987
Property:		
Land	$ 194,456	$ 157,157
Buildings	408,152	346,591
Leasehold improvements	690,799	702,305
Fixtures and equipment	818,724	683,444
Transport equipment	74,427	52,414
Property under capital leases	317,776	359,012
	2,504,334	2,300,923
Less accumulated depreciation and amortization	472,169	280,170
Total property, net	$2,032,165	$2,020,753

Note A. Summary of Significant Accounting Policies (in part):
Property and Depreciation. Property is stated at historical cost. Depreciation is computed on the straight-line method using the following lives:

Stores and other buildings	10–30 years
Fixtures and equipment	2–12 years
Transport equipment	4–14 years

Leasehold improvements include buildings constructed on leased land and improvements to leased buildings. Leasehold improvements are amortized on the straight-line method over the shorter of the remaining terms of the lease or the estimated useful lives of the assets.

Property under capital leases is amortized on the straight-line method over the remaining terms of the leases. Depreciation and amortization expense for property was $263,419 in 1988 and $420,494 in 1987.

Preopening Costs. Costs related to opening new stores are expensed as incurred.
Note J. Taxes on Income (in part):
A primary component of deferred income tax benefit was depreciation of $20,243.

Required 1. Explain how each property item relates to Safeway's business. Has Safeway been expanding its property in the last year? If so, has it been buying or leasing the new property assets? Approximately how old are its property assets? (Consider the cost of the leased assets as the price paid to buy equivalent purchased assets.)

2. Assess the impact of a change in depreciation methods on the following ratios for 1988. Use the deferred tax amount for depreciation to calculate an accelerated depreciation amount. Assume an income tax rate of 34%.

   a. Profit margin equals net income ($27,613,000) divided by net sales ($13,612,393,000).

   b. Return on assets equals net income divided by average total assets ($4,371,686,000).

3. Do you agree with Safeway's treatment of preopening costs? Assume that preopening costs were $40,000,000 in 1988 and that such costs are amortized over the 20-average-year life of a grocery store rather than being expensed. Is there a material impact on the two ratios given in part 2 from capitalizing preopening costs?

4. Reconcile the different net income amounts (derived from the various accounting methods chosen in parts 2 and 3) to the same cash flow from operations amount for 1988.

77. Depreciation and Intangibles. The following excerpts are from IBM's 1988 annual report relating to plant and depreciation (in millions of dollars):

	1988		1987
Current assets		$35,343	$34,369
Plant and other property	$41,761		$40,320
Less: accumulated depreciation	(19,711)		(18,234)
	$22,050		$22,086
Rental machines and parts	$ 3,121		2,755
Less: accumulated depreciation	(1,745)		1,874)
	$ 1,376		$ 881
Total		23,426	22,967
Software, investments and other assets		14,268	12,693
Total assets		$73,037	$70,029

Significant Accounting Policies (in part):
Depreciation. Plant, rental machines, and other property are carried at cost and depreciated over their estimated useful lives using the straight-line method.
Software. Costs related to the conceptual formulation and design of licensed programs are expensed as research and development. Costs incurred subsequent to establishment of technological feasibility to produce the finished product are generally capitalized. The annual amortization is the greater of the amount computed based on the estimated revenue distribution over the revenue-producing lives or the straight-line method, but not in excess of six years. Ongoing costs to support or service licensed programs are expensed.
Management Discussion of 1988 Results and Other Footnotes (in part):
Depreciation was $3,871 and amortization of software was $893. The 1987 amounts were $3,534 and $863, respectively. Production costs of software products capitalized were $1,300. Principal deferred income tax items included $100 for depreciation in 1988 and $535 for depreciation in 1987.

Required 1. Assess the impact if accelerated depreciation was used on the following ratios for 1988 and 1987:

   a. Profit margin equals net income divided by net sales.
   b. Return on assets equals net income divided by average total assets.

Use the following data (in millions) in computing these ratios:

	1988	1987
Net income	$ 5,806	$ 5,258
Net sales	59,681	55,256

Use ending, rather than average, total assets, since the 1986 total asset amount was not given. Use the deferred tax amount for depreciation to calculate an accelerated depreciation amount. Assume an income tax rate of 34%.

2. Assess the impact of capitalizing the costs of software products since the beginning of 1987 on the same ratios from part 1. Assume that the 1987 program products expenditures were the same amount as in 1988. Do you agree with management in capitalizing these costs?

3. Combine the two analyses from parts 1 and 2. Is the impact of these accounting method choices material?

4. Reconcile the two different net income amounts calculated in part 3 to the same cash flow from operations amount for 1988.

78. Property, Plant, and Equipment, and Intangibles. Scott Paper Company is the world's leading manufacturer and marketer of sanitary tissue paper products. The following excerpts are from its 1988 financial statements relating to property, plant, and equipment, and intangible assets (in millions of dollars):

Income statement:		
Net income		$400.9
Balance sheet:		
Plant assets, at cost		
Land	$ 43.8	
Buildings	634.8	
Machinery and equipment	4,490.0	
	5,168.6	
Accumulated depreciation	(2,159.5)	$3,009.1
Timber resources, at cost less timber harvested		103.5
Patents, goodwill, and other assets		161.4
Total assets		$5,156.3
Notes:		
Depreciation of buildings, machinery, and equipment		$ 265.7
Cost of timber harvested		3.9
Amortization of logging roads		1.9
Total		$ 271.5
Deferred taxes on depreciation		$ 49.1

Reforestation costs as well as expenditures for renewals and betterments which increase the useful life or capacity of plant assets are capitalized. Costs for repairs and maintenance are expensed.

On most retirements or sales, the cost of plant assets is removed from the asset account and charged to the related depreciation reserve account. Amounts realized from such dispositions are credited to the reserve account.

The Company capitalizes start-up costs which exceed $3.0 on any single domestic capital project. The capitalized costs are amortized over a period of 60 months.

Depreciation is principally calculated by the straight-line method based on the estimated useful lives of the assets which are generally 3 to 25 years for machinery and equipment and 20 to 50 years for buildings. For certain major capital additions, depreciation is calculated by the units-of-production method during the learning curve phase of the project. Depreciation on capital lease assets is calculated by the straight-line method.

The cost of timber harvested is determined by calculating that portion of the investment in timber which the current year's harvest bears to the total standing timber.

Amortization of logging roads is absorbed in costs as timber is harvested and is based on the estimated recoverable timber in areas serviced by the roads.

Required **1.** Discuss the strengths of Scott's property and intangible asset accounting, including depreciation and amortization.

2. Discuss the weaknesses of the same accounting methods.

79. Repairs and Maintenance and Disposals. Rockwell International is a large aerospace manufacturer with many U.S. government contracts. On its 1988 balance sheet it shows total property of $5,527 million and net property of $2,640 million. The following note to its financial statements relates to property and depreciation:

Property is stated at cost. Depreciation of property is provided based on estimated useful lives generally using accelerated and straight-line methods. Significant renewals and betterments are capitalized, and replaced units are written off. Maintenance and repairs, as well as renewals of minor amount, are charged to expense. Maintenance and repairs were $256.4 million in 1988, $247.2 million in 1987 and $244 million in 1986.

When assets are sold or retired, accumulated depreciation is charged with the portion thereof applicable to such assets. The resulting gain or loss is recorded in income in the year of sale or retirement, except as to certain assets for which gains (to the extent of accumulated depreciation) and losses are recorded in overhead accounts (which are included in the cost of inventory) in conformity with United States Government contract cost principles.

Required **1.** Assume that the maintenance and repairs of $256.4 million in 1988 were instead significant renewals and betterments with average lives of ten years for straight-line depreciation. Show the impact on the 1988 accounting equation with T-accounts. Ignore income taxes.

2. Assume that there is an unrecorded $15 million sale of a plant asset that cost $50 million with accumulated depreciation of $40 million. Show the impact on the 1988 accounting equation with T-accounts under both generally accepted accounting principles and U.S. contract cost principles. Ignore income taxes.

80. Intangibles. Westinghouse Corporation is a large conglomerate in the United States. The following excerpts are from its 1988 financial statements relating to intangible assets (in millions of dollars):

Note 10. Intangible and other noncurrent assets (in part):

	1988	1987
Goodwill and other acquired intangible assets	$ 592.4	$ 490.4
Uranium settlement assets	80.9	112.2
Other	510.0	439.1
	$1,183.3	$1,041.7

Uranium settlement assets relate to uranium inventory awaiting delivery and settlement items being produced under uranium supply contract settlement agreements. Inventory and other settlement items expected to be delivered within one year are included in other current assets.

Note 1. Summary of significant accounting policies (in part):
Amortization of Intangibles. Goodwill and other acquired intangible assets are amortized over their estimated lives, but not in excess of 40 years.

Required 1. Compute amortization for Westinghouse in 1988 and 1987. Assume that goodwill and other acquired intangible assets and other assets are amortized over 40 years. Assume amounts given are gross, not net, of amortization.

2. Recompute amortization for Westinghouse in 1988 and 1987, using 5, rather than 40, years for the items mentioned in part 1. Is the difference material to net income ($822.8 million in 1988 and $900.5 million in 1987)? Ignore income taxes.

3. Reconcile the two different net income amounts calculated in parts 1 and 2 to the same cash flow from operations for 1988.

81. Depreciation and Income Taxes. Pillsbury Company is one of the largest consumer foods companies in the United States. The following excerpts are from its 1988 financial statements relating to property (in millions of dollars):

Note 10 (in part):
The components of property, plant, and equipment are as follows:

Land and improvements	$ 286.4
Buildings and improvements	1,398.9
Machinery and equipment	1,278.9
	2,964.2
Less accumulated depreciation	(1,163.8)
	1,800.4

Note 1 (in part):
Property, plant, and equipment. Owned property, plant, and equipment is stated at cost. Depreciation is computed using the straight-line method for financial statement purposes and accelerated methods for tax purposes.
Note 8 (in part):
Income taxes. Deferred taxes result from timing differences in the recognition of revenue and expense for tax and financial statement purposes. The effects of those differences include: Excess of tax over book depreciation of $22.3.

Required 1. Is it acceptable to use one method of depreciation for financial accounting purposes and another for tax purposes? If so, did Pillsbury make the right choices?

2. The 1988 depreciation expense amount is $219.4 million. The net income for 1988 is $69.3 million. If accelerated depreciation had been used for financial accounting purposes, would there have been a material impact on net income?

82. **Depreciation, Interest Capitalization, and Intangibles.** The following excerpts (in thousands of dollars) were taken from the Coca-Cola Company's 1988 annual report.

	1988	1987
Land	$ 116,726	$ 112,741
Buildings and improvements	853,252	763,317
Machinery and equipment	1,645,652	1,492,583
Containers	293,277	275,120
	$2,908,907	$2,643,761
Less allowance for depreciation	(1,149,832)	(1,042,233)
Net plant, property, and equipment	$1,759,075	$1,601,528
Goodwill and other intangible assets	$ 56,546	$ 74,155
Total assets	$7,450,612	$8,605,546
Net operating revenues	$8,337,831	$7,658,341
Depreciation and amortization	169,768	154,525
U.S. deferred income tax charge	14,857	32,466
Net income	$1,044,703	$ 916,136

Property, plant, and equipment is stated at cost, less allowance for depreciation. Depreciation expense is determined principally by the straight-line method. The annual rates of depreciation are 2% to 10% for buildings and improvements and 7% to 34% for machinery, equipment, and containers. Interest capitalized as part of the cost of acquisition or construction of major assets was $8,000, $6,000, and $12,000 in 1988, 1987, and 1986, respectively. Deferred taxes are provided principally for depreciation, certain employment related expenses, and certain capital transactions which are recognized in different years for financial statement and income tax purposes.

Required 1. Convert Coca-Cola's net income from being computed by the straight-line depreciation method to accelerated depreciation by doubling the entire deferred tax amount. Is there a significant impact on the 1988 profit margin? Why or why not?

2. Show the impact on the accounting equation of capitalizing interest in 1988. Assume that this interest related to buildings with a 10% depreciation rate. Was there a material impact on net income in 1988? Ignore income taxes.

3. Why doesn't Coca-Cola show its secret production formula for "Coca-Cola Classic" as an intangible asset?

83. **Property, Plant and Equipment, and Intangibles Conversions.** Baxter International is a leading supplier of health-care products, systems and services. The following excerpts are from its 1988 annual report (in millions of dollars):

Property, plant and equipment, at cost	$2,935
Accumulated depreciation	(911)
Net property, plant and equipment	$2,024
Goodwill	$2,473
Average total costs	$8,550

Net sales	$6,861
Depreciation	314
Goodwill amortization	22
Net income	$ 388

| Deferred income tax expense for depreciation | $ 23 |

Baxter uses straight-line depreciation for financial reporting purposes and accelerated depreciation for income tax purposes. Goodwill is amortized over a 40-year period, except that goodwill incurred before 1970 is not amortized.

Required 1. Compute profit margin and return on total assets ratios for Baxter in 1988. Then, recompute these two ratios, assuming that accelerated depreciation and a 10-year goodwill write-off period are used. Round to the nearest million dollars and ignore income taxes. Were these conversions material?

2. Reconcile the net income differences from the two above approaches to the same cash flows from operations amount.

84. **Computer Software Costs and Goodwill.** Unisys Corporation is one of the world's largest designers, manufacturers, and marketers of computer-based information systems and related products and services. The following excerpts are from its 1988 financial statements (in millions of dollars):

Note 1. Summary of significant accounting policies (in part):
Cost in excess of net assets acquired:
    Cost in excess of net assets acquired principally represents the excess of cost over fair value of the net assets of Sperry Corporation, which is being amortized on the straight-line method over 40 years.
Software capitalization:
    The cost of development of computer software to be sold or leased is capitalized and amortized to cost of net sales over the estimated revenue producing lives of the products, but not in excess of three years following product release. Unamortized marketable software costs (which are included in other assets) at December 31, 1988 and 1987 were $314.5 and $195.1, respectively; related amortization for 1988, 1987, and 1986 was $64.2, $30.7, and $5.8, respectively.
Note 3. Acquisitions (in part):
    In 1986, the Company acquired the entire equity interest of Sperry in a transaction valued at $4,818.0, including $1,431.7 of convertible preferred stock. The acquisition was accounted for by the purchase method. The excess of the total acquisition cost over the fair value of the net assets acquired was $1,391.1.

Required 1. In the highly competitive, "hi-tech" computer industry, you are questioning the use of 40- and 3-year lives for goodwill and software amortization, respectively. For 1988, convert Unisys to 10- and 2-year lives for goodwill and software amortization, respectively. Is there a material impact on the 1988 net income of $680.6 million? Unisys's effective income tax rate is 29% for 1988.

2. What is the impact on cash flows from operations? Include calculations in your answer.

85. Adjustments for Restructuring. Manville Corporation now has three operating groups, Fiber Glass, Forest, and Specialty Products and has completely withdrawn from the asbestos industry. The following excerpts are from its 1988 financial statements (in millions of dollars):

Note 15. Restructuring of operations.

In 1988, the $139.2 charge to restructuring of operations is made up of provisions totaling $103.1 for environmental cleanup costs, principally related to asbestos at certain former manufacturing sites, and $36.1 for other restructuring activities, including the planned shutdown of certain equipment because of process changes and the establishment of additional reserves associated with prior disinvestments.

While the Company feels that it has made adequate provisions for environmental cleanup costs based on current environmental laws and regulations, there is no assurance that future changes in environmental laws, regulations, and their application could not ultimately result in additional cost to the Company. The Company attempts to comply with all local, state, and federal environmental laws and regulations.

Restructuring of operations in 1987 is comprised principally of $20.6 of gains on the sales of the Company's interest in two real estate joint ventures and the liquidation of a long-term receivable, offset by an $18 charge providing for the disposition of certain U.S. operations.

During 1986, the Company recorded a $47 restructuring charge to cover the cost of reducing the Company's overall work force and the related relocation of employees. The charge also includes a provision for the anticipated disposition of certain assets, including the Company's former headquarters building.

Required 1. For each year and for each item disclosed in the note, discuss the impact of the restructuring of operations upon specific accounts in the accounting equation. Since all charges are calculated before income tax considerations, ignore income taxes in the analysis.

2. If current environmental laws for cleanup of manufacturing sites become stricter in the future, what would be the impact on the accounting equation?

86. Adjustments for Restructuring. Unisys is one of the world's largest designers, manufacturers, and marketers of computer-based information systems and related products and services. The following excerpts are from its 1988 financial statements (in millions of dollars except earnings per share amounts):

Note 5. Significant 1986 fourth quarter charges:

In December 1986, the Company recorded certain adjustments which reduced net income by $280.0, or $2.03 per common share. These adjustments reflected (a) provisions for consolidation of operations, reduction of employment levels, and divestiture of operations which reduced net income by $201.0, or $1.46 per common share, and (b) provisions for discontinuance of nonstrategic programs, and for excess assets, investment, and other asset valuation adjustments, debt redemption and other charges, which reduced net income by $79.0, or $0.57 per common share.

Required 1. Discuss the impact of the two adjustments on the accounting equation.

2. Did these restructuring adjustments have a material impact on 1986 earning per share of $(0.54)? How did these adjustments affect the trend in earnings per share which were $2.93 in 1987 and $3.27 in 1988? (1986 was the year Burroughs and Sperry corporations merged to become Unisys.)

Current Liabilities; Present and Future Value; Mortgages, Notes, and Bonds

After reading this chapter, you should understand

- Characteristics and valuation of various current liabilities
- Contingencies
- The concepts of present value and future value
- Mortgages payable
- Long-term notes payable and receivable
- The nature of bonds
- Why bonds might be issued rather than stock being sold
- Accounting for bonds sold at par, a premium, or a discount

- The effective interest method of amortizing a premium or discount
- Retirement of bonds at maturity or prior to maturity
- Conversion of bonds into common stock
- The straight-line method of amortization
- Troubled debt restructurings (Appendix)

Various current liabilities have already been, or will be, discussed. For example, accounts and notes payable, interest payable, salaries payable, unearned rent, and income taxes payable have been discussed in earlier chapters and dividends payable is discussed in Chapter 10. Other current liabilities are not discussed because it is unlikely that they would appear as a material item in the financial statements. For example, sales taxes, management bonuses, payroll taxes, property taxes, and their related liabilities are not discussed. In the first section of the chapter, various other current liabilities are discussed.

Noncurrent liabilities involve payments that will occur more than one year in the future. In such circumstances, it is necessary to consider the time value of money. The concepts of present and future value are discussed. An understanding of these concepts is essential when evaluating decisions and understanding financial statement categories that involve amounts of money received or paid at different time periods. In addition, the concept of present value is used in several areas of financial accounting, three of which, mortgages, notes, and bonds payable, are discussed in this chapter.

SECTION A Current Liabilities

■ NATURE AND DEFINITION OF CURRENT LIABILITIES

The specific meaning, nature, and classification of current liabilities, which are considered in the following sections, are very important to users of financial statements.

Current liabilities are obligations whose liquidation is reasonably expected to require the use of existing current assets or the creation of other current liabilities within one year or the operating cycle, whichever is longer. The usual criterion is one year. For certain businesses, however, where the **operating cycle— from cash to inventory to receivables and back to cash**—extends beyond the year, the length of the operating cycle determines the classification of the liability, as discussed in Chapter 1.

Currently, most corporations present current liabilities at the top of the first classification under Liabilities. A few corporations (3 out of 600 companies surveyed in the 1989 *Accounting Trends and Techniques*) offset current liabilities against the current assets to report working capital. Items within the current liability section are typically listed in the order of average length of the maturities, according to amount (largest to smallest), or in the order of liquidation preferences—that is, in the order of their legal claims against assets. Those liabilities having legal priority would be shown first, secured obligations second, and unsecured third.

As discussed in Chapter 1, an attribute of a liability (and also an asset) is its liquidity. **Liquidity refers to a liability's nearness to cash**. The FASB has become increasingly concerned about reporting the liquidity of liabilities and assets because investors, creditors, and other decision makers use future cash flows in their decision-making processes.[1] In part, *these future cash flows are predicted based on the nearness to cash of liabilities and assets.*

Alternative methods of reporting the liquidity of both liabilities and assets include (1) continuing the current practice for classifying current liabilities and assets (mixture of operating-cycle and maturity-date approach), (2) classifying current liabilities and assets using the "pure" operating-cycle approach, (3) classifying current liabilities and assets under the maturity approach only, (4) adopting a different classification scheme, possibly using more classes, and (5) leaving the balance sheet unclassified but arranging in order of liquidity. Each method has certain advantages and disadvantages in terms of revealing liquidity, but they are beyond the scope of this book.

The FASB observed that the principal objective of financial reporting—that of providing information useful in assessing the amount, timing, and uncertainty of future cash flows—rests on a sound knowledge of the liquidity of liabilities and assets. The FASB, in examining the classification of liabilities and assets, studied ways of relating these items to each other and of relating them to other financial statement data to obtain information about liquidity and to determine what relationships might be the best predictors of failure of a company. Five "liquidity" ratios were listed as providing information to lending institutions, creditors, and other external users of financial information: (1) cash flow to total debt, (2) net income to total assets, (3) total debt to total assets, (4) current assets to current liabilities, and (5) cash to current liabilities. Four of the five require information about liabilities; two require information about current liabilities. Since ratio analysis is discussed in Chapter 14, these ratios are not discussed here.

As stated in Chapter 1, **financial flexibility refers to an entity's ability to use its financial resources to adapt to change.** This ability primarily involves the management of cash and other resources to achieve certain financial advantages from both an offensive and defensive point of view. In part, too, it involves the potential to create new current and long-term liabilities, to restructure existing debt, and to manage debt in other ways. These features relating to financial flexibility are covered later in this chapter and in other chapters.

■ VALUATION OF CURRENT LIABILITIES

Ideally, all liabilities should be recorded (and later valued for balance sheet presentation) at the present value of the future outlays they require (as discussed later in the chapter) and should be reported in a manner that will enhance disclosure about their liquidity. Most current liabilities in practice, however, are measured and recorded at their maturity or face amount. The difference between

· · · · · · · · · · · · · · · · · · · ·

[1]"An Analysis of Issues Related to Reporting Funds Flows, Liquidity, and Financial Flexibility," *FASB Discussion Memorandum* (Stamford, Conn.: FASB, 1980).

the maturity amount and the present value of the maturity amount is usually not material because of the short time period involved (usually one year or less). While a slight overstatement of liabilities will result from the recording of these liabilities at their maturity amount, this overstatement is justified on the basis of materiality and the cost/benefit relationship.

■ CHARACTERISTICS OF VARIOUS CURRENT LIABILITIES

The current liabilities discussed in this chapter are those that, in addition to the ones covered in other chapters, are likely to have a material impact on the financial statements or be disclosed in the notes and therefore be most important for the users of the statements. Included are the currently maturing portion of long-term debt, classifications of obligations that are callable by the creditor, advances and refundable deposits, accrued liability for compensated absences, disclosure of off-balance sheet financing obligations, liabilities from product financing arrangements, unearned items, and warranty obligations.

Currently Maturing Portion of Long-Term Debt

As a general rule, although not directly related to the operating cycle, the currently maturing portion of long-term debt is classified as a current liability. Two different situations are involved here. First, any long-term debt requiring the use of current assets for its retirement will become a current liability on the balance sheet prepared immediately before the year of retirement. If a company has issued 20-year bonds and these are scheduled to become due on July 1, 1993, they should be shown as current liabilities on the December 31, 1992 balance sheet. The second situation involves the issuance of serial bonds—that is, bonds payable that are retired in periodic installments. For example, assume that on July 1, 1989, Rexlow Corporation issues 11% serial bonds (discussed later in the chapter) with a face value of $1 million. These bonds are to be retired in serial installments of $100,000 beginning on July 1, 1993, and each year thereafter until all bonds are retired. A December 31, 1992, balance sheet would show as a current liability the currently maturing installment of $100,000 and a long-term liability item of $900,000 (the remaining installments due after July 1, 1993).

The currently maturing amounts of the long-term debt are *not* included in current liabilities if they have been refinanced on a long-term basis. The liabilities are *excluded* from current liabilities if there is both an intention by the company to refinance on a long-term basis and an ability to refinance.[2] The ability to

....
[2]"Classification of Short-Term Obligations Expected to Be Refinanced," *FASB Statement of Financial Accounting Standards No. 6* (Stamford, Conn.: FASB, 1975), par. 9–11.

refinance must be demonstrated by the fact that the company has already issued long-term debt or equity securities after the date of the balance sheet but before the balance sheet is issued, or has entered into a bona fide long-term financing agreement that clearly permits the company to refinance the maturing obligations on a long-term basis.

Classification of Obligations That Are Callable by the Creditor

A long-term obligation should be classified as a current liability if (1) the debtor is in violation of a provision of a long-term debt agreement (a requirement in the debt indenture or contract) at the balance sheet date, and the violation makes the liability callable by the creditor within one year (or operating cycle, if longer) from the balance sheet date, or (2) the violation, if not remedied (or cured) within a specified grace period, *will make* the liability callable within one year from the balance sheet date (or operating cycle, if longer).[3] An exception to this requirement is a callable obligation that meets the following conditions: (1) the creditor has waived or subsequently lost the right to request repayment for more than one year (or operating cycle, if longer) from the balance sheet date, or (2) it is probable that the violation of a debt agreement for a long-term obligation containing a grace period will be cured within that grace period, thus preventing it from being callable. The circumstances surrounding an obligation under item 2 must be disclosed in the notes to the financial statements.

The preceding rules indicate that the FASB concluded that the current liability classification is intended to include obligations that, by their terms, are due on demand or will be due on demand within one year (or the operating cycle, if longer) from the balance sheet date, *even though liquidation may not be expected within that period.* As indicated by the italicized phrase in the preceding sentence, this Statement does not conform to the requirement that a current liability be "reasonably expected to require either the use of existing current assets or the creation of other current liabilities within a year or the operating cycle, whichever is longer." Rather, it substitutes a notion that obligations should be classified as current when they are legally callable within one year, whether or not they are likely to be called. In dissenting to this Statement, three Board members stated that:

> . . . It is asserted that this amendment will improve comparability. It will, in fact, cause situations to appear the same even when underlying facts and circumstances are sufficiently different to justify different reasonable expectations. This is not comparability; it is substituting an arbitrary rule for judgment.[4]

....

[3] "Classification of Obligations That Are Callable by the Creditor," *FASB Statement of Financial Accounting Standards No. 78* (Stamford, Conn.: FASB, 1983), par. 5.
[4] *Ibid.*

Advances and Refundable Deposits

Many utility and other companies require customers and employees to make deposits as guarantees to cover equipment used by the customer, to cover payments that may arise in the future, or to guarantee performance of a contract or service. Since these deposits either are refundable or are subject to be offset against a trade accounts receivable, they are a special type of liability. The accounting for these deposits involves a receipt of cash and recording a liability appropriately describing the nature of the refundable deposit. For example, the liability for a refundable deposit received by a public utility may be called Refundable Deposits Received from Customers. The law frequently requires that interest be paid on these deposits; therefore, most utilities refund the deposits as soon as good credit standing is established by customers. Any related interest must be accounted for by the utility on a regular accrual basis. Thus, another current liability, Interest Payable, would arise.

Accrued Liability for Compensated Absences

Compensated absences include vacation, holiday, illness, or other activities for which the employee is paid. They do not include such items as severance pay, stock options, or long-term fringe benefits. An expense and a liability for employees' compensation for future absences are recognized if all the following conditions are met:

1. The employer's obligation relating to the employee's rights to receive compensation for future absences is attributable to the employee's services already rendered.
2. The obligation relates to rights that vest or accumulate.
3. Payment of the compensation is probable.
4. The amount can be reasonably estimated. If the employer meets the first three conditions and does not accrue a liability because the last condition is not met, the known facts about compensated absences must be disclosed in the notes to the financial statements.[5]

Two of the terms used in the preceding paragraph require additional explanation. **A vested right exists when an employer has an obligation to make payment to an employee even if that individual's employment ceases.** Vested rights, then, are not contingent on employees' future services. **Accumulated rights are those that can be carried forward by the employee to future periods if not taken in the period in which they are earned.** The most common type of this right is vacation time that is allowed to accumulate and for which payment is probable. Even if these rights are not vested, they do accumulate and therefore the employer must recognize an expense and a liability. The liability is reduced

....
[5]"Accounting for Compensated Absences," FASB *Statement of Financial Accounting Standards No. 43* (Stamford, Conn.: FASB, 1980).

when the employee is paid during the vacation. No salary expense is recognized because the employee is not providing a service while on vacation.

The second most frequent compensated absence is sick pay, which is accounted for in a manner different from vacation pay. If sick pay benefits vest and have not been used by the end of the period, then an expense and a liability must be recognized. If sick pay benefits *accumulate* but do not vest, recognition is optional. The reason for this exception to the general rule of recognition is that employers administer sick pay in at least two different ways. Some companies permit employees to accumulate unused sick pay and take compensated time off from work even though they are not ill. A current liability must be accrued for this type of sick pay because it is probable that it will be paid in the future regardless of whether or not the employees are ill. Other companies require that employees receive accumulated sick pay only if they are absent from work because of illness. In this case, accrual is optional because payment is less likely to be considered probable and measurement of the amount is less reliable.

Disclosure of Off-Balance Sheet Financing Obligations

Off-balance sheet financing obligations are those obligations of the company that are not recorded as liabilities under generally accepted accounting principles. Several are discussed in this book. For example, an unconditional purchase obligation is a purchase obligation that requires transfer of funds in the future for fixed or minimum amounts or quantities of goods or services at fixed or minimum prices. However, the obligation is not recorded as a liability because no transaction has occurred. If the unconditional purchase obligation is (1) non-cancelable, (2) is negotiated as part of arranging financing for facilities to provide the contracted items, and (3) contains a term in excess of one year, certain disclosures are required regardless of whether the obligation and related asset are reported on the balance sheet. These disclosures include, for example, information about required payments over the next five years.[6] The intent is to enhance the prediction of future cash outflows.

In 1990, the FASB issued a Statement that requires disclosure about financial instruments that have an off-balance sheet risk.[7] **Financial instruments** are cash, evidence of an ownership interest in an entity or a contract that gives the company a right to receive cash or another financial instrument from another entity, or an obligation to deliver cash or a financial instrument to another party. Companies are required to report selected information about financial instruments having a risk of loss that exceeds the amount recognized, and about financial instruments with concentrations of credit risk. These complex disclosures include

....

[6]"Disclosure of Long-Term Obligations," *FASB Statement of Financial Accounting Standards No. 47* (Stamford, Conn.: FASB, 1981).

[7]"Disclosure of Information about Financial Instruments with Off-Balance Sheet Risk and Financial Instruments with Concentrations of Credit Risk," *FASB Statement of Financial Accounting Standards No. 105* (Norwalk, Conn.: FASB, 1990).

such items as the contract amount, the nature and terms, the amount of loss that the company would incur if the other entity failed to perform, the collateral posted, and significant concentrations of credit risk, such as in a single industry, geographic region, U.S. dollars, or foreign currencies.

Liabilities from Product Financing Arrangements

A product financing arrangement is an agreement in which a company sells inventory and agrees to repurchase it (perhaps additionally processed) at a specified price. The company must not record the transaction as a sale or remove the inventory from its balance sheet. The company, however, must record a liability for the original "selling" price, which is eliminated at the time of repurchase.[8] If a company has another entity purchase a product on its behalf, it must record the asset (often an inventory item) and related liability when the product is purchased by the other entity. A part or all of both of the foregoing liabilities are likely to be reported as current liabilities on the company's balance sheet.

Unearned Items

Unearned items include amounts collected in advance that have not yet been earned and recorded as revenues. Although often erroneously classified under the balance sheet caption Deferred Credits, these items should receive more appropriate classifications as current or long-term liabilities.

Examples of unearned items that could be classified as either current or long-term liabilities are revenues collected in advance such as interest, rent, magazine subscriptions, royalties, airline tickets, tokens, gift certificates, and service contracts. Most of these items are current liabilities; a few, however, may be long-term liabilities. If more than one year (or the operating cycle, if longer) is required in the earning process and if noncurrent assets are primarily used in order to earn the revenue, then the unearned item should be classified as a long-term liability. On the other hand, unearned interest included on the face of notes receivable should be classified as a contra account to Notes Receivable on the balance sheet.

As illustrated in Chapter 3, the accounting for these unearned items involves an increase in Cash and an increase in a liability account. An adjustment is then made at the end of the fiscal period to state correctly the amount of revenue earned and the remaining liability amount.

Warranty Obligations

Another current liability arises out of product warranties. These agreements require the seller, over a specified period of time after the sale, to correct any deficiency in quality, quantity, or performance of the merchandise sold, to replace the item, or refund the selling price.

....
[8]"Accounting for Product Financing Arrangements," *FASB Statement of Financial Accounting Standards No. 49* (Stamford, Conn.: FASB, 1981), par. 6 and 7.

The period of the warranty may span two or more accounting periods. Adherence to the matching principle requires that **the warranty expense be recorded in the period in which the sale is made,** because the flaws in the merchandise are assumed to be present at the time of the sale and because it is assumed that the existence of the warranty facilitated the sale to the customer. The actual use of cash and other resources to correct the defects in the merchandise, however, may be made in a subsequent period. Consequently, a recognition of the warranty expense in the period of sale and the corresponding current liability requires an estimate of all costs that will be incurred after the sale to correct the defects and deficiencies. For example, the Fedders Corporation recorded a liability, "Accrued Warranty Expense," of $1,813,000 in its 1988 balance sheet and made the following disclosure in the notes:

> The company's warranty policy provides five-year coverage for compressors and one-year coverage on all parts and labor related to the room air conditioners sold in the United States and Canada. The policy with respect to sales returns provides that a distributor may not return inventory except at the company's option.

Executory Contracts

An **executory contract** is an agreement in which two parties agree to a future exchange of resources or services. Examples of executory contracts include unused lines of credit, purchase commitments, agreements to pay future compensation, and commitments for plant expansion. Since no exchange of resources or services has occurred in an executory contract (sometimes called an unexecuted contract), no liability (or asset reduction) or contingent liability exists. However, when an executory contract has a likely material impact on the future cash flows of a company, disclosure should be made in the notes to the financial statements.

■ CONTINGENCIES

A contingency is an existing condition that involves uncertainty as to a possible gain or loss to a company that will ultimately be resolved when a future event occurs (or fails to occur).[9] This definition includes three primary characteristics of contingencies: (1) an existing condition, (2) uncertainty as to the ultimate effect of this condition, and (3) the resolution of the uncertainty depending on a future event. Generally accepted accounting principles focus on *loss* contingencies. Two of these have already been discussed in this book—the uncollectibility of accounts receivable (Chapter 5) and the obligations related to product warranties (earlier in this chapter). In each case there is an existing condition (the receivable is owed by the customer and the warranty is in effect); there is uncertainty as to the ultimate effect of this condition (the amount to be collected and the amount to be paid); and the resolution depends on a future event

....

[9]"Accounting for Contingencies," *FASB Statement of Financial Accounting Standards No. 5* (Stamford, Conn.: FASB, 1975), par. 1.

(payment does or does not occur). Less familiar loss contingencies include the risk of loss or damage of property by fire, explosion, or other hazards, threat of expropriation of assets, pending or threatened litigation, actual or possible claims and assessments, guarantees of indebtedness of others, and agreement to repurchase receivables that have been sold.

When a loss contingency exists, the likelihood of the future event occurring to confirm the loss and the related impairment of an asset (e.g., reduce accounts receivable) or the incurrence of a liability (e.g., increase warranty liability) can vary widely. *FASB Statement No. 5* defines three levels as follows:

1. *Probable.* The chance of the future event occurring is *likely.*
2. *Reasonably possible.* The chance of the future event occurring is *more* than remote but *less* than likely.
3. *Remote.* The chance of the future event occurring is *slight.*

The two methods of accounting for loss contingencies depend on the degree of certainty that is associated with the future event, as follows:[10]

1. **Recognition in the Financial Statements.** An estimated loss from a loss contingency *is* reported in the financial statements as a reduction of income (loss or expense) and the reduction in an asset or increase in a liability if *both* of the following conditions are met:
   a. It is *probable* that an asset has been impaired or a liability incurred at the date of the financial statements.
   b. The amount of the loss can be *reasonably estimated.*

   If a liability is recorded in this process, it is not necessary to know the exact payee or the exact date that it is to be paid.

2. **Disclosure in the Notes to the Financial Statements.** An estimated loss from a loss contingency is reported in the notes if it is *reasonably possible* that an asset has been impaired or a liability incurred. However, amounts are often not disclosed.

The discussion that follows is concerned with the accounting for the recognition of loss contingencies, disclosure in financial statement notes of loss contingencies, and disclosure in financial statement notes of gain contingencies.

Recognition of Loss Contingencies

As discussed earlier, certain loss contingencies are *usually* reported in the financial statements because they ordinarily meet both criteria stated in the preceding section, such as the noncollectibility of receivables and obligations related to product warranties. Several other loss contingencies *may be* reported provided that they meet the two stated criteria. These include the threat of expropriation of assets, pending or threatened litigation, actual or possible claims and assess-

....
[10]*Ibid.,* par. 3.

ments, guarantees of indebtedness of others, and agreements to repurchase receivables (or the related property) that have been sold. On the other hand, at least three contingencies are *usually not* reported in the financial statements. These include the uninsured risk of loss or damage of company property by fire, explosion, or other hazards, general or unspecified business risks, and risk of loss from catastrophes assumed by property and casualty insurance companies including reinsurance companies. This latter group of items reveals that the mere exposure to risk does not mean that an asset is impaired or that a liability has been incurred. The impairment occurs when the event causing the loss occurs.

When a loss contingency is recognized, an *expense* or *loss* is recorded. Also a liability, or the reduction of an asset (or increase in a contra asset), is recorded. Consider the example of recording bad debts: Bad Debts Expense is increased (debited) and Allowance for Doubtful Accounts (contra-asset account) is increased (credited).

Disclosure in Notes of Loss Contingencies

If a loss contingency is not recognized in the financial statements because one or both of the criteria for recognition are not met, disclosure of the contingency must be made when there is at least a reasonable possibility that a loss or an additional loss may have been incurred. According to the FASB, a loss contingency is reasonably possible when the chance is more than remote but less than likely that the future event or events will confirm the loss or impairment of an asset or the incurrence of a liability. Most of the examples of loss contingencies listed earlier could fall into this category, particularly the threat of expropriation of assets, pending or threatened litigation, and actual or possible claims and assessments. When reporting this type of loss contingency, the disclosure should indicate the nature of the contingency and give an estimate of the possible loss or range of loss or indicate that such an estimate cannot be made.

The FASB also states that the long-standing practices of disclosure of those loss contingencies where the possibility of loss is only remote should be continued. Examples of loss contingencies that are remote (the chance of the future event or events occurring is slight) include direct and indirect guarantees of indebtedness of others, obligations of commercial banks under "standby letters of credit," and guarantees to repurchase receivables that have been sold or otherwise assigned. The disclosure of this group of guarantees must include the nature and amount of the guarantee and, if estimable, the value of any recovery that could be expected to result. This latter requirement would result from the guarantor's right to proceed against an outside party.

Disclosure in Notes of Gain Contingencies

Provided that the three characteristics are present (as stated in the definition of contingencies), a gain contingency could exist. This kind of contingency would result in a potential increase in assets or decrease in liabilities. Adhering to the convention of conservatism, the FASB concluded that these gains should not be reported in the financial statements; rather, they should be disclosed in the notes to the financial statements. *FASB Statement No. 5* states:

(a) Contingencies that might result in gains usually are not reflected in the accounts since to do so might be to recognize revenue prior to its realization.
(b) Adequate disclosure shall be made of contingencies that might result in gains, but care shall be exercised to avoid misleading implications as to the likelihood of realization.[11]

An example of a gain contingency is the case where a company is suing another company for patent infringement and the probability of winning the suit is excellent. A second example is the case of a probable expropriation of property by a foreign government if the expected reimbursement will exceed the book value of the property.

Evaluation of Accounting for Contingencies

As we have seen, some contingencies are routinely recorded in the financial statements because they are both probable and measurable. Others are not recorded because the probability of loss is remote. It is the middle group of contingent items, those that may or may not be recorded, which cause the greatest difficulty in financial reporting and the understanding of financial statements. The most common of these occurs with litigation.

In the current legal and economic environment, companies are exposed to numerous lawsuits. With each lawsuit, the management must decide whether to record any loss associated with the litigation and the related liability, and the auditors must agree with the decision. Consideration should be given to the opinion of legal counsel, the nature of the litigation, precedent experience of the company and other companies in similar cases, and management reaction to the lawsuit. Theoretically, if the loss of the lawsuit is probable and if the loss amount can be estimated, the loss should be recorded. However, companies generally do not record such items.

This procedure can be justified for three reasons, two of which relate to accounting principles. First, it may be reasonable for the management and its lawyers to argue that the threshold of "probable" has not been reached and that they are continuing to defend the lawsuit in the expectation that the company will be found not guilty. Second, it may be reasonable to argue that the amount of any potential loss is not measurable because each lawsuit is unique and is subject to the decisions of a particular judge and jury. Third, the company would be extremely reluctant to record the contingent loss in the financial statements because that might be considered as an admission of guilt (although not admissible evidence in a court). Therefore, the user of the financial statements should not expect the company to have recorded in the financial statements any con-

· · · · · · · · · · · · · · · · · · ·

[11] *Ibid.*, par. 17.

tingent loss and liability associated with a lawsuit. Instead, a discussion of the lawsuit will be found in the notes to the financial statements.

In Chapter 4, modified audit opinions were discussed. The auditor may issue this opinion when it believes a *material* uncertainty is associated with the financial statements. Therefore, the auditor may agree that the contingent loss and related liability should not be recorded in the financial statements but still modify its opinion because the size of any judgment against the company would have a material impact on the financial statements. This decision is often extremely difficult to make because the modified opinion will probably have a negative effect on the company and its stock price. The auditor is essentially trying to determine the likelihood and the possible amount of the loss in order to evaluate the potential effect on the company. For example, Manville Corporation declared bankruptcy in 1982 because of claims being made against it for asbestos-related injuries. At that time, Manville estimated that it would receive 52,700 claims totaling $2 billion. Prior to declaring bankruptcy, the auditor had issued a modified opinion, but no liability (and related loss) was recorded for contingencies even though the company had already lost numerous cases (legal fees and judgments paid were recorded as expenses when incurred).

In contrast, in 1985 A. H. Robins did recognize a liability and a loss of $615 million to cover expected losses from thousands of suits related to its Dalkon Shield contraceptive device. This recognition resulted in a $461.6 million loss, and the company's net worth was eliminated. Since the company had already settled 8,300 claims at a cost of $314.6 million and more than 4,000 cases were pending and new claims were still being filed, the company decided that the requirements for recognition of an accounting contingency had been met.

To illustrate the difficulty of deciding whether to issue a modified opinion in connection with a contingency, the auditor issued modified opinions for UAL Inc., the parent of United Airlines, from 1978 to 1983. The modification was caused by a class action employment discrimination suit brought by flight attendants. Eventually, UAL paid only $38 million in damages, hardly a material amount for UAL. In contrast, the auditor did not issue a modified opinion in 1979 for AMR Corp., the parent of American Airlines, after its DC-10 had crashed in Chicago, resulting in 275 deaths and numerous lawsuits. The auditor did not issue a modified opinion because it was satisfied that AMR had sufficient insurance to cover any lawsuits.

Many companies are faced with increasing insurance premiums and, in some cases, the inability to obtain insurance for certain risks. Therefore, many companies have chosen to "self-insure." This situation does not create a contingency because an exposure to risk does not mean that an asset has been impaired or a liability incurred. A loss only arises when an accident occurs in the future. Thus, a company that pays insurance premiums has an expense each period, whereas a company that self-insures has a loss whenever an accident occurs.

Illustration of Contingency Disclosures

The contingency disclosures of several companies are shown in Exhibit 8–1. These disclosures include two loss contingencies and one gain contingency. The

EXHIBIT 8–1   Disclosure of contingencies

· · · · · · · · · · · · · · · · · ·

WESTINGHOUSE
NOTES TO THE FINANCIAL STATEMENTS (in part):

*Note 19 Commitments
and Contingent Liabilities (in part):*

The Corporation had previously provided for all estimated future costs associated with the resolution of all uranium supply contract suits and related litigation. The net liability for estimated future costs of $39 million at December 31, 1989, is deemed adequate considering all facts and circumstances known to management. The future obligations require providing specific quantities of uranium and products and services over a period extending beyond the year 2010. The net costs of meeting these obligations and other related settlement transactions are applied to the balance of the liability and are not reflected in results of operations. Variances from estimates which may occur will be considered in determining if an adjustment of the liability is necessary.

DuPONT
NOTES TO THE FINANCIAL STATEMENTS (in part):

*Note 22 Commitments
and Contingent Liabilities (in part):*

(in millions)
The company has indirectly guaranteed various debt obligations under agreements with certain affiliated and other companies to provide specified minimum revenues from shipments or purchases of products. At December 31, 1989, these indirect guarantees totaled $110. In addition, at December 31, 1989, the company had directly guaranteed $153 of the obligations of certain affiliated companies and others. No material loss is anticipated by reason of such agreements and guarantees.

---

loss contingencies involve litigation against Westinghouse, and guarantees of the indebtedness of others by DuPont. The gain contingency involves claims against other companies by Apple Computer.

SECTION B   Present and Future Value, Mortgages, and Notes

■ PRESENT VALUE AND FUTURE VALUE

The previous section of the chapter has included a discussion of current liabilities. Noncurrent liabilities involve more complex valuation issues because of the longer period of time until the cash flows occur. These valuation issues require an understanding of present value and future value concepts.

Would you rather receive $1 today or $1 next year? The answer to this question should be that you would rather receive $1 today because a dollar held today is

EXHIBIT 8–1   *(continued)*

················ ————————————

APPLE COMPUTER, INC.
NOTES TO THE FINANCIAL STATEMENTS (in part):

Litigation (in part):

In March 1988, Apple filed suit against Microsoft Corporation (Microsoft) and Hewlett-Packard Company (HP) alleging that their computer programs Microsoft Windows 2.03 and HP NewWave infringe Apple's registered audiovisual copyrights protecting the Macintosh user interface. Microsoft and HP each filed separate answers setting forth affirmative defenses and counterclaims against Apple, seeking declaratory relief and unspecified monetary damages (including punitive damages). In May 1988, the Court granted a motion by Microsoft to bifurcate the suit and litigate first Microsoft's asserted defense that Apple's claims against Windows 2.03 are barred by a 1985 license agreement between Apple and Microsoft relating to Windows Version 1.0. In rulings in March and July 1989, the Court ruled that the 1985 agreement does not constitute a complete defense to Apple's claims because the visual displays of Windows 2.03 are fundamentally different from those of Windows version 1.0; the visual display elements of Windows Version 1.0 which are used in Windows 2.03 are licensed; and the visual displays in Windows 2.03 that are not licensed are those relating to the use of overlapping main application windows and the appearance and manipulation of icons. The Court also confirmed that the license does not extend to visual displays added by HP in its NewWave software, which operates in conjunction with Windows 2.03. The case will now proceed to determine whether Apple's copyrights exhibit originality and are valid, and whether the use by Microsoft and HP of unlicensed visual displays in combination with licensed visual displays infringes Apple's copyrights.

---

worth more than a dollar to be received a year from now. The difference between the two amounts is *interest*, or more generally, there is a *time value of money*. The components of the interest rate are discussed later in the chapter; they are the factors that cause money to have a time value.

To illustrate the time value of money, suppose that Peter Cameron has $100 on January 1, 1993, and can invest it at 10%. This money will grow over the next three years as shown in the following table:

	Principal Amount at Beginning of the Year	Interest at 10%	Principal Amount at End of the Year
1993	$100	$10.00	$110.00
1994	110	11.00	121.00
1995	121	12.10	133.10

Therefore, a person would rather have $100 today than $100 in one year, because the $100 today grows to $110 in one year. Alternatively, the analysis tells us that the following amounts, given the 10% interest rate and their respective dates, have *equivalent* values:

- $100 at the beginning of 1993.
- $110 at the end of 1993.
- $121 at the end of 1994.
- $133.10 at the end of 1995.

Since these amounts have equivalent values, if you were asked which amount you wanted to receive, you would be indifferent among the four alternatives, given the 10% rate. It is essential to note, however, that the dollar amounts have a time attached to them. Whenever we are considering the time value of money, we must always know the date at which the dollar amount is measured. A dollar received or paid in 1993 does not have the same value as a dollar received or paid in 1994.

Definitions of Present Value and Future Value

Two important terms are widely used whenever the value of money is being considered. **Present value is the value today of a certain number of dollars measured in the future.** The present value concept can be used analytically by either the payor or receiver of money. In the preceding example, therefore, $100 is the present value at the beginning of 1993 of $133.10 at the end of 1995 if the interest rate is 10%. **Future value is the value at a future date of a certain number of dollars measured today.** Therefore, $133.10 at the end of 1995 is the future value of $100 at the beginning of 1993 if the interest rate is 10%. Again, this analytical concept can be used by either the payor or receiver.

Although present value and future value are both widely used concepts, present value is a much more useful accounting concept than future value because it is often necessary to include in the financial statements the value of cash flows that will occur in the future. Therefore, the discussion in this chapter concentrates on present value although future value is also discussed.

Simple Interest and Compound Interest

Simple interest is calculated by the formula:

$$\text{Interest} = \text{Principal} \times \text{Rate} \times \text{Time}$$

Therefore simple interest on $100 for three years at 10% would be:

$$\text{Interest} = \$100 \times 10\% \times 3 \text{ years}$$
$$= \$30$$

This simple interest is different from the interest in our previous example, which amounted to $33.10 ($133.10 − $100.00), because the example uses compound interest. **Compound interest is interest that accrues on both the principal and past accrued (unpaid) interest.** Thus, during 1993 interest of 10% is accrued on the principal of $100, making a total of $110 at the end of 1993. In 1994 interest of 10% is accrued on the principal of $100 *and* the 1993 interest of $10, or on a total of $110. The interest amounts to $11 in 1994. In 1995 interest is similarly accrued on the principal of $100 plus the interest for 1993 and 1994 of $21. The interest on the $121 is $12.10. Thus, the total compound interest is $33.10 ($10 + $11 + $12.10) compared to the simple interest of $30. Compound interest is the process that underlies the concepts of present and future value.

Calculations of present and future values are essential in many situations. If a company enters into a transaction which creates an obligation to pay a certain number of dollars in the future, the present value of those dollars should be disclosed as a liability in the balance sheet. Application of this present value concept in accounting for mortgages, notes, and bonds is discussed later in this chapter. Accounting for leases and pensions also utilizes present value concepts; these topics are discussed in Chapter 9. In addition, present and future values are necessary for many types of investment decisions, such as the acquisition of property, plant, and equipment. To assist these types of accounting disclosures and management decisions, formulas and tables are frequently used.

Formulas and Tables

Instead of preparing a year-by-year calculation of present and future values, a formula or a table may be used. The general relationship between present and future value is as follows:

$$FV = PV(1 + i)^n \text{ or } PV = \frac{FV}{(1 + i)^n}$$

where

PV = Present value
FV = Future value
i = Interest rate
n = Number of periods

Using the same example of 10% and three years, if we know the present value of $100, the future value is calculated as follows:

$$FV = PV(1 + i)^n$$
$$= \$100(1 + 0.10)^3$$
$$= \$100(1.331)$$
$$= \$133.10$$

Alternatively, if the future value of $133.10 is known, the present value is calculated as follows:

$$PV = \frac{FV}{(1 + i)^n}$$

$$= \frac{\$133.10}{(1 + 0.10)^3}$$

$$= \frac{\$133.10}{1.331}$$

$$= \$100$$

Tables have been developed that simplify the calculation process even more. Table 1 in Appendix B is entitled the Future Value of $1. **Table 1 is used to compute the future value of a single amount when the present value is known.** A future value is computed by using the table as follows:

$$FV = PV \times \textbf{Future Value of \$1 Factor}$$

A *factor* is a specific amount for a certain time period and rate. Thus, each specific amount included in Table 1 is a future value factor for a certain time period and rate. If you look up the factor for 10% and three periods in Table 1, you will find that it is 1.331000. Therefore the future value at the end of three years of $100 received or paid today using a 10% interest rate is as follows:

$$FV = PV \times \text{Future Value of \$1 Factor for 3 Periods at 10\%}$$
$$= \$100 \times 1.331000$$
$$= \$133.10$$

Table 2 in Appendix B is entitled the Present Value of $1. **Table 2 is used to compute the present value of a single amount when the future value is known.** A present value is computed by using the table as follows:

$$PV = FV \times \textbf{Present Value of \$1 Factor}$$

If you look up the factor for 10% and three periods in Table 2, you will find that it is 0.751315. Therefore, the present value of $133.10 received or paid at the end of three years, using a 10% interest rate, is:

$$PV = FV \times \text{Present Value of \$1 Factor for 3 Periods at 10\%}$$
$$= \$133.10 \times 0.751315$$
$$= \$100$$

The process of converting a future value to a lower present value is known as *discounting* and the rate used is often called the *discount rate*. Thus, the $133.10 future value is discounted to the $100 present value by multiplying it times the 0.751315 factor for 3 periods at the 10% discount rate.

Tables 1 and 2 follow exactly the same procedures as the formulas. They simply provide the answers that would be obtained by using the formulas for the various rates and time periods. Thus, the Future Value of $1 table is based on the formula $(1 + i)^n$ and the Present Value of $1 table is based on the formula $1/(1 + i)^n$.

In summary, the Present Value of $1 table is used to convert (discount) a future value back to the present. Note that all numbers in the table are less than 1.0. The calculation of the present value can be diagrammed as follows:

$$\begin{array}{ccc} \text{Present} & = \text{Present Value} & \times \text{Future} \\ \text{Value} & \text{of \$1 Factor} & \text{Value} \end{array}$$

$$\longleftarrow\!|$$

The Future Value of $1 table is used to convert a present value to a future value.

Note that all the numbers in the table are greater than 1.0. The calculation of the future value may be diagrammed as follows:

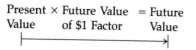

$$\text{Present} \times \text{Future Value} = \text{Future}$$
$$\text{Value} \quad \text{of \$1 Factor} \quad \text{Value}$$

An Annuity

In many situations we are not concerned with the present or future value of a single amount as in the previous examples, but with an annuity. **An annuity is a series of equal periodic cash flows.** These cash flows may be either received or paid. For example, a three-year $100 annuity consists of a cash flow of $100 per year for three years. In this book we will assume that the first cash flow in an annuity occurs at the *end* of the first time period. Thus, if an annual annuity begins on January 1, 1993, the first cash flow occurs on December 31, 1993.

We could compute the present value on January 1, 1993, of a three-year $100 annuity at 10% by treating it as three separate single amounts and using the factors from Table 2 as follows:

PV of $100 paid or received on Dec. 31, 1993 = $100 × 0.909091 = $ 90.9091
PV of $100 paid or received on Dec. 31, 1994 = $100 × 0.826446 =   82.6446
PV of $100 paid or received on Dec. 31, 1995 = $100 × 0.751315 =   75.1315
PV of $100, 3-year annuity at 10% on Jan. 1, 1993   = $248.6852

This computation can also be illustrated by using a time diagram as follows:

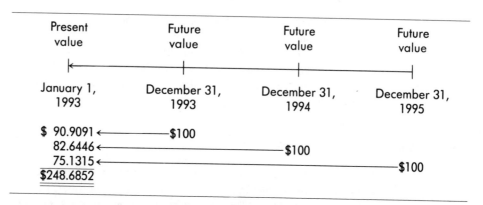

Instead of using Table 2 and completing the numerous calculations shown, use of Table 4 in Appendix B makes the calculation process much simpler. The table is entitled Present Value of Ordinary Annuity of $1 and is developed on the basis of the assumption that the present value is computed one period before the first cash flow. **Table 4 is used to compute the present value of an annuity.** The present value is computed by using the table as follows:

PV of Annuity = Periodic Amount of the Annuity × Present Value of Annuity Factor

If you look up the factor for 10% and three periods in Table 4, you will find that it is 2.486852. Therefore, the present value of the annuity of $100 received or paid at the end of each year for three years using a 10% interest rate is as follows:

$$PV \text{ of Annuity} = \text{Annuity} \times \text{Present Value of Annuity for 3 Periods at 10\%}$$
$$= \$100 \times 2.486852$$
$$= \$248.6852$$

Another way of saying this is that the annuity of $100 received or paid at the end of each year for three years is discounted to a present value of $248.6852. This process enables the present value to be computed by a single multiplication rather than three multiplications and an addition. It is important to realize, however, that exactly the same present value concept is involved. The purpose of Table 4 is to simplify the calculations.

Table 3 in Appendix B is entitled Future Value of Ordinary Annuity of $1 and is developed on the basis of the assumption that the future value is computed on the date of the last cash flow. **Table 3 is used to compute the future value of an annuity.** The future value is computed by using the table as follows:

FV of Annuity = Periodic Amount of the Annuity × Future Value of Annuity Factor

The future value of a three-year annuity of $100 received or paid at the end of each year for three years using a 10% interest rate is calculated by looking up the factor for three periods at 10% in Table 3, which is 3.310000:

$$FV \text{ of Annuity} = \text{Annuity} \times \text{Future Value of Annuity for 3 Periods at 10\%}$$
$$= \$100 \times 3.310000$$
$$= \$331.00$$

Many electronic calculators have the capacity to compute present and future values. The calculation process follows exactly the same concepts as discussed. The calculator uses formulas to determine each factor whenever a calculation is made (we have not illustrated the formulas for the annuity calculations), rather than looking up the factor in a table as is usually done when a calculator is not available.

Interest Periods Other Than One Year

It is often necessary to calculate present and future values for situations in which interest periods other than one year are used. Remember, however, that **interest rates are expressed in terms of an annual rate unless specified otherwise.** For example, a savings account may pay 8% interest, compounded quarterly. This means that the interest is 2% each quarter and that the interest accrues each quarter on the principal plus interest of the previous quarters. Thus, in this example, if we are computing a present value or future value for a three-year period, we would look up in the appropriate table the factor for 2% for 12 periods (3 years × 4 quarters) rather than 8% for three years. **The general rule is that if there are n compounding periods in the year, the interest rate per period is the annual interest rate divided by n and the number of interest periods is the number of years multiplied by n.**

To illustrate, suppose that we need to compute the present value of $1,000 that will be received at the end of four years. The annual interest rate is 10%, but interest accrues *semiannually.* Therefore, the appropriate rate to use is 5% (10% ÷ 2) per period; and there are 8 (4 years × 2) time periods. The calculation (using the factor from Table 2) is as follows:

$$\text{Present Value} = \text{Future Value} \times \text{Present Value of \$1 Factor}$$
$$\text{for 8 Periods at 5\%}$$
$$= \$1,000 \times 0.676839$$
$$= \$676.84 \text{ (rounded)}$$

In contrast, the present value calculated with *annual* compounding would be as follows:

$$\text{Present Value} = \text{Future Value} \times \text{Present Value of \$1 Factor}$$
$$\text{for 4 Periods at 10\%}$$
$$= \$1,000 \times 0.683013$$
$$= \$683.01 \text{ (rounded)}$$

It should be expected that the semiannual compounding would result in a lower *present value* ($676.84 as compared with $683.01) than would annual compounding because of the added interest that will accrue. That is, a smaller present value will accrue to the same future value when interest is compounded more often. Similarly, if the future value is being calculated from a present value, compounding more frequently than once a year will result in a higher future value.

An Analysis of Present Value Principles in Financial Reporting

Accounting principles without a unifying objective or rationale have evolved for when present value techniques should, and should not, be used. Among the issues are the use of present value for the initial valuation of assets and liabilities, the amortization of those assets and liabilities, and any subsequent revaluation based on current interest rate.

Present value techniques are used in generally accepted accounting principles for certain monetary items. A **monetary item** is money or a claim to money that is not affected by changes in the prices of specific goods or services. For example, a note payable is a monetary item whereas a warranty payable is a nonmonetary item. Those monetary items for which present value techniques are used in accounting principles including mortgages, bonds payable and bond investments, long-term notes payable and receivable, leases, and postretirement benefits. Present value is not used for troubled debt restructuring and deferred income taxes. Some users argue that present value should be used for nonmonetary items including property, plant, and equipment. However, accounting principles have not been extended to the use of present value for such nonmonetary items. Therefore, present value principles are not used for warranties, unearned revenue, compensated absences, and nonmonetary assets. Each of the topics mentioned above is discussed in this book.

Most users argue that the use of present value creates a *relevant* accounting measurement because the present value amounts are more relevant than, say, the total of the undiscounted cash flows. However, the use of present value may create measurements that are less *reliable* because the computation requires:

1. The estimation of the future cash flows, including the timing, amount, and risk of those cash flows.

2. The estimation of the interest rate. Interest rates that could be used include the historical rate, the current rate, the average expected rate, the weighted average cost of capital, or the incremental borrowing rate.

3. The degree to which the cash flows from the individual assets may be added (and the liabilities subtracted) to give a measure of the value of the company.

In summary, present value is used in financial reporting but without a basic concept that determines its use or nonuse. There will be considerable discussion in the next few years because the FASB has announced its intention to evaluate the use of present value in financial reporting. Mortgages, notes, and bonds are discussed in this chapter, and leases and pensions in the next chapter. Present value is generally not used for current assets and current liabilities because of the relatively short time until the cash flow occurs.

■ MORTGAGES PAYABLE

A mortgage payable is a long-term debt for which the lender has a specific claim against an asset of the borrower. For example, most homeowners purchase their homes by issuing a mortgage. That is, they borrow the money from a lender and the lender is assigned a secured claim on the home. Companies also acquire assets through mortgages.

The typical mortgage requires equal monthly payments (an annuity), and these payments are determined according to present value principles as follows:

Monthly Payment = Amount Borrowed ÷ Present Value of Annuity Factor Based on the Interest Rate and the Life of the Mortgage

Each payment consists of two components: (1) interest expense based on the periodic interest rate and the book value of the loan at the beginning of the period and (2) a portion of the principal balance. These components are calculated as follows:

Interest Expense = Periodic Interest Rate × Book Value of Loan at the Beginning of the Period

Repayment of Principal = Monthly Payment − Interest Expense

To illustrate how to account for a mortgage, suppose that the Joma Company purchases a building for $100,000. It agrees to pay $20,000 at acquisition and to pay the remainder under the terms of a 30-year mortgage at 12%. The acquisition is recorded as follows:

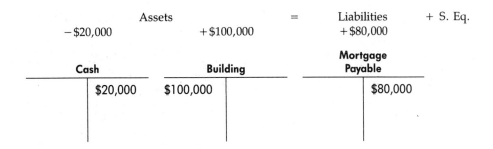

Since the payments are to be monthly, the annual rate of 12% and time period of 30 years must be converted into their monthly equivalents of 1% and 360 periods. This factor is not included in Table 4 of Appendix B but it is 97.218331. The monthly payment is computed as follows:

$$\text{Monthly Payment} = \text{Amount Borrowed} \div \text{Present Value of Annuity Factor}$$
$$= \$80,000 \div 97.218331$$
$$= \$822.89$$

The interest expense for the *first* month is calculated as follows:

$$\text{Interest Expense} = \text{Periodic Interest Rate} \times \text{Book Value of Loan at the Beginning of the Month}$$
$$= 1\% \times \$80,000$$
$$= \$800$$

The remaining portion of the monthly payment is $22.89 ($822.89 − $800.00) and is the reduction of the principal. The first monthly payment is recorded as follows:

Assets	=	Liabilities	+	Stockholders' Equity
−$822.89		−$22.89		−$800

Cash		Mortgage Payable		Interest Expense	
	$822.89	$22.89		$800	

The balance of the mortgage payable is the present value of the remaining cash payments discounted at 1% per month.

The interest expense for the second month is calculated as follows:

$$\text{Interest Expense} = 1\% \times (\$80,000 - \$22.89)$$
$$= 1\% \times \$79,977.11$$
$$= \$799.77 \text{ (rounded)}$$

The second monthly payment is recorded as follows:

Assets	=	Liabilities	+	Stockholders' Equity
− $822.89		− $23.12		− $799.77

Cash		Mortgage Payable		Interest Expense	
$822.89		$23.12		$799.77	

Each month the balance of the Mortgage Payable is reduced so that the balance is eliminated when the final monthly payment is made.

At the end of each year, depreciation is recorded on the building in the usual manner. The depreciation expense and interest expense are reported on the Joma Company's income statement in the Operating Expenses and Other Revenues and Expenses sections, respectively. The mortgage payable is split into the current liability and long-term liability amounts on the company's year-end balance sheet.

To illustrate a misconception that often arises over present value, consider a 15-year and a 30-year mortgage of $100,000 at 12%. On the 30-year mortgage the monthly payment is $1,029, whereas on the 15-year mortgage the monthly payment is $1,200 (the larger monthly payment on the 15-year mortgage results from the quicker repayment of the principal). The misconception arises when the total amounts of the monthly payments are computed and compared. On the 30-year mortgage, the total interest is $270,301, whereas the total interest on the 15-year loan is $116,030. A comparison of these two total amounts is misleading. The error is that when such totals are computed, amounts from different time periods have been added together, thereby ignoring the basic principle of present value that there is a time value to money. In other words, an interest rate of 0% has been assumed, which is obviously inconsistent with the mortgage rate of 12%! It should be understood that if the present value of the payments required under either loan is computed using a discount rate of 12%, the present value is $100,000. Thus, the differing payments for differing time periods in the future have the same present value if the loan amount and the interest rate are the same.

■ LONG-TERM NOTES PAYABLE AND RECEIVABLE

Long-term notes payable represent a future obligation to repay debt, and in many cases no collateral backs the note; that is, the note is unsecured. A long-term note generally includes a provision for interest on the borrowed funds, and the rate of interest charged will depend on such factors as the credit standing of the borrower and the amount of current debt.

Notes payable that are classified as current liabilities were discussed in Chapter 3. Notes payable are classified as long-term liabilities if they are not expected to be paid within one year, or the operating cycle, whichever is longer. A note payable represents an obligation to repay a certain amount (the *face value*) at a specified date (the *maturity date*) in the future and also includes a requirement to pay interest each period on the amount borrowed.

When a long-term note payable is issued, cash (or another asset) is received and the note is recorded at its face value as a noncurrent liability (Notes Payable). Subsequently, each interest payment is recorded as interest expense and a reduction in cash. Prior to maturity, the face value of the noncurrent note payable is reported as a long-term liability on the issuing company's balance sheet. Upon payment of the note at maturity, the Notes Payable is eliminated and the cash payment is recorded.

The company that lends the money and receives the long-term note follows similar accounting procedures to those just discussed for its long-term note receivable. It records a noncurrent asset (Notes Receivable) when it lends the cash. Subsequently, when it receives and records each cash interest payment, it also records interest revenue. Prior to maturity, the lending company reports the noncurrent note receivable in the Investments section of its balance sheet. Upon settlement of the note at maturity, the Notes Receivable is eliminated and the cash receipt is recorded. Since the recording and reporting of interest-bearing long-term notes receivable and payable are very similar to the accounting for current notes payable, discussed in Chapter 3, no further discussion is presented here.

Noninterest-Bearing Notes

A noninterest-bearing note may be issued in exchange for cash or in exchange for an asset or services rendered. **When a long-term note is exchanged solely for cash, the note is assumed to have a present value equal to the cash proceeds, and the appropriate interest rate is determined by comparing the cash exchanged with the face value of the note. Any difference between the proceeds and the note's face value is accounted for as a discount and amortized over the life of the note by the effective interest method.** To illustrate, assume that in January of the current year Johnson Corporation issues a three-year, noninterest-bearing note with a face value of $8,000. A noninterest-bearing note is similar to a zero coupon bond (discussed later) because no interest is paid during the life of the note and a single payment is made on the maturity date. The value of the note is the present value of the face value. If we assume the appropriate discount rate is 12%, the present value of $5,694.24 ($8,000 × 0.711780) is the amount of cash exchanged for the note. The issuance of the note is recorded as follows:

Assets	=	Liabilities		+ Stockholders' Equity
+$5,694.24		+$8,000	−$2,305.76	

Cash		Notes Payable	Discount on Notes Payable	
$5,694.24		$8,000	$2,305.76	

The discount account is a contra account and is subtracted from the Notes Payable on the balance sheet. The interest expense of $683.31 for the first year is computed by multiplying the book value of $5,694.24 ($8,000 − $2,305.76) by 12% and is recorded as follows:

Assets =	Liabilities	+ Stockholders' Equity
	+$683.31	−$683.31

	Discount on Notes Payable	Interest Expense	
	$683.31	$683.31	

As a result the book value of the note has increased to $6,377.55 ($5,694.24 + $683.31). The interest expense of $765.31 in the second year is computed by multiplying this new book value by 12% and is recorded as follows:

Assets =	Liabilities	+ Stockholders' Equity
	+$765.31	−$765.31

	Discount on Notes Payable	Interest Expense	
	$765.31	$765.31	

As a result, the book value of the note has increased to $7,142.86 ($6,377.55 + $765.31). The interest expense of $857.14 in the third year is computed by multiplying this new book value by 12% and is recorded as follows:

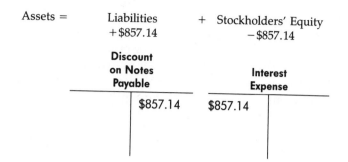

The balance in the discount account is now zero and the repayment of the note is recorded by reducing Cash and Notes Payable by $8,000.

A similar situation arises when a noninterest-bearing note is issued as payment for an asset or services received. The note must be discounted to its present value, and that value is assigned to the asset or services. For example, if a lawyer accepts an $8,000 noninterest bearing three-year note for services rendered, the value of the services is only $5,694.24 if the market rate of interest is 12%.

SECTION C Bonds and Disclosure

■ BONDS PAYABLE

When companies borrow large amounts of money for a long period of time, it usually involves the issuance of bonds by the company. **A bond is a type of note in which a company agrees to pay the holder the face value at the maturity date and to pay interest periodically at a specified rate on the face value.** Thus, the company that issues the bonds is borrowing money from the holder of the bonds, who is the lender. **The face value (also called the par value) is the amount of money that the issuer promises to pay at maturity.** It is the same concept as the principal of a note. **The maturity date is the date on which the issuer of the bond promises to pay the face value to the holder.** The issuer usually also agrees to pay interest each period. **The contract rate is the rate at which the issuer of the bond pays interest each period until maturity.** The contract rate is also called the *stated or nominal* rate. This information is printed on a bond certificate, which is held by the owner of the bond. **A bond certificate is a serially numbered legal document that specifies the face value, the annual interest rate, the maturity date, and other characteristics of the bond issue.** Since bond issues are usually intended to borrow large amounts of money, corporations (and government entities) are the most common issuers of bonds. Each bond issue usually has a bond indenture. **A bond indenture is a document that defines the rights of the bondholders.** Corporate bonds are nearly always issued so that each bond has a face value of $1,000. The entire bond issue may be sold to one purchaser or to numerous individual purchasers. Thus, a $1 million dollar bond issue will consist of 1,000 bonds, each with a $1,000 face value. In addition, interest is usually paid twice each year (semiannually), although the interest rate is expressed in annual terms. Therefore, the annual rate must be halved to obtain the interest rate per semiannual period. For example, a 10%, $1,000 bond will pay interest of $100 (10% × $1,000) per year in two installments of $50 (10% × 1/2 × $1,000) every six months. A face value of $1,000 per bond and semiannual interest payments will be assumed throughout this chapter.

Why Bonds Are Issued

There are two primary ways in which a corporation can obtain large amounts of money (capital) for long periods of time. One is by selling common stock (or preferred stock), which is discussed briefly in Chapter 1 and more fully in Chapter 10. Selling common stock provides the corporation with permanent capital since there is no obligation to repay the stockholders. In addition, there is no legal obligation to make periodic dividend payments although many companies choose to do so. Because the stockholders are owners, selling additional stock spreads ownership, voting rights, and the earnings over more shares. The second way of obtaining long-term capital is to issue bonds, which obligates the corporation to repay the amount borrowed and also to pay interest each period. The payment of interest is a legal obligation, and if the corporation issuing the bonds (the borrower) fails to pay the interest on the principal, the holder of the bonds (the lender) can take legal action to enforce payment, which may cause the borrower to declare bankruptcy. The bondholders are creditors of the company (not owners) and have no voting rights.

The primary reason why the management of a corporation may decide to issue bonds instead of common stock is that the earnings available to the common stockholders can be increased through leverage. **Leverage is the use of borrowing by a corporation to increase the return to common stockholders.** It is also called *trading on equity*. If a corporation can borrow money by issuing bonds and using the money to invest in a project that provides greater income than the interest that must be paid on the bonds, the corporation and its stockholders will be better off (they will earn a higher income). One measure of the return to common stockholders is earnings per share, which is discussed in Chapter 10. When a corporation successfully uses leverage, earnings per share will increase.

To illustrate this concept, assume that a corporation currently has 10,000 shares of common stock outstanding, income before interest and income taxes of $100,000, and an income tax rate of 30%. The management has decided to expand its operations by building a factory for $200,000. The factory will provide additional pretax income of $40,000 per year. The corporation is considering selling 5,000 additional shares for $40 each or issuing bonds at par with a face value of $200,000 and a 10% interest rate. The effects of the two alternatives are illustrated in Exhibit 8–2.

The interest expense on the bonds is an expense on the income statement, and therefore income before income taxes is reduced when bonds are used for

EXHIBIT 8–2 Use of leverage

	Before Expansion	Bond Financing	Stock Financing
Income before interest and income taxes	$100,000	$140,000	$140,000
Interest expense	—	(20,000)	—
Income before income taxes	$100,000	$120,000	$140,000
Income tax expense	(30,000)	(36,000)	(42,000)
Net income	$ 70,000	$ 84,000	$ 98,000
Earnings per share	$7.00	$8.40	$6.53

financing. Income tax expense is also reduced so that the net effect of the bond financing alternative is that net income is increased by $14,000 ($84,000 − $70,000) when bond financing is used. When stock financing is used, although net income increases by $28,000 ($98,000 − $70,000), the number of common shares is increased to 15,000 so that earnings per share declines from $7.00 to $6.53 ($98,000 ÷ 15,000 = $6.53, rounded). The corporation may choose to pay dividends to the stockholders, but the payments do not affect the computation of net income and may not be deducted in the computation of income taxes. When bond financing is used, earnings per share increases to $8.40 ($84,000 ÷ 10,000 = $8.40). Therefore, although financing by issuing bonds does not increase net income by as much as selling common stock, in this case it has a more favorable impact on earnings per share of present stockholders and is of greater benefit to the stockholders.

The reason for this advantageous result is that the new factory is expected to earn a pretax return (earnings ÷ investment) of 20% ($40,000 ÷ $200,000), whereas the pretax interest cost on the bonds is only 10%. Borrowing money at 10% to earn a return of 20% provides the leverage that is advantageous to the owners of the corporation. While it may be advantageous to borrow money, there is a limit to the amount of money a company can borrow. As the amount of money borrowed increases, the risk of default increases and therefore the interest rate the company will have to pay increases. At some point the interest rate will exceed the rate that can be earned from an investment, lenders will refuse to lend more money, or management will decide the risk of borrowing has become too high. Thus, all companies have a limit on the amount of borrowing that they can undertake.

It should be recognized that the issuing of bonds can result in lower earnings per share if the project is not successful. For example, suppose that the expansion turns out to be disastrous and the income before interest and income taxes is reduced to $50,000. The earnings per share if stock financing is used is reduced to $2.33 ($35,000 ÷ 15,000), whereas if bond financing is used earnings per share is only $2.10 ($21,000 ÷ 10,000) as shown in Exhibit 8–3.

EXHIBIT 8–3 Lower earnings per share through bond financing

	Bond Financing	Stock Financing
Income before interest and income taxes	$50,000	$50,000
Interest expense	(20,000)	—
Income before income taxes	$30,000	$50,000
Income tax expense	(9,000)	(15,000)
Net income	$21,000	$35,000
Earnings per share	$2.10	$2.33

Characteristics of Bonds

Companies issue bonds that may have different characteristics. Some of the more common types of bonds and their characteristics are:

1. **Debenture bonds are bonds that are not secured by specific property.** The holder of the bonds (the lender of the money) is considered as a general creditor with the same rights as others creditors if the issuer fails to pay the interest or principal and declares bankruptcy.

2. **Mortgage bonds are bonds that are secured with specific property.** The lender has a priority right to the specific property if the company fails to pay the interest or principal.

3. **Registered bonds are bonds whose ownership is registered with the company.** The company maintains a record of the holder of each bond, and therefore payment of the interest and principal can be made without such payment being requested by the holder.

4. **Coupon bonds are unregistered bonds on which interest is claimed by the holder presenting a coupon to the company.** Currently, coupon bonds are rarely issued because bonds issued after December 31, 1982, must be registered for the related interest expense to be deductible for income tax purposes.

5. **Zero-coupon bonds are bonds on which the interest is not paid until the maturity date.** The bonds are sold at a price considerably below their face value, interest accrues until maturity, and then the bondholders are paid the face value, which includes the interest, at maturity. U.S. savings bonds, Series E, are examples of zero-coupon bonds.

6. **Serial bonds are bonds issued at one time, but portions of the total face value mature at different future dates.** For example, a bond issued in 1993 may have a face value of $50,000 and bonds with a face value of $10,000 mature each year from 2000 through 2004.

7. **Sinking fund bonds are bonds for which the company must pay into a sinking fund over the life of the bonds.** The amount paid in should be

sufficient to retire the bonds at maturity. Sinking fund is the term used to describe the account into which the cash is paid.

8. **Callable bonds are bonds that are callable by the company at a predetermined price for a specified period.** The company has a right to require the holder to return the bonds before the maturity date, with the company paying the predetermined price and interest to date.

9. **Convertible bonds are bonds that are convertible into a predetermined number of shares.** The owner of each bond has the right to exchange it for a predetermined number of shares of the corporation.

10. **Junk bonds are bonds that have high risk and high interest rates.** These bonds are typically issued at the time of a major financial restructuring, or the takeover, of a company. Many junk bonds are zero coupon bonds or satisfy the interest obligation "in kind" by issuing more debt rather than paying cash. Often, the issuing company may have a significant amount of debt outstanding already, and there may be some uncertainty about the repayment of the junk bonds. Thus, there is often high risk associated with these bonds, and high interest rates are needed to attract investors.

The characteristics of a particular bond issue are listed on the bond certificates for that issue. Although companies may issue bonds with these various characteristics, we focus on the accounting for debenture bonds in this chapter.

Bonds Issued at Par

If bonds are sold at par (i.e., at face value), the accounting is relatively simple because the cash received from the sale equals the face value. The semiannual interest expense also equals the interest paid.

Suppose that the Homestake Company issues 10%, 5-year, bonds with a face value of $100,000 for $100,000. The sale of the bonds is recorded as follows:

Assets	=	Liabilities	+ Stockholders' Equity
+$100,000		+$100,000	

Cash		Bonds Payable	
$100,000			$100,000

The bonds payable are reported as a noncurrent liability in the balance sheet.

The interest must be computed on each interest payment date. Since bonds pay interest semiannually, the semiannual interest payment is computed as follows:

$$\text{Semiannual Interest Payment} = \text{Face Value of Bonds} \times \left(\frac{\text{Annual Contract Rate}}{} \div \frac{\text{Number of Interest Payments per Year}}{} \right)$$

For the Homestake Company, the calculation is as follows:

$$\text{Semiannual Interest Payment} = \$100,000 \times (10\% \div 2)$$
$$= \$5,000$$

The semiannual interest expense and cash payment are recorded as follows:

Assets	= Liabilities + Stockholders' Equity
−$5,000	− $5,000

Cash		Interest Expense	
$5,000		$5,000	

The interest expense is included in the Other Revenues and Expenses section in the income statement.

Interest Rates

In the preceding example of a bond issued at par, it was assumed that a 10% interest rate is appropriate. The determination of an appropriate interest rate depends on several factors and may vary significantly from the 10% rate assumed for our example.

An interest rate determines the amount received when money is loaned for a period of time. Therefore, it is the price charged for the service of making a loan and changes frequently just as other prices in the economy change in response to changes in supply and demand. Some of the factors that affect interest rates are the policies of the Federal Reserve Board as it manages the supply and demand for money in the U.S. economy, federal regulations, and the fiscal policy of the federal government. Also, interest rates are affected by several additional factors.

1. The **risk-free rate** is the interest rate that would exist in a situation where there is no risk of borrower default and no expected inflation. This rate is the basic time value of money. It is the rate paid by a borrower to obtain money now, and the rate received by the lender as compensation for giving up the rights to the money for an agreed length of time.

2. The amount of **risk** associated with the loan will affect the interest rate. The **risk premium** is the additional interest that must be paid when there is a possibility of borrower default. The higher the risk of default, of course, the higher the risk premium. For example, the lowest interest rate that a bank charges to its largest, most secure customers (such as large corporations) is known as the **prime rate**. The bank will charge a higher rate to its smaller and less secure customers. Also, many credit cards charge interest of 1½% a month because of the greater risk associated with those loans.

3. Interest rates are affected by the length of the loan because risk increases as the length of the loan increases. For example, if you deposit money in a savings account that gives you the right of immediate withdrawal, you would receive interest of approximately 6% at the time of writing this book. However, if you are willing to loan the bank the money for a longer period, such as 6 months, a year, or even five years, the interest rate could go as high as 9%. A bank issuing a 30-year mortgage would receive interest of about 10%.

4. The **expected inflation rate** over the life of the loan will affect the interest rate. Additional interest is paid by the borrower to compensate for the expected inflation over the life of the loan. Inflation causes the value of the dollar to be repaid to have less purchasing power than the dollar that was originally lent. The added interest compensates for this decline.

To illustrate the nature of these four components, at the time of writing this book the following rates, called *yields* (discussed later), were being incurred on selected borrowings:

Maturity Date	Borrower	Yield
1996	Federal government	8.05%
1996	Chevron	8.8%
2005	Chevron	9.1%
1996	Union Carbide	13.7%

Since the United States is not inflation free, there are no situations in which only risk-free borrowings occur. Thus, we can see only the effect of the risk-free rate plus the expected inflation rate. This situation is illustrated by borrowings of the federal government, which are considered to be risk free but occur in an inflationary environment. Thus, the risk-free rate plus the inflation expectation is 8.05%. Since Chevron does have some risk of default, the risk premium associated with the borrowing that will mature in 1996 is 0.75%. The risk premium for the 2005 borrowing of Chevron is 1.05% because there is a longer time period in which Chevron can have financial problems. The risk premium for Union Carbide is 5.65%, which indicates the higher likelihood that Union Carbide rather than Chevron will default. While it is not expected that the reader will be able to compute an interest rate for a particular situation, an understanding of the components should increase the understanding of bonds and the present and future value calculations later in the chapter.

Bonds Issued at a Discount or Premium

When a company issues bonds, it may offer them to the public or privately to an institution such as an insurance company or a pension fund. When the bonds are offered to the public, the company usually deals with a securities broker (or an investment banker). The broker, or a group of brokers, agrees on a price for the bonds and pays the company for them. The broker then sells the bonds to its clients. The broker, of course, hopes to make a profit on this service, but the company issuing the bonds avoids the problem of having to find the purchasers and be involved in cash transactions with each purchaser.

There are certain steps a company must follow when it issues bonds. The company must receive approval from the regulatory authorities such as the Securities and Exchange Commission. It must also set the terms of the bond issue such as the contract rate and the maturity date. It must also make a public announcement of its intent to sell the bonds on a particular date and print the bond certificates. At the time of the sale the broker negotiates with the company to determine an appropriate selling price. The selling price is based on the terms of the bond issue and the components of the interest rate as discussed earlier. The broker determines the rate that it believes best reflects current market conditions for the particular bond issue. This market rate of interest is called a yield. **The yield is the market rate at which the bonds are issued.**[12] The yield is also sometimes called the *effective rate.* The yield on the bonds may be different from the contract rate set by the company and printed on the bond certificates. The interest rate on the bonds is determined by management, whereas the yield is determined by the marketplace. Often the interest rate and the yield are equal, in which case the bonds sell at par (face value). However, often they are not equal, in which case the bonds sell at a discount or premium. The difference between the contract rate and the yield may result from a difference of opinion between the broker and the company about the yield at which the bonds will be sold, or a change of economic conditions between the date the company announced the bond issue, set the contract rate and had the rate printed on the bond certificates, and the date it was issued.

Once the terms of the bond issue have been set and the yield determined, the selling price of the bonds may be calculated, as discussed in the next section. **If the yield is *more* than the contract rate, the purchasers of the bonds will pay *less* than the face value of the bonds; that is, the bonds are sold at a *discount*.** Alternatively, **if the yield is *less* than the contract rate, the purchasers of the bonds will pay *more* than the face value of the bonds; that is, the bonds are sold at a *premium*.** The issuance price of bonds sold at a premium or discount is usually quoted as a percentage of the face value. For example, bonds with a face value of $10,000 that are quoted at 102 (i.e., 102% of the face value) sell for $10,200 ($10,000 × 1.02), whereas bonds with a face value of $20,000 that are quoted at 97 sell for $19,400 ($20,000 × 0.97).

It is important to understand why bonds sell at a price different from the face value when the yield is different from the contract rate. The difference between the price paid and the face value enables the purchaser to earn a return on the bonds equal to the yield required by the market at the date of purchase. For instance, bonds are sold at a discount because the yield is higher than the

---

[12]After bonds have been issued, the yield on them will fluctuate in the bond market as changes occur in the risk premium and expected inflation rate. It is the yield at the time of issuance, however, that is relevant to a company in accounting for the bonds.

contract rate. The "savings" (i.e., the discount) between the lower selling price and the face value, coupled with the contract interest received by the purchaser each interest period, results in a return equal to the higher yield. Alternatively, bonds are sold at a premium because the yield is lower than the contract rate. The "excess" (i.e., the premium) between the higher selling price and the face value, coupled with the contract interest received by the purchaser each interest period, results in a lower yield.

Because purchasers of bonds are effectively earning a yield either higher (for bonds sold at a discount) or lower (for bonds sold at a premium) than the contract rate, the interest *expense* recorded by the issuing company each period is different from the interest *paid*. When bonds are sold at a *discount* the interest expense is *more* than the interest paid. When bonds are sold at a *premium* the interest expense is *less* than the interest paid. The difference between the interest expense and the interest payment is the amount of the discount or premium amortized in the period (discussed later).

■ BOND SELLING PRICES AND THE EFFECTIVE INTEREST METHOD

The selling price of a bond issue may be calculated by present value computations if the maturity date, the face value, the contract rate, and the yield are known. **The selling price is the present value of the cash flows that the company is committed to pay under the terms of the bond issue.** The cash flows consist of the semiannual interest payments and the face value at the end of the life of the bonds. The selling price is calculated as follows:

$$\text{Selling Price of the Bond Issue} = \text{Present Value of Face Value} + \text{Present Value of Interest Payments}$$

The present value of the face value is computed as follows:

$$\text{Present Value of Face Value} = \text{Face Value} \times \text{Present Value of \$1 Factor}$$

The present value of the interest payments is computed as follows:

$$\text{Present Value of Interest Payments} = \text{Periodic Interest Payment} \times \text{Present Value of Annuity Factor}$$

and

$$\text{Periodic Interest Payment} = \text{Face Value of Bonds} \times \text{Periodic Interest Rate}$$

and

$$\text{Periodic Interest Rate} = \text{Annual Contract Rate} \div \text{Number of Interest Payments per Year}$$

The present value factors in each calculation are based on the *yield* and the life of the bonds. Recall from our earlier discussion that the yield on the bonds is the market rate of interest when the bonds are *issued*; it is the return that will be earned by the purchaser of the bonds on the purchase price and is also the cost to the company of the money it borrows. Although bond yields are stated in terms of annual rates, in reality the actual yield for each interest period is half the annual yield because bonds pay interest semiannually. Thus, the semiannual yield is determined as follows:

$$\text{Semiannual Yield} = \text{Annual Yield} \div 2$$

Since the yield is stated in terms of a semiannual rate, the periods must also be semiannual as follows:

$$\text{Number of Semiannual Periods} = \text{Life of the Bonds in Years} \times 2$$

Therefore, the cash payments to which the company is committed are discounted at the semiannual yield for the number of semiannual periods in the life of the bonds.

Selling Price Less Than Face Value (Discount)

To illustrate the calculation of the selling price of a bond issue by using present value concepts, consider the Homestake Company, which issues bonds with the following characteristics:

Date of sale:	January 1, 1993
Maturity date:	December 31, 1997
Face value:	$100,000
Contract rate:	10%
Interest payment dates:	June 30 and December 31

The selling price of the 10% bonds is the present value of the future cash payments to which Homestake is committed. These payments are the face value of $100,000 at the maturity date and the interest payment of $5,000 ($100,000 × 10% × 1/2) every six months.

If the bonds are sold to yield 12%, the cash payments to which Homestake is committed should *not* be discounted at 12% per year for five years. They should instead be discounted at 6% per semiannual period for ten semiannual periods. The present value is calculated as follows:

Present Value of Face Value = Face Value × Present Value of $1 Factor
for 10 Periods at 6%
= $100,000 × 0.558395 (from Table 2)
= $55,839.50

Present Value of Semiannual = Semiannual Interest × Present Value of Annuity Factor
Interest Payments   Payment   for 10 Periods at 6%
= $5,000 × 7.360087 (from Table 4)
= $36,800.43

Selling Price of the Bonds = Present Value of + Present Value of Semiannual
Face Value   Interest Payments
= $55,839.50 + $36,800.43
= $92,639.93

In this case the bonds sell at a discount, that is, at a selling price that is *less* than the face value. The discount occurs because the yield is *higher* than the contract rate. The purchasers of the bonds are obtaining a 12% return (6% semiannually) on the $92,639.93 they are lending the company, and the company is borrowing $92,639.93 at a cost of 12% (6% semiannually).

The liability for the bonds is separated into two accounts when the sale is recorded. The face value is recorded in the Bonds Payable account, and the difference between the face value and the selling price is recorded in the Discount on Bonds Payable account. The Discount on Bonds Payable is a contra-liability account and is subtracted from the Bonds Payable account in the balance sheet to determine the book value of the bonds. The issue of the Homestake Company bonds on January 1, 1993, is recorded as follows:

Assets	=	Liabilities		+ Stockholders' Equity
+ $92,639.93		+ $100,000	− $7,360.07	

Cash		Bonds Payable		Discount on Bonds Payable	
$92,639.93			$100,000	$7,360.07	

Interest Expense and Interest Payment

The Homestake Company makes its first interest payment of $5,000 on June 30, 1993, as indicated earlier. This amount is *not* the interest expense for the period, however. **The effective interest method is a method of recognizing interest expense in which the expense is based on the amount of money borrowed and the rate (yield) at which it is borrowed. Under the effective interest method, the interest expense for a period is calculated by multiplying the book value of the bonds at the beginning of the period by the yield per period.** The yield per period is computed by dividing the annual yield by the number of interest periods in the year. For the Homestake Company, the book value at the beginning of the first period is the issuance price and the yield is 6% (12% ÷ 2) per semiannual interest period. **When the bonds are sold at a discount the interest expense each period is greater than the interest paid.** The semiannual interest expense for the first period is calculated as follows:

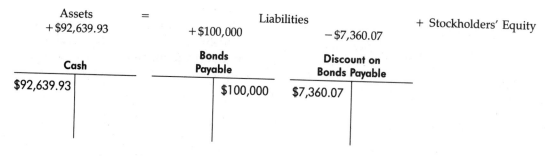

$$\begin{aligned}\text{Semiannual Interest Expense} &= \left(\text{Annual Yield} \div \begin{array}{c}\text{Number of Interest}\\ \text{Payments per Year}\end{array}\right) \times \begin{array}{l}\text{Book Value of the}\\ \text{Bonds at the}\\ \text{Beginning of the}\\ \text{Period}\end{array}\end{aligned}$$

$$= (12\% \div 2) \times (\$100,000 - \$7,360.07)$$
$$= 6\% \times \$92,639.93$$
$$= \$5,558.40$$

Since the company has an interest *expense* of $5,558.40 but is only *paying* interest of $5,000, it is increasing its liability by the difference of $558.40. The company increases its bond liability by amortizing a portion of the discount. **Amortization is the process of writing off the discount (or premium) as an adjustment of interest expense over the life of the bonds.** Using the effective interest method the amount of the amortization may be expressed as follows:

$$\text{Semiannual Discount Amortization} = \begin{array}{c}\text{Semiannual}\\ \text{Interest}\\ \text{Expense}\end{array} - \begin{array}{c}\text{Semiannual Interest}\\ \text{Payment}\end{array}$$

$$= \$5,558.40 - \$5,000$$
$$= \$558.40$$

The amount of the discount amortization is subtracted from (credited to) the Discount on Bonds Payable account, thereby increasing the book value of the liability. The interest expense, discount amortization, and interest payment on June 30, 1993, using the effective interest method, are recorded as follows:

Assets	=	Liabilities	+	Stockholders' Equity
−$5,000		+$558.40		−$5,558.40

Cash	Discount on Bonds Payable	Interest Expense
$5,000	Bal. $7,360.07 $558.40	$5,558.40
	Bal. $6,801.67	

At this point the Discount on Bonds Payable account has a balance of $6,801.67 ($7,360.07 − $558.40) and the book value of the bonds has increased from $92,639.93 to $93,198.33 ($100,000 − $6,801.67).

The second interest payment is made on December 31, 1993. The semiannual interest expense is computed as follows:

$$\begin{array}{l}\text{Semiannual Interest}\\ \text{Expense}\end{array} = (12\% \div 2) \times (\$100,000 - \$6,801.67)$$
$$= 6\% \times \$93,198.33$$
$$= \$5,591.90$$

Since the interest payment is $5,000, the discount amortization is $591.90. Therefore, the interest expense is recorded as follows:

Assets	=	Liabilities	+ Stockholders' Equity
− $5,000		+ $591.90	− $5,591.90

Cash	Discount on Bonds Payable	Interest Expense

Cash		Discount on Bonds Payable		Interest Expense
	$5,000	Bal. $6,801.67	$591.90	$5,591.90
		Bal. $6,209.77		

The balance in the Discount on Bonds Payable account is now $6,209.77 ($6,801.67 − $591.90), and the book value of the bonds is $93,790.23. These amounts would be reported on the December 31, 1993, balance sheet as follows:

10% Bonds payable, due 12/31/1997	$100,000.00
Less: discount on bonds payable	(6,209.77)
	$ 93,790.23

The total interest expense of $11,150.30 ($5,558.40 + $5,591.90) is shown on the income statement for 1993 in the Other Revenues and Expenses section.

To summarize the interest expense each six-month period, a schedule can be prepared as shown in Exhibit 8–4. (The information can be prepared using spreadsheet software.) At the end of the life of the bonds on December 31, 1997, the discount has been completely amortized so that the book value of the bonds is equal to the face value of $100,000 and the bonds are retired (as discussed later in the chapter).

Selling Price More Than Face Value (Premium)

As we saw in the above example, a bond may be sold at a price below its face value. A bond may also be sold at a price above its face value, that is, at a premium. This situation will occur when the yield required by investors is less than the contract rate.

To illustrate a bond sold at a premium consider the same bond issue by the Homestake Company, except that now the yield is 8%, or 4% each six months. The selling price of the 10% bonds is computed as follows:

$$\text{Present Value of Face Value} = \text{Face Value} \times \text{Present Value of \$1 Factor}$$
$$\text{for 10 periods at 4\%}$$
$$= \$100,000 \times 0.675564$$
$$= \$67,556.40$$

EXHIBIT 8–4

....

HOMESTAKE COMPANY
Schedule for Bonds Sold at a Discount
Effective Interest Method
(10% bonds to yield 12%)

Date	Cash Paid[a] (credit)	Interest Expense[b] (debit)	Amortization of Discount on Bonds Payable[c] (credit)	Book Value of Bonds[d]
1/1/1993				$ 92,639.93
6/30/1993	$5,000	$5,558.40	$558.40	93,198.33
12/31/1993	5,000	5,591.90	591.90	93,790.23
6/30/1994	5,000	5,627.41	627.41	94,417.64
12/31/1994	5,000	5,665.06	665.06	95,082.70
6/30/1995	5,000	5,704.96	704.96	95,787.66
12/31/1995	5,000	5,747.26	747.26	96,534.92
6/30/1996	5,000	5,792.10	792.10	97,327.02
12/31/1996	5,000	5,839.62	839.62	98,166.64
6/30/1997	5,000	5,890.00	890.00	99,056.64
12/31/1997	5,000	5,943.36[e]	943.36	100,000.00

[a]Face Value × (Annual Contract Rate ÷ Number of Interest Payments per Year), or $100,000 × (10% ÷ 2).
[b](Annual Yield ÷ Number of Interest Payments per Year) × Book Value of Bonds at Beginning of Period (from previous line); at 6/30/1993, (12% ÷ 2) × $92,639.93.
[c]Interest Expense − Cash Paid; at 6/30/1993, $5,558.40 − $5,000.00.
[d]Book Value of Bonds from Previous Line + Amortization of Discount on Bonds Payable (this is equal to the face value of the bonds payable − the unamortized discount on bonds payable); at 6/30/1993, $92,639.93 + $558.40.
[e]Adjusted for rounding error of $.04.

Present Value of Semiannual = Semiannual Interest × Present Value of Annuity
Interest Payments   Payment   Factor for 10 Periods at 4%
             = $5,000 × 8.110896
             = $40,554.48

Selling Price of the Bonds = Present Value of + Present Value of Semiannual
                  Face Value   Interest Payments
             = $67,556.40 + $40,554.48
             = $108,110.88

As discussed earlier the liability for the bonds is separated into two accounts when the sale is recorded. The face value is recorded in the Bonds Payable account and the excess of the selling price over the face value is recorded in the Premium on Bonds Payable account, which is an adjunct account to the Bonds Payable account. **An adjunct account is added to another account to determine the book value.** The sale of the bonds on January 1, 1993, is recorded as follows:

Assets	=	Liabilities		+ Stockholders' Equity
+$108,110.88		+$100,000	+$8,110.88	

Cash	Bonds Payable	Premium on Bonds Payable
$108,110.88	$100,000	$8,110.88

Immediately after issuing the bonds, the Homestake Company would disclose its liability as follows:

10% Bonds payable, due 12/31/1997	$100,000.00
Plus: premium on bonds payable	8,110.88
	$108,110.88

The interest expense using the effective interest method and the related premium amortization are computed in a similar way as for a discount as follows:

$$\text{Semiannual Interest Expense} = \left(\text{Annual Yield} \div \begin{array}{c}\text{Number of Interest} \\ \text{Payments per Year}\end{array} \right) \times \begin{array}{c}\text{Book Value of} \\ \text{the Bonds at} \\ \text{the Beginning} \\ \text{of the Period}\end{array}$$

$$\text{Semiannual Interest Payment} = \text{Face Value} \times \left(\begin{array}{c}\text{Annual Contract} \\ \text{Rate}\end{array} \div \begin{array}{c}\text{Number of Interest} \\ \text{Payments per Year}\end{array} \right)$$

$$\begin{array}{ccc}\text{Semiannual Premium} & = \text{Semiannual Interest} & - \quad \text{Semiannual Interest} \\ \text{Amortization} & \text{Payment} & \text{Expense}\end{array}$$

A schedule may be prepared for these bonds as is shown in Exhibit 8–5. We can see from the exhibit that the interest expense on June 30, 1993, is recorded as follows:

Assets	=	Liabilities	+	Stockholders' Equity
−$5,000		−$675.56		−$4,324.44

Cash	Premium on Bonds Payable	Interest Expense
$5,000	$675.56 Bal. $8,110.88	$4,324.44
	Bal. $7,435.32	

When bonds are sold at a premium the interest expense each period is less than the interest paid. Therefore, the company is repaying some of its liability

EXHIBIT 8–5

....

HOMESTAKE COMPANY
Schedule for Bonds Sold at a Premium
Effective Interest Method
(10% bonds to yield 8%)

Date	Cash Paid[a] (credit)	Interest Expense[b] (debit)	Amortization of Premium on Bonds Payable[c] (debit)	Book Value of Bonds[d]
1/1/1993				$108,110.88
6/30/1993	$5,000	$4,324.44	$675.56	107,435.32
12/31/1993	5,000	4,297.41	702.59	106,732.73
6/30/1994	5,000	4,269.31	730.69	106,002.04
12/31/1994	5,000	4,240.08	759.92	105,242.12
6/30/1995	5,000	4,209.68	790.32	104,451.80
12/31/1995	5,000	4,178.07	821.93	103,629.87
6/30/1996	5,000	4,145.19	854.81	102,775.06
12/31/1996	5,000	4,111.00	889.00	101,886.06
6/30/1997	5,000	4,075.44	924.56	100,961.50
12/31/1997	5,000	4,038.50[e]	961.50	100,000.00

[a]Face Value × (Annual Contract Rate ÷ Number of Interest Payments per Year), or $100,000 × (10% ÷ 2).
[b](Annual Yield ÷ Number of Interest Payments per Year) × Book Value of Bonds at Beginning of Period (from previous line); at 6/30/1993, (8% ÷ 2) × $108,110.88.
[c]Cash Paid − Interest Expense; at 6/30/1993, $5,000 − $4,324.44.
[d]Book Value of Bonds from Previous Line − Amortization of Premium on Bonds Payable (this is equal to the face value of the bonds payable + the unamortized premium on bonds payable); at 6/30/1993, $108,110.88 − $675.56.
[e]Adjusted for rounding error of $.04.

with each interest payment. This repayment is recognized by reducing the amount in the Premium on Bonds Payable account, which in turn reduces the book value of the liability (Bonds Payable plus Premium on Bonds Payable).

The second interest payment is made on December 31, 1993. The semiannual interest expense is computed as follows:

$$\text{Semiannual Interest Expense} = (8\% \div 2) \times (\$100,000 + \$7,435.32)$$
$$= 4\% \times \$107,435.32$$
$$= \$4,297.41$$

Since the interest payment is $5,000, the premium amortization is $702.59 ($5,000 − $4,297.41). Therefore, the interest expense is recorded as follows:

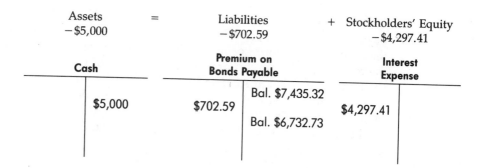

Assets	=	Liabilities	+	Stockholders' Equity
−$5,000		−$702.59		−$4,297.41

At the end of the life of the bonds on December 31, 1997, the premium is completely amortized. At this point the book value of the bonds equals the face value of $100,000, and the bonds are retired (as discussed later in the chapter).

Recording Accrued Interest Under Effective Interest Method

An interest payment date may not coincide with the end of a company's accounting period. In such a case, the company records the expense and the discount or premium amortization on a proportional basis. For example, if the end of the fiscal year is two months after the last interest payment date, the company records 2/6 of the amounts computed in the preceding examples. Of course, no cash is paid, so the company records a current liability, Interest Payable.

■ ADDITIONAL CONSIDERATIONS

Several additional aspects of bonds need to be discussed. Bonds are frequently issued between interest payment dates; some bonds pay no interest (zero coupon); bonds are retired either at the maturity date or earlier; some bonds are convertible into common stock; some bonds require the establishment of sinking funds and bonds may be accounted for under the straight-line method, if not materially different from the effective interest method. Each of these topics is discussed in the following sections.

Bonds Issued Between Interest Payment Dates

As we have seen, the dates on which the company issuing bonds agrees to pay interest are included in the terms of the bond and are printed on the bond certificate. These payments are usually semiannual, and at the end of each semiannual period the company pays a full six months interest. **A company may issue the bonds between the specified interest dates because of the time that may elapse between the announcement of the bond issue and the actual sale of the bonds.** In such a case the purchasers of bonds are entitled to receive interest only for the period the bonds are owned, which on the first interest payment date is the period from the purchase date to the first interest payment date. To reduce record keeping and to allow the company to make a complete interest payment to each purchaser, **at the time of issuance, the purchasers of the bonds pay accrued interest in addition to the purchase price of the bond.** The accrued interest is the interest that has accumulated from the interest payment date preceding the sale of the bonds to the date of the sale of the bonds. At the next interest payment date the company then pays the full six months interest.

To illustrate, suppose that on March 1, 1993, the Lowland Company sells five-year, 10% bonds with a face value of $24,000 at par value plus accrued interest. The bonds pay interest on June 30 and December 31. Two months have elapsed, therefore, between the interest payment date preceding the sale (December 31) and the date of the sale (March 1). On March 1 accrued interest of $400 ($24,000 × 10% × 2/12) is paid by the purchasers of the bonds in addition to the par value of $24,000. The sale on March 1 is recorded as follows:

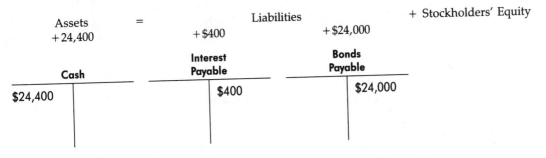

The accrued interest is recorded as a liability because it will be paid on June 30, 1993, when the next semiannual interest payment is made. This payment will be $1,200 ($24,000 × 10% × 6/12), although only $800 is the interest expense for the four months the bonds have been outstanding while the remaining $400 is the payment of the liability recorded on March 1. The first semiannual interest payment on June 30, 1993, is recorded as follows:

Assets	=	Liabilities	+	Stockholders' Equity
− $1,200		− $400		− $800

	Cash		Interest Payable		Interest Expense	
	$1,200	$400		$800		

The above sequence of events may be illustrated by the following diagram:

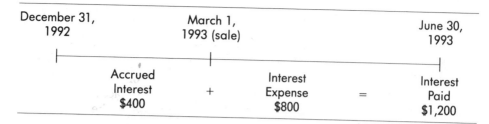

It may seem confusing for a company to charge bond purchasers for accrued interest and then return this accrued interest when the first interest payment is made. The primary purpose for this practice is that if the bonds were sold on different dates to different purchasers and the company did not charge accrued interest, it would have to record separately the date of each sale and calculate the exact amount of interest it has to pay each purchaser on the first interest payment date. By charging accrued interest at the time of the sale, the company can make a full semiannual interest payment to all purchasers. It should also be noted that for amortizing any premium or discount (none, in this example), the bonds will not be outstanding for the full five years, but only for four years and ten months.

Zero Coupon Bonds

In recent years, many companies have issued zero coupon bonds. As the name implies, zero coupon bonds are bonds that *pay* no interest each period. That is, the only cash flow associated with the bonds is the payment of the principal amount on the maturity date. However, even though the bonds *pay* no interest, the company must still recognize an interest *expense* because it has incurred a cost each period on the amount borrowed.

The calculation of the selling price follows the principles discussed earlier; that is, it is the present value of the face value. The discount is the difference between the selling price and the face value. The interest expense is computed, as discussed earlier, by multiplying the yield by the book value of the bonds at the beginning of the period. Since there is no cash payment for interest, the total interest expense is recognized as a decrease in the discount (and therefore raises the book value of the bonds). Similarly, although the purchaser receives no interest, interest revenue is earned each period.

Retirement of Bonds at Maturity

As discussed earlier in the chapter, the process of computing the interest expense and amortizing the discount or premium over the life of the bonds means that at the maturity date the balance in the Discount or Premium account will have been eliminated. On the maturity date, therefore, the Bonds Payable account is the only account with a remaining balance and reflects the maturity value, which is the amount of cash that must be paid to the holders of the bonds. The retirement of the bonds of the Homestake Company on December 31, 1997, is recorded as follows:

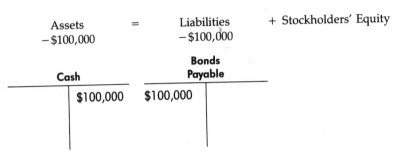

Assets	=	Liabilities	+ Stockholders' Equity
− $100,000		− $100,000	

Cash		**Bonds Payable**
	$100,000	$100,000

Retirement of Bonds Prior to Maturity

As mentioned earlier in the chapter, bonds may be issued with a call provision that allows a company to retire *(call)* the bonds before they mature by paying an amount to the holders that was specified at the time the bonds were sold. Alternatively, if the bonds are being traded on a bond market, the company can purchase the bonds and retire them.

Before accounting for the retirement, the company must first accrue the interest expense and pay the interest for the period since the last interest payment or accrual. As explained earlier, the semiannual interest and the amortization of the discount or premium is calculated in the normal way, and this amount is multiplied by the fraction of the six months that has passed.

After recognizing the interest expense the company has to account for the retirement of the bonds. **When the cash used to retire the bonds is *less* than the book value of the bonds, the company recognizes a *gain* on the retirement. Or, if the cash payment is *greater* than the book value of the bonds, the company recognizes a *loss*.** If such gains and losses are material, they must be classified as *extraordinary* items on the income statement (discussed in Chapter 10), even though they do not meet the criteria of being unusual in nature and occurring infrequently.[13]

To illustrate the early retirement of bonds suppose that a company calls bonds with a face value of $10,000 when they have a book value of $9,800 (we will assume that the recording of interest is up to date). The cost to retire the bonds is $10,200. This can be stated as *a call price* of 102 because, as discussed earlier, bond prices are quoted as a percentage of the face value. The face value of $10,000 multiplied by the call price of 102 gives the cost of retiring the bonds ($10,000 × 1.02 = $10,200). The extraordinary loss on retirement of the bonds is the cost of retiring the bonds minus the book value of the bonds ($10,200 − $9,800), and is recorded as follows:

....
[13]"Reporting Gains and Losses from Extinguishment of Debt," *FASB Statement of Financial Accounting Standards No. 4* (Stamford, Conn.: FASB, 1975), par. 8.

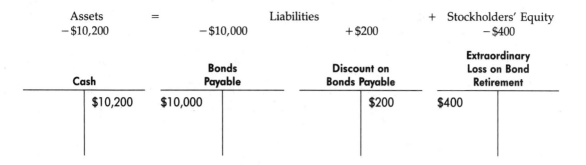

The extraordinary loss would be disclosed, net of applicable income taxes, in a separate section of the income statement, as discussed in Chapter 10.

Instead of retiring the debt, a company may place assets in an irrevocable trust and eliminate its liability. This action is known as **defeasance of debt**. In such situations, both the assets placed in trust and the liability are removed from the debtor's accounting records. An extraordinary gain or loss is recorded when the cost of the assets placed in trust is less than or greater than the book value of the liability. Additionally, specific requirements about the nature of the assets held in trust are required as follows:[14]

1. The trust must be restricted to owning only monetary assets that are essentially risk free as to the amount, timing, and collection of interest and principal. These monetary assets generally are limited to investments in direct obligations of the U.S. government or obligations guaranteed by the U.S. government.

2. The monetary assets must provide cash flows (from interest and principal) that are similar, as to timing and amount, to the scheduled interest and principal payments on the debt being extinguished.

To determine the amount of debt considered to be extinguished when assets are placed in an irrevocable trust, only the expected cash inflows (i.e., interest and principal) from assets initially held by the trust (net of any trust costs) should be considered. For reporting purposes, as long as the debt remains outstanding the notes to the debtor's financial statements at the end of each period should include a general description of the transaction and disclose the amount of the debt considered to be extinguished.

To illustrate defeasance of debt, assume that on January 1, 1991, Holmes Company issued $200,000 of five-year, 12% bonds to yield 10%. On December 31, 1993, these bonds have a book value of $207,092. At this time, Holmes invests $193,225 in $200,000, 12% U.S. government bonds currently yielding 14% and maturing on December 31, 1995, and places them in an irrevocable trust to be

. . . .

[14]"Extinguishment of Debt," *FASB Statement of Financial Accounting Standards No. 76* (Stamford, Conn.: FASB, 1983), par. 3.

used to satisfy its debt obligations. Since the cash inflows associated with the government bonds equal the cash outflows associated with the company's bonds, defeasance has occurred. The Holmes Company would recognize an extraordinary gain of $13,867 ($207,092 − $193,225) as it eliminated the bonds payable from its balance sheet with the payment of $193,225.

Relationship Between Market Value and the Discount Rate.   As we have seen, other things being equal, the higher the yield on the bonds the lower their selling price. Conversely, the lower the yield on the bonds, the higher their selling price. As we have also seen, accounting for the bonds in the periods after their issuance utilizes the original yield at which the bonds were sold. The *market prices* of bonds, however, change in response to changing market conditions, principally changes in expected rates of inflation and changes in the perceived riskiness of the bonds.

The market price of bonds can always be determined if the yield is known. The market price is *the present value of the remaining cash flows discounted at the current yield*. If we assume, for simplicity, that a company has issued bonds at par, the following relationships may be stated:

If the current market yield is higher than the yield at issuance, the bonds will be trading at less than par value.

If the current market yield is lower than the yield at issuance, the bonds will be trading at more than par value.

Therefore, in a period in which the yields on bonds rise (fall), the market price of the bonds will fall (rise).

Suppose that a company issued bonds with a face value of $50,000 in a period when yields were lower than they are in the current period. Assume that the rise in the yield has lowered the market price to $40,000. Therefore, the company could retire the bonds and show an extraordinary gain as follows:

Assets	=	Liabilities	+	Stockholders' Equity
− $40,000		− $50,000		+ $10,000

Cash		Bonds Payable		Extraordinary Gain on Bond Retirement
	$40,000	$50,000			$10,000

If the company now chose to issue new bonds at the current higher market rate, it would have replaced lower cost debt with higher cost debt and shown a gain in the income statement. It was this type of situation that led the FASB to require that such gains (and losses) be disclosed as extraordinary items, thereby making it less likely that the users of the financial statements would be misled by such refinancings.

Conversion of Bonds

To make a bond issue more attractive to purchasers, the bonds may be convertible into common stock. **Convertible bonds enable the purchaser to acquire a bond that has some characteristics of common stock.** This is similar to convertible preferred stock discussed in Chapter 10. For example, suppose that the Teague Company sells a $1,000 bond for $1,040 that is convertible into 20 shares of $10 par common stock. At the time of the sale the stock is selling for $35 per share. The common stock price at which conversion becomes attractive is $52 per share ($1,040 ÷ 20 shares), and therefore at the time of the sale of the bond the purchaser owns an investment that has the characteristics of a bond. Once the price of the common stock rises above $52 per share, however, the bond price will tend to change in proportion to any change in the stock price. It would be expected to sell for approximately 20 times the common stock price. Therefore, the owner of the bond is able to participate in the rise in the stock price while at the same time having the safety of a bond. A purchaser pays for this privilege, however, because a convertible bond is issued at a lower yield than a nonconvertible bond, other things being equal.

When convertible bonds are issued, they are recorded in exactly the same manner as nonconvertible bonds, as discussed earlier. Similarly, the subsequent interest expense and discount or premium amortization are accounted for in the same ways as nonconvertible bonds. When convertible bonds are converted, any accrued interest since the last interest payment date must be recorded and paid. Then the common stock issued is recorded at the book value of the bonds retired. For example, if a $1,000 bond with a book value of $1,020 (we will assume that the recording of interest is up to date) is converted into 20 shares of common stock with a par value of $10 per share, the conversion is recorded as follows:

Assets =	Liabilities	+	Stockholders' Equity	
	− $1,000	− $20	+ $200	+ $820
	Bonds Payable	**Premium on Bonds Payable**	**Common Stock**	**Additional Paid-in Capital**
	$1,000	$20	$200	$820

The book value of the bonds is replaced by an equivalent amount of contributed capital. This procedure is consistent with accounting for the conversion of preferred stock discussed in Chapter 10.

Sinking Fund

Many bonds have a sinking fund provision that requires the company issuing the bonds to set aside enough cash over a specified period so that sufficient

cash will be available at maturity to retire the bonds. This cash is transferred to a sinking fund account. For example, if a company issues $100,000, 20-year bonds, there might be a provision to make an annual payment at the end of each year into a sinking fund starting after ten years. Therefore the company will make ten payments into the fund, which must amount to $100,000 at the maturity date of the bonds. If the company can earn 6% on the money it invests in the sinking fund, how much must each annual payment be? This is a future value problem in which we must find the value of a ten-period annuity at 6% that has a future value of $100,000:

$$\text{Future Value of Annuity} = \begin{array}{c}\text{Periodic Amount of} \\ \text{the Annuity}\end{array} \times \begin{array}{c}\text{Future Value} \\ \text{of Annuity Factor}\end{array}$$

$$\$100,000 = \begin{array}{c}\text{Periodic Amount of} \\ \text{the Annuity}\end{array} \times 13.180795 \text{ (from Table 3)}$$

$$\text{Periodic Amount of the Annuity} = \frac{\$100,000}{13.180795}$$

$$= \$7,586.80$$

Therefore the company must put $7,586.80 into the sinking fund at the end of each year for ten years as follows:

	Assets		= Liabilities + Stockholders' Equity
− $7,586.80		+ $7,586.80	

Cash	Bond Sinking Fund
$7,586.80	$7,586.80

The bond sinking fund is shown as a noncurrent asset in the balance sheet under the category of Long-Term Investments. The cash deposited in the sinking fund will be invested, and the interest or dividends received on these investments will be added (debited) to the Bond Sinking Fund account. These additions, along with the annual deposits, will amount to $100,000 at the maturity date of the bonds if the fund earns 6% each year. At maturity, the cash from the bond sinking fund is used to retire the bonds.

Straight-Line and Effective Interest Methods

In this chapter we have focused on the use of the effective interest method of computing interest expense. Accounting principles require the use of the effective interest method. An alternative method, the straight-line method of amortization, may be used, however, if its use does not produce material differences from the effective interest method. The effective interest method focuses on the computation of the interest expense with the amortization being the balancing amount. In contrast, the straight-line method focuses on the computation of the amortization with the interest expense being the balancing amount.

To illustrate the straight-line method, refer to the Homestake Company example. When the bonds were sold for $92,639.93, there was a discount of $7,360.07. Under the straight-line method, an equal amount of the discount is amortized each period. Since the bonds have a life of ten semiannual periods, $736.01 ($7,360.07 ÷ 10, rounded) of the discount is amortized each period as follows:

Assets	=	Liabilities	+	Stockholders' Equity
− $5,000		+ $736.01		− $5,736.01

Cash		Discount on Bonds Payable		Interest Expense	
	$5,000		$736.01	$5,736.01	

When the bonds were sold for $108,110.88, there was a premium of $8,110.88. Under the straight-line method, $811.09 ($8,110.88 ÷ 10, rounded) is amortized each period as follows:

Assets	=	Liabilities	+	Stockholders' Equity
− $5,000		− $811.09		− $4,118.91

Cash		Premium on Bonds Payable		Interest Expense	
	$5,000	$811.09		$4,118.91	

Since the two methods do not produce material differences for bonds issued at a value close to par, many companies use the straight-line method. The advantage of using the straight-line method is that it is simpler to apply because the same amounts are recorded every semiannual period. It does not lead to a rational measure of interest expense, however, because the expense stays constant even though the book value of the bonds increases (decreases) each period as the discount (premium) is amortized. Therefore the *effective rate* of interest changes each period.

In contrast, the effective interest method records an interest expense each semiannual period that is based on the yield and the book value of the bonds. Since the yield represents the interest rate on the money borrowed by the company and the book value is the outstanding balance of the amount borrowed

EXHIBIT 8–6   Example of disclosure of short-term and long-term debt

---

NIKE, INC.

Note 6—Short-term borrowings and credit lines:

Notes payable to banks and interest-bearing accounts payable to Nissho Iwai American Corporation (NIAC) are summarized below:

| | Banks | | | | NIAC | |
| | Domestic Operations | | Foreign Operations | | | |
	Borrowings	Interest Rate	Borrowings	Interest Rate	Borrowings	Interest Rate
	(in thousands)					
May 31, 1989	$12,606	9½%	$26,564	9⅞%	$25,204	11.0%
May 31, 1988	$94,855	7¾%	$40,330	7⅜%	$20,404	8¼%

At May 31, 1989, NIKE had no outstanding borrowings under its $100 million unsecured multiple option facility with nine banks. There was $25 million in outstanding borrowings under this agreement at May 31, 1988. This agreement contains optional borrowing alternatives consisting of a committed revolving loan facility, an uncommitted short-term advance facility and an uncommitted euronote facility. The interest rate charged on this agreement is determined by the borrowing option and is based on the London Interbank Offered Rate (LIBOR). The borrowing rate under the committed revolving loan facility is LIBOR plus ⅛%. The agreement provides for annual fees of .15% of the total commitment plus fees based upon usage under the committed revolving loan facility. Under the agreement, the Company must maintain, among other things, certain minimum specified financial ratios and balances. A domestic subsidiary has $25 million in separate unsecured revolving credit agreements of which $7,606,000 was outstanding at May 31, 1989. This subsidiary had $9,885,000 outstanding under a similar secured agreement at May 31, 1988. Total domestic borrowings also included $5 million and $60 million at May 31, 1989 and 1988, respectively, under unsecured, uncommitted short-term credit facilities with several banks.

During 1989, the Company received approval and ratings to issue up to $100 million in commercial paper which is required to be supported by committed or uncommitted lines of credit. At May 31, 1989, there were no amounts outstanding under this arrangement.

The Company has outstanding loans at interest rates at various spreads above the banks' cost of funds for financing foreign operations.

Accounts payable to NIAC are generally due up to 115 days after shipment from the foreign port. Interest on such accounts payable accrues at a bank's prime rate as of the beginning of the month of the invoice date, less ½%.

---

during the period, the interest expense is a rational measure of the cost of borrowing money for the period. The interest expense increases (decreases) as the book value of the bonds increases (decreases) as the discount (premium) is amortized.

In summary, under the straight-line method the amount of the semiannual interest expense is calculated by adding (subtracting) the discount (premium) amortized to the cash paid. Under the effective interest method, the semiannual interest expense is computed by multiplying the semiannual yield times the book value of the bonds and the difference between the interest expense and the cash payment is the amount of the discount or premium amortization.

EXHIBIT 8–6 *(continued)*

....

Note 7—Long-term debt:
Long-term debt includes the following:

	May 31,	
	1989	1988
	(in thousands)	
8.45% unsecured term loan, due July 1993	$25,000	$25,000
8.25% capital equipment purchase agreement payable in installments through 1991	1,870	2,659
8.0%–8.8% industrial revenue bonds, secured by certain real estate	—	1,661
14% assumed loan, secured by certain real estate, due in installments through February 1991	2,482	—
12.25% assumed loan, secured by certain real estate, due in installments through February 1991	5,303	—
Other	1,280	2,559
Total	35,935	31,879
Less current maturities	1,884	1,573
	$34,051	$30,306

The $25 million term loan agreement requires, among other things, the maintenance of specified financial ratios and balances and contains limits on the amount of investments and sales of assets.

Amounts of long-term maturities in each of the five fiscal years 1990 through 1994, respectively, are $1,884,000, $8,822,000, $146,000, $8,000, and $25,075,000.

■ **DISCLOSURE**

Nike's disclosure of its short-term and long-term debt is illustrated in Exhibit 8–6 (leases are discussed in Chapter 9). These disclosures can help the user assess the financial flexibility of a company by analyzing the future cash outflows to retire debt (or the need to refinance debt). Inability to repay debt may have serious consequences, including bankruptcy. Other disclosures, such as the availability of unused lines of credit, also help assess financial flexibility.

■ **APPENDIX: TROUBLED DEBT RESTRUCTURING**

A troubled debt restructuring occurs when the creditor, for economic or legal reasons related to the debtor's financial difficulties, grants a concession to the debtor that it would not otherwise consider.[15] A troubled debt restructuring may include any combination of the following:

....

[15]"Accounting by Debtors and Creditors for Troubled Debt Restructurings," *FASB Statement of Financial Accounting Standards No. 15* (Stamford, Conn.: FASB, 1977), par. 2.

1. Modification of terms of a debt such as:
   a. Reduction of the stated interest rate for the remaining original life of the debt
   b. Extension of the maturity date or dates at a stated interest rate lower than the current market rate for new debt with similar risk
   c. Reduction of the face amount or maturity amount of the debt
   d. Reduction of accrued interest
2. Issuance or other granting of an equity interest to the creditor by the debtor
3. A transfer from the debtor to the creditor of assets, such as receivables from third parties or real estate

Modification of Terms

When a restructuring agreement involves only a modification of terms, the carrying value of the payable (face value of the debt plus any unpaid interest owed) is compared to the total future cash payments specified by the new terms. One of the two following situations occurs:

1. The future cash payments are greater than, or equal to, the current carrying value of the liability; therefore, the debtor recognizes no gain.
2. The future cash payments are less than the current carrying value of the liability; therefore, the debtor recognizes a gain.

No Gain Recognized by the Debtor.   When a modification of terms results in the cash to be repaid equalling or exceeding the current carrying value of the debt, no adjustment is made to the carrying value of the debt. Subsequently, annual interest expense is calculated by the effective interest method. **The interest rate used is the rate that equates the total amount of cash to be paid with the current carrying value of the debt.** In this situation, a portion of each cash payment is recorded as interest expense and the remainder is recorded as a reduction in the carrying value of the liability.

For example, assume that on December 31, 1993, Chapin Company restructures a $1,400,664 debt with its bank (a note payable of $1,200,000 plus interest payable of $200,664). The bank (1) forgives the $200,664 of interest payable and $200,000 of principal, (2) extends the maturity date from December 31, 1993, to December 31, 1998, and (3) reduces the interest rate from 16.72% to 13%. The total future cash payments under the new terms are $1,650,000 (principal of $1,000,000 at the end of five years and interest of $130,000 at the end of each year for five years). Since the amount of the principal and interest to be paid ($1,650,000) exceeds the current carrying value of the debt ($1,400,664), no gain is recognized. The difference of $249,336 between the amount of the principal plus the stated interest and the current carrying value of the debt is recorded as interest expense over the next five years by using the effective interest method. The interest expense each period is determined by multiplying the effective interest rate by the carrying value at the beginning of the period.

The effective interest rate is the rate which discounts the principal of $1,000,000 and the five interest payments of $130,000 to the $1,400,664 carrying value of the note. This discounting procedure involves two present value calculations as follows:

12/31/93   12/31/94 12/31/95 12/31/96 12/31/97 12/31/98

PV of
principal   ⟵—————————————————————————————— $1,000,000

    +
PV of
interest   ⟵———— $130,000–$130,000–$130,000–$130,000–$130,000
= Carrying value of debt on 12/31/93 ($1,400,664)

This rate is found by trial-and-error procedures (or a "present value" calculator) to be 4% as follows:

Present value of interest payments	
(Present value of an ordinary annuity $n = 5$, $i = 0.04$)	$130,000 \times 4.451822 = \$\ 578,737$
Present value of principal	
(Present value of $1 $n = 5$, $i = 0.04$)	$1,000,000 \times 0.821927 = \underline{821,927}$
Current carrying value of the debt	$\underline{\underline{\$1,400,664}}$

On December 31, 1993, the Interest Payable balance is transferred to the Notes Payable account by the Chapin Company as follows:

Assets =   Liabilities   + Stockholders' Equity
                       − $200,664   + $200,664

         Interest   Notes
         Payable   Payable
   $200,664 | | $200,664
            | |
            | |
            | |

After this entry, the Notes Payable account contains the entire $1,400,664 carrying value of the note. The amount of interest expense to be recorded in each period is then determined by applying the effective interest rate of 4% to the carrying value of the note each year. Exhibit 8–7 illustrates the computation of the interest expense and principal reduction for each year of the Chapin Company's restructuring agreement.

In reviewing Exhibit 8–7, note that each cash payment is split into its principal and interest components by multiplying the carrying value of the note in each year times the interest rate implicit in the agreement (4% in this case).

EXHIBIT 8–7

CHAPIN COMPANY
Debt Restructuring Agreement
Schedule to Compute Interest Expense

Date	Cash (Credit)[a]	Interest Expense (Debit)[b]	Notes Payable (Debit)[c]	Carrying Value of Note[d]
12/31/1993				$1,400,664.00
12/31/1994	$ 130,000	$56,026.56	$ 73,973.44	1,326,690.56
12/31/1995	130,000	53,067.62	76,932.38	1,249,758.18
12/31/1996	130,000	49,990.33	80,009.67	1,169,748.51
12/31/1997	130,000	46,789.94	83,210.06	1,086,538.45
12/31/1998	1,130,000	43,461.55[e]	1,086,538.45	-0-

[a]From terms of restructuring agreement.
[b]Previous carrying value × 0.04.
[c]Amount from footnote a − amount from footnote b.
[d]Previous carrying value − amount from footnote c.
[e]Difference due to $0.01 rounding error.

Chapin Company records the difference between the interest expense and each cash payment as a reduction in the carrying value of the note payable. For example, Chapin Company records the following at the end of 1994 and 1995:

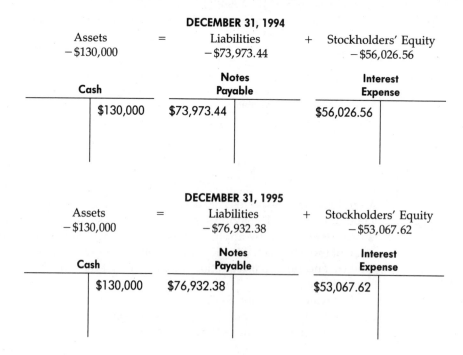

DECEMBER 31, 1994

Assets	=	Liabilities	+	Stockholders' Equity
−$130,000		−$73,973.44		−$56,026.56

Cash		Notes Payable		Interest Expense	
$130,000		$73,973.44		$56,026.56	

DECEMBER 31, 1995

Assets	=	Liabilities	+	Stockholders' Equity
−$130,000		−$76,932.38		−$53,067.62

Cash		Notes Payable		Interest Expense	
$130,000		$76,932.38		$53,067.62	

Gain Recognized by the Debtor.   An adjustment to the carrying value of the liability is required if the current carrying value of the debt exceeds the aggregate future principal and interest payments specified under the new terms. The debtor recognizes an *extraordinary* gain (discussed in Chapter 10) equal to the excess of the carrying value (face value + accrued interest) over the sum of the future payments.

For example, assume that the Chapin Company was allowed the terms stated above (reduction of principal by $200,000, forgiving of $200,664 of interest payable, and extension of repayment period by five years), except that the stated interest rate was reduced to 3%. The aggregate future cash payments in this case total $1,150,000 ($1,000,000 principal and $30,000 interest per year for five years). This amount is $250,664 less than the current carrying value of $1,400,664 ($1,200,000 face value + $200,664 interest payable). Chapin Company would reduce the carrying value of the liability by $250,664 and report this amount as an extraordinary gain in 1993. To do so, the amount of the interest payable is removed from the accounting records, and the difference between the gain and the interest payable ($250,664 − $200,664) is subtracted from the Notes Payable account. Subsequently, each future cash payment reduces the carrying value of the payable and no interest expense is recognized, since the effective interest rate is 0%. That is, since the amount to be repaid is less than the original carrying value of the debt, the creditor is, in effect, accepting repayment without an accompanying interest charge.

Chapin Company would record the following under these terms for the first two years.

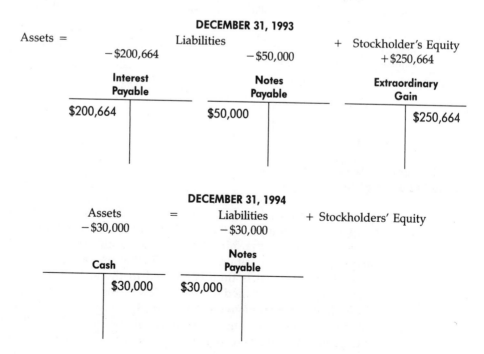

After the December 31, 1993 entry, the Notes Payable account has a balance of $1,150,000. The reduction of the Notes Payable account by $30,000 each year for five years will reduce this account to $1,000,000. This amount will then be removed at the time of the lump-sum principal payment at the end of the fifth year.

Satisfaction of the Debt Through an Asset or Equity Exchange

When a debtor exchanges an asset or an equity interest to satisfy a liability, the transfer is recorded on the basis of the fair market value of the asset or equity interest transferred, unless the fair market value of the debt satisfied is more clearly evident. It is also necessary to compare the fair market value of the asset or equity interest with the carrying value of the liability to determine if the debtor should recognize a gain on the exchange. Any gain is reported as an extraordinary item.

For example, assume that on December 31, 1993, the Chapin Company satisfies the note payable and the accrued interest totaling $1,400,664 by issuing 35,000 shares of its own common stock to the bank. The shares have a par value of $10 per share and are currently selling at $30 per share on the open market. The stock would be recorded at the total market value of $1,050,000, the liability reduced by $1,400,664, and an extraordinary gain of $350,664 would be recognized as follows:

Assets =	Liabilities	+		Stockholders' Equity	
− $200,664	− $1,200,000		+ $350,000	+ $700,000	+ $350,664
Interest Payable	Notes Payable		Common Stock	Additional Paid-in Capital	Extraordinary Gain
$200,664	$1,200,000		$350,000	$700,000	$350,664

Asset or Equity Swap Combined with a Modification of Terms

In some situations, a troubled debt restructuring will include an asset or equity swap as well as a modification of terms. In this case the asset or equity transfer is first recorded at the fair market value as already discussed. The *remaining* carrying value of the liability after deducting the fair market value of the assets or equity transferred is then compared to the aggregate future principal and interest payments specified under the new terms. If the remaining carrying value is less than the total payments, no gain is recognized and a new effective rate is calculated. If the remaining carrying value is greater than the total payments, an extraordinary gain is recognized and no interest is recorded in future periods.

The accounting procedures to be followed in these two situations are the same as discussed earlier.

Financial Reporting by the Creditor

The creditor (bank) would report the three examples discussed earlier as follows:

Modification of Terms With No Loss. In the first example, the bank would report no loss on the restructuring. The first cash receipt of $130,000 at the end of 1994 would result in the bank recognizing Interest Revenue of $56,026.56 and a reduction of its Notes Receivable of $73,973.44.

Modification of Terms With a Loss Recognized. In the second example, the bank would recognize an *ordinary* loss of $250,664, a reduction of Interest Receivable of $200,664 and a reduction of Notes Receivable of $50,000. The first cash receipt of $30,000 at the end of 1994 would result in the bank recognizing a reduction of its Notes Receivable of $30,000. No interest is recognized in this situation.

Satisfaction of the Debt Through an Asset or Equity Exchange. In the third example, the bank would recognize an *ordinary* loss of $350,664, a reduction of Interest Receivable of $200,664, a reduction of Notes Receivable of $1,200,000, and an Investment of $1,050,000.

Evaluation of Accounting for Troubled Debt Restructurings

Some users (and accountants) have criticized the procedures used for troubled debt restructuring involving a modification of terms. They argue that the procedures (i.e., a limited, or no, gain or loss) lead to inconsistencies in recording events with similar economic substance. They view a modification of terms as an economic event that should always be recorded based on the fair value. Under this approach, the principal and interest payments would be discounted to the present value using the debtor's incremental borrowing rate. The restructured note would be recorded at this present value and the gain for the debtor (and the loss for the creditor) would be the difference between the present value and the book value. Accounting for a restructuring involving a modification of terms would then be consistent with a restructuring involving an equity interest or asset exchange. The effect would be that the creditor and debtor would recognize lower asset and liability amounts, respectively, on their balance sheets and a (larger) gain and loss, respectively, would be recognized.

These same critics consider that FASB was unduly influenced by the lobbying of financial institutions (banks). These banks argued that the recognition of large losses by them would undermine the public's confidence in the banking system and have an adverse effect on the economy. Others have countered these arguments by pointing out that the FASB was being conservative in its approach in order to minimize the gain recognized by debtors in a restructuring.

QUESTIONS

1. Why is the liquidity of liabilities important in the accounting for liabilities?

2. Why is a liability created when cash is received in advance for rent charged on a building that is being leased to others?

3. If a company offers a warranty on a product it sells, why may a liability exist at the end of the accounting period?

4. What are compensated absences? How should these be accounted for?

5. A company selling inventory and agreeing to repurchase it later neither records the transaction as a sale nor removes the inventory from the balance sheet. Does a current liability arise? How is its amount measured?

6. What two criteria must be met before a short-term debt expected to be refinanced can be classified as a noncurrent liability?

7. How does a company demonstrate the ability to refinance currently maturing short-term debt? By what date must this ability be demonstrated?

8. Define a contingency. What exactly is the company uncertain about—whether a future event will take place giving rise to a liability, or whether a future event will take place that will confirm that a liability exists from an event that has already taken place?

9. How do the matching principle and the conservatism convention enter into the accounting for contingencies?

10. What two criteria must be met before a loss contingency can be accrued in the accounts?

11. What conditions would have to be met in order to accrue the loss from an unfiled lawsuit?

12. Define a gain contingency. Describe the accounting requirements for a gain contingency.

13. What is meant by the time value of money?

14. What is the difference between present value and future value?

15. What is an annuity? Why is an annuity a useful financial concept?

16. In calculating compound interest, how are the number of periods and the interest rate computed for interest periods other than one year?

17. What are the two components of each monthly mortgage payment? How is each calculated?

18. Define the following terms as they relate to bonds: (a) face value, (b) maturity date, and (c) contract rate.

19. Why would a company issue bonds when it is obliged to pay interest each period instead of issuing stock for which dividend payments are discretionary?

20. Distinguish between the following types of bonds: (a) debenture and mortgage bonds, (b) registered and coupon bonds, (c) serial bonds and callable bonds.

21. Why may a bond's contract rate differ from its yield?

22. What are the factors that affect an interest rate?

23. Under what condition will a bond be sold at a discount? At a premium?

24. What type of accounts are the Discount on Bonds Payable account and the Premium on Bonds Payable account? How is each included in the financial statements?

25. If a bond is retired prior to its maturity date, under what condition will the issuing company report a loss on its income statement? A gain? Is the loss or gain ordinary or extraordinary?

26. What are convertible bonds? When can it be expected that conversion will occur?

27. How is the conversion of bonds into common stock recorded?

28. What is a sinking fund bond? Why do many bond issues require the establishment of a sinking fund? How is a sinking fund disclosed on the financial statements?

PROBLEMS AND CASES

. . . .

29. Subscriptions Received in Advance. On June 20 the Madison Company received $90 for a two-year subscription to a monthly magazine. The first copy is delivered on July 10.

Required Record the effects on the accounting equation of the receipt of the cash, and the adjustment necessary at the end of the year. Where would any resulting liability be disclosed?

30. Warranties. During 1993 the Ryan Company sold electric toasters with one-year warranties. It was expected that 600 of the toasters would be returned for repair and that each repair would cost $7. By the end of the year, 200 toasters had been repaired at an average cost of $7 each.

Required 1. Record the effects on the accounting equation of the above events for 1993.

2. What is the amount of the liability at the end of the year? Where would it be disclosed?

31. Short-Term Debt Expected to Be Refinanced. On December 31, 1992, Excello Electric Company had $1 million of notes payable due February 8, 1993. On January 15, 1993, the company issued bonds with a face value of $900,000 at 98; brokerage fees and other costs of issuance were $3,450. On January 22, 1993, the proceeds from the bond issue plus additional cash held by the company on December 31, 1992, were used to liquidate the $1 million of short-term notes. The December 31, 1992, balance sheet is prepared on February 10, 1993.

Required Prepare a partial balance sheet as of December 31, 1992, showing how the $1 million of short-term notes payable should be disclosed. Include an appropriate note for proper disclosure.

32. Short-Term Debt Expected to Be Refinanced. On December 31, 1992, Carrboro Textile Company had short-term debt in the form of notes payable totaling $600,000. These notes were due on June 1, 1993. On February 2, 1993, Carrboro entered into an agreement with Worldwide Life Insurance Company whereby Worldwide will lend Carrboro $475,000, payable in five years at 14%. The money will be available to Carrboro on May 20, 1993. Carrboro issues its December 31, 1992, year-end financial statements on March 1, 1993.

Required Show how the $600,000 notes payable will be classified on Carrboro Textile Company's balance sheet on December 31, 1992.

33. Loss Contingency. On December 3, 1992, Dan Johnson, delivery truck driver for Farmers Products, Inc., ran a stop sign and collided with another vehicle. On January 8, 1993, the driver of the other vehicle filed suit against Farmers Products for damages to the vehicle. Estimated damages to this vehicle were $3,455. The dairy issued its 1992 financial statements on March 1, 1993.

Required Prepare the disclosures that Farmers Products should make in preparation of its December 31, 1992, financial statements.

34. Gain Contingency. On December 31, 1992, Braino Tech., Inc. learned that its competitor had introduced a product making use of an accessory over which Braino Tech. has exclusive patent rights. Braino Tech planned to file suit and in all likelihood, its attorneys felt, Braino should recover at least $100,000. Braino Tech.'s December 31, 1992, year-end financial statements were issued March 1, 1993, and Braino Tech. still planned to file suit even though it had not yet done so.

Required Discuss the accounting treatment in regard to the 1992 financial statements of Braino Tech.

35. Present Value of a Single Sum. The following amounts are to be received or paid in the future:

1. $3,000 to be received at the end of 3 years; interest rate of 6%.

2. $5,000 to be received at the end of 5 years; interest rate of 8%.

3. $10,000 to be paid at the end of 10 years; interest rate of 12%.

4. $20,000 to be paid at the end of 15 years; interest rate of 5%.

5. $3,000 to be received at the end of 8 years; interest rate of 6%.

Required Compute the present value of each amount.

36. Future Value of a Single Sum. The following are present value amounts, numbers of periods, and interest rates:

1. $2,000; 3 years; interest rate of 6%.

2. $5,500; 5 years; interest rate of 8%.

3. $10,000; 10 years; interest rate of 12%.

4. $20,000; 15 years; interest rate of 5%.

5. $3,000; 8 years; interest rate of 6%.

Required Compute the future value of each amount at the end of the given number of periods.

37. Present Value of an Annuity. The following annuities are to be received or paid in the future:

1. A 3-year annuity of $2,000 at 6%.

2. A 5-year annuity of $5,400 at 8%.

3. A 10-year annuity of $10,000 at 12%.

4. A 15-year annuity of $20,000 at 5%.

5. An 8-year annuity of $3,000 at 6%.

Required Compute the present value of each annuity.

38. Future Value of an Annuity. Use the information in Problem 37.

Required Compute the future value of each annuity.

39. Present and Future Values. Listed below are four independent situations:

1. Jane Seymour invests $4,500 on January 1, 1993, in a savings account that earns interest at 6% compounded quarterly. How much will be in the account on December 31, 1997?

2. David Jones wants to put enough money in a fund to pay for his son's college education for four years. The fund will pay $3,000 every six months, starting September 1, 1993, and it is expected that the fund can be invested to earn 10% compounded semiannually. How much money must be put in the fund on March 1, 1993?

3. Peter Morgan is saving to buy a house. On December 31, 1993, a relative dies and leaves him $20,000, which he immediately puts into a savings account. He believes he can also put $4,000 per year into the account starting on December 31, 1994. If the savings account pays 6% compounded annually, how much will Peter Morgan have available on January 1, 1999?

4. Anne Boleyn purchases a ten-year annuity on January 1, 1993, for $100,000. The annuity will pay her an equal amount each year for ten years. If she wants an 8% return on her investment, how much will each annuity payment be? Assume that the annuity is paid once each year beginning on December 31, 1993.

Required Use the appropriate present and future value tables to solve each of these situations.

40. Present and Future Values. The following are four independent situations:

1. Steve Stunning is saving to build a weight room in his home. On July 1, 1993, he sells his motorcycle for $1,000 and immediately puts the money into his savings account. He believes that he can also put $900 per year into this account starting on July 1, 1994. If the savings account pays 8% compounded annually, how much will Steve have in the account on July 1, 1997?

2. Laurie Lightly purchases a 20-year annuity on January 1, 1993, for $200,000. The annuity will pay her an equal amount each year for 20 years. If she wants a 6% return on her investment, how much will the annuity payment be each December 31 if the first payment is received on December 31, 1993?

3. Rhonda Ritz puts $400,000 in a savings account on June 1, 1993. If the account pays 10% interest compounded annually, how much will be in the account on May 31, 1998?

4. Brian Bright wants to put enough money in a fund to pay for his daughter's college education for four years. The fund will pay $3,500 every four months starting September 1, 1993, and the fund will earn 12% compounded every four months. How much money must Brian put in the fund on May 1, 1993?

Required Use the appropriate present and future value tables to solve each of the above situations.

41. Mortgage. The Holliday Company purchased a building for $220,000 and paid 20% down. The remainder was financed by a 20-year mortgage at 12%, with payments to be made monthly. The present value of an annuity of 1% for 240 periods is 90.819416.

Required 1. Compute the amount of the monthly mortgage payment.

2. Record the effects on the accounting equation of the acquisition of the building and each of the first two mortgage payments.

42. **Mortgage.** On November 1, 1993, the Williams Company purchased a building for $120,000 and paid 30% down. The remainder was financed by a 25-year mortgage at 12% with payments to be made monthly. The present value of an annuity of 1% for 300 periods is 94.946551. The building has an estimated service life and residual value of 40 years and $19,000, respectively. The company uses the straight-line depreciation method.

Required 1. Compute the amount of the monthly mortgage payment.

2. Record the effects on the accounting equation of all the events for the building and the mortgage in 1993.

3. Prepare the required disclosures in the financial statements for 1993.

43. **Mortgage.** On November 1, 1993, the Blossom Company purchased a building for $100,000 and paid 10% down. The remainder was financed by a 15-year mortgage at 15% with payments to be made monthly. The present value of an annuity of 1.25% for 180 periods is 71.449643. The building has an estimated service life and residual value of 30 years and $12,000, respectively. The company uses the straight-line depreciation method.

Required 1. Compute the amount of the monthly mortgage payment.

2. Record the effects on the accounting equation of all the events for the building and the mortgage in 1993.

3. Prepare the required disclosures in the financial statements for 1993.

44. **Long-Term Notes Payable.** During 1993 the Ruiz Company engaged in the following transactions:

1. On January 1 the company purchased a machine for $30,000. It paid 10% down and gave a 12%, three-year note for the balance. Interest on the note is due each December 31.

2. On May 1, the company borrowed $14,000 by issuing a 10%, two-year note. Interest payments are to be made each April 30.

Required Record the effects of the preceding information on the accounting equation for 1993.

45. **Long-Term Notes Receivable.** During 1993 the Bobong Company engaged in the following transactions:

1. On January 1 the company sold a parcel of land for $20,000. It received 30% down and accepted a 15%, four-year note for the balance. Interest on the note is due each December 31.

2. One June 1 the company loaned $7,000 and received a 12%, two-year note. Interest payments are due each May 31.

Required Record the effects of the preceding information on the accounting equation for 1993.

46. Note Issued in Exchange for an Asset. On January 1, 1993, the Sanders Corporation purchased equipment having a fair market value of $75,131.50 by issuing a noninterest-bearing $100,000, three-year note due December 31, 1995.

Required Record the effects on the accounting equation of (1) the purchase of the equipment, (2) the annual interest charges over the life of the note, and (3) the repayment of the note. (Use the present value table to determine the effective interest rate.)

47. Bonds Sold at Par. On January 1, 1993, the Miles Company issued 20-year, 9% bonds with a face value of $200,000 at par. Interest is to be paid semiannually on June 30 and December 31.

Required **1.** How much interest expense is recorded in 1993?

2. What is the book value of the bonds in the December 31, 1993, balance sheet? Show how this is disclosed.

48. Bonds Sold at a Discount. On January 1, 1993, the Loveland Company issued ten-year, 8% bonds with a face value of $110,000. The bonds pay interest semiannually and were issued to yield 10%. The company uses the effective interest method.

Required **1.** What is the selling price of the bonds? What is the amount of the discount?

2. How much interest expense does the Loveland Company record in 1993?

3. What is the book value of the bonds in the December 31, 1993, balance sheet? Show how this is disclosed.

49. Bonds Sold at a Premium. Use the same information as in Problem 48, except that the bonds were issued to yield 3%. The company uses the effective interest method.

Required **1.** What is the selling price of the bonds? What is the amount of the premium?

2. How much interest expense does the Loveland Company recognize in 1993?

3. What is the book value of the bonds in the December 31, 1993, balance sheet? Show how this is disclosed.

50. Determining the Proceeds from Bond Issues. The Madison Corporation is authorized to issue $800,000 of five-year bonds dated June 30, 1993, with a face rate of interest of 11%. Interest on the bonds is payable semiannually and the bonds are sold on June 30, 1993.

Required Determine the proceeds that will be received if (1) the bonds are sold to yield 14% and (2) the bonds are sold to yield 8%.

51. Effective Interest Amortization of Premium or Discount. The Taylor Company issued $100,000 of 13% bonds on January 1, 1993. The bonds pay interest semiannually on June 30 and December 31 and are due December 31, 1995.

Required **1.** Assume the bonds are sold for $102,458.71 to yield 12%. Record the effects on the accounting equation of:

a. The sale of the bonds.
b. Each semiannual interest payment and premium amortization, using the effective interest method.

2. Assume the bonds are sold for $97,616.71 to yield 14%. Record the effects on the accounting equation of:

   a. The sale of the bonds.
   b. Each semiannual interest payment and discount amortization, using the effective interest method.

52. Effective Interest Method of Amortization. On January 1, 1993, the Mussel Company issued 9% bonds with a face value of $60,000. Interest on the bonds is paid on June 30 and December 31 each year, and the bonds mature on December 31, 1998. The bonds are sold to yield 8%, and the company uses the effective interest method of amortization.

Required **1.** Compute the selling price of the bonds.

2. Prepare an amortization schedule for the premium or discount.

3. Record the effects on the accounting equation of all the events for the bonds in 1993 and of retiring the bonds at the maturity date.

53. Effective Interest Method of Amortization. Use the same information as in Problem 52, except that the bonds were sold to yield 10%.

Required **1.** Compute the selling price of the bonds.

2. Prepare an amortization schedule for the premium or discount.

3. Record the effects on the accounting equation of all the events for the bonds in 1993 and of retiring the bonds at the maturity date.

54. Effective Interest Method of Amortization. On January 1, 1993, the Adobe Company issued 10% bonds with a face value of $80,000. Interest on the bonds is paid on June 30 and December 31 each year, and the bonds mature on December 31, 1998. The bonds were sold to yield 8%, and the company uses the effective interest method of amortization.

Required **1.** Compute the selling price of the bonds.

2. Prepare an amortization schedule for the premium or discount.

3. Record the effects on the accounting equation of all the events for the bonds in 1993 and of retiring the bonds at the maturity date.

55. Effective Interest Method of Amortization. Use the same information given in Problem 54, except that the bonds were sold to yield 12%.

Required **1.** Compute the selling price of the bonds.

2. Prepare an amortization schedule for the premium or discount.

3. Record the effects on the accounting equation of all the events for the bonds in 1993 and of retiring the bonds at the maturity date.

56. Conversion of Bonds. The Derek Company issued 10% bonds with a face value of $50,000 at 102 on January 1, 1990. The bonds pay interest every June 30 and December 31. Each $1,000 bond is convertible into 60 shares of $11 par common stock. The bonds have a book value of $50,700 on January 1, 1993. At that time all the bonds are converted.

Required **1.** How many shares of common stock does the company issue upon conversion?

2. Record the effects on the accounting equation of the conversion.

57. Conversion of Bonds. At the end of the Robbins Company's fiscal year on June 30, 1993, its balance sheet included the following information:

6% Bonds payable, due June 30, 1998 (each $1,000 bond is convertible into 30 shares of $6 par common stock)	$20,000
Add: premium on bonds payable	500
	$20,500

Interest on the bonds is paid on June 30 and December 31. The company uses the straight-line method of amortization. On July 1, 1993, all the bonds were converted. At this time the $6 par common stock was selling for $40 per share.

Required **1.** Record the effects of the conversion on the accounting equation.

2. Does it appear that the owners of the bonds who converted them made a rational decision? Why or why not?

58. Straight-Line Amortization. On January 1, 1993, the Myrtle Company issued ten-year, 8% bonds with a face value of $100,000 at 98. Interest is paid on June 30 and December 31 each year. The company uses the straight-line method of amortization.

Required **1.** Prepare an amortization schedule for the discount or premium.

2. Record the effects on the accounting equation of all the events for the bonds during 1993.

3. What is the book value of the bonds on the December 31, 1993, balance sheet? Show how it is disclosed.

4. What is the interest expense for 1993? Show how it is disclosed on the 1993 income statement.

59. Straight-Line Amortization. On January 1, 1993, the Golden Company sold five-year, 10% bonds with a face value of $500,000 at 102. Interest is paid on June 30 and December 31 each year. The company uses the straight-line method of amortization.

Required **1.** Prepare an amortization schedule for the discount or premium.

2. Record the effects on the accounting equation of all the events for the bonds during 1993.

3. What is the book value of the bonds on the December 31, 1993, balance sheet? Show how it is disclosed.

4. What is the interest expense for 1993? Show how it is disclosed on the 1993 income statement.

60. Retirement of Bonds Before Maturity. The Porter Company has 10% bonds outstanding with a face value of $40,000. The bonds pay interest on June 30 and December 31. On July 1, 1993, when the bonds have a book value of $40,600, the Porter Company calls them at 101.

Required Record the effects on the accounting equation of the redemption of the bonds.

61. Retirement of Bonds Before Maturity. The Hill Corporation issued $1,500,000 of 11% bonds at 98 on January 1, 1990. Interest is paid semiannually on June 30 and December 31. The bonds had a ten-year life from the date of issue, and the discount is being amortized by use of the straight-line method. On March 31, 1993, the bonds are recalled at the call price of 106 plus accrued interest.

Required Record the effects on the accounting equation of the reacquisition (recall) of the Hill Corporation bonds.

62. Extinguishment of Bonds Prior to Maturity. On December 1, 1990, the Cone Company issued its 10%, $2 million face value bonds for $2.2 million, plus accrued interest. Interest is payable on November 1 and May 1. On December 31, 1992, the book value of the bonds, inclusive of the unamortized premium, was $2.1 million. On July 1, 1993, Cone reacquired the bonds at 99, plus accrued interest. Cone appropriately uses the straight-line method for the amortization of bond premium because the results do not materially differ from those of the interest method.

Required Prepare a schedule to compute the gain or loss on this extinguishment of debt. Show supporting computations in good form. *(AICPA adapted)*

63. Retirement of Bonds Before Maturity. On December 31, 1993, the following information appeared in the balance sheet of the Zoom Company:

7% Bonds payable, due December 31, 1999	$50,000
Less: discount on bonds payable	(1,200)
	$48,800

Interest is paid on June 30 and December 31. The bonds were originally sold to yield 8%. On January 1, 1994, the Zoom Company retired bonds with a face value of $20,000 by purchasing them at 101 on the bond market. On July 1, 1994, the company called the remaining bonds at 103. The company uses the effective interest method.

Required 1. Record the effects on the accounting equation of all the events for the bonds during 1994.

2. Prepare a partial income statement for 1994 for the Zoom Company.

64. Retirement of Bonds Before Maturity. On December 31, 1993, the following information appeared in the balance sheet of the Bix Company:

9% Bonds payable, due December 31, 2011	$75,000
Plus: premium on bonds payable	3,000
	$78,000

Interest on the bonds is paid June 30 and December 31. The bonds were originally sold to yield 8%. On July 1, 1994, the Bix Company retired bonds with a face value of $25,000 by purchasing them at 98 on the bond market. On December 31, 1994, the company called the remaining bonds at 102. The company uses the effective interest method.

Required 1. Record the effects on the accounting equation of all events for the bonds during 1994.

2. Prepare a partial income statement for 1994 for the Bix Company.

65. Defeasance of Debt. On December 31, 1989, Webster Company issued $100,000 of ten-year, 13% bonds at a premium. On December 31, 1993, the remaining unamortized premium on these bonds amounts to $4,292. At this time, Webster purchases, for $96,029, U.S. government bonds with a face value of $100,000 and a 13% stated interest rate. These bonds are placed in an irrevocable trust to be used to satisfy the Webster Company's bond obligations. The U.S. government bonds mature on December 31, 1999, and pay interest on the same dates as do the Webster Company bonds.

Required Record the effects on the accounting equation of the December 31, 1993 transaction.

66. Bond Sinking Fund. The Crawford Company issued ten-year bonds with a face value of $110,000 on January 1, 1993. The terms of the bond issue require the establishment of a sinking fund. The company believes that it can earn a return of 8% on the money invested in the sinking fund.

Required 1. How much must the company invest in the sinking fund each year if the first payment is made on December 31, 1993?

2. Record the effects on the accounting equation of the first payment on December 31, 1993.

3. Where would the sinking fund be disclosed in the financial statements?

67. Short-Term Debt Expected to Be Refinanced. Below is the current liability section of Hollo Hardware Company on December 31, 1993:

CURRENT LIABILITIES

Accounts payable, trade	$ 50,000
Notes payable, 16%, due February 20, 1994	70,000
Unearned interest and revenue	12,000
Total current liabilities	$132,000

On January 15, 1994, Hollo enters into an agreement with the local bank to receive a line of credit for $60,000 available for the next two years with payment due two years after the date of the loan. Interest at 1% above the prime rate will be charged quarterly. On February 15, 1994, Hollo borrows the money to refinance the short-term note due in five days.

Required **1.** Does this agreement allow Hollo to exclude any of the short-term note from current liabilities on the December 31, 1993, balance sheet? If so, how much? Discuss.

2. Would the result be the same if Hollo borrowed the money on February 25, 1994?

68. The Absence of an Insurance Disclosure. Blue Cab Company has been in operation for 30 years. Due to the type of business it has carried accident insurance on its cabs. Past experience has shown that the average amount of claims per year is $3,000 for accidents caused by Blue Cab's drivers. Because of a temporary cash flow problem, Blue Cab decided not to renew its policy for the period July 1, 1993 to June 30, 1994. Blue Cab was sued for and paid $1,200 worth of claims from July 1 until December 31, 1993.

Required Discuss the accounting treatment, if any, Blue Cab should give the lack of insurance in its December 31, 1993, financial statements.

69. Pending Damage Suit Disclosure. On January 15, 1993, a truck driver for Cork Transfer Company negligently rounded a curve which was also a bridge covering several local merchant shops. The truck jumped the guardrail and fell 30 feet onto one of the shops, causing highly flammable chemicals in the truck to explode. Although by February 20, 1993 (the date Cork's financial statements for 1992 are issued), no claims had been filed against Cork, it fully expected some to be filed in the future.

Required Discuss the accounting treatment, if any, Cork should give the contingent loss occurring from the wreck in the December 31, 1992, financial statements.

70. Estimate Liability Arising from Loss Contingency. Worldwide Motors has produced "Stallions" for 10 years as of December 31, 1993. In a civil judgment against it on July 20, 1993, it was found that for the period of January 1, 1990, until the present, Worldwide was negligent in the design of the cars because the gasoline tank was positioned in the rear in such a way that it would explode upon impact of another car. On December 30, 1993, Worldwide estimated that its ultimate liability on the Stallions would total $6 million.

Required Discuss fully the accounting treatment Worldwide should give to the contingency on its financial statements as of December 31, 1993.

71. Short-Term Debt Expected to Be Refinanced. The 1993 financial statements of Warder Corporation did not include the following in their current liabilities on the December 31, 1993, balance sheet:

1. Convertible bonds maturing in 60 days that were never converted.

2. Note payable due two months after balance sheet date, with refinancing agreement entered into four weeks after balance sheet date.

3. Notes payable of Warder's completely owned subsidiary due its stockholders and payable on demand.

4. Deposits from customers on equipment ordered by them from Warder.

Required Discuss the assumptions needed for Warder to correctly exclude the above items from the December 31, 1993, current liabilities. The balance sheet was issued on March 1, 1994.

72. Loss Contingencies. *Part a.* The two basic requirements for the accrual of a loss contingency are supported by several basic concepts of accounting. Three of these concepts are periodicity (time periods), measurement, and objectivity.

Required Discuss how the two basic requirements for the accrual of a loss contingency relate to the three concepts listed above.

Part b. The following three independent sets of facts relate to (1) the possible accrual or (2) the possible disclosure by other means of a loss contingency.

Situation I

A company offers a one-year warranty for the product that it manufactures. A history of warranty claims has been compiled and the probable amount of claims related to sales for a given period can be determined.

Situation II

Subsequent to the date of a set of financial statements, but prior to the issuance of the financial statements, a company enters into a contract which will probably result in a significant loss to the company. The amount of the loss can be reasonably estimated.

Situation III

A company has adopted a policy of recording self-insurance for any possible losses resulting from injury to others by the company's vehicles. The premium for an insurance policy for the same risk from an independent insurance company would have an annual cost of $2,000. During the period covered by the financial statements, there were no accidents involving the company's vehicles which resulted in injury to others.

Required Discuss the accrual and/or type of disclosure necessary (if any) and the reason(s) why such disclosure is appropriate for each of the three independent sets of facts in the situations described here. Complete your response to each situation before proceeding to the next situation. *(AICPA adapted)*

73. Financing by Stocks or Bonds. The Underhill Company has been operating at a very stable level, consistently earning a pretax income of $250,000. The company is evaluating the possibility of expanding its operations. It has calculated that it would cost $1 million to build a new plant. It is expected that pretax income would increase by $150,000 as a result of the expansion. The company currently has 100,000 shares of $10 par value common stock outstanding. Its income tax rate is 40%. The company is considering whether to finance the expansion by selling 10% bonds at par or by selling 70,000 shares of common stock to obtain the $1 million.

Required 1. How much will earnings per share be, using each of the alternative methods of financing?

2. Which method of financing would you recommend?

74. Sale of Bonds at a Premium or Discount. At a board meeting of the Temple Company to discuss the issuance of bonds with a face value of $100,000, the following comments were made:

"At current market rates, I think the bonds will sell to yield 10%. Therefore, we should have a contract rate of 11% so that the bonds will sell at a premium. Like anyone else, investors view premiums as favorable, and we should do anything we can to get favorable reactions."

"I agree that the yield will be 10%, but I think we should have a contract rate of 8%, so that the bonds will be sold at a discount. We all know people like to get a good deal, and if they can buy the bonds for less than the face value, I'm sure they will sell very easily."

"If the yield is 10%, we should have a contract rate of 10%. Since we need exactly $100,000 to finance our expansion, that is the best alternative."

Required Critically evaluate each of the comments.

75. Convertible Bonds. The Brooks Company needs to raise capital of $1 million. It is considering selling 10% debenture bonds, 8% convertible bonds, or $10 par common stock.

Required Discuss the advantages and disadvantages of each method of financing from the perspective of the company. Include in your discussion an analysis of the effect of each method on the financial statements at the time of the sale of the bonds and the stock, and also in subsequent years.

76. Appendix: Troubled Debt Restructuring. On January 1, 1993, Northfield Corporation becomes delinquent on a $100,000, 16% note to the First National Bank on which $22,201 of interest has accrued. On January 2, 1993, the bank agrees to restructure the note. It forgives the accrued interest, extends the repayment date to December 31, 1995, and reduces the interest rate to 12%.

Required Prepare a schedule for Northfield Corporation to compute the annual interest expense in regard to the above note for each year of the restructuring agreement.

77. Appendix: Troubled Debt Restructuring. The Oakwood Corporation is delinquent on a $2,400,000, 14.42% note to the Second National Bank that was due January 1, 1993. At that time Oakwood owed the principal amount plus $346,075.50 of accrued interest. Oakwood enters into a debt-restructuring agreement with the bank on January 2, 1993.

Required Record the effects on the accounting equation for Oakwood to record the restructuring agreement and all subsequent interest payments, assuming:

1. The bank extends the repayment date to December 31, 1996, forgives the accrued interest owed, reduces the principal by $200,000, and reduces the interest rate to 12%.

2. The bank extends the repayment date to December 31, 1996, forgives the accrued interest owed, reduces the principal by $200,000, and reduces the interest rate to 6%.

3. The bank accepts 175,000 shares of Oakwood's $5 par value common stock that is currently selling for $14.50 per share in full settlement of the debt.

ANNUAL REPORT PROBLEMS
. . . .

78. Litigation Settlement. The following excerpts are from Exxon's 1985 annual report (in millions of dollars):

	1983	1984	1985
Revenue	$94,734	$97,288	$92,869
Costs and other deductions (summarized)	89,756	91,760	87,051
Hawkins provision*	—	—	948
Total costs and other deductions	$89,756	$91,760	$87,999
Net income	$ 4,978	$ 5,528	$ 4,870

*Results for 1985 include a provision for $948, or $545 net of income taxes, related to the Hawkins Field unit litigation.

Note 10:
On January 27, 1986, the U.S. Supreme Court announced its decision not to review Exxon's appeal of the judgment in the Hawkins case favoring the Department of Energy (DOE). The litigation related to the pricing of crude oil produced from the Hawkins Field in East Texas between 1975 and the end of price controls in 1981. As a result, on February 27, 1986, Exxon, as unit operator, paid about $2,100 to the U.S. Treasury, representing an $895.5 judgment plus accrued interest. The estimated potential net cost to Exxon was reflected in provisions against earnings in 1985 and earlier periods and allows for recovery of applicable windfall profits taxes, severance and income tax, as well as recovery from other interest owners in the field.

Required 1. Show the impact on Exxon's accounting equation for 1985 from this item.

2. Show the impact on Exxon's accounting equation for 1986 from this item.

3. In your opinion, was this item sufficiently material to show as a separate line item in Exxon's 1985 income statement?

79. Current Liabilities and Litigation. Westinghouse is a large diversified manufacturing company. The following excerpts are from its 1988 annual report relating to current liabilities (in millions of dollars):

Short-term debt:	
commercial paper	$1,842
bank loans	113
Accounts payable	738
Accrued employee compensation	335
Accrued product warranty	127
Income taxes currently payable	183
Estimated future costs of uranium settlement (note 17)	16
Restructuring costs	97
Total	$3,451

Note 17 (in part):
The Corporation had previously provided for all estimated future costs associated with the resolution of all uranium supply contract suits and related litigation. The net liability for estimated future costs of $69.6 at December 31, 1988, is deemed adequate considering all acts and circumstances known to management. The future obligations require providing specific quantities of uranium and products and services over a period extending beyond the year 2010. The net costs of meeting these obligations and other related settlement transactions are applied to the balance of the liability and are not reflected in results of operations. Variances from estimates which may occur will be considered in determining if an adjustment of the liability is necessary.

Required **1.** Describe each of the current liability accounts and use T-accounts to show the origin of each current liability.

2. Assume the estimated future costs of the uranium settlement were $5 million too high in 1988. What is the impact on the financial statements, using T-account analysis? What if the long-term estimate was found to be $20 million too high in 1988? Ignore income taxes.

80. Contingencies. Manville Corporation is a diversified international manufacturing and natural resources supplier. The following excerpts (in thousands of dollars) are from its 1985 annual report relating to liabilities when it was under Chapter 11 of the Bankruptcy Act.

Audit Report (in part):
As discussed in Note 1 to the consolidated financial statements, Manville Corporation and certain of its subsidiaries are defendants in a substantial number of asbestos health legal actions and may be liable for asbestos removal property damage claims and other claims. On August 26, 1982, Manville Corporation and substantially all of its United States and Canadian subsidiaries filed separate petitions for reorganization under Chapter 11 of the Bankruptcy Reform Act of 1978 because of contingent liabilities resulting from pending and potential litigation related to the asbestos health issue. The ultimate liability resulting from these matters cannot presently be reasonably estimated.

In our opinion, the financial statements referred to above fairly present the consolidated results of operations and changes in financial position of Manville Corporation for each of the three years in the period ended December 31, 1985, and, subject to the effects of adjustments that might have been required had the outcome of the uncertainties referred to in the preceding paragraph been known, the consolidated financial position of Manville Corporation at December 31, 1985 and 1984, in conformity with generally accepted accounting principles applied on a consistent basis.

Balance Sheet (in part)

	1985
Liabilities	
Total current liabilities (note 7)	$ 286,021
Long-term debt (note 7)	91,730

Liabilities subject to Chapter 11 proceedings (note 7)	577,913
Other noncurrent liabilities (note 7)	114,777
Deferred income taxes	143,780
Total liabilities	$1,214,221
Contingencies and Commitments (note 1)	0
Preferred stock	300,800
Total common shareholders' equity	878,226
Total liabilities and shareholders' equity	$2,393,247

Note 1 (in part):
The debtor corporations are alleged to be liable, to some as yet unascertained extent, for claims for damages asserted by or on behalf of owners of property in which asbestos-containing products are located (for which approximately 9,230 proofs of claim aggregating approximately $80.2 million have been filed through March 10, 1986, in the reorganization proceedings).

Note 7 (in part):
The current liabilities, long-term debt and other noncurrent liabilities reflected on the Company's consolidated balance sheets relate to post-petition liabilities of the corporations then under protection of the Chapter 11 filing and/or obligations not subject to Chapter 11 proceedings. The liabilities subject to Chapter 11 proceedings of $577,913 at December 31, 1985, are in default and were immediately due and payable upon the Chapter 11 filing under the terms of the various borrowing agreements. Most such debt, however, cannot be paid or restructured until the conclusion of the Chapter 11 proceedings.

Required 1. Discuss the audit report with respect to *FASB Statement No. 5* concerning loss contingencies. Which financial statements have an unqualified audit opinion and why?

2. Use T-accounts to assess the financial statement impact of the following scenarios:

 a. The company becomes fully liable for the claims discussed in note 1.

 b. All the debt discussed in note 7 is extinguished by the company paying 40 cents on each dollar; cash and marketable securities are $320,350.

3. What would be the impact on the following ratios if the liabilities subject to Chapter 11 proceedings were reclassified as current liabilities?

 a. Current ratio equals current assets ($817,043) divided by current liabilities.

 b. Debt to equity ratio equals total debt divided by total shareholders' equity.

81. Contingencies. Southern California Edison (SCE) serves 10 million people with electricity from nine energy resources, more than any other electric utility in the world. The following excerpts are from its 1988 annual report (in millions of dollars):

Cash and equivalents	$ 23
Receivables — net	691
Cash flows from operating activities	1,388
Cash flows from financing activities	(431)
Cash flows from investing activities	(966)
Decrease in cash and equivalents	(9)

Net income	731
Net sales	5,933
Total liabilities	8,756
Total assets	13,910

Note 9. Contingencies:
Nuclear Insurance

On August 22, 1988, Congress amended the Price-Anderson Act, extending it until August 1, 2002. It increased—to $7,600 from $720—the limit on public liability claims that could arise from a nuclear incident. Participants in the San Onofre and Palo Verde nuclear power plants have purchased the maximum private insurance available, which currently is $200. The balance is to be covered by the industry's retrospective rating plan, using deferred premium charges. This secondary level of financial protection is required by the Nuclear Regulatory Commission (NRC). The maximum amount of the deferred premium that may be charged for each nuclear incident is $63 per reactor, but not more than $10 per reactor may be charged in any one year for each incident. The Company could be required to pay a maximum of $183.6 per nuclear incident, on the basis of its ownership interests in San Onofre and Palo Verde, but it would have to pay no more than $29.1 per incident in any one year.

Required **1.** Assume that a nuclear incident occurred in 1988 from an earthquake, and SCE was required to pay costs of $183.6 million. However, SCE only had to pay a maximum of $29.1 million per year, starting in 1988. Would there be a material impact on the following ratios (ignore income taxes and deferred insurance premiums):

    a. Profit margin
    b. Debt ratio

2. Could SCE afford to pay this hypothetical $183.6 million?

82. Zero Coupon Debt and Bonds. The following excerpts are from Sara Lee's 1988 financial statements relating to debt, specifically zero coupon notes and early debt retirement (in millions of dollars):

	1988	1987
Zero coupon notes due 2014 and 2015	$6.273	$5.626
8.75% Debentures due 2016	$150	$150

The zero coupon notes are net of unamortized discounts of $117.563 in 1988 and $118.210 in 1987. Principal payments of $18.836 and $105 are due in 2014 and 2015, respectively. The 8.75% debentures require sinking fund payments of $6 from 1997 through 2015, with the balance due in 2016.

Required **1.** Analyze the 1988 zero coupon debt and the 2015 principal payment transactions, using the T-account approach. What is the total face amount of the zero coupon notes now outstanding. What was the net expense to Sara Lee in 1988 from using zero coupon debt as a source of financing?

2. Analyze the 1988 and the 2016 principal payment transactions for the debentures, using the T-account approach. Assume that interest is paid annually.

83. **Zero Coupon Debt and Debt Defeasance.** Exxon is one of the world's largest oil companies. Excerpts from its 1988 financial statements relating to zero coupon notes follow:

During 1985, an affiliate issued at a discount $1,146 million of zero coupon notes due in 2004. The affiliate received $127 million as proceeds from these notes. No payment of interest is provided for by zero coupon notes. At maturity, the $1,146 million will be paid to note holders. At December 31, 1988, these notes were included in the United States dollars category of other consolidated subsidiaries as follows (in millions):

	1988	1987
Principal	$1,146	$1,146
Less unamortized discount	(947)	(967)
Total	$ 199	$ 179

In 1982, debt totaling $515 million was removed from the balance sheet as a result of the deposit of U.S. Government securities in irrevocable trusts. The principal and interest of the securities deposited with the trustee were sufficient to fund the scheduled principal and interest payments of these Exxon debt issues.

In 1987, Exxon placed an additional $172 million of Government securities in the trusts. As a result of improved matching of maturity dates between the Government securities in the trusts and the corresponding Exxon debt, the addition of $172 million of Government securities permitted the removal of $240 million from the balance sheet, and 1987 net income was increased by $40 million after tax. The face value of outstanding debt in these trusts at year end 1988 was $897 million.

Required 1. Analyze the 1988 impacts on the financial statements from these zero coupon notes, using the T-account approach.

2. Did Exxon use the effective interest or straight-line amortization approach for the zero coupon notes in 1988? Is there a material impact on 1988 income of $5,260 million? Is there a violation of generally accepted accounting principles?

3. Analyze the 1987 impacts on the financial statements from the debt defeasance transaction using T accounts.

4. Discuss the advantage of using debt defeasance with the irrevocable trust (as discussed) in terms of the following ratio: Debt to equity ratio equals total debt divided by total shareholders' equity.

84. **Bonds and Notes.** The following excerpts are from General Electric's 1988 financial statements relating to bonds and other long-term borrowings (in millions of dollars):

	1988	1987	Due Date	Sinking Fund Prepayment Period
Long-term borrowings:				
4½ to 8% Euro-dollar notes[a]	$1,494	$1,494	Various	
5.30% Debentures	28	34	1992	1973–91
8⅝% Debentures	300	300	2016	1977–95
8½% Debentures	217	217	2004	1985–03
Industrial Development Bonds	262	225	Various	
All other notes	2,029	2,221		
	$4,330	$4,491		

[a]Interest rates are subject to annual adjustment at the Company's option. At annual rate adjustment dates, notes are redeemable in whole or in part at the Company's option or repayable at the option of the holders at face value plus accrued interest.

Long-term borrowing maturities during the next five years, including the portion classified as current, are $1,233 in 1989, $51 in 1990, $24 in 1991, $572 in 1992 and $952 in 1993. These amounts are after deducting debentures which have been reacquired for sinking fund needs.

Required **1.** Using T-accounts, analyze the following items:

    a. Assume $50 million of debentures are reacquired with sinking fund assets with no gain or loss involved.

    b. Assume that the 8½% $200 million debentures were issued for $220 million at an effective rate of interest of 7.2% on January 1, 1987 (ignore the $217 million listed above). Analyze the 1987 and 1988 transactions for this debenture using the effective interest method. Assume that interest is paid twice a year. Why isn't a bond premium account used?

2. Is there a material difference between using the effective interest method and the straight-line method of amortization for the 8½% debentures? Net income was $3,386 million and $2,915 million in 1988 and 1987, respectively.

3. Why are the next five years of long-term borrowing maturities disclosed?

4. What are advantages of borrowing with Euro-dollar notes to GE?

85. Bonds. Colgate-Palmolive is a large consumer products company in the United States. The following excerpt is from its 1988 annual report relating to bonds payable (in millions of dollars):

	1988	1987
Debentures:		
$150 face amount debentures due 2017 at an effective interest rate of 9.98%	$146.465	$146.340

Assume that the bonds were issued on January 1, 1987 for $146 million at a coupon interest rate of 9.6% and that interest is paid semiannually. Net income was $318 million in 1988.

Required 1. Analyze all the 1987 and 1988 transactions for this bond, using T-accounts and the effective interest method. Ignore the $146.465 million and the $146.340 million listed above.

2. Is there a material difference in 1988 net income between using the effective interest method and the straight-line method? Why isn't a bond discount account used by Colgate-Palmolive?

86. Long-Term Debt. Westinghouse is a large manufacturing company in the United States. The following excerpts are from its 1988 financial statements relating to long-term debt (in millions of dollars):

	Interest Rate	Year of Maturity	1988	1987
Long-term debt:				
Notes	7¾%	1996	$300.0	$300.0
Debentures	5⅜%	1992	38.8	38.8
New Zealand dollar notes	16½%	1991	117.2	51.2
Australian dollar notes	13½%	1990	43.8	35.3
Variable rate notes	10%	2007	219.3	216.8
Convertible subordinated debentures	9%	2009	113.4	115.6
Other long-term debt	7.1%	2003	59.8	65.6
Total			$892.3	$823.3

The Corporation has entered into interest rate and foreign currency swap agreements which fully hedge the exposures related to the interest and principal payments of the New Zealand dollar issues and $24.8 of the Australian dollar notes. In each case, the swaps result in a U.S. dollar variable rate of interest below the Federal Reserve Board index for commercial paper.

The 9 percent subordinated debentures are convertible into common stock at a conversion price of $31 per share. The debt matures on August 15, 2009, and is subject to a mandatory annual sinking fund requirement of $10 commencing in 1995. Conversions, which have reduced the debt outstanding by $86.6 at December 31, 1988, may be applied against the sinking fund obligation.

Required 1. Describe each item in Westinghouse's long-term debt.

2. Compute the total 1988 interest expense on the long-term debt, assuming all changes in this debt took place on December 31, 1987. Does your calculation agree with the 1988 interest expense of $220.1 million on the income statement? If not, why?

3. What is the impact on the 1988 net income of $822.8 million if there is a 10% loss on the unhedged foreign notes? Ignore income taxes. Why is the additional information on the interest rate and foreign currency swap agreements disclosed?

4. Use T-accounts to analyze the assumed conversion of the remaining debentures into common stock which has a $1.00 par value.

87. **Financial Flexibility and Risk with Long-term Debt.** Colgate-Palmolive Company is one of the world's leading consumer products companies, marketing its products in over 100 countries, with subsidiaries in 60 countries. The following excerpts are from its 1988 financial statements relating to long-term debt and credit facilities (in thousands of dollars):

	1988	1987
$150,000 face amount debentures due 2017 at an effective interest rate of 9.98%	$146,465	$146,340
8.4% notes with various maturities through 1998	112,500	125,000
$100,000 face amount Euro-dollar notes due 1996 at 9.5%	98,845	98,685
European Currency Unit notes due 1991 at 7.7%	75,474	75,300
$62,400 face amount dual currency bonds due 1995 at 10.3%	56,416	55,373
Swiss frank notes due 1993 at 8.9%	50,000	50,000
Australian currency notes due 1991 at 10%	47,500	47,500
Domestic term loan due 1990 at 10.25%	37,500	37,500
French franc notes with various maturities	26,317	11,289
Obligations under capital leases	2,861	23,423
Other (principally overseas)	41,618	48,744
	695,496	719,154
Less: current portion of long-term debt	21,205	25,024
	$674,291	$694,130

Scheduled maturities of long-term debt outstanding at December 31, 1988, exclusive of capitalized lease obligations are as follows: 1989—$19,067; 1990—$87,325; 1991—$138,248; 1992—$15,812; 1993—$67,310.

On July 2, 1987, the company filed a registration statement on Form S-3 with the Securities and Exchange Commission under which the company will offer for sale from time to time up to $300,000 of unsecured indebtedness. Under this registration statement, the company sold $150,000 of 30 year debentures on July 20, 1987.

At December 31, 1988, the company had unused credit facilities amounting to $918,000. No borrowings were outstanding under these credit agreements at December 31, 1988. Commitment fees related to credit facilities are not material.

Required 1. Assume that Colgate-Palmolive decided to take advantage of business opportunities to expand its markets in Europe (see problem 14-40). How much financial flexibility does the company have currently (in terms of its unused borrowing capacity under existing agreements)? What would be the impact upon its debt ratio (total debt of $2,066,940,000 divided by total shareholders' equity of

$1,150,627,000) if it used all of its remaining borrowing capacity under existing agreements?

2. No additional information was given about hedging or interest rate swaps to reduce the risk of long-term borrowings. Assume that the dollar weakens by 10% before any long-term debt is paid off. What is the potential loss to Colgate-Palmolive? Would there be a material impact on 1988 net income of $317,801,000?

88. Financial Instruments. H.J. Heinz is a large consumer products company. The following excerpts are from its 1989 financial statements (in thousands of dollars):

Note 4. Debt (in part):

	Interest	Maturity	1989	1988
Foreign currencies (U.S. dollar equivalents):				
Promissory notes:				
Australian dollars	12.1	1991	$ 29,660	$26,311
Italian lire	6.8–17.2	1990–97	9,061	15,496
New Zealand dollars	Variable	1990–94	99,495	—
Australian dollars	Variable	1992	79,000	—
Other	7.4–23.2	1990–97	33,701	34,292
Total			$250,917	$76,099

In June 1988, the company issued Australian $100,000 of 12.75% unsecured notes due in 1992. The proceeds of this issue were swapped into floating rate U.S. dollar debt based on commercial paper rates. The effective interest rate at May 3, 1989 (the end of the fiscal year) was 9.4%.

In August 1988, the company's United Kingdom subsidiary completed the borrowing of New Zealand $150,000 in the form of 13.8% bank loans due 1991 through 1994. The loans are guaranteed by the company and have been swapped into floating rate sterling debt that is based on the sterling borrowing rate (13.6% as of May 3, 1989).

Required 1. Did the 1988 interest rate swaps save money for Heinz? Assess the impact on the 1989 interest expense of $77,694,000 and on the 1989 income before income taxes of $724,891,000.

2. What is Heinz's exposure to a devaluation of the dollar? Assume a 10% weakening in the dollar at the time the foreign currency debt is due and that dollars are used to pay off these debts. Assess the impact on the 1989 income before taxes of $724,891,000.

89. Financial Instruments. McDonald's sold its 70 billionth hamburger in 1988. The following excerpts are from its 1988 financial statements relating to a debt financing footnote (in thousands of dollars):

Debt obligations (in part):

The following table summarizes the company's debt obligations, incurred principally through various public offerings and bank loans as of December 31, 1988.

Debt	Maturity Date	Interest Rate	Amount Outstanding
Short-term notes payable in various currencies		9.4	$ 114,490
Long-term notes, including current maturities:			
Notes due next year in various currencies	1989	9.5	496,241
135 million New Zealand dollar notes	1990	16.7	85,169
225 million Australian dollar borrowings	1990–4	13.0	193,731
187 million Pound sterling notes	1990–8	9.8	340,827
$475 million notes	1991–5	9.8	476,750
25 billion Yen notes	1992	6.4	200,025
150 million Canadian dollar notes	1992–3	8.5	127,277
150 million Netherlands guilder notes	1993	4.9	60,761
250 million Deutsche mark borrowings	1993–4	6.2	140,950
$85 million Euro-dollar notes	1994	7.9	65,862
$86 million zero coupon notes	1994	12.6	46,353
Dual currency 20 billion yen/$96 million*	1995	8.6	86,805
100 million zero coupon Pound sterling notes	1996	8.2	99,526
Mortgage and installment notes	through 2014	8.5	83,561
$200 million debentures	2016–7	9.4	198,078
Other		9.8	344,251
Currency exchange agreements—net liability positions			108,098
Total debt obligations			$3,268,755

*Notes have interest paid in yen and principal due in U.S. dollars.

Exchange agreements (in part):

The company has entered into long-term currency exchange agreements with certain financial institutions and financial companies, whereby the company has exchanged various currencies, which included the exchange of interest payments. Certain of these agreements, as well as additional interest rate exchange agreements, effectively converted certain fixed-rate into floating-rate obligations, and certain floating-rate into fixed-rate obligations. The exchange agreements provide for an effective right of offset, and therefore, the related receivable and liability are offset in the company's financial statements. These agreements expire from 1989 to 1996.

The following table summarizes the company's fixed-rate and floating-rate obligations, by major currencies, including the effects of currency and interest rate exchange agreements at December 31, 1988:

Debt	Interest Rate	Amount Outstanding
Fixed-rate in U.S. dollars	9.6	$717,979
Floating-rate in U.S. dollars	8.3	614,084
Fixed-rate in Pound sterling	9.9	543,748
Fixed-rate in Deutsche marks	5.5	303,938
Fixed-rate in French francs	8.6	185,855
Fixed-rate in Yen	6.4	100,013
Fixed-rate in various currencies	12.1	226,063
Floating-rate in various currencies	10.4	477,903
Debt obligations including the effects of currency and interest rate exchange agreements		$3,169,583
Net asset positions of currency exchange agreements (included in miscellaneous other assets)		99,172
Total debt obligations		$3,268,755

Required Assess the impact on financing risk from the exchange agreements by analyzing the following questions. How was the total interest expense affected by the exchange of interest payments? Concerning the debt principal repayments, how was the exposure to currency rate changes affected by the long-term currency exchange agreements (use a 10% devaluation or weakening of the U.S. dollar as an example in your calculations)? Would there have been a material effect on McDonald's 1988 net income of $645,863,000 if such exchange agreements had not been undertaken and the above assumptions had occured?

Leases, Income Taxes, and Postemployment Benefits

After reading this chapter, you should understand

- Leasing
- Accounting for capital leases and operating leases
- Sale–leaseback transactions
- Permanent and temporary differences
- Deferred income taxes

- Operating loss carrybacks and carryforwards
- Accounting for pensions
- Accounting for other postemployment benefits (Appendix)

Leasing of assets is becoming an increasingly common method by which a company may obtain the use of assets for its operating activities without acquiring legal ownership. In many cases, leases result in the recording of an asset and a liability by the company, whereas in other cases neither an asset nor a liability is recorded. Similarly, many companies lease, rather than sell, an asset to another company. The different methods of accounting for leases can have significant impacts on the financial statements.

Many of the rules used for computing a company's pretax accounting income are different from the rules used to compute its taxable income. Some of these differences cause deferred income taxes to be reported on a company's balance sheet. When a company incurs an operating loss, for income tax purposes it may carry back and/or carry forward the loss for computing its income tax liability. In addition, many companies include their employees under a pension plan in order to provide those employees with a retirement income. The accounting for a company's pension plan also requires certain disclosures on the company's financial statements. Each of these topics is discussed in this chapter. In the Appendix to the chapter, accounting for other postemployment benefits is discussed.

SECTION A Leases

A lease is an agreement conveying the right to use property, plant, or equipment without transferring legal ownership of the item. For example, when a company leases a computer from IBM the company acquires the right to use the computer for the period of the lease, but it does not acquire legal ownership. IBM remains the legal owner of the computer. **The lessee is the company that acquires the right to use the property, plant, or equipment. The lessor is the company that gives up the use of the property, plant, or equipment.** (For instance, IBM is the lessor in the above example.)

Note that a lease is an agreement conveying the right to use property, plant, and equipment and not an agreement to perform services. For example, if a coal exporting company signs an agreement with a shipping company to use specific ships for a period of time to transport the coal, a lease exists. If the agreement is only for the shipping company to transport an agreed volume of coal on whichever ships it chooses, a lease does not exist. Although this may be a narrow distinction, in the second case there is no agreement conveying the right to use *specific* property. In addition, as discussed below the risks and benefits of ownership of the ships have not been transferred from the shipping company to the coal company.

Before discussing how to account for leases, it is useful to compare leasing an asset to purchasing an asset on credit. For example, if a company purchases a building for use in its operations by issuing a 30-year mortgage, there is no doubt about how the transaction should be recorded. An operating asset, the building, and a noncurrent liability, the mortgage payable, are both reported on the balance sheet. Although the company owns the building, the mortgage company has a legally secured interest in the building to protect its financial interests.

Now suppose that another company leases a building for 30 years for use in its operations. It does not acquire legal ownership of the building but agrees to make lease payments for 30 years. In both the lease and the mortgage situations, the company purchasing the building and the company leasing the building will use the building in their operations and each is committed to make payments for 30 years. Should financial statements focus on the legal difference so that there is no asset for a lease because there is no legal ownership even though in both instances the buildings were acquired for use in operations? Does that mean there is no liability for the lessee despite the 30-year commitment to make lease payments? Or should financial statements focus on the economic substance of the transaction so that both the purchaser of the building and the lessee of the building have engaged in substantially similar economic transactions to acquire operating assets? If so, the lease should result in the lessee recording both an operating asset and a noncurrent liability. As shown later, accounting principles require that the recognition of the asset and liability depend on the particular terms of each lease.

■ ADVANTAGES OF LEASING

The lease arrangement does have certain shortcomings—it is, for example, usually more expensive in the long run to lease than to buy. However, judging by its tremendous growth in popularity, the advantages of leasing for some companies must outweigh the disadvantages. For example, U.S. companies leased over $100 billion of productive equipment in 1988.

Advantages of Leasing from Lessee's Viewpoint

From the lessee's point of view, the commonly discussed advantages are that

1. The lease provides 100% financing so that the lessee acquires the asset without having to make a substantial down payment. Because cash flow is critical to the survival and growth of a business, its management is of paramount importance.

2. Under some circumstances, the leasing arrangement may reduce the risk of obsolescence and inadequacy; in these cases, the risk is borne by the lessor.

3. For tax purposes, the lessee, by deducting lease payments, can write off the full cost of the asset, including the part that relates to land. The tax deduction may be accelerated since it is often spread over the period of the lease rather than the life of the property.

4. As a financing device, the lease contract may contain fewer restrictive provisions and be more flexible than other debt agreements.

5. For certain contract-type work, leasing may permit higher charges because the interest element contained in the rental payments is allowed as a contract charge whereas interest on borrowed money to purchase assets usually is not.

6. The leasing arrangement creates a claim that is against only the leased equipment and not against all assets.

7. In certain cases (for operating leases), the lease does not add a liability to the balance sheet, and does not affect certain financial ratios, such as rate of return on total investment. The resulting higher rate of return and other ratios (particularly the ratio of debt to assets or stockholders' equity) that tend to be inflated because of the omission of the leased asset and liability from the balance sheet may add to the borrowing capacity of the lessee firm.

Advantage number 7 is critical to some companies. The crux of this issue is that certain leases are legal devices enabling lessees to acquire substantially all the rights and privileges normally accorded to owners of assets (these leases are called capital leases and will be defined more fully later). If a company can in substance acquire an asset by altering the terms and provisions of the lease contract yet place neither it nor the liability on its books, then those key ratios mentioned above can be improved substantially. The company would then be practicing what is commonly referred to as "off-balance sheet financing" (as discussed in Chapter 8).

Advantages of Leasing from Lessor's Viewpoint

From the lessor's point of view, the chief advantages are that leasing provides (1) a way of indirectly making a "sale" and (2) an alternative means of obtaining a profit opportunity by engaging in a transaction that enables the lessor company to transfer an asset by the lease agreement. This financial-type transfer permits the lessor to earn a normal rate of return in the form of interest on the cost of the asset acquired and leased.

■ ACCOUNTING FOR LEASES

Accountants have generally concluded that **economic substance is more important than legal form**. Therefore, generally accepted accounting principles require that the lessee record an operating asset and a noncurrent liability (a capital lease) when the lease transfers substantially all the risks and benefits of ownership from the lessor to the lessee. Otherwise, the lessee records neither an operating asset nor a noncurrent liability (an operating lease). The specific criteria used to determine whether the risks and benefits have transferred are as follows:[1]

1. The lease transfers ownership of the property to the lessee by the end of the lease term.
2. The lease contains a bargain purchase option. (A bargain purchase option is an option granted to the lessee to purchase the leased property at the end of the lease at a price so favorable that the exercise of the option appears, at the inception of the lease, to be reasonably assured).
3. The lease term is equal to 75% or more of the estimated economic life of the leased property.
4. The present value of the minimum lease payments is equal to 90% or more of the fair value of the leased property to the lessor. The minimum lease payments are the payments that are required to be made over the life of the lease.

A lease is recorded as a capital lease by the *lessee* if it meets any one of the four criteria for the transfer of the risks and benefits of ownership. Alternatively, **a lease is recorded as an operating lease by the *lessee* if it does not meet any one of the four criteria for the transfer of the risks and benefits of ownership.**

....
[1]"Accounting for Leases," *FASB Statement of Financial Accounting Standards No. 13 as Amended and Interpreted through January 1990* (Norwalk, Conn.: FASB, 1990).

In addition to the four criteria for the transfer of the risks and benefits of ownership, there are two revenue recognition criteria that apply to the lessor:

1. The collectibility of the minimum lease payments is reasonably assured.

2. No important uncertainties surround the amount of unreimbursable costs yet to be incurred by the lessor under the lease. For example, the lessor may have to incur significant costs to complete the asset and the amount of the costs is uncertain, in which case it could not record a capital lease.

A lease is recorded as a capital lease by the *lessor* if it meets any one of the four criteria for the transfer of the risks and benefits of ownership and both criteria for revenue recognition. A lease is recorded as an operating lease by the *lessor* if it does not meet any one of the four criteria for the transfer of the risks and benefits of ownership or does not meet both revenue recognition criteria.

Although the four criteria for the transfer of the risks and benefits of ownership are somewhat arbitrary, you should recognize that if any one of them is satisfied, the lessee has accepted the major risks and benefits of ownership. Accounting for capital and operating leases for both the lessee and the lessor is discussed in the following sections. This discussion focuses only on the basic principles involved, because accounting for leases is a very complex area involving numerous rules that are beyond the scope of this book.

Lessee Accounting for a Capital Lease

If the lease meets any one of the criteria for a capital lease, the lessee records an asset and a liability. **Both the asset and the liability are valued at the present value of the minimum lease payments.** Determination of the appropriate interest rate to use in the present value calculation is a complex procedure beyond the scope of this book, and therefore a rate will always be assumed.[2] For example, suppose that the Adams Company enters into a capital lease for a computer from the Binary Company under the following terms:

Inception of lease:	January 1, 1993
Life of lease:	8 years
Annual lease payments at the end of each year:	$5,000
Date of first payment:	December 31, 1993
Interest rate:	10%

....
[2]The interest rate is usually the lessor's implicit rate. The implicit rate is the interest rate that equates the present value of the sum of the minimum lease payments and any unguaranteed residual value to the fair value of the leased property.

The value at which to record the asset and liability is computed as follows:

$$\begin{aligned} \textbf{Present Value of} &= \textbf{Annual Payment} \times \textbf{Present Value of} \\ \textbf{Lease Payments} & \qquad\qquad\qquad\qquad \textbf{Annuity Factor for} \\ & \qquad\qquad\qquad\qquad \textbf{8 Periods at 10\%} \end{aligned}$$

$$= \$5,000 \times 5.334926$$
$$= \$26,675 \text{ (rounded)}$$

The asset and liability are recorded by the lessee (Adams Company) on January 1, 1993, as follows:

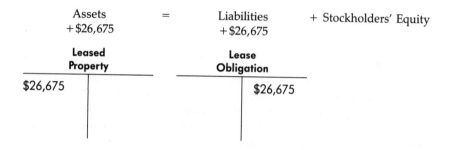

	Assets	=	Liabilities	+ Stockholders' Equity
	+$26,675		+$26,675	

The leased property is listed in the Property, Plant, and Equipment section of the balance sheet. The present value of the portion of the Lease Obligation liability to be paid in the next year is included as a current liability, with the remaining portion classified as a noncurrent liability.[3]

Since the Adams Company has recorded an asset, the cost must be amortized as an expense over its useful life (the term *amortization* is used more commonly than *depreciation* for leased property but the concept is exactly the same). The life of the lease is eight years, and if it is assumed that straight-line amortization is used with no residual value, the amortization each year is calculated as follows:

$$\textbf{Annual Amortization} = \frac{\textbf{Cost of Leased Property} - \textbf{Estimated Residual Value}}{\textbf{Estimated Life}}$$

$$= \frac{\$26,675 - \$0}{8}$$

$$= \$3,334 \text{ (rounded)}$$

. . . .

[3]The inclusion of the present value of the amount payable in the next year produces the same current liability each year for a given lease and is a logically sound method. Some companies, however, include as a current liability the change in the present value of the lease payments over the next year. This procedure results in a different amount being recognized as a current liability in each year. In this book, we will only use the present value of next year's payments approach. For a further discussion of this topic, see R. J. Swieringa, "When Current Is Noncurrent and Vice Versa!" *The Accounting Review* (January 1984), pp. 123–130.

The Adams Company records this amortization in the normal manner on December 31, 1993, as follows:

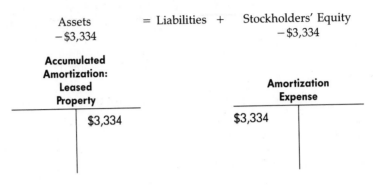

Assets	= Liabilities +	Stockholders' Equity
− $3,334		− $3,334

This entry would be repeated for each year of the asset's life. Note that the asset would be depreciated over its *economic* life if the lease transfers ownership or includes a bargain purchase option. The amortization expense is classified as an operating expense on the income statement. The accumulated amortization is deducted from the Leased Property on the balance sheet to show the remaining book value of the asset.

As in other annuity situations involving compound interest, each $5,000 lease payment consists of a payment of both interest and principal. Every year when the Adams Company records the payment, it must separate the payment into the Interest Expense portion and the portion involving a reduction in the Lease Obligation liability. The procedure used for this purpose is the effective interest method described in Chapter 8, except that if the lease payment is made annually as assumed in this example, the *annual* interest rate is used in the interest expense computation. The use of a payment made at the end of each year is a simplifying assumption. It is much more likely that a lease would require payments at the beginning of each month, but such a different payment schedule is unlikely to have a material impact on the financial statements.

The interest expense and the reduction in the liability for 1993 are computed as follows:

$$\text{Interest Expense} = \text{Interest Rate} \times \text{Book Value of Liability}$$
$$= 10\% \times \$26,675$$
$$= \$2,667 \text{ (rounded)}$$

$$\text{Reduction of Liability} = \text{Cash Payment} - \text{Interest Expense}$$
$$= \$5,000 - \$2,667$$
$$= \$2,333$$

Therefore, the lease payment is recorded by the Adams Company on December 31, 1993, as follows:

Assets	=	Liabilities	+	Stockholders' Equity
− $5,000		− $2,333		− $2,667

EXHIBIT 9–1 Interest expense and amortization expense for lessee

Date	Lease Obligation[a]	Interest Expense[b]	Cash Payment[c]	Reduction in Lease Obligation[d]	Amortization Expense[e]	Total Expenses[f]
01/01/1993	$26,675					
12/31/1993	26,675	$2,667	$5,000	$2,333	$3,334	$6,001
12/31/1994	24,342	2,434	5,000	2,566	3,334	5,768
12/31/1995	21,776	2,178	5,000	2,822	3,334	5,512
12/31/1996	18,954	1,895	5,000	3,105	3,334	5,229
12/31/1997	15,849	1,585	5,000	3,415	3,334	4,919
12/31/1998	12,434	1,243	5,000	3,757	3,334	4,577
12/31/1999	8,677	868	5,000	4,132	3,334	4,202
12/31/2000	4,545	455[g]	5,000	4,545	3,337[h]	3,792

[a]Lease obligation from previous line less reduction in lease obligation; at 12/31/94, $26,675 − $2,333.
[b]Interest Rate × Lease Obligation (rounded); at 12/31/93, 10% × $26,675.
[c]Defined by the lease.
[d]Cash Payment − Interest Expense; at 12/31/93, $5,000 − $2,667.
[e](Cost of Leased Property − Residual Value) ÷ Life; ($26,675 − $0) ÷ 8 (rounded).
[f]Interest Expense + Amortization Expense; at 12/31/93, $2,667 + $3,334.
[g]Adjusted for rounding error of $1.
[h]Adjusted for rounding error of $3.

Cash		Lease Obligation		Interest Expense	
	$5,000	$2,333		$2,667	

The book value of the liability is now $24,342 ($26,675 − $2,333), and this amount is reported on the balance sheet. The present value of the amount payable in the next year is included as a current liability and the remaining portion as a noncurrent liability. The interest expense is included in the Other Revenues and Expenses section of the income statement.

The computation of the interest expense, reduction of the liability, and amortization expense for each of the years of the lease is shown in Exhibit 9–1. The calculation of the interest expense and reduction in liability for 1994 is as follows:

$$1994 \text{ Interest Expense} = \text{Interest Rate} \times \text{Book Value of Liability}$$
$$= 10\% \times \$24,342$$
$$= \$2,434 \text{ (rounded)}$$

$$1994 \text{ Reduction of Liability} = \text{Cash Payment} - \text{Interest Expense}$$
$$= \$5,000 - \$2,434$$
$$= \$2,566$$

This procedure is followed every year for the remaining life of the lease, and the recording of the final lease payment will cause the book value of the liability, Lease Obligation, to be reduced to zero.

Lessor Accounting for a Capital Lease

Since the lessee records the "purchase" of an asset when there is a capital lease that meets any one of the four criteria for the transfer of the risks and benefits of ownership, it is consistent for the lessor to record the "sale" of the asset if one of the four criteria is met. In addition, for the lessor to record a capital lease, both of the revenue recognition criteria must be satisfied. Since the lessee has recorded the payments to be made as a liability, to be consistent the lessor should record the payments to be received as an asset. Therefore **a lessor records a capital lease as a sale on credit.**

In the previous example the Binary Company is the lessor. Since it has agreed to receive a series of lease payments that have a present value of $26,675, that is the value assigned to the asset and the sales revenue. The Binary Company records the inception of the lease on January 1, 1993, as follows:

Assets	= Liabilities +	Stockholders' Equity
+$26,675		+$26,675

Lease Receivable		Sales	
$26,675			$26,675

At the same time the Binary Company records the cost of the computer as an expense (cost of goods sold). For example, if the computer cost $15,000, the Binary Company records the following:

Assets	= Liabilities +	Stockholders' Equity
−$15,000		−$15,000

Inventory		Cost of Goods Sold	
	$15,000	$15,000	

The Binary Company will receive $5,000 per year for the next eight years. The interest revenue for the lessor is computed by multiplying the book value of the receivable at the beginning of the period by the interest rate. In the first year, the revenue is $2,667 (10% × $26,675, rounded). Therefore, the Binary Company records the cash receipt on December 31, 1993, as follows:

	Assets	= Liabilities +	Stockholders' Equity
+ $5,000	− $2,333		+ $2,667
Cash	**Lease Receivable**		**Interest Revenue**
$5,000	$2,333		$2,667

This entry should be compared with the recognition of the interest expense for the Adams Company given earlier where the cash was decreased by $5,000, the liability was decreased by $2,333, and an expense of $2,667 was recognized.

In each subsequent period Interest Revenue is calculated by multiplying the interest rate times the net book value of the asset. In 1994, the amount is calculated as follows:

$$\begin{aligned} \text{1994 Interest Revenue} &= 10\% \times \text{Book Value of Receivable} \\ &= 10\% \times \$24{,}342 \\ &= \$2{,}434 \text{ (rounded)} \end{aligned}$$

The present value of the amount receivable in the next year is included as a current asset and the remaining portion as a noncurrent asset. The interest revenue is included in the Other Revenues and Expenses section of the income statement.

The lease just described is a sales-type lease. **A sales-type lease is a lease in which the lessor has a manufacturer's or dealer's profit (or loss).** In other words, the present value of the lease payments ($26,675) exceeds the cost or carrying value of the property ($15,000). Alternatively, when the lessor does not record a profit, the lease is a **direct financing lease**. In such situations, the lessor is usually a financial institution such as a bank. For a direct financing lease, the lessor records the lease in the same way as for a sales-type lease, except that it does not record the sales or the cost of goods sold. To illustrate, assume that a bank purchased the computer from the Binary Company for $26,675 and recorded it as Equipment. When the bank leases the computer to the Adams Company, it would record the signing of the lease as follows:

	Assets	= Liabilities + Stockholders' Equity
+ $26,675	− $26,675	
Lease Receivable	**Equipment**	
$26,675	$26,675	

CA
NON CA

The bank removes the asset, Equipment, from its balance sheet because it does not use the asset in its operations. Its revenue is generated by the receivable. In each subsequent period, the bank would recognize interest revenue in the same way as illustrated for the situation in which the Binary Company was the lessor.

Operating Lease

When a lease does not meet any of the criteria for a capital lease, it is classified as an operating lease. The lessee does not record the "purchase" of an asset or the incurrence of a liability, and the lessor does not record the "sale" or a receivable.

Lessee. If the lease of the computer was considered an operating lease, the Adams Company would record nothing at the inception of the lease. When the payment is made each December 31, the company would record the payment as an expense, commonly called Rent Expense, because the lease is being accounted for as a rental. The payment on December 31, 1993 (and each successive year) would be recorded as follows:

Assets	= Liabilities +	Stockholders' Equity
− $5,000		− $5,000

Cash		Rent Expense
$5,000		$5,000

The rent expense is included as an operating expense in the income statement.

Lessor. The Binary Company would record the receipt as rent revenue as follows:

Assets	= Liabilities +	Stockholders' Equity
+ $5,000		+ $5,000

Cash		Rent Revenue
$5,000		$5,000

When an asset is leased to another company under an *operating* lease, it is desirable for the lessor to classify the asset separately in the balance sheet under a caption such as Property Leased to Others, and therefore the Binary Company would record the following on January 1, 1993:

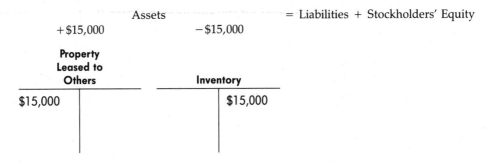

Assets = Liabilities + Stockholders' Equity

+$15,000 −$15,000

Property Leased to Others		Inventory	
$15,000			$15,000

In addition, the Binary Company would depreciate the computer since it is now included as an operating asset on its balance sheet. If it is assumed that the life of the computer is eight years with no residual value and straight-line depreciation is used, the Binary Company would record depreciation of $1,875 ($15,000 ÷ 8) on December 31 (and each successive year) as follows:

Assets = Liabilities + Stockholders' Equity

−$1,875 −$1,875

Accumulated Depreciation: Property Leased to Others		Depreciation Expense	
	$1,875	$1,875	

If it is assumed that the Binary Company is in the business of leasing, the rent revenue and the depreciation expense would both be included in operating income in the income statement.

Impact of the Criteria on the Lease Classification

Recall that four criteria are used to determine if a lease is classified as a capital lease or an operating lease. The first criterion, transfer of ownership at the end of the life of the lease, will be included in the lease agreement if both parties want such a transfer to occur. The second criterion, a bargain purchase option, will be included for a similar reason, although some uncertainty may arise as to what constitutes a bargain, and therefore whether the criterion is met. Since there is an option rather than an explicit purchase agreement, there is some possibility that the option will not be exercised and the original intent of the parties will not be met. Thus, the lessor accepts more of the risk in this situation. The third criterion will be met if the lease term is for at least 75% of the economic life of the property. The life of the lease will be based on the agreement of the two parties. However, the economic life is an estimate, and there may be a motivation to make the estimated life sufficiently long to avoid this criterion and not record a capital lease. Whether the fourth criterion is met is often dependent on whether the residual value of the property at the end of the life of the lease is guaranteed by the *lessee* or is unguaranteed. The minimum lease payments are defined to include a *guaranteed* residual value but to exclude an *unguaranteed* residual value. Therefore, if the residual value is guaranteed by the lessee, it is included in the present value calculation and it is much more likely that the 90% threshold will be met and a capital lease recorded. This is a reasonable situation because the agreement of the lessee to guarantee the residual value of the property represents a significant addition to the risk born by the lessee. Similarly, the existence of an unguaranteed residual value imposes much more of the risk on the lessor, and therefore an operating lease is more likely.

Effects of Capital and Operating Leases on the Financial Statements

As a summary of accounting for capital and operating leases it is useful to emphasize the effects of the two types of leases on the financial statements. These effects are shown in Exhibit 9-2.

Many lessees structure a lease transaction to avoid recording a capital lease because it has two negative effects on the financial statements. For a capital lease, the lessee initially records an asset and a liability of equal amounts. This procedure makes the company appear to be less strong financially because the ratio of total debt to total assets or to stockholders' equity has increased. Ratios are discussed in Chapter 14, but to illustrate the effect of a capital lease, assume that before signing the lease discussed earlier in the chapter the Adams Company had total liabilities of $50,000 and total assets of $100,000 so that its debt ratio (liabilities ÷ assets) was 50% ($50,000 ÷ $100,000). After recording the capital lease, the company's total liabilities are $76,675 ($50,000 + $26,675) and its total assets are $126,675 ($100,000 + $26,675). Therefore the company's debt ratio is now 61% ($76,675 ÷ $126,675, rounded). The worsening of the ratio might suggest to a user of the financial statements that the financial strength of the company has weakened.

The second negative impact on the financial statements concerns the impact of a capital lease on the income statement. Again, refer to the Adams Company example. In the first year of the lease, the company has an amortization expense of $3,334 and an interest expense of $2,667 for a total of $6,000 (rounded). In comparison, if the lease were classified as an operating lease, the company's rent expense would only be $5,000. Therefore, we see that the capital lease reduces the company's income before income taxes by $1,000. Therefore, any

EXHIBIT 9–2 Effects of leases on the financial statements

····················

CAPITAL LEASE	
LESSEE Income Statement	**LESSOR** Income Statement

Operating expenses:
    Amortization expense
	Revenues:
	    Sales revenue (in the year of
	        inception of a sales-type lease)
	Expenses:
	    Cost of goods sold (in the year of
	        inception of a sales-type lease)

Other revenues and expenses:
    Interest expense
	Other revenues and expenses:
	    Interest revenue

Balance Sheet	**Balance Sheet**

Property, plant, and equipment:
    Leased property
    Less: accumulated amortization
Current liabilities:
    Lease obligation
        (payable within one year)
Noncurrent liabilities:
    Lease obligation
        (payable after one year)
	Current assets:
	    Lease receivable (receivable
	        within one year)
	Noncurrent assets:
	    Lease receivable (receivable after
	        one year)

OPERATING LEASE	
LESSEE Income Statement	**LESSOR** Income Statement

Operating expenses:
    Rent expense
	Revenues:
	    Rent revenue
	Operating expenses:
	    Depreciation expense

Balance Sheet	**Balance Sheet**

No asset or liability	Noncurrent assets:
	    Property leased to others
	    Less: accumulated depreciation

evaluation that uses income might suggest to the user of the financial statements that the profitability of the company has worsened.

In each subsequent year the interest expense under the capital lease is reduced so that the differential becomes less. Eventually, the total expenses under a capital lease become less than the rent expense under an operating lease. Over the life of the lease the total expenses are the same ($40,000) under both lease classifications. Therefore, the general rule is that a capital lease as compared to an operating lease decreases income before income taxes early in the life of the lease and increases income before income taxes later in the life of the lease, but total lifetime income before income taxes is the same. Note that these impacts are on the financial statements and that the effect on taxable income and income taxes paid may not be the same because the tax rules are not the same as the accounting rules.

In summary, many managers are reluctant to record a capital lease because of the negative effect it has on both the balance sheet and income statement of the lessee. For reasons that are beyond the scope of the book, it is often relatively easy to design a lease agreement so that it is not classified as a capital lease. Therefore, the user of financial statements should be aware that many leases that might reasonably be considered as capital leases in substance are classified by many lessees as operating leases in accordance with accounting principles. In such cases, the disclosures for the leases by the lessee assume a greater importance. Among the required disclosures are the following:

1. For capital leases, future minimum lease payments for each of the next five years, the total lease payments to which the company is committed, and the amount of the interest necessary to reduce the minimum lease payments to their present value. For example, the Adams Company would disclose the following in the notes accompanying its December 31 balance sheet:

Year Ending December 31	
1994	$ 5,000
1995	5,000
1996	5,000
1997	5,000
1998	5,000
Later years	10,000
	$35,000
Less: Interest	(10,658)
	$24,342

2. For operating leases, future rental payments for each of the next five years, and the total rental payments to which the company is committed.

If a company has operating leases that have large dollar commitments or commitments that appear to extend for a long period into the future, the user of financial statements may find it desirable to study the impact on the financial statements of converting the operating leases to capital leases for comparability and a better understanding of the economic substance of the company. For example, the disclosure by Nike of its lease commitments is illustrated in Exhibit 9–3. A simple averaging process would indicate that these lease commitments for years beyond 1994 continue for 3.5 years [($78,284,000 − $12,996,000 − $9,754,000 − $8,762,000 − $7,838,000 − $8,651,000) ÷ 8,651,000, rounded] into

EXHIBIT 9–3   Example of disclosure of lease obligations

········

L-T debt
34.1 million

NIKE, INC.

Note 13—Commitments and contingencies (in part):
The Company leases space for its offices, warehouses, and retail stores under leases expiring from one to ten years after May 31, 1989. Rent expense aggregated $12,179,000, $11,605,000 and $11,608,000 for the years ended May 31, 1989, 1988, and 1987 respectively. Amounts of minimum future annual rental commitments under non-cancellable operating leases in each of the five fiscal years 1990 through 1994 are $12,996,000, $9,754,000, $8,762,000, $7,838,000, $8,651,000 and in aggregate $78,284,000.

operate lease

1997. Thus the company has signed eight-year leases, which are classified by the company as operating leases, and no liability or asset is recorded in the financial statements. (Of course, a declining trend in each year's payments would extend the apparent maximum life of the leases to the ten years disclosed by Nike.) By assuming a reasonable discount rate, the user can compute an approximate present value of these commitments. It is also interesting to note that Nike's long-term debt is $34.1 million and the inclusion of the present value of the $78,284,000 would have a significant impact on its long-term liabilities.

The lessor has similar disclosure requirements to those of the lessee. Generally, lessors are less concerned with the classification of a lease as an operating or capital lease because the lessor never records a liability. The user of financial statements may still be interested in performing a similar adjustment of converting the operating leases to capital leases if it appears that a company has operating leases that have large dollar receivables or receivables that appear to extend for a long period into the future.

Off-Balance Sheet Financing

The difference in the financial statement effects illustrated in Exhibit 9–2 provides another example of *off-balance sheet financing*. When the lease is classified as an operating lease, the lessee has obtained the use of the equipment without paying cash for it at the time of acquisition or showing a liability for future payments. Thus, the equipment has been acquired by using financing that does not appear as a liability on the balance sheet.

In recent years there has been an increasing trend to structure transactions in such a way that an obligation does not appear on the balance sheet as a liability. The avoidance of a liability is considered desirable by the company acquiring the use of an asset because many financial analysts and banks consider the amount of the liabilities in proportion to the total assets to be a useful indicator of the financial stability of the company. Therefore, keeping the liabilities lower will reflect favorably on the company by keeping measures such as the return on total assets and the debt ratio higher than they otherwise would be. This topic is discussed further in Chapter 14. Many accountants and users, however, consider off-balance sheet financing to be undesirable because the economic substance of the transaction is ignored. The required disclosures for companies that use off-balance sheet financing have been increased in recent years. The disclosures are included in the notes to each company's financial statements.

Sale–Leaseback

A sale–leaseback occurs when a company sells an asset that it owns (often land and buildings) and leases it back from the buyer. The transaction is advantageous because the lessee (the seller) receives needed cash from the sale and the lessor (the purchaser) acquires a profitable investment.

If the lease is a capital lease, the seller–lessee records the lease (as discussed earlier). Any profit on the sale is deferred and amortized in proportion to the amortization of the leased asset. If the lease is an operating lease, the profit is also deferred and is amortized in proportion to the lease payments. Alternatively, any loss on the sale is recognized in the period of the transaction, in accordance with the conservatism principle. There are no new issues for the purchaser–lessor.

To illustrate, assume that on January 1, 1993, the Milan Company sold its office building for $700,000 and leases it back for 15 years. The building had an original cost of $750,000 and a book value of $400,000. The Milan Company records the sale of the building as follows:

	Assets			= Liabs. + S. Eq.
+$700,000	−$750,000	+$350,000	−$300,000	

Cash	Building	Accumulated Depreciation: Building	Deferred Gain on Sale–Leaseback
$700,000	$750,000	$350,000	$300,000

The deferred gain should be reported as a contra-account to the building recorded under the capital lease (see below) but some companies would include it as a liability. The company records the lease as follows:

Assets	=	Liabilities	+ Stockholders' Equity
+ $700,000		+$700,000	

Building	Lease Obligation
$700,000	$700,000

The lease payment and the annual amortization on the building are recorded in the normal manner. If the company uses the straight-line method, the deferred gain is recognized at the rate of $20,000 ($300,000 ÷ 15 years) each year as follows:

Assets	= Liabilities +	Stockholders' Equity
+$20,000		+$20,000

Deferred Gain on Sale–Leaseback		Gain on Sale–Leaseback	
$20,000			$20,000

The gain on the sale–leaseback is included in Other Revenues and Expenses on the income statement.

SECTION B Income Taxes

■ ACCOUNTING FOR INCOME TAXES

The earnings (net income) of sole proprietorships and partnerships are not subject to income taxes because, for tax purposes, these business entities are not considered to be independent of their owners. The owners of sole proprietorships and partnerships are, of course, taxed as individuals on their personal earnings from the business. A corporation, on the other hand, is considered to be a legal entity that is separate and distinct from its owners. Consequently, the earnings of a corporation are subject to federal and, in many cases, state and foreign income taxes. Since the maximum federal corporate income tax rate is 34% at the time of writing, it is not unusual for a corporation's income tax rate to approach or exceed 40% of its income before income taxes. Because actual income tax computations are very complex, for simplicity we will assume an income tax rate in this book. Also we will only discuss the U.S. federal income tax.

Financial accounting practices may be influenced by the procedures adopted for income tax reporting. For example, under the provisions of the Internal Revenue Code a corporation may only use the LIFO method of inventory valuation for income tax reporting if it also uses LIFO for financial accounting reporting. Because of such influences, and in an effort to save costs, some companies attempt to minimize the effect of the Code on their accounting systems by using similar practices for both financial accounting and income tax purposes.

Some users have maintained that the accounting procedures adopted for financial reporting and for income tax reporting should be the same. However, this conformity would result in the use of procedures that are chosen for their acceptability under the Internal Revenue Code, because reports filed for income taxation purposes must comply with the statutory provisions of the tax code. Moreover, since companies try to legally avoid or postpone taxes, the conformity of financial accounting and income taxation reporting procedures would result in a tendency to select practices that minimize or delay income taxes without considering the usefulness of the practices for financial reporting.

The objectives of financial reporting and the Internal Revenue Code are quite different. The objective of generally accepted accounting principles for financial reporting is to provide useful information to decision makers about companies—information that will enable investors to make the *buy-hold-sell* decisions discussed in Chapter 1. The overall objective of the Internal Revenue Code, on the other hand, is to obtain funds, in an equitable manner, to operate the federal government. Additionally, tax laws frequently have been used to stimulate and regulate the economy (for example, the Modified Accelerated Cost Recovery System). In view of these different goals, most accountants and users favor the conformity of financial accounting and income tax reporting procedures *only* when the goals are equally applicable. For instance, when a cost represents both an expense and a tax deduction, it is deducted from revenue to arrive at both pretax financial accounting and taxable income.

As a result of their differing objectives, financial accounting is governed by generally accepted accounting principles and income tax reporting is governed by the Internal Revenue Code. If items of revenue and expense are coincidentally reported simultaneously, there is no issue. If they are not, it is necessary to determine (1) the income tax obligation based on the company's taxable income (2) the amount of the deferred income tax liability or asset, and (3) the income tax expense to be reported in regard to the pretax accounting income on the income statement. It is very unlikely that the income tax expense and obligation will be equal. That is, the income tax expense in the income statement is usually not equal to the income taxes paid to the federal, state, and other governments. In this chapter, we limit the discussion to the impact of federal income taxes on financial reporting.

■ OVERVIEW AND DEFINITIONS

Consider the condensed income statements and income tax returns for the Freese Corporation for 1993 and 1994 shown in Exhibit 9–4.

Causes of Differences

Several differences between the Freese Corporation's income statements and income tax returns in Exhibit 9–4 should be noted: (1) the amounts of revenue recognized in each year are different, (2) the expenses deductible as cost of goods sold differ in each year, and (3) other expenses differ in 1993. The causes of differences between pretax financial accounting income and taxable income (and

EXHIBIT 9–4

FREESE CORPORATION
Income Statement and Income Tax Return
Years Ended December 31, 1993 and 1994

	INCOME STATEMENT		INCOME TAX RETURN	
	1993	1994	1993	1994
Revenue	$180,000	$200,000	$170,000	$210,000
Cost of goods sold	(75,000)	(85,000)	(70,000)	(90,000)
Gross profit	$105,000	$115,000	$100,000	$120,000
Other expenses	(60,000)	(50,000)	(60,000)	(60,000)
Pretax income from continuing operations	$ 45,000	$ 65,000	$ 40,000	$ 60,000
Income taxes	(8,000)	(16,000)	(3,200)	(11,300)
Net income	$ 37,000	$ 49,000	$ 36,800	$ 48,700

potentially between income tax expense and income taxes payable) can be categorized into five groups:

1. *Permanent Differences.* Some items of revenue and expense reported for financial accounting purposes are never reported for income tax purposes under
the provisions of the Internal Revenue Code. Moreover, other items classified
as allowable deductions for income tax accounting do not qualify as expenses
under generally accepted accounting principles. These items result in permanent differences between pretax accounting income and taxable income.

2. *Temporary Differences.* Some items of revenue and expense are reported in one
period for financial reporting purposes but are reported in an earlier or later
period for income tax purposes. These items result in temporary (timing)
differences between pretax accounting income and taxable income (also known
as interperiod income tax allocation).

3. *Operating Loss Carrybacks and Carryforwards.* When an operating loss is reported,
the Internal Revenue Code allows the corporation's taxable income to be offset
over a number of years for taxation purposes. The amount of the loss in any
one year may be carried back 3 years and forward 15 years to offset previous
or subsequent reported taxable income.

4. *Intraperiod Tax Allocation.* This topic is discussed in Chapter 10.

5. *Tax Credits.* To stimulate certain investments or to provide tax relief in certain
circumstances, the Internal Revenue Code provides specific tax credits that
may be deducted in the computation of the income taxes owed. Examples
include "research and developmental" and foreign tax credits. Although a
tax credit does not cause a difference between pretax accounting income and
taxable income, it may cause a difference between income tax expense and
income taxes payable. Further discussion is beyond the scope of this book.

■ PERMANENT DIFFERENCES AND TEMPORARY DIFFERENCES

Differences between pretax accounting income and taxable income arise because of both permanent and temporary differences. Permanent differences do not require interperiod income tax allocation procedures, whereas temporary differences ultimately reverse and currently require such allocation. Each of these differences is discussed in the following section.

Permanent Differences

A permanent difference is a difference between pretax accounting income and taxable income in an accounting period that will never reverse in a later accounting period. Permanent differences between pretax accounting income and taxable income frequently arise because of economic policy making or because the U.S. Congress perceives a need to partially offset a provision of the tax code that may impose too heavy a tax burden on a particular segment of the economy. There are three types of permanent differences between pretax accounting income and taxable income:

1. Revenues are recognized for financial accounting reporting purposes that are never taxable. For example:
   a. Interest on municipal bonds. For income tax purposes, the Internal Revenue Code provides that receipt of interest on municipal bonds by an investor corporation is generally never recognized as revenue. The provision enables municipalities to offer bonds that carry a relatively lower rate of interest than corporate bonds of a similar quality, thus reducing the cost of borrowing for these municipalities.
   b. Life insurance proceeds payable to a corporation upon the death of an insured employee. For income tax purposes, the proceeds received are not considered revenue to the corporation but rather as partial compensation for the loss of the employee.

2. Expenses are recognized for financial accounting reporting purposes that are never deductible for income tax purposes. For example:
   a. Life insurance premiums on officers. For income tax purposes, the periodic premiums for life insurance policies on officers are not deductible as expenses. This procedure is consistent with the treatment of the insurance proceeds discussed above.
   b. Amortization of goodwill. For income tax purposes, the indeterminability of the estimated future period of benefit has resulted in the legislative decision not to allow a deduction of the amortization of goodwill, unless there is evidence of a limited life or a decline in value.

3. Deductions are allowed for income tax purposes that do not qualify as expenses under generally accepted accounting principles. For example:

a. Percentage depletion in excess of cost depletion. For income tax purposes, certain corporations that own wasting assets are allowed to deduct from their revenues a percentage depletion in excess of the cost depletion on a wasting asset. This provision of the tax code was designed to encourage exploration for natural resources.

b. Special dividend deduction. For income tax purposes, a special deduction (usually 80%) for certain dividends from investments in equity securities is allowed.

Permanent differences affect either reported pretax accounting income or taxable income, but not both. They do not require interperiod income tax allocation because subsequent events will not alter the fact that generally accepted accounting principles and the tax code differ on the items of revenue and expense to be recognized. A corporation that has nontaxable revenue or additional deductions for income tax reporting purposes will report a relatively lower taxable income as compared to pretax accounting income than it would have if these items were not present, whereas a corporation with expenses that are not tax deductible will report a relatively higher taxable income. The income tax expense is based on the pretax accounting income *excluding* the permanent differences. For example, if a company has pretax accounting income of $100,000 that includes municipal bond interest of $10,000, the income tax expense is computed as a percentage of $90,000. Permanent differences cause the effective tax rate (income tax expense divided by pretax accounting income) to be different than the statutory tax rate. Permanent differences are disclosed in the notes to the financial statements as illustrated later in the chapter.

Foreign Tax Credits and the Effective Tax Rate. In the existing income tax environment, tax rates in foreign countries are frequently higher than the U.S. corporate income tax rate of 34%. Companies with foreign-source taxable income may have an effective tax rate higher than the statutory rate.

To illustrate, assume the following situation (amounts in millions):

	U.S.	Foreign
Taxable income	$70	$30
Tax rate (assumed)	30%	40%
Income taxes payable	$21	$12

On its U.S. income tax return the company would report a total taxable income of $100 ($70 + $30), receiving a foreign tax credit based on the foreign taxes paid. However, the amount of the foreign tax credit cannot exceed an amount equal to the U.S. income tax imposed on the foreign-source income. Therefore, its foreign tax credit is the lesser of $12, the foreign tax imposed, or $9 ($30 × 30%), the U.S. tax imposed on foreign income. The company pays $21 [($100 × 30%)–$9] to the U.S. government. However, the total income tax paid by the company is $33 ($21 + $12) which is also its income tax expense (assuming there are no temporary differences). In the notes to the financial statements, the company would disclose that there is a difference between the statutory tax rate in the U.S. of 30% and its effective tax rate of 33%.

Temporary Differences

A temporary difference is a difference between pretax accounting income and taxable income that originates in an accounting period and reverses in some future accounting period(s). Furthermore, **an originating temporary difference is the initial difference between pretax accounting income and taxable income.** On the other hand, **a reversing temporary difference is a difference between pretax accounting income and taxable income that occurs because an originating temporary difference from a previous period has reversed.** Temporary differences relate to individual items and may be classified into four general groups. The first two groups result in pretax accounting income exceeding taxable income in the year of origination, and the last two result in taxable income exceeding pretax accounting income in the originating year of the temporary difference.

Pretax Accounting Income Originally Greater Than Taxable Income.

1. *Revenues or Gains Are Recognized in the Current Period for Financial Accounting Purposes and in a Subsequent Period for the Determination of Taxable Income.* For example, gross profit on installment sales normally is recognized at the point of sale for financial accounting purposes but, in certain situations, as cash is collected for income tax purposes. Another example is the recognition of investment revenue under the equity method for financial accounting purposes (as discussed in Chapter 11) but in a subsequent period as dividends are received for tax purposes.

2. *Expenses and Losses Are Deducted to Arrive at Taxable Income Prior to the Time They Are Charged Against Revenue for Financial Accounting Purposes.* For example, a fixed asset may be depreciated by the Modified Accelerated Cost Recovery System (MACRS) over the tax life (discussed in Chapter 7) for income tax purposes and by the straight-line method over a longer period for financial accounting purposes. Also, interest and taxes on a self-construction project may be deducted as incurred in arriving at taxable income but may be capitalized in certain instances as a part of the cost of the fixed asset for financial accounting.

Taxable Income Originally Greater Than Pretax Accounting Income.

3. *Revenues and Gains Are Included in Taxable Income Prior to Their Inclusion for Financial Accounting Purposes.* For example, such items as rent, interest, and royalties received in advance are taxable when received but are not reported for financial accounting purposes until the service actually has been provided. Additionally, gains on "sales and leasebacks" are taxed at the date of sale but reported over the life of the lease contract for financial accounting purposes.

4. *Expenses or Losses Are Charged Against Pretax Accounting Income Earlier Than They Are Allowed in the Determination of Taxable Income.* For example, product

warranty costs, bad debts, and losses on temporary investments in equity securities and inventories may be estimated and recorded as expenses in the current year for financial accounting purposes but deducted as actually incurred in a later year for the determination of taxable income. Or a contingent liability is expensed for financial accounting purposes if a loss is deemed probable but is deducted in arriving at taxable income as it is actually paid.

■ DEFERRED INCOME TAXES

A company's income tax *obligation* is based on the revenues and expenses that are recognized under the Internal Revenue Code. **The amount of the deferred income taxes reported on the balance sheet is the effect of temporary differences that will reverse in the future.** The income tax *expense* is the sum of the income tax obligation and the deferred income tax for the year.[4] Generally the deferred income tax is a liability. The liability arises because a company's temporary differences usually cause it to have taxable amounts in future periods. That is, the company has deferred paying its taxes until a later period. If the deferred income tax is an asset, the income tax expense is equal to the income tax obligation minus the deferred income tax for the year.

Temporary Difference: Taxable Amounts in Future Years

To illustrate the concepts and procedures underlying deferred income taxes, three examples are discussed. In each example it is assumed that the company was formed in 1993 or had no previous temporary differences. First, suppose that the Booton Company reports $280,000 of pretax financial income (income before income taxes) in 1993, as illustrated in Exhibit 9–5. Included in that income is an accounting expense of $20,000 that is not deductible for income tax purposes (a permanent difference such as the amortization of goodwill). Therefore the company's taxable financial income is $300,000 ($280,000 + $20,000). The company has only one temporary difference resulting from the recognition of gross profit on installment sales of $80,000. This amount is included in financial income but is excluded from taxable income in 1993. It will, however, be taxable in future years as cash is received. Therefore the company's taxable income is only $220,000 and the company records an income tax obligation of $88,000 ($220,000 × 40%).

The gross profit on the installment sales will be included in taxable income in the years 1994 to 1997, as illustrated in Exhibit 9–5. Since accounting principles are based on transactions and events that have occurred, they do not allow the assumption that future income will be earned. Therefore, it is assumed that zero financial income is earned in those years and that the only source of taxable income is the gross profit amounts (it is assumed in this example that there is only one temporary difference). These future taxable amounts create a liability

· ·

[4]"Accounting for Income Taxes," *FASB Statement of Financial Accounting Standards No. 96* (Stamford, Conn.: FASB, 1987).

EXHIBIT 9–5

[handwritten: amortization good will]

[handwritten: pre tax > Tax Income]

BOOTON COMPANY
Temporary Difference: Taxable Amounts

	1993	1994	1995	1996	1997
Pretax financial income	$280,000				
Nondeductible expense	20,000				
Taxable financial income	$300,000	$ 0	$ 0	$ 0	$ 0
Temporary differences					
Gross profit on installment sales	80,000				
Taxable amount (reversals)		14,000	36,000	18,000	12,000
Taxable income (loss)	$220,000	$14,000	$36,000	$18,000	$12,000
Enacted tax rate (assumed)	40%	35%	32%	30%	28%
Income tax obligation	$ 88,000				
Deferred tax liability					
Current		$(4,900)			
Noncurrent			$(11,520)	$(5,400)	$(3,360) = $(20,280)

[handwritten: because →]

---

for the company in 1993. The amount of the liability is computed using the **currently enacted tax rates for the future years**. These rates are assumed as indicated in Exhibit 9–5. The *current* deferred tax liability of $4,900 is the taxable amount for 1994 ($14,000) multiplied by the currently enacted tax rate (35%) for that year. The *noncurrent* deferred tax liability of $20,280 is the taxable amounts for 1994 to 1997, multiplied by the currently enacted tax rate for each of those years. Note that in all three examples it is assumed that the company has not made estimated tax payments during the year and will make its tax payment in the next year. Therefore, the income taxes payable is equal to the income tax obligation for the year. The company's income taxes for 1993 are recorded as follows:

Assets =		Liabilities			+ Stockholders' Equity
$88,000	+	$4,900	+	$20,280	− $113,180

Income Taxes Payable	Deferred Income Taxes: Current	Deferred Income Taxes: Noncurrent	Income Tax Expense
$88,000	$4,900	$20,280	$113,180

[handwritten: 因為 115 不付稅到明年]

The income statement for 1993 includes the following:

Income before income taxes		$ 280,000
Income tax expense:		
Currently payable	$88,000	
Deferred amount	25,180	
		(113,180)
Net income		$ 166,820

pre tax < Tax Income

EXHIBIT 9–6

warranty ...

	1993	1994	1995	1996	1997
CLARK COMPANY					
Temporary Difference: Deductible Amounts					
Pretax financial income	$280,000				
Nondeductible expense	20,000				
Taxable financial income	$300,000	$ 0	$ 0	$ 0	$ 0
Temporary differences					
Estimated warranty payments in future years	(80,000)				
Taxable amount (reversals)		(14,000)	(36,000)	(18,000)	(12,000)
Taxable income (loss)	$380,000	$(14,000)	$(36,000)	$(18,000)	$(12,000)
Enacted tax rate (assumed)	40%				
Income tax obligation	$152,000				
Deferred tax asset					
Current		$ 5,600			
Noncurrent			$ 14,400	$ 7,200	= $21,600

Of the total $113,180 income tax expense, $88,000 is payable based on the company's taxable income and tax rate. The remaining $25,180 is deferred because the company will pay additional taxes in future years on the taxable income from the reversal of the temporary differences that are recognized in those years. Each of the deferred income tax liabilities is included on the December 31, 1993, balance sheet.

warranty => F I

Not. T I

Temporary Difference: Deductible Amounts in Future Years

For the second example, suppose that the Clark Company reports pretax financial income of $280,000 in 1993, as illustrated in Exhibit 9–6. Included in that income is a nondeductible expense of $20,000. Therefore the company's taxable financial income is $300,000. The company has only one temporary difference resulting from the recognition of warranty expense of $80,000. This amount is deducted in the computation of financial income but is not deducted from taxable income in 1993. It is deductible only when the warranty costs are paid in future years. Therefore the company's taxable income is $380,000, and the company records an income tax obligation of $152,000 ($380,000 × 40%).

The warranty payments will be deducted in the computation of taxable income in the years 1994 to 1997, as illustrated in Exhibit 9–6. Since accounting principles do not allow the assumption that future income will be earned, these deductible amounts in future years represent a taxable loss in those years (it is assumed in this example that there is only one temporary difference). Under the terms of the Internal Revenue Code, operating losses may be carried back three years and (forward 15 years) discussed in greater detail later in the chapter. Therefore the losses caused by the warranty payments in the next three years would be carried back to 1993. If such losses actually occurred, the company would carry them back to 1993 and claim a refund. Therefore, these losses in the next three years create an asset in 1993. (Note that the deductible amount in 1997 does not create a deferred income tax asset in 1993 because the loss in that year cannot be carried back four years.[5]) The amount of the asset is computed using the tax rate of the *current* year. This rate is used because that is the rate that would be used to calculate the amount of the refund claimed under the Internal Revenue Code. The *current* deferred tax asset of $5,600 is the deductible amount for 1994 ($14,000) multiplied by the tax rate for 1991 (40%). The *noncurrent* deferred tax asset of $21,600 ($14,400 + $7,200) is the taxable amounts for the remaining two years for which losses may be carried back, 1995 and 1996, multiplied by the tax rate for 1993. The company's income taxes for 1993 are recorded as follows:

Assets		=	Liabilities	+	Stockholders' Equity
+ $5,600	+ $21,600		+ $152,000		− $124,800
Deferred Income Taxes: Current	**Deferred Income Taxes: Noncurrent**		**Income Taxes Payable**		**Income Tax Expense**
$5,600	$21,600		$152,000	$124,800	

The income statement for 1993 includes the following:

Income before income taxes		$280,000
Income tax expense:		
Currently payable	$152,000	
Deferred amount	(27,200)	
		(124,800)
Net income		$155,200

Of the total $124,800 income tax expense, $152,000 is payable based on the company's taxable income and tax rate. The difference of $27,200 is deferred because the company will pay fewer taxes in future years on the lower taxable income that results from the reversal of the temporary differences that are recognized in those years. Each of the deferred income tax assets is included on the December 31, 1993, balance sheet.

Temporary Difference: Depreciation

Since depreciation is usually the temporary difference that has the most significant impact on financial statements, the third example illustrates the effects of

....

[5] At the time of writing this book, the FASB was considering revising the rules so that the deductible amount in 1997 may, under certain circumstances, create a deferred tax asset.

depreciation. To illustrate, assume that the Allee Company purchases an asset costing $200,000 at the beginning of January, 1993. The asset has an estimated economic life of eight years and straight-line depreciation is used. The asset has a defined tax (MACRS) life of five years. (The MACRS system was discussed in Chapter 7.) These facts and the amounts of depreciation are summarized in Exhibit 9–7. In 1993, the company had a pretax financial income of $100,000. The temporary difference because of depreciation is $15,000 ($40,000 − $25,000) and therefore the company's taxable income is $85,000 and its tax obligation is $34,000 ($85,000 × 40%). The taxable loss in 1994 is carried back to 1993 and creates a current deferred tax asset of $15,600. The "apparent" noncurrent deferred tax asset created by the taxable loss in 1995 is offset against the deferred tax liability resulting from the taxable income in the years 1996 to 2000. The company's income taxes for 1993 are recorded as follows:

Assets	=	Liabilities		+	Stockholders' Equity
+$15,600		+$21,600	+$34,000		−$40,000

Deferred Income Taxes: Current		Deferred Income Taxes: Noncurrent		Income Taxes Payable		Income Tax Expense	
$15,600			$21,600		$34,000	$40,000	

The income statement for 1993 includes the following:

Income before income taxes		$100,000
Income tax expense:		
Currently payable	$34,000	
Deferred amount	6,000	
		(40,000)
Net income		$60,000

While the net amount deferred of $6,000 ($21,600 − $15,600) is reported in the income statement, the current deferred income tax asset of $15,600 and the noncurrent deferred income tax liability of $21,600 are separately recorded in the December 31, 1993, balance sheet.

In 1994, the Allee Company's asset is in its second year of depreciation. If we assume that the company's pretax financial income is again $100,000, its taxable income is $61,000 because the temporary difference for the year caused by the depreciation is $39,000 ($64,000 − $25,000), as shown in Exhibit 9–7. Therefore the company's tax obligation is $24,400 ($61,000 × 40%) as shown in Exhibit 9–8. The taxable loss in 1995 is carried back to 1993[6] and creates a current deferred tax asset of $5,360. The existing current deferred tax asset balance from 1993 is $15,600 and therefore has to be reduced by $10,240 ($15,600 − $5,360).

. . . .

[6]If the company had taxable income in 1992, the loss would be carried back the full three years to that year.

EXHIBIT 9-7

ALLEE COMPANY, 1993
Temporary Difference: Depreciation

Asset purchased:	January 1, 1993
Cost:	$200,000
Economic life:	8 years 25000 .
Depreciation method:	Straight line
MACRS life:	5 years
MACRS depreciation method:	200% declining balance
Residual value:	Zero
Income tax rate:	40%

	1993	1994	1995	1996
Financial depreciation	$25,000	$25,000	$25,000	$25,000
Tax (MACRS) depreciation	40,000	64,000	38,400	23,040
Pretax financial income	$100,000	$ 0	$ 0	$ 0
Temporary difference due to depreciation	(15,000)	(39,000)	(13,400)	1,960
Taxable income (loss)	$ 85,000	$(39,000)	$(13,400)	$ 1,960
Enacted tax rate (assumed)	40%	40%	40%	40%
Income tax obligation	$ 34,000			
Deferred tax asset Current		$ 15,600		
Deferred tax liability Noncurrent			$ 5,360	$ (784)

The noncurrent deferred tax liability resulting from the taxable amounts in the years 1996 to 2000 is $26,960. The existing noncurrent deferred tax liability balance from 1993 is $21,600 and therefore has to be increased by $5,360 ($26,960 − $21,600). The company's income taxes for 1994 are recorded as follows:

Assets	=	Liabilities		+	Stockholders' Equity
−$10,240		+$5,360	+$24,400		−$40,000

Deferred Income Taxes: Current	Deferred Income Taxes: Noncurrent	Income Taxes Payable	Income Tax Expense
$10,240	$5,360	$24,400	$40,000

The income statement for 1994 includes the following:

Income before income taxes		$100,000
Income tax expense:		
Currently payable	$24,400	
Deferred amount	15,600	
		(40,000)
Net income		$ 60,000

EXHIBIT 9–7 *(continued)*

1997	1998	1999	2000
$25,000	$25,000	$25,000	$25,000
23,040	11,520	0	0
$ 0	$ 0	$ 0	$ 0
1,960	13,480	25,000	25,000
$ 1,960	$13,480	$25,000	$25,000
40%	40%	40%	40%

| $ (784) | $ (5,392) | $(10,000) | $(10,000) | = $(21,600) |

The current deferred income tax asset balance of $5,360 and the noncurrent deferred income tax liability balance of $26,940 are included on the December 31, 1994 balance sheet.

Note that in each year the Allee Company's total income tax expense is $40,000 which is equal to the pretax financial income ($100,000) multiplied by the income tax rate (40%). The user of the financial statements can also understand the amount of the tax obligation (the cash paid for the current year's income taxes) by examining the breakdown of the income tax expense given in the income statement or in the notes.

Evaluation of Deferred Income Taxes

The basic principles of accounting for deferred income taxes are logical, but some of the specific rules have created considerable controversy. As illustrated in Exhibit 9–10, the income tax disclosures are complex. Also, the requirements for scheduling out a company's future taxable and deductible amounts require difficult predictions and complex calculations that impose a significant cost on the company. Consequently, some companies have argued that the *cost/benefit* constraint has not been satisfied. They also argue that the computations are not *reliable* because of the assumptions that have to be made in the scheduling.

EXHIBIT 9–8

···············

ALLEE COMPANY, 1994
Temporary Difference: Depreciation

	1993	1994	1995	1996
Pretax financial income	$100,000	$100,000	$ 0	$ 0
Temporary difference due to depreciation	(15,000)	(39,000)	(13,400)	1,960
Taxable income (loss)	$ 85,000	$ 61,000	$(13,400)	$1,960
Enacted tax rate (assumed)	40%	40%	40%	40%
Income tax obligation		$ 24,400		
Deferred tax asset				
Current			$ 5,360	
Deferred tax liability				
Noncurrent				$ (784)

	Ending Balance	Beginning Balance	Adjustment
Deferred tax asset			
Current	$ 5,360	$15,600	$10,240 decrease
Deferred tax liability			
Noncurrent	26,960	21,600	5,360 increase

However, many users agree with the principles and commend the FASB for taking a strong, if not popular, position. They argue that the information is relevant and reliable.

The assumption that income in future years cannot be anticipated is certainly consistent with the basic concepts of accounting that require that financial statements be based on transactions and events that have occurred, and not on what may happen in the future. In a situation where the temporary difference causes future taxable amounts, the measurement of the liability is appropriate because it does measure the incremental cash outflows that will occur in the future.

When the temporary difference results in future deductible amounts, there is less agreement about the meaning of the results. The restriction that the asset be valued based on the carryback of three years, as allowed by tax law, means that many companies are restricted in the amount of the asset that they can recognize. Thus companies may not reflect the benefits of the deductible amounts that will occur beyond three years. It is argued, therefore, that their assets are understated. Certainly, the measurement of assets and liabilities is not consistent because the liability is based on all future years while the asset is based on three years. Also, the three examples above are based on U.S. federal income tax. Since the rules for carrybacks and carryforwards vary among states and foreign countries, the amounts of the asset and liability also have to be computed for each tax jurisdiction based on its particular rules.

EXHIBIT 9–8 *(continued)*

1997	1998	1999	2000
$ 0	$ 0	$ 0	$ 0
1,960	13,480	25,000	25,000
$1,960	$13,480	$25,000	$25,000
40%	40%	40%	40%
$ (784)	$ (5,392)	$(10,000)	$(10,000) = $(26,960)

The intent of the principles for deferred income taxes is to provide an appropriate measure of the deferred tax asset or liability based on expectations of future cash flows. It may be argued, then, that the amounts should be discounted. Many liabilities and assets are valued at the present value of the future cash flows, such as mortgages, bonds, leases, notes, and pensions. However, two major difficulties would arise if discounting were required. First, a discount rate would have to be specified, and there is no defined market rate that could be used as there is in the other situations. Second, the actual years in which each of the future taxable and deductible amounts occur would have to be defined with considerable precision. While this process might be relatively easy for depreciation where the lives and depreciation methods are usually well-defined, it would be less easy for many other temporary differences such as bad debts and warranties. For both these reasons, discounting would make the amounts reported in the financial statements less *reliable* even though many users would argue that they would be more *relevant*.

Since the rules for the computation of the liability are based on currently enacted tax rates for future years, the financial statements of companies will be affected when there is a change in those tax rates. For example, suppose that Congress enacts a law that increases the tax rates for corporations in future years. Companies would have to recompute the amount of their deferred tax liabilities based on the higher future tax rates. The increased amount of the liability would also have to be included as a component of income tax expense for the current year—the year in which the change in the future tax rates is enacted. Thus companies will include the effects of future tax increases (and decreases) in the current year's financial statements. It will be interesting to see if these financial reporting rules influence the lobbying activities of companies as Congress considers tax rate changes.

Considerable controversy surrounds deferred income tax accounting because of the effects the procedures can have over many years. Typically, over time a company increases its assets that are subject to depreciation either because the company is growing and requires more assets, or because it replaces its assets at a higher cost, or both. In such cases, the deferred income tax liability balance will increase over time.

The general rule is that **an increase in the total cost of depreciable assets in the balance sheet will cause an increase in the deferred income tax liability** (although depending on the lives of the assets and depreciation methods used, there may be occasional decreases). Therefore, the income taxes paid are always less than the income tax expense and the deferred income taxes will never be paid. For this reason, many users argue that deferred income taxes should not be recorded as a liability and that deferred income tax procedures should not be used. Instead, they suggest that the income tax expense recorded in the income statement should be equal to the income tax obligation for the year.

■ OPERATING LOSSES

The Internal Revenue Code allows a corporation reporting an operating loss for income tax purposes in any period to carry the loss back or carry it forward to offset previous or future taxable income. A corporation may first carry such a reported operating loss back three years (in sequential order, starting with the earliest of the three years). This procedure is called an **operating loss carryback**. In such a case, the corporation files amended income tax returns showing lower taxable income for those years and receives a refund of income taxes previously paid. If the taxable income for the past three years is not enough to offset the amount of the currently reported operating loss, the loss is then sequentially carried forward 15 years and offset against future taxable income, should there be any. This procedure is called an **operating loss carryforward**. The corporation then pays lower income taxes in the future based on lower future taxable income. A diagram of the operating loss carryback and carryforward sequence in shown in Exhibit 9–9. A corporation may also elect to forgo the carryback and, instead, only carry forward an operating loss. Most corporations do not make this election because an operating loss carryback will result in a definite and immediate income tax refund, whereas a carryforward will reduce the income tax obligation in subsequent years only to the extent that taxable income is earned.

The generally accepted accounting principles for operating loss carrybacks and carryforwards are as follows:

EXHIBIT 9–9   Diagram of operating loss carrybacks and carryforwards

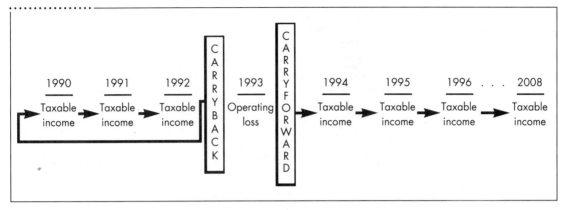

1. The tax benefits of an operating loss **carryback** are recognized in the period of the loss as a current receivable on the balance sheet and as a reduction of the operating loss on the income statement. The tax benefits are based on the prior applicable tax rates.

2. The tax effects of an operating loss **carryforward** are *not* recognized in the period of the loss. Instead, the tax effects are recognized in the period when they are realized, as a reduction of income taxes payable at the then current tax rates.

Illustration

To illustrate the effects of operating loss carrybacks and carryforwards, assume that the Tucker Corporation reported a pretax operating loss of $150,000 for both accounting and income tax purposes in 1993, and that reported pretax accounting and taxable income for the previous three years had been: 1990—$20,000 (tax rate 20%); 1991—$40,000 (tax rate 25%); 1992—$50,000 (tax rate 30%). If Tucker carries back its 1993 operating loss, the reported operating loss will result in a tax refund of $29,000 and a $40,000 operating loss carryforward because only $110,000 of the $150,000 loss was offset by previously reported pretax income. The amount of the refund is calculated as follows:

Year	Reported Pretax Accounting Income and Taxable Income	Tax Rate	Tax Refund
1990	$ 20,000	0.20	$ 4,000
1991	40,000	0.25	10,000
1992	50,000	0.30	15,000
	$110,000		$29,000

At the end of 1993, the company records the refund as follows:

Assets	= Liabilities +	Stockholders' Equity
+$29,000		+$29,000

Income Tax Refund Receivable		Operating Loss Carryback Refund	
$29,000			$29,000

This refund would be reflected on Tucker's 1993 income statement as follows:

Pretax loss from continuing operations	$(150,000)
Less: income tax operating loss carryback refund	29,000
Net loss	$(121,000)

The Income Tax Refund Receivable is included in the current assets of the Tucker Company's 1993 ending balance sheet. The note to the 1993 financial statements might read: "The company has a $40,000 operating loss carryforward which can be used within 15 years to offset future taxable income and reduce income taxes."

Assume that in 1994 Tucker reported pretax accounting and taxable income of $30,000 and was subject to a tax rate of 30%. The company would use $30,000 of its $40,000 operating loss carryforward and therefore would not pay any taxes. Tucker's 1994 income statement would include income tax expense of $9,000 ($30,000 × 0.30) and an offsetting $9,000 income tax operating loss carryforward credit, and its net income would be $30,000. The remaining operating loss carryforward of $10,000 would be disclosed in a note.

Now assume that in 1995 Tucker reported pretax accounting and taxable income of $52,000 and was subject to a tax rate of 30%. A tax savings of $3,000 ($10,000 × 30%) would result from the remaining $10,000 operating loss carryforward, and therefore the company would have a tax liability of $12,600 [($52,000 − $10,000) × 30%]. The carryforward credit is reported as a reduction of income tax expense on the company's 1995 income statement as follows:

Pretax operating income		$52,000
Less: income tax expense	$(15,600)	
income tax operating loss carryforward credit	3,000	(12,600)
Net income		$39,400

Note that the income tax operating loss carryforward credit causes the effective tax rate to be different from the statutory rate. In summary, Tucker has received tax benefits from its operating loss by carrying its loss back three years and forward two years.

■ DISCLOSURE OF INCOME TAXES

The disclosure of income taxes by Nike is illustrated in Exhibit 9–10.[7] The company discloses its income tax obligation for the year, its provision for income taxes, and the amount deferred. The total expense in the income statement is "the provision for income taxes" ($103,600,000 in 1989) of which some is deferred ($4,404,000 in 1989). The causes of the deferrals are disclosed next, followed by the reasons for the difference between the effective rate (38.3% in 1989) and the statutory rate (37.6% federal and state in 1989).

SECTION C Pensions

A company may provide various postemployment benefits to its employees. The two major types are pensions, which are discussed in the chapter, and other postemployment benefits, which are discussed in the Appendix to the chapter.

■ CHARACTERISTICS OF PENSION PLANS

A person who retires typically has three sources of income: savings, social security, and a pension. Many companies, especially large ones, have a pension plan for their employees. **A pension plan is an agreement between a company and its employee group whereby the company promises to provide income to its retired employees in return for the services that were provided by the employees during their employment.** This retirement income, which normally is paid monthly, is often determined on the basis of the employee's income and length of service with the company. For instance, under the retirement plan of one major corporation, employees who retire at age 65 receive annual retirement income according to the following formula: Average of last five years' salary × number of years of service × 0.0257. Thus, an individual who worked for this company for 30 years, and had an average salary of $35,000 for the last five years of service, would receive annual pension benefits of $26,985 ($35,000 × 30 × 0.0257). A pension plan of this type is a **defined benefit plan** because the plan specifically states either the *benefits* to be received by employees after retirement or the method of determining such benefits. In contrast, a pension plan is a **defined contribution plan** when the employer's *contribution* is determined based on a specified formula. Any future benefits are limited to those that can be provided by the contributions and the returns earned on the investment of those contributions. This type of plan occurs more frequently in nonprofit organizations. The two types of plans involve different risks to the company and the employees. With a defined benefit plan, most of the risks lie with the company because the

· · · · · · · · · · · · · · · · · · ·

[7]These disclosures are prepared under old rules that existed prior to the principles discussed in the chapter. The form of the disclosures is similar to those under the new rules, although the amounts will be different. The new rules are required for fiscal years beginning after December 15, 1991.

EXHIBIT 9–10   Example of disclosure of income taxes

·················

NIKE, INC.

Note 8 — Income taxes:
Income before income taxes and the provision for income taxes are as follows:

	YEAR ENDED MAY 31,		
	1989	1988	1987
	(in thousands)		
Income before income taxes:			
United States	$207,815	$124,519	$44,315
Foreign	62,832	41,676	29,364
	$270,647	$166,195	$73,679
Provision for income taxes:			
Current:			
United States			
Federal	$ 72,785	$ 43,830	$16,172
State	15,720	8,296	3,702
Foreign	19,499	14,019	6,030
	108,004	66,145	25,904
Deferred:			
United States			
Federal	(2,663)	(1,583)	11,910
State	(788)	(265)	(120)
Foreign	(953)	203	106
	(4,404)	(1,645)	11,896
	$103,600	$ 64,500	$37,800

As of May 31, 1989 the Company has utilized all foreign tax credits.
The sources and amounts of the provision (credit) for deferred income taxes were as follows:

	YEAR ENDED MAY 31,		
	1989	1988	1987
	(in thousands)		
Inventory adjustment to market	$ 130	$ 1,907	$ (1,310)
Reserves and accrued liabilities	(1,754)	756	—
Tax basis adjustments to inventory	(2,236)	(2,050)	—
Purchased tax benefits	(362)	(293)	4,311
Deferred compensation	(1,735)	(644)	622
Barter credits	1,120	(1,583)	(491)
Undistributed earnings of foreign subsidiaries	1,784	258	8,087
Bad debts	(915)	(36)	(411)
Other, net	(436)	40	1,088
	$(4,404)	$(1,645)	$11,896

EXHIBIT 9–10 *(continued)*

....

NIKE, INC.

A reconciliation from the U.S. statutory federal income tax rate to the effective income tax rate follows:

	YEAR ENDED MAY 31,		
	1989	1988	1987
	(in thousands)		
U.S. federal statutory rate	34.0%	35.0%	46.0%
State income taxes, net of federal benefit	3.6	3.3	2.4
Recalculation of purchased tax benefit liability	—	—	(2.3)
Tax impact of foreign losses	—	(1.7)	.8
Taxes on foreign earnings	—	—	1.0
Other, net	.7	2.2	3.4
Effective income tax rate	38.3%	38.8%	51.3%

During 1982, the Company purchased future tax benefits for $15,277,000. Tax benefits of $8,136,000 in excess of the purchase price have been recognized as of May 31, 1989 and are classified as a long-term liability. In Fiscal 1987, the Company recognized $3,700,000 in non-taxable other income as a result of recalculating the effect of the 1986 Tax Reform Act on its purchased tax benefit liability.

payments to the retired employees have been defined and the company has the responsibility of ensuring that those amounts are paid. In contrast, with a defined contribution plan most of the risks lie with the employees because the company's responsibilities essentially end once the required contribution for the period has been made by the company. Defined benefit plans raise many complex accounting issues, which are the primary focus of this chapter. Defined contribution plans are briefly discussed later in the chapter.

Pension plans may be either **funded** or **unfunded**. Under a funded plan, the company makes periodic payments to a *funding agency* that assumes the responsibility for safeguarding and investing the pension assets to earn a return on the investments for the pension plan, and for making payments to the recipients of benefits. An unfunded plan is one in which no periodic payments are made to an external agency; the pension payments to retired employees are made from current company resources. Although the *Employee Retirement Income Security Act of 1974* (ERISA) has eliminated unfunded plans for corporations, many plans are only partially funded, as we shall discuss later in the chapter. Also, many governmental plans are unfunded. The amounts needed to fund a pension plan are determined (estimated) by **actuaries**, individuals trained in actuarial science who use compound interest techniques, with projections of future events and *actuarial funding methods* to calculate current contributions by the company.

Pension plans may also be either **contributory** or **noncontributory**. Under a contributory plan, employees bear part of the cost of the plan and make contributions from their salary into the pension fund. With noncontributory plans, the entire pension cost is borne by the employer. We are concerned with noncontributory plans in this chapter.

In addition, most companies design their pension plans to meet the Internal Revenue Code qualifications, which allow:

1. Employer contributions to be deductible for income tax purposes

2. Pension fund earnings not to be subject to income taxes

3. Employer contributions to the pension fund not to be taxable to the employees until pension benefits are actually received

4. Employee contributions to the pension fund not to be taxable until pension benefits are actually received

In addition to pensions, many employers provide other postemployment benefits to their employees. These benefits, and the FASB's proposed accounting for them, are discussed in the Appendix to this chapter.

ILLUSTRATION OF CALCULATIONS FOR PENSION PLANS

The determination of the pension expense and the amount that the company funds are complex. The basic characteristics of these calculations are illustrated by a simple diagram and example based on the following information for the Lonetree Company in 1993:

Number of employees:	10
Years to retirement at December 31, 1993:	20 years
Years of life expectancy after retirement:	12 years
Annual pension benefits earned during 1993:	$2,000 per employee
Discount rate:	8%

Note that the $2,000 earned per employee is the annual pension benefit that has been earned during 1993 as a result of the services performed by each employee during the year. This amount will be received each of the 12 years that each employee is retired. Thus, if each employee does continue to work for the next 20 years, each will have earned an annual retirement income of $40,000 ($2,000 × 20). When the preceding amounts have been estimated, the company calculates its cost for 1993 by using present value principles. The cash flows (i.e., the annuity) that were earned during 1993 and that will be paid to the employees during their retirement are $20,000 (10 employees × $2,000) per year. These cash flows will start in 20 years and will be paid for 12 years. Therefore, the company needs to calculate the cost in 1993 of these future cash flows; that is, the company

P V   *CF*

must compute the present value of the cash flows. This is a two-step process, as shown in the following diagram:

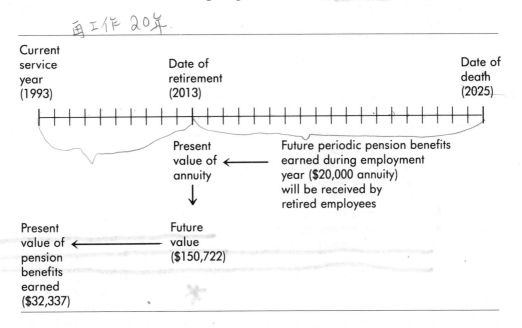

由工作 20年.

Current service year (1993) — **Date of retirement (2013)** — **Date of death (2025)**

Present value of annuity ← Future periodic pension benefits earned during employment year ($20,000 annuity) will be received by retired employees

Present value of pension benefits earned ($32,337) ← Future value ($150,722)

The diagram reads from right to left. Initially, the present value of the future periodic pension benefits earned during the current year (1993) is computed as of the date of retirement (2013). The present value of the $20,000 per year from 2013 to 2025 is the present value of a 12-year annuity discounted at 8% as follows:

Present Value = Periodic Amount of × Present Value of Annuity
of Annuity   the Annuity   for 12 Years at 8%

= $20,000 × 7.536078 (from Table 4) $(20,000)(PVIFA_{12n\,8\%})$

= $150,722 (rounded) $=150,722$.

Thus, in 2013 the funding agency must have $150,722 to pay out $20,000 each year for 12 years (2013 to 2025) to employees in retirement.

The second step is to compute the present value in the current year (1993) of the amount needed at retirement (2013). The present value of the $150,722 in 2013 is the present value of a single sum discounted at 8% as follows:

Present Value = Future Value × Present Value of $1 Factor
for 20 Years at 8%

= $150,722 × 0.214548 (from Table 2)

service cost ⟹ = $32,337 (rounded)

This amount is known as the **service cost** and is a component of pension expense, as discussed later. It is important to understand the effects of different interest rates on this (and other) present value calculations. Suppose the company had chosen a rate of 10%. The service cost in 1993 would have been calculated as follows:

$$\text{Present Value} = \begin{array}{c}\text{Periodic Amount} \\ \text{of the Annuity}\end{array} \times \begin{array}{c}\text{Present Value of} \\ \text{Annuity for 12} \\ \text{Years at 10\%}\end{array} \times \begin{array}{c}\text{Present Value} \\ \text{of \$1 Factor for} \\ \text{20 Years at 10\%}\end{array}$$

$$= \$20,000 \times 6.813692 \times 0.148644$$

$$= \$20,256 \text{ (rounded)}$$

A difference in the rate of 2 percentage points changes the service cost by 60% ($32,337 ÷ $20,256 = 1.60, rounded). Thus, a major issue arising in accounting for pensions is that the selection of the rate can have a significant influence on the amount of the service cost computed by the company. The criteria used for the selection of the rate are discussed later, and they do allow some interpretation by management.

Another accounting issue arises when a company increases (or decreases) the pension payments it is committed to making to its employees. This may happen when a company negotiates a new union contract with its employees, when it has been exceptionally profitable (or unprofitable), or when it compensates for excessive inflation. To illustrate, suppose that at the end of 1995 the Lonetree Company agrees to increase the benefits that will be paid to its ten employees during retirement by $5,000 per year per employee, thereby increasing the total cash flow to its ten employees by $50,000 per year during their retirement. Note that the employees do not have to perform any future services to receive these payments during their retirement. Again, the company calculates the cost of these increased future benefits by present value calculations. First, the present value, at the time the employees start their retirement, of the $50,000 per year is calculated. Then the present value of that amount at the end of 1995 is calculated as follows:

$$\text{Present Value} = \begin{array}{c}\text{Periodic Amount} \\ \text{of the Annuity}\end{array} \times \begin{array}{c}\text{Present Value of} \\ \text{Annuity for 12} \\ \text{Years at 8\%}\end{array} \times \begin{array}{c}\text{Present Value} \\ \text{of \$1 Factor for} \\ \text{18 Years at 8\%}\end{array}$$

$$= \$50,000 \times 7.536078 \times 0.250249$$

$$= \$94,295 \text{ (rounded)}$$

This amount is known as the **prior service cost**. A similar procedure is followed when a company initiates a pension plan. A company often assigns immediate pension benefits to its employees as a reward for the services they have performed before the adoption of the plan. The cost of these benefits is also known as the prior service cost. As illustrated later, the prior service cost is amortized in future periods and is *not* shown as a liability in the current period's balance sheet. Thus, the reader of those financial statements should realize that a company may be committed to a potentially large future cash outflow that is not recorded as a liability. Information about these amounts may be found in the notes to the financial statements.

■ ACCOUNTING PRINCIPLES FOR DEFINED BENEFIT PENSION PLANS

The generally accepted accounting principles to be used by an employer in accounting for its defined benefit pension plans are very complex and only the basic elements are included in the following discussion.[8] The computation of periodic pension expense, liabilities and assets, rates of return, and disclosures are each discussed. It should be noted that these items are defined by generally accepted accounting principles, whereas the minimum amount funded by the employer is defined by ERISA and is discussed later.

Pension Expense

The net periodic pension expense recognized by a company includes five components: service cost, interest cost, actual return on plan assets, amortization of unrecognized prior service cost, and gain or loss.[9] However, companies are only required to disclose separately the first three components, with the last two being combined in a single amount. Each of these disclosures is discussed below.

1. **Service Cost. The service cost is the actuarial present value of the benefits attributed by the pension benefit formula to services rendered by the employees during the current period.** The measurement of the benefits attributed to the period was discussed earlier and the discount rate is discussed later.

2. **Interest Cost. The interest cost is the increase in the projected benefit obligation due to the passage of time.** Thus, it is the projected benefit obligation at the beginning of the period multiplied by the discount rate used by the company. Since the pension plan is a deferred compensation agreement in which future payments are discounted to their present values, interest accrues due to the passage of time. The interest cost is added in the computation of pension expense.   *PBO*

    The projected benefit obligation is the actuarial present value, at a specified date, of all the benefits attributed by the pension benefit formula to employee service rendered prior to that date. The amount includes *future increases in compensation* that the company projects that it will pay to employees during the remainder of their employment, if the pension benefit formula is based on those future compensation levels.

3. **Actual Return on Plan Assets. The actual return on plan assets is the difference between the fair value of the plan assets at the end of the period and the fair value at the beginning of the period, adjusted for contributions by the company and payments of benefits to retired employees during the**

· · · · · · · · · · · · · · · · · · · ·

[8]"Employers' Accounting for Pensions," *FASB Statement of Financial Accounting Standards No. 87* (Stamford, Conn.: FASB, 1985).

[9]A sixth component is the amortization of any unrecognized net liability or asset that existed at the initial application of *FASB Statement No. 87.* This item is a result of the transition from the requirements of *APB Opinion No. 8* and is not discussed.

period. Plan assets are held by the funding agency and consist of investments such as stocks, bonds, and real estate. If the plan assets earn a positive return, this amount is subtracted in the computation of pension expense, but is added if a negative return occurs.

4. **Amortization of Unrecognized Prior Service Cost and Net Gain or Loss.** The prior service cost is not recognized (i.e., not recorded in the financial statements) in total in the period granted because it is assumed that the company will realize benefits such as reduced employee turnover in future periods. **The unrecognized prior service cost is amortized by assigning an equal amount to each future period of service of each active, participating employee at the date of the amendment who is expected to receive future benefits under the plan.** Alternatively, straight-line amortization over the average remaining service life of active employees may be used for simplicity. Note that employees hired after the date of the amendment, or the plan adoption, are not included in either calculation. In the usual case, the plan amendment increases the projected benefit obligation and therefore the amortization is added in the computation of pension expense. However, there have been several instances in recent years of companies in financial difficulty or facing increasing competition which have amended their pension plans to reduce the projected benefit obligation, in which case the amortization is subtracted in the computation.

Note that the amount of the prior service cost is *not* included as a liability or asset. Therefore, this amount is referred to as the *unrecognized* prior service cost. It is important to understand that the prior service cost is unrecognized because it is not included in the financial statements but, of course, it has been "recognized" by the actuaries as a relevant cost.

The computation of the gain or loss is very complex and beyond the scope of this book. However, two important points should be understood. First, one element of the gain or loss is the difference between the actual and expected return on plan assets and the *total* pension expense is therefore based on a deduction of the *expected* return on plan assets. The actual return is explicitly deducted in the computation of pension expense as the third element. However, since the difference between the actual and expected return is also included in pension expense, the net result is a reduction of the expected return in the computation of pension expense. This adjustment effectively means that pension expense is based on management's estimate of the average long-term return on assets in the pension fund rather than the actual amount earned in any particular period. Second, the gain or loss (other than the difference just discussed) is not recognized in the period in which it occurs but is amortized over future periods in a manner similar to the prior service cost.

Pension Liabilities and Assets

The amount of the net periodic pension expense may be different from the assets contributed by the company to the pension plan (the amount funded). These two amounts may be different because they are defined by different sets of rules.

The expense is defined by *FASB Statement No. 87*, whereas the funding must be consistent with the rules of ERISA, as discussed later. Therefore, a liability, **unfunded accrued pension cost**, is recognized and reported on the company's balance sheet if the net periodic pension expense recognized to date is greater than the amount funded to date. Alternatively, an asset, **prepaid pension cost**, is recognized and reported on the company's balance sheet if the net periodic pension expense to date is less than the amount funded to date. This asset or liability is similar to the numerous assets and liabilities that arise from the use of the accrual basis of accounting.

An additional liability may also have to be recognized on the company's balance sheet if the *accumulated* benefit obligation is greater than the fair value of the plan assets at the end of the period. The **accumulated benefit obligation is the actuarial present value of all the benefits attributed by the pension benefit formula to employee service rendered before a specified date.** The amount is based on *current and past compensation levels* of employees and therefore includes *no* assumptions about future pay increases (in contrast to the projected benefit obligation, which includes anticipated future pay increases). The **unfunded accumulated benefit obligation** is the accumulated benefit obligation minus the fair value of the plan assets, and is the minimum liability that the company must recognize. The total pension-related liability recognized (including any unfunded accrued pension cost) must be at least equal to the unfunded accumulated benefit obligation. The unfunded accumulated benefit obligation provides information about the liability a company would have if its pension plan were discontinued. Alternatively, if the plan is continued, it provides a minimum measure of the additional funds that a company will have to contribute in future periods.

If this additional liability is recognized, an intangible asset, **deferred pension cost**, of an equal amount is also recognized and reported on the company's balance sheet. The reason for recognizing an intangible asset is that there is an expectation of enhanced future performance by employees from such factors as reduced turnover and higher productivity. The amount of the intangible asset, however, must not exceed the amount of any unrecognized prior service cost. In the case where the additional liability exceeds the unrecognized prior service cost, the excess (debit) is reported as a reduction of stockholders' equity. Whenever a subsequent balance sheet is prepared, the amount of the additional liability would be recomputed and the related intangible asset or separate component of stockholders' equity would be adjusted or eliminated as necessary.

In summary, the pension amounts that may be reported, depending on the circumstances, on a company's balance sheet include:

Assets	Liabilities
1. Prepaid pension cost	1. Unfunded accrued pension cost
2. Deferred pension cost (intangible asset)	2. Additional pension liability

Stockholders' Equity
1. Excess of additional pension liability over unrecognized prior service cost (negative element)

Rates of Return

In computing the actuarial present value of the benefits, the company must use a discount rate that reflects the rates at which the pension benefits could be effectively settled. For example, if the company could settle its obligation by purchasing an annuity from an insurance company for each employee, the rate on that annuity could be used as the appropriate discount rate. The rate of return on high-quality fixed-income investments currently available and expected to be available in the future could also be used. However determined, this same discount rate is used to compute the interest cost component of pension expense.

On the other hand, the expected (assumed) long-term rate of return on plan assets used to compute the expected return on assets (for the computation of the net gain or loss) should reflect the average rate of earnings expected on the funds invested or to be invested. Actual experience should be considered along with the rates of return expected to be available in the future.

In a survey of 1987 financial statements, the average discount rate used by companies was 8.73%, with a range from 6% to 11.25%. The average long-term rate of return on plan assets was 9.03%.

Additional Disclosures

To provide users with additional relevant information, a company with a defined benefit pension plan makes the following disclosures:

1. A description of the plan including employee groups covered, type of benefit formula, funding policy, and types of assets held

2. The amount of the pension expense showing separately the service cost component, the interest cost component, the actual return on assets for the period, and the net total of other components

3. A schedule reconciling the funded status of the plan with amounts reported in the company's balance sheet, showing separately:
   a. The fair value of plan assets
   b. The projected benefit obligation identifying the accumulated benefit obligation and the vested benefit obligation
   c. The amount of unrecognized prior service cost
   d. The amount of unrecognized gain or loss
   e. The amount of any remaining unrecognized net obligation or net asset existing at the transition from *APB Opinion No. 8* to *FASB Statement No. 87*
   f. The amount of any additional liability recognized.
   g. The amount of net pension asset or liability recognized in the balance sheet (the net of the previous six items)

4. The weighted average discount rate and rate of compensation increase used to measure the projected benefit obligation and the weighted average expected long-term rate of return on plan assets

5. The amounts and types of securities included in plan assets

■ EXAMPLES OF ACCOUNTING FOR PENSIONS

As noted earlier, many of the amounts used in pension accounting are computed by actuaries and are based on actuarial assumptions. For simplicity, various situations related to accounting for defined benefit pension plans are illustrated in this section using assumed amounts.

Example 1: Pension Expense Equal to Pension Funding

Assume the following facts for the Carlisle Company:

1. The company adopts a pension plan on January 1, 1993. No retroactive benefits were granted to employees.
2. The service cost each year is: 1993 $400,000
                            1994   420,000
                            1995   432,000
3. The projected benefit obligation at the beginning of each year is: 1994 $400,000
                                                             1995   840,000
4. The discount rate is 10%.
5. The actual rate of return on plan assets is 10%.
6. The expected rate of return on plan assets is 10%.
7. The company adopts a policy of funding an amount equal to the pension expense and makes the payment to the funding agency at the end of each year.
8. Plan assets are based on the amounts contributed each year, plus a return of 10% per year, less an assumed payment of $20,000 at the end of each year to retired employees (beginning in 1994).

Based on this information, the only component of the pension expense in 1993 is the $400,000 service cost. This situation occurs because (1) there is no interest cost or actual return on plan assets since the funding was made at the end of the first year, (2) there is no prior service cost, and (3) there is no gain or loss because the actual and expected rates of return are equal. Since the company funds an amount equal to the pension expense, the following amounts are recorded on December 31, 1993:

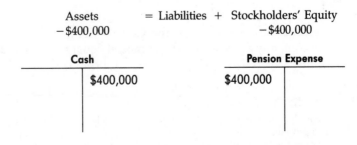

Assets	= Liabilities +	Stockholders' Equity
− $400,000		− $400,000

Cash		Pension Expense	
$400,000		$400,000	

The calculation of the pension expense for 1994 is more complex because it now has three components: service cost, interest cost, and actual return on plan assets. The service cost is assumed to be $420,000. Since the projected benefit obligation at January 1, 1994 is assumed to be $400,000 (the service cost for 1993), the interest cost is $40,000 (the projected benefit obligation of $400,000 multiplied by the discount rate of 10%). The actual return on the plan assets is the $400,000 invested by the funding agency for the pension fund at the beginning of the year multiplied by the 10% actual rate of return. Therefore, the pension expense for 1994 is computed as follows:

Service cost (assumed)	$420,000
Interest cost ($400,000 × 10%)	40,000
Actual return on plan assets ($400,000 × 10%)	(40,000)
Pension expense	$420,000

For 1995, the service cost is assumed to be $432,000. The projected benefit obligation at the beginning of 1995 is assumed to be $840,000. The assets at the beginning of 1995 are $840,000 ($400,000 invested at the end of 1993 + $40,000 actual return in 1994 − $20,000 payment to retired employees at the end of 1994 + $420,000 invested at the end of 1994). Therefore, the pension expense for 1995 is computed as follows:

Service cost (assumed)	$432,000
Interest cost ($840,000 × 10%)	84,000
Actual return on plan assets ($840,000 × 10%)	(84,000)
Pension expense	$432,000

Note that the interest cost and the return on the plan assets offset each other in this example. This occurs because the discount rate and the actual rate of return on plan assets are both 10% and because the company funds an amount equal to the expense.

Example 2: Pension Expense Greater Than Pension Funding

Assume the same facts for the Carlisle Company as in Example 1, except that the company does not fund an amount equal to the pension expense but instead funds $385,000 in 1993, $400,000 in 1994, and $415,000 in 1995.[10] Since the

• • • • • • • • • • • • • • • • • • • •

[10]For illustrative purposes, the amount funded is less than the service cost. In some circumstances, this procedure might be a violation of the minimum funding requirements of ERISA. However, the amount funded may be less than the *total* pension expense.

company provides *fewer* assets to the pension fund, the return on those assets each period is less, and therefore the pension expense must be larger to compensate for the lower actual return. The company's pension expense in 1993 is the $400,000 service cost and is recorded on December 31, 1993 as follows:

Assets	=	Liabilities	+	Stockholders' Equity
− $385,000		+ $15,000		− $400,000

Cash	Unfunded Accrued Pension Cost	Pension Expense
$385,000	$15,000	$400,000

Since the company funds only $385,000 in 1993 when the expense is $400,000, a liability of $15,000 is recognized. The classification of this liability as current or noncurrent in the balance sheet follows the normal rules.

In 1994, the only difference from the previous example in the computation of the pension expense is the reduced return on the plan assets. Since only $385,000 was contributed by the company on December 31, 1993, a return of only $38,500 was earned in 1994. The pension expense for 1994 is computed as follows:

Service cost	$420,000
Interest cost ($400,000 × 10%)	40,000
Actual return on plan assets ($385,000 × 10%)	(38,500)
Pension expense	$421,500

Since the company funds $400,000 in 1994, a liability of $21,500 is also recognized. The balance in the liability account at the end of 1994 is $36,500 ($15,000 + $21,500).

In 1995, the computation of the pension expense is again affected by the reduced return on the plan assets. Since only $400,000 was contributed by the company, the assets of the pension fund on January 1, 1995 are $803,500 ($385,000 invested at the end of 1993 + $38,500 actual return in 1994 − $20,000 payment to retired employees at the end of 1994 + $400,000 invested at the end of 1994), and a return of $80,350 on those assets is earned during 1995. Therefore the pension expense for 1995 is computed as follows:

Service cost	$432,000
Interest cost ($840,000 × 10%)	84,000
Actual return on plan assets ($803,500 × 10%)	(80,350)
Pension expense	$435,650

Since the company funds $415,000 in 1995, a liability of $20,650 is also recognized. The balance in the liability account at the end of 1995 is $57,150 ($36,500 + $20,650).

Example 3: Pension Expense Less Than Pension Funding

Assume the same facts for the Carlisle Company as in Example 1, except that the company does not fund an amount equal to the pension expense but instead funds $415,000 in 1993, $425,000 in 1994, and $440,000 in 1995. Since the company provides *more* assets to the pension fund, the return on those assets each period is greater, and therefore the pension expense must be less to compensate for the higher actual return. The company's pension expense in 1993 is the $400,000 service cost and the entry on December 31, 1993 is:

Assets		= Liabilities +	Stockholders' Equity
− $415,000	+ $15,000		− $400,000

Cash		Prepaid Pension Cost		Pension Expense	
	$415,000	$15,000		$400,000	

Since the company funds $415,000 in 1993 when the expense is $400,000, an asset of $15,000 is recognized. The classification of this asset as current or non-current in the balance sheet follows the normal rules.

In 1994, the only difference in the computation of the pension expense from Example 1 is the increased return on the plan assets. Since $415,000 was contributed by the company on December 31, 1993, a return of $41,500 was earned in 1994. The pension expense for 1994 is computed as follows:

Service cost	$420,000
Interest cost ($400,000 × 10%)	40,000
Actual return on plan assets ($415,000 × 10%)	(41,500)
Pension expense	$418,500

Since the company funds $425,000 in 1994, an asset of $6,500 is also recognized. The balance in the asset account at the end of 1994 is $21,500 ($15,000 + $6,500).

In 1995, the computation of the pension expense is again affected by the increased return on the plan assets. Since $425,000 was contributed by the company, the assets of the pension fund on January 1, 1995 are $861,500 ($415,000 invested at the end of 1993 + $41,500 actual return in 1994 − $20,000 payment to retired employees in 1994 + $425,000 invested at the end of 1994), and a return of $86,150 on those assets is earned during 1995. Therefore, the pension expense for 1995 is computed as follows:

Service cost	$432,000
Interest cost ($840,000 × 10%)	84,000
Actual return on plan assets ($861,500 × 10%)	(86,150)
Pension expense	$429,850

Since the company funds $440,000 in 1995, an asset of $10,150 is also recognized. The balance in the asset account at the end of 1995 is $31,650 ($21,500 + $10,150).

Example 4: Pension Expense Including Amortization of Unrecognized Prior Service Cost

The previous three examples illustrated relatively simple computations of pension expense and the related pension liability (unfunded accrued pension cost) or pension asset (prepaid pension cost). The remaining examples deal with more complex issues. Recall that an amendment to a pension plan frequently includes provisions that grant increased retroactive benefits based on services performed by employees in prior periods. The cost of providing these benefits is called a prior service cost. A prior service cost may also arise when a plan is adopted. A prior service cost causes an increase in the projected benefit obligation. The prior service cost, however, is not recognized in the financial statements in the year of the amendment or plan adoption. Instead, the prior service cost is amortized as a component of pension expense.

To illustrate this amortization, assume the same facts for the Carlisle Company as in Example 2, except that the company awarded retroactive benefits to the employees when it adopted the pension plan on January 1, 1993. The unrecognized prior service cost was computed by the company's actuary to be $200,000 and therefore created a projected benefit obligation of that amount on January 1, 1993. To fund this projected benefit obligation, the company decided to increase its contribution by $17,000 per year. For simplicity, it is also assumed that the unrecognized prior service cost is amortized by the straight-line method over the remaining 20-year service life of the company's active employees. Thus, the amount of the amortization is $10,000 ($200,000 ÷ 20) per year.

The company's pension expense in 1993 now has three components. In addition to the service cost of $400,000, both the interest cost on the $200,000 projected benefit obligation and the $10,000 amortization of the unrecognized prior service cost must be recognized. Therefore, the pension expense for 1993 is computed as follows:

Service cost	$400,000
Interest cost ($200,000 × 10%)	20,000
Amortization of unrecognized prior service cost	10,000
Pension expense	$430,000

Since the company funds $402,000 ($385,000 + $17,000) in 1993, the following is recorded on December 31, 1993:

Assets   =   Liabilities   +   Stockholders' Equity
− $402,000   + $28,000   − $430,000

Cash	Unfunded Accrued Pension Cost	Pension Expense	
$402,000	$28,000	$430,000	

Note that the unrecognized prior service cost of $200,000 is *not* recorded in the financial statements but is included in the disclosures.

On January 1, 1994, the projected benefit obligation is assumed to be $620,000. Therefore, the pension expense for 1994 is computed as follows:

Service cost	$420,000
Interest cost ($620,000 × 10%)	62,000
Actual return on plan assets ($402,000 × 10%)	(40,200)
Amortization of unrecognized prior service cost	10,000
Pension expense	$451,800

Since the company funds $417,000 ($400,000 + $17,000) in 1994, a liability of $34,800 is also recognized.

On January 1, 1995, the projected benefit obligation is assumed to be $1,082,000, the plan assets are $839,200 ($402,000 + $40,200 + $417,000 − $20,000 paid to retired employees), and the pension expense for 1995 is computed as follows:

Service cost	$432,000
Interest cost ($1,082,000 × 10%)	108,200
Actual return on plan assets ($839,200 × 10%)	(83,920)
Amortization of unrecognized prior service cost	10,000
Pension expense	$466,280

Since the company funds $432,000 ($415,000 + $17,000) in 1995, a liability of $34,280 is also recognized. Thus, at the end of 1995 the total liability reported by the company is $97,080 ($28,000 + $34,800 + $34,280).

Example 5: Recognition of Additional Pension Liability

The previous examples focused primarily on the computation of pension expense and the related pension liability or asset. This example deals with the recognition of an additional pension liability that may arise when the accumulated benefit obligation is greater than the fair value of the plan assets. To illustrate the recognition of the additional liability, assume the following facts for the Devon Company at the end of 1993:

Projected benefit obligation	$2,000,000
Accumulated benefit obligation	1,200,000
Plan assets (fair value)	1,000,000
Unfunded accrued pension cost	50,000

Remember that the difference between the two benefit obligations is that the *projected* benefit obligation includes assumed future pay increases whereas the *accumulated* benefit obligation is based on current pay levels. The unfunded *accumulated* benefit obligation is computed as the difference between the accumulated benefit obligation and the fair value of the plan assets as follows:

Accumulated benefit obligation	$1,200,000
Plan assets (fair value)	(1,000,000)
Unfunded accumulated benefit obligation	$ 200,000

This unfunded accumulated benefit obligation of $200,000 is the minimum liability that the company must recognize. Since the company already has recorded a liability (unfunded accrued pension cost) in the amount of $50,000, the *additional* liability of $150,000 to be recognized at the end of 1993 is calculated as follows:

Unfunded accumulated benefit obligation	$200,000
Unfunded accrued pension cost	(50,000)
Additional pension liability	$150,000

Besides recognizing the additional liability, the company also recognizes an intangible asset of an equal amount. Since no title is suggested by the FASB, we will call it Deferred Pension Cost. The intangible asset and the increase the pension liability from $50,000 to $200,000 are recorded on December 31, 1993, as follows:

Assets	=	Liabilities	+ Stockholders' Equity
+$150,000		+$150,000	

Deferred Pension Cost	Additional Pension Liability
$150,000	$150,000

On the 1993 year-end balance sheet the Devon Company reports the Deferred Pension Cost account balance of $150,000 as an intangible asset. The balances of the Additional Pension Liability and Unfunded Accrued Pension Cost are combined to report a total pension liability of $200,000 on the balance sheet. However, the additional liability must be included in the pension plan disclosures.

A different entry would be made if the preceding facts remained the same except that the company had a prepaid pension cost (asset) of $40,000 instead of the unfunded accrued pension cost (liability) of $50,000. In this case, the minimum liability must still be $200,000 but a $40,000 asset exists. Consequently, it is necessary to record a liability and an intangible asset of $240,000. The balances of the Additional Pension Liability and Prepaid Pension Cost would be combined to report a net pension liability of $200,000 on the balance sheet.

The above situations have assumed that the additional liability does not exceed the unrecognized prior service cost. In other words, it is likely that the need for the recognition of the additional liability arose because of amendments to the plan which increased the accumulated benefit obligation but have not yet been funded by the company.

Another complexity in the recognition of the additional liability occurs if it exceeds the unrecognized prior service cost. Typically, this situation arises because there have been negative returns on the plan assets. Since it would be inappropriate to record such declines in value of the plan assets as an intangible asset of the company, stockholders' equity is reduced instead. To illustrate this situation, assume the same facts as originally given for the Devon Company, but in addition the company has an unrecognized prior service cost of $120,000. The same additional liability of $150,000 must be recognized but the intangible asset cannot exceed the unrecognized prior service cost of $120,000. Therefore, the $30,000 difference is subtracted from stockholders' equity. The entry by the Devon Company is as follows:

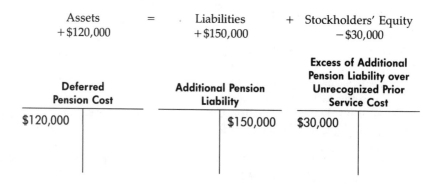

In this case, on the year-end balance sheet of the Devon Company the $120,000 balance in Deferred Pension Cost is reported as an intangible asset, the Unfunded Accrued Pension Cost of $50,000 and the Additional Pension Liability of $150,000 is combined in a single amount, and the $30,000 excess is reported in the stockholders' equity section as follows (other amounts assumed):

STOCKHOLDERS' EQUITY

Common stock	$600,000
Additional paid-in capital	230,000
Retained earnings	170,000
Excess of additional pension liability over	
unrecognized prior service cost	(30,000)
Total stockholders' equity	$970,000

It should be noted that the additional liability, the intangible asset, and the reduction in stockholders' equity are *not* amortized. The appropriate amounts are computed each year and included in the balance sheet for that year. For example, refer back to the original facts for the Devon Company. In that situation, the additional liability was recorded at $150,000 at the end of 1993. Now suppose that at the end of 1994 the following information was available:

Accumulated benefit obligation	$1,300,000
Plan assets (fair value)	1,220,000
Unfunded accrued pension cost	60,000

The unfunded accumulated benefit obligation is $80,000 ($1,300,000 − $1,220,000) and the required additional liability at the end of 1994 is $20,000 ($80,000 − $60,000). The entry on December 31, 1994, to adjust the additional liability is as follows:

Assets	=	Liabilities	+ Stockholders' Equity
−$130,000		−$130,000	

Deferred Pension Cost	Additional Pension Liability
$130,000	$130,000

This entry reduces the existing account balances of $150,000 by $130,000 to $20,000. Thus, the changes in the account balances have no effect on the income statement.

■ ADDITIONAL ISSUES

Accounting for Defined Contribution Plans

As explained earlier, some pension plans are **defined contribution plans** because the employer's contribution is determined based on a specified formula, and any future benefits paid to retired employees are limited to those that can be provided by the contributions and the earnings on those contributions. Accounting for defined contribution plans is very straightforward and is specified in *FASB Statement No. 87.*

The pension expense recorded by a company is equal to the contribution that the company is required to make in that period. Thus, the company would record Pension Expense and reduce Cash for the annual contribution. A liability is recognized only in the rare situation that the contribution for a given year has not been paid.

The company is also required to disclose the following:

1. A description of the plan including employee groups covered, the basis for determining contributions, and the nature and effect of significant matters affecting the comparability of the information for all periods presented
2. The amount of the pension expense recognized during the period

Disclosures by Funding Agencies

A company typically makes its periodic pension plan payments to a funding agency that administers the plan. A funding agency may be a specific corporate or individual trustee or an insurance company. These agencies issue financial statements that summarize the financial aspects of a company's pension plan, aimed primarily toward providing financial information about the pension plan's ability to pay benefits when due. The annual financial statements issued by a funding agency for a company's pension plan must include (1) a financial statement (on an accrual accounting basis) presenting information about the net assets (at fair value) available for benefits at the end of the plan year, (2) a financial statement presenting information about the changes during the year in the net assets available for benefits, (3) information regarding the actuarial present value of accumulated plan benefits as of either the beginning or end of the plan year, and (4) information regarding the significant effects of factors affecting the year-to-year change in the actuarial present value of accumulated plan benefits.[11] Although these funding agency financial statements are beyond the scope of this book, certain of this information must be disclosed in the notes to the financial statements of the *company* sponsoring the pension plan as discussed earlier.

Employee Retirement Income Security Act of 1974

The **Employee Retirement Income Security Act of 1974** (ERISA), alternatively known as the *Pension Reform Act of 1974*, mentioned earlier in this chapter, is based on recommendations made by various individuals and organizations. Its primary aim is to create standards for the operation and maintenance of pension

. . . .

[11]"Accounting and Reporting by Defined Benefit Pension Plans," *FASB Statement of Financial Accounting Standards No. 35* (Stamford, Conn.: FASB, 1980), par. 5 and 6.

funds in an effort to correct reported abuses in the handling of these funds. Also, it attempted to increase the protection given to employees covered by such plans. For example, at the Congressional Hearings it was revealed that some companies in which service until the age of 65 was a requirement for pension eligibility routinely followed a policy of terminating employees at ages 60 to 62, thereby greatly minimizing the company's pension liabilities and depriving these employees of pension income on their retirement.

The *Pension Reform Act of 1974* provides guidelines for employee participation in pension plans, vesting provisions, minimum funding requirements, financial statement disclosure, and the administration of the plan. In addition, the administrators of pension plans are required to file annual reports with the Department of Labor that include a description of the plan and copies of the relevant financial statements.

The Act also created the Pension Benefit Guaranty Corporation (PBGC). The purpose of the PBGC is to provide benefits to employees covered by plans that have been terminated (usually because of the bankruptcy of the sponsoring company). The PBGC receives an annual fee for every employee covered by a pension plan that is subject to the PBGC. The PBGC can also impose a lien against 30% of the net assets of the company. This lien has the status of a tax lien and therefore ranks above the claims of most other creditors. Since the company may be bankrupt, however, this lien may not result in many assets being received by the PBGC.

Pension Plan Settlements and Curtailments

In recent years, many companies have either settled (terminated) or curtailed their defined benefit pension plans. Some have settled their defined benefit pension plans and substituted defined contribution plans. Others have reduced (curtailed) the benefits to be paid to employees, while continuing the defined benefit pension plans. In each situation, the company is likely to "recapture" the excess plan assets. For example, a company may decide to terminate its pension plan and buy from an insurance company an annuity for each of its employees that provides the same expected benefits during retirement. If the plan assets exceed the costs of the annuities, the excess assets revert to the general use of the company. The net gain or loss from a settlement or curtailment is included in the net income of the period.[12]

Termination Benefits Paid to Employees

When a company wishes to reduce the size of its work force without firing employees, it may provide special benefits for a period of time in the hope of encouraging some employees to terminate voluntarily. These benefits may include

....

[12]"Employers' Accounting for Settlements and Curtailments of Defined Benefit Pension Plans and for Termination Benefits," *FASB Statement of Financial Accounting Standards No. 88* (Stamford, Conn.: FASB, 1985), par. 9–14.

lump-sum cash payments, payments over future periods, or similar induce-
ments. A company records a loss and a liability for these *termination benefits*
when the following two conditions are met:[13]

1. The employee accepts the offer.

2. The amount can be reasonably estimated.

The amount of the loss includes the amount of any lump-sum payments and
the present value of any expected future benefits.

■ APPENDIX: OTHER POSTEMPLOYMENT BENEFITS

In addition to providing pensions to their employees, many companies also offer
other postemployment benefits (OPEBs). Healthcare benefits are the most significant of these OPEBs, but some companies also provide dental benefits, eye
care, tuition assistance, life insurance, legal services, and financial advisory
services. Our discussion focuses on accounting for healthcare benefits because
they are usually the largest dollar amount, present the greatest measurement
difficulties, and are controversial.

New accounting principles have been established for OPEBs, and they are
effective in 1993. For previous years, the following disclosures are required:

1. A description of the benefits offered and the employee groups covered

2. The cost of those benefits included in net income for the period

3. A description of the accounting and funding policies

4. Any significant matters that affect comparability among periods[14]

Companies have typically accounted for OPEBs by recording the costs as
they are paid. This cash basis of accounting was accepted originally because the
liability was thought to be immaterial and because the benefits were considered
to be revocable. However, the business and societal environments have changed
in recent years.

Many healthcare plans were formulated in the 1960s after the passage of
Medicare. Companies generally agreed to pay the cost of the retired employees'
healthcare that was not covered by Medicare. At that time, these plans were not
very costly. However the costs of the plans have increased significantly in recent
years because (1) inflation in healthcare costs has significantly exceeded general
inflation, (2) Medicare reimbursements have been decreasing leaving a larger
portion to be covered by companies, (3) the number of retired employees has
increased both absolutely and relative to the number of current employees as
companies have matured and life expectancies have increased, and (4) many
companies have encouraged early retirement and their healthcare programs

....
[13] *Ibid.*, par. 15.
[14] "Disclosure of Postretirement Healthcare and Life Insurance Benefits," *FASB Statement of Financial
Accounting Standards No. 81* (Stamford, Conn.: FASB, 1984), par. 6.

cover the entire healthcare costs of the retired employees until age 65 when Medicare is available.

In reaction to these changes, in 1990 the FASB issued a *Statement* on employers' accounting for OPEBs that will be effective in 1993.[15] The objectives of this *Statement* are

1. To enhance the relevance of reported income by recognizing the cost of OPEBs over the period they are earned by employees

2. To enhance the relevance of the balance sheet by including a measure of the obligation to provide OPEBs

3. To enhance the ability of users to understand the extent and effects of an employer's promise to provide OPEBs

4. To improve the understandability and comparability of amounts reported by mandating a single method for measuring the cost and obligation

The *Statement* requires that companies accrue the cost of OPEBs during the periods in which the employees earn the benefits. That is, accounting principles require the use of the accrual basis rather than the cash basis and use principles similar to those for pensions. (The principles are discussed later.) These new accounting principles will have a dramatic impact on the financial statements of many companies. Preliminary studies have indicated that the expense of the healthcare plan for a company's retired employees may be as much as 7 times the expense recognized under the current cash basis.[16] Furthermore, estimates of the total liabilities of all U.S. companies have ranged from $169 billion to $2 trillion. Estimates of the liability for some steel companies, which average two retired employees for every active employee, range from 20% to 100% of stockholders' equity. Based on such estimates, the profits of the Fortune 100 companies may be reduced by approximately 25%. For instance, General Motors adds $600 to the cost of each car it makes to cover health costs of workers, retirees, and dependents.

These varied estimates indicate that many companies have provided OPEBs without computing the long-term costs involved. It is interesting, for example, that companies have generally refused to index pension payments because of the inflation risk involved. However, healthcare benefits are essentially indexed because companies have committed to benefits in terms of *services* rather than to a specific dollar amount for those services. Also healthcare benefits are surprisingly egalitarian, because they are usually *not* based on length of service or salary, but rather on some minimum length of service after which the same benefits are provided equally to every employee.

Since pensions and OPEBs are both postemployment benefits, it is logical to consider their similarities and differences in developing accounting principles for OPEBs.

....

[15]"Employers' Accounting for Postretirement Benefits Other Than Pensions," *FASB Statement of Financial Accounting Standards No. 106* (Norwalk, Conn.: FASB, 1990).

[16]M. Akresh, B. Bald, and H. Danker, *Retiree Health Benefits: Field Test of the FASB Proposal* (Morristown, N.J., 1988: Financial Executives Research Foundation).

Similarities To and Differences From Pensions

The basic argument that accounting for OPEBs should be similar to the principles used for pensions involves the concept of a liability. As discussed in Chapter 1, a liability is a "probable future sacrifice of economic benefits arising from present obligations of a particular entity to transfer assets or provide services to other entities in the future as a result of past transactions or events."[17] The term "obligations" encompasses more than "legal obligations." It not only includes legal duties defined in a contract, but also equitable and constructive obligations based on promises or moral responsibility.

Many OPEBs do not have the same explicit legal contract as a pension agreement, and the obligation of the company to continue to provide benefits is not as clear. Some people argue there is no liability because the company has the right to withdraw the benefits. However, recent court decisions have not allowed companies to withdraw rights from retired employees, and there are indications that it may be difficult to withdraw rights already earned by current employees. The concept of a liability, therefore, appears to have been satisfied.

However, if a liability does exist prior to employees' retirement, it can be argued that a liability only exists when employees become eligible for the benefits. OPEB plans typically specify a minimum number of years of active service before the employees are eligible for the benefits. Vesting for these plans is called "cliff" vesting because vesting occurs when the requirements are met and not gradually over a period of years.

Another argument is that a company offering OPEBs is essentially providing deferred compensation to employees because the benefits received during retirement were earned during the period of employment. The company, therefore, incurs an obligation as its employees provide services. The new accounting principles follow this viewpoint.

The major differences between OPEBs and pensions are summarized in Exhibit 9–11, with the focus on the exhibit being healthcare benefits. While the beneficiary of a pension plan is generally the retired employee, OPEBs are often provided to the retired employee, spouse, and dependents up to age 21. The pension benefit is defined as a fixed dollar amount that is paid monthly. The OPEB, however, is usually not limited in amount because benefits are paid no matter how long or serious the illness and are paid as used, with the amount varying geographically. Also, an estimation of the amount is difficult because it is necessary to predict the future cost of healthcare including the impacts of new illnesses, such as AIDS, and new treatments. Finally, while pension plans are funded with the contributions tax deductible, OPEBs are generally not funded because there are no legal requirements for them and the contributions are *not* tax deductible.

New Accounting Principles

The new accounting principles require that companies follow procedures for OPEBs that closely parallel those for pensions. (It is assumed that the reader

- - - - - - - - - - - - - - - - - - - -

[17]*FASB Statement of Financial Accounting Concepts No. 6*, (Stamford, Conn.: FASB, 1985).

EXHIBIT 9-11 Major differences between postretirement healthcare benefits and pensions

Item	Pensions	Healthcare
Beneficiary	Retired employee (some residual benefit to surviving spouse)	Retired employee, spouse, and dependents
Benefit	Defined, fixed dollar amount, paid monthly	Not limited, paid as used, varies geographically
Funding	Funding legally required and tax deductible	Usually not funded because not legally required and not tax deductible

has studied the discussion of accounting for pensions so that the explanation in this section may be simplified. Also, it may be helpful to review those principles as the OPEB principles are discussed.)

Before discussing the accounting for OPEBs, two concepts need to be understood. The **expected postretirement benefit obligation** is the actuarial present value on a particular date of the benefits expected to be paid under the terms of the postretirement benefit plan. The amount is measured based on the benefits that employees will receive after their expected retirement dates. The **accumulated postretirement benefit obligation** is the actuarial present value of the benefits attributed to employee service rendered to a specific date. Prior to an employee's full eligibility date, the accumulated postretirement benefit obligation is the portion of the expected postretirement benefit obligation attributed to that employee's service rendered to that date; on or after the full eligibility date, the accumulated and expected postretirement benefit obligations for an employee are the same. Thus the difference between the expected and accumulated postretirement benefit obligation is that the accumulated amount is based on benefits earned to date, whereas the expected amount is based on all benefits expected to be paid to employees. In contrast, the difference between the projected and accumulated benefit obligation for pensions is the inclusion of expected salary increases in the projected amount.

OPEB Expense

The net postretirement benefit expense[18] includes the following components:

1. **Service Cost. The service cost is the actuarial present value of the expected postretirement benefit obligation attributed to services rendered by the employees during the current period.** The discount (interest) rate used to

. . . .

[18]The FASB prefers this term to the more commonly used term, OPEB, because other benefits such as layoff benefits may be paid after employment but before retirement.

calculate the service cost is the rate of return on high-quality fixed-income investments.

2. **Interest Cost. The interest cost is the increase in the accumulated post-retirement benefit obligation due to the passage of time.** Since the OPEB is a deferred compensation plan in which future payments are discounted to their present values, interest accrues because of the passage of time. Thus, the interest cost is the accumulated postretirement benefit obligation at the beginning of the period multiplied by the discount rate. The interest rate used to calculate the accumulated postretirement benefit obligation is the same rate as used for the service cost. The interest cost is added in the computation of the postretirement benefit expense.

3. **Actual Return on Plan Assets. The actual return on plan assets is the difference between the fair value of the plan assets at the end of the period and the fair value at the beginning of the period, adjusted for contributions by the company and payments of benefits to retired employees during the period.** Since OPEBs usually have *not* been funded, this component is not discussed further.

4. **Amortization of Unrecognized Prior Service Cost and Net Gain or Loss.** The prior service cost is the increase in the accumulated postretirement benefit obligation that results from plan amendments (and at the initiation of the plan) and that is not recognized in total in the period granted. **The unrecognized prior service cost is amortized by assigning an equal amount to each remaining year of service until full eligibility for benefits is reached for each plan participant active at the date of amendment.** Straight-line amortization over the average remaining years of service to full eligibility is also allowed for simplicity. The amortization amount is added in the computation of the postretirement benefit expense.

   The computation of the gain or loss is very complex and beyond the scope of this book. The gain or loss may be recognized in the period in which it occurs or amortized over future periods in a manner similar to the prior service cost.

5. **Recognition of the Obligation Existing at the Date of the Initial Adoption of the *Statement*.** The obligation is known as the **transition obligation** and is equal to the accumulated postretirement benefit obligation (less the fair value of the plan assets which are assumed to be zero). The transition obligation is either recognized in full in the year in which the *statement* is adopted or recognition is delayed and the unrecognized transition obligation is amortized on a straight-line basis over the average remaining service life of active plan participants or 20 years, whichever is greater. The amount of the transition obligation recognized in any year is added in the computation of the postretirement benefit expense.

OPEB Liability or Asset

The new accounting principles also address the calculation of the OPEB liability or asset because the amount of the net postretirement benefit expense to date may be different than the amount funded to date. Since the plan is usually not funded, a liability, **unfunded accrued postretirement benefit cost**, would be increased each period by an amount equal to the expense. It would, of course, be decreased by payments made to retired employees. However, in contrast to accounting for pensions, there is *no* provision for recognizing an **additional liability.**

Transition

Adoption of the *Statement* is required for fiscal years beginning after December 15, 1992.

Disclosures

The *Statement* provides for disclosures that are very similar to those for pensions. Some key differences are discussed later.

Differences from Accounting for Pensions

It can be seen from the preceding discussion that the accounting principles for OPEBs closely parallel the accounting for pensions. The major differences are:

1. There is no provision for recognizing a minimum liability for OPEBs and the related intangible asset.
2. The interest component of the net postretirement benefit expense is based on the accumulated postretirement benefit obligation whereas the interest component of the pension expense is based on the projected benefit obligation.
3. Two additonal disclosures are required:
   a. the amortization of the transition obligation, if any, and
   b. the effect of a 1% increase in the healthcare cost trend rate on the measurement of the accumulated postretirement benefit obligation and on the combined service and interest cost components of the postretirement benefit expense.

■ ILLUSTRATION OF ACCOUNTING FOR OPEBs

To illustrate the basic principles for OPEBs, the following simplified example is used. Assume that the Livingston Company has been using the cash basis of accounting and adopts the requirements for accruing the cost of its healthcare plan for retired employees on January 1, 1992. At that time the company has two employees and one retired employee as shown in Exhibit 9–12. Based on the information in the exhibit, the company records the following expense and liability at the end of 1992:

EXHIBIT 9–12

·················

LIVINGSTON COMPANY
Accrual of Postretirement Healthcare Benefits

BASIC INFORMATION

The plan is not funded
The discount rate is 10%
All employees were hired at age 25
All employees become eligible for full benefits at age 55
Employee C was paid $1,500 postretirement healthcare benefits in 1992
The company chooses to amortize the transition obligation
Additional information on January 1, 1992:

Employee	Status	Age	Expected Retirement Age	Expected Postretirement Benefit Obligation[a]	Accumulated Postretirement Benefit Obligation
A	Employee	40	65	$ 30,000	$ 15,000[a]
B	Employee	60	65	60,000	60,000[b]
C	Retired	70	—	25,000	25,000[b]
				$115,000	$100,000[c]

[a]Actuarially determined at January 1, 1992.
[b]Expected and accumulated postretirement benefit obligations are equal because employees are past the date for full eligibility which occurred at age 55.
[c]The transition amount (because there are no plan assets).

COMPUTATION OF POSTRETIREMENT BENEFIT EXPENSE FOR 1992

1. Service Cost	$ 1,100[a]
2. Interest cost	10,000[b]
3. Actual return on plan assets	0
4. Amortization of unrecognized prior service cost and gain or loss	0
5. Amortization of transition obligation	5,000[c]
	$16,100

[a]Actuarially determined. Note that there is no service cost for B and C because they have passed the date for full eligibility.
[b]Accumulated postretirement benefit obligation at January 1, 1992 × discount rate, or $100,000 × 10%.
[c]$100,000 ÷ 20, or $5,000. Employees A, B, and C have 25, 5, and 0 years remaining service, respectively. Therefore, the average remaining service period is (25 + 5) ÷ 3 = 10 years. The company uses the alternative 20-year period.

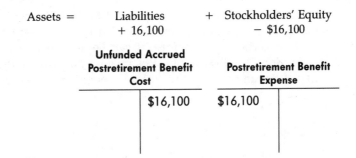

The company also records the payments of retirement benefits as follows:

Assets	=	Liabilities	+ Stockholders' Equity
− $1,500		− $1,500	

Cash		Unfunded Accrued Postretirement Benefit Cost	
	$1,500	$1,500	

■ ACCOUNTING FOR OPEBs: AN EVALUATION

Since the new principles are based on accrual accounting, little controversy over the issue might be expected. However, several aspects have been questioned by critics.

Relevance and Reliability

It can easily be argued that accrual accounting is more *relevant* than cash basis accounting because costs are matched as expenses against revenues in the period in which the benefits are earned. For OPEBs the benefits are earned while the employee is working, not when retired. Some have argued, however, that OPEB costs cannot be measured with sufficient *reliability* to offset the increased relevance because of the numerous assumptions about future events that are required. The measurement of the various amounts used in accounting for OPEBs are even more difficult than for pensions. For example, healthcare plans agree to pay some or all of the cost of a service, the amount and cost of which are unknown, whereas pension payments are tied to more predictable variables of length of service and pay levels. Also healthcare plans require an estimate of such items as the medical cost trend rate and marital and dependency status during retirement.

Those who favor the new principles argue that knowledge of these costs is essential for rational decision making by management and that accounting includes many estimates. Also, they argue that this OPEB cost information is useful for lending and investment decisions of users and that such decisions are never based on certainty. Therefore, it can be argued that it is better to record the information based on the best estimates and provide disclosures of the subjectivity of the amounts, rather than to report only cash payments.

Differences in Funding

There are few differences between pension and OPEB accounting. However, there will be some differences in the practical impacts because the OPEB plans are generally not funded. Suppose for example that one company has an unfunded OPEB plan that is expected to provide exactly the same cash payments to retired employees as a funded pension plan of another company. The expense for the OPEB would be higher because the actual return on plan assets is not subtracted. It can, of course, be argued that this difference is appropriate because the company with the unfunded OPEB will have to pay more assets in the future whereas the company with the pension plan has already paid the assets into a fund which is earning a return on those assets.

Transition Obligation

The principles require that the transition obligation be recognized either immediately or prospectively over 20 years. Some argue that a period longer than 20 years should be used in order to reduce the impact on company income statements.

Interaction with Deferred Income Taxes

Recognizing a postretirement benefit expense for financial reporting without a related deduction for income tax reporting will create a temporary difference. Because the tax deduction will occur in the periods when the benefits are paid which will often be beyond the 15-year carryforward period, a deferred tax benefit (asset) will usually not be recognized for the full amount of the current period expense.

Minimum Liability

As discussed earlier, there is no requirement to recognize a minimum liability for OPEBs in contrast to the accounting for pensions. The FASB decided that a minimum liability was not required because users would obtain sufficient information from the disclosures. Also, it may be argued that the only liability is the difference between the expense and the funding if the company has no legal obligation to pay postretirement benefits. Therefore recognition of the minimum liability would be inappropriate. Also, the corresponding intangible asset is conceptually questionable and may not be properly understood by users. However, it may also be argued that the difference between accounting for pensions and OPEBs is undesirable because the same concept is accounted for in the financial statements for pensions and by disclosure for OPEBs. The requirement to recognize the minimum liability for pensions was based on the belief that most pension plans were adequately funded. The purpose of the minimum liability provision is to identify those relatively rare situations in which the plan is significantly underfunded. In contrast, virtually all OPEB plans are significantly underfunded and recognition of a minimum liability would not serve to identify exceptions. Instead, information about the funded status is provided in the notes to the financial statements.

Social Impacts

While accounting for OPEBs, as required by the new principles, will have a significant impact on the income statement, balance sheet, and related notes, it has no impact on the cash flow statement. Even in the absence of a cash flow impact there are some potential social impacts. Although the accounting issues and their impacts on the financial statements are important, the ability of companies to fulfill their obligations under existing plans is more important. The required computations should help in understanding the OPEB commitments and the ability of companies to pay them.

It is possible that when companies understand the full costs of their commitments, they may decide to curtail the benefits. Although this action may appear to be undesirable, surely it is preferable that companies curtail the benefits now rather than declare bankruptcy in the future because of an inability to pay costs that have not been recognized.

It is also likely that companies will exert pressure on Congress to allow the funding of OPEB plans to be tax deductible, but they will probably not be successful in the current situation of federal budget deficits. Some people may also argue that the new principles will place U.S. companies at a competitive disadvantage with foreign companies.

A qualitative characteristic of accounting information is *neutrality*. Accounting information is not intended to encourage or discourage particular decisions such as the offering of OPEBs, their funding, their tax deductibility, or their impacts on foreign trade. Instead, its purpose is to provide useful information for those types of decisions. Accrual accounting does not change the nature and extent of the OPEB promise. However, it will require companies to report the effects of their commitments on the financial statements.

There will be a cost of implementing the accounting principles for OPEBs. Whether the benefits exceed the costs will, of course, never be known with certainty. However, the FASB, many accountants, many users of financial statements, and many company executives believe that benefits will exceed costs.

QUESTIONS

••

1. List seven advantages for the lessee of leasing as compared with purchasing an asset.

2. Define a lease. Under what conditions is a lease considered a capital lease? An operating lease?

3. Describe briefly the accounting procedures followed by the lessor and by the lessee for an operating lease.

4. Describe briefly the procedures followed by the lessee to account for a capital lease.

5. If there is a capital lease for a building, does the lessee or the lessor include the building and amortization (depreciation) expense in its financial statements?

6. If there is a capital lease, how does the lessee compute its interest expense? How does the lessor compute its interest revenue? How does the lessee compute the reduction in its liability? How does the lessor compute the reduction in its receivable?

7. Assume that a lessee leases equipment and insists on terms that qualify it as an operating lease, barely escaping the qualification as a capital lease. Discuss the impact that such an operating lease will have on financial statements and related financial information as compared to the effect that a capital lease would have.

8. The Owens Company leased equipment for four years at $50,000 a month, with an option to renew the lease for six years at $2,000 per month or to purchase the equipment for $25,000 (a price considerably less than the expected fair market value) after the initial lease term of four years. How should this transaction be recorded in the accounts of the Owens Company?

9. McFarland Corporation leased equipment under a lease calling for the payment of $50,000 a year in rent. At the end of the current year, when the capital lease had a remaining term of 20 years, McFarland Corporation subleased the asset for a rental of $75,000 a year for 20 years. The new lease is acceptable to the lessor, who agrees that McFarland Corporation has completed its primary obligation. When will

the gain from this transaction be reported by McFarland Corporation? Explain.

10. What is off-balance sheet financing? Why do some companies find such financing attractive?

11. How does a temporary difference occur? If a company's MACRS depreciation is greater than its straight-line depreciation, describe the differences between the company's financial statements and income tax calculations.

12. Where are deferred income taxes disclosed on a company's financial statements? Why do some accountants disagree with this disclosure?

13. Distinguish between the objectives of financial reporting and the Internal Revenue Code.

14. Identify the five groups of possible differences between pretax accounting income and taxable income (or between income tax expense and income taxes payable).

15. What is a permanent difference? Give two examples.

16. What is a temporary difference? Give two examples.

17. Describe an operating loss carryback. Describe an operating loss carryforward.

18. What is a pension plan? Explain how yearly income of retired employees is determined under a defined benefit pension plan.

19. Distinguish between a defined benefit pension plan and a defined contribution pension plan.

20. Distinguish between funded and unfunded pension plans; between contributory and noncontributory pension plans.

21. What is service cost? How does this differ from prior service cost?

22. Define projected benefit obligation. How does this differ from an accumulated benefit obligation?

23. List and briefly define the components of pension expense.

24. What is an unfunded accrued pension cost and when does it arise? What is a prepaid pension cost and when does it arise?

25. When would an additional pension liability be recorded for a pension plan?

26. List the additional disclosures a company must make for its defined benefit pension plan.

27. What are the similarities and differences between pensions and other postemployment benefits?

PROBLEMS AND CASES
. . . .

28. Expense and Income from Capital Lease. On January 1, 1993, the Thompson Company leased a computer from the Hexad Company. The lease was a capital lease, and the asset and liability were recorded by the Thompson Company at $96,000 based on a 10% interest rate and a 12-year life. The lease payment of $14,089 is made at the end of each year. The company uses the straight-line amortization (depreciation) method for the leased asset and no residual value is expected.

Required **1.** Compute the interest expense for the Thompson Company.

2. Compute the annual amortization expense.

29. Capital Lease—Lessee. On January 1, 1993, the Eton Company leased a Rolls Royce from Elite Cars for the president's use. The lease specified that $25,000 was to be paid at the end of each year for five years. The lease was classified as a capital lease. The interest rate is 12%. The straight-line amortization (depreciation) method and a zero residual value are used.

Required **1.** Show how the leased asset would be reported on the balance sheet of the Eton Company at December 31, 1993.

2. What is the amount of the liability on the balance sheet of the Eton Company at December 31, 1993?

30. Operating Lease—Lessee and Lessor. On January 1, 1993, the Meyers Company leased a jet from the Harris Aviation Company. The jet cost the Harris Aviation Company $500,000 to build. The company uses the straight-line amortization (depreciation) method with an estimated life of ten years and an estimated residual value of $50,000. The lease is for seven years and requires a payment of $155,000 on December 31 each year. The lease is classified as an operating lease.

Required **1.** Record the effects on the accounting equation of the lease for the Meyers Company during 1993.

2. Prepare a partial income statement for 1993 for the Meyers Company.

3. Record the effects on the accounting equation of the lease for the Harris Aviation Company during 1993.

4. Prepare a partial income statement for 1993 and a partial balance sheet at December 31, 1993, for the Harris Aviation Company.

31. Capital Lease—Lessee. On January 1, 1993, the Ventrello Company leased a jet from the Cate Aviation Company. The lease is for six years and requires a payment of $230,000 on December 31 each year. The lease is classified as a capital lease and the interest rate is 12%. The company uses the straight-line amortization (depreciation) method and no residual value is expected.

Required 1. Record the effects on the accounting equation of the lease for the Ventrello Company during 1993.

   2. Prepare a partial income statement for 1993 and a partial balance sheet at December 31, 1993, for the Ventrello Company in regard to the lease.

32. Capital Lease—Lessor. Use the information in Problem 31. The jet cost the Cate Aviation Company $450,000 to build.

Required 1. Record the effects on the accounting equation of the lease for the Cate Aviation Company during 1993.

   2. Prepare a partial income statement for 1993 and a partial balance sheet at December 31, 1993, for the Cate Aviation Company in regard to the lease.

33. Capital Lease—Lessee. On January 1, 1993, the Odoms Company leased a building from the Weese Development Company. The lease is for 20 years and requires a payment of $12,000 on December 31 of each year. An interest rate of 10% is used and the lease is classified as a capital lease. The company uses the straight-line amortization (depreciation) method and no residual value is expected.

Required 1. Record the effects on the accounting equation of the lease for the Odoms Company during 1993.

   2. Prepare a partial income statement for 1993 and a partial balance sheet at December 31, 1993, for the Odoms Company relating to the lease, including current and noncurrent amounts.

34. Capital Lease—Lessor. Use the information in Problem 33. The building cost the Weese Development Company $60,000 to construct.

Required 1. Record the effects on the accounting equation of the lease for the Weese Development Company during 1993.

   2. Prepare a partial income statement for 1993 and a partial balance sheet at December 31, 1993, for the Weese Development Company relating to the lease, including current and noncurrent amounts.

35. Determining Type of Lease and Subsequent Accounting. On January 1, 1993, the Caswell Company signs a ten-year agreement to lease a storage building from the Wake Company. The following information pertains to this lease agreement:

   1. The agreement requires rental payments of $100,000 at the end of each year.

   2. The fair value of the building on January 1, 1993, is $2 million.

   3. The building has an estimated economic life of 50 years, with no residual value. The Caswell Company depreciates similar buildings according to the straight-line method.

   4. The lease does not contain a renewable option clause. At the termination of the lease, the building reverts to the lessor.

   5. The interest rate is 14% per year.

Required Determine if the lease is an operating or capital lease and record the effects on the accounting equation of the signing of the lease agreement and the payments and expenses related to this lease for the years 1993 and 1994.

36. Lessee Accounting Issues. The Sax Corporation signs a lease agreement dated January 1, 1993, that provides for it to lease computers from the Appleton Corporation beginning January 1, 1993. The lease terms, provisions, and related events are as follows:

1. The lease term is five years; the lease is noncancelable and requires equal rental payments to be made at the end of each year.

2. The cost, and also fair value, of the computers to Appleton at the inception of the lease is $500,000; the computers have an estimated life of five years and have a zero estimated residual value at the end of this time.

3. The lease contains no renewal or bargain purchase option.

4. The annual rental is set by Appleton on the basis of an interest rate of 14%.

5. Sax Corporation uses the straight-line method to record depreciation on similar equipment.

Required Determine if the lease is an operating or capital lease and:

1. Calculate the amount of the equal rental payments.

2. Prepare a table summarizing the lease payments and interest expense.

3. Record the effects on the accounting equation of the lease for the Sax Corporation for the years 1993 and 1994.

37. Lessor Accounting Issues. The Rexon Corporation leases equipment to Ten-Care Corporation beginning January 1, 1993. The lease terms, provisions, and related events are as follows:

1. The lease term is eight years; the lease is noncancelable and requires equal rental payments to be made at the end of each year.

2. The cost, and also fair value, of the equipment is $600,000; the equipment has an estimated life of eight years and has a zero estimated value at the end of that time.

3. The lease contains no renewal or bargain purchase option.

4. The interest rate implicit in the lease is 14%.

5. The collectibility of the rentals is reasonably assured, and there are no important uncertainties surrounding the amount of unreimbursable costs yet to be incurred by the lessor.

Required 1. Calculate the amount of the equal rental receipts.

2. Prepare a table summarizing the lease receipts and interest revenue earned by Rexon.

3. Record the effects on the accounting equation of the lease for Rexon for the years 1993 and 1994.

38. Lessor Accounting Issues. Ramallah Corporation leases heavy equipment to Terrell, Inc., on January 2, 1993, on the following terms:

1. Forty-eight lease rentals of $2,000 at the end of each month are to be paid by Terrell, Inc.

2. The cost of the heavy equipment to Ramallah Corporation was $75,948.

3. The difference between total rental receipts ($2,000 × 48 = $96,000) and the cost of the equipment ($75,948) was computed to yield a return of 1% per month over the lease term.

4. The collectibility of the rentals is reasonably assured, and there are no important uncertainties surrounding the amount of unreimbursable costs yet to be incurred by the lessor.

Required Record the effects on the accounting equation of the lease for the Ramallah Corporation (the lessor) to record the lease contract and the receipt of the first lease rental on January 31, 1993. Record the interest earned during the first month and carry calculations to the nearest dollar.

39. **Lessor Accounting.** The Berne Corporation, the lessor, enters into a lease with Fox Corporation to lease equipment to Fox beginning January 1, 1993. The lease terms, provisions, and related events are as follows:

1. The lease term is four years; the lease is noncancelable and requires annual rental payments of $90,000 to be made at the end of each year.

2. The cost of the equipment is $200,000; the equipment has an estimated life of four years and an estimated residual value at the end of the lease term of zero.

3. The interest rate implicit in the lease is 16%.

4. The collectibility of the rentals is reasonably assured, and there are no important uncertainties surrounding the amount of unreimbursable costs yet to be incurred by the lessor.

Required 1. Calculate the selling price and assume that this is also the fair value.

2. Prepare a table summarizing the lease receipts and interest revenue earned by the lessor.

3. Record the effects on the accounting equation of the lease for the Berne Corporation, the lessor, for the years 1993 and 1994.

40. **Lease Income and Expense.** Reuben Company retires a machine from active use on January 2, 1993, for the express purpose of leasing it. The machine had a carrying value of $900,000 after 12 years of use and is expected to have 10 more years of economic life. The machine is depreciated on a straight-line basis. On March 1, 1993, Reuben Company leases the machine to Owens Company for $180,000 a year for a five-year period ending February 28, 1998. Under the provisions of the lease, Reuben Company incurs total maintenance and other related costs of $20,000 relating to the year ended December 31, 1993. Owens Company pays $180,000 to Reuben Company on March 1, 1993. The lease was properly classified as an operating lease.

Required 1. Compute the income before income taxes derived by Reuben Company from this lease for the calendar year ended December 31, 1993.

2. Compute the amount of rent expense incurred by Owens Company from this lease for the calendar year ended December 31, 1993.

41. **Leases and Subsequent Accounting.** The Ravis Rent-A-Car Company leases a car to Ira Reem, an employee, on January 1, 1993. The term of the noncancelable lease is four years. The following information about the lease is provided:

1. Title to the car passes to Ira Reem upon the termination of the lease with no additional payment required by the lessee.

2. The cost and fair value of the car to the Ravis Rent-A-Car Company is $8,400. The car has an economic life of five years.

3. The lease payments are determined at an amount that will yield Ravis Rent-A-Car Company a rate of return of 14% on its net investment.

4. Collectibility of the lease payments is reasonably assured.

5. There are no important uncertainties surrounding the amount of unreimbursable costs yet to be incurred by the lessor.

6. Equal annual lease payments are due at the end of each year.

Required 1. Prepare a table summarizing the lease receipts and interest revenue earned by the Ravis Rent-A-Car Company for the four-year lease term.

2. Record the effects on the accounting equation for 1993 and 1994 of the lease agreement, the lease receipts, and the recognition of income for Ravis Rent-A-Car Company.

42. Leasing. The Byrne Company is planning to acquire some office machinery. It is considering three different methods of acquiring the machinery, which has a six-year life and no residual value.

1. Buy the machinery for $100,000, pay $20,000 down, and borrow the balance from a bank at 10% for six years. Interest is to be paid on December 31 each year.

2. Lease the machinery under a six-year lease, which would be classified as a capital lease. The lease would require a payment of $30,000 at the end of each year. There is no option to buy the machinery included in the lease.

3. Lease the machinery under a one-year lease, which would be classified as an operating lease. The company intends to renew the lease each year for six years. The lease payment, which is due when the lease is signed, is $30,000.

Required 1. Prepare an analysis (using assumptions that you think are appropriate) of the cash flows the company would pay over the six years under each alternative.

2. Explain how each of the alternatives would affect the financial statements.

3. Which alternative would you recommend?

43. Various Lease Issues. McClain Transfer contracts with manufacturers of consumer goods to provide delivery services throughout the United States. In order to serve so large an area, McClain must operate 100 tractor-trailer units. In the past, instead of buying the trailers outright, McClain leased them under the following terms:

1. Payments of $81,739 were due at the end of each year, starting in the year of the lease, for ten years.

2. A bargain purchase option on the trailers at the end of the tenth year for $1,000 was included. Estimated economic life of the trailers is 15 years.

Prior to *FASB Statement No. 13*, McClain simply treated the lease payments as an operating expense and did not capitalize the lease until the bargain purchase option was exercised. With the adoption of *FASB Statement No. 13*, McClain must now capitalize the lease at its present value and record the resultant liability. The president of McClain is quite upset about this requirement, because the company's debt/equity ratio, current ratio (part of the liability is current), and return on investment will all be less favorable. During 1993, 100 trailers were leased under the above terms, with an interest rate of 14%. At December 31, 1993, McClain's balance sheet shows Leased Equipment—Net of $2,800,000 and Obligations Under Leases of $2,806,718. When the president sees these figures, he is infuriated and will not accept the fact that the carrying value of the liability exceeds the carrying value of the asset.

Required   1. How is it possible that the carrying value of the liability exceeds the carrying value of the asset at the end of the first year of the lease? Discuss fully.

2. What simple restructuring of the payments will avoid this situation?

44. Disclosure of Leases and Related Issues. United Manufacturing Company manufactures and leases computers to its customers. During 1993, the following lease transaction takes place: On January 1, a computer is leased to Superior Microelectronics Industries and is guaranteed by United against obsolescence. The present value of the lease payments is greater than 90% of the fair market value of the computer to both United and Superior.

Required   On whose financial statements will the computer leased in the transaction be shown?

45. Sale–Leaseback. On January 1, 1993, the Stimpson Company sells land to the Barker Company for $2.5 million and leases it back. The land had cost Stimpson $2 million. The lease is a capital lease and has a term of 25 years.

Required   Compute the effects of the above events on the accounting equation during 1993.

46. Sale–Leaseback. On January 1, 1993, the Orr Company sells a building to the Foible Company for $3 million and leases it back. The building had cost Orr $2.1 million and had a book value of $1.7 million. The lease is a capital lease and has a term of ten years.

Required   Compute the effects of the above events on the accounting equation during 1993.

47. Single Temporary Difference. At the end of 1993, Holden Company reported taxable income of $9,000 and pretax financial income of $10,600. The difference is due to depreciation for tax purposes in excess of depreciation for financial reporting purposes. The income tax rate for the current year is 35%, but Congress has enacted tax rates of 32% for 1994 and 30% for 1995 and beyond.

Holden Company has calculated the excess of its financial depreciation over its tax depreciation for future years as follows: 1994, $600; 1995, $700; and 1996, $300. Prior to 1993, the company had no deferred tax liability or asset.

Required   Compute the effects on the accounting equation at the end of 1993.

48. Temporary Difference. At the end of 1993, Durn Company reported taxable income of $9,800 and pretax financial income of $12,500, due to a single temporary difference. The income tax rate for the current year is 30%, but Congress has enacted a 40% tax rate for 1994 and beyond.

Because of this one temporary difference, the Durn Company has calculated that its future taxable income will exceed its pretax financial income by the following amounts in the years 1994 through 1997:

1994	$1,000
1995	800
1996	600
1997	300

Required Compute the effects on the accounting equation at the end of 1993.

49. Multiple Temporary Differences. Wilcox Company has prepared the following reconciliation of its pretax financial income with its taxable income for 1993:

Pretax financial income	$4,650
Add: estimated warranty expense deducted for financial reporting in excess of actual warranty costs deducted for income taxes	100
Less: additional accelerated depreciation deducted for income taxes	(1,800)
Taxable income	$2,950

The current tax rate is 30%, and no change in the tax rate has been enacted for future years. The company anticipates that actual warranty costs will exceed estimated warranty expense and that financial depreciation will exceed tax depreciation by the following amounts for the years 1994 through 1966:

	Difference in Warranty Amounts[a]	Difference in Depreciation Amounts[b]
1994	$50	$ 300
1995	30	300
1996	20	1,200

[a]Tax warranty cost in excess of financial warranty expense
[b]Financial depreciation in excess of tax depreciation

Required Compute the effects on the accounting equation at the end of 1993.

50. Multiple Temporary Difference. Vickers Company reports taxable income of $4,500 for 1993. The company has two temporary differences between pretax financial income and taxable income. The first difference is expected to result in taxable amounts as follows: 1994, $820; 1995, $900; 1996, $500; 1997, $250. The second difference is expected to result in deductible amounts as follows: 1994, $600; 1995, $460; 1996, $300. The company has a deferred tax liability of $369 at the beginning of 1993. The current tax rate is 30%, and no change in the tax rate has been enacted for future years.

Required Compute the effects on the accounting equation at the end of 1993. Do not separate the deferred income taxes into current and noncurrent components.

51. Net Deduction Carryback. Magner Company reports taxable income of $8,300 for 1993. The company has two temporary differences between pretax financial income and taxable income. The first difference is due to the use of MACRS depreciation for income taxes and units-of-production depreciation for financial reporting. In future years, it estimates that financial deprecation will exceed tax depreciation by the following amounts:

1994	$1,200
1995	1,500
1996	1,800
1997	2,100

For the second difference, the company expects to have a tax deduction of $5,400 in 1997 for an expense that it estimated and deducted from pretax financial income in 1993. The company had a deferred tax liability of $210 at the beginning of 1993. The current tax rate is 30%, and no change in the tax rate has been enacted for future years.

Required Compute the effects on the accounting equation at the end of 1993. Do not separate the deferred income taxes into current and noncurrent components.

52. **Net Deduction Carryback and Carryforward.** In 1993 and prior years, the Grant Company used the accrual method to recognize gross profit for financial reporting and the installment method to recognize gross profit for income taxes. As a result, in future years it estimates that the gross profit recognized for income tax purposes will exceed the gross profit recognized for financial reporting by the following amounts:

1994	$ 600
1995	900
1996	1,500
1997	2,000
1998	2,500

In 1993, the company also recorded estimated legal expense (and a related liability) of $6,200 for financial reporting. It expects to pay this liability in 1997. At that time the company will deduct the payment from its taxable income. The company is subject a current tax rate of 30%; no change in the tax rate has been enacted for future years. The company's taxable income for 1993 is $10,000 and it has a deferred income tax balance at the beginning of the year of $2,250.

Required Compute the effects on the accounting equation at the end of 1993. Do not separate the deferred income taxes into current and noncurrent components.

53. **Deferred Tax Asset.** In 1993, its first year of operations, the Sallee Company reports taxable income of $8,000, but a pretax financial loss of $1,200, because of two temporary differences. The first difference is the result of $13,600 tax depreciation in excess of financial depreciation. Consequently, in future years financial depreciation is expected to be greater than tax depreciation by the following amounts: 1994, $3,000; 1995, $3,200; 1996, $3,500; 1997, $3,900.

The second difference is due to a $22,800 estimated expense deducted for financial reporting but not for income taxes. The expense is expected to be deducted from taxable income when it is paid in 1996. The company is subject to a current tax rate of 30%; no change in the tax rate has been enacted for future years.

Required 1. What is the net operating loss carryforward (if any) for financial reporting purposes at the end of 1993?

2. Compute the effects on the accounting equation at the end of 1993. Do not separate the deferred income taxes into current and noncurrent components.

54. Deferred Tax Asset and Liability. Wicks Company began operations on January 1, 1993. At the end of 1993, the company reported taxable income of $7,800. To determine its deferred taxes, the company prepared the following schedule of expected future taxable and deductible amounts:

	1994	1995	1996	1997
Taxable amounts	$2,900	$2,200	$ 2,600	$2,100
Deductible amount			(15,500)	

The current income tax rate is 30%, and no change in the tax rate has been enacted for future years.

Required Compute the effects on the accounting equation at the end of 1993.

55. Interperiod Tax Allocation. Klerk Company has four temporary differences between its pretax financial income and its taxable income, as follows:

1. Gross profit on certain installment sales is recognized under the accrual method for financial reporting and under the installment method for income taxes.

2. MACRS depreciation is used for income taxes; a different depreciation method is used for financial reporting.

3. Rent receipts are included in taxable income when collected in advance; rent revenue is recognized under the accrual method for financial reporting.

4. Warranty expense is estimated for financial reporting; warranty costs are deducted as incurred for income taxes.

The company earned taxable income of $260,000 for 1993. The company has prepared the following schedule to determine the future taxable and deductible amounts at the end of 1993 for its four temporary differences:

Year	Taxable Amounts #1	#2	Deductible Amounts #3	#4
1994	$20,500	$50,000	$11,000	$14,700
1995	20,000	59,000	11,000	14,200
1996	19,100	65,000	—	13,600
1997	18,300	67,000	—	12,800

The income tax rate for the current year is 40%, but Congress has enacted a 30% tax rate for future years.

Required 1. Compute the effects on the accounting equation at the end of 1993.

2. Show the income tax disclosures on Klerk Company's December 31, 1993, balance sheet.

56. Comprehensive: Deferred Tax Asset and Liability. Gire Company began operations at the beginning of 1993, at which time it purchased a depreciable asset for $60,000. For 1993 through 1996 the asset was depreciated on the straight-line basis over a four-year life (no residual value) for financial reporting. For income tax purposes, the asset was depreciated using MACRS over a three-year life.

For 1993 through 1996, the company reported pretax financial income of the following amounts (the differences are due solely to the depreciation temporary differences):

Year	Pretax Financial Income
1993	$23,998
1994	38,670
1995	27,886
1996	29,446

Over the entire four-year period, the company was subject to an income tax of 30%, and no change in the tax rate had been enacted for future years.

Required 1. Prepare a schedule that shows for each year (1993 through 1996), the (a) MACRS depreciation, (b) straight-line depreciation, and (c) depreciation temporary difference.

2. Prepare a schedule to compute the deferred tax liability and deferred tax asset at the end of 1993.

3. Compute the effects on the accounting equation at the end of 1993.

4. Show the income tax disclosures on the December 31, 1993, balance sheet.

5. Compute the effects on the accounting equation at the end of (a) 1994, (b) 1995, and (c) 1996.

57. Operating Loss Carryback. The Sawyer Company has reported the following amounts of pretax accounting income and taxable income for the past three years: 1990— $60,000 (tax rate 20%); 1991—$80,000 (tax rate 25%); 1992—$100,000 (tax rate 30%). In 1993 Sawyer had a pretax operating loss of $260,000.

Required 1. Prepare the lower portion of the 1993 income statement.

2. Prepare a note in regard to the loss carryforward.

58. Operating Loss Carryforward. During 1993 the Hight Company reports a pretax operating loss of $60,000 for financial accounting and income tax purposes, which it carries forward. In 1994, the company reports pretax accounting income and taxable income of $100,000 when its tax rate is 30%.

Required 1. Prepare the lower portion of the 1994 income statement.

2. Prepare a note for inclusion in the 1994 financial statements.

59. Deferred Income Taxes, Pensions, and Liabilities. In Chapter 1 liabilities are defined as economic obligations (debts) of a company. Two situations arise in accounting that may appear to be contradictory. First, when a company has a temporary difference between depreciation for its financial statements and MACRS depreciation for its income tax reporting, the company records a liability. Second, when a company improves the pension benefits already earned by its employees (for example, to compensate them for higher than expected inflation), a liability for the additional future payments is generally not recorded by the company.

Required For each of these situations discuss whether or not a liability should be recorded.

60. Pension Expense. The Bailey Company has had a defined benefit pension plan for several years. At the end of 1993, the company's actuary provided the following information for 1993 regarding the pension plan: (1) service cost, $120,000; (2) actual return on plan assets, $14,000; (3) interest cost on projected benefit obligation, $16,000; and (4) amortization of unrecognized prior service cost, $4,000. The company decides to fund an amount at the end of 1993 equal to its pension expense.

Required Compute the amount of Bailey Company's pension expense for 1993.

61. Components of Pension Expense. On December 31, 1993, the Robey Company accumulated the following information for 1993 in regard to its defined benefit pension plan.

Service cost	$105,000
Interest cost on projected benefit obligation	12,000
Actual return on plan assets	11,000
Amortization of unrecognized prior service cost	3,000

On its December 31, 1992 balance sheet, the company had reported an unfunded accrued pension cost liability of $14,000.

Required 1. Compute the amount of Robey Company's pension expense for 1993.

2. Record the effects on the accounting equation of Robey's 1993 pension expense if it funds the pension plan in the amount of: (a) $109,000, (b) $100,000, (c) $112,000.

62. Interest Cost and Return on Assets. On December 31, 1993, the Palmer Company determined that the 1993 service cost on its defined benefit pension plan was $120,000. At the beginning of 1993, Palmer Company had pension plan assets of $520,000 and a projected benefit obligation of $600,000. Its discount rate (and actual rate of return on plan assets) for 1993 was 10%. There are no other components of Palmer Company's pension expense; the company had an unfunded accrued pension cost liability at the end of 1992.

Required 1. Compute the amount of Palmer Company's pension expense for 1993.

2. Record the effects on the accounting equation of Palmer's 1993 pension expense if it funds the pension plan in the amount of: (a) $128,000, and (b) $122,000.

63. Pension Expense Different Than Funding: One Year. The Verna Company has had a defined benefit pension plan for several years. At the end of 1993, the company accumulated the following information: service cost for 1993, $127,000; projected benefit obligation, 1/1/1993, $634,000; discount rate, 9%; plan assets, 1/1/1993, $589,000; actual rate of return on plan assets, 9%. There are no other components of Verna Company's pension expense; the company had an unfunded accrued pension cost liability at the end of 1992. The company contributed $128,000 to the pension plan at the end of 1993.

Required Compute the amount of Verna Company's pension expense for 1993.

64. Pension Expense Different Than Funding: Multiple Years. Baron Company adopted a defined benefit pension plan on January 1, 1992. The following information pertains to the pension plan for 1993 and 1994.

	1993	1994
Service cost	$160,000	$172,000
Projected benefit obligation (1/1)	120,000	289,600
Plan assets (1/1)	120,000	279,600
Company contribution (funded 12/31)	150,000	160,000
Discount rate	8%	8%
Actual rate of return on plan assets	8%	8%

There are no other components of Baron Company's pension expense.

Required Compute the amount of Baron Company's pension expense for 1993 and 1994.

65. Determination of Projected Benefit Obligation. Several years ago the Hazelrigg Company established a defined benefit pension plan for its employees. The following information is available for 1993 in regard to its pension plan: discount rate, 10%; service cost, $142,000; plan assets (1/1), $659,000; and actual return on plan assets, $65,900. There is no amortization of unrecognized prior service cost. On December 31, 1993 the company contributed $140,000 to the pension plan, resulting in increase to Unfunded Accrued Pension Cost of $6,200.

Required Compute the amount of Hazelrigg Company's projected benefit obligation on January 1, 1993.

66. Pension Expense Different Than Funding: Multiple Years. Carli Company adopted a defined benefit pension plan on January 1, 1992 and funded the entire amount of its 1992 pension expense. The following information pertains to the pension plan for 1993 and 1994.

	1993	1994
Service cost	$200,000	$215,000
Projected benefit obligation (1/1)	180,000	396,200
Plan assets (1/1)	180,000	408,200
Company contribution (funded 12/31)	212,000	220,000
Discount rate	9%	9%
Actual rate of return on plan assets	9%	9%

There are no other components of Carli Company's pension expense.

Required 1. Compute the amount of Carli Company's pension expense for 1993 and 1994.

2. Compute the amount of any asset or liability at the end of each year.

67. Unrecognized Prior Service Cost. On January 1, 1993, the Smith Company adopted a defined benefit pension plan. At that time the company awarded retroactive benefits to its employees, resulting in an unrecognized prior service cost that created a projected benefit obligation of $125,000 on that date. The company decided to amortize the unrecognized prior service cost by the straight-line method over the 20-year average remaining service life of its active participating employees. The company's actuary has also provided the following additional information for 1993 and 1994.

Service cost: 1993, $147,000; 1994, $152,000; actual return on plan assets: 1994, $17,000; and projected benefit obligation: 1/1/1994, $284,500. The discount rate was 10% in both 1993 and 1994. The company contributed $170,000 and $175,000 to the pension fund at the end of 1993 and 1994, respectively. There are no other components of Smith Company's pension expense; disregard any additional pension liability.

Required Compute the amount of Smith Company's pension expense for 1993 and 1994.

68. Appendix: Accounting for an OPEB Plan. On January 1, 1992, Flash and Dash Company adopted the requirements for accruing the cost of its healthcare plan for retired employees, instead of the cash basis of accounting that it had been using. On December 31, 1992, the following information was obtained:

Service cost	$ 30,000
Accumulated postretirement benefit obligation	100,000
Accumulated postretirement benefit obligation for employees fully eligible to receive benefits	40,000
Actual return on plan assets	0
Amortization of unrecognized prior service cost and net gain	0
Amortization of unrecognized transition obligation	12,000
Payments to retired employees	5,000
Interest rate	10%
Average remaining service period of active plan participants	12 years

Required 1. Compute the OPEB expense for 1992 if the company uses the maximum amortization period.

2. Show the effects on the accounting equation for 1992 if the plan is not funded.

69. Appendix: Accounting for an OPEB Plan. On January 1, 1992, the Vasby Software Company adopted the requirements for accruing the cost of its healthcare plan instead of the cash basis of accounting that it had been using. The service cost for 1992 is $8,000. The plan is not funded and the discount rate is 10%. All employees were hired at age 28 and become eligible for full benefits at age 58. Employee C was paid $7,000 postretirement healthcare benefits in 1992. On December 31, 1992, the accumulated postretirement benefit obligation for Employees B and C were $77,000 and $41,500, respectively. Additional information on January 1, 1992:

Employee	Status	Age	Expected Retirement Age	Expected Postretirement Benefit Obligation	Accumulated Postretirement Benefit Obligation
A	Employee	38	65	$ 42,000	$ 14,000
B	Employee	62	65	70,000	70,000
C	Retired	67	—	45,000	45,000
				$157,000	$129,000

Required 1. Compute the OPEB expense for 1992 if the company uses the maximum amortization period.

2. Show the effects on the accounting equation for 1992 if the plan is not funded.

ANNUAL REPORT PROBLEMS

• •

70. Leases and Off-Balance Sheet Financing. The following excerpts are from Kimberly-Clark's 1988 annual report related to leases (in millions of dollars):

Note 7. Leases

Future minimum rental payments under operating leases as of December 31, 1988 were:

Year Ending December 31:	
1989	$ 19.9
1990	16.0
1991	13.1
1992	9.4
1993	5.7
Thereafter	45.3
Total minimum rental payments	$109.4

Consolidated rental expense under operating leases was $56.5 in 1988, $52.5 in 1987 and $48.0 in 1986.

Required **1.** Using T-accounts to analyze off-balance sheet financing, compute the effect on the balance sheet at December 31, 1988, and the income statement for 1989 if the operating leases were capitalized. Assume each year's payments are made at the end of the year. Use a 10% interest rate and straight-line amortization. Assume the "thereafter" payments are due in equal amounts over the next three years after 1993. From Note 2, Kimberly-Clark's effective tax rate is 39.4%.

2. Concerning this off-balance sheet financing, is there a material impact on the following ratios:

a. Return on total assets (use 1988 net income of $378.6 million and total assets of $4,267.6 million).

b. Debt/equity ratio (use 1988 total liabilities of $2,402.0 million and total stockholders' equity of $1,865.6 million).

71. Leases and Off-Balance Sheet Financing. Southern California Edison Company is the major utility company serving the Los Angeles area. The following excerpts are from its 1988 annual report relating to leases:

Note 8—Leases

The Company leases automotive, computer, office, and miscellaneous equipment through operating rental agreements with varying terms, provisions, and expiration dates. At December 31, 1988, estimated remaining rental commitments for noncancelable operating leases consisted of the following:

	(in thousands)
Year Ended December 31,	
1989	$ 28,284
1990	25,227
1991	22,354
1992	18,926
1993	14,637
For Periods Thereafter (3yr)	16,266
Total Future Rental Commitments	$125,694

Required **1.** Compute the net present value of the total operating lease payments. Use a 10% interest rate and assume the "thereafter" payments are due in equal amounts over the next three years after 1993.

2. Compute the debt/equity ratio in 1988 with and without off-balance sheet financing. Use the 1988 total liabilities of $3,542,858 thousand and total stockholders' equity of $10,367,041 thousand. Is there a material difference?

3. Which lease method would a utility generally prefer for rate-setting purposes? For financial reporting purposes? Do the lease cash payments change depending on whether the lease is recorded as a capital or operating lease? no

72. Leases and Liabilities. Squibb Corporation is a major manufacturer of pharmaceutical products. The following are excerpts from its financial statements and related notes (in millions of dollars):

	1988	1987	1986
Net income	$ 425	$ 358	$ 396
Current assets	1,856	1,743	1,505
Total assets	3,083	2,782	2,408
Current liabilities	1,449	1,029	750
Total liabilities	1,683	1,256	1,050

Notes to the Financial Statements
Long-Term Debt:
In 1987, $100 of notes were redeemed. Although these notes were classified as long-term debt at December 31, 1986, changing economic conditions resulted in the Corporation refinancing the notes in 1987 with short-term debt of commercial paper.
Leases:
The Corporation was obligated at December 31, 1988, under long-term operating leases for various types of property and equipment, with minimum aggregate rentals totaling $138. Total rental expense for operating leases in 1988 was $36. The Corporation's obligations under capital leases are not material.

Required **1.** If the $100 million of long-term debt notes had been reclassified as short-term as of December 31, 1986, would there have been a material impact on the following ratios:

a. 1986 current ratio
b. 1986 debt ratio

2. Did Squibb's use of this off-balance sheet financing for leases have a material impact upon the following ratios (ignore net present value adjustments to the aggregate rentals and ignore any adjustments to expenses):

a. 1988 debt ratio
b. 1988 return on average total assets

73. Leases and Off-Balance Sheet Financing. The following excerpts are from Scott Paper's 1988 annual report relating to leases (in millions of dollars):

Leases
A capital lease transfers substantially all of the benefits and risks of ownership of the leased property to the Company. On the Company's consolidated balance sheet the following amounts of capitalized leases are included in plant assets and the related obligations are included in debt:

	1988	1987
Plant assets under capital leases	$51.4	$50.6
Accumulated depreciation	(22.7)	(21.4)
Net capital leases	$28.7	$29.2
Current lease obligations	$ 4.6	$ 4.8
Long-term lease obligations	21.5	22.6
Capital lease obligations	$26.1	$27.4

All leases other than capital leases are operating leases and are accounted for as operating expenses. The rental expense for operating leases was $35.8 and $30.4 for 1988 and 1987, respectively. Future obligations for operating leases total $131.9.

Required **1.** Use T-accounts to analyze the 1988 lease transactions and account changes shown. Use a single T-account for all capital lease obligations and assume a 10% effective interest rate on the lease obligations. Also assume that no plant assets under capital leases were retired and that no capital lease obligations were canceled.

2. Concerning this off-balance sheet financing, is there a material impact on the following ratios:

a. Return on total assets (use 1988 net income of $400.9 million and total assets of $5,156.3 million).
b. Debt/equity ratio (use 1988 total liabilities of $3,211.5 million and total stockholders' equity of $1,944.8 million).

Assume the net present value of the $131.9 million of future operating lease payments is $90 million. Use Scott's effective tax rate of 40% and a 10 year life.

74. Deferred Income Taxes and Depreciation. The following excerpts are from Pillsbury's 1988 annual report relating to deferred income taxes (in millions of dollars):

	1988	1987
Long-Term Liabilities:		
Deferred taxes on income	$221.6	$255.8

Note 8 (in part):
Deferred taxes result from timing differences in the recognition of revenue and expense for tax and financial statement purposes. Tax effects of those differences are as follows:

	1988
Excess of tax over book depreciation	$ 22.3
Change in reserves not currently deductible for taxes	(52.6)
Installment sales	(2.8)
Unremitted earnings of consolidated foreign subsidiaries[a]	0
Other, net	(1.1)
Total	$(34.2)

Income tax expense consists of current $120.9 less the $34.2 deferred income taxes for a total of $86.7.

[a]At May 31, 1988, federal taxes are not provided on approximately $113 of unremitted earnings of foreign subsidiaries which management intends to reinvest indefinitely.

Required 1. Describe each item in the Deferred Taxes on Income account for 1988.

2. Using T-accounts, reconcile the Deferred Taxes on Income account for 1988 based on the information disclosed.

3. What is the amount of tax depreciation? Use the statutory 34% income tax rate. The financial statement depreciation was $219.4 million.

4. What is the impact on net income if accelerated, rather than straight-line, depreciation was used?

75. **Deferred Income Taxes.** Honeywell is an international corporation specializing in automation and control systems. The following excerpts are from its 1988 financial statements relating to income taxes (in millions of dollars):

	1988	1987
Income Taxes:		
Current	$422.3	$142.8
Deferred	(188.3)	14.9
Total	$234.0	$157.7

Deferred income taxes are provided for the temporary differences between the financial reporting basis and the tax basis of Honeywell's assets and liabilities.

	1988	1987
Excess of tax over book depreciation	$ 8.7	$ 24.2
Gain on installment sales, conversion sales, sales-type leases and long-term contracts deferred for tax purposes	(121.3)	3.8
Unrecorded tax benefits related to future tax deductions	163.1	0
Accruals and restructuring reserves	(187.5)	(9.8)
Employee benefits	(25.2)	(5.8)
Other	(26.1)	2.5
Total	$(188.3)	$ 14.9

The combined effective income tax rate differs from the U.S. federal statutory rate as follows:

	1988	1987
U.S. federal statutory rate	34%	34%
Additional taxes on foreign dividends	15	0
Variation in tax rates on foreign income	8	2
Capital loss carryforward	(10)	0
Unrecorded tax benefits related to future tax deductions	20	0
Other	2	2
Effective rate	69%	38%

Required 1. Explain each item that affected deferred taxes in 1988 and 1987. Honeywell adopted *Statement No. 96* in 1988.

2. Use T-accounts to analyze the income tax expense, the income tax payable, and the deferred income tax impacts on the financial statements for both 1988 and 1987.

3. Explain why Honeywell had effective tax rates of 69% and 38% in 1988 and 1987, respectively, when the statutory rate was 34%.

76. **Pensions and Early Adoption.** Herman Miller, Inc., is a furniture manufacturer located in Grand Rapids, Michigan. The following excerpts are from its May 31, 1986, financial statements related to pensions (in thousands of dollars):

Employee Benefit Plans
The company has a noncontributory defined benefit pension plan which covers substantially all employees. Benefits under this plan are based upon the employees years of service and the average earnings for the five highest consecutive years of service during the ten years immediately preceding retirement. The company has consistently funded amounts which are actuarially determined to provide the plan with sufficient assets to meet future benefit payment requirements.

The company elected to adopt *Statement No. 87*, "Employers' Accounting for Pensions," with respect to this plan effective June 2, 1985. As required by *Statement No. 87*, the company changed the actuarial cost method of calculating pension cost to the "Projected Unit Credit" method from the "Entry Age Normal" method used previously. Adoption of *Statement No. 87* reduced pension cost by approximately $2,200 in 1986.

Pension cost in 1986 included the following components:

$2,399	Service cost-benefits earned during the year
2,189	Interest cost on projected benefits obligations
	Return on assets:
(7,520)	Actual
3,667	Deferred
(319)	Net amortization
$ 416	Net pension cost

The assumptions used in the determination of pension cost were as follows:

	1984	1985	1986
Discount rate	8.0%	8.0%	9.0%
Rate of salary progression	5.5%	5.5%	5.5%
Long-term rate of return on assets	8.0%	8.0%	10.0%

During 1986, the company changed its estimate of the assumed rate of return from 8 percent to an assumed long-term rate of return on plan assets of 10 percent and an assumed discount rate of 9 percent. The change in assumed rates reduced pension cost by approximately $1,900. Pension cost charged against income was $4,972 in 1985 and $4,661 in 1984. These amounts have not been restated for the effects of *Statement No. 87.*

Income Statement (in part):

	June 2, 1984	June 1, 1985	May 31, 1986
Net income	$28,564	$40,922	$37,818
Earnings per share	$ 1.14	$ 1.63	$ 1.53

Audit Report (in part):

In our opinion, the financial statements referred to above present fairly the financial position of Herman Miller, Inc. and subsidiaries as of May 31, 1986, and June 1, 1985, and the results of their operations and the changes in their financial position for each of the three years in the period ended May 31, 1986, in conformity with generally accepted accounting principles applied on a consistent basis.

Required **1.** Without knowing all the technical accounting provisions of *Statement No. 87*, how can the user determine if this complex pension pronouncement has been properly followed by Herman Miller?

2. Did the early adoption of *Statement No. 87* by Herman Miller have a material impact on its income statements? Include calculations in your answer.

3. What were the major causes of the pension expense change in the 1986 financial statements? Were the related assumptions reasonable?

4. Are the 1984 and 1985 income statements comparable with the 1986 income statement? If not, how could they be made comparable?

77. **Pensions and Postretirement Benefits.** The following excerpts are from Campbell Soup's 1989 annual report (in millions of dollars):

Pension Plans and Retirement Benefits Note (in part):
Substantially all of the employees of the Company are covered by noncontributory defined benefit pension plans. Plan benefits are generally based on years of service and employees' compensation during the last years of employment. Benefits are paid from funds previously provided to trustees and insurance companies or are paid directly by the Company. Actuarial assumptions and plan provisions are reviewed regularly by the Company and its independent actuaries to assure that plan assets will be adequate to provide pension and survivor benefits. Plan assets consist primarily of shares in common stock, fixed income, real estate, and money market funds.

Effective March 1, 1988, certain improvements to the plans were made which increased 1988 pension expense by $2.7. Certain actuarial assumptions were changed in 1987 resulting in a net decrease in 1986 pension expense of $6.1.

Pension expense included the following:

	1989	1988	1987
Service cost-benefits earned during the year	$ 17.2	$ 16.3	$ 20.4
Interest cost on projected benefit obligation	58.8	49.8	45.3
Actual return on plan assets	(113.8)	(25.9)	(68.2)
Net amortization and deferral	57.8	(27.5)	11.9
Net pension expense	$ 20.0	$ 12.7	$ 9.4

The funded status of the plans was as follows:

	1989	1988
Actuarial present value of benefit obligations:		
Vested	$(593.4)	$(502.8)
Non-vested	(26.2)	(26.5)
Accumulated benefit obligation	(619.6)	(529.3)
Effect of projected future salary increases	(79.9)	(81.9)
Projected benefit obligation	$(699.5)	$(611.2)
Plan assets at market value	$ 751.6	$ 605.3
Projected benefit obligation (in excess of) or less than plan assets	$ 52.1	$ (5.9)
Unrecognized net loss	28.8	37.0
Unrecognized prior service cost	49.6	44.1
Unrecognized net assets at July 29, 1985	(43.2)	(47.3)
Prepaid pension expense	$ 87.3	$ 27.9
Principal actuarial assumptions were:		
Measurement of projected benefit obligation:		
Discount rate	9.0%	9.0%
Long-term rate of compensation increase	5.0%	5.0%
Long-term rate of return on plan assets	9.0%	9.0%

The Company also provides certain health care and life insurance benefits to substantially all retired employees and their dependents. The cost of these retiree health and life insurance benefits are expensed as claims are paid and amounted to $11.0 in 1989, $9.0 in 1988 and $6.4 in 1987.

Required **1.** What is the impact on Campbell's normal earnings from operations before taxes of $449.5 million in 1989, $429.2 million in 1988, and $417.9 million in 1987 from its pension plans and retirement benefits?

2. Would you expect this impact to continue in the future for Campbell? By how much would 1989 pension and postretirement expenses have to increase in order to impact normal earnings from operations before taxes by 10%?

78. Postretirement Benefits. General Electric's goal is to run businesses that are number one or two in their global markets or, in the case of services that have a substantial position, are of a scale and potential appropriate to a $50 billion enterprise. The following excerpts are from its 1988 annual report (in millions of dollars):

Note 7. Principal retiree health care and life insurance plans:
GE sponsors a number of plans providing retiree health care and life insurance benefits. GE's aggregate cost for the principal plans, which cover substantially all employees in the United States, was $302 in 1988, $278 in 1987 and $84 in 1986. The costs for 1988 and 1987 were significantly higher than for 1986 due to favorable nonrecurring changes in 1986 when the assumed discount rate used to determine the present value of future life and health benefits was increased.

Generally, employees who retire after qualifying for optional early retirement under the GE Plan are eligible to participate in retiree health care and life insurance plans. Health care benefits for eligible retirees under age 65 and eligible dependents are included in costs as covered expenses are actually incurred. For eligible retirees and spouses over age 65, the present value of future health care benefits is funded or accrued and is included in costs in the year the retiree becomes eligible for benefits. The present value of future life insurance benefits for eligible retirees is funded and is included in costs in the year of retirement.

Most retirees outside the United States are covered by government health care programs, and GE's cost is not significant.

Note 27. All Other Liabilities (in part):
For GE, this account includes noncurrent compensation and benefit accruals at year-ends 1988 and 1987 of $1,516 and $1,449, respectively.

Required **1.** Assuming that 1988 and 1987 levels of postretirement benefits are normal, was there a material impact on 1986 net income before taxes of $3,127 million from the "favorable nonrecurring changes" in the 1986 postretirement benefit expenses? Would it have affected the trend in net income before taxes which was $3,227 million in 1987 and $4,721 million in 1988?

2. It may be difficult to compare GE with its competitors if different accounting methods are used for postretirement benefits. Which methods are used by GE for which groups of employees? Assuming that its competitors have not adopted the related FASB proposal, convert GE to the method used by its competitors in 1988, using the data in Note 27. Is there a material impact on either net income before taxes or the change in such income from 1987 to 1988?

Stockholders' Equity and Components of the Income Statement

After reading this chapter, you should understand

- The characteristics, advantages, and disadvantages of a corporation
- Accounting for the issuance of stock
- Accounting for donated capital, the conversion of preferred stock to common stock, and stock subscriptions
- Stock splits and stock dividends
- Treasury stock
- Cash dividends
- Appropriation of retained earnings
- The components of an income statement, including income from contin-

uing operations, results of discontinued operations, extraordinary gains and losses, and the cumulative effects of a change in accounting principle
- Prior period adjustments
- Stock option plans
- Simple earnings per share
- Primary and fully diluted earnings per share (Appendix 1)
- Alternative revenue and expense recognition methods (Appendix 2)

Although the issuance of common stock by a corporation was first discussed in Chapter 1, the characteristics of a corporation are explored in more detail in this chapter. The stockholders' equity section of a corporation's balance sheet includes contributed capital and retained earnings components. Contributed capital reports the total amount of the investments made by the stockholders into the corporation. To accumulate sufficient capital to finance its activities, a corporation may enter into many different transactions involving the issuance of common and preferred stock, the receipt of donated capital, and stock subscriptions. The components of stockholders' equity may also be affected by conversion of preferred stock to common stock. Additional stock may be issued to stockholders by means of a stock split or stock dividend. A corporation may decrease (and increase) its outstanding stock by acquiring (and reselling) treasury stock. Retained earnings includes the lifetime earnings of the corporation not distributed as dividends to stockholders. Cash dividends may be declared and distributed to both preferred and common stock. Retained earnings may also be affected by corrections of errors made in the computation of previous earnings, by appropriations, and by some changes in accounting principles.

Corporate earnings include intraperiod allocation of income taxes, discontinued operations, extraordinary items, and some changes in accounting principles. Also, earnings per share must be disclosed on the face of the income statement by public companies. Furthermore, stock options may be granted by the corporation to employees. Each of these topics is discussed in the chapter. In Appendix 1, more complex computations of earnings per share are discussed. It has been assumed throughout this book that revenue is recognized at the point of sale. Alternative revenue (and expense) recognition principles are discussed in Appendix 2.

SECTION A Stockholders' Equity

■ CORPORATE FORM OF ORGANIZATION

In 1819 Chief Justice John Marshall defined a corporation as "an artificial being, invisible, intangible, and existing only in contemplation of the law." Today, although a corporation is a collection of individual owners, it is treated as a separate entity according to the law. **A corporation is a separate legal entity, with a continuous life, that is separate from and independent of its individual owners.** Thus, ownership in a corporation may be transferred from one individual to another. An owner has no personal liability for the corporation's debts and frequently plays no active part in the management of the corporation. As a result, the success of the corporation depends on its ability to attract large amounts of capital (often from a diverse set of owners), which is controlled by its professional management group for an indefinite period of time.

To operate as a corporation in the United States, a business entity must incorporate in one of the states. **Incorporation is the process of filing the necessary documents and obtaining permission to operate as a corporation.** Each state has its own laws of incorporation; many of these laws are uniform throughout the country, whereas others are not. Normally, one or more individuals may apply to the appropriate state officials for approval to form a corporation. The application includes the names of the individual incorporators; the corporate name, address, and nature of business; the types, legal value (if any), and number of capital shares to be authorized for issuance; and any other information required by the state's laws. The application may also include the names and addresses of the initial subscribers (subscriptions are discussed later) to the capital stock, the number of subscribed shares, the subscription price, and the down payment (if any). **The articles of incorporation (or corporate charter) is an approved application to form a corporation.** A meeting may then be held at which the initial issuance of capital stock is made to the incorporators, a board of directors is elected, a set of rules (bylaws) regulating the corporate operations is established, and the board appoints the executive officers (i.e., the *top management*) of the corporation. These terms are discussed more fully later in the chapter.

In order for a corporation to conduct its operations, the state gives it various rights and powers, including the right to enter into contracts, to hold, buy, and sell property, to sue and be sued, and to have a continuous life. These rights and powers are accompanied by a number of responsibilities. A corporation may engage only in the activities for which it was established; it must safeguard the corporate capital; it must adhere to all state and federal laws; it must adhere to state regulations concerning the distribution of net income; it must pay its debts; and it must pay local, state, and federal taxes.

Ownership and Management of a Corporation

Capital stock is the ownership unit in a corporation. A stock certificate is evidence of ownership in a corporation. **A stock certificate is a serially numbered legal document that indicates the number of shares of capital stock owned by a stockholder and the par (legal) value, if any.** It may also include additional information concerning the method of transferring the capital stock to any other owner. **The owners of a corporation are referred to as the stockholders (or shareholders).**

Since shares of stock are transferable between individuals, the owners of a corporation may be a diverse set of stockholders who are not involved in the management of the corporation. Because of this separation of ownership and management, each stockholder may be given five rights. These rights are:

1. The right to attend stockholders' meetings and to vote in setting and approving major policies and actions of the corporation. Included are policies and actions concerning such items as mergers with other companies, acquisitions of other companies, sales of major portions of the corporation, and the authorization of additional stock and bonds.

2. The right to vote in the election of the board of directors. **A board of directors is a group of individuals that has the responsibility and authority to supervise the corporation's ordinary business activities, make future plans, and take whatever action is necessary in the current management of the corporation.** Voting to elect the board of directors (and the *chairman of the board*) also takes place at the stockholders' meetings.

3. The right to share in net income by receiving dividends from the corporation. The payment of dividends, however, is determined by the board of directors.

4. The right to purchase additional capital stock if it is issued. This is called the preemptive right. **The preemptive right is the right to maintain a proportionate percentage of ownership of the corporation by purchasing a proportionate (pro rata) share of additional capital stock if it is issued.** This right is often very important for small, privately held companies for which

control is very important. However, it may be waived by a stockholder, for example, to allow the corporation to acquire another company by issuing a large number of additional shares of stock.

5. The right to share in the distribution of the assets of the corporation if it is liquidated (terminated). If a corporation is terminated, creditors are given first priority in the collection of their claims; any remaining assets are then distributed to stockholders.

Stockholders vote on major corporate policies and actions. They also vote in the election of the board of directors, thus indirectly influencing the supervision of the corporation's business activities. The board of directors appoints the president, who is usually the top (chief) executive officer in the organization. The president is responsible for the planning and control of all the corporate activities. In large corporations, the responsibilities of president, chief executive officer, and chief operating officer may be assigned to different people. Several vice presidents usually assist the president in the planning and control of operations, as illustrated in Exhibit 10–1. The vice president of finance, or chief financial officer, may oversee both the treasurer and controller. The treasurer is responsible for short- and long-term financing, credit and collections, and short- and long-term investments. The controller is responsible for the general supervision of accounting, internal auditing and internal control, and management of corporate taxes. The secretary is responsible for the corporate records, including keeping the minutes of the stockholders' meetings and the board of directors' meetings, corresponding with stockholders, and maintaining the stockholders' records.

Because stock certificates may be transferred from one individual to another, state laws require that each corporation maintain records of its stockholders. **The stockholders' ledger contains a record for each stockholder that shows the stockholders' name, address, and number of shares held.** This information enables the corporation to notify stockholders of all stockholders' meetings and to pay the correct amount of dividends to the proper stockholders. Whenever new shares are issued or shares are exchanged between stockholders, the stockholders' ledger must be updated. Exchanges of stock are initially recorded in a stock transfer journal. **A stock transfer journal contains the names and addresses of the new and former stockholders involved in each stock transfer, the date of exchange, the stock certificate numbers, and the number of shares exchanged.** Many corporations employ an independent *transfer agent* to issue the stock certificates as well as a *registrar* to maintain the stockholder records.

Companies may be public or private. A **public** company is one whose shares are publicly traded on a stock exchange or over-the-counter. A public company is subject to many reporting requirements imposed by the SEC, the stock exchange, and similar organizations. A **private** (or nonpublic) company does not allow its stock to be publicly traded and thereby avoids many reporting requirements. Private companies are also exempt from disclosing earnings per share (discussed later in this chapter) and segment information (discussed in Chapter 14).

A special type of corporation is an "S corporation." Under the Internal Rev-

EXHIBIT 10−1 Typical organization chart

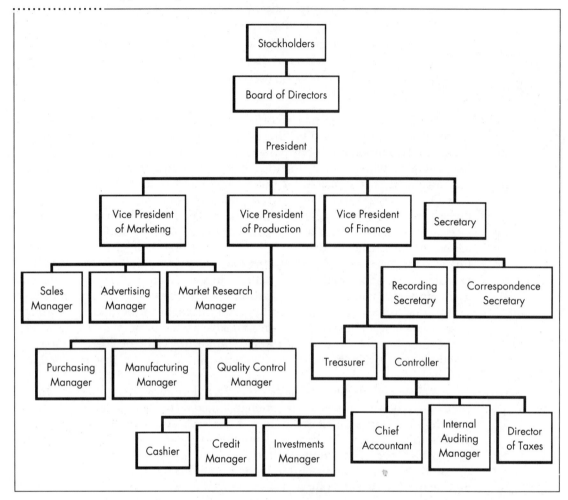

enue Code, an S corporation is not taxed, but is treated like a partnership with income passed through to the shareholders. In order to qualify, the corporation must, among other requirements, have only one class of stock outstanding and have no more than 35 shareholders. The S corporation combines the advantages of limited liability without double taxation.

Advantages of a Corporation

The corporation has become so prominent because it offers five primary advantages:

1. *Limited Liability.* Under the law a corporation is a separate legal entity, independent of its owners, and responsible for paying its obligations. Stockholders cannot be held personally responsible for the corporation's debts. This dif-

ference is the most important advantage over sole proprietorships and partnerships, in which creditors may be able to satisfy their claims by use of the owners' personal assets.

2. *Ease of Transferability of Ownership.* The capital stock of many corporations sells on organized stock markets like the New York Stock Exchange and the American Stock Exchange. Because shares of stock are transferable, it is relatively easy for an owner to dispose of his or her ownership should the need arise. This is not the case in a sole proprietorship or partnership.

3. *Ability to Attract Large Amounts of Ownership Capital.* The operation of a major corporation requires a large amount of capital invested by owners. Because ownership in a corporation is transferable and stockholders have limited liability, corporations usually are able to attract the large amounts of capital necessary for their operations.

4. *Ability to Attract Top-Quality Management.* Most owners of corporations have neither the talent nor desire to manage its operations. These owners willingly give these management duties to the corporation's board of directors. The directors, in turn, can hire the highest-quality management team necessary to ensure successful operations.

5. *Continuity of Life.* As a separate legal entity a corporation has a continuous life. In contrast to a sole proprietorship or partnership, the activities of a corporation are normally not affected or disrupted by the death or withdrawal of an owner.

Disadvantages of a Corporation

Although the advantages of a corporation generally are very important, there are three primary disadvantages:

1. *Significant Taxation.* Sole proprietorships and partnerships, as business entities, are not subject to income taxes. The owners of a sole proprietorship or partnership are taxed on their personal income from the business. Corporations, however, are treated as separate legal entities subject to federal and state income taxes. Since the maximum federal income tax rate for corporations is currently 34%, and many of them pay state income taxes, it is not unusual for income taxes to approach or exceed 40% of a corporation's income before income taxes. When the earnings of the corporation are distributed to stockholders as dividends, the stockholders may again be taxed on this personal income. This is referred to as *double taxation* and is the most significant disadvantage of a corporation.

2. *Government Control and Regulation.* In order to protect creditors and stockholders, laws have been enacted to control and regulate corporations. For instance, the payment of dividends by a corporation is usually limited to a specified amount established by the laws of the state in which it is incorporated. In addition, corporations are restricted in the purchase of their own stock. Public corporations must file numerous reports with the SEC. Addi-

tional reports are required to be filed for such items as employees' safety and health and the corporation's environmental activities.

3. *Restricted Ability to Attract Creditor Capital.* For a sole proprietorship or partnership, the creditors may use the personal assets of the owners to satisfy their claims. The owners of a corporation have limited liability, however. As a result, a corporation (particularly a smaller one) may find it more difficult to borrow money on a short- or long-term basis because creditors may perceive their investment to be less safe.

The advantages of a corporation usually exceed the disadvantages when a business grows to a reasonable size. Because a corporation's management has the responsibility to abide by state and federal laws and to safeguard and ensure the proper use of capital invested by a diverse set of owners, accounting for the invested capital has become an important activity in itself. In view of the recent trend of many corporations to become private (often with a leveraged buyout in which large amounts of debt are issued), it is important to realize that these organizations remain as corporations. The difference is that the stockholders may now be a small group of investors, and therefore the corporation avoids many reporting requirements.

It is also important to be aware that statements in this book relating to the typical characteristics of classes of stock or typical legal requirements are general statements. In any particular state, or for any particular company, these generalities may not hold. This is especially true as companies develop more complex and innovative ways of raising capital.

■ CORPORATE CAPITAL STRUCTURE

There are usually many owners of a corporation and frequent changes in ownership. State laws require special accounting procedures for the stockholders' equity of a corporation; these laws have been established to protect the absentee owners of a corporation as well as its creditors. **The stockholders' equity on a corporation's balance sheet is usually separated into two components: contributed capital and retained earnings.**

The total amount of investments made by stockholders into the corporation is reported in the contributed capital section. Each of the components (Capital Stock and Additional Paid-in Capital) and the information about the number of shares (authorized, issued, and outstanding) included in this section are discussed in the following section. **The retained earnings reports the total lifetime corporate earnings that have been reinvested in the corporation and not distributed to stockholders as dividends.** The accounting issues relating to retained earnings are discussed later in the chapter.

Capital Stock and Legal Capital

Capital stock refers to the ownership units in the corporation. Capital stock may be issued by the corporation for cash, in installment sales, in noncash exchanges, and in other transactions. The dollar amount recorded as Capital Stock for each transaction depends on the laws of the state in which it is incorporated. Because capital stockholders have a *limited liability,* to protect creditors state laws usually set a legal capital for all corporations. **Legal capital is the amount of stockholders' equity that cannot be distributed to stockholders.** A corporation may not pay dividends or reacquire capital stock if these activities will reduce the legal capital. The definition of legal capital varies from state to state. In most states, however, the total par value or stated value of the issued capital stock is the legal capital.

Par Value Stock. Historically, the usual way legal capital has been established is by requiring that all capital stock have a par value. **The par value of capital stock is a monetary amount that is designated as the legal capital per share in the articles of incorporation and is printed on each stock certificate.** The total legal capital of a corporation is determined by multiplying the par value per share times the number of shares issued. Generally, states require that a separate accounting be made of the legal capital. Consequently, as we will see shortly, for each issuance of capital stock the total dollar amount of the par value is recorded as capital stock.

No-Par Stock. Most states also allow the issuance of no-par capital stock. **No-par capital stock does not have a par value.** When no-par stock is issued, some states require that the entire proceeds received by the corporation for the issued shares be designated as legal capital, and accounting practices have been established for this situation. Many states, however, allow the corporation's board of directors to establish a stated value per share of no-par stock. **The stated value of no-par stock is the legal capital per share of stock.** The stated value per share, when multiplied times the number of shares issued, is the total amount of legal capital. Accounting for stated value, no-par stock is very similar to accounting for par value stock, and the total dollar amount of the stated value is recorded as capital stock.

The concept of legal capital has had a significant impact on corporate accounting practices, particularly as they apply to stockholders' equity. Capital stock accounts are established to record the legal capital, and additional paid-in capital accounts are used for the remainder of the total amount of capital contributed by stockholders.

Additional Paid-in Capital

The par value of a share of capital stock often is set very low—perhaps $10, $1, or even less per share. Since capital stock normally is issued at a price far in excess of par value, the legal capital is usually only a small part of the total proceeds received. The total proceeds received is the *market* value, the price at which the stock is issued. It is very important to understand that the par value of capital stock has *no* direct relationship to its market value at any time.

A corporation may issue capital stock in a variety of transactions. In addition to following state laws for recording the par or stated value in a capital stock account, it is also sound accounting practice (as well as state law in certain states) to record the excess value received. The excess value received is called additional paid-in capital. **Additional paid-in capital is the difference between the market value and the par (or stated) value in each stock transaction.** It is alternatively entitled *Additional Paid-in Capital on Capital Stock, Additional Paid-in Capital in Excess of Par (or Stated) Value, Premium on Capital Stock,* or *Contributed Capital in Excess of Par (or Stated) Value.* Additional paid-in capital sometimes arises from transactions not involving the original issuance of capital stock. These transactions are discussed later in the chapter.

Classes of Capital Stock

Corporations may issue two classes of capital stock, common stock and preferred stock. If a corporation issues only one class of capital stock, it is generally referred to as common stock. **Common stock is capital stock that shares in all the stockholders' rights.** Some companies have issued more than one type of common stock. Each type has different characteristics, such as different voting rights. If a corporation issues more than one class of stock, the other class of stock (in addition to common stock) is called preferred stock. **Preferred stock is capital stock for which certain additional rights are given to the stockholders in exchange for giving up some of the usual stockholders' rights.** The additional rights may include:

1. *Preference for Dividends.* The right to receive a dividend before any dividend is paid to common stockholders.
2. *Preference in Liquidation.* The right to receive in liquidation repayment of the capital contributed before any distributions are made to common stockholders.
3. *Stated Dividend.* The right to receive a fixed dividend amount per share, if dividends are paid. This amount is usually stated as a percentage of the par value, or as a specific dollar amount.
4. *Cumulative.* The right to receive any unpaid dividends from previous periods before dividends are paid to common stockholders.
5. *Convertible.* The right to convert each share into a predetermined number of common shares.

The right to vote is usually given up in exchange for the additional rights.

Preferred stock is typically issued with a par value. When a corporation issues both common stock and preferred stock, it will report the Common Stock and Preferred Stock separately to disclose the legal capital of each kind of stock. It will also report the Additional Paid-in Capital on Common Stock and Additional Paid-in Capital on Preferred Stock as the differences between the market values received and the par values of each type of stock. When a corporation issues both classes of stock, the contributed capital component of stockholders' equity would include the following items (using assumed numbers of shares and dollar amounts):

STOCKHOLDERS' EQUITY

Contributed capital		
Preferred stock, $100 par, 2,000 shares authorized,		
600 shares issued and outstanding	$60,000	
Common stock, $10 par, 30,000 shares authorized,		
9,000 shares issued and outstanding	90,000	
Additional paid-in capital on preferred stock	72,000	
Additional paid-in capital on common stock	43,000	
Total contributed capital		$265,000
Retained earnings		173,000
Total Stockholders' Equity		$438,000

Redeemable Preferred Stock

Certain issues of preferred stock are redeemable. That is, under certain specified conditions, the corporation will reacquire the stock and repay the owners. Redeemable preferred stock that is subject to mandatory redemption or to redemption at the option of the holder (in contrast to redemption at the option of the issuing company) must follow special SEC disclosure rules. Redeemable preferred stock has some of the characteristics of debt because there is a likelihood of a cash outflow in the future that the company has no ability to prevent. For SEC reports, the amounts of redeemable preferred stock, nonredeemable preferred stock, and common stock must be segregated. The general heading "Stockholders' Equity" and a total dollar amount of equity securities (common and preferred stock) cannot include redeemable preferred stock. Therefore, the redeemable preferred stock is usually reported on the balance sheet between liabilities and stockholders' equity. To illustrate, Nike disclosed the following:

Note 9—Redeemable Preferred Stock:
NIAC is the sole owner of the Company's authorized Redeemable Preferred Stock, $1 par value, which is redeemable at the option of NIAC at par value aggregating $300,000. A cumulative dividend of $.10 per share is payable annually on May 31 and no dividends may be declared or paid on the Common Stock of the Company unless dividends on the Redeemable Preferred Stock have been declared and paid in full. There have been no changes in the Redeemable Preferred Stock in the three years ended May 31, 1989. As the holder of the Redeemable Preferred Stock, NIAC does not have general voting rights but does have the right to vote as a separate class on the sale of all or substantially all of the assets of the Company and its subsidiaries, on merger, consolidation, liquidation or dissolution of the Company or on the sale or assignment of the NIKE trademark for athletic footwear sold in the United States.

Callable Preferred Stock

Callable preferred stock may be recalled by the corporation at its option. The call price, usually several dollars above the issuance price, is stated on the stock certificate. Stockholders owning *nonconvertible* callable preferred stock must give up their shares when called by the corporation. This type of stock is very similar to preferred stocks that are redeemable at the option of the company. Stockholders owning *convertible* callable preferred stock usually have the choice of conversion or recall.

When the preferred stock is called, the par value of the stock and the related additional paid-in capital are eliminated. Since the cash paid (the call price) is usually greater than the original issuance price, the difference reduces Retained Earnings. Note that a loss is *not* recorded because losses (and gains) are not recorded from transactions with shareholders. For example, assume that a company had issued 50 shares of $100 par callable preferred stock for $120 per share. When the corporation calls these shares at the call price of $125 per share, the following is recorded:

Assets	= Liabilities +		Stockholders' Equity	
− $6,250		− $5,000	− $1,000	− $250

Cash		Preferred Stock		Additional Paid-in Capital		Retained Earnings	
$6,250		$5,000		$1,000		$250	

■ CAPITAL STOCK TRANSACTIONS

Common stock is authorized for issuance in the articles of incorporation after which it may be issued for cash, by subscription, or in exchange for noncash assets.

Authorization

The corporate charter contains the authorization to issue capital stock. This authorization lists the classes of stock that may be issued, the par or stated value, the number of authorized shares, and in the case of preferred stock, any preference provisions. Once a corporation has issued all of its authorized stock, it must reapply to the state for approval to issue more shares and obtain shareholder approval. Consequently, a corporation usually obtains authorization to issue more stock than it initially plans to sell.

It is important to understand the difference between authorized capital stock and issued capital stock. **Authorized capital stock is the number of shares of capital stock (both common and preferred) that the corporation *may* legally issue. Issued capital stock is the number of shares of capital stock that a corporation *has* legally issued to its stockholders on a specific date.** As shown earlier, the numbers of shares authorized and issued for each class of stock are reported in the stockholders' equity section of a corporation's balance sheet.

Issuance for Cash

Capital stock may be issued with a par value, as no-par stock with a stated value, or as true no-par stock. An example of the issuance of par value stock was given in Chapter 1. To review, the total cash proceeds are divided into the par value of the stock issued and the additional paid-in capital. For example, a company would record the issuance of 1,000 shares of $20 par value common stock for $50 per share as follows:

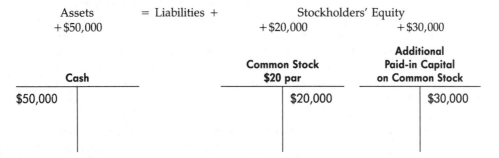

| Assets | = Liabilities + | | Stockholders' Equity | |
| + $50,000 | | | + $20,000 | + $30,000 |

	Cash		Common Stock $20 par		Additional Paid-in Capital on Common Stock	
$50,000				$20,000		$30,000

If the company issued no-par stock with a stated value of $20, it would record the issuance of 1,000 shares as above with the stated value of $20,000 recorded in a Common Stock $20 Stated Value account.

Alternatively, the company may be authorized to issue no-par stock without a stated value. In this case the entire amount of the cash received is the legal capital and is recorded in the capital stock account. Although typically prohibited, capital stock could be issued at a price *below* its par or stated value. In this case the stock sells at a *discount*, and the original stockholder may be required to pay into the corporation the amount of the discount should the corporation be unable to meet its financial obligations.

Miscellaneous costs may be incurred for the issuance of common stock. They include legal fees, accounting fees, stock certificate costs, and other costs. As discussed in Chapter 7, these costs associated with the *initial* issuance of stock at incorporation should be recorded as an intangible asset entitled Organization Costs. When these costs are associated with *subsequent* issuances of common stock, they reduce the proceeds received and are subtracted from Additional Paid-in Capital.

Stock Subscriptions

Investors sometimes agree to purchase capital stock on an "installment" basis. In this case the corporation and the future stockholder enter into a legally binding subscription contract. **In a subscription contract the subscriber (investor) agrees to buy a certain number of shares at a set price, with the payment spread over a specified time period.** The contract often requires a down payment and should contain provisions for any defaults (nonpayments) by the subscriber. The shares of capital stock are not issued to a subscriber until the subscriber has completed full payment of the subscription price. Such transactions are most frequent when a corporation is initially incorporated and are often part of employment agreements with top management personnel and with major stockholders.

The subscription is recorded by increasing Subscriptions Receivable and increasing Capital Stock Subscribed (and Additional Paid-in Capital if necessary). The SEC requires that the Subscriptions Receivable be subtracted from stockholders' equity in the balance sheet. The subscription, therefore, does not increase total stockholders' equity. It can be argued that this accounting is appropriate because capital that is not paid in should not be considered as capital since no assets are available to the corporation, and there is no asset because collection is uncertain or perhaps is contingent on certain future events. Also, receivables from a subscription are different from normal trade receivables because no goods or services have been provided in the normal course of business.

The classification of subscriptions receivable by a private company (which does not report to the SEC) as an asset is not uncommon. When such reporting occurs, the user of the financial statements should examine the terms of the subscription contract with care. For example, the receivable could be from an officer of the company, not be payable for ten years, and only be expected to be paid if there is a takeover by another company.

Occasionally, a subscriber will not make the entire payments required by the subscription contract. When a default occurs the accounting is determined by the subscription contract provisions, such as (1) return to the subscriber the entire amount paid in; (2) return to the subscriber the amount paid in, less any costs incurred by the corporation to reissue the stock; (3) issue to the subscriber a lesser number of shares based on the total amount of payment received; or (4) require the forfeiture of all amounts paid in. If the subscription contract does not include a provision for subscription defaults, the laws of the state in which the corporation is incorporated usually provide for one of these alternatives.

Noncash Issuance of Stock

Sometimes capital stock is issued for assets other than cash or for services performed. When this occurs a correct value must be used to record the transaction. This is a thorny issue when it involves intangible assets such as patents, copyrights, or organization costs because of the difficulty in valuing these assets. **The general rule is to record the transaction at the fair market value of the stock issued or the assets received, whichever is more reliable.** For instance, at the time of the transaction the stock may be selling on the stock market at a specified price. In this case the stock has a known value (the stock market price), and therefore this value would be used to record the transaction.

Alternatively, the corporation's stock may not be actively traded on a stock market. In this case the fair market value of the assets received may be more reliable and should be used to record the transaction. This value may be based on a review of recent transactions involving similar assets or on an appraisal by a competent, independent appraiser.

Sometimes shares of capital stock are issued by a corporation as payment for legal or accounting services performed in its incorporation process. The costs of these services are recorded as an intangible asset, Organization Costs, because these services will benefit the corporation in the future. The transaction should be recorded at the agreed-upon contract price for the services by increasing Organization Costs for the contract price, increasing Common Stock for the par value of the shares issued, and recording the difference between the contract price and the par value as an increase to Additional Paid-in Capital.

It is important to understand the impact on the financial statements of an error in recording the noncash issuance of capital stock. Suppose, for instance, that stock was issued for equipment and the transaction was recorded at too high a value. In this case both the assets and stockholders' equity of the corporation would be overstated. In addition, since equipment is a depreciable asset, the initial error would cause an overstatement each year in the depreciation expense, resulting in an understatement of net income. The financial statements would be correct only at the end of the asset's useful life. If the equipment was initially recorded at too low a value, opposite errors would result. Good judgment must be used in recording noncash issuances of capital stock to avoid errors in the financial statements of current and later periods.

■ OTHER CHANGES IN CONTRIBUTED CAPITAL

Several other items may affect contributed capital. These items include donated capital, the conversion of preferred stock to common stock, stock splits, and stock dividends. Each of these items is discussed in the sections that follow.

Donated Capital

In a few instances, a corporation may increase contributed capital for events not related to the issuance of capital stock. These increases are rare and are recorded at the fair market value. For example, it is possible for a corporation to receive donated assets, such as a plant site, to induce it to locate in an "industrial park" of a community. Some communities do this to increase the employment opportunities for their citizens and to increase the collection of property taxes. In this case the corporation records the donation as follows (amounts assumed):

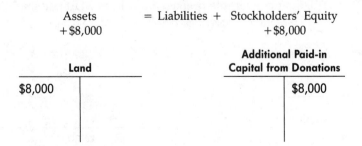

This accounting is appropriate because the assets of the corporation have increased without an increase in liabilities; the entire value belongs to the stockholders. Note that the transaction does not affect the income statement.

Whether cash or noncash assets are received as a result of donations, the balance of the Additional Paid-in Capital from Donations account is listed as an item in the contributed capital section of the balance sheet. It is added to the balances of the capital stock and other additional paid-in capital accounts to determine the total contributed capital.

Conversion of Preferred Stock to Common Stock

Earlier we mentioned that a corporation may issue two classes of stock, common and preferred. One of the preferences that might be extended to preferred stockholders is the right to exchange (convert) the preferred stock for common stock at a later date. This feature allows the preferred stockholder to participate in increases in the price of the common stock. **Convertible preferred stock is preferred stock that is exchangeable into common stock.** Usually, the number of common shares into which each preferred share is convertible is established at the time the preferred stock is issued.

Another feature of preferred stock involves the right to a set dividend. Both the conversion preference and the dividend feature are advantages to the preferred stockholder. Since the preferred stock is convertible into a specified amount of common stock, the market price of the convertible preferred stock tends to rise in proportion to any rise in the market price of the common stock. When the market price of the common stock is falling, however, the right to a set dividend on the preferred stock tends to stabilize the market value of the preferred stock.

The issuance of preferred stock (whether or not it is convertible) is accounted for in the same manner (except for changes in account titles) as the issuance of common stock. The conversion feature is disclosed in the notes to the financial statements. Accounting for the conversion of preferred to common stock is very straightforward. The par value of the converted preferred stock and the additional paid-in capital on the preferred stock are eliminated and replaced with the par value of the common stock and the additional paid-in capital on the common stock.

To illustrate, assume that a corporation had previously issued 40 shares of $100 par convertible preferred stock for $110 per share. At the time of issuance the corporation recorded the following:

Assets	=	Liabilities	+ Stockholders' Equity
− $1,500		− $1,500	

Cash		Preferred Stock		Additional Paid-in Capital on Preferred Stock
$4,400		$4,000		$400

Assume that each share of preferred stock is convertible into 6 shares of $10 par common stock and that 30 shares are converted. The company reduces Preferred Stock and the Additional Paid-in Capital by a total of $3,300 (30 × $110) and records Common Stock of $1,800 (30 × 6 × $10 par) and Additional Paid-in Capital on Common Stock of $1,500 ($3,300 − $1,800) as follows:

A. = L. +

Stockholders' Equity

+$1,800	+$1,500	−$3,000	−$300

Common Stock	Additional Paid-in Capital on Common Stock	Preferred Stock	Additional Paid-in Capital on Preferred Stock
$1,800	$1,500	$3,000	$300
		Bal: $1,000	Bal: $100

Note that the conversion of preferred stock to common stock affects the components of contributed capital but it does not affect the total contributed capital. The $3,300 contributed capital for the preferred stock was simply replaced by an equal amount of contributed capital for the common stock as shown below:

Before Conversion		After Conversion	
Contributed capital		Contributed capital	
Preferred stock, $100 par, 100 shares authorized, 40 shares issued and outstanding	$4,000	Preferred stock, $100 par, 100 shares authorized, 10 shares issued and outstanding	$1,000
Additional paid-in capital on preferred stock	400	Additional paid-in capital on preferred stock	100
Common stock, $10 par, 10,000 shares authorized, 500 shares issued and outstanding	5,000	Common stock, $10 par, 10,000 shares authorized, 680 shares issued and outstanding	6,800
Additional paid-in capital on common stock	15,000	Additional paid-in capital on common stock	16,500
Total contributed capital	$24,400	Total contributed capital	$24,400

Stock Splits

Sometimes the market price of a corporation's common stock increases to the point where it is not as attractive to certain investors. Many corporations believe a wide distribution of ownership increases the demand for their stock, improves their public image, and increases their product sales to their stockholders. To reduce the market price so that it falls within the *trading range* (the price per share investors are willing to pay for common stock) of most investors, the board of directors may authorize a stock split. **A stock split is a decrease in the par** value per share of stock and a proportional increase in the number of shares authorized and issued.

Since a stock split affects the number of authorized shares and the legal capital, each stock split must be approved by the state in which the corporation is incorporated. To illustrate a stock split, suppose a corporation that has issued 50,000 shares of $10 par common stock declares a 2 for 1 stock split with a reduction to a $5 par value. After the split a total of 100,000 shares of $5 common stock have been issued. A stockholder who previously owned 40 shares of $10 par common stock will own 80 shares of $5 par common stock after the stock split. The additional number of shares participating in the same amount of corporate earnings will cause a proportional decrease in the market price per share.

A stock split has no impact on the dollar amount of any element of stockholders' equity and consequently it has no effect on total stockholders' equity. In the previous example the total par value of the common stock is $500,000 before and after the stock split as shown below:

Before Stock Split		After Stock Split	
Contributed capital		Contributed capital	
Common stock, $10 par, 80,000 shares authorized, 50,000 shares issued and outstanding	$500,000	Common stock, $5 par, 160,000 shares authorized, 100,000 shares issued and outstanding	$500,000
Additional paid-in capital on common stock	150,000	Additional paid-in capital on common stock	150,000
Total contributed capital	$650,000	Total contributed capital	$650,000

Stock Dividends

Occasionally, a corporation may declare and distribute a stock dividend. **A stock dividend is a pro rata (proportional) distribution of additional shares of a corporation's own stock to its stockholders.**

A stock dividend usually consists of the same class of shares; that is, a common stock dividend is declared on common stock outstanding (the number of shares currently held by stockholders, as discussed later). Stock dividends most frequently are issued out of authorized but unissued shares, although treasury stock shares may be used. Unlike cash dividends, the declaration of a stock dividend usually can be legally rescinded by the corporation.

A stock dividend differs from a cash dividend in that **no corporate assets are distributed**. After a stock dividend, each stockholder holds the same percentage of ownership in the corporation as was held prior to the distribution. For instance, assume that a corporation has 10,000 common shares outstanding, one stockholder owns 2,000 shares, and the corporation issues a 10% stock dividend. After the stock dividend 11,000 shares will be outstanding (10,000 × 1.10), and the stockholder will now own 2,200 (2,000 × 1.10) shares. The stockholder owned 20% of the outstanding common stock *both prior to and after* the stock dividend. What occurs, from an accounting standpoint, is a rearrangement of stockholders' equity. Total stockholders' equity does not change, but retained earnings is decreased by the amount of the dividend and contributed capital is increased by the same amount because of the additional number of shares issued. A stock dividend also differs from a stock split because the par value of the shares is not changed. Although both transactions increase the number of shares outstanding and neither causes any change in total stockholders' equity, a stock dividend does not affect the par value, whereas a stock split does not affect total retained earnings or total contributed capital.

Stock dividends are often viewed favorably by stockholders even though (1) they receive no corporate assets; (2) theoretically, the total market value of their investment will not increase because the increased number of shares will be offset by a decrease in the stock market price per share due to a larger number of shares participating in the same corporate earnings; and (3) future cash dividends may be limited because retained earnings is decreased by the amount of the stock dividend, and most states set legal dividend restrictions based on positive retained earnings. Some stockholders, however, welcome stock dividends because (1) the corporation may announce that it will continue to pay the same cash dividend per share, in which case stockholders will receive higher total dividends; (2) the market price may decrease to a lower trading range, making the stock more attractive to additional investors; (3) other investors may also look favorably on the stock dividends and purchase the stock, causing the stock market price *not* to decrease proportionally; and (4) they see them as evidence of corporate growth and sound financial policy.

In accounting for a stock dividend by a corporation, a distinction is made between a *small* and a *large* stock dividend, and generally accepted accounting principles have been established for each of them. **A small stock dividend is less than or equal to 20% of the previously outstanding common shares.**[1] It is argued that for a small stock dividend the size of the dividend does not significantly affect the stock market price of the outstanding shares. Thus, the "value" of the stock issued in the stock dividend is considered to be the current stock market price, and therefore the stock dividend is recorded at this price. For a small stock dividend, retained earnings is reduced and contributed capital is increased by an amount equal to the current market value on the date of declaration for the additional shares of the stock dividend.

A large stock dividend is greater than 20% of the previously oustanding common shares. The size of a large stock dividend is likely to cause a substantial decrease in the stock market price of the outstanding shares. Therefore, the current market price is *not* appropriate for recording such a stock dividend. The *par* (or *stated*) value of the stock is used instead. For a large stock dividend, retained earnings is reduced and contributed capital is increased by the total par value for the additional shares of the stock dividend.

....

[1]Generally accepted accounting principles state that a small stock dividend is less than 20% to 25%. For simplicity, we will use 20%.

The following diagram shows the effect of a small and large stock dividend on the various items of stockholders' equity.

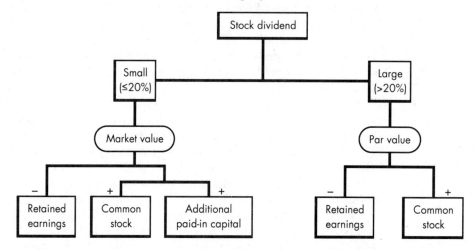

To illustrate the accounting for the two sizes of stock dividends, assume that a corporation has the following stockholders' equity prior to a stock dividend:

STOCKHOLDERS' EQUITY	
Contributed capital	
Common stock, $10 par, 40,000 shares authorized,	
10,000 shares issued and outstanding	$100,000
Additional paid-in capital on common stock	70,000
Total contributed capital	$170,000
Retained earnings	80,000
Total stockholders' equity	$250,000

Small Stock Dividend. Assume that the corporation declares and issues a 10% stock dividend. On the date of declaration the stock is selling for $19 per share. The 1,000 share (10,000 shares × 10%) stock dividend is recorded at the current market value of $19,000 as follows:

Assets = Liabilities + Stockholders' Equity

+$10,000		+$9,000	−$19,000

Common Stock	Additional Paid-in Capital	Retained Earnings
$10,000	$9,000	$19,000

The resulting stockholders' equity is as follows:

STOCKHOLDERS' EQUITY

Contributed capital
  Common stock, $10 par, 40,000 shares authorized,
    11,000 shares issued and outstanding $110,000
  Additional paid-in capital on common stock 70,000
  Additional paid-in capital from stock dividend 9,000
    Total contributed capital $189,000
Retained earnings 61,000
  Total stockholders' equity $250,000

Note that there is no difference in the $250,000 total stockholders' equity prior to and after the stock dividend. Only the components are changed, with retained earnings decreasing by $19,000 and contributed capital increasing by the same amount (and the issued shares increasing to 11,000).

Large Stock Dividend. Assume, *instead,* that the corporation declares and issues a 30% stock dividend when the stock is selling for $19 per share. In this case the market value is disregarded, and the par value of $30,000 for the 3,000 shares (10,000 shares × 30% × $10 par) is used to record the stock dividend as follows:

Assets = Liabilities +	Stockholders' Equity	
	+$30,000	−$30,000
	Common Stock	**Retained Earnings**
	$30,000	$30,000

10 X 10%

The resulting stockholders' equity is as follows:

STOCKHOLDERS' EQUITY

Contributed capital
  Common stock, $10 par, 40,000 shares authorized,
    13,000 shares issued and outstanding $130,000
  Additional paid-in capital on common stock 70,000
    Total contributed capital $200,000
Retained earnings 50,000
  Total stockholders' equity $250,000

Again there is no difference between the $250,000 total stockholders' equity prior to and after the stock dividend. Only the components are changed, with retained earnings decreasing by $30,000 and contributed capital increasing by the same amount (and the number of issued shares increasing by 3,000 to 13,000). Note that because the par value is used, there is no increase in additional paid-in capital for a *large* stock dividend.

■ TREASURY STOCK

In most states a corporation may reacquire its own previously issued capital stock, after which the stock is held by the corporation in its treasury. **Treasury stock is a corporation's own capital stock that (1) has been fully paid for by stockholders, (2) has been legally issued, (3) is reacquired by the corporation, and (4) is being held by the corporation.**

A corporation may acquire treasury stock for various reasons:

1. To have shares available for employee purchase plans
2. To issue stock in the conversion of convertible preferred stock
3. To invest excess cash and help to maintain the market price of its stock
4. To issue stock in the acquisition of other companies
5. To reduce the number of shares outstanding and increase the earnings per share
6. To use in the issuance of a stock dividend
7. To concentrate ownership of the shares to assist in the defense against a hostile takeover

Each of these transactions is subject to legal, governmental, and stock exchange regulations.

Treasury stock is clearly *not* an asset; a corporation cannot own itself. A corporation cannot recognize a gain or loss when reacquiring its own stock, which restricts a corporation from influencing its net income by buying and selling its own stock. Consequently, treasury stock is accounted for as a reduction of stockholders' equity. Treasury stock generally does not have the stockholders' rights discussed earlier; it has no voting or preemptive rights, cannot participate in dividends, and has no rights at liquidation. It does participate in stock splits, however, since the par value must be reduced. When treasury stock is acquired, the amount of retained earnings available for dividends must ordinarily be restricted by the cost of the treasury stock held so that the payment of dividends will not reduce contributed capital, as discussed later.

To illustrate, suppose that a corporation has previously issued 5,000 shares of $10 par common stock for $12 per share. The corporation decides to reacquire 400 shares of this common stock, and it purchases these shares on the stock market at a cost of $14 per share. The reacquisition of the stock for $5,600 (400 × $14) is recorded as follows:

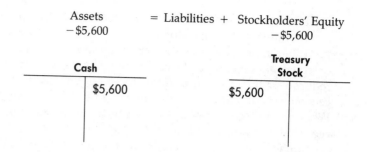

Note that the treasury stock was recorded at its *cost* per share and that the stock's original par value was disregarded.[2] If the corporation prepared a balance sheet before reissuing these shares, the stockholders' equity would appear as follows:

STOCKHOLDERS' EQUITY

Contributed capital
  Common stock, $10 par, 40,000 shares authorized,
    5,000 shares issued, 4,600 shares outstanding $50,000
  Additional paid-in capital on common stock   10,000
    Total contributed capital $60,000
Retained earnings (assumed) [see *Note*]   35,000
    Total contributed capital and retained earnings $95,000
Less: treasury stock (400 shares at $14 per share)   (5,600)
    Total stockholders' equity $89,400

Note: Retained earnings are restricted regarding dividends in the amount of $5,600, the cost of the treasury stock.

In the example the $5,600 cost of the treasury stock is subtracted from the $95,000 total of contributed capital and retained earnings to determine the $89,400 total stockholders' equity. The numbers of shares authorized, issued, and outstanding are disclosed. The amount of retained earnings available for dividends must be restricted by the amount of the cost of the treasury stock so that the payment of dividends will not reduce contributed capital. This is typically disclosed by means of a note as shown.

It is important to understand the difference between issued capital stock and outstanding capital stock. Recall that issued capital stock is the number of shares that a corporation has issued to stockholders. **Outstanding capital stock is the number of shares that have been issued to stockholders and that are still being held by them as of a specific date.** Thus, the difference between *issued*

. . . .
[2]This cost method is the most common way of accounting for treasury stock. The par value method is sometimes used, but is much less common and is not discussed in this book.

capital stock and *outstanding* capital stock is the number of shares being held by a corporation as *treasury* stock.

When treasury stock is reissued it may be reissued at a price above, below, or equal to the cost of reacquisition. Upon reissuance the Treasury Stock is reduced by the *cost* of the shares reissued, and the difference between the proceeds received and this cost is treated as an adjustment of stockholders' equity. When the proceeds exceed the cost of the reissued treasury stock, the excess is recorded as Additional Paid-in Capital from Treasury Stock. The balance of this account is included in the contributed capital section in the balance sheet. If the proceeds are less than the cost, the Additional Paid-in Capital from Treasury Stock is reduced by the amount of the difference. If this account does not exist or has a balance too small to absorb the difference, the remainder should be recorded as a reduction in retained earnings.

To illustrate the reissuance, assume that 300 shares of the treasury stock from our earlier example are reissued at $15 per share. The reissuance of the treasury stock that originally cost $4,200 (300 × $14) for $4,500 (300 × $15) is recorded as follows:

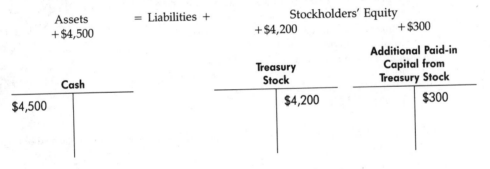

Assets	= Liabilities +	Stockholders' Equity	
+ $4,500		+ $4,200	+ $300

Cash		Treasury Stock	Additional Paid-in Capital from Treasury Stock
$4,500		$4,200	$300

After this transaction the stockholders' equity appears as follows:

STOCKHOLDERS' EQUITY

Contributed capital		
Common stock, $10 par, 40,000 shares authorized, 5,000 shares issued, 4,900 shares outstanding	$50,000	
Additional paid-in capital on common stock	10,000	
Additional paid-in capital from treasury stock	300	
Total contributed capital		$60,300
Retained earnings (assumed) [see *Note*]		35,000
Total contributed capital and retained earnings		$95,300
Less: treasury stock (100 shares at $14 per share)		(1,400)
Total stockholders' equity		$93,900

Note: Retained earnings are restricted regarding dividends in the amount of $1,400, the cost of the treasury stock.

In this stockholders' equity section observe that the Additional Paid-in Capital from Treasury Stock is included in contributed capital. As long as this account has an ending balance, it is included in contributed capital even if a company has reissued all of its treasury stock. This is because stockholders have contributed more to the company than the company paid for its treasury stock and this excess is a part of contributed capital. Also observe that the number of shares outstanding has increased (to 4,900) from the previous example.

To continue, suppose that the remaining 100 shares of treasury stock were reissued at $13 per share. This reissuance of the treasury stock that originally cost $1,400 (100 × $14) for $1,300 (100 × $13) is recorded as follows:

Assets	= Liabilities +	Stockholders' Equity	
+$1,300		+$1,400	−$100

Cash		Treasury Stock		Additional Paid-in Capital from Treasury Stock	
$1,300			$1,400	$100	

In this case the $1,300 proceeds were less than the $1,400 cost of the treasury stock and therefore Additional Paid-in Capital from Treasury Stock was reduced by the $100 difference.

Summary of Treasury Stock Characteristics

For treasury stock the following items are important:

1. Treasury stock is not an asset; it is accounted for as a reduction in stockholders' equity.

2. Treasury stock has no vote, has no preemptive right, does not share in dividends, does not participate in assets at liquidation, but does participate in stock splits.

3. Treasury stock transactions do not result in gains or losses on the income statement so that a corporation cannot influence its net income by buying and selling its own stock.

4. Treasury stock reissuances increase additional paid-in capital when the proceeds exceed the cost of the reissued shares.

5. Treasury stock reissuances decrease additional paid-in capital (and occasionally retained earnings) when the proceeds are less than the cost of the reissued shares.

6. The cost of treasury stock is deducted from the sum of contributed capital and retained earnings to determine total stockholders' equity on the balance sheet.

7. Retained earnings usually must be restricted as to dividends by the cost of treasury stock held.

■ CASH DIVIDENDS

A corporation may distribute cash dividends on its common stock and its preferred stock. (Stock dividends are another "type" of dividend, discussed earlier in the chapter.) Whereas net income increases the assets of the corporation and this increase is recorded in retained earnings, the distribution of cash dividends has the opposite effect. The distribution reduces the *assets* of the corporation and is also recorded as a reduction in retained earnings. Thus, the phrase "retained earnings paid out in dividends," which is often used in discussing dividends, is somewhat misleading. Cash dividends are paid out of *cash* and retained earnings are reduced because the payment is a return *of* capital to the stockholders.

In order to pay cash dividends a company must meet legal requirements and have enough cash available. The setting of a corporation's dividend policy is the responsibility of the board of directors. The board determines the amount and timing of the dividends, considering legal requirements, compliance with contractual agreements, and the financial well-being of the corporation.

Legal requirements vary from state to state, with states typically requiring a positive (credit) balance in retained earnings before dividends may be declared and limiting dividends to the amount of the balance. (**A deficit is the term used to describe a *negative* retained earnings balance.** This occurs when the company's accumulated prior net losses or dividends are in excess of prior earnings.) Usually the amount of retained earnings available for dividends is also restricted by the cost of the treasury shares held (as discussed earlier).

Consideration should be given to the impact of the payment of a dividend on cash, current assets, and working capital, the ability to finance corporate expansion projects with the remaining assets, and the effect of the dividend on the stock market price per share. The payment of dividends may also be restricted by other factors, such as a debt covenant. Payment of dividends should be in the financial long- and short-term best interests of the corporation and its stockholders.

There may be many stockholders of a corporation, and therefore extensive record keeping may be required by the corporation for its dividends. As a result the dividend process is usually spread out over a period of several weeks. Three dates are significant for a cash dividend (or any type of dividend): (1) the date of declaration, (2) the date of record, and (3) the date of payment.

On the date of declaration, the board of directors formally declares that a dividend will be paid to stockholders of record on a specified future date, typically four to six weeks later. On the declaration date the corporation becomes legally liable to pay the future dividend, retained earnings is reduced and the current liability is recorded. It normally takes a corporation some time to process the dividend checks and for investors to determine whether they desire to buy or sell the stock based on the dividends. Thus, a *cut-off* date is needed—the date of record. **On the date of record, only investors listed as stockholders of the corporation (the stockholders of record) can receive the dividend.** The date of record usually occurs several weeks after the declaration date and several weeks before the payment date, as specified in the dividend provisions. On the date of record no entry is necessary, although the corporation may make a memorandum entry in the general journal indicating that the date of record has been reached; it also begins processing the dividend checks. **On the date of payment, the corporation distributes the dividend checks.** An entry is also made on this date to eliminate the liability and reduce the cash.

Dividends are normally declared on a *per share basis*. That is, a set dollar amount per common share outstanding is established at the time of declaration. The total amount of the dividend liability is determined by multiplying the dividends per share times the number of common shares *outstanding* on the date of declaration.

To illustrate, assume that on November 15, 1993, a corporation declared a 60¢ per share dividend on its 4,000 outstanding common shares. These dividends are payable on December 30, 1993, to stockholders of record as of December 15, 1993. The declaration of the dividends of $2,400 (4,000 × $0.60) is recorded as follows:

Assets =	Liabilities	+	Stockholders' Equity
	+$2,400		−$2,400

Dividends Payable		Retained Earnings	
	$2,400	$2,400	

The payment of the dividends is recorded as follows:

Assets	=	Liabilities	+ Stockholders' Equity
−$2,400		−$2,400	

Cash		Dividends Payable	
	$2,400	$2,400	

If the accounting period had ended between the date of declaration and the date of payment, the Dividends Payable would be classified as a current liability on the balance sheet.

Dividends on Preferred Stock

As we indicated earlier in the chapter, some investors consider certain stockholder rights to be more important than others. To appeal to these investors, preferred stock may be issued. The rights of preferred stockholders are included on the stock certificate. Two of these rights are important for dividends: (1) a preference to dividends and (2) accumulation of dividends. Preferred stock may be issued with one or both of these rights. Each of these rights is discussed next.

Preference as to Dividends.   Holders of preferred stock usually have a preference as to dividends. **A dividend preference is a right of preferred stockholders to receive a dividend before a dividend can be paid to common stockholders.** Preferred stock is usually issued with a par or stated value, and the dividends are expressed as a percentage of this value. For instance, assume that a corporation has outstanding 1,000 shares of 10%, $50 par preferred stock. The corporation must pay $5 per share ($50 par × 10%), which totals $5,000 ($5 × 1,000 shares), as dividends to preferred stockholders before it can pay *any* dividends to common stockholders.

Such a preference to dividends does *not* guarantee that a preferred dividend will be paid in any given year since the board of directors can decide not to pay any dividends. To protect preferred stockholders further, a provision may be included on the preferred stock certificate that requires the accumulation of dividends.

Cumulative Preferred Stock.   Stockholders are not legally entitled to share in dividends unless these dividends have been declared by the board of directors. If dividends are not declared in a given year, a holder of noncumulative preferred stock will never be paid that dividend. For this reason noncumulative preferred stock is seldom issued, because investors consider this feature to be a distinct disadvantage.

Most preferred stock is cumulative. **Cumulative preferred stock is preferred stock that must be paid all dividends of the current and past periods before any dividends can be paid to common stockholders. Any dividends not declared on cumulative preferred stock in a given period become dividends in arrears.** Dividends in arrears accumulate from period to period. The dividends in arrears are *not* a liability to the corporation because no liability exists until the dividend declaration. Any dividends in arrears, however, are very important to investors and other interested parties and should be disclosed in a note to the financial statements.

To illustrate dividends in arrears, assume that a corporation has 2,000 shares of 8%, $100 par cumulative preferred stock outstanding. Each share of stock is entitled to an $8 annual dividend. If dividends are not declared in 1992 and 1993, preferred stockholders would be entitled to dividends in arrears of $16,000 (2,000 × $8) at the end of 1992 and $32,000 (2,000 × $8 × 2 years) at the end of 1993. If dividends are declared at the end of 1994, $48,000 (for 3 years) would have to be paid to preferred stockholders before any dividend payments could be made to common stockholders.

■ APPROPRIATIONS OF RETAINED EARNINGS

When setting dividend policy the board of directors of a corporation should consider both legal requirements and sound financial practice. Stockholders sometimes look at only the legal requirements, and as the retained earnings balance increases, they may expect to receive more dividends. The *assets* of the corporation, however, must be used for a variety of corporate activities, including financing ongoing operations and long-term expansion projects, meeting principal and interest payments on bonds, and making dividend payments.

To indicate that a part of retained earnings is unavailable for dividends, a corporation may appropriate (restrict) retained earnings. **An appropriation of retained earnings is the restriction of an amount of retained earnings by the board of directors so that this amount is not available for the declaration of dividends.** It is important to note that such a policy does *not* directly restrict the use of any assets; it merely requires that the corporation not distribute any assets that would reduce the restricted retained earnings. A corporation may still declare and pay dividends, reducing unappropriated retained earnings.

Reasons for Appropriations

A board of directors may appropriate retained earnings (1) to meet *legal* requirements, (2) to meet *contractual* restrictions, or (3) because of *discretionary* actions. States usually require restrictions of retained earnings when a corporation reacquires its own stock as treasury stock, the appropriation of retained earnings being an amount equal to the cost of the treasury shares. The argument for this appropriation is that the corporation, by acquiring treasury stock, reduces the amount of invested (permanent) capital. By restricting retained earnings for an equal amount, permanent capital is protected.

Retained earnings may also be restricted as a result of a contractual agreement. Such an agreement is often made when a corporation issues long-term bonds. To provide some assurance that excessive dividends will not be distributed which would endanger bondholders' claims, the bond provisions may require the periodic appropriation of a certain amount of retained earnings.

Finally, retained earnings may be appropriated as a result of management discretion. This type of restriction may be related to planning for future expansion. That is, a company may be planning to build a new plant or to add to existing facilities. It may be desirable to finance this activity through internally generated funds (i.e., funds that the corporation already holds or will receive from operations in the near future) rather than seek external funding from creditors or through the issuance of more capital stock. To indicate that these internal funds are being held as assets within the corporation for this purpose and are unavailable for dividends, the board of directors may appropriate a portion of retained earnings.

Accounting for Appropriations

Appropriations of retained earnings may be accounted for by (1) adjusting accounts or (2) reporting the restrictions in a note to the financial statements. In the first case, an *Appropriated Retained Earnings* account is established and the Retained Earnings account is reduced. On the balance sheet, retained earnings would be shown as follows (amounts assumed):

Retained earnings, unappropriated	$160,000
Retained earnings appropriated for treasury stock	40,000
Total retained earnings	$200,000

A major disadvantage of using formal entries to disclose appropriations of retained earnings is that users still may be confused about the availability of dividends. In the last example, for instance, when stockholders see "Retained Earnings, Unappropriated" in the amount of $160,000 on the balance sheet, they may expect dividends to be paid in that amount. In order to improve the reporting of retained earnings appropriations, most companies now report this information by means of a note to the financial statements. When a note is used, a clear description of the legal, contractual, or discretionary provisions and the amount of the appropriation are necessary. To illustrate, the $200,000 retained earnings balance from above and the note for the treasury stock would appear as follows:

Retained earnings (see *Note A*)	$200,000

Note A: Retained earnings are restricted regarding dividends in the amount of $40,000, the cost of the treasury stock.

SECTION B   Corporate Earnings

■ CORPORATE EARNINGS

The income statement of a corporation may have several major components. The following outline lists these components and the items within each component:

1. Income from continuing operations
   a. Operating income
   b. Nonoperating income (other revenues and expenses and gains and losses)
   c. Income tax expense related to continuing operations

2. Results of discontinued operations
   a. Income (loss) from operations of a discontinued segment (net of income taxes)
   b. Gain (loss) on disposal of a discontinued segment (net of income taxes)

3. Extraordinary gains or losses (net of income taxes)
4. The cumulative effect of a change in an accounting principle
5. Net income (the net amount of items 1, 2, 3, and 4)
6. Earnings per share

Not every income statement contains each of these components. An example of an income statement that includes each component is shown in Exhibit 10–2. The purpose of these components is to increase the usefulness of the income statement to users. In addition to the increased information, the income from continuing operations should have greater predictive ability than net income. Many companies use a more condensed form of the income statement and provide the detailed information in the notes to the financial statements.

Income from Continuing Operations

Income from continuing operations includes the income statement items discussed in the previous chapters. Included here is operating income, determined by subtracting cost of goods sold from net sales to obtain gross profit, and then deducting the selling expenses and general and administrative expenses. Also included is the nonoperating income (or expense), which is the sum of the other revenues and expenses. These other revenues and expenses include significant recurring items such as interest expense and revenue which are not part of the corporation's primary operations. They also include ordinary (as opposed to extraordinary) gains and losses such as those related to the sale of equipment.

Intraperiod Income Tax Allocation

The components of income tax expense are separately reported on the income statement by intraperiod income tax allocation. **Intraperiod income tax allocation is the process of matching a portion of the total income tax expense against the pretax: (1) income from continuing operations, (2) income (loss) from the operations of a discontinued segment, (3) gain (loss) from the disposal of a discontinued segment, (4) gain (loss) from an extraordinary item, and (5) the cumulative effect of a change in accounting principle.** The reason for intraperiod income tax allocation is quite simple: the allocation is necessary to give a fair presentation of the after-tax impact of the major components of net income.

The portion of the income tax expense for continuing operations is listed as a separate item on the income statement and is deducted from pretax income from continuing operations (or income before income taxes if there are no additional components of net income) to determine income from continuing operations. (If there are no additional components, the resulting amount is the net income.) As shown on Exhibit 10–2 for the Glanton Corporation, the $3,600 income tax expense of continuing operations, as computed in Exhibit 10–3, is deducted from the $12,000 pretax income from continuing operations to determine the $8,400 income from continuing operations.

Any items included in the results from discontinued operations, as extraordinary items, or as changes in accounting principle, are shown *net* of income

EXHIBIT 10–2

GLANTON CORPORATION
Income Statement
For Year Ended December 31, 1993

Sales (net)		$100,000
Cost of goods sold		(60,000)
Gross profit		$ 40,000
Operating expenses		
Selling expenses	$16,000	
General and administrative expenses	13,000	
Total operating expenses		(29,000)
Operating income		$ 11,000
Other revenues and expenses		
Gain on sale of equipment	$ 500	
Interest revenue	700	
Interest expense	(200)	
Nonoperating income		1,000
Pretax income from continuing operations		$ 12,000
Income tax expense of continuing operations		(3,600)
Income from continuing operations		$ 8,400
Results of discontinued operations		
Loss from operations of discontinued		
Segment X (net of $150 income tax credit)	$ (350)	
Gain on sale of discontinued Segment X		
(net of $450 income tax expense)	1,050	700
Income before extraordinary loss		$ 9,100
Extraordinary loss from tornado (net of $600		
income tax credit)		(1,400)
Income before effect of change in depreciation		
method		$ 7,700
Cumulative effect of change in depreciation		
method (net of $2,100 income tax)		4,900
Net income		$ 12,600
Earnings per common share (see *Note A*)		
Income from continuing operations		$ 3.13
Results of discontinued operations		.30
Extraordinary loss from tornado		(.61)
Change in depreciation method		2.13
Earnings per common share		$ 4.95

Note A: Preferred dividends of $1,200 were deducted from net income and income from continuing operations in computing earnings per share. The weighted average number of common shares outstanding is 2,300 shares.

EXHIBIT 10–3

....

GLANTON CORPORATION					
Computation of Income Taxes for 1993					
	Pretax Amount	×	Income Tax Rate	=	Income Taxes
Income from continuing operations	$12,000	×	.30	=	$3,600
Loss from operations of discontinued segment	(500)	×	.30	=	(150)
Gain on sale of discontinued segment	1,500	×	.30	=	450
Extraordinary loss	(2,000)	×	.30	=	(600)
Cumulative effect of change in depreciation method	7,000	×	.30	=	2,100
Taxable income and income taxes	$18,000	×	.30	=	$5,400

taxes. That is, for each of these items the income tax expense (or income tax credit, in the case of a loss) is deducted directly from (or added to) each item, and only the after-tax amount is included in the computation of net income. To illustrate, assume that in 1993 the Glanton Corporation reports pretax income from continuing operations of $12,000, a pretax loss from operations of discontinued Segment X of $500, a pretax gain on the sale of discontinued Segment X of $1,500, a pretax extraordinary loss of $2,000, and a cumulative effect of a change in depreciation method of $7,000. It computes its total income tax expense and the income taxes related to each item as shown in Exhibit 10–3 (assuming a 30% income tax rate). Note that the two items of loss reduced the income taxes in the amounts of $150 and $600, respectively. These amounts are called *income tax credits*.

The income tax expense or credit for those items included below income from continuing operations is shown parenthetically on the income statement. In Exhibit 10–2 the loss from operations of discontinued Segment X is shown at its after-tax amount of $350 ($500 less the income tax credit of $150 from Exhibit 10–3), the gain on sale of discontinued Segment X is listed at $1,050 ($1,500 − $450), the extraordinary loss at $1,400 ($2,000 − $600), and the cumulative effect of the change in accounting principle at $4,900 ($7,000 − $2,100).

Results of Discontinued Operations

The term **discontinued operations** refers to the operations of a segment that has been sold, abandoned, spun off, or otherwise disposed of. **A segment is a component of a company whose activities represent a separate *major* line of business or class of customer.**[3] This segment might be a subsidiary, division, or department provided that its assets, results of operations, and activities can

....

[3]"Reporting the Results of Operations," *APB Opinion No. 30* (New York: AICPA, 1973).

be clearly distinguished physically, operationally, and for financial reporting purposes, from the remainder of the company.

The disposal of a segment is distinguished from the disposal of assets related to part of a line of business, the shifting of a particular line of business from one location to another, or the phasing out of a product line or class of service. It is sometimes difficult to determine what is a disposal of a segment and what is not. Several examples of transactions involving the disposal of a segment include (1) the sale by a diversified company of a major division that represents the company's only activities in the electronics industry, (2) the sale by a meat packing company of its 20% interest in a professional football team, (3) the sale by a communications company of its radio stations but none of its television stations, and (4) the disposal by a food distributor of its wholesale supermarket division while maintaining its wholesale fast-foods restaurants division. Transactions which should *not* be considered as disposals of segments include (1) the sale by a diversified company of one of its two furniture manufacturing subsidiaries, (2) the disposal by a manufacturer of children's wear of its foreign children's wear designing, selling, and manufacturing division, and (3) the sale by an apparel manufacturer of a woolen suit manufacturing plant in order to concentrate on the manufacture of suits from synthetic products.[4]

The disposal of a discontinued segment is an important event for a corporation because the disposal potentially affects its future earnings potential. For this reason certain information about the discontinued segment is reported separately on the income statement. This information includes: **(1) the income (or loss) from the operations of the discontinued segment for the accounting period up to the measurement date or the disposal date and (2) the gain or loss from the disposal of the discontinued segment**. The disclosure of discontinued operations is illustrated in Exhibit 10–4.

When a segment has operated for part of a year before it is discontinued, the operating income or loss from the discontinued segment is reported separately from the income from continuing operations of the company. Thus, each component of revenue and expense relating to the discontinued segment is "pulled out" of the income from continuing operations and included in the income or loss from operations of the discontinued segment as the first component of the Results of Discontinued Operations.

The gain or loss from the disposal of the assets and liabilities of the segment is also reported. The gains and losses are computed in the normal way as the difference between the selling price and book value and are included in the second component. This second component also includes the operating income or loss during the phase-out period from the measurement date to the disposal date and any costs associated with the disposal.

If the company expects the second component to be a net loss, the loss should be reported on the **measurement date** (the date on which the management of the company commits itself to a formal plan to dispose of the segment). If a

---

[4]"These examples were taken from *Accounting Interpretations of APB Opinion No. 30* (New York: AICPA, 1973).

EXHIBIT 10−4 Discontinued operations

BFGOODRICH
(in millions)

Income Statement (in part):	For Year Ended December 31		
	1989	1988	1987
Income from continuing operations	$171.2	$205.1	$80.8
Income (loss) from discontinued operations—net	1.2	(12.1)	(1.6)

NOTES TO CONSOLIDATED FINANCIAL STATEMENTS (in part):

Note C. Discontinued Operations

During 1989, BFGoodrich sold the elastomers business unit of its Specialty Chemicals segment and decided to sell the marine products and services business unit of its Aerospace Products segment.

In 1988, BFGoodrich sold its 50 percent interest in The Uniroyal Goodrich Tire Company ("UGTC") to UGTC Holding Corporation, a Delaware corporation formed by a group of investors organized by Clayton & Dubilier, Inc. UGTC had been formed on August 1, 1986, when BFGoodrich and Uniroyal Holdings, Inc. ("Uniroyal") combined their tire business (except aircraft tires) into a joint-venture partnership owned equally by subsidiaries of BFGoodrich and Uniroyal. In connection with the sale, BFGoodrich received $225.0 in cash, plus a warrant to purchase common stock of UGTC Holding Corporation representing 10 percent of its initial equity on a fully diluted basis, which effectively represents up to 7 percent of the equity of UGTC on a fully diluted basis. BFGoodrich has not recorded any value for the warrant. In September 1989, Groupe Michelin agreed to acquire UGTC, which agreement is subject to various conditions and government approvals. If the transaction is consummated as proposed, BFGoodrich expects to realize a pretax gain of approximately $30.0 from exercising or tendering the warrant.

Also during 1988, BFGoodrich sold substantially all of the assets and businesses of its Industrial Products business segment; sold its engineered rubber product business unit; and entered into an agreement to sell its aircraft tire business unit (such sale being consummated on January 24, 1989). The engineered rubber products and aircraft tire business units had been part of the Company's Aerospace Products business segment.

The results of operations of these businesses are accounted for as discontinued operations in the Consolidated Statement of Income. A summary of income statement information relating to discontinued operations is as follows:

	1989	1988	1987
Sales	$70.2	$193.6	$225.4
Costs and expenses	63.3	198.5	232.3
Operating income (loss)	6.9	(4.9)	(6.9)
Equity in earnings of UGTC	—	1.8	11.6
Other income (loss)—net	—	(.7)	—
Income (loss) from operations before income taxes	6.9	(3.8)	4.7
Income tax expense	(1.4)	(.3)	(1.6)
Income (loss) from operations	5.5	(4.1)	3.1
Loss on disposition of discontinued operations (net of income tax expense of $1.4 in 1989 and tax benefits of $3.7 in 1988 and $3.1 in 1987)	(4.3)	(8.0)	(4.7)
Income (loss) from discontinued operations—net	$ 1.2	$ (12.1)	$ (1.6)

The loss on disposition of discontinued operations includes provisions of $4.0 ($3.2 net of income taxes), in the second quarter of 1989 and in the fourth quarter of 1987, respectively, to cover estimated costs of environmental matters related to previously disposed discontinued operations.

gain is expected, it is reported on the **disposal date** (the date the disposal is completed). Thus, a company anticipating a loss includes that loss (based on estimates) in its income statement before the disposal has actually occurred. This distinction is an example of conservatism. When comparative income statements are presented, for each prior income statement the income from the discontinued segment is shown separately from the income from continuing operations of that period.

Extraordinary Items

For some companies certain "extraordinary" events or transactions may occur that result in material gains or losses. **An extraordinary item is an event or a transaction that is unusual in nature *and* occurs infrequently.**[5] *Both* of the following criteria must be met for a company to classify an event or a transaction as an extraordinary item:

1. **Unusual Nature. The underlying event or transaction should possess a high degree of abnormality and be of a type clearly unrelated to, or only incidentally related to, the ordinary and typical activities of the company, taking into account the environment in which the company operates.**

2. **Infrequency of Occurrence. The underlying event or transaction should be of a type that would not reasonably be expected to recur in the foreseeable future, taking into account the environment in which the company operates.**

In considering the **unusual nature** criterion, the environment in which a company operates is a primary consideration. This environment includes such factors as the characteristics of the industry in which the company operates, its geographical location(s), and the nature and extent of government regulation. An event may be unusual in nature for one company but not for another because of differences in their respective environments. Similarly, the determination of whether an event is **infrequent** in occurrence should consider the operating environment of the company. An event might be considered infrequent for one company and frequent for another because of different probabilities of recurrence within each respective operating environment.

To illustrate, a loss from an explosion in an office building may be classified as extraordinary, while a loss from an explosion in a munitions factory may *not* be considered extraordinary because the nature of the event is not unusual. Other examples of events that may give rise to extraordinary gains or losses include earthquakes, tornadoes, floods, expropriation of assets by a foreign country, and a prohibition under a newly enacted law or regulation, provided each event is *both* unusual and infrequent. Furthermore, material gains or losses from the extinguishment of debt are always reported as extraordinary items, as discussed in Chapter 8. Of the extraordinary items reported by 600 companies in 1988, 26 were for debt extinguishment, and 12 met the criteria of unusual and infrequent.[6] The disclosure of extraordinary items is illustrated in Exhibit 10–5.

....
[5]"Reporting the Results of Operations," *op. cit.*

EXHIBIT 10–5 Extraordinary items

....

REYNOLDS METALS COMPANY
(in millions)

Income Statement (in part):	Years Ended December 31,		
	1989	1988	1987
Income before income taxes and extraordinary item	$758.3	$658.7	$265.2
Taxes on income	225.6	176.7	64.5
Income before extraordinary item	$532.7	$482.0	$200.7
Extraordinary item	—	—	18.8
Net Income	$532.7	$482.0	$219.5

Notes to Consolidated Financial Statements (in part):

Note B—Extraordinary Item

The extraordinary item consists of utilization of tax loss carryforwards—$21.2; loss on extinguishment of debt—$10.5; and a gain on insurance settlement—$8.1.

In order to clarify further the distinction between extraordinary and nonextraordinary items, events or transactions that would meet both criteria and should be reported as *extraordinary items* include the following cases:[7]

1. A large portion of a tobacco manufacturer's crops is destroyed by a hailstorm. Severe damage from hailstorms in the locality where the manufacturer grows tobacco is rare.

2. A steel-fabricating company sells the only land it owns. The land was acquired ten years ago for future expansion, but shortly thereafter the company abandoned all plans for expansion and held the land for appreciation.

3. A company sells an investment in a block of common stock of a publicly traded firm. The block of shares, which represents less than 10% of the publicly held firm, is the only security investment the company has ever owned.

4. An earthquake destroys one of the oil refineries owned by a large multinational oil company.

Those events or transactions that do not meet both criteria and should *not* be reported as extraordinary items include these examples:

1. A citrus grower's Florida crop is damaged by frost. Frost damage is normally experienced every three to four years. The criterion of infrequency of occurrence taking into account the environment in which the company operates would not be met since the history of losses caused by frost damage provides

....

[6] *Accounting Trends and Techniques* (New York: AICPA, 1989), p. 309.
[7] *"Accounting Interpretations of APB Opinion No. 30,"* op. cit.

evidence that such damage may reasonably be expected to recur in the fore-seeable future.

2. A company that operates a chain of warehouses sells the excess land surrounding one of its warehouses. When the company buys property to establish a new warehouse, it usually buys more land than it expects to use for the warehouse with the expectation that the land will appreciate in value. In the past five years there have been two instances in which the company sold such excess land. The criterion of infrequency of occurrence has not been met since past experience indicates that such sales may reasonably be expected to recur in the foreseeable future.

3. A large diversified company sells a block of shares from its portfolio of securities which it has acquired for investment purposes. This is the first sale from its portfolio of securities. Since the company owns several securities for investment purposes, it should be concluded that sales of such securities are related to its ordinary and typical activities in the environment in which it operates, and thus the criterion of unusual nature would not be met.

4. A textile manufacturer with only one plant moves to another location. It has not relocated a plant in 20 years and has no plans to do so in the foreseeable future. Notwithstanding the infrequency of occurrence of the event as it relates to this particular company, moving from one location to another is an occurrence that is a consequence of customary and continuing business activities. Therefore, the criterion of unusual nature has not been met.

The decision whether to classify a gain or loss as extraordinary is often very difficult to make and can lead to conflict between the management of the company and the auditors. The user of financial statements only knows about a material gain or loss classified as extraordinary and is not necessarily aware of one not classified as extraordinary. However, a material gain or loss that arises from an event that is *either* unusual in nature *or* infrequent in occurrence *but not both* is reported as a separate component of income from continuing operations. Because these items are a component of income from continuing operations for which a related income tax expense is computed, unusual or infrequent gains or losses are *not* shown net of income taxes. Examples of such items are those previously cited that are not classified as the disposal of a segment or as not extraordinary.

Effects of Accounting Changes

Occasionally, a company must make an accounting change. Accounting changes include (1) a change in an accounting principle, (2) a change in an accounting estimate, and (3) prior period adjustments.[8] The appropriate accounting for each of these changes is complex and is only discussed briefly.

....
[8]"Accounting Changes," *APB Opinion No. 20* (New York: AICPA, 1971).

Change in Accounting Principle. A change in accounting principle occurs when a company adopts a generally accepted accounting principle different from the one which it has previously been using in its financial reporting. Here the term *accounting principle* includes not only principles but also accounting practices and the methods of application. It was suggested in Chapter 4 that the consistent use of accounting principles from period to period improves intracompany comparability. Consequently, there is a presumption that once an accounting principle is adopted, it continues to be used for similar transactions. However, consistent use of an accounting principle does not preclude a change in that principle when this change results in more informative financial statements. The burden of justifying a change in accounting principle rests with the company. Examples of changes in principles include a change in the inventory cost flow assumption, such as from first-in, first-out (FIFO) to average cost, and a change in the depreciation *method* for previously recorded assets (such as a switch from double-declining-balance to straight-line depreciation).

In most instances, to report a material change in accounting principle the cumulative effect of the change upon *prior* periods' income is included in the net income for the *period of the change*. That is, the related existing asset or liability account balance at the *beginning* of the current period is recalculated and a *new* balance determined under the assumption that the new accounting principle had been applied during prior periods. The account is adjusted to bring its balance to the required amount, and the offsetting amount is the cumulative effect of the change in accounting principle on *prior* periods' earnings and is included in net income. For instance, suppose a company acquired certain equipment in 1989 and has been depreciating it using the double-declining-balance method. At the beginning of 1993, it decides to change to the straight-line method for this equipment. The company calculates its total depreciation to date under the straight-line method. The difference in total depreciation between the two methods is recorded as a decrease in the Accumulated Depreciation balance at the beginning of 1993 because of the lesser depreciation charges in prior years, had the straight-line method been applied during those years. These lesser depreciation charges in prior years have resulted in increased earnings in those years. The cumulative increase in the prior earnings (net of income taxes) is disclosed on the income statement. This disclosure is illustrated in Exhibit 10–2 for the Glanton Corporation.

The new accounting principle is then applied during the current year in the normal fashion. The effect of adopting the new principle on income from continuing operations, net income, and earnings per share for the *current* period is disclosed in a note to the financial statements. This note includes an explanation and justification for the adoption of the new accounting principle. In our example the effect on net income due to the difference in depreciation expense for 1993 from using the straight-line method instead of the double-declining-balance method would be disclosed in such a note. Changes in accounting principles that have a material effect on income are relatively rare.

A change in accounting principle is also required when the FASB issues a *Statement* that defines a new principle. The accounting method to be used for the change is specified in the *Statement* but is usually a prior period adjustment, which is discussed later.

Change in Accounting Estimate.   Because financial statements are presented on a periodic basis, accounting estimates are necessary, and changes in these estimates frequently occur. Examples include changes in estimates of uncollectible receivables, inventory obsolescence, service lives and residual values of depreciable or depletable assets, and warranty costs. These changes may arise because of the occurrence of new events, as additional experience is acquired, or as more information is obtained. Note that they are *not* corrections of errors (which are prior period adjustments, discussed later), but rather they are changes due to additional facts not known at the time the original estimate was made. **When a change in an accounting estimate occurs, it is accounted for in the period of change and in future periods if the change affects both.** For instance, suppose in 1993 due to new information a company determines that a machine it owns has a remaining life of five years instead of its original estimate of an eight-year remaining life. The depreciation on the machine in 1993 and future years is based on the shorter five-year life (as discussed in Chapter 7). As a result, a higher depreciation expense is shown on the company's current and future income statements. No cumulative effect or restatement of the prior years' financial statements is made. However, in the period of the change in estimate a note is included in the financial statements that shows the effect of the change on that period's income before extraordinary items, net income, and earnings per share.

Prior Period Adjustments.   Three items are accounted for and reported as prior period adjustments: (1) the correction of a material error in the financial statements of a prior period, (2) certain changes in accounting principles, and (3) changes in an accounting entity.

Most errors are found before the financial statements are issued, or are not material. However, a company may occasionally make an error in the financial statements of one accounting period which is not discovered until a subsequent period. The error may be due to such items as mathematical mistakes, the incorrect use of existing facts, oversights, or the use of an accounting principle that is not generally accepted. The correction of a material error is accounted for as a prior period adjustment to the beginning retained earnings balance in the period of correction. The asset or liability balance in error at the beginning of the period is corrected, and the offsetting amount recorded directly in retained earnings. For instance, suppose that during 1993 a company found that it had inadvertently not recorded depreciation expense on a building in 1992. Thus, in 1992 depreciation expense was too low, accumulated depreciation was too low, and net income (which was added to retained earnings) was too high. The correction in 1993 entails a reduction in retained earnings and an increase in accumulated depreciation for the amount of the misstated depreciation. Any related impact upon income taxes is similarly recorded. The prior period adjustment (net of income taxes) is appropriately described and reported as an adjust-

EXHIBIT 10–6

```
BANNER CORPORATION
Statement of Retained Earnings
For Year Ended December 31, 1993
```

Retained earnings, January 1, 1993	$68,150
Add: prior period adjustment, correction of understatement of 1992 ending inventory (net of $2,000 income taxes)	3,000
Adjusted retained earnings, January 1, 1993	$71,150
Add: net income	9,300
	$80,450
Less: cash dividends, $0.50 per share	(2,500)
Retained earnings, December 31, 1993	$77,950

ment to the beginning retained earnings on the statement of retained earnings. As a result, the adjusted beginning retained earnings balance is the amount of retained earnings that *would have been* reported if the error had not been made. Corrections of material errors are relatively rare. The prior period adjustment for the Banner Corporation due to an error in counting the 1992 ending inventory is shown in Exhibit 10–6 (amounts assumed).

Certain changes in accounting principles are accounted for by prior period adjustment. The three most important examples are (1) the adoption of a newly mandated generally accepted accounting principle following the issuance of a *Statement* by the FASB, (2) a change *from* the LIFO inventory costing method, and (3) a change to or from the "full cost" method that is used in the extractive industries. The effect of the change on all previous accounting periods is included as an adjustment to the beginning balance of retained earnings, in a similar manner to that of an error. In addition, all the previous financial statements that are presented for comparative purposes are restated to reflect the assumed use of the new accounting principle in those periods. Note that the effect of the prior period adjustment on the financial statements of prior periods is a "re-editing" of the previously issued statements.

When the FASB adopts a new accounting principle, it specifies the date by which the principle must be adopted. This future date allows companies time to make any modifications to their accounting systems and collect relevant data. The date may be more than one year after the publication of the new principle. Therefore a company may be able to choose the year in which it adopts the principle. This situation creates a lack of comparability as different companies adopt the new principle in different years. A company may also choose the year of adoption because of the effect the principle will have on its earnings. In other words, the company may use the timing of the adoption to "manage" its earnings.

A change in a reporting entity is also accounted for by prior period adjustment. For example, when one company obtains control over another one (as discussed in Chapter 11), the previous periods' financial statements are restated to reflect the results that would have occurred if the combination had been in existence in those periods.

Using the cumulative effect method of accounting protects the integrity of the previously issued financial statements by requiring that all of the effect of the change be included in net income of the period of the change. In contrast, the prior period adjustment method enhances the comparability of the financial statements by requiring all the financial statements presented be prepared on the basis of the same accounting principles.

■ STOCK OPTION PLANS

Corporations often institute programs that enable employees to acquire ownership in the corporation through the purchase of shares of stock, often at a price less than the current market price. These programs are commonly referred to as **stock option plans**. The degree of allowed participation in a stock option plan does vary. At one extreme, the plan will be extended only to key officers and managers within the corporation; at the other extreme, all employees may be eligible to participate. Such plans are established for various reasons: (1) the need to attract more equity capital, (2) the belief that employee ownership will lead to a greater commitment to corporate activities, and (3) the desire to provide further compensation for certain employees. An important distinction is between noncompensatory and compensatory stock option plans.

Noncompensatory Stock Option Plans

A noncompensatory stock option plan is one that is designed to raise capital or to obtain more widespread employee ownership of the corporate stock rather than to provide additional compensation for certain employees. Four characteristics are identified as essential in a plan of this type:

1. Substantially all full-time employees who meet limited employment qualifications are able to participate in the plan.

2. Stock is offered to eligible employees on an equal basis or on a basis related to a uniform percentage of salaries.

3. The time permitted for exercise of the option by the employees is limited to a reasonable period.

4. The discount from the market price is not greater than that which would be reasonable in an offer of stock to stockholders or others.

If **all** these characteristics are met, the plan is defined as **noncompensatory** and the accounting is very straightforward. No compensation is considered to be extended to employees under such a plan and the increase in stockholders' equity is recorded when the shares are issued.

■ COMPENSATORY STOCK OPTION PLANS

Any stock option plan that does *not* possess all the preceding four characteristics is defined as a compensatory plan. **A compensatory stock option plan is typically extended to selected key officers or managers within the corporation to provide them with additional compensation.** The terms of a compensatory plan are generally very complex and related to such items as the number of shares to which each employee is entitled and the option price (both of which may depend on some future event), the period of service the employee must complete before becoming eligible, the date the option can first be exercised, and the date of expiration (if any).

Since a compensatory stock option plan may affect both the income statement and balance sheet, several issues must be addressed regarding compensatory plans.[9] These include determination of (1) the compensation cost (if any), (2) the accounting period(s) to which the compensation cost applies as an expense, and (3) the proper accounting for and disclosure of the compensatory stock option plan.

Compensation Cost.

Compensation cost is a function of the fair value of the stock option plan. There are various methods of determining the plan's fair value (and compensation cost). A reliable method is to consider that the compensation cost incurred consists of the difference between the amount of proceeds the corporation will receive from the issuance of the shares related to the stock option plan and the amount of proceeds that it could receive if the stock were issued on the open market. The difference represents the proceeds (or fair value) forgone by the corporation in lieu of paying higher cash salaries. The question arises, however, as to when this difference should be measured. It could be measured at any number of dates, including (1) the date of the adoption of the plan, (2) the date on which an option is granted to a particular employee, (3) the date on which the employee has satisfied any conditions related to the option, (4) the date when the employee may first exercise the option, (5) the date on which the option is exercised, or (6) the date on which the employee disposes of the acquired stock.

General accepted accounting principles have resolved the above issues by requiring that **the total compensation cost related to the stock option plan is the excess of the quoted market price over the option price on the measurement date. The measurement date is defined as the first date on which are known *both* (1) the number of shares an individual employee is entitled to receive and (2) the option or purchase price, if any.** For many plans, both the number of shares and the option price are known on the date that the option is *granted* to the employee. Then the date of grant is the date of measurement. For those plans with terms dependent on future events, a later measurement date is used.

....
[9]"Accounting for Stock Issued to Employees," *APB Opinion No. 25* (New York: AICPA, 1972).

Note that in cases where the option price is equal to, or higher than, the market price on the measurement date, *no* compensation cost is incurred. Prior to 1976, in many stock option plans the option price was equal to the market price because it provided the employee with significant federal income tax advantages (for example, the tax was generally deferred until the recipient *sold* the stock, at which time any gain was taxed at the lower long-term capital gains rate). These plans were referred to as *qualified stock option plans.* While qualified stock option plans were advantageous to the employee, they were a disadvantage to the corporation because it could not deduct any related cost as an expense. However, the Tax Reform Act of 1976 repealed most of these tax incentives for the employees. This action made *nonqualified stock option plans* (when the option price is less than the market price on the measurement date) more attractive to corporations. Under these plans, a corporation is entitled to a deduction based on the difference between the market price and the option price when the option is exercised. Under this type of plan, however, the employee is taxed on the difference between the option price and the market price when the option is exercised. Then, in the 1981 Economic Recovery Tax Act, Congress reinstated qualified stock option plans in a new, more liberal form to provide an incentive device for corporations to attract and retain key executives. The 1986 Tax Reform Act eliminated the preferential tax rate for capital gains.

Compensatory Stock Option Plans: Date of Measurement Is Date of Grant and Market Price Is Equal To, or Less Than, Option Price

When the measurement date is the date of the grant of the stock option, the market price may be less than, equal to, or greater than the option price. **When the market price on the measurement date is equal to, or less than, the option price the company recognizes no expense.** Thus, there is no compensation cost to the company even though the executives obtain a benefit by purchasing shares for less than the market price at the date of exercise. When the option is exercised, the company records the issuance of the stock at the *option price* in the normal manner.

Compensatory Stock Option Plans: Date of Measurement Is Date of Grant and Market Price Is Greater Than Option Price

In accounting for a compensatory stock option plan when the market price is greater than the option price on the measurement date and the measurement date is the date of grant, the compensation cost is recognized as an expense over the years in which the company receives the benefit of the employee's services. These years are referred to as the **service period.** The following items must be recorded: (1) the total compensation cost, (2) the annual compensation expense related to the plan, and (3) the issuance of the stock when the option is exercised.

To illustrate, assume that on December 31, 1993, a corporation grants to a key executive, Anthony Paul, the nontransferable right to acquire 1,000 shares of $10 par common stock for $27 per share. The market price on that date is $29 per share, and the service period is four years. The rights terminate at the end of seven years or if the executive leaves the corporation. The total compensation cost is $2,000 [($29 market price − $27 option price) × 1,000 shares] and is recorded as follows:

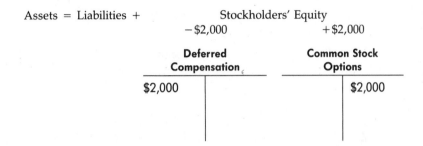

The Deferred Compensation is treated as a negative (contra) component of stockholders' equity on the balance sheet, and its balance is subtracted from the Common Stock Options in the contributed capital section. Therefore, there is no net effect on stockholders' equity.

The total deferred compensation cost is subsequently allocated as compensation expense to each year in the service period by use of the straight-line approach. In this example, the annual compensation expense ($500) is computed by dividing the total compensation cost ($2,000) by the number of years of required service (four years) and is recorded each year from 1994 to 1997 as follows:

Assets = Liabilities +   Stockholders' Equity

+ $500   − $500

Deferred Compensation		Compensation Expense	
	$500	$500	

At the end of the service period, the entire amount of Deferred Compensation will have been reported as Compensation Expense, but the Common Stock Options balance remains. If the option were exercised in 1999, the company would receive $27,000 (1,000 × $27) from Anthony Paul, the Common Stock Options would be reduced by $2,000 (1,000 × $2), and the balance of $29,000 (the market price on the date of grant of the option) would be recorded as contributed capital as follows:

Assets	= Liabilities +	Stockholders' Equity	
+$27,000	+$10,000	+$19,000	−$2,000

Cash		Common Stock	Additional Paid-in Capital	Common Stock Options
$27,000		$10,000	$19,000	$2,000

Note that the net increase in stockholders' equity of $27,000 is equal to the option price and *not* the market price of the stock issued.

Disclosure

Each year, the Compensation Expense is included on the income statement. The Common Stock Options balance offset by the Deferred Compensation balance is listed on the balance sheet as an element of contributed capital. To illustrate the balance sheet disclosure, the following items (among others) would appear in contributed capital, on December 31, 1994.

Common stock options	$2,000	
Less: deferred compensation	(1,500)	$500

The terms of the stock option plan, including the number of shares under option, the option price, the shares exercisable, and any shares exercised (along with the exercise price) must also be disclosed in the notes to the financial statements. For illustrative purposes, the preceding example involved only one executive. In reality, it is likely that many executives of a corporation would be involved in its compensatory stock option plan, and the accounting would follow the same principles as discussed for this one executive.

The total compensation given to each of the top executives through salary and stock options is often not included in the annual report to shareholders. It is a required disclosure in the Form 10-K filed with the SEC.

Stock Appreciation Rights

Although nonqualifying compensatory stock option plans provide key executives with the opportunity to acquire shares of stock with a market value in excess of the option price, these plans do have disadvantages. At the time of exercise, the executive must have sufficient cash to pay both the option price and the income taxes on the excess of the market price over the option price. This may place a significant cash flow burden on the executive. To remedy part of this problem, companies have developed compensation plans involving stock appreciation rights. **Stock appreciation rights** (SARs) are rights that enable executives to receive cash or stock (or a combination) that is equal to the *excess* of the market value over the option price. SARs are advantageous to an executive because the excess can be received on the date of exercise, thereby avoiding the cash outflow to actually acquire the stock. Furthermore, the executive may use the cash received from the SARs to pay the income taxes on the excess.

For stock appreciation rights plans, the date of measurement is usually deferred until the date the rights are *exercised*. Since the exercise date normally falls after the service period, (1) estimates of the total compensation cost must be made at the end of each year, (2) compensation expense must be recorded over the service period on the basis of these estimates (and any corrections of previous estimation errors), and (3) because corrections of estimates are *not* made retroactively, additional adjustments to compensation expense must be made each year *after* the service period has expired, up to the date of exercise.

Junior Stock Plans

Some companies have established "junior stock plans" for their key employees. **Junior stock** is stock of a corporation that generally does not have voting, liquidation, or dividend rights and is convertible in the future into the corporation's regular common stock if certain corporate performance goals are achieved. Junior stock is usually not transferable and has a lower market value than the regular corporate common stock because of the restrictions of stockholders' rights and the uncertainty of conversion. Under a **junior stock plan**, key employees are allowed to purchase a certain number of shares of junior stock at the lower market price with the expectation that they will convert at some future conversion ratio to regular common stock (with a higher market value) when the performance goals are met.

For purposes of measuring the total compensation cost, the measurement date is the first date on which are known both the number of shares of regular common stock that an employee is entitled to receive in exchange for the junior stock and the option price, if any. Prior to the measurement date, compensation cost is estimated and allocated to expense over the service period when it becomes probable that the performance goals will be achieved. If the junior stock becomes convertible to regular common stock after the measurement date, compensation expense is recognized each period until the date the junior stock becomes convertible, if this is later than the end of the service period.

The disclosure by Nike of its stock option plan, including stock appreciation rights, is illustrated in Exhibit 10–7. The company's profit sharing plan is also disclosed.

■ EARNINGS PER SHARE

All the information included in the financial statements and the related notes should be useful to external decision makers. Most users, however, focus on selected items that they consider to be of greatest relevance. Earnings per share

EXHIBIT 10–7 Example of disclosure of stock options and profit sharing plan

················ ———————————————————————

NIKE, INC.

Note 10—Common Stock:

The authorized number of shares of Class A Common Stock no par value and Class B Common Stock no par value are 20,000,000 and 50,000,000 respectively. Each share of Class A Common Stock is convertible into one share of Class B Common Stock. Voting rights of Class B Common Stock are limited in certain circumstances with respect to the election of directors.

During fiscal 1988, NIKE purchased and retired 1,362,100 shares of its own common stock at a total cost of $21.9 million.

The Company's Employee Incentive Compensation Plan (Option Plan) provides for the issuance of a maximum of 1,680,000 shares of the Company's Common Stock. Options granted must not be at a price less than the fair market value of the Class B Common Stock at the date of grant and can be issued in either Class A or Class B Common Stock. The Option Plan is administered by a committee of the Board of Directors which has the authority to determine optionees, the number of shares to be covered by each option, the dates upon which each option is exercisable, the method of payment, and certain other terms. The Option Plan has a stock appreciation feature which gives the committee authority to allow a specified holder to surrender his option in exchange for (1) the cash value of the difference between the option price and the fair market value of the common stock subject to option at the date of surrender, (2) the number of shares having such cash value or (3) a combination of the above. The Option Plan expires in 1990.

The following summarizes the Option Plan transactions for the two years ended May 31, 1989:

	Shares (in thousands)	Option Price Per Share ($)
Options outstanding May 31, 1987	442	9.50 to 19.75
Exercised	(93)	9.50 to 19.75
Surrendered	(41)	9.50 to 21.25
Granted	91	17.06 to 22.19
Options outstanding May 31, 1988:	399	9.50 to 22.19
Exercised	(144)	9.50 to 22.19
Surrendered	(18)	9.50 to 21.69
Granted	209	21.12 to 39.31
Options outstanding May 31, 1989:	446	9.50 to 39.31
Options exercisable at May 31:		
1989	150	9.50 to 22.06
1988	148	9.50 to 19.75

In addition to the Option Plan, the Company has several agreements outside of the Plan with certain directors and employees. As of May 31, 1989, 848,000 options with exercise prices ranging from $.417 per share to $25.00 per share had been granted. The aggregate compensation expense related to these agreements is $4,521,000 and is being amortized over vesting periods from October 1980 through December 1993. These agreements expire from September 1993 through December 1998.

EXHIBIT 10-7 *(continued)*

················

NIKE, INC.

The following summarizes transactions outside the Option Plan for the two years ended May 31, 1989:

	Shares (in thousands)	Option Price Per Share ($)
Options outstanding May 31, 1987	378	.417 to 9.50
Exercised	(190)	.417 to 9.50
Surrendered	—	—
Granted	8	9.50
Options outstanding May 31, 1988:	196	.417 to 9.50
Exercised	(53)	.417 to 9.50
Surrendered	—	—
Granted	60	25.00
Options outstanding May 31, 1989:	203	.417 to 25.00
Options exercisable at May 31:		
1989	69	.417 to 9.50
1988	34	9.50

Note 11—Profit Sharing Plan:

The Company has a profit sharing plan available to substantially all employees. The terms of the plan call for annual contributions by the Company as determined by the Board of Directors. Contributions of $4,700,000, $3,000,000 and $1,300,000 to the plan are included in other expense in the consolidated financial statements for the years ended May 31, 1989, 1988, and 1987.

(EPS) is one measure that is considered to be very important by most users. It is often considered to be the one single measure that best summarizes the performance of the company, particularly for common shareholders.

The amount of earnings per share, the change in earnings per share from the previous period, and the trend in earnings per share are all important indicators of the success, or failure, of the company. Many investors are also interested in the cash flow per share generated by the company. Although companies are prohibited from reporting cash flow per share, the earnings per share may be considered to be a long-run indicator of cash flow per share.

Earnings per share is also divided into the price per share of the common stock to compute the price/earnings ratio, as discussed in Chapter 14. For example, at the time of writing this book, General Motors, Ford, and Chrysler had price/earnings ratios of 6, 4, 3, respectively. General Motors' price/earnings ratio of 6 indicates that the stock is selling for a price of 6 times the most recent year's earnings per share. Based on this data, investors apparently are more optimistic about the future of General Motors and expect that it will experience a higher growth in earnings per share.

Investors are also interested in predicting earnings per share for future periods. While accountants generally do not provide information about the future, two earnings per share calculations are intended to indicate the potential impacts of possible future events. When a company has issued common stock options (discussed in this chapter), convertible debt (discussed in Chapter 8), or convertible preferred stock (discussed in this chapter), additional common shares will be issued when the options are exercised or the securities converted, thereby affecting earnings per share. Primary and fully diluted earnings per share include the potential effects of such conversions and are discussed in Appendix 1 of this chapter.

Earnings per share is a corporation's net income per share available to its common stockholders. In its simplest form, earnings per share is computed by dividing the corporation's net income by the number of common shares outstanding throughout the entire year. Many corporations, however, report several components of net income and have preferred stock outstanding that has first priority to dividends. They also may have shares of common stock outstanding for only a portion of a year as a result of stock issuances during the year or treasury stock may have been acquired or reissued. Earnings per share computations can be very complicated. In this section, the calculation of simple earnings per share is discussed. Two other measures of earnings per share— primary earnings per share and fully diluted earnings per share—are discussed in Appendix 1 of this chapter. The **simple earnings per share** computation may be expressed as follows:

$$\text{Earnings per Common Share Outstanding} = \frac{\text{Net Income} - \text{Preferred Dividends}}{\text{Weighted Average Number of Common Shares Outstanding}}$$

Net Income and Preferred Dividends

Common stockholders are considered to be the *residual* owners of the corporation. Therefore, earnings per share applies *only* to common shares, and only the earnings available to common stockholders are used in the numerator of the earnings per share computation. If a corporation has no preferred shares outstanding, the net income is used as the numerator in computing earnings per share. If there is outstanding preferred stock, however, the preferred dividends for the current period are deducted from the net income to determine the earnings available to common stockholders. To illustrate the computation of the numerator, suppose that the Glanton Corporation (from Exhibit 10–2) had preferred stock outstanding during all of 1993 and the dividends on this preferred stock amounted to $1,200. The numerator of the Glanton Corporation's 1993 earnings per share is $11,400, computed by subtracting the $1,200 preferred dividends from the $12,600 net income, as illustrated in Exhibit 10–9.

Weighted Average Common Shares

Since a corporation earns its net income over the entire year, the earnings should be related to the weighted average number of common shares outstanding during

EXHIBIT 10–8 Weighted average common shares

Months Shares Are Outstanding	Shares Outstanding	×	Fraction of Year Outstanding	=	Weighted Average
January–July	1,800		$\frac{7}{12}$		1,050
August–December	3,000		$\frac{5}{12}$		1,250
		Total Weighted Average Common Shares		=	2,300

EXHIBIT 10–9 Computation of earnings per share

Earnings per share	$4.95	$= \dfrac{\$12,600 - \$1,200}{2,300}$
Components:		
Income from continuing operations	$3.13	$= \dfrac{\$8,400 - \$1,200}{2,300}$
Results of discontinued operations	.30	$= \dfrac{\$700}{2,300}$
Extraordinary loss from tornado	(.61)	$= \dfrac{\$(1,400)}{2,300}$
Change in depreciation method	2.13	$= \dfrac{\$4,900}{2,300}$
	$4.95	

the year. If a corporation has not issued any common shares during the year, the common shares outstanding for the entire year are used as the denominator. When common shares have been issued during the year, these shares are multiplied times the fraction of the year (in months) they are outstanding. The result is added to the beginning number of shares to determine the weighted average number of common shares outstanding during the year. This number is used as the denominator in the earnings per share calculation.

To illustrate, assume that the Glanton Corporation had 1,800 common shares that were outstanding during 1993, until August 1, 1993, when it issued an additional 1,200 common shares so that it had 3,000 common shares outstanding at the end of the year. Its weighted average number of common shares outstanding during 1993 is 2,300 as shown in Exhibit 10–8, and used in the calculations illustrated in Exhibit 10–9.

Computation and Disclosure

The simple earnings per share figure is computed by dividing the earnings available to common stockholders (i.e., net income less preferred dividends) by the weighted average number of common shares outstanding. This earnings per share figure is disclosed on the income statement directly below net income. In addition, the earnings per share related to the major components of net income are also disclosed. The earnings per share for the income from continuing operations is calculated by subtracting the preferred dividends from the income from continuing operations and dividing the result by the weighted average common shares. The earnings per share figures for the results of discontinued operations, extraordinary items, and changes in an accounting principle are computed by dividing the respective amounts (disregarding the preferred dividends) by the weighted average common shares. The amount of the preferred dividends deducted from the numerator and the weighted average number of common shares used in the denominator should be disclosed in a note to the income statement.

The simple earnings per share of the Glanton Corporation for 1993 are $4.95, as shown in Exhibit 10–9. Also shown are the earnings per share for each component of the income statement. The earnings per share figures total $4.95 and are shown in Exhibit 10–2. The note to the Glanton Corporation income statement discloses the preferred dividends and weighted average shares.

■ STATEMENT OF CHANGES IN STOCKHOLDERS' EQUITY

As can be seen from the discussion in this chapter, in a single accounting period a corporation may have many transactions affecting some component of contributed capital. In addition, the retained earnings of a corporation are increased by the net income and decreased by the dividends of the accounting period. To disclose its corporate capital activities, each corporation reports the changes in the different classes of capital stock (including the number of shares issued), in each additional paid-in capital account, in capital stock subscribed, in treasury stock, and in retained earnings. Most corporations disclose this information on a statement of changes in stockholders' equity. **A statement of changes in stockholders' equity is a supporting schedule to the stockholders' equity section of the balance sheet.**

The statement of changes in stockholders' equity of the Barth Corporation is shown in Exhibit 10–10, using assumed figures. In the exhibit each of the transactions that affected the components of stockholders' equity is briefly explained. The shares issued and dollar amounts are also included. For instance, the second line indicates that the $18,000 proceeds received from issuing 1,000 shares of common stock were allocated in the amounts of $10,000 to the common stock account and $8,000 to additional paid-in capital. Note that the amounts in the treasury stock column are listed in parentheses because treasury stock is a negative component of stockholders' equity. The columns are then totaled, and

EXHIBIT 10–10

BARTH CORPORATION
Statement of Changes in Stockholders' Equity
Schedule A
For Year Ended December 31, 1993

Explanation	COMMON STOCK Shares Issued	COMMON STOCK $10 Par Value	Common Stock Subscribed	ADDITIONAL PAID-IN CAPITAL On Common Stock	ADDITIONAL PAID-IN CAPITAL From Treasury Stock	ADDITIONAL PAID-IN CAPITAL From Donations	Retained Earnings	Treasury Stock
Balances, 1/1/1993	6,000	$60,000	-0-	$24,000	$2,000	-0-	$67,000	$(4,500)
Issued for cash	1,000	10,000		8,000				
Reissued treasury stock (100 shares at $17, cost $15)					200			1,500
Subscription to 500 shares at $18 per share			$5,000	4,000				
Accepted donated land for plant site						$6,000		
Net income							49,000	
Dividends							(20,000)	
Balances, 12/31/1993	7,000	$70,000	$5,000	$36,000	$2,200	$6,000	$96,000	$(3,000)

EXHIBIT 10–11

BARTH CORPORATION
Stockholders' Equity
December 31, 1993

Contributed capital (see Schedule A)
Common stock, $10 par, 30,000 shares authorized, 7,000 shares issued, 6,800 shares outstanding	$70,000	
Common stock subscribed (500 shares)	5,000	
Additional paid-in capital on common stock	36,000	
Additional paid-in capital from treasury stock	2,200	
Additional paid-in capital from donations (land)	6,000	
Total contributed capital		$119,200
Retained earnings (see *Note* and Schedule A)		96,000
Total contributed capital and retained earnings		$215,200
Less: treasury stock (200 shares at a cost of $15 per share)		(3,000)
Total stockholders' equity		$212,200

Note: Retained earnings are restricted regarding dividends in the amount of $3,000, the cost of the treasury stock.

the column headings and totals are included in the stockholders' equity section of the balance sheet, as shown in Exhibit 10–11. Note that the items and amounts listed in stockholders' equity in Exhibit 10–11 correspond to the columns and totals in Exhibit 10–10. Nike's Statement of Shareholders' Equity is illustrated in Appendix A at the end of the book.

If a statement of changes in stockholders' equity is not presented because the only item that changed was retained earnings, a statement of retained earnings may be prepared as a separate schedule to the balance sheet or as a schedule directly beneath the income statement. When shown separately, the statement reports on the impact of net income, dividends, and prior period adjustments for the accounting period on retained earnings. Exhibit 10–12 provides an illustration of a retained earnings statement (all amounts are assumed).

■ APPENDIX 1: EARNINGS PER SHARE— ADDITIONAL ISSUES

The computation of **simple** earnings per share was discussed in the chapter. Many corporations have a more complex capital structure, including such items as convertible preferred stock and bonds and stock options. Each of these is potentially a common stock equivalent (to be defined later). Holders of these securities are likely to participate in the appreciation of the common stock resulting primarily from the earnings of the corporation. Logically, then, they should be considered in computing earnings per share.

Instead of a single, simple earnings-per-share disclosure, **corporations with complex capital structures are required to make equally prominent dual pre-**

EXHIBIT 10–12

....

SLUSHER CORPORATION
Statement of Retained Earnings
For Year Ended December 31, 1993

Retained earnings, January 1, 1993		$ 78,000
Add: Correction of understatement in 1992 net income due to overstatement of depreciation (net of $2,000 income tax expense)		3,000
Adjusted retained earnings, January 1, 1993		$ 81,000
Add: Net income		39,000
		$120,000
Less: Cash dividend on common stock ($4 per share)	$9,300	
Cash dividend on preferred stock ($6 per share)	7,200	
Stock dividend on common stock	2,500	(19,000)
Retained earnings, December 31, 1993		$101,000

---

sentations on the face of the income statement. The two amounts are known as primary earnings per share and fully diluted earnings per share. **Primary earnings per share** is based on the outstanding common shares and the common stock equivalents that have a dilutive effect. **Fully diluted earnings per share** reflects the dilution of earnings per share which would have occurred if *all* contingent issuances of common stock that would have individually reduced earnings per share had taken place.[10] The computations and disclosures of primary and fully diluted earnings per share are considered in the following sections.

▮ PRIMARY EARNINGS PER SHARE

In computing primary earnings per share for a complex capital structure, the potential impact of common stock equivalents must be considered in addition to the calculations included in simple earnings per share.

A common stock equivalent is a security that is not in the form of a common stock, but which contains provisions that enable its holder to acquire common stock. Because of the terms and circumstances under which the security was first issued, it is in substance equivalent to a common stock. The security has not been converted into common stock; the critical issue is whether an evaluation (discussed later) of the security's provisions determines it to be a common stock equivalent. This determination is made when the security is *issued* and is not changed so long as it remains outstanding. However, to be included in the primary earnings-per-share calculation, the common stock equivalent must have a *dilutive* effect on (that is, decrease) earnings per share. Thus, a common

....

[10]"Earnings Per Share," *APB Opinion No. 15* (New York: AICPA, 1969).

stock equivalent may be included in the primary earnings-per-share computation in one accounting period and not in another depending on whether or not it is determined to be dilutive.

Stock Options

Stock options were discussed in the chapter. **Stock options are *always* considered to be common stock equivalents.** However, they are included in primary earnings per share only if they are *dilutive*. Since the exercise of stock options would not normally affect net income, the focus is on the earnings-per-share denominator. **The treasury stock method is used to determine the change in the number of shares.** In this method, the impact on common shares is computed under the assumption (for earnings-per-share computations) that the options were exercised at the beginning of the period (or at the time of the issuance of the options if later) and that the assumed proceeds obtained from the exercise were used by the corporation to reacquire common stock at the average market price during the period. The intent is to approximate the impact on the corporate capital structure had all stock options being exercised. **Under the treasury stock method, the change in the number of shares is the difference between the assumed shares issued and the assumed shares reacquired and is added to the denominator of the earnings-per-share calculation.** This relationship is illustrated by the following diagram:

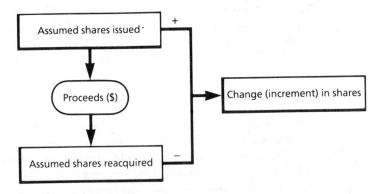

Whenever shares issued exceed shares reacquired, the effect is a dilution of earnings per share. This situation occurs whenever **the average market price is greater than the option price.** In this case, it is assumed that fewer shares are acquired as treasury stock than are issued via the exercise of the option. Should the average market price be less than the option price, the assumed exercise would be antidilutive and the options would be *excluded* from the primary earnings-per-share computation. The normal steps necessary to implement the treasury stock method may be summarized as follows:

1. Determine the average market price of common shares during the period (if less than the option price, there is no need to continue; the assumed exercise of the options and warrants would be antidilutive).

2. Compute the shares issued from the assumed exercise of all options.
3. Compute the proceeds received from the assumed exercise by multiplying the number of shares by the option price.
4. Compute the assumed shares reacquired by dividing the proceeds (step 3) by the average market price (step 1).
5. Compute the incremental common shares (the results of step 2 minus step 4).

To illustrate, assume a corporation has 10,000 common shares and options to purchase 1,000 common shares at $20 per share outstanding the entire year, and that the average market price for the common stock during the year was $25 per share. The net increase in the denominator would be 200 shares, which would have a dilutive effect on earnings per share. The share calculation is shown below.

Shares Assumed Issued per Assumed Exercise		1,000
Shares Assumed Reacquired:		

$$\frac{\text{Proceeds}}{\text{Average Market Price per Share}} = \frac{1,000 \times \$20}{\$25} = \frac{\$20,000}{\$25} = \underline{800}$$

Assumed Increment in Common Shares for
  Computing Primary Earnings per Share   <u>200</u>

Once the number of incremental shares resulting from the assumed exercise of the options is computed, the increase is added to the denominator of the simple earnings per share. The original numerator is then divided by the new denominator to determine the tentative primary earnings per share. If no other common stock equivalents are outstanding, this tentative figure is the final primary earnings per share.

Convertible Securities

Convertible bonds and convertible preferred stock may contain provisions that, at the time of issuance, make them essentially equivalent to common stock. To make this evaluation consistently and objectively, the FASB established an "effective yield test."

Effective Yield Test. Convertible securities are issued at a lower interest rate and/or at a higher selling price than nonconvertible securities, the difference being due to the value of the conversion feature. Thus, the greater the difference, the more valuable the conversion feature and the more likely it will be exercised. To evaluate the likelihood of conversion, the effective yield test was developed. **A convertible security is a common stock equivalent if, at the time of issuance, it has an effective yield of less than 66 2/3 percent of the then current average Aa corporate bond yield.**[11]

· · · · · · · · · · · · · · · · · · · ·

[11] "Yield Test for Determining Whether a Convertible Security Is a Common Stock Equivalent," *FASB Statement of Financial Accounting Standards No. 85* (Stamford, Conn.: FASB, 1985).

The designation *Aa* refers to the rating given to the quality of bonds by financial institutions and investor information services such as *Moody's* or *Standard & Poors*. The *average* Aa corporate bond yield should be based on bond yields for a brief period of time, say, one week including or immediately preceding the security issuance date.

The effective yield is to be based on the convertible security's stated annual interest or dividend payments, stated maturity date, and any original issuance premium or discount. Generally, semiannual compounding of interest should be assumed. In the case of a convertible security (such as convertible preferred stock) that does *not* have a stated maturity date, the effective yield should be computed by dividing the annual cash interest or dividend by the market price at the time of issuance. The **effective yield test** (or simply **yield test**) may be formulated as follows:

$$\text{If:} \quad \text{Effective yield at issuance} < \left(66\frac{2}{3}\% \times \frac{\text{Average Aa corporate}}{\text{bond yield at issuance}} \right)$$

Then: The security is a common stock equivalent

As noted earlier, once a security is determined to be a common stock equivalent at the date of issuance, it is *always* considered a common stock equivalent. To illustrate, suppose a corporation issued convertible bonds at a price that resulted in an effective yield of 9.5%. On the same date it also issued 9%, $100 par convertible preferred stock at $120 per share. At the time of these issuances, the average Aa corporate bond yield rate was 13%. The convertible bonds have an effective yield of 9.5% as given, while the effective yield on the convertible preferred stock is 7.5% [(0.09 × $100) ÷ $120]. Since 66⅔% of the 13% Aa corporate bond yield is 8.67% (0.667 × 0.13), the convertible bonds will *never* be considered a common stock equivalent and the convertible preferred stock will *always* be considered a common stock equivalent, as shown below:

Convertible bonds:
   9.5% > (66⅔% × 13%);   Not a common stock equivalent

Convertible preferred stock:
   $$\frac{\$9}{\$120} < (66\frac{2}{3}\% \times 13\%); \quad \text{Common stock equivalent}$$

In this illustration, the convertible bonds would be excluded from the primary earnings-per-share computation. The convertible preferred stock would be included, but *only* if it had a dilutive effect on earnings per share.

Although the effective yield test is an objective way of evaluating common stock equivalents, many users are critical of this test for several reasons. First, the use of 66⅔% is arbitrary and has no direct correlation to the economic value of a conversion feature. Second, each corporation's bond yield (and bond market price) is established based on its perceived risk, so that a comparison to the average Aa corporate bond yield is often inappropriate. Third, a comparison of a convertible preferred stock effective yield to the average Aa corporate bond yield is also inappropriate. Finally, use of the effective yield test may lead to the unrealistic inclusion (or exclusion) of certain securities in earnings per share. That is, because of changed financial conditions, the conversion option of a convertible security that initially satisfied the effective yield test may not be currently perceived as valuable by investors, and so ultimate conversion is unlikely. Likewise, the conversion feature of a security initially not classified as a common stock equivalent may become more valuable because of changed conditions, so that conversion is likely. Nonetheless, once a security is classified on the date of issuance as either a common stock equivalent or not a common stock equivalent by the effective yield test, that classification may never be changed for earnings-per-share calculations regardless of future events.

Determination of Dilutive Convertible Securities That Are Common Stock Equivalents.

As discussed earlier, stock options are always considered to be common stock equivalents and are the first to be included (assuming they are dilutive) in primary earnings per share. Other common stock equivalents are also included in primary earnings per share after stock options, but only if their inclusion also has a dilutive impact on the earnings per share.

Each common stock equivalent is *assumed* (for purposes of computing primary earnings per share) to have been converted into common stock at the beginning of the earliest period reported (or at the date of issuance of the security, if this date is later). This assumed conversion causes two changes in the earnings-per-share calculation: an increase in the denominator and an increase in the numerator. The denominator increases by the number of shares applicable to the assumed conversion. If bonds are assumed to be converted into common stock, the numerator increases because the corporate net income is larger, since the interest expense (net of income taxes) associated with the converted bonds would not have been incurred. On the other hand, if preferred stock is assumed to be converted into common stock, the preferred dividends would not have been declared and the earnings available to common stockholders is increased.

The numerical value impact on primary earnings per share (PEPS) for each common stock equivalent is computed by dividing the change in the numerator by the change in the denominator, as shown in the following equation:

$$\text{Impact on PEPS} = \frac{\text{Change in Earnings-per-Share Numerator}}{\text{Change in Earnings-per-Share Denominator}}$$

Exhibit 10–13 illustrates the calculation of the impact of each common stock equivalent on primary earnings per share, assuming that a corporation has four common stock equivalents outstanding the entire year (amounts assumed). Each common stock equivalent is dilutive if the impact on primary earnings per share is *less* than the most recently computed value of earnings per share (that is, after including the impact of stock options). For example, if the most recently computed value of earnings per share in Exhibit 10–13 is $1.90, securities A and C are dilutive, whereas securities B and D are antidilutive (that is, including them in the computations would increase earnings per share).

EXHIBIT 10–13 Computation of impact of common stock equivalents on primary earnings per share

A. SUMMARY OF COMMON STOCK EQUIVALENTS

Security	Description
A	9% convertible preferred stock. Dividends of $5,400 were declared during the year. The preferred shares are convertible into 3,000 shares of common stock.
B	10% convertible bonds. Interest expense (net of income taxes) of $4,800 was recorded during the year. The bonds are convertible into 1,920 shares of common stock.
C	8% convertible preferred stock. Dividends of $8,000 were declared during the year. The preferred shares are convertible into 5,000 shares of common stock.
D	12% convertible bonds. Interest expense (net of income taxes) of $10,800 was recorded during the year. The bonds are convertible into 5,400 shares of common stock.

B. COMPUTATIONS

Security	Impact	
A	$1.80 =	$\dfrac{\$\ 5,400}{3,000}$
B	$2.50 =	$\dfrac{\$\ 4,800}{1,920}$
C	$1.60 =	$\dfrac{\$\ 8,000}{5,000}$
D	$2.00 =	$\dfrac{\$10,800}{5,400}$

Computation of Tentative and Final Primary Earnings per Share

As indicated earlier, the computation of primary earnings per share begins with determining the increment in shares from the assumed exercise of stock options. This increment is added to the denominator from the simple earnings per share and an initial tentative primary earnings per share is calculated. Next, the remaining common stock equivalents are included in primary earnings per share if they are dilutive. The final primary earnings per share contains all the dilutive common stock equivalents.

Exhibit 10–14 illustrates the computation of primary earnings per share for a corporation assuming (1) stock options are outstanding, (2) both convertible bonds and convertible preferred stock are outstanding, and (3) the preferred stock and one of the bond issues is a common stock equivalent, but (4) the convertible bonds are dilutive whereas the convertible preferred stock is anti-dilutive. The computations result in primary earnings per share of $1.90.

■ FULLY DILUTED EARNINGS PER SHARE

The purpose of disclosing fully diluted earnings per share is to show the *maximum* potential dilution of current earnings per share that would have occurred if all dilutive contingent issuances had taken place. This is an example of the application of the conservatism principle. It is possible for a security designated as a common stock equivalent to be dilutive when included in primary earnings per share but antidilutive if included in fully diluted earnings per share. Furthermore, stock options may have a more dilutive impact than that assumed in primary earnings per share. Thus, an entirely new set of computations must be made for fully diluted earnings per share. However, the sequence of steps is very similar to that for primary earnings per share.

The fully diluted earnings-per-share computations begin with the simple earnings-per-share numerator and denominator. Next, the incremental shares from the assumed exercise of stock options are added to the denominator. If the average market price during the period is the same as or higher than the ending market price, the incremental shares for fully diluted earnings per share are the *same* as those used in computing primary earnings per share. However, if the end-of-the-period market price of the common stock is *higher* than the average market price during the period, this *ending* market price must be used in the *treasury stock method* (discussed earlier) to determine the assumed number of common shares reacquired with the proceeds from the assumed option exercise. To illustrate, assume the corporation, as in the earlier example, has outstanding 10,000 common shares and options to purchase 1,000 common shares at a price of $20 per share. The average and ending market prices per share of the stock are $25 and $40, respectively. The incremental shares for computing primary earnings per share total 200 (as computed earlier), but the incremental shares total 500 for computing fully diluted earnings per share because of the higher ending market price. This latter calculation is shown below.

Shares Issued per Assumed Exercise		1,000
Shares Assumed Reacquired:		
$\dfrac{\text{Proceeds}}{\text{Ending Market Price per Share}} = \dfrac{\$20{,}000}{\$40} =$		500
Assumed Increment in Common Shares for Computing Fully Diluted Earnings per Share		500

Instead of the 200 shares, these 500 shares would be included in the denominator for computing an initial tentative fully diluted earnings per share. Next, the impact on fully diluted earnings per share of the assumed conversion of each convertible security is calculated as illustrated in primary earnings per share.

EXHIBIT 10–14 Computation of primary and fully diluted earnings per share (options, convertible bonds, and convertible preferred stock are outstanding)

1. Information:
   a. Net income for 1993 is $2,800.
   b. The income tax rate is 30%.
   c. 900 shares of common stock have been outstanding the entire year.
   d. Options are outstanding the entire year. The assumed exercise of these options results in an increment of 85 shares of common stock for primary earnings per share, and 100 shares for fully diluted earnings per share.
   e. 100 shares of 8%, $100 par (and issuance price) convertible preferred stock have been outstanding the entire year. $800 dividends were declared on this stock in 1993. The average Aa corporate bond yield was 14% at time of issuance. The preferred stock is a common stock equivalent [8% < (66⅔% × 14%)]. Each share of preferred stock is convertible into 3 shares of common stock.
   f. 10% convertible bonds, $5,000 face value (and issuance price) have been outstanding the entire year. Interest expense on the bonds in 1993 was $500. The average Aa corporate bond yield was 16% at time of issuance. The bonds are common stock equivalents [10% < (66⅔% × 16%)]. Each $1,000 bond is convertible into 50 shares of common stock.
   g. 12% convertible bonds, $10,000 face value (and issuance price), have been outstanding the entire year. Interest expenses on the bonds in 1993 was $1,200. The average Aa corporate bond yield was 14% at the time of issuance. The bonds are *not* common stock equivalents [12% > (66⅔% × 14%)]. Each $1,000 bond is convertible into 84 shares of common stock.

2. Primary earnings per share:
   a. Impact of common stock equivalents on primary earnings per share:

Security	Impact
Preferred	$2.67 = $\dfrac{\$800}{100 \times 3}$
10% Bonds	$1.40 = $\dfrac{\$500 \times (1 - 0.3)}{5 \times 50}$

   b. Primary earnings-per-share computations:

Explanation	Earnings (Adjustments)	÷	Shares (Adjustments)	=	Earnings Per Share
Simple earnings per share	$2,000[a]	÷	900		= $2.22 Simple
Increment in shares (options)			85		
	$2,000	÷	985		= $2.03
Savings in interest expense (bonds)	350[b]				
Increment in shares (bonds)			250[c]		
Primary earnings and shares	$2,350	÷	1,235		= $1.90 Primary

[a] $2,000 = $2,800 net income less $800 preferred dividends.
[b] $350 = $500 pretax interest expense savings × (1 − 0.3). *Note:* The bonds were issued at their face value, so there is no discount or premium amortization.
[c] 250 = 5 bonds × 50 common shares.

   c. Evaluation of dilutive effect:
      1. The $2.67 impact on primary earnings per share of the convertible preferred stock is more than $1.90; therefore, inclusion of the preferred stock in primary earnings per share would be antidilutive.

EXHIBIT 10–14 *(continued)*

2. $1.40 is less than $2.03; therefore, the 10% convertible bonds' common stock equivalents are dilutive and are included in primary earnings per share.
  d. Primary earnings per share is $1.90.
3. Fully diluted earnings per share:
  a. Impact of convertible securities on fully diluted earnings per share:

Security	Impact
Preferred	$2.67 = $\dfrac{\$800}{100 \times 3}$
10% Bonds	$1.40 = $\dfrac{\$500 \times (1 - 0.3)}{5 \times 50}$
12% Bonds	$1.00 = $\dfrac{\$1,200 \times (1 - 0.3)}{10 \times 84}$

  b. Fully diluted earnings-per-share computations:

Explanation	Earnings (Adjustments)	÷	Shares (Adjustments)	=	Earnings Per Share
Simple earnings per share	$2,000	÷	900		= $2.22 Simple
Increment in shares (options)			100		
	$2,000	÷	1,000		= $2.00
Savings in interest expense (10% bonds)	350				
Increment in shares (10% bonds)			250		
Savings in interest expense (12% bonds)	840[a]				
Increment in shares (12% bonds)			840[b]		
Fully diluted earnings and shares	$3,190		2,090		= $1.53 Fully Diluted

[a]$840 = $1,200 pretax interest expense savings $\times$ (1 − 0.3). *Note:* The bonds were issued at their face value so there is no discount or premium amortization.
[b]840 = 10 bonds $\times$ 84 common shares.

  c. Evaluation of dilutive effect:
    1. The $2.67 impact on primary earnings per share of the convertible preferred stock is more than $1.53; therefore, inclusion of the preferred stock in fully diluted earnings per share would be antidilutive.
    2. $1.40 is less than $2.00; therefore, the 10% convertible bonds are dilutive and are included in fully diluted earnings per share.
    3. $1.00 is less than $2.00; therefore, the 12% convertible bonds are dilutive and are included in fully diluted earnings per share.
  d. Fully diluted earnings per share is $1.53.
4. Application of the 3% Rule:
  Fully diluted earnings per share is less than 97% of simple earnings per share ($1.53 < 0.97 $\times$ $2.22). Therefore, the company must report the following on its income statement:
    Primary earnings per share: $1.90
    Fully diluted earnings per share: $1.53

The only difference is that *all* convertible securities are included, whereas primary earnings per share included only common stock equivalents. Finally, each convertible security is included in fully diluted earnings per share. The computation of fully diluted earnings per share is shown in the illustration in Exhibit 10–14.

■ ADDITIONAL CONSIDERATIONS

The 3% Rule

To provide "relief" from the complex analysis involved in computing primary and fully diluted earnings per share, *APB Opinion No. 15* indicates that any reduction in earnings per share due to dilutive convertible securities may be ignored if it is less than 3% in the aggregate. Unfortunately, this evaluation usually must be made *after* all the complex calculations have been completed. This materiality criterion may be expressed as follows: if the aggregate dilution from all the dilutive securities is less than 3% of the simple earnings per common share outstanding, it is not necessary to disclose primary or fully diluted earnings per share. Thus, **if fully diluted earnings per share is more than 97% of simple earnings per common share outstanding,** *only* simple earnings per common share outstanding need be disclosed. Alternatively, **if fully diluted earnings per share is less than or equal to 97% of simple earnings per share, then** *both* **primary and fully diluted earnings per share must be disclosed** (and simple earnings per share is *not* disclosed). This disclosure is illustrated in Exhibit 10–14.

Stock Dividends or Splits

When the common shares outstanding increase as a result of a stock dividend or stock split, *retroactive* recognition must be given to these events for all comparative income statements presented. This retroactive adjustment results in comparable earnings-per-share amounts for all periods expressed in terms of the most recent capital structure.

The simplest way of giving effect to this retroactive recognition is to assume (for earnings-per-share computations) that the stock dividend or split occurred at the *beginning* of the earliest comparative period and that all stock transactions between this beginning date and the *actual* date of the stock dividend or split included the additional shares resulting from the assumed dividend or split. Assume, for example, that a corporation begins operations in January 1993 and issues 5,000 shares of common stock that are outstanding during all of 1993. On December 31, 1993, it issues a 2 for 1 stock split. At the end of 1993, the weighted average number of shares to be used in the earnings-per-share computation for 1993 is 10,000 (5,000 × 200% × $^{12}\!/_{12}$) because the 2 for 1 stock split is *assumed* to have occurred on January 1, 1993. On May 29, 1994, the company issues 5,000 shares of common stock; on August 1, 1994, it issues a 20% stock dividend; and

EXHIBIT 10–15 Comparative weighted average shares

Months Shares Are Outstanding	Shares Outstanding	× Fraction of Year Outstanding	= Equivalent Whole Units
1993			
January–December	12,000 (5,000 × 200% × 120%)	12/12	12,000
1994			
January–May	12,000 (10,000 × 120%)	5/12	5,000
June–September	18,000 (15,000 × 120%)	4/12	6,000
October–December	20,000 (15,000 × 120% + 2,000)	3/12	5,000
			16,000

on October 4, 1994, it issues 2,000 shares of stock. At the end of 1994, when presenting comparative earnings per share for 1993 and 1994, the weighted average numbers of shares to be used in the computation are 12,000 shares for 1993 and 16,000 shares for 1994, as shown in Exhibit 10–15.

For comparative purposes at the end of 1994, the 2 for 1 stock split actually issued on December 31, *and* the 20% stock dividend actually issued on August 1, 1994, are both *assumed* to have been issued on January 1, 1993. Under this assumption, 12,000 shares of stock would have been outstanding during all of 1993. Similarly, during 1994, 12,000 initially would have been outstanding. The 5,000 shares issued on May 29 would have increased by 20% to 6,000 shares, resulting in 18,000 shares outstanding until October 4, 1994. The 2,000 shares issued on October 4, 1994, would *not* have increased, because this issuance occurred *after* the actual stock dividend. The resulting weighted average number of shares is 16,000 at the end of 1994. Remember that the assumptions discussed above, although not reflecting the actual timing of the transactions, are necessary to compute comparable earnings-per-share amounts for all income statements presented.

Concluding Comments

There are three measures of earnings per share but only two reporting alternatives. Either simple earnings per share or both primary and fully diluted earnings per share are reported. The calculations can be even more complex than those illustrated here.[12] Since the user of financial statements often bases some analyses of a company on earnings-per-share trends over time and a comparison among companies on earnings per share or its derivatives (such as the price-earnings ratio), it is important to have a general understanding of the calculations involved in the various measures.

....

[12]For a more comprehensive discussion, see Nikolai and Bazley, *Intermediate Accounting*, 5th ed. (Boston: PWS-Kent Publishing Co., 1991).

■ APPENDIX 2: ALTERNATIVE REVENUE AND EXPENSE RECOGNITION METHODS

As discussed in Chapter 2, revenues are *recognized* when two criteria have been met: (1) realization has taken place and (2) the revenues have been earned. Normally, these criteria are met in the period of the sale but in certain situations recognition of revenues (and expenses) may be advanced or deferred (or no recognition given). The decision as to when to recognize revenue focuses on three factors:

1. **The Economic Substance of the Event Takes Precedence over the Legal Form of the Transaction.** Usually an exchange (sale) is considered to have taken place at the time of the legal transaction at which title to the property is transferred. However, if economic "reality" is substantially distorted by dependence on the legalities of a transaction, the recognition of revenues may be advanced to a period prior to the sale or deferred to a period after the sale. For example, as discussed in Chapter 9, the gross profit on a sales-type lease is recognized by the lessor even though it retains legal title. As discussed later, gross profit may be recognized on long-term construction contracts each year during the contract instead of when the construction is completed, even though title has not passed.

2. **The Collectibility of the Receivable from the Sale.** If the collectibility is *not* reasonably certain, then realization has not occurred and the earning process is not complete, so the recognition of revenue should be deferred. This is the case when there is an inability to predict whether customers will pay their accounts or when significant collection efforts may be required. Deferral of revenue recognition may also be appropriate when future refunds or returns cannot be reasonably estimated.

3. **The Risks and Benefits of Ownership Have Been Transferred to the Buyer.** For revenue to be recognized, the risks and benefits of ownership must have been substantially transferred from the seller to the buyer. For example, sales-type leases require the recognition of revenue by the lessor because the transfer of the risks and benefits of ownership are considered to have transferred even though a legal sale has not taken place. Similarly, revenue may be recognized during a long-term construction contract because the risks and benefits are deemed to be transferred to the buyer.

Once it has been decided when to recognize revenues (during, before, or after the period of sale), then a particular accounting method must be selected. Expenses are matched against the revenues recognized. As discussed in Chapter 2, some expenses, including cost of goods sold, are recognized on the basis of an association of cause and effect. The recognition of these expenses will be affected by the revenue recognition method used. The revenue recognition alternatives and the methods used are briefly summarized:

1. **Revenue Recognition in the Period of Sale.** This rule is the one that is generally used. This approach is appropriate when realization has taken place and revenues have been earned at the time of sale. The accrual method of

accounting is used in which revenues (accomplishments) are recognized at the time of the sales transaction and expenses (sacrifices) are matched against the revenues in the period of sale. The reduction in inventory and the cost of goods sold are recorded at cost, and the resulting accounts receivable and revenue are recorded at the selling price.

2. **Revenue Recognition Prior to the Period of Sale.** This approach is appropriate in order to reflect economic substance instead of legal form so that economic reality is not distorted. For example, the "percentage-of-completion" method may be used for long-term construction contracts. In this method, revenue and certain expenses are recognized based on the percentage completed during the period. The inventory for a long-term construction project is recorded at cost until revenue is recognized, at which time it is raised to net realizable value by adding the gross profit recognized.

3. **Revenue Recognition at the Completion of Production.** This approach has been advocated for certain precious metals and farm products with immediate marketability at quoted prices, unit interchangeability, and an inability of the producer to determine unit acquisition costs. This approach has become less appropriate over time as markets with fixed prices become less common. Also, since mining and agricultural companies generally recognize revenue in the period of the sale, this method is not discussed further.

4. **Revenue Recognition After the Period of the Sale.** This approach is appropriate when the collectibility of the receivable is highly uncertain or there is no reliable basis for estimating the collectibility. The "installment" method may be used to defer revenue recognition. In this method, revenue is recognized as cash is received, and a portion of the total gross profit is recognized in proportion to the cash received. The accounts receivable, less the deferred gross profit, are recorded at their cost until the revenue is recognized.

5. **Revenue Recognition Delayed Until a Future Event Occurs.** This approach is appropriate when there has been an insignificant transfer of the risks and benefits of ownership and no revenue can be recognized either at the time of the sale or as cash is received. The "deposit" method is used in this situation and all cash receipts are recorded as deposits until an event occurs that transfers sufficient risks and benefits to the buyer so that revenue may be recognized. Related assets are recorded at their cost or book value until the revenue recognition occurs.

The accounting issues involved in the recognition of revenue and expenses in the period of sale have been discussed in numerous places throughout this book and will not be discussed further here. The two most commonly used alternative methods, the percentage-of-completion method and the installment method, are discussed in more detail.

■ PERCENTAGE-OF-COMPLETION METHOD

As indicated earlier, the percentage-of-completion method is used for certain long-term construction contracts in order to recognize revenue prior to the completion of the contract. In such cases, recognition of revenue at the time of sale (**completed contract**) can lead to a distortion of the economic substance of a company's operations. For instance, if a company agrees to construct an item over a period of three years, under the completed contract method of accounting no revenue and no cost of goods sold would be recognized in years 1 and 2, while all the revenue and cost of goods sold would be recognized in year 3. In fact, if the company recognizes any operating expenses in the first two years, it might report operating losses in these years with a disproportionate operating profit in the third year. In order to better reflect economic reality, the percentage-of-completion method is used. The percentage-of-completion method should be used whenever an enforceable contract has been signed, the seller and buyer are expected to fulfill their obligations, and dependable estimates can be made of the work completed, the revenues, and the costs.

Under the percentage-of-completion method, each year a company recognizes the gross profit on its construction contracts based on the percentage of each contract completed during the year. The percentage completed may be determined by an "input" measure or an "output" measure. For instance, an input measure might be the costs incurred during the period compared to the total expected costs to complete the contract. An output measure might be the number of floors of a building completed during the year compared to the total number of floors to be contained in the building. Once the percentage completed for the year is determined, it is applied to the total expected gross profit from the contract to determine the gross profit to be recognized for that year.

To illustrate, assume Company A agrees to construct a manufacturing plant for Company B. The contract price is $500,000 and Company A's estimated and actual construction costs are $350,000, so that its total gross profit is $150,000. The plant takes three years to complete. The costs incurred and percentage complete each year are:

1993	$175,000	50%
1994	122,500	35%
1995	52,500	15%

For simplicity, we are disregarding operating expenses. Exhibit 10–16 shows the amount of gross profit that Company A would recognize in each of the three years under the percentage-of-completion method as compared to the completed contract method of accounting. As may be seen in the exhibit, in the case of long-term construction contracts the percentage-of-completion method better reflects economic reality than does the completed contract method because it relates a measure of the benefits and sacrifices (i.e., the gross profit) to the years in which the gross profit is earned rather than to the year when the contract is completed.

It is important to understand the effects of the percentage-of-completion method on the financial statements. In 1993 Company A records the $175,000

EXHIBIT 10–16 Gross profit recognition: percentage-of-completion versus completed contract

	PERCENTAGE-OF-COMPLETION		
	Revenue	Expense[d]	Gross Profit
1993	$250,000[a]	$175,000	$ 75,000
1994	175,000[b]	122,500	52,500
1995	75,000[c]	52,500	22,500
	$500,000	$350,000	$150,000

	COMPLETED CONTRACT		
	Revenue	Expense	Gross Profit
1993	$0	$0	$0
1994	0	0	0
1995	500,000	350,000	150,000
	$500,000	$350,000	$150,000

[a]$500,000 × 0.50.
[b]$500,000 × 0.35.
[c]$500,000 × 0.15.
[d]The expense each period is equal to the contract costs incurred.

construction costs incurred as an inventory, Construction in Progress, in the usual manner. The revenue and expense for the year are then recorded as follows:

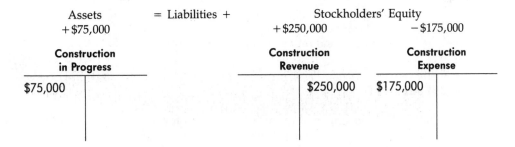

Assets	= Liabilities +	Stockholders' Equity	
+$75,000		+$250,000	−$175,000

Note that this entry has raised the balance in Construction in Progress from its cost of $175,000 to its selling price of $250,000 ($175,000 + $75,000). Since the project is now 50% complete, this amount represents 50% of the selling price of $500,000.

In 1994 the costs of $122,500 are added to the Construction in Progress and the gross profit of $52,500 is also added as the revenue and expense are recorded. In the December 31, 1994, balance sheet, the Construction in Progress has a balance of $425,000 ($175,000 + $75,000 + $122,500 + $52,500), which is equal to the percentage of the selling price of the project that is completed (85% × $500,000).

This procedure, in principle, is the same as accounting for any sale. In more typical situations, the cost of the inventory is removed and the cash (or accounts receivable) is recorded at the selling price. The net assets, however, have increased by the amount of the gross profit (selling price − cost) just as with the construction in progress.

Most long-term contracts allow the contractor to bill the customer during the construction period in order to provide financing for the project. If we assume that Company A bills Company B for $140,000 in 1993, it would record the following:

Assets		= Liabilities + Stockholders' Equity
+$140,000	−$140,000	

Accounts Receivable		Partial Billings	
$140,000			$140,000

The partial billings is a contra asset to construction in progress. The net amount of the asset in the balance sheet represents the costs incurred on the project plus the profit recognized less the amount billed to the customer; thus, it is the net investment of the contractor in the project. The balance sheet disclosure at December 31, 1993, is as follows:

Construction in progress	$250,000
Less: partial billings	(140,000)
Costs and recognized profit not yet billed	$110,000

■ INSTALLMENT METHOD

Retail firms have engaged in installment sales for many years. Installment sales involve a financing agreement whereby the customer signs a contract, makes a small down payment, and agrees to make periodic payments for the merchandise over an extended period, often several years. Installment sales are common for such items as large appliances, furniture, and automobiles. Typically, the customer accepts possession of the merchandise when the contract is signed (thereby enjoying its use during the payment period), while the seller retains legal title to the merchandise until the payments are complete. Before the establishment of "credit bureaus" and improved techniques for establishing, evaluating, and maintaining records of individuals' "credit ratings," installment sales contracts were often used because the collection of the installment payments was highly uncertain. Today, installment sales contracts may still be used because of a customer's lower credit rating, but the risk of noncollection is less because customers realize that nonpayment may jeopardize their credit rating.

Normally, installment *sales* are recognized in the usual manner. That is, the revenue and expense are recognized at the time the sales agreement is signed. There are exceptional cases, however, such as certain real estate sales where receivables are collected over an extended period and where the terms of the transaction provide no reasonable basis for estimating the degree of collectibility. In these exceptional cases, the installment *method* is used. **Under the installment method, revenue is recognized as cash is collected.** That is, as each payment is received from the customer, a portion of the gross profit (revenue less cost) on the sale is recognized (based on the gross profit percentage in the year of the sale), so that by the final payment the entire gross profit has been recorded.

For income tax purposes, the installment method is acceptable in certain situations. Furthermore, in recent years there has been an increase in complex sales transactions where the recognition of revenue at the time of sale is inappropriate. This is the case in regard to certain franchise fees for the franchisor and certain retail land sales, where use of the installment method is appropriate.

Illustration of Installment Method

Assume that the Bart Company opens for business in 1993 and sells merchandise under terms which make the use of the installment method required. The following is a summary of the sales, costs, and collections for 1993.

Installment sales	$100,000
Cost of installment sales (%)	(70,000) (70%)
Gross profit (%)	$ 30,000 (30%)
Cash collections during:	
1993	$ 28,000
1994	40,000
1995	32,000

To use the installment method, the gross profit percentage for the year's total sales must be computed. For the Bart Company the gross profit percentage is 30% ($30,000 ÷ $100,000) in 1993. The company records the contracts as follows:

	Assets	= Liabs. + S. Eq.
+$100,000	−$30,000	−$70,000

Accounts Receivable		Deferred Gross Profit		Inventory	
$100,000			$30,000		$70,000

The deferred gross profit is a contra asset to accounts receivable. Note that the net value of the receivable is $70,000 ($100,000 − $30,000) and is equal to the cost of the inventory. This value is appropriate because no profit has yet been recognized. Some companies report the deferred gross profit as a liability, but this procedure may be misleading because the company is not obligated to pay $30,000.

The company collects $28,000 in 1993 and recognizes this in the normal manner by increasing cash and reducing accounts receivable. The company also recognizes revenue of $28,000. Since the cost of the installment sales is 70% of the selling price, cost of goods sold of $19,600 (70% × $28,000) is also recognized. The difference between the revenue and the cost of goods sold is the deferred gross profit that is recognized in 1993 and is equal to 30% of the installment sales (30% × $28,000 = $8,400). These amounts are recorded as follows:

Assets	= Liabilities +		Stockholders' Equity	
+$8,400			+$28,000	−$19,600

Deferred Gross Profit			Revenue	Cost of Goods Sold	
$8,400			$28,000	$19,600	

At December 31, 1993, the net value of the receivable is shown as follows:

Accounts receivable	$72,000 [a]
Less: Deferred gross profit	(21,600) [b]
	$50,400

[a]$100,000 − $28,000.
[b]$30,000 − $8,400.

In 1994 the company collects $40,000 and therefore recognizes revenue of $40,000 and cost of goods sold of $28,000 (70% × $40,000), and the deferred gross profit is reduced by $12,000 (30% × $40,000). Finally in 1995 when the remaining $32,000 is collected, revenue of $32,000 and cost of goods sold of $22,400 (70% × $32,000) are recorded. The reduction in the deferred gross profit of $9,600 eliminates the balance in that account. In summary, under the installment sales method, revenue is recognized as cash is received and the appropriate expense is matched against the revenue. In this example, 70 cents of expense is recognized for each $1 of revenue.

QUESTIONS

1. What information is contained in a corporation's articles of incorporation?

2. List the basic rights of a stockholder. Which do you consider to be the most important?

3. What is the meaning of the following terms: (a) authorized capital stock, (b) issued capital stock, (c) outstanding capital stock, and (d) treasury stock? What is the difference between issued and outstanding capital stock?

4. What is *legal capital* and why is it important?

5. How does preferred stock differ from common stock?

6. Define the following terms regarding preferred stock:

   a. Dividend preference

   b. Cumulative

   c. Convertible

   d. Redeemable

7. Why is a preferred stock similar to a long-term bond? Why is it similar to common stock?

8. What is a stock subscription? How is Subscriptions Receivable classified on the balance sheet?

9. If capital stock is issued for an asset other than cash, what amount would you use to record the transaction?

10. What are the two segments of contributed capital and what might be included in each segment?

11. What is a stock dividend? Distinguish between a large and a small stock dividend and explain what amounts are used to record the declaration of each dividend.

12. (a) What is treasury stock? (b) Why might a corporation wish to acquire treasury stock?

13. What does it mean when preferred dividends are "in arrears"?

14. What are the three dates of importance in regard to dividends?

15. What is an appropriation of retained earnings? For what reasons would retained earnings be appropriated?

16. What is a segment of a corporation? What information for a discontinued segment is disclosed on an income statement and where is it disclosed?

17. What is an extraordinary item? Where and how are gains or losses from extraordinary items disclosed on an income statement?

18. What is intraperiod income tax allocation? Why is it necessary?

19. (a) What are the characteristics of a noncompensatory stock option plan? (b) How does a compensatory plan differ from a noncompensatory plan? (c) What is the intent of a noncompensatory plan? A compensatory plan?

20. (a) What is the measurement date of a compensatory stock option plan? (b) Why might the measurement date occur after the date of grant of the stock option?

21. For each of the following independent compensatory stock option plans, determine the compensation cost involved, the accounting periods to which this cost would be charged as expense, and the measurement date of the compensation cost.

   a. On December 31, 1993, a corporation grants a key executive the nontransferable right to acquire 500 shares of $5 par common stock for $11 per share. The current market price of the stock is $16 per share, but the option may not be exercised until three years of service have been performed.

   b. On December 31, 1993, a corporation grants to a key executive the right to acquire 1,000 shares of $10 par common stock for $20 per share. The current market price for the stock is $27 per share, but the option may not be exercised until four years of continuous service from the date of grant have been performed.

   c. On December 31, 1993, a corporation grants to a key executive the right to obtain 2,000 shares of $10 par common stock for $25 per share. The current market price of the stock is $24 per share, but the option may not be exercised until two years of service have been performed.

22. How is simple earnings per common share outstanding computed? How is it disclosed on a corporate income statement?

23. Appendix 1: On what date are stock dividends and splits considered to be issued for computing earnings per share?

24. Appendix 1: What two earnings-per-share figures are shown for a company with a complex capital structure? Besides common shares outstanding, what additional securities are included in each earnings-per-share calculation?

25. Appendix 1: What is a common stock equivalent? When is it included in earnings per share?

26. Appendix 1: What is the "effective yield test" and how is it applied?

27. Appendix 2: What three factors are important in determining whether revenue should be recognized in a period other than the period of sale?

28. Appendix 2: What are the reasons for recognizing revenue (a) in the period of sale, (b) during production, and (c) after the period of sale?

PROBLEMS AND CASES

29. **Par Value and No-Par Stock Issuance.** Ryland Corporation is authorized to issue 100,000 shares of common stock. It sells 30,000 shares at $12 per share.

Required Record the effects on the accounting equation of the sale of the common stock, given the following independent assumptions:

1. The stock has a par value of $7 per share.

2. The stock is no-par stock but has been assigned a stated value of $4 per share.

3. The stock has no par and no stated value.

30. **Stock Subscription.** On July 1 the Mark Corporation enters into a subscription contract with subscribers for 9,000 shares of $4 par common stock at a price of $6 per share. The contract requires a down payment of $2 per share, with the remaining balance to be paid in full on December 1. The stock will be issued to each subscriber upon full payment.

Required Record the effects on the accounting equation of the following:

1. The July 1 receipt of the down payment on the signing of the contract.

2. The December 1 receipt of the remaining balance of $4 per share.

3. The issuance of the stock on full payment.

31. **Noncash Issuance of Stock.** The Antley Company issued 200 shares of $100 par preferred stock in exchange for 5 acres of land.

Required Record the effects on the accounting equation of the acquisition of the land for each of the following independent situations:

1. The preferred stock is currently selling on the market for $145 per share. No appraisal is available on the land.

2. The land is appraised at $27,000. The preferred stock is not actively traded on the stock market.

32. **Stock Transactions.** The Cary Company is authorized to issue 100,000 shares of $7 par common stock. At the beginning of 1993, 18,000 shares of common stock were issued and outstanding. These shares had been issued at $14 per share. During 1993 the company entered into the following transactions:

Date	Transaction
Jan. 16	Issued 1,300 shares of common stock at $15 per share.
Mar. 21	Exchanged 12,000 shares of common stock for a building. The common stock was selling at $17 per share.
May 7	Reacquired 500 shares of its common stock at $16 per share.
July 1	Accepted subscriptions to 1,000 shares of common stock at $18 per share. The contract called for a 10% down payment, with the balance due December 1.
Sept. 20	Sold 500 shares of treasury stock at $19 per share.
Dec. 1	Collected the balance due on the July 1 subscriptions and issued the stock.

Required **1.** Record the effects on the accounting equation of the above transactions.

2. Prepare the stockholders' equity section of the December 31, 1993, balance sheet (assume ending retained earnings for 1993 is $122,000).

33. Stock Transactions. The Crane Corporation was organized and started business on January 1, 1993. It is authorized to issue 100,000 shares of $2 par common stock and 50,000 shares of $100 par preferred stock. During 1993 the Crane Corporation entered into the following stock transactions:

Date	Transaction
Jan. 1	Issued 20,000 shares of common stock at $16 per share and 10,000 shares of preferred stock at $127 per share.
Jan. 5	Issued 10,000 shares of common stock in payment of various organization costs totaling $150,000. Since the stock had not been on the market long enough to establish a price, the total amount of $150,000 was used to record the transaction.
Mar. 6	Issued 30,000 shares of common stock at $18 per share and 15,000 shares of preferred stock at $130 per share.
June 24	Purchased land by issuing 1,000 shares of common stock and 500 shares of preferred stock. Common and preferred stock were selling on the market at $16 and $129 per share, respectively, and these prices were used to record the purchase.
Sept. 11	Issued 5,000 shares of common stock at $17 per share.
Oct. 18	Issued 600 shares of preferred stock at $130 per share.

Required Prepare the contributed capital section of the December 31, 1993, balance sheet.

34. Various Transactions. Sapp Company is authorized to issue 20,000 shares of no-par, $5 stated-value common stock and 5,000 shares of 9%, $100 par noncumulative preferred stock. It enters into the following transactions.

1. Accepts a subscription contract to 7,000 shares of common stock at $40 per share and receives a 30% down payment.

2. Collects the remaining balance of the subscription contract and issues the common stock.

3. Acquires a building by paying $23,000 cash and issuing 2,000 shares of common stock and 600 shares of preferred stock. Common stock is currently selling at $46 per share; preferred stock has no current market value. The building is appraised at $180,000.

4. Sells 1,000 shares of common stock at $47 per share.

5. Sells 900 shares of preferred stock at $115 per share.

6. Declares a 2 for 1 stock split on the common stock, reducing the stated value to $2.50 per share.

Required 1. Record the effects on the accounting equation of the above transactions.

2. Compute the annual dividends to be distributed to preferred and common stockholders (assume $28,000 is available for dividends).

35. **Convertible Preferred Stock.** On January 1, 1993, the Gasser Corporation issued 75 shares of $100 par convertible preferred stock at $103 per share. Each share of preferred stock is convertible into three shares of $5 par common stock. On January 12, 1994, all of the preferred stock was converted to common stock.

Required Record the effects on the accounting equation of the issuance of the preferred stock on January 1, 1993 and the conversion of the preferred stock to common stock on January 12, 1994.

36. **Convertible Preferred Stock.** On January 1, 1993, the Bray Corporation issues 900 shares of $100 par, convertible preferred stock for $115 per share. On January 5, 1994, all the preferred stockholders convert their shares to common stock.

Required 1. Record the effects on the accounting equation at January 1, 1993, for the issuance of the preferred stock.

2. Record the effects on the accounting equation at January 5, 1994, for the conversion, assuming

   a. Each share of preferred stock is convertible into three shares of $25 par common stock.

   b. Each share of preferred stock is convertible into five shares of $25 par common stock.

37. **Stock Split.** Bloom Company is authorized to issue 30,000 shares of $4 par common stock. To date it has issued 10,000 shares for $10 per share. On May 8, 1993, the board of directors authorized a 2 for 1 stock split with a reduction in par value to $2 per share.

Required What is the effect on the components of stockholders' equity as a result of the stock split?

38. **Stock Dividend.** The stockholders' equity section of the January 1, 1993, balance sheet for the Turner Corporation follows:

Contributed capital
  Common stock, $10 par, 60,000 shares authorized,
    30,000 shares issued and outstanding $300,000
  Additional paid-in capital on common stock   100,000
    Total contributed capital $400,000
Retained earnings   325,000
    Total stockholders' equity $725,000

On June 1, 1993, the corporation declared and issued a 15% stock dividend. The market value of the stock on June 1 is $16 per share. No additional shares of common stock were issued between January 1 and June 1, 1993.

Required 1. Record the effects on the accounting equation of the stock dividend.

2. Prepare the stockholders' equity section of the July 15, 1993 balance sheet for the Turner Corporation after the issuance of the stock dividend.

39. Stock Dividend. The stockholders' equity section of the January 1, 1993, balance sheet for the Rutler Corporation follows:

Contributed capital
  Common stock, $5 par, 80,000 shares authorized,
    40,000 shares issued and outstanding $200,000
  Additional paid-in capital on common stock   370,000
    Total contributed capital $570,000
Retained earnings   320,000
    Total stockholders' equity $890,000

On June 1, 1993, the corporation declared and issued a 25% stock dividend. On the date of declaration the stock had a current market value of $22 per share. No additional shares of common stock were issued between January 1 and June 1, 1993.

Required 1. Record the effects on the accounting equation of the stock dividend.

2. Prepare the stockholders' equity section of the July 1, 1993, balance sheet for the Rutler Corporation after the issuance of the stock dividend.

40. Treasury Stock. On January 1, 1993, the Amitroy Company had 10,000 shares of $5 par common stock outstanding. These shares were originally issued at a price of $12 per share. During 1993 the following stock transactions occurred:

1. March 3: The company reacquired 2,000 shares of its common stock at a cost of $11 per share.

2. April 23: The company sold 1,000 shares of the treasury stock for $12 per share.

3. July 25: The company sold the remaining 1,000 shares of the treasury stock for $10.75 per share.

Required Record the effects on the accounting equation of the above transactions.

41. Treasury Stock and Stockholders' Equity. On January 1, 1993, the Rollo Corporation had 5,000 shares of $10 par common stock outstanding. These shares were originally issued at $25 per share. During 1993 the Rollo Corporation entered into the following transactions:

1. Reacquired 2,500 shares of its common stock for $24 per share.
2. Sold 1,250 shares of the treasury stock for $26 per share.
3. Sold 750 shares of the treasury stock for $21.50 per share.

Required Prepare, in good form, the stockholders' equity section of the Rollo Corporation's balance sheet at December 31, 1993 (assume 40,000 shares are authorized and retained earnings is $40,000).

42. Treasury Stock. Mulky Company reported the following data on its December 31, 1993 balance sheet:

Preferred stock, $100 par (4,000 shares authorized)	$100,000
Additional paid-in capital on preferred stock	9,000
Common stock, $10 par (30,000 shares authorized)	70,000
Additional paid-in capital on common stock	32,000
Retained earnings	112,000

During 1994 the company entered into the following transactions:

1. Reacquired 200 shares of its own preferred stock at $110 per share.
2. Reacquired 500 shares of its own common stock at $16 per share.
3. Sold 100 shares of preferred treasury stock at $112 per share.
4. Sold 300 shares of common treasury stock at $19 per share.
5. Sold 200 shares of common treasury stock at $13.50 per share.

The company maintains separate treasury stock accounts and related additional paid-in capital accounts for each class of stock.

Required 1. Record the effects on the accounting equation of the above treasury stock transactions.

2. Assuming the company earned a net income in 1994 of $30,000 and declared and paid dividends of $10,000, prepare the stockholders' equity section of the balance sheet at December 31, 1994.

43. Stockholders' Equity. The following list of balances was taken from the accounting records of the Dean Company on December 31, 1993:

Additional paid-in capital on preferred stock	$ 7,500
Common stock	80,000
Subscriptions receivable: preferred stock	6,750
Additional paid-in capital from treasury stock	1,500
Preferred stock	50,000
Treasury stock	6,000

Preferred stock subscribed	10,000
Additional paid-in capital on common stock	40,000
Retained earnings	200,000

Additional Information:

1. Common stock has a $10 par value, 10,000 shares are authorized, 8,000 shares have been issued and are outstanding.

2. Preferred stock has a $100 par value, 1,000 shares are authorized, 500 shares have been issued and are outstanding. One hundred shares have been subscribed at $120 per share.

3. During 1993, 1,500 shares of common stock were reacquired at $12 per share; 1,000 shares were reissued at $13.50 per share.

Required Prepare the stockholders' equity section of the December 31, 1993, balance sheet for the Dean Company.

44. Stockholders' Equity. A partial list of balances of the Harley Company on December 31, 1993, is shown as follows:

Accounts payable	$ 9,000
Common stock subscribed	30,000
Accounts receivable	125,000
Additional paid-in capital on common stock	390,000
Additional paid-in capital from treasury stock	3,000
Common stock	150,000
Subscriptions receivable: common stock	95,000
Additional paid-in capital on preferred stock	94,500
Preferred stock	350,000
Retained earnings	850,000

Additional Information:

1. Common stock is no-par, with a stated value of $5 per share; 80,000 shares are authorized, 30,000 shares have been issued and are outstanding, and 6,000 shares have been subscribed at a price of $19 per share.

2. 500 shares of common stock were reacquired in 1993 at $18 per share and reissued later at $24 per share.

3. Preferred stock has a $100 par value; 7,000 shares are authorized, and 3,500 shares have been issued and are outstanding.

Required Prepare the stockholders' equity section of the December 31, 1993, balance sheet for the Harley Company.

45. Changes in Stockholders' Equity. Filter Company is authorized to issue 10,000 shares of $10 par common stock. On January 1, 1993, 5,800 shares of common stock were outstanding. These shares had been issued at $21 per share. The retained earnings has a beginning balance of $93,000. During 1993 the following transactions took place:

Date	Transaction
Jan. 15	Issued 400 shares of common stock at $23 per share.
Mar. 30	Purchased land by issuing 2,100 shares of common stock. The stock had a current market price of $22 per share, which was used to record the transaction.
June 10	Reacquired 250 shares of common stock at $21 per share.

Required Prepare a statement of changes in stockholders' equity for the year ended December 31, 1993 (assume net income for 1993 was $15,000 and dividends were $2,600).

46. Changes in Stockholders' Equity. Clook Corporation is authorized to issue 25,000 shares of $5 stated value common stock. At the beginning of 1993, 12,000 shares were outstanding. These shares had been issued at $35 per share. The retained earnings has a beginning balance of $510,000. During 1993 the following transactions took place:

Date	Transaction
Jan. 14	Issued 1,000 shares of common stock for $38 per share.
Apr. 17	Reacquired 850 shares of its common stock for $39 per share.
July 25	Issued 1,200 shares of common stock in exchange for a patent. The stock was selling at $40 per share on the market, and this price was used to record the transaction.
Sept. 12	Sold 850 shares of the treasury stock for $42 per share.

Required 1. Prepare a statement of changes in stockholders' equity for the year ended December 31, 1993 (assume net income was $94,000 and dividends were $44,000).

2. Prepare the stockholders' equity section of the December 31, 1993, balance sheet for the Clook Corporation.

47. Changes in Stockholders' Equity. The Dought Corporation is authorized to issue 2,000 shares of $100 par preferred stock and 50,000 shares of $5 stated value common stock. As of December 31, 1993, Dought's stockholders' equity accounts showed the following balances:

Preferred stock, $100 par	$150,000
Common stock, $5 stated value	125,000
Additional paid-in capital on preferred stock	19,500
Additional paid-in capital on common stock	400,000
Retained earnings	75,000

During 1994 Dought entered into the following transactions affecting stockholders' equity:

1. Issued 200 shares of preferred stock at $115 per share.

2. Reacquired 500 shares of common stock for $20 per share.

3. Sold 250 shares of the treasury stock for $20 per share.

4. Issued 1,300 shares of common stock in exchange for 10 acres of land. At this time the common stock was selling for $23 per share, and no appraisal value was available for the land.

Required 1. Prepare a statement of changes in stockholders' equity for the year ended December 31, 1994 (assume 1994 net income was $113,000 and dividends were $22,500).

2. Prepare the stockholders' equity section of the December 31, 1994, balance sheet for the Dought Corporation.

48. Stockholders' Equity. Wake Manufacturing Corporation completed the following transactions during its first year of operation, 1993:

1. The state authorized the issuance of 30,000 shares of $5 par common stock; 15,000 shares were issued at $23 per share.

2. The state authorized the issuance of 6,000 shares of $50 par preferred stock. All 6,000 shares were issued at $70 per share.

3. The Clear Valley Regional Development Authority donated land with a fair market value of $18,000, in the Clear Valley Industrial Park, to Wake as inducement for Wake's building a plant on the land and beginning operations in Clear Valley.

4. Wake reacquired 1,000 shares of its own outstanding common stock at $18 per share.

5. Wake sold 500 shares of treasury stock for $23 per share.

6. Net income for the first year of operations was $16,500. No dividends were declared.

Required Prepare the stockholders' equity section of the Wake Manufacturing Corporation balance sheet as of December 31, 1993.

49. Cash Dividends. On October 1, 1993, the Sewel Corporation declared a cash dividend on its 1,500 outstanding shares of 9%, $100 par preferred stock. These dividends are payable on December 1, 1993, to stockholders of record as of November 15, 1993. On November 1, 1993, the company declared an 85¢ per share cash dividend on its 9,000 outstanding shares of common stock. These dividends are payable on December 15, 1993, to stockholders of record as of November 30, 1993.

Required Record the effects on the accounting equation of the declaration and the payment of each of these dividends.

50. Dividends in Arrears. The Ithaca Corporation has 3,000 shares of 11%, $100 par cumulative preferred stock outstanding. Dividends on this stock have *not* been declared for the past four years. This year the corporation wishes to pay dividends to its common stockholders.

Required What amount of preferred dividends must be paid before the Ithaca Corporation can pay dividends on common stock? Show your calculations.

51. Cash and Stock Dividends. The stockholders' equity of the Quiser Corporation on January 1, 1993, includes the following items:

Preferred stock, 9%, $100 par (5,000 shares authorized)	$100,000
Common stock, $10 par (80,000 shares authorized)	200,000
Additional paid-in capital on preferred stock	12,000
Additional paid-in capital on common stock	37,000
Retained earnings	172,000
	$521,000

The company entered into the following transactions during 1993:

Date	Transaction
Jan. 1	Declared the annual cash dividend on the outstanding preferred stock and a 90¢ per share dividend on the outstanding common stock. These dividends are to be paid on February 15, 1993.
Feb. 15	Paid the cash dividend declared on January 1.
May 15	Declared and issued a 16% stock dividend on the common stock outstanding on this date. The common stock is currently selling for $18 per share.
July 1	Split the common stock 2 for 1, reducing the par value to $5 per share and increasing the authorized shares to 160,000.
Aug. 5	Declared and issued a 35% stock dividend on the common stock outstanding on this date.
Dec. 31	Discovered that the 1992 depreciation expense had been understated by $2,500.

Required 1. Record the effects on the accounting equation of the above transactions (the corporation is subject to a 30% income tax rate).

2. Prepare the stockholders' equity section of the December 31, 1993, balance sheet for the Quiser Corporation (assume that 1993 net income was $101,500).

52. Cash and Stock Dividends. The stockholders' equity of the Kahler Corporation on January 1, 1993, includes the following items:

Preferred stock, 8%, $100 par (8,000 shares authorized)	$ 300,000
Common stock, $10 par (200,000 shares authorized)	450,000
Additional paid-in capital on preferred stock	28,000
Additional paid-in capital on common stock	255,000
Retained earnings	400,000
	$1,203,000

The company entered into the following transactions during 1993:

Date	Transaction
Jan. 1	Declared the annual cash dividend on the outstanding preferred stock and an 85¢ per share dividend on the outstanding common stock, to be paid on January 30, 1993.
Jan. 30	Paid the cash dividend declared on January 1.
Mar. 1	Declared and issued a 35% stock dividend on the common stock outstanding on this date.
May 15	Split the common stock 2 for 1, reducing the par value to $5 per share and increasing the authorized shares to 400,000.
June 1	Declared and issued a 10% stock dividend on the common stock outstanding on this date. The common stock is currently selling for $15 per share.
Dec. 31	Discovered that an error was made in calculating the 1992 depreciation e pense. This error understated 1992 net income by $3,000 (pretax).

Required 1. Record the effects on the accounting equation of these transactions (the corporation is subject to a 30% income tax rate).

2. Prepare the stockholders' equity section of the December 31, 1993, balance sheet for the Kahler Corporation (assume that the 1993 net income was $320,500).

53. **Cash and Stock Dividends.** The Small Corporation shows the following items of stockholders' equity:

Common stock, $10 par (40,000 shares authorized, 10,000 shares issued and outstanding)	$100,000
Additional paid-in capital on common stock	80,000
Retained earnings	160,000

The company's common stock is currently selling for $20 per share on the stock market. The board of directors is considering the following *alternative* actions in regard to "dividends":

1. Payment of a $2.50 per share cash dividend.

2. Distribution of a 15% stock dividend.

3. Distribution of a 40% stock dividend.

4. Distribution of a 2 for 1 stock split, reducing the par value to $5 per share.

The board has always paid a cash dividend and is not very familiar with stock dividends and stock splits. It is also unsure of the effect of each of these alternatives on stockholders' equity and has asked for your advice.

Required 1. Explain what is meant by a stock dividend and a stock split, including which, if any, is really a "dividend."

2. Explain what is likely to happen to the market price per share of common stock as a result of a stock dividend or stock split.

3. For each *alternative,* determine the amount of each item of stockholders' equity for the Small Corporation immediately *after* the cash payment or the issuance of the common stock. Show your calculations for each amount that changed.

54. Appropriations. On January 1, 1993, the Bloner Corporation had a retained earnings balance of $125,000. On June 1, 1993, the corporation acquired treasury stock at a cost of $29,000. The treasury stock is still being held at the end of 1993.

Required 1. If the corporation makes formal entries to recognize appropriations of retained earnings, record the effects on the accounting equation of the treasury stock.

2. If the corporation, instead, recognizes appropriations of retained earnings by means of notes, prepare the note to accompany the December 31, 1993, balance sheet.

3. During 1994 all of the treasury stock was reissued and the appropriation of retained earnings was canceled. How would the cancellation be recorded if (a) the company had used an entry to recognize the appropriation or (b) the company had recognized the appropriation by means of a note?

55. Appropriations. The December 31, 1993, stockholders' equity for the Benzer Corporation follows:

Contributed capital	
Common stock, $10 par, 90,000 shares authorized,	
50,000 shares issued and outstanding	$ 500,000
Additional paid-in capital on common stock	800,000
Total contributed capital	$1,300,000
Retained earnings	1,400,000
Total stockholders' equity	$2,700,000

On this date the board of directors voted to appropriate $400,000 of retained earnings for future expansion.

Required 1. Assuming that the Benzer Corporation makes entries to recognize appropriations, (a) record the effects on the accounting equation of the above appropriation and (b) prepare the stockholders' equity section of the December 31, 1993, balance sheet for the Benzer Corporation after the appropriation.

2. If, instead, the corporation discloses appropriations by means of a note, prepare the note and the stockholders' equity section of the December 31, 1993, balance sheet after the above appropriation.

56. Income Statement. The records of the Gliten Corporation for the year ended December 31, 1993, show the following items:

Operating income	$15,000
Nonoperating income	3,000

Additional Information:

1. The weighted average number of common shares outstanding for the year is 6,000 shares.

2. The company is subject to a 33% income tax rate.

3. There is no preferred stock outstanding and the company has no discontinued operations or extraordinary items.

Required Prepare the lower portion of the income statement of the Gliten Corporation for 1993, starting with operating income. Be sure to include simple earnings per share.

57. Income Statement. The records of the Crowney Corporation for the year ended December 31, 1993, show the following items:

Pretax income from continuing operations	$87,500
Loss from operations of discontinued Segment Z (pretax)	(2,000)
Gain on sale of discontinued Segment Z (pretax)	2,200
Extraordinary loss from flood (pretax)	(30,000)

Additional Information:

1. The corporation had 10,000 shares of common stock outstanding during all of 1993.

2. There is no preferred stock outstanding.

3. The corporation is subject to a 30% income tax rate.

Required Prepare the lower portion of the income statement of the Crowney Corporation for 1993, starting with pretax income from continuing operations. Be sure to include earnings per share.

58. Income Statement. The records of the Stringer Corporation show the following items on December 31, 1993:

Cost of goods sold	$42,000
Extraordinary loss from tornado (pretax)	1,500
General and administrative expenses	8,000
Interest revenue	700
Interest expense	200
Gain on sale of discontinued Segment R (pretax)	1,000
Loss from operations of discontinued Segment R (pretax)	3,000
Selling expenses	13,000
Sales	80,000

Additional Information:

1. There were 2,000 shares of common stock outstanding on January 1, 1993. On July 1, 1993, the corporation issued 4,000 common shares.

2. The corporation paid dividends for the current year on 200 shares of 8%, $100 par preferred stock outstanding. No dividends were paid to common stockholders.

3. The corporation is subject to a 31% income tax rate.

Required Prepare the income statement of the Stringer Corporation for 1993.

59. Income Statement, Lower Portion. On January 1, 1993, the Eshroe Corporation had 2,200 shares of common stock outstanding and a retained earnings balance of $59,600. On June 1, 1993, another 2,400 shares of common stock were issued. On December 31, 1993, the company's records showed the following items:

Operating income	$22,000
Nonoperating income	4,500
Loss from operations of discontinued Segment Y (pretax)	2,000
Gain on sale of discontinued Segment Y (pretax)	2,500
Extraordinary loss from flood (pretax)	3,500
Dividends declared and paid: preferred stock	3,000
Dividends declared and paid: common stock	2,880

During 1993 it was discovered that the depreciation expense for 1992 had been overstated by $3,000 (pretax). Corrections were made for the error and related income taxes.

Required Assuming the Eshroe Corporation is subject to a 30% income tax rate, prepare:

1. The lower portion of the income statement for 1993 starting with operating income.

2. A statement of retained earnings for 1993.

60. Income Statement, Lower Portion. On January 1, 1993, the Conler Corporation had 3,600 shares of common stock outstanding and a retained earnings balance of $82,100. On April 1, 1993, another 1,600 shares of common stock were issued. During 1993 it was discovered that the depreciation expense for 1992 had been understated by $1,500 (pretax). Corrections were made for the error and related income taxes. On December 31, 1993, the company's records showed the following items:

Operating income	$41,000
Nonoperating income	3,500
Income from operations of discontinued Segment C (pretax)	1,950
Loss on sale of discontinued Segment C (pretax)	2,750
Extraordinary loss from earthquake (pretax)	4,500
Dividends declared and paid: preferred stock	4,200
Dividends declared and paid: common stock	5,000

Required Assuming the Conler Corporation is subject to a 30% income tax rate, prepare:

1. The lower portion of the income statement for 1993 starting with operating income.
2. A statement of retained earnings for 1993.

61. Prior Period Adjustment. In 1993 the Closel Corporation discovered that it had not recorded $5,000 of depreciation expense in 1992. The corporation is subject to a 30% income tax rate.

Required 1. Record the effects on the accounting equation in 1993 of the correction to the accounting records.

2. Where would the correction be disclosed in the corporation's financial statements for 1993?

62. Compensatory Stock Options. On December 31, 1993, Remley Research Corporation grants to Mr. Thaddeus Basham, a key executive, the nontransferable right to acquire 1,000 shares of $10 par common stock for $41 per share. At that date, the market price of the stock is $50 per share. The grant is contingent upon Mr. Basham's completing three years of continuous service to Remley subsequent to December 31, 1993. The corporation is on a calendar year accounting period.

Required Record the effects on the accounting equation of the grant, the 1994, 1995, and 1996 annual compensation expense, and the issuance of the stock, assuming Basham exercises his option on May 15, 1997. Show how the stock option would be disclosed on the December 31, 1994, balance sheet.

63. Stock Options, One Executive. Ms. Ellen Hugmann, a top executive, was granted a stock option by her company on December 31, 1993, when the market price of the company's common stock was $60 per share. The stock option allows her to acquire 2,000 shares of $10 par common stock for $57 per share, after completing a two-year service period. The option expires on December 31, 1996. On April 15, 1996, Ms. Hugmann exercises her option. No other transactions involving this stock option occurred during 1993 through 1996. The company's fiscal year ends December 31.

Required Record the effects on the accounting equation for 1993 through 1996 in regard to this stock option.

64. Weighted Average Shares. At the beginning of the current year the Stepher Corporation had 2,000 shares of $10 par common stock outstanding. During the year it engaged in the following transactions related to its common stock:

Date	Transaction
Apr. 1	Issued 800 shares of stock
July 1	Issued 460 shares of stock

Required Determine the weighted average number of common shares outstanding for computing the earnings per share.

65. Computation of Simple Earnings per Share. The Neese Corporation reported net income in 1993 of $44,600. The company paid dividends for the current year on 200 shares of 7%, $100 par preferred stock and had 12,000 shares of common stock outstanding for the entire year.

Required Compute the earnings per share of the Neese Corporation for 1993.

66. Simple Earnings per Share. Burke Company shows the following condensed income statement information for the year ended December 31, 1993.

Income before extraordinary items	$27,216
Less: Extraordinary loss (net of income tax credit)	(2,176)
Net income	$25,040

The company declared dividends of $6,000 on preferred stock and $17,280 on common stock. At the beginning of 1993, 10,000 shares of common stock were outstanding. On May 4, 1993, the company issued 2,000 additional common shares, and on October 18, 1993, it issued a 20% stock dividend on its common stock. The preferred stock is not convertible.

Required 1. Compute the earnings per common share outstanding.

2. Show the income statement disclosure of earnings per share.

3. What information should be included in the note disclosures.

67. Disclosure of Earnings per Share. The Rondale Corporation reported net income in 1993 of $28,600, consisting of income from continuing operations of $27,000, results of discontinued operations (net of tax) of $4,000, and an extraordinary *loss* (net of tax) of $2,400. The corporation paid dividends for the current year on 100 shares of 8%, $100 par preferred stock and had 10,000 shares of common stock outstanding for the entire year.

Required Compute the earnings per share of the Rondale Corporation for 1993 and show how it would be reported on the income statement.

68. Retained Earnings. The records of the Warner Corporation show the following items as of December 31, 1993:

Income from continuing operations	$39,000
Loss from operations of discontinued Segment P (net of tax)	3,000
Gain on sale of discontinued Segment P (net of tax)	6,500
Extraordinary loss from expropriation of assets (net of tax)	2,500
Dividends declared and paid: preferred stock	3,800
Dividends declared and paid: common stock	7,900
Prior period adjustment: overstatement of 1992 depreciation (net of $1,360 income tax)	3,240
Additional paid-in capital: treasury stock	10,000
Stock dividend declared and issued	20,000
Treasury stock	12,000

Required Prepare a statement of retained earnings for the Warner Corporation for the year ended December 31, 1993 (assume that the beginning retained earnings balance for 1993 was $74,350).

69. **Income and Retained Earnings Statements.** The Grotwohl Corporation lists the following items on December 31, 1993:

Cost of goods sold	$142,000
Extraordinary loss from earthquake (net of tax)	4,000
General and administrative expenses	11,000
Interest revenue	1,750
Interest expense	650
Gain on sale of discontinued Segment L (net of tax)	1,200
Loss from operations of discontinued Segment L (net of tax)	400
Selling expenses	24,900
Sales (net)	270,000

Additional Information:

1. There were 18,000 shares of common stock outstanding on January 1, 1993. On September 1, 1993, the company issued 6,000 more common shares.

2. The company paid current cash dividends on 850 shares of 8%, $100 par preferred stock outstanding and an 80¢ per share dividend on the common stock outstanding on December 31, 1993.

3. During 1993 a mathematical error was discovered in the computation of a gain on the sale of machinery recorded in 1992. The 1992 gain was understated by $900 (net of tax). The correcting entry was made for the error and related income taxes.

Required 1. Prepare the income statement of the Grotwohl Corporation for the year ended December 31, 1993. Include earnings per share information (assume a 30% income tax rate).

2. Prepare a statement of retained earnings for the year ended December 31, 1993 (assume the beginning retained earnings for 1993 was $72,000).

70. **Misclassifications.** The bookkeeper for the Cortez Company prepared the following income statement and retained earnings statement for the year ended December 31, 1993:

CORTEZ COMPANY
December 31, 1993
Expense and Profits Statement

Sales (net)	$220,000
Less: selling expenses	(27,200)
Net sales	$192,800
Add: interest revenue	1,300
Add: gain on sale of equipment	4,900
Gross sales revenues	$199,000

Less: costs of operations		
Cost of goods sold	$139,100	
Correction of overstatement in last year's income due to error (net of $825 income tax credit)	3,300	
Dividend costs ($0.50 per share for 8,300 common shares outstanding the entire year)	4,150	
Extraordinary loss due to earthquake (net of $900 income tax credit)	3,600	(150,150)
		$ 48,850
Taxable revenues		(8,200)
Less: income tax on continuing income		$ 40,650
Net income		
Miscellaneous deductions:		
Loss from operations of discontinued Segment L (net of $450 income tax credit)	$ 1,800	
Administrative expenses	17,800	(19,600)
Net revenues		$ 21,050

CORTEZ COMPANY
Retained Revenues Statement
For Year Ended December 31, 1993

Beginning retained earnings	$65,000
Add: gain on sale of Segment L (net of $675 income tax expense)	2,700
Recalculated retained earnings	$67,700
Add: net revenues	21,050
	$88,750
Less: interest expense	(1,100)
Ending retained earnings	$87,650

You determine that the given amounts are correct but, in certain instances, have been incorrectly titled or classified.

Required 1. Review both statements and indicate where each incorrectly classified item should be classified. Also indicate any other errors you find.

2. Prepare a corrected 1993 income statement and retained earnings statement for the Cortez Company.

71. **Extraordinary Items.** Generally accepted accounting principles have established two narrow criteria which must be met in order for an event or transaction to be classified as an extraordinary item.

Required 1. Identify and discuss each criterion.

2. Develop examples of events which might be extraordinary to one company but not extraordinary to another, such as

  a. An earthquake
  b. A flood
  c. A tornado
  d. A severe frost

Justify your reasoning.

3. Discuss how the following should be disclosed on the income statement:
   a. An extraordinary item
   b. An event or transaction that does not meet both criteria

72. Appendix 1: Convertible Securities and Earnings per Share. Walker Company has 15,000 shares of common stock outstanding during all of 1993. It also has two convertible securities outstanding at the end of 1993.

1. Convertible preferred stock: 1,000 shares of 9%, $100 par preferred stock were issued in 1992 for $120 per share. The average Aa corporate bond yield at the date of issuance was 12%. Each share of preferred stock is convertible into 3.5 shares of common stock. The current dividends have been paid. To date, no preferred stock has been converted.

2. Convertible bonds: Bonds with a face value of $100,000 and an interest rate of 10% were issued at par on July 1, 1993. The average Aa corporate bond yield at that time was 13%. Each $1,000 bond is convertible into 30 shares of common stock. To date, no bonds have been converted.

The company earned net income of $54,000 during 1993. Its income tax rate is 30%.

Required Compute primary earnings per share and fully diluted earnings per share. What amount(s) would be disclosed on the income statement?

73. Appendix 1: Convertible Securities and Earnings per Share. Caldwell Company has 20,000 shares of common stock outstanding during all of 1993. It also has two convertible securities outstanding at the end of 1993.

1. Convertible preferred stock: 2,000 shares of 9.5%, $50 par preferred stock were issued on January 1, 1993, for $58 per share. The average Aa corporate bond yield at the date of issuance was 12%. Each share of preferred stock is convertible into three shares of common stock. Current dividends have been declared. To date, no preferred stock has been converted.

2. Convertible bonds: Bonds with a face value of $200,000 and an interest rate of 9.2% were issued at par in 1992. The average Aa corporate bond yield at that time was 14%. Each $1,000 bond is convertible into 36 shares of common stock. To date, no bonds have been converted.

The company earned net income of $59,100 during 1993. Its income tax rate is 30%.

Required Compute primary earnings per share and fully diluted earnings per share. What amount(s) would be disclosed on the income statement?

74. Appendix 1: Stock Options, EPS. Butler Company has 30,000 shares of common stock outstanding during all of 1993. This common stock has been selling at an average market price of $45 per share. The ending market price is $50 per share. The company also has outstanding a $15,000 note payable on which it is paying interest at a 12% annual rate. During 1993, Butler Company earned income of $39,000 after income taxes of 30%.

Required 1. Assuming that stock options to purchase 4,000 shares of common stock at $35 per share are outstanding the entire year, compute the primary and fully diluted earnings per share.

2. Repeat your analysis, assuming instead that the stock options allowed the purchase of 8,000 shares.

75. Appendix 1: Stock Splits, Convertibles, EPS. On January 1, 1993, Early Company had 10,000 shares of $10 par common stock and 1,000 shares of 9.7%, $100 par convertible preferred stock outstanding. On that date each share of preferred stock was convertible into 2.5 shares of common stock. These convertible preferred shares are common stock equivalents. On August 2, 1993, the company issued a 2 for 1 stock split, reducing the par value to $5 per share. This resulted in 20,000 shares of common stock outstanding at the end of 1993. During 1993 the company earned net income of $90,000.

Required Compute the primary and fully diluted earnings per share.

76. Appendix 1: Weighted Average Shares. At the beginning of the current year, Heath Company had 22,000 shares of $10 par common stock outstanding. During the year, it engaged in the following transactions related to its common stock, so that at year end it had 66,000 shares outstanding.

Date	Transaction
April 2	Issued 5,000 shares of stock
June 4	Issued 3,000 shares of stock
July 1	Issued a 10% stock dividend
September 28	Issued a 2 for 1 stock split, reducing the par value to $5 per share
October 3	Reacquired 1,000 shares as treasury stock
November 27	Reissued the 1,000 shares of treasury stock

Required Determine the weighted average number of shares outstanding for computing the earnings per share.

77. Appendix 1: Comparative Earnings per Share. Ryan Company shows net income of $5,125 for the year ended December 31, 1993, its first year of operations. On January 1, 1993, the company issued 9,000 shares of common stock. On August 3, 1993, it issued an additional 3,000 shares of stock, resulting in 12,000 shares outstanding at year end.

During 1994, Ryan Company earned net income of $16,400. It issued 2,000 additional shares of stock on March 1, 1994, and declared and issued a 2 for 1 stock split on November 1, 1994, resulting in 28,000 shares outstanding at year-end.

During 1995, Ryan Company earned net income of $23,520. The only common stock transaction during 1995 was a 20% stock dividend issued on July 1, 1995.

Required 1. Compute the earnings per common share outstanding that would be disclosed in the 1993 annual report.

2. Compute the 1993 and 1994 comparative earnings per common share outstanding that would be disclosed in the 1994 annual report.

3. Compute the 1993, 1994, and 1995 comparative earnings per common share outstanding that would be disclosed in the 1995 annual report.

78. Appendix 2: Percentage-of-Completion Method. In 1993, Tarlo Company agrees to construct a highway for Brice County over a three-year period (1993 through 1995). The contract price is $1,200,000, and the construction costs (both actual and estimated) total $705,000 for the three years. The percentage completed at the end of each year is as follows: 1993, 20%; 1994, 70%; 1995, 100%.

Required 1. Prepare a schedule showing the amount of gross profit that Tarlo Company would recognize each year using the percentage-of-completion method.

2. Prepare a schedule showing the amount of gross profit that Tarlo Company would recognize each year using the completed contract method.

79. Appendix 2: Percentage-of-Completion Method. The Koolman Construction Company began work on a contract in 1993. The contract price is $3,000,000, and the company uses the percentage-of-completion method. Other information relating to the contract is as follows:

	1993	1994
Costs incurred during the year	$ 500,000	$ 700,000
Estimated costs to complete, December 31	1,500,000	1,300,000
Billings during the year	400,000	850,000
Collections during the year	350,000	800,000

Required 1. Compute the gross profit or loss to be recognized in 1993 and 1994.

2. Prepare the appropriate sections of the income statement and ending balance sheet for each year.

80. Appendix 2: Installment Sales. The following information is available for the Butler Company, which began its operations in 1993:

	1993	1994
Total credit sales (including installment sales)	$100,000	$160,000
Total cost of goods sold (including installment cost of goods sold)	72,000	105,000
Installment sales	60,000	80,000
Installment cost of goods sold	42,000	52,000
Cash receipts on installment sales		
1993 sales	25,000	26,000
1994 sales		30,000

Required 1. Prepare a partial income statement and a partial balance sheet for 1993.

2. Prepare a partial income statement and a partial balance sheet for 1994.

81. Appendix 2: Installment Sales. Anibonita Company began operations in 1993. It sells goods on installment sales contracts; these transactions are considered to be exceptional, so it uses the installment method to recognize gross profit. Listed below is a summary of the installment sales, costs of installment sales, operating expenses, and collections for 1993 and 1994.

	1993	1994
Installment sales	$80,000	$90,000
Costs of installment sales	52,000	59,400
Operating expenses	13,000	15,000
Cash collections from:		
1993 installment sales	42,000	21,000
1994 installment sales		41,000

Required Using the installment method to recognize gross profits, prepare 1993 and 1994 condensed income statements for the Anibonita Company.

82. Appendix 2: Revenue Recognition Alternatives. The following are the operating activities of two different companies.

Company A: Engages in long-term construction contracts. Uses the percentage-of-completion method to recognize gross profits. Started contract X in 1993, contract Y in 1994, and contract Z in 1995. The total gross profit (estimated and actual) and the percentage completed for each contract during 1994 through 1996 are:

	Contract X	Contract Y	Contract Z
Gross profit	$600,000	$400,000	$500,000
% completed during:			
1994	60%	45%	—
1995	25%	35%	30%
1996	—	20%	50%

Company B: Sells goods on the installment basis. Uses the installment method (because these are exceptional cases) to recognize gross profits. Below is a summary of the installment sales, costs of installment sales, operating expenses, and collections for 1993 and 1994:

	1993	1994
Installment sales	$80,000	$100,000
Costs of installment sales	48,000	65,000
Operating expenses	17,000	20,000
Cash collections from:		
1992 installment sales		
(1992 gross profit is 39%)	58,000	—
1993 installment sales	56,000	24,000
1994 installment sales	—	68,000

Required 1. Prepare a schedule which shows Company A's gross profit for 1994, 1995, and 1996.

2. Prepare 1993 and 1994 condensed income statements for Company B.

83. Appendix 2: Revenue Recognition Alternatives. The following are the operating activities of two different companies.

Company Y: Sells goods on the installment basis. Uses the installment method (because these are exceptional cases) to recognize gross profits. The following is a summary of the installment sales, gross profit, operating expenses, and collections for 1993 and 1994.

	1993	1994
Installment sales	$90,000	$110,000
Gross profit	35,100	45,100
Operating expenses	18,000	21,000
Cash collections from:		
1992 installment sales		
(1992 gross profit is 40%)	35,000	—
1993 installment sales	67,000	23,000
1994 installment sales	—	80,000

Company Z: Engages in long-term construction contracts. Uses the percentage-of-completion method to recognize gross profits. Started contract 1 in 1993, contract 2 in 1994, and contract 3 in 1995. The total gross profit (estimated and actual) and the percentage complete for each contract at the end of 1994 through 1996 are:

	Contract 1[a]	Contract 2	Contract 3
Gross profit	$800,000	$350,000	$600,000
% complete at the end of:			
1994	75%	40%	—
1995	100%	70%	35%
1996	—	100%	80%

[a]30% was complete at the end of 1993.

Required 1. Prepare 1993 and 1994 condensed income statements for Company Y.

2. Prepare a schedule which shows Company Z's gross profit for 1994, 1995, and 1996.

84. Appendix 2: Timing of Revenue Recognition. Revenue is usually recognized at the point of sale. Under special circumstances, however, bases other than the point of sale are used for the timing of revenue recognition.

Required 1. Why is the point of sale usually used as the basis for the timing of revenue recognition?

2. Disregarding the special circumstances when bases other than the point of sale are used, discuss the merits of each of the following objections to the sales basis of revenue recognition:

   a. It is too conservative because revenue is earned throughout the entire process of production.

   b. It is not conservative enough because accounts receivable do not represent disposable funds; sales returns and allowances may be made; and collection and bad debt expenses may be incurred in a later period.

3. Revenue may also be recognized (a) during production and (b) when cash is received. For each of these two bases of timing revenue recognition, give an example of the circumstances in which it is properly used and discuss the accounting merits of its use in lieu of the sales basis. *(AICPA adapted)*

85. **Appendix 2: Exchanges and Revenue Recognition Issues.** Certain business "exchanges" are very complex and may qualify as exceptional cases in which the related revenues and expenses should be advanced or deferred. Four such cases follow:

    1. Franchisor grants a franchise to a franchisee; it collects part of the initial franchise fee and agrees to perform related initial services over an extended period.

    2. Land development company acquires land for future development into a "sports retirement community," subdivides the land into lots, and sells the lots on "credit" with payment to be made on a long-term basis.

    3. Lessor leases equipment to a lessee on a long-term noncancelable lease; the fair value of the leased item is greater than the cost, and the ownership of the leased item is transferred to the lessee by the end of the lease life.

    4. A construction company builds bridges; it enters into a contract to construct a bridge for Rice County over a two-year period.

Required For each of the above situations, (a) indicate the revenue recognition issues involved, and (b) discuss when the revenue should be recognized and by what method.

ANNUAL REPORT PROBLEMS

86. **Stockholders' Equity.** Baxter International is a leading supplier of health care products, systems, and services. Listed in random order are all the accounts used for equities and liabilities in its 1988 balance sheet (in millions of dollars):

Common stock in treasury, at cost	$ (1)
Long-term debt and lease obligations	2,233
Income taxes payable	232
Cumulative convertible exchangeable preferred stock	541
Convertible subordinated debentures	78
Adjustable rate preferred stock	339
Notes payable to banks	324
Additional contributed capital	1,174
Current maturities of long-term debt and lease obligations	206

Common stock	246
Deferred income taxes and noncurrent liabilities	377
Accounts payable and accrued liabilities	1,124
Retained earnings	1,654
Foreign currency adjustment	23

Required 1. Prepare the stockholders' equity section of the balance sheet as of December 31, 1988. (Include the foreign currency adjustment in stockholders' equity.)

2. Calculate the debt ratio (which is total liabilities divided by total assets) and include a list of current and long-term liabilities in support of your answer.

87. Stockholders' Equity. The following excerpts are from Kimberly-Clark's 1988 annual report related to stockholders' equity (in millions of dollars except par values):

Stockholders' Equity (in part)	1988	1987
Preferred stock—no-par value—authorized 20,000,000 shares; issued and outstanding—none	$ —	$ —
Common stock—$1.25 par value—authorized 300,000,000 shares; issued 81,000,000 shares	101.2	101.2
Additional paid-in capital	135.4	144.5
Cost of common stock in treasury	(21.8)	(39.3)
Unrealized currency translation adjustments	(50.5)	(85.9)
Retained earnings	1,701.3	1,451.4
	$1,865.6	$1,571.9

Note 8. Stockholders' Equity (in part):
On April 16, 1987, the stockholders approved (a) an increase in the authorized shares of common stock from 100 million to 300 million shares and in the authorized shares of preferred stock from 10 million to 20 million shares; (b) a reduction of the par value of the common stock from $2.50 to $1.25 per share; and (c) a split of each issued share of common stock into two shares. Numbers of common shares and per share data in this report reflect the additional shares distributed in the stock split.

384,215 shares of treasury stock costing $19.4 were used for the exercise of stock options in 1988 and 34,228 shares costing $1.9 million were purchased for treasury stock in 1988. During 1987, the Corporation completed the acquisition of 12 million shares of treasury stock for $631.6. On December 17, 1987, the board of directors announced the retirement of 14.5 million shares of treasury stock, which became authorized but unissued shares, for $650.4. On June 21, 1988, the board of directors declared a distribution of one preferred share purchase right at $200 par for each outstanding share of the Corporation's common stock to stockholders of record as of July 1, 1988. These rights are intended to protect the stockholders against abusive takeover tactics. Under certain circumstances, a right will entitle its holder either to acquire shares of the Corporation's stock or shares of the acquiring firm's common stock, in either event having a market price of twice the exercise price of the stock.

Note 6. Equity Participation Plan (in part):
Stock options are granted at not less than market value and become exercisable

a period of three years from date of grant. The period of each option is limited to not more than 10 years.

The Compensation Committee has granted stock appreciation rights (SARs) to certain participants. SARs allow the participants, in lieu of option exercise, to receive cash equal to the difference between the option price and the market price of the Corporation's common stock at the date of conversion. As a condition to SAR conversion, a participant is required to exercise an equal number of option shares. At December 31, 1988, 2,259,846 shares of common stock were available for additional grants of participation shares and stock options. Amounts expensed under the Plan in 1988 and 1987 were $10.3 and $8.8, respectively.

Required 1. Use T-accounts to analyze the 1987 stockholders' equity changes concerning the stock split, the increase in number of shares authorized, and the treasury stock transactions.

2. Use T-accounts to analyze all the 1988 stockholders' equity changes, except for the unrealized translation adjustment account, which will be discussed in Chapter 13. Cash dividends for 1988 were $128.7 million. Were any rights used in 1988 to protect stockholders against "abusive takeover tactics"?

88. Discontinued Items. The following excerpts are from Honeywell's 1988 annual report (in millions of dollars):

Note 5. Nonrecurring Items:
In 1986, Honeywell announced plans to realign its operations and to focus on its core business. As a result of the implementation of these plans, Honeywell recorded nonrecurring charges of $219.4, reducing income from continuing operations $134.4 ($2.98 per share) during the fourth quarter of 1986.

Charges resulting from the business reorganizations, plant consolidations and relocation, termination of operations, and revaluation of goodwill amounted to $165.4, reducing income from continuing operations $107.1 ($2.37 per share).

Termination costs related to a work force reduction of 3,200 employees amounted to $54.0, reducing income from continuing operations $27.3 ($0.61 per share).

Note 6. Discontinued Product Lines:
In 1988, Honeywell sold Training and Control Systems Division, a provider of electronic simulation-based military training systems, for $114.0. Also sold in 1988 were a protection services subsidiary in the U.K. for $51.9, and the water management systems business of a U.S. subsidiary for $13.5.

In 1988, Honeywell announced its intention to sell its Electro-Optics Division, Defense Communications and Production Division, Signal Analysis Center, and its semiconductor operations. These planned sales reflect Honeywell's resolve to continue focusing on core businesses where it has a competitive advantage. The income statement pretax loss of $150.8 ($3.54 per share) on discontinuance of product lines includes the profits on the sale of product lines in 1988 and provisions for the anticipated losses on disposition of the other product lines currently held for sale.

Required 1. Why did Honeywell treat the nonrecurring items and discontinued product lines losses as part of continuing operations, rather than as discontinued operations?

2. Assume that you want to analyze Honeywell's performance of its core businesses. If you eliminate the effects of the nonrecurring items and the discontinued product

lines as noncore businesses, how is the trend affected for earnings per share from continuing operations, which were $4.72 in 1988, $5.75 in 1987, and $0.28 in 1986?

89. **Discontinued Operations and Extraordinary Items.** HNG/InterNorth is a diversified energy company. The following excerpts are from its 1985 financial statements related to nonoperating items (in millions of dollars):

Statement of Income (in part):

Income from continuing operations before income taxes and extraordinary charge	$ 165.8
Income (loss) from discontinued operations (note 4)	38.1
Income before extraordinary charge	$ 203.9
Extraordinary charge (note 3)	(218.0)
Net income (loss)	$ (14.1)
Preferred stock dividends	48.5
Earnings (loss) on common stock	$ (62.6)

Note 3. Peruvian Operations (in part):

On August 29, 1985, the Peruvian government unilaterally canceled certain exploration and production agreements between the government-owned oil company and various foreign companies including Belco Petroleum Corporation of Peru (BPCP), a wholly owned subsidiary of the Corporation. On December 27, 1985, the Peruvian government nationalized the operations of BPCP. The corporation intends to pursue all avenues to achieve adequate and effective compensation for its nationalized property which had a book value of $393, and has held preliminary discussions with its insurance companies and with the Government of Peru. The Corporation charged earnings in the amount of $218 for its estimated loss, which is net of estimated recoveries from insurance, the Peruvian government and the possible return of some property and provides for anticipated future expenses related to the recovery process. No income tax benefits were realized on the loss. This charge has been accounted for as an extraordinary item.

Note 4. Discontinued Operations (in part):

For accounting purposes, the Corporation's retail natural gas operation, coal properties and two LPG transport ships have been classified as discontinued operations.

The retail natural gas operations were sold on December 20, 1985. The sales price of approximately $250 resulted in an after tax gain of $42.0 or $.95 per share. In December 1985, the Corporation wrote off its remaining investment in the coal properties. This charge reduced the Corporation's 1985 earnings by $10.2 or $.23 per share.

Summary operating results of these discontinued operations are as follows for 1985:

Operating earnings	$ 6.3
Gain realized on sale of retail natural gas operations (net of income tax expense)	42.0
Loss recognized on write off of investment in coal properties (net of income tax benefits)	(10.2)
Income (loss) from discontinued operations	$38.1

Required 1. Do the economic events discussed in this problem properly qualify as discontinued operations and extraordinary items as opposed to nonrecurring items from continuing operations?

2. Use T-accounts to reconcile the retained earnings account which had year-end balances of $1,082.6 million and $910.2 million in 1984 and 1985, respectively. Show the discontinued operations and extraordinary items separately and use a property, plant, and equipment summary account for these items. Ignore income tax effects.

3. Were any preferred or common stock dividends paid in 1985? If so, why were they paid when the company had a net loss in 1985? The preferred stock is cumulative and redeemable in various amounts annually.

90. Common Stock. General Signal is a large diversified company. The following excerpts are from its 1988 annual report related to shareholders' equity (in thousands of dollars):

Shareholders' Equity	1988	1987
Common stock—Authorized 75,000,000 shares (par value $1 per share); issued: 1988—30,737,505 shares; 1987—29,584,000 shares	$ 41,842	$ 40,692
Additional paid-in capital	295,916	236,818
Common stock held in treasury, at cost: 1988—11,677,913 shares; 1987—2,112,379 shares	(579,876)	(88,697)
Cumulative foreign exchange translation adjustments	(2,062)	(12,662)
Retained earnings	705,226	731,000
Total capital stock and other shareholders' equity	$ 461,046	$ 907,151

Statement of Retained Earnings		
Years ended December 31		
Balance at beginning of year	$731,000	$712,323
Net income (loss)	25,198	69,378
Common stock dividends	(50,972)	(50,701)
Balance at end of year	$705,226	$731,000

Note 6. Capital Stock (in part):
Common Stock:
On April 21, 1969, the par value of the company's common stock was changed from $6.67 to $1.00. The 1,959,559 common shares outstanding on April 18, 1969, are carried at a stated value of $6.67 per share, aggregating $13,070, and shares issued since then are carried at the par value of $1.00 per share.

Self-tender Offer (in part):
On November 17, 1988, the company commenced a "Dutch Auction" self-tender offer to shareholders for the repurchase of 9 million shares of its own common stock, subject to increase at the company's discretion. Under the offer terms, share-

holders were invited to tender their shares by December 15, 1988, at prices ranging from $44 to $51 per share as specified by each shareholder.

At the conclusion of the offer, approximately 10.9 million shares had been tendered, of which the company repurchased 9,572,627 shares at $51 per share for a total cost of approximately $491,000, including legal and financial consulting fees. The total shares repurchased represent approximately one-third of the outstanding shares at that date. The transaction was financed through existing cash and $400,000 in long-term debt.

	Common Stock	Additional Paid-in Capital	Treasury Stock
Balance, December 31, 1987	$40,692	$236,818	$ (88,697)
Share repurchase	—	—	(490,661)
Common stock issued for acquisitions	980	50,621	—
Exercise of stock options	170	7,655	(624)
Other	—	822	106
Balance, December 31, 1988	$41,842	$295,916	$(579,876)

Required 1. Why would the company have both a $6.67 stated value and a $1.00 par value for its common stock? Can the number of these shares and amounts be reconciled to the balance sheet from the note 6 common stock information?

2. Use T-accounts to analyze all the 1988 changes in the stockholders' equity accounts as described above. Ignore the cumulative foreign exchange translation adjustment account, which is discussed in Chapter 13.

3. What might be the "other" adjustment? What is a "Dutch Auction"? Why would the company repurchase one-third of its common shares and incur $400 million in debt?

91. **Reorganization: Stockholders' Equity and Liabilities.** Manville Corporation was incorporated in 1981 to continue businesses begun by the predecessors of Johns-Manville Corporation in 1858. It has three groups of businesses, fiber glass products, forest products, and specialty products. In November, 1988, the company emerged from reorganization under Chapter 11 of the Bankruptcy Code. It had been operating under Chapter 11 since August, 1982. Below are excerpts from its 1988 financial statements and related notes (in millions of dollars):

	1988	1987
Total assets	$ 2,393	$2,753
Long-term debt (notes 1 and 2)	$ 869	$ 223
Liabilities subject to Chapter 11 proceedings (note 1)	0	547
Total liabilities	1,595	1,382
Redeemable $5.40 Series preferred stock (note 3)	$ 0	$ 301
Series A convertible preferred stock (note 2)	418	0
Series B cumulative preference stock (note 2)	89	0

Common stock ($.01 par in 1988; $2.50 par in 1987) (notes 2, 3 and 4)	3	60
Capital in excess of par value or APIC	759	178
Retained earnings (deficit)	(479)	820
Cumulative translation adjustment	8	12
Total stockholders' equity	$ 798	$1,070
Net income from operations	$ 96	$ 64
Extraordinary charge, net of tax (notes 1 and 2)	(1,288)	(91)
Cumulative effect of change in income tax accounting	(107)	0
Net income (loss)	$(1,299)	$ 73

Notes (in part):

Note 1: Concerning the $547 liabilities subject to Chapter 11 proceedings, banks and other commercial creditors received $455 in principal which consisted of $250 in cash; 12%, 3 year notes of $170 in principal; and 9%, 20 year bonds of $35 in principal.

Note 2: The extraordinary charge of $1,380 does not include any information from Note 1. It does include all other costs to implement the plan of reorganization as follows:

$ 441	increase in long-term debt
418	issuance of Series A preferred stock
89	issuance of Series B preference stock
1	issuance of shares of $.01 par common stock to creditors
222	increase in APIC related to $.01 par common stock
209	cash paid out as part of reorganization expenses
$1,380	

Note 3: The Redeemable $5.40 Series preferred stock was canceled in exchange for shares of the new $.01 par common stock with $1 par value.

Note 4: All the shares of the old $2.50 common stock were canceled in exchange for shares of the new $.01 par common stock with $1 par value.

Required **1.** Show the impact upon the accounting equation from the information in the previous four notes of Manville. These four notes relate to Manville's reorganization and emergence form Chapter 11 bankruptcy. They can be used to reconcile the beginning and ending balances in all the individual liability and stockholders' equity accounts shown in the case. Ignore income taxes and the cumulative translation adjustment.

2. The actual and potential distribution of the 120 million new shares of $.01 par common stock related to the above notes is as follows (in millions of shares):

Actual:

24	to personal injury trust for asbestos claims
11	to unsecured creditors
10	to holders of old $5.40 Series preferred stock
3	to holders of old $2.50 par common stock
48	total actual shares of new $.01 par common stock issued

Potential:

72   to personal injury trust if it converts the new Series A convertible preferred stock into the new common stock

120   total actual and potential shares of new $.01 par common stock

    a. What is the actual ownership interest (in a percentage) of the original shareholders right after restructuring, but before any potential conversions of the 72 million new common shares?

    b. What is potential ownership interest dilution (in a percentage) to the original shareholders if the additional 72 million shares of common stock are issued? Who really owns Manville now?

3. Excerpts from Manville's lease note (in millions of dollars): At December 31, 1988, minimum rental commitments under long-term noncancellable operating leases are $71. Total rental expense was $26 in 1988 and $22 in 1987. Did Manville's use of this off-balance sheet financing for leases have a material impact upon the following ratios (ignore net present value adjustments to the aggregate rentals and ignore any adjustments to expenses):

    a. 1988 debt/equity ratio

    b. 1988 return on total assets

92. **Insurance Recovery.** PPG Industries is a large industrial company with major business segments of glass, coatings and resins, and chemicals. An excerpt from its 1985 statement of earnings (in millions of dollars) follows:

	1985	1984	1983
Other earnings (see note 11)	$75.3	$55.6	$58.1
Note 11 (complete)			
Interest income	$ 8.3	$11.0	$ 8.6
Royalty income	19.5	20.8	17.7
Gain from insurance recovery	21.2	—	—
Other	26.3	23.8	31.8
Total	$75.3	$55.6	$58.1

Management Discussion and Analysis (in part):

    An increase in net earnings of about $10 resulted from an insurance recovery in excess of book value related to the loss of the S.S. *Puerto Rican,* a PPG chemical tanker that suffered extensive damage late in 1984.

Required 1. Using T-accounts or the accounting equation, analyze the impact of the insurance recovery on the 1985 accounts of PPG. Assume that the book value of the tanker was $15 million.

    2. Why wasn't this item recorded in 1984? Why does a financial statement reader have to look in three different places in the annual report to discover why other earnings increased significantly in 1985?

93. Financing Expansion. The following are excerpts from McDonald's 1988 shareholder's equity (in thousands of dollars):

Long-term debt	$3,111,053
Preferred stock, no par value	–0–
Common stock, no par value	23,083
Additional paid-in capital	168,409
Retained earnings	3,935,222
Average total assets	7,570,500
Net income	645,863
Net income per share	3.43

Required Assume that McDonald's desires to raise $1 billion for an expansion program into Eastern Europe. Also assume that it can continue to earn the same return on assets (net income divided by average total assets) on this $1 billion that it earned in 1988. Use McDonald's effective income tax rate of 40%. Analyze the impact on net earnings available to each share of common stock under the following forms of financing:

1. Twenty-year debentures with a 10% interest rate.

2. Nonconvertible preferred stock similar to the preferred stock already available; assume the issue price is $100 per share and $2 per share dividends are required.

3. Common stock similar to the common stock already issued; assume the issue price is $50 per share.

94. Appendix 1: User Analysis of EPS Trends. Champion International Corporation's goal is to be a superior low-cost producer of pulp and paper. The following excerpts are from its 1988 annual report (in millions of dollars except earnings per share):

	1988	1987	1986
Income statement (in part):			
Income before income taxes	$730	$620	$313
Income taxes	274	238	118
Net income	$456	$382	$195
Average number of common shares			
outstanding (in millions)	95	95	94
Earnings per share:			
Primary	$4.80	$4.03	$2.08
Fully diluted	$4.65	$3.92	$2.05

Notes to Financial Statements (in part):

Note 3. Inventories (in part):
    Effective January 1, 1987, the company refined the elements of cost included in inventory by including certain general and administrative expenses relating to the procurement or production of inventory. This change was made to conform to the company's inventory accounting policies to the extent permitted by generally accepted accounting principles, to conform to the uniform cost capitalization policies included in the Tax Reform Act of 1986, and to better reflect the cost of pro-

duction. The cumulative effect of this change was to increase 1987 net income by approximately $4 or $0.04 per share. The effect on 1987 earnings was not material. Beginning in 1988, these costs, which under former company practice would have been reported as general and administrative expense, are reported as cost of products sold as the inventory is sold. The corresponding 1987 amounts have been reclassified to conform to the current year's presentation.

Note 4. Property, Plant, and Equipment (in part):
    Effective January 1, 1987, the company revised the useful lives of certain depreciable assets. The effect of this revision was to reduce depreciation expense for 1987 by approximately $14.

Note 11. Other (Income) Expense—Net (in part):

	1988	1987	1986
Gain of sale of investments in Stone and U.S. Plywood corporations	$—	$(143)	$—
1988 St. Regis merger related—net(a)	23	—	—
Miscellaneous—net(b,c)	(4)	(21)	(16)

(a) In 1988, the company provided $35 reflecting its agreement to partially fund unexpected losses incurred by the divested former St. Regis insurance operations and $16.4 for unfavorable developments on preacquisition St. Regis matters, primarily environmental liabilities. Also, the company provided $29.9 for additional expenditures to further integrate the companies into a single management methodology. Finally, the company resolved various preacquisition St. Regis liabilities for $58 less than the recorded amounts.
(b) In connection with the sale of the company's investment in U.S. Plywood Corporation, Miscellaneous—net for 1987 includes income of $11.8 resulting from an adjustment of reserves established as part of the company's wood products restructuring program.
(c) Miscellaneous—net for 1986 includes gains attributable to favorable settlements of certain preacquisition St. Regis obligations. The Tax Reform Act of 1986 reduced the tax benefits that will become available when certain liabilities associated with the St. Regis acquisition are paid. The reduction was largely offset by other factors affecting these and similar liabilities.

Note 12. Income Taxes (in part):
    The adjustment to prior years' income taxes for 1987 is primarily attributable to the recognition of energy tax credits on black liquor recovery boilers constructed in prior years. Recognition for financial reporting purposes was delayed pending resolution by the Internal Revenue Service of the qualification of recovery boilers as energy property. [Effective tax rates for 1987 and 1988 were reduced 3.3% (or $20.4) and 2.1% (or $15.3), respectively, for adjustments to prior years' income taxes. Without these adjustments, the effective tax rate for the last three years averaged 40%.]

Note 15. Quarterly Results of Operations (Unaudited) (in part):
(a) 1987 fully diluted earnings per share includes gains resulting from the sale of the company's investments in Stone and U.S. Plywood Corporations totaling $0.89 per share. In connection with the U.S. Plywood sale, fully diluted earnings per share also includes $0.07 resulting from an adjustment of reserves established in connection with the company's wood products restructuring program.

(b) Effective January 1, 1987, the company revised the useful lives of certain depreciable assets. The effect of this revision on the third quarter of 1987 was to increase fully diluted earnings per share by $0.07, $0.04 of which relates to the first two quarters of 1987. The first and second quarters' results have not been restated due to immateriality. The impact of the change for the full year 1987 was $0.09 per share.
(c) Results for 1988 include $23.3 of net other expenses principally related to both favorable and unfavorable resolutions of certain preacquisition St. Regis liabilities. The provision for income taxes includes a related tax benefit of $28.8 which reflects the favorable resolutions not being taxable.

Management's Discussion and Analysis (in part):
Results of Operations (in part):

Results for 1988 were significantly above the levels for both 1987 and 1986. For 1988, fully diluted earnings per share were a record $4.65, up from $3.92 in 1987 and $2.05 in 1986. The 1987 figure included one-time gains totaling $0.89 per share from the sale of investments in Stone and U.S. Plywood Corporations. Net income for 1988 was $456, up from $382 in 1987 (including one-time gains) and $195 in 1986. Net sales of $5,100 were up from $4,600 and $4,400 in 1987 and 1986, respectively.

The substantial improvement over 1987 and 1986 was attributable principally to strong demand for pulp and paper, which is the company's primary business. The wood products segment, however, suffered both from generally lower prices for lumber and plywood and from a 13-week strike at five western U.S. manufacturing facilities.

Required What is the impact on the three-year trend in fully diluted earnings per share if the nonrecurring items and the accounting method changes are eliminated? Do you agree with management that "results for 1988 were significantly above the levels for both 1987 and 1986"?

95. Appendix 1: Earnings per Share. Rockwell is a large aerospace company. The following excerpts are from its 1988 annual report related to earnings per share:

Note 19 (in part):
Primary earnings per share of common stock, after recognition of the Series A and B preferred stock dividend requirements, are based on the weighted average number of common shares outstanding during each year (266,605,000 in 1988, 280,035,000 in 1987 and 296,517,000 in 1986). The computation does not include a negligible dilutive effect of stock options and stock appreciation rights.

Fully diluted earnings per share of common stock are based on the assumption that all preferred stocks and convertible debentures were converted at the beginning of the year and all dilutive stock options were exercised at the beginning of the year or date of grant, if later. The computation assumes the elimination of preferred dividends and convertible debenture interest expense (net of tax).

	1988	1987	1986
Net income (in millions)	$811.9	$635.1	$611.2
Earnings per common share:			
Primary	?	?	?
Fully diluted	$ 3.01	$ 2.23	$ 2.03
Average market price (fourth quarter)	$ 21	$ 27	$ 31

Required 1. Compute the primary earnings per share for all three years.

2. How many potential dilutive shares exist in each of the three years?

3. Would there be a material impact in any of the three years on the price earnings ratio, assuming all the potential dilutions occur? (The price earnings ratio is the market price divided by the earnings per share.)

96. Appendix 2: Revenue Recognition and Extraordinary Items. Public Service Company of Colorado is the largest utility company in Colorado. The following excerpts are from its 1988 annual report (in millions of dollars except earnings per share amounts):

Note 1. Summary of Significant Accounting Policies (in part):
Change in method of revenue recognition:

Effective January 1, 1987, the Company adopted a change in accounting method which provides for the accrual of estimated unbilled revenues. Unbilled revenues represent the estimated amount customers will be billed for service delivered from the time meters were last read to the end of the accounting period. Customers' meters are read on a cycle basis and, prior to the change in accounting method, revenues were recognized concurrently with customer billings. The new accounting method results in a better matching of expenses with the related revenues. The after-tax effect of the accounting change for the twelve months ended December 31, 1987 was an increase in net income of $31.3 ($0.60 earnings per share). This increase is a combination of an increase of $29.6 ($0.56 earnings per share) attributable to the cumulative effect of the accounting change to January 1, 1987, and an increase of $1.7 ($0.04 earnings per share) in the 1987 results of operations.

Note 2. Fort St. Vrain Nuclear Generating Station (in part):
During 1986, the Company recognized an extraordinary loss of $101.4 (net of $101.5 in related income taxes and net earnings per share decrease of $1.93) which resulted from writing down a substantial portion of the total investment in Fort St. Vrain, recognizing estimated future defueling and decommissioning expenses, and recognizing estimated unrecoverable operating and capital expenditures. The amount of the write-off was based on the assumption that the plant would remain operational until all existing fuel in the reactor and on-site was utilized and that the reactor would then be decommissioned and the plant converted to a fossil-fuel-burning plant.

Whether the Company will realize its remaining investment in Fort St. Vrain (approximately $65.7 at December 31, 1988) and whether the Company will be able to avoid future operating and capital expenditures are dependent on future events. Approximately $35.6 in unrecoverable operating and capital expenditures were recorded during 1988 ($0.39 earnings per share). In 1987, approximately $24.5 in such unrecoverable costs were recorded reducing net income by $13.3 or $0.25 earnings per share.

At the time the extraordinary loss was recorded in 1986, the Company estimated the cost of defueling and decommissioning Fort St. Vrain, based upon a study prepared by the Company in 1982, to be approximately $95.4. The study, however, assumed several circumstances that do not reflect those which it now appears will exist at the time defueling and decommissioning is commenced. Thus, additional cost studies were prepared, and the Company determined the present value of the estimated liability at December 31, 1988, to be $159.2. Therefore, the additional unrecoverable expense of $63.8 ($1.09 earnings per share) was recognized to reflect this revision in the liability and reported as part of regular operating activities.

Required 1. Do you agree that the change in revenue recognition method was an improvement in financial reporting?

2. In connection with the Fort St. Vrain nuclear plant (which uses the same technology as the Chernoble nuclear plant in Russia), why would the 1986 expenses be reported as extraordinary items and the 1987 and 1988 expenses included in regular operating income?

3. The reported earnings per share after all the above adjustments were $2.14 in 1988, $3.05 in 1987, and $0.13 in 1986. How would the trend in earnings per share over these three years change if all above major revenue and expense items were eliminated?

4. Would there be a material impact on 1988 earnings per share if the Company had to write off its remaining investment in Fort St. Vrain? Assume the net earnings per share impact is $0.67.

Additional Aspects of Financial Reporting

Marketable Securities, Long-Term Investments, and Acquisitions of Other Companies

After reading this chapter, you should understand

- Lower of cost or market method for current and noncurrent marketable securities—stocks
- Accounting for current marketable securities—bonds
- How the percentage of ownership in the common stock of another company affects the accounting method

- used for a noncurrent investment
- Equity method
- Consolidations under the purchase and pooling methods
- Accounting for noncurrent investments in bonds
- Minority interest (Appendix 2)

A company may make various types of investments. For example, a company often has excess cash that it invests in current (short-term) marketable securities, such as stocks or bonds of other companies. A company may also acquire noncurrent marketable securities because excess cash is available for more than one year. A noncurrent investment in bonds of other companies may be acquired, either to develop a financial relationship with another company, or to obtain a relatively safe source of continuing revenue.

Noncurrent investments in the stocks of other companies may be purchased. These acquisitions may be made either because they appear to be more profitable than investing in property, plant, or equipment, or for operating reasons. For example, a company can obtain a certain degree of influence, or even control, over the operations of other companies from which it purchases inventory or to which it sells products by purchasing common stock of these companies, voting at the stockholders' meetings, and being represented on the boards of directors. A company may also invest in the stocks of companies that have a long-term business cycle different from its own. The income earned on the stock may help to offset any declines in the income from the company's own business, resulting in a smoother trend of earnings. A company may acquire control of another company in order to achieve its growth objectives, instead of purchasing assets to expand its own activities. Each of these situations is discussed in this chapter.

■ HOW THE INVESTMENT IS MADE

Before discussing the various methods of accounting for investments, it is important to understand the relationship between the investor and the investee. **The investor is the company purchasing the investment. The investee is the company whose stock or bonds are being purchased.** In most situations the investor buys the shares or bonds of the investee on the stock market from existing owners who are willing to sell their investment. This transaction has no direct effect on the investee company whose shares or bonds are being purchased or sold, and therefore there is no effect on its financial statements. (The investee company, or its agent, does have to record the name and address of the new owners, however, so that dividend or interest checks and other information can be correctly mailed.)

Occasionally, an investor company purchases shares or bonds that are newly issued. Because the investee company receives the proceeds from the transaction, its financial statements are affected, as discussed in Chapters 8 and 10. In this chapter it is assumed that the investor company is purchasing shares or bonds that are already outstanding. Therefore, the transaction has no effect on the financial statements of the investee company.

No matter how the acquisition is made, the investor company records an asset for the cost of acquisition, which includes the purchase price, commissions to the stockbroker, and any transfer taxes that are imposed. The title used for the asset usually varies according to the type of acquisition.

SECTION A Marketable Securities

When a company acquires stocks or bonds of other companies it may intend to sell them soon or hold them for a longer period. If a company has temporary excess cash, it may not wish to invest in long-term physical assets or reduce liabilities because the company will need the money in the near future for operations. Instead of investing the excess cash in cash equivalents (discussed in Chapter 5) that earn relatively low interest, many companies invest in marketable securities that may provide a higher rate of return. **Marketable securities are investments in common stocks or bonds that are readily saleable.** (Marketable securities may also include preferred stocks but, for simplicity, these are not discussed in this book.)

These securities are classified as *current* when the company's intent is to sell the securities (or the securities mature) to obtain extra cash within one year or the operating cycle, whichever is longer. These securities are classified as *non-current* if the intent is to hold the security for *more* than one year or the normal operating cycle, whichever is longer. The classification as current or noncurrent is simply based on management intent. Also, since the classification is only important when the financial statements are issued, the criterion of a year extends from the balance sheet date.

Two general issues arise in accounting for marketable securities. First, how should the asset be reported in the balance sheet? Second, when is the revenue from the investment recognized? The answers to both questions unfortunately vary between stocks and bonds. Marketable securities—stocks are reported in the balance sheet at the lower of cost or market, whereas current marketable securities—bonds are reported at cost.[1] Dividends paid on stock issued by the investee are recorded as revenue by the investor when the dividends are received. Interest paid on bonds issued by the investee is recorded as revenue by the investor for the period they are owned. To put it simply, interest on bonds accrues continuously over time, whereas dividends on stock are discretionary, periodic payments.

In the first part of the chapter, accounting for current and noncurrent marketable securities—stocks is discussed. Next current marketable securities—bonds are discussed. Later in the chapter, the equity method for investments in stocks is explained. Accounting for a controlling interest under the purchase and pooling methods is discussed. Finally noncurrent investments in bonds are discussed.

Market Prices of Stocks and Bonds

An investment in stocks or bonds of publicly traded companies can be made very easily by dealing through a stockbroker. The stocks and bonds of large companies are traded on organized securities exchanges, such as the New York Stock Exchange or the American Stock Exchange. The stocks and bonds of smaller companies are traded in the over-the-counter market in which brokers deal directly with each other rather than through a stock exchange.

The market prices of such stocks and bonds are quoted daily and reported in many newspapers. For example, the stock of IBM was recently listed as follows:

| 52 Weeks | | Dividend | Yield % | Price/ Earnings | Sales, 100s | High | Low | Close | Net Change |
High	Low								
130⅞	93⅜	4.84	4.8	11	24187	100⅜	98⅞	100	+1⅛

· · · · · · · · · · · · · · · · · · · ·

[1]Current marketable securities—bonds may also be reported at lower of cost or market. In this book, however, we assume that these securities are reported at cost.

This information indicates that the stock has sold at a high of $130⅞ per share and a low of $93⅜ per share in the last 52 weeks. The annual dividend is $4.84 per share, which is a yield of 4.8% (the dividend as a percentage of the market price) on the closing market price. The price of a share is 11 times the earnings per share. On the date of this quotation, 2,418,700 shares were traded, the high price for the day was $100⅜ per share, the low price $98⅞ per share, and the closing price $100 per share, which was an increase in price of $1⅛ over the closing price of the previous day.

Bonds of IBM were also listed as follows:

Bonds	Current Yield	Volume	Close	Net Change
9⅜ 04	9.2	239	102⅛	+⅜

This information indicates that the bonds have an interest rate of 9⅜% and mature in the year 2004. The bonds currently yield 9.2% (the annual interest as a percentage of the market price) and on the date of this quotation 239 bonds were traded. The closing price was 102⅛, which represents an increase of ⅜ from the closing price of the previous day. The bond price is quoted as a percentage of the face value of the bond and not as a dollar amount. Since bonds have a face value of $1,000, this quote represents a price of $1,021.25 (102⅛% × $1,000).

These quoted market prices indicate the price an investor company would have to pay to purchase the securities or the price at which they can be sold. In addition, it would have to pay a fee to the stockbroker to make a purchase or a sale, and for bonds the investor company will also have to pay accrued interest since the last interest payment date, as discussed in Chapter 8.

■ CURRENT MARKETABLE SECURITIES—STOCKS

Accounting for the acquisition, valuation, revenue from, and sale of current and noncurrent marketable securities—stocks is discussed in the following sections.

Acquisition of Current Marketable Securities—Stocks

All marketable securities are recorded at the cost of acquisition. To illustrate, suppose that on October 1, 1993, the Lennon Company purchases 100 shares of the common stock of General Motors when the market price is $40 per share and 50 shares of the common stock of United Airlines when the market price is $20 per share. Stockbroker's fees and transfer taxes are ignored in this example. The total acquisition cost of $5,000 [(100 × $40) + (50 × $20)] is recorded as follows:

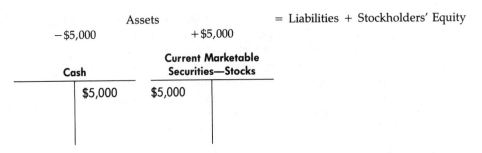

Thus, the Lennon Company has exchanged one current asset, cash, for another current asset, marketable securities.

Subsequent Valuation of Current Marketable Securities—Stocks: Lower of Cost or Market Method

On each balance sheet date, the current marketable securities—stocks must be properly valued for inclusion as a current asset on the balance sheet. This valuation of current marketable securities—stocks uses the lower of cost or market method based on the current portfolio of stocks owned.[2] **A company's portfolio includes all of its investments in stock of other companies. The current portfolio includes only those investments in stock that are classified as current, and is valued at the lower of its original cost or its current market value.** That is, if the total cost of the current portfolio is less than the total market value of the portfolio on the balance sheet date, the Current Marketable Securities—Stocks is reported at cost. Alternatively, if the market value of the portfolio is less than the cost of the portfolio, the Current Marketable Securities—Stocks are reported at market value. This procedure is consistent with the conservatism principle, discussed in Chapter 4.

To illustrate the application of the lower of cost or market method, suppose that the Lennon Company's current investments in capital stock had the following values at December 31, 1993, determined from current stock market prices:

Company	Number of Shares	Cost per Share	Market Value per Share	Total Cost	Total Market Value
General Motors	100	$40	$30	$4,000	$3,000
United Airlines	50	20	25	1,000	1,250
				$5,000	$4,250

Since the total market value of the current portfolio is $4,250 and the cost was $5,000, the portfolio must be valued at $4,250 in the balance sheet and a loss of $750 ($5,000 − $4,250) included in the income statement. These amounts are recorded as follows:

••••••••••••••••••••••
[2]"Accounting for Certain Marketable Securities," *FASB Statement of Financial Accounting Standards No. 12* (Stamford, Conn.: FASB, 1975).

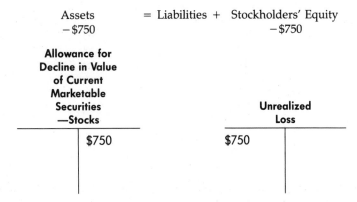

$$\text{Assets} = \text{Liabilities} + \text{Stockholders' Equity}$$
$$-\$750 \qquad\qquad\qquad -\$750$$

Allowance for Decline in Value of Current Marketable Securities —Stocks		Unrealized Loss	
	$750	$750	

The Unrealized Loss on the decline in the value of the current marketable securities is the loss from holding the securities that has *not* been realized through a sale. Therefore, the loss is called an *unrealized loss*. A loss is reported because there is a decline in the value of an asset, which reduces the value of the company to the owners. The loss should be included in the Other Revenues and Expenses section of the income statement.

The Allowance for Decline in Value of Current Marketable Securities is a contra asset and therefore reduces the value of the asset in the balance sheet. The cost of the portfolio is often reported on the face of the balance sheet so that users of the financial statements know both the cost and the market value. For example, the Lennon Company might disclose its current marketable securities as follows:

Current Assets	
Marketable securities—stocks, at cost	$5,000
Less: Allowance for decline in value	(750)
Marketable securities—stocks, at lower of cost or market	$4,250

If the market price of the portfolio continues to fall, a loss must again be recognized at the end of the next period. The loss would be equal to the additional decline in value and would be the amount necessary to obtain the correct balance in the Allowance account. The general rule is that the loss in any period is equal to the decline in the recorded value of the portfolio during the period under the lower of cost or market method. For example, suppose that the Lennon Company is preparing its quarterly financial statements on March 31, 1994, and the portfolio has the following market values:

Company	Number of Shares	Cost per Share	Market Value per Share	Total Cost	Total Market Value
General Motors	100	$40	$27	$4,000	$2,700
United Airlines	50	20	26	1,000	1,300
				$5,000	$4,000

Note that although the market price of the United Airlines stock went up from $25 to $26 per share, it is the *total* market value of the current portfolio that is compared to the previously recorded value of the portfolio. Since the previously recorded market value was $4,250, the additional decline in value to $4,000 is recorded as follows:

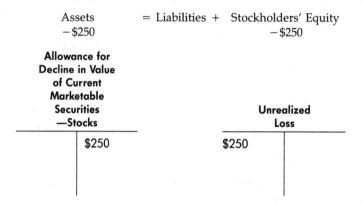

Assets   = Liabilities +   Stockholders' Equity
  − $250   − $250

Allowance for Decline in Value of Current Marketable Securities —Stocks	Unrealized Loss
$250	$250

If the market price of the portfolio subsequently rises, the gain (loss recovery) in value is recognized at the end of the next period, but the gain cannot exceed previously recognized losses. That is, the portfolio cannot be valued above cost. The general rule is that the gain in any period is equal to the increase in the recorded value of the portfolio during the period provided that the recorded value does not exceed cost. For example, suppose that the Lennon Company is preparing its quarterly financial statements on June 30, 1994. At this time the portfolio has the following market values:

Company	Number of Shares	Cost per Share	Market Value per Share	Total Cost	Total Market Value
General Motors	100	$40	$33	$4,000	$3,300
United Airlines	50	20	26	1,000	1,300
				$5,000	$4,600

Before discussing the entry required on June 30, 1994, let us review the entries that have been made in the following relevant accounts:

Current Marketable Securities—Stocks	Allowance for Decline in Value of Current Marketable Securities—Stocks
10/1/93 $5,000	12/31/93 $750
	3/31/94 250

Since the Current Marketable Securities account has a balance of $5,000 and the Allowance account has a balance of $1,000, the book value of the portfolio of current marketable securities in stock is $4,000. At June 30, 1994, the $4,600 market value of the portfolio is still less than the $5,000 cost, and therefore the securities should be carried at their market value of $4,600 in the balance sheet. This requires an ending balance in the Allowance account of $400 ($5,000 − $4,600). Since the existing balance is $1,000, this balance has to be reduced by the amount of the market value recovery of $600 ($1,000 − $400) to $400 on June 30, 1994, as follows:

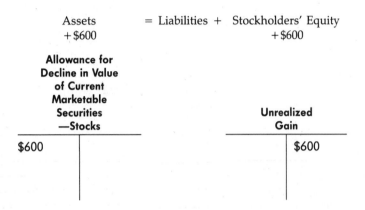

Note that because the Allowance is a contra asset, the $600 reduction has the net effect of increasing the value reported in the balance sheet. The gain of $600 appears in the income statement for the quarterly period in the Other Revenues and Expenses section. Alternatively, the gain could be called a **loss recovery**. The balance sheet includes the value of the portfolio as follows:

Current Assets	
Marketable securities—stocks, at cost	$5,000
Less: allowance for decline in value	(400)
Marketable securities—stocks, at lower of cost or market	$4,600

When additional cash is needed for a company's operations, an individual security included in current marketable securities—stocks may be sold. The gain or loss on the sale is measured by the difference between the proceeds from the sale and the *cost* of the stock and therefore is not affected by the balance in the Allowance account. The gain or loss is *not* measured as the difference between the proceeds from the sale and the market value of the common stock on the last balance sheet date because *individual* stocks are not carried at their market value. It is the *total portfolio* that is being carried at the lower of cost or market. On August 10, 1994, the Lennon Company sold 20 shares of General Motors (which originally cost $40 per share) for $35 per share. Thus, there is a loss on the sale of $100 [20 shares × ($40 − $35)], which would be recorded on August 10, 1994, as follows:

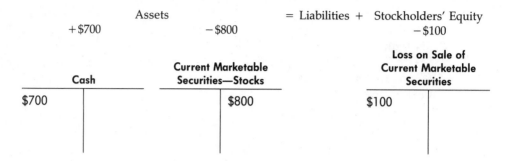

Assets = Liabilities + Stockholders' Equity

+$700   −$800   −$100

Cash	Current Marketable Securities—Stocks	Loss on Sale of Current Marketable Securities
$700	$800	$100

The loss should be included in the Other Revenue and Expenses section of the income statement. On September 30, 1994, the securities owned by the Lennon Company had the following values:

Company	Number of Shares	Cost per Share	Market Value per Share	Total Cost	Total Market Value
General Motors	80	$40	$37	$3,200	$2,960
United Airlines	50	20	22	1,000	1,100
				$4,200	$4,060

Before discussing the entry required, let us review the entries that have been made in the relevant accounts as follows:

Current Marketable Securities—Stocks		Allowance for Decline in Value of Current Marketable Securities—Stocks	
10/1/93 $5,000			12/31/93 $750
	8/10/94 $800		3/31/94 250
		6/30/94 $600	

Since the Current Marketable Securities account has a balance of $4,200 ($5,000 − $800) and the Allowance account has a balance of $400 ($750 + $250 − $600), the book value of the portfolio of current marketable securities is $3,800 ($4,200 − $400).

At September 30, 1994, the $4,060 market value of the portfolio is still less than the $4,200 cost, and therefore the portfolio should be carried at its market value in the balance sheet. This requires an ending balance in the Allowance account of $140 ($4,200 − $4,060). Since the existing balance is $400, this balance has to be reduced by $260 ($400 − $140), thereby raising the asset value from $3,800 to $4,060. An unrealized gain of $260 is also recognized as follows:

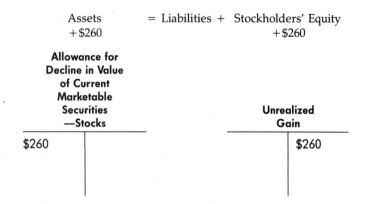

If the total market value of the current marketable securities (stocks) is $4,500 on December 31, 1994, when the next quarterly financial statements are prepared, a gain of only $140 is recorded to eliminate the Allowance account. That is, when the market value of the portfolio goes *above* the cost, the gain is computed by the company as the difference between the previous market value ($4,060) and the cost ($4,200) of the portfolio. Therefore, the marketable securities are now recorded at their cost of $4,200 and *not* at the market value of $4,500 because the market value is *higher* than the cost. The Lennon Company would disclose the following information in its balance sheet:

Current Assets	
Marketable securities—stocks, at cost	
(market value is $4,500)	$4,200

In the annual income statement for 1994, the company would include a net amount for the quarterly unrealized gains and losses. This net amount would be $750 (−$250 + $600 + $260 + $140). The realized loss on the sale of $100 would also be included on the income statement.

Revenue on Current Marketable Securities—Stocks

A corporation has no obligation to pay dividends on its issued stock. Dividends are a discretionary payment that must be voted by the board of directors, as discussed in Chapter 10. Thus, the purchaser of stock has no right to receive dividends, and therefore records no revenue, until the dividends are *declared* by the corporation. When a corporation decides to pay dividends it first declares that it will pay dividends. This act creates a legal obligation to pay the dividends. The dividends are actually paid about a month later. The reasons for different declaration and payment dates are discussed in Chapter 10. Most companies recognize revenue when the dividend is received. Suppose United Airlines pays a dividend of $1 per share. The Lennon Company now has revenue of $50 (50 shares × $1), which is recorded as follows:

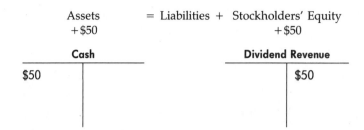

The Dividend Revenue should be included in the Other Revenues and Expenses section in the income statement. Some companies record dividend revenue when the dividend is declared by the investee company. Then Dividends Receivable and Dividend Revenue are recorded when the dividend is declared. Cash is increased and Dividends Receivable is reduced to zero when the cash is received.

■ NONCURRENT MARKETABLE SECURITIES— STOCKS

As mentioned earlier, accounting for the noncurrent portfolio of marketable securities—stocks is very similar to that used for the current portfolio. That is, the noncurrent portfolio of securities that are intended to be held for *more* than one year (or the operating cycle, whichever is longer) is initially recorded at the acquisition cost. Furthermore, the portfolio is valued on the balance sheet at the lower of its cost or market value. The one difference is that the decline in the value of the noncurrent portfolio is *not* included in the income statement as an unrealized loss but is included directly as a reduction of stockholders' equity on the balance sheet. The term "loss" should not be used with the noncurrent portfolio because "loss" is an income statement term. Therefore, an alternative title such as "unrealized decline" is appropriate. This difference is illustrated in the following diagram:

Decline in Asset Value (−)	Income Statement	Stockholders' Equity (−)
Current portfolio————————→	Unrealized loss or gain ————————→	Retained earnings
Noncurrent portfolio—————————————————————————————————————→		Unrealized decline

For a current portfolio, the unrealized loss or gain is included in the income statement and therefore affects retained earnings in the balance sheet. In contrast, the unrealized decline for a noncurrent portfolio is not included in the income statement (and therefore does not affect retained earnings) but is included as a reduction of stockholders' equity in the balance sheet. The totals for assets and stockholders' equity are the same under both methods. Income and the components of stockholders' equity are different, however.

The reason for not including the reduction in market value of a noncurrent portfolio in the income statement is that, since the portfolio is to be held for at least a year, there is a reasonable possibility that the decline will be reversed before a sale is made. In other words, it is less likely that the decline will ever be recorded as a loss from the actual sale of the investment. Including these declines and reversals in the income statement might tend to distort the results of the ongoing operating activities of the company. It seems just as likely, however, that the user of the financial statements will be confused by the placement of this decline on noncurrent marketable securities in the stockholders' equity section of the balance sheet. Accounting principles, however, require this form of disclosure.

As with the current marketable securities—stocks, the Allowance account balance is subtracted from the cost of the noncurrent marketable securities—stocks to report the market value of these securities in the balance sheet. The unrealized decline in the value of the securities that is included in stockholders' equity would be reported in the balance sheet in the following manner (amounts assumed):

STOCKHOLDERS' EQUITY

Contributed capital		
Common stock, $5 par	$10,000	
Additional paid-in capital	25,000	
Total contributed capital		$35,000
Retained earnings		42,000
Total contributed capital and retained earnings		$77,000
Less: unrealized decline in value of noncurrent		
marketable securities—stocks		(2,000)
Total stockholders' equity		$75,000

As discussed earlier, recoveries in the market value *up to* the cost of the portfolio are recognized. Remember that marketable securities—stocks cannot be carried at a value in excess of their cost. This recovery of value for noncurrent marketable securities—stocks, in contrast to current marketable securities—stocks, is *not a gain* reported on the income statement. Instead, this full or partial recovery of value would simply be recognized by the full or partial *reduction* of the unrealized decline on the balance sheet. The balances in the Allowance account and the Unrealized Decline account would both be reduced (or eliminated if total market value goes above total cost), and therefore the asset value and the stockholders' equity on the balance sheet would both be increased.

To illustrate the application of the lower of cost or market method to noncurrent marketable securities—stocks, we shall use the facts given earlier in the chapter for the Lennon Company's investment in current marketable securities but instead assume that the portfolio is classified as noncurrent. On October 1, 1993, the Lennon Company purchased securities for $5,000, which are recorded as follows:

Assets   = Liabilities + Stockholders' Equity
− $5,000   + $5,000

Cash	Noncurrent Marketable Securities—Stocks
$5,000	$5,000

On December 31, 1993, the portfolio is valued at $4,250 and the decline in value is recorded as follows:

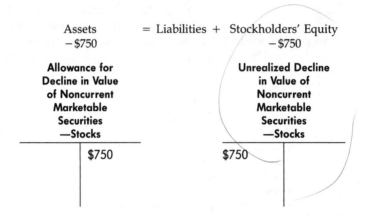

Assets   = Liabilities + Stockholders' Equity
− $750   − $750

Allowance for Decline in Value of Noncurrent Marketable Securities —Stocks	Unrealized Decline in Value of Noncurrent Marketable Securities —Stocks
$750	$750

On March 31, 1994, the portfolio is valued at $4,000 and the additional decline in value is recorded as follows:

Assets   = Liabilities + Stockholders' Equity
− $250   − $250

Allowance for Decline in Value of Noncurrent Marketable Securities —Stocks	Unrealized Decline in Value of Noncurrent Marketable Securities —Stocks
$250	$250

On June 30, 1994, the portfolio is valued at $4,600 and the increase in value is recorded as follows:

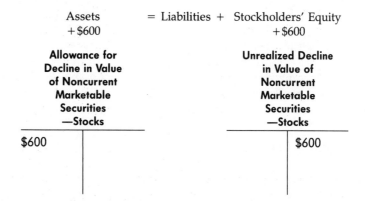

| | Assets | = Liabilities + | Stockholders' Equity |
| | + $600 | | + $600 |

| **Allowance for Decline in Value of Noncurrent Marketable Securities —Stocks** | | **Unrealized Decline in Value of Noncurrent Marketable Securities —Stocks** |
| $600 | | | $600 |

Note that the balance in both the Allowance and the Unrealized Decline accounts is now $400. On August 10, 1994, shares that originally cost $800 are sold for $700. The loss of $100 is recognized as follows:

| | Assets | | = Liabilities + | Stockholders' Equity |
| + $700 | | − $800 | | − $100 |

| **Cash** | | **Noncurrent Marketable Securities—Stocks** | | **Loss on Sale of Noncurrent Marketable Securities** |
| $700 | | | $800 | | $100 |

The loss should be included in the Other Revenues and Expenses section of the income statement because it is now realized. On September 30, 1994, the portfolio is valued at $4,060 and the increase in the value of the portfolio from $3,800 ($4,200 − $400) is recorded as follows:

| | Assets | = Liabilities + | Stockholder's Equity |
| | + $260 | | + $260 |

| **Allowance for Decline in Value of Noncurrent Marketable Securities —Stocks** | | **Unrealized Decline in Value of Noncurrent Marketable Securities —Stocks** |
| $260 | | | $260 |

On December 31, 1994, the portfolio is valued at $4,500, which is greater than the cost of $4,200. Therefore the balances of $140 in the Allowance and Unrealized Decline accounts are eliminated and the noncurrent portfolio is recorded at cost.

Revenue from dividends on noncurrent marketable investments in stock is recognized in exactly the same way as for current investments. That is, revenue is generally recognized as the dividends are received from the investee by increasing assets (cash) and stockholders' equity (dividend revenue).

■ ADDITIONAL CONSIDERATIONS

Sometimes there is a change in management's intent about the length of time a security should be owned and it is transferred between the portfolios. The transfer is recorded at the lower of cost or market, and any loss is considered to be a realized loss and is reported on the income statement. The lower of cost or market value becomes the new cost of the security. Therefore, management cannot avoid losses by transferring a security from one portfolio to the other.

A decline in value of a security may be considered to be "other than temporary." For example, the investee has declared bankruptcy. A new cost basis is established for that security based on the market value, and the amount of the write-down is considered a realized loss and reported on the income statement.

Income Tax Rules for Marketable Securities—Stocks

Federal income tax rules do not allow the use of the lower of cost or market method for income tax reporting purposes. Thus, an unrealized loss on a decline in the value of marketable securities is not a tax deduction, and subsequent gains up to the original cost are not taxable income. The realized gain or loss on the sale of current marketable securities for tax purposes is the difference between the selling price and the cost and therefore is the same amount as we discussed in this chapter. Such a gain is taxable income, and a loss is deducted from taxable income.

Evaluation of the Lower of Cost or Market Method

The lower of cost or market method is consistent with the historical cost and conservatism concepts. Many users of financial statements criticize this method, however, and argue that marketable securities—stocks should always be reported in a company's balance sheet at their market value and cost should be ignored. If such market values were recognized, gains in value above cost would have to be recognized. Since such a gain can easily be realized through a sale, many users argue that it should be included in the income statement of the period in which the market value increased. The major arguments in favor of using market values are:

1. The current market price is a better indicator than cost of the eventual amount of cash to be received from the sale.

2. The market value of the securities may be realized easily through a sale without interfering with the productive operations of the company.

3. Changes in market value are an indicator of the success of the investment strategy of the management of the company, and the resulting gains and losses should be reported in the income statement.

4. The market price can be easily determined and is reliable.

Although companies are not allowed to use market value (when it is above the cost) in the financial statements,[3] the market value of the total current marketable securities should be disclosed in the financial statements, as shown earlier. The market value may be disclosed in parentheses on the face of the balance sheet or in the notes to the financial statements.

Those who support the lower of cost or market method suggest that including the asset at market value would violate the historical cost concept and confuse the users of financial statements by valuing different assets in different ways. In addition, it is argued that an increase in value should not be recognized until there is a transaction (the sale of the stock), so that the increase in value can be measured with more reliability. Also, it may be argued that the use of the lower of cost or market method may be less relevant for the noncurrent portfolio because the intent is for the company to own the investment for at least a year. Therefore the current market value may not be a relevant indicator of the expected selling price at some future date.

■ CURRENT MARKETABLE SECURITIES—BONDS

Acquisition of Current Marketable Securities—Bonds

As with stocks an investment in Current Marketable Securities—Bonds is recorded at the acquisition cost. For example, suppose that on August 30, 1993, the Lennon Company purchased 12 Exxon Company bonds when they were selling at 98. Remember that, as discussed in Chapter 8, bonds have a face value of $1,000 and the selling price is quoted as a percentage of the face value. Thus, the company is purchasing bonds with a face value of $12,000 for 98% of the face value, or $11,760. If stockbroker's fees of $150 are also paid, the cost of the bonds is $11,910. An additional complication arises with the acquisition of bonds, however, because interest on the bonds accrues continuously but is paid periodically. Therefore, when purchasing the bonds the Lennon Company will be charged by the previous owner for the interest that has accrued to the owner since the last interest payment date. Suppose that the Exxon Company bonds have an annual interest rate of 10% and pay interest semiannually on June 30 and December 31. On August 30 (the purchase date) two months of interest has accrued since June 30, which amounts to $200 ($12,000 \times 10\% \times 2/12$). The previous

---

[3]Some companies in special industries, such as mutual funds and brokerage companies, report investments in securities at their current market value.

owner of the bonds has earned the interest for two months, but the Lennon Company will receive the interest payment for the entire six months at December 31, 1993. Therefore, the Lennon Company pays the previous owner of the bonds for the two months interest and would pay a total of $12,110 ($11,910 + $200). The acquisition is recorded as follows:

	Assets		= Liabs. + S. Eq.
− $12,110	+ $200	+$11,910	
Cash	Interest Receivable	Current Marketable Securities—Bonds	
$12,110	$200	$11,910	

The interest is recorded as a receivable because the interest accrues over time and the Lennon Company will receive the interest when Exxon makes the next interest payment on December 31. Note that in accordance with the accrual basis of accounting the Lennon Company is recognizing interest *revenue* on a separate basis from interest *received*.

Subsequent Valuation of Current Marketable Securities—Bonds

On each balance sheet date, the current marketable securities—bonds must be properly valued for inclusion as a current asset on the balance sheet. The accounting principles used for this valuation and reporting of Current Marketable Securities—Bonds are not as clearly defined as the principles for stocks. Most companies use the *cost method*, which simply means that the investment is reported in the balance sheet at the acquisition cost no matter whether the market value is higher or lower. Therefore, no adjustment is required at the end of the period. The lower of cost or market method, however, is allowed for current investments in bonds in which case the adjustment procedure described for stocks would be used. In this book we use the cost method. Thus, on the December 31, 1993, balance sheet the investment in the Exxon bonds would be shown as follows:

Current Assets	
Marketable securities—bonds, at cost	$11,910

In addition, the market value of the bonds should be disclosed. Since the interest receivable on the bonds will have been collected on December 31, 1993 (as discussed in the following section), it is not shown as a current asset.

Revenue on Current Marketable Securities—Bonds

Interest on bonds accrues continuously over time, and therefore the investor in Current Marketable Securities—Bonds earns revenue continuously. Whenever financial statements are prepared the investor must recognize the correct amount of interest revenue for the period. Continuing with the example in the previous section, Exxon will pay six months interest of $600 ($12,000 × 10% × 6/12) on December 31, 1993, to the Lennon Company. Since the Lennon Company has owned the bonds for only four months, however, interest for only four months is recognized as revenue. The receipt of the other two months interest is payment of the Interest Receivable recorded at the time of acquisition. The receipt of the interest on December 31, 1993, is recorded as follows:

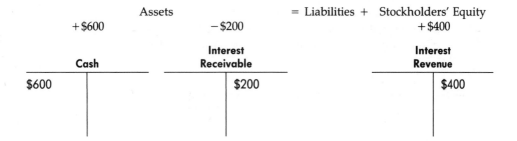

Assets		= Liabilities +	Stockholders' Equity
+ $600	− $200		+ $400

Cash	Interest Receivable	Interest Revenue
$600	$200	$400

Thus, of the $600 cash received only $400 is included in the revenue of the period, and the remaining $200 is receipt of an asset recognized at the time of the acquisition of the bonds. The Interest Revenue is included in the Other Revenues and Expenses section of the income statement.

Sale of Current Marketable Securities—Bonds

When additional cash is needed for the operations of a company a current investment in bonds may be sold. Because interest accrues over time, it is necessary to recognize the interest earned between the last interest payment date and the date of sale. Suppose that the Lennon Company sells its investment in the Exxon bonds on January 31, 1994, at 102 plus accrued interest. The company will receive $12,240 ($12,000 × 1.02) for the bonds plus the interest that has been earned since the last payment date. The company has earned interest of $100 ($12,000 × 10% × 1/12) since the last interest payment on December 31, 1993. Since the company sells the bonds for $12,240 plus accrued interest and interest revenue of $100 had been earned during January, total cash of $12,340 is received. Because the bonds were being carried at their cost of $11,910, the Lennon Company has a gain of $330 on the sale ($12,240 − $11,910). The sale on January 31, 1994, is recorded as follows:

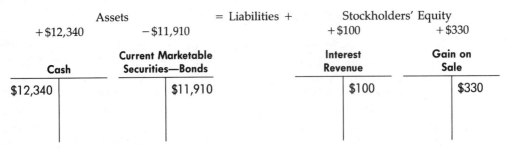

The net increase in the assets of $430 arises from both the Gain on Sale and the Interest Revenue, which are included in the Other Revenues and Expenses section on the income statement. It is important to differentiate between the two amounts because they result from different causes. The gain on the sale is the result of advantageous buying and selling decisions, whereas the interest revenue is the amount earned on the investment over time.

The treatment of the interest at the acquisition of the bond, during its ownership, and at its sale may be summarized as follows:

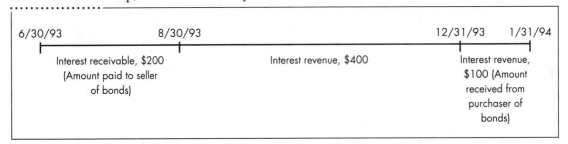

SECTION B Equity Method

■ NONCURRENT INVESTMENTS IN STOCK

Earlier we discussed investments in noncurrent marketable securities—stocks for which the lower of cost or market method is used. There we were assuming that the investment did not provide significant influence. However, acquisitions of stock may allow the investor to exercise significant influence over the investee. Accounting for these acquisitions is complex, but can be made easier if it is understood that the accounting method used by the investor for a particular acquisition depends on the extent to which the investor can or cannot influence the investee. Accounting principles distinguish between three levels of influence: control, significant influence, and less than significant influence:

Level of Influence	Accounting Method Used
Less than significant influence	Lower of cost or market
Significant influence	Equity
Control	Consolidation

The lower of cost or market method is used when less than 20% of the outstanding common stock of the investee company is owned by the investor company. This method was discussed earlier in this chapter. **The equity method is used when the investor company has significant influence over the investee company. Significant influence is presumed to exist when 20% or more of the outstanding common stock is owned by the investor company.** Significant influence, however, can be indicated by other factors, such as representation on the board of directors, participation in the policy-making process, significant intercompany transactions, interchange of managerial personnel, or technological dependency. If the other evidence outweighs the ownership interest, the 20% rule can be ignored. For example, a company with 10% of the common stock might be able to elect four of the ten members of the board of directors, in which case it would be appropriate to use the equity method. In this book we will use the equity method only when the ownership interest is 20% or more. Ownership of more than 50% of the outstanding common stock allows the investor company to control the investee company, and *consolidated* financial statements are prepared. (The investor does account for its investment under the equity method, but this balance is eliminated as the consolidated financial statements are prepared, as discussed later.)

■ THE EQUITY METHOD

The equity method of accounting for noncurrent investments in common stock is used when the investor company has the ability to exercise significant influence over the investee company but does not have control. Significant influence is presumed to exist when the ownership interest is at least 20% of the common stock of the investee until control can be exercised.

At this level of ownership there are several reasons why the lower of cost or market method is not appropriate.

1. It can be expected that the investment will be for a long period of time and therefore the cost may become outdated.

2. The market value of the shares of the investee company will not necessarily represent a good measure of the total value of the investment. The price of a share on the stock market on any given day is the result of the supply and demand on that day. The sale of over 20% of the shares of a company would almost certainly be at a different market price than the sale of a small quantity of shares.

3. Income is not best measured by the dividends received. For example, suppose that an investee company earns $40,000 and pays dividends of $4,000. If an investor company owns 25% of the shares, it would receive dividends of $1,000, but this amount does not represent the income accumulation of the investor company in the sense that it is not the best measure of the increase in its wealth. Since the investee has earned $40,000 and the investor owns 25% of the income, the investor should instead recognize income of $10,000.

4. The investor may be able to influence the dividend policy and thereby affect the cash payments received. Therefore, recognition of income on an accrual basis (equity method) is preferable to the recognition of income on the basis of the cash dividends received (lower of cost or market method).

The equity method uses a different approach for recording the value of the investment and recognizing income than the lower of cost or market method. The investor company accounts for the investment and income as follows:

$$\textbf{Investment = Cost + Income Earned − Dividends Received}$$

where: $$\textbf{Income Earned = Investee's Net Income × Ownership \%}$$

and: $$\textbf{Dividends Received = Total Dividends Paid by Investee × Ownership \%}$$

The investor company recognizes as income its share of the investee company's net income. When this income is recognized, the value of the asset is increased by the same amount. The receipt of dividends does *not* involve recognition of income but instead the investor company records this receipt as a *reduction* in the book value of the Investment. That is, **the accounting by the investor company parallels the accounting by the investee company**. When the investee company earns income its stockholders' equity is increased, and when it pays dividends its stockholders' equity is decreased. The book value of the investor company's Investment account is increased as its share of the investee company's stockholders' equity increases (as income is earned) and is decreased as its share of the investee company's stockholders' equity decreases (as dividends are received). Dividends are the actual distribution of net income; for the investor company to record dividends as income would involve double counting because the investor has already recorded its share of the income that is now being distributed.

Illustration of Equity Method

To illustrate the equity method, suppose that the Davis Company purchases 25% of the outstanding common shares of the Bristol Company on January 1, 1993, for $50,000. The investment would be recorded by the Davis Company on this date as follows:

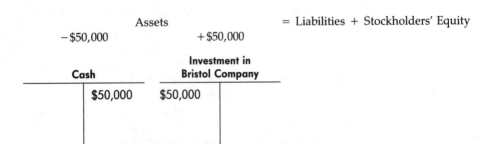

	Assets		= Liabilities + Stockholders' Equity
−$50,000		+$50,000	

Cash		Investment in Bristol Company	
$50,000	$50,000		

EXHIBIT 11–1

BRISTOL COMPANY
Balance Sheet
January 1, 1993

ASSETS		LIABILITIES	
Current assets	$120,000	Current liabilities	$ 40,000
Noncurrent assets	280,000	Noncurrent liabilities	160,000
		Total liabilities	$200,000
		STOCKHOLDERS' EQUITY	
		Common stock, no par	$ 30,000
		Retained earnings	170,000
		Total stockholders' equity	$200,000
Total assets	$400,000	Total liabilities and stockholders' equity	$400,000

On January 1, 1993, the Bristol Company's condensed balance sheet was as shown in Exhibit 11–1.

At the end of 1993 the Bristol Company reported net income of $60,000 and paid dividends of $20,000. The income from the investment that is included in the Davis Company's income statement is:

$$\text{Income Earned} = \text{Investee's Net Income} \times \text{Ownership \%}$$
$$= \$60,000 \times 25\%$$
$$= \underline{\$15,000}$$

The dividends that are received by the Davis Company are:

$$\text{Dividends Received} = \text{Total Dividends Paid by the Investee} \times \text{Ownership \%}$$
$$= \$20,000 \times 25\%$$
$$= \underline{\$5,000}$$

The Davis Company recognizes its share of the Bristol Company's net income as follows:

Assets	= Liabilities +	Stockholders' Equity
+$15,000		+$15,000

Investment in Bristol Company		Investment Income	
$15,000			$15,000

The receipt of the dividends from Bristol Company is recorded by the Davis Company as follows:

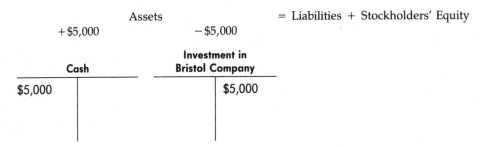

The book value of the Davis Company's investment at the end of 1993 is:

Cost of investment	$50,000
+ Share of Bristol Company's net income (25% × $60,000)	15,000
− Dividends received (25% × $20,000)	(5,000)
Book value of investment at year-end	$60,000

In order to further emphasize the rationale of the equity method, consider the balance sheet of the Bristol Company (the investee) after the above events have been recorded. The investment by the Davis Company has no effect on the balance sheet of the Bristol Company because the Davis Company purchased 25% of the *existing* outstanding shares. The earning of income and the payment of dividends by the Bristol Company do affect its balance sheet. By using the basic accounting equation we can examine the effect of these events. For simplicity, we will assume that liabilities remain unchanged. The income and dividends have the following impact on the Bristol Company:

	Assets	= Liabilities	+ Stockholders' Equity
Earning income	+ $60,000 =	0	+ $60,000
Payment of dividends	− 20,000 =	0	− 20,000
Net effect	+ $40,000 =	0	+ $40,000

The net effect is an increase in the assets and the stockholders' equity of the Bristol Company of $40,000. The assets of the Bristol Company are now $440,000 ($400,000 at the beginning of the period plus the increase of $40,000) and the liabilities are $200,000 (it is assumed they remain unchanged), and therefore the net assets (stockholders' equity) are $240,000 ($440,000 − $200,000). Since the Davis Company owns 25% of the Bristol Company, it effectively owns 25% of the net assets of the company. The value of this 25% share is $60,000 (25% ×

$240,000). Note that this is exactly the balance of the Davis Company's account, Investment in Bristol Company.

The fact that the book value in the Investment account of the investor company parallels the book value of the ownership interest in the net assets (stockholders' equity) of the investee company is the primary justification for the equity method. It should be recognized that the values are *equal* only because the Davis Company made the original purchase of the shares at a cost ($50,000) that was equal to the book value of the ownership interest in the net assets of the Bristol Company on January 1, 1993 [25% × ($30,000 common stock + $170,000 retained earnings) or 25% × ($400,000 assets − $200,000 liabilities)]. That is, the market price of Bristol's shares was equal to the book value on that date. If the Davis Company had made the purchase for an amount different from $50,000, the book value of the Investment in the Bristol Company account at year-end would not be equal to the ownership interest in the net assets of the Bristol Company. The increase in the book value of the Investment account ($10,000), however, would be equal to the Davis Company's share of the increase in the net assets of the Bristol Company (25% × $40,000).

Evaluation of Equity Method

Some users of financial statements criticize the equity method because the investor company recognizes income in excess of the cash received as dividends (assuming that the investee's income is more than the dividends it pays). They argue that the cash received from dividends is a more useful measure of the investor company's income. This criticism is not consistent with the accrual concept, which has such a strong influence on accounting. In accrual accounting, income is recognized in the period in which it is earned, and therefore income flows and cash flows are seldom, if ever, equal. The equity method is another example of the recognition of income on the accrual basis. An understanding of the above discussion of the equity method should enable the reader to recognize why generally accepted accounting principles require the use of the equity method when the investor company can exercise significant influence over the investee company.

Since the determination of significant influence is somewhat subjective, it is important to compare the impacts on the income statement of the lower of cost or market method and the equity method. If the investee's income is larger than the dividends distributed, the equity method will enable the investor to report a higher income under the equity method (percent of investee's net income) than under the lower of cost or market method (dividends received). Alternatively, if the investee reports a loss and pays no dividends, the equity method will require the investor to report its share of the loss whereas the lower of cost or market method would require that no income (or loss) be reported. Therefore the investor may influence its income by selecting a level of ownership based on the expected performance of the investee.

It is also important to understand that the income recognized under the equity method is different than the cash dividends received that are recognized in the cash flow statement (assuming that the investee does not pay dividends equal to its income). This topic is discussed in Chapter 12. It should also be noted that for income tax purposes, the equity method is not allowed. Instead, taxable income is recognized on the basis of the cash dividends received.

SECTION C Consolidated Financial Statements

■ ACCOUNTING FOR A CONTROLLING INTEREST

An investor company that owns more than 50% of the voting common stock of another company has control over that investee and consolidated financial statements are prepared. *Effective* control, however, may exist at a lower ownership percentage but consolidated financial statements are *not* prepared and the equity method is used. **The parent company is the investor company that controls the investee. The subsidiary company is the investee company that is controlled by the investor.** The two companies remain separate legal entities and maintain separate accounting records during the accounting period. A major advantage of this continued separate legal identity is that the principle of limited liability applies to each corporation. Thus, the parent company is not responsible for the debts of the subsidiary. There may also be other reasons for maintaining separate legal entities, such as tax advantages and conformity with foreign government regulations.

The financial statement user, however, is interested in financial statements that report the activities of the parent company and all the entities in which the parent company has a controlling interest. At the end of the accounting period, therefore, the results of operations and the ending financial position are accounted for in the parent company's annual report as if the separate legal entities were a single accounting entity. That is, a single set of financial statements is published. They are called consolidated financial statements. **Consolidated financial statements are the financial statements prepared by the parent company that controls one or more subsidiary companies.** The financial statements are the result of bringing together, or consolidating, the financial statements of the separate companies. For simplicity, we will assume in the following discussion that the parent company owns 100% of the subsidiary. Situations with less than 100% ownership are discussed in Appendix 2 of this chapter.

As an example, the Ford Motor Company's financial statements represent the consolidated results of at least 45 separate companies. The financial statement user does not receive (or want) financial statements that report separately on the activities of each of the 45 companies. Instead, a single set of consolidated financial statements is prepared; **the separate legal entities are treated as a single accounting entity for financial reporting.** Ideally, the investor or creditor should receive a set of financial statements that would be identical to the single set of statements that would be prepared if the entire operations of Ford consisted of only one company. Although the consolidated financial statements are not identical, the principles used ensure that the consolidated financial statements are essentially the same as if there were only one company.

In principle, the consolidated financial statements are the sum of the financial statements of the separate companies. Therefore, the assets and liabilities of the separate companies are added together in the consolidated balance sheet, and the revenues and expenses of the separate companies are combined in the consolidated income statement (except for the items discussed below). It is common, however, for the parent and subsidiary to buy and sell from each other and engage in other kinds of intercompany transactions. Since they are separate legal entities, they would record these transactions in their own accounting records. To avoid double counting, certain items that are included in the separate financial statements must be eliminated (excluded) from the consolidated financial statements.

Since each company mantains its own accounting records, there is no set of consolidated financial records. The consolidated financial statements are prepared by combining the financial statements of the parent and subsidiaries, with certain items being eliminated. **Eliminations are items that must be removed from the financial statements of the investor and the investee to avoid double counting in the consolidated financial statements.**

To summarize, the consolidated financial statements are prepared by adding together the financial statements of the various entities as adjusted for the eliminations. The eliminations do not affect the financial records of the individual companies but are used only for the preparation of the consolidated financial statements. A diagram of these relationships is shown below:

Parent	Subsidiary		Consolidated Financial Statements
Balance Sheet	*Balance Sheet*		*Balance Sheet*
Assets	+ Assets		= Assets
Liabilities	+ Liabilities	− Eliminations	Liabilities
Stockholders' Equity	+ Stockholders' Equity		Stockholders' Equity
Income Statement	*Income Statement*		*Income Statement*
Revenues	+ Revenues	− Eliminations	Revenues
Expenses	+ Expenses		= Expenses
Net Income	Net Income		Net Income

The Basic Principles of Consolidation

To illustrate the basic principles of consolidation, consider the balance sheets of the Parent Company and the Subsidiary Company in Exhibit 11–2. It is assumed that Parent Company purchased 100% of the shares of Subsidiary Company for $100,000 on December 31, 1993; that is, the two balance sheets are prepared immediately after the acquisition. Parent Company includes the cost of the acquisition as an Investment on its balance sheet. Note that the balance sheet of Subsidiary Company is unaffected by the acquisition.

EXHIBIT 11–2

PARENT COMPANY AND SUBSIDIARY COMPANY
Consolidated Balance Sheet

	Parent Company Balance Sheet Dec. 31, 1993	Subsidiary Company Balance Sheet Dec. 31, 1993	Eliminations	Parent Company and Subsidiary Consolidated Balance Sheet Dec. 31, 1993
Cash	$ 60,000	$ 20,000		$ 80,000
Accounts receivable	30,000	40,000		70,000
Inventory	90,000	30,000		120,000
Property, plant, and equipment (net)	200,000	80,000		280,000
Investment in subsidiary	100,000		−$100,000	
	$480,000	$170,000		$550,000
Accounts payable	$ 25,000	$ 20,000		$ 45,000
Bonds payable	100,000	50,000		150,000
Common stock (no par)	150,000	60,000	−$60,000	150,000
Retained earnings	205,000	40,000	−$40,000	205,000
	$480,000	$170,000		$550,000

To prepare the consolidated balance sheet, the amounts in each category on the balance sheet of Parent Company are added to the amount in Subsidiary Company's balance sheet. The Investment in the Parent Company's balance sheet must be eliminated to avoid double counting, however, because it represents the purchase of the net assets of the Subsidiary Company. Furthermore, the stockholders' equity of the Subsidiary Company is entirely owned by Parent. Therefore, to include the stockholders' equity of both companies in the consolidated balance sheet would also result in double counting. Since the consolidated financial statements are prepared for the use of the stockholders of Parent, the stockholders equity of Subsidiary is eliminated. In summary, to avoid double counting, Parent Company's Investment and Subsidiary Company's stockholders' equity must not be included in (they must be eliminated from) the consolidated balance sheet. Note that the consolidated balance sheet includes the cash, accounts receivable, inventory, property, plant, and equipment, accounts payable, and bonds payable of both companies, whereas only Parent Company's stockholders' equity is included.

Two methods are used to account for consolidations: **the purchase method** and **the pooling method**. The consolidated financial statements can be significantly different depending on which method is appropriate to account for the acquisition of a subsidiary. The criteria that determine the use of each method are discussed later.

■ THE PURCHASE METHOD

To illustrate the preparation of consolidated financial statements under the purchase method, assume that on January 1, 1993, the Hunt Company purchases all the voting common stock of the Elm Company for $200,000 cash. This cash acquisition is consistent with the purchase method.

The Consolidated Balance Sheet

The balance sheet of the Hunt Company on December 31, 1992, *before* the acquisition, is illustrated in Exhibit 11–3. Note that the company has no-par common stock (discussed in Chapters 1 and 10), which simply means that the entire proceeds from the sale of the stock are reported as one amount rather than two separate amounts. The acquisition on January 1, 1993, of Elm Company's voting common stock is recorded as a reduction of cash and an increase in an investment; therefore, the total assets of Hunt are unaffected. (As discussed earlier, the balance sheet of Elm is unaffected because it is assumed that the shares are purchased by Hunt from Elm's existing shareholders.)

To illustrate the preparation of the consolidated balance sheet, assume that it is prepared on January 1, 1993. The Investment account of Hunt and the stockholders' equity of the Elm Company must be eliminated. In this example, however, a more realistic situation arises because these two amounts are not equal. The investment is $200,000, whereas the stockholders' equity of Elm is $120,000. There are two reasons for this difference. First, the market value of the net assets of Elm exceeds their book value. The net assets of Elm that are being acquired by Hunt are recorded in the normal manner, that is, at their purchase price (cost), which is the fair market value on the date of the transaction. This process is similar to a lump-sum purchase discussed in Chapter 7. The important aspect to understand is that the assets acquired are recorded at their costs to the purchaser and *not* at the book value of the company being acquired. In this example, it is assumed that the fair market value of Elm's property, plant, and equipment is $30,000 greater than their book value and therefore must be increased from $140,000 to $170,000. It is also assumed that the book values of the other assets and liabilities equal their market values. Therefore, the fair market value of the net assets of Elm is $150,000 (assets with a book value of $220,000 + the excess of fair market value over book value of $30,000 − liabilities of $100,000).

The second reason for the difference between the purchase price and the book value of Elm is that the Hunt Company has purchased the goodwill of the Elm Company. **Goodwill is recorded as the difference between the purchase price of the company and the fair market value of the net assets acquired** (goodwill was discussed in Chapter 7). The goodwill of the Elm Company is the purchase price of $200,000 less the fair market value of the net assets of $150,000 ($250,000 − $100,000), or $50,000.

These calculations may be summarized as follows:

EXHIBIT 11–3

HUNT COMPANY AND ELM COMPANY
Consolidated Balance Sheet: The Purchase Method

	Hunt Company Balance Sheet Dec. 31, 1992	Transaction Jan. 1, 1993	Hunt Company Balance Sheet Jan. 1, 1993	Elm Company Balance Sheet Jan. 1, 1993	Eliminations	Hunt Company and Subsidiary Consolidated Balance Sheet Jan. 1, 1993
Cash	$250,000	−$200,000	$ 50,000	$ 20,000		$ 70,000
Notes receivable	30,000		30,000	20,000		50,000
Inventory	70,000		70,000	40,000		110,000
Property, plant, and equipment (net)	300,000		300,000	140,000	+$ 30,000ª (Consolidated)	470,000
Goodwill					+$ 50,000ᵇ (Consolidated)	50,000
Investment in Elm		+$200,000	200,000		−$200,000 (Hunt)	
	$650,000		$650,000	$220,000		$750,000
Notes payable	$ 25,000		$ 25,000	$ 30,000		$ 55,000
Bonds payable	200,000		200,000	70,000		270,000
Common stock (no par)	175,000		175,000	70,000	−$70,000 (Elm)	175,000 (Hunt)
Retained earnings	250,000		250,000	50,000	−$50,000 (Elm)	250,000 (Hunt)
	$650,000		$650,000	$220,000		$750,000

ªFair market value of Elm's property, plant, and equipment is $170,000, or $30,000 greater than the book value.
ᵇPurchase price of $200,000 less the fair market value of Elm's net assets acquired of $150,000.

Price paid by Hunt Company		$200,000
Less: Book value of net assets of Elm	$120,000	
Excess of fair market value over book value of Elm's net assets	30,000	
Fair market value of Elm's net assets		(150,000)
Value of goodwill		$ 50,000

The Hunt Company and Subsidiary consolidated balance sheet is then prepared by adding together the two separate balance sheets, adding the extra $30,000 to the property, plant, and equipment and the $50,000 of goodwill. (Note that these two amounts are *not* recorded on the individual balance sheets of either company.) The Investment in Elm and the stockholders' equity accounts of Elm are also subtracted (eliminated). The Hunt Company and Subsidiary consolidated balance sheet has total assets of $750,000, liabilities of $325,000, and stockholders' equity of $425,000 (which is Hunt's stockholders' equity).

In certain circumstances, the purchase price of a company may be less than the fair market value of the net assets. For example, the shares of a publicly traded company may be selling at such a low price. In such circumstances, "negative goodwill" is not recorded. Instead, the negative amount is subtracted from the fair market value of the property, plant, and equipment.

The Consolidated Income Statement

The consolidated income statement is the sum of the income statements of the individual companies, subject to certain adjustments. When the consolidated balance sheet was prepared, additional value was recorded for the property, plant, and equipment and goodwill was recognized. These additional values must be depreciated and amortized, respectively. First, the excess of the fair market value of the subsidiary's property, plant, and equipment over its book value must be depreciated over the remaining lives of the assets. Second, the goodwill that is recognized must be amortized. Most companies use the maximum life of 40 years, as discussed in Chapter 7. An elimination is also required because the parent company includes in its income statement the investment income earned from the subsidiary in conformity with the equity method. This amount must be eliminated to avoid double counting.

These eliminations are not especially significant to users of financial statements. Once the user is aware that the eliminations occur, it should be understood that the assets, liabilities, revenues, expenses, gains, and losses are all recognized according to the principles that have been discussed throughout the book as they should be applied to the *consolidated* entity.

The preparation of the consolidated income statement for the Hunt Company and the Elm Company is illustrated in Appendix 1 of this chapter. The preparation of the consolidated balance sheet at the end of the year is also illustrated.

◼ THE POOLING METHOD

The essence of a pooling is not that one company is acquiring another, but that two previously independent companies are merging, and especially that the interests of the shareholders of the two companies are being merged. In other words, the two companies have decided to pool their resources and the shareholder interests have merged. Thus, the transaction must be essentially a single transaction in which common stock (and not cash) is exchanged and the stockholders of both companies continue as stockholders of the combined companies. In contrast, under the purchase method the stockholders of the purchasing company remain as the only shareholders of the combined companies and the shareholders of the acquired company have sold their interests.

For a pooling to occur, 12 criteria must be satisfied.[4] The details of these criteria are beyond the scope of the book, but the two most important ones are (1) the combination is completed in a single transaction or in accordance with a specific plan within one year, and (2) a corporation issues only common stock with the same rights as those of its outstanding voting common stock in exchange for at least 90% of the voting common stock of another company.

Although purchase transactions may involve both the payment of cash and the issuance of common stock and a pooling may involve a small amount of cash, in this book we will assume for simplicity that transactions are all cash (a purchase) or all common stock (a pooling). Note that management cannot choose a method. If the 12 criteria are met, the transaction is a pooling; if not, it is a purchase. However, transactions may be deliberately structured in order to qualify for one method or the other. It is appropriate to refer to an acquisition that is accounted for as a *pooling* by the term *merger,* and one that is accounted for as a *purchase* by the term *acquisition.* These terms, however, are widely used and often not with these precise meanings.

Consolidated Balance Sheet

Since one company has not *acquired* another company, the market values inherent in the transaction are *not* recorded in a pooling. In other words, there has been no exchange transaction to establish a new valuation basis, in contrast to a purchase in which the acquired assets and liabilities are recorded at their market values at the date of acquisition. Instead, in a pooling the balance sheet values of the two companies are carried forward at their book values because the two companies have combined their resources, which are already being accounted for appropriately on the basis of the original acquisition cost for that company.

Accounting for a pooling is illustrated using the Hunt and Elm companies, but now assume that the companies merge. On January 1, 1993, the Hunt Company issued 10,000 common shares (of Hunt) to the common shareholders

······················
[4]"Business Combinations," *APB Opinion No. 16* (New York: AICPA, 1970), par. 45–48.

of Elm Company in exchange for their shares in Elm. Thus, the shareholders have received shares of Hunt in exchange for their shares of Elm. In a pooling, this investment and the shares issued are both valued by the Hunt Company at the book value of Elm of $120,000 ($220,000 − $100,000). Therefore, the transaction increases the assets and stockholders' equity of the Hunt Company by $120,000, as illustrated in Exhibit 11–4. When the balance sheets of the two companies are consolidated, the Investment in Elm on the Hunt Company balance sheet is eliminated against the Common Stock (no par) of Elm.[5] Since the two amounts are equal, there are no additional adjustments to make. Note that the consolidated retained earnings includes the Elm Company's retained earnings. This procedure is consistent with the philosophy of pooling in which the interests of both groups of shareholders are merged.

Consolidated Income Statement

The consolidated income statement is simply the sum of the income statements of the two individual companies, with the parent company's investment income earned from the subsidiary eliminated to avoid double counting. Because all the assets are recorded at their book values, no adjustments are required for additional depreciation on property, plant, and equipment or for amortization of goodwill that was necessary under the purchase method. Note, therefore, that the consolidated income under the pooling method is higher than for the purchase method. Over the maximum amortization period used, it will be higher by the total difference between the fair market value of the shares issued by the parent company and the book value of the subsidiary. Therefore, any ratio that uses net income is affected. For example, the return on total assets for a pooling company is higher because income (the numerator) is higher and the total amount of the assets (the denominator) is lower.

The preparation of the consolidated income statement for the Hunt Company and the Elm Company is illustrated in Appendix 1 of this chapter. The preparation of the consolidated balance sheet at the end of the year is also illustrated.

■ ADDITIONAL CONSIDERATIONS

Intercompany Transactions

Parent and subsidiary companies often engage in transactions with each other. **Intercompany transactions are transactions between a parent and a subsidiary**

· ·

[5]When the common stock of the two companies have par values, adjustments are made between the common stock balance and the additional paid-in capital. These adjustments are beyond the scope of this book. It is important to focus on the sum of the balances of these two accounts, which would be equal to the balance of the common stock (no par) used in this example. That is, the consolidated stockholders' equity is the sum of the individual stockholders' equity of the merging companies.

EXHIBIT 11–4

HUNT COMPANY AND ELM COMPANY
Consolidated Balance Sheet: The Pooling Method

	Hunt Company Balance Sheet Dec. 31, 1992	Transaction Jan. 1, 1993	Balance Sheet Jan. 1, 1993	Elm Company Balance Sheet Jan. 1, 1993	Eliminations	Hunt Company and Subsidiary Consolidated Balance Sheet Jan. 1, 1993
Cash	$250,000		$250,000	$ 20,000		$270,000
Notes receivable	30,000		30,000	20,000		50,000
Inventory	70,000		70,000	40,000		110,000
Property, plant, and equipment (net)	300,000		300,000	140,000		440,000
Investment in Elm		+ $120,000	120,000		– $120,000 (Hunt)	
	$650,000		$770,000	$220,000		$870,000
Notes payable	$ 25,000		$ 25,000	$ 30,000		$ 55,000
Bonds payable	200,000		200,000	70,000		270,000
Common stock (no par)	175,000	+ $120,000	295,000	70,000	– $120,000	245,000
Retained earnings	250,000		250,000	50,000		300,000
	$650,000		$770,000	$220,000		$870,000

company. These transactions must be eliminated when preparing consolidated financial statements.

Intercompany Loans. One company may lend money to the other, or one company may owe money as a result of a transaction. For example, suppose that in addition to the purchase of the common stock the Hunt Company lent $10,000 to the Elm Company. Therefore, the Elm Company has a note payable of $10,000 and the Hunt Company has a note receivable of $10,000. Whereas each individual company has an asset and a liability, the consolidated entity has neither an asset nor a liability because no cash receipt or payment has occurred with an outside entity. To avoid double counting, both the note payable and the note receivable must be eliminated by reducing the notes payable of the Elm Company and reducing the notes receivable of the Hunt Company.

Sales of Goods Between the Parent and Subsidiary. When a sale of goods is made between the parent and subsidiary, the sale must be eliminated from the consolidated income statement. This elimination is required because no sale has occurred for the consolidated entity. It is only when a sale has been made outside the consolidated entity that sales revenue is recognized. Along with the elimination of the sale, the cost of the inventory recorded as cost of goods sold must also be eliminated.

For example, suppose that the Hunt Company purchases inventory for $5,000 from the Elm Company and sells it to other entities for $9,000. The Elm Company had originally purchased the inventory for $3,000. On their separate income statements, the two companies would include the following information:

	Hunt	Elm
Sales	$9,000	$5,000
Cost of goods sold	5,000	3,000
Gross Profit	$4,000	$2,000

For the consolidated entity, however, the sales to other entities are only $9,000 and the cost of the goods sold to other entities is only $3,000. Therefore, when the consolidated income statement is prepared by adding together the income statements of the two companies, sales of $5,000 and cost of goods sold of $5,000 must be eliminated to avoid double counting.

Although sales between parent and subsidiary companies are usually the most significant elimination in the consolidated income statement, other eliminations may also be necessary. For example, interest revenue and interest expense on a loan between the companies would also have to be eliminated. Again, these eliminations are not especially significant to users of financial statements because the generally accepted accounting principles that have been discussed throughout the book are applied to the *consolidated* entity.

A Comparison of Purchase and Pooling

As we have seen, an *acquisition* accounted for by the *purchase* method is based on the market value of the transaction, with the net assets acquired being valued at their individual acquisition costs and goodwill being recognized. In contrast, a *merger* accounted for by the *pooling* method is based on book values.

To contrast the balance sheets under each method, consider Exhibits 11–3 (purchase) and 11–4 (pooling). Because the transaction is structured so differently in each situation, the balance sheets are substantially different. The pooling method has resulted in larger equity and more cash because stock was issued rather than cash being paid. Note that in this example it was assumed that the Hunt Company had sufficient cash to make the purchase, whereas many companies borrow some or all of the cash necessary for an acquisition. Furthermore, many companies make a purchase by issuing large amounts of stock, without satisfying the criteria for a pooling.

In addition to the structure of the transaction, the major difference that results from the use of different methods is the revaluation of the net assets. The property, plant, and equipment of Elm is being acquired by Hunt and therefore is recorded in the normal way—that is, at the amount paid, which is the fair market value on that date. The goodwill is also recognized because it represents an asset acquired by Hunt (it may be helpful to refer to Chapter 7 for the discussion of goodwill). Therefore, the purchase method has resulted in the net assets (other than cash, which is affected by the structure of the acquisition transaction) on the consolidated balance sheet being higher by $80,000 (the excess of the purchase price of $200,000 over the book value of the net assets acquired of $120,000).

The difference in the income statements between purchase and pooling results directly from the recognition of the market values of the net assets acquired. The increase in the property, plant, and equipment is expensed over the lives of the respective assets, and the goodwill is amortized over a maximum of 40 years. Therefore, the purchase method results in a lower income than the pooling method. This lower income will continue until the excess has been completely expensed. These differences are illustrated in Exhibits 11–5 and 11–7 in Appendix 1.

In the chapter examples, we have assumed that the acquisitions occurred at the beginning of the year. When an acquisition occurs during the year, there is another difference between a purchase and a pooling. In a purchase, only the income of the subsidiary since the date of acquisition is included in the consolidated income statement. In contrast, in a pooling the consolidated income statement includes the entire year's income of the subsidiary. Also, in a pooling the financial statements for the previous years are restated to retroactively report on the effects of the consolidation, whereas in a purchase no restatement occurs but pro-forma information is presented.

An Evaluation of Purchase and Pooling

There is little criticism of purchase accounting, except for the appropriateness of the 40-year amortization period for goodwill used by most companies, as discussed in Chapter 7. It should also be recognized that there are many practical problems in the determination of the fair market values of each of the net assets acquired. The management of a company may tend to favor allocating higher values to those assets that have longer lives and to goodwill so as to reduce the amount of the additional expenses that must be recorded each year following the acquisition. The calculation of income taxes payable, however, would suggest just the opposite, with a preference for allocating higher values to those assets that have shorter tax lives, and not to goodwill because the amortization is not tax deductible.

Pooling was very popular during the 1960s, and many people argued that allowing the method encouraged mergers that would not otherwise have occurred. The 12 criteria for pooling were introduced in 1970 and reduced the number of poolings. Some still argue that pooling is an inappropriate accounting method because of its reliance on book value and accounting for the acquisition at the seller's cost rather than the buyer's cost (the fair market value). Also it is argued that subsequent income amounts are overstated because of the undervaluation of the assets.

Accounting principles require that the acquisition of an *individual* asset is recorded at the cost of acquisition (the fair market value on that date) and is never recorded at the seller's cost (or book value). Therefore, it is argued that the method of acquisition of an entire company should not affect the accounting principles used. The *substance* of the transaction is that one company is acquired and the *form* of the transaction is the method of compensating the stockholders of the company being acquired. It is argued that the substance (market value) should take precedence over the form (meeting the pooling criteria).

Those who support the pooling method argue that an acquisition has not occurred because all the stockholders of the two companies are still the stockholders of the merged companies. Therefore, it may be arbitrary to say that one company has acquired the other. For example, if two companies of approximately equal size merge, the new board of directors consists of directors selected from the boards of both companies, and the new management includes officers from both companies, then it may *not* be reasonable to argue that an acquisition has occurred and that the net assets of one of the companies must be revalued.

In summary, it is important that managers understand the differences between the two methods because such knowledge may affect the way in which they choose to structure a transaction. Similarly, users of financial statements also need to understand the differences because of the potentially material impact on the financial statements.

Exception to Consolidation

There is one exception to the general rule that consolidation occurs when there is majority ownership.[6] This exception involves those situations in which control

••••••••••••••••••••••

[6]"Consolidation of All Majority Owned Subsidiaries," *FASB Statement of Financial Accounting Standards No. 94* (Stamford, Conn.: FASB, 1987). It is expected that the FASB will eventually substitute the concept of effective control for majority ownership. Thus, consolidation would occur in those situations in which effective control could be exercised with less than 50% ownership.

is temporary or does not rest with the majority owner. Consolidation is inappropriate if the parent company cannot exercise financial and operating control over the subsidiary. Such a lack of control may exist, for example, if the subsidiary is in bankruptcy, or for *some* foreign subsidiaries, when the payment of dividends to the parent is highly restricted, the operations of the subsidiary are severely regulated, or expropriation of the assets is likely.

Note that in this situation in which consolidation does not occur, the investor accounts for its investment in the investee by the cost method. For example, contrast a parent that owns 100% of a subsidiary and prepares consolidated financial statements with a situation in which the same company accounts for its 100% ownership by the cost method. The consolidated net income is different in the two situations. With the cost method, only the dividends received by the parent from the subsidiary are included in the parent company's income statement. With consolidation, each category in the consolidated income statement includes the total amounts from each category of each company's individual income statements.

The structure of the balance sheets is different in the two cases. With the cost method, the investment is recorded as a line item in the parent company's balance sheet. With consolidation, each category of assets and liabilities includes the total amounts for both companies. This is a very important distinction. Under consolidation, the liabilities of the subsidiary are included in the consolidated balance sheet. Under the cost method, the liabilities of the subsidiary are *not* included in the investor's balance sheet. Thus, nonconsolidation of a subsidiary is another example of off-balance sheet financing (discussed in Chapter 9).

SECTION D Noncurrent Investments in Bonds

■ NONCURRENT INVESTMENTS IN BONDS

Accounting for noncurrent investments in bonds does not follow the same principles as for current marketable securities—bonds but instead parallels the accounting for bonds payable discussed in Chapter 8. A noncurrent investment in bonds is classified as such if management's intent is *not* to sell the bonds within one year or the operating cycle, whichever is longer.

An investor company would purchase the bonds of another company as a noncurrent investment to acquire a relatively safe source of continuing revenue or to establish a financial relationship with another company, perhaps a company whose stock it already owns. Insurance companies and companies with investments in pension funds often purchase bonds for the former reason. Because they can plan their cash payments to the insurance policyholders or the recipients of the pensions over a long period of time, they can plan to hold the bonds until maturity and avoid having to sell the bonds if their market price should become depressed.

Bonds Purchased at a Discount or Premium

Bonds are purchased at the current market price as an investment in order to earn periodic interest revenue and receive the face value on the maturity date. Bonds purchased at a discount or premium (i.e., at an amount below or above face value) are recorded at their acquisition cost, which includes the cost of the bonds, broker's fees, and transfer taxes. **The cost is recorded as an Investment in Bonds and no separate discount or premium is usually recorded.**

Even though a separate discount or premium is not recorded, the discount or premium (the difference between the purchase price and the face value) is amortized as an adjustment to interest revenue over the remaining life of the bonds. Thus, the balance of the Investment account will increase (in the case of a purchase at a discount) or decrease (in the case of a purchase at a premium) over the life of the bonds until the balance equals the face value on the maturity date of the bonds. As with accounting for bonds payable **the effective interest method should be used, although the straight-line method is acceptable if the results are not materially different.** The related interest revenue is recognized periodically when cash is received and must also be accrued at the end of the accounting period. The interest revenue is included in the Other Revenues and Expenses section in the income statement.

To illustrate the accounting for a bond investment assume that the Wilkens Company purchased bonds issued by the Homestake Company with the following characteristics:

Date of purchase:	January 1, 1993
Maturity date:	December 31, 1997
Face value:	$100,000
Contract rate:	10%
Interest payment dates:	June 30 and December 31
Yield:	12%

Accounting for these bonds by the Homestake Company was discussed in Chapter 8, and it may be useful to refer to that chapter and compare the accounting by the Wilkens Company and the Homestake Company.

The purchase price of the bonds is $92,639.93, as discussed in Chapter 8 (brokerage fees and transfer taxes are ignored in this example).[7] The Wilkens Company records the acquisition on January 1, 1993, as follows:

· ·

[7]The present value of the bonds is computed as follows:

Present Value = Present Value of Face Value + Present Value of Interest Payments
$$= (\$100{,}000 \times 0.558395) + (\$5{,}000 \times 7.360087)$$
$$= \$55{,}839.50 + \$36{,}800.43$$
$$= \$92{,}639.93$$

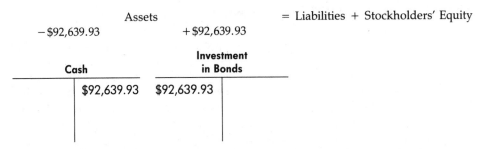

Usually for bond investments, the total purchase price is recorded as a single amount, instead of the two accounts used by the Homestake Company. Although not recorded separately, there is a discount of $7,360.07 ($100,000 − $92,639.93), which is amortized by either the effective interest method or the straight-line method each time the interest revenue is recorded.

Effective Interest Method

When a company uses the effective interest method for an investment in bonds, the semiannual interest revenue, the amount of the semiannual interest receipt, and the semiannual discount (premium) amortization, are computed as follows:

$$\text{Semiannual interest revenue} = \left(\frac{\text{Annual}}{\text{yield}} \div \frac{\text{Number of interest}}{\text{receipts per year}}\right) \times \begin{array}{l}\text{Book value of the}\\ \text{bond investment}\\ \text{at the beginning}\\ \text{of the period}\end{array}$$

$$\text{Semiannual interest receipt} = \frac{\text{Face}}{\text{value}} \times \left(\begin{array}{l}\text{Annual contract} \quad \text{Number of}\\ \text{rate} \qquad\qquad \div \text{ interest receipts}\\ \qquad\qquad\qquad \text{per year}\end{array}\right)$$

$$\text{Semiannual discount amortization} = \frac{\text{Semiannual interest}}{\text{revenue}} - \frac{\text{Semiannual interest}}{\text{receipt}}$$

or

$$\text{Semiannual premium amortization} = \frac{\text{Semiannual interest}}{\text{receipt}} - \frac{\text{Semiannual interest}}{\text{revenue}}$$

If the Wilkens Company uses the effective interest method, the interest revenue recognized on June 30, 1993, is $5,558.40 [(12% ÷ 2) × $92,639.93], the cash received is $5,000 [(10% ÷ 2) × $100,000], and the difference of $558.40 is the amortization of the discount that increases the book value of the Investment in Bonds. The entry on June 30, 1993, to record the interest revenue is:

	Assets		= Liabilities +	Stockholders' Equity
+$5,000		+$558.40		+$5,558.40

Cash		Investment in Bonds		Interest Revenue	
$5,000		$558.40			$5,558.40

At December 31, 1993, the Wilkens Company recognizes interest revenue for the second six-month period. The interest revenue is $5,591.90 [(12% ÷ 2) × ($92,639.93 + $558.40)]. Since the interest received is $5,000 [(10% ÷ 2) × $100,000], the increase in the value of the Investment is $591.90 ($5,591.90 − $5,000). The entry to record this interest on December 31, 1993, is recorded as follows:

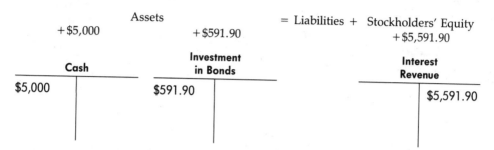

Assets = Liabilities + Stockholders' Equity
+ $5,000   + $591.90   + $5,591.90

Cash	Investment in Bonds	Interest Revenue
$5,000	$591.90	$5,591.90

At the end of the year the Investment account is included in the Long-term Investments section on the balance sheet at a book value of $93,790.23 ($92,639.93 + $558.40 + $591.90). Interest revenue of $11,150.30 ($5,558.40 + $5,591.90) is included in the Other Revenues and Expenses section of the 1993 income statement. Recognition of interest revenue in subsequent years would parallel the recording of the Homestake Company's interest expense. To facilitate the recording of the interest revenue each period the Wilkens Company could prepare a schedule similar to Exhibits 8–4 and 8–5, except that the headings would be labeled Cash Received (debit), Interest Revenue (credit), Increase (Decrease) in Investment (debit or credit), and Book Value of Investment.

Straight-Line Method

When a company uses the straight-line method to amortize a premium or discount for an investment in bonds, the amount of the semiannual interest receipt, the semiannual discount (premium) amortization, and the semiannual interest revenue are computed as follows:

$$\text{Semiannual interest receipt} = \text{Face value} \times \left(\text{Annual contract rate} \div \text{Number of interest receipts per year} \right)$$

$$\text{Semiannual discount (premium) amortization} = \text{Total discount (premium) at purchase of bonds} \div \left(\text{Number of years in life of bonds} \times \text{Number of interest receipts per year} \right)$$

$$\text{Semiannual interest revenue} = \text{Semiannual interest receipt} + \text{Semiannual discount amortization}$$

$$\text{or} - \text{Semiannual premium amortization}$$

If the Wilkens Company amortizes the discount by using the straight-line method, the discount of $7,360.07 would be amortized evenly over ten semiannual periods, or $736.01 ($7,360.07 ÷ 10, rounded) each period. Since the interest received on June 30, 1993, is $5,000 [$100,000 × (10% ÷ 2)], the interest revenue is $5,736.01 ($5,000 + $736.01). The receipt of the first interest payment on June 30, 1993, is recorded as follows:

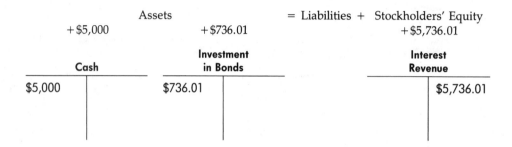

	Assets		= Liabilities +	Stockholders' Equity
+$5,000		+$736.01		+$5,736.01
	Cash	**Investment in Bonds**		**Interest Revenue**
$5,000		$736.01		$5,736.01

When the straight-line method is used, the Wilkens Company recognizes the same amount of interest revenue each semiannual period. At the end of the year the Investment in Bonds is included in the Long-Term Investments section of the balance sheet at a book value of $94,111.95 ($92,639.93 + $736.01 + $736.01). Interest revenue of $11,472.02 ($5,736.01 + $5,736.01) is included in the Other Revenues and Expenses section of the 1993 income statement.

Under either the effective interest or straight-line methods, the book value of the bonds in the balance sheet will increase (for bonds purchased at a discount) or decrease (for bonds purchased at a premium) until the book value equals the face value on the maturity date. The book value of the bonds under either method is not affected by any changes in the market value of the bonds. Remember that, as discussed in Chapter 8, the straight-line method may be used only as long as it does not produce material differences from the effective interest method.

■ APPENDIX 1: PREPARATION OF THE CONSOLIDATED INCOME STATEMENT AND THE BALANCE SHEET AT THE END OF THE YEAR

Using the Hunt Company and Elm Company example from the chapter, the preparation of the consolidated income statement for 1993 and the consolidated balance sheet at December 31, 1993, is illustrated for both the purchase method and the pooling method.

The Consolidated Income Statement: The Purchase Method

During 1993 the two companies engage in their operating activities and therefore prepare their individual income statements, illustrated in Exhibit 11–5. The con-

EXHIBIT 11–5

HUNT COMPANY AND ELM COMPANY
Consolidated Income Statement for 1993:
The Purchase Method

	Hunt Company 1993	Elm Company 1993	Adjustments	Hunt Company and Subsidiary Consolidated Income Statement for the Year Ended Dec. 31, 1993
Revenue	$600,000	$380,000		$980,000
Cost of goods sold	(200,000)	(140,000)		(340,000)
Selling and administrative expenses	(300,000)	(160,000)	+$ 3,000[b]	(463,000)
Goodwill amortization			+$ 1,250[c]	(1,250)
Investment income	56,000[a]		–$56,000	
Income before income taxes	$156,000	$ 80,000		$175,750
Income tax expense	(30,000)	(24,000)		(54,000)
Net income	$126,000	$356,000		$121,750

[a]Elm's net income of $56,000.
[b]$30,000 ÷ 10 years.
[c]$50,000 ÷ 40 years.

solidated income statement is the sum of the income statements of the two companies, subject to certain adjustments. First, the excess of the fair value of the Elm Company's property, plant, and equipment over its book value ($30,000) must be depreciated over the remaining lives of the assets. In this example, we assume that the life is ten years, and therefore $3,000 additional depreciation expense must be recognized in the consolidated income statement. Second, the goodwill of $50,000 that is recognized must be amortized. Since most companies use the maximum life of 40 years (as discussed in Chapter 7), we will use that life. Therefore, amortization expense of $1,250 must also be recognized in the consolidated income statement. (Note that the increase in each expense is indicated by a "+" but that it decreases net income.) Third, the Hunt Company includes in its individual income statement the investment income earned from Elm of $56,000 in conformity with the equity method. Since this amount is equal to the net income of Elm (because of the 100% ownership), it must be eliminated to avoid double counting. For simplicity it is assumed that the income tax expense of Hunt is based on income excluding the investment income and that the consolidated income tax expense is the sum of the two separate income tax expenses. The consolidated net income is the sum of Hunt's net income of $70,000 after excluding the investment income of $56,000, plus Elm's net income of $56,000, less the additional depreciation of $3,000 and the goodwill amortization of $1,250.

The Consolidated Balance Sheet at the End of the Year: The Purchase Method

The preparation of the consolidated balance sheet at December 31, 1993, is illustrated in Exhibit 11–6. The balance sheets of the two companies are simplified by assuming that the total liabilities of each company are unchanged since January 1, 1993, and that all the assets, except the Investment in Elm, are combined.

The consolidated balance sheet is the sum of the two individual balance sheets with the adjustments for the necessary eliminations. There are two stages in this elimination process. First, the Investment in Elm and the stockholders' equity of Elm must be eliminated with the recognition of the $30,000 excess of the fair market value over the book value of Elm and the goodwill of $50,000. Note that Hunt's Investment in Elm, under the equity method, has increased from its cost of $200,000 to $256,000 because Elm earned a net income of $56,000. Similarly, Elm's retained earnings has increased by $56,000. Second, the assets and the goodwill must be reduced by the amounts of the additional depreciation expense and goodwill amortization that is recorded in the consolidated income statement. These amounts must also be subtracted from the consolidated retained earnings balance. Note that the consolidated retained earnings is the retained

EXHIBIT 11–6

. . . .

	HUNT COMPANY AND ELM COMPANY Consolidated Balance Sheet for December 31, 1993: The Purchase Method			
	Hunt Company Balance Sheet Dec. 31, 1993	Elm Company Balance Sheet Dec. 31, 1993	Eliminations	Hunt Company and Subsidiary Consolidated Balance Sheet Dec. 31, 1993
Assets other than investment	$520,000	$276,000	+$ 30,000 − $3,000	$823,000
Goodwill			+$ 50,000 − $1,250	48,750
Investment in Elm	256,000ᵃ		−$256,000	
	$776,000	$276,000		$871,750
Liabilities	$225,000	$100,000		$325,000
Common stock (no par)	175,000	70,000	−$ 70,000	175,000
Retained earnings	376,000ᵇ	106,000ᶜ	−$106,000 − $4,250	371,750
	$776,000	$276,000		$871,750

ᵃBeginning balance of $200,000 + Elm's net income of $56,000.
ᵇBeginning balance of $250,000 + Hunt's net income of $126,000.
ᶜBeginning balance of $50,000 + Elm's net income of $56,000.

earnings of Hunt at January 1, 1993, plus the consolidated net income for 1993 ($250,000 + $121,750 = $371,750).

Consolidated Income Statement: The Pooling Method

The consolidated income statement in Exhibit 11–7 is simply the sum of the income statements of the two separate companies, with the Hunt Company's investment income eliminated to avoid double counting. Because all the assets are recorded at their book values, no adjustments are required for the additional depreciation and amortization of goodwill as were necessary under the purchase method. Note, therefore, that the consolidated income under the pooling method is higher than for the purchase method. Over the period of amortization of the goodwill and depreciation of the property, plant, and equipment, the consolidated income will be higher by a total of $80,000.

The Consolidated Balance Sheet at the End of the Year: The Pooling Method

The preparation of the consolidated balance sheet at December 31, 1993, is illustrated in Exhibit 11–8. The balance sheets of the two companies are simplified by assuming that the total liabilities of each company are unchanged and that all the assets, except the Investment in Elm, are combined.

EXHIBIT 11–7

HUNT COMPANY AND ELM COMPANY
Consolidated Income Statement for 1993:
The Pooling Method

	Hunt Company 1993	Elm Company 1993	Adjustments	Hunt Company and Subsidiary Consolidated Income Statement for the Year Ended Dec. 31, 1993
Revenue	$600,000	$380,000		$980,000
Cost of goods sold	(200,000)	(140,000)		(340,000)
Selling and administrative expenses	(300,000)	(160,000)		(460,000)
Investment income	56,000[a]		− $56,000	
Income before income taxes	$156,000	$ 80,000		$180,000
Income tax expense (30%)	(30,000)	(24,000)		(54,000)
Net income	$126,000	$ 56,000		$126,000

[a]Elm's net income of $56,000.

EXHIBIT 11–8

HUNT COMPANY AND ELM COMPANY
Consolidated Balance Sheet For December 31, 1993:
The Pooling Method

	Hunt Company Balance Sheet Dec. 31, 1993	Elm Company Balance Sheet Dec. 31, 1993	Eliminations	Hunt Company and Subsidiary Consolidated Balance Sheet Dec. 31, 1993
Assets other than investment	$720,000	$276,000		$996,000
Investment in Elm	176,000[a]		−$176,000	
	$896,000	$276,000		$996,000
Liabilities	$225,000	$100,000		$325,000
Common stock (no par)	295,000	70,000	−$120,000	245,000
Retained earnings	376,000[b]	106,000[c]	−$ 56,000	426,000
	$896,000	$276,000		$996,000

[a]Beginning balance of $120,000 + Elm's net income of $56,000.
[b]Beginning balance of $250,000 + Hunt's net income of $126,000.
[c]Beginning balance of $50,000 + Elm's net income of $56,000.

As before, the consolidated balance sheet is the sum of the two individual balance sheets with the adjustments for the necessary elimination. The only elimination required is the Investment in Elm of $176,000 (the value assigned to the shares issued by Hunt in exchange for all Elm's stock) against Common Stock (no par) of $120,000 and Retained Earnings of $56,000. Note that the consolidated retained earnings is the sum of the beginning retained earnings of both companies plus the consolidated net income for 1993 ($250,000 + $50,000 + $126,000 = $426,000).

■ **APPENDIX 2: MINORITY INTEREST**

All the examples in the chapter have assumed that the parent company purchased 100% of the common stock of the subsidiary company. When the parent exercises control but owns less than 100% of the voting common stock, consolidated financial statements are prepared by using the same general principles. In such cases, however, the subsidiary has other stockholders who own a minority interest in its net assets. **Minority interest is the ownership of other stockholders when the parent company owns less than 100% of the common stock**

of the subsidiary company. It may also be referred to as Outside Stockholders' Interest in Subsidiaries or a similar title.

The minority interest affects both the consolidated balance sheet and the consolidated income statement. In the balance sheet, the amount of the minority interest is usually computed by multiplying the percentage ownership interest of the minority stockholders by the total stockholders' equity of the subsidiary.[8] The minority interest is often listed in the stockholders' equity section of the consolidated balance sheet, although it is sometimes listed in a separate section between liabilities and stockholders' equity. In the consolidated income statement the amount of the subsidiary's income attributable to the minority is subtracted.

The minority interest under the purchase method is illustrated using the information regarding purchase price and fair market values for the Hunt and Elm companies example earlier in the chapter. It is now assumed that on January 1, 1993, the Hunt Company purchases 70% of the outstanding voting common stock of Elm for $140,000 (70% × $200,000) cash. The consolidated balance sheet on January 1, 1993, is shown in Exhibit 11–9. The elimination involves the removal of the Investment in Elm of $140,000, the stockholders' equity of Elm of $120,000, and recording the minority interest of $36,000 (30% × the stockholders' equity of Elm of $120,000). These amounts are not equal because Hunt has also purchased 70% of the excess of the fair market value over the book value of the property, plant, and equipment, and goodwill. The total excess of the fair market value over book value is $30,000, so $21,000 ($30,000 × 70%) is recorded. Since 70% of the book value of Elm's net assets is $84,000 ($120,000 × 70%), the fair market value of the 70% of Elm's net assets being acquired by Hunt is $105,000 ($84,000 + $21,000). The total goodwill is the purchase price of $140,000 less the fair market value of 70% of the net assets of $105,000, or $35,000. These calculations may be summarized as follows:

Price paid by Hunt Company		$140,000
Less: book value of 70% of the net assets of Elm	$84,000	
70% of the excess of the fair market value over		
the book value of Elm's net assets	21,000	
Fair market value of 70% of Elm's net assets		(105,000)
Value of goodwill		$ 35,000

The consolidated income statement under the purchase method is shown in Exhibit 11–10. The excess of the fair market value over the book value of the property, plant, and equipment of $21,000 is depreciated over its life of ten years, and the goodwill of $35,000 is amortized over 40 years. The investment income

....

[8]In some circumstances, which are beyond the scope of this book, the minority interest may not be exactly equal to this amount. The difference, however, is unlikely to be material.

EXHIBIT 11–9

HUNT COMPANY AND ELM COMPANY
Minority Interest
Consolidated Balance Sheet:
The Purchase Method

	Hunt Company Balance Sheet Dec. 31, 1992	Hunt Company Transaction Jan. 1, 1993	Hunt Company Balance Sheet Jan. 1, 1993	Elm Company Balance Sheet Jan. 1, 1993	Eliminations	Hunt Company and Subsidiary Consolidated Balance Sheet Jan. 1, 1993
Cash	$250,000	–$140,000	$110,000	$ 20,000		$130,000
Notes receivable	30,000		30,000	20,000		50,000
Inventory	70,000		70,000	40,000		110,000
Property, plant, and equipment (net)	300,000		300,000	140,000	+$ 21,000[a] (Consolidated)	461,000
Goodwill					+$ 35,000[b] (Consolidated)	35,000
Investment in Elm		+$140,000	140,000		–$140,000 (Hunt)	
	$650,000		$650,000	$220,000		$786,000
Notes payable	$ 25,000		$ 25,000	$ 30,000		$ 55,000
Bonds payable	200,000		200,000	70,000		270,000
Common stock (no par)	175,000		175,000	70,000	–$70,000 (Elm)	175,000 (Hunt)
Retained earnings	250,000		250,000	50,000	–$50,000 (Elm)	250,000 (Hunt)
Minority interest					+$36,000[c] (Consolidated)	36,000
	$650,000		$650,000	$220,000		$786,000

[a] 70% × (excess of fair market value of Elm's property, plant, and equipment of $170,000 over their book value of $140,000), or 70% × $30,000.
[b] 70% × purchase price of $200,000 less the fair market value of net assets acquired of $150,000.
[c] 30% × stockholders' equity of Elm, or 30% × ($70,000 + $50,000).

EXHIBIT 11–10

. . . .

HUNT COMPANY AND ELM COMPANY
Minority Interest
Consolidated Income Statement for 1993:
The Purchase Method

	Hunt Company 1993	Elm Company 1993	Adjustments	Hunt Company and Subsidiary Consolidated Income Statement for the Year Ended Dec. 31, 1993
Revenue	$600,000	$380,000		$980,000
Cost of goods sold	(200,000)	(140,000)		(340,000)
Selling and administrative expenses	(300,000)	(160,000)	+$ 2,100[b]	(462,100)
Goodwill amortization			+$ 875[c]	(875)
Investment income	39,200[a]		−$39,200	
Income before income taxes	$139,200	$ 80,000		$177,025
Income tax expense	(30,000)	(24,000)		(54,000)
				$123,025
Minority interest in Elm's income			+$16,800[d]	(16,800)
Net Income	$109,200	$ 56,000		$106,225

[a]70% × Elm's net income of $56,000.
[b]$21,000 ÷ 10 years.
[c]$35,000 ÷ 40 years.
[d]30% × Elm's net income of $56,000.

in Hunt's income statement is eliminated, and the minority interest in Elm's net income is recorded as $16,800 (30% × $56,000).

The consolidated balance sheet at the end of the year is shown in Exhibit 11–11. The Investment in Elm is eliminated along with the stockholders' equity of Elm, and the minority interest of $52,800 (30% × $176,000) is included in the consolidated balance sheet. The excess of the fair market value over the book value of $21,000 and the goodwill of $35,000 are also recorded. The additional depreciation of $2,100 and the goodwill amortization of $875 must also be subtracted from the assets in the consolidated balance sheet and will reduce consolidated retained earnings by $2,975.

The minority interest under the pooling method is not illustrated because for a pooling to occur at least 90% of the voting common stock must have been acquired. Therefore, the existence of a minority interest in a pooling is rare. If a minority interest did occur, however, it would be valued at the minority percentage multiplied by the stockholders' equity of the subsidiary. Further discussion is beyond the scope of this book.

EXHIBIT 11–11

HUNT COMPANY AND ELM COMPANY
Minority Interest
Consolidated Balance Sheet for December 31, 1993:
The Purchase Method

	Hunt Company Balance Sheet Dec. 31, 1993	Elm Company Balance Sheet Dec. 31, 1993	Eliminations	Hunt Company and Subsidiary Consolidated Balance Sheet Dec. 31, 1993
Assets other than investment	$580,000	$276,000	+$ 21,000 −$2,100	$874,900
Goodwill			+$ 35,000 −$ 875	34,125
Investment in Elm	179,200^a		−$179,200	
	$759,200	$276,000		$909,025
Liabilities	$225,000	$100,000		$325,000
Common stock (no par)	175,000	70,000	−$ 70,000	175,000
Retained earnings	359,200^b	106,000^c	−$106,000 −$2,975	356,225
Minority interest			+$ 52,800^d	52,800
	$759,200	$276,000		$909,025

^{a}Beginning balance of $140,000 + 70% × Elm's net income of $56,000.
^{b}Beginning balance of $250,000 + Hunt's net income of $109,200.
^{c}Beginning balance of $50,000 + Elm's net income of $56,000.
^{d}30% × stockholders' equity of Elm of $70,000 + $106,000.

QUESTIONS

1. Why do companies purchase securities of other business organizations?

2. What are the determining factors in classifying an investment as either current or noncurrent?

3. Why does a company invest in current marketable securities? Give examples of the securities in which a company might invest.

4. How is a current investment in marketable securities (stocks) accounted for subsequent to acquisition? A current investment in marketable securities—bonds?

5. What is the Unrealized Loss on Decline in Value of Current Marketable Securities—Stocks and where is it disclosed on the financial statements?

6. What is the Allowance for Decline in Value of Current Marketable Securities—Stocks and where is it disclosed on the financial statements?

7. How is revenue on a current investment in stocks reported? Revenue on a current investment in bonds?

8. How is the gain or loss on the sale of an investment in stocks determined? An investment in bonds?

9. Why does a purchaser of bonds pay for "accrued interest" whereas a purchaser of stocks does not pay for "accrued dividends"?

10. Briefly describe the accounting for long-term investments in stock under the lower of cost or market method.

11. When using the lower of cost or market method in recording and reporting long-term investments in stock, how does the accounting treatment for a decline in value that is other than temporary differ from the accounting treatment for a temporary decline in value?

12. What are the three methods that may be used to account for a noncurrent investment in the common stock of another company? When is each used?

13. What characteristics may be used to indicate that the investor company has significant influence over the investee company?

14. An investor may purchase shares on the stock market or from the investee company itself. How does each of these methods of acquisition affect the investee company's financial statements?

15. Why do some users criticize the lower of cost or market method?

16. Why is the equity method considered to be a better accounting method than the lower of cost or market method for certain types of investments?

17. When the equity method is used, how does the investor company record the value of its investment? How does the investor company record the income earned on its investment?

18. When the equity method is used, what is the relationship between the change in the balance of the investor company's investment account and the change in the balance sheet of the investee company?

19. Under what circumstances is the purchase method used? The pooling method?

20. What are the principal differences that appear in the financial statements if pooling is used instead of purchasing?

21. When a consolidated balance sheet is prepared, why is it necessary to eliminate certain items? Give two examples of items that might be eliminated.

22. When a consolidated income statement is prepared, why is it necessary to eliminate certain items? Give two examples of items that might be eliminated.

23. Appendix 2: What is minority interest? Where would it appear in a consolidated balance sheet? How is it computed?

PROBLEMS AND CASES
. . . .

24. Current Marketable Securities—Stocks. The Castle Company purchased a portfolio of current marketable securities that were all capital stocks on January 14, 1993. The company bought and sold shares during the next year, and the portfolio had the following costs and market values at the end of each quarter during the year:

	Cost	Market Value
March 31, 1993	$87,500	$88,200
June 30, 1993	82,000	80,000
September 30, 1993	93,000	87,000
December 31, 1993	64,000	65,000

Required **1.** How much unrealized loss or gain will be reported in each of the quarterly income statements prepared on the above dates?

2. At what value will the marketable securities be recorded in each of the quarterly balance sheets prepared on the above dates?

25. Current Marketable Securities—Stocks. On January 5, 1993, the Belford Company purchased for $42,000 a portfolio of current marketable securities that were all common stocks. At the end of the company's fiscal year on June 30, 1993, the market value of the portfolio was $35,000. On August 25, 1993, the company sold one of the stocks in its portfolio, which had cost $10,500, for $12,000. On June 30, 1993, this security had a market value of $9,500.

Required How much income will the Belford Company recognize from January 5, 1993, through August 25, 1993, as a result of these events?

26. **Current Marketable Securities—Stocks.** The Wilson Company invests its temporary excess funds in marketable securities. At the end of 1992 Wilson's portfolio of current marketable securities (capital stock) is as follows:

Security	Number of Shares	Cost per Share	Market Value per Share
Bierstadt Company	500	$25	$28
Lindsey Company	400	35	37
Pyramid Company	900	20	20

During the first quarter of 1993 the company engaged in the following transactions:

Date	Transactions
Feb. 10	Sold one-half of the Pyramid shares for $26 per share.
Mar. 18	Purchased 700 shares of Maroon Company stock for $18 per share.
Mar. 31	Received dividends of $1,400 on the marketable securities during the period for which the market values on this date are:

Security	Market Value per Share
Bierstadt Company	$24
Lindsey Company	31
Pyramid Company	22
Maroon Company	17

During the second quarter of 1993 the company engaged in the following transactions:

Date	Transactions
Apr. 18	Purchased 300 shares of the Huron Company stock for $30 per share.
May 15	Sold the Lindsey Company shares for $37 per share.
June 30	Received dividends of $1,700 on the marketable securities during the period for which the market values on this date are:

Security	Market Value per Share
Bierstadt Company	$26
Pyramid Company	19
Maroon Company	21
Huron Company	32

Required 1. Record the effects on the accounting equation of all the above events. The company records dividend revenue when the cash is received.

2. Show how the income recognized each quarter and the value of the marketable securities reported in the balance sheet at the end of each quarter would be disclosed on the interim financial statements.

27. **Current Marketable Securities—Stocks.** The Streeter Company invests its temporary excess funds in marketable securities. At the end of 1992 Streeter's portfolio of current marketable securities (capital stock) is as follows:

Security	Number of Shares	Cost per Share		Market Value per Share	
Parham Company	500 *250*	$20	*5000*	$23	*11500*
Beckman Company	400	*30*	*12000*	32	*12800*
Traub Company	800	15	*12000*	15	*12000*
	700	*10*	*7000*		*36300*
			26000		

During the first quarter of 1993 the company engaged in the following transactions:

Date	Transactions
Mar. 11	Sold one-half of the Parham shares for $23 per share. *unrealized gain 750* *divided revenue 1500*
Mar. 17	Purchased 700 shares of the Gilman Company for $10 per share.
Mar. 31	Received dividends of $1,500 on the marketable securities during the period, and the market values on this date are:

Security		Market Value per Share	
Parham Company	*250*	$18	*4500*
Beckman Company	*400*	(28)	*11200*
Traub Company	*800*	17	*13600*
Gilman Company	*700*	9	*6300*
			35600

During the second quarter of 1993 the company engaged in the following transactions:

Date	Transactions
May 16	Purchased 300 shares of the Hagge Company stock for $25 per share.
June 9	Sold the Beckman Company stock for $32 per share.
June 30	Received dividends of $2,100 on the marketable securities during the period, and the market values on this date are:

Security			Market Value per Share	
Parham Company *$20*	*250*		$21	*250*
Traub Company *$15*	*800*		14	*(800)*
Gilman Company *$10*	*700*		13	*2100*
Hagge Company *$25*	*300*		27	*600*
				2150

Required 1. Record the effects of these events on the accounting equation. The company records dividend revenue when cash is received.

2. Show how the income recognized each quarter and the value of the marketable securities reported in the balance sheet at the end of each quarter would be disclosed on the interim financial statements.

28. **Current Marketable Securities—Stocks.** At the beginning of 1993, the Ferris Corporation adopted a policy of investing idle cash in marketable securities. The following transactions relate to Ferris' Temporary Investment account during the first two quarters of 1993:

January 5	Purchased 100 shares of A Company common stock at $70 per share.
January 15	Purchased 300 shares of R Company common stock at $37½ per share.
February 10	Purchased 200 shares of T Company common stock at $62 per share.
March 31	Dividends received during the first quarter were:

A, $3.00 per share
R, $1.30 per share
T, $1.85 per share

On this date the following information on quoted market prices is also available:

A, $72 per share
R, $36 per share
T, $61 per share

April 9	Sold the R Company shares at $36½ per share.
April 21	Purchased 200 shares of K Company common stock at $43 per share.
June 30	Dividends received during the second quarter were:

A, $3.00 per share
T, $1.80 per share
K, $1.55 per share

On this date the following information on quoted market prices is also available:

A, $75 per share
T, $61 per share
K, $45 per share

Required 1. Record the effects on the accounting equation of all of the above information. The company records dividend revenue when the cash is received.

2. What amounts of income or loss would Ferris have recognized as a result of these transactions during the first and second quarters of 1993?

29. **Current Marketable Securities—Stocks.** On June 30, 1993, Reagan Corporation acquired the following equity securities as temporary investments:

Security	Cost
500 shares of I Co.	$40,000
400 shares of O Inc.	22,000
600 shares of U Corp.	36,000

On September 30, 1993, the end of Reagan's third quarter, the following information is available:

Security	Market Value
I	$41,000
O	19,000
U	36,000

On October 15, 1993, all the I shares are sold for $41,500, and on December 31, 1993, the following information is available:

Security	Market Value
O	$21,000
U	$37,500

On January 5, 1994, the investment in O Company securities is reclassified from current to noncurrent. The market value is $21,300 on this date.

Required Record the effects on the accounting equation of all of the above information.

30. Current Marketable Securities—Stocks. The Noonan Corporation invests its excess funds in marketable securities. At the end of 1993, Noonan's portfolio of temporary investments consisted of the following equity securities:

Security	Number of Shares	Cost per Share	Market Value per Share
Keene Company	500	$60	$60
Sachs, Inc.	800	40	41
Bacon Company	400	70	72

During the first half of 1994, Noonan engaged in the following temporary investment transactions:

January 5	Sold one-half of the Sachs shares for $41 per share.
February 1	Purchased 700 shares of Jackson Corporation common stock for $45 per share.
March 31	Dividends of $2,600 were received on temporary investments, and the following information is available on market prices:

Security	Market Value per Share
Keene Company	$59
Sachs, Inc.	42
Bacon Company	70
Jackson Corporation	43

April 14	Purchased 300 shares of Quinn Company preferred stock for $52 per share.
May 10	Sold the remainder of the Sachs shares for $43 per share.
June 30	Dividends of $2,800 were received on temporary investments, and the following information is available:

Security	Market Value per Share
Keene Company	$60
Bacon Company	69
Jackson Corporation	46
Quinn Company	50

July 2	Decided to reclassify the investment in Bacon Company equity securities from current to noncurrent. The market value was $69 per share.

Required 1. Record the effects on the accounting equation of the above transactions for January 5 through July 2, 1994.

2. What amount of income or loss from temporary investment transactions should Noonan report for the first and second quarters of 1994?

31. Noncurrent Marketable Securities—Stocks. On September 15, 1993, the Morton Corporation purchased shares of common stock (all less than 20% of the outstanding stock) in three companies as a long-term investment. No dividends were declared or received on any of the shares during 1993. The costs and the market values on December 31, 1993, were as follows:

	Number of Shares	Cost per Share	Market Value per Share
Moses Company	100	$20	$23
Upchurch Company	250	40	41
Jensen Company	500	11	8

Required Show all of the items that will appear in the Morton Corporation's financial statements in 1993 relating to the investment.

32. Noncurrent Marketable Securities—Stocks. Use the same information as in Problem 31. Assume that the Morton Corporation sold the shares of the Jensen Company on December 10, 1994, for $9 per share.

Required 1. How much is the gain or loss that is recognized on the sale?

2. If the prices of the shares in the other two companies have not changed since December 31, 1993, show all of the items that will appear in the Morton Corporation's 1994 financial statements relating to the investment.

33. Noncurrent Marketable Securities—Stocks. The Prestridge Corporation uses the lower of cost or market method to account for its noncurrent investments in common stock. The following information is available for its noncurrent investment account:

January 1, 1993. Purchased common stock as follows:
  Wright Company, 700 shares for $20 per share   14000
  Armstrong Company, 500 shares for $30 per share   15000
  Keyworth Company, 1,000 shares for $15 per share   15000

December 31, 1993:   44000

	Cost per Share	Market Value per Share	Dividends Received per Share
Wright Company	$20	$19	$1
Armstrong Company	30	28	2
Keyworth Company	(15)	16	2

June 10, 1994. Sold 500 shares of Wright Company for $19 per share. (−500)

August 15, 1994. Sold 400 shares of Keyworth Company for $17 per share. (+800)

December 31, 1994:

	Cost per Share	Market Value per Share	Dividends Received per Share
Wright Company	$20	$21	$1
Armstrong Company	30	35	2
Keyworth Company	15	17	1

Required 1. Record the effects on the accounting equation of the above events for the Prestridge Corporation. The corporation records dividend revenue when the cash is received.

2. Prepare partial income statements for 1993 and 1994 and also partial balance sheets at December 31, 1993, and December 31, 1994, relating to the above events for the Prestridge Corporation.

34. Noncurrent Marketable Securities—Stocks. The Adams Corporation uses the lower of cost or market method to account for its noncurrent investments in common stock. The following information is available for its noncurrent investment account:

March 21, 1993. Purchased common stock as follows:
  Stephens Company, 300 shares for $30 per share
  Wheaton Company, 800 shares for $15 per share
  White Company, 500 shares for $20 per share

December 31, 1993:

	Cost per Share	Market Value per Share	Dividends Received per Share
Stephens Company	$30	$32	$2
Wheaton Company	15	13	1
White Company	20	18	1.50

July 2, 1994. Sold 100 shares of Stephens Company stock for $33 per share.

September 9, 1994. Sold 400 shares of White Company stock for $16 per share.

December 31, 1994:

	Cost per Share	Market Value per Share	Dividends Received per Share
Stephens Company	$30	$33	$2
Wheaton Company	15	14	1
White Company	20	16	1

Required 1. Record the effects on the accounting equation of the above events for the Adams Corporation. The corporation records dividend revenue when the cash is received.

2. Prepare partial income statements for 1993 and 1994 and partial balance sheets at December 31, 1993, and December 31, 1994, relating to the above events for the Adams Corporation.

35. **Recording Changes in Market Value.** On December 31, 1993, the Peck Corporation purchased the following securities as a long-term investment. Each of these investments was small in relation to the total number of shares outstanding, and no other investments are held.

A Corporation Common	$10 par 3,000 shares @ $35 = $105,000
B Corporation Common	$ 5 par 5,000 shares @ $15 = $ 75,000
C Corporation Common	$ 5 par 8,000 shares @ $20 = $160,000

This was the only investment security transaction during the year. At the end of 1994 and 1995 the following information is available:

	1994		1995	
	Cost	Market	Cost	Market
A Corporation Common	$105,000	$125,000	$105,000	$118,000
B Corporation Common	75,000	70,000	75,000	80,000
C Corporation Common	160,000	140,000	160,000	140,000

Required 1. Assuming the declines in value are temporary, record the effects on the accounting equation at the end of 1994 and 1995 to reflect Peck Corporation's investment in common stock.

2. Instead, record the effects for 1994 and 1995 if the decline in value of C Corporation Common was assumed to be other than temporary during 1994.

36. Lower of Cost or Market Method. On January 1, 1993, Marsh Company had 1,000 shares of X Company common stock in its long-term investments portfolio. The stock had cost $15 per share and has a current market value of $13 per share. The January 1, 1993, balance sheet showed the following:

ASSETS

Long-term investments in stock	$15,000
Less: allowance to reduce noncurrent equity investments to market	(2,000)
	$13,000

STOCKHOLDERS' EQUITY

Unrealized decline in market value of noncurrent equity investments	($2,000)

During 1993, as long-term investments, the company acquired 900 shares of Y Company common stock for $18 per share and 800 shares of Z Company common stock for $23 per share. At the end of 1993 the respective market values per share were: X—$14, Y—$16, and Z—$21.

Required Prepare the December 31, 1993, balance sheet items.

37. Market Value Method. The Gates Investment Fund uses the market value method to account for its investments. On January 1, 1993, Gates' investment account had a balance of $32,400—an amount that exceeds the original cost. The following information is available concerning Gates' investment securities for 1993.

Dividends and interest received	$ 4,500
Market value of investment securities 12/31/93	34,500

Required 1. Record the effects on the accounting equation during 1993 to account for Gates' investments under the market value method.

2. What is the balance in Gates' investment account on December 31, 1993?

3. How would your answer have differed if Gates were using the lower of cost or market method? Why?

38. Current Marketable Securities—Bonds. On February 1, 1993, the Grays Company purchased eight Torres Company 8% $1,000 bonds at 105 plus accrued interest, and paid stockbroker's fees of $200. The bonds pay interest on June 30 and December 31 each year. On August 31, 1993, the company sold the bonds at 107 plus accrued interest.

Required **1.** Compute the total amount paid for the bonds.

   2. Compute the interest earned on the bonds by the Grays Company during 1993.

   3. For the sale of the bonds, compute the amount received and the gain or loss.

39. Current Marketable Securities—Bonds. On March 1, 1993, the Harsh Company purchased Elm Company bonds with a face value of $6,000. The bonds pay interest at a 10% annual interest rate on June 30 and December 31 each year. The Harsh Company paid 97 plus accrued interest, plus a stockbroker's commission of $150. The Harsh Company sold the bonds on November 1, 1993, at 102 plus accrued interest.

Required **1.** Compute the amount paid for the bonds.

   2. Compute the interest earned on the bonds by the Harsh Company during 1993.

   3. For the sale of the bonds, compute the amount received and the gain or loss.

40. Temporary Investments in Bonds. The following information concerns the Ball Corporation's temporary investments in bonds during 1993.

March 1	Purchased $100,000 face value 10% bonds of the York Corporation at 90 plus accrued interest. Interest on these bonds is payable each June 30 and December 31.
May 1	Purchased $200,000 face value 12% bonds of the Newton Corporation at 101, plus accrued interest. Interest on these bonds is payable each June 30 and December 31.
June 30	Received the semiannual interest on the York and Newton bonds.
August 1	Sold the York bonds at 88 plus accrued interest.
October 1	Purchased $100,000 face value 13% bonds of the Hill Corporation at 103 plus accrued interest. Interest on these bonds is payable each June 30 and December 31.
December 31	Received the semiannual interest on the Newton and Hill bonds.

Required **1.** Record the effects on the accounting equation of the above transactions using the cost method.

   2. What amount of income or loss would Ball have recognized as a result of these events in each quarter of 1993?

41. Equity Method. On January 1, 1993, the Jackson Company purchased 10,000 shares of the Rizzo Company, which represented 45% of its outstanding common stock. On that date the book value of the net assets of the Jackson Company was $125,000. The total cost of the shares was $50,000. At the end of 1993 the Rizzo Company reported net income of $30,000 and paid total dividends of $15,000.

Required **1.** How much does the Jackson Company recognize as income for 1993?

   2. What is the book value of the investment reported in the balance sheet of the Jackson Company on December 31, 1993?

42. **Equity Method.** On January 1, 1993, the Foley Company purchased 20,000 shares of the Preston Company for $100,000. This represents 26% of the Preston Company's outstanding shares. On that date the book value of the net assets of the Preston Company was $400,000. On December 31, 1993, the Foley Company reported a balance in its investment account of $120,000. The Preston Company did not pay dividends during 1993.

Required 1. How much did the Foley Company report as 1993 income on its investment?

2. What was the total net income of the Preston Company during 1993?

43. **Equity Method.** The Carter Company purchased, on the stock market, 40,000 of the 120,000 outstanding shares of the Chavous Company on January 1, 1993, for $200,000. The condensed balance sheet of the Chavous Company on January 1, 1993, is as follows:

CHAVOUS COMPANY
Balance Sheet
January 1, 1993

ASSETS		LIABILITIES	
Current assets	$ 400,000	Current liabilities	$ 100,000
Noncurrent assets	600,000	Noncurrent liabilities	300,000
		Total liabilities	$ 400,000
		STOCKHOLDERS' EQUITY	
		Common stock, no par	$ 250,000
		Retained earnings	350,000
		Total stockholders' equity	$ 600,000
		Total liabilities and	
Total assets	$1,000,000	stockholders' equity	$1,000,000

At the end of 1993 the Chavous Company reported net income of $150,000 and paid dividends of $45,000.

Required 1. Record the effects on the accounting equation of the above events in 1993 for the Carter Company.

2. Prepare a partial income statement for 1993 and a partial balance sheet at December 31, 1993, for the Carter Company relating to the above events.

3. Assuming that noncurrent assets increased by $55,000 and liabilities and common stock are unchanged, prepare a condensed balance sheet for the Chavous Company at December 31, 1993.

4. What is the relationship between the change in the balance of the Investment account of the Carter Company since the purchase of the investment and the change in the balance sheet of the Chavous Company?

44. **Equity Method.** The Wild Company purchased, on the stock market, 80,000 of the 200,000 outstanding shares of the Dynan Company on January 1, 1993, for $360,000. The condensed balance sheet of the Dynan Company on January 1, 1993, is as follows:

DYNAN COMPANY
Balance Sheet
January 1, 1993

ASSETS		LIABILITIES	
Current assets	$ 600,000	Current liabilities	$ 200,000
Noncurrent assets	900,000	Noncurrent liabilities	400,000
		Total liabilities	$ 600,000
		STOCKHOLDERS' EQUITY	
		Common stock, no par	$ 400,000
		Retained earnings	500,000
		Total stockholders' equity	$ 900,000
		Total liabilities and	
Total assets	$1,500,000	stockholders' equity	$1,500,000

At the end of 1993 the Dynan Company reported net income of $300,000 and paid dividends of $60,000.

Required **1.** Record the effects on the accounting equation of the above events in 1993 for the Wild Company.

2. Prepare a partial income statement for 1993 and a partial balance sheet at December 31, 1993, for the Wild Company relating to the investment.

3. Assuming that noncurrent assets increased by $100,000 and that liabilities and common stock are unchanged, prepare a condensed balance sheet for the Dynan Company at December 31, 1993.

4. What is the relationship between the change in the balance of the Investment account of the Wild Company since the purchase of the investment and the change in the balance sheet of the Dynan Company?

45. Equity Method. The Miller Corporation acquired 30% of the outstanding common stock of the Crowell Corporation for $160,000 on January 1, 1993. (The purchase price of the shares was equal to their book value.) During 1993 the following information is available for Crowell:

March 31, 1993	Declared and paid a cash dividend of $40,000.
June 30, 1993	Reported semiannual earnings of $100,000 for the first half of 1993.
September 30, 1993	Declared and paid a cash dividend of $40,000.
December 31, 1993	Reported semiannual earnings of $120,000 for the second half of 1993.

Required **1.** Record the effects on the accounting equation of the above information.

2. What is the balance in Miller's investment account on December 31, 1993? (Show your computations.)

46. Consolidated Balance Sheet. On January 1, 1993, the Kyle Company had total assets of $300,000, including cash of $20,000, a note receivable of $35,000, inventory of $75,000, property, plant, and equipment of $120,000, and investment in the Swensen

Company of $50,000; liabilities of $200,000; and stockholders' equity of $100,000. The Swensen Company had assets of $125,000, consisting of cash of $15,000, inventory of $40,000, and property, plant, and equipment of $70,000; liabilities of $75,000; and stockholders' equity of $50,000. The Kyle Company owns 100% of the outstanding common stock of the Swensen Company.

Required Prepare a consolidated balance sheet on January 1, 1993, for the Kyle Company and its subsidiary.

47. Consolidated Income Statement. During 1993 the Merman Company had sales of $50,000, cost of goods sold of $24,000, and operating expenses of $15,000. During 1993 the Harrison Company had sales of $40,000, cost of goods sold of $19,000, and operating expenses of $10,000. The Merman Company owns 100% of the outstanding common stock of the Harrison Company. Included in the sales were goods costing the Harrison Company $6,000 which it sold to the Merman Company for $9,000. The Merman Company has resold the goods to its outside customers.

Required Prepare a consolidated income statement for the Merman Company and its subsidiary for 1993.

48. Minority Interest. On January 1, 1993, the Norel Company purchased 80% of the common stock of the Weir Company for $104,000. At that date the Weir Company had common stock of $50,000 and retained earnings of $80,000.

Required How much is the minority interest on the January 1, 1993, consolidated balance sheet?

49. Consolidation. On June 30, 1993, the Milo Company purchased 100% of the common stock of the Alpha Company. In addition, on the same date the Alpha Company borrowed $20,000 from the Milo Company by issuing a note. After these transactions the balance sheet accounts of the two companies on June 30, 1993, were as follows:

	Milo Company	Alpha Company
ASSETS		
Cash	$ 10,000	$ 9,000
Accounts receivable	30,000	8,000
Notes receivable	50,000	30,000
Inventory	80,000	40,000
Investment in Alpha Company	70,000	—
Property, plant, and equipment (net)	120,000	80,000
Total assets	$360,000	$167,000
LIABILITIES AND STOCKHOLDERS' EQUITY		
Accounts payable	$ 55,000	$ 27,000
Notes payable	65,000	70,000
Common stock, no par	100,000	40,000
Retained earnings	140,000	30,000
Total liabilities and stockholders' equity	$360,000	$167,000

Required Prepare the consolidated balance sheet for the Milo Company and its subsidiary at June 30, 1993, if the purchase method is used.

50. Consolidation. On January 1, 1993, the Bashor Company purchased 100% of the common stock of the Cohen Company. It paid $120,000, which was equal to the book value of the Cohen Company at that time. During the year the Cohen Company earned income of $30,000 and no dividends were paid. In addition, the Bashor Company sold goods costing $10,000 to the Cohen Company for $15,000 on account. The account has not yet been paid. The Cohen Company sold these goods to its outside customers for $25,000 cash. At December 31, 1993, the balance sheets of the two companies were as follows:

	Bashor Company	Cohen Company
ASSETS		
Cash	$ 30,000	$ 15,000
Accounts receivable	52,000	25,000
Notes receivable	43,000	13,000
Inventory	90,000	57,000
Investment in Cohen Company	150,000	—
Property, and equipment (net)	100,000	75,000
Total assets	$465,000	$185,000
LIABILITIES AND STOCKHOLDERS' EQUITY		
Accounts payable	$ 75,000	$ 20,000
Notes payable	45,000	15,000
Common stock, no par	120,000	60,000
Retained earnings	225,000	90,000
Total liabilities and stockholders' equity	$465,000	$185,000

Required 1. Prepare the consolidated balance sheet for the Bashor Company and its subsidiary on December 31, 1993, if the company uses the purchase method.

2. What items would be eliminated on a consolidated income statement for 1993?

51. Purchase Method. On January 1, 1993, Oak Company acquired 100% of the voting common stock of Bat Company for $90 million cash. On December 31, 1992, each company had the following balance sheets (in millions):

	Oak	Bat
Cash	$120	$ 10
Accounts receivable	40	15
Inventory	60	25
Property, plant, and equipment (net)	180	50
	$400	$100
Accounts payable	$ 30	$ 18
Bonds payable	70	22
Common stock (no par)	100	33
Retained earnings	200	27
	$400	$100

Required 1. Prepare the individual balance sheets of Oak Company and Bat Company on January 1, 1993 (after the acquisition).

2. Prepare the consolidated balance sheet on January 1, 1993, if the fair market values of the net assets of Bat Company are equal to their book values. Oak Company uses the purchase method.

3. How much goodwill would be amortized each year if the maximum life is used?

52. **Purchase Method.** On January 1, 1993, Oak Company acquired 100% of the voting common stock of Bat Company for $90 million cash. On December 31, 1992, each company had the following condensed balance sheets (in millions):

	Oak	Bat
Cash	$120	$ 10
Accounts receivable	40	15
Inventory	60	25
Property, plant, and equipment (net)	180	50
	$400	$100
Accounts payable	$ 30	$ 18
Bonds payable	70	22
Common stock (no par)	100	33
Retained earnings	200	27
	$400	$100

On January 1, 1993, the fair market value of the property, plant, and equipment of Bat Company was $60 million. Each company uses the straight-line method for depreciation and amortization.

Required 1. Prepare the consolidated balance sheet on January 1, 1993. Oak Company uses the purchase method.

2. If the estimated remaining life of the equipment is ten years and the maximum amortization period is used for goodwill, how much additional depreciation expense and goodwill amortization is recognized in 1993?

53. **Purchase and Pooling.** On January 1, 1993, Oak Company sold shares for $90 million cash and acquired 100% of the voting common stock of Bat Company for $90 million cash. On December 31, 1992, each company had the following condensed balance sheets (in millions):

	Oak	Bat
Cash	$120	$ 10
Accounts receivable	40	15
Inventory	60	25
Property, plant, and equipment (net)	180	50
	$400	$100
Accounts payable	$ 30	$ 18
Bonds payable	70	22
Common stock (no par)	100	33
Retained earnings	200	27
	$400	$100

On January 1, 1993, the fair market value of the property, plant, and equipment of Bat Company was $60 million.

Required 1. Prepare the individual balance sheets of Oak Company and Bat Company on January 1, 1993 (after the acquisition).

2. Prepare the consolidated balance sheet on January 1, 1993. Oak Company uses the purchase method.

3. Assume that instead of selling shares for $90 million, Oak Company issued additional common shares to the stockholders of Bat Company in exchange for their shares. The market value of the shares issued was $90 million. Prepare the consolidated balance sheet on January 1, 1993. Oak Company uses the pooling method.

4. Explain the reasons for the differences between the two balance sheets.

54. Noncurrent Investment in Bonds and the Effective Interest Method. On January 1, 1993, the Robinson Company purchased 10%, ten-year bonds with a face value of $100,000 for $113,590.33. At this price the bonds yield 8%. Interest on the bonds is paid on June 30 and December 31. The company uses the effective interest method of amortization.

Required 1. Compute the interest revenue recorded during 1993.

2. What would be the balance of the Investment in Bonds account on the Robinson Company's December 31, 1993, balance sheet?

55. Noncurrent Investments in Bonds and the Effective Interest Method. On January 1, 1993, the Nairne Company purchased noncurrent investments in the bonds of two companies:

	Simon Company	**Fraser Company**
Face value	$40,000	$30,000
Maturity date	Dec. 31, 1998	Dec. 31, 2002
Contract rate	9%	7%
Yield	8%	8%

Both bonds pay interest on June 30 and December 31. The company uses the effective interest method to amortize any premiums or discounts in regard to the investments in bonds.

Required 1. Compute the purchase price of each bond issue.

2. Record the effects on the accounting equation of all the events for the investments during 1993.

3. Compute the book value of each investment at December 31, 1993.

56. Noncurrent Investments in Bonds and the Effective Interest Method. On January 1, 1993, the Winfrey Company purchased noncurrent investments in the bonds of two companies:

	Bates Company	Clevett Company
Face value	$80,000	$60,000
Maturity date	Dec. 31, 1997	Dec. 31, 2002
Contract rate	9%	11%
Yield	10%	10%

Both bonds pay interest on June 30 and December 31. The company uses the effective interest method to amortize any premium or discount in regard to the investments in bonds.

Required 1. Compute the purchase price of each bond issue.

2. Record the effects on the accounting equation of all of the events for the investments during 1993.

3. Compute the book value of each investment at December 31, 1993.

57. Noncurrent Investments in Bonds and the Straight-Line Method. On January 1, 1993, the Andrews Company purchased noncurrent investments in the bonds of two companies:

	Damar	Ackerman
Cost	$88,000	$66,000
Face value	$90,000	$60,000
Maturity date	Dec. 31, 2000	Dec. 31, 1998
Contract rate	9%	12%

Both bonds pay interest on June 30 and December 31. The company uses the straight-line method to amortize any premiums or discounts in regard to the investments in bonds.

Required 1. Record the effects on the accounting equation of all the events for the investments in 1993.

2. Show how the balance of the Investments account would be reported on the December 31, 1993, balance sheet of the Andrews Company.

58. Noncurrent Investments in Bonds and the Straight-Line Method. On January 1, 1993, the Gooch Company purchased noncurrent investments in the bonds of two companies:

	Tanner	Carew
Cost	$45,800	$96,000
Face value	$50,000	$90,000
Maturity date	Dec. 31, 1999	Dec. 31, 2004
Contract rate	8%	11%

Both bonds pay interest on June 30 and December 31. The company uses the straight-line method to amortize any premium or discount in regard to the investments in bonds.

Required 1. Record the effects on the accounting equation of all of the events for the investments during 1993.

2. Show how the balance of the Investments account would be reported on the December 31, 1993, balance sheet of the Gooch Company.

59. **Current Marketable Securities.** The Board of Directors of the Oxford Company is discussing the method that should be used for the valuation of the company's current marketable securities. Some of the comments are as follows:

"We should use cost, because until we sell the securities, we don't know if we have made any money."

"If we use cost, we are effectively lying to the shareholders, and as a member of the Board of Directors I don't feel I'm fulfilling my responsibilities."

"Market value is too pessimistic. If the price is up in one period and down in the next, we will report a loss in the second period although we may have a profit overall. That's misleading."

Required Describe what the speaker of each of these comments means and prepare a counterargument for each of them. (Ignore the requirements of generally accepted accounting principles.)

60. **Investments in Common Stock.** When a company buys common stock of another company the acquisition can be accounted for under one of four alternative methods: lower of cost or market with the loss on the decline in market value included in the income statement; lower of cost or market with the "loss" included in stockholders' equity; the equity method; or consolidation. Each method results in different amounts appearing in various sections of the financial statements.

Required 1. In what situation is each of the four methods used?

2. Explain how the results of the four methods appear on the financial statements.

3. Explain the justification for requiring the use of each of the four different methods from the perspective of the user of the financial statements.

61. **Marketable Securities.** The following three *unrelated* situations involve marketable equity securities:

Situation I

A noncurrent portfolio with an aggregate market value in excess of cost includes one particular security whose market value has declined to less than one-half of the original cost. The decline in value is considered to be other than temporary.

Situation II

A marketable equity security, whose market value is currently less than cost, is classified as noncurrent but is to be reclassified as current.

Situation III

A company's noncurrent portfolio of marketable equity securities consists of the common stock of one company. At the end of the prior year the market value of the security was 50% of original cost, and the effect was properly reflected in a valuation allowance account. However, at the end of the current year the market value of the security had appreciated to twice the original cost. The security is still considered noncurrent at year-end.

Required What is the effect on classification, carrying value, and earnings for each of the above situations? *(AICPA adapted)*

62. Appendix 1: Purchase and Subsequent Year. On January 1, 1993, Oak Company sold shares for $90 million cash and acquired 100% of the voting common stock of Bat Company for $90 million cash. On December 31, 1992, each company had the following condensed balance sheets (in millions):

	Oak	Bat
Cash	$120	$ 10
Accounts receivable	40	15
Inventory	60	25
Property, plant, and equipment (net)	180	50
	$400	$100
Accounts payable	$ 30	$ 18
Bonds payable	70	22
Common stock (no par)	100	33
Retained earnings	200	27
	$400	$100

On January 1, 1993, the fair market value of the property, plant, and equipment of Bat Company was $60 million. In 1993 each company had the following income statements (in millions):

	Oak	Bat
Revenue	$200	$90
Cost of goods sold	(80)	(30)
Selling and administrative expenses	(87)	(50)
Investment income	7	
Income before income taxes	$ 40	$10
Income tax expense	(12)	(3)
Net income	$ 28	$ 7

The life of the property, plant, and equipment is ten years and the maximum amortization period is used for goodwill. Each company uses the straight-line method for depreciation and amortization. Oak Company uses the purchase method.

Required 1. Prepare the consolidated income statement for 1993. Assume that the consolidated income tax expense is the sum of the income tax expense of each company.

2. Prepare the balance sheet for each company at December 31, 1993. For simplicity, combine the assets, except the Investment, into a single amount and assume that the liabilities of each company remain unchanged.

3. Prepare the consolidated balance sheet at December 31, 1993.

63. **Appendix 1: Pooling and Subsequent Year.** On January 1, 1993, Oak Company issued additional common shares to the stockholders of Bat Company in exchange for their shares. On December 31, 1992, each company had the following condensed balance sheets (in millions):

	Oak	Bat
Cash	$120	$ 10
Accounts receivable	40	15
Inventory	60	25
Property, plant, and equipment (net)	180	50
	$400	$100
Accounts payable	$ 30	$ 18
Bonds payable	70	22
Common stock (no par)	100	33
Retained earnings	200	27
	$400	$100

In 1993, each company had the following income statements (in millions):

	Oak	Bat
Revenue	$200	$90
Cost of goods sold	(80)	(30)
Selling and administrative expenses	(87)	(50)
Investment income	7	
Income before income taxes	$ 40	$10
Income tax expense	(12)	(3)
Net income	$ 28	$ 7

Oak Company uses the pooling method.

Required 1. Prepare the consolidated income statement for 1993. Assume that the consolidated income tax expense is the sum of the income tax expense of each company.

2. Prepare the balance sheet for each company at December 31, 1993. For simplicity, combine the assets, except the Investment, into a single amount and assume that the liabilities of each company remain unchanged.

3. Prepare the consolidated balance sheet at December 31, 1993.

64. **Appendix 2: Minority Interest.** On January 1, 1993, Oak Company acquired 80% of the voting common stock of Bat Company for $72 million cash. On December 31, 1992, each company had the following condensed balance sheets (in millions):

	Oak	Bat
Cash	$120	$ 10
Accounts receivable	40	15
Inventory	60	25
Property, plant, and equipment (net)	180	50
	$400	$100
Accounts payable	$ 30	$ 18
Bonds payable	70	22
Common stock (no par)	100	33
Retained earnings	200	27
	$400	$100

On January 1, 1993, the fair market value of the property, plant, and equipment of Bat Company was $60 million.

Required 1. Prepare the individual balance sheets of Oak Company and Bat Company at January 1, 1993 (after the acquisition).

2. Prepare the consolidated balance sheet at January 1, 1993. Oak Company uses the purchase method.

65. Appendix 2: Minority Interest and Subsequent Year. On January 1, 1993, Oak Company acquired 80% of the voting common stock of Bat Company for $72 million cash. On December 31, 1992, each company had the following condensed balance sheets (in millions):

	Oak	Bat
Cash	$120	$ 10
Accounts receivable	40	15
Inventory	60	25
Property, plant, and equipment (net)	180	50
	$400	$100
Accounts payable	$ 30	$ 18
Bonds payable	70	22
Common stock (no par)	100	33
Retained earnings	200	27
	$400	$100

On January 1, 1993, the fair market value of the property, plant, and equipment of Oak Company was $60 million. In 1993 each company had the following income statements (in millions):

	Oak	Bat
Revenue	$200.0	$90.0
Cost of goods sold	(80.0)	(30.0)
Selling and administrative expenses	(87.0)	(50.0)
Investment income	5.6	
Income before income taxes	$ 38.6	$10.0
Income tax expense	(12.0)	(3.0)
Net income	$ 26.6	$ 7.0

The life of the property, plant, and equipment is ten years and the maximum amortization period is used for goodwill. Each company uses the straight-line method for depreciation and amortization. Oak Company uses the purchase method.

Required **1.** Prepare the consolidated income statement for 1993. Assume that the consolidated income tax expense is the sum of the income tax expense of each company.

2. Prepare the balance sheet for each company at December 31, 1993.

3. Prepare the consolidated balance sheet at December 31, 1993. For simplicity, combine the assets, except the Investment, into a single amount and assume that the liabilities of each company remain unchanged.

ANNUAL REPORT PROBLEMS

66. Equity Method. The following excerpts are from Scott Paper's 1988 annual report relating to equity method investments (in millions of dollars):

Accounting Policies Note (in part):
Scott primarily uses the equity method of accounting for its investments in unconsolidated international and supplier affiliates. Scott's share of the earnings of its supplier affiliates is reflected by applying its share of the pretax income of such affiliates as a reduction of product costs, and by including its share of the affiliates' income taxes in taxes on income.

Investments in Supplier Affiliates
Supplier affiliates supply Scott with pulp, logs and chemicals primarily for use in its pulp and paper operations. The statement below shows Scott's investment in its supplier affiliates using the equity method of accounting.

| | December 31 | |
	1988	1987
Cost	$ 43.0	$ 9.5
Equity in undistributed earnings	.1	29.8
	$ 43.1	$39.3

Changes	1988	1987
Share of earnings	$ 3.8	$ 6.2
Cash dividends paid to Scott	(149.1)	(6.3)
New investments	191.1	0
Disposition	(42.0)	0
Increase in investment	$ 3.8	$ (.1)

Investment in International Equity Affiliates

The international affiliates are mostly joint ventures owned by Scott together with local owners in each country. The international affiliates are principally engaged in the manufacture and sale of sanitary paper products similar to those sold domestically. The statements below show Scott's investment in and share of the earnings of the unconsolidated international affiliates using the equity method of accounting. However, due to the pending sales or impaired value of Scott's investments in certain countries, the cost method was adopted for the Company's investments in Korea and Argentina.

Investments in International Equity Affiliates

	December 31	
	1988	1987
Cost	$ 63.9	$ 65.8
Equity in undistributed earnings	146.8	119.2
	$210.7	$185.0

Changes	1988	1987
Share of earnings	$ 37.0	$ 38.8
Cash dividends paid to Scott	(18.2)	(2.4)
Reinvested earnings	18.8	36.4
New investments	0.2	9.9
Dispositions and other—net	1.5	—
Transfers to consolidated operations	—	(3.3)
Foreign currency translation	5.2	5.6
Increase in investment	$ 25.7	$ 48.6

Required 1. Analyze all the 1988 impacts on the financial statements from investments in supplier affiliates using T-accounts. There was a gain before taxes of $207.3 million on the disposition. The proceeds received were ten-year notes receivable.

2. Analyze all the 1988 impacts on the financial statements from investments in international equity affiliates using T-accounts. Add the foreign currency translation (discussed in Chapter 13) to the investment account. Assume no gain or loss on the dispositions.

3. Do you agree with the switch from the equity to cost method for various foreign investments?

67. Unconsolidated Subsidiaries. Southern California Edison is the largest utility serving the Los Angeles area. The following excerpts are from its 1988 annual report relating to unconsolidated subsidiary investments (in thousands of dollars):

	1988	1987
Investments in partnerships (Note 2)	$480,027	$128,858

Note 2. Summary of Significant Accounting Policies (in part):
Consolidation Policy. The Company uses the equity method of accounting to report investments of 50% or less in partnerships primarily engaged in cogeneration, geothermal, and other energy-related facilities which are exempt from utility regulation. All significant intercompany transactions have been eliminated, except intercompany profits from energy sales to Edison by unregulated, energy-producing affiliates, which are allowed in rates.

Required **1.** Use T-accounts to analyze the 1988 impacts of the regular equity investments on the financial statements. Assume that there were no cash dividends and that unregulated intercompany profits were $10 million.

2. Why did the company not eliminate unregulated intercompany profits for this partnership investment account?

68. Various Accounting Methods for Investments. The following excerpts are from the 1988 annual report of American Express relating to investment securities (in millions of dollars):

	1988	1987
Investment securities—at cost		
Total (market: 1988, $28,625; 1987, $23,166)	$28,929	$23,167
Investment securities—at lower of aggregate cost or market (LCM)		
Total (cost: 1988, $2,638; 1987, $2,402)	2,514	2,265
Investment securities—at market		
Total	17,704	15,939
Shareholders' equity		
Net unrealized security losses	(74)	(41)

Note 1. Summary of Significant Accounting Policies (in part):
Investment Securities. Debt securities and investment mortgage loans, other than trading securities of Shearson Lehman Hutton Holdings Inc., are carried at amortized cost, except where there is a permanent impairment of value, in which case they are carried at estimated realizable value. All trading securities owned by Shearson and all nonredeemable preferred and common stocks owned by the life insurance subsidiaries are carried at market. Other preferred and common stocks are generally carried at the lower of aggregate cost or market. Unrealized appreciation or depreciation on Shearson's trading securities are included in net income.

Required **1.** Explain why American Express uses three different accounting methods for its investment securities.

2. Use T-accounts to explain all the 1988 changes in the investment security accounts listed. Assume that there was only one aggregate sale of $800 million investment securities (carried at market) for $900 million cash and that $1,000 million investment interest income was earned in 1988. Also assume 1988 purchases of $282 million and $2,381 million of investment securities at LCM and at market, respectively.

69. Accounting for Investments. The Transamerica Corporation is an insurance and finance company. The following excerpts are from its 1988 annual report relating to investment securities (in millions of dollars):

	1988	1987
Fixed investment maturities, at amortized cost: Bonds (market, $11,660; $9,456)	$11,838	$9,716
Equity securities, at market: Common stocks (cost $269; $193)	294	204
Short-term investments	454	612
Net unrealized gains on equity securities	16	7

Note 1. Summary of significant accounting policies (in part):
Investments. Fixed maturities are carried at amortized cost and generally held to maturity. Equity securities are carried at market values as of the balance sheet date.

Realized investment gains and losses are reported in net income based upon specific identification of the investments sold as of the trade date.

Net unrealized investments gains and losses on equity securities, net of related taxes, are reflected directly in shareholders' equity.

Required 1. Use T-accounts to analyze the impact on the financial statements in 1988 of all the given investment activities. Assume that the only investment sale in 1988 was for short-term investments with a sales price of $200 million.

2. What type of account is the "net unrealized gains on equity securities"?

70. Investments. In 1985 Combustion Engineering (CE) wrote off $108 million of oilfield equipment owned by its Vetco subsidiary. The company also put up another $435 million of assets for sale, but after more than a year on the market, the best bid was less than $100 million. Since the company's net worth was $664 million, the second write-off would have been very significant. To avoid the write-off, the company merged Vetco with the Hughes Offshore subsidiary of Hughes Tool Company. The new company, Vetco Gray, is owned 19.9% by CE and 80.1% by Hughes. CE contributed $270 million in assets to the new company and was paid with $110 million in cash, the common stock, and $100 million in preferred stock. Vetco Gray also accepted $30 million of CE's debt. The new company arranged for $140 million of bank loans and pledged all its assets as collateral. The bank also required that CE and Hughes guarantee $60 million and $20 million of the new company's debt, respectively, and that Hughes pledge $60 million of its assets. (These facts are based on an article in *Business Week*, November 17, 1986, p. 68.)

Required 1. Record the effects of the given events on the consolidated financial statements of CE, Hughes, and Vetco Gray, assuming that no gains or losses were recognized after the initial write-off.

2. What disclosures would be appropriate for CE, Hughes, and Vetco Gray?

3. At what amount did the bank value the assets?

4. Assume that Vetco Gray had a net loss of $50 million in its first year of operations. Record the effects on the accounting equation for CE and Hughes.

71. Classified and Comparative Financial Statements. General Motors and Ford are two of the largest auto manufacturers in the world. The following excerpts are from their 1988 annual reports:

General Motors: Note 1. Significant Accounting Policies (in part):
In the fourth quarter of 1988, the Corporation adopted Statement of Financial Accounting Standards (SFAS) No. 94, Consolidation of All Majority-owned Subsidiaries, as required by the Financial Accounting Standards Board (FASB). SFAS No. 94 significantly altered the format of the basic financial statements. Under prior accounting policies (e.g., the equity method), the net investment in nonmanufacturing type companies (e.g., General Motors Acceptance Corporation—GMAC) was reflected as a single line item on the Consolidated Balance Sheet, and the net income of these operations was reflected as a single line item on the Statement of Consolidated Income.

However, as required by SFAS No. 94, the accounts of GMAC and other more than 50% wholly owned finance and insurance subsidiaries, have been added, account by account, to those of the statements of GM and its manufacturing, marketing, defense, electronics, and computer service subsidiaries.

As a result, it is no longer meaningful to prepare a Consolidated Balance Sheet in which current and noncurrent assets and liabilities are displayed. Instead, the unclassified format utilized by banking and finance companies has been adopted. Furthermore, the Statement of Consolidated Income no longer reflects Operating Income amounts.

Ford: Note 1. Accounting Policies (in part):
The Company's financial services and real estate subsidiaries, previously accounted for by the equity method, have been consolidated in 1988 as required under SFAS No. 94. The consolidated financial statements reflect the assets, liabilities, operating results, and cash flows for two broad business segments: Automotive and Financial Services. In accordance with industry practice, the assets and liabilities of the Automotive segment are classified as current or noncurrent, and those of the Financial Services segment are unclassified.

Required **1.** Do you agree with GM that "it is no longer meaningful to prepare a Consolidated Balance Sheet in which current and noncurrent assets and liabilities are displayed. Instead, the unclassified format utilized by banking and finance companies has been adopted"? Be sure to consider finance receivables (for the car loans) which are the major asset of the financial services business segment in your answer.

2. How would you compare the liquidity of GM and Ford, given the above approaches to preparing the balance sheets?

3. How would you compare the operating performance of GM and Ford, given the above approaches to preparing the income statements?

72. Acquisitions. The following excerpts are from Amoco Corporation's 1988 annual report:

Note 2. Acquisitions (in part):
On September 1, 1988, Amoco Canada Petroleum Company Ltd., a wholly owned subsidiary of Amoco, acquired all of the outstanding stock and certain indebtedness of Dome Petroleum Ltd. for total consideration of $4.2 billion. The acquisition was

accounted for as a purchase, and the results of Dome operations have been consolidated with those of Amoco since September 1, 1988. The purchase price, including cash and Amoco Canada debt securities, has been allocated to Dome's assets and liabilities based on estimated fair values. The final purchase price allocation may differ from the preliminary allocation as a result of further appraisals and evaluations of Dome's assets and liabilities.

Unaudited pro forma consolidated results of operations for the years 1988 and 1987 presented as though Dome had been acquired at the beginning of each year show earnings per share of $3.72 in 1988 and $2.41 in 1987.

Required **1.** Did the acquisition of Dome have a material impact upon Amoco's total assets of $29,919 million as of December 31, 1988? In reviewing Amoco's 1988 balance sheet, no goodwill has been recorded for the Dome purchase. Why not? Is there any chance that goodwill may yet be recorded for the Dome purchase? If so, would such subsequent goodwill be in accordance with generally accepted accounting principles?

2. Did Dome have profitable operations over the last two years? (Amoco's earnings per share were $4.00 for 1988 and $2.65 for 1987.) If not, why did Amoco purchase Dome?

73. Consolidations. General Electric's goal is to run businesses that are number one or two in their global markets or, in the case of services that have a substantial position, are of a scale and potential appropriate to a $50 billion enterprise. The following excerpts are from its 1988 annual report (in millions of dollars):

Statement of Earnings (in part):			
	Consolidated	GE	GEFS
Revenues	$50,089	$40,292	$10,655
Costs and expenses	45,368	35,810	9,628
Earnings before income taxes	4,721	4,482	1,027
Provision for income taxes	1,335	1,096	239
Net earnings	$ 3,386	$ 3,386	$ 788

Note 1. Summary of Significant Accounting Policies (in part): In 1988, GE was required to adopt Statement of Financial Accounting Standards (SFAS) No. 94—"Consolidation of All Majority-Owned Subsidiaries." The consolidated financial statements now represent the adding together of all companies in which GE directly or indirectly has a majority ownership or otherwise controls (affiliated companies). In the past, results of financial services affiliates—the principal one being General Electric Financial Services, Inc. (GEFS)—were included on the equity basis as one line in total earnings and net assets. This was permissible under prior rules and, because financial services operations are so different in nature from and essential to operations of other GE businesses, management believed that financial statements were more understandable if GEFS statements were shown separately.

Management believes it is important to preserve as much as possible the identity of the principal financial data and related measurements to which share owners and others have become accustomed over the years. Accordingly, consolidated financial statements and notes now are generally presented in a format that includes data grouped basically as follows: GE, GEFS, and Consolidated. The Consolidated columns represent the adding together of GE and GEFS. However, it is necessary to remove the effect of transactions except between GE and GEFS to arrive at a consolidated total. The eliminations are $858 for total revenues; $70 for total costs and expenses; and $788 for net earnings. Many products financed by GEFS are manufactured by companies other than GE.

Required   Do you agree with GE's new presentation and disclosure strategies generated by SFAS No. 94, "Consolidation of All Majority-Owned Subsidiaries"? Reconcile the three columns of the Statement of Earnings. Is this reporting issue material to operations?

74. Purchase and Pooling Methods. Transamerica is a major provider of specialized financial and insurance services. The following excerpts are from its 1988 annual report, relating to acquisitions (in thousands of dollars):

Note E. Acquisitions
On October 31, 1987, the outstanding common shares of BWAC Inc., whose businesses included Borg-Warner Acceptance Corporation, a commercial lending operation subsequently renamed Transamerica Commercial Finance Corporation, were acquired for $787,979 in cash, including acquisition costs. The transaction has been accounted for as a purchase and the operations of Transamerica Commercial Finance Corporation included in the consolidated statement of income from November 1, 1987. Had the acquisition been accomplished as of January 1, 1986, net income would have been $429,135 ($5.50 per share) in 1987 and $304,529 ($3.92 per share) in 1986. Goodwill amounted to $414,818 and is being amortized over a 40-year period.

On May 21, 1987, Transamerica Corporation acquired Fairmont Financial, Inc., a provider of workers' compensation insurance, for $97,234 in Transamerica common stock (3,003,380 shares) in a transaction accounted for as a pooling of interests. In addition, holders of Fairmont options and convertible debentures acquired the right to receive 1,127,373 Transamerica shares. Amounts in 1986 have been restated to include the operating results of Fairmont. The effect of the restatement was to increase net income for 1986 by $8,457 and decrease earnings per share by $0.03.

On October 31, 1988, Transamerica Corporation acquired TIFCO Inc., an insurance premium financing company for $73,750. The transaction has been accounted for as a purchase and its operations are included in the consolidated statement of income from November 1, 1988.

Required   **1.** Is the use of both business combination methods by Transamerica a violation of the consistency principle of accounting? Why or why not?

2. If the BWAC Inc. purchase had been accomplished as of January 1, 1986, would there have been a material impact on earnings per share for 1987 ($5.47) and 1986 ($3.54)? Why is such data disclosed for the BWAC Inc. purchase and not for the TIFCO Inc. purchase?

3. How can net income be increased for 1986, while earnings per share be decreased in relation to the Fairmont acquisition?

75. Purchase and Pooling Methods. Bell Atlantic is the eastern regional phone company created by the split-up of AT&T. The following excerpt is from its 1985 annual report related to its business combinations (in millions of dollars):

Note 11. Acquisitions (in part):

In January 1985 the Company acquired Sorbus Services which provides third-party computer maintenance throughout the United States. This acquisition has been accounted for by the purchase method and accordingly, the results of operations of the acquired companies have been included in the consolidated financial statements since the date of acquisition. The purchase price of the acquisition ($235) has been allocated to the fair market value of the assets acquired and liabilities assumed.

In June 1985 the Company acquired CompuShop, a computer specialty retail chain marketing microcomputers, peripheral equipment and software. This acquisition was accomplished through the issuance of approximately 257,100 shares of the Company's common stock and accounted for as a pooling of interests. Periods prior to the acquisition have not been restated because the effect on the consolidated financial statements is not material.

Required **1.** Use the T-accounts of total assets, total liabilities, and total stockholders' equity to assess the impacts of the two business combinations. Assume goodwill of $40 million and a 40-year straight-line amortization period. Assume that the company's common stock was selling at $50 per share in June 1985. Assume that the liabilities for the two acquired companies were $50 million and $10 million, respectively. Also assume that the historical cost of the pooled company's total assets were $20 million at time of acquisition.

2. Is the use of both business combination methods in 1985 a violation of the consistency principle of accounting? Why or why not?

76. Divestiture of Subsidiary. Santa Fe Southern Pacific (SFSP) is a diversified railroad company. The following excerpts are from its 1985 annual report relating to business combinations (in millions of dollars):

Report of Independent Accountants (in part):

As discussed in Note 2, the accompanying financial statements include the assets and operations of the trusteed Southern Pacific Transportation Company. These financial statements do not include adjustments which may be necessary should the Interstate Commerce Commission require disposal of a portion of Santa Fe Southern Pacific Corporation's railroad and trucking assets and operations.

In our opinion, subject to effects on the financial statements of such adjustments, if any, as might have been required had the outcome of the matter referred to in the preceding paragraph been known, the financial statements examined by us present fairly the financial position of Santa Fe Southern Pacific Corporation and its subsidiary companies at December 31, 1985 and 1984, and the results of their operations and changes in their financial position for each of the two years in the period ended December 31, 1985, in conformity with generally accepted accounting principles consistently applied.

Financial Statements (in part):

	1985	1984
Total revenues	$ 6,438.0	$ 6,661.8
Operating and other expenses	5,968.4	6,171.0
Net income	469.6	490.8
Total assets	11,807.6	11,648.7
Total liabilities	6,043.4	5,880.2
Total shareholders' equity	5,764.2	5,768.5

Note 2. Business Combination (in part):

On December 23, 1983, Santa Fe Industries, Inc. (Santa Fe) and Southern Pacific Company (Southern Pacific) became wholly owned subsidiaries of SFSP. The business combination was accounted for as a pooling of interests and the results of operations of prior periods are reported on a combined basis.

The prior approval of the Interstate Commerce Commission (ICC) is required to combine the railroad and trucking operations of Santa Fe and Southern Pacific under the control of SFSP. To permit consummation of the combination of Santa Fe and Southern Pacific pending receipt of ICC approval, the common stock of the Southern Pacific Transportation Company (SPT) has been deposited in an independent voting trust. The terms of the voting trust provide that SFSP, Santa Fe and Southern Pacific will not control SPT until ICC approval is obtained. While there is no assurance of ICC approval, because of the ICC's recent approval of other major rail combinations, management is confident that ICC approval will be obtained; accordingly, the financial statements include all assets and operations of SPT. Should the ICC not approve the combination of the railroad and trucking operations, SFSP may be required to dispose of all or part of the trusteed operations or SFSP's other railroad operations. At this time SFSP is unable to identify the assets and operations, if any, which may be required to be disposed of, and the financial statements do not include any adjustments which might be necessary should the ICC require such a disposal. Summary financial information of SPT follows:

	1985	1984
Operating revenues	$2,545.8	$2,713.5
Operating and other expenses	2,427.7	2,572.1
Net income	118.1	141.4
Total assets	4,792.4	4,678.5
Total liabilities	2,530.1	2,534.3
Total shareholders' equity	2,262.3	2,144.2

Required **1.** Use the T-accounts of total assets, total liabilities, and total shareholders' equity to assess the impact of complete divestiture of SPT as of December 31, 1985, assuming rejection of the business combination by the ICC. Also assume a $40 million loss on this divestiture from additional cash expenses.

2. Would there be any differences in the answer to question 1 if the purchase method of accounting for business combinations had been used instead of the pooling method?

3. Are the potential impacts of this possible divestiture material enough to justify the audit report qualification, assuming no divestiture gain or loss?

Statement of Cash Flows

After reading this chapter, you should understand

- The need for a statement of cash flows
- The uses of the statement
- The direct method and the indirect method of computing the net cash flow from operating activities
- Cash flows from investing activities

- Cash flows from financing activities
- The items included in the statement of cash flows
- Investing and financing transactions not affecting cash
- Preparation of the statement (Appendix)

Throughout this book we have studied two major financial statements: the income statement, which summarizes the results of the operating activities of a company during the accounting period, and the balance sheet, which shows the financial position of the company at a specific time. With just these two financial statements, a vital link between the company's activities and the information reported to the users of accounting information is missing. A financial statement is needed to report the impacts on cash flows of a company's operating, financing, and investing activities during the accounting period. This statement should report such items as how much cash was increased because of operations, what proceeds were received from the issuance of stocks or bonds, and how the acquisition of equipment was financed. This financial statement, known as the statement of cash flows, is the subject of this chapter.

■ BACKGROUND AND CURRENT REPORTING REQUIREMENTS

Companies have prepared versions of the statement of cash flows for a long time. These reports were mainly used to assist the managers of the business in its day-to-day operations, however. These statements were referred to by many names, including the "sources and uses statement," the "cash flow statement," and the "funds statement." Prior to 1987, companies were required to include a "statement of changes in financial position" whenever a balance sheet or income statement was issued for external users. Then, the Financial Accounting Standards Board required that a "statement of cash flows" be included instead.[1] As discussed in Chapter 2, the statement of cash flows is required because of the importance that users attach to information about a company's cash flows.

A statement of cash flows is a financial statement that shows the impacts on the cash flows of the operating, investing, and financing activities of a company during an accounting period in a manner that reconciles the beginning and ending cash balances. This information is very useful to financial statement users in making economic decisions. It is important, therefore, to have an agreement about what to include in the statement. The statement of cash flows should clearly show the following information:

1. The cash provided or used in the company's operating activities. This amount may be computed under either the direct method or the indirect method (discussed later in the chapter). The FASB encourages the use of the direct method, however.

2. The cash provided or used in the company's investing activities.

3. The cash provided or used in the company's financing activities.

4. A reconciliation of the beginning cash balance to the ending cash balance.

5. The results of other important investing and financing activities, regardless of whether cash was affected (these items are included in either a separate schedule or a narrative description).

As we will see, most of the important investing and financing activities do affect cash; we will discuss those activities that do not in a later section of the chapter.

As discussed in Chapter 5, many companies invest excess cash in short-term, highly liquid investments, such as treasury bills, commercial paper, and money market funds. These investments are called *cash equivalents*. Then, instead of reporting "Cash" on its balance sheet, the company reports "Cash and Cash Equivalents." When a company reports in this manner, the purpose of the statement of cash flows is to explain the change during the period in cash and cash equivalents. For convenience, in this chapter we will focus only on changes in cash.

■ OVERVIEW OF STATEMENT OF CASH FLOWS

A company cannot continue operating without sufficient cash to do so. The assumption of continued operations is the basis of the going-concern (continuity) assumption discussed in Chapter 4. The FASB stated that the primary purpose of a statement of cash flows is to provide information about the cash receipts and cash payments of a company during a period. A secondary purpose is to

· · · · · · · · · · · · · · · · · · · ·

[1] "Statement of Cash Flows," *FASB Statement of Financial Accounting Standards No. 95* (Stamford, Conn.: FASB, 1987), par. 3.

provide information about the investing and financing activities of the company during the period.

The information in a statement of cash flows, if used with information in the income statement and balance sheet, should help external users to assess (1) the company's ability to generate positive future net cash flows, (2) the company's ability to meet its obligations and pay dividends and its needs for external financing, (3) the reasons for differences between income and associated cash receipts and payments, and (4) both the cash and noncash aspects of the company's investing and financing transactions during the period.

The statement of cash flows is intended to provide useful information to external users about the above items. Owners, potential investors, creditors, and potential creditors may use the information in the statement to evaluate how effectively the management of the company obtains and uses its cash. To help in such an evaluation, the statement of cash flows is divided into three sections: (1) Cash Flows from Operating Activities, (2) Cash Flows from Investing Activities, and (3) Cash Flows from Financing Activities.

Operating activities include all transactions and other events that are not investing and financing activities. These include, for instance, transactions that involve acquiring, producing, selling, and delivering goods for sale, as well as providing services. Cash inflows from operating activities include cash receipts from the sale of goods or services and collections of accounts receivable, as well as collection of interest on loans and receipt of dividends on investments. Cash outflows for operating activities include cash payments on accounts payable, to employees, for taxes, to lenders for interest, and to other suppliers for various expenses.

Investing activities include transactions involving lending money and collecting on those loans, acquiring and selling investments, and acquiring and selling property, plant, and equipment. Cash inflows from investing activities include cash receipts from repayments by borrowers of loan principal amounts, sales of investments in other entities (e.g., stocks and bonds), and sales of property, plant, and equipment. Cash outflows for investing activities include cash payments for loans made to borrowers, investments, and acquisitions of property, plant and equipment.

Financing activities include transactions involving the obtaining of resources from owners and providing them with a return on, and of, their investment as well as obtaining resources from creditors and repaying the amounts borrowed. Cash inflows from financing activities include cash receipts from the issuance of common and preferred stock, from bonds, from mortgages, and from notes. Cash outflows for financing activities include payments for dividends, to repurchase the company's common or preferred stock (treasury stock), and for repayments of amounts borrowed (except liabilities such as accounts payable, interest payable, and salaries payable, which are operating activities).

Particularly relevant are the classifications of certain cash flows. The cash flows associated with interest expense, interest revenue, and dividends earned are included in the computation of the net cash flow from operating activities. The cash flows associated with borrowing and repaying cash are included in the cash flows from financing activities, and the cash flows from investing activities include the cash flows associated with lending and repaying cash, investments in other companies, and the sale of those investments. These apparent inconsistencies occur because the interest expense, interest revenue, and dividends earned are included in the income statement, and therefore the net cash flow from operating activities is based on the same items that are included in the income statement.

A typical statement of cash flows is illustrated in Exhibit 12–1 using the direct method for cash flows from operating activities. The results of a company's operating activities appear in a separate section of the statement of cash flows. Most likely, a company will not continue to be successful unless it is able to obtain most of its cash from its operating activities. This occurs when the cash received from selling goods or services exceeds the cash needed to provide the goods or services. Generating cash from operating activities generally is considered to be the most important cash flow activity of a company. The Rainey Corporation provided $13,000 of its cash from operating activities during 1993, as shown in Exhibit 12–1. The company received $50,000 cash from sales to its customers and an additional $1,000 from interest and dividends. The company paid $28,000 cash to its suppliers and employees (purchasing inventory and services and paying employees), $3,000 cash for interest, and $7,000 cash for income taxes. Users can compare the company's net cash flow from operating activities for a given year with the same information from previous years in order to detect favorable or unfavorable trends in the company's operating activities. This information can also be compared with the same information from other companies for the same purpose.

In addition, a company obtains or uses cash as a result of its investing activities. The results of these investing activities are reported in a separate section of the statement of cash flows. During 1993 the Rainey Corporation had a net cash outflow of $6,000 for its investing activities. It used $8,000 cash to purchase property, plant, and equipment and received $2,000 from the sale of property, plant, and equipment.

A company also obtains or uses cash as a result of its financing activities. The results of these financing activities are reported in a separate section of the statement of cash flows. During 1993 the Rainey Corporation had a net cash outflow of $4,000 for its financing activities. It obtained $4,000 cash by issuing common stock and $5,000 by issuing bonds payable. It used $7,000 for the payment of a mortgage and $6,000 for the payment of dividends.

The $13,000 cash provided by operating activities combined with the $6,000 cash used for investing activities and the $4,000 cash used for financing activities resulted in a net increase in cash of $3,000 for the Rainey Corporation in 1993. This increase reconciles the $7,000 beginning cash balance to the $10,000 ending cash balance.

By reviewing the investing and financing sections of the statement of cash flows, users can see how (in addition to operating activities) a company obtained and used its cash. They can also compare the relative amounts in each section to see if important changes have occurred. For instance, the investing activities show that the Rainey Corporation purchased and sold property, plant, and

EXHIBIT 12–1

················

RAINEY CORPORATION
Statement of Cash Flows
For Year Ended December 31, 1993

Cash flows from operating activities		
Collections from customers	$50,000	
Interest and dividends collected	1,000	
Cash provided by operating activities		$51,000
Payments to suppliers and employees	$28,000	
Payments of interest	3,000	
Payments of income taxes	7,000	
Cash disbursed for operating activities		(38,000)
Net cash flow from operating activities		$13,000
Cash flows from investing activities		
Purchases of property, plant, and equipment	$ (8,000)	
Proceeds from disposal of property, plant, and equipment	2,000	
Net cash used by investing activities		(6,000)
Cash flows from financing activities		
Proceeds from issuing common stock	$ 4,000	
Proceeds from issuing bonds	5,000	
Payments on mortgage	(7,000)	
Dividends paid	(6,000)	
Net cash used by financing activities		(4,000)
Net increase in cash		$ 3,000
Plus: cash balance, January 1, 1993		7,000
Cash balance, December 31, 1993		$10,000

equipment in 1993 and may indicate a change in its operating capability. In addition, the financing activities show the issuance of both bonds and common stock by the Rainey Corporation in 1993 and indicate a change in its capital structure and may indicate a change in its financial flexibility and risk. A comparison with other companies can reveal, for instance, whether the company is obtaining or using a greater proportion of its cash from investing or financing activities than from operating activities. This may be important in assessing the company's relative risk. Users can also evaluate the likelihood of future cash dividends as well as the need for additional cash to finance existing operations or the expansion of operations. They can also evaluate the ability of the company to pay current obligations, make continual interest payments, and pay off long-term debt when it reaches its maturity date.

Management, as an internal user, is able to use the information in the statement of cash flows in much the same way as an external user. Management can determine whether the net cash flow from operating activities is large enough to finance existing operations, whether excess cash from operating activities may be sufficient to finance expansion projects, or whether additional cash must be obtained from external sources. In addition, management uses a form of the statement of cash flows in its budgeting process.

■ CASH INFLOWS AND OUTFLOWS

Before discussing the preparation of the statement of cash flows, it is helpful to understand the major inflows and outflows of cash from a company's operating, investing, and financing activities during an accounting period. These flows of cash are shown in Exhibit 12–2.

Inflows of Cash

There are three categories of inflows (increases) of cash:

1. *Decreases in Assets Other Than Cash.* The sale of assets other than cash results in an inflow of cash because cash is usually received in exchange for the assets.

2. *Increases in Liabilities.* The incurrence of liabilities results in an inflow of cash because cash is usually received in exchange for the liabilities. Alternatively,

EXHIBIT 12–2   Major inflows and outflows of cash

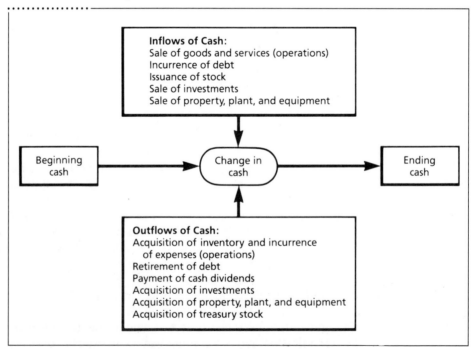

the increase in a liability such as accounts payable causes an increase in cash because of a smaller cash outflow.

3. *Increases in Stockholders' Equity.* Stockholders' equity increases mainly because of net income and additional investments by owners. Additional investments result in an inflow of cash because cash is usually received in exchange for the stock issued. Net income is slightly more complicated because the inflows and outflows of cash for operating activities do not usually equal the revenues and expenses included in net income (this topic is discussed later).

Outflows of Cash

There are also three categories of outflows (decreases) of cash:

1. *Increases in Assets Other Than Cash.* The acquisition of assets other than cash results in an outflow of cash because cash is paid in exchange for the assets. Alternatively, the increase in an asset such as accounts receivable causes a decrease in cash because of a smaller cash inflow.

2. *Decreases in Liabilities.* The payment of liabilities results in an outflow of cash because cash is usually paid to satisfy the liabilities.

3. *Decreases in Stockholders' Equity.* Stockholders' equity may decrease as a result of several transactions. Two common transactions are the payment of dividends and the acquisition of treasury stock. In each case a decrease in stockholders' equity is usually accompanied by an outflow of cash.

To summarize, inflows of cash are the results of decreases in assets other than cash and increases in liabilities and/or in stockholders' equity during an accounting period. Outflows of cash are the results of increases in assets other than cash and decreases in liabilities and/or in stockholders' equity during the period. The difference between the inflows and outflows is the change in the cash during the accounting period. This relationship is further illustrated by the equations shown in Exhibit 12–3. Note that these relationships derive from the basic accounting equation. Each equation is a modification of the previous equation to show the eventual increases and decreases of cash. In the statement of cash flows, these increases and decreases are separated into the three categories discussed earlier (i.e., operating, investing, and financing activities) in order to summarize the relevant cash flows for users.

Classifications of Cash Flows

The categories of inflows and outflows of cash discussed in the previous sections can be further classified as relating to operating, investing, and financing activities.

1. *Cash flows from operating activities:*
   a. *Inflows:* Increases in stockholders' equity (i.e., retained earnings) because of certain revenues, adjusted for changes in certain current assets and current liabilities that are related to the operating cycle.

EXHIBIT 12–3   Equations for change in cash

$$\text{Assets} = \text{Liabilities} + \text{Stockholders' Equity}$$

$$\text{Change in Assets} = \text{Change in Liabilities} + \text{Change in Stockholders' Equity}$$

$$\text{Change in Cash} + \text{Change in Assets Other than Cash} = \text{Change in Liabilities} + \text{Change in Stockholders' Equity}$$

$$\text{Change in Cash} = \text{Change in Liabilities} + \text{Change in Stockholders' Equity} - \text{Change in Assets Other than Cash}$$

$$\text{Change in Cash} = \text{Increase in Cash} - \text{Decrease in Cash}$$

where:

$$\text{Increase in Cash} = \text{Increase in Liabilities} + \text{Increase in Stockholders' Equity} + \text{Decrease in Assets Other than Cash}$$

and:

$$\text{Decrease in Cash} = \text{Decrease in Liabilities} + \text{Decrease in Stockholders' Equity} + \text{Increase in Assets Other than Cash}$$

b. *Outflows:* Decreases in stockholders' equity (i.e., retained earnings) because of certain expenses, adjusted for changes in certain current assets and current liabilities that are related to the operating cycle.

2. *Cash flows from investing activities:*
   a. *Inflows:* Decreases in noncurrent assets and certain current assets (e.g., notes receivable and marketable securities).
   b. *Outflows:* Increases in noncurrent assets and certain current assets (e.g., notes receivable and marketable securities).

3. *Cash flows from financing activities:*
   a. *Inflows:* Increases in noncurrent liabilities, stockholders' equity, and certain current liabilities (e.g., notes payable).
   b. *Outflows:* Decreases in noncurrent liabilities, stockholders' equity, and certain current liabilities (e.g., notes payable).

Changes in assets other than cash, liabilities, and stockholders' equity may also result from investing and financing activities *not* affecting cash, as discussed later.

■ NET CASH FLOW FROM OPERATING ACTIVITIES

The generation of positive cash flows from operating activities is critical to the continuity of a company. Therefore, it is useful to understand the relationships between sales revenues, expenses, and cash flows within a company's operating cycle. The calculation of the net cash flow from operating activities, however, is usually the most complex part of the statement of cash flows. For these reasons, additional discussion of this section of the statement is presented here.

A company initially purchases (or produces) inventory for cash or on account. It incurs general and administrative expenses during the period and either pays cash, incurs current liabilities, or eliminates a prepaid asset. To generate sales (cash or credit), it incurs selling expenses and either pays cash or incurs current liabilities. Finally, the company collects its accounts receivable, thereby converting them back into cash. These revenues, expenses, and related cash flows in the operating cycle are illustrated in Exhibit 12–4.

As seen in Exhibit 12–4 each phase of the operating cycle has an impact on both net income and the net cash flow from operating activities. The impact is not likely to be the same for both items, however, because of differences between

EXHIBIT 12–4 Operating cycle: revenues, expenses, and related cash flows

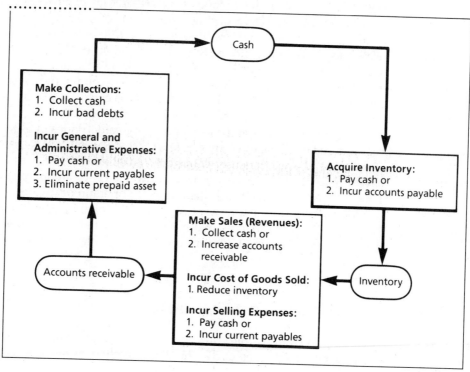

the recognition of revenues and the matching of expenses, and the timing of cash flows. For instance, when inventory is purchased for cash, an outflow of cash occurs, but no expense is recorded. A purchase of inventory on credit increases accounts payable (a current liability) but involves no immediate expense or cash outflow. Later, when the accounts payable is paid, no expense is recorded but a cash outflow occurs. The expense is recorded (as cost of goods sold) when the inventory is sold even though no cash outflow occurs at that time. When a cash sale is made, revenue is recorded and there is a cash inflow. However, when a credit sale is made, both revenue and accounts receivable (a current asset) are increased but no inflow of cash occurs. Later, when the accounts receivable is collected, no revenue is recorded but a cash inflow occurs. Some accounts receivable are not collected so an expense (bad debts) is incurred even though no cash outflow occurs. In addition, throughout the accounting period when selling expenses and general and administrative expenses are paid in cash, expenses are recorded and cash outflows occur. However, when these expenses are accrued at the end of the period, both the expenses and current payables are recorded, but no cash outflows occur. The cash outflows are made in the next accounting period when the liabilities are paid. Furthermore, cash outflows for some of these expenses may occur and be recorded as a current asset in the accounting period before the expenses are recorded (e.g., prepaid insurance).

The basic differences between revenues and cash inflows from operating activities, and between expenses and cash outflows for the operating activities that are discussed in this section, are illustrated in Exhibit 12–5. For example, assume for simplicity that during its first year of operations a company made cash sales of $30,000 and credit sales of $42,000 and collected $37,000 of the related accounts receivable. At the end of the year, the Sales Revenue would be $72,000 and the Accounts Receivable would have a balance of $5,000. As shown in Exhibit 12–6, an analysis of the related T-accounts shows $67,000 in cash provided by operating activities. (This $67,000 is equal to the cash sales of $30,000 plus the collections on accounts receivable of $37,000.)

Similarly, assume that the same company paid salaries of $13,000 during the year and recorded salaries payable of $1,000 at the end of its first year of operations. The Salaries Expense would be $14,000 and the Salaries Payable would have a balance of $1,000. As shown in Exhibit 12–6, an analysis of the related T-account shows $13,000 cash disbursed for operating activities. This company would report a net cash flow of $54,000 from operating activities ($67,000 − $13,000). Additional changes in other current asset and current liability accounts that affect the net cash flow from operating activities are discussed later in the chapter.

Disclosure of Net Cash Flow from Operating Activities

According to *FASB Statement No. 95,* when a company reports its net cash flow from operating activities under the direct method, it must report its operating

EXHIBIT 12–5 Differences between revenues, expenses, and operating cash flows

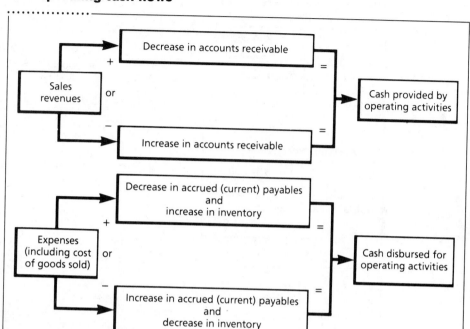

cash inflows separately from its operating cash outflows. Also, certain categories should be used, as discussed in the following sections.

Cash Inflows from Operating Activities

Under the direct method a company should report its cash inflows from operating activities in three categories: (1) collections from customers, (2) interest and dividends collected, and (3) other operating receipts, if any. Generally these cash inflows from operating activities are calculated by an analysis of income statement and balance sheet items as follows:

1. *Collections from customers.* Sales revenue, plus (minus) decrease (increase) in accounts receivable, and plus (minus) increase (decrease) in unearned revenues.

2. *Interest and dividends collected.* Interest revenue and dividend revenue, plus (minus) decrease (increase) in interest or dividends receivable, and plus (minus) amortization of premium (discount) on investment in bonds.

3. *Other operating receipts.* Other revenues and gains, minus gains on disposals of assets and liabilities, and minus (plus) investment income (losses) recognized under the equity method.

EXHIBIT 12–6 Calculation of operating cash flows

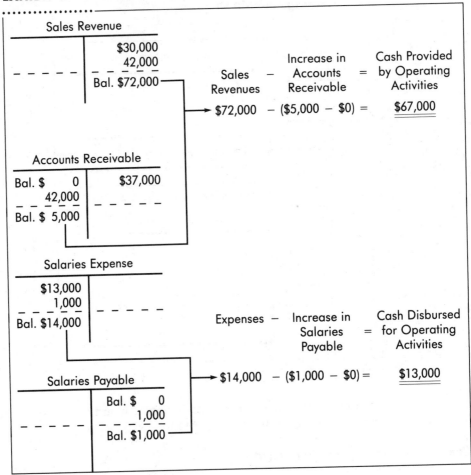

Cash Outflows from Operating Activities

A company should report its cash outflows from operating activities in four categories: (1) payments to suppliers and employees, (2) payments of interest, (3) other operating payments (if any), and (4) payments of income taxes. Generally these cash outflows from operating activities are calculated by an analysis of income statement and balance sheet items as follows:

1. *Payments to suppliers and employees.* Cost of goods sold plus wage expense plus salaries expense, plus (minus) increase (decrease) in inventory, plus (minus) decrease (increase) in accounts payable, wages payable, and/or salaries payable.

2. *Payments of interest.* Interest expense, plus (minus) decrease (increase) in interest payable, plus (minus) amortization of premium (discount) on bonds payable.

EXHIBIT 12–7 Major adjustments to convert income statement amounts to cash flows from operating activities

Income Statement Amounts	Adjustments	Cash Flow
	Cash Inflows from Operating Activities	
Sales revenue	+ Decrease in accounts receivable or − Increase in accounts receivable + Increase in unearned revenues or − Decrease in unearned revenues	= Collections from customers
Interest revenue and dividend revenue	+ Decrease in interest receivable or − Increase in interest receivable + Amortization of premium on investment in bonds − Amortization of discount on investment in bonds	= Interest and dividends collected
Other revenues and gains	− Gains on disposals of assets and liabilities[b] − Investment income (equity method) or + Investment losses (equity method)	= Other operating receipts
	Cash Outflows from Operating Activities	
Cost of goods sold, wage expense, and salaries expense	+ Increase in inventory or − Decrease in inventory + Decrease in accounts payable or − Increase in accounts payable + Decrease in wages and salaries payable or − Increase in wages and salaries payable	= Payments to suppliers and employees[a]
Interest expense	+ Decrease in interest payable or − Increase in interest payable + Amortization of premium on bonds payable − Amortization of discount on bonds payable	= Payments of interest
Other expenses and losses	+ Increase in prepaid expenses or − Decrease in prepaid expenses − Depreciation, depletion, and amortization expense[b] − Losses on disposals of assets and liabilities[b]	= Other operating payments
Income tax expense	+ Decrease in income taxes payable or − Increase in income taxes payable + Decrease in deferred income taxes or − Increase in deferred income taxes	= Payment of income taxes

[a]For a manufacturing company, it is also necessary to subtract the depreciation included in cost of goods sold.
[b]Unless listed as separate items on the income statement

3. *Other operating payments.* Other expenses and losses, plus (minus) increase (decrease) in prepaid expenses, minus depreciation, depletion, and amortization expense, and minus losses on disposals of assets and liabilities.

4. *Payments of income taxes.* Income tax expense, plus (minus) decrease (increase) in income taxes payable, plus (minus) decrease (increase) in deferred income taxes.

These adjustments are further discussed and illustrated later in the chapter. They are also summarized in Exhibit 12–7. These adjustments may have to be modified depending on the manner in which a company reports the related items in its financial statements and the industry in which it operates. For example, the above adjustments have been based on a retail company. For a manufacturing company the cost of goods sold would include depreciation in addition to wage and inventory costs. The depreciation component would therefore have to be subtracted from the cost of goods sold in the computation of the cash payments to suppliers and employees. Also, a retail company would be able to separate payments to suppliers from payments to employees and might choose to report the two amounts separately.

■ PREPARATION OF THE STATEMENT OF CASH FLOWS

Although the user of financial statements is not required to prepare the statement of cash flows, the capability provides additional understanding of the statement. The preparation also helps provide an understanding of the relationships between the cash flow statement and the income statement and the beginning and ending balance sheets included in the annual reports of companies. Furthermore, there may be situations in which the user has only partial information and wants to develop cash flow data. In this section, an informal approach to the preparation is used. More formal methods are illustrated in the Appendix to this chapter.

The preparation of the statement of cash flows is illustrated using the information for the Kit Company in Exhibit 12–8. The balance sheets for December 31, 1992, and 1993, and the income statement for 1993 are presented. To prepare the statement of cash flows, we need to examine the changes in all the items that cause inflows and outflows of cash (i.e., assets other than cash, liabilities, and stockholders' equity) between the two balance sheets and consider the effects of these changes on cash. The Kit Company's statement of cash flows for 1993 is presented in Exhibit 12–9; an explanation of each item from that statement follows.

Net Cash Flow from Operating Activities

The net cash flow from operating activities for the Kit Company includes the collections from customers, the payments to suppliers and employees, the payments of interest, and the payments of taxes.

Collections from Customers. The Kit Company had sales of $600,000 during 1993. Since accounts receivable increased by $6,000 (from $28,000 to $34,000), sales must have exceeded cash collections by $6,000. Therefore, cash received from customers was $594,000. Since this is the only cash flow related to operating activities, it is the total cash provided by operating activities.

Payments to Suppliers and Employees. The Kit Company had cost of goods sold of $200,000 during 1993. Since inventory increased by $15,000 (from $40,000 to $55,000), purchases must have exceeded cost of goods sold by $15,000. Therefore, purchases must have been $215,000. Furthermore, accounts payable increased by $5,000 (from $30,000 to $35,000), indicating that payments were less than purchases. Therefore, cash payments for purchases must have been $210,000. General and administrative expenses were $334,000 during 1993. Since salaries payable decreased by $2,000 (from $5,000 to $3,000), cash payments exceeded the general and administrative expenses. Therefore, the cash payments must have been $336,000. The total payments to suppliers and employees were $546,000 ($210,000 + $336,000). Note that depreciation expense is *not* included in the cash flows because it does not represent either a cash inflow or outflow (as discussed in Chapter 7).

Payments of Interest. The Kit Company incurred interest expense of $6,000 in 1993. Since the premium on bonds payable decreased (which reduces interest expense) by $1,000 (from $5,000 to $4,000) during the year, the cash paid for interest must have exceeded the interest expense. Therefore, the cash payments must have been $7,000.

Payments of Income Taxes. The income tax expense was $15,000 in 1993. Since deferred income taxes increased (which reduces income taxes paid) by $2,000 during the year, the income taxes paid must have been less than the expense. Therefore, the cash payments must have been $13,000. (Note that if the company had income taxes payable, an adjustment for the change in the balance would also have been necessary.)

Summary. The cash provided by operating activities totaled $594,000. The $566,000 cash disbursed for operating activities includes the $546,000 cash paid to suppliers and employees, the $7,000 cash paid for interest, and the $13,000 paid for income taxes. The net cash flow from operations of $28,000 is the cash provided by operating activities less the cash disbursed for operating activities ($594,000 − $566,000).

Cash Flows from Investing Activities

The cash flows from investing activities of the Kit Company consist only of the purchase of property, plant, and equipment.

Purchases of Property, Plant, and Equipment. The property, plant, and equipment increased by $30,000 (from $100,000 to $130,000) because an acquisition

EXHIBIT 12–8

	KIT COMPANY		
	December 31, 1992		December 31, 1993
BALANCE SHEETS			
Current assets			
Cash	$ 27,000		$ 42,000
Accounts receivable	28,000		34,000
Inventory	40,000		55,000
		$ 95,000	$131,000
Noncurrent assets			
Property, plant, and equipment	$100,000		$130,000
Less: accumulated depreciation	(40,000)		(50,000)
		60,000	80,000
Total assets		$155,000	$211,000
Current liabilities			
Accounts payable	$ 30,000		$ 35,000
Salaries payable	5,000		3,000
		$ 35,000	$ 38,000
Noncurrent liabilities			
Bonds payable	$ 50,000		$ 70,000
Premium on bonds payable	5,000		4,000
	$ 55,000		$ 74,000
Deferred income taxes	10,000		12,000
		65,000	86,000
Stockholders' equity			
Common stock, no par	$ 40,000		$ 47,000
Retained earnings	15,000		40,000[a]
		55,000	87,000
Total liabilities and stockholders' equity		$155,000	$211,000

INCOME STATEMENT
FOR YEAR ENDED DECEMBER 31, 1993

Sales	$600,000	
Cost of goods sold	(200,000)	
Gross profit		$400,000
Other expenses		
Depreciation expense	$ 10,000	
General and administrative expenses	334,000	
Interest expense	6,000	
		(350,000)
Income before income taxes		$ 50,000
Income tax expense		(15,000)
Net income		$ 35,000

[a]Balance, 12/31/1992, $15,000 + net income $35,000 − dividends $10,000.

EXHIBIT 12-9

....

KIT COMPANY
Statement of Cash Flows
For Year Ended December 31, 1993

Cash flows from operating activities		
Collections from customers	$594,000	
Cash provided by operating activities		$594,000
Payments to suppliers and employees	$546,000	
Payments of interest and taxes	7,000	
Payments of income taxes	13,000	
Cash disbursed for operating activities		(566,000)
Net cash flow from operating activities		$ 28,000
Cash flows from investing activities		
Purchases of property, plant, and equipment	$(30,000)	
Net cash used by investing activities		(30,000)
Cash flows from financing activities		
Proceeds from issuing common stock	$ 7,000	
Proceeds from issuing bonds	20,000	
Dividends paid	(10,000)	
Net cash provided by financing activities		17,000
Net increase in cash		$ 15,000
Plus: cash balance, January 1, 1993		27,000
Cash balance, December 31, 1993		$ 42,000

occurred (it is assumed that there were no disposals during the year). This amount is a cash outflow for investing activities. Since this is the only cash outflow, the net cash used by investing activities is also $30,000.

Cash Flows from Financing Activities

The cash flows from financing activities for the Kit Company include cash inflows from the issuance of common stock and the issuance of bonds, and cash outflows from the payment of dividends.

Proceeds from Issuing Common Stock. The common stock, no par, increased by $7,000 (from $40,000 to $47,000) because common stock was issued during the year. This amount is a cash inflow from financing activities. It is assumed that no treasury stock was acquired during the year.

Proceeds from Issuing Bonds Payable. The bonds payable increased by $20,000 (from $50,000 to $70,000) because bonds were issued during the year (it is assumed that there were no retirements of bonds). This amount is a cash inflow from financing activities.

Dividends Paid. The Kit Company paid dividends of $10,000. This amount is a cash outflow for financing activities.

The net cash provided by financing activities is $17,000. This amount includes the $7,000 cash received from issuing stock plus the $20,000 cash received from issuing bonds less the $10,000 cash paid for dividends.

The statement of cash flows in Exhibit 12–9 shows a $15,000 net increase of cash, consisting of the net cash flow from operating activities of $28,000, the net cash used by investing activities of $30,000, and the net cash provided by financing activities of $17,000. This calculated increase of $15,000 agrees with the actual increase in cash from $27,000 to $42,000 during the period, as disclosed in the beginning and ending balance sheets and reconciled at the bottom of the statement.

Note that the analysis to prepare the statement of cash flows included the changes in each of the assets other than cash, the liabilities, and the stockholders' equity as follows:

Account Change	Statement of Cash Flows
Accounts receivable	Collections from customers
Inventory	Payments to suppliers
Property, plant, and equipment	Cash flows from investing activities
Accounts payable	Payments to suppliers and employees
Salaries payable	Payments to suppliers and employees
Bonds payable	Cash flows from financing activities
Premium on bonds payable	Payments of interest
Deferred income taxes	Payments of income taxes
Common stock, no par	Cash flows from financing activities
Retained earnings	
Net income	Cash flows from operating activities, which are:
Sales	Collections from customers
Cost of goods sold	Payments to suppliers and employees
General and administrative expenses	Payments to suppliers and employees
Interest expense	Payments of interest
Income tax expense	Payments of income taxes
Dividends paid	Cash flows from financing activities

In the above table, it can be seen that retained earnings was affected by two items, the earning of net income and the payment of dividends. Under this method of calculating cash flows from operating activities, the net income amount is not included in the statement of cash flows, but each component is included as indicated. The one exception is that the depreciation expense of $10,000 is not included because it does not relate to cash flows. Similarly, this list of items does not include the balance sheet item "accumulated depreciation" because the increase of $10,000 (from $40,000 to $50,000) was caused by the recording of depreciation for the period (it is assumed that there are no disposals of property, plant, and equipment). A summary of the amounts affecting the three financial statements is shown in Exhibit 12–10.

When a company uses the direct method for reporting the net cash flow from operating activities, as illustrated so far in this chapter, it must also present a schedule reconciling its net income to its cash flows provided by (used in) operating activities. Effectively, this schedule is the indirect method of computing the net cash flow from operating activities.

■ NET CASH FLOW FROM OPERATING ACTIVITIES: INDIRECT METHOD

As we have seen, the net cash flow from operating activities is the cash provided by operating activities less the cash disbursed for operating activities. As illustrated for the Kit Company, this information may be obtained by adjusting each element (revenues and expenses) of the company's income statement by the changes in the relevant balance sheet account balances. This approach is known as the *direct* method.

An alternative format, the *indirect* method, may be used by companies instead. In this alternative, the net income is adjusted for those items included in the income statement that did *not* result in an inflow or outflow of cash from operating activities. Thus, any noncash transactions are eliminated from net income to determine the net cash flow from operating activities. Also, there are differences between the amounts included in net income and the related cash flows, as discussed earlier in the chapter.

To illustrate this reconciliation, consider the Kit Company income statement and balance sheet information in Exhibit 12–8. The net cash flow from operating activities is reported by beginning with net income and adjusting for differences between income flows and cash flows from operating activities as follows:

Net income	$35,000
Adjustments for differences between income flows and cash flows from operating activities	
Depreciation expense	10,000
Increase in deferred income taxes	2,000
Increase in accounts receivable	(6,000)
Increase in inventory	(15,000)
Increase in accounts payable	5,000
Decrease in salaries payable	(2,000)
Amortization of bond premium	(1,000)
Net cash flow from operating activities	$28,000

Note that the net cash flow from operating activities of $28,000 is the same as shown in Exhibit 12–9. An explanation of each of the adjustments to net income follows.

EXHIBIT 12–10   Relationships among the three financial statements when the net cash flow from operating activities is prepared under the direct method

KIT COMPANY

Beginning Balance Sheet		Income Statement		Cash Flow Statement
Accounts receivable	$28,000	Revenue	$600,000	Collections from customers
Inventory	40,000	Cost of goods sold	(200,000)	Payments to suppliers
PPE (net)	60,000	Depreciation expense	(10,000)	Purchase of PPE
Accounts payable	30,000			
Salaries payable	5,000	G&A expense	(334,000)	Payments to employees
Bonds payable	50,000			Issue bonds
Premium on bonds payable	5,000	Interest expense	(6,000)	Payments of interest
Deferred income taxes	10,000	Income tax expense	(15,000)	Payments of income tax
Common stock, no par	40,000			Issue common stock
Retained earnings	15,000	Net income	$ 35,000	Dividends paid
Cash	27,000			Net increase in cash

Depreciation Expense.   It is important to understand that depreciation expense is not a source of cash. Because the expense of $10,000 was subtracted in the computation of net income but there was no outflow of cash, it must be added back to net income in the computation of net cash flow from operating activities.

Increase in Deferred Income Taxes.   Deferred income taxes increased by $2,000 during the year. Since the income tax expense is $15,000, the income taxes paid must have been $13,000 (in this example there are no income taxes payable). Because the expense of $15,000 was subtracted in the computation of net income but only $13,000 of cash was used, the difference of $2,000 must be added back to net income in the computation of net cash flow from operating activities.

Increase in Accounts Receivable.   Accounts receivable increased by $6,000 during the year, indicating that sales exceeded cash collections. Since the sales of $600,000 were included in the computation of net income but $6,000 less cash was collected, the difference of $6,000 is subtracted from net income in the computation of net cash flow from operating activities.

Increase in Inventory and Increase in Accounts Payable.   Inventory increased by $15,000, indicating that purchases exceeded cost of goods sold. Since the cost of goods sold was $200,000, purchases must have been $215,000. Accounts pay-

EXHIBIT 12–10 *(continued)*

···················

Cash Flow Statement

Operating Activities	Investing Activities	Financing Activities	Ending Balance Sheet	
$594,000			Accounts receivable	$34,000
(210,000)ᵃ			Inventory	55,000
	$(30,000)		PPE (net)	80,000
ᵃ			Accounts payable	35,000
(336,000)			Salaries payable	3,000
		$20,000	Bonds payable	70,000
			Premium on bonds	
(7,000)			payable	4,000
(13,000)			Deferred income taxes	12,000
		7,000	Common stock, no par	47,000
		(10,000)	Retained earnings	40,000
$ 28,000	$(30,000)	$17,000		
	15,000		Cash	42,000

ᵃPurchases = Cost of goods sold + Increase (− Decrease) in Inventory
Payments = Purchases − Increase (+ Decrease) in Accounts payable
$210,000 = $200,000 + ($55,000 − $40,000) − ($35,000 − $30,000)
Note: The parentheses indicate subtractions in the vertical columns (i.e., they indicate neither debits and credits, nor subtractions in the horizontal rows).

able increased by $5,000, indicating that payments were less than purchases. Since purchases were $215,000, payments must have been $210,000. Because cost of goods sold (of $200,000) was subtracted in the computation of net income but $10,000 more cash was used, the difference of $10,000 must be subtracted from net income in the computation of the net cash flow from operating activities. This net subtraction is accomplished by subtracting the $15,000 increase in inventory and adding the $5,000 increase in accounts payable.

Decrease in Salaries Payable. Salaries payable decreased by $2,000, indicating that cash payments were greater than general and administrative expenses. Since these expenses were $334,000, payments must have been $336,000. Because the expenses were subtracted in the computation of net income, but $336,000 cash was used, the difference of $2,000 must be subtracted from net income in the computation of the net cash flow from operating activities.

Decrease in Premium on Bonds Payable. The premium on bonds payable decreased by $1,000 during the year. Since the bond interest expense was $6,000, the cash paid for interest must have been $7,000. Because the expense was subtracted in the computation of net income but $7,000 cash was used, the difference of $1,000 must be subtracted from net income in the computation of the net cash flow from operating activities.

EXHIBIT 12–11   Relationships among the three financial statements when the net cash flow from operating activities is prepared under the indirect method

KIT COMPANY

Beginning Balance Sheet		Income Statement		Cash Flow Statement
Accounts receivable	$28,000	Revenue	$600,000	Increase in A/R
Inventory	40,000	Cost of goods sold	(200,000)	Increase in inventory
PPE (net)	60,000	Depreciation expense	(10,000)	Depreciation expense
				Purchase of PPE
Accounts payable	30,000			Increase in A/P
Salaries payable	5,000	G&A expense	(334,000)	Decrease in S/P
Bonds payable	50,000			Issue bonds
Premium on bonds				
payable	5,000	Interest expense	(6,000)	Amortization of premium
Deferred income taxes	10,000	Income tax expense	(15,000)	Increase in DIT
Common stock, no par	40,000			Issue common stock
Retained earnings	15,000	Net income	35,000	Net income
				Dividends paid
Cash	27,000			Net increase in cash

A summary of the amounts affecting the three financial statements is shown in Exhibit 12-11. Under the indirect method, other items that did not result in an inflow or outflow of cash for *operating* activities may also be adjustments to net income. The more common items and the chapter in which each is discussed are listed in Exhibit 12–12. A complete cash flow statement with the cash flow from operating activities computed under the indirect method is illustrated in Exhibit 12–17.

Before the FASB adopted the requirement that the statement of cash flows must be reported, a statement of changes in financial position was presented instead. In this statement, the indirect method was used almost exclusively in the published financial reports of companies. Companies may select either the direct or indirect method for the statement of cash flows, but past experience indicates that the indirect approach will be more popular. While either method is allowed, if a company uses the direct method it must also include a separate schedule that reconciles its net income to its cash flows provided by (or used in) operating activities (i.e., the indirect method). Because of the previous use of the indirect method and the extra disclosures required under the direct method, most companies use the indirect method. In a recent survey, over 97% of companies used the indirect method.[2] It is possible, however, that more companies

[2]"Accounting Trends and Techniques" (New York: AICPA, 1989), p. 372.

EXHIBIT 12–11   *(continued)*

Cash Flow Statement				
Operating Activities	**Investing Activities**	**Financing Activities**	**Ending Balance Sheet**	
$ (6,000)			Accounts receivable	$34,000
(15,000)			Inventory	55,000
10,000			⎰ PPE (net)	80,000
	$(30,000)		⎱	
5,000			Accounts payable	35,000
(2,000)			Salaries payable	3,000
		$20,000	Bonds payable	70,000
			Premium on bonds	
(1,000)			payable	4,000
2,000			Deferred income taxes	12,000
		7,000	Common stock, no par	47,000
35,000			⎰ Retained earnings	40,000
		(10,000)	⎱	
$28,000	$(30,000)	$17,000		
	15,000		Cash	42,000

Note: The parentheses indicate subtractions in the vertical columns (i.e., they indicate neither debits and credits, nor subtractions in the horizontal rows).

will use the direct method as they become familiar with it, and the FASB encourages the use of the *direct* method.

One of the reasons for the popularity of the indirect method is that it "ties" the net income reported on a company's income statement to the net cash provided by operating activities reported on the company's statement of cash flows. Also, the indirect method shows how the change in the elements of a company's operating cycle (current assets and current liabilities) affected its operating cash flow. Thus it may be argued that the indirect method shows the "quality" of income by providing information about intervals of leads and lags between income and operating cash flows.

■ ADDITIONAL EXAMPLES

In the preceding examples, only one item caused the change in each balance sheet item (except retained earnings). However, more than one transaction or event often causes the change in the balance sheet amounts and there may be one or more related cash flows. Two examples of these more complex situations are discussed here.

Cash Flows Related to Property, Plant, and Equipment

The typical transactions and events that affect property, plant, and equipment and the related accumulated depreciation are acquisitions, disposals, and rec-

EXHIBIT 12–12   Adjustments to net income to convert to net cash flow from operating activities

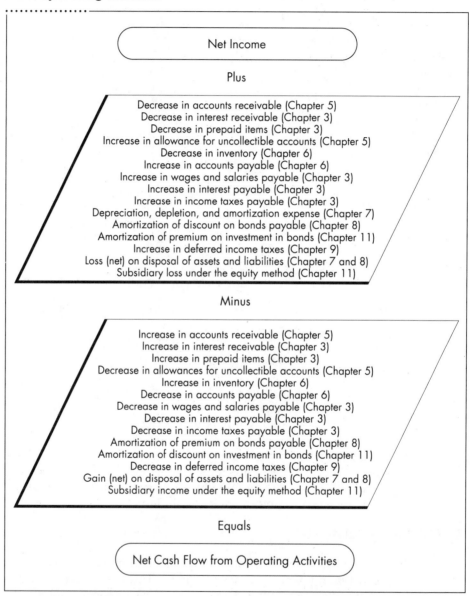

Net Income

Plus

Decrease in accounts receivable (Chapter 5)
Decrease in interest receivable (Chapter 3)
Decrease in prepaid items (Chapter 3)
Increase in allowance for uncollectible accounts (Chapter 5)
Decrease in inventory (Chapter 6)
Increase in accounts payable (Chapter 6)
Increase in wages and salaries payable (Chapter 3)
Increase in interest payable (Chapter 3)
Increase in income taxes payable (Chapter 3)
Depreciation, depletion, and amortization expense (Chapter 7)
Amortization of discount on bonds payable (Chapter 8)
Amortization of premium on investment in bonds (Chapter 11)
Increase in deferred income taxes (Chapter 9)
Loss (net) on disposal of assets and liabilities (Chapter 7 and 8)
Subsidiary loss under the equity method (Chapter 11)

Minus

Increase in accounts receivable (Chapter 5)
Increase in interest receivable (Chapter 3)
Increase in prepaid items (Chapter 3)
Decrease in allowances for uncollectible accounts (Chapter 5)
Increase in inventory (Chapter 6)
Decrease in accounts payable (Chapter 6)
Decrease in wages and salaries payable (Chapter 3)
Decrease in interest payable (Chapter 3)
Decrease in income taxes payable (Chapter 3)
Amortization of premium on bonds payable (Chapter 8)
Amortization of discount on investment in bonds (Chapter 11)
Decrease in deferred income taxes (Chapter 9)
Gain (net) on disposal of assets and liabilities (Chapter 7 and 8)
Subsidiary income under the equity method (Chapter 11)

Equals

Net Cash Flow from Operating Activities

ording depreciation. To illustrate, suppose that between the beginning and ending balance sheet a company's property, plant, and equipment increased from $150,000 to $180,000 and the increase was caused by an acquisition of an asset for $60,000 and a sale of another asset which had originally cost $30,000. Also, suppose that the accumulated depreciation increased from $70,000 to $80,000 and the increase was caused by recording depreciation expense of $35,000 and the elimination of accumulated depreciation on the asset sold of $25,000. These situations would have four impacts on the statement of cash flows and its related schedules. The acquisition would be a cash outflow for investing activities of $60,000. The disposal would result in a cash inflow from investing activities. The book value of the asset sold was $5,000 ($30,000 − $25,000), but the amount of the cash received would be affected by any gain or loss on the sale. If we assume that there was a gain of $4,000, the cash inflow would be $9,000. The depreciation expense and the gain do not affect the statement of cash flows under the direct method. However, they are added and subtracted, respectively, to net income if the indirect method is used.

This example may be summarized as follows:

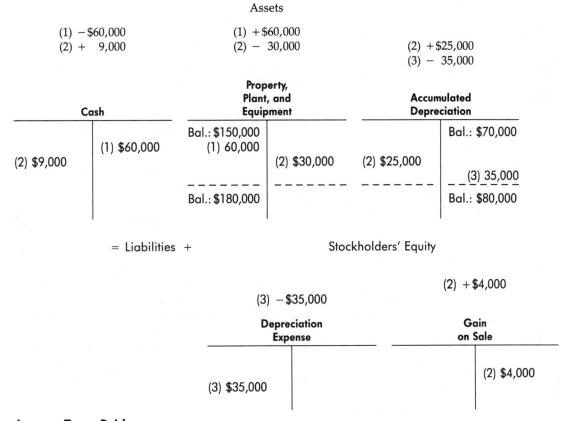

Assets

(1) − $60,000
(2) + 9,000

(1) + $60,000
(2) − 30,000

(2) + $25,000
(3) − 35,000

Cash

(2) $9,000

(1) $60,000

Property, Plant, and Equipment

Bal.: $150,000
(1) 60,000

(2) $30,000

Bal.: $180,000

Accumulated Depreciation

Bal.: $70,000

(2) $25,000

(3) 35,000

Bal.: $80,000

= Liabilities +

Stockholders' Equity

(2) + $4,000

(3) − $35,000

Depreciation Expense

(3) $35,000

Gain on Sale

(2) $4,000

Income Taxes Paid

Accounting for income taxes affects income tax expense, income taxes payable, and deferred income taxes. To illustrate, suppose that between the beginning and ending balance sheets income taxes payable decreased from $40,000 to $35,000 while deferred income taxes increased from $55,000 to $75,000. Suppose also that the company reported an income tax expense of $100,000 in its income statement. The income tax expense ($100,000) minus the increase in the deferred income taxes ($20,000) gives the amount of the income tax obligation for the year ($80,000). Since the company owes $5,000 less at the end of the year than it did at the beginning, during the year it has paid $5,000 more than its obligation for the year. Therefore, the company paid income taxes of $85,000 and the statement of cash flows would include a cash outflow from operating activities for income taxes paid of this amount under the direct method. The decrease in the income taxes payable and the increase in the deferred income taxes would be subtracted and added, respectively, to net income if the indirect method is used.

ADDITIONAL TOPICS

Companies using the indirect method of reporting operating cash flows must also disclose their interest *paid* and income taxes *paid*. These disclosures are often included in the related note. Thus, the income taxes paid may be included in the income tax disclosure note rather than being related to the cash flow statement. These disclosures are computed in the same way as discussed for the direct method earlier in the chapter and summarized in Exhibit 12–7. These disclosures provide useful information without requiring the user to make computations.

Banks, brokers, and dealers in securities, and similar companies often hold loans for resale on a short-term basis or carry securities in a trading account. A **trading account** includes securities that are acquired specifically for resale and are turned over very quickly. In these situations, the cash flows from the purchases and sales of these securities are reported in the operating activities section of the cash flow statement.[3] This disclosure is different than that for other companies for which the cash flows are reported as investing activities. The rationale for this disclosure difference is that these types of assets for financial institutions are similar to inventory for other companies, and therefore are part of the operating cycle.

Generally, companies are *not* allowed to net cash outflows against cash inflows for reporting the results of related investing or financing activities. An exception is made for certain activities of banks and other financial institutions.[4] These companies are allowed to report the net cash flows for (1) deposits and withdrawals with other financial institutions, (2) time deposits accepted and repaid, and (3) loans made to customers and principal collections of these loans. This difference is allowed because showing these items on a "gross" basis provides information that is of limited value to users and is costly for the company to accumulate.

· ·

[3]"Statement of Cash Flows—Exemption of Certain Enterprises and Classification of Cash Flows from Certain Securities Acquired for Resale," *FASB Statement of Financial Accounting Standards No. 102* (Norwalk, Conn.: FASB, 1989).
[4]"Statement of Cash Flows—Net Reporting of Certain Cash Receipts and Cash Payments and Classification of Cash Flows from Hedging Transactions," *FASB Statement of Financial Accounting Standards No. 104* (Norwalk, Conn.: FASB, 1989).

A separate item included in the cash flow statement is the effect of changes in foreign exchange rates on cash balances held in foreign currencies. For example, if a company held 1,000 British pounds while the exchange rate changed from $1.40 to $1.60 per pound, it has an increase in the amount of equivalent dollars it holds from $1,400 to $1,600. This increase, or gain, of $200 is included as a separate category in the cash flow statement.

■ NONCASH INVESTING AND FINANCING ACTIVITIES

In addition to the analysis we have used for the statement of cash flows, it is necessary to disclose other items that are important aspects of a company's investing and financing activities, even though cash was not *directly* affected. In other words, it is necessary to report on the results of *all* investing and financing activities. Therefore, a separate schedule of the investing and financing activities that did not affect cash inflows or cash outflows is included with the statement of cash flows. Alternatively, a narrative description in the notes to the financial statements is often used.

For example, suppose that a company acquires land by issuing common stock. This transaction does not affect cash but is disclosed because of its importance to the investing and financing activities. The issuance of the common stock is a financing activity not affecting cash, and the acquisition of the land is an investing activity not affecting cash. Another example is the signing of a capital lease resulting in the acquisition of a noncurrent asset (investing activity) and the incurrence of a noncurrent liability (financing activity). Similarly, the conversion of bonds or preferred stock into common stock results in the reduction of bonds payable or preferred stock (financing activity) and the issuance of common stock (financing activity). Examples of the inclusion of these noncash investing and financing activities in the preparation of a statement of cash flows and accompanying schedule are included in the Appendix to this chapter and illustrated in Exhibit 12–17.

■ APPENDIX: PREPARATION OF A STATEMENT OF CASH FLOWS — PROCEDURES

The preparation of a statement of cash flows is illustrated for both the direct and indirect methods. A different example is used in each situation. So that either (or both) method may be selected for study, there is a certain amount of duplication in the various explanations.

■ PREPARATION OF A STATEMENT OF CASH FLOWS: THE DIRECT METHOD

When beginning the preparation of the statement of cash flows for a company, it is helpful to remember that the statement has three sections: (1) the cash flows from operating activities, (2) the cash flows from investing activities, and (3) the cash flows from financing activities.

Information Requirements

When preparing the statement of cash flows, it is necessary to analyze the changes in the assets other than cash, the liabilities, and stockholders' equity. For the direct method, the analysis is normally prepared on an eight-column worksheet (see Exhibit 12–13). Information from the following financial statements of the current period is required for this analysis:

1. The beginning and ending balance sheets
2. The income statement
3. Other supplemental information concerning the reasons for the changes in the accounts

Steps in Preparation

After gathering the preceding information several steps must be completed to prepare the statement of cash flows. These steps are summarized next, after which a comprehensive example is used to explain each step.

Step 1.   Enter the titles of all the assets, liabilities, and stockholders' equity and list each beginning and ending balance. Compute the debit or credit change in each account (see Exhibit 12–13). List each revenue and expense from the income statement.

Step 2.   Add the following headings to the lower part of the worksheet:

a. Cash Flows from Operating Activities
b. Cash Flows from Investing Activities
c. Cash Flows from Financing Activities
d. Noncash Investing and Financing Activities (if necessary)

Step 3.   Account for all the changes in the relevant (noncash) accounts that occurred during the current period. *Reconstruct* the entries that caused the changes in each account directly on the worksheet, making certain modifications to show the effects on cash flows. *Remember* that the actual entries that caused the changes have already been recorded. In this step we are simply reconstructing the entries on the worksheet to prepare the statement of cash flows. In the upper part of the worksheet, the relevant accounts are analyzed. In the lower part, the effects on cash flows are recorded.

The following general rules should be used for reconstructing the entries:

A. **Start with the revenues and expenses.** The amounts in these accounts during the year represent potential operating cash inflows and outflows. Therefore, for revenues, the entry on the worksheet is to increase (debit) the related operating cash inflow in the Cash Flows from Operating Activities in the lower part of the worksheet and to increase (credit) the revenue account in the upper part of the worksheet. For expenses, the entry is to increase (credit) the related operating cash *outflow* in the Cash Flows from Operating Activities in the lower part of the worksheet and to increase (debit) the expense account in the upper part of the worksheet.

Note that there are two exceptions to these procedures. First, the worksheet entries for any *noncash* revenues and expenses (e.g., depreciation expense) are recorded only in the upper part of the worksheet and therefore not included in the statement of cash flows. Second, worksheet entries are *not* prepared at this time for gains or losses. These are accounted for when the investing and financing transactions to which they relate are analyzed.

B. **Account for the changes in the current assets other than cash and the current liabilities.** Since most of these changes are part of the operating cycle, their impacts are listed as adjustments to the related cash inflow or outflow from operating activities. Review each account and determine the entry responsible for its change. If the entry affects cash, the entry on the worksheet is to show the increase (debit) in the current asset other than cash, or the decrease (debit) in the current liability in the upper part and a decrease (credit) in the cash inflows from, or an increase (credit) in the cash outflows. Similarly, a decrease (credit) in a current asset other than cash, or an increase (credit) in a current liability, is accompanied by an increase (debit) in the cash inflows or a decrease (debit) in the cash outflows.

Note that there is an exception to this procedure for changes in current notes receivable and payable, marketable securities, and dividends payable. These changes are the results of investing and financing activities.

C. **Account for the changes in the remaining current assets (except cash) and current liabilities, noncurrent assets, noncurrent liabilities, and stockholders' equity.** Review each account and determine the entry responsible for its change. If the entry affects cash, the entry on the worksheet is to show the increase (debit) in the asset in the upper part and a decrease (credit) in the Cash Flows from Investing Activities in the lower part. Alternately, the entry is to show the decrease (debit) in the liability or stockholders' equity in the upper part and a decrease (credit) in the Cash Flows from Financing Activities. Similarly, a decrease (credit) in the asset in the upper part is accompanied by an increase (debit) in the Cash Flows from Investing Activities, and an increase (credit) in a liability or stockholders' equity is accompanied by an increase (debit) in the Cash Flows from Financing Activities.

Note the distinction between the recording of the current items and the noncurrent items. Most of the current items affect the net cash flow from operations, whereas all the noncurrent items affect the cash from either investing activities or financing activities.

D. **If the investing or financing activity does not affect cash, it is a noncash investing or financing activity.** For this type of transaction, "expanded" entries are necessary. One entry shows the increase in investing or financing activities, whereas the other entry shows the decrease in investing or financing activities.

EXHIBIT 12–13

COPELAND COMPANY
Worksheet for Statement of Cash Flows
For Year Ended December 31, 1993

Accounts	12/31/92 Balance Sheet Debit	Credit	12/31/93 Balance Sheet and 1993 Income Statement Debit	Credit	Change Debit	Credit	Worksheet Entries Debit	Credit
Cash	5,300		9,800		4,500		(r) 4,500	
Accounts receivable	9,600		10,900		1,300		(i) 1,300	
Inventory	12,500		11,000			1,500		(i) 1,500
Investments	22,000		20,000			2,000		(n) 2,000
Property and equipment	82,600		107,300		24,700		(o) 24,700	
Accumulated depreciation		32,800		41,900		9,100		(h) 9,100
Accounts payable		10,300		12,100		1,800		(k) 1,800
Salaries payable		1,100		800	300		(l) 300	
Interest payable		300		500		200		(m) 200
Notes payable		34,000		34,000		—		
Common stock, no par		30,000		40,000		10,000		(p) 10,000
Retained earnings		23,500		20,000	3,500		(q) 3,500	
Sales				98,700		98,700		(a) 98,700
Interest revenue				2,500		2,500		(b) 2,500
Gain on sale of investments				800		800		(n) 800
Cost of goods sold			51,000		51,000		(c) 51,000	
Salaries expense			23,000		23,000		(d) 23,000	
Depreciation expense			9,100		9,100		(h) 9,100	
Interest expense			4,000		4,000		(e) 4,000	
Other expenses			1,900		1,900		(f) 1,900	
Income tax expense			3,300		3,300		(g) 3,300	
Totals	132,000	132,000	251,300	251,300	126,600	126,600	126,600	126,600

EXHIBIT 12–13 *(continued)*

	Worksheet Entries		
Accounts		**Debit**	**Credit**
Cash flows from operating activities			
Collections from customers	(a)	98,700	(i)	1,300
Interest and dividends collected	(b)	2,500		
Other operating receipts		—		
Payments to suppliers and employees	(j)	1,500	(c)	51,000
	(k)	1,800	(d)	23,000
			(l)	300
Payments of interest	(m)	200	(e)	4,000
Other operating payments			(f)	1,900
Payments of income taxes			(g)	3,300
Cash flows from investing activities				
Proceeds from sale of investments	(n)	2,800		
Payment for purchase of equipment			(o)	24,700
Cash flows from financing activities				
Proceeds from issuance of common stock	(p)	10,000		
Payment of dividends			(q)	3,500
Net increase in cash			(r)	4,500
Totals		117,500		117,500

Step 4.   The final entry on the worksheet records the change in cash. The net increase (or decrease) in cash must be equal to the change in cash balance between the beginning and ending balance sheet.

Before we illustrate these four steps in an example, recall the equation developed in Exhibit 12–3:

$$\begin{array}{ccccc} \text{Change in} & = & \text{Change in} & + & \text{Change in} & - & \text{Change in} \\ \text{Cash} & & \text{Liabilities} & & \text{Stockholders'} & & \text{Assets Other} \\ & & & & \text{Equity} & & \text{than Cash} \end{array}$$

The right-hand side of the equation includes the accounts analyzed in the upper part of the worksheet. The change in cash on the left-hand side of the equation is the net increase (or decrease) in cash in the lower part of the worksheet. Another way to consider the relationship is to think of the right-hand side of the equation as the *causes* of the changes in cash and the left-hand side as the *effects* on cash.

Comprehensive Example: Direct Method

The preparation of the worksheet for the statement of cash flows of the Copeland Company is illustrated. The information from the beginning balance sheet and the income statement and balance sheet at the end of the year is presented directly on the worksheet in Exhibit 12–13 and the Statement of Cash Flows is presented in Exhibit 12–14. In this example, there are no noncash investing and financing activities. The following information was also obtained from the Copeland Company's accounting records for 1993:

a. Investments costing $2,000 were sold for $2,800.

b. Equipment was purchased at a cost of $24,700.

c. Common stock was issued for $10,000.

d. Dividends of $3,500 were declared and paid.

After entering the accounts and amounts, the changes in the accounts are entered in the appropriate change column of the worksheet. Then, based on the preceding information, entries (a) through (r) are entered on the worksheet. Each of the worksheet entries is briefly explained below.

Entries (a) and (b) account for the sales and interest revenue and record the potential collections from customers and receipts of interest. (There are no other operating receipts.) Entries (c), (d), (e), (f), and (g) account for the cost of goods sold, salaries expense, interest expense, other expenses, and income tax expense; and record the "potential" payments to suppliers and employees, payments of interest, other operating payments, and payments of income taxes. Entry (h) accounts for the depreciation expense and increase in accumulated depreciation. Note that it is made in the upper portion of the worksheet, and therefore has no impact on the operating cash flows. The entry is necessary, however, to help account for the changes in all the income statement and balance sheet accounts.

Entries (i) through (m) account for the impact of the changes in the current

EXHIBIT 12–14

COPELAND COMPANY Statement of Cash Flows For Year Ended December 31, 1993		
Cash flows from operating activities		
Cash inflows:		
Collections from customers	$ 97,400	
Interest and dividends collected	2,500	
Cash inflows from operating activities		$99,900
Cash outflows:		
Payments to suppliers and employees	$(71,000)	
Payments of interest	(3,800)	
Other operating payments	(1,900)	
Payments of income taxes	(3,300)	
Cash outflows for operating activities		(80,000)
Net cash provided by operating activities		$19,900
Cash flows from investing activities		
Proceeds from sale of investments	$ 2,800	
Payment for purchase of equipment	(24,700)	
Net cash used for investing activities		(21,900)
Cash flows from financing activities		
Proceeds from issuance of common stock	$ 10,000	
Payment of dividends	(3,500)	
Net cash provided by financing activities		6,500
Net increase in cash		$ 4,500
Plus: cash balance, January 1, 1993		5,300
Cash balance, December 31, 1993		$ 9,800

assets and current liabilities upon the "potential" operating cash flows recorded earlier. Entry (i) reduces the collections from customers because of the increase in accounts receivable. Entries (j) and (k) reduce the payments to suppliers and employees because of the decrease in inventory and the increase in accounts payable. Entry (l) increases the payments to suppliers and employees because of the decrease in salaries payable. Finally, entry (m) reduces the interest payments because of the increase in interest payable. There are no adjustments to the other operating payments or to the payments of income taxes in this example.

Entries (n) through (q) record the investing and financing cash flows. Entry (n) records the $2,800 investing cash inflow from the sale of investments costing $2,000. Note that the $800 gain is recorded in the usual manner and accounts for that respective income statement item. Entry (o) records the investing cash outflow for the purchase of equipment. Entry (p) records the financing cash inflow from the sale of common stock. Entry (q) records the financing cash outflow for the payment of dividends.

Entry (r) is the final entry and records the increase in cash. The debit and credit columns in the upper and lower portions are totaled to check for equality and the worksheet is complete. The statement of cash flows of the Copeland Company, prepared from the worksheet in Exhibit 12–13, is shown in Exhibit 12–14.

■ PREPARATION OF A STATEMENT OF CASH FLOWS: THE INDIRECT METHOD

When beginning the preparation of the statement of cash flows for a company, it is helpful to remember that the statement has three sections: (1) the cash flow from operating activities, (2) the cash flows from investing activities, and (3) the cash flows from financing activities. Note also that a schedule of the noncash investing and financing activities is included in this example.

Information Requirements

When preparing the statement of cash flows, it is necessary to analyze the changes in the assets other than cash, the liabilities, and stockholders' equity. For the indirect method, the analysis is normally prepared on a five-column worksheet (see Exhibit 12–16). Information from the following financial statements of the current period is required for this analysis:

1. The beginning and ending balance sheets
2. The income statement
3. The retained earnings statement
4. Other supplemental information concerning the reasons for the changes in the accounts

Steps in Preparation

After gathering the preceding information, several steps must be completed to prepare the statement of cash flows. These steps are summarized next, after which a comprehensive example is used to explain each step.

Step 1.   Enter the titles of all the assets, liabilities, and stockholders' equity and list each beginning and ending balance. Those accounts with debit balances are listed first, followed by those with credit balances. Compute the debit or credit change in each account. (see Exhibit 12–16).

Step 2.   Add the following headings to the lower part of the worksheet:

a. Cash Flows from Operating Activities
b. Cash Flows from Investing Activities
c. Cash Flows from Financing Activities
d. Noncash Investing and Financing Activities (if necessary)

Step 3. Account for all the changes in the relevant (noncash) accounts that occurred during the current period. *Reconstruct* the entries that caused the changes in each account directly on the worksheet, making certain modifications to show the effects on cash flows. *Remember* that the actual entries that caused the changes have already been recorded. In this step we are simply reconstructing the entries on the worksheet to prepare the statement of cash flows. In the upper part of the worksheet, the relevant accounts are analyzed. In the lower part, the effects on cash flows are recorded.

The following general rules should be used for reconstructing the entries:

A. **Start with net income.** The net income is a summary of all the entries from operations affecting cash and retained earnings. Consequently, the entry on the worksheet is to show the net income as an increase (debit) in the Cash Flows from Operating Activities in the lower part of the worksheet and an increase (credit) in Retained Earnings in the upper part of the worksheet. Alternately, if there is a net loss, the entry on the worksheet is to show the net loss as a decrease (credit) in the Cash Flows from Operating Activities in the lower part of the worksheet and a decrease (debit) in Retained Earnings in the upper part of the worksheet.

B. **Account for the changes in the current assets other than cash and the current liabilities.** Review each account and determine the entry responsible for its change. If the entry affects cash, the entry on the worksheet is to show the increase (debit) in the current asset other than cash or the decrease (debit) in the current liability in the upper part and a decrease (credit) in the Cash Flows from Operating Activities. Similarly, a decrease (credit) in a current asset other than cash or an increase (credit) in a current liability is accompanied by an increase (debit) in the Cash Flows from Operating Activities. Note that there is an exception to this procedure for changes in current notes receivable and payable, marketable securities, and dividends payable. These changes are the results of investing and financing activities.

C. **Account for the changes in the remaining current assets (except cash) and current liabilities, noncurrent assets, noncurrent liabilities, and stockholders' equity.** Review each account and determine the entry responsible for its change. If the entry affects cash, the entry on the worksheet is to show the increase (debit) in the asset in the upper part and a decrease (credit) in the Cash Flows from Investing Activities in the lower part. Alternately, the entry is to show the decrease (debit) in the liability or stockholders' equity in the upper part and a decrease (credit) in the Cash Flows from Financing Activities. Similarly, a decrease (credit) in the asset in the upper part is accompanied by an increase (debit) in the Cash Flows from Investing Activities and an increase (credit) in a liability or stockholders' equity is accompanied by an increase (debit) in the Cash Flows from Financing Activities.

Note the distinction between the recording of the current items and the noncurrent items. Most of the current items affect the net cash flow from operating activities, whereas all the noncurrent items affect the cash flow from either investing activities or financing activities.

D. **If the entry affects a noncash income statement item** (e.g., depreciation expense, gains, or losses), the entry on the worksheet is to show the effect on the appropriate accounts in the upper part (e.g., credit accumulated depreciation) and include it as an adjustment (e.g., debit depreciation expense) to the Cash Flows from Operating Activities in the lower part of the worksheet.

E. **If the entry does not affect cash, it is a noncash investing or financing activity.** For this type of transaction, "expanded" entries are necessary. One entry shows the increase in the cash flow from investing or financing activities, whereas the other entry shows the decrease in the cash flow from investing or financing activities.

Step 4. The final entry on the worksheet records the change in cash. The net increase (or decrease) in cash must be equal to the change in cash balance between the beginning and ending balance sheet.

Before we illustrate these four steps in an example, recall the equation developed in Exhibit 12–3:

$$\begin{array}{ccccc} \text{Change in} = & \text{Change in} + & \text{Change in} & - & \text{Change in} \\ \text{Cash} & \text{Liabilities} & \text{Stockholders'} & & \text{Assets Other} \\ & & \text{Equity} & & \text{than Cash} \end{array}$$

The right-hand side of the equation includes the accounts analyzed in the upper part of the worksheet. The change in cash on the left-hand side of the equation is the net increase (or decrease) in cash in the lower part of the worksheet. Another way to consider the relationship is to think of the right-hand side of the equation as the *causes* of the changes in cash and the left-hand side as the *effects* on cash.

Comprehensive Example: Indirect Method

The preparation of the worksheet for the statement of cash flows of the Symes Company is illustrated. The condensed financial information is presented in Exhibit 12–15. The worksheet is presented in Exhibit 12–16 and the Statement of Cash Flows is presented in Exhibit 12–17. The entries to account for the changes in the various accounts are entered on the worksheet. Each worksheet entry is discussed next and is listed (a) through (l) for reference.

The analysis begins with a worksheet entry to record net income as the initial source of cash from operating activities. The net income is a summary amount including cash flows from operating activities. Net income caused an increase in both cash and retained earnings. The increase (credit) in Retained Earnings of $4,300 is recorded in the upper part of the worksheet and the increase (debit) in the Cash Flows from Operating Activities in the lower part of the worksheet (item a).

The accounts receivable decreased $400 during the year. This occurred because cash collections exceeded credit sales by this amount. To show the additional cash inflow from operating activities, the decrease (credit) in Accounts Receivable is recorded in the upper part of the worksheet and the increase (debit) of $400

EXHIBIT 12–15

SYMES COMPANY
Condensed Financial Information

1. Balance sheet information:

	Balances	
Accounts	**12/31/92**	**12/31/93**
Cash	$ 500	$ 1,500
Accounts receivable	1,400	1,000
Inventory	2,000	3,800
Land	5,200	7,200
Equipment	23,700	28,200
Accumulated depreciation	(1,000)	(1,300)
	$31,800	$40,400
Accounts payable	$ 2,100	$ 1,200
Salaries payable	400	600
Bonds payable	-0-	4,000
Common stock, $10 par	8,000	8,500
Additional paid-in capital	16,000	17,500
Retained earnings	5,300	8,600
	$31,800	$40,400

2. Income statement information:

Sales		$ 7,000
Operating expenses:		
Depreciation expense	$ 700	
Other operating expenses	2,200	(2,900)
Operating income		$ 4,100
Other revenues:		
Gain on sale of equipment		200
Net income		$ 4,300

3. Retained earnings information:

Beginning retained earnings	$ 5,300
Add: net income	4,300
	$ 9,600
Less: dividends	(1,000)
Ending retained earnings	$ 8,600

4. Supplemental information for 1993 (including data from the income statement and retained earnings statement above and from a review of the transactions affecting various accounts during the year):
   a. Net income is $4,300.
   b. Dividends declared and paid are $1,000.
   c. Equipment was purchased at a cost of $5,600.
   d. Ten-year bonds payable with face value of $4,000 were issued for $4,000.
   e. Depreciation expense for the year is $700.
   f. Land was acquired through the issuance of 50 shares of $10 par common stock when the stock was selling at a market price of $40 per share.
   g. Equipment with a cost of $1,100 and a book value of $700 was sold for $900.

EXHIBIT 12–16

SYMES COMPANY
Worksheet for Statement of Cash Flows
For Year Ended December 31, 1993

Account Titles	Balances 12/31/1992	Balances 12/31/1993	Change	Worksheet Entries Debit		Worksheet Entries Credit	
Debits							
Cash	$ 500	$ 1,500	$1,000	(l)	$ 1,000		
Noncash Accounts:							
Accounts receivable	1,400	1,000	(400)			(b) $	400
Inventory	2,000	3,800	1,800	(c)	1,800		
Land	5,200	7,200	2,000	(k-1)	2,000		
Equipment	23,700	28,200	4,500	(f)	5,600	(g)	1,100
Totals	$32,800	$41,700	$8,900				
Credits							
Accumulated depreciation	$ 1,000	$ 1,300	$ 300	(g)	400	(h)	700
Accounts payable	2,100	1,200	(900)	(d)	900		
Salaries payable	400	600	200			(e)	200
Bonds payable	-0-	4,000	4,000			(i)	4,000
Common stock, $10 par	8,000	8,500	500			(k-2)	500
Additional paid-in capital	16,000	17,500	1,500			(k-2)	1,500
Retained earnings	5,300	8,600	3,300	(j)	1,000	(a)	4,300
Totals	$32,800	$41,700	$8,900		$12,700		$12,700

				Debit		Credit	
Cash flows from operating activities							
Net income				(a)	$ 4,300		
Decrease in accounts receivable				(b)	400		
Increase in inventories				(c)		$ 1,800	
Decrease in accounts payable				(d)		900	
Increase in salaries payable				(e)	200		
Gain on sale of equipment				(g)		200	
Depreciation expense				(h)	700		
Cash flows from investing activities							
Purchases of property, plant, and equipment				(f)		5,600	
Sale of equipment				(g)	900		
Cash flows from financing activities							
Proceeds from issuing bonds				(i)	4,000		
Dividends paid				(j)		1,000	
Investing and financing activities not affecting cash							
Acquisition of land by issuance of common stock				(k-1)		2,000	
Proceeds from issuing common stock for land				(k-2)	2,000		
Net increase in cash				(l)		1,000	
					$12,500		$12,500

EXHIBIT 12–17

....

SYMES COMPANY
Statement of Cash Flows
For Year Ended December 31, 1993

Cash flows from operating activities		
Net income	$ 4,300	
Adjustments for differences between income		
flows and cash flows from operating activities		
Depreciation expense	700	
Decrease in accounts receivable	400	
Increase in inventories	(1,800)	
Decrease in accounts payable	(900)	
Increase in salaries payable	200	
Gain on sale of equipment	(200)	
Net cash flow from operating activities		$2,700
Cash flows from investing activities		
Purchases of property, plant, and equipment	$(5,600)	
Sale of equipment	900	
Net cash used by investing activities		(4,700)
Cash flows from financing activities		
Proceeds from issuing bonds	$ 4,000	
Dividends paid	(1,000)	
Net cash provided by financing activities		3,000
Net increase in cash (see Schedule 1)		$ 1,000
Plus: cash balance, January 1, 1993		500
Cash balance, December 31, 1993		$ 1,500
Schedule 1		
Noncash investing and financing activities		
Investing activities		
Acquisition of land by issuance of common stock		$(2,000)
Financing activities		
Proceeds from issuing common stock for land		$ 2,000

in the Cash Flows from Operating Activities in the lower part of the worksheet (item b).

Inventory increased by $1,800 during the year, indicating that purchases exceeded the cost of goods sold. To show the additional cash outflow from operating activities due to the purchase of inventory, the Cash Flows from Operating Activities must be decreased. The increase (debit) in Inventory is recorded in the upper part of the worksheet and the decrease (credit) of $1,800 in the Cash Flows from Operating Activities is recorded in the lower part of the worksheet (item c).

Accounts Payable decreased by $900 during the year, indicating that cash payments for operating activities exceeded expenses recorded in the income statement. This additional cash outflow for operations must be shown as a decrease in the Cash Flows from Operating Activities. The $900 decrease (debit) in Accounts Payable is recorded in the upper part of the worksheet and the decrease (credit) of $900 in the Cash Flows from Operating Activities in the lower part of the worksheet (item d).

Salaries Payable increased by $200 during the year, indicating that less cash was paid than that shown as salaries expense for the year. The increase (credit) in Salaries Payable is recorded in the upper part of the worksheet and the increase (debit) of $200 in the Cash Flows from Operating Activities is recorded in the lower part of the worksheet (item e).

The purchase of the new equipment involved a cash outflow. The increase (debit) in Equipment of $5,600 is recorded in the upper part of the worksheet and the outflow as a decrease (credit) in the Cash Flows from Investing Activities (item f).

When the company sold the equipment, it recorded an increase of $900 in Cash, a decrease in Accumulated Depreciation for $400 ($1,100 − $700), and a decrease in Equipment of $1,100. Since the proceeds were more than the book value, it also recorded a Gain on Sale of Equipment of $200. As shown on the income statement, this gain caused net income to increase even though there was no cash inflow from *operating activities*. The decrease (debit) in Accumulated Depreciation and the decrease (credit) in Equipment are recorded in the upper part of the worksheet, the sale price is recorded as an increase (debit) of $900 in the Cash Flows from Investing Activities, and the gain is recorded as an adjustment (subtraction or credit) of $200 to Net Cash Flow from Operating Activities (item g).[5]

During the year Depreciation Expense was increased by $700, and this amount was shown as a deduction to determine net income. The contra-asset account, Accumulated Depreciation, was also increased by $700. Although the depreciation expense reduced net income, there was no outflow of cash. This depreciation deduction must therefore be *added back* to net income to show correctly the cash flow from operating activities. To do this, Accumulated Depreciation is increased (credit) by $700 in the upper part of the worksheet and the increase (debit) in the Cash Flows from Operating Activities of $700 is recorded in the lower part of the worksheet (item h). It should be remembered that depreciation is not a source of cash! It is added back to net income because when depreciation was originally deducted in computing the amount of net income, there was no corresponding outflow of cash.

....

[5]If the equipment had been sold at a loss, the loss would have decreased net income even though there was no outflow of cash from operating activities. In this case the worksheet entry is recorded as discussed, except that the loss is added back to net income in a manner similar to depreciation expense.

After recording the worksheet entries affecting Equipment and Accumulated Depreciation, it may be seen that the $300 change (increase or credit) in Accumulated Depreciation and the $4,500 change (increase or debit) in the Equipment account have now been accounted for. It is often necessary to record the results of two (or more) unrelated transactions before accounting for the change in an account.

The issuance of bonds caused a cash inflow. The increase (credit) in Bonds Payable of $4,000 is recorded in the upper part of the worksheet and the increase (debit) in the Cash Flows from Financing Activities is recorded in the lower part of the worksheet (item i).

Retained earnings and cash were reduced by the declaration and payment of cash dividends. The decrease (debit) in Retained Earnings of $1,000 is recorded in the upper part of the worksheet, and the decrease (credit) in the Cash Flows from Financing Activities is recorded in the lower part of the worksheet (item j). The increase in Retained Earnings resulting from net income of $4,300, reduced by the decrease of $1,000 for dividends, accounts for the $3,300 change in retained earnings.

When the company issued shares of its common stock in exchange for land, the exchange was recorded at the market price of the 50 shares of stock. At that time the Land account was increased by $2,000; the Common Stock, $10 par account was increased for the par value of $500; and the Additional Paid-in Capital account was increased for the excess of market value over par value, $1,500. Although this transaction did not affect cash, it did involve both an investing and financing activity. The company invested in land and financed this investment by the issuance of common stock. Both the investing and financing information should be included in the worksheet and disclosed in a separate schedule accompanying the statement of cash flows. To do so, the original transaction is "expanded" into two transactions, an investing transaction and a financing transaction. The increase (debit) in the Land is recorded in the upper part of the worksheet and the decrease (credit) of $2,000 in the Cash Flows from Investing Activities in the lower part of the worksheet (item k-1). The increases (credit) in the Common Stock and the Additional Paid-in Capital are recorded in the upper part of the worksheet and the increase (debit) of $2,000 in the Cash Flow from Financing Activities is recorded in the lower part of the worksheet (item k-2).

At this point a double check should be made to determine that all the changes in the noncash accounts have been accounted for. The final entry is made to record the increase in cash (the final amount on the statement of cash flows) and to bring the worksheet debit and credit columns into balance. The increase of $1,000 to Cash is recorded in the upper part of the worksheet and the Net Increase in Cash of $1,000 is recorded in the lower part of the worksheet (item l).

The worksheet may now be used to prepare the statement of cash flows as shown in Exhibit 12–17. This worksheet approach is very efficient because the lower portion of the worksheet is nearly identical to the statement. The disclosure of the amounts paid for interest and for income taxes is not illustrated in this example, and is not included in the problems and cases.

QUESTIONS

1. What is a statement of cash flows? What are the three major sections of the statement?

2. When used with other financial statements, what does the statement of cash flows help users assess?

3. What are the three types of activities that a statement of cash flows reports on for a company? Provide examples of transactions for each type of activity.

4. What is usually the most important section of the statement of cash flows? Why do you think this is the case?

5. Which changes in balance sheet accounts result in cash inflows? Give an example of each.

6. Which changes in balance sheet accounts result in cash outflows? Give an example of each.

7. What is a financing activity that does not result in a cash flow? Give an example.

8. What is an investing activity that does not result in a cash flow? Give an example.

9. What are the most common adjustments to net income to determine net cash flow from operating activities?

10. Indicate how each of the following items would be reported on a statement of cash flows:
    a. Purchase of land
    b. Sale of used equipment at a loss
    c. Depreciation expense
    d. Sale of common stock
    e. Issuance of common stock in exchange for a building

11. Indicate how each of the following items would be reported on a statement of cash flows:
    a. Purchase of equipment
    b. Sale of land at a gain
    c. Patent amortization expense
    d. Sale of preferred stock
    e. Issuance of common stock in exchange for land

12. How would (a) the payment of accounts payable and (b) the payment of dividends by a company be reported on the company's statement of cash flows? If your answers to (a) and (b) are different, why are they different?

13. If the T. R. Hough Co. reports a net income of $25,000, depreciation expense of $6,000, a decrease in accounts payable of $5,000, and no changes in the remaining current assets and liabilities, what would be the net cash flow from operating activities?

14. Designate which of the following events are inflows, which are outflows, and which do not affect cash.
    a. Company acquisition of treasury stock
    b. Sale of used equipment at its book value
    c. Write-off of an uncollectible account by reducing the Allowance for Uncollectible Accounts
    d. Sale of common stock
    e. Conversion of noncurrent convertible bonds payable into common stock

15. Perry Company sold a machine in 1993. The machine cost $20,000 and was 60% depreciated. Perry Company received $10,000 cash. What adjustment to net income must be made to determine the net cash flow from operating activities under the indirect method? Explain.

16. XYZ Company reports a net income of $250,000, which includes $150,000 depreciation expense, $4,000 amortization of premium on bonds payable, and a $6,000 loss on the sale of a long-term investment. What is the net cash flow from operating activities under the indirect method?

PROBLEMS AND CASES

....

17. Impact on Statement of Cash Flows. Several transactions of a company follow:

   1. Purchase of machinery for $5,000

   2. Declaration and payment of 60¢ per share dividend on 8,000 shares of common stock

   3. Issuance of $10,000, five-year bonds at face value

   4. Depreciation expense of $4,000

   5. Sale of equipment for $2,000 The equipment had originally cost $6,000 and had a book value of $2,200 at the time of sale

   6. Purchase of a $7,000 machine by issuance of a two-year note payable for the same amount

Required Indicate how (and the amount) each of the above transactions would be reported on the company's statement of cash flows.

18. Net Cash Flow from Operating Activities Under the Direct Method. Items taken from the records of the Wilson Company for 1993 follow:

1. Sales, $51,000
2. Cost of goods sold, $20,000
3. Wage expense, $15,900
4. Purchase of land, $4,000
5. Increase in accounts receivable, $1,800
6. Depreciation expense, $2,000
7. Gain on sale of equipment, $700
8. Issuance of $8,000 bonds at face value
9. Increase in accounts payable, $2,600
10. Patent amortization expense, $1,300
11. Decrease in inventory, $1,000
12. Loss on sale of land, $500
13. Decrease in wages payable, $300
14. Declaration and payment of dividends, $3,400

Required Prepare the net cash flow from operating activities section under the direct method.

19. Net Cash Flow from Operating Activities Under the Direct Method. The following list of accounting information was taken from the records of the Fox Corporation for 1993:

1. Issuance of common stock, $16,000
2. Loss on sale of equipment, $3,700
3. Purchase of land, $22,000
4. Decrease in accounts receivable, $3,400
5. Depreciation expense, $18,000
6. Increase in inventory, $7,300
7. Gain on sale of land, $4,900
8. Decrease in accounts payable, $5,500
9. Increase in machinery, $2,400
10. Increase in salaries payable, $900
11. Issuance of long-term note payable, $6,000
12. Decrease in unearned rent revenue, $500
13. Declaration and payment of dividends, $19,000
14. Decrease in prepaid rent, $1,100
15. Sales, $150,000
16. Cost of goods sold, $40,000
17. Salaries expense, $45,000
18. Rent revenue, $6,000
19. Rent expense, $5,000
20. Patent amortization expense, $4,200

Required Prepare the net cash flow from operating activities section under the direct method.

20. Net Cash Flow from Operating Activities: Direct Method. The following changes in account balances occurred for the Woodrail Company for 1993:

Sales	$73,000
Interest revenue	4,300
Cost of goods sold	37,500
Salaries expense	13,600
Interest expense	5,400
Income tax expense	3,000

In addition, the following changes occurred in selected accounts during 1993:

Accounts receivable	$ 6,100	decrease
Inventory	9,800	increase
Accounts payable	7,000	increase
Salaries payable	900	decrease
Interest payable	400	increase

Required Using the direct method, prepare the cash flows from operating activities section of the 1993 statement of cash flows for the Woodrail Company. Compute separate amounts for payments to suppliers and payments to employees.

21. Statement of Cash Flows: Direct Method. The following is a list of items to be included in the 1993 statement of cash flows of the Thomas Company:

1. Payments to suppliers, $31,500
2. Other operating receipts, $1,200
3. Payments of dividends, $4,000
4. Payments of income taxes, $5,000
5. Collections from customers, $68,500
6. Payments for purchase of equipment, $18,500
7. Payments to employees, $19,300
8. Interest and dividends collected, $7,100
9. Other operating payments, $900
10. Proceeds from issuance of bonds, $11,300
11. Payments of interest, $8,400
12. Proceeds from sale of investments, $6,000
13. Cash balance, January 1, $12,000

Required Prepare the statement of cash flows, using the direct method for operating cash flows.

22. Statement of Cash Flows: Direct Method. A list of the items to be included in the preparation of the 1993 statement of cash flows for the Yellow Company is presented below:

1. Proceeds from sale of land, $2,100
2. Payments of interest, $5,000
3. Equipment acquired by capital lease, $7,200
4. Proceeds from issuance of preferred stock, $11,000
5. Other operating payments, $1,300
6. Interest and dividends collected, $4,800
7. Payments to employees, $19,800
8. Payment for purchase of investments, $13,300
9. Collections from customers, $55,300
10. Payments of income taxes, $2,900
11. Payments of dividends, $5,200
12. Other operating receipts, $1,600
13. Payments to suppliers, $29,500

Required Prepare the statement of cash flows, using the direct method for operating cash flows. The cash balance on January 1, 1993, is $6,000.

23. Statement of Cash Flows: Direct Method. The following changes in account balances occurred for the Walson Company at the end of 1993.

	Increase (Decrease)
Cash	$ 1,800
Accounts receivable	9,000
Inventory	(2,500)
Land	(1,900)
Buildings and equipment	10,400
Accumulated depreciation	6,800
Accounts payable	(4,500)
Salaries payable	800
Income taxes payable	1,000
Common stock, no par	9,000
Retained earnings	(4,000)
Sales	75,000
Cost of goods sold	40,000
Salaries expense	17,200
Depreciation expense	6,800
Income tax expense	3,300

In addition, the following information was obtained from the company's records:

1. Land was sold, at cost, for $1,900.

2. Dividends of $4,000 were declared and paid.

3. Equipment was purchased for $10,400.

4. Common stock was issued for $9,000.

5. Cash balance, January 1, $7,100.

Required Prepare a 1993 statement of cash flows for the Walson Company, using the direct method for operating cash flows. Compute separate amounts for payments to suppliers and payments to employees.

24. Statement of Cash Flows: Direct Method. The following increases (decreases) occurred in the balance sheet accounts of the Frye Company during 1993:

	Increase (Decrease)
Cash	$4,000
Accounts receivable	2,000
Inventory	(1,000)
Accounts payable	6,000
Land	6,000
Buildings and equipment	13,000
Accumulated depreciation	5,000
Bonds payable	4,000
Common stock, no par	2,000
Retained earnings	7,000

Additional Information for 1993:

1. Sales, $135,000.

2. Cost of goods sold, $44,000.

3. Depreciation expense, $5,000.

4. General and administrative expenses, $65,600.

5. Interest expense, $400.

6. Income tax expense, $5,000.

7. Land that had been acquired in 1983 at a cost of $3,000 was sold for $3,000.

8. Additional land was purchased for $9,000.

9. Equipment was purchased at a cost of $13,000.

10. Two hundred shares of common stock were sold for $10 per share.

11. Ten-year, $4,000 bonds were issued at face value.

12. Dividends of $8,000 were declared and paid.

13. Cash balance, January 1, $15,100.

Required Prepare a 1993 statement of cash flows for the Frye Company under the direct method.

25. **Statement of Cash Flows: Direct Method.** The following increases (decreases) in account balances for 1993 were taken from the accounting records of the Ment Company:

	Increase (Decrease)
Cash	$15,000
Accounts receivable	(4,000)
Inventory	(6,000)
Land	3,000
Plant and equipment	7,200
Accumulated depreciation	1,200
Accounts payable	2,800
Salaries payable	1,000
Bonds payable	2,000
Common stock, no par	1,400
Retained earnings	6,800

Additional Information for 1993:

1. Sales, $70,000.

2. Cost of goods sold, $30,800.

3. Depreciation expense, $1,200.

4. General and administrative expenses, $25,000.

5. Interest expense, $1,000.

6. Income tax expense, $3,000.

7. Dividends declared and paid totaled $2,200.

8. Plant and equipment were purchased at a cost of $7,200. No plant and equipment were sold during the year.

9. Land was purchased at a cost of $3,000.

10. One hundred shares of common stock were sold for $14 per share.

11. Five-year, $2,000 bonds were issued at face value.

12. Cash balance, January 1, $3,100.

Required Prepare a statement of cash flows for 1993 under the direct method.

26. **Statement of Cash Flows: Direct Method.** The following accounts were taken from the balance sheets of the Hawkins Company.

	Account Balances	
	January 1, 1993	December 31, 1993
Cash	$ 2,400	$ 3,400
Accounts receivable (net)	2,800	2,690
Marketable securities (short-term)	1,700	3,000
Inventories	7,100	6,910
Prepaid items	1,300	1,710
Investments (long-term)	7,000	5,400
Land	15,000	15,000
Buildings and equipment	32,000	46,200
Discount on bonds payable	—	290
	$69,300	$84,600
Accumulated depreciation	$16,000	$16,400
Accounts payable	3,800	4,150
Income taxes payable	2,400	2,504
Wages payable	1,100	650
Interest payable	—	400
10% convertible bonds	9,000	—
Note payable (long-term)	3,500	—
12% bonds payable	—	10,000
Deferred income taxes	800	1,196
Common stock, $10 par	14,000	21,500
Additional paid-in capital	8,700	13,700
Retained earnings	10,000	14,100
	$69,300	$84,600

Additional information for the year:

1. Sales $39,930
   Cost of goods sold (19,890)
   Depreciation expense (2,100)
   Wages expense (11,000)
   Other operating expenses (1,000)
   Bond interest expense (410)
   Dividend revenue 820
   Gain on sale of investments 700
   Loss on sale of equipment (200)
   Income tax expense (2,050)
   Net income $ 4,800

2. Dividends declared and paid totaled $700.

3. On January 1, 1993, the 10% convertible bonds that had originally been issued at their face value were converted into 500 shares of common stock. The book value method was used to account for the conversion.

4. Long-term investments that cost $1,600 were sold for $2,300.

5. The long-term note payable was paid by issuing 250 shares of common stock at the beginning of the year.

6. Equipment with a cost of $2,000 and a book value of $300 was sold for $100. The company uses one Accumulated Depreciation account for all depreciable assets.

7. Equipment was purchased at a cost of $16,200.

8. The 12% bonds payable were issued on September 1, 1993, at 97. They mature on September 1, 2003. The company uses the straight-line method to amortize the discount.

9. Taxable income was less than pretax accounting income, resulting in a $396 increase in deferred income taxes.

10. Short-term marketable securities were purchased at a cost of $1,300.

Required Prepare the statement of cash flows, using the direct method. Compute separate amounts for payments to suppliers and payments to employees.

27. **Net Cash Flow from Operating Activities: Direct and Indirect Methods.** The Dean Company reported the following condensed income statement for 1993:

Sales		$100,000
Cost of goods sold		(58,000)
Gross profit		$ 42,000
Operating expenses		
Depreciation expense	$ 8,000	
Other operating expenses	12,000	(20,000)
Income before income taxes		$ 22,000
Income tax expense		(8,900)
Net income		$ 13,100

During 1993, the following changes occurred in the company's current assets and current liabilities:

	Increase (Decrease)
Cash	$ 3,700
Accounts receivable	(4,000)
Inventory	8,900
Accounts payable (purchases)	(4,600)
Salaries payable	1,700

Required 1. Prepare the net cash flow from operating activities of the Dean Company's 1993 statement of cash flows under the indirect method.

2. Prepare the net cash flow from operating activities section of the Dean Company's 1993 statement of cash flows under the direct method.

28. Net Cash Flow from Operating Activities: Indirect Method. The following information relates to the Hyde Company's activities for 1993:

1. Amortization of premium on bonds payable, $600
2. Purchase of equipment, $7,000
3. Depreciation expense, $7,000
4. Decrease in accounts receivable, $800
5. Decrease in accounts payable, $2,800
6. Issuance of long-term note, $4,200
7. Increase in inventories, $7,500
8. Gain on sale of land, $8,000
9. Increase in prepaid assets, $500
10. Declaration of cash dividends, $1,800
11. Increase in wages payable, $300
12. Patent amortization expense, $1,000
13. Net income, $10,000

Required Prepare the net cash flow from operating activities under the indirect method.

29. Net Cash Flow from Operating Activities: Indirect Method. The following items involve the statement of cash flows of the Jensen Company for 1993:

1. Net income, $18,000
2. Accounts receivable increased by $2,000
3. Deferred income taxes increased by $5,000
4. Depreciation expense, $2,000
5. Inventory decreased by $3,100
6. Accounts payable decreased by $4,000

Required Prepare the net cash flow from operating activities for the statement of cash flows of the Jensen Company for 1993 under the indirect method.

30. Net Cash Flow from Operating Activities: Indirect Method. The following accounting items were taken from the records of the Watson Company for 1993:

1. Net income, $20,000
2. Purchase of land, $4,500
3. Retirement of bonds, $6,000
4. Depreciation expense, $7,500
5. Issuance of common stock, $7,000
6. Patent amortization expense, $2,000
7. Bond payable discount amortization, $1,000
8. Increase in accounts receivable, $3,400
9. Payment of dividends, $5,000
10. Decrease in accounts payable, $2,600

Required Prepare the net cash flow from operating activities for the Watson Company's 1993 statement of cash flows under the indirect method.

31. Cash Flow Statement with Net Cash Flow from Operating Activities Under the Indirect Method. The following items involve the cash flow activities of the Rocky Company for 1993:

1. Net income, $37,000
2. Payment of dividends, $12,000
3. Ten-year, $26,000 bonds payable were issued at face value
4. Depreciation expense, $11,000
5. Building was acquired at a cost of $43,000
6. Accounts receivable decreased by $2,000
7. Accounts payable decreased by $4,000
8. Equipment was acquired at a cost of $8,100
9. Inventories increased by $7,000

Required Prepare the cash flow statement with the net cash flow from operating activities under the indirect method.

32. Statement of Cash Flows: Indirect Method. The following items involve the cash flow activities of the Jones Company for 1993:

1. Net income, $56,400
2. Issuance of common stock, $25,000
3. Purchase of equipment, $41,500
4. Purchase of land, $19,600
5. Depreciation expense, $20,500
6. Patent amortization expense, $1,200
7. Payment of dividends, $21,000
8. Decrease in salaries payable, $2,600
9. Increase in accounts receivable, $10,300
10. Cash balance, January 1, $4,100

Required Prepare the statement of cash flows of the Jones Company for 1993 using the indirect method.

33. Statement of Cash Flows: Indirect Method. A list of selected items involving the cash flow activities of the Topps Company for 1993 follows:

1. Patent amortization expense, $3,500
2. Machinery was purchased for $44,500
3. At year-end, bonds payable with a face value of $20,000 were issued for $17,000
4. Net income, $48,500
5. Dividends paid, $16,000
6. Depreciation expense, $12,900
7. Preferred stock was issued for $10,100
8. Long-term investments were acquired for $21,000
9. Accounts receivable increased by $4,300
10. Land was sold at cost, $11,000
11. Inventories increased by $15,400
12. Accounts payable increased by $2,700

Required Prepare the statement of cash flows of the Topps Company for 1993 under the indirect method. The cash balance on January 1 was $1,100.

34. Statement of Cash Flows: Indirect Method. The following items involve the cash flow activities of the Mueller Company for 1993:

1. Net income, $56,000
2. Increase in accounts receivable, $4,400
3. Issuance of common stock, $12,300
4. Depreciation expense, $11,800
5. Dividends paid, $24,500
6. Purchase of building, $57,000
7. Bond payable discount amortization, $600
8. Sale of long-term investments at cost, $8,400
9. Purchase of equipment, $5,000
10. Issuance of preferred stock, $30,000
11. Increase in income taxes payable, $3,500
12. Purchase of land, $9,700
13. Decrease in accounts payable, $2,900
14. Increase in inventories, $10,300

Required Prepare the statement of cash flows of the Mueller Company for 1993 under the indirect method. The cash balance on January 1 was $9,100.

35. Statement of Cash Flows. The following are the beginning and ending balance sheet accounts of the Anita Company for 1993:

	1/1/1993	12/31/1993
Cash	$ 2,000	$ 3,500
Accounts receivable	4,000	7,000
Inventory	7,000	6,500
Land	6,000	10,500
Equipment	30,000	30,000
Accumulated depreciation	(10,000)	(11,000)
Totals	$39,000	$46,500
Accounts payable	$ 2,000	$ 2,500
Bonds payable	-0-	3,000
Common stock, no par	17,000	18,500
Retained earnings	20,000	22,500
Totals	$39,000	$46,500

Additional Information for 1993:

1. Net income was $5,000. Included in net income were sales of $40,000, cost of goods sold of $11,800, depreciation expense of $1,000, general and administrative expenses of $20,000, interest expense of $200, and income tax expense of $2,000.
2. Dividends were $2,500.
3. Land was purchased for $4,500.
4. Ten-year, $3,000 bonds payable were issued at face value.
5. Two hundred shares of no par common stock were issued for $7.50 per share.

Required 1. Prepare a statement of cash flows of the Anita Company for 1993 under the direct method.

2. Prepare the net cash flow from operating activities under the indirect method.

36. Statement of Cash Flows. The beginning and ending balance sheet accounts of the Tyler Company for 1993 are shown:

	1/1/1993	12/31/1993
Cash	$ 4,000	$ 6,500
Accounts receivable	5,000	4,700
Inventory	6,000	7,200
Property and equipment	70,000	70,000
Accumulated depreciation	(12,000)	(13,400)
Totals	$73,000	$75,000
Accounts payable	$ 5,000	$ 3,500
Common stock, $5 par	12,000	12,250
Additional paid-in capital	36,000	36,750
Retained earnings	20,000	22,500
Totals	$73,000	$75,000

Additional Information for 1993:

1. Net income was $7,000, including sales of $90,000, cost of goods sold of $39,600, depreciation expense of $1,400, general and administrative expenses of $39,000, and income tax expense of $3,000.
2. Fifty shares of common stock were issued for $20 per share.
3. Dividends of $4,500 were declared and paid.

Required 1. Prepare a statement of cash flows of the Tyler Company for 1993 under the direct method.

2. Prepare the net cash flow from operating activities under the indirect method.

37. Statement of Cash Flows. The following are the beginning and ending balance sheet accounts of the Henley Corporation for 1993:

	1/1/1993	12/31/1993
Cash	$ 2,000	$ 3,600
Accounts receivable	2,000	3,000
Inventory	5,000	6,000
Land	12,000	8,000
Equipment	30,000	46,000
Accumulated depreciation	(8,000)	(10,600)
Totals	$43,000	$56,000
Bonds payable (due 2003)	$ -0-	$ 4,000
Common stock, $10 par	10,000	11,000
Additional paid-in capital	18,000	19,000
Retained earnings	15,000	22,000
Totals	$43,000	$56,000

Additional Information for 1993:

1. Net income was $10,000, including sales of $100,000, cost of goods sold of $25,000, depreciation expense of $2,600, and wage expense of $63,600.

2. Cash dividends declared and paid were $3,000.

3. Land that originally cost $4,000 was sold for $5,200.

4. Equipment was purchased at a cost of $16,000.

5. Ten-year, $4,000 bonds payable were issued at face value.

6. One hundred shares of common stock were sold for $20 per share.

Required 1. Prepare a statement of cash flows of the Henley Corporation for 1993 under the direct method.

2. Prepare the net cash flow from operating activities under the indirect method.

38. Statement of Cash Flows. The following list of accounting information is from the Bartle Company for 1993:

1. Net income, $22,000
2. Equipment was acquired at a cost of $14,000
3. Dividends of –?– were declared and paid
4. Three hundred shares of $10 par common stock were issued for $20 per share
5. Depreciation expense, $8,200
6. Twenty-year, $8,000 bonds payable were issued at face value
7. Land was acquired in exchange for 100 shares of $10 par common stock when the stock was selling for $22 per share

8. Patent amortization expense, $2,600
9. Land with a cost of $800 was sold for $1,000
10. A building was acquired at a cost of $30,000
11. Cash decreased by $1,900
12. Sales, $100,000
13. Cost of goods sold, $30,000
14. General and administrative expenses, $37,400
15. Cash balance, January 1, $13,000

Required 1. Prepare a statement of cash flows of the Bartle Company for 1993 under the direct method.

2. Prepare the net cash flow from operating activities under the indirect method.

39. Statement of Cash Flows. A list of selected accounting information of the Floye Company for 1993 is presented:

1. Copyright amortization expense was $3,000
2. Machinery was purchased for $13,600
3. Bonds payable with a face value and book value of $10,000 were retired for $10,000
4. Depreciation expense was $9,800
5. Six hundred shares of $5 par common stock were issued for $15 per share
6. A building valued at $32,000 was acquired by issuing 2,000 shares of $5 par common stock. The stock was selling for $16 per share

7. Net income was $28,000
8. Dividends declared and paid were $15,000
9. Equipment with a cost of $11,000 and a book value of $4,500 was sold for $6,700
10. Land was purchased at a cost of –?–
11. Cash increased by $8,500
12. Sales, $130,000
13. Cost of goods sold, $50,400
14. General and administrative expenses, $41,000
15. Cash balance, January 1, $18,000

Required 1. Prepare a statement of cash flows of the Floye Company for 1993 under the direct method.

2. Prepare the net cash flow from operating activities under the indirect method.

40. Statement of Cash Flows. A list of selected items involving the statement of cash flows of the Roering Company for 1993 is presented:

1. Depreciation expense, $9,000
2. Equipment was acquired for $15,000
3. Common stock was issued for $8,000
4. Dividends declared and paid, $5,000
5. Net income, $32,000
6. Patent amortization expense, $4,000
7. Land was sold for $7,000; a gain of $2,000 was recorded on the sale
8. At year end, 20-year bonds payable with a face value of $11,000 were issued for $12,000

9. Building was purchased for $41,000
10. Increase in deferred income taxes, $3,000
11. Sales, $113,000
12. Cost of goods sold, $40,000
13. General and administrative expenses, $20,000
14. Income tax expense, $10,000
15. Cash balance, January 1, $14,100

Required 1. Prepare the statement of cash flows of the Roering Company for 1993 under the direct method.

2. Prepare the net cash flow from operating activities under the indirect method.

41. Statement of Cash Flows: Indirect Method. The following increases in account balances were taken from the accounting records of Gordon Company:

Cash	$2,500
Accounts receivable	6,400
Accounts payable	3,000
Land	5,000
Plant and equipment	9,200
Accumulated depreciation	2,000
Other current liabilities	2,800
Long-term note payable	5,000
Common stock, no par	3,300
Retained earnings	7,000

Net income for 1993 was $13,000. Dividends declared and paid totaled $6,000. Plant and equipment were purchased at a cost of $9,200. No plant and equipment were sold during the year. Land was acquired by issuing a long-term note payable. One hundred shares of common stock were sold for $33 per share.

Required Prepare a statement of cash flows for the Gordon Company for 1993 under the indirect method. The cash balance on January 1 was $6,100.

42. **Balance Sheet from Statement of Cash Flows.** Gibb Company prepared the following balance sheet at the *beginning* of 1993:

GIBB COMPANY
Balance Sheet
January 1, 1993

ASSETS		LIABILITIES AND STOCKHOLDERS' EQUITY	
Cash	$ 2,600	Accounts payable	$ 4,000
Accounts receivable (net)	2,900	Salaries payable	1,100
Inventory	4,700		$ 5,100
Land	9,800	Common stock, $10 par	13,500
Buildings and equipment	68,300	Additional paid-in capital	11,200
Less: accumulated		Retained earnings	44,400
depreciation	(14,100)		
		Total liabilities and	
Total assets	$74,200	stockholders' equity	$74,200

At the *end* of 1993 it prepared the following statement of cash flows:

GIBB COMPANY
Statement of Cash Flows
For Year Ended December 31, 1993

Net cash flow from operating activities		
Net income	$ 4,000	
Adjustments for differences between income flows and cash flows from operating activities		
Add: Depreciation expense	1,900	
Decrease in inventory	500	
Increase in salaries payable	400	
Less: Increase in accounts receivable (net)	(1,100)	
Decrease in accounts payable	(1,000)	
Net cash provided by operating activities		$ 4,700
Cash flows from investing activities		
Purchase of building	$(13,900)	
Proceeds from sale of land	3,000	
Net cash used for investing activities		(10,900)
Cash flows from financing activities		
Payment of dividends	$ (3,100)	
Issuance of bonds	5,700	
Issuance of common stock	4,500	
Net cash provided by financing activities		7,100
Net increase in cash		$ 900

Additional information related to the statement of cash flows:

1. The long-term bonds have a face value of $6,000 and were issued on December 31, 1993.

2. The building was purchased on December 29, 1993.

3. The land was sold at its original cost.

4. The common stock which was sold totaled 300 shares and had a par value of $10 per share.

Required Prepare a classified balance sheet for the Gibb Company as of December 31, 1993. (*Hint:* Review the information on the statement of cash flows and the balances in the beginning balance sheet accounts to determine the impact on the ending balance sheet accounts.)

43. **Erroneous Statement.** The president of Tide Corporation has come to your bank for a loan. He states: "Each of the last three years our cash has gone down. This year we need to increase our cash by $7,000. We have never borrowed any money on a long-term basis and are reluctant to do so. However, we definitely need to purchase some new, more advanced equipment to replace the old equipment we are selling this year. We also want to acquire some treasury stock because it would be a good investment. We also would like to pay dividends of 50% of net income instead of our usual 40%. Given our expected net income and the money we will receive from our depreciation expense and the gain on the sale of the old equipment, I estimate we will have to borrow $12,000, based on the following schedule."

SCHEDULE OF CASH FLOWS

Inflows of cash		
Inflows from net income		$20,000
Other inflows:		
Depreciation expense		4,000
Gain on sale of old equipment		3,000
Proceeds from sale of old equipment		8,000
Bank loan (estimated)		12,000
Total inflows		$47,000
Outflows of cash		
Purchase equipment	$30,000	
Pay dividends (50% of net income)	10,000	
Total outflows		(40,000)
Increase in cash		$ 7,000

The president explains that the $5,000 expected cost of acquiring the treasury stock was not included because it would involve only a transaction between the corporation and the existing stockholders and would be of no interest to "outsiders." He also states that "if his figures are off a little bit," the most the corporation wants to borrow is $16,000. You determine that the amounts he has listed for each item (except the bank loan) are accurate.

Required 1. Prepare a statement of cash flows for the Tide Corporation that shows the bank loan necessary to increase cash by $7,000.

2. Explain to the president why his $12,000 estimate of the bank loan is incorrect.

3. Suggest ways to reduce the necessary bank loan and still increase cash.

44. Noncash Financing and Investing Activities. The statement of cash flows is normally a required basic financial statement for each period for which an earnings statement is presented. The statement should include a separate schedule listing the noncash financing and investing activities.

Required 1. What are noncash financing and investing activities?

2. What are two types of noncash financing and investing activities?

3. What effect, if any, would each of the following seven items have on the statement of cash flows?

   a. Accounts receivable
   b. Inventory
   c. Depreciation
   d. Deferred income taxes
   e. Issuance of long-term debt in payment for a building
   f. Payoff of current portion of debt
   g. Sale of a fixed asset resulting in a loss *(AICPA adapted)*

45. Statement of Cash Flows (Indirect Method). Alfred Engineering Company is a young and growing producer of electronic measuring instruments and technical equipment. You have been retained by Alfred to advise it in the preparation of a statement of cash flows. For the fiscal year ended October 31, 1993, you have obtained the following information concerning certain events and transactions of Alfred:

1. The amount of reported earnings for the fiscal year was $800,000.

2. Depreciation expense of $240,000 was included in the earnings statement.

3. Uncollectible accounts receivable of $30,000 were written off against the allowance for uncollectible accounts. Also, $37,000 of bad debts expense was included in determining earnings for the fiscal year, and the same amount was added to the allowance for uncollectible accounts.

4. A gain of $4,700 was realized on the sale of a machine; it originally cost $75,000 of which $25,000 was undepreciated on the date of sale.

5. On July 3, 1993, building and land were purchased for $600,000; Alfred gave in payment $100,000 cash, $200,000 market value of its unissued common stock, and a $300,000 mortgage.

6. On August 3, 1993, $700,000 face value of Alfred's 6% convertible debentures were converted into $140,000 par value of its common stock. The bonds were originally issued at face value.

7. The board of directors declared a $320,000 cash dividend on October 20, 1993, payable on November 15, 1993, to stockholders of record on November 5, 1993.

Required For each of the seven items, explain whether each is an inflow or outflow of cash and explain how it should be disclosed in Alfred's statement of cash flows for the fiscal year ended October 31, 1993. The company uses the indirect method. If any item is neither an inflow nor outflow of cash, explain why it is not and indicate the disclosure, if any, that should be made of the item in Alfred's statement of cash flows for the fiscal year ended October 31, 1993. *(AICPA adapted)*

46. Appendix: Worksheet: Direct Method. The following are the December 31, 1992 balance sheet and the December 31, 1993 trial balance of the Adair Company:

	12/31/92 Balance Sheet		12/31/93 Trial Balance	
	Debit	Credit	Debit	Credit
Cash	$ 2,700		$ 3,100	
Accounts receivable	7,200		7,000	
Inventory	8,100		9,900	
Investments	10,100		18,700	
Property and equipment	105,300		135,300	
Accumulated depreciation		$42,400		$49,200
Accounts payable		8,100		9,200
Salaries payable		1,300		700
Interest payable		-0-		300
Notes payable		-0-		9,000
Common stock, no par		43,600		60,100
Retained earnings		38,000		31,500
Sales				89,000
Cost of goods sold			48,800	
Depreciation expense			6,800	
Salaries expense			12,000	
Other operating expenses			1,700	
Interest revenue				1,200
Interest expense			900	
Income tax expense			6,000	
Totals	$133,400	$133,400	$250,200	$250,200

A review of the accounting records reveals the following additional information for 1993:

1. Investments were purchased for $8,600.
2. A building was purchased for $30,000.
3. A note payable was issued for $9,000.
4. Common stock was issued for $16,500.
5. Dividends of $6,500 were declared and paid.

Required 1. Using the direct method for operating cash flows, prepare a worksheet to support the 1993 statement of cash flows for the Adair Company.

2. Prepare the statement of cash flows.

47. Appendix: Complex Worksheet: Direct Method. Shown below for the Heinz Company is the balance sheet of December 31, 1992, and the trial balance as of December 31, 1993.

	12/31/1992 Balance Sheet		12/31/1993 Trial Balance	
Cash	$ 2,700		$ 3,820	
Accounts receivable (net)	5,900		6,215	
Inventories	15,300		15,530	
Prepaid items	1,400		1,000	
Investments (long-term)	8,300		7,300	
Land	16,300		19,000	
Buildings	68,700		60,700	
Accumulated depreciation:				
buildings		$ 35,000		$ 34,500
Equipment	29,600		25,600	
Accumulated depreciation:				
equipment		14,200		14,700
Patents (net)	8,700		9,185	
Accounts payable		8,900		9,195
Interest payable		630		300
Wages payable		2,500		2,600
Bonds payable		23,000		17,000
Discount on bonds				
payable	0		715	
Common stock, $10 par		22,000		22,650
Additional paid-in capital		15,320		15,970
Retained earnings		35,350		35,350
	$156,900	$156,900		
Sales (net)				50,000
Cost of goods sold			23,800	
Wages expense			16,510	
Other operating expenses			1,100	
Depreciation expense:				
buildings			2,700	
Depreciation expense:				
equipment			3,100	
Patent amortization			815	
Interest expense			1,715	
Loss (ordinary) on sale of				
investments			200	
Interest revenue				790
Gain (ordinary) on				
exchange of dissimilar				
assets				1,300
Income tax expense			650	
Extraordinary loss (net of				
income taxes)			2,600	
Dividends declared			2,100	
Totals			$204,355	$204,355

A review of the accounting records reveals the following additional information:

1. Bonds payable with a face value, book value, and market value of $14,000 were retired on June 30, 1993.

2. Bonds payable with a face value of $8,000 were issued at 90.25 on August 1, 1993. They mature on August 1, 1998. The company uses the straight-line method to amortize bond discount.

3. A tornado completely destroyed a small building that had an original cost of $8,000 and book value of $4,800. Settlement with the insurance company resulted in after-tax proceeds of $2,200 and an extraordinary loss (net of income taxes) of $2,600.

4. Equipment with a cost of $4,000 and a book value of $1,400 was exchanged for an acre of land valued at $2,700. No cash was exchanged. The transaction was properly considered to be a dissimilar asset exchange.

5. Long-term investments with a cost of $1,000 were sold for $800.

6. Sixty-five shares of common stock were exchanged for a patent. The common stock was selling for $20 per share at the time of the exchange.

Required Prepare a worksheet to support a statement of cash flows for 1993, under the direct method.

48. **Appendix: Worksheet: Indirect Method.** The following information is presented for the Harris Company.

HARRIS COMPANY
Comparative Balance Sheets

	January 1, 1993	December 31, 1993
Cash	$ 700	$1,140
Accounts receivable	450	300
Inventory	350	400
Land	300	500
Equipment	1,600	1,800
Less: Accumulated depreciation	(200)	(150)
Total assets	$3,200	$3,990
Accounts payable	$ 600	$ 750
Bonds payable (due 1/1/98)	1,000	1,000
Common stock, $10 par	900	1,400
Retained earnings	700	840
Total liabilities and stockholders' equity	$3,200	$3,990

HARRIS COMPANY
Condensed Income Statement
For Year Ended December 31, 1993

Revenues	$ 9,000
Cost of goods sold	(6,000)
Expenses	(2,000)
Loss on sale of equipment	(260)
Gain on sale of land	400
Net income	$ 1,140

Partial additional information:

1. The equipment that was sold for cash had cost $400 and had a book value of $300.
2. Land that was sold brought a cash price of $600.
3. Fifty shares of stock were issued at par.

Required Making whatever additional assumptions are necessary:

1. Prepare a worksheet to support a statement of cash flows for 1993 using the indirect method.
2. Prepare the statement of cash flows.

49. **Appendix: Worksheet: Indirect Method.** The following is a list of increases and decreases that occurred in the balance sheet accounts of the Pierce Company for 1993:

Accounts	Increase (Decrease)
Cash	$ 5,300
Accounts receivable	(1,000)
Inventory	4,900
Prepaid insurance	700
Land	4,400
Buildings and equipment	16,400
Accumulated depreciation	5,100
Accounts payable	2,300
Other current payables	(600)
Bonds payable	6,000
Common stock, $10 par	5,000
Additional paid-in capital	3,500
Retained earnings	9,400

Additional Information for 1993:

1. Net income was $18,600, which included $5,100 of depreciation.
2. Dividends of $9,200 were declared and paid.
3. Land and equipment were purchased at $8,400 and $16,400, respectively.
4. Long-term bonds were issued at their face value of $6,000.
5. Five hundred shares of $10 par common stock were issued at $17 per share.
6. Land that had cost $4,000 was sold for $3,100.

Required 1. Prepare a worksheet for the 1993 statement of cash flows using the indirect method. The cash balance on January 1 was $10,000.

2. Prepare the statement of cash flows for 1993.

50. **Appendix: Complex Worksheet: Indirect Method.** The following are the comparative condensed balance sheets and the condensed income statement of the McVey Company for 1993:

McVEY COMPANY
Comparative Balance Sheets

	January 1, 1993	December 31, 1993
Cash	$ 3,200	$ 6,900
Accounts receivable	6,800	11,600
Inventory	8,000	8,400
Land	9,200	15,200
Buildings	75,100	100,300
Accumulated depreciation: buildings	(26,700)	(30,600)
Equipment	33,900	34,600
Accumulated depreciation: equipment	(10,300)	(11,100)
Patents (net)	8,500	7,800
Total assets	$ 107,700	$ 143,100
Accounts payable	$ 11,000	$ 17,300
Accrued current payables	700	500
Bonds payable (due 12/31/2003)	-0-	9,000
Premium on bonds payable	-0-	400
Common stock, $10 par	22,000	27,500
Additional paid-in capital	31,000	38,100
Retained earnings	43,000	50,300
Total liabilities and stockholders' equity	$ 107,700	$ 143,100

McVEY COMPANY
Income Statement
For Year Ended December 31, 1993

Sales	$ 73,000
Cost of goods sold	(43,800)
Depreciation expense: buildings	(3,900)
Depreciation expense: equipment	(2,100)
Patent amortization expense	(700)
Other operating expenses	(7,900)
Operating income	$ 14,600
Loss on sale of equipment	(1,500)
Net income	$ 13,100

Additional Information for 1993:

1. Dividends declared and paid total $5,800.

2. Three hundred shares of $10 par common stock were sold for $22 per share.

3. Equipment and a building were purchased for $8,700 and $25,200, respectively.

4. Equipment with a cost of $8,000 and accumulated depreciation of $1,300 was sold for $5,200.

5. Ten-year bonds payable with a face value of $9,000 were issued for $9,400 on December 31, 1993. (*Hint:* Record the issuance of the bonds at a premium in the usual manner.)

6. Two hundred and fifty shares of $10 par common stock with a current market value of $24 per share were issued in exchange for land.

Required 1. Prepare a worksheet for a 1993 statement of cash flows using the indirect method.

2. Prepare the statement of cash flows for 1993.

51. **Appendix: Complex Worksheet: Indirect Method.** Presented are condensed balance sheets, a condensed income statement, and the retained earnings statement of the Fite Company for 1993:

FITE COMPANY
Comparative Balance Sheets

	1/1/1993	12/31/1993
Cash	$ 2,700	$ 3,100
Receivables (short-term)	7,100	8,900
Inventory	8,200	7,900
Land	10,100	18,700
Buildings and machinery	105,300	135,300
Accumulated depreciation	(42,400)	(45,000)
Copyrights (net)	9,400	8,000
Total assets	$100,400	$136,900
Accounts payable	$ 8,100	$ 9,200
Salaries payable	1,300	1,000
Note payable (due 12/31/1998)	-0-	8,600
Bonds payable	-0-	10,000
Common stock, $5 par	25,000	30,000
Additional paid-in capital	29,000	36,000
Retained earnings	38,000	45,300
Treasury stock	(1,000)	(3,200)
Total liabilities and stockholders' equity	$100,400	$136,900

FITE COMPANY
Income Statement
For Year Ended December 31, 1993

Sales	$ 81,000
Cost of goods sold	(48,800)
Depreciation expense	(6,800)
Copyright amortization expense	(1,400)
Other expenses	(12,300)
Operating income	$ (11,700
Gain on sale of machinery	1,700
Net income	$ 13,400

FITE COMPANY
Retained Earnings Statement
For Year Ended December 31, 1993

Beginning retained earnings	$ 38,000
Add: net income	13,400
	$ 51,400
Less: cash dividends	(6,100)
Ending retained earnings	$ 45,300

Additional Information for 1993:

1. Long-term bonds were issued at their face value of $10,000.

2. A building was purchased at a cost of $42,200.

3. Machinery with a cost of $12,200 and accumulated depreciation of $4,200 was sold for $9,700.

4. One thousand shares of $5 par common stock were issued for $12 per share.

5. On December 31, 1993, a five-year note for $8,600 was issued in exchange for an acre of land.

6. Two hundred shares of the company's common stock were reacquired as treasury stock for $11 per share.

Required 1. Prepare a worksheet for the 1993 statement of cash flows using the indirect method.

2. Prepare the statement of cash flows for 1993.

ANNUAL REPORT PROBLEMS

52. General Motors. Review the financial statements and related notes of General Motors in Appendix A.

Required Answer the following questions and indicate on what page of the financial report you located the answer. (*Note:* All answers may be found in the annual report and no calculations are necessary.)

1. What was the amount of the increase or decrease in cash and cash equivalents during 1989?

2. What was the amount of the net cash provided by operating activities during 1989?

3. What was the amount of the source of cash due to the increase in long-term debt during 1989?

4. How much cash was used for the expenditures for real estate, plants, and equipment during 1989?

5. What was the amount of the cash dividends paid to stockholders during 1989?

6. What was the amount of the total cash and cash equivalents at the end of 1989?

7. What was the amount of the increase or decrease in inventories during 1989?

8. What was the amount of the increase or decrease in the accounts payable during 1989?

9. What was the amount of the net cash used in investing activities during 1989?

53. Statement of Cash Flows: Direct and Indirect Methods. The following relevant information is needed to prepare Boeing's 1988 statement of cash flows (in millions of dollars):

	1988	1987
INCOME STATEMENT		
Sales	$16,962	$15,505
Costs and expenses	16,514	15,146
Interest and dividend income	378	308
Interest expense	6	9
Federal taxes on income	206	178
Net earnings	$ 614	$ 480
BALANCE SHEET (SUMMARIZED)		
Cash and certificates of deposit	$ 3,544	$ 2,197
Short-term investments	419	1,238
Accounts receivable	1,559	1,546
Inventories	2,947	3,509
Customer financing	1,131	1,215
Property, plant, and equipment	6,385	5,813
Accumulated depreciation	(3,682)	(3,259)
Goodwill	305	307
Total assets	$12,608	$12,566
Accounts payable and accrued liabilities	$ 4,697	$ 4,434
Advances and progress billings in excess of related costs	1,304	846
Deferred taxes on income	945	2,029
Long-term debt	258	270
Common shares, issued at stated value	1,341	1,335
Retained earnings	4,137	3,760
Treasury shares, at cost	(74)	(108)
Total liabilities and stockholders' equity	$12,608	$12,566

Additional Information:

1. Cash dividends of $237 were paid in 1988.

2. No stock dividends were declared in 1988.

3. Old equipment costing $118 with a zero net book value was scrapped for no cash.

4. $6 of debentures were converted into common shares.

Required 1. Prepare a statement of cash flows using the direct method for 1988. Use T-accounts to reconcile any account that has more than one increase or decrease, based on the given information. Note: You may not be able to use exactly the same categories discussed in the text.

2. Prepare the net cash flow from operating activities under the indirect method.

54. **Statement of Cash Flows: Direct and Indirect Methods.** Hershey Foods is one of the largest manufacturers and marketers of chocolate, confectionery and pasta products in the world. The following information is necessary to prepare its 1988 statement of cash flows (in thousands of dollars):

	1988	1987
INCOME STATEMENT		
Net sales	$2,168,048	$1,863,816
Other operating income (net)	39,489	1,684
Cost of goods sold	1,326,458	1,149,663
Selling and administrative expenses	575,515	468,062
Income tax expense	91,615	99,604
Net income	$ 213,949	$ 148,171
BALANCE SHEET (SUMMARIZED)		
Cash and cash equivalents	$ 70,073	$ 7,771
Accounts receivable (net)	166,789	121,528
Inventories	308,755	263,156
Other current assets	73,480	329,510
Total current assets	$ 619,097	$ 721,965
Investments	38,270	31,850
Property, plant, and equipment	1,018,871	810,352
Accumulated depreciation	(282,859)	(245,880)
Intangibles	371,286	226,067
Total assets	$1,764,665	$1,544,354
Loans payable to banks	$ 54,875	$ 29,684
Accounts payable and accrued expenses	273,112	210,675
Accrued taxes on income	17,394	16,414
Total current liabilities	$ 345,381	$ 256,773
Long-term debt	233,025	280,900
Deferred taxes	132,429	131,136
Other noncurrent liabilities	47,964	43,135
Common stock	90,186	90,186
Additional paid-in capital	51,285	51,285
Cumulative foreign currency adjustments	20,075	2,038
Retained earnings	844,320	688,901
Total liabilities and stockholders' equity	$1,764,665	$1,544,354

Additional Information:

1. Equipment was sold for $12,564 cash. Its original cost was $7,689 with accumulated depreciation of $4,807.

2. Amortization of intangibles was $8,197.

3. There were cash dividends on common stock of $58,530.

Required 1. Prepare a 1988 statement of cash flows for Hershey Foods using the direct approach. Use T-accounts to reconcile any account that has more than one increase or decrease, based on the given information. Note: You may not be able to use exactly the same categories discussed in the text. Include the cumulative foreign currency adjustment as a separate item in the statement.

2. Prepare the net cash flow from operating activities under the indirect method.

55. **Statement of Cash Flows: Direct and Indirect Methods.** The following excerpts are from Kimberly-Clark's 1988 annual report (in millions of dollars):

	1988	1987
CONSOLIDATED INCOME AND RETAINED EARNINGS		
Sales	$5,393.5	$4,884.7
Cost of sales	3,404.2	3,065.9
Selling and administrative expenses	1,348.7	1,232.7
Interest income	11.2	7.2
Other income	70.2	61.5
Interest expense	80.6	65.6
Other expenses	33.0	33.5
Provision for income taxes	229.8	230.5
Net income	$ 378.6	$ 325.2
Retained earnings at beginning of year	1,451.4	1,251.3
Cash dividends	(128.7)	(125.1)
Retained earnings at end of year	$1,701.3	$1,451.4
CONSOLIDATED BALANCE SHEET (IN PART)		
Current assets		
Cash	$ 84.1	$ 89.7
Accounts receivable	584.9	519.9
Inventories	566.5	525.4
	$1,235.5	$1,135.0
Current liabilities		
Accounts payable and accrued liabilities	$ 747.9	$ 619.9
Income taxes payable	88.4	96.7
Dividends payable	32.2	29.5
Short-term debt	110.9	250.0
	$ 979.4	$ 996.1
STATEMENT OF CASH FLOWS (IN PART)		
Noncash items included in income	$ 228.2	
Cash flows from operating activities	?	
Cash flows from investing activities		
Capital spending	(438.2)	
Disposals of property, plant, and equipment	13.7	
Other	(3.6)	
Net cash used by investment activities	$(428.1)	
Cash flows from financing activities		
Long-term debt issued	67.2	
Others	?	

Required 1. Prepare a 1988 statement of cash flows for Kimberly-Clark using the direct method. Assume that the noncash items were for selling and administrative items.

2. Prepare the net cash flow from operating activities under the indirect method.

56. Statement of Cash Flows: Direct and Indirect Methods. The following excerpts are from Scott Paper's 1988 annual report (in millions of dollars):

	1988	1987
CONSOLIDATED INCOME AND RETAINED EARNINGS		
Sales	$4,726.4	$4,122.0
Cost of sales	3,115.3	2,713.6
Selling and administrative expenses	878.8	965.9
Taxes on income	237.8	117.1
Other income	53.9	47.4
Interest expense	147.5	139.0
Net income	400.9	233.8
Retained earnings at beginning of year	1,606.1	1,422.4
Cash dividends	(55.2)	(49.6)
Stock dividends	(452.8)	(0.5)
Retained earnings at end of year	$1,499.0	$1,606.1
CONSOLIDATED BALANCE SHEET (IN PART)		
Current assets		
Cash	$ 373.8	$ 72.6
Accounts receivable	610.7	589.3
Inventories	630.4	530.3
	$1,614.9	$1,192.2
Current liabilities		
Payable to suppliers and others	$ 920.3	$ 796.4
Short-term debt	129.4	94.2
Accrued taxes on income	97.4	55.6
	$1,147.1	$ 946.2
STATEMENT OF CASH FLOWS (IN PART)		
Noncash items included in net income	$ 105.2	
Cash flows from operating activities	?	
Cash flows from investing activities		
Investments in plant assets	(508.7)	
Business acquisitions	(119.4)	
Proceeds from asset sales	312.4	
Net cash used by investing activities	$(315.7)	
Cash flows from financing activities		
Long-term debt issuance	$ 303.0	
Repayments of long-term debt	(216.4)	
Others	?	

Required 1. Prepare a 1988 statement of cash flows for Scott Paper using the direct method. Assume the noncash items included in net income relate to selling and administrative expenses.

2. Prepare the net cash flow from operating activities under the indirect method.

57. Cash Flow Statement: Analysis. The following excerpts are from General Motors' 1988 Statement of Consolidated Cash Flows (in millions of dollars):

	December 31, 1988
STATEMENT OF CONSOLIDATED CASH FLOWS (SUMMARIZED)	
Net income	$ 4,632.1
Depreciation and amortization	7,037.2
Net loss on sale of plants	78.7
Provision for financing losses	820.8
Share of net earning of equity affiliates	(1,539.5)
Dividends paid	(1,657.5)
Expenditures for property and equipment	(5,626.5)
Proceeds from disposals of property and equipment	296.5
Foreign currency translation	(35.5)
Change in investing assets:	
Finance receivables – acquisitions	(91,031.1)
Finance receivables – liquidations	88,901.0
Other – investments	(1,297.6)
Acquisitions of companies	(675.2)
Additions to long-term debt	7,689.9
Reductions of long-term debt	(11,153.0)
Purchase of common stock	(786.5)
Issuance of common stock	253.0
Cash and cash equivalents:	
at beginning of year	3,723.0
at end of year	5,800.3
Increase (Decrease) in Operating Assets and Liabilities	
Receivables	$(3,145.8)
Inventories	(263.5)
Other current assets	240.7
Other liabilities	93.6
Accounts payable	635.9
Income taxes	(370.9)
Short-term loans payable	2,643.3

Required **1.** Convert the given information into a statement of cash flows using the indirect method. (*Hint:* The foreign currency translation amount should be shown as a separate category entitled "Effect of Exchange Rates on Cash.")

2. Compare GM's Statement of Cash Flows with Ford's in Problem 58. (*Hint:* Over the last three years, GM's sales have increased about $8 billion to $123.6 billion, while Ford's sales have increased about $22 billion to $92.4 billion.)

58. Cash Flow Statement: Analysis. The following excerpts are from Ford Motor Company's 1988 Consolidated Statement of Cash Flows (in millions of dollars):

	December 31, 1988
CONSOLIDATED STATEMENT OF CASH FLOWS (SUMMARIZED)	
Net income	$ 5,300.2
Depreciation and amortization	3,792.3
Provision for credit losses	1,248.9
Provision for deferred income taxes	(81.6)
Capital expenditures	(4,781.8)
Acquisition of other companies	(406.5)
Acquisition of finance receivables	(85,510.1)
Collections of finance receivables	79,254.5
Equity in earnings of subsidiaries	(101.2)
Other investments – loans	(9,605.1)
Long-term debt principal payments	(17,360.9)
Long-term debt issuance	22,837.9
Common stock purchase	(816.0)
Cash dividends	(1,113.5)
Short-term debt issuance	6,641.2
Foreign currency translation	480.5
Cash and cash equivalents:	
at beginning of year	5,919.2
at end of year	6,724.9
Increase (Decrease) in Current Assets and Liabilities: (Summarized)	
Accounts receivable	$2,005.0
Inventory	439.9
Other current assets	(574.4)
Accounts payable and accrued liabilities	1,493.2
Accrued taxes	1,404.2

Required 1. Convert the given information into a statement of cash flows using the indirect method. (*Hint:* The foreign currency translation amount should be shown as a separate category entitled "Effect of Exchange Rates on Cash".)

2. Compare Ford's Statement of Cash Flows with GM's in Problem 57. (*Hint:* Over the last three years, Ford's sales have increased about $22 billion to $92.4 billion, while GM's sales have increased about $8 billion to $123.6 billion.)

59. Interpretation of Statement of Cash Flows. Bristol-Myers is a major manufacturer of products related to health and health care. Its 1988 and 1987 Statements of Cash Flows are presented below (in millions of dollars):

	1988	1987
CASH FLOWS FROM OPERATING ACTIVITIES:		
Net income	$ 829.0	$ 709.6
Adjustments:		
Depreciation and amortization	127.9	115.9
Other operating items	8.8	30.7
Receivables	(121.1)	(92.0)
Inventories	(74.6)	4.4
Prepaids	(19.1)	(1.4)
Accounts payable	76.7	(38.0)
Accrued expenses and income taxes	73.5	65.4
Other assets and liabilities	79.5	28.3
Net cash provided by operating activities	$ 980.6	$ 822.9
CASH FLOWS FROM INVESTING ACTIVITIES:		
Proceeds from sales of time deposits and marketable securities	$5,050.3	$8,242.1
Purchases of time deposits and marketable securities	(4,349.7)	(8,774.7)
Additions to fixed assets	(249.1)	(186.5)
Other, including sales of businesses in 1987	(35.3)	148.3
Net cash provided by (used in) investing activities	$ 416.2	$ (570.8)
CASH FLOWS FROM FINANCING ACTIVITIES:		
Short-term borrowings	$ (45.3)	$ (35.9)
Long-term debt	(3.5)	24.2
Proceeds from stock options exercised	37.1	24.0
Purchase of treasury stock	(71.0)	(.9)
Dividends paid	(483.8)	(402.1)
Net cash used in financing activities	$ (566.5)	$ (390.7)
Effect of exchange rates on cash	$ 2.5	$ (1.0)
Increase (decrease) in cash and equivalents	$ 832.8	$ (139.6)
Cash and equivalents at beginning of year	353.4	493.0
Cash and equivalents at end of year	$1,186.2	$ 353.4

Required 1. List the major reasons for the increase in cash and equivalents in 1988 versus the decrease in 1987 by type of activity:

    a. Operating

    b. Investing

    c. Financing

2. Is Bristol-Myers more of an "income" stock (primarily dividend returns to investors) or a "growth" stock (primarily market price appreciation returns to investors)? Include the dividend yield and price earnings ratios in your answer. Use the average market price in your calculations. The following information from the annual report may be relevant:

	1988	1987	1986
Dividends per common share	$1.68	$1.40	$1.06
Earnings per common share	$2.88	$2.47	$2.07
Market prices	High Low	High Low	High Low
of common shares	$47 $38	$56 $28	$44 $30

3. Are there any apparent inconsistencies between this "income" or "growth" profile that you identified and management's apparent strategy of increasing cash and equivalents over the last year?

60. **User Analysis of Cash Flows.** Colgate-Palmolive Company is one of the world's leading consumer products companies, marketing its products in over 100 countries, with subsidiaries in 60 countries. The following excerpts are from its 1988 financial statements relating to the Consolidated Statement of Cash Flows and long-term debt (in thousands of dollars):

	1988	1987	1986
Operating activities:			
Income	$152,667	$ 886	$114,847
Noncash adjustments and operating assets and liabilities-net	(28,166)	97,882	55,747
Net cash provided by continuing operations	124,501	98,768	170,594
Discontinued operations	(169,443)	(16,781)	144,803
Net cash flow from operating activities	(44,942)	81,987	315,397
Investing activities:			
Capital expenditures	(238,717)	(285,791)	(220,911)
Payment for acquisitions	(174,582)	(115,646)	(63,334)
Proceeds from business sales	953,323	223,170	232,182
Other-net	(60,120)	(17,286)	16,030
Net cash flow from investing activities	479,904	(195,553)	(36,033)
Financing activities:			
Debt payments	(154,998)	(36,882)	(538,330)
Debt issuance	19,378	261,270	308,774
Dividends paid	(101,569)	(96,176)	(95,880)
Common stock purchase	(2,615)	(96,299)	(37,965)
Other-net	6,921	5,799	7,002
Net cash flow from investing activities	(232,883)	37,712	(356,399)
Effect of exchange rate changes	(12,394)	15,424	4,562
Net increase (decrease) in cash	$189,685	$ (60,430)	$ (72,473)
Total long-term debt	$695,496	$719,154	
Less: current portion of long-term debt	21,205	125,024	
	$674,291	$694,130	

Scheduled maturities of long-term debt outstanding at December 31, 1988, exclusive of capitalized lease obligations are as follows: 1989—$19,067; 1990—$87,325; 1991—$138,248; 1992—$15,812; 1993—$67,310.

Required Assume that Colgate-Palmolive decided to take advantage of business opportunities to expand its markets in Europe (see problem 14-40). Also, assume it used its financial flexibility and borrowed the $1 billion of its unused borrowing capacity under existing agreements at a 10% interest rate (see problem 8-87). Would it be able to pay its existing long-term debt as the debt came due? Would it be able to generate sufficient cash to pay off the $1 billion in 10 years without refinancing? Assume that Colgate-Palmolive's current cash flow on European assets is 9.9%.

61. **User Analysis of Statement of Cash Flows.** H.J. Heinz is a large consumer products company. The following excerpts are from its 1989 financial statements (in thousands of dollars except per share amounts):

CONSOLIDATED STATEMENT OF CASH FLOWS			
	1989	1988	1987
Operating Activities:			
Net income	$440,230	$386,014	$338,506
Adjustments to reconcile net income to cash provided by operating activities:			
Depreciation and amortization	148,104	133,348	109,868
Deferred tax provision	65,271	27,560	82,763
Other items, net	(45,454)	(10,595)	20,109
Changes in current assets and liabilities net of effects from acquisitions and divestitures:			
Receivables	(69,818)	(72)	18,254
Inventories	(134,582)	(12,251)	(3,723)
Other current assets	(13,650)	19,908	(30,314)
Accounts payable	25,290	38,145	(11,240)
Accrued liabilities	19,855	18,940	44,645
Income taxes	(18,929)	(33,837)	(62,267)
Cash provided by operating activities	416,317	567,160	506,601
Investing Activities:			
Capital expenditures	(323,325)	(238,265)	(184,730)
Acquisitions, net of cash acquired	(167,470)	(287,597)	(85,918)
Proceeds from divestitures	72,712	18,880	—
Purchase of short-term investments	(382,550)	(513,408)	(434,328)
Sales and maturities of short-term investments	412,365	666,272	311,198
Other items, net	12,627	5,005	(48,079)
Cash used for investing activities	(375,641)	(349,113)	(441,857)

Financing Activities:

Proceeds from long-term debt	227,291	45,108	322,777
Payments on long-term debt	(34,683)	(165,832)	(4,400)
Proceeds (payments) on short-term debt	49,110	(41,305)	(5,354)
Dividends	(178,474)	(154,573)	(132,455)
Purchase of treasury stock	(97,508)	(123,519)	(236,165)
Exercise of stock options	30,393	23,463	9,118
Other items, net	(1,590)	1,589	3,169
Cash (used for) financing activities	(5,461)	(415,069)	(43,310)
Effect of exchange rate changes on cash and cash equivalents	(8,098)	280	(3,727)
Net increase (decrease) in cash and cash equivalents	27,117	(196,742)	17,707
Cash and cash equivalents at beginning of year	75,488	272,230	254,523
Cash and cash equivalents at end of year	$102,605	$ 75,488	$272,230

Management's Financial Review (in part):
Liquidity and Capital Resources (in part):

Cash provided by operating activities in 1989 was $416,300, compared to $567,200 in 1988. Receivables increased $69,800, primarily because of higher sales. An additional $134,600 was spent on building inventory in 1989 to support higher sales volume and the restructuring of operations, particularly pet food.

Investing activities in 1989 required $375,600, compared to $349,100 in 1988. Capital expenditures increased $85,100 to $323,300 and were directly related to productivity improvements and growth-related expansion at existing facilities. It is expected that capital expenditures in 1990 will continue at present levels. Cash totaling $167,500 was spent on acquisitions in 1989, compared to $287,600 in 1988. Divestitures provided $72,700 of cash in 1989, compared to $18,900 in the previous year.

Cash used for financing activities declined by $409,600 to $5,500 in 1989. The change is primarily attributable to a net increase in cash from both long- and short-term borrowings of $241,700 in 1989, compared to a net reduction of $162,000 in 1988 (as a result of the repayment of debt using short-term investments).

During the year, the board of directors authorized an increase in the quarterly dividends for common stock from 31 cents per share to 36 cents per share and also authorized the repurchase of up to 5 million shares of common stock. $178,500 was spent in fiscal 1989 to pay dividends, an increase of $23,900 over 1988. $97,500 was spent in fiscal 1989 to repurchase 2.1 million shares of common stock. The company intends to reissue repurchased shares upon the exercise of stock options and conversion of preferred stock. In 1988, the company repurchased 2.7 million shares of common stock for $123,500 under a previously authorized share repurchase program.

As of May 3, 1989, the company had $347,000 in unused lines of credit (cancelable only after 390 days written notice), which are maintained primarily to support domestic commercial paper and bank borrowings. Accordingly, $273,500 of commercial paper and bank debt supported by such agreements was classified as long-term debt. In addition, the company has $550,000 of foreign and other domestic lines of credit available at year-end. The ratio of debt to invested capital was 35.1% in 1989, 32.9% in 1988 and 38.6% in 1987.

The company's financial position continues to remain strong, enabling it to meet cash requirements for operations, capital expansion programs and dividends to shareholders.

Note 4. Debt (in part):

The amount of long-term debt, excluding commercial paper, required to be retired in each of the four years succeeding 1990 (when $229,000 is due) is $50,200 in 1991, $98,600 in 1992, $52,900 in 1993, and $114,900 in 1994.

Required In its financial review, Heinz stated that "the company's financial position continues to remain strong, enabling it to meet cash requirements for operations, capital expansion programs, and dividends to shareholders." Analyze whether Heinz's financial position will enable it to meet cash requirements for long-term debt repayment in the next five years.

62. **User Analysis of Statement of Cash Flows.** Southland Corporation is one of the leading specialty retailers in the United States and is the country's largest operator and franchisor of convenience stores, doing business principally under the name 7-Eleven. The following excerpts are from its 1988 annual report (in thousands of dollars except per share amounts):

CONSOLIDATED STATEMENT OF CASH FLOWS

	1988	1987	1986
Operating Activities:			
Net income	$(216,231)	$ (74,854)	$178,577
Adjustments to reconcile net income to cash provided by operating activities:			
Depreciation and amortization	294,723	219,131	161,945
Noncash interest expense	167,704	29,137	—
Other items, net	(45,423)	(13,486)	(68,460)
Changes in current assets and liabilities:			
Receivables	(30,625)	(15,156)	(49,539)
Inventories	(119,062)	76,725	(46,054)
Other current assets	(15,050)	(24,908)	(22,932)
Accounts payable	(5,545)	146,523	52,703
Accrued liabilities	(8,973)	5,717	(45,109)
Income taxes	(34,437)	(54,528)	(26,538)
Cash provided by (used in) operating activities	(12,919)	294,301	134,593
Investing Activities:			
Capital expenditures	(131,413)	(492,834)	(590,029)
Acquisitions	(25,557)	(15,151)	(59,020)
Proceeds from divestitures	633,406	156,367	526,540
Equity purchased for JT merger		(1,762,525)	
Revaluation of assets and liabilities for merger		(1,932,783)	
Other items, net	(10,694)	5,206	65,246
Cash provided by (used for) investing activities	465,742	(4,041,720)	(57,263)

Financing Activities:

Proceeds from long-term debt	342,837	4,876,508	9,495
Payments on long-term debt	(882,578)	(756,567)	(26,289)
Proceeds (payments) on short-term debt	—	(415,291)	(31,329)
Dividends	—	(34,722)	(63,877)
Proceeds from stock issuance	—	152,995	31,530
Proceeds of revolving credit	110,000	25,000	—
Debt issuance costs	(17,389)	(155,611)	(37)
Cash provided by (used for) financing activities	(447,130)	3,692,312	(80,507)
Net increase (decrease) in cash and cash equivalents	5,693	(55,107)	(3,177)
Cash and cash equivalents at beginning of year	16,090	71,197	74,374
Cash and cash equivalents at end of year	$ 21,783	$ 16,090	$ 71,197

Note 1: Merger with JT Acquisition Corporation (in part):

On July 3, 1987, Southland Corporation entered into a plan of merger with JT Acquisition Corporation in a two-step transaction. In the first-step tender offer, on August 1, 1987, JT accepted for payment 31,500,000 shares of the company's common stock at $77 per share in cash and 2,418,949 shares of the company's preferred stock at $90.27 per share in cash. JT already owned 2,597,403 shares of the company's common stock, giving it control of approximately 70% of the then outstanding common shares and 97% of the then outstanding preferred shares. In the second-step merger, which was consummated on December 15, 1987, JT was merged into the company with the company continuing as the surviving corporation. As a result of the merger, each remaining common share of the company was converted into $61.32 in cash and 0.67 of a share of a new preferred stock. Each remaining share of the old preferred stock was canceled and exchanged for $90.27 in cash. As a result of the above, the results of operations of the company subsequent to the merger are not comparable to those of any period prior to the merger.

Note 11. Debt (in part):

The company is obligated under a Bank Credit Agreement which includes a Senior Term Loan and a Divestiture Term Loan. At December 31, 1988, the unpaid balances of the Senior Term Loan and the Divestiture Term Loan were $1,400,000 and $272,508 respectively. The Credit Agreement also provides a $450,000 revolving credit facility of which $135,000 was outstanding at December 31, 1988.

The Senior Term Loan must be fully paid on December 31, 1995. A payment of $100,000 was made in January 1989, and the remainder is to be paid through minimum quarterly installments ranging from $37,500 to $75,000 commencing March 31, 1990 through September 30, 1995. The Divestiture Term Loan balance is payable in full on December 31, 1989. The $450,000 available under the revolving credit facility will be reduced to $400,000 on December 31, 1990 and to $350,000 on December 31, 1991. The revolving credit facility will expire, and all amounts outstanding will be due and payable in full on December 31, 1992.

As of December 31, 1988, long-term debt scheduled maturities, which include capital lease obligations and sinking fund requirements, are as follows:

1989	$ 527,174
1990	270,297
1991	171,703
1992	265,357
1993	224,376
Thereafter	2,855,845
	$4,314,752

The Senior Term Loans, the Divestiture Term Loans and the Revolving Credit Facility under the credit agreement are collectively known as the "Permanent Financing Facility."

Required Will Southland be able to repay its "Permanent Financing Facility" as it comes due?

Accounting for Changing Prices and International Operations

818-819
832-837

After reading this chapter, you should understand

- General price-level changes and the constant purchasing power adjustment process
- Specific price changes and the current cost adjustment process
- Constant purchasing power financial statements
- The nature of the purchasing power gain or loss on net monetary items
- Current cost financial statements

- The nature of holding gains and losses
- Exit prices
- Accounting for international operations
- The conversion of a foreign subsidiary's financial statements into dollars
- Supplementary disclosures (Appendix)

The dollar is the basic measuring unit in U.S. financial statements. It is well known, of course, that the value of the dollar does change. In this chapter, three effects of changes in the value of the dollar are explained.

First, changes in the overall value of the dollar are caused by inflation. Second, the specific prices of individual goods and services change. The basic principles underlying these alternatives are discussed in this chapter. These changes in value are not explicitly recognized under GAAP (except when the lower of cost or market method is used). However, companies are encouraged, but not required, to disclose certain effects of inflation and the changes in the prices of individual goods or services. These discretionary disclosures are discussed in the Appendix to this chapter.

The third change in the value of the dollar is recognized under GAAP. It is the change in the value of the dollar with respect to foreign currencies. When a transaction is expressed in a foreign currency or a company owns a foreign subsidiary, the foreign currency amounts must be converted into U.S. dollars to be included in the company's financial statements. These topics are also discussed in this chapter.

SECTION A Accounting for Changing Prices

◼ ALTERNATIVE MEASURES OF INCOME

Suppose that a company purchased land at the beginning of 1993 for $50,000. A year later, after there has been inflation of 10%, the land is sold for $65,000. What is the profit on the sale of the land? There are three different answers depending on how profit is measured. Before we discuss the three alternatives, however, we should have a clear understanding of what is meant by the term *profit* or *income*.

A common definition in economics is that income is the amount that could be paid to the owners of the company during a period of time and still enable the company to be as well off at the end of the period as it was at the beginning. The issue, therefore, is the measurement of the wealth of the company at the beginning and the end of the period.

One answer to the earlier question is that the profit is $15,000 ($65,000 − $50,000). This is the answer if profit is measured according to the generally accepted accounting principles discussed in this book. In this case profit is being measured as the difference between the dollars received from the sale and the historical dollars used to acquire the item being sold. The wealth at the beginning of the period is measured as the *nominal* dollars used to acquire the land, and therefore the profit of $15,000 is the increase in the nominal dollars during the period. **Nominal dollars are dollars that have not been adjusted to reflect changes in prices.** Nominal dollars are used in the historical cost financial statements that have been discussed throughout this book because they are the basis for generally accepted accounting principles.

A second answer is that the profit is $10,000. This is the answer if the wealth at the beginning of the period is measured in terms of the purchasing power at the end of the period of the dollars that were originally used to buy the land. **Purchasing power is the measure of the ability of dollars to purchase goods and services.** Since the land cost $50,000 and there has been inflation of 10% since the purchase, the $50,000 historical dollars have the same value, or purchasing power, as $55,000 ($50,000 × 1.10) at the end of the period. Therefore, the purchasing power of the owner of the land has increased by $10,000 ($65,000 − $55,000). This is the measure of profit when the wealth at the beginning of the period is measured in terms of the purchasing power of the dollars at the end of the period, or more generally, when profit is measured in terms of constant purchasing power. **Constant purchasing power amounts (constant dollars) are historical (nominal) dollars that have been adjusted for changes in the general purchasing power.**

A third answer is that the profit is zero. If it is accepted that the owner of the land needs to replace it with land of equivalent capacity (e.g., same size and location), there is no profit because the $65,000 obtained from the sale is needed to replace the land. A similar piece of land of the same size and location would, of course, cost $65,000 and therefore there is no profit. This is the measure of profit when the wealth at the beginning of the period is measured in terms of the current cost of the item being sold. **Current cost is the amount that would have to be paid at a certain point in time (e.g., the current period) to purchase an identical, or similar, item.**

Companies may prepare certain constant purchasing power or current cost information for both internal decision making and external reporting. Before discussing this information, it is useful to examine additional characteristics of these two alternative methods of measurement.

The Nature of Price Changes

As all of us are aware the price of virtually everything that is bought and sold changes each year. In recent times most of the price changes have been increases rather than decreases. It can easily be seen that price changes vary with the type of item. However, some prices rise much faster than others. For instance the prices of energy and housing have tended to fluctuate, whereas the prices of computers and calculators have tended to fall.

A price change is either a specific price change or a general price change. **A specific price change is the measure of the change in the price of a *particular* good or service.** Examples are the price changes in such items as a gallon of unleaded gas or a pound of lean hamburger. Current cost accounting is based on changes in specific prices. **A general price change is the weighted average of the changes in the individual prices of a *group* of goods and services.** This measure of the change in prices indicates the general inflation rate and therefore the change in the purchasing power of the dollar. **A general price-level index is a measure of general price changes over a period of time stated as an index rather than in dollar amounts.** Constant purchasing power accounting is based on changes in the general price level as measured by a general price-level index.

To illustrate the difference between the two concepts of price changes further, consider a general price-level (GPL) index made up of four individual items. To simplify the illustration we are including only four items, whereas the available indexes (discussed later) include hundreds of items. The items are included in the index by using amounts that reflect average buying patterns. For example, if the average household buys 40 pounds of hamburger per year, the price of 40 pounds of hamburger will be included when the index is computed. The price per unit of each of the four items and the average amounts purchased per year are used to compute the average total price as follows:

Item	Price per Unit in 1993	Average Amounts Purchased	Average Total Price in 1993
A	$ 2	40 units	$ 80
B	5	30	150
C	10	20	200
D	40	10	400
Total			$830

In 1994 the prices of the individual items and the average amounts purchased are used to compute the average total price as follows:

Item	Price per Unit in 1994	Average Amounts Purchased	Average Total Price in 1994
A	$ 3	40 units	$120
B	6	30	180
C	12	20	240
D	40	10	400
Total			$940

The change in prices between 1993 and 1994 may be summarized as follows:

Item	Percent Change in Prices	Calculations
A	50%	($3 − $2) ÷ $2 = 0.50
B	20	($6 − $5) ÷ $5 = 0.20
C	20	($12 − $10) ÷ $10 = 0.20
D	0	($40 − $40) ÷ $40 = 0
Overall	13.25%	($940 − $830) ÷ $830 = 0.1325

The prices of individual items, that is, the specific prices, have increased in the range from zero (item D) to 50% (item A), whereas the general price change indicates an average increase of 13.25%.

Although this is a very simple measure of the change in the general price level, it is possible to use it to develop a general price-level index. If the price of the items in 1993 is assigned an index number of 100, the general price level in 1994 has an index of 113.25:

$$\text{GPL Index in 1994} = \frac{\text{Average Total Price in 1994}}{\text{Average Total Price in 1993}} \times \text{Index in 1993}$$

$$= \frac{\$940}{\$830} \times 100$$

$$= 113.25$$

To illustrate the index concept further, suppose that in 1995 the average total price for the four items is $1,020. The index in 1995 would be:

$$\text{GPL Index in 1995} = \frac{\text{Average Total Price in 1995}}{\text{Average Total Price in 1993}} \times \text{Index in 1993}$$

General price level.

$$= \frac{\$1,020}{\$830} \times 100$$

$$= 122.89$$

Alternatively, the index in 1995 could be calculated as follows:

$$\text{GPL Index in 1995} = \frac{\text{Average Total Price in 1995}}{\text{Average Total Price in 1994}} \times \text{Index in 1994}$$

$$= \frac{\$1,020}{\$940} \times 113.25$$

$$= 122.89$$

A *specific* price-level index of a particular item can be developed in the same way as the general price-level index, based on a comparison of the specific prices of an individual item in each year. For example, the price of item A has risen from $2.00 in 1993 to $3.00 in 1994. If the price of $2.00 in 1993 is assigned an index number of 100, the specific price-level index for item A in 1994 is 150 [($3.00 ÷ $2.00) × 100].

1994 $\frac{300}{200}$ ×100 = 150
1993

Available Price-Level Indexes

Numerous price-level indexes are developed by various groups and are publicly available. The largest developer of price-level indexes is the federal government, which publishes over 2,700 different indexes. Most of them are specific price-level indexes, although many of them measure the change in the general price level. Of the latter type, there are three indexes that are widely publicized—the Wholesale Price Index, the Gross National Product Implicit Price Deflator, and the Consumer Price Index. The Consumer Price Index is prepared for various types of consumers. **The Consumer Price Index for All Urban Consumers (CPI–U) is used for the constant purchasing power supplementary disclosures discussed later in the Appendix to the chapter.** We use the CPI–U as the general price-level index throughout this chapter.

CPI – U = General price Index.

■ COMPREHENSIVELY RESTATED FINANCIAL STATEMENTS

F/S ⇒ use history cost

In the introductory paragraphs to this chapter the basic principles underlying the historical cost, constant purchasing power, and current cost methods of accounting were discussed. A company is required to use the historical cost method to prepare its financial statements. However, a company may prepare a complete set of constant purchasing power or current cost financial statements for use in its internal decision making or for supplementary disclosures in its annual report. Furthermore, companies are encouraged to disclose selected information prepared according to constant purchasing power and current cost principles as discussed in the Appendix to the chapter. To illustrate these three alternatives further, consider the following example of a series of simplified events for a corporation. Some of the situations and amounts discussed are very simple so that the reader can more easily focus on the concepts and not be distracted by complex arithmetic.

1. The Triad Company was formed by selling no-par common stock for $100 when the CPI–U index was 100.

2. The company purchased a building for $30 with a two-year life and no residual value when the CPI–U index was 100.

3. The company purchased three units of inventory for $10, $12, and $14 each when the CPI–U index was 100, 110, and 120, respectively.

4. The company sold two units of inventory for $30 each when the CPI–U index was 110. A FIFO cost flow assumption is used.

5. The average CPI–U index for the year was 110.

6. The current cost at year-end was $14 for the inventory and $40 for the building. The CPI–U index at year-end was 120.

7. Income taxes are disregarded.

Historical Cost Financial Statements

The income statement and ending balance sheet prepared under the three alternatives are presented in Exhibits 13–1 and 13–2. In Exhibit 13–1 the historical cost (or nominal dollar) net income is $23 because sales are $60, the cost of goods sold on a FIFO basis is $22, and the depreciation expense, computed on a straight-line basis, is $15. In Exhibit 13–2 the total assets, measured on a historical cost (nominal dollar) basis, are $123, consisting of cash of $94, inventory of $14, and the building with a book value of $15. In this simple example there are no liabilities. Common stock is $100 and the retained earnings are equal to the net income of the period because there were no beginning retained earnings or dividends paid during the year. The remaining items in the exhibits expressed in constant purchasing power and current costs are discussed in the next section.

Constant Purchasing Power Financial Statements

The underlying principle of constant purchasing power financial statements is to adjust historical costs into dollars of constant purchasing power. The general formula for this adjustment is:

$$\text{Constant Purchasing Power} = \text{Historical Cost} \times \frac{\text{General Price-Level Index in Current Period}}{\text{General Price-Level Index at Time of Historical Cost Transaction}}$$

EXHIBIT 13–1

TRIAD COMPANY
Income Statement
for Current Year

	Historical Cost	Constant Purchasing Power	Current Cost
Sales revenue	$60[a]	$60.00[d]	$60.00[g]
Cost of goods sold	(22)[b]	(23.00)[e]	(24.00)[h]
Depreciation expense	(15)[c]	(16.50)[f]	(17.50)[i]
Net income	$23	$20.50	$18.50

[a] 2 units × $30.

[b] Since a FIFO cost flow assumption is used, the cost of the first two units ($10 + $12) is included in the cost of goods sold.

[c] (Cost − Residual Value) ÷ Life = ($30 − $0) ÷ 2.

[d] It is assumed that the sales were made at the average general price level for the year, or $60 × $\frac{110}{110}$ = $60.

[e] $\left(\$10 \times \frac{110}{100}\right) + \left(\$12 \times \frac{110}{110}\right) = \$23.$

[f] $\$15 \times \frac{110}{100}.$

[g] The sales revenue does not require adjusting.

[h] Average Current Cost × Number of Units Sold = $\frac{\$14 + \$10}{2} \times 2.$

[i] (Average Current Cost − Residual Value) ÷ Life = $\left(\frac{\$40 + \$30}{2} - \$0\right) \div 2.$

For example, in the illustration used at the beginning of the chapter the land was purchased for $50,000 and there was inflation of 10%, which is equivalent to a general price-level index increasing from, for example, 150 to 165 (150 × 1.10 = 165). Therefore, the cost of the land in constant purchasing power is measured by:

$$\text{Constant Purchasing Power Cost of Land} = \$50,000 \times \frac{165}{150}$$

$$= \$55,000$$

This approach has been used to calculate the constant purchasing power amount of the sales, cost of goods sold, depreciation expense, cash, inventory, building, accumulated depreciation, and common stock for the Triad Company. The amount in the retained earnings account is calculated differently, as is discussed later. In this example the price-level index in the current period that is used for the numerator of the general price-level calculation is the *average* index for the current period, or 110. The average index is used because the financial statements report on the activities of the company for a year. The computations of the constant purchasing power income statement items in Exhibit 13–1 are discussed next.

EXHIBIT 13–2

·················

TRIAD COMPANY
Balance Sheet
at End of Current Year

	Historical Cost	Constant Purchasing Power	Current Cost
Cash	$ 94[a]	$ 86.17[d]	$ 94[a]
Inventory	14[b]	12.83	14[i]
Building	30	33.00	40[k]
Less: accumulated depreciation	(15)	(16.50)[g]	(20)[l]
Total assets	$123	$115.50	$128
Common stock, no par	$100	$110.00[h]	$100
Retained earnings[c]	23	5.50[i]	28[m]
Total liabilities and stockholders' equity	$123	$115.50	$128

[a]$100 (Sale of Common Stock) − $30 (Building) − $36 (Inventory) + $60 (Sales).
[b]Since a FIFO cost flow assumption is used, the cost of the last unit purchased is included in inventory.
[c]Since the beginning retained earnings is assumed to be zero and no dividends are paid, the retained earnings in the ending balance sheet is equal to the results of the calculations in notes i and m.
[d]$94 × (110 ÷ 120).
[e]$14 × (110 ÷ 120).
[f]$30 × (110 ÷ 100).
[g]$15 × (110 ÷ 100).
[h]$100 × (110 ÷ 100).
[i]Net Income ($20.50) − Purchasing Power Loss ($15.00).
[j]1 Unit × Ending Current Cost of $14.
[k]Current cost at year end.
[l](Current Cost − Residual Value) ÷ Life = ($40 − $0) ÷ 2 = $20.
[m]Net Income ($18.50) + Holding Gains ($9.50).

Sales. The sales were made when the CPI–U index was 110 and therefore do not need adjusting. Alternatively, the formula for the adjustment could be used as follows:

$$\$60 \times \frac{110}{110} = \$60 \text{ sales}$$

Cost of Goods Sold. Under the FIFO cost flow assumption the cost of goods sold included units with historical costs of $10 and $12, which were purchased when the CPI–U index was 100 and 110, respectively. The cost of goods sold is adjusted as follows:

$$\left(\$10 \times \frac{110}{100}\right) + \left(\$12 \times \frac{110}{110}\right) = \$23 \text{ cost of goods sold}$$

Note that if the average cost flow assumption had been used, the average historical cost per unit would be $12 [($10 + $12 + $14) ÷ 3] and the cost of goods sold on a historical cost basis would be $24 (2 units × $12). It would be typical

No need to adj when using average price

to assume that the cost of goods sold on an average cost basis was measured in terms of the average price level for the year and therefore would not need adjusting. The constant purchasing power cost of goods sold would be $24 [$24 × (110 ÷ 110)].

Depreciation Expense. For historical cost depreciation expense the original cost of the asset is depreciated over its expected life (two years in this example), and therefore depreciation expense is measured in terms of the historical dollars at the time of acquisition of the asset and not in a constant purchasing power amount. Thus, the historical cost depreciation of $15 is measured in terms of a CPI–U index of 100 and needs to be adjusted as follows:

$$\$15 \times \frac{110}{100} = \$16.50 \text{ depreciation expense}$$

Other expenses included in the income statement (such as selling expenses, general and administrative expenses, and income tax expense) are typically assumed to occur at the average price level for the year and therefore do not need adjusting. The computations of the constant purchasing power balance sheet items in Exhibit 13–2 are discussed next.

Cash. The cash in the historical cost balance sheet is measured in terms of the CPI–U index at that time, which is the year-end index of 120. Therefore, the cash needs to be adjusted to the average price level of the year as follows:

$$\$94 \times \frac{110}{120} = \$86.17 \text{ cash}$$

Other "monetary" assets (defined later), such as accounts receivable, would be adjusted to the average price level by using the same adjustment factor.

Inventory. Under the FIFO cost flow assumption the unit in the ending inventory cost $14; it was purchased when the index was 120 and is adjusted as follows:

$$\$14 \times \frac{110}{120} = \$12.83 \text{ inventory}$$

Building and Accumulated Depreciation. The building was purchased for $30 and accumulated depreciation of $15 has been recorded. Since both of these amounts are measured in terms of the CPI–U index of 100, they have to be adjusted as follows:

$$\$30 \times \frac{110}{100} = \$33.00 \text{ building}$$

$$(\$15) \times \frac{110}{100} = (\$16.50) \text{ accumulated depreciation}$$

Liabilities. The Triad Company has no "monetary" liabilities (defined later), but if they did these monetary liabilities would be adjusted in the same way as cash. That is, they are included in the historical cost balance sheet at the price level of the end of the year, and they must be adjusted to the average price level.

Common Stock. The common stock was sold when the CPI–U index was 100 and therefore is adjusted as follows:

$$\$100 \times \frac{110}{100} = \$110 \text{ common stock}$$

Purchasing Power Gain or Loss on Net Monetary Items. During a period of inflation, holding cash results in a loss of purchasing power. For example, $10 cash when hamburger is $2 per pound enables you to buy five pounds of hamburger. When the price of hamburger rises to $2.50 per pound, $10 will buy only four pounds of hamburger. Therefore, holding the $10 cash during the period of inflation has resulted in the loss of purchasing power of one pound of hamburger. This loss is 25% of the purchasing power needed to buy four pounds of hamburger at the end of the period. This loss can also be measured as 25% of the cash held or $2.50 ($10 × 0.25 = $2.50). This result also can be obtained by noting that at the end of the period it takes $12.50 (or an increase of 25%) to buy five pounds of hamburger. *The purchasing power of cash declines as inflation in the prices of all goods and services occurs.* When constant purchasing power financial statements are prepared this loss of general purchasing power must be recognized.

Cash is only one monetary asset. There are several monetary assets (and liabilities) that a company can own (or owe). A **monetary asset is money or a claim to receive a fixed amount of money in the future.** The principal monetary assets are cash, accounts receivable, and notes receivable. Holding monetary assets during a period of inflation results in a purchasing power loss. A **monetary liability is an obligation to repay a fixed amount of money in the future.** The principal monetary liabilities include accounts payable, notes payable, and bonds payable. Holding a monetary *liability* during a period of inflation results in a purchasing power gain because inflation reduces the purchasing power of the dollars needed to repay these liabilities. The reduction in the purchasing power owed results in a purchasing power gain. **Net monetary items are monetary assets less monetary liabilities.** The purchasing power gain or loss is the combined gain or loss in purchasing power that occurs when net monetary items are held during a period in which the general price level changes. The computation of the purchasing power gain or loss is made more complex because the net monetary items are changed during the period by some of a company's transactions.

In the Triad Company example cash is the only monetary item. The cash balance has decreased from $100 to $94 during the period. The company has incurred a purchasing power loss that is computed as follows. First, all the cash transactions are adjusted to the constant purchasing power represented by the average CPI–U index of 110:

Depreciation Expense. The depreciation expense is based on the average current cost of the building as follows:

$$\text{Depreciation Expense} = \frac{\text{Average Current Cost} - \text{Residual Value}}{\text{Life}}$$

$$= \frac{\left(\dfrac{\$30 + \$40}{2}\right) - \$0}{2}$$

$$= \$17.50$$

Other expenses typically included in the income statement (such as selling expenses, general and administrative expenses, and income tax expense) are assumed to occur at the average cost for the year and therefore do not need adjusting. The computations of the current cost balance sheet items in Exhibit 13–2 are discussed next.

Cash. Cash does not need adjustment, because it is already stated in terms of its value at the end of the year. Similarly, all other monetary assets and monetary liabilities are not adjusted.

Inventory. The inventory in the balance sheet is valued at the current cost of the units in the inventory at year-end. In our example the ending inventory of $14 is computed as follows:

$$\text{Ending Inventory} = \text{Number of Units} \times \text{Ending Current Cost}$$

$$= 1 \times \$14$$

$$= \$14$$

Building and Accumulated Depreciation. The building is valued at the current cost at year-end ($40) less accumulated depreciation based on this year-end value. Since the life of the building is half over, the accumulated depreciation is half the current cost:

Building $= \$40$

$$\text{Accumulated Depreciation} = \left(\begin{array}{c}\text{Current Cost at the} \\ \text{End of the Period}\end{array} - \begin{array}{c}\text{Residual} \\ \text{Value}\end{array}\right) \times \frac{\text{Number of Years Owned}}{\text{Life}}$$

$$= (\$40 - \$0) \times \frac{1}{2}$$

$$= \$20$$

Common Stock. The common stock is not adjusted because there is no reliable measure of the amount for which all the common stock outstanding could be sold in the current period.

Holding Gains and Losses. When current cost financial statements are being prepared, holding gains and losses arise. **A holding gain (loss) is the increase**

(decrease) in the current cost of a nonmonetary asset during the period. Holding gains (losses) may be realized or unrealized. A realized holding gain (loss) is a gain (loss) that has been recognized on an item that has been included in the historical cost income statement. On the other hand, an unrealized holding gain (loss) is a gain (loss) on an item that has not yet been recognized in the historical cost income statement. In general, the realized and unrealized holding gains (losses) are measured as follows:

Realized Holding Gain (Loss) = Current Cost Expense − Historical Cost Expense

Unrealized Holding Gain (Loss) = Current Cost Asset Value − Historical Cost Asset Value

Holding gains in the Triad Company example arise on the inventory and the building. Therefore, the realized and unrealized holding gains are calculated as follows:

average cost × # of unit sold × 2 life

Realized Holding Gain (Inventory)	= Current Cost of the Cost of Goods Sold	− Historical Cost of the Cost of Goods Sold
	= $24 *14+10/2 × 2 = 24* − $22	*10 + 12 = 22*
	= $2	

Realized Holding Gain (Building)	= Current Cost Depreciation Expense	− Historical Cost Depreciation Expense
	= $17.50	− $15.00
	= $2.50	

Unrealized Holding Gain (Inventory)	= Current Cost of Inventory	− Historical Cost of Inventory
	= $14	− $14
	= $0	

Unrealized Holding Gain (Building)	= Net Current Cost of Building	− Net Historical Cost of Building
	= ($40 − $20)	− ($30 − $15)
	= $5	

result from rasing price

The total holding gains are $9.50 ($2 + $2.50 + $0 + $5). There is disagreement about whether holding gains and losses should be included in income. In this example the holding gains are *excluded* from income, but they are *added* to retained earnings. No matter how holding gains and losses are included in financial statements it is important to recognize the nature of these gains. They result simply from the rise in price of the respective assets, and they do not increase the wealth of the company if it is agreed that the assets will have to be replaced at the higher cost. It is difficult to argue that the company is better off, because it will have to replace assets at the higher cost.

Retained Earnings. Since there is no beginning balance of retained earnings and no dividends were paid, the amount in the balance sheet is the net income for the period ($18.50) plus the holding gain ($9.50), or $28. Examples of the adjustments to additional items not included in the above example are included in the discussion of the supplementary disclosures.

chasing power amounts is clearly defined because ~~~~~~~~~~~~~ used, and this index is prepared by the federal government.

The method of computing the current cost supplementary disclosures, in contrast, is much less well defined. The current cost of *inventory* is the current cost of purchasing or producing the goods concerned. The current cost of *property, plant,* and *equipment* is the current cost of acquiring the same service potential (indicated by operating costs and physical output capacity) as embodied by the asset owned. The current cost of property, plant, and equipment may be determined by either (1) the current cost of a used asset of the same age and in the same condition as the asset owned, (2) the current cost of a new asset with the same service potential as the used asset had when new, less a deduction for depreciation, or (3) the current cost of a new asset with a different service potential, less a deduction for depreciation, and adjusted for the cost of the difference in service potential due to differences in life, output capacity, and nature of service, including any operating cost savings. There are three basic methods of finding the current cost of inventory and property, plant, and equipment.

Direct Pricing

The current cost of the asset is determined directly by using the most recent invoice price, a supplier's price list, or other quotations or estimates, or by using standard manufacturing costs. This is an appropriate measurement technique for assets that are frequently purchased or manufactured or that have an established market price, such as inventory and office equipment.

Functional or Unit Pricing

The current cost is calculated by estimating the construction (or acquisition) cost per unit (such as per square foot of building space) and multiplying this figure by the number of units in the asset. For example, if a company owns a building with 5,000 square feet and current construction costs are $100 per square foot, the current cost of the building would be $500,000.

Specific Price Index

The current cost is calculated by adjusting the historical cost by a specific price index appropriate to the asset. Since the federal government publishes more than 2,700 price indexes, it should be possible to find an index that is appropriate for each particular asset or component of an asset. The adjustment process is the same as that used for a general price index:

$$\frac{\text{Current}}{\text{Cost}} = \frac{\text{Historical}}{\text{Cost}} \times \frac{\text{Specific Price Index in Current Period}}{\text{Specific Price Index at Time of Historical Cost Transaction}}$$

The second two methods are more likely to be appropriate for property, plant, and equipment. Since any of the methods may be used for any asset, however, and the second two methods do not necessarily result in accurate measures of current cost, there is likely to be much variation in the current cost figures developed by companies. This potential variation is one of the major criticisms of any supplementary current cost disclosures.

■ DISCRETIONARY SUPPLEMENTARY DISCLOSURES

The earlier illustration of the preparation of comprehensive constant purchasing power and current cost financial statements was based on very simple historical cost financial statements. In practice, however, financial statements are much more complex. No companies are required to prepare *comprehensively* adjusted financial statements, although they may voluntarily disclose the information. Beginning in 1979, however, selected companies were required to make certain supplementary disclosures of the effects of changing prices.[1] The original disclosures were simplified in 1984.[2] In 1986, the *requirement* for the disclosures was suspended and companies were instead *encouraged* to make them.[3] These discretionary disclosures include selected information for the current year as well as for five years. The selected disclosures for the current year are

1. Income from continuing operations based on current cost

2. Purchasing power gain or loss on net monetary items (excluded from income from continuing operations)

3. Current cost amounts of inventory and of property, plant, and equipment at the end of the current year

4. Increase or decrease in the current cost amounts of inventory and of property, plant, and equipment, before and after eliminating the effects of inflation (excluded from income from continuing operations)

The selected disclosures for the five-year summary are:

1. Net sales and other operating revenues

2. Income from continuing operations (and related earnings per share) based on current cost

. . . .

[1] "Financial Reporting and Changing Prices," *FASB Statement of Financial Accounting Standards No. 33* (Stamford, Conn.: FASB, 1979).

[2] "Financial Reporting and Changing Prices: Elimination of Certain Disclosures," *FASB Statement of Financial Accounting Standards No. 82* (Stamford, Conn.: FASB, 1984).

[3] "Financial Reporting and Changing Prices," *FASB Statement of Financial Accounting Standards No. 89* (Stamford, Conn.: FASB, 1986).

3. Net assets at year-end based on current cost

4. Increase or decrease in the current cost amounts of inventory and of property, plant, and equipment, after eliminating the effects of inflation

5. Purchasing power gain or loss on net monetary items

6. Cash dividends declared per common share

7. Market price per common share at year-end

The methods of computing this information are discussed in the Appendix to this chapter.

EVALUATION OF THE ALTERNATIVE METHODS

most conservative. but not during the time of inflation

As has been explained throughout this chapter the three methods are based on different concepts. The historical cost method is based on nominal dollars, the constant purchasing power method is based on dollars of the same purchasing power, and the current cost method is based on productive capacity. Since the methods are alternatives, and *not* substitutes, for each other, it is not realistic to state that one is the best. The user of the information needs to understand the meaning of the information presented under each alternative and therefore decide which method yields the most useful information for any particular purpose.

The historical cost method has the advantage of being the most reliable and widely understood method. It is also the most conservative in terms of the balance sheet valuations, but as we have seen, it does not necessarily produce the most conservative, or lowest, measure of income during periods of inflation. It is difficult to see that it is most relevant to the needs of users of financial statements, however. The user only knows that there has been a net inflow of nominal dollars (assuming the company has a positive net income) and that the company's capital measured in nominal dollars has increased. The user has no assurance that the purchasing power of the company's capital is being maintained or that the company can continue to operate at the same capacity level.

Ensuring that the company maintains the purchasing power of its capital would probably be considered relevant by most stockholders. They contributed a certain number of dollars to the company when they invested in it, and are probably more concerned about the purchasing power of those dollars than about the number of dollars originally contributed. Constant purchasing power income statements ensure that the purchasing power of the capital is maintained before income is earned.

In addition, the usefulness of the constant purchasing power balance sheet is increased in two ways. First, the values of all the items in the balance sheet are reported in terms of dollars of constant purchasing power. Thus, the amounts can be meaningfully compared. In contrast, the historical cost balance sheet includes costs incurred at many different times, and therefore these costs are very difficult, if not impossible, to compare. For example, the purchasing power of the cash, which is measured in current period dollars, cannot be compared with the purchasing power of the dollars invested in the land, which was purchased in a previous period and is therefore measured in dollars of that period. Second, the comparability of historical cost balance sheets over time is very limited for the same reasons. For example, a valid comparison between a 1989 and a 1993 balance sheet cannot be made because each includes costs of very different purchasing powers. When both balance sheets are converted to 1993 constant purchasing power dollars, a meaningful comparison can be made.

A company needs specific assets to conduct its operations, and it is possible that the company could be maintaining the general purchasing power of its capital but not its ability to replace those assets. This situation arises when the costs of the particular assets that the company is using rise faster than the general price level. Use of the current cost concept ensures that the operating capacity of the company is maintained before income is earned. In addition, the current value of the assets reported in the balance sheet represents the value of these assets at that particular balance sheet date, which many users of financial statements consider to be more relevant than a report of the number of nominal dollars that the asset originally cost.

When the three alternatives are compared, many users of financial statements argue that the current cost method of preparing financial statements is conceptually the most desirable and therefore much more relevant. It must be recognized that the amounts may be less reliable than those produced under the historical cost or constant dollar methods, but it is very difficult to evaluate a tradeoff between relevance and reliability.

An additional consideration is the cost/benefit relationship. There is little doubt that some users of financial statements did find the additional supplementary information beneficial. Companies that provided the information did incur a cost, however. For example, du Pont reported that it spent $100,000 initially to implement a system for preparing the supplementary disclosures.[4] It is problematical whether the users of du Pont's financial statements did, over the years, obtain more than $100,000 of benefits.

Evaluation of the Elimination of the Disclosures on the Effects of Changing Prices

When supplementary disclosures about the effects of changing prices were first adopted in 1979, it was intended that the requirement would be reviewed after a period of not more than five years. Consequently, the FASB sponsored and monitored research to help assess the usefulness of the information. In 1986 the FASB voted to eliminate the requirement for the remaining disclosures by a 4 to 3 majority.

There were several arguments in favor of eliminating the required disclosures. First, there was evidence that the disclosures were not widely used. Among the reasons for the lack of use were concerns about the relevance of the information. It was argued that the concept of current cost (the cost of replacing

....

[4] *Wall Street Journal*, July 19, 1984.

existing service potential) is not relevant because many companies intend to replace their assets with others that have a different service potential. It was also argued that applying a specific price index to the historical cost does not provide a relevant value because technological change may not be appropriately reflected in the index. The lack of use also resulted from concerns about the *reliability* of the information. For example, the determination of the current cost when an asset with equivalent service potential was not available required significant judgment and therefore could be considered unreliable. Furthermore, since the disclosures were labeled "unaudited" and "supplementary," they were considered to lack reliability.

Second, there was concern that the *costs of providing the information exceeded the benefits*. Although both the costs and the benefits could not be accurately measured, it is appropriate for the FASB to suspend disclosure requirements if preparers and users perceive that costs exceed benefits. Third, it was argued that the disclosures lacked *comparability*. This situation resulted from the degree of flexibility in methods of application, by differences in the quality of the raw data used to prepare the disclosures, and by failure to disclose the assumption used. Fourth, concern was expressed that the disclosures lacked *understandability* because they were overly complex. It was argued that the disclosures were difficult to understand because they were not adequately explained and did not include comprehensive financial statements.

Fifth, many users of financial statements indicated that they used information about changing prices in their decisions but had developed their own methods for making the adjustments. Therefore, additional disclosures might not be useful because users had information that was better or different from that required. The final argument against continuing the required disclosures was that interest in the disclosures had decreased because prices were changing much less than in previous years. Therefore, other concerns were more important, such as the ability of the company to finance replacements of productive capacity or the effects of changing interest rates on monetary assets and liabilities.

There were also several arguments in favor of continuing the required disclosures. First, it was argued that the basic concept underlying the disclosures (inflation causes historical cost financial statements to show illusory profits and to mask erosion of capital) is virtually undisputed. Second, although there was evidence of limited use of the disclosures, five years is an insufficient time to assess the usefulness of the information. Therefore, effort should be provided to improve the shortcomings of the information.

Third, suspension of the required disclosures would encourage companies to remove the systems used to develop the information. Therefore, information would no longer be available for research on the relevance and reliability of the information. The final argument against the elimination of the required disclosures was that the FASB will be asked to require supplementary disclosures of the effects of changing prices when inflation rates increase at some time in the future and that the effort required will be as difficult, time-consuming, and costly as the implementation of the original disclosures in 1979. The due process required for adoption of a new Statement at that time may delay its adoption until a lack of credibility arises for both the FASB and financial reporting.

EXHIBIT 13–3

TRIAD COMPANY
Financial Statements Using Exit Values

INCOME STATEMENT FOR CURRENT YEAR

Purchasing margin:	
Inventory	$56[a]
Building	0
Holding gain:	
Inventory	0
Building	(10)[b]
Net income	$46

[a]($30 − $10) + ($30 − $12) + ($32 − $14)
[b]$20 − $30

BALANCE SHEET AT END OF CURRENT YEAR

Cash	$ 94[c]	Common stock, no par	$100[c]
Inventory	32[d]	Retained earnings	46
Building	20[e]		
	$146		$146

[c]From Exhibit 13–2
[d]1 unit × exit price of $32
[e]Exit price at year end

■ EXIT VALUES

The three alternative measurement methods that have been discussed in this chapter use *entry*, or input values. An historical cost is, of course, the cost measured at the time of the acquisition of the item. A constant purchasing power amount is an adjusted historical cost amount. A current cost is the amount that would have to be paid to purchase an item. In contrast, some users of financial statements argue that it would be more appropriate to use exit values. An exit value is the net cash amount that a company would receive if it sold the item. An exit value is often referred to as the *net realizable value* because it is the net amount to be received from the sale after deducting costs associated with the sale, such as transportation costs and sales commissions. The basic argument in favor of the use of exit values is that the company will have to dispose of each item at some point in the future and therefore the current measure of the cash to be received from such sales is relevant to users of financial statements.

The use of exit values is illustrated in Exhibit 13–3 using the facts for the Triad Company given earlier in Exhibits 13–1 and 13–2. In addition, it is assumed that at the date of acquisition the exit values of the three units of inventory were $30, $30, and $32, respectively. The exit values of the inventory and building at the end of the year are $32 and $20, respectively. There are two components of income. The first is the purchasing margin which is the sum of the differences between the exit values and the acquisition costs of the assets on the date of acquisition. The cost of the units of inventory were $10, $12, and $14 whereas the exit values at the dates of acquisition were $30, $30, and $32, respectively. Therefore the increases of $20, $18, and $18 are included in net income. (It is assumed that there was no purchasing margin for the building.)

The second component of income is the holding gain or loss which is the sum of the changes in the exit values of the assets. The decrease in the exit value of the building from $30 to $20 is included in net income. (It is assumed that there is no holding gain or loss for the inventory.) The exit values of the inventory and building are included in the balance sheet.

Many people argue that the use of exit values would not provide relevant information, however. Consider two examples. If a company used an exit value for its inventory, it would record that inventory at its selling price (less costs of disposal) before any sale transaction occurred and therefore would recognize income simply by acquiring inventory. Second, suppose that a company acquired a specialized machine for use in its activities. If the machine has no value to another company, its value would immediately be recorded as zero and its entire purchase price expensed in the period of acquisition even though the company intends to use the machine for several years.

Alternatively, it can be argued that in certain situations exit values have more relevance than input values. For example, if a company is to be liquidated then exit values are more relevant. Of course, the going concern (continuity) assumption is no longer relevant either. Also when a company is being sold in its entirety, many purchasers are interested in exit values because they may intend to sell some of the assets. However, few users argue that exit values should be the basis of accounting principles for financial statements used for most investment and lending decisions.

SECTION B Accounting for International Operations

As U.S. companies expand their operations, they frequently become involved in transactions with customers and suppliers in other countries. For example, a U.S. company may decide that it can purchase inventory at a lower cost or acquire machinery that is more efficient from a company based in a foreign country. Or, a U.S. company may decide to expand its revenue opportunities by selling its products in foreign countries. In each of these situations, the accounting for the transaction by the U.S. company is complicated by the need to record the transaction in U.S. dollars while the price may be expressed in terms of a foreign currency. Furthermore, as a U.S. company expands its operations in a foreign country it often sets up (or buys) a foreign subsidiary company, whose financial statements must be consolidated into the U.S. parent company's financial statements, as discussed in Chapter 11. These types of transactions and events are becoming more common; therefore a basic understanding of international accounting issues is important for those entering today's business world and for users of the financial statements of such companies.

Two situations concerning international accounting issues are discussed in the following sections: (1) accounting for the kinds of foreign currency transactions just described and (2) procedures for converting a foreign subsidiary's financial statements (expressed in terms of a foreign currency) into U.S. dollars.

Before we discuss these two situations, it is important to understand the meaning of exchange rates. An exchange rate measures the value of one currency in terms of another currency. Unfortunately, some exchange rates are commonly expressed in U.S. dollars whereas others are expressed in terms of the number of foreign units that are equal to the U.S. dollar. To illustrate, recently the British pound was quoted at a rate of $1.60. This rate means that it would take $1.60 to buy 1 British pound; that is, the pound is a larger unit than the U.S. dollar. In contrast, the West German mark was recently quoted at a rate of 1.90 marks to the U.S. dollar. This rate means that it would take 1.90 marks to buy $1; that is, the mark is a smaller unit than the dollar. To avoid confusion, in this book we will always quote exchange rates in terms of the number of U.S. dollars that is equivalent to 1 unit of foreign currency. Therefore, regarding the British pound and the West German mark, we will use exchange rates of $1.60 for the pound and $0.53 (1 ÷ 1.90) for the mark. The general rule is that a foreign currency is converted into U.S. dollars as follows:

$$\begin{array}{l} \text{Amount in} \\ \text{U.S. Dollars} \end{array} = \begin{array}{l} \text{Foreign Currency} \\ \text{Amount} \end{array} \times \begin{array}{l} \text{Exchange Rate} \\ \text{(stated in dollars)} \end{array}$$

Some recent exchange rates are illustrated in Exhibit 13–4.

Strong   Weak
(rising) (falling)

Since an exchange rate represents the price of one currency in terms of another, rates change continuously as supply and demand for currencies change. These changes are often described by terms such as strong (rising) and weak (falling). To illustrate, consider the exchange rate for the pound of $1.61 in Exhibit 13–4. If the dollar is weakening against the pound, the price (exchange rate) of the pound rises when stated in terms of the dollar. For example a change in the rate to $1.70 would be a weakening of the dollar, because it now takes more dollars to buy 1 pound. To say that the dollar is weakening is the same as saying that the pound is strengthening.

■ FOREIGN CURRENCY TRANSACTIONS

As explained earlier, many U.S. companies conduct transactions with customers and suppliers in foreign countries. Sometimes the transaction is expressed in U.S. dollars. For example, most purchases and sales of crude oil are expressed in terms of the U.S. dollar. In these situations, there is no accounting issue; the transaction is recorded just as we have discussed in the previous chapters of this book. For example, if a U.S. oil company purchases 10,000 barrels of crude oil from Saudi Arabia, the price would be quoted in dollars and not in the equivalent amount of riyals. If the price is $20 per barrel, the company would

EXHIBIT 13–4 Selected foreign exchange rates

Country (currency)	Price in U.S. dollars
Britain (pound)	$1.61
Canada (dollar)	0.86
France (franc)	0.17
Israel (shekel)	0.53
Japan (yen)	0.0070
Mexico (peso)	0.00038
Saudi Arabia (riyal)	0.27
Switzerland (franc)	0.64
West Germany (mark)	0.58

Source: The *Wall Street Journal* (December 22, 1989).

record a purchase of inventory and the related payment of $200,000 ($20 × 10,000).

In many situations, however, the transaction is expressed in terms of the foreign currency. In these cases the transaction must be recorded by the company in U.S. dollars. Therefore, the foreign currency amount must be converted into dollars at the exchange rate on the day of the transaction. For example, suppose a U.S. company purchases inventory of electronic components from a Japanese company for 50 million yen (Y) when the exchange rate is $0.007 (1 yen = $0.007). Assume that the U.S. company pays cash of $350,000 (Y50,000,000 × $0.007) on the same day to purchase yen to settle the transaction, which is recorded by the U.S. company as follows:

	Assets		= Liabilities + Stockholders' Equity
− $350,000		+ $350,000	

Cash (Cr)		Inventory (Dr)	
$350,000	$350,000		

More often, transactions between companies in different countries involve credit terms, if only to allow time for the processing of the orders and payment across international borders. In addition, currency exchange rates change continuously. As a result, the exchange rate is likely to have changed between the date the U.S. company records, say, a purchase transaction and the date it makes the payment. On the date of the payment, then, the company must record an exchange gain or loss to account for the difference between the purchase price and the amount of the payment. **An exchange gain or loss is caused by a change in the exchange rate between the date of a purchase or sale on account and the** *decline => take more money to buy ___*

date of the payment or receipt. More specifically, exchange gains and losses occur for purchases or sales on account as follows:

1. An exchange *gain* occurs when the exchange rate *declines* between the date a *payable* is incurred and the date of the cash *payment.*

2. An exchange *gain* occurs when the exchange rate *increases* between the date a *receivable* is acquired and the date of the cash *receipt.*

3. An exchange *loss* occurs when the exchange rate *increases* between the date a *payable* is incurred and the date of the cash *payment.*

4. An exchange *loss* occurs when the exchange rate *declines* between the date a *receivable* is acquired and the date of the cash *receipt.*

U.S. make purchase

To illustrate an exchange gain that occurs when the exchange rate declines between the date a credit purchase is recorded and the date of the cash payment, suppose that in the preceding example the U.S. company made the purchase of the electronic components on account. Because the inventory was purchased when the exchange rate was $0.007, the acquisition is recorded as follows:

Went to buy — time. (beg)

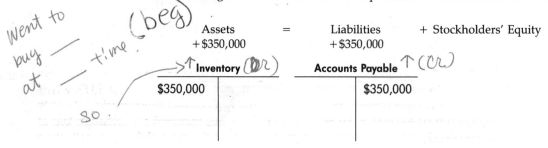

Assets	=	Liabilities	+ Stockholders' Equity
+ $350,000		+ $350,000	

Inventory (Dr)		Accounts Payable ↑ (Cr)	
$350,000		$350,000	

at 80:

The Japanese company has a right to receive 50 million yen, and the U.S. company is obligated to pay sufficient dollars that will convert to 50 million yen on the date that the payment is made. Now assume that the exchange rate on the date of payment is $0.0068 (1 yen = $0.0068). In this case, since only $0.0068 now buys 1 yen, the U.S. company will have to pay fewer dollars to buy 50 million yen. That is, the yen has become less expensive. More specifically, the U.S. company has to pay only $340,000 (Y50,000,000 × $0.0068). Therefore, the company has incurred an exchange *gain* of $10,000 ($350,000 − $340,000), which it records at the time of payment as follows:

FYI beg $.007 → yen now only pay $ .0068 → yen -time

US company.

(end)

Assets	=	Liabilities	+ Stockholders' Equity
− $340,000		− $350,000	+ $10,000

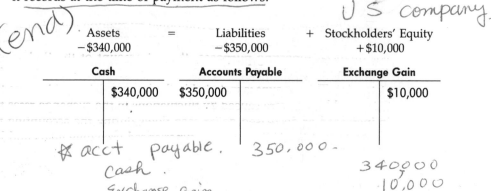

Cash		Accounts Payable		Exchange Gain	
$340,000		$350,000			$10,000

☆ acct payable.   350,000 −
Cash .   *340,000*
Exchange gain   *10,000*

The exchange gain occurs because the U.S. company has to pay only $340,000 to settle its debt originally recorded at $350,000. The gain can also be computed by multiplying the amount owed by the change in the exchange rate [Y50,000,000 × ($0.007 − $0.0068) = $10,000]. Remember that the Japanese company still receives 50 million yen; it is the U.S. company that has the exchange gain.

To illustrate an exchange loss that occurs when the exchange rate declines between the date a credit sale is recorded and the date of the cash receipt, suppose that a U.S. company sells computer equipment to a West German company on account and agrees to a price of 300,000 marks (DM) rather than a price in dollars. On the date of the sale, the exchange rate is $0.61 (1 mark = $0.61), and therefore the U.S. company records the sale of $183,000 (DM300,000 × $0.61) as follows:

	Assets	= Liabilities +	Stockholders' Equity
	+$183,000		+$183,000

Accounts Receivable		Sales Revenue	
$183,000			$183,000

The West German company has an obligation to pay 300,000 marks regardless of the exchange rate on the date of payment. If the exchange rate is $0.59 when it pays the amount owed, the U.S. company can convert those marks into only $177,000 (DM300,000 × $0.59). As a result, it has incurred an exchange *loss* of $6,000 ($177,000 − $183,000), which it records at the time of the cash collection as follows:

	Assets		= Liabilities +	Stockholders' Equity
+$177,000		−$183,000		−$6,000

Cash		Accounts Receivable		Exchange Loss	
$177,000		$183,000		$6,000	

The exchange loss can also be computed by multiplying the amount receivable by the change in the exchange rate [DM300,000 × ($0.61 − $0.59) = $6,000]. For financial reporting purposes, the net amount of the Exchange Gains and Losses is reported in the Other Revenues and Expenses section of the income statement. This amount is included in the income statement because the exchange gains and losses were caused by fluctuations in the exchange rates that resulted in increased or decreased dollar cash flows during the accounting period.

Note that the U.S. company experienced exchange gains and losses in the preceding situations because it agreed to transactions expressed in terms of foreign currencies. In such situations, the U.S. company accepts the risks associated with exchange rate changes. When the transactions are expressed in U.S. dollars, the foreign company accepts, and the U.S. company avoids, the risks associated with exchange rate changes.

■ CONVERSION OF THE FINANCIAL STATEMENTS OF A FOREIGN SUBSIDIARY INTO U.S. DOLLARS

Many U.S. companies establish or purchase foreign companies. If a foreign subsidiary is controlled by a U.S. parent company, the subsidiary company's financial statements must be included in the consolidated financial statements of the U.S. parent company (as discussed in Chapter 11). The subsidiary company's financial statements must be prepared according to U.S. generally accepted accounting principles before consolidation occurs. Since we are assuming that the foreign subsidiary's financial statements are prepared in foreign currency amounts, they must be converted into U.S. dollars for consolidation.

Before we can explain the process of converting the foreign currency amounts into U.S. dollars, we must distinguish between the reporting currency of the subsidiary and the functional currency. **The reporting currency is the currency that a company uses for its financial statements.** Thus, a U.S. parent company uses the dollar as its reporting currency. Generally, however, a foreign subsidiary of the U.S. parent company uses the foreign currency as its reporting currency. **The functional currency is the currency of the location in which a company primarily operates.**[5] Normally, it is the currency in which the company primarily receives and pays cash. Thus, a U.S. parent company uses the dollar as its functional currency. For a foreign subsidiary, the functional currency is the *same* as the reporting currency (i.e., the *foreign currency*) when the subsidiary's operations are relatively self-contained—that is, when the foreign subsidiary primarily receives and pays foreign currency. In contrast, the functional currency of a foreign subsidiary is the *U.S. dollar* when the subsidiary's operations are directly related to, or an extension of, the parent company (e.g., a branch office)— that is, when the subsidiary primarily receives and pays U.S. dollars. Note, however, that even though the functional currency of a foreign subsidiary may be the U.S. dollar, the subsidiary's financial statements may still be expressed in a foreign currency. The decision to use a particular reporting currency is made by management for the convenience of the operation of its accounting system. In contrast, the decision regarding the functional currency is determined by generally accepted accounting principles.[6]

· ·

[5]If a foreign country has a "highly inflationary economy" (defined as cumulative inflation of approximately 100% or more over a three-year period), the functional currency is defined to be the U.S. dollar.

[6]"Foreign Currency Translation," *FASB Statement of Financial Accounting Standards No. 52* (Stamford, Conn.: FASB, 1981).

The definition of the functional currency of the foreign subsidiary is important because it determines the method used to convert the reporting currency of the foreign subsidiary into U.S. dollars. **If a foreign currency is used for both the reporting currency and the functional currency of the foreign subsidiary, the financial statements of the foreign subsidiary are** *translated* **into U.S. dollars.** After translation into U.S. dollars, the financial statements of the foreign subsidiary are combined with those of the U.S. parent company into consolidated financial statements. Assets and liabilities of the foreign subsidiary are translated using the *current* exchange rate at the date of the consolidated balance sheet. The common stock is translated at the appropriate historical rate at the time the stock was issued. The retained earnings is computed in the normal way as the sum of the beginning balance plus the translated amount of the net income less the translated amount of the dividends distributed. The common stock and retained earnings are eliminated during the consolidation process. The translation of the asset and liability amounts from the foreign currency into U.S. dollars results in *translation adjustments*. The amount of the translation adjustments is included directly in the stockholders' equity section of the consolidated balance sheet. Revenues, expenses, gains, and losses of the foreign subsidiary are translated at the *average* exchange rate for the period of the consolidated income statement.

If a foreign subsidiary's reporting currency is a foreign currency but its functional currency is the U.S. dollar, the subsidiary's financial statements are *remeasured* **into U.S. dollars.** (Note the use of the term *remeasured* instead of *translated*, which is used when the functional currency is a foreign currency.) After the remeasurement into U.S. dollars, the financial statements of the foreign subsidiary are combined with those of the U.S. parent company into consolidated financial statements. In this case, the *monetary assets* and *monetary liabilities* of the foreign subsidiary are remeasured at the *current* exchange rate at the date of the consolidated balance sheet. A monetary asset is money or a claim to receive a fixed amount of money in the future. The principal monetary assets include cash, accounts receivable, and notes receivable. A monetary liability is an obligation to repay a fixed amount of money in the future. The principal monetary liabilities include accounts payable, notes payable, and bonds payable. Monetary assets and liabilities were discussed in greater detail earlier in the chapter.

Nonmonetary assets and *nonmonetary liabilities* of the foreign subsidiary are remeasured at the *historical exchange* rate at the time the asset was acquired or the liability incurred. The common stock of the foreign subsidiary is remeasured at the appropriate historical rate, and the retained earnings is computed in the normal way as the sum of the beginning balance plus the remeasured amount of the net income less the remeasured amount of the dividends distributed. The common stock and retained earnings are eliminated during the consolidation process. The remeasurement of the monetary assets and liabilities from the foreign currency into U.S. dollars results in *transaction gains and losses,* which are included in the consolidated income statement. Revenues, expenses, gains, and losses of the foreign subsidiary are remeasured at the *average* exchange rate for the period of the consolidated income statement unless they can be related to the acquisition of a specific asset at an *historical* rate. For example, cost of goods sold and depreciation expense are remeasured at the historical rate at which the inventory and the property, plant, and equipment of the foreign subsidiary were acquired, respectively. The two alternative situations just discussed and the appropriate exchange rates to translate or remeasure are summarized in Exhibit 13–5. The reasons for the two methods are discussed later in the chapter.

Example of the Conversion of Financial Statements into U.S. Dollars

An example of the conversion of a foreign subsidiary's financial statements is illustrated in Exhibits 13–6 and 13–7. We explain the conversion of the financial statements of the Tenden Company, a foreign subsidiary of a U.S. parent company, from the foreign currency (marks) into U.S. dollars for each of the two methods. After the conversion of the financial statements into dollars, any intercompany transactions would be eliminated and the consolidation procedures discussed in Chapter 11 would be followed. For simplicity, we will not discuss the consolidation of the Tenden Company's financial statements into the statements of its U.S. parent company. The exchange rate was $0.50 when the company was acquired and the dollar weakened until the exchange rate was $0.62 at December 31, 1992. The dollar then strengthened during 1993 and the exchange rate was $0.60 at December 31, 1993.

Functional Currency Is the West German Mark.   The translation of the financial statements of the Tenden Company (foreign subsidiary) when the functional currency is the West German mark is illustrated in Exhibit 13–6. All the items (except for the common stock, retained earnings, and translation adjustment) in the company's December 31, 1992, and 1993, balance sheets are *translated* at the current exchange rate on those dates of $0.62 and $0.60, respectively.

The common stock is translated at the historical rate when the stock was initially acquired by the parent. The retained earnings in the beginning balance sheet is the same amount as the balance in the example where the functional currency is the U.S. dollar. This equality is very unlikely to occur in practice but is assumed in this situation to assist in the understanding of the different effects of the two methods. The translation adjustment included in stockholders' equity at December 31, 1992, is a balancing amount. The retained earnings at the end of the year is the beginning balance plus the net income less the dividends translated at the average rate for the year. (Both the common stock and the retained earnings of the company would be eliminated if we had completed the consolidation process.)

The amount of the translation adjustment in the balance sheet is the *cumulative* total of each year's translation adjustments and is caused by the exchange rate change on the company's net assets (assets minus liabilities).[7] The change

----

[7]The amount tends to be added to stockholders' equity when the exchange rates in the countries where the subsidiaries are located have risen (the dollar has weakened) and be subtracted when those rates have fallen (the dollar has strengthened).

EXHIBIT 13–5 Summary of translation and remeasurement process

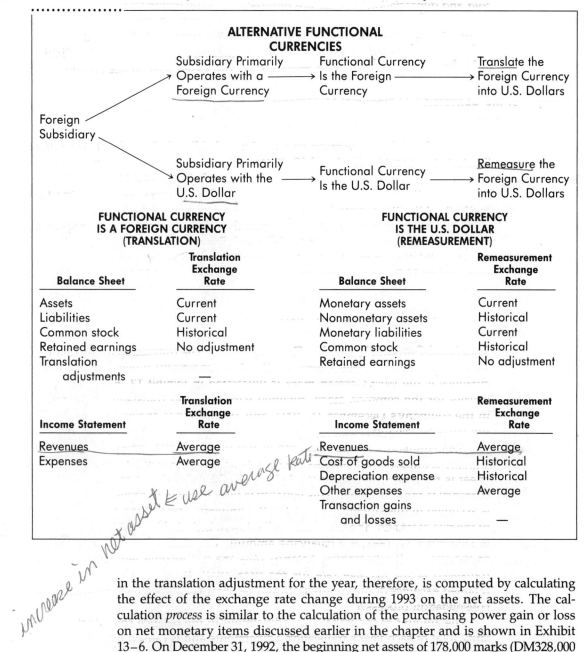

ALTERNATIVE FUNCTIONAL CURRENCIES

Foreign Subsidiary →

Subsidiary Primarily Operates with a Foreign Currency → Functional Currency Is the Foreign Currency → Translate the Foreign Currency into U.S. Dollars

Subsidiary Primarily Operates with the U.S. Dollar → Functional Currency Is the U.S. Dollar → Remeasure the Foreign Currency into U.S. Dollars

FUNCTIONAL CURRENCY IS A FOREIGN CURRENCY (TRANSLATION)

Balance Sheet	Translation Exchange Rate
Assets	Current
Liabilities	Current
Common stock	Historical
Retained earnings	No adjustment
Translation adjustments	—

Income Statement	Translation Exchange Rate
Revenues	Average
Expenses	Average

FUNCTIONAL CURRENCY IS THE U.S. DOLLAR (REMEASUREMENT)

Balance Sheet	Remeasurement Exchange Rate
Monetary assets	Current
Nonmonetary assets	Historical
Monetary liabilities	Current
Common stock	Historical
Retained earnings	No adjustment

Income Statement	Remeasurement Exchange Rate
Revenues	Average
Cost of goods sold	Historical
Depreciation expense	Historical
Other expenses	Average
Transaction gains and losses	—

[handwritten annotation: increase in net asset ← use average rate]

in the translation adjustment for the year, therefore, is computed by calculating the effect of the exchange rate change during 1993 on the net assets. The calculation *process* is similar to the calculation of the purchasing power gain or loss on net monetary items discussed earlier in the chapter and is shown in Exhibit 13–6. On December 31, 1992, the beginning net assets of 178,000 marks (DM328,000 − DM150,000) were valued at $110,360 (DM178,000 × exchange rate of $0.62 on December 31, 1992). The increase in net assets of DM52,000 in 1993 is valued at $31,720 (DM52,000 × average exchange rate of $0.61). Therefore, the total expected value of the net assets is $142,080 ($110,360 + $31,720). However, the ending net assets of 230,000 marks (DM390,000 − DM160,000) are valued at

EXHIBIT 13–6

TENDEN COMPANY (FOREIGN SUBSIDIARY)
Conversion of Financial Statements from
German Marks into U.S. Dollars
(Functional Currency Is the Mark)

	Marks	Exchange Rate	U.S. Dollars
BALANCE SHEET			
DECEMBER 31, 1992			
Cash	DM 18,000	$0.62[a]	$ 11,160
Accounts receivable	50,000	0.62	31,000
Inventory	80,000	0.62	49,600
Property and equipment	250,000	0.62	155,000
Less: accumulated depreciation	(70,000)	0.62	(43,400)
Total assets	DM328,000		$203,360
Accounts payable	DM 90,000	0.62	$ 55,800
Bonds payable	60,000	0.62	37,200
Common stock, no par	140,000	0.50[b]	70,000
Retained earnings[c]	38,000	—	28,560
Translation adjustment (cumulative)[d]	—		11,800[e]
Total liabilities and stockholders' equity	DM328,000		$203,360
BALANCE SHEET			
DECEMBER 31, 1993			
Cash	DM 50,000	$0.60[f]	$ 30,000
Accounts receivable	70,000	0.60	42,000
Inventory	120,000	0.60	72,000
Property and equipment	250,000	0.60	150,000
Less: accumulated depreciation	(100,000)	0.60	(60,000)
Total assets	DM390,000		$234,000
Accounts payable	DM100,000	0.60	$ 60,000
Bonds payable	60,000	0.60	36,000
Common stock, no par	140,000	0.50	70,000
Retained earnings	90,000	—	60,280
Translation adjustment (cumulative)	—		7,720[g]
Total liabilities and stockholders' equity	DM390,000		$234,000

Net asset = (Total L and SH E) — payayable

$138,000 (DM230,000 × exchange rate of $0.60 on December 31, 1993). Therefore, there has been a reduction in the translation adjustment of $4,080 ($142,080 − $138,000) as the dollar strengthened in 1993. The cumulative translation adjustment in the December 31, 1993, balance sheet ($7,720) is the beginning balance ($11,800) less the reduction ($4,080).

All items in the Tenden Company's 1993 income statement are translated at

EXHIBIT 13-6   *(continued)*

average exchange rate

INCOME STATEMENT
FOR YEAR ENDED DECEMBER 31, 1993

	Marks	Exchange Rate	U.S. Dollars
Sales	DM400,000	$0.61^h	$244,000
Cost of goods sold	(170,000)	0.61	(103,700)
Gross profit	DM230,000		$140,300
Operating expenses			
Depreciation expense	(30,000)	0.61	(18,300)
Selling and administrative expenses	(80,000)	0.61	(48,800)
Transaction gain	—		—
Income before income taxes	DM120,000		$ 73,200
Income tax expense	(48,000)	0.61	(29,280)
Net income	DM 72,000		$ 43,920

STATEMENT OF CHANGES IN RETAINED EARNINGS
FOR YEAR ENDED DECEMBER 31, 1993

Retained earnings, 12/31/92	$28,560
Net income	43,920
	$72,480
Less: Dividends (DM20,000 × $0.61)	(12,200)
Retained earnings, 12/31/93	$60,280

CHANGE IN TRANSLATION ADJUSTMENT
FOR YEAR ENDED DECEMBER 31, 1993

Net assets, 12/31/92	DM178,000 × 0.62^a =	$110,360
Increase	52,000 × 0.61^h	31,720
		$142,080
Net assets, 12/31/93	DM230,000 × 0.60^f	(138,000)
Change in translation adjustment		$ 4,080

^{a}Exchange rate on December 31, 1992.
^{b}Exchange rate on the date the stock was initially sold.
^{c}Assumed amounts.
^{d}Cumulative lifetime adjustment.
^{e}Balancing amount.
^{f}Exchange rate on December 31, 1993.
^{g}Beginning balance of $11,800 − $4,080.
^{h}Average exchange rate for 1993.

the average exchange rate of $0.61 for 1993. Note that there is no gain or loss in the income statement, because all *translation* adjustments are included in the stockholders' equity section of the company's balance sheet when the functional currency is a foreign currency. (An exchange gain or loss would be included in the income statement, as discussed earlier.) For convenience, it is also assumed that the income tax expense is not affected by any foreign currency items.

Functional Currency Is the U.S. Dollar. The remeasurement of the financial statements of the Tenden Company when the functional currency is the U.S. dollar is illustrated in Exhibit 13–7. The monetary assets and liabilities (cash, accounts receivable, accounts payable, and bonds payable) in the company's December 31, 1992, and 1993, balance sheets are *remeasured* at the current exchange rate on those dates of $0.62 and $0.60, respectively. The nonmonetary assets are remeasured at the appropriate historical rate. We assume that the inventory transactions were as follows:

Inventory, 12/31/92	DM 80,000	× 0.63	=	$ 50,400
Purchases	210,000	× 0.61		128,100
	DM290,000			$178,500
Inventory, 12/31/93	120,000	× 0.605		(72,600)
Cost of goods sold	DM170,000			$105,900

The December 31, 1992, inventory was purchased when the exchange rate was $0.63. The purchases (or production) during the period are assumed to occur evenly over the period; therefore the average exchange rate is used. The ending inventory was purchased when the exchange rate was $0.605. The property and equipment was acquired when the exchange rate was $0.55; therefore this rate is used to remeasure the property and equipment and the related accumulated depreciation in both balance sheets. The common stock is remeasured at the historical rate when the stock was initially acquired by the parent. The retained earnings in the December 31, 1992, balance sheet is a balancing amount. The retained earnings in the December 31, 1993, balance sheet is the beginning balance plus the remeasured net income less the dividends remeasured at the average rate for the year. Note that there is no *translation* adjustment in the company's balance sheet because all *transaction* gains and losses are included in the company's income statement when the U.S. dollar is the functional currency.

In the 1993 income statement, the sales, selling and administrative expenses, and the income tax expense are all remeasured at the average rate for 1993 of $0.61. The items for which an historical rate is appropriate—cost of goods sold and depreciation expense—are remeasured at their appropriate historical rates. The computation of the cost of goods sold was illustrated earlier. The depreciation expense is remeasured at $0.55, the rate at which the related asset was purchased. The transaction gain from the strengthening of the dollar in 1993 is also included in the company's income statement and is caused by the exchange rate change on the company's net monetary assets (monetary assets less monetary liabilities). The calculation *process* is similar to the calculation of the purchasing power gain or loss on net monetary items discussed earlier in the chapter and is shown in Exhibit 13–7. The company has negative net monetary items, or net monetary liabilities, in both balance sheets. On December 31, 1992, the beginning net monetary liabilities of 82,000 marks (DM68,000 − DM150,000) were valued at $50,840 (DM82,000 × exchange rate of $0.62 on December 31, 1992). The decrease in the net monetary liabilities (i.e., the increase in net monetary items of DM42,000) is valued at $25,620 (DM42,000 × average exchange rate of $0.61). Therefore, the total expected value of the net monetary liabilities is $25,220 ($50,840 − $25,620). The ending net monetary liabilities of 40,000 marks (DM120,000 −

DM160,000) are valued at $24,000 (DM40,000 × exchange rate of $0.60 on December 31, 1993). Therefore, the company has experienced a transaction gain on the remeasurement of its net monetary liabilities of $1,220.[8]

Note that in this example, for simplicity, we have assumed that the company has not made any foreign currency transactions that resulted in exchange gains and losses (as discussed earlier). If the company had such gains and losses, they would have been included in its income statement. For convenience, it is also assumed that the income tax expense is not affected by any foreign currency items.

Evaluation of the Conversion of Financial Statements into U.S. Dollars

The two methods of converting the financial statements of a foreign subsidiary from the foreign currency into U.S. dollars may at first seem arbitrary. However, they are based on a logic that relates to the definition of the functional currency. When the functional currency is the foreign currency, the subsidiary is relatively self-contained. The foreign currency net cash flows that the foreign subsidiary generates may be either reinvested in the subsidiary or converted into U.S. dollars and paid as dividends to the U.S. parent company. For this type of foreign subsidiary, it is appropriate to exclude the translation adjustments from the consolidated income statement because the foreign subsidiary is self-contained and its cash flows and income-producing activities do not directly affect the cash flows and income-producing activities of the U.S. parent. Instead, they affect the subsidiary's net assets and the parent's investment, and therefore the adjustments are recorded directly in the stockholders' equity of the consolidated balance sheet.

In contrast, when the functional currency is the U.S. dollar, the foreign subsidiary is an extension of the U.S. parent company. Therefore, the changes in the foreign subsidiary's assets and liabilities have a direct impact on the U.S. parent company's cash flows and income-producing activities in U.S. dollars, and so the transaction gain or loss is included in the consolidated income statement. The remeasurement process attempts to include the subsidiary in the consolidated financial statements as if there had been no foreign currency transactions. Indeed, if the subsidiary chose to keep its financial records in U.S. dollars, its financial statements could be consolidated directly without any need for remeasurement.

International Accounting Principles

As discussed in Chapter 1, financial statements are prepared to assist external users in making investment and credit decisions. With the continuing growth

....

[8]Most companies have monetary liabilities that exceed monetary assets. Such companies will tend to have a transaction gain when the exchange rates in the countries where subsidiaries are located have fallen (the dollar has strengthened) and have a transaction loss when those rates have risen (the dollar has weakened).

EXHIBIT 13–7

TENDEN COMPANY (FOREIGN SUBSIDIARY)
Conversion of Financial Statements from
German Marks into U.S. Dollars
(Functional Currency
Is the U.S. Dollar)

	Marks	Exchange Rate	U.S. Dollars
BALANCE SHEET DECEMBER 31, 1992			
Cash	DM 18,000	$0.62ᵃ	$ 11,160
Accounts receivable	50,000	0.62	31,000
Inventory	80,000	0.63ᵇ	50,400
Property and equipment	250,000	0.55ᶜ	137,500
Less: accumulated depreciation	(70,000)	0.55	(38,500)
Total assets	DM328,000		$191,560
Accounts payable	DM 90,000	0.62	$ 55,800
Bonds payable	60,000	0.62	37,200
Common stock, no par	140,000	0.50ᵈ	70,000
Retained earnings	38,000	—	28,560ᵉ
Total liabilities and stockholders' equity	DM328,000		$191,560
BALANCE SHEET DECEMBER 31, 1993			
Cash	DM 50,000	$0.60ᶠ	$ 30,000
Accounts receivable	70,000	0.60	42,000
Inventory	120,000	0.605ᵍ	72,600
Property and equipment	250,000	0.55	137,500
Less: accumulated depreciation	(100,000)	0.55	(55,000)
Total assets	DM390,000		$227,100
Accounts payable	DM100,000	0.60	$ 60,000
Bonds payable	60,000	0.60	36,000
Common stock, no par	140,000	0.50	70,000
Retained earnings	90,000	—	61,100
Total liabilities and stockholders' equity	DM390,000		$227,100

of international business activities, more and more investors and creditors are making decisions about companies operating in foreign countries. For example, many U.S. investors purchase shares of European and Japanese companies. Such investors would prefer that companies in all countries use the same accounting principles. Unfortunately, very little conformity exists from country to country. The lack of conformity has been caused by such factors as the different ways the accounting profession in each country has developed, the different legal systems, and the different goals of the governments. In addition, differences in

EXHIBIT 13–7 *(continued)*
················

INCOME STATEMENT
FOR YEAR ENDED DECEMBER 31, 1993

Sales	DM400,000	$0.61[h]	$244,000
Cost of goods sold	(170,000)	—	(105,900)
Gross profit	DM230,000		$138,100
Operating expenses			
Depreciation expense	(30,000)	0.55	(16,500)
Selling and administrative expenses	(80,000)	0.61	(48,800)
Transaction gain			1,220
Income before income taxes	DM120,000		$ 74,020
Income tax expense	(48,000)	0.61	(29,280)
Net income	DM 72,000		$ 44,740

STATEMENT OF CHANGES IN RETAINED EARNINGS
FOR YEAR ENDED DECEMBER 31, 1993

Retained earnings, 12/31/92	$ 28,560
Net income	44,740
	$ 73,300
Less: dividends (DM20,000 × $0.61)	(12,200)
Retained earnings, 12/31/93	$ 61,100

TRANSACTION GAIN
FOR YEAR ENDED DECEMBER 31, 1993

Net monetary items, 12/31/92	DM(82,000) × 0.62[a] =	$ (50,840)
Increase	42,000 × 0.61[h]	25,620
		$ (25,220)
Net monetary items, 12/31/93	DM(40,000) × 0.60[f]	(24,000)
Transaction gain		$(1,220)

INVENTORY CALCULATIONS

Inventory, 12/31/92	DM 80,000 × 0.63 =	$ 50,400
Purchases	210,000 × 0.61	128,100
	DM290,000	$178,500
Inventory, 12/31/93	(120,000) × 0.605	(72,600)
Cost of goods sold	DM170,000	$105,900

[a]Exchange rate on December 31, 1992.
[b]Exchange rate when the inventory was purchased.
[c]Exchange rate when the property and equipment was purchased.
[d]Exchange rate on the date the stock was initially sold.
[e]Balancing amount.
[f]Exchange rate on December 31, 1993.
[g]Exchange rate when the inventory was purchased.
[h]Average exchange rate for 1993.

tax laws cause differences in financial reporting. Some countries require that financial statements be prepared according to tax rules, whereas other countries, including the United States, have financial accounting principles that are not directly related to tax rules.[9]

Two organizations are directly concerned with international accounting activities. The International Accounting Standards Committee (IASC) was formed in 1972 with the intent of developing international accounting principles. By 1988, 100 accounting organizations representing 74 countries were participating in the Committee. To date, the IASC has issued 26 International Accounting Standards. Members of the IASC have committed themselves to introducing these standards in their respective countries. The IASC has no enforcement powers, however, and so the use of these standards is not universal.

The main objective of the International Federation of Accountants (IFAC), which was founded in 1977, is to establish international standards of auditing, ethics, education, and training. By 1988, 100 professional accounting organizations representing 74 countries were members of the IFAC. Like the IASC, the IFAC also has no enforcement powers, but its members are committed to enhancing the quality of accounting in their respective countries.

We hope that through the continued efforts of the IASC and the IFAC a greater uniformity of accounting principles and practices will be developed throughout the world.

■ APPENDIX: SUPPLEMENTARY DISCLOSURES

Companies are encouraged to make supplementary disclosures of the effects of changing prices in the notes to the financial statements. These disclosures are encouraged because they should assist users of financial statements to understand the impacts of changing prices and to reduce the limitations of historical cost financial statements, which ignore such changes. As summarized in the chapter, when the disclosures are made the following information for the current year should be presented:

1. Income from continuing operations (and related earnings per share) based on current cost

2. Purchasing power gain or loss on net monetary items

3. Current cost amounts of inventory and of property, plant, and equipment at the end of the current year

4. Increase or decrease in the current cost amounts of inventory and of property, plant, and equipment, before and after eliminating the effects of inflation

The illustrations in the chapter of the preparation of comprehensive constant purchasing power and current cost financial statements were based on very

....

[9]For a more detailed discussion of international accounting issues, see AlHashim and Arpan, *International Dimensions of Accounting*, Second Edition, (Boston: PWS-KENT Publishing Co., 1988).

EXHIBIT 13–8

· · · · · · · · · · · · · · · · · ·

COLONIAL COMPANY
Historical Cost Income Statement
For Year Ended December 31, 1993

Sales		$300,000
Cost of goods sold		
Inventory, December 31, 1992	$ 40,000	
Purchases	132,000	
Inventory, December 31, 1993	(60,000)	
Cost of goods sold		(112,000)
Gross profit		$188,000
Operating expenses		
Depreciation expense	$ 50,000	
Selling and administrative expenses	80,000	
Total operating expenses		(130,000)
Income before income taxes		$ 58,000
Income tax expense (at 40%)		(23,200)
Net income		$ 34,800

COLONIAL COMPANY
Historical Cost Balance Sheets

	December 31, 1992	December 31, 1993
Cash	$ 20,000	$ 59,800
Accounts receivable	50,000	80,000
Inventory	40,000	60,000
Equipment	400,000	400,000
Less: accumulated depreciation	(150,000)	(200,000)
Total assets	$360,000	$399,800
Accounts payable	$ 40,000	$ 45,000
Bonds payable	150,000	150,000
Common stock, no par	100,000	100,000
Retained earnings	70,000	104,800
Total liabilities and stockholders' equity	$360,000	$399,800

Additional information:

CPI–U index December 1992: 260
             Average   1993: 273
             December 1993: 286

Inventory: Beginning inventory: 10,000 units at $4 each = $40,000
             Ending inventory: 12,000 units at $5 each = $60,000
             Purchases during the year: 30,000 units
             Average current cost during the year: $4.75 per unit
             Current cost at the end of the year: $5.25 per unit
             Current cost at the beginning of the year: $4.25 per unit

EXHIBIT 13–8   *(continued)*

Equipment: Purchased January 1, 1990
             Residual value: Zero
             Estimated life: 8 years
             Depreciation method: straight line
             Current cost, December 31, 1992: $500,000
             Current cost, December 31, 1993: $650,000

simple historical cost financial statements. In practice, however, financial statements are much more complex.

To illustrate the relationship between the basic financial statements and the selected disclosures for the current year listed above, consider the Colonial Company's historical cost income statement and balance sheet in Exhibit 13–8 along with the additional information. The supplementary disclosures as well as information that helps to relate the supplementary disclosures to the historical cost income statement are shown in Exhibit 13–9.

Income from Continuing Operations

Income from continuing operations is disclosed under the current cost basis. In this example income from continuing operations under the historical cost basis is the same as net income because there are no gains or losses from discontinued operations, extraordinary items, or changes in accounting principle. The only two items that are typically adjusted to compute income from continuing operations under the current cost basis are the cost of goods sold and depreciation expense. The other items are not adjusted because it is assumed that they are already at the average current cost for the period. The cost of goods sold and the depreciation expense are adjusted as follows:

COST OF GOODS SOLD (CURRENT COST)

Units Sold = Units in Beginning Inventory + Units Purchased − Units in Ending Inventory

$$= 10{,}000 + 30{,}000 - 12{,}000$$

$$= 28{,}000$$

Average Current Cost of Goods Sold = Units Sold × Average Current Cost per Unit

$$= 28{,}000 \times \$4.75$$

$$= \$133{,}000$$

DEPRECIATION EXPENSE (CURRENT COST)

Current Cost Depreciation Expense = (Average Current Cost − Residual Value) ÷ Life

$$= \left(\frac{\$500{,}000 + \$650{,}000}{2} - \$0\right) \div 8$$

$$= \$71{,}875$$

Because of the higher cost of goods sold and depreciation expense on a current cost basis, the Colonial Company incurred an $8,075 loss from continuing oper-

EXHIBIT 13–9

COLONIAL COMPANY
Supplementary Disclosure of the Effects of Changing Prices
For Year Ended December 31, 1993

	As Reported in the Historical Cost Income Statement	Adjusted for Changes in Specific Prices (current costs)
Sales	$300,000	$300,000
Cost of goods sold	(112,000)	(133,000)
Depreciation expense	(50,000)	(71,875)
Selling and administrative expenses	(80,000)	(80,000)
Income tax expense	(23,200)	(23,200)
Income (loss) from continuing operations	$ 34,800	$ (8,075)
Gain from increase in purchasing power of net monetary items		$ 8,509

	Inventory	Equipment
Current cost:		
Specific price (current cost) at year-end	$ 63,000	$325,000
Increases or decreases in current costs:		
Increase in specific prices, including inflation	$ 21,500	$ 84,375
Inflation component	(4,989)	(30,398)
Increase in specific prices after inflation	$ 16,511	$ 53,977

ations on a current cost basis. The disclosure of this loss is shown in Exhibit 13–9.

Purchasing Power Gain or Loss on Net Monetary Items

Instead of analyzing each individual cash flow as we did in the example in the chapter, a simplified method of calculating the purchasing power gain or loss on net monetary items is usually used. The beginning and ending historical cost net monetary items (monetary assets minus monetary liabilities) are calculated, and the net increase or decrease is the difference between the two amounts. The beginning net monetary items are adjusted to the average price level (i.e., to constant purchasing power). The net increase or decrease for the year is assumed to have occurred at the average price level for the year so that no adjustment is necessary to express it in terms of the constant purchasing power amount. This is in contrast to our example in the main part of the chapter where the amount and timing of *each* change in the net monetary items was adjusted by multiplying it times an appropriate adjustment factor. The balance of the beginning net monetary items (in constant purchasing power) is added to the increase in net monetary items to determine the balance of the ending net monetary items (in constant purchasing power). The balance of the ending net monetary items (at historical cost) is computed in a similar way and then adjusted to the average price level. The purchasing power gain or loss is calculated by deducting the historical ending net monetary items (adjusted to the average price level) from the constant purchasing power ending net monetary items.

In the Colonial Company example the beginning and ending net monetary items are both negative; that is, monetary liabilities exceed monetary assets. In our example the net monetary liabilities are calculated in a schedule as follows:

SCHEDULE OF NET MONETARY ITEMS

	December 31, 1992 (beginning)	December 31, 1993 (ending)
Cash	$ 20,000	$ 59,800
Accounts receivable	50,000	80,000
Less: accounts payable	(40,000)	(45,000)
bonds payable	(150,000)	(150,000)
Net monetary items	$(120,000)	$ (55,200)

The decrease in the net monetary liabilities (or an increase in net monetary items) is $64,800 ($120,000 − $55,200) and is assumed to occur at the average price level for the year. Since the company has held net monetary liabilities, there is a purchasing power *gain* calculated as follows:

SCHEDULE TO COMPUTE PURCHASING POWER GAIN OR LOSS

	Historical Cost	Adjustment	Constant Purchasing Power
Beginning net monetary items	$(120,000) ×	$\dfrac{273}{260}$ =	$(126,000)
Increase in net monetary items	64,800		64,800
Ending net monetary items unadjusted	$ (55,200)		
Constant purchasing power ending balance (at average price level)			$ (61,200)
Historical ending balance adjusted to average price level $\left[\$(55,200) \times \dfrac{273}{286} \right]$			(52,691)
Purchasing power gain (at average price level)			$ (8,509)

The historical cost measure of the ending net monetary *liabilities* is $55,200, which is adjusted to a constant purchasing power amount of $52,691. The constant purchasing power measure of the ending net monetary *liabilities*, giving consideration to the changes that have occurred during the year, is $61,200. Therefore, the company has a purchasing power *gain* of $8,509 ($61,200 − $52,691), as shown above. The disclosure of the purchasing power gain is shown in Exhibit 13–9.

Current Cost at End of Current Fiscal Year

The current cost of the inventory and property, plant, and equipment at the end of the current fiscal year is disclosed. The inventory at the end of 1993 consists of 12,000 units. The current cost of the inventory at the end of the year is $5.25 per unit, and therefore the total current cost is $63,000 (12,000 × $5.25), as shown in Exhibit 13–9.

The equipment at the end of 1993 is shown at the current cost at the year-end ($650,000) less the accumulated depreciation based on that current cost. The equipment was purchased on January 1, 1990, and has an eight-year life. Therefore, at the end of 1993 it is one-half (4 ÷ 8) depreciated. The current cost (specific price) is $325,000 [$650,000 − ($650,000 × 1/2)], as shown in Exhibit 13–9.[10]

Increases or Decreases in Current Cost, Before and After Eliminating the Effects of Inflation

The increases or decreases in the current cost of the inventory and property, plant, and equipment, before and after eliminating the effects of inflation, are disclosed. The beginning current cost of the inventory and property, plant, and equipment (less accumulated depreciation) are computed in the same way as above:

INVENTORY

$$\text{Current Cost of Beginning Inventory} = \text{Units} \times \text{Current Cost per Unit}$$
$$= 10,000 \times \$4.25$$
$$= \$42,500$$

EQUIPMENT

$$\text{Current Cost of Equipment} = \text{Beginning Current Cost} - \text{Accumulated Depreciation}$$
$$= \$500,000 - (\$500,000 \times 3/8)$$
$$= \$500,000 - \$187,500$$
$$= \$312,500$$

At the beginning of the year, the equipment was three years old and therefore was 3/8 depreciated. The increase or decrease (*before* inflation) in the current cost of the inventory and equipment is computed as follows:

$$\begin{matrix} \text{Increase or} \\ \text{Decrease} \\ \text{(unadjusted} \\ \text{for inflation)} \end{matrix} = \begin{matrix} \text{Current Cost} \\ \text{Ending Balance} \end{matrix} - \left(\begin{matrix} \text{Current Cost} \\ \text{Beginning} \\ \text{Balance} \end{matrix} \begin{matrix} \text{Additions} \\ + \text{During the} \\ \text{Year} \end{matrix} \begin{matrix} \text{Reductions} \\ - \text{During the} \\ \text{Year} \end{matrix} \right)$$

To illustrate, the inventory increase is computed as follows:

····················

[10]The accumulated depreciation included in the current cost disclosures is *not* the sum of the current cost depreciation expense calculated each year of the asset's life. The accumulated depreciation is based on the current cost of the asset at the end of the particular year and the length of time the asset has been owned, whereas the depreciation expense each year is based on the average current cost for that year.

EXHIBIT 13–10 Computation of the increase or decrease in the current cost, before and after adjusting for the effects of inflation

	Current Cost (Unadjusted)	Adjustment	Current Cost (Constant Purchasing Power)
	INVENTORY		
Balance, 12/31/92	$ 42,500	273 ÷ 260	$ 44,625
Additions	132,000		132,000
Reductions	(133,000)		(133,000)
	$ 41,500		$ 43,625
Balance, 12/31/93	63,000	273 ÷ 286	60,136
Increase (decrease)	$ 21,500		$ 16,511
	EQUIPMENT		
Balance, 12/31/92	$312,500	273 ÷ 260	$328,125
Additions	—		—
Reductions	(71,875)		(71,875)
	$240,625		$256,250
Balance, 12/31/93	325,000	273 ÷ 286	310,227
Increase (decrease)	$ 84,375		$ 53,977

$$\text{Increase} = \$63,000 - (\$42,500 + \$132,000 - \$133,000)$$
$$= \$63,000 - \$41,500$$
$$= \$21,500$$

The current cost ending balance ($63,000) and the beginning balance ($42,500) were computed earlier based on the number of units on hand and the current cost per unit at that time. The additions during the year are the purchases of inventory. For simplicity it is assumed that the historical cost paid for the purchases is equivalent to the average current cost for the year. The reductions during the year are the current cost amount of the cost of goods sold as computed earlier. The same calculations are made for the property, plant, and equipment and are shown in Exhibit 13–10. The beginning and ending current cost net balances of the equipment are based on the current cost of each asset at that time less the related accumulated depreciation. The additions would again be acquisitions (there are none in this example). The reductions are the current cost depreciation expense (calculated earlier for income from continuing operations) and disposals (there are no disposals in this example, but they would be included at current cost less related accumulated depreciation).

To calculate the increase (decrease) in the current cost, after eliminating the effects of inflation, each of the components in the calculation of the increase (decrease) unadjusted for inflation must be adjusted to the constant purchasing power amount. Since the beginning and ending balances computed above are measured in current costs at the beginning and end of the period, respectively, these amounts must be adjusted to the average price level for the period by multiplying times an adjustment factor of the average CPI–U divided by the CPI–U at the time of measurement of the current cost. It should be noted that the denominator of the factor is the CPI–U at the time of *measurement* and *not* the CPI–U at the time of acquisition of the asset. Thus, for example, the beginning balance of the inventory is adjusted by a factor of 273 (average CPI–U) divided by 260 (beginning CPI–U). Any additions or reductions are assumed to take place at the average price level for the year and therefore do not need adjusting. The increase or decrease, net of inflation, is computed as follows:

$$\begin{aligned}
\text{Increase or Decrease, After Inflation} =& \left(\frac{\text{Current Cost}}{\text{Ending Balance}} \times \frac{\text{Adjustment}}{\text{Factor}}\right) \\
&- \left[\left(\frac{\text{Current Cost}}{\text{Beginning Balance}} \times \frac{\text{Adjustment}}{\text{Factor}}\right) + \frac{\text{Additions}}{\text{During the Year}} - \frac{\text{Reductions}}{\text{During the Year}}\right]
\end{aligned}$$

To illustrate, the increase (decrease) in the current cost of inventory, after inflation (i.e., in constant purchasing power), is computed as follows:

$$\begin{aligned}
\text{Increase} =& [\$63,000 \times (273 \div 286)] - [(\$42,500 \times 273 \div 260) + \$132,000 - \$133,000] \\
=& \$60,136 - (\$44,625 + \$132,000 - \$133,000) \\
=& \$60,136 - \$43,625 \\
=& \underline{\underline{\$16,511}}
\end{aligned}$$

The increase, after inflation, indicates that the increase in the current cost of the inventory exceeded the increase in the general price level as measured by the CPI–U.

The difference between the unadjusted increase (decrease) in the current cost (specific prices) and the increase (decrease) in the current cost, net of inflation, is referred to as the inflation component. The inflation component for the inventory is computed as follows:

$$\begin{aligned}
\text{Inflation Component} =& \text{Increase in Current} - \text{Increase in Current Cost} \\
& \text{Cost (unadjusted)} \quad\quad \text{After Inflation} \\
& \quad\quad\quad\quad\quad\quad\quad\quad (\text{i.e., in constant purchasing power}) \\
=& \$21,500 - \$16,511 \\
=& \underline{\underline{\$4,989}}
\end{aligned}$$

This calculation reinforces the fact that the current cost of the inventory increased faster than inflation, since inflation accounted for only $4,989 of the $21,500 unadjusted current cost increase. The reporting of the increase in the current cost (unadjusted), the increase in the current cost in constant purchasing power, and the inflation component for the inventory of the Colonial Company is illustrated in Exhibit 13–9. Similar disclosures are made for equipment as shown in Exhibit 13–9.

The Five-Year Summary Included in the Supplementary Disclosures on the Effects of Changing Prices

If a company presents the supplementary disclosures for the current year, a five-year summary of the following information should also be provided:

1. Net sales and other operating revenues
2. Income from continuing operations based on current cost (including amounts for earnings per share)
3. Net assets at year-end, based on current cost
4. Increase or decrease in the current cost amounts of inventory and of property, plant, and equipment, after eliminating the effects of inflation
5. Purchasing power gain or loss on net monetary items
6. Cash dividends declared and market price at year-end, per common share

To illustrate the five-year summary, we continue our example of the Colonial Company discussed earlier. The data as *originally* reported in *each* of the five years is shown in Exhibit 13–11. Some of this information is taken from the historical cost financial statements, some from the supplementary disclosures of the effects of changing prices, and some of it is additional data. Since the data for each year are measured in terms of dollars of that year, each year's amounts are measured in terms of different purchasing powers. Therefore, the five-year summary is adjusted to dollars of constant purchasing power so that a realistic comparison of the data can be made. There are two alternatives for the value of the CPI–U index that may be used for adjusting the five-year summary. Either alternative may be chosen by the company.

Average Index for the Current Year

All the dollar amounts from the different years may be adjusted to the average CPI–U index for the current year (273 as shown in Exhibit 13–11 for this example). If this alternative is used, the dollars from each past year are adjusted forward to the purchasing power of the current period. Therefore, the dollar amounts for four of the years in the five-year summary are larger (assuming inflation) than when they were originally measured and reported in the financial statements of past years. The five-year summary of Exhibit 13–11 adjusted to the average index for the current year (1993) is illustrated in Exhibit 13–12.

Base Period Index

The second alternative is to adjust all the historical dollars to the CPI–U index of the base period. **The base period is the year for which the index value is 100.** For the CPI–U index the base period is 1967, and it is usually written as 1967 = 100. If this alternative is used, the historical dollars in the five-year summary are adjusted back to the purchasing power of 1967. Therefore, each dollar amount in the five-year summary is smaller than when it was originally measured (assuming inflation) and reported in the financial statements for the particular year.

To illustrate this alternative consider the net sales and other operating revenues from Exhibit 13–11. Each of these items would be adjusted to the 1967 base index of 100 as follows:

1993	$300,000	× 100/273	=	$109,890
1992	$280,000	× 100/250	=	$112,000
1991	$250,000	× 100/235	=	$106,383
1990	$200,000	× 100/220	=	$ 90,909
1989	$180,000	× 100/200	=	$ 90,000

EXHIBIT 13–11

	COLONIAL COMPANY Data for Five-Year Summary as Originally Reported				
	1993	1992	1991	1990	1989
Net sales and other operating revenues	$300,000[a]	$280,000	$250,000	$200,000	$180,000
Income from continuing operations:					
Current cost	(8,075)[a]	5,420	27,618	45,000	42,300
Earnings per share[b]	(0.81)	0.54	2.76	4.50	4.23
Net assets at year-end:					
Current cost	332,800[c]	210,000	200,000	190,000	145,000
Increase or decrease in the current cost amount of inventory, after eliminating the effects of inflation	16,511[a]	18,000	16,000	15,000	12,000
Increase or decrease in the current cost amount of equipment, after eliminating the effects of inflation	53,977[a]	(18,000)	20,000	33,000	(8,000)
Purchasing power gain on net monetary items	8,509[a]	3,000	2,750	4,120	2,300
Cash dividends declared per share	—	1.00	1.00	1.00	1.00
Market price of common stock at year-end	17	12	15	18	12

All amounts are assumed except for those calculated in the footnotes below.

[a]Calculated in earlier analysis
[b]Assuming 10,000 shares outstanding
[c]Cash ($59,800) + Accounts Receivable ($80,000) + Inventory (12,000 × $5.25 = $63,000) + Equipment ($325,000) − Accounts Payable ($45,000) − Bonds Payable ($150,000)
Additional Information:
CPI–U Index: Average 1993 = 273
           Average 1992 = 250
           Average 1991 = 235
           Average 1990 = 220
           Average 1989 = 200
                 1967 = 100

EXHIBIT 13–12

....

COLONIAL COMPANY
Five-Year Summary in Constant Purchasing Power
(average 1993 dollars CPI–U = 273)

	1993[a]	1992[b]	1991[c]	1990[d]	1989[e]
Net sales and other operating revenues	$300,000	$305,760	$290,426	$248,182	$245,700
Income from continuing operations:					
Current cost	(8,075)	5,919	32,084	55,841	57,740
Earnings per share	(0.81)	0.59	3.21	5.58	5.77
Net assets at year-end:					
Current cost	332,800	229,320	232,340	235,773	197,925
Increase or decrease in the current cost amount of inventory, after eliminating the effects of inflation	16,511	19,656	18,587	18,614	16,380
Increase or decrease in the current cost amount of equipment, after eliminating the effects of inflation	53,977	(19,656)	23,234	40,950	(10,920)
Purchasing power gain on net monetary items	8,509	3,276	3,195	5,113	3,140
Cash dividends declared per share	—	1.09	1.16	1.24	1.37
Market price of common stock at year-end	17.00	13.10	17.43	22.34	16.38

[a]Exhibit 13–6 data for 1993

[b]Exhibit 13–6 data for 1992 $\times \dfrac{273}{250}$

[c]Exhibit 13–6 data for 1991 $\times \dfrac{273}{235}$

[d]Exhibit 13–6 data for 1990 $\times \dfrac{273}{220}$

[e]Exhibit 13–6 data for 1989 $\times \dfrac{273}{200}$

The adjusted amounts would be reported in the five-year summary, and each of the other items in the five-year summary would be adjusted in the same way.

Understanding the Two Alternatives

A comparison of the two alternative presentations of "net sales and other operating revenues" should provide an understanding of the differences between the two methods. The historical dollar amounts of the sales in 1989 and 1993 are not comparable because they are calculated in terms of dollars of different purchasing power. For example, a conclusion that the company had experienced a growth in net sales of 67% ($300,000 ÷ $180,000 = 1.67) would be misleading. Instead, the conclusion should be that net sales have increased by 22% ($300,000 ÷ $245,700 = 1.22; or $109,890 ÷ 90,000 = 1.22) after allowing for the effects of inflation.

As another example consider the disclosure of the market price of the common stock at year-end. The market price in 1989 was $12. At that time the CPI–U index was 200, whereas in 1993 it is 273. Therefore, the $12 in 1989 has an equivalent purchasing power of $16.38 [$12 × (273 ÷ 200)] in 1993 as disclosed in Exhibit 13–12. On the other hand, the base year index was 100 in 1967 and thus the $12 in 1989 has an equivalent purchasing power of $6 [$12 × (100 ÷ 200)] in 1967. The five-year summary allows users of the financial statements to make better comparisons of the financial results over time, and therefore their evaluations of the success of the company should be improved.

QUESTIONS

1. Define the following terms: (a) nominal dollars; (b) constant purchasing power dollars, and (c) current cost.

2. Distinguish between a general price-level change and a specific price change. What, if any, is the relationship between them?

3. Describe how historical costs are adjusted to constant purchasing power.

4. Define monetary assets and monetary liabilities. Give two examples of each.

5. During a period of inflation does holding net monetary assets result in a purchasing power gain or loss? Why?

6. Is the base year of a price index significant? Why or why not?

7. What is a holding gain? Distinguish between a realized and an unrealized holding gain.

8. Why is a current cost income statement prepared in terms of the average current costs for the year, whereas a current cost balance sheet is prepared in terms of the current costs at the end of the year?

9. Are companies required to include supplementary disclosures of the effect of changing prices in their annual financial statements?

10. Consider the major items included in the income statement. Which are most nearly measured on a current cost basis on historical cost financial statements? Which are least?

11. What is the major argument in favor of constant purchasing power financial statements? Of current cost financial statements?

12. How may historical cost net income include a return of capital in income?

13. What methods may be used to determine the current cost of inventory, and property, plant, and equipment? Give an example of an asset for which each method is appropriate.

14. When supplementary information about the effects of changing prices is disclosed, what information about the current year should be included?

15. When supplementary information about the effects of changing prices is disclosed, what information should be included in the five-year summary?

16. Explain what causes an exchange gain or loss and when each occurs.

17. Explain the meaning of the terms *reporting currency* and *functional currency.*

18. Distinguish between translation and remeasurement.

PROBLEMS AND CASES

19. Income Measurement. A company purchased land for $22,500. Three years later the current cost of the land is $31,000. During the three years the general price level rose from 120 to 150.

Required **1.** If the company sells the land, how much income would be computed at the time of the sale under each of the following concepts:

    a. Historical cost
    b. Constant purchasing power
    c. Current cost

    2. What is the concept of income used in each of the alternatives?

20. General Price-Level Index. January 1990 is the base period for a general price-level index. For simplicity, it will be assumed that the price index includes only five items. The average amounts purchased and the prices of the items in January 1990, January 1993, and January 1994 follow:

Item	Average Amounts Purchased	Price per Unit in January 1990	Price per Unit in January 1993	Price per Unit in January 1994
A	30 units	$ 3.00	$ 3.80	$ 4.20
B	25	5.00	5.40	5.20
C	20	8.00	9.25	10.00
D	15	21.00	23.00	23.60
E	10	50.00	58.30	60.00

Required **1.** What is the general price-level index in January 1993 and in January 1994?

    2. What is the percentage change in the average total price between January 1993 and January 1994?

    3. What would be the general price-level index in each of the three years if January 1993 was the base period?

    4. What is the purpose of the average amounts purchased? (*Hint:* Compute the general price-level index in January 1993, using January 1990 as the base period, if no amounts are used in either year.)

21. Specific Price-Level Indexes. Use the information in Problem 20.

Required Compute a specific price-level index for each of the five items if January 1990 is the base period for each index.

22. Constant Purchasing Power Income Statement. The Abaco Company is preparing a comprehensively adjusted constant purchasing power income statement for the year at the average CPI–U index of 132. The historical cost amounts and the index when the amount was recorded follow:

	Amount	Index
Sales	$80,000	132
Cost of goods sold	37,000	—
Depreciation expense	10,000	—
Selling expenses	12,000	132
Administrative expenses	16,000	132

The depreciation expense was calculated on a straight-line basis for assets purchased when the index was 110. The cost of goods sold was calculated on a FIFO basis. It included inventory that was purchased for $24,000 when the index was 128 and for $13,000 when the index was 130. The CPI–U index at the end of the year is 136.

Required Prepare a comprehensively adjusted constant purchasing power income statement for the Abaco Company using the average CPI–U index. Round each amount to the nearest dollar.

23. **Constant Purchasing Power Balance Sheet.** The Marsh Company is preparing a comprehensively adjusted constant purchasing power balance sheet at the end of the year in terms of the average CPI–U index for the year of 132. The CPI–U index at the end of the year is 136. The historical cost amounts in the various balance sheet accounts and the index when the amount was recorded follow:

	Amount	Index
Cash	$13,600	136
Accounts receivable	17,000	136
Inventory	25,750	—
Machinery	37,000	110
Accumulated depreciation: machinery	14,000	—
Accounts payable	20,400	136
Common stock, no par	30,000	100
Retained earnings	28,950	—

The machinery is being depreciated on a straight-line basis with no residual value. The company used the FIFO inventory method and the ending inventory for the year included units that had cost $16,750 when the index was 134 and $9,000 when the index was 135.

Required Prepare a comprehensively adjusted constant purchasing power balance sheet for the Marsh Company using the average CPI–U index. Round each amount to the nearest dollar. (*Hint:* Use the retained earnings as a balancing amount.)

24. **Purchasing Power Gain or Loss.** The Shire Company had the following beginning and ending historical cost balances for the current year in selected accounts:

	Beginning Balance	Ending Balance
Cash	$ 6,000	$ 8,000
Accounts receivable	27,000	28,000
Inventory	35,000	38,000
Accounts payable	9,000	11,000
Bonds payable	20,000	20,000

The beginning, average, and ending CPI–U index for the year was 144, 153, and 160, respectively.

Required Prepare (1) a schedule of net monetary items and (2) a schedule to compute the purchasing power gain or loss for the year. In part 2 use the method that assumes that the increase or decrease in all the net monetary items during the year occurred at the average price level for the year. Round each amount to the nearest dollar.

25. **Purchasing Power Gain or Loss.** At the beginning of the year the Baker Company had net monetary assets of $42,000. At the end of the year the net monetary assets were $50,000. During the year the following transactions affected the net monetary assets:

1. Sales of $100,000, which occurred evenly throughout the year

2. Purchases of inventory of $44,000, which occurred when the CPI–U index was 122

3. Payment of wages of $30,000, which occurred evenly throughout the year

4. Purchase of a building for $18,000, which occurred when the CPI–U index was 125

The beginning, average, and ending CPI–U indexes for the year were 120, 124, and 128, respectively.

Required Prepare a schedule to compute the purchasing power gain or loss for the year at the average price level. Use the method that requires an analysis of the time at which each increase or decrease in net monetary items occurred. Round each amount to the nearest dollar.

26. **Current Cost Income Statement.** The Powell Company is preparing a comprehensively adjusted current cost income statement using average current costs for the current year. The following items are the historical cost amounts in selected accounts:

Sales	$90,000
Cost of goods sold	40,000
Depreciation expense	12,000
Selling expenses	16,000
Administrative expenses	18,000

The cost of goods sold consisted of 10,000 units at $4 each. The cost of the inventory at the beginning of the year was $3.70 per unit and rose by 20% during the year. Selling and administrative expenses were incurred at average costs for the year. The depreciation was calculated by using straight-line depreciation on an asset that cost

$60,000, with a five-year life and no expected residual value. The cost of an equivalent asset at the beginning of the year was $78,000 and rose by 15% during the year.

Required Prepare a comprehensively adjusted current cost income statement for the current year.

27. **Current Cost Balance Sheet.** The Erikson Company is preparing a comprehensively adjusted current cost balance sheet using ending current costs for the period. The following items are the historical cost amounts in selected accounts:

Cash	$ 8,000
Marketable securities	10,000
Inventory	16,000
Machinery	40,000
Accumulated depreciation: machinery	5,000

The following additional information is available:

1. The market value of the marketable securities at the end of the year is $9,000.

2. The inventory consists of 10,000 units purchased at an average cost of $1.60 per unit. The current cost of the inventory at the beginning and end of the year was $1.50 and $1.75 per unit, respectively.

3. The machinery was purchased at the beginning of the year and is being depreciated on a straight-line basis over an expected life of eight years with no residual value. At year end the current cost is $46,000.

Required At what amount should each item be included in the current cost balance sheet of the Erikson Company?

28. **Constant Purchasing Power Financial Statements.** The historical cost financial statements of the Newport Company are shown as follows:

NEWPORT COMPANY
Income Statement
For Year Ended December 31, 1993

Sales		$82,000
Cost of goods sold		
Beginning inventory	$21,000	
Purchases	54,000	
Cost of goods available for sale	$75,000	
Less: ending inventory	(27,000)	
Cost of goods sold		(48,000)
Gross profit		$34,000
Operating expenses		
Depreciation expense	$ 6,000	
Other operating expenses	18,000	
Total operating expenses		(24,000)
Net income		$10,000

NEWPORT COMPANY
Balance Sheets

	December 31, 1992	December 31, 1993
Cash	$ 14,000	$ 17,000
Accounts receivable	16,000	22,000
Inventory	21,000	27,000
Property and equipment	80,000	80,000
Less: accumulated depreciation	(24,000)	(30,000)
Total assets	$107,000	$116,000
Accounts payable	$ 5,000	$ 4,000
Bonds payable	16,000	16,000
Common stock, no par	40,000	40,000
Retained earnings	46,000	56,000
Total liabilities and stockholders' equity	$107,000	$116,000

The following additional information is available:

1. Sales and other operating expenses occurred evenly throughout the year.

2. Inventory is valued on a FIFO cost flow assumption. Ending inventory each year was purchased in September of that year. Purchases were made at the average price level for the year.

3. The property and equipment consists of land that was purchased for $20,000 in January 1985 and a building that cost $60,000 on January 1, 1989, and is being depreciated using the straight-line method over a ten-year life with no residual value.

4. The common stock was sold when the company was formed in January 1985.

5. The CPI–U index was as follows:

January 1985	160
January 1989	210
September 1992	270
December 1992	275
Average for 1993	290
September 1993	295
December 1993	300

6. Net monetary items were affected by sales, purchases, and other operating expenses.

Required Prepare (1) a comprehensively adjusted income statement for 1993, (2) a schedule of net monetary items and a schedule to compute the purchasing power gain or loss, and (3) a balance sheet at December 31, 1993, all in terms of the average index for 1993. Ignore income taxes. Round each amount to the nearest dollar. (*Hint:* In the balance sheet, use the retained earnings as a balancing amount.)

29. Current Cost Financial Statements. Use the historical cost financial statements for the Newport Company in Problem 28. The following additional information is available:

1. Sales and other operating expenses occurred evenly throughout the year.

2. The ending inventory each year included 10,000 units. The cost of goods sold in 1993 was composed of 20,000 units. The current cost of the inventory was as follows:

December 1992	$2.25 per unit
Average 1993	2.50 per unit
December 1993	2.75 per unit

3. The property and equipment includes the following items:

		Current Cost of Equivalent New Assets		
Item	Cost	December 1992	December 1993	Depreciable Life
Land	$20,000	$50,000	$55,000	—
Building	60,000	80,000	95,000	10 years (no residual value)

Required 1. Prepare a comprehensively adjusted current cost income statement in terms of the average current costs for the year. Ignore income taxes and holding gains or losses.

2. Prepare a current cost balance sheet at December 31, 1993, in terms of the current costs at that time. (*Hint:* Use the retained earnings as a balancing amount.)

30. Constant Purchasing Power Financial Statements. The following are the historical cost financial statements of the Basin Company:

BASIN COMPANY
Income Statement
For Year Ended December 31, 1993

Sales		$155,000
Cost of goods sold		
Beginning inventory	$ 41,000	
Purchases	101,000	
Cost of goods available for sale	$142,000	
Less: ending inventory	(70,000)	
Cost of goods sold		(72,000)
Gross profit		$ 83,000
Operating expenses		
Depreciation expense	$ 20,000	
Other operating expenses	36,000	
Total operating expenses		(56,000)
Net income		$ 27,000

BASIN COMPANY
Balance Sheets

	December 31, 1992	December 31, 1993
Cash	$ 23,000	$ 48,000
Accounts receivable	36,000	50,000
Inventory	41,000	70,000
Property and equipment	200,000	200,000
Less: accumulated depreciation	(80,000)	(100,000)
Total assets	$220,000	$268,000
Accounts payable	$ 12,000	$ 33,000
Bonds payable	70,000	70,000
Common stock, no par	50,000	50,000
Retained earnings	88,000	115,000
Total liabilities and stockholders' equity	$220,000	$268,000

The following additional information is available:

1. Sales and other operating expenses occurred evenly throughout the year.

2. Inventory is valued on a FIFO cost flow assumption. The ending inventory each year was purchased in October of that year. Purchases were made at the average price level for 1993.

3. The property and equipment consist of land that was purchased for $60,000 in May 1984 and a machine that cost $140,000 on January 1, 1989 and is being depreciated using the straight-line method over a seven-year life with no residual value.

4. The common stock was sold when the company was formed in May 1984.

5. The CPI–U index was as follows:

May 1984	140
January 1989	200
October 1992	265
December 1992	270
Average for 1993	285
October 1993	290
December 1993	295

6. The net monetary items were affected by the sales, the purchases, and the other operating expenses.

Required Prepare (1) a comprehensively adjusted income statement for 1993, (2) a schedule of net monetary items and a schedule to compute the purchasing power gain or loss for 1993, and (3) a balance sheet at December 31, 1993, all in terms of the average CPI–U index for 1993. Ignore income taxes. Round each amount to the nearest dollar. (*Hint:* In the balance sheet, use the retained earnings as a balancing amount.)

31. **Current Cost Financial Statements.** Use the historical cost financial statements for the Basin Company in Problem 30. The following additional information is available for the company:

1. Sales and other operating expenses occurred evenly throughout the year.

2. The ending inventory for 1992 and 1993 included 5,000 units and 7,000 units, respectively. The cost of goods sold in 1993 was composed of 8,000 units. The current cost of the inventory was as follows:

December 1992	$ 8.60 per unit
Average 1993	9.50 per unit
December 1993	10.40 per unit

3. The property and equipment includes the following items:

Item	Cost	Current Cost of Equivalent New Asset December 31, 1992	December 31, 1993	Depreciable Life
Land	$ 60,000	$ 95,000	$100,000	—
Building	140,000	180,000	191,000	7 years (no residual value)

Required 1. Prepare a comprehensively adjusted current cost income statement in terms of the average current costs for the year. Ignore income taxes and holding gains or losses.

2. Prepare a current cost balance sheet at December 31, 1993, in terms of the current costs at that time. (*Hint:* Use the retained earnings as a balancing amount in the balance sheet.)

32. **Alternative Income Concepts.** Alan Pierce owns and operates a small company. He has heard about supplementary disclosures of the effects of changing prices that can be prepared by companies and is interested in having the disclosures prepared for his company. During a meeting to discuss the disclosures, he makes the following comments:

1. "I understand these alternatives are measuring different types of income because they assume different things about how to measure wealth. I don't understand how that can be, because I invested $50,000 in my business five years ago and nobody can change that."

2. "This purchasing power loss is very strange. How can I have a loss when I haven't paid money out, sold something, or had a debit or credit in the accounting system?"

3. "How can it be useful to know the current cost of the building when I have no intention of replacing the building for at least ten years?"

4. "Net income, after income taxes at 40%, this year was $20,000. Dividends paid by the company to me were $15,000. I thought that the company was $5,000 better

off. Now you say that the current cost income before income taxes is $12,000. I still have to pay the taxes, but the company seems to be heading for trouble. . . ."

Required Prepare a response to each comment made by Mr. Pierce.

33. Measuring Current Cost. A company is preparing its supplementary disclosures on the effects of changing prices. The accountant who has been assigned the task of calculating the current cost of the assets has come to you for help.

"For example," she says, "think about the building we're sitting in. The company paid $60,000 for it when it was brand new three years ago. I can go to a real estate agency and find out what they think it's worth. But they're always optimistic. I could go to a builder and ask what it would cost to build today. But they don't build them quite the same way today; different materials, better insulation, and so on. I could look up a government-prepared index for building prices, but that's only an overall average. Or I could apply functional pricing. This building has 2,000 square feet, and I could find out the cost per square foot to build now. But that wouldn't be the same building, and what about all of the improvements the company has made. What should I do?"

Required Clearly describe the alternative methods of calculating current costs. Describe the advantages and disadvantages of each method in the context of a building. How would you recommend the current cost of the building be determined?

34. Current Value and Fair Presentation of Financial Statements. The total assets of the Sunset Land Company were $2½ million on December 31, 1993, including land of $150,000. Net income was negligible because no land sales took place and none were planned.

The land consisted of 50,000 acres valued at its acquisition cost in the early part of the century of $3 per acre. The market value of the land is now believed to exceed $15 million.

The auditor's opinion attached to the financial statements states, in part, "The financial statements present fairly the financial position of the Sunset Land Company . . . in conformity with generally accepted accounting principles."

Required Does the use of generally accepted accounting principles enable the financial position of the Sunset Land Company to be presented fairly?

35. Exchange Gains and Losses. On January 15, 1993, the Searle Company, a U.S. company, acquired machinery on account from a British company for 12,000 pounds. The company paid for the machine on January 30, 1993. The exchange rates on January 15 and 30 were $1.85 and $1.80, respectively.

Required Record the effects on the accounting equation of the acquisition and payment by the Searle Company.

36. Exchange Gains and Losses. On June 20, 1993, the Livingston Company, a U.S. company, sold merchandise on account to a Swiss company for 25,000 francs. The company received payment for the merchandise on July 10, 1993. The exchange rates on June 20 and July 10 were $0.69 and $0.68, respectively.

Required Record the effects on the accounting equation of the sale and collection by the Livingston Company.

37. **Translation.** The Rozman Company, a foreign subsidiary of a U.S. company, had prepared the following income statement and balance sheet in terms of West German marks:

ROZMAN COMPANY
Income Statement
For Year Ended December 31, 1993

Sales	DM700,000
Cost of goods sold	(300,000)
Gross profit	DM400,000
Operating expenses	
Depreciation expense	(60,000)
Selling and administrative expenses	(80,000)
Income before income taxes	DM260,000
Income tax expense	(104,000)
Net income	DM156,000

ROZMAN COMPANY
Balance Sheet
December 31, 1993

Cash	DM 300,000
Accounts receivable	400,000
Inventory	600,000
Property and equipment	900,000
Less: accumulated depreciation	(100,000)
Total assets	DM2,100,000
Accounts payable	DM 300,000
Bonds payable	700,000
Common stock, no par	800,000
Retained earnings	300,000
Total liabilities and stockholders' equity	DM2,100,000

The following additional information is available:

1. The functional currency of the Rozman Company is the West German mark.

2. The average exchange rate for 1993 was $0.52.

3. The exchange rate on December 31, 1993, was $0.54.

4. The common stock was issued when the exchange rate was $0.45.

Required Prepare the 1993 income statement and ending balance sheet of the Rozman Company in terms of U.S. dollars. Assume that the company has a cumulative translation adjustment of $30,000. Use the retained earnings as a balancing amount.

38. Remeasurement. The Groski Company, a foreign subsidiary of a U.S. company, had prepared the following income statement and balance sheet in terms of British pounds:

GROSKI COMPANY
Income Statement
For Year Ended December 31, 1993

Sales	£400,000
Cost of goods sold	(100,000)
Gross profit	£300,000
Operating expenses	
Depreciation expense	(20,000)
Selling and administrative expenses	(50,000)
Income before income taxes	£230,000
Income tax expense	(92,000)
Net income	£138,000

GROSKI COMPANY
Balance Sheet
December 31, 1993

Cash	£ 100,000
Accounts receivable	200,000
Inventory	500,000
Property and equipment	700,000
Less: accumulated depreciation	(200,000)
Total assets	£1,300,000
Accounts payable	200,000
Bonds payable	300,000
Common stock, no par	600,000
Retained earnings	200,000
Total liabilities and stockholders' equity	£1,300,000

The following additional information is available:

1. The functional currency of the Groski Company is the U.S. dollar.

2. The average exchange rate for 1993 was $1.90.

3. The exchange rate on December 31, 1993, was $1.85.

4. The inventory was purchased when the exchange rate was $1.88.

5. The property and equipment was purchased when the exchange rate was $2.10.

6. The common stock was issued when the exchange rate was $2.20.

7. The transaction loss for 1993 was $5,000.

Required Prepare the 1993 income statement and ending balance sheet of the Groski Company in terms of U.S. dollars. Use the retained earnings as a balancing amount.

39. Translation. The Fowler Grain Company, a Canadian subsidiary of a U.S. company, had prepared the following income statement and balance sheet in Canadian dollars:

FOWLER GRAIN COMPANY
Income Statement
For Year Ended December 31, 1993

Sales	C$750,000
Cost of goods sold	(400,000)
Gross profit	C$350,000
Operating expenses	
Depreciation expense	(40,000)
Selling and administrative expenses	(150,000)
Income before income taxes	C$160,000
Income tax expense	(64,000)
Net income	C$ 96,000

FOWLER GRAIN COMPANY
Balance Sheet
December 31, 1993

Cash	C$ 40,000
Accounts receivable	200,000
Inventory	300,000
Property and equipment	240,000
Less: accumulated depreciation	(120,000)
Total assets	C$660,000
Accounts payable	C$ 50,000
Obligations under capital leases	180,000
Common stock, no par	100,000
Retained earnings	330,000
Total liabilities and stockholders' equity	C$660,000

The following additional information is available:

1. The functional currency of the Fowler Grain Company is the Canadian dollar.

2. The average exchange rate for 1993 was $0.83.

3. The exchange rate on December 31, 1993, was $0.81.

4. The common stock was issued when the exchange rate was $0.90.

Required Prepare the 1993 income statement and ending balance sheet of the Fowler Grain Company in terms of U.S. dollars. Assume that the company has a cumulative translation adjustment of $22,000. Use the retained earnings as a balancing amount.

40. Remeasurement. The Chambers Pharmaceutical Company, a French subsidiary of a U.S. company, had prepared the following income statement and balance sheet in francs:

CHAMBERS PHARMACEUTICAL COMPANY
Income Statement
For Year Ended December 31, 1993

Sales	Fr900,000
Cost of goods sold	(150,000)
Gross profit	Fr750,000
Operating expenses	
Depreciation expense	(80,000)
Selling and administrative expenses	(320,000)
Income before income taxes	Fr350,000
Income tax expense	(140,000)
Net income	Fr210,000

CHAMBERS PHARMACEUTICAL COMPANY
Balance Sheet
December 31, 1993

Cash	Fr 50,000
Accounts receivable	150,000
Inventory	270,000
Property and equipment	500,000
Less: accumulated depreciation	(160,000)
Total assets	Fr810,000
Accounts payable	Fr100,000
Obligations under capital leases	300,000
Common stock, no par	200,000
Retained earnings	210,000
Total liabilities and stockholders' equity	Fr810,000

The following additional information is available:

1. The functional currency of the Chambers Pharmaceutical Company is the U.S. dollar.

2. The average exchange rate for 1993 was $0.17.

3. The exchange rate on December 31, 1993 was $0.15.

4. The inventory was purchased when the exchange rate was $0.16.

5. The property and equipment was purchased when the exchange rate was $0.20.

6. The common stock was issued when the exchange rate was $0.25.

7. The transaction loss for 1993 was $12,000.

Required Prepare the 1993 income statement and ending balance sheet of the Chambers Pharmaceutical Company in terms of U.S. dollars. Use the retained earnings as a balancing amount.

41. **Translation.** The Rye Company is a British subsidiary of a U.S. company. The financial statements of the company for 1993 follow:

RYE COMPANY
Balance Sheets

	12/31/92	12/31/93
Cash		£ 40,000
Accounts receivable	60,000	75,000
Inventory	75,000	95,000
Property and equipment	300,000	300,000
Less: accumulated depreciation	(100,000)	(140,000)
Total assets	£360,000	£370,000
Accounts payable	£ 40,000	£ 30,000
Bonds payable	90,000	90,000
Common stock, no par	150,000	150,000
Retained earnings	80,000	100,000
Total liabilities and stockholders' equity	£360,000	£370,000

Income Statement
For Year Ended December 31, 1993

Sales	£480,000
Cost of goods sold	(260,000)
Gross profit	£220,000
Operating expenses	
Depreciation expense	(40,000)
Selling and administrative expenses	(80,000)
Income before income taxes	£100,000
Income tax expense	(30,000)
Net income	£ 70,000

Statement of Changes in Retained Earnings
For Year Ended December 31, 1993

Retained earnings, 12/31/92	£ 80,000
Net income	70,000
	£150,000
Less: dividends	(50,000)
Retained earnings, 12/31/93	£100,000

The functional currency of the Rye Company is the British pound. The common stock was issued when the exchange rate was $1.80, the retained earnings balance at December 31, 1992 was $120,000, and the cumulative translation adjustment at December 31, 1992, was $(68,000). The exchange rates are as follows:

12/31/92	$1.40
Average for 1993	1.45
12/31/93	1.50

Required Prepare the financial statements of the Rye Company in U.S. dollars.

42. Remeasurement. Use the financial statements for the Rye Company in Problem 41. Assume now that the functional currency is the U.S. dollar. The company's purchases of inventory of £280,000 were made at the average exchange rate for the year. The ending inventory each year was purchased in October of that year. The property and equipment was purchased in January 1990. The retained earnings balance at December 31, 1992, was $129,000. The exchange rates are as follows:

1/1/90	$1.80
10/1/92	1.36
12/31/92	1.40
Average for 1993	1.45
10/1/93	1.48
12/31/93	1.50

Required Prepare the financial statements of the Rye Company in U.S. dollars.

43. **Appendix: Supplementary Disclosures: Inventory.** The Winans Company shows the following cost of goods sold section on its 1993 income statement:

Inventory, December 31, 1992	$ 80,000
Purchases	230,000
Cost of goods available for sale	$310,000
Less: Inventory, December 31, 1993	(112,500)
Cost of goods sold	$197,500

Additional Information:
Inventory, December 31, 1992: 4,000 units at $20 per unit
Inventory, December 31, 1993: 4,500 units at $25 per unit
Purchases during 1993: 10,000 units
Average current cost for 1993: $23.50 per unit
Current cost, December 31, 1992: $21 per unit
Current cost, December 31, 1993: $26 per unit

Required Compute the following amounts for the 1993 supplementary disclosures:

1. Cost of goods sold on a current cost basis

2. Current cost of the inventory

44. **Appendix: Supplementary Disclosures: Equipment.** The Stuart Company shows the following on its 1993 income statement and December 31, 1993, balance sheet:

Depreciation expense	$30,000
Equipment	$90,000
Less: Accumulated depreciation	(42,000)
	$48,000

Additional Information:

1. Manufacturing equipment: Purchased on January 1, 1988
    Cost: $60,000
    Depreciation method: straight line
    Residual value: zero

Estimated life: 12 years
Current cost, December 1992: $92,000
Current cost, December 1993: $100,000

2. Selling equipment: Purchased on January 1, 1990
   Cost: $30,000
   Depreciation method: straight line
   Residual value: zero
   Estimated life: 10 years
   Current cost, December 1992: $40,000
   Current cost, December 1993: $46,000

Required Compute the following amounts for the 1993 supplementary disclosures:

1. Depreciation expense on a current cost basis

2. Current cost of the equipment

45. Appendix: Supplementary Disclosures. The historical cost income statement of the Searle Company is shown as follows:

SEARLE COMPANY
Income Statement
For Year Ended December 31, 1993

Sales		$100,000
Cost of goods sold		
Inventory, December 31, 1992	$20,000	
Purchases	55,000	
Inventory, December 31, 1993	(30,000)	
Cost of goods sold		(45,000)
Gross profit		$ 55,000
Operating expenses		
Depreciation expense	$10,000	
Selling and administrative expenses	20,000	
Total operating expenses		(30,000)
Income before income taxes		$ 25,000
Income tax expense		(10,000)
Net income		$ 15,000

Additional Information:

1. Inventory:
   Beginning inventory: 4,000 units at $5 per unit
   Ending inventory: 5,000 units at $6 per unit
   Purchases during the year: 10,000 units
   Average current cost during the year: $5.70 per unit

2. Equipment:
   Purchased January 1, 1987, for $100,000
   Residual value: zero
   Estimated life: 10 years

Depreciation method: straight line
Average current cost during the year: $170,000

Required Prepare the supplementary disclosures of income from continuing operations for 1993.

46. Appendix: Supplementary Disclosures. The historical cost financial statements of the Chandler Company follow:

CHANDLER COMPANY
Income Statement
For Year Ended December 31, 1993

Sales		$120,000
Cost of goods sold		
Inventory, December 31, 1992	$20,000	
Purchases	63,000	
Cost of goods available for sale	$83,000	
Less: inventory, December 31, 1990	(25,000)	
Cost of goods sold		(58,000)
Gross profit		$ 62,000
Operating expenses		
Depreciation expense	$12,000	
Selling and administrative expenses	20,000	
Total operating expenses		(32,000)
Income before income taxes		$ 30,000
Income tax expense		(12,000)
Net income		$ 18,000

CHANDLER COMPANY
Balance Sheets

	December 31, 1992	December 31, 1993
Cash	$ 22,000	$ 35,000
Accounts receivable	30,000	38,000
Inventory	20,000	25,000
Equipment	96,000	96,000
Less: accumulated depreciation	(48,000)	(60,000)
Total assets	$120,000	$134,000
Accounts payable	$ 18,000	$ 14,000
Bonds payable	30,000	30,000
Common stock, no par	50,000	50,000
Retained earnings	22,000	40,000
Total liabilities and stockholders' equity	$120,000	$134,000

The following additional information is available:

1. Inventory:
   Inventory, December 31, 1992: 10,000 units purchased at $2.00 each.
   Inventory, December 31, 1993: 10,000 units purchased at $2.50 each.
   Purchases: 30,000 units in 1993.
   Average current cost for the year is $2.30 per unit.
   Current cost at the beginning of the year is $2.05 per unit.
   Current cost at the end of the year is $2.55 per unit.

2. Equipment:
   Purchased on January 1, 1989.
   Depreciation method: straight line
   Residual value: zero
   Estimated life: 8 years
   Current cost, December 1992: $110,000
   Current cost, December 1993: $150,000

3. CPI–U index:
   December 1992: 255
   Average for 1993: 265
   December 1993: 275

Required Prepare a schedule that would be included in the notes to the financial statements of the Chandler Company to report the 1993 supplementary disclosures. Round each amount to the nearest dollar. Include the related historical cost information for income from continuing operations.

47. **Appendix: Supplementary Disclosures.** The historical cost financial statements of the Barnes Company follow:

BARNES COMPANY
Income Statement
For Year Ended December 31, 1993

Sales		$215,000
Cost of goods sold		
Inventory, December 31, 1992	$ 35,000	
Purchases	110,000	
Cost of goods available for sale	$145,000	
Less: inventory, December 31, 1993	(40,000)	
Cost of goods sold		(105,000)
Gross profit		$110,000
Operating expenses		
Depreciation expense	$ 10,000	
Selling and administrative expenses	47,000	
Total operating expenses		(57,000)
Income before income taxes		$ 53,000
Income tax expense		(21,200)
Net income		$ 31,800

BARNES COMPANY
Balance Sheets

	December 31, 1992	December 31, 1993
Cash	$ 41,000	$ 56,000
Accounts receivable	54,000	68,000
Inventory	35,000	40,000
Equipment	90,000	90,000
Less: accumulated depreciation	(30,000)	(40,000)
Total assets	$190,000	$214,000
Accounts payable	$ 24,000	$ 15,000
Bonds payable	36,000	36,000
Common stock, no par	75,000	75,000
Retained earnings	55,000	88,000
Total liabilities and stockholders' equity	$190,000	$214,000

The following additional information is available:

1. Inventory:
   Inventory, December 31, 1992: 5,000 units at $7.00 each.
   Inventory, December 31, 1993: 5,000 units at $8.00 each.
   Purchases: 14,765 units in 1993.
   Average current cost for the year is $7.65 per unit.
   Current cost at the beginning of the year is $7.10 per unit.
   Current cost at the end of the year is $8.20 per unit.

2. Equipment:
   Purchased on January 1, 1991
   Depreciation method: straight line
   Residual value: zero
   Estimated life: 9 years
   Current cost, December 1992: $100,000
   Current cost, December 1993: $123,000

3. CPI–U index:
   December 1992: 270
   Average for 1993: 280
   December 1993: 290

Required   Prepare a schedule that would be included in the notes to the financial statements of the Barnes Company to report the 1993 supplementary disclosures. Round each amount to the nearest dollar. Include the related historical cost information for income from continuing operations.

48. **Appendix: The Five-Year Summary Included in the Supplementary Disclosures.** The following selected items were prepared for the Clark Company for inclusion in the five-year summary prepared as part of the supplementary disclosures of

the effects of changing prices. Selected data reported in each year's financial statements are as follows:

	1993	1992	1991	1990	1989
Net sales and other operating revenues	$98,000	$90,000	$76,000	$78,000	$70,000
Income from continuing operations—current cost	16,000	18,000	13,000	11,000	14,000

The average CPI–U index for each year is: 1993 = 300, 1992 = 288, 1991 = 279, 1990 = 270, 1989 = 262.

Required Prepare a five-year summary of the above items for the Clark Company in terms of the average index for 1993. Round each amount to the nearest dollar.

49. Appendix: Five-Year Summary. The Young Company has reported supplementary information on the effects of changing prices for the last five years. The information that has been reported each year over the last five years follows:

	1993	1992	1991	1990	1989
Net sales and other operating revenues	$200,000	$220,000	$180,000	$160,000	$120,000
Income from continuing operations					
Current cost	27,650	42,500	36,000	35,000	21,500
Earnings per share	2.77	4.25	3.60	3.50	2.15
Net assets at year-end					
Current cost	590,000	570,000	520,000	450,000	370,000
Increase or decrease in the current cost amount of inventory, net of inflation	29,000	24,500	21,750	18,420	19,600
Increase or decrease in the current cost amount of property, plant, and equipment, net of inflation	32,000	60,000	48,000	41,200	40,100
Purchasing power loss on net monetary items	6,050	4,100	8,000	4,200	3,750
Cash dividends declared per share	2.00	1.50	1.50	1.25	1.25
Market price of common stock at year-end	21	26	22	19	18
Average CPI–U index	290	270	250	235	220

Required Prepare a five-year summary of supplementary disclosures in terms of the average CPI–U index for 1993. Round each amount to the nearest dollar except for the earnings per share, the cash dividends per share, and the market price per share.

50. Appendix: Five-Year Summary. The Vento Company has reported supplementary information on the effects of changing prices for the last five years. The information that has been reported each year over the last five years follows:

	1993	1992	1991	1990	1989
Net sales and other operating revenues	$ 400,000	$440,000	$375,000	$340,000	$310,000
Income from continuing operations					
Current cost	51,000	57,900	48,250	39,100	30,400
Earnings per share	5.10	5.79	4.82	3.91	3.04
Net assets at year-end					
Current cost	1,500,000	950,000	795,000	660,000	600,000
Increase or decrease in the current cost amount of inventory, net of inflation	52,000	47,500	40,250	34,900	30,000
Increase or decrease in the current cost amount of property, plant, and equipment, net of inflation	58,400	70,300	67,600	60,100	57,600
Purchasing power loss on net monetary items	10,500	8,400	7,600	12,500	9,750
Cash dividends declared per share	4.00	3.00	3.00	2.50	2.50
Market price of common stock at year-end	42	52	44	38	36
Average CPI–U index	300	285	270	260	250

Required Prepare a five-year summary of supplementary disclosures in terms of the average CPI–U index for 1993. Round each amount to the nearest dollar except for the earnings per share, the cash dividends per share, and the market price per share.

ANNUAL REPORT PROBLEMS

51. Foreign Currency Analysis. The following excerpts are from Kimberly Clark's 1988 annual report relating to foreign currency translation (in millions of dollars):

	1988	1987
BALANCE SHEET		
Stockholders' Equity		
Unrealized currency translation adjustments (note 5)	$(50.5)	$(85.9)

Note 5. Foreign currency translation:
Assets and liabilities of foreign operations are translated into U.S. dollars at period-end exchange rates except for operations in the hyper-inflationary economies of Mexico, Brazil and Colombia where the functional currency for U.S. accounting purposes is the U.S. dollar. Gains and losses on such translation are reflected as unrealized

currency translation adjustments in stockholders' equity. Income and expense accounts are translated into U.S. dollars at rates of exchange in effect each month.

UNREALIZED CURRENCY TRANSLATION ADJUSTMENTS

	1988	1987
Balance, January 1	$ (85.9)	$(163.8)
Canadian dollar	34.7	21.3
British pound	(5.3)	30.6
French franc	(8.3)	12.3
German mark	(3.7)	5.5
Other	18.0	8.2
Total	35.4	77.9
Balance, December 31	$ (50.5)	$ (85.9)

Net currency exchange losses reflected in net income amounted to $5.2 in 1988, and $13.4 in 1987, compared to a gain of $0.7 in 1986.

Required 1. Explain the foreign currency translations and currency exchange transactions in relation to the strength or weakness of the U.S. dollar in 1988 and 1987. Why aren't such translations reflected in the income statement?

2. Analyze the foreign currency performance of Kimberly-Clark in 1988. (No impacts on the Statement of Cash Flows were disclosed.)

52. Foreign Currency Analysis. The following excerpts are from Campbell Soup's 1989 annual report relating to foreign currency translation (in millions of dollars):

Foreign Currency Translation Note:
Fluctuations in foreign exchange rates resulted in the following decreases in net earnings:
Foreign exchange losses, net:

	Translation in Latin America	Other Foreign Currency Transactions	Total	Income tax effect	Net earnings
1989	$20.0	$(0.7)	$19.3	$(0.2)	$19.1
1988	17.5	(0.9)	16.6	0.1	16.7
1987	6.7	(1.9)	4.8	0.8	5.6

The balances in the cumulative translation adjustments account in Stockholders' Equity are the following:

	1989	1988	1987
Europe	$(3.5)	$ 8.8	$18.4
Canada	(2.5)	(2.5)	(7.9)
Australia	7.3	21.1	0.6
Other	0.8	1.1	0.8
	$ 2.1	$28.5	$11.9

Required 1. Are the treatments of the above items in accordance with generally accepted accounting principles?

2. Analyze the foreign currency performance of Campbell Soup Company in 1989 and 1988. [The effect of exchange rate changes on cash in the Statement of Cash Flows were $(12.1) million in 1989 and $(10.8) million in 1988.]

53. **Foreign Currency Analysis.** Colgate-Palmolive Company is one of the world's leading consumer products companies, marketing its products in over 100 countries, with subsidiaries in 60 countries. The following excerpts are from its 1988 annual report relating to overseas operations (in thousands of dollars):

Overseas income before income taxes was $231,423 in 1988, $107,438 in 1987 and $124,237 in 1986. The 1987 decline in overseas income before income taxes relates to the provision for restructured operations recorded during the year. Included in income from continuing operations were foreign currency changes, resulting from the translation of balance sheets of subsidiaries operating in highly inflationary environments and from foreign currency transactions, of $22,412 in 1988, $18,381 in 1987 and $5,659 in 1986.

The following is an analysis of the changes in the separate component of shareholders' equity for cumulative foreign currency translation adjustments:

	1988	**1987**	**1986**
Balance, January 1	$(184,610)	$(256,198)	$(273,582)
Aggregate translation adjustments	(44,159)	58,152	17,384
Reduction due to disposition of certain operations	3,475	13,436	—
Balance, December 31	$(225,294)	$(184,610)	$(256,198)

Required Evaluate Colgate's overseas operations performance over these three years. Total income from continuing operations before income taxes was $250,219,000 in 1988, $40,394,000 in 1987 (when a $250,700,000 provision for restructured operations was included), and $195,521,000 in 1986.

54. **Foreign Currency Analysis.** Bristol-Myers is a large drug and consumer products company. The following excerpts are from its 1988 financial statements relating to foreign currency items (in millions of dollars):

Note 2. Foreign Currency Translation
Cumulative translation adjustments which represent the effect of translating assets and liabilities of the company's non-U.S. operations, except those in highly inflationary economies, were

	1988	**1987**	**1986**
Balance, January 1	$(84.2)	$(147.3)	$(181.7)
Effect of balance sheet translations:			
Amount	6.1	61.4	31.6
Tax effect	.3	1.7	2.8
Balance, December 31	$(77.8)	$ (84.2)	$(147.3)

Transaction losses resulting from foreign currency transactions and translation adjustments relating to non-U.S. entities operating in highly inflationary economies, principally Brazil and Mexico, of $31.4, $16.0, and $12.1, net of applicable income taxes, are reflected in net income for 1988, 1987, and 1986 respecitvely.

Required If the cumulative translation adjustments were included in net income, rather than just a separate stockholders' equity account, would there be a material impact on the company's net income? For 1988, 1987, and 1986, the net income was $829.0 million, $709.6 million, and $589.5 million, respectively. Would there be a material impact on net income if the transaction losses were not included in net income?

55. Foreign Currency Analysis. The following excerpts are from IBM's 1988 annual report (in millions of dollars):

Non-U.S. Operations Note (in part):

Non-U.S. subsidiaries which operate in a local currency environment account for approximately 90% of the company's non-U.S. revenue. The remaining 10% of the company's non-U.S. revenue is from subsidiaries and branches which operate in U.S. dollars or whose economic environment is highly inflationary.

As the value of the dollar weakens, net assets recorded in local currencies translate into more U.S. dollars than they would have at the previous year's rates. Conversely, as the dollar becomes stronger, net assets recorded in local currencies translate into fewer U.S. dollars than they would have at the previous year's rates. The translation adjustments, resulting from the translation of net assets, amounted to $1,917 at December 31, 1988, $2,865 at December 31, 1987, $307 at December 31, 1986, and $(1,466) at December 31, 1985. The changes in translation adjustments since the end of 1985 are a reflection of the weakening of the dollar in 1986 and 1987 and the strengthening in 1988.

Required **1.** Are IBM's translation adjustments from the non-U.S. subsidiaries which comprise 90% of the non-U.S. revenue or from the ones that account for the other 10%? Specify in which years IBM had translation adjustment gains or losses.

2. If the translation adjustments had been included in net income, would there have been material impacts? IBM's net income was $5,806 million, $5,258 million, and $4,789 million in 1988, 1987, and 1986, respectively.

56. Different International Accounting Principles. Transamerica Corporation is a large provider of specialized financial and insurance services. The following excerpts are from its 1988 financial statements (in thousands of dollars):

Note H. Foreign Investments (in part):

On August 30, 1985, Transamerica exchanged Fred S. James & Co., Inc. for a 39% interest in Sedgwick Group plc, a London based international insurance brokerage firm. The consolidated statement of income includes Transamerica's equity in the earnings of Sedgwick.

The principal differences between United Kingdom accounting principles and those generally accepted in the United States are primarily due to differences in accounting for business combinations. Sedgwick, in accounting for its acquisition of James, wrote off all goodwill immediately against equity. Had Sedgwick followed U.S. accounting principles and accounted for the acquisition as a purchase transaction, it would have recognized goodwill as an asset to be amortized over a period not to exceed 40 years, and its equity would have been greater by the amount of that goodwill. These differences do not affect the consolidated financial statements, because the goodwill and related amortization are included in Transamerica's financial statements. Goodwill amounts to $430,000 and is being amortized over a 40-year period. Transamerica's share of Sedgwick's net income, after the amortization of goodwill and the provision for U.S. taxes on Sedgwick's distributed and undistributed income, amounted to $24,134 in 1988, $29,698 in 1987, and $31,063 in 1986.

Required **1.** Would there be a material impact upon Transamerica's net income if it followed United Kingdom accounting principles for goodwill, concerning its equity investment? Transamerica's net income was $346,436 thousand in 1988, $427,247 thousand in 1987, and $275,998 thousand in 1986.

2. Would there be a material impact upon Transamerica's net income from the foreign investment in Sedgwick?

57. Appendix: Changing Prices Calculations. Safeway Stores is one of the nation's largest grocery store chains. The following excerpts are from its 1985 financial statements relating to inflation accounting and choices of accounting methods (in millions of dollars):

Supplementary Financial Data Adjusted for the Effects of Changing Prices Note (in part):

	As Reported in the Consolidated Statement of Income (Historical Cost)	Adjusted for Changes in Specific Prices (Current Cost)
Sales	$19,650	$19,650
Cost of sales	14,872	14,903
Other expenses, net	4,425	4,461
Income before provision for income taxes	353	286
Provision for income taxes	122	122
Net income	$ 231	$ 164
Gain from the change in purchasing power of net monetary liabilities		$ 103
Depreciation and amortization expense[a]	$ 333	$ 422

[a]Allocated between cost of sales and other expenses in the determination of net income.

At year-end 1985, the current cost of merchandise inventories was $1,900 and the current cost of net property was $3,800.

BALANCE SHEET [IN PART]

Merchandise inventories
FIFO cost	$1,878
Less LIFO reductions	(313)
LIFO inventory	$1,565

Property, Plant and Equipment

Total cost	$4,640
Less accumulated depreciation	(2,003)
Net property	$2,637
Total assets	$4,841

Notes (in part)

Straight-line depreciation is used for financial statement purposes. A primary component of 1985 deferred income tax expense was accelerated depreciation of $24 which was 70% of the total 1985 deferred income tax expense. The cumulative deferred income taxes were $82 at the end of 1985 with the statutory federal income tax rate of 46%.

Required 1. Using the following accounting methods, prepare a brief comparative performance analysis in 1985 for Safeway by computing the return on assets (net income divided by average total assets; use ending total assets since the 1984 amounts were not given):

    a. The inventory (LIFO) and depreciation (straight-line) methods used by Safeway in its annual report.

    b. The alternative methods of FIFO and accelerated depreciation (assume that the LIFO reserve at the beginning of 1985 was $300 million).

    c. The inflation accounting method.

2. What are the major impacts of inflation and accounting method choices (inventory and depreciation) with respect to the return on assets calculations?

58. Appendix: Changing Prices Calculations. Kimberly-Clark and Scott Paper are major competitors in the sanitary tissue paper products industry. The following excerpts are from their 1985 financial statements related to inflation and historical cost accounting for inventory and property accounting (in millions of dollars):

	KIMBERLY-CLARK		SCOTT PAPER	
	As Reported	Restated Current Costs	As Reported	Restated Current Costs
Net sales	$4,072.9	$4,072.9	$3,049.5	$3,049.5
Cost of products sold	2,387.2	2,392.0	1,866.0	1,861.5
Depreciation	140.3	190.0	167.3	258.7
Other expenses, net	1,106.1	1,106.1	787.0	787.0
Income before income taxes	439.3	384.8	229.2	142.3
Provision for income taxes	189.4	189.4	75.4	75.4
Income before other items	249.9	195.4	153.8	66.9
Other income	17.2	17.2	47.3	47.3
Net income	$ 267.1	$ 212.6	$ 201.1	$ 114.2

Inventories

FIFO	$ 288.0			
Average cost			$ 129.0	
LIFO	189.1		166.6	
Total	$ 477.1	$ 587.4	$ 295.6	$ 394.3
Net property	$2,156.0	$2,744.5	$2,133.6	$2,900.0
Total assets	$3,503.8		$3,517.3	
Total stockholders' equity	$1,743.9		$1,183.4	

Accounting Policies Note (in part):
Kimberly-Clark used both FIFO and LIFO inventory methods as shown above. Scott Paper used both average cost and LIFO inventory methods as shown above. Kimberly-Clark used the straight-line and unit-of-production methods of depreciation in the financial statements. Scott Paper principally used the straight-line method of depreciation in the financial statements.

Required 1. Evaluate the profit performance of both competitors under their existing historical cost financial statements and under the inflation accounting notes, using the following ratios:

    a. Profit margin (net income divided by net sales).
    b. Return on assets (net income divided by average total assets).
    c. Return on stockholders' equity (net income divided by average stockholders' equity) (use ending, rather than average, amounts for total assets and stockholders' equity since 1984 amounts were not given).

  2. Which accounting method provides more meaningful comparisons of performance?

59. Appendix: Changing Prices Calculations. Exxon, Mobil, Amoco, and Phillips are all major competitors in the oil industry. Listed below are excerpts from their 1985 financial statements relating to inflation and historical cost accounting (in millions of dollars, except per share amounts):

	Exxon	Mobil	Amoco	Phillips
Net income				
Historical cost	$4,870	$1,040	$1,953	$ 418
Current cost	2,174	(408)	1,455	(455)
Earnings per share (historical cost)	6.46	2.55	7.42	1.44
Dividends per share	3.45	2.20	4.80	0.95
Income tax expense	4,688	3,269	1,858	1,213

Required 1. Compute the following inflation-based ratios for the four oil companies:

    a. Current cost net income per share
    b. Dividend payout rate (dividends per share divided by the current cost net income per share
    c. Effective tax rate (income tax expense divided by current cost net income before income tax expense).

2. Which companies were affected the most significantly by inflation in terms of the three ratios calculated above?

60. Appendix: Overview of Changing Prices. Pillsbury is a large consumer goods company. The following excerpts are from its 1985 financial statements related to inflation accounting:

Financial statements are prepared using historical costs as required by generally accepted accounting principles. As a result, these financial statements may not reflect the full impact of specific price changes (current cost) and general inflation.

The supplementary disclosures attempt to remeasure certain historical financial information to recognize the effects of changes in specific prices using current cost indices. For comparative purposes, the current cost information is then expressed in average fiscal 1985 dollars to reflect the effects of general inflation based on the U.S. Consumer Price Index. This involves the use of assumptions and estimates and therefore should not be interpreted as a highly reliable indicator of the effects of inflation. Furthermore, comparisons between companies may not be valid.

Net earnings has only been adjusted for remeasured depreciation expense in fiscal 1985. Because the Company now uses the LIFO method for valuing substantially all U.S. inventories, except grain inventories which are stated on the basis of market prices, the fiscal 1985 cost of sales is already reported in current costs. Prior to fiscal 1985, an adjustment to historical FIFO basis cost of sales under the current cost method was also required. No adjustments have been made to net sales, other operating expenses or the provisions for income taxes. The effective tax rates are therefore higher than reported in the primary financial statements. If taxes on income were adjusted (using the primary statement effective tax rate of 43.6 percent), net earnings would increase $10.6 million (25 cents per share) under current cost remeasurement.

Required Note any points of possible disagreement or elaboration concerning the above disclosures.

Additional Aspects of Financial Reporting and Financial Analysis

After reading this chapter, you should understand

- Purposes of financial reporting
- Financial analysis comparisons
- Financial reporting for business segments
- Interim financial statements
- Management's discussion and analysis
- Horizontal and vertical analysis of financial statements
- Financial ratios
- SEC reports

A company's financial statements are intended to summarize its various financial activities and operations. The information contained in the statements is examined, synthesized, and related to other information by external users for a variety of reasons. Current stockholders, for example, are concerned about their investment income, as well as about the company's overall profitability, stability, and sound capital structure necessary for continued successful operations. Some potential investors are interested in "solid" companies, ones whose financial statements indicate stable earnings and dividends with limited or moderate growth. Others prefer companies whose financial statements indicate financial flexibility, rapid growth, and diversification into different lines of business. Short-term creditors are interested in a company's short-run liquidity, its ability to pay current obligations as they mature. Long-term creditors are concerned about the long-term security of their interest income and the company's ability to maintain successful earnings and cash flows to meet continuing financial commitments. And these are only a few of the users, and uses, of financial statements that could be discussed.

This book is designed for users of **general-purpose** financial statements—statements that serve the needs of a diverse set of external users. The information contained in these statements should be comprehensible to those users who have a reasonable understanding of business and economic activities and who are willing to examine the information with reasonable diligence.[1] There are two purposes for this chapter. The first is to help complete the understanding of financial reporting, including segment reporting, interim reports, and SEC reporting. The second purpose is to discuss various aspects of financial analysis, including horizontal analysis, vertical analysis, and ratio analysis.

SECTION A Additional Aspects of Financial Reporting

■ PURPOSES OF FINANCIAL REPORTING

The objectives of financial reporting were discussed in Chapter 4. The broad purpose of financial reporting is to provide useful information to present and potential investors, creditors, and other users in making rational decisions. On a more specific level, a company's financial statements should provide information to help external users in assessing the amounts, timing, and uncertainty of the future cash flows of the company. In determining what constitutes "useful" information, the FASB identified several qualitative characteristics, the two primary ones being relevance and reliability (as discussed in Chapter 4). Several "ingredients" of the primary qualities were also identified. In regard to relevance, these include (1) **predictive value**, the quality of information that helps decision makers to forecast the outcome of past or present events; (2) **feedback value**, the quality of information that enables decision makers to confirm or correct prior expectations; and (3) **timeliness**—that is, having information available to decision makers before it loses its capacity to influence decisions. In regard to reliability, these include (1) **verifiability**, the ability of measures to agree that the selected accounting method has been used without error or bias; (2) **representational faithfulness**, a high degree of correspondence between the reported accounting measurements or descriptions and the actual transactions or events; and (3) **neutrality**, the absence of bias along with the completeness of information. A secondary characteristic of useful accounting information is **comparability**, that "interactive" quality which enables decision makers to identify and explain similarities and differences between two (or more) sets of economic information.

Several types of information that are helpful to external users in making predictions of a company's future cash flows are:

1. *Return on Investment.* Shareholders (stockholders) invest capital for a share of the equity (stockholders' equity) of a company. These investors are concerned with a return *on* capital. Before a company can provide a return on capital, its capital must be maintained or recovered (i.e., there must first be a return of capital to the company). Once a company's capital is maintained, then the return on capital may be distributed to investors or may be retained

....
[1]"Objectives of Financial Reporting by Business Enterprises," *FASB Statement of Financial Accounting Concepts No. 1* (Stamford, Conn.: FASB, 1978), par. 34.

by the company for reinvestment. Whether the return on capital is distributed or retained, return on investment provides a measure of overall company performance.

2. *Risk.* Risk is the uncertainty or unpredictability of the future results of a company. The wider the range expected for future results, the greater the risk associated with an investment in or extension of credit to the company. Risk is caused by numerous factors including, for example, high rates of technological change, uncertainty about demand, exposure to the effects of price changes, and political changes in the U.S. and foreign governments. In general, the greater the risk associated with an investment in a particular company, the higher the rate of return expected by investors (or the higher the rate of interest charged by creditors).

3. *Financial Flexibility.* Financial flexibility is the ability of a company to take effective actions to change the amounts and timing of cash flows. Financial flexibility is important because it enables a company to respond to unexpected needs and opportunities. Financial flexibility comes from the ability of a company to (a) adapt operations to increase net operating cash inflows, (b) raise new capital through, for instance, the sale of debt or stock securities at short notice, and (c) obtain cash by selling assets without disrupting on-going operations. Financial flexibility affects risk as well as cash flows. It reduces the risk of failure in the event of a shortage in net cash flows from operations.

4. *Liquidity.* Liquidity is the term used to describe the amount of time until an asset is converted into cash or a liability is paid. For operating assets, liquidity relates to the timing of cash flows in the normal course of business. For nonoperating assets, liquidity refers to marketability. The liquidity of a company is an indication of its ability to meet its obligations when they come due. Liquidity is positively related to financial flexibility but negatively related to both risk and return on investment. A more liquid company is likely to have a superior ability to adapt to unexpected needs and opportunities and a lower risk of failure. On the other hand, liquid assets often offer lower rates of return than nonliquid assets.

5. *Operating Capability.* Operating capability refers to the ability of a company to maintain a given physical level of operations. This level of operations may be indicated by the quantity of goods or services (e.g., inventory) of a specified quality produced in a given period or by the physical capacity of the fixed assets (e.g., property, plant, and equipment). Information about operating capability is helpful in understanding a company's past performance and in predicting future changes in its volume of activities. Operating capability may be affected by changes in methods of operations, changes in product lines, and by the timing of the replacement of the service potential used up in operations.[2]

....

[2]"Reporting Income, Cash Flows, and Financial Position of Business Enterprises," *FASB Proposed Statement of Financial Accounting Concepts* (Stamford, Conn.: FASB, 1981), par. 7–33.

EXHIBIT 14–1   Types of information used in external decision making

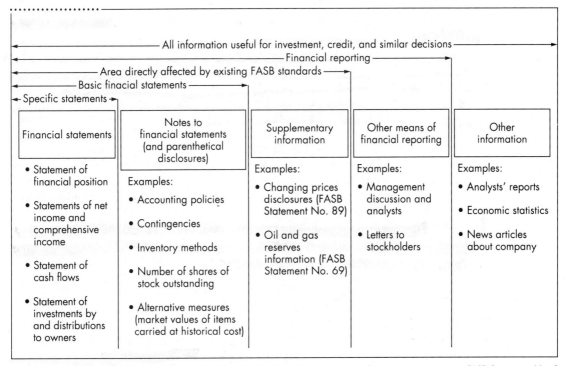

Adapted from diagram in "Recognition and Measurement in Financial Statements of Business Enterprises," *FASB Statement No. 5* (Stamford, Conn.: FASB, 1985), p.5.

Throughout this book, we have discussed the reporting of the above types of accounting information in the financial statements (i.e., income statement, balance sheet, statement of cash flows). Not all accounting information, however, is disclosed in these financial statements. The FASB notes that ". . . some useful information is better provided by financial statements and some is better provided, or can only be provided, by notes to the financial statements or by supplementary information, or other means of financial reporting."[3] Exhibit 14–1 illustrates the types of information used in investment, credit, and similar decisions. In the following sections we discuss additional financial reporting to help external users evaluate a company's returns, risk, financial flexibility, liquidity, and operating capability, but first we briefly discuss the efficiency of the capital markets in our economy.

• • • • • • • • • • • • • • • • • • • •

[3]"Recognition and Measurement in Financial Statements of Business Enterprises," *FASB Statement of Financial Accounting Concepts No. 5* (Stamford, Conn.: FASB, 1985), par. 7.

Market Efficiency

Over the past three decades, researchers have engaged in **efficient markets research** based on an efficient markets hypothesis.[4] Evidence from this research tends to show that (1) the prices of securities traded in the capital markets fully reflect all *publicly* available information, and (2) these prices are adjusted based on new information almost *instantaneously* and in an *unbiased* manner. That is, as soon as a new item of information becomes publicly available, it is interpreted, analyzed, and incorporated into the market prices. Information about companies becomes publicly available in a variety of ways, including reports filed with the SEC, news releases, management forecasts, interim financial statements, and annual reports. The market prices adjust instantaneously in an unbiased manner because of the communication system in the market place and because sophisticated investors, security analysts, and stockbrokers continuously gather, interpret, analyze, and process information.

An efficient capital market means that an individual investor should not be able to use published information to earn an "abnormal" return on security investments with a given amount of risk. In an efficient market, all securities with a similar amount of risk will yield the same rate of return; only through the use of "insider information" can abnormal returns be made. If the efficient markets hypothesis is valid, how does the related research impact financial reporting and the related financial analysis?

For financial reporting, it can be argued that since the market efficiently processes many types of financial information, **full disclosure** of financial information is important for two reasons. First, full public disclosure helps to prevent the illegal use of insider information to earn abnormal returns. Second, full disclosure (at a reasonable cost) in the financial statements and related notes helps the market to operate efficiently and in a cost effective manner.

One of the reasons markets tend to be efficient is because users interpret and analyze the financial information. Financial analysis techniques are useful when an investor is considering the investment potential of a company whose securities are *not* traded in an organized capital market, when a financial institution is considering lending money to a company, or when a company must be monitored to ensure that it is adhering to any financial restrictions imposed by lending agreements. Finally, not all investors believe in the efficient markets hypothesis and continue to use financial analysis techniques to improve their investment decisions.

· · · · · · · · · · · · · · · · · · · ·

[4]For a more complete discussion of efficient capital markets research and its implications, see T. R. Dyckman and D. Morse, *Efficient Capital Markets and Accounting: A Critical Analysis*, 2nd ed., (Englewood Cliffs, N.J.: Prentice-Hall, 1986), R. W. Watts and J. R. Zimmerman, *Positive Accounting Theory* (Englewood Cliffs, N.J.: Prentice-Hall, 1986), or W. H. Beaver, *Financial Reporting: An Accounting Revolution* (Englewood Cliffs, N.J.: Prentice-Hall, 1981).

■ FINANCIAL ANALYSIS COMPARISONS

Before discussing the disclosure of the various additional financial data, it is helpful to point out how this information is used. The decision process employed by external users may be summarized as follows: (1) the external users examine the various data of importance to them in financial reports; (2) they look for criteria to assist them in analyzing the results and making decisions; usually, although not exclusively, they make comparisons with a particular company's past results as well as with similar companies within the same or related industries; and (3) they make their decision. Of importance to the present discussion are the comparisons made in the financial analysis. Of course, investors and creditors also use information from other sources in making their decisions.

Intracompany Comparisons   *⟵ time seriously analysis*

within company.

Intracompany comparison is a method of evaluating a company's current financial performance and condition by comparing them with the company's past results. An important factor in such comparisons is the evidence of **trends**—indications that a company's performance is stable, is improving, or is deteriorating, not only in the short run but also in the longer run. Public companies must present at least two years of balance sheets and three years of income statements and cash flow statements, and many also include 5-, 10-, or 15-year summaries of key financial data.

Intercompany Comparisons   *⟵ Compare one company to other company*

Intercompany comparison is a method of evaluating a company's financial performance and condition by comparing them with individual competitors, with the industry as a whole, or with the results in related industries. The comparison(s) may be made for a single period or for several past periods. Individual competitors' financial information may be drawn from their respective financial statements. Information on the performance of the industry as a whole or of related industries may be based on compilations of financial information by such financial analysis companies as Moody's Investors Service, Standard and Poor's, Dun and Bradstreet, and Robert Morris and Associates. These companies not only provide a wealth of information from annual reports but also publish periodic updates and supplements. Other organizations and trade associations supply similar information on a more selective basis.

Anyone using financial analysis information for intercompany comparisons must be concerned not only with consistency over time, but also with comparability of data across firms. As discussed in Chapter 4, any lack of consistency over time caused by a material change in accounting principle is explicitly disclosed in the audit opinion and related disclosures. Comparability of data between firms is much more difficult because of such factors as different classifications used in the financial statements, different definitions of segments and geographical areas in the supplementary disclosures, and the use of alternative generally accepted accounting principles (for example, LIFO versus FIFO for inventory costing or accelerated versus straight-line depreciation). When using financial accounting data, the user should be aware of the potential consistency and comparability problems.

■ SEGMENT REPORTING

The financial statements of many multidivisional companies are prepared on a "consolidated" basis; that is, the accounting results of various legal segments are *aggregated* into a set of financial statements encompassing the entire economic entity (as discussed in Chapter 11). Although investors and creditors recognize the importance of consolidated statements in evaluating overall company performance, they suggest that the *disaggregation* of the financial data can also be important in their financial analysis.

The evaluations of risk and return are significant factors in investment and credit decisions. Risk results from, among other factors, (1) the nature and current status of the industries in which the company operates, (2) the changing conditions in the geographic areas within which the corporation operates, (3) the characteristics of its major customers, and (4) the national and international economic and political factors that may affect its operations. The profitability, or return, offered by a company is also affected by its types of industrial segments, the relationships between the revenues and expenses of its industrial segments, its major customers, and national and international factors.

Financial analysis information on risk and return is improved through the presentation of disaggregated segment financial information. In light of the need for such data, a public company's financial statements must include information about its operations in different industries, its foreign operations and export sales, and its major customers.[5] The intent of this disaggregation is to improve the *predictive value* and *feedback value* of financial statement information. Non-public companies, those whose securities are not traded publicly or that are not required to file financial statements with the SEC, are not required to report segment information.

Reporting on Segments

An industry segment is a component of an enterprise that provides a product or service or a *group* of related products and services, primarily to unaffiliated customers, for a profit. To determine its industry segments, a company may use the Standard Industrial Classification (SIC is a federal system for classifying businesses according to the type of economic activity in which they are engaged);

· · · · · · · · · · · · · · · · · · · ·

[5]"Financial Reporting for Segments of a Business Enterprise," *FASB Statement of Financial Accounting Standards No. 14* (Stamford, Conn.: FASB, 1976).

look internally at its "profit centers"; or consider (1) the nature of the product, (2) the nature of the production process, and (3) its markets and marketing methods.

Reportable Segments.   A company need not provide financial information about all these segments, however. Materiality determines whether or not a segment is a **reportable segment**—one whose operations are significant enough that its financial activities must be reported. **An industry segment is considered significant and is defined as a reportable segment if it satisfies at least *one* of the three following tests:**

1. *Revenue Test.* Its revenues (*including* intersegment sales or transfers) are 10% or more of the combined revenues of all the enterprise's industry segments.

2. *Operating Profit Test.* The absolute amount of its operating profit (loss) is 10% or more of the combined operating profits of all industry segments that did not incur an operating loss.[6]

3. *Asset Test.* Its identifiable assets are 10% or more of the combined identifiable assets of all industry segments.

The terms *revenues, operating profits and losses,* and *identifiable assets* are defined in the next section.

   In addition to the above, an overall materiality test states that the reportable segments must constitute a substantial portion of the enterprise's total operations. That is, enough reportable segments must be disclosed so that their combined revenues (*excluding* intersegment sales) constitute at least 75% of the entire company's revenues (*excluding* intersegment sales). Should a company operate predominantly or exclusively in a single industry, it need not disclose segment information; however, it must identify the industry. This situation occurs when a single dominant segment's revenues, operating profit (or loss), and identifiable assets each constitute more than 90% of the combined totals for all industry segments.

Information to Be Reported.   The following financial information is to be reported separately for each reportable segment:

1. *Revenues.* The revenues of a reportable industry segment include those from sales to unaffiliated customers and from intersegment sales or transfers. Intersegment sales or transfers are those between one segment and another segment within the company. *Excluded* from revenues are revenues earned at the corporate level (e.g., interest revenue on corporate investments) and the equity in income or loss from unconsolidated subsidiaries.

2. *Operating Profit or Loss.* The operating profit or loss of a reportable industry segment is its revenues (defined above) minus all operating expenses. Oper-

....

[6]If the combined operating losses of all industry segments that incurred an operating loss exceed the combined operating profits as calculated above, the combined operating loss amount would be used for this 10% test.

ating expenses include (a) traceable expenses that relate to revenues from sales (external and intersegment) and (b) those operating expenses incurred by a company that are allocable on a reasonable basis among those industry segments for whose benefit the expenses were incurred. *Excluded* from operating expenses are such items as general corporate expenses (e.g., certain administrative expenses), interest expense, income taxes, results from discontinued operations, extraordinary items, and the cumulative effects of changes in accounting principles.

3. *Identifiable Assets.* The identifiable assets of a reportable industry segment are the tangible and intangible assets that are used by the segment, including (a) those used exclusively by that segment and (b) a reasonably allocated portion of assets used jointly by two or more segments. *Excluded* from identifiable assets are those maintained for general corporate purposes, intersegment loans and advances, and investments in unconsolidated subsidiaries.

4. *Other Related Disclosures.* Several other disclosures must be made in regard to each reportable industry segment. The primary ones include (a) the aggregate amount of depreciation, depletion, and amortization expense included in the computation of operating profit; (b) its capital expenditures for property, plant, and equipment; (c) the types of products and services from which its revenue is derived; and (d) the accounting policies relevant to the segment's data.

This same information is also reported for the rest of the enterprise's insignificant industry segments that have not met at least one of the criteria for reportable segments. That is, the remaining insignificant industry segments are combined and their combined revenues, operating profits (or losses), and identifiable assets are reported. A **reconciliation** also is necessary. The revenues listed for the reportable industry segments and the other aggregated industry segments must be reconciled to the total revenue reported in the company's income statement, the operating profit or loss of the segments reconciled to the pretax income from continuing operations, and the identifiable assets of the segments reconciled to the company's total assets. Any unallocated revenues, expenses, and assets should be separately identified in the reconciliation. Note that there are no requirements to disclose the cash flows of the segments.

In summary, a company's consolidated financial statements are "broken down" into segment reports to provide more useful information. These segment reports include information on each industry segment's revenues, operating profit, and identifiable assets. In computing these items, information on general corporate revenues, expenses, and assets is *excluded*, as illustrated in Exhibit 14–2.

Problems in Measurement. The measurement problems are similar to those encountered in the development of an internal managerial performance evaluation system. They primarily involve transfer pricing methods related to intersegment sales and operating expense allocations.

A transfer price is the charge made to a segment of a company that "purchases" a good or service from another company segment. Several transfer

EXHIBIT 14–2   Relationship of consolidated financial statements to segment reports

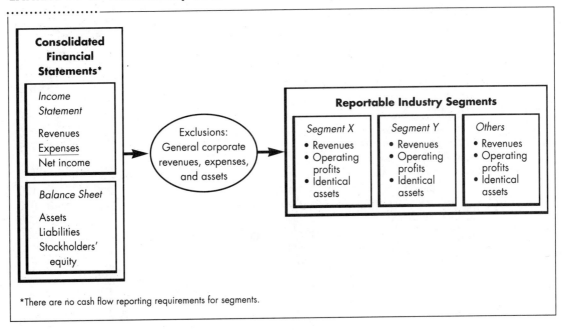

*There are no cash flow reporting requirements for segments.

pricing methods are in use, including charging the purchasing segment on the basis of market (external selling) prices, the "full" costs of the producing segment, the variable cost, or a negotiated price. The use of any transfer price method is allowed for the determination of intersegment sales included in segment revenues, as long as the method is the same as that used for internal accounting purposes. Whenever a significant amount of intersegment sales occur, the lack of specificity regarding transfer pricing may lead to a lack of comparability of segment information between companies. For instance, two similar companies, one using a transfer price based on the market price and the other using a transfer price based on variable cost, would report different revenues and operating profits simply because of the different transfer prices.

An even greater issue exists regarding the allocation of operating expenses. Only those that are allocable to the benefiting segments on a "reasonable" basis are included in the computation of operating profits. General corporate expenses are excluded. The identification of allocable operating expenses and the selection of an allocation method can have a significant effect on the comparability of operating income across companies as well as among segments of the same company. What one company considers an allocable operating expense, another may consider a general corporate expense.

The allocation of operating expenses to segments may be made on various bases, including sales, contribution margins, assets or investments, numbers of employees, and physical measures such as square footages. The basis or bases

EXHIBIT 14–3

CLINE COMPANY
Consolidated Income Statement
For Year Ended December 31, 1993

Sales		$3,800
Cost of goods sold	$2,470	
Selling, general, and administrative expenses	620	
Operating expenses		(3,090)
Pretax operating profit		$ 710
Other revenues and expenses		
Interest expense	$ (80)	
Equity in net income of Y Company (25% owned)	200	120
Pretax income from continuing operations		$ 830
Income taxes		(300)
Income from continuing operations		$ 530
Results of discontinued operations		
Loss from operations of discontinued West Coast division (net of income tax effect of $50)	$ 80	
Loss on disposal of West Coast division (net of income tax effect of $100)	130	(210)
Income before extraordinary items		$ 320
Extraordinary gain (net of income tax effect of $60)		90
Net income		$ 410

(Earnings per share are not shown)

for allocation may depend on the sophistication of a company's management information system. Selection from several alternative bases for allocation of operating expenses may lead to different operating results across segments as well as noncomparable operating results for similar segments in different companies. Issues of this type also exist regarding the exclusion from and allocation of identifiable assets to industry segments.

Illustration.   To illustrate the presentation of reportable industry segment financial information, assume the Cline Company presents the income statement shown in Exhibit 14–3. In addition, the Cline Company reports total assets of $19,000 on its December 31, 1993, balance sheet.

Cline Company discloses its reportable segment information in a supplemental schedule. In developing the information to be included in this schedule, the information shown in Exhibit 14–4 was prepared. Five industry segments were identified and the revenues, operating expenses (which include depreciation), and identifiable assets were allocated to each segment as shown. Next, the reportable industry segments were determined. The revenue test was applied first. Segment B met the 10% test but the others did not. After deducting operating expenses from revenues, it was determined that Segment C's $105 operating

EXHIBIT 14–4

CLINE COMPANY
Working Paper for Segment Reporting
For Year Ended December 31, 1993
All Industry Segments

	A	B	C	D	E	Segment Totals	Unallocated	Totals
Total revenues (sales)	$ 300	$ 2,530a	$ 370	$ 280	$ 320	$ 3,800	$ 0	$ 3,800
Operating expenses								
Cost of goods sold	$ 190	$ 1,685	$ 210	$ 185	$ 200	$ 2,470	$ 0	$ 2,470
Selling, general, and administrative expenses	40	350	55	30	45	520	100	620
Total operating expenses	$ (230)	$ (2,035)	$ (265)	$ (215)	$ (245)	$ (2,990)	$ (100)	$ (3,090)
Operating profit	$ 70	$ 495	$ 105 b	$ 65	$ 75	$ 810	$ (100)	$ 710
Identifiable assets	$ 1,800 c	$ 9,400	$ 2,000	$ 1,300 d	$ 1,500 d	$ 16,000	$ 3,000	$ 19,000

a Segment B meets the revenue test.
b Segment C meets the operating profit test. (Segment B also meets this test.)
c Segment A meets the asset test. (Segments B and C also meet this test.)
d Segments D and E meet none of the tests and are combined for reporting purposes.

EXHIBIT 14–5

··················

Reconciled.

CLINE COMPANY
Industry Segment Financial Results
For Year Ended December 31, 1993

D + E

	Reportable Industry Segments			Other Industry Segments	Total Results
	A	B	C		
Total revenue (sales)	$ 300	$2,530	$ 370	$ 600	$ 3,800
Operating profit	$ 70	$ 495	$ 105	$ 140	$ 810
General corporate expenses					(100)
Equity in net income of Y Company					200
Interest expense					(80)
Pretax income from continuing operations					$ 830
Identifiable assets at December 31, 1993	$1,800	$9,400	$2,000	$2,800	$16,000
Investment in net assets of Y Company					800
Corporate assets					2,200
Total assets at December 31, 1993					$19,000

Note:

The company operates principally in three industries, A, B, and C. Operations in Industry A involve production and sale of (describe types of products and services). Operations in Industry B involve production and sales of (describe types of products and services). Operations in Industry C involve production and sales of (describe types of products and services). Total revenue by industry segment includes sales to unaffiliated customers. The company makes no intersegment sales.

Operating profit is total revenue less operating expenses. In computing operating profit, none of the following items have been added or deducted: general corporate expenses, interest expense, income taxes, equity in income from unconsolidated investee, loss from discontinued operations of the West Coast division (which was a part of the company's operations in Industry B), or extraordinary gain (relating to the company's operations in Industry C).

Depreciation for Industries A, B, and C, was $20, $300, and $40, respectively. Capital expenditures for the three industries were $100, $400, and $200, respectively. Identifiable assets by industry are those assets that are used in the company's operations in each industry. Corporate assets are principally cash and marketable securities.

The company has a 25% interest in Y Company, whose operations are in the United States and are vertically integrated with the company's operations in Industry A. Equity in net income of Y Company was $200; investment in net assets of Y Company was $800.

Contracts with a U.S. government agency account for $600 of the sale to unaffiliated customers of Industry B.

profit (and also Segment B's) was at least 10% of the $810 total operating profit of all the segments. Finally, Segment A has $1,800 of identifiable assets that are more than 10% of the $16,000 combined identifiable assets of all the industry segments. (The identifiable assets of Segments B and C also meet this test.) Thus, Segments A, B, and C all qualify as reportable segments, whereas Segments D and E are to be combined for reporting purposes. It should be noted that the $3,200 ($300 + $2,530 + $370) revenues from Segments A, B, and C exceed 75% of the $3,800 total revenues from all the operating segments so that enough reportable segments have been included.

Exhibit 14–5 shows the schedule that Cline Company includes in its annual report. Note that the revenues and operating profits of the industry segments are reconciled to the appropriate totals on the consolidated income statement by including the nonreportable segments in the disclosure. Segment revenues are reconciled to total sales. The segment operating profits are reconciled to the pretax income from continuing operations by adding the equity income and deducting the general corporate expenses and interest expense. Similarly, the industry segment identifiable assets are reconciled to the total corporate assets.

Reporting on Foreign Operations and Export Sales

The financial statements of a company must also report on significant foreign operations. Foreign operations are defined as those revenue-producing operations that are located outside the United States and that are generating revenue either from sales to unaffiliated customers or to other intracompany segments. Revenue and asset tests are used to define significant foreign operations. That is, if either (1) revenue generated by the foreign operations from sales to unaffiliated customers is at least 10% of total company revenues or (2) identifiable assets of the company's foreign operations are at least 10% of total company assets, then certain foreign and domestic financial information as discussed below must be disclosed. Furthermore, importance is given to activities in significant foreign geographic areas. If, in a particular foreign geographic area, a company's revenues from sales to unaffiliated customers or its identifiable assets are 10% or more of *total* company revenues or assets, respectively, it is considered a "significant" geographic area and additional geographic financial information must be disclosed.

Information to Be Reported. The financial information to be reported concerning foreign operations is similar to the disclosure requirements for industry segments. That is, for both domestic and foreign operations (1) revenues, (2) operating profits or loss (or net income or some measure of profitability between operating profits or loss and net income), and (3) identifiable assets (as defined earlier) are disclosed separately. In addition, should the foreign operations include one or more significant geographic areas, the foreign revenues, operating profits or losses, and identifiable assets of these geographic areas are separately disclosed. Finally, if the *domestic* operations make 10% or more of their sales to unaffiliated customers in foreign countries, that amount of *export* sales are separately reported in the aggregate and by geographic areas when these area sales are significant. All the preceding information is presented in U.S. dollar amounts; corresponding percentages may be shown as well. Geographic areas are identified and revenues, operating profits or loss, and identifiable assets are reconciled to totals reported on the company's financial statements.

Illustration. To illustrate the presentation of the foreign and domestic financial information, the Cline Company example is continued in Exhibit 14–6. The information used to prepare the disclosures in Exhibit 14–6 is not presented here, but would be similar to that shown in Exhibit 14–4. In Exhibit 14–6, the income statement information from Exhibit 14–3 is disaggregated to report on Cline Company's foreign activities.

EXHIBIT 14–6

CLINE COMPANY
Foreign Geographic Operating Results
For Year Ended December 31, 1993

	United States	Foreign Geographic Area A	B	Total Results
Total revenue (sales)	$ 2,430	$ 750	$ 620	$ 3,800
Operating profit	$ 500	$ 180	$ 130	$ 810
General corporate expenses				(100)
Equity in net income of Y company				200
Interest expense				(80)
Pretax income from continuing operations				$ 830
Identifiable assets at December 31, 1993	$11,300	$2,600	$2,100	$16,000
Investment in net assets of Y company				800
Corporate assets				2,200
Total assets at December 31, 1993				$19,000

Note:
Operating profit is total revenues less operating expenses. In computing operating profit, none of the following items have been added or deducted: general corporate expenses, interest expense, income taxes, equity in income from unconsolidated investee, loss from discontinued operations of West Coast division (which was part of the company's U.S. operations), or extraordinary gain (which relates to the company's operations in Geographic Area B). The company makes no intersegment sales.
   Identifiable assets are those assets of the company that are identified with the operations in each geographic area. Corporate assets are principally cash and marketable securities.
   Of the $2,430 U.S. sales, $470 were export sales, principally to Geographic Area A.

The foreign financial information is separated into Geographic Areas A and B, since revenues in each area constitute more than 10% of total company revenues. The revenues, operating profit, and identifiable assets are reconciled with the related amounts in the company's financial statements. The note includes the amount of export sales made by its domestic operations. It should be observed that since Cline Company has reportable industry segments as well as significant foreign operations, Exhibit 14–6 is *not* a substitute for Exhibit 14–5. Instead, *both* schedules would be shown as supporting information in the company's financial statements.

Information About Major Customers

If at least 10% of a company's revenue is derived from sales to a single customer, that fact and the amount of revenue from each such customer is disclosed, together with the identity of the industry segment or segments making the sales. A single customer is defined as a group of entities under common control, the federal government, a state government, a local government, or a foreign government. Such a disclosure is made in the notes to Exhibit 14–5.

The disclosure by Nike of its operations by geographic area is illustrated in Exhibit 14–7. Since the company operates in only one segment, no segment disclosures were required. However, the company did disclose its revenues from each type of product in the "Management Discussion and Analysis" section of its annual report, as shown in Exhibit 14–7.

Uses of Segment Information

Segment information increases the *relevance* of financial information by increasing the amount of information available to users of financial statements and by indicating the industries in which the company operates. Intracompany comparisons of revenues and operating profits of each reportable industry segment can be made. These comparisons can show the relative performance of each segment. For example, in Exhibit 14–5, Segment A earned an operating profit of $70 using assets of $1,800 for a 3.9% return, while Segment B earned $495 using $9,400 assets, a 5.3% return. Alternatively the results of one segment for several years can be compared to identify any trends in its operating performance.

Intercompany comparisons can also be made, but care must be taken because valid comparisons may not be possible because of the lack of *comparability*. For example, companies in the same industry may define their segments and geographical areas differently. Also the segment and related information is not audited. However, segment reporting may be the only way to compare an independent company (such as Avis) with a competitor that is a subsidiary of another company (such as Hertz).

■ INTERIM FINANCIAL REPORTS

External users often want more frequent accounting information than that provided in the company's annual report. **Interim financial statements are reports for periods of less than a year.** Typically, interim reports are sent to shareholders quarterly. Their purpose is to improve the timeliness of accounting information. These reports must be issued by all companies whose stock is being traded on the New York or American Stock Exchange and by most companies filing with the SEC.

Sometimes it is difficult to determine meaningful operating results for intervals of less than a year. Revenues of some businesses are seasonal and fluctuate widely across interim periods. Some companies incur high costs in one interim period that benefit the operating activities in other periods. Other companies must estimate costs that will not be paid until subsequent interim periods but that benefit the current one. Estimates also must be made of such items as inventories and income taxes if the interim reports are to be relevant and reliable.

In resolving such accounting measurement issues, **each interim period is viewed primarily as an integral part of an annual period** and a company con-

EXHIBIT 14–7 Example of disclosure of operations by geographic areas and additional disclosures

·················

NIKE, INC.

Note 14—Operations by geographic areas:

The Company operates predominantly in one industry segment, that being the design, production and marketing of athletic and casual footwear, apparel and accessories. During 1989 and 1988, sales to one major customer amounted to 16% and 12% of total sales, respectively. In 1987, no single customer's sales exceeded 10% of total sales. Information about the Company's operations in the United States and foreign areas is presented below. Inter-geographic revenues and assets have been eliminated to arrive at the consolidated amounts. Expenses and assets not identifiable with the operations of a specific geographic segment have been listed separately.

	Year Ended May 31,		
	1989	**1988**	**1987**
	(in thousands)		
Revenues from unrelated entities:			
United States	$1,362,148	$ 900,417	$641,603
Europe	241,380	233,402	191,358
Other foreign	107,275	69,621	44,396
	$1,710,803	$1,203,440	$877,357
Inter-geographic revenues:			
United States	$ 1,757	$ 725	$ 2,043
Europe	—	—	—
Other foreign	4,323	5,008	5,540
	$ 6,080	$ 5,733	$ 7,583
Total revenues:			
United States	$1,363,905	$ 901,142	$643,646
Europe	241,380	233,402	191,358
Other foreign	111,598	74,629	49,936
Less inter-geographic revenues	(6,080)	(5,733)	(7,583)
	$1,710,803	$1,203,440	$877,357
Operating income:			
United States	$ 230,156	$ 114,046	$ 48,755
Europe	35,376	37,036	27,529
Other foreign	30,173	13,075	2,723
Less corporate, interest and other income (expense) and eliminations	(25,058)	2,038	(5,328)
	$ 270,647	$ 166,195	$ 73,679
Assets:			
United States	$ 600,629	$ 499,707	$288,689
Europe	102,744	94,900	85,869
Other foreign	50,756	51,784	25,063
Total identifiable assets	754,129	646,391	399,621
Corporate cash and eliminations	71,281	62,704	112,222
Total assets	$ 825,410	$ 709,095	$511,843

EXHIBIT 14–7 *(continued)*

....

Management discussion and analysis (in part):
The approximate breakdown of revenues by product category that follows contains certain amounts restated to conform with 1989 classifications:

	Year Ended May 31,		
	1989	**1988**	**1987**
	(in thousands)		
Footwear			
Basketball	$ 414,600	$ 287,300	$178,000
Fitness	237,800	129,000	92,500
Running	202,600	177,900	123,800
Racquet	58,400	60,700	38,500
Other	153,200	102,600	77,200
Non-athletic	87,300	—	—
Total footwear	1,153,900	757,500	510,000
Apparel	208,200	142,900	130,700
Athletic equipment	—	—	900
Total United States	1,362,100	900,400	641,600
Foreign			
Europe	241,400	233,400	191,400
Canada	52,200	31,500	20,300
Other	55,100	38,100	24,100
Total foreign	348,700	303,000	235,800
Total NIKE	$1,710,800	$1,203,400	$877,400

tinues to use the generally accepted accounting principles that were used in the preparation of its most recent annual report. However, certain principles are modified for interim reporting purposes so that the results will be more informative and articulate better with the annual results. When publicly traded companies report interim summaries of financial information to their security holders, the following data are reported at a minimum:[7]

1. Sales or gross revenues, income taxes, the cumulative effect of a change in accounting principle, and net income

2. Primary and fully diluted (or simple) earnings per share for each period presented

3. Seasonal revenues, costs, and expenses

4. Significant changes in estimates of income taxes

5. Results of discontinued operations and extraordinary, unusual or infrequent items

6. Contingent items

....

[7]"Interim Financial Reporting," *APB Opinion No. 28* (New York: AICPA, 1973)

7. Changes in accounting principles or estimates

8. Significant changes in financial position

When the above information is presented on a quarterly basis, current year-to-date information, along with comparable data from the previous year, should be provided as well. The FASB also encourages companies to provide condensed balance sheet and cash flow data for the interim periods to assist users in their financial analysis related to *financial flexibility* and *liquidity*. When this information is not presented, significant changes since the last reporting date in liquid assets, working capital, long-term liabilities, and stockholders' equity should be reported. Segment information is not required to be disclosed in interim reports. It is also important to note that interim financial information is *not* audited.

Revenues

Revenues from products or services should be recognized during an interim period in the same manner as during the annual accounting period. For example, when the percentage-of-completion method is used to recognize long-term construction contracts, revenues should be recognized on the basis of the percent completed during that interim period. In cases where revenues are subject to seasonal variations, the company should disclose the seasonal nature of its activities and should consider presenting supplemental information regarding revenues for previous periods.

Costs and Expenses Associated with Revenues

The costs and expenses that can be directly associated with or allocated to product sales or to the provision of services should be matched against interim revenues. These include such items as material costs, wages, manufacturing overhead, and warranties. With regard to inventories for interim reporting, companies generally should use the same inventory pricing methods (for example, LIFO, FIFO, average) and make provisions for write-downs to market in the same way as they do for annual reporting, with the following exceptions:

1. Companies that utilize a periodic inventory system and use estimated gross profit rates (or other estimation methods) to determine the cost of goods sold during interim periods (instead of taking a costly physical inventory four times a year) should disclose the method used and any significant adjustments that result from reconciliation with the annual physical inventory.

2. If a company using the LIFO method encounters a temporary partial liquidation of its inventory that is expected to be replaced by year-end, cost of goods sold should include the expected cost to replace the liquidated inventory and the inventory at the interim reporting date should *not* take the liquidation into account. Assuming rising prices, this requirement avoids the possibility of showing abnormally high interim period income because of temporary LIFO "liquidation profits."

3. Permanent losses due to inventory market declines should be recognized in accordance with the lower of cost or market procedures, discussed in Chapter 6, in the interim period during which the decline occurred. Any recovery of such losses in subsequent interim periods within the same year should be recognized as gains (not to exceed the previously recognized losses) in those later periods. Temporary market declines need not be recognized in interim periods.

4. Gains and losses that occur in an interim period and that would not be deferred at year-end should be recognized in the interim period of occurrence. For example, a gain on the sale of land or a loss on the disposal of equipment should be recognized in the interim period.

5. Materiality should be determined on the basis of a relationship of the item to the estimated income for the entire *year* and not to the interim period results.

Income Taxes

To present fairly the results of operations, at the end of *each* interim period the company should make its best estimate of the effective income tax rate expected to be applicable for the *entire* year. Consequently, each quarter the company must estimate its annual income and, based on this annual income, estimate its annual income taxes to derive an effective annual income tax rate. The effective rate should then be used to provide for income taxes related to income on a year-to-date basis. The amount of income taxes applicable to the current interim period is the difference between the income tax computed on year-to-date income and the related income taxes reported on previous interim reports of the accounting period.

To illustrate, assume a corporation reported pretax income of $20,000 at the end of the first quarter and estimated its income tax on this income to be $6,900 (this estimate was derived at the end of the first quarter, using the technique discussed above). The corporation is now preparing an interim income statement at the end of the second quarter for that quarter and the first six months. It has determined that its pretax income for the second quarter is $26,000 and anticipates it will earn $25,000 and $29,000 in each of the next two quarters, respectively. Assume further a hypothetical corporate income tax structure entailing a 20% tax rate on the first $25,000 of earnings and a 30% tax rate on earnings in excess of $25,000. As shown in Exhibit 14–8, based on an estimated effective income tax rate of 27.5%, the corporation would report income tax expense of $12,650 for the first six months and $5,750 for the second quarter of operations.

In the case of an *established* pattern of seasonal revenues that result in an earlier interim period operating loss that is offset by income in later periods, the income tax effects (that is, the income tax credit) of the earlier loss should be recognized in that interim period and offset against the income taxes incurred on the income of the subsequent interim periods.

EXHIBIT 14–8   Computation of interim income taxes

1. Estimation of annual income:

First quarter:	$ 20,000	Actual income
Second quarter:	26,000	Actual income
Third quarter:	25,000	Estimated income
Fourth quarter:	29,000	Estimated income
	$100,000	Estimated annual income

2. Estimated effective income tax rate:

$$20\% \times \$25,000 = \$ 5,000$$
$$30\% \times (\$100,000 - \$25,000) = \underline{22,500}$$
$$\text{Estimated total tax} = \$27,500$$
$$27.5\% \text{ Effective income tax rate} = \frac{\$27,500 \text{ Estimated income tax}}{\$100,000 \text{ Estimated income}}$$

3. Estimated income tax for first 6 months:

$$\$46,000 \times 27.5\% = \underline{\$12,650} \text{ Estimated income tax on first 6 months'}$$
income

4. Estimated income tax for second quarter:

$12,650	Estimated income tax on first 6 months of income
(6,900)	Estimated income tax on first-quarter income
$ 5,750	Estimated income tax on second-quarter income

Uses of Interim Financial Statements

Interim reports increase the *relevance* of financial information by increasing the timeliness of the information available for users. Publicly held companies must file their *Form 10-Q* within 45 days of the end of the quarter. The same inter- and intracompany comparisons can be made with interim reports as with annual reports, provided sufficient information is available. This more timely information reduces the risk associated with investing in or lending to a company. For instance, trends in a company's sales, operating expenses, and earnings over time can be more quickly detected in interim reports. Or for seasonal industries, the current sales and earnings of a company can be compared either to its own past results or to the results of other companies in the interim "peak sales" and "low volume" interim periods to identify differences in operating activities. It should also be noted that interim reports are not audited.

It is often argued that there is too much emphasis placed on interim financial information. The management may feel pressured to achieve a certain level of interim earnings at the expense of developing an appropriate strategy for long-term growth of the company. Also if a company makes significant adjustments in the fourth quarter, the results from the first three quarters will be less useful as predictors of the annual results.

■ MANAGEMENT'S DISCUSSION AND ANALYSIS

The SEC requires certain information to be included in the *Form 10-K* annual report filed with it. One of these reporting requirements involves **the management's discussion and analysis (MD&A)** of the company's financial condition, and results of operations. The focus of the MD&A is on "forward looking" information, such as plans for capital expenditures, dividends, debt financing, and product lines. The intent is to give investors the opportunity to look at the company "through the eyes of management" by providing both a short-term and long-term analysis of the company's business. Thus, the MD&A is to provide a narrative explanation of the financial statements so that investors can judge the "quality" of earnings and the likelihood that past performance is indicative of future performance in regard to cash flows from operations and from outside sources.

In its MD&A, a company must provide information regarding liquidity, capital resources, and the results of operations, as well as other information necessary to an understanding of its financial condition and changes in its financial condition. This disclosure includes descriptions and amounts of items that would have an impact on future operations but that did not affect past operations, as well as amounts of items that affected past operations but are not expected to have an impact on future operations. Furthermore, when knowledge of segment information is useful to understanding a company's business, the discussion should focus on each relevant, reportable segment, as well as the whole company.

The following is a brief discussion of the major disclosure issues required to be discussed in the MD&A.

Liquidity

A company is to identify any known trends or demands, commitments, events, or uncertainties that are likely to result in an increase or decrease in its short-term and long-term liquidity. If a significant deficiency in liquidity is identified, the company is to indicate the actions it expects to take to remedy the situation. The company must also identify and separately describe its internal and external sources of liquidity (such as unused lines of credit available to the company), and discuss any major unused sources of liquid assets.

Capital Resources

A company is to describe its commitments for capital expenditures at the end of the current period, as well as indicate the purpose of these commitments and the anticipated sources of funds needed to fulfill the commitments. The company must describe favorable or unfavorable trends in its capital resources. This description is to include a discussion of expected significant changes in the mix of capital resources and the relative cost. The discussion must also explain any changes between debt and equity financing, and off-balance sheet financing arrangements.

Results of Operations

A number of disclosures are necessary regarding income from continuing operations. First, a company is to describe any significant, unusual, or infrequent transactions and their effect on income from continuing operations. This description should include the impact on the various affected revenues and expenses. Second, a description must also be included of any known trends or uncertainties that are likely to affect favorably or unfavorably income from continuing operations. Third, if a significant change in the relationship between costs and revenues is expected to occur, the change is to be described. Fourth, if there is a significant increase in net sales revenues, a discussion must be included to explain whether the increase was due to increased selling prices, increased volume, or the introduction of new products or services. Finally, a discussion must be included of the impact of inflation and changing prices on net sales revenues and income from continuing operations.

An illustration of a portion of Gerber Products MD&A is shown in Exhibit 14–9.

SECTION B Analysis of Financial Statements

■ PERCENTAGE ANALYSIS

The interpretation of current results and the comparison of a company's operating results, cash flows, and financial position across several periods or with other companies may be enhanced by converting the monetary relationships within the financial statements to percentage relationships. The three types of analyses that use percentage relationships are referred to as horizontal analysis, vertical analysis, and ratio analysis. The first two are discussed in this section; ratio analysis is discussed in the following section.

Horizontal Analysis

In horizontal analysis, changes in a company's operating results and financial position *over time* **are expressed in terms of percentages as well as in absolute amounts.** This method is used most frequently in conjunction with the income statement. It may also be used for balance sheet comparisons but is used less frequently in the analysis of the statement of cash flows because of the lack of regularity with which items recur on this statement.

When only two years of comparative data are disclosed in percentages, the earlier year is used as the base year and the amount of change in each item is expressed as a percentage of that item's base-year amount. When data are shown for more than two years, two alternative approaches may be used. In the first

EXHIBIT 14–9

....

GERBER PRODUCTS COMPANY
Management's Discussion and Analysis (in part)
Results of Operations—1989 Compared to 1988

Consolidated net sales and revenues increased by $102,572,000 or 10.6%. Gerber Products Division food sales increased by $75,082,000 or 16.6% as brand share gains, higher consumption per birth and an increased number of births resulted in a 10.6% increase in unit sales volume. Higher net selling prices also contributed to the increase in sales. Sales of Gerber Division general merchandise product lines, other than Atlanta Novelty plush toys, increased by 14%. Sales of products marketed by Atlanta Novelty, which was liquidated in the first quarter of fiscal 1989, amounted to $6,384,000 in 1989 compared to $16,227,000 in 1988. Increased sales volume and to a lesser extent price increases which more than offset moderately higher costs, improved gross margin. Marketing expense increased due primarily to higher advertising and promotional expenses for baby food and costs associated with reduction of the sales force. As a percent of net sales, marketing expense declined from 13.5% in 1988 to 12.8% in 1989 as sales force expense increased at a much lower rate than net sales. Increased baby food sales volume caused warehouse and shipping expense to rise. Operating profit of the Gerber division increased $44,597,000 or 55.1% over last year. Fiscal 1988 included a $5,000,000 provision for loss on disposal of Atlanta Novelty, Inc.'s plush toy operations.

Higher Buster Brown playwear sales volume was partially offset by an expected reduction in sleepwear sales volume to produce a $11,638,000 or 3.4% increase in Apparel Group sales. Gross margin dollars increased as a result of the larger proportion of higher margin branded products included in the sales mix, price increases, and improvements in inventory control and manufacturing systems which reduced write-downs of product due to obsolescence or late delivery to customers. Selling expenses for Buster Brown branded playwear increased due to expanded promotional efforts. Marketing and administrative expenses for Gerber Childrenswear declined due primarily to staff reductions. Provisions for estimated losses totalling $2,900,000 for disposal of certain fixed assets were recognized in the current year. Operating profit increased by $7,685,000 or 37.9% over last year.

Increased sales and revenues for the Other segment resulted from higher sales volumes in international markets, particularly Canada, continued expansion of child care centers, and growth of both life and health insurance business. Start-up losses from new child care centers, and inclusion last year of a gain from sales of a Canadian manufacturing facility, offset in part by improved results of insurance operations, resulted in a decrease in operating profit.

Lower short-term borrowings and repayment of $16,982,000 of long-term debt resulted in a decrease in interest expense. Higher cash balances and short-term investments generated increased interest income. General corporate expense increased due primarily to higher unallocated insurance expense and a reduction in earnings on advance deposits to an employee welfare benefit trust.

Earnings from continuing operations increased by $32,809,000 or $1.67 per share.

EXHIBIT 14–9 *(continued)*

Liquidity and Capital Resources

Cash provided from continuing operations in 1989 amounted to $117,885,000 compared with $61,305,000 in 1988 and $60,296,000 in 1987. Other major sources of cash in 1989 included proceeds from the sale of discontinued furniture operations of $30,152,000 and sale of the discontinued transportation operation's equipment, certain terminals, and other assets, which generated approximately $45,000,000 of cash. These funds were used to reduce short-term borrowings and repay $16,982,000 of long-term debt. Also, the Company used $50,209,000 for a stock repurchase program, paid dividends of $28,929,000 and expended $33,015,000 for capital additions.

The increased cash flow from continuing and discontinued operations significantly improved the financial condition of the Company. Working capital improved $28,868,000 during 1989 and the current ratio increased from 1.7 to 1 at March 31, 1988 to 2.3 to 1 at March 31, 1989. Current liabilities declined $69,826,000 during 1989 and the ratio of total debt to total capitalization declined from 39% at March 31, 1988 to 32% at March 31, 1989, even though total capitalization was reduced by the stock repurchase program.

Management believes the Company's present liquidity, in combination with cash flow from future operations, will be more than adequate to fund continuing operating requirements in the foreseeable future. If unusual events were to occur, the Company has numerous sources of short-term financing available, including commercial paper, bank lines of credit and short-term credit facilities. Short-term borrowing arrangements are disclosed in Note F of Notes to Consolidated Financial Statements. Further, because of the Company's strong financial condition, management believes it has substantial long-term debt capacity.

Capital Additions

Additions to land, buildings and equipment (unrelated to purchased companies and discontinued operations) were $33,015,000 in 1989, $45,462,000 in 1988 and $55,634,000 in 1987. Major expenditures in 1989 included expansion of waste treatment and food warehouse facilities and additional child care centers. Other capital expenditures were mainly for renewals and replacements to improve or maintain existing capacity. Expenditures in 1988 and 1987 were primarily for the expansion and addition of manufacturing, warehouse and distribution facilities for apparel operations, expansion of food research and warehouse facilities and additional child care centers. Capital additions for 1990 are expected to approximate $50,000,000 and will be primarily for renewals and replacements to improve existing food manufacturing and warehousing facilities.

Inflation

Inflation has not had a significant impact on the Company over the past three years nor is it expected to have a significant impact in the foreseeable future. The Company continuously attempts to minimize the effect of inflation through cost reductions and improved productivity.

approach, the preceding year is used as the base year for each subsequent year and the percentage change from year to year is shown. This "year-to-year" approach is illustrated for the Cooper Company in column (1) of Exhibit 14–10. Although this approach has the advantage of identifying and highlighting year-to-year changes, it does not allow for an easy analysis of the relative changes over an extended period. Because different years are used as bases, it is not possible to add the changes from year to year to derive the total cumulative change. When such an analysis is desired, a second approach may be utilized. Here, the *initial* year is used as the base year, and the cumulative results from subsequent years are compared with the initial year to determine the cumulative percentage changes. This "base-year-to-date" approach is illustrated for the Cooper Company in column (2) of Exhibit 14–10.

Whenever horizontal analysis is used, care must be taken in computing and interpreting percentage changes. If a base figure is zero or negative, although an *amount* of the change may be shown, *no percentage* change may be validly expressed. Furthermore, in cases where changes are expressed as percentages, no vertical addition or subtraction of the percentages (as discussed in the next section) can be made because the percentage changes result from the use of different bases. Finally, for items of small base amounts, a relatively small dollar change may result in a very high percentage change, thus potentially attaching more significance to the item than may be warranted. For example, selection of a weak initial year can make the cumulative percentage changes appear stronger than may be warranted.

Vertical Analysis

In vertical analysis, the monetary relationships between items on the financial statements of a particular period are expressed in terms of percentages as well as dollars. When vertical analysis is used for comparisons of financial statements from several periods, trends or changes in the relationships between items are more easily identified. Financial statements expressed in percentages only are referred to as **common-size statements**.

Vertical analysis may be used in conjunction with the income statement, retained earnings statement, balance sheet, or the statement of cash flows. In the case of the income statement, net sales usually are expressed as 100% and all other components are expressed accordingly. On the balance sheet, total assets represent 100%; on the retained earnings statement, beginning retained earnings is 100%; and in the case of the statement of cash flows, the increase in cash is usually expressed as 100%. Vertical analyses for the Cooper Company are illustrated in Exhibits 14–11 and 14–12.

Both vertical and horizontal analysis may be used to a limited extent in conjunction with interim reports and reports of the results of business segments. Vertical and horizontal analyses are also used in conjunction with ratio analysis.

EXHIBIT 14—10

COOPER COMPANY
Comparative Income Statements
(Horizontal Analysis)

| | For Years Ended December 31, | | | (1) Year-to-Year Increase (Decrease) | | | | (2) Base-Year-to-Date Increase (Decrease) | |
| | | | | 1992 to 1993 | | 1991 to 1992 | | 1991 to 1993 | |
	1993	1992	1991	Amount	Percent	Amount	Percent	Amount	Percent
Sales	$138,000	$130,000	$109,500	$ 8,000	6.2	$20,500	18.7	$28,500	26.0
Sales returns	(8,000)	(10,000)	(9,500)	(2,000)	(20.0)	500	5.3	(1,500)	(15.8)
Sales (net)	$130,000	$120,000	$100,000	$10,000	8.3	$20,000	20.0	$30,000	30.0
Cost of goods sold	(74,100)	(67,200)	(58,000)	6,900	10.3	9,200	15.8	16,100	27.8
Gross profit	$ 55,900	$ 52,800	$ 42,000	$ 3,100	5.9	$10,800	25.7	$13,900	33.1
Selling expenses	14,900	14,300	10,800	600	4.2	3,500	32.4	4,100	40.0
General expenses	19,700	20,600	15,000	(900)	(4.4)	5,600	37.3	4,700	31.3
Interest expense	3,000	2,400	2,400	600	25.0	0	0.0	600	25.0
Total expenses	$ (37,600)	$(37,300)	$ (28,200)	$ 300	0.8	$ 9,100	32.3	$ 9,400	33.3
Pretax continuing income	$ 18,300	$ 15,500	$ 13,800	$ 2,800	18.1	$ 1,700	12.3	$ 4,500	32.6
Income tax expense	(5,490)	(4,650)	(4,140)	840	18.1	510	12.3	1,350	32.6
Net income	$ 12,810	$ 10,850	$ 9,660	$ 1,960	18.1	$ 1,190	12.3	$ 3,150	32.6
Number of common shares	5,400	4,800	4,000	600	12.5	800	20.0	1,400	35.0
Earnings per share*	$2.15	$2.01	$2.12	$.14	7.0	$(.11)	(5.2)	$.03	1.4

*Earnings per share = $\dfrac{\text{Net income} - \text{Preferred dividends ($1,200)}}{\text{Average common shares outstanding}}$

EXHIBIT 14–11

COOPER COMPANY
Comparative Income Statements
(Vertical Analysis)
For Years Ended December 31, 1993 and 1992

	1993		1992	
	Amount	Percent	Amount	Percent
Sales	$138,000	106.2	$130,000	108.3
Sales returns	(8,000)	6.2	(10,000)	8.3
Sales, net (70% on credit)	$130,000	100.0	$120,000	100.0
Cost of goods sold	(74,100)	57.0	(67,200)	56.0
Gross profit	$ 55,900	43.0	$ 52,800	44.0
Selling expenses	14,900	11.5	14,300	11.9
General expenses	19,700	15.1	20,600	17.2
Interest expense	3,000	2.3	2,400	2.0
Total expenses	$ (37,600)	28.9	$ (37,300)	31.1
Pretax continuing income	$ 18,300	14.1	$ 15,500	12.9
Income tax expense	(5,490)	4.2	(4,650)	3.9
Net income	$ 12,810	9.9	$ 10,850	9.0
Number of common shares	5,400		4,800	
Earnings per share	$2.15		$2.01	

Comparative Retained Earnings Statements
(Vertical Analysis)
For Years Ended December 31, 1993 and 1992

	1993		1992	
	Amount	Percent	Amount	Percent
Beginning retained earnings	$33,150	100.0	$28,300	100.0
Net income	12,810	38.6	10,850	38.3
	$45,960	138.6	$39,150	138.3
Preferred dividends, $8/share	(1,200)	(3.6)	(1,200)	(4.2)
Common dividends, $1/share	(5,400)	(16.3)	(4,800)	(17.0)
Ending retained earnings	$39,360	118.7	$33,150	117.1

■ RATIO ANALYSIS

Another form of percentage analysis involves the use of financial ratios. Ratios, which entail the division of one or more items on the financial statements by another related item or items, are frequently employed to evaluate the financial aspects (i.e., return, risk, financial flexibility, liquidity, and operating capability) of a particular company. Many ratios have become standardized; they have been recognized as useful indicators of financial performance and are routinely com-

EXHIBIT 14–12

....

COOPER COMPANY
Comparative Condensed Balance Sheets
(Vertical Analysis)
December 31, 1993 and 1992

	1993		1992	
	Amount	Percent	Amount	Percent
Cash	$ 1,900	1.5	$ 2,100	1.9
Marketable securities				
(short-term)	2,000	1.5	2,700	2.4
Receivables (net)	7,600	5.9	8,600	7.7
Inventories	8,900	6.9	10,100	9.0
Prepaid items	1,000	.8	1,200	1.1
Total current assets	$ 21,400	16.6	$ 24,700	22.1
Noncurrent assets (net)	107,800	83.4	87,300	77.9
Total assets	$129,200	100.0	$112,000	100.0
Accounts payable	$ 5,000	3.9	$ 7,000	6.3
Other current liabilities	3,240	2.5	4,850	4.3
Long-term liabilities (12%)	25,000	19.3	20,000	17.9
Total liabilities	$ 33,240	25.7	$ 31,850	28.5
Preferred stock, 8%,				
$100 par*	$ 15,000	11.6	$ 15,000	13.4
Common stock, $5 par**	27,000	20.9	24,000	21.4
Additional paid-in capital	14,600	11.3	8,000	7.1
Retained earnings	39,360	30.5	33,150	29.6
Total stockholders' equity	$ 95,960	74.3	$ 80,150	71.5
Total liabilities and stockholders'				
equity	$129,200	100.0	$112,000	100.0

*The 150 shares of preferred stock are noncumulative and have a liquidation value of $140 per share.
**December 31, 1993, market price is $14.25 per share.

puted and published on a company and industry basis by financial analysis companies. These ratios become "benchmarks" against which to compare a company's results to evaluate its performance. The ratios are used in intracompany and intercompany comparisons for a variety of economic decisions. Other ratios are developed by individual users or user groups for their own specific needs.

More than 30 different ratios or variations of ratios have been discussed in the financial analysis literature. However, we shall focus on the primary standard ratios. These may be classified into five groups: (1) stockholder profitability ratios, (2) company profitability ratios, (3) liquidity ratios, (4) activity ratios, and (5) stability ratios. The intended use of each ratio and its proper computation are discussed briefly in the following sections. The 1993 data for the computation of these ratios can be obtained from Exhibits 14–11 and 14–12 for the Cooper Company. Since the numerical calculations of these ratios are not discussed in

EXHIBIT 14–13 Stockholder profitability ratios

Ratio	Formula	Cooper Company Calculations (1993)
1. Earnings per share	$$\frac{\text{Net income} - \text{Preferred dividends}}{\text{Average common shares outstanding}}$$	$$\frac{\$12,810 - \$1,200}{5,400} = \$2.15$$
2. Price/earnings	$$\frac{\text{Market price per common share}}{\text{Earnings per share}}$$	$$\frac{\$14.25}{\$\ 2.15} = 6.6$$
3. Dividend yield	$$\frac{\text{Dividends per common share}}{\text{Market price per common share}}$$	$$\frac{\$\ 1.00}{\$14.25} = 7.0\%$$

the text, reference should be made to these exhibits to identify the proper information inputs for each ratio.

Stockholder Profitability Ratios

Stockholder profitability ratios have been developed to serve as indicators of how effective a company has been in meeting the profit (i.e., return) objectives of its owners. Several stockholder profitability ratios have been developed; these are shown in Exhibit 14–13, along with the calculations for the Cooper Company.

Earnings per Share. The earnings-per-share information is probably the most frequently cited ratio in financial analysis. It is considered important enough to be a required disclosure on the face of the income statement. As its name indicates, it shows the amount of earnings attributable to each share of common stock held by stockholders. Corporations with complex capital structures are required to disclose both primary and fully diluted earnings-per-share amounts, as discussed in Chapter 10.

Price/Earnings. Although not precisely a stockholder profitability ratio, actual and potential stockholders use the price/earnings ratio to evaluate the attractiveness of an investment in a particular stock. A higher price/earnings ratio compared to other similar companies may indicate that investors perceive expansion potential for the company. Care must be taken, however, that the comparison is made to other "similar" companies. The price/earnings ratios for companies in certain "growth" industries, such as the electronics industry, are likely to be higher than for, say, companies in the automobile or steel industries. Interpretation of the ratio is also affected by investors' perceptions of the company's quality and trend of earnings, relative risk, use of alternative accounting methods, and other factors. Primary (or simple) earnings per share based on income from continuing operations is usually used as the denominator.

Dividend Yield. The market value of the stock represents the value a stockholder must forgo in order to continue holding the security. Stockholders are interested in their individual rates of return based upon the actual dividends received as compared with the ending market price (or market price on another particular date) of the stock. The dividend yield provides this information. The dividend yield, combined with the percentage change in the market price of the stock held during the period, is often considered the total annual return on the stockholders' investment.

The price earnings ratio and dividend yield are published in daily stock market listings. This daily reporting indicates the importance attached to these measures.

Company Profitability Ratios

Profitability ratios are used as indicators of how effective a company has been in meeting its overall profit (return) objectives, particularly in relation to the resources invested. Several overall company profitability ratios are shown in Exhibit 14–14, along with the calculations for the Cooper Company.

Profit Margin. The relationship of net income to net sales is commonly used to evaluate a company's efficiency in controlling costs and expenses in relation to sales. That is, the lower a company's expenses relative to sales, the higher the sales dollars remaining for other activities. Income from continuing operations typically is used in the numerator. The reporting of industry and foreign segment information permits a variation of this ratio to be computed for the reportable segments of a company. For each segment, the profit margin *before* income taxes can be computed by dividing the segment's operating profits by its revenues. A weakness of the ratio is that it does not consider the investment (the total assets or stockholders' equity) necessary to generate the sales and income.

Return on Total Assets. The amount of net income earned in relation to total assets is an indicator of a company's efficiency in the use of its economic resources. When a comparison is made of the return on total assets of one company to another, consideration should be given to the age of the assets of each company for two reasons. First, the return on a company's assets will get higher as the assets become older because the denominator will decrease each year because of the increase in accumulated depreciation. Second, the price increases because of inflation will result in a company that uses recently purchased assets showing a relatively lower return on these assets. Typically, extraordinary items, results of discontinued operations, and the effects of changes in accounting principles are excluded from the numerator because they are the result of infrequent events not directly related to the ongoing economic resources used in a company's operations. Interest expense (after income taxes)[8] is added back to net income

.................،..........
[8]After-tax interest expense is usually computed by multiplying the pretax interest expense by 1 minus the effective income tax rate. In the case of the Cooper Company, the effective tax rate is 30% ($5,490 ÷ $18,300), so that the $3,000 pretax interest expense is multiplied by 70% (1 − 0.30) to determine the after-tax results.

EXHIBIT 14–14   Company profitability ratios

Ratio	Formula	Cooper Company Calculations (1993)
1. Profit margin	$\dfrac{\text{Net income}}{\text{Net sales}}$	$\dfrac{\$12,810}{\$130,000} = 9.9\%$
2. Return on total assets	$\dfrac{\text{Net income} + \text{Interest expense (net of tax)}}{\text{Average total assets}}$	$\dfrac{\$12,810 + (\$3,000 \times 0.7)}{\dfrac{\$129,200 + \$112,000}{2}} = 12.4\%$
3. Return on stockholders' equity	$\dfrac{\text{Net income}}{\text{Average stockholders' equity}}$	$\dfrac{\$12,810}{\dfrac{\$95,960 + \$80,150}{2}} = 14.5\%$

because it is a financial cost paid to creditors to acquire the assets as opposed to a cost of generating sales. Since net income is earned over the entire period, the *average* total assets (beginning plus ending assets divided by two) for the period is used as the denominator. Some users argue, however, that it is preferable to use the amount from the ending balance sheet rather than an average. The ending balance sheet amount is the most recent amount available and therefore may be the most relevant comparison. Averaging this amount with the beginning balance may tend to "hide" changes that have occurred during the year. Reporting the results of industry and foreign segments permits the computation of a variation of this ratio for the reportable segments of a company. For each segment the *pretax* return on identifiable assets can be computed by dividing the segment's operating profit by its identifiable assets.

Return on Stockholders' Equity.   Net income may also be divided by stockholders' equity to reflect the residual return on the owners' equity. When this return is higher than the return on total assets, the company has favorable financial leverage (that is, it is trading on the equity, discussed in Chapter 8 and later). A weakness of the return on stockholders' equity ratio (as well as the return on total assets ratio), however, is that it does not consider the current value of the capital invested, since financial statements are based primarily on historical cost dollar amounts. Extraordinary items, results of discontinued operations, and changes in accounting principles usually are excluded from the numerator, and *average* stockholders' equity is usually used for the denominator. Some companies deduct preferred dividends from net income and use only common stockholders' equity in this ratio; they argue that preferred stock is more similar in nature to long-term liabilities than it is to common stock.

Liquidity Ratios

Liquidity ratios are used to evaluate a company's ability to pay its currently maturing financial obligations. These ratios generally involve all or most of the

EXHIBIT 14–15 Liquidity ratios

Ratio	Formula	Cooper Company Calculations (1993)
1. Current ratio	$\dfrac{\text{Current assets}}{\text{Current liabilities}}$	$\dfrac{\$21,400}{\$5,000 \ + \ \$3,240} = 2.60$
2. Acid-test ratio	$\dfrac{\text{Quick assets}}{\text{Current liabilities}}$	$\dfrac{\$11,500}{\$5,000 \ + \ \$3,240} = 1.40$

components of a company's **working capital**, its current assets less its current liabilities. Current assets include cash, short-term marketable securities, receivables, inventories, and prepaid items. Among current liabilities are such items as accounts payable incurred in the normal acquisition of goods or services; accruals for wages, taxes, and interest payable; short-term notes payable; advance collections of unearned revenues; and the current maturing portion of long-term debt. The common liquidity ratios are shown in Exhibit 14–15, along with the calculations for the Cooper Company.

Current Ratio.   The current ratio is probably the most commonly used indicator of a company's short-run liquidity. Sometimes it is referred to as the *working capital ratio*. It is considered to be a better indicator of a company's current debt-paying ability than simply working capital because working capital shows only the absolute difference between a company's current assets and its current liabilities. By computing the current ratio, the relative relationship between the current assets and current liabilities is known, so that comparisons of different sized companies can be made. In the past, as a "rule of thumb," a 2.0 current ratio was considered satisfactory. Today, however, more attention is given to (1) industry practices, (2) the length of a company's operating cycle, and (3) the mix of the current assets. Too *high* a current ratio relative to similar companies within the same industry may indicate inefficient management of current assets. The shorter a company's operating cycle, the less likely that it will need a substantial amount of working capital or as high a current ratio to operate efficiently. A company's operating cycle position is evaluated through the use of activity ratios, discussed in the next section. The proportion of different items that make up the total current assets is referred to as the mix of the current assets. This mix has an effect on how quickly the current assets can be converted into cash. As an extreme, a high proportion of prepaid items within current assets may indicate a weak liquidity position, since prepaid assets are consumed within the operating cycle rather than converted back into cash. For this reason, the acid-test ratio was developed, and the mix of a firm's current assets and the impact on its liquidity are considered in this ratio.

Acid-Test Ratio.   The acid-test or *quick* ratio is a more severe test of a company's short-term debt-paying abilities. In this ratio, only the current assets that may be readily converted into cash are used in the calculation. These, referred to as **quick assets**, generally consist of cash, short-term marketable securities, accounts receivable, and short-term notes receivable. Inventories are excluded because their salability is uncertain and they are frequently sold on credit; thus, they cannot be quickly converted into cash. Prepaid items are excluded because they are not convertible into cash. Since short-term marketable securities are shown on a company's balance sheet at their lower of cost or market value, if the market value is *higher* than cost, this market value should be included (instead of cost) in the computation. The acid-test ratio highlights potential liquidity problems attributable to an inadequate mix of current assets. For instance, the use of this ratio will usually reveal the lower liquidity of a company having a significant investment in inventories that would not be revealed in the current ratio. However, care must be taken to consider which assets to include. Even though inventories are usually excluded from the acid-test ratio, sometimes these are, in fact, more liquid than certain receivables. A quick ratio of 1.0 used to be a general rule of thumb. Today, as with the current ratio, greater consideration is given to such factors as industry practices and the company's typical operations.

Activity Ratios

Activity ratios are used to provide a general idea regarding the length of various segments of a company's operating cycle in order to evaluate the liquidity of certain current assets. The ratios are also indicators of the efficiency with which the company uses its short-term economic resources. The three common activity ratios are shown in Exhibit 14–16, along with the calculations for the Cooper Company.

Inventory Turnover.   Inventories are acquired, sold, and replenished in the normal course of a company's operations during its accounting period. Dividing a company's cost of goods sold for the period by its average inventory indicates the number of times the inventory is "turned over" or sold during that period. As a general rule, the higher the inventory turnover, (1) the more effective the company is in its operations, (2) the lesser the amount of investment that must be tied up in inventories, and (3) the shorter the operating cycle necessary to replenish cash. A company with a higher inventory turnover than others in the same industry is usually using its purchasing, receiving, and sales departments more efficiently. It is also minimizing the chance of having obsolete inventory. The lesser amount needed for investment in inventory means the company either needs less capital or can invest its capital in other earnings activities. However, *too* high an inventory turnover may indicate lost sales as a result of insufficient inventory on hand.

   Often the inventory turnover is divided into the number of operating days in a "business" year (365, 300, or 250, depending on the industry) so that the inventory segment of the operating cycle may be expressed in days. Care should be taken in developing the average inventory; seasonal factors can affect this average substantially. Furthermore, when a comparison is made of one company

EXHIBIT 14–16 Activity ratios

Ratio	Formula	Cooper Company Calculations (1993)
1. Inventory turnover	$\dfrac{\text{Cost of goods sold}}{\text{Average inventory}}$	$\dfrac{\$74,100}{\dfrac{\$8,900 + \$10,100}{2}} = 7.8$ times or 47 days*
2. Receivables turnover	$\dfrac{\text{Net credit sales}}{\text{Average net receivables}}$	$\dfrac{\$130,000 \times 0.70}{\dfrac{\$7,600 + \$8,600}{2}} = 11.2$ times or 33 days*
3. Payables turnover	$\dfrac{\text{Cost of goods sold}}{\text{Average accounts payable}}$	$\dfrac{\$74,100}{\dfrac{\$5,000 + \$7,000}{2}} = 12.35$ times or 30 days*

*365-day business year.

to another, both companies should be using similar inventory costing methods. In periods of rising prices, no valid comparison of inventory turnovers can be made when one company is using FIFO and another company is using LIFO. The company using LIFO will show a higher cost of goods sold and lower inventory than the FIFO company, even though their operations are similar.

Receivables Turnover. Once inventories have been sold on credit, the company must collect the receivables. Dividing net credit sales by average net trade receivables indicates how many times receivables are "turned over" or collected each period. The receivables turnover is an indicator of the efficiency with which the company collects its receivables and converts them back into cash. As a general rule, the higher the turnover the better, because the company has fewer resources tied up in receivables, collects these resources at a faster pace, and usually has fewer uncollectible accounts. When net credit sales information is not readily available, net sales are used in the calculations. Care should be taken to consider seasonal factors and to exclude nontrade receivables in developing the average receivables.

The receivables turnover often is divided into the number of days in the business year to show the average collection period in days. A comparison of a company's average collection period to the days in its typical credit terms gives an indication of how aggressively the company's credit department collects overdue accounts.

Payables Turnover. The payables turnover ratio measures the number of times accounts payable turn over during the year. The higher the turnover, the shorter the time between the purchase of inventory and the cash payment. However, too high a turnover may indicate that the company is making payments too quickly and losing the "free" credit provided by accounts payable. Alternatively, if a company's payables turn over slower than the average for its industry, it may indicate that the company is having financial difficulty. It may be preferable to compute the ratio by using purchases as the numerator, in which case purchases can be computed by adding the ending inventory to the cost of goods sold and subtracting the beginning inventory. The payables turnover ratio may also be divided into the number of days in the business year to show the average payment period in days.

The three turnover ratios may be analyzed together to assess the total number of days in the company's operating cycle from payment of cash to buy inventory to the collection of cash from sales. This period may be computed by adding the number of days in the receivables turnover to the number of days in the inventory turnover and subtracting the number of days in the payables turnover. For example, in Exhibit 14–16, the Cooper Company's operating cycle is 50 (47 + 33 − 30) days.

Stability Ratios

Stability ratios are used as indicators of the long-run solvency and stability of the company. They provide evidence of the safety (risk) of the investments in the company by long-term bondholders, preferred stockholders, and common stockholders. Several stability ratios are shown in Exhibit 14–17, along with the calculations for the Cooper Company.

Debt Ratio. The debt ratio indicates the percentage of total assets contributed by creditors. Subtraction of this ratio from 100% yields the percentage of total assets (or *equity* ratio) contributed by stockholders. Sometimes, when a company has issued a significant amount of preferred stock (which has characteristics of both debt and common stock), the equity ratio is further divided into a preferred equity ratio and a common equity ratio. The appropriate relationship (or "mix") between the debt and equity ratios depends on the industry. In general, creditors prefer to see a lower debt ratio because, in the event of business decline, their interests are better protected and there is less risk. Up to a point, stockholders prefer a higher debt ratio, particularly when the company is favorably "trading on the equity," or applying favorable "financial leverage." This occurs when the company borrows money from creditors at an interest rate (net of income taxes) that is lower than the return the company can earn in its operations. However, an extremely high debt ratio is likely to be a disadvantage when a company wishes to attract additional external capital. Investors in both long-term bonds and stocks usually consider a highly leveraged company a relatively unstable and more risky investment.

Another version of the debt ratio, often called the debt/equity ratio is computed by dividing total liabilities by total stockholders' equity. This ratio expresses the relationship between the capital contributed by creditors and that contributed by owners.

EXHIBIT 14–17 Stability ratios

Ratio	Formula	Cooper Company Calculations (1993)
1. Debt ratio	$\dfrac{\text{Total liabilities}}{\text{Total assets}}$	$\dfrac{\$33,240}{\$129,200} = 26\%$
2. Debt/equity ratio	$\dfrac{\text{Total liabilities}}{\text{Total stockholders' equity}}$	$\dfrac{\$33,240}{\$95,960} = 35\%$
3. Times interest earned	$\dfrac{\text{Pretax operating income} + \text{Interest expense}}{\text{Interest expense}}$	$\dfrac{\$18,300 + \$3,000}{\$3,000} = 7.1$
4. Book value per common share	$\dfrac{\text{Common stockholders' equity}}{\text{Outstanding common shares}}$	$\dfrac{\$95,960 - (\$140 \times 150)}{5,400} = \$13.88$ per common share

Times Interest Earned. The times interest earned ratio (sometimes called the *interest coverage* ratio) is used as an indicator of the ability of a company to cover its interest obligations through its annual earnings. As such, it is a measure of the safety of creditors' (particularly long-term) investments in the company. As a general rule, the higher the ratio the better able the company is to meet its interest obligations. While interest obligations are legal commitments, it is also true that continued interest payments are endangered by low earnings over an extended period of time. Because both earnings and interest expense are based on accrual accounting, the times interest earned ratio is slightly inaccurate, since it should include only cash outflows for interest and cash inflows from earnings. Such refinements are rarely made to this ratio, however.

The numerator of the times interest earned ratio is usually a form of pretax *operating* income—that is, pretax continuing income to which interest expense is added back. If a company has preferred stock outstanding, a similar calculation may be made to evaluate the safety of preferred dividends. The *preferred dividends coverage ratio* would be computed by dividing net income by the annual preferred dividends.

Book Value. The book value per common share reflects the net assets per share of stock. It is sometimes referred to as the liquidation value per share. This title is inappropriate because the liquidation value may be very different from the book value. Although the book value per common share is frequently computed, for several reasons it is not very useful as an indicator of a company's financial stability. First, most companies are going concerns and a related liquidation value is of no consequence. Second, even if a liquidation value were of importance, the book value per share is based on assets recorded primarily in terms of historical costs and thus has no relation to the liquidation value per share. Third, of concern in evaluating a company's stability is the market value per share of its common stock. Since book value is based on historical costs, it also has no direct relation to this market value. However, should the market price of a company's common stock fall below its book value per common share, some investors would attach unfavorable significance to this event.

When book value per share is computed and the company has both preferred and common stock outstanding, the equity relating to the common stock must be determined first. This necessitates separating stockholders' equity into its preferred and common stock components on the basis of the legal claims of each class upon liquidation. Typically, preferred stock is allocated its par value unless the stock's characteristics include a liquidation value, in which case the latter value is used. When preferred dividends are cumulative and in arrears, an appropriate portion of retained earnings is also assigned as preferred stock-holders' equity. The residual amount of stockholders' equity is then assigned as common stockholders' equity. The book value per common share is computed by dividing this residual stockholders' equity by the number of common shares outstanding. A book value per share of preferred stock also may be computed on the basis of the preferred stockholders' equity and the number of preferred shares outstanding.

Cash Flow Ratios

Cash flow ratios are used as indicators of the solvency and liquidity of a company. For example, cash flow from operating activities may be divided by the amount of long-term debt maturing in the next year. Since cash flow from operating activities is usually the primary source of cash for a company, this ratio measures the ability of the company to service principal payments. It is also an indicator of whether the company has the capacity to incur additional debt. This ratio is not calculated because the Cooper Company's cash flow statement is not presented. Other cash flow ratios include cash flow from operating activities divided by cash operating expenses, total assets, or total liabilities.

Ratios Summary

Only the primary standard ratios were identified and discussed in this section. Exhibit 14–18 summarizes these ratios and their computations. The reader interested in further discussion of how users employ these ratios in their decision-making process or how additional ratios are computed should consult the ratio analysis section of a standard financial analysis book.

■ SEC REPORTS

The Securities and Exchange Commission (SEC) was created to administer various securities acts under powers provided by Congress in the Securities Act of 1933 and the Securities Exchange Act of 1934. The intent of Congress was to regulate the disclosure of all significant financial information provided by companies issuing publicly traded securities (e.g., stocks and bonds). The SEC has

EXHIBIT 14–18 Summary of ratios

Ratio	Formula
STOCKHOLDER PROFITABILITY RATIOS	
1. Earnings per share	$\dfrac{\text{Net income} - \text{Preferred dividends}}{\text{Average common shares outstanding}}$
2. Price/earnings	$\dfrac{\text{Market price per common share}}{\text{Earnings per share}}$
3. Dividend yield	$\dfrac{\text{Dividends per common share}}{\text{Market price per common share}}$
COMPANY PROFITABILITY RATIOS	
1. Profit margin	$\dfrac{\text{Net income}}{\text{Net sales}}$
2. Return on total assets	$\dfrac{\text{Net income} + \text{Interest expense (net of tax)}}{\text{Average total assets}}$
3. Return on stockholders' equity	$\dfrac{\text{Net income}}{\text{Average stockholders' equity}}$
LIQUIDITY RATIOS	
1. Current ratio	$\dfrac{\text{Current assets}}{\text{Current liabilities}}$
2. Acid-test ratio	$\dfrac{\text{Quick assets}}{\text{Current liabilities}}$

the legal authority to prescribe accounting principles and reporting practices for these regulated companies.

The SEC is a large organization with its headquarters in Washington, D.C. It is administered by five commissioners, each of whom is appointed to a five-year term by the President of the United States after approval by the Senate. One commissioner is designated to be chair of the SEC.

The SEC is organized along several administrative offices, five divisions, and nine regional offices. Among the administrative offices, the **Office of the Chief Accountant** is of particular interest because it is responsible for providing the SEC with advice concerning accounting and auditing. The *Chief Accountant* helps in the establishment of administrative policies regarding accounting matters, is directly responsible for *Regulation S–X* (which establishes the form and content of financial statements filed with the SEC), and is primarily responsible for the *Financial Reporting Releases*[9] (which prescribe accounting principles for

[9]Prior to 1982, these documents were referred to as *Accounting Series Releases*. The name was changed to better reflect their nature.

EXHIBIT 14–18 *(continued)*

Ratio	Formula
ACTIVITY RATIOS	
1. Inventory turnover	$\dfrac{\text{Cost of goods sold}}{\text{Average inventory}}$
2. Receivables turnover	$\dfrac{\text{Net credit sales}}{\text{Average net receivables}}$
3. Payables turnover	$\dfrac{\text{Cost of goods sold}}{\text{Average accounts payable}}$
STABILITY RATIOS	
1. Debt ratio	$\dfrac{\text{Total liabilities}}{\text{Total assets}}$
2. Debt/equity ratio	$\dfrac{\text{Total liabilities}}{\text{Total stockholders' equity}}$
3. Times interest earned	$\dfrac{\text{Pretax operating income} + \text{Interest expense}}{\text{Interest expense}}$
4. Book value per common share	$\dfrac{\text{Common stockholders' equity}}{\text{Outstanding common shares}}$
CASH FLOW RATIO	
1. Cash flow to maturing debt	$\dfrac{\text{Cash flow from operating activities}}{\text{Long-term debt maturing next year}}$

regulated companies). Among the divisions, the **Division of Corporation Finance** is also important. This division is responsible for assisting in the establishment of reporting standards (except those directly pertaining to financial statements, which are the responsibility of the Chief Accountant) and the requirements for adherence to these standards by regulated companies. The division is also responsible for reviewing the financial reports submitted to the SEC by these companies.[10]

Numerous forms are required to be filed with the SEC under various circumstances by regulated (public) companies. Of primary concern to users of financial statements are:

- *Form 10-K.* An annual report
- *Form 10-Q.* A quarterly report of operations

---

[10]For a more extensive discussion of the history and administrative responsibilities of the various segments of the SEC, see K. F. Skousen, *An Introduction to the SEC,* Fourth Edition (Cincinnati, Ohio: South-Western Publishing Company, 1987).

The similarities and differences between the SEC annual and quarterly reports and a company's annual and interim reports (where GAAP is regulated by the FASB and its predecessors) issued to stockholders are briefly discussed as follows.

Form 10-K is the most common SEC annual report form. It must be filed with the SEC within 90 days of a company's fiscal year-end. The current Form 10-K consists of four major parts, as summarized in Exhibit 14–19.

Prior to 1980, Form 10-K required the inclusion of considerably more and different information than that presented in a company's published annual report. In 1980, the SEC adopted several amendments intended to minimize the differences between documents filed with it and those sent to stockholders. As a result, the SEC now separates its required financial information into two types: (1) information that must be reported in *both* annual reports filed with the SEC and annual reports issued to stockholders and (2) information required to be filed only with the SEC.

Information of the first type is included in part II of Exhibit 14–19. This information, as well as any or all of the part I information, can now be included in the Form 10-K by *reference* to the company's published annual report issued to stockholders. Note, however, that all the information in part II *must* now be included in the latter report. Thus, for instance, many companies are now including a management discussion and analysis, as well as three years of comparative financial statements, in their stockholders' annual reports.

The second type of information (required to be filed with the SEC only) is considered to be important primarily to a limited and sophisticated group of users (e.g., security analysts). This type includes the information contained in parts I, III, and IV of Exhibit 14–19.

Form 10-Q is used to report a company's quarterly financial information to the SEC and is required to be filed within 45 days of the end of each of the company's first three fiscal quarters. It contains similar disclosures to that of Form 10-K but includes only quarterly and year-to-date information and is not audited. The accounting principles discussed earlier in the chapter are used to prepare the Form 10-Q financial statement disclosures, so that this financial information is very similar to that provided in a company's quarterly report to stockholders. However, it may be more extensive because the SEC *requires* the presentation of comparative interim income statements, balance sheets, and statements of cash flows.

■ CONCLUSIONS

The dedicated student will have learned a great deal about generally accepted accounting principles and financial reporting by a thorough study of this book. Unfortunately, even if the student retained 100% of the material included here, there would still be some gaps in his or her knowledge. Many of the areas covered in this book have additional complexities that were not discussed. Some areas, particularly those relating to specialized industries, are beyond the scope of this text, and various federal and state reporting requirements have not been included. For example, the Federal Farm Credit Banks are including in income

EXHIBIT 14–19   SEC Form 10-K required disclosures

Part	Item	Heading	Summary of Contents
I	1	Business	Description of business. History. Recent developments. Industry segments. Principal products and services.
	2	Properties	Location and general character of plants and other physical properties. Industry segments using properties.
	3	Legal proceedings	Description of pending legal proceedings, including principal parties, dates, allegations, and relief sought.
	4	Security ownership	Listing of beneficial owners and management owners of corporation's securities.
II	5	Market for common stock	Identification of market(s) where corporation's common stock is traded. Number of shares, frequency, and amount of dividends.
	6	Selected financial data	Five-year summary of net sales, income (loss) from continuing operations (and EPS), total assets, long-term obligations, and cash dividends.
	7	Management's discussion and analysis	Discussion of information regarding liquidity, capital resources, results of operations, and impact of inflation necessary to understand the corporation's financial position, changes in financial position, and operating results.
	8	Financial statements and supplementary data	Consolidated financial statements, including balance sheet (2 years), income statement and statement of cash flows (3 years). Statement of changes in stockholders' equity (3 years), selected quarterly information. Auditor's opinion.
III	9	Directors and officers	Listing of names, ages, and positions of directors and executive officers.
	10	Management remuneration and transactions	Listing of names, positions, salaries, stock options, and other benefits.
IV	11	Exhibits, schedules, and reports	Detailed supporting schedules, such as marketable securities, property, plant, and equipment (and related depreciation), and short-term borrowings. Listing of subsidiaries. Computation of ratios.
		Signatures	Signatures of chief executive, financial, and accounting officers, and majority of board of directors.

accrued interest on loans that are as much as four years delinquent. This procedure would be a violation of GAAP but is allowed under the appropriate federal regulations.

There are also some situations in which GAAP is not appropriately applied. For example, several problems with financial reporting to the SEC have occurred recently:

1. Inadequate justification for treating costs incurred as assets in situations where there were cost overruns on contracts.

2. Use of an oral offer to avoid a write-down to the quoted market price of marketable securities when GAAP requires use of a price quoted on an exchange.

3. Nonrecognition of losses on advances to "nonsubsidiary subsidiaries" (a company created solely for the benefit of a sponsoring company). The sponsoring company does not own any of the new company's stock but may hold notes convertible into a majority of the new company's shares, provides the sole means of financing, effectively controls the new company, and plans to acquire the new company when it becomes profitable.

4. Companies "shopping" to find an auditor to agree to an unusual accounting practice, and thereby avoid a modified opinion.

5. Capitalizing virtually all legal costs, not just those incurred for patents.

6. Recording as sales items shipped to dealers and salespersons before they have been "sold" to the ultimate customers (perhaps before they have even been ordered by a customer).

7. Including costs of defective tools and dies in property, plant, and equipment.

8. Arbitrarily increasing the cost of inventory to avoid the recognition of losses for scrapped inventories.

9. Not disclosing related party transactions.

Many of these situations have led to a company's being required to restate previously issued financial statements. The appropriate accounting would be a prior period adjustment, as discussed in Chapter 10.

The reader should understand that financial reporting is neither static nor perfect. The user of financial statements should always be aware of the possibility of an unusual transaction(s) being recorded in an unexpected manner. The management that prepares the financial statements should also be aware that its responsibility is directly to the shareholders as well as indirectly to the public through the SEC. Therefore, the statements should be prepared in the clearest and most understandable manner, with informative disclosures of all items that would be considered material by users.

While expressing these relevant concerns, we also emphasize that a large majority of companies do routinely follow GAAP without any intent to conceal or distort. The difficulty for the reader is to discern those financial reports that require special attention. However, it should also be clear to the reader that even the routine application of GAAP requires judgment by the company and by the auditor. Similarly, interpretation by the user also requires judgment.

QUESTIONS

1. List and briefly discuss the five types of information that are helpful in making predictions about a company's future cash flows.

2. What two types of comparisons may external users make in their financial decision making?

3. Why do investors and creditors desire financial information concerning the operating segments of a company?

4. Briefly describe the three alternative tests used to determine a "reportable segment."

5. Briefly describe the three major items of information that must be reported for each reportable industry segment.

6. What financial information must be reported regarding a company's (a) foreign operations, (b) export sales, and (c) major customers?

7. What are interim financial statements and why are they issued?

8. What specific principles should be applied to the reporting of inventories in interim financial reports?

9. What principles should be applied to the accounting for costs (other than product) and expenses during an interim period?

10. Briefly explain how the accounting procedures for preparing interim reports are (a) similar and (b) dissimilar to those used in preparing annual reports.

11. What is horizontal analysis and how is it prepared?

12. What is vertical analysis and how does it differ from horizontal analysis?

13. What is ratio analysis and how is it used?

14. Briefly describe how each of the stockholder profitability ratios is computed.

15. Briefly describe how each of the company profitability ratios is computed.

16. Which financial ratios may be used to evaluate the effectiveness and efficiency of a company's reportable industry segments?

17. Briefly describe how each of the liquidity ratios is computed.

18. Briefly describe how each of the activity ratios is computed.

19. Briefly describe how each of the stability ratios is computed.

PROBLEMS AND CASES

20. **Segment Reporting.** Mory Conglomerate Company has total assets of $140,000 at the end of 1993 and lists the following condensed income statement for 1993.

MORY CONGLOMERATE COMPANY
Income Statement
For Year Ended December 31, 1993

Sales	$110,000
Operating expenses	(75,000)
Income before income taxes	$ 35,000
Income tax expense	(14,000)
Net income	$ 21,000

The company has two reportable industry segments, A and B, and has developed the information listed below:

| | Segments | | Other | |
	A	B	Segments	Total
Sales	$50,000	$35,000	$25,000	$110,000
Operating expenses	30,000	24,000	21,000	75,000

The company's assets are assigned to the segments as follows: $67,000 to Segment A; $44,000 to Segment B; and $29,000 to the other segments.

Required Prepare a schedule to report on the 1993 revenues, operating profits, and identifiable assets of Segments A and B and the other industry segments of the Mory Conglomerate Company.

21. **Determination of Reportable Industry Segments.** In preparing its segment reporting schedule, the Loxer Diversified Company has developed the following information for each of its five segments:

| | Segments | | | | | |
	1	2	3	4	5	Totals
Sales	$3,520	$3,000	$3,880	$25,800	$3,800	$40,000
Operating expenses	2,200	1,800	1,700	15,480	2,820	24,000
Identifiable assets	6,300	7,500	6,200	40,000	5,000	65,000

Required Determine which of these segments are reportable industry segments and which should be combined for segment reporting.

22. **Segment Reporting.** York Company has two reportable industry segments, A and B. A 1993 condensed income statement for the entire company follows:

YORK COMPANY
Income Statement
For Year Ended December 31, 1993

Sales	$90,000
Cost of goods sold	(50,000)
Gross profit	$40,000
Operating expenses	(18,000)
Income before income taxes	$22,000
Income tax expense	(8,800)
Net income	$13,200

Additional Information:

1. Sales are made as follows: Segment A, $52,000; Segment B, $26,000; other segments, $12,000 of the total.

2. Cost of goods sold for each segment is as follows: Segment A, $30,000; Segment B, $12,500; other segments, $7,500.

3. Operating expenses are identified with the segments as follows: Segment A, $10,000; Segment B, $4,500; other segments, $3,500.

4. The company has $110,000 total assets as of December 31, 1993. These assets are assigned to the segments as follows: Segment A, $49,500; Segment B, $38,500; other segments, $22,000.

Required Prepare a schedule that reports on the 1993 revenues, operating profits, and identifiable assets of Segments A and B and the other segments of the York Company.

23. **Segment Reporting.** The Doxy Diversified Company has total assets of $115,000 at the end of 1993 and the following condensed income statement for 1993:

DOXY DIVERSIFIED COMPANY
Income Statement
For Year Ended December 31, 1993

Sales	$80,000
Operating expenses	(57,600)
Income before income taxes	$22,400
Income tax expense (40%)	(8,960)
Net income	$13,440

The company has two reportable industry segments, A and B, and has developed the following information to prepare its segmental reporting schedule:

	Segments			
	A	B	Other	Totals
Sales	$51,360	$14,360	$14,280	$ 80,000
Operating expenses	36,780	10,400	10,420	57,600
Identifiable assets	70,320	22,720	21,960	115,000

Required 1. Based on the above information prepare a schedule that reports on the 1993 revenues, operating profits, and identifiable assets of Segments A and B and the other segments of the Doxy Diversified Company.

2. Compute the profit margin *before* income taxes for Segments A and B, and for the other segments. What do these ratio results reveal?

24. **Segment Reporting.** Steinoff Industries has total assets of $171,000 at the end of 1993 and the following condensed income statement for 1993:

STEINOFF INDUSTRIES
Income Statement
For Year Ended December 31, 1993

Sales	$125,000
Operating expenses	(86,400)
Income before income taxes	$ 38,600
Income tax expense (40%)	(15,440)
Net income	$ 23,160

The company has two reportable industry segments, Q and R, and has developed the following information in preparing its segmental reporting schedule:

| | Segments | | | |
	Q	R	Other	Totals
Sales	$ 79,560	$30,400	$15,040	$125,000
Operating expenses	55,170	20,800	10,430	86,400
Identifiable assets	110,000	33,000	28,000	171,000

Required 1. On the basis of the above information prepare a schedule that reports on the 1993 revenues, operating profits, and identifiable assets of Segments Q and R, and the other segments of Steinoff Industries.

2. Compute the *pretax* return on ending *identifiable* assets for Segments Q and R, and for the other segments. What do these ratio results reveal?

25. **Interim Reporting.** The Campbell Company prepares quarterly and year-to-date interim reports. Its interim income statement for the quarter ended March 31, 1993, follows:

CAMPBELL COMPANY
Income Statement
For First Quarter Ended March 31, 1993

Sales (net)		$80,000
Cost of goods sold		(44,000)
Gross profit		$36,000
Operating expenses		
Selling expenses	$11,500	
General expenses	10,800	(22,300)
Operating income		$13,700
Other revenues and expenses		
Interest revenue	$ 300	
Interest expense	(500)	(200)
Income before income taxes		$13,500
Income tax expense		(5,400)
Net income		$ 8,100
Earnings per share (10,000 shares)		$ .81

On June 30, 1993, the following have been recorded for the first six months of the year:

Sales (net)	$175,000
Interest revenue	650
Cost of goods sold	94,000
Selling expenses	24,000
General expenses	20,000
Interest expense	1,050
Income tax expense	14,640

In addition, 10,000 shares of common stock have been outstanding for the entire six months.

Required Based on the above information for the Campbell Company, prepare

1. A year-to-date interim income statement for the first six months of 1993
2. An interim income statement for the second quarter of 1993

26. Interim Reporting, Gross Profit Method. The Jolsh Corporation listed the following items on its interim worksheet for the second quarter, ended June 30, 1993:

Inventory (beginning)	$ 4,000
Purchases	22,000
Sales	28,000
Sales returns and allowances	3,000

Based on experience Jolsh Corporation estimates its gross profit is 30% of net sales.

Required 1. Compute the estimated cost of goods sold of the Jolsh Corporation for the second quarter of 1993 using the gross profit method.

2. Based on your answer to requirement 1, compute the estimated ending inventory on June 30, 1993.

27. Interim Reporting. The Ziegler Corporation presented the following interim income statement for the first quarter of 1993:

ZIEGLER CORPORATION
Income Statement
For First Quarter Ended March 31, 1993

Sales (net)		$320,000
Cost of goods sold		
Inventory (1-1-1993)	$ 38,400	
Purchases (net)	192,000	
Cost of goods available for sale	$230,400	
Less: inventory (3-31-1993, estimated)	(54,400)	
Cost of goods sold		(176,000)
Gross profit		$144,000
Operating expenses		
Selling expenses	$ 52,000	
General and administrative expenses	32,000	
Total operating expenses		(84,000)
Income before income taxes		$ 60,000
Income tax expense		(24,000)
Net income		$ 36,000
Earnings per share (12,000 shares)		$ 3.00

On June 30, 1993, the following information was available:

Cash	$ 54,400
Accounts receivable	32,300
Notes receivable (due 12-31-1993)	16,000
Inventory (1-1-1993)	38,400
Property and equipment	100,000
Accumulated depreciation	22,500
Accounts payable	16,000
Common stock, no par	56,000
Retained earnings	22,600
Sales (net)	600,000
Purchases (net)	320,000
Selling expenses	97,500
General and administrative expenses	58,500
Interest receivable	400
Interest revenue	400
Income tax expense	45,760
Income taxes payable	45,760

The company uses the gross profit method to estimate its interim inventory. Historical gross profit has averaged 45% of net sales. No common stock has been issued or retired in 1993.

Required 1. Prepare interim income statements for the periods April 1 to June 30, 1993, and January 1 to June 30, 1993.

2. Prepare a June 30, 1993, interim balance sheet.

3. For both the first quarter (January 1 to March 31, 1993) and the second quarter (April 1 to June 30, 1993) compute the following ratios: (a) earnings per share, (b) inventory turnover, and (c) profit margin. What do your ratio results reveal?

28. **Interim Reporting.** The Renax Company prepared the following interim income statement for the first quarter of 1993.

RENAX COMPANY
Income Statement
For First Quarter Ended March 31, 1993

Sales (net)		$480,000
Cost of goods sold		
Inventory (1-1-1993)	$ 57,600	
Purchases (net)	288,000	
Cost of goods available for sale	$345,600	
Less: inventory (3-31-1993, estimated)	(81,600)	
Cost of goods sold		(264,000)
Gross profit		$216,000

Operating expenses
   Selling expenses $ 78,000
   General and administrative expenses   48,000
   Total operating expenses   (126,000)
Income before income taxes $ 90,000
Income tax expense   (36,000)
Net income $ 54,000
Earnings per share (22,000 shares) $ 2.45

The following information was available on June 30, 1993:

Cash	$ 77,600
Accounts receivable	48,450
Notes receivable (due 12-31-1993)	24,000
Inventory (1-1-1993)	57,600
Property and equipment	150,000
Accumulated depreciation	33,750
Accounts payable	24,000
Common stock, no par	84,000
Retained earnings	33,900
Sales (net)	920,000
Purchases (net)	500,000
Selling expenses	148,500
General and administrative expenses	89,500
Interest receivable	600
Interest revenue	600
Income tax expense	70,640
Income taxes payable	70,640

No common stock has been issued or retired in 1993. The company uses the gross profit method to estimate its interim inventory. Historical gross profit has averaged 45% of net sales.

Required 1. Prepare interim income statements for the periods April 1 to June 30, 1993, and January 1 to June 30, 1993.

2. Prepare a June 30, 1993, interim balance sheet.

3. For both the first quarter (January 1 to March 31, 1993) and the second quarter (April 1 to June 30, 1993) compute the following ratios: (a) earnings per share, (b) inventory turnover, and (c) profit margin. What do your ratio results reveal?

29. Horizontal Analysis. The Clovland Company presents the following condensed comparative income statements for 1993 and 1994:

CLOVLAND COMPANY
Comparative Income Statements

	For Years Ended December 31	
	1994	1993
Sales (net)	$110,000	$90,000
Cost of goods sold	(60,000)	(45,000)
Gross profit	$ 50,000	$45,000
Operating expenses	(22,000)	(20,000)
Income before income taxes	$ 28,000	$25,000
Income tax expense	(11,200)	(10,000)
Net income	$ 16,800	$15,000
Number of common shares	7,100	7,600
Earnings per share	$ 2.37	$ 1.97

Required Based on the above information prepare a horizontal analysis for the years 1993 and 1994. Calculate the profit margin for the company for the two years. What is this ratio generally used for and what does it indicate about the Clovland Company?

30. **Horizontal Analysis.** The Taboue Corporation showed the following information for the years 1993 and 1994:

TABOUE CORPORATION
Comparative Income Statements

	For Years Ended December 31		Year-to-Year Increase (decrease) 1993 to 1994	
	1994	1993	Amount	Percent
Sales (net)	$65,000	$60,000	$ (a)	(b)%
Cost of goods sold	(c)	(33,600)	(d)	(e)
Gross profit	$27,950	$26,400	$ (f)	(g)
Operating expenses	(19,050)	(h)	400	(i)
Income before income taxes	$ 8,900	$ (j)	$1,150	(k)
Income tax expense	(3,560)	(3,100)	(l)	(m)
Net income	$ (n)	$ 4,650	$ (o)	(p)
Number of common shares	2,600	(q)	(r)	13.0
Earnings per share	$ 2.05	$ 2.02	$ (s)	(t)

Required Determine the appropriate percentages and amounts for the blanks lettered (a) through (t). Round to the nearest tenth of a percent. Briefly comment on what your analysis reveals.

31. **Horizontal Analysis and Ratios.** The Shulz Company presents the following comparative income statements for 1993 and 1994:

SHULZ COMPANY
Comparative Income Statements

	For Years Ended December 31,	
	1994	**1993**
Sales (net)	$100,000	$85,000
Cost of goods sold	(56,000)	(45,000)
Gross profit	$ 44,000	$40,000
Selling expenses	(12,000)	(10,000)
General expenses	(8,000)	(8,000)
Operating income	$ 24,000	$22,000
Interest revenue	500	200
Interest expense	(1,000)	(500)
Income before income taxes	$ 23,500	$21,700
Income tax expense	(9,400)	(8,680)
Net income	$ 14,100	$13,020
Average number of common shares	5,500	5,000

Additional Information:

1. There were no shares of preferred stock outstanding in 1993 or 1994.

2. As of December 31, 1994, the company's common stock had a market price of $12.50 per share. The market price on December 31, 1993, was $15.00 per share.

3. Dividends in the amount of $6,000 and $7,500 were paid to common stockholders in 1994 and 1993, respectively.

Required 1. Prepare a horizontal analysis for the Shulz Company for 1993 and 1994.

2. Compute the following ratios for the company for 1993 and 1994:
   a. Earnings per share
   b. Price/earnings
   c. Profit margin
   d. Dividend yield
   e. Times interest earned

3. Briefly discuss any important changes in operating results revealed by your horizontal and ratio analyses.

32. **Horizontal Analysis and Ratios.** Howale Corporation presented the following comparative income statements for 1993 and 1994.

HOWALE CORPORATION
Comparative Income Statements

	For Years Ended December 31,	
	1994	1993
Sales (net)	$250,000	$262,000
Cost of goods sold	(150,000)	(129,400)
Gross profit	$100,000	$132,600
Selling expenses	(28,000)	(25,500)
General expenses	(23,500)	(21,000)
Operating income	$ 48,500	$ 86,100
Interest revenue	500	400
Interest expense	(1,500)	(500)
Income before income taxes	$ 46,500	$ 86,000
Income tax expense	(19,000)	(34,400)
Net income	$ 28,500	$ 51,600
Average number of common shares	15,000	15,000

Additional Information:

1. Dividends in the amounts of $20,250 and $53,100 were paid to common stock-holders in 1994 and 1993, respectively.

2. There were no preferred shares outstanding in either year.

3. As of December 31, 1994, the company's common stock had a market price of $15.00 per share. On December 31, 1993, the stock had a market price of $29.55 per share.

Required 1. Prepare a horizontal analysis for the Howale Corporation for 1993 and 1994.

2. Compute the following ratios for the corporation for 1993 and 1994:

   a. Earnings per share
   b. Price/earnings
   c. Profit margin
   d. Dividend yield

3. Briefly discuss any important changes in operating results revealed by your horizontal and ratio analyses.

33. **Vertical Analysis.** The Cooke Company presents the following condensed balance sheet information for 1993:

COOKE COMPANY
Balance Sheet
December 31, 1993

Cash	$ 2,600
Accounts receivable	3,400
Inventory	6,500
Long-term investments	10,000
Property and equipment (net)	37,500
Total assets	$60,000

Current liabilities	$ 5,000
Bonds payable, 8%	20,000
Total liabilities	$25,000
Common stock, $2 par	$ 6,000
Additional paid-in capital	9,000
Retained earnings	20,000
Total stockholders' equity	$35,000
Total liabilities and stockholders' equity	$60,000

Required Based on the above information prepare a vertical analysis of the Cooke Company balance sheet for 1993. Round to the nearest tenth of a percent. What is the company's current ratio? Based on the "rule of thumb," is it satisfactory?

34. **Vertical Analysis.** The Anton Company presents the following condensed income statement for 1993:

ANTON COMPANY
Income Statement
For Year Ended December 31, 1993

Sales (net)	$140,000
Cost of goods sold	(76,000)
Gross profit	$ 64,000
Operating expenses	(32,750)
Income before income taxes	$ 31,250
Income tax expense	(12,500)
Net income	$ 18,750
Earnings per share	$ 3.00

In addition, the average inventory for 1993 was $10,000.

Required Based on the above information prepare a vertical analysis of the income statement for 1993. What is the company's inventory turnover and what does this ratio tell us about a company?

35. **Vertical Analysis and Ratios.** The Koeppen Company operates a high-volume retail outlet. Comparative financial statements for the company for 1993 and 1994 are shown:

KOEPPEN COMPANY
Comparative Income Statements

	For Years Ended December 31,	
	1994	1993
Sales	$180,000	$150,000
Cost of goods sold	(108,000)	(85,500)
Gross profit	$ 72,000	$ 64,500
Operating expenses	(44,600)	(37,500)
Income before income taxes	$ 27,400	$ 27,000

	For Years Ended December 31,	
	1994	**1993**
Income tax expense (40%)	(10,960)	(10,800)
Net income	$ 16,440	$ 16,200
Earnings per share (6,000 shares)	$ 2.74	$ 2.70

KOEPPEN COMPANY
Comparative Balance Sheets

	December 31,	
	1994	**1993**
Cash	$ 4,100	$ 3,000
Marketable securities (short-term)	2,100	2,100
Accounts receivable (net)	8,600	6,400
Inventory	11,300	9,700
Noncurrent assets (net)	129,900	118,800
Total assets	$156,000	$140,000
Current liabilities	$ 13,000	$ 12,400
Long-term liabilities (10%)	40,000	35,000
Total liabilities	$ 53,000	$ 47,400
Common stock, $3 par	$ 18,000	$ 18,000
Additional paid-in capital	30,000	30,000
Retained earnings	55,000	44,600
Total stockholders' equity	$103,000	$ 92,600
Total liabilities and stockholders' equity	$156,000	$140,000

Additional Information:

1. At the beginning of 1993 the company had outstanding accounts receivable (net) of $7,600.

2. On January 1, 1993, the inventory totaled $9,500.

3. The beginning balance of stockholders' equity for 1993 was $83,400.

4. Sixty percent of the company's sales were on credit.

Required 1. Prepare vertical analyses of the Koeppen Company income statements and balance sheets for 1993 and 1994.

2. Compute the following ratios for 1993 and 1994:

   a. Current
   b. Inventory turnover (in days, assuming a 365-day business year)
   c. Accounts receivable turnover (in days, assuming a 365-day business year)
   d. Return on stockholders' equity

3. Briefly discuss any important changes revealed by your vertical and ratio analyses.

36. **Vertical Analysis and Ratios.** The Tuscumber Company presented the following comparative financial statements for 1993 and 1994:

TUSCUMBER COMPANY
Comparative Income Statements

	For Years Ended December 31,	
	1994	1993
Sales	$200,000 (100%)	$185,000 100%
Cost of goods sold	(120,000) (60%)	(124,000)(67%)
Gross profit	$ 80,000 (40%)	$ 61,000 33%
Operating expenses	(52,400) (26.2)	(38,800) 21%
Income before income taxes	$ 27,600 13.8%	$ 22,200 12%
Income tax expense	(11,040) (5.5%)	(8,880) 4.8%
Net income	$ 16,560 8.28	$ 13,320 7.2%
Earnings per share (6,000 shares)	$ 2.76	$ 2.22

TUSCUMBER COMPANY
Comparative Balance Sheets

	December 31,	
	1994	1993
Cash	$ 12,100	$ 10,500
Marketable securities (short-term)	7,900	8,300
Accounts receivable (net)	10,400	13,300 11600
Inventory	17,600	12,000 18,000
Noncurrent assets (net)	106,000	105,900
Total assets	$154,000	$150,000
Current liabilities	$ 25,100	$ 34,700
Long-term liabilities (12%)	52,300	47,300
Total liabilities	$ 77,400	$ 82,000
Common stock, $3 par	$ 18,000	$ 18,000
Additional paid-in capital	20,000	20,000
Retained earnings	38,600	30,000
Total stockholders' equity	$ 76,600	$ 68,000 64000
Total liabilities and stockholders' equity	$154,000	$150,000

Additional Information:

1. At the beginning of 1993 the company had outstanding accounts receivable (net) of $11,600.

2. On January 1, 1993, the inventory totaled $18,000.

3. The beginning balance of stockholders' equity for 1993 was $64,000.

4. Seventy percent of the company's sales were on credit.

Required 1. Prepare vertical analysis of the Tuscumber Company income statements and balance sheets for 1993 and 1994.

2. Compute the following ratios for 1993 and 1994:

   a. Current

   b. Inventory turnover (in days, assuming a 300-day business year)

    c. Accounts receivable turnover (in days, assuming a 300-day business year)

    d. Return on stockholders' equity

  3. Briefly discuss any important changes revealed by your vertical and ratio analyses.

37. Ratios. The Lobe Company presents the following condensed income statement for 1993 and condensed December 31, 1993, balance sheet:

LOBE COMPANY
Income Statement
For Year Ended December 31, 1993

Sales (net)		$400,500
Less: Cost of goods sold	$240,000	
Operating expenses	88,950	
Interest expense	11,550	
Income taxes	24,000	
Total expenses		(364,500)
Net income		$ 36,000

LOBE COMPANY
Balance Sheet
December 31, 1993

Cash	$ 7,600
Marketable securities (short-term)	14,900
Accounts receivable (net)	23,000
Inventory	86,500
Long-term investments	45,000
Property and equipment (net)	423,000
Total assets	$600,000
Current liabilities	$ 60,000
Bonds payable, 7%	190,000
Common stock, $10 par	180,000
Additional paid-in capital	87,500
Retained earnings	82,500
Total liabilities and stockholders' equity	$600,000

Additional Information:

1. Common stock was outstanding the entire year and dividends of $1.80 per share were declared and paid in 1993. The common stock is selling for $24 per share on December 31, 1993.

2. Credit sales for the year totaled $260,325.

3. Average net accounts receivable for the year were $26,500.

4. Average stockholders' equity for the year was $343,000.

5. The company operates on a 365-day business year.

Required On the basis of the above information, compute the following ratios for the Lobe Company:

1. Earnings per share
2. Dividend yield
3. Return on stockholders' equity
4. Current
5. Acid-test
6. Accounts receivable turnover (in days)
7. Times interest earned
8. Book value per common share

On the basis of applicable "rules of thumb," what information is revealed by the acid-test ratio for the company that is not disclosed by its current ratio?

38. Ratios. The following are a condensed income statement for 1993 and a December 31, 1993, balance sheet for the Mea Company:

MEA COMPANY
Income Statement
For Year Ended December 31, 1993

Sales (net)	$152,200
Cost of goods sold	(91,300)
Gross profit	$ 60,900
Operating expenses	(40,100)
Interest expense	(2,800)
Income before income taxes	$ 18,000
Income taxes	(7,200)
Net income	$ 10,800

MEA COMPANY
Balance Sheet
December 31, 1993

Cash	$ 3,100
Marketable securities (short-term)	2,000
Accounts receivable (net)	6,350
Inventory	9,650
Property and equipment (net)	97,900
Total assets	$119,000
Current liabilities	$ 12,400
Bonds payable, 8%	35,000
Common stock, $10 par	40,000
Additional paid-in capital	12,250
Retained earnings	19,350
Total liabilities and stockholders' equity	$119,000

Additional Information:

1. The common stock was outstanding the entire year and is selling for $20.25 per share at year-end.

2. On January 1, 1993, the inventory was $10,750, the total assets were $112,000, and the total stockholders' equity was $65,400.

3. The company operates on a 300-day business year and is subject to a 40% income tax rate.

Required Compute the following ratios for the Mea Company:

1. Price/earnings
2. Profit margin
3. Return on total assets
4. Return on stockholders' equity
5. Current
6. Inventory turnover (in days)
7. Debt

Is the company favorably "trading on its equity"? Explain.

ANNUAL REPORT PROBLEMS ....

39. **General Motors.** Review the financial statements and related notes of General Motors in Appendix A.

Required Answer the following questions and indicate on what page of the financial report you located the answer. (*Note:* All answers may be found in the annual report; no calculations are necessary.)

1. What was the net income for 1989? What were the related earnings-per-share amounts on each type of stock?

2. What was the amount of the total assets on December 31, 1989?

3. What was the amount of the total stockholders' equity on December 31, 1989? How much of this total was capital surplus?

4. What was the amount of the total increase or decrease in cash and cash equivalents in 1989? How much of this total was from operating activities?

5. Where does the company summarize its accounting policies?

6. How are inventories valued? For what inventory is LIFO used?

7. What depreciation method does the company use?

8. How are goodwill and other intangible assets being amortized?

9. How much R&D was expensed in 1989?

10. What was the amount of the LIFO liquidation profit in 1989?

11. What was the amount of the finance receivables at December 31, 1989?

12. What was the amount of insurance expense in 1989?

13. What was the total cost of machinery and equipment at December 31, 1989?

14. How many shares of $1⅔ par value common stock were issued in 1989 as a result of the exercise of stock options? What was the range of option prices for these exercised options?

15. What was the amount of the total pension expense in 1989? What was the amount of the projected benefit obligation (in excess of) or less than plan assets for U.S. plans at December 31, 1989?

16. What amount of the total income taxes for 1989 was (a) currently payable and (b) deferred?

17. For the fourth quarter of 1989, what was the amount of the (a) net sales and revenues, (b) income or loss before income taxes, and (c) net income. How much was the related earnings per share on each class of common stock?

18. What were the principal lines of business of the company in 1989?

19. What was the amount of the total net sales and revenue from (a) the United States and (b) Latin America in 1989?

20. What was the amount of the total assets of General Motors Acceptance Corporation at December 31, 1989?

21. What was the net income of General Motors Acceptance Corporation for 1989?

22. What was the amount of the net income as a percent of net sales and revenues in 1989?

23. What were the payments for benefit plans during 1989?

24. How is the $5 preferred stock redeemable?

25. What dollar amount is disclosed for contingent liabilities at December 31, 1989?

26. What was the high and low stock price in 1989 for the $1⅔ par value common stock?

27. In which year did the company distribute a 100% stock dividend?

28. What foreign currency translation amounts were included in stockholders' equity at December 31, 1989?

40. Segment Reporting. Colgate-Palmolive Company is one of the world's leading consumer product companies, marketing its products in over 100 countries, with subsidiaries in 60 countries. The following excerpts are from its 1988 annual report relating to segment reporting (in thousands of dollars):

Industry Segment Data (in part):
The following business segments accounted for these percentages of worldwide sales for the past three years:

	1988	1987	1986
Household and Personal Care	90%	91%	92%
Specialty Marketing	10%	9%	8%

Scope of Business (in part):

Principal products in each of the business segments are as follows:

Household and Personal Care products include laundry and dishwashing detergents, fabric softeners, cleaners and cleansers, toothpastes, toothbrushes, bar and liquid soaps, hair care and shave products, and other items. Laundry and dishwashing detergents and oral care products accounted for the following percentages of worldwide sales for the past three years:

	1988	1987	1986
Laundry and dishwashing detergents	38%	40%	40%
Oral care products	21%	21%	20%

Specialty Marketing products include food and medical products for pets, crystal tableware and portable fuel and related equipment for warming food.

Geographic Area Data (in part):

	1988	1987	1986
Net sales:			
United States	$1,687,173	$1,513,544	$1,322,569
Europe	1,508,207	1,487,291	1,284,201
Western Hemisphere	909,841	844,781	717,049
Far East and Africa	629,104	520,071	444,879
	$4,734,325	$4,365,687	$3,768,698
Operating profit:			
United States	$ 67,974*	$ 83,574**	$ 106,838
Europe	99,917	12,284**	58,346
Western Hemisphere	114,054	90,459**	81,150
Far East and Africa	55,770	15,673**	18,098
	$ 337,715*	$ 201,990**	$ 264,432
Identifiable assets:			
United States	$1,272,097	$1,112,778	$ 869,508
Europe	880,368	758,996	581,580
Western Hemisphere	386,671	341,228	264,689
Far East and Africa	316,044	279,083	215,635
Discontinued operations	—	703,142	774,091
	$2,855,180	$3,195,227	$2,705,503

*Operating profit for the United States geographic area in 1988 includes renegotiation expense of $59,000 for a service agreement.

**Operating profit for geographic areas in 1987 includes the effect of the charge for restructured operations of $205,700. The effects on geographic area data were to reduce the operating profit of the United States, Europe, Western Hemisphere, and the Far East and Africa by $37,700, $69,000, $6,000 and $21,600, respectively. Unallocated expenses include $71,400.

Required Is Colgate-Palmolive in a position to take advantage of the business opportunities created by the ongoing changes in Western and Eastern Europe? Include profitability ratios by geographic areas in your answer. (Use ending, rather than average, total assets in your calculations since no 1985 data is given.) What additional data would you analyze in answering this question?

41. Ratio Analysis and Intercompany Comparison. Several commercial data bases of ratios are available for comparative purposes. One such data base is the Robert Morris

Annual Financial Statement Survey. Ratios are grouped by five major categories: liquidity, coverage, leverage, operating, and specific expense items. These types of ratios are computed for standard industry classifications (SIC) and by the upper quartile (UQ), or top 25%, of the companies; the median (M), or top 50% of the companies; and the lower quartile (LQ), or top 75% of the companies. It also further divides each SIC by asset sizes of four ranges: $0 to $1 million, $1 to $10 million, $10 to $50 million, and $50 million to $100 million.

Although seventeen ratios are provided in the data base, for simplicity, one common ratio is provided for each of five categories as follows:

1. Liquidity:

$$\text{Current Ratio} = \frac{\text{Current Assets}}{\text{Current Liabilities}}$$

2. Coverage (or Stability):

$$\text{Times Interest Earned} = \frac{\text{Pretax Operating Income} + \text{Interest Expense}}{\text{Interest Expense}}$$

3. Leverage (or Stability):

$$\text{Debt/Equity Ratio} = \frac{\text{Total Liabilities}}{\text{Total Stockholders' Equity}}$$

4. Operating (or Profitability):

$$\text{Return on Stockholders' Equity} = \frac{\text{Pretax Operating Income}}{\text{Total Stockholders' Equity}}$$

5. Specific Expense:

$$\text{Depreciation to Sales} = \frac{\text{Depreciation Expense}}{\text{Net Sales}}$$

For the SIC number 1311, which is for crude petroleum producers, the five ratios listed above are provided in 1988 for all companies:

	UQ	M	LQ
Current ratio	1.8	1.1	0.5
Times interest earned	4.3	2.1	(0.6)
Debt to equity ratio	0.8	1.6	2.9
Return on stockholders' equity	0.26	0.06	(0.05)
Depreciation to sales	0.05	0.14	0.30

The following data are from the 1988 annual reports of four major crude petroleum producers: Exxon, Mobil, Amoco, and Phillips (in millions of dollars):

	Exxon	Mobil	Amoco	Phillips
Current assets	$14,846	$11,178	$ 5,393	$ 3,062
Current liabilities	17,479	10,255	5,468	2,468
Pretax operating income	8,384	3,461	3,307	1,115
Interest expense	944	907	468	688
Total liabilities	42,526	23,134	16,577	9,855

	Exxon	Mobil	Amoco	Phillips
Total assets	74,293	38,820	29,919	11,968
Stockholders' equity	31,767	15,686	13,342	2,113
Depreciation expense	4,415	2,683	2,318	868
Net sales	87,252	53,322	21,150	11,304

Required 1. Assume that a very conservative investor would only invest in a company that is in the top 25% of its industry in all five ratio categories listed above. Do any of the companies qualify?

2. Assume that a speculative investor is looking for "turn-around" investment opportunities of companies in the lower 50% of the industry in all five ratio categories listed above. Do any of the companies qualify?

3. Would you recommend any of these companies for an investment?

42. **Ratio Analysis and Intercompany Comparison.** Kimberly-Clark and Scott Paper are major competitors in the sanitary tissue products market. The following excerpts are from the 1988 annual reports of the two companies (in millions of dollars):

	Kimberly-Clark	Scott Paper
Current assets	$1,235.5	$1,614.9
Current liabilities	979.4	1,147.1
Inventories	566.5	522.2
Prepaid expenses	—	108.2
Income before income taxes	583.9	601.7
Interest expense	80.6	147.5
Net income	378.6	400.9
Depreciation expense	187.6	283.0
Current portion of long-term debt	110.9	129.4
Net fixed assets	2,575.3	3,009.1
Stockholders' equity	1,865.6	1,944.8
Total liabilities	2,402.0	3,211.5
Total assets	4,267.6	5,156.3
Net sales	5,393.5	4,726.4

Required 1. For the following categories, compute the listed ratios for both companies:

    a. Liquidity: current ratio, acid-test ratio
    b. Stability: times interest earned, debt ratio
    c. Company profitability: profit margin, return on stockholders' equity, return on total assets

    Use a 40% income tax rate and use ending, rather than average, amounts since the 1987 amounts are not given.

2. Evaluate the performance of the two companies in the three categories.

43. **Performance Analysis With Industry Ratios.** Several commercial databases of ratios are available for comparative analyses. One such database is the Robert Morris *Annual Financial Statement Survey*. It groups ratios by the following categories. It computes

these ratios by standard industry classifications (SIC) and by the upper quartile (UQ) or top 25% of the companies, the median (M) or top 50%, and the lower quartile (LQ) or top 75%. The following seven ratios from this database are provided for the SIC number 1311 for integrated oil companies, such as Exxon.

Type of Ratio	UQ	M	LQ
Company profitability:			
1. Profit margin	0.075	0.043	0.014
2. Return on stockholders' equity	0.146	0.090	0.043
Liquidity:			
3. Current ratio	1.7	1.3	1.0
Activity:			
4. Inventory turnover	65.0	44.2	15.0
5. Receivables turnover	10.5	7.8	4.7
Stability:			
6. Debt	0.4	0.8	1.4
7. Times interest earned	5.9	2.7	1.1

Required Use the data in Problem 3–45 for Exxon. (Note that these amounts are for 1 month whereas the industry ratios are based on an annual period.) Analyze Exxon's performance for January, 1989 by computing these seven ratios and comparing them to the above industry numbers.

1. Company Profitability:

   a. Profit margin
   b. Return on stockholders' equity (use ending, not average, stockholders' equity to be consistent with the Robert Morris database calculations)
   c. Industry comparison for company profitability

2. Liquidity:

   a. Current ratio
   b. Industry comparison for liquidity

3. Activity:

   a. Inventory turnover (use ending, not average, inventory to be consistent with the Robert Morris database calculations)
   b. Receivables turnover (use ending, not average, receivables to be consistent with the Robert Morris database calculations)
   c. Industry comparison for activity

4. Stability:

   a. Debt ratio (use stockholders' equity, not total assets, to be consistent with the Robert Morris database calculations)
   b. Times interest earned
   c. Industry comparison for stability

5. Summary of comparisons and performance evaluation for Exxon

44. Performance Analysis with Industry Ratios. Several commercial databases of ratios are available for comparative analyses. One such database is the Robert Morris *Annual*

Financial Statement Survey. Ratios are grouped by the categories listed below. These ratios are computed by standard industry classifications (SIC) and by the upper quartile (U) or top 25% of the companies, the median (M) or top 50%, and the lower quartile (L) or top 75%.

The following seven ratios from this database are provided for the SIC number 3571 for manufacturers of electronic computers and/or major components for computer systems, such as MiniScribe Corporation. These ratios are provided for the last three years, 1988, 1987, and 1986, by the three quartiles. These ratios have also been calculated for MiniScribe in 1987 and 1986.

Type of Ratio	1988		1987		1986	
	All Cos.	Mini-Scribe	All Cos.	Mini-Scribe	All Cos.	Mini-Scribe
Company profitability:						
1. Profit margin						
(U)-top 25%	0.08	?	0.06	0.09	0.04	0.12
(M)-top 50%	0.06		0.03		0.02	
(L)-top 75%	0.04		0.02		0.01	
2. Return on stockholders' equity						
(U)-top 25%	0.36	?	0.27	0.28	0.30	0.31
(M)-top 50%	0.20		0.12		0.06	
(L)-top 75%	0.10		(0.02)		(0.09)	
Liquidity:						
3. Current ratio						
(U)-top 25%	5.1	?	6.9		3.7	
(M)-top 50%	2.9		3.6		3.1	
(L)-top 75%	1.7		1.9	2.6	1.9	2.2
Activity:						
4. Inventory turnover						
(U)-top 25%	4.1	?	2.9	3.2	4.3	
(M)-top 50%	2.9		2.3		2.3	3.1
(L)-top 75%	2.4		1.9		1.6	
5. Receivables turnover						
(U)-top 25%	8.2	?	5.0	6.3	6.4	
(M)-top 50%	5.2		4.3		4.2	4.7
(L)-top 75%	4.3		3.3		3.3	
Stability:						
6. Debt						
(U)-top 25%	0.3	?	0.3		0.3	
(M)-top 50%	0.6		0.7		0.5	
(L)-top 75%	1.2		1.1	1.7	1.1	1.1
7. Times interest earned						
(U)-top 25%	23.3	?	11.6		17.0	
(M)-top 50%	15.6		5.4	6.4	3.3	11.8
(L)-top 75%	9.5		(1.4)		(3.2)	

In order to calculate these seven ratios for MiniScribe in 1988, the following income statement and balance sheet information has been compiled from estimates of original 1988 numbers in the financial press since no 1988 financial statements had been issued by MiniScribe by November, 1989. The amounts are in millions of dollars.

1988 Estimated Income Statement:	
Net credit sales	$603
Cost of sales	(446)
Gross profit	$157
Interest expense (net)	(11)
Other expenses (net)	(115)
Net income before taxes	$ 31
Income tax expense	(5)
Net income	$ 26

1988 Estimated Balance Sheet	
Current assets	
Cash	$ 51
Accounts receivable	173
Inventory	141
Total current assets	$365
Property and equipment, net	75
Other assets	10
Total assets	$450
Current liabilities	$223
Long-term debt	100
Total liabilities	$323
Stockholders' equity	127
Total	$450

Required Compute the following seven ratios for MiniScribe in 1988. Analyze MiniScribe's performance by comparing the trends of these seven ratios over the last three years and by comparing these ratios to the above industry numbers.

1. Company Profitability:

   a. Profit margin
   b. Return on stockholders' equity (use ending, not average, stockholders' equity in your calculations to be consistent with the Robert Morris database calculations)
   c. Summary comments: MiniScribe's performance concerning company profitability

2. Liquidity:

   a. Current ratio
   b. Summary comments: MiniScribe's performance concerning liquidity

3. Activity

   a. Inventory turnover (use ending, not average, inventory in your calculations to be consistent with the database calculations)
   b. Receivables turnover (use ending, not average, receivables in your calculations to be consistent with the database calculations)
   c. Summary comments: MiniScribe's performance concerning activity

4. Stability:

   a. Debt ratio (use stockholders' equity, not total assets, in your calculations to be consistent with the database calculations)
   b. Times interest earned
   c. Summary comments: MiniScribe's performance concerning stability

5. From your ratio analysis, in which year did possible problems or "red flags" emerge concerning MiniScribe's performance? Why?

45. Alternative Accounting Methods. Safeway Stores is one of the nation's largest grocery store chains. The following excerpts are from its 1988 annual report relating to its choice of accounting methods (in millions of dollars):

Inventories at FIFO	$ 1,136
Less LIFO reductions	(27)
	$ 1,109
Net property	2,032
Total assets	4,372
Stockholders' equity	(368)
Deferred income tax expense item: accelerated depreciation	
(statutory tax rate of 34%)	20
Sales	13,612
Cost of sales	10,177
Other expenses, net	3,404ª
Net income	$ 31

ªIncludes straight-line depreciation of $263, pre-opening costs of $10, and payment of post-retirement benefits of $2.

Use the following assumptions: the increase in the LIFO reserve in 1988 was $18 million; preopening costs of $10 million could be deferred over four years starting in 1988; the other postemployment benefits were on a pay-as-you-go (cash) basis, but if on the accrual basis, the present value of postretirement benefits obligations would be $50 million in 1988; ignore any changes in income tax expense and ignore any potential prior period adjustments; use ending, rather than average, amounts since the 1987 amounts are not given.

Required 1. Choose inventory, depreciation, pre-opening, and other postemployment benefits accounting methods to calculate:

    a. Maximization of net income
    b. Minimization of net income

2. Were Safeway's choices of accounting methods nearer the income maximization or minimization approaches? Assess the impact of your choices on cash flow from operations and on the following company profitability ratios:

    a. Profit margin
    b. Return on stockholders' equity
    c. Return on total assets

46. Alternative Accounting Methods. The following excerpts are from Eastman Kodak's 1988 annual report (in millions of dollars):

Inventories	
At average cost	$ 4,001
Less: LIFO reserve	(976)
	$ 3,025
Depreciation	
Accelerated in U.S. and straight-line outside U.S.	$ 1,058
Deferred income tax expense item:	
depreciation (statutory tax rate of 34%)	59
Amortization of goodwill	

25-year amortization of $4,600 goodwill (primarily from
purchase of Sterling Drug in 1988)   184

Sales	$17,034
Cost of goods sold	9,601
Selling and administrative expenses	4,495
Other expenses, net	1,541
Net income	$ 1,397
Stockholders' equity	$ 6,780
Total assets	$22,964

The increase in LIFO reserve from 1987 to 1988 was $42 million. Assume that the
goodwill could have been amortized over a ten-year life instead of a 25-year life.
Ignore any changes in income tax expense and ignore any potential prior period
adjustments. Use ending, rather than average, amounts since the 1987 amounts were
not given.

Required 1. Choose accounting methods for inventory, depreciation, and goodwill to calculate:

   a. Maximization of net income
   b. Minimization of net income

2. Were Kodak's choices of accounting methods nearer the income maximization or
minimization approaches? Assess the impact of your choices on cash flow from
operations and on the following company profitability ratios:

   a. Profit margin
   b. Return on stockholders' equity
   c. Return on total assets

47. **Ratios Provided in Annual Reports.** United States Tobacco is a leading producer and
marketer of smokeless tobacco products. Financial ratios from its 1988 annual report
are provided as follows:

	1988	1987	1986
Primary earnings per common share	$ 1.41	$ 1.13	$ 0.92
Dividends per common share	0.74	0.60	0.49
Price/earnings ratio per common share:			
High	14.9	14.3	12.4
Low	8.6	8.6	8.2
Market price per common share:			
High	21	16	11
Low	12	10	7
Current ratio	4.2	4.1	4.1
Shareholders' equity per common share	$ 4.12	$ 3.64	$ 3.33
Percent of long-term debt to shareholders' equity	4.8%	9.3%	12.7%
Return on average shareholders' equity	38.0%	33.9%	29.9%
Return on average assets	28.3%	24.4%	21.0%
Return on net sales	26.2%	22.7%	20.1%

Required Evaluate the performance of United States Tobacco using the ratio categories discussed in this chapter:

1. Stockholder profitability
2. Company profitability
3. Liquidity
4. Activity
5. Stability

What additional ratios not provided by United States Tobacco would be helpful in evaluating performance in each of these categories?

48. Ratios Provided in Annual Reports. Wendy's International Inc., has nearly 3,800 restaurants worldwide. The following ratios are provided by the company in its 1988 financial statements:

	1988	1987	1986
Earnings per share—primary	$0.30	$0.05	$(0.05)
Book value per share	4.36	4.29	4.45
Dividends per share	0.24	0.24	0.21
Market price of common stock at year-end	5.75	5.63	10.25
Company restaurant operating profit margin	11.0%	8.3%	13.1%
Pretax profit margin	4.1%	—	1.3%
Return on average assets[a]	8.5%	2.1%	4.8%
Return on average stockholders' equity	6.9%	1.1%	—
Current ratio	1.00	0.75	0.81
Debt to equity	46%	47%	53%
Debt to total capitalization	31%	32%	34%

[a]Income before income taxes and interest charges was used in the computation of these ratios.

Required Evaluate the performance of Wendy's using the ratio categories discussed in this chapter:

1. Stockholder profitability
2. Company profitability
3. Liquidity
4. Activity
5. Stability

What additional ratios not provided by Wendy's would be helpful in evaluating performance in each of these categories?

49. Impacts of Accounting Method Choices. Champion International is a large producer of various types of papers and newsprint pulp. The following excerpts are from its 1988 financial statements and related notes (in millions of dollars):

Inventories (note 1)	$ 412
Property, Plant and Equipment (note 2)	5,124
Less: Accumulated depreciation	(1,422)
Net Amount	$3,702
Other Assets and Deferred Charges (note 3)	431
Total Assets	$6,700
Net Sales	$5,129
Cost of goods sold	3,988
Depreciation	202
Amortization	0
Other expenses	209
Income before taxes	$ 730
Income taxes	274
Net income	$ 456

Note 1:
At December 31, 1988 and 1987, inventories using the last-in, first-out (LIFO) method, representing approximately 20% and 22% of total inventories, were $81 and $93, respectively. If the lower of average cost or market method (which approximates current cost) had been utilized for inventories carried at LIFO, inventory balances would have been increased by $64 and $55 at December 31, 1988 and 1987, respectively.

Note 2:
For financial reporting purposes, plant and equipment are depreciated on the straight-line method over the estimated service lives of the individual assets. (Excerpt from the income tax footnote: The major deferred income tax item was the excess of tax over financial depreciation expense of $93. The 1988 statutory federal income tax rate was 34%.)

Note 3:
Preoperating expenses and start-up costs incurred with the construction of major properties are deferred until such properties become operational. These items are then amortized over a five-year period. (Assume that none of these construction projects were completed in 1988 and that the costs were incurred in 1988.)

Required 1. What choices of the following accounting methods would a company make to maximize its net income (assuming inflation)?

   a. FIFO or LIFO
   b. Straight-line depreciation or accelerated depreciation
   c. Deferral or immediate write-off of start-up costs

2. If Champion were converted to the FIFO inventory method, would there be a material impact on its profit margin? Use the statutory income tax rate of 34% and round to the nearest million dollars.

3. If Champion were converted from its existing straight-line depreciation method and capitalization of start-up costs to an accelerated depreciation method and no deferral of start-up costs, would there be a material impact on its return on total assets? Use the statutory income tax rate of 34% and round to the nearest million dollars.

4. Reconcile the differences in performance in question 3 by converting net income to cash flow from operating activities for both approaches.

5. Considering materiality, are Champion's choices of accounting methods closer to maximizing net income or minimizing net income?

■ APPENDIX A

■ Nike, Inc. 1989 Annual Report: Financial Section

■ General Motors 1989 Annual Report: Financial Section

■ NIKE, INC.

Included in Appendix A are the parts of the financial section of the annual report of Nike, Inc. that have *not* been included in the text. The following excerpts are included in the text:

1. Statement of management responsibilities (Chapter 4).
2. Note 2, Inventories (Chapter 6).
3. Note 5, Property, plant, and equipment (Chapter 7).
4. Note 6, Short-term borrowings (Chapter 8).
5. Note 7, Long-term debt (Chapter 8).
6. Note 8, Income taxes (Chapter 9).
7. Note 9, Redeemable preferred stock (Chapter 10).
8. Note 10, Common stock (Chapter 10).
9. Note 11, Profit sharing plan (Chapter 10).
10. Note 13 (in part), Commitments and contingencies (Chapter 9).
11. Note 14, Operations by geographic areas (Chapter 14).

HIGHLIGHTS

Selected Financial Data

	1989	1988	1987	1986	1985
	(in thousands, except per share data)				
Year Ended May 31:					
Revenues	$1,710,803	$1,203,440	$877,357	$1,069,222	$946,371
Net income	167,047	101,695	35,879	59,211	10,270
Net income per common share	4.45	2.70	.93	1.55	.27
Cash dividends declared per common share	.55	.40	.40	.40	.40
At May 31:					
Working capital	$422,478	$298,816	$325,200	$278,784	$217,849
Total assets	825,410	709,095	511,843	476,838	503,966
Long-term debt	34,051	30,306	35,202	15,300	7,573
Redeemable Preferred Stock	300	300	300	300	300
Common shareholders' equity	561,804	411,774	338,017	316,846	271,668

Selected Quarterly Financial Data

	1st Quarter		2nd Quarter		3rd Quarter		4th Quarter	
	1989	1988	1989	1988	1989	1988	1989	1988
	(in thousands, except per share data)							
Revenues	$510,686	$282,828	$322,033	$234,408	$464,663	$331,787	$413,421	$354,417
Gross profit	185,536	95,402	116,922	70,943	171,739	106,397	161,775	127,318
Net income	56,986	25,081	24,775	18,547	48,828	27,599	36,458	30,468
Net income per common share	1.52	.65	.66	.50	1.30	.74	.97	.81
Dividends declared per common share	.10	.10	.15	.10	.15	.10	.15	.10
Price range of common stock								
High	29⅛	22⅝	34⅜	24¾	33¼	23	39¾	26½
Low	23⅛	16¼	24¾	14	24⅜	14⅞	29⅝	21⅛

The Company's Class B Common Stock is traded in the NASDAQ National Market System under the NASDAQ symbol NIKE. At May 31, 1989, there were 33 security dealers making a market in the stock and there were approximately 3,900 shareholders of record.

MANAGEMENT DISCUSSION AND ANALYSIS

Highlights

 • Consolidated revenues exceeded $1.7 billion, a 42% improvement over the Company's previous high achieved in 1988 and a 95% increase over 1987.

 • Consolidated net income of $167 million or $4.45 per share represents record earnings for the second consecutive year, an increase of 64% over 1988 net income of $101.7 million or $2.70 per share and a 365% increase over 1987 net income of $35.9 million or $.93 per share.

Results of Operations

 Increased revenues and improved gross margins highlighted the earnings growth in 1989. Domestic footwear pairage shipments in 1989 rose 12% over the previous year, while the average sales price per pair increased 23%. The increase in sales price is attributable to a larger percentage of sales of high-end products and to a general increase in prices resulting from higher production costs. Domestic apparel revenues rose 46% over the previous year primarily because of increased product demand. Foreign revenue growth resulted from increased product demand partially offset by the translation effect of a stronger U.S. dollar. The approximate breakdown of revenues by product category that follows contains certain amounts restated to conform with 1989 classifications:

	Year Ended May 31,		
	1989	1988	1987
		(in thousands)	
Footwear			
Basketball	$ 414,600	$ 287,300	$178,000
Fitness	237,800	129,000	92,500
Running	202,600	177,900	123,800
Racquet	58,400	60,700	38,500
Other	153,200	102,600	77,200
Non-athletic	87,300	—	—
Total footwear	1,153,900	757,500	510,000
Apparel	208,200	142,900	130,700
Athletic equipment	—	—	900
Total United States	1,362,100	900,400	641,600
Foreign			
Europe	241,400	233,400	191,400
Canada	52,200	31,500	20,300
Other	55,100	38,100	24,100
Total foreign	348,700	303,000	235,800
Total NIKE	$1,710,800	$1,203,400	$877,400

 Gross margin improvement was primarily attributable to increased sales of higher margin products, increased management focus on improving product margins and inventory management. Fiscal 1988 earnings were also characterized by increased revenues and an improved margin, as well as a lower effective tax rate and revenue from other sources. In fiscal 1987, net income declined primarily due to decreased revenues caused by reduced quantities sold.

 Selling and administrative expenses in 1989 exceeded those in each of the previous two years due to increases in sales volume related expenses and in advertising. Total selling and administrative expenses as a percentage of revenues were 20.7% compared to 20.5% in 1988 and 23.3% in 1987.

 The funding of the acquisition of Cole Haan and construction of the Company's world headquarters building resulted in an increase in interest expense in 1989 and a reduction of interest income. Interest income is included in other income and separately disclosed in Note 12 of the financial statements. In 1988 and 1987, interest income increased due to an increased investment of cash in short-term instruments. Included as other income in 1988 is $9.3 million of interest income and $14 million received from the U.S. Government in settlement of litigation related to U.S. Customs duty, the latter increasing earnings per share by $.23. Other income in 1987 included a $3.7 million non-taxable gain partially offset by profit sharing expense and by the loss on disposition of two subsidiaries.

As a result of the Tax Reform Act of 1986, the Company's effective income tax rate for fiscal 1989 was 38% compared to 39% in 1988 and 51% in 1987. The tax rate exceeds the top statutory federal rate primarily due to state income taxes.

"Futures" orders booked for domestic delivery of footwear from June through November 1989 are approximately 9% higher in units and 23% higher in dollars than such orders booked in the comparable period of the prior year. "Futures" orders received are not necessarily indicative of total revenues for subsequent periods because: (1) the mix of "futures" and "at once" shipments may vary significantly from quarter to quarter and from year to year, and (2) they do not include orders for U.S. apparel, Cole Haan or for foreign operations, areas which management feels represent significant growth opportunities.

Liquidity and Capital Resources

The Company's financial condition remains strong. Assets at May 31, 1989 total $825 million, up from $709 million at the end of the previous year. Cash and equivalents at May 31, 1989 totalled $86 million, compared to $75 million at May 31, 1988. Working capital at May 31, 1989 was $124 million more than the previous year, a 41% rise, primarily because of increases in accounts receivable and inventory and a decrease in notes payable. The current ratio at May 31, 1989 was 3.0:1 compared to 2.2:1 at May 31, 1988.

The increase in inventory over the previous year is attributable to a higher footwear average unit cost and to an increased level of apparel and foreign inventories. Footwear quantities at May 31, 1989 are comparable to the quantities on hand at May 31, 1988. Inventory turned 5.1 times in 1989 compared to 5.0 times in 1988. Accounts receivable have increased in proportion to 1989 revenue growth and notes payable have decreased because of cash generated by operations.

Capital expenditures for 1989 aggregated $42 million. They are primarily attributable to the construction of a new world headquarters facility, the acquisition of the formerly leased eastern regional distribution facility, and electronic data processing equipment purchases. In 1988 and 1987, capital expenditures were $25 million and $12 million respectively. A significant portion of the 1988 expenditures were related to the construction of a new western regional distribution facility. Construction of the Company's new world headquarters building, which began in the fall of 1988, is being financed internally. This structure will be used to consolidate offices now occupying seven leased facilities, and it will cost an estimated $70 million. To date, the Company has expended $22 million on the project and there are current construction commitments of approximately $20 million. The Company has little invested in manufacturing plant and equipment because most of the manufacturing of NIKE products is done on a contract basis through independent factories.

The quarterly cash dividend of $.10 per share, initially declared in February 1984, was increased to $.15 in the second quarter of 1989. Dividends were declared in all four quarters during fiscal 1989. Based upon currently projected earnings and cash flow requirements, the Company anticipates continuing a dividend.

During 1989, the Company received ratings from Standard and Poor's Corporation and from Moody's Investors Service for a $100 million commercial paper program which was unused at May 31, 1989. The program was rated A2 by Standard and Poor's and P2 by Moody's. At May 31, 1989, the Company has $117 million in committed unused lines of credit available on its multiple option facility and revolving credit agreements. See note 6 of the Consolidated Financial Statements for further details concerning the Company's short-term borrowings. In May 1988, the Company borrowed

$85 million from available credit lines to help fund the acquisition of Cole Haan. NIKE's ratio of debt to equity at May 31, 1989 is .5:1 compared to .7:1 at May 31, 1988 and .5:1 at May 31, 1987. Management believes that funds generated by operations, together with currently available resources, will adequately finance 1990 working capital expenditures.

REPORT OF INDEPENDENT ACCOUNTANTS

Portland, Oregon
July 10, 1989

To the Board of Directors and
Shareholders of NIKE, Inc.

In our opinion, the accompanying consolidated balance sheet and the related consolidated statements of income, of cash flows and of shareholders' equity present fairly, in all material respects, the financial position of NIKE, Inc. and its subsidiaries at May 31, 1989 and 1988, and the results of their operations and their cash flows for each of the three years in the period ended May 31, 1989, in conformity with generally accepted accounting principles. These financial statements are the responsibility of the Company's management; our responsibility is to express an opinion on these financial statements based on our audits. We conducted our audits of these statements in accordance with generally accepted auditing standards which require that we plan and perform the audit to obtain reasonable assurance about whether the financial statements are free of material misstatement. An audit includes examining, on a test basis, evidence supporting the amounts and disclosures in the financial statements, assessing the accounting principles used and significant estimates made by management, and evaluating the overall financial statement presentation. We believe that our audits provide a reasonable basis for the opinion expressed above.

Price Waterhouse

NIKE, INC.
CONSOLIDATED STATEMENT OF INCOME *(in thousands, except per share data)*

	Year Ended May 31,		
	1989	1988	1987
Revenues	$1,710,803	$1,203,440	$877,357
Costs and expenses:			
Cost of sales	1,074,831	803,380	596,662
Selling and administrative	354,825	246,583	204,742
Interest (Notes 6 and 7)	13,949	8,004	8,475
Other (income) expense (Notes 4, 8, 11, and 12)	(3,449)	(20,722)	(6,201)
	1,440,156	1,037,245	803,678
Income before income taxes	270,647	166,195	73,679
Income taxes (Note 8)	103,600	64,500	37,800
Net income	$ 167,047	$ 101,695	$ 35,879
Net income per common share (Note 1)	$ 4.45	$ 2.70	$ .93
Average number of common and common equivalent shares (Note 1)	37,572	37,639	38,393

The accompanying notes to consolidated financial statements are an integral part of this statement.

NIKE, INC.
CONSOLIDATED BALANCE SHEET *(in thousands)*

Assets	May 31, 1989	1988
Current Assets:		
Cash and equivalents	$ 85,749	$ 75,357
Accounts receivable, less allowance for doubtful accounts of $7,824 and $6,164	296,350	258,393
Inventories (Note 2)	222,924	198,470
Deferred income taxes (Note 8)	18,504	8,569
Prepaid expenses	14,854	12,793
Total current assets	638,381	553,582
Property, plant and equipment (Notes 5 and 7)	154,314	112,022
Less accumulated depreciation	64,332	54,319
	89,982	57,703
Goodwill (Notes 1 and 3)	81,899	84,747
Other assets	15,148	13,063
	$825,410	$709,095

Liabilities and Shareholders' Equity		
Current Liabilities:		
Current portion of long-term debt (Note 7)	$ 1,884	$ 1,573
Notes payable to banks (Note 6)	39,170	135,215
Accounts payable (Note 6)	71,105	50,288
Accrued liabilities	76,543	59,073
Income taxes payable	27,201	8,617
Total current liabilities	215,903	254,766
Long-term debt (Note 7)	34,051	30,306
Non-current deferred income taxes and purchased tax benefits (Note 8)	13,352	11,949
Commitments and contingencies (Note 13)	—	—
Redeemable Preferred Stock (Note 9)	300	300
Shareholders' equity (Note 10):		
Common Stock at stated value:		
Class A convertible — 14,295 and 14,453 shares outstanding	171	173
Class B — 23,004 and 22,650 shares outstanding	2,700	2,696
Capital in excess of stated value	74,227	69,737
Foreign currency translation adjustment	(2,156)	(1,157)
Retained earnings	486,862	340,325
	561,804	411,774
	$825,410	$709,095

The accompanying notes to consolidated financial statements are an integral part of this statement.

NIKE, INC.
CONSOLIDATED STATEMENT OF CASH FLOWS *(in thousands)*

| | Year Ended May 31, | | |
	1989	1988	1987
Cash provided (used) by operations:			
Net income	$167,047	$101,695	$ 35,879
Income charges (credits) not affecting cash:			
Depreciation	14,775	14,020	12,078
Deferred income taxes and purchased tax benefits	(8,532)	(211)	8,486
Other	3,752	432	2,494
Changes in certain working capital components:			
(Increase) decrease in inventory	(24,454)	(60,082)	59,542
(Increase) decrease in accounts receivable	(37,957)	(64,187)	1,174
(Increase) decrease in other current assets	(2,061)	(5,624)	4,331
Increase in accounts payable, accrued liabilities and income taxes payable	56,871	32,976	8,462
Cash provided by operations	169,441	19,019	132,446
Cash provided (used) by investing activities:			
Additions to property, plant and equipment	(42,022)	(25,513)	(11,874)
Disposals of property, plant and equipment	2,565	8,863	1,728
Acquisition of Cole Haan:			
Goodwill	—	(82,044)	—
Net assets acquired	—	(13,086)	—
Additions to other assets	(1,014)	(1,445)	(930)
Cash used by investing activities	(40,471)	(113,225)	(11,076)
Cash provided (used) by financing activities:			
Additions to long-term debt	—	12	30,332
Reductions in long-term debt including current portion	(4,019)	(11,693)	(10,678)
Increase (decrease) in notes payable to banks	(96,045)	82,185	(18,489)
Proceeds from exercise of options	2,517	2,262	1,911
Issuance of common stock	—	5,813	—
Dividends—common and preferred	(20,510)	(14,904)	(15,188)
Purchase and retirement of common stock	—	(21,890)	—
Cash (used) provided by financing activities	(118,057)	41,785	(12,112)
Effect of exchange rate changes on cash	(521)	911	(529)
Net increase (decrease) in cash and equivalents	10,392	(51,510)	108,729
Cash and equivalents, beginning of year	75,357	126,867	18,138
Cash and equivalents, end of year	$ 85,749	$ 75,357	$126,867
Supplemental disclosure of cash flow information:			
Cash paid during the year for:			
Interest (net of amount capitalized)	$ 14,700	$ 9,300	$ 7,100
Income taxes	90,700	65,800	15,700
Supplemental schedule of noncash investing and financing activities:			
During August 1988 the Company purchased its eastern distribution facility which previously was under lease. In conjunction with the purchase, long-term liabilities were assumed as follows:			
Cost of eastern distribution facility	$ 9,519		
Cash paid	(1,444)		
Long-term liabilities assumed	$ 8,075		

The accompanying notes to consolidated financial statements are an integral part of this statement.

NIKE, INC.
CONSOLIDATED STATEMENT OF SHAREHOLDERS' EQUITY *(in thousands)*

	Common Stock				Capital In Excess of Stated Value	Foreign Currency Translation Adjustment	Retained Earnings	Total
	Class A		Class B					
	Shares	Amount	Shares	Amount				
Balance at May 31, 1986	15,051	$180	22,721	$2,697	$81,633	$ (507)	$232,843	$316,846
Stock options exercised			166	2	1,909			1,911
Conversion to Class B Common Stock	(453)	(6)	453	6				—
Translation of statements of foreign operations						(1,431)		(1,431)
Net income—year ended May 31, 1987							35,879	35,879
Dividends on Redeemable Preferred Stock							(30)	(30)
Dividends on Common Stock							(15,158)	(15,158)
Balance at May 31, 1987	14,598	174	23,340	2,705	83,542	(1,938)	253,534	338,017
Stock options exercised	174	2	109	1	2,259			2,262
Conversion to Class B Common Stock	(319)	(3)	319	3				—
Translation of statements of foreign operations						781		781
Net income—year ended May 31, 1988							101,695	101,695
Dividends on Redeemable Preferred Stock							(30)	(30)
Dividends on Common Stock							(14,874)	(14,874)
Purchase and retirement of Common Stock			(1,362)	(16)	(21,874)			(21,890)
Issuance of Common Stock			244	3	5,810			5,813
Balance at May 31, 1988	14,453	173	22,650	2,696	69,737	(1,157)	340,325	411,774
Stock options exercised	30	—	166	2	4,490			4,492
Conversion to Class B Common Stock	(188)	(2)	188	2				—
Translation of statements of foreign operations						(999)		(999)
Net income—year ended May 31, 1989							167,047	167,047
Dividends on Redeemable Preferred Stock							(30)	(30)
Dividends on Common Stock							(20,480)	(20,480)
	14,295	$171	23,004	$2,700	$74,227	$(2,156)	$486,862	$561,804

The accompanying notes to consolidated financial statements are an integral part of this statement.

NIKE, INC.
NOTES TO CONSOLIDATED FINANCIAL STATEMENTS

Note 1 — Summary of significant accounting policies:

Basis of consolidation:

The consolidated financial statements include the accounts of the Company and its subsidiaries. All significant intercompany transactions and balances have been eliminated. To facilitate the timely preparation of the consolidated financial statements, the accounts of certain foreign operations have been consolidated for fiscal years ending in April.

Recognition of revenues:

Revenues recognized include sales plus fees earned on sales by licensees.

Cash and equivalents:

Cash and equivalents represent cash and short-term, highly liquid investments with maturities of essentially three months or less.

Inventory valuation:

Inventories are stated at the lower of cost or market. Cost is determined using the last-in first-out (LIFO) method for substantially all inventories.

Property, plant and equipment and depreciation:

Property, plant and equipment are recorded at cost. Depreciation for financial reporting purposes is determined on a straight-line basis for buildings and leasehold improvements and principally on a declining balance basis for machinery and equipment.

Goodwill:

At May 31, 1989 the Company's excess of purchase cost over the fair value of net assets of businesses acquired was $81,899,000, net of amortization of $5,533,000. This excess is being amortized on a straight-line basis over periods of eight and forty years.

Foreign currency translation:

Assets and liabilities of foreign operations are translated into U.S. dollars at current exchange rates. Income and expense accounts are translated into U.S. dollars at average rates of exchange prevailing during the period. Adjustments resulting from translating foreign functional currency financial statements into U.S. dollars are taken directly to a separate component of shareholders' equity. Foreign currency transaction gains and losses are included in income.

Forward exchange contracts:

The Company enters into forward exchange contracts in order to reduce the impact of foreign currency fluctuations on primarily non-U.S. purchases of inventory. Gains or losses on these transactions are matched to inventory purchases and charged or credited to cost of sales as such inventory is sold.

Income taxes:

Deferred income taxes are recognized for timing differences between income for financial reporting purposes and taxable income. Income taxes are provided currently on earnings of foreign subsidiaries expected to be repatriated.

In December 1987 and 1988, the Financial Accounting Standards Board issued new standards on accounting for income taxes which require the use of the liability method for computing deferred income taxes. One of the principal differences from the deferred method used in these financial statements is that changes in tax rates and laws will be reflected in income from continuing operations in the period such changes are enacted; whereas under the deferred method such changes were reflected over time, if at all. The Company plans to adopt this statement in fiscal 1991, as permitted under the transition rules, but has not yet quantified the effect adoption will have on the consolidated financial statements.

Net income per common share:

Net income per common share is computed based on the weighted average number of common and common equivalent (stock option) shares outstanding for the periods reported.

Note 3 — Acquisition of Cole Haan Holdings, Inc.:

On May 24, 1988, NIKE acquired substantially all the stock of Cole Haan Holdings, Inc. (Cole Haan) and its subsidiaries. Cole Haan is a leading designer and marketer of high quality casual and dress shoes. The acquisition was accounted for using the purchase method of accounting. The purchase price was $80 million plus repayment of debt of $15 million. The Company paid for the purchase with $89.2 million in cash and by issuing 243,713 shares of NIKE stock, with a market value of $5.8 million, for the remainder.

Cole Haan's assets and liabilities have been recorded in the Company's consolidated balance sheet at their fair values at the acquisition date. At May 31, 1988, assets of the newly acquired company totalled $35 million, exclusive of goodwill. Since Cole Haan was acquired so close to NIKE's fiscal year end, its operating results for the few days of NIKE ownership were not material and are not included in the Company's 1988 consolidated statement of income. The excess of cost over the fair value of net assets acquired totalled approximately $82 million and has been accounted for as goodwill, which is being amortized over forty years.

The following unaudited combined pro forma information shows the results of the Company's operations as though the acquisition had occurred on June 1, 1987 and 1986:

	1988	1987
Revenues (in thousands)	$1,268,430	$924,461
Net income (in thousands)	$99,299	$34,220
Earnings per share	$2.64	$.89

The pro forma results of operations are not necessarily indicative of the actual results of operations that would have occurred had the purchase been made at the beginning of the respective periods, or of results which may occur in the future.

Note 4 — Customs Settlement:

During 1988, the Company settled a customs duty dispute with the U.S. Government relating to valuation methods used for certain NIKE imports from 1979 to 1981. This settlement resulted in a refund of duties and interest to the Company of approximately $14 million. The settlement proceeds are included in other income in the consolidated financial statements for the year ended May 31, 1988.

Note 12 — Interest income:

Included in other income for the three years ended May 31, 1989, 1988, and 1987 is interest income of $7,694,000, $9,321,000, and $7,230,000.

Note 13—Commitments and contingencies (in part):

In the fall of 1988, the Company began construction of a new world headquarters facility. The expected cost of the facility including land, buildings and improvements is approximately $70 million. The Company has expended $22 million to date, and has construction commitments of approximately $20 million as of May 31, 1989.

■ **GENERAL MOTORS**

Operating And Financial Review

Earnings

GM's net income was $4,224.3 million in 1989, down 13.0% from 1988. Net income per share of $1-2/3 par value common stock was $6.33, down 11.7%. Sales and revenues increased 2.7% to $126.9 billion.

Net income declined in 1989 from record 1988 results, due primarily to lower volume in the North American automotive market in the fourth quarter of the year and increased sales incentives due to competitive pressures.

In 1988, net income of $4,856.3 million was 36.8% higher than in 1987. Net income of $7.17 per share of $1-2/3 par value common stock in 1988 was up 42.5%.

Net income for 1988 included $0.35 per share of $1-2/3 par value common stock and $0.05 per share of Class H common stock resulting from an accounting change, adopted January 1, 1988, to include in inventory certain manufacturing overhead costs previously charged directly to expense.

Net income for 1989 and 1988 was also favorably affected by a lower statutory tax rate, a net tax credit reflecting the continuing amortization of investment tax credits earned in prior years, and tax benefits, amounting to $220.7 million and $353.9 million, or $0.36 and $0.58 per share, respectively, of $1-2/3 par value common stock, related to the utilization of loss carryforwards at certain overseas operations.

Dollar sales and revenues include price adjustments of $1.8 billion in 1989, $1.1 billion in 1988, and $3.2 billion in 1987.

Earnings on common stocks as a percent of average common stockholders' equity (including common stock subject to repurchase) was 12.0% in 1989, compared with 14.6% in 1988 and 11.3% in 1987.

Profit margin (net income as a percent of net sales and revenues), with GMAC on an equity basis, was 3.8% in 1989 and 4.4% in 1988. Cost of sales and other operating charges as a percent of net sales and revenues

of General Motors operations was 84.3% in 1989 and 84.8% in 1988.

Automotive Business

General Motors once again sold more automobiles than any other manufacturer in the world. Worldwide factory sales of vehicles to GM dealers totaled 7,946,000 units in 1989, down 2.0% from 1988. GM unit sales declined 6.6% in the United States and 0.1% in Canada, partially offset by an increase of 8.2% overseas, including a rise of 9.8% in Europe.

GM's worldwide factory sales of cars in 1989 were 5,735,000 units, down 2.5%. Truck sales, which account for over one-fourth of the Corporation's annual unit volume, were 2,211,000 units, down 0.7% from 1988.

In the United States, industry sales of cars and light-duty trucks declined 6.0% in 1989 to 14.9 million units. Industry sales were below 15 million units for the first time since 1984. In Europe, by contrast, industry sales remained strong throughout 1989.

GM's share of total U.S. retail vehicle sales declined to 34.6% in 1989 from 35.2% in 1988 and 34.7% a year earlier. GM's share of domestic car sales was 35.1%, compared with 36.2% in 1988 and 36.6% in 1987. GM dealers sold 1.7 million light-duty trucks, despite lower industry volume, and GM increased its market share to 34.9% in 1989 from 34.3% in 1988 and 31.5% in 1987. Trucks account for approximately one-third of GM's total unit sales in the U.S.

Of the 20 top-selling cars in the United States, nine were GM name-

plates, more than any other manufacturer. Of the 15 top-selling trucks, six were GM nameplates, also more than any other manufacturer.

Although 1989 income was down from 1988, GM's North American operating groups continued to be profitable, permitting a minimum payout of $50 per employe, or $22.1 million, under the profit sharing plan. Costs during the year included $1.5 billion in sales incentives.

GM's primary goal in North America is to profitably raise its market share. Doing so will require continued product innovation, quality improvement, cost reductions, and effective marketing programs.

GM is in the midst of an aggressive new product program, introducing as many new 1990 model cars and trucks as Ford, Chrysler, Toyota, and Honda combined. Between the 1990 and 1994 model years, GM plans to update 99% of its domestic car volume and almost 60% of its domestic truck volume.

The Corporation is also making significant strides in the area of product quality. In the 1989 J. D. Power Sales Satisfaction Index, GM was ranked as the top domestic manufacturer among car owners and GMC Truck as the top manufacturer among compact-truck owners. Moreover, in the 1989 J. D. Power Initial Quality Survey, the Buick LeSabre was the highest-ranked American model for trouble-free cars and was second among 154 domestic and import models. For the third straight year, Cadillac was the top domestic

WORLDWIDE FACTORY SALES

(Units in Thousands)	CARS			TRUCKS			TOTAL		
	1989	1988	1987	1989	1988	1987	1989	1988	1987
United States	3,238	3,516	3,592	1,599	1,661	1,520	4,837	5,177	5,112
Canada	414	411	344	323	327	238	737	738	582
Overseas*	2,083	1,955	1,857	289	238	214	2,372	2,193	2,071
TOTAL	5,735	5,882	5,793	2,211	2,226	1,972	7,946	8,108	7,765

*Includes units which are manufactured overseas by other companies and which are imported and sold by General Motors and affiliates.

Operating And Financial Review *(continued)*

nameplate for combined product quality and dealer service in the 1989 J. D. Power Customer Satisfaction Index.

Our Action Plan to reduce costs is resulting in noticeable improvement. The plan is designed to yield permanent annual cost savings of up to $13 billion by the end of 1990, reducing GM's break-even point and making it possible to earn a profit on lower volume levels. Permanent annual cost reductions in excess of $3 billion were achieved in 1989 through the plan, raising total cost savings from this plan to $11.5 billion since 1987.

The 1989 financial and operating performance of GM's overseas automotive businesses was once again very strong. Vehicle sales increased in Europe, Latin America, and Asia/Pacific markets, and overseas earnings were at a record level. Earnings

of $2,663.7 million in 1989 represented a 1.6% gain from $2,621.6 million in 1988. Overseas business units paid cash dividends of $1,820.1 million to GM in 1989 and $1,194.1 million in 1988.

In November 1989, the Corporation sold 20 million shares of Isuzu Motors Limited stock to a number of Japanese financial institutions. The sale reduced the Corporation's interest in Isuzu from 40.2% to 38.2% and favorably affected earnings by $82.8 million, or $0.14 per share of $1-2/3 par value common stock. The 38.2% interest exceeds GM's initial 34.2% interest in Isuzu. The strong commercial relationship between the two organizations in product manufacturing, development, and marketing is important to both parties and will further expand in new areas worldwide.

Prospects for the automotive industry over the next decade are discussed in the section titled "The 1990s: A Continuing Challenge" in the Message to Stockholders on page 2 of this Report.

General Motors Acceptance Corporation

GMAC's 1989 earnings of $1,110.7 million were down 6.5% from $1,187.6 million in 1988, due primarily to higher borrowing costs which narrowed interest rate margins. The 1989 earnings include $50.7 million resulting from the sale to Isuzu Motors Limited of GMAC's 51% interest in Isuzu Motors Finance Co., Ltd. Gross revenue was a record $14,503.8 million, up $1,004.2 million from 1988, as GMAC continued to expand its programs to serve the financing and insurance needs of GM customers and dealers.

Total financing revenue amounted to $11,215.5 million, up $570.9 million from 1988. Retail and lease financing revenue, the largest segment of GMAC's business, was $7,488.4 million, up $325.2 million from the prior year level. Revenue from leasing operations decreased 2.7% to $2,187.0 million. Wholesale financing revenue increased 24.8% to $1,540.1 million. Other income totaled $2,131.9 million in 1989, compared with $1,648.1 million in 1988. The increase was due primarily to interest earned on notes receivable from General Motors Corporation.

Insurance premiums earned by Motors Insurance Corporation decreased to $1,156.4 million in 1989 from $1,206.9 million in 1988.

Interest and discount expense rose 19.1% to $7,908.3 million in 1989, reflecting increased borrowing costs. Total earning assets of GMAC were a record $102.2 billion at December 31, 1989, up 4.7% from $97.6 billion at December 31, 1988. GMAC's total borrowings were $86.9 billion at December 31, 1989, a 6.1% increase over year-end 1988. Approximately 84% of 1989 borrowings supported United States operations.

Another Record Year for EDS

Electronic Data Systems Corporation (EDS) had another excellent year, achieving separate consolidated

RETAIL UNIT SALES OF CARS AND TRUCKS WORLDWIDE

(Units in Thousands)	1989	1988	Change from '88
Worldwide Industry	44,600	44,130	470
GM	7,979	8,265	(286)
As % of worldwide	17.9%	18.7%	(0.8 pts.)
United States:			
Industry	14,855	15,799	(944)
GM: cars	3,437	3,822	(385)
trucks	1,708	1,741	(33)
total	5,145	5,563	(418)
As % of U.S.	34.6%	35.2%	(0.6 pts.)
Foreign sponsored	4,071	4,215	(144)
As % of U.S.	27.4%	26.7%	0.7 pts.
Canada:			
Industry	1,480	1,562	(82)
GM	510	559	(49)
As % of Canada	34.5%	35.8%	(1.3 pts.)
International:			
Industry	28,265	26,769	1,496
GM: cars	2,023	1,863	160
trucks	301	280	21
total	2,324	2,143	181
As % of international	8.2%	8.0%	0.2 pts.
GM cars & trucks:			
Europe	1,595	1,450	145
West Germany	472	441	31
United Kingdom	395	348	47
As % of Europe	10.5%	10.0%	0.5 pts.
Latin America	361	342	19
Brazil	212	195	17
Mexico	72	48	24
Venezuela	7	36	(29)
Africa	29	37	(8)
Middle East	52	65	(13)
Asia/Pacific	287	249	38
Australia	98	92	6

Operating And
Financial Review*(continued)*

net income of $435.3 million in 1989, up 13.3% from 1988. Earnings per share attributable to Class E common stock on a post-split basis were $1.81, up from $1.57 in 1988 and $1.33 in 1987, and are based on the Available Separate Consolidated Net Income of EDS (described in Note 9 to the Financial Statements).

EDS is the world leader in systems integration and communication services. Sales to sources outside GM and its affiliates rose 25.0% in 1989 to $2,384.6 million, reflecting EDS's success in obtaining new business as well as growth through acquisitions. In addition, EDS continued to assist GM in a variety of automation projects being implemented in the Corporation's factories and offices.

EDS financial statements do not include the $2,179.5 million cost to GM of EDS customer contracts, computer software programs, and other intangible assets, including goodwill, arising from the acquisition of EDS by GM in 1984. This cost, plus the $343.2 million cost of contingent notes purchased in 1986, less certain income tax benefits, was assigned principally to intangible assets, including goodwill, and is being amortized by GM over the estimated useful lives of the assets acquired. Such amortization was $348.9 million in 1989, $386.6 million in 1988, and $385.7 million in 1987.

For the purpose of determining earnings per share and amounts available for dividends on common stocks, such amortization is charged against earnings attributable to GM's $1-2/3 par value common stock. The effect of EDS operations on the earnings attributable to $1-2/3 par value common stock was a net charge of $225.1 million in 1989, $286.1 million in 1988, and $257.0 million in 1987, consisting of the previously described amortization less related income tax benefits, profit on intercompany transactions, and the earnings of EDS attributable to $1-2/3 par value common stock. The net charge does not reflect any estimate of the savings realized by GM from the installation of new computer systems within GM operations.

SUMMARY FINANCIAL DATA–GMAC

Condensed Statement of Separate Consolidated Net Income

(Dollars in Millions)	1989	1988	1987
Financing Revenue:			
Retail and lease financing	$ 7,488.4	$ 7,163.2	$ 7,234.4
Leasing	2,187.0	2,247.0	2,397.7
Wholesale	1,540.1	1,234.4	1,229.8
Total financing revenue	11,215.5	10,644.6	10,861.9
Insurance premiums earned	1,156.4	1,206.9	1,176.4
Other income	2,131.9	1,648.1	1,362.4
Gross Revenue	14,503.8	13,499.6	13,400.7
Interest and discount	7,908.3	6,641.9	6,118.3
Other expenses	5,044.0	5,060.0	4,906.0
Total Expenses	12,952.3	11,701.9	11,024.3
Income before income taxes	1,551.5	1,797.7	2,376.4
Income taxes	440.8	610.1	923.2
Separate Consolidated Net Income	$ 1,110.7	$ 1,187.6	$ 1,453.2
Dividends paid to GM	$ 600.0	$ 1,000.0	$ 900.0

Condensed Consolidated Balance Sheet

(Dollars in Millions)	December 31, 1989	1988
Cash and investments in securities	$ 3,142.6	$ 3,272.0
Finance receivables–net	79,120.1	74,230.8
Notes receivable from General Motors Corporation	14,460.5	14,840.0
Other assets	6,839.2	6,698.1
Total Assets	$103,562.4	$99,040.9
Short-term debt	$ 54,415.4	$54,505.0
Accounts payable and other liabilities (including GM and affiliates–$2,897.7 and $3,515.5)	8,912.0	9,960.3
Long-term debt	32,453.0	27,370.4
Stockholder's equity	7,782.0	7,205.2
Total Liabilities and Stockholder's Equity	$103,562.4	$99,040.9

SUMMARY FINANCIAL DATA–EDS

(Dollars in Millions Except Per Share Amounts)	1989	1988	1987
Revenues:			
Systems and other contracts:			
GM and affiliates	$2,988.9	$2,837.0	$2,883.3
Outside customers	2,384.6	1,907.6	1,444.8
Interest and other income	93.3	99.5	99.6
Total Revenues	5,466.8	4,844.1	4,427.7
Costs and Expenses	4,786.5	4,254.7	3,903.4
Income Taxes	245.0	205.3	201.2
Separate Consolidated Net Income	$ 435.3	$ 384.1	$ 323.1
Available Separate Consolidated Net Income*	$ 171.0	$ 160.3	$ 139.1
Average number of shares of Class E common stock outstanding (in millions)**	94.5	101.8	105.2
Earnings Attributable to Class E Common Stock on a Per Share Basis**	$1.81	$1.57	$1.33
Cash dividends per share of Class E common stock**	$0.48	$0.34	$0.26

*Separate consolidated net income of EDS multiplied by a fraction, the numerator of which is the weighted average number of shares of Class E common stock outstanding and the denominator of which is currently 238.7 million shares (post-split). The denominator during 1988 and 1987 was 243.8 million shares (post-split). Available Separate Consolidated Net Income is determined quarterly.
**Adjusted to reflect the two-for-one stock split in the form of a 100% stock dividend declared February 5, 1990, payable to Class E common stockholders on March 10, 1990.

Operating And Financial Review *(continued)*

GM Hughes Electronics

Earnings of GM Hughes Electronics Corporation (GMHE) declined 2.6% to $781.2 million, while revenues increased 1.0% to $11,359.0 million. Earnings per share attributable to Class H common stock were $1.94 in 1989, compared with $2.01 in 1988 and $1.67 in 1987, and are based on the Available Separate Consolidated Net Income of GMHE (described in Note 9 to the Financial Statements).

Results for 1989 include a nonrecurring charge of $30.8 million, or $0.08 per share of Class H common stock, for costs associated with Hughes Aircraft employment reductions in anticipation of U.S. defense spending cutbacks, partially offset by a gain of $17.2 million, or $0.04 per share of Class H common stock, from the sale of a portion of Hughes Aircraft's stock

holdings in Nippon Avionics Co., Ltd.

GMHE is the world leader in defense electronics sales. In addition, GMHE serves commercial customers in such areas as automobile electronics and satellite communications. GMHE also provides direct support to GM through projects to automate the Corporation's factories and by supplying components and technologies for GM vehicles. GMHE is working with GM on approximately 150 projects to adapt aerospace technology to automotive products and operations.

For the purpose of determining earnings per share and amounts available for dividends on common stocks, the amortization of intangible assets arising from the acquisition of Hughes in 1985 is charged against earnings attributable to GM's $1-2/3

par value common stock. The effect of GMHE operations on the earnings attributable to $1-2/3 par value common stock was a net credit of $17.8 million in 1989 and a net charge of $31.6 million and $55.3 million in 1988 and 1987, respectively, consisting of amortization of the intangible assets, profit on intercompany transactions, and the earnings of GMHE attributable to $1-2/3 par value common stock. The net credit/charge does not reflect any estimate of the savings and improvements in product development or plant operation resulting from the application of GMHE technology to GM's operations.

Cash Flow

One of General Motors' underlying financial strengths is its substantial cash flow from operations. Net cash provided by operating activities with GMAC on an equity basis was $11,553.4 million in 1989, compared with $11,093.1 million in 1988. Net cash provided by operating activities, including GMAC, was $13,005.8 million in 1989, $14,476.6 million in 1988, and $13,596.4 million in 1987. Cash flow is expected to remain strong in 1990.

Cash and cash equivalents at December 31, 1989 with GMAC on an equity basis totaled $4,999.8 million, compared with $5,578.7 million a year earlier. The decrease in 1989 was due to an excess of net cash used in investing (primarily property expenditures) and financing (primarily repurchases of common stocks and cash dividends paid to stockholders) activities over net cash provided by operating activities. Including GMAC, cash and cash equivalents were $5,169.5 million at December 31, 1989, $5,800.3 million a year earlier, and $3,723.0 million at the end of 1987. The 1989 decrease was due primarily to an excess of net cash used in investing activities (primarily property expenditures and finance receivable acquisitions net of liquidations) over the amount of cash provided by operating and financing (primarily the net increase in long-term debt) activities.

GM's liquidity can also be measured by its current ratio (current assets to current liabilities with

SUMMARY FINANCIAL DATA–GMHE

(Dollars in Millions Except Per Share Amounts)	Years Ended December 31,		
	1989	**1988**	**1987**
Revenues:			
Net sales:			
Outside customers	$ 7,647.7	$ 7,518.2	$ 7,273.2
GM and affiliates	3,521.8	3,482.8	3,134.4
Other income-net	189.5	242.6	73.4
Total Revenues	11,359.0	11,243.6	10,481.0
Costs and Expenses	10,371.3	10,259.7	9,581.8
Income Taxes	355.3	349.3	378.1
Income before cumulative effect of accounting change	632.4	634.6	521.1
Cumulative effect of accounting change	–	18.7*	–
Separate Consolidated Net Income	632.4	653.3	521.1
Available Separate Consolidated Net Income:			
Adjustments to exclude the effect of purchase accounting**	148.8	148.8	148.8
Earnings of GMHE, Excluding Purchase Accounting Adjustments	$ 781.2	$ 802.1	$ 669.9
Available Separate Consolidated Net Income*	$ 188.1	$ 256.9	$ 219.2
Average number of shares of Class H common stock outstanding (in millions)	95.7	127.9	130.8
Earnings Attributable to Class H Common Stock on a Per Share Basis:			
Before cumulative effect of accounting change	$1.94	$1.96	$1.67
Cumulative effect of accounting change	–	0.05	–
Net earnings attributable to Class H common stock	$1.94	$2.01	$1.67
Cash dividends per share of Class H common stock	$0.72	$0.44	$0.36

*Effective January 1, 1988, accounting procedures at Delco Electronics were changed to include in inventory certain manufacturing overhead costs previously charged directly to expense.
**Amortization of intangible assets arising from the acquisition of Hughes Aircraft Company.
***Earnings of GMHE, excluding purchase accounting adjustments, multiplied by a fraction, the numerator of which is the weighted average number of shares of Class H common stock outstanding and the denominator of which is currently 400 million shares. Available Separate Consolidated Net Income is determined quarterly.

Operating And Financial Review *(continued)*

GMAC on an equity basis). At December 31, 1989 and 1988, the current ratio was 1.72 and 1.78, respectively.

Debt Changes

GM and its subsidiaries maintained a very strong balance sheet, providing substantial financial flexibility for the Corporation.

Long-term debt of GM and its subsidiaries with GMAC on an equity basis was $4,254.7 million at the end of 1989, an increase of $11.6 million during the year. The ratio of long-term debt to the total of long-term debt and stockholders' equity (excluding common stock subject to repurchase) was 10.8% at December 31, 1989, up from 10.6% at the end of 1988. The ratio of long-term debt and short-term loans payable to the total of this debt and stockholders' equity (excluding common stock subject to repurchase) was 15.8% at the end of 1989 compared to 14.8% at year-end 1988.

During 1989, notes and loans payable of GM and its subsidiaries, including GMAC (as detailed in Note 14 to the Financial Statements), increased 6.0% to $93,424.8 million at year-end from $88,130.1 million at December 31, 1988. This increase was due to an increase in long-term borrowing needs reflecting a decrease in net cash provided by operating activities. GM's fully consolidated ratio of debt to stockholders' equity (excluding common stock subject to repurchase) was 2.67 to 1 at December 31, 1989 compared to 2.47 to 1 a year earlier.

During 1988, notes and loans payable declined $563.3 million to $88,130.1 million at December 31, 1988. This decline was attributable to a reduction in long-term borrowing needs reflecting an increase in net cash provided by operating activities in 1988.

The senior long-term debt of GM and GMAC continues to be rated Aa3 by Moody's and AA– by Standard & Poor's. GMAC commercial paper retains the highest possible rating.

At year-end, GM and its subsidiaries, including GMAC, had unused short-term credit lines totaling approximately $19.0 billion and unused long-term credit agreements of approximately $1.3 billion.

Capital Spending

GM's worldwide capital expenditures were $7.5 billion in 1989, $5.6 billion in 1988, and $7.2 billion in 1987. Expenditures in 1989 were focused primarily on product development, in support of the Corporation's programs to continue to improve product quality and establish a more distinctive product identity for each of its divisions.

Worldwide expenditures for real estate, plants, and equipment were $4.6 billion in 1989, compared with $3.4 billion in 1988 and $4.8 billion in 1987. Of the 1989 expenditures, approximately 78% were in the United States (74% in 1988 and 79% in 1987), 7% in Canada (12% in 1988 and 10% in 1987), and 15% overseas (14% in 1988 and 11% in 1987).

Worldwide expenditures for special tools were $2.9 billion in 1989, $2.2 billion in 1988, and $2.4 billion in 1987.

Commitments for capital spending, including special tools, were $4.3 billion at December 31, 1989. Estimated capital expenditures of $6.5 billion in 1990 are expected to be financed primarily from cash flows provided by operating activities.

Stock Repurchase Program

GM's stock repurchase program is aimed at enhancing shareholder value. Under this program, the Corporation in March 1987 began to use a portion of its cash flow to repurchase up to 128 million shares of its $1-2/3 par value common stock and as many as five million shares of Class E common and ten million shares of Class H common stocks through open market purchases. The initially announced repurchase of the five million shares of Class E common stock was completed and two additional repurchase programs of five million shares each on a pre-split basis were announced in May 1988 and February 1990, respectively.

Through 1989, repurchases through

EMPLOYMENT, PAYROLLS, AND BENEFITS

	1989	1988	1987
Average worldwide employment			
GM (excluding units listed below)	628,500	624,000	673,100
GMAC	18,400	18,500	18,200
EDS	55,000	47,500	44,600
Hughes	73,200	75,700	77,500
Average number of employes	775,100	765,700	813,400
Worldwide payrolls (in millions)	$28,337.9	$27,548.6	$27,145.7
Average U.S. hourly employment*	299,800	309,700	344,700
U.S. hourly payrolls* (in millions)	$13,165.9	$13,242.0	$12,841.5
Average labor cost per hour worked— U.S. hourly*	$29.50	$27.90	$25.90
North American employment at December 31 (excluding GMAC, EDS, and Hughes)			
Salaried	100,700	99,900	106,500
Hourly	328,500	343,600	366,000
Total	429,200	443,500	472,500
Payments for benefit plans—U.S. (in billions)*			
Pensions	$ —**	$0.8	$1.4
Health care	2.9	3.0	2.9
Other	1.8	1.9	1.8
Total	$4.7	$5.7	$6.1
Equal employment opportunity*:			
Minorities as % of GM U.S. work force	21%	21%	21%
White-collar	15%	14%	14%
Blue-collar	23%	23%	23%
Women as % of GM U.S. work force	19%	19%	19%
White-collar	27%	27%	27%
Blue-collar	16%	17%	17%

*Excludes EDS and Hughes.
**Contribution not required by ERISA.

Operating And Financial Review *(continued)*

this program totaled 37.6 million $1-2/3 par value common shares, 9.8 million Class E common shares (pre-split), and 4.0 million Class H common shares. In 1989, the Corporation purchased a total of 9,856,604 $1-2/3 par value common shares at an average price of $42.76 per share, 2,951,709 Class E common shares at an average price of $50.53 per share on a pre-split basis, and 1,035,297 Class H common shares at an average price of $27.22 per share.

In addition to the stock repurchase program, the Corporation purchased $1-2/3 par value common, Class E common, and Class H common shares on the open market to satisfy share requirements for the incentive and benefits plans of the Corporation and its subsidiaries.

Dividend Policy

The Corporation's policy is to dis-tribute dividends on $1-2/3 par value common stock based on the outlook and indicated capital needs of the business. With respect to Class E common and Class H common stocks, the Corporation's current policy is to pay cash dividends approx-imately equal to 30% and 35% of the Available Separate Consolidated Net Income of EDS and GMHE, respec-tively, for the prior year.

On March 31, 1989, GM distributed a two-for-one stock split in the form of a 100% stock dividend on its $1-2/3 par value common stock.

Book Value

Book value per share of $1-2/3 par value common stock was $52.32 at the end of 1989, up from $48.92 a year earlier and $44.55 at the end of 1987. On a post-split basis, book value per share of Class E common stock increased to $13.41 from $12.54 and $11.41 at the end of 1988 and 1987, respectively. Book value per share of Class H common stock increased to $26.18 from $24.48 and $22.30 at the end of 1988 and 1987, respectively. Excluding common stock subject to repurchase, book value per share of Class H common stock would be $20.22 at the end of 1989.

Accounting Standards

During 1989, the Financial Account-ing Standards Board delayed imple-mentation of Statement of Financial Accounting Standards (SFAS) No. 96, Accounting for Income Taxes, until January 1, 1992, while continu-ing to encourage earlier voluntary adoption. GM has not adopted SFAS No. 96. The effect of the adoption of SFAS No. 96 is expected to be favorable to net income, but in an amount that the Corporation is unable to quantify at this time.

General Motors Operations with GMAC on an Equity Basis

The following presents financial data of the Corporation's manufacturing, wholesale marketing, defense, electronics, and computer service operations with the financing and insurance operations reflected on an equity basis consistent with reporting prior to 1988.

Statement of Consolidated Income (Dollars in Millions)	Years Ended December 31,	
	1989	**1988**
Net Sales and Revenues		
Manufactured products	$109,893.9	$108,075.9
Computer systems services	2,639.3	2,152.6
Total Net Sales and Revenues	112,533.2	110,228.5
Costs and Expenses		
Cost of sales and other operating charges, exclusive of items below	94,913.9	93,486.7
Selling, general, and administrative expenses	7,240.0	6,655.3
Depreciation and amortization of property	5,087.6	4,950.5
Amortization of intangible assets	505.5	545.1
Total Costs and Expenses	107,747.0	105,637.6
Operating Income	4,786.2	4,590.9
Other income less income deductions—net	2,331.2	1,847.4
Interest expense	(2,228.4)	(1,537.3)
Income before Income Taxes	4,889.0	4,901.0
Income taxes	1,733.2	1,492.5
Income after Income Taxes	3,155.8	3,408.5
Earnings of nonconsolidated affiliates	1,068.5	1,223.6
Income before cumulative effect of accounting change	4,224.3	4,632.1
Cumulative effect of accounting change	—	224.2
Net Income	$ 4,224.3	$ 4,856.3

Certain amounts for 1988 have been reclassified to conform with 1989 classifications.

Operating And
Financial Review*(continued)*

General Motors Operations with GMAC on an Equity Basis *(continued)*

Consolidated Balance Sheet (Dollars in Millions) ASSETS	December 31,	
	1989	**1988**
Current Assets		
Cash and cash equivalents	$ 4,999.8	$ 5,578.7
Other marketable securities	2,070.9	1,258.0
Total cash and marketable securities	7,070.7	6,836.7
Accounts and notes receivable:		
Trade	18,037.4	17,337.1
Nonconsolidated affiliates	3,758.8	3,742.5
Inventories	7,991.7	7,984.3
Contracts in process	2,073.3	2,035.4
Prepaid expenses and deferred income taxes	2,374.4	2,475.8
Total Current Assets	41,306.3	40,411.8
Equity in Net Assets of Nonconsolidated Affiliates	9,000.1	8,331.8
Other Investments and Miscellaneous Assets	5,761.8	5,636.0
Property	33,895.2	31,832.4
Intangible Assets	6,801.7	5,013.1
Total Assets	$96,765.1	$91,225.1

LIABILITIES AND STOCKHOLDERS' EQUITY		
Current Liabilities		
Accounts payable	$ 7,659.2	$ 7,750.2
Loans payable	2,301.7	1,930.9
Income taxes payable	706.4	157.4
Accrued liabilities	13,409.2	12,844.4
Total Current Liabilities	24,076.5	22,682.9
Long-Term Debt	4,254.7	4,243.1
Payable to GMAC	14,460.5	14,840.0
Capitalized Leases	311.0	292.6
Other Liabilities	15,584.3	11,795.6
Deferred Credits	1,445.6	1,699.2
Common Stock Subject to Repurchase	1,650.0	—
Stockholders' Equity	34,982.5	35,671.7
Total Liabilities and Stockholders' Equity	$96,765.1	$91,225.1

Certain amounts for 1988 have been reclassified to conform with 1989 classifications.

Operating And
Financial Review*(concluded)*

General Motors Operations with GMAC on an Equity Basis *(concluded)*

Statement of Consolidated Cash Flows (Dollars in Millions)	Years Ended December 31,	
	1989	1988
Cash Flows from Operating Activities		
Income before cumulative effect of accounting change	$ 4,224.3	$ 4,632.1
Adjustments to reconcile income before cumulative effect of accounting change to net cash provided by operating activities:		
Depreciation and amortization of property	5,087.6	4,950.5
Amortization of intangible assets	505.5	545.1
Net (gain) loss on sale of real estate, plants, and equipment	(3.1)	78.7
Net gain on sale of partial interest in Isuzu Motors Limited	(82.8)	—
Deferred income taxes and undistributed earnings of nonconsolidated affiliates	(107.6)	233.6
Change in operating assets and liabilities:		
Accounts receivable	(94.7)	2,193.6
Inventories excluding effect of accounting change	(7.4)	311.6
Contracts in process	(37.9)	(48.1)
Prepaid expenses	558.1	(698.3)
Accounts payable	(91.0)	662.4
Income taxes payable excluding effect of accounting change	512.2	(350.6)
Other liabilities	732.8	101.8
Other	357.4	(1,519.3)
Net Cash Provided by Operating Activities	11,553.4	11,093.1
Cash Flows from Investing Activities		
Investment in companies, net of cash acquired	(198.1)	(675.2)
Expenditures for real estate, plants, and equipment	(4,457.5)	(3,289.0)
Proceeds from disposals of real estate, plants, and equipment	379.0	296.5
Expenditures for special tools	(2,927.8)	(2,194.4)
Change in investing assets:		
Other marketable securities	(812.9)	100.5
Notes receivable	(355.7)	340.9
Accounts receivable	(266.2)	(1,420.0)
Net Cash Used in Investing Activities	(8,639.2)	(6,840.7)
Cash Flows from Financing Activities		
Net increase (decrease) in loans payable	370.8	(947.8)
Increase in long-term debt	967.1	1,074.9
Decrease in long-term debt	(955.5)	(781.2)
Net increase (decrease) in payable to GMAC	(379.5)	859.0
Repurchases of common stocks	(1,655.1)	(786.5)
Proceeds from issuing common stocks	173.2	253.0
Cash dividends paid to stockholders	(1,964.1)	(1,657.5)
Net Cash Used in Financing Activities	(3,443.1)	(1,986.1)
Effect of Exchange Rate Changes on Cash and Cash Equivalents	(50.0)	(35.5)
Net increase (decrease) in cash and cash equivalents	(578.9)	2,230.8
Cash and cash equivalents at beginning of the year	5,578.7	3,347.9
Cash and cash equivalents at end of the year	$ 4,999.8	$ 5,578.7

Responsibilities For Consolidated Financial Statements

The following consolidated financial statements of General Motors Corporation and subsidiaries were prepared by management which is responsible for their integrity and objectivity. The statements have been prepared in conformity with generally accepted accounting principles and, as such, include amounts based on judgments of management. Financial information elsewhere in this Annual Report is consistent with that in the financial statements.

Management is further responsible for maintaining a system of internal accounting controls, designed to provide reasonable assurance that the books and records reflect the transactions of the companies and that its established policies and procedures are carefully followed. From a stockholder's point of view, perhaps the most important feature in the system of control is that it is continually reviewed for its effectiveness and is augmented by written policies and guidelines, the careful selection and training of qualified personnel, and a strong program of internal audit.

Deloitte & Touche, independent auditors, are engaged to audit the consolidated financial statements of General Motors Corporation and its subsidiaries and issue reports thereon. Their audit is conducted in accordance with generally accepted auditing standards which comprehend a review of internal accounting controls and a test of transactions. The Independent Auditors' Report appears below.

The Board of Directors, through the Audit Committee (composed entirely of non-employe Directors), is responsible for assuring that management fulfills its responsibilities in the preparation of the financial statements. The Committee selects the independent auditors annually in advance of the Annual Meeting of Stockholders and submits the selection for ratification at the Meeting. In addition, the Committee reviews the scope of the audits and the accounting principles being applied in financial reporting. The independent auditors, representatives of management, and the internal auditors meet regularly (separately and jointly) with the Committee to review the activities of each, to ensure that each is properly discharging its responsibilities, and to assess the effectiveness of the system of internal accounting controls. It is management's conclusion that the system of internal accounting controls at December 31, 1989 provides reasonable assurance that the books and records reflect the transactions of the companies and that its established policies and procedures are complied with. To ensure complete independence, Deloitte & Touche have full and free access to meet with the Committee, without management representatives present, to discuss the results of their audit, the adequacy of internal accounting controls, and the quality of the financial reporting.

Chairman

Chief Financial Officer

Independent Auditors' Report

Deloitte & Touche

Renaissance Center
Detroit, Michigan 48243

February 14, 1990

General Motors Corporation, its Directors, and Stockholders:

We have audited the Consolidated Balance Sheet of General Motors Corporation and subsidiaries as of December 31, 1989 and 1988 and the related Statements of Consolidated Income and Consolidated Cash Flows for each of the three years in the period ended December 31, 1989. These financial statements are the responsibility of the Corporation's management. Our responsibility is to express an opinion on these financial statements based on our audits.

We conducted our audits in accordance with generally accepted auditing standards. Those standards require that we plan and perform the audit to obtain reasonable assurance about whether the financial statements are free of material misstatement. An audit includes examining, on a test basis, evidence supporting the amounts and disclosures in the financial statements. An audit also includes assessing the accounting principles used and significant estimates made by management, as well as evaluating the overall financial statement presentation. We believe that our audits provide a reasonable basis for our opinion.

In our opinion, such financial statements present fairly, in all material respects, the financial position of General Motors Corporation and subsidiaries at December 31, 1989 and 1988 and the results of their operations and their cash flows for each of the three years in the period ended December 31, 1989 in conformity with generally accepted accounting principles.

As discussed in Note 1 to the Financial Statements, effective January 1, 1988 the Corporation changed its method of accounting for certain manufacturing overhead costs.

Consolidated Financial Statements

Statement of Consolidated Income

For the Years Ended December 31, 1989, 1988, and 1987
(Dollars in Millions Except Per Share Amounts)

	1989	1988	1987
Net Sales and Revenues (Note 1)			
Manufactured products	$109,610.3	$107,815.2	$ 99,912.7
Financial services	11,216.9	10,664.9	10,920.8
Computer systems services	2,384.6	1,907.6	1,444.8
Other income (Note 2)	3,720.1	3,253.9	2,592.1
Total Net Sales and Revenues	126,931.9	123,641.6	114,870.4
Costs and Expenses			
Cost of sales and other operating charges, exclusive of items below (Note 7)	94,682.6	93,241.9	86,996.5
Selling, general, and administrative expenses	8,583.2	7,999.9	7,180.0
Interest expense (Note 14)	8,757.2	7,232.9	7,080.4
Depreciation of real estate, plants, and equipment (Note 1)	5,157.8	5,047.0	5,039.7
Amortization of special tools (Note 1)	1,441.8	1,432.1	2,155.5
Amortization of intangible assets (Note 1)	568.6	601.9	631.7
Other deductions (Note 2)	1,342.4	1,351.0	1,378.1
Total Costs and Expenses	120,533.6	116,906.7	110,461.9
Income before Income Taxes	6,398.3	6,734.9	4,408.5
United States, foreign, and other income taxes (Note 8)	2,174.0	2,102.8	857.6
Income before cumulative effect of accounting change	4,224.3	4,632.1	3,550.9
Cumulative effect of accounting change (Note 1)	–	224.2	–
Net Income	4,224.3	4,856.3	3,550.9
Dividends on preferred and preference stocks (Note 17)	34.2	26.0	13.7
Earnings on Common Stocks	$ 4,190.1	$ 4,830.3	$ 3,537.2
Earnings Attributable to Common Stocks:			
$1-2/3 par value before cumulative effect of accounting change	$ 3,831.0	$ 4,195.0	$ 3,178.9
Cumulative effect of accounting change	–	218.1	–
Net earnings attributable to $1-2/3 par value	$ 3,831.0	$ 4,413.1	$ 3,178.9
Class E	$ 171.0	$ 160.3	$ 139.1
Class H before cumulative effect of accounting change	$ 188.1	$ 250.8	$ 219.2
Cumulative effect of accounting change	–	6.1	–
Net earnings attributable to Class H	$ 188.1	$ 256.9	$ 219.2
Average number of shares of common stocks outstanding (in millions):			
$1-2/3 par value	604.3	615.7	631.5
Class E on a post-split basis (Note 16)	94.5	101.8	105.2
Class H	95.7	127.9	130.8
Earnings Per Share Attributable to Common Stocks (Note 9):			
$1-2/3 par value before cumulative effect of accounting change	$6.33	$6.82	$5.03
Cumulative effect of accounting change	–	0.35	–
Net earnings attributable to $1-2/3 par value	$6.33	$7.17	$5.03
Class E on a post-split basis (Note 16)	$1.81	$1.57	$1.33
Class H before cumulative effect of accounting change	$1.94	$1.96	$1.67
Cumulative effect of accounting change	–	0.05	–
Net earnings attributable to Class H	$1.94	$2.01	$1.67

Certain amounts for 1988 have been reclassified to conform with 1989 classifications. Reference should be made to notes on pages 29 through 44.

Consolidated Balance Sheet

December 31, 1989 and 1988 (Dollars in Millions Except Per Share Amounts)	1989	1988
ASSETS		
Cash and cash equivalents (Note 10)	$ 5,169.5	$ 5,800.3
Other marketable securities	5,043.8	4,381.1
Total cash and marketable securities (Note 10)	10,213.3	10,181.4
Finance receivables—net (Note 11)	92,354.6	87,476.9
Accounts and notes receivable (less allowances)	5,447.4	4,540.6
Inventories (less allowances) (Note 1)	7,991.7	7,984.3
Contracts in process (less advances and progress payments of $2,630.7 and $2,174.4) (Note 1)	2,073.3	2,035.4
Net equipment on operating leases (Note 13)	5,131.1	5,005.1
Prepaid expenses and deferred charges	3,914.7	5,156.6
Other investments and miscellaneous assets (less allowances)	5,050.2	4,482.1
Property (Note 1):		
Real estate, plants, and equipment—at cost (Note 13)	63,390.7	60,806.5
Less accumulated depreciation (Note 13)	34,849.7	32,794.7
Net real estate, plants, and equipment	28,541.0	28,011.8
Special tools—at cost (less amortization)	5,453.5	3,918.9
Total property	33,994.5	31,930.7
Intangible assets—at cost (less amortization) (Note 1)	7,126.3	5,270.0
Total Assets	$173,297.1	$164,063.1

LIABILITIES AND STOCKHOLDERS' EQUITY		
Liabilities		
Accounts payable (principally trade)	$ 7,707.8	$ 7,896.9
Notes and loans payable (Note 14)	93,424.8	88,130.1
United States, foreign, and other income taxes (Note 8)	5,671.4	4,930.3
Capitalized leases	261.5	294.8
Other liabilities (Note 15)	28,195.2	25,520.6
Deferred credits (including investment tax credits—$915.4 and $1,160.4)	1,403.9	1,618.7
Total Liabilities	136,664.6	128,391.4
Common Stock Subject to Repurchase (Note 1)	1,650.0	—
Stockholders' Equity (Notes 3, 4, 5, 16, and 17)		
Preferred stocks ($5.00 series, $153.0; $3.75 series, $81.4)	234.4	234.4
Preference stocks (E $0.10 series, $1.0; H $0.10 series, $1.0)	2.0	2.0
Common stocks:		
$1-2/3 par value (issued, 605,683,572 and 306,456,671 shares)	1,009.5	510.7
Class E (issued, 48,830,764 and 50,646,603 shares)	4.9	5.1
Class H (issued, 35,162,664 and 128,388,969 shares)	3.5	12.8
Capital surplus (principally additional paid-in capital)	2,614.0	6,235.2
Net income retained for use in the business	31,230.7	28,970.5
Subtotal	35,099.0	35,970.7
Accumulated foreign currency translation and other adjustments	(116.5)	(299.0)
Total Stockholders' Equity	34,982.5	35,671.7
Total Liabilities and Stockholders' Equity	$173,297.1	$164,063.1

Certain amounts for 1988 have been reclassified to conform with 1989 classifications. Reference should be made to notes on pages 29 through 44.

Statement of Consolidated Cash Flows

For the Years Ended December 31, 1989, 1988, and 1987 (Dollars in Millions)	1989	1988	1987
Cash Flows from Operating Activities			
Income before cumulative effect of accounting change	$ 4,224.3	$ 4,632.1	$ 3,550.9
Adjustments to reconcile income before cumulative effect of accounting change to net cash provided by operating activities:			
Depreciation of real estate, plants, and equipment	3,680.3	3,561.0	3,454.4
Depreciation of equipment on operating leases	1,477.5	1,486.0	1,585.3
Amortization of special tools	1,441.8	1,432.1	2,155.5
Amortization of intangible assets	568.6	601.9	631.7
Amortization of discount and issuance costs on debt issues	263.2	256.5	217.0
Provision for financing losses	841.9	820.8	671.0
Pension expense net of cash contributions	810.4	(300.3)	327.3
Net (gain) loss on sale of real estate, plants, and equipment	(3.1)	78.7	156.6
Net gain on sale of partial interest in Isuzu Motors Limited and its affiliates	(133.5)	–	–
Other investments, miscellaneous assets, and deferred credits	(350.9)	(1,661.3)	(580.8)
Change in operating assets and liabilities:			
Accounts receivable	(856.3)	3,145.8	(1,629.0)
Inventories excluding effect of accounting change	(7.4)	311.6	(704.6)
Contracts in process	(37.9)	(48.1)	(110.3)
Prepaid expenses and deferred charges	273.5	(240.7)	(924.9)
Real estate mortgages held for sale	(114.3)	(79.9)	403.7
Accounts payable	(189.1)	635.9	782.2
Income taxes excluding effect of accounting change	678.2	(370.9)	1,893.7
Other liabilities	700.4	(45.1)	1,961.4
Other	(261.8)	260.5	(244.7)
Net Cash Provided by Operating Activities	13,005.8	14,476.6	13,596.4
Cash Flows from Investing Activities			
Investment in companies, net of cash acquired	(121.3)	(675.2)	(110.0)
Expenditures for real estate, plants, and equipment	(4,577.3)	(3,432.1)	(4,804.4)
Proceeds from disposals of real estate, plants, and equipment	490.6	296.5	385.5
Expenditures for special tools	(2,927.8)	(2,194.4)	(2,346.2)
Change in investing assets:			
Other marketable securities	(662.7)	(284.8)	234.2
Finance receivables–acquisitions	(100,688.9)	(89,472.6)	(96,260.5)
Finance receivables–liquidations	94,957.7	88,727.9	92,407.7
Proceeds from sales of receivables	–	–	2,393.8
Finance receivables–other	11.6	(1,558.5)	(7,717.5)
Notes receivable	(50.5)	173.1	(152.0)
Equipment on operating leases	(1,603.5)	(932.9)	(602.0)
Net Cash Used in Investing Activities	(15,172.1)	(9,353.0)	(16,571.4)
Cash Flows from Financing Activities			
Net increase (decrease) in short-term loans payable	844.7	2,643.3	(540.3)
Increase in long-term debt	14,422.1	7,689.9	14,333.7
Decrease in long-term debt	(10,235.3)	(11,153.0)	(8,774.6)
Repurchases of common stocks	(1,655.1)	(786.5)	(729.8)
Proceeds from issuing common and preference stocks	173.2	253.0	1,152.3
Cash dividends paid to stockholders	(1,964.1)	(1,657.5)	(1,667.9)
Net Cash Provided by (Used in) Financing Activities	1,585.5	(3,010.8)	3,773.4
Effect of Exchange Rate Changes on Cash and Cash Equivalents	(50.0)	(35.5)	(118.9)
Net increase (decrease) in cash and cash equivalents	(630.8)	2,077.3	679.5
Cash and cash equivalents at beginning of the year	5,800.3	3,723.0	3,043.5
Cash and cash equivalents at end of the year	$ 5,169.5	$ 5,800.3	$ 3,723.0

Certain amounts for 1988 and 1987 have been reclassified to conform with 1989 classifications. Reference should be made to notes on pages 29 through 44.

Notes To
Financial Statements

NOTE 1. Significant Accounting Policies

Principles of Consolidation

The consolidated financial statements include the accounts of General Motors Corporation (General Motors, GM, or the Corporation) and domestic and foreign subsidiaries which are more than 50% owned. The accounts of General Motors Acceptance Corporation (GMAC), GM's wholly owned finance subsidiary and its subsidiaries, including Motors Insurance Corporation (MIC), have been added, account by account, to those of the statements of GM and its manufacturing, marketing, defense, electronics, and computer service subsidiaries. General Motors' share of earnings or losses of associates in which at least 20% of the voting securities is owned is included in consolidated income under the equity method of accounting (see Note 2).

Revenue Recognition

Sales are generally recorded by the Corporation when products are shipped to independent dealers. Provisions for normal dealer sales incentives and returns and allowances are made at the time of sale. Costs related to special sales incentive programs are recognized as sales reductions when these programs are determinable.

Certain sales under long-term contracts, primarily in the defense business, are recorded using the percentage-of-completion method of accounting. Under this method, sales are recorded equivalent to costs incurred plus a portion of the profit expected to be realized on the contract, determined based on the ratio of costs incurred to estimated total costs at completion. Profits expected to be realized on contracts are based on the Corporation's estimates of total sales value and cost at completion. These estimates are reviewed and revised periodically throughout the lives of the contracts, and adjustments to profits resulting from such revisions are recorded in the accounting period in which the revisions are made. Estimated losses on contracts are recorded in the period in which they are identified.

Effective with finance receivables acquired on or after January 1, 1988, earnings are accounted for over the terms of the receivables on the interest method as required by Statement of Financial Accounting Standards No. 91, Accounting for Nonrefundable Fees and Costs Associated with Originating or Acquiring Loans and Initial Direct Costs of Leases. The effect of this change was not material. In the case of finance receivables in which the face amount includes the finance charge (principally retail financing), prior to 1988, earnings were accounted for over the terms of the receivables on the sum-of-the-digits (rule of 78ths) basis. On finance receivables in which the face amount represents the principal (principally wholesale, interest-bearing financing, and leasing), the interest is taken into income as accrued; unpaid interest accrued at the balance sheet date is included in Finance receivables—net.

Insurance premiums are earned on a basis related to coverage provided over the terms of the policies (principally pro rata). Commission costs and premium taxes incurred in acquiring new business are deferred and amortized over the terms of the related policies on the same basis as premiums are earned. The liability for losses and claims includes a provision for unreported losses, based on past experience, net of the estimated salvage and subrogation recoverable.

Provision for Financing Losses

Losses arising from repossession of the collateral supporting doubtful accounts are charged off as soon as disposition of the collateral has been effected and the amount of the deficiency has been determined. Where repossession has not been effected, losses are charged off as soon as it is determined that the collateral cannot be repossessed, generally not more than 150 days after default.

Loss allowances on finance receivables are maintained in amounts considered by management to be appropriate in relation to receivables outstanding.

Inventories

Effective January 1, 1988, accounting procedures were changed to include in inventory certain manufacturing overhead costs previously charged directly to expense. The effect of this change on 1988 earnings was a favorable adjustment of $0.35 per share of $1-2/3 par value common stock and $0.05 per share of Class H common stock.

Inventories are stated generally at cost, which is not in excess of market. The cost of substantially all domestic inventories other than the inventories of GM Hughes Electronics Corporation (GMHE) is determined by the last-in, first-out (LIFO) method. If the first-in, first-out (FIFO) method of inventory valuation had been used for inventories valued at LIFO cost, such inventories would have been $2,445.4 million higher at December 31, 1989 and $2,525.3 million higher at December 31, 1988. As a result of decreases in U.S. LIFO inventories, certain LIFO inventory quantities carried at lower costs prevailing in prior years, as compared with the costs of current purchases, were liquidated in 1989 and 1988. These inventory adjustments favorably affected income before income taxes by approximately $244.8 million in 1989 and $20.5 million in 1988. The cost of inventories outside the United States and of GMHE is determined generally by FIFO or average cost methods.

Major Classes of Inventories (Dollars in Millions)	1989	1988
Productive material, work in process, and supplies	$3,816.9	$3,958.7
Finished product, service parts, etc.	4,174.8	4,025.6
Total	$7,991.7	$7,984.3

(continued)

Notes To
Financial Statements *(continued)*

NOTE 1. *(continued)*

Contracts in Process

Contracts in process are stated at costs incurred plus estimated profit less amounts billed to customers and advances and progress payments received. Engineering, tooling, manufacturing, and applicable overhead costs, including administrative, research and development, and selling expenses, are charged to costs and expenses when they are incurred. Under certain contracts with the United States Government, progress payments are received based on costs incurred on the respective contracts. Title to the inventories relating to such contracts (included in contracts in process) vests with the United States Government.

Depreciation and Amortization

Depreciation is provided based on estimated useful lives of groups of property generally using accelerated methods, which accumulate depreciation of approximately two-thirds of the depreciable cost during the first half of the estimated useful lives.

Expenditures for special tools are amortized over their estimated useful lives. Amortization is applied directly to the asset account. Replacement of special tools for reasons other than changes in products is charged directly to cost of sales.

GMAC provides for depreciation of automobiles and other equipment on operating leases or in company use generally on a straight-line basis.

Income Taxes

Investment tax credits are generally deferred and amortized over the lives of the related assets (the "deferral method") for General Motors Corporation, GMAC, and Electronic Data Systems Corporation (EDS). GMHE recognizes investment tax credits as a reduction of income tax expense in the year that the assets which give rise to the credits are placed in service (the "flow-through method").

The tax effects of timing differences between pretax accounting income and taxable income (principally related to depreciation, sales and product allowances, vehicle instalment sales, benefit plans expense, profits on long-term contracts, lease transactions, provision for financing losses, and policy and warranty) are deferred. Provisions are made for estimated United States and foreign income taxes, less available tax credits and deductions, which may be incurred on remittance of the Corporation's share of subsidiaries' undistributed earnings less those deemed to be indefinitely reinvested.

Product-Related Expenses

Expenditures for advertising and sales promotion and for other product-related expenses are charged to costs and expenses as incurred; provisions for estimated costs related to product warranty are made at the time the products are sold. Expenditures for research and development are charged to expenses as incurred and amounted to $5,247.5 million in 1989, $4,753.8 million in 1988, and $4,361.2 million in 1987.

Foreign Currency Translation

Exchange and translation losses included in net income in 1989, 1988, and 1987 amounted to $105.0 million, $8.9 million, and $21.0 million, respectively.

Related-Party Transactions

At December 31, 1989 and 1988, $1,246.4 million and $743.2 million, respectively, of interest-bearing loans were outstanding to various affiliates of General Motors Corporation and its subsidiaries.

Acquisitions and Intangible Assets

Effective December 31, 1985, the Corporation acquired Hughes Aircraft Company (Hughes) and its subsidiaries for $2.7 billion in cash and cash equivalents and 100 million shares of General Motors Class H common stock having an estimated total value of $2,561.9 million and which carried certain guarantees. On February 28, 1989, the Corporation and the Howard Hughes Medical Institute (Institute) reached agreement to terminate the Corporation's then-existing guarantee obligations with respect to the Institute's holding of Class H common stock. Under terms of the agreement: (i) the Corporation purchased 35 million shares of Class H common stock from the Institute on February 28, 1989; (ii) the Institute received put options exercisable under most circumstances at $30 per share on March 1, 1991, 1992, 1993, and 1995 for 20 million, 10 million, 10 million, and 15 million shares, respectively; (iii) the Corporation will have the option to call the Institute's shares from March 1, 1989 until February 28, 1991, 1992, 1993, and 1995 for 20 million, 10 million, 10 million, and 15 million shares, respectively, at a call price of $35 per share for all shares except for the 15 million shares callable until February 28, 1995, for which the call price is $37.50 per share; and (iv) the Corporation paid to the Institute $675 million in cash and approximately $300 million in notes (the aggregate value of the cash and notes was charged to capital surplus).

The acquisition of Hughes was accounted for as a purchase. The purchase price exceeded the net book value of Hughes by $4,244.7 million, which was assigned as follows: $500.0 million to patents and related technology, $125.0 million to the future economic benefits to the Corporation of the Hughes Long-Term Incentive Plan (LTIP), and $3,619.7 million to other intangible assets, including goodwill. The amounts assigned to the various intangible asset categories are being amortized on a straight-line basis: patents and related technology over 15 years, the future economic benefits of the Hughes LTIP over five years, and other intangible assets over 40

(continued)

Notes To
Financial Statements *(continued)*

NOTE 1. *(concluded)*

years. Amortization is applied directly to the asset accounts.

For the purpose of determining earnings per share and amounts available for dividends on common stocks, the amortization of intangible assets arising from the acquisition of Hughes is charged against earnings attributable to $1-2/3 par value common stock. The effect on the 1989, 1988, and 1987 earnings attributable to $1-2/3 par value common stock was a net credit (charge) of $17.8 million, ($31.6) million, and ($55.3) million, respectively, consisting of the amortization of the intangible assets arising from the acquisition, the profit on inter-company transactions, and the earnings of GMHE attributable to $1-2/3 par value common stock.

On October 18, 1984, the Corporation acquired EDS and its subsidiaries for $2,501.9 million. The acquisition was consummated through an offer to exchange EDS common stock for either (a) $44 in cash or (b) $35.20 in cash plus two-tenths of a share of Class E common stock plus a nontransferable contingent promissory note issued by GM. This note is payable seven years after closing in an amount equal to .2 times the excess of $62.50 ($31.25 post-split) over the market price of the Class E common stock at the maturity date of the note. Contingent notes were issued in denominations termed "Note Factors," each of which represents five contingent notes. Holders were allowed to tender their notes for prepayment at discounted amounts beginning in October 1989.

If the market price of Class E common stock at the maturity date of the notes were to equal the market price at December 31, 1989, $54.63 a share (pre-split), the aggregate additional consideration for contingent notes outstanding at December 31, 1989 would be $82.5 million. Any additional consideration would be charged to goodwill and amortized over the remaining life of that asset.

The acquisition of EDS was accounted for as a purchase. The purchase price in excess of the net book value of EDS, $2,179.5 million, was assigned principally to existing customer contracts, $1,069.9 million, computer software programs developed by EDS, $646.2 million, and other intangible assets, including goodwill, $290.2 million. The cost assigned to these assets is being amortized on a straight-line basis over five years for computer software programs, about seven years for customer contracts, ten years for goodwill, and varying periods for the remainder. Amortization is applied directly to the asset accounts.

For the purpose of determining earnings per share and amounts available for dividends on common stocks, the amortization of these assets is charged against earnings attributable to $1-2/3 par value common stock. The effect on the 1989, 1988, and 1987 earnings attributable to $1-2/3 par value common stock was a net charge of $225.1 million, $286.1 million, and $257.0 million, respectively, consisting of the amortization of the intangible and other assets arising from the acquisition less related income tax effects, the profit on intercom-

pany transactions, and the earnings of EDS attributable to $1-2/3 par value common stock.

The intangible assets of GMAC mortgage operations, related to the acquisition of mortgage servicing rights, are amortized over periods that generally match future net servicing revenues.

NOTE 2. Other Income and Other Deductions

(Dollars in Millions)	1989	1988	1987
Other Income:			
Insurance premiums	$ 570.4	$ 697.7	$ 720.2
Interest income	1,980.4	1,793.9	1,319.8
Other	1,211.7	731.2	535.6
Equity in earnings (losses) of associates	(42.4)	31.1	16.5
Total Other Income	$3,720.1	$3,253.9	$2,592.1

Interest income reflects nonfinancing interest income, while other income primarily relates to gains recognized by GMAC on the sale of finance receivables, mortgage servicing revenue, and MIC investment income.

	1989	1988	1987
Other Deductions:			
Insurance losses and loss adjustment expenses	$ 442.3	$ 546.5	$ 616.5
Provision for financing losses	841.9	820.8	671.0
Other	58.2	(16.3)	90.6
Total Other Deductions	$1,342.4	$1,351.0	$1,378.1

NOTE 3. General Motors Incentive Program

The General Motors Incentive Program consists of the General Motors 1987 Stock Incentive Plan and the General Motors 1987 Performance Achievement Plan. The Program is administered by the Incentive and Compensation Committee of the Board of Directors (the Committee).

Stock Incentive Plan

Under the 1987 Stock Incentive Plan (the Plan), the Committee may grant options and other rights (including stock appreciation rights, restricted stock units, and contingent payment rights) to key employes during the period from June 1, 1987 through May 31, 1992. The aggregate number of shares for which options and other rights may be granted under the Plan is 50 million shares of $1-2/3 par value common stock, 10 million shares (post-split) of Class E common stock, and 10 million shares of Class H common stock.

Incentive and nonqualified stock options granted under the Plan generally are exercisable one-half after one year and one-half after two years from the dates of grant; the option prices are 100% of fair market value on the dates of grant. The options generally expire ten years from the dates of grant and are subject to earlier termination under certain conditions.

(continued)

Notes To
Financial Statements *(continued)*

NOTE 3. *(concluded)*

Changes in the status of outstanding options were as follows:

$1-2/3 par value common stock	Option Prices	Shares Under Option
Outstanding at		
January 1, 1987	$19.13-$38.60	8,103,608
Granted	40.85	2,346,480
Exercised: Options	19.13-38.60	(1,202,576)
SARs	19.13-38.60	(353,660)
Terminated	23.25-40.85	(153,704)
Outstanding at		
December 31, 1987	19.13-40.85	8,740,148
Granted	37.47	3,198,420
Exercised: Options	19.13-40.85	(715,306)
SARs	19.13-38.60	(175,350)
Terminated	23.25-40.85	(122,440)
Outstanding at		
December 31, 1988	19.13-40.85	10,925,472
Granted	41.50	3,060,195
Exercised: Options	19.13-40.85	(2,628,417)
SARs	19.13-38.60	(407,222)
Terminated	25.00-41.50	(115,378)
Outstanding at		
December 31, 1989	$19.13-$41.50	10,834,650

Stock appreciation rights (SARs) have been granted to certain officers of the Corporation in prior years, but no SARs or contingent payment rights were granted in 1989, 1988, or 1987. SARs provide holders with the right to receive cash equal in value to the appreciation in the Corporation's common stock over the option price of the shares under option. They may be exercised only upon surrender of the related options and expire with the related options.

The Corporation intends to continue to deliver newly issued $1-2/3 par value common stock upon the exercise of the stock options. Options for 6,226,870 shares were exercisable at December 31, 1989; the maximum number of shares for which additional options and other rights may be granted under the Plan was 29,876,785 shares of $1-2/3 par value common stock, 6,126,788 shares (post-split) of Class E common stock, and 6,333,743 shares of Class H common stock at December 31, 1989.

Each restricted stock unit (Unit) relates to one share of $1-2/3 par value common stock, Class E common stock, or Class H common stock, as determined by the Committee at the time of grant. The Units entitle the employe to receive, without payment to the Corporation, shares of common stock in consideration for services performed. Such Units vest over specified periods generally ranging up to three years from the date of grant. In 1989, the Committee granted Units relating to 3,632,924 shares of $1-2/3 par value common stock, 1,043,596 shares (post-split) of Class E common stock, and 1,375,725 shares of Class H common stock.

Performance Achievement Plan

Under the provisions of the 1987 Performance Achievement Plan, the Committee established target awards for the four-year period ending in 1992. Awards are established based on targeted relationships between Corporation earnings and worldwide industry sales during the award periods; the percentages of the target awards ultimately distributed to the participants are determined by the Committee based on actual results in relation to the established goals and individual performance.

NOTE 4. EDS Incentive Plans

The GM Board of Directors approved and adopted the 1984 Electronic Data Systems Corporation Stock Incentive Plan in accordance with stockholder approval obtained in connection with GM's acquisition of EDS. Under this Plan, shares, rights, or options to acquire up to 80 million shares (post-split) of Class E common stock may be granted or sold during the ten-year life of the Plan.

The EDS incentive and compensation committee has granted to key employes a total of 19,495,458 shares (post-split) of Class E common stock at prices up to $0.05 per share (post-split). The Class E common shares granted under the Plan are subject to restrictions and generally vest over a ten-year period from the date the stock rights are granted.

In 1985, the committee also granted incentive stock options under the provisions of the 1984 Plan. The option price is equal to 100% of the fair market value of Class E common stock on the date the options were granted. These incentive stock options expire six years from the date of grant and are subject to earlier termination under certain conditions. Changes in the status of outstanding options (on a post-split basis) were as follows:

Class E common stock	Option Prices	Shares Under Option
Outstanding at		
January 1, 1987	$17.91	7,575,500
Exercised	17.91	(154,902)
Terminated	17.91	(445,698)
Outstanding at		
December 31, 1987	17.91	6,974,900
Exercised	17.91	(270,958)
Terminated	17.91	(169,228)
Outstanding at		
December 31, 1988	17.91	6,534,714
Exercised	17.91	(2,233,062)
Terminated	17.91	(286,426)
Outstanding at		
December 31, 1989	$17.91	4,015,226

Options for 4,015,226 shares of Class E common stock (post-split) were exercisable at December 31, 1989; the maximum number of shares for which additional shares, rights, or options may be granted under the Plan was 54,434,306 shares (post-split) at December 31, 1989.

Notes To
Financial Statements *(continued)*

NOTE 5. GMHE Incentive Plans

In 1985, stockholder approval was obtained in connection with GM's acquisition of Hughes for a GMHE Incentive Plan. Under this Plan, shares, rights, or options to acquire up to 20 million shares of Class H common stock may be granted during the ten-year life of the Plan.

The GM Incentive and Compensation Committee may grant options and other rights to acquire shares of Class H common stock under the provisions of the GMHE Plan. The option price is equal to 100% of the fair market value of Class H common stock on the date the options were granted. These nonqualified options generally expire ten years from the dates of grant and are subject to earlier termination under certain conditions.

Changes in the status of outstanding options were as follows:

Class H common stock	Option Prices	Shares Under Option
Outstanding at		
January 1, 1987	$19.75	78,910
Granted	24.34-24.69	764,100
Terminated	24.34	(4,400)
Outstanding at		
December 31, 1987	19.75-24.69	838,610
Granted	30.00-30.25	818,375
Exercised	19.75-24.60	(44,530)
Terminated	24.34-30.25	(72,510)
Outstanding at		
December 31, 1988	19.75-30.25	1,539,945
Granted	27.57	994,765
Exercised	19.75-24.60	(42,576)
Terminated	27.57-30.00	(106,850)
Outstanding at		
December 31, 1989	$19.75-$30.25	2,385,284

Options for 98,457 shares of Class H common stock were exercisable at December 31, 1989; the maximum number of shares for which additional options and other rights may be granted under the Plan was 16,919,336 shares at December 31, 1989.

NOTE 6. Pension Program and Postemployment Benefits

The Corporation and its subsidiaries have a number of defined benefit pension plans covering substantially all employes. Plans covering U.S. and Canadian represented employes generally provide benefits of negotiated stated amounts for each year of service as well as significant supplemental benefits for employes who retire with 30 years of service before normal retirement age. The benefits provided by the plans covering its U.S. and Canadian salaried employes, and employes in certain foreign locations, are generally based on years of service and the employe's salary history. The Corporation and its subsidiaries also have certain nonqualified pension plans covering executives which are based on targeted wage replacement percentages and are generally unfunded.

Plan assets are primarily invested in United States government obligations, equity and fixed income securities, commingled pension trust funds, GM preference stock valued at approximately $866.1 million as of the measurement date in 1989, and insurance contracts. The Corporation's funding policy with respect to its qualified plans is to contribute annually not less than the minimum required by applicable law and regulation nor more than the maximum amount which can be deducted for Federal income tax purposes.

Total pension expense of the Corporation and its subsidiaries amounted to $810.8 million in 1989, $544.4 million in 1988, and $714.6 million in 1987. Net periodic pension cost (credit) for 1989, 1988, and 1987 of U.S. plans and plans of subsidiaries outside the United States included the components shown below.

1989	U.S. Plans	Non-U.S. Plans
	(Dollars in Millions)	
Benefits earned during the year	$ 661.2	$ 90.7
Interest accrued on benefits earned in prior years	3,331.6	335.4
Return on assets		
—Actual	($6,443.9)	($532.2)
—Less deferred gain	3,025.6 (3,418.3)	204.5 (327.7)
Net amortization	87.0	(7.9)
Net periodic pension cost	$ 661.5	$ 90.5
1988		
Benefits earned during the year	$ 616.6	$ 83.1
Interest accrued on benefits earned in prior years	3,190.3	301.4
Return on assets		
—Actual	$ 56.1	$ 25.7
—Plus deferred loss	(3,420.2)(3,364.1)	(394.2) (368.5)
Net amortization	74.9	(47.0)
Net periodic pension cost (credit)	$ 517.7	($ 31.0)
1987		
Benefits earned during the year	$ 798.2	$ 27.7
Interest accrued on benefits earned in prior years	2,718.0	150.9
Return on assets		
—Actual	($7,436.6)	($586.0)
—Less deferred gain	4,608.4 (2,828.2)	304.5 (281.5)
Net amortization	122.5	(74.9)
Net periodic pension cost (credit)	$ 810.5	($177.8)

(continued)

Notes To
Financial Statements *(continued)*

NOTE 6. *(concluded)*

(Dollars in Millions)	U.S. Plans				Non-U.S. Plans			
	1989		1988		1989		1988	
	Assets Exceed Accum. Benefits	Accum. Benefits Exceed Assets	Assets Exceed Accum. Benefits	Accum. Benefits Exceed Assets	Assets Exceed Accum. Benefits	Accum. Benefits Exceed Assets	Assets Exceed Accum. Benefits	Accum. Benefits Exceed Assets
Actuarial present value of benefits based on service to date and present pay levels								
Vested	$14,300.3	$16,948.5	$12,967.7	$16,506.2	$1,969.9	$1,261.0	$1,971.1	$1,063.1
Nonvested	614.9	3,731.4	644.2	3,097.8	161.1	38.1	274.2	30.0
Accumulated benefit obligation	14,915.2	20,679.9	13,611.9	19,604.0	2,131.0	1,299.1	2,245.3	1,093.1
Additional amounts related to projected pay increases	1,553.6	78.5	1,500.1	69.9	154.7	225.9	146.5	241.4
Total projected benefit obligation based on service to date	16,468.8	20,758.4	15,112.0	19,673.9	2,285.7	1,525.0	2,391.8	1,334.5
Plan assets at fair value	21,166.0	18,885.9	18,932.4	17,477.9	3,174.2	8.6	3,538.4	—
Projected benefit obligation (in excess of) or less than plan assets	4,697.2	(1,872.5)	3,820.4	(2,196.0)	888.5	(1,516.4)	1,146.6	(1,334.5)
Unamortized net amount resulting from changes in plan experience and actuarial assumptions	(915.0)	(1,093.7)	(93.9)	(72.4)	120.3	(221.0)	246.6	(22.4)
Unamortized prior service cost	16.5	1,612.8	20.9	1,745.9	334.0	203.3	347.2	—
Unamortized net obligation or (asset) at date of adoption	(1,946.1)	1,480.0	(2,139.4)	1,614.0	(696.1)	417.6	(1,045.6)	429.3
Adjustment for unfunded pension liabilities	—	(1,920.6)	—	—	—	(180.4)	—	—
Net prepaid pension cost (accrued liability) recognized in the Consolidated Balance Sheet	$ 1,852.6	($ 1,794.0)	$ 1,608.0	$ 1,091.5	$ 646.7	($1,296.9)	$ 694.8	($ 927.6)

The table above reconciles the funded status of the Corporation's U.S. and non-U.S. plans with amounts recognized in the Corporation's Consolidated Balance Sheet at December 31, 1989 and 1988.

Measurement dates used for the Corporation's principal U.S. plans are October 1 for GM's plans (including Delco Electronics Corporation) and EDS, and December 1, 1989 and 1988 and December 31, 1987 for Hughes plans. For non-U.S. plans, the measurement dates used are October 1 for certain foreign plans and December 1 for Canadian plans.

The weighted average discount rate used in determining the actuarial present values of the projected benefit obligation shown in the table for U.S. plans was 9.5% at December 31, 1989 and 10.0% at December 31, 1988 and for non-U.S. plans was 9.8% at December 31, 1989 and 10.1% at December 31, 1988. The rate of increase in future compensation levels of applicable U.S. employes was 5.4% at December 31, 1989 and 5.6% at December 31, 1988 and of applicable non-U.S. employes was 5.5% at December 31, 1989 and 5.1% at December 31, 1988. Benefits under the hourly plans are generally not based on wages and therefore no benefit escalation beyond existing negotiated increases was included. The expected long-term rate of return on assets used in determining pension expense for U.S. plans was 10.1% for 1989 and 10.0% for 1988 and for non-U.S. plans was 10.5% for 1989 and 10.7% for 1988. The assumptions for non-U.S. plans were developed on a basis consistent with that for U.S. plans, adjusted to reflect prevailing economic conditions and interest rate environments.

In addition to providing pension benefits, the Corporation and certain of its subsidiaries provide certain health care and life insurance benefits for retired employes. Substantially all of the Corporation's employes, including employes in some foreign countries, may become eligible for those benefits if they reach normal retirement age while working for the Corporation. The Corporation recognizes the cost of providing those benefits primarily by expensing the cost as incurred. The cost of such benefits amounted to $1,067.4 million in 1989, $1,130.6 million in 1988, and $982.8 million in 1987.

A program for early retirement or special separation was offered to certain salaried employes. Expenses accrued in connection with the program were $144.8 million in 1989, $144.1 million in 1988, and $437.7 million in 1987.

Notes To
Financial Statements *(continued)*

NOTE 7. Special Provision for Scheduled Plant Closings and Other Restructurings

In 1986, the Corporation announced plans to close certain manufacturing and assembly plants over the next three years and to restructure certain other operations. The 1986 results of operations included a special provision of $1,287.6 million for costs associated with these scheduled plant closings and other restructurings that were reasonably estimable at the time. This provision included $802.9 million for scheduled plant closings in the U.S. and $484.7 million for various other restructurings of foreign operations. During 1989, 1988, and 1987, a net of $148.1 million, $218.6 million, and $151.3 million, respectively, was charged against this reserve for costs incurred related to the plant closings.

NOTE 8. United States, Foreign, and Other Income Taxes

(Dollars in Millions)	1989	1988	1987
Taxes estimated to be payable currently:			
United States Federal	$1,017.0	$1,628.3	($ 626.1)
Foreign	1,180.3	552.6	(176.8)
State and local	93.6	76.8	92.7
Total	2,290.9	2,257.7	(710.2)
Taxes deferred—net:			
United States Federal	(314.3)	(172.9)	1,210.0
Foreign	472.0	253.4	506.6
State and local	(28.5)	44.3	83.8
Total	129.2	124.8	1,800.4
Investment tax credits deferred—net:			
United States Federal	(225.3)	(263.2)	(243.9)
Foreign	(20.8)	16.5)	11.3
Total	(246.1)	(279.7)	(232.6)
Total taxes	$2,174.0	$2,102.8*	$ 857.6

*Excluding effect of accounting change.

Investment tax credits entering into the determination of taxes estimated to be payable currently amounted to $30.9 million in 1989, $13.5 million in 1988, and $155.1 million in 1987.

The deferred taxes (credit) for timing differences consisted principally of the following: 1989—$797.3 million for depreciation, $5.6 million for sales and product allowances, ($111.8) million for vehicle instalment sales, ($547.0) million for benefit plans expense, ($159.9) million for profits on long-term contracts, ($340.0) million for lease transactions, ($58.4) million provision for financing losses, and ($63.4) million for policy and warranty; 1988—$602.6 million for depreciation, $100.5 million for sales and product allowances, ($217.2) million for vehicle instalment sales, ($329.6) million for benefit plans expense, ($290.0) million for profits on long-term contracts, ($126.8) million for lease

transactions, ($102.8) million provision for financing losses, ($242.5) million for policy and warranty, and $190.2 million for uniform capitalization of inventory costs; and 1987—$1,306.3 million for depreciation, $156.9 million for sales and product allowances, $676.7 million for vehicle instalment sales, $99.8 million for benefit plans expense, ($246.4) million for profits on long-term contracts, $305.7 million for lease transactions, ($105.6) million for sales of finance receivables, and ($85.4) million provision for financing losses.

Income before income taxes included the following components:

(Dollars in Millions)	1989	1988	1987
Domestic income	$2,967.3	$3,170.8	$2,470.3
Foreign income	3,431.0	3,564.1	1,938.2
Total	$6,398.3	$6,734.9	$4,408.5

The consolidated income tax was different than the amount computed using the United States statutory income tax rate for the reasons set forth in the following table:

(Dollars in Millions)	1989	1988	1987
Expected tax at U.S. statutory income tax rate	$2,175.4	$2,289.9	$1,763.4
State and local income taxes	45.7	95.2	100.0
Investment tax credits amortized	(277.0)	(293.2)	(387.7)
Utilization of loss carry-forwards at certain foreign operations	(220.7)	(353.9)	(297.9)
Tax effect of foreign dividends	345.6	206.9	2.1
Tax rate changes on reversing timing differences	(117.9)	(126.6)	(161.5)
Research and experimentation credit	(28.6)	–	(63.3)
Other adjustments	251.5	284.5	(97.5)
Consolidated income tax	$2,174.0	$2,102.8*	$ 857.6

*Excluding effect of accounting change.

NOTE 9. Earnings Per Share Attributable to and Dividends on Common Stocks

Earnings per share attributable to common stocks have been determined based on the relative amounts available for the payment of dividends to holders of $1-2/3 par value common, Class E common, and Class H common stocks. The effect on earnings per share of $1-2/3 par value common stock resulting from the assumed exercise of outstanding options, the delivery of stock awards, and the assumed conversion of the preference shares discussed in Note 17 is not material. The operations of the EDS and GMHE Incentive Plans and the assumed conversion of the preference shares do not have a material dilutive effect on earnings per share of Class E common or Class H common stocks, respectively, at this time.

(continued)

Notes To
Financial Statements *(continued)*

NOTE 9. *(concluded)*

Dividends on the $1-2/3 par value common stock are declared out of the earnings of GM and its subsidiaries, excluding the Available Separate Consolidated Net Income of EDS and GMHE.

Dividends on the Class E common stock are declared out of the Available Separate Consolidated Net Income of EDS earned since the acquisition of EDS by GM. The Available Separate Consolidated Net Income of EDS is determined quarterly and is equal to the separate consolidated net income of EDS, excluding the effects of purchase accounting adjustments arising from the acquisition of EDS, multiplied by a fraction, the numerator of which is the weighted average number of shares of Class E common stock outstanding during the period and the denominator of which is currently 238.7 million shares (post-split). The denominator decreases as shares are purchased by EDS and increases as shares are used for EDS employe benefit plans. The denominator during 1988 and 1987 was 243.8 million shares (post-split).

Dividends on the Class H common stock are declared out of the Available Separate Consolidated Net Income of GMHE earned since the acquisition of Hughes by GM. The Available Separate Consolidated Net Income of GMHE is determined quarterly and is equal to the separate consolidated net income of GMHE, excluding the effects of purchase accounting adjustments arising from the acquisition of Hughes, multiplied by a fraction, the numerator of which is the weighted average number of shares of Class H common stock outstanding during the period and the denominator of which is currently 400 million shares.

The denominators used in determining the Available Separate Consolidated Net Income of EDS and GMHE are adjusted as deemed appropriate by the Board of Directors to reflect subdivisions or combinations of the Class E common and Class H common stocks and to reflect certain transfers of capital to or from EDS and GMHE.

Dividends may be paid on common stocks only when, as, and if declared by the Board of Directors in its sole discretion. The Board's policy with respect to $1-2/3 par value common stock is to distribute dividends based on the outlook and the indicated capital needs of the business. The current policy of the Board with respect to the Class E common and Class H common stocks is to pay cash dividends approximately equal to 30% and 35% of the Available Separate Consolidated Net Income of EDS and GMHE, respectively, for the prior year.

NOTE 10. Cash and Marketable Securities

(Dollars in Millions)	1989 Cost	1989 Market Value	1988 Cost	1988 Market Value
Cash, time deposits, and certificates of deposit	$ 3,916.4	$ 3,916.7	$ 3,258.6	$ 3,258.6
Bonds, notes, and other securities:				
United States government and other governmental agencies and authorities	1,110.8	1,118.8	2,858.8	2,858.5
States, municipalities, and political subdivisions	1,354.7	1,400.2	2,008.6	2,027.2
Other	3,168.1	3,227.3	1,499.7	1,533.5
Total bonds, notes, and other securities	5,633.6	5,746.3	6,367.1	6,419.2
Preferred stocks with mandatory redemption terms	71.5	72.5*	91.8	92.5*
Common stocks:				
Public utilities	34.9	75.7	34.9	53.0
Banks, trust and insurance companies	14.3	29.4	11.8	21.9
Industrial and miscellaneous	200.8	486.7	193.7	389.0
Total common stocks	250.0	591.8	240.4	463.9
Total cash and marketable securities	9,871.5	$10,327.3	9,957.9	$10,234.2
Adjustment to value common stocks at market	341.8		223.5	
Book value of cash and marketable securities	$10,213.3		$10,181.4	

*Based on estimated market value.

Cash equivalents are defined as short-term, highly liquid investments with original maturities of 90 days or less.

Supplemental disclosure of cash flow information is as follows:

(Dollars in Millions)	1989	1988	1987
Cash paid (refunded) during the years for:			
Interest	$8,613.8	$7,406.3	$6,908.5
Income taxes	1,540.1	(177.0)	(453.0)
Noncash investing and financing activities—capital leases	67.0	47.4	142.9

Notes To
Financial Statements *(continued)*

NOTE 11. Finance Receivables—Net

The distribution of maturities of finance receivables outstanding at December 31, 1989 and 1988 is summarized as follows:

(Dollars in Millions)	1989	1988
Retail, lease financing, and leasing receivables		
Past due		
Over 30 days	$ 187.0	$ 118.0
30 days or less	503.6	472.3
Due in following year	40,411.3	40,534.6
Due in second following year	21,138.3	20,223.1
Due thereafter	25,938.5	22,567.5
Total	88,178.7	83,915.5
Wholesale receivables (principally due on demand)	10,526.4	9,629.3
Term loans to dealers and others	3,488.3	3,075.6
Other	1,534.8	1,176.7
Total finance receivables	103,728.2	97,797.1
Less:		
Unearned income	10,082.8	9,145.2
Allowance for financing losses	1,290.8	1,175.0
Total finance receivables—net	$ 92,354.6	$87,476.9
Repossessions (included above)	$345.5	$343.4

The aggregate amount of total receivables maturing in each of the five years following December 31, 1989 is as follows: 1990—$54,433.8 million; 1991—$21,857.3 million; 1992—$15,026.5 million; 1993—$8,587.4 million; 1994—$2,942.3 million; and 1995 and thereafter—$880.9 million.

The following table presents an analysis of the allowance for financing losses for 1989, 1988 and 1987.

(Dollars in Millions)	1989	1988	1987
Allowance for financing losses at beginning of the year	$1,175.0	$ 979.4	$726.7
Provision for financing losses			
Non-recourse increment—			
retail	563.8	332.8	282.1
Other	278.1	488.0	388.9
Total	841.9	820.8	671.0
Charge-offs	(827.1)(	695.2)(	493.5)
Recoveries and other	101.0	70.0	75.2
Allowance for financing losses at end of the year	$1,290.8	$1,175.0	$979.4

The Corporation's finance subsidiary's recourse liability under the limited guaranties connected with the sale in prior years of certain retail finance receivables is generally 5% of the outstanding balances in the pools. The amount recorded for this potential liability totaled $22.8 million at December 31, 1989 and $69.5 million at December 31, 1988. GMAC's retail instalment obligations servicing portfolio at December 31, 1989 amounted to $1.4 billion, compared with $3.8 billion at December 31, 1988. The gains or losses on the sales of receivables are recorded as other income.

NOTE 12. General Motors Acceptance Corporation and Subsidiaries

Condensed Consolidated Balance Sheet (Dollars in Millions)	1989	1988
Cash and investments in securities	$ 3,142.6	$ 3,272.0
Finance receivables—net	79,120.1	74,230.8
Notes receivable from General Motors Corporation	14,460.5	14,840.0
Other assets	6,839.2	6,698.1
Total Assets	$103,562.4	$99,040.9
Short-term debt	$ 54,415.4	$54,505.0
Accounts payable and other liabilities (including GM and affiliates—$2,897.7 and $3,515.5)	8,912.0	9,960.3
Long-term debt	32,453.0	27,370.4
Stockholder's equity	7,782.0	7,205.2
Total Liabilities and Stockholder's Equity	$103,562.4	$99,040.9

Condensed Statement of Separate Consolidated Net Income (Dollars in Millions)	1989	1988	1987
Gross Revenue	$14,503.8	$13,499.6	$13,400.7
Interest and discount	7,908.3	6,641.9	6,118.3
Other expenses	5,044.0	5,060.0	4,906.0
Total Expenses	12,952.3	11,701.9	11,024.3
Income before income taxes	1,551.5	1,797.7	2,376.4
Income taxes	440.8	610.1	923.2
Separate Consolidated Net Income	$ 1,110.7	$ 1,187.6	$ 1,453.2
Dividends paid to GM	$ 600.0	$ 1,000.0	$ 900.0

Notes To
Financial Statements *(continued)*

NOTE 13. Real Estate, Plants, and Equipment and Accumulated Depreciation

(Dollars in Millions)	1989	1988
Real estate, plants, and equipment (Note 14):		
Land	$ 673.2	$ 627.1
Land improvements	1,711.5	1,687.7
Leasehold improvements—less amortization	185.6	203.0
Buildings	12,445.3	12,161.4
Machinery and equipment	41,125.6	40,034.5
Furniture and office equipment	2,843.2	2,653.6
Satellites and related facilities	504.6	336.0
Capitalized leases	1,170.2	1,045.3
Construction in progress	2,731.5	2,057.9
Total	$63,390.7	$60,806.5
Accumulated depreciation:		
Land improvements	$ 968.7	$ 942.6
Buildings	5,731.0	5,579.8
Machinery and equipment	25,468.1	23,978.3
Furniture and office equipment	1,849.0	1,578.6
Satellites and related facilities	192.1	150.6
Capitalized leases	640.8	564.8
Total	$34,849.7	$32,794.7

Foreign currency translation adjustments had the effect of increasing gross property by $268.7 million in 1989 and increasing net property by $92.4 million.

The gross book value of equipment on operating leases was $8,197.0 million at the end of 1989 and $8,491.0 million at the end of 1988. The accumulated depreciation for equipment on operating leases was $3,065.9 million at the end of 1989 and $3,485.9 million at the end of 1988.

The lease payments applicable to equipment on operating leases maturing in each of the five years following December 31, 1989 are as follows: 1990–$1,729.2 million; 1991–$1,371.3 million; 1992–$851.9 million; 1993–$210.2 million; and 1994–$5.6 million.

NOTE 14. Notes and Loans Payable

(Dollars in Millions)	Weighted Average Interest Rate	1989	1988
Notes, loans, and debentures:			
Payable within one year	Various	$56,717.1	$56,516.1
Payable beyond one year:			
U.S. Dollars:			
1990	–	–	6,888.9
1991	9.6%	8,702.7	5,207.8
1992	9.3%	6,545.8	3,852.7
1993	8.4%	4,118.2	2,819.7
1994	8.7%	3,410.6	956.9
1995 and after	9.1%	8,210.2	6,892.5
Other currencies	Various	6,846.8	6,305.9
Subordinated indebtedness	Various	182.5	207.0
Unamortized discount		(1,309.1)(	1,517.4)
Total		$93,424.8	$88,130.1

The Corporation and its subsidiaries maintain bank lines of credit that are supported by bank commitment fees and compensating balances against certain lines of credit. Compensating balances, which are not subject to withdrawal restrictions, are maintained at a level required to provide the same income that a fee would generate. Commitment fees incurred by the Corporation amounted to $15.3 million in 1989, $22.5 million in 1988, and $18.3 million in 1987. Compensating balances maintained by the Corporation averaged $31.2 million for 1989 and $102.7 million for 1988.

At December 31, 1989, the Corporation and its subsidiaries had unused short-term credit lines of approximately $19.0 billion and unused long-term credit agreements of approximately $1.3 billion.

Short-term borrowings are primarily entered into by GMAC. Commercial paper is offered in the United States, Canada, and Europe in varying terms ranging up to 270 days. The weighted average interest rates on commercial paper at December 31, 1989, 1988, and 1987 were 9.05%, 9.22%, and 7.68%, respectively. Master notes represent borrowings on a demand basis arranged generally under agreements with trust departments of certain banks. The weighted average interest rates on master notes at December 31, 1989, 1988, and 1987 were 8.39%, 9.14%, and 7.09%, respectively. Commercial paper and master notes obligations were $33,816.9 million and $4,536.8 million, respectively, at December 31, 1989 and $34,573.2 million and $4,751.8 million, respectively, at December 31, 1988.

Short-term borrowing amounts during the years shown were as follows:

(Dollars in Millions)	1989	1988	1987
Maximum amount outstanding at any month-end	$48,686.3	$47,376.5	$46,806.9
Average borrowings outstanding during the year	$47,161.0	$44,304.6	$45,819.3
Weighted average short-term interest rates*	9.37%	7.67%	6.99%
Weighted average commercial paper rates**	9.46%	7.66%	6.78%

*Based on the approximate average aggregate amount outstanding during the year and the cost of borrowings.
**Rates have been determined by relating commercial paper costs for each year to the daily average dollar amounts outstanding.

In 1981, the Corporation and a subsidiary arranged a private financing of $500 million in 14.7% notes due 1991. An option to acquire certain real estate in 1991 was also granted. The option holder may deliver the notes in payment for the real estate.

Total interest cost incurred in 1989, 1988, and 1987 amounted to $8,859.4 million, $7,297.8 million, and $7,177.9 million, respectively, of which $102.2 million, $64.9 million, and $97.5 million, related to certain real estate, plants, and equipment acquired in those years, was capitalized.

Notes To
Financial Statements *(continued)*

NOTE 15. Other Liabilities

(Dollars in Millions)	1989	1988
Taxes, other than income taxes	$ 1,202.2	$ 1,204.6
Payrolls	1,839.8	1,955.6
Employe benefits	3,298.1	1,632.4
Warranties, dealer and customer allowances, claims, discounts, etc.	6,801.5	7,561.7
Unpaid insurance losses, loss adjustment expenses, and unearned insurance premiums	2,144.5	2,217.2
Interest	1,372.4	1,255.4
Other	11,536.7	9,693.7
Total	$28,195.2	$25,520.6

NOTE 16. Class E Common Stock Split

On February 5, 1990, the Board of Directors declared a two-for-one stock split in the form of a 100% stock dividend for Class E common stock, payable March 10, 1990 to shareholders of record on February 16, 1990. At delivery, the balance sheet will be adjusted for the stock split by increasing Class E common stock and reducing capital surplus by approximately $4.9 million. All per share data have been adjusted for the stock split.

NOTE 17. Stockholders' Equity

The preferred stock is subject to redemption at the option of the Board of Directors on any dividend date on not less than 30 days' notice at the redemption prices stated on the following page, plus accrued dividends.

On September 14, 1987, 19,573,836 shares of $0.10 par value convertible, nonvoting preference stock, valued at $1,039.9 million, were contributed to GM's U.S. pension plans for hourly-rate and salaried employes with respect to the 1986 plan year. The contribution consisted of six separate series of 3,262,306 shares each: (1) Series E-I, E-II, and E-III shares will pay dividends equivalent to twice the dividends declared and paid on Class E common stock and are convertible on a one-for-two fixed basis into Class E common shares three, four, and five years after issuance, respectively (on a post-split basis); and (2) Series H-I, H-II, and H-III shares will pay dividends equivalent to twice the dividends declared and paid on Class H common stock and are convertible on a one-for-two fixed basis into Class H common shares three, four, and five years after issuance, respectively.

Preference Stock Series	Redemption Price/Share	Redemption Date
E-I	$57.25	October 1, 1990
E-II	62.00	September 15, 1991
E-III	67.25	September 15, 1992
H-I	63.50	October 1, 1990
H-II	69.00	September 15, 1991
H-III	74.75	September 15, 1992

Holders of the preference shares will be able to elect to require GM to redeem the shares at the prices on the dates indicated in the preceding table. The redemption prices indicated represent the liquidation values of such shares.

On or after each series' redemption date, quarterly preferential dividends will be payable of $0.715 per share on Series E shares and $0.795 per share on Series H shares. After September 15, 1993, any or all of the preference shares not converted could be redeemed by GM at its option at the applicable redemption prices, although preference shareholders will first have the right to convert if GM exercises its redemption option.

Holders of $1-2/3 par value common stock, Class E common stock, and Class H common stock are entitled to one, one-quarter (post-split), and one-half vote per share, respectively, on all matters submitted to the stockholders for a vote. The liquidation rights of common stockholders are based on per share liquidation units of the various classes and are subject to certain adjustments if outstanding common stock is subdivided, by stock split or otherwise, or if shares of one class of common stock are issued as a dividend to holders of another class of common stock. At December 31, 1989, each share of $1-2/3 par value common, Class E common, and Class H common stock was entitled to a liquidation unit of approximately one, one-quarter (post-split), and one-half, respectively.

After December 31, 1994 or December 31, 1995, the Board of Directors may exchange $1-2/3 par value common stock for Class E common stock or for Class H common stock, respectively, if the Board has declared and paid certain minimum cash dividends during each of the five years preceding the exchange. If GM should sell, liquidate, or otherwise dispose of substantially all of EDS, Hughes, or the other business of GMHE, the Corporation will be required to exchange $1-2/3 par value common stock for Class E common or Class H common stock, respectively. In the event of any exchange, the Class E common or Class H common stockholders will receive $1-2/3 par value common stock having a market value at the time of the exchange equal to 120% of the market value of the Class E common or Class H common stock exchanged.

The Certificate of Incorporation provides that no cash dividends may be paid on the $1-2/3 par value common stock, Class E common stock, Class H common stock, or any series of preference stock so long as current assets (excluding prepaid expenses) in excess of current liabilities of the Corporation are less than $75 per share of outstanding preferred stock. Such current assets (with inventories calculated on the FIFO basis) in excess of current liabilities were greater than $75 in respect of each share of outstanding preferred stock at December 31, 1989 and 1988.

(continued)

Notes To
Financial Statements *(continued)*

NOTE 17. *(continued)*

(Dollars in Millions Except Per Share Amounts)	1989	1988	1987
Capital Stock:			
Preferred Stock, without par value, cumulative dividends (authorized, 6,000,000 shares):			
$5.00 series, stated value $100 per share, redeemable at Corporation option at $120 per share—outstanding at beginning and end of the year (1,530,194 shares)	$ 153.0	$153.0	$153.0
$3.75 series, stated value $100 per share, redeemable at Corporation option at $100 per share—outstanding at beginning and end of the year (814,100 shares)	81.4	81.4	81.4
Preference Stock, $0.10 par value (authorized, 100,000,000 shares):			
E series, convertible one-for-two (post-split) at fixed dates into Class E common stock: Issued in conjunction with pension plan contribution (9,786,918 shares issued and outstanding)	1.0	1.0	1.0
H series, convertible one-for-two at fixed dates into Class H common stock: Issued in conjunction with pension plan contribution (9,786,918 shares issued and outstanding)	1.0	1.0	1.0
Common Stock, $1-2/3 par value (authorized, 1,000,000,000 shares):			
Issued at beginning of the year (306,456,671 shares in 1989, 312,654,018 in 1988, and 319,383,830 in 1987)	510.7	521.1	532.3
Reacquired on the open market (9,856,604 shares in 1989, 6,555,000 in 1988, and 8,049,495 in 1987)	(16.4)	(11.0)	(13.4)
Newly issued shares sold under provisions of the GM Incentive Program (Note 3) and, in 1987, the Dividend Reinvestment Plan (2,138,166 shares in 1989, 357,653 in 1988, and 1,319,683 in 1987)	3.6	.6	2.2
Two-for-one stock split in the form of a 100% stock dividend (306,945,339 shares)	511.6	–	–
Issued at end of the year (605,683,572 shares in 1989, 306,456,671 in 1988, and 312,654,018 in 1987)	1,009.5	510.7	521.1
Class E Common Stock, $0.10 par value (authorized, 190,000,000 shares):			
Issued at beginning of the year (50,646,603 shares in 1989, 51,601,687 in 1988, and 53,507,119 in 1987)	5.1	5.2	5.4
Issued in the acquisition of MTech Corp (3,266,284 shares)	–	.3	–
Issued in the acquisition of M&SD Corp. (703,200 shares)	–	.1	–
Reacquired on the open market (3,581,949 shares in 1989, 5,819,978 in 1988, and 3,381,258 in 1987)	(.4)	(.6)	(.3)
Issued in conjunction with EDS Incentive Plans (Note 4) and other employe stock plans (1,766,110 shares in 1989, 895,410 in 1988, and 1,475,826 in 1987)	.2	.1	.1
Issued at end of the year (48,830,764 shares in 1989, 50,646,603 in 1988, and 51,601,687 in 1987)	4.9	5.1	5.2
Class H Common Stock, $0.10 par value (authorized, 600,000,000 shares):			
Issued at beginning of the year (128,388,969 shares in 1989, 65,434,936 in 1988, and 66,585,332 in 1987)	12.8	6.5	6.6
Issued in conjunction with GMHE Incentive Plans (Note 5) and other employe stock plans (57,180 shares in 1989, 2,052,212 in 1988, and 574,783 in 1987)	–	.2	.1
Two-for-one stock split in the form of a 100% stock dividend (65,653,841 shares)	–	6.6	–
Reacquired on the open market (3,283,485 shares in 1989, 4,752,020 in 1988, and 1,725,179 in 1987)	(.3)	(.5)	(.2)
Purchased from the Howard Hughes Medical Institute (35,000,000 shares)	(3.5)	–	–
Reclassification of shares subject to repurchase from the Institute (55,000,000 shares)	(5.5)	–	–
Issued at end of the year (35,162,664 shares in 1989, 128,388,969 in 1988, and 65,434,936 in 1987)	3.5	12.8	6.5
Total capital stock at end of the year	$1,254.3	$765.0	$769.2

(continued)

Notes To
Financial Statements *(continued)*

NOTE 17. *(concluded)*

(Dollars in Millions Except Per Share Amounts)	1989	1988	1987
Capital Surplus (principally additional paid-in capital):			
Balance at beginning of the year	$ 6,235.2	$ 6,764.6	$ 6,332.6
Preference stock:			
Amount in excess of par value of shares contributed to GM's U.S. pension plans	–	–	1,037.9
$1-2/3 par value common stock:			
Repurchase price in excess of par value of shares reacquired on the open market	(410.0)(	484.5)(	575.1)
Amounts in excess of par value of newly issued shares used for the			
GM Incentive Program and the Dividend Reinvestment Plan	93.4	36.7	71.6
Amount transferred to $1-2/3 par value common stock in conjunction with the			
two-for-one stock split in the form of a 100% stock dividend	(511.6)	–	–
Class E common stock:			
Repurchase price in excess of par value of shares reacquired on the open market	(161.9)(	199.7)(	101.5)
Amounts in excess of par value:			
Issued in the acquisition of MTech Corp and M&SD Corp.	–	165.0	–
Issued in conjunction with EDS Incentive Plans and other employe stock plans	74.5	32.0	49.7
Class H common stock:			
Repurchase price in excess of par value:			
Shares reacquired on the open market	(90.7)(	134.4)(	77.3)
Shares purchased from the Howard Hughes Medical Institute	(971.9)	–	–
Reclassification of shares subject to repurchase from the Institute	(1,644.5)	–	–
Amounts in excess of par value of shares issued in conjunction with GMHE			
Incentive Plans and other employe stock plans	1.5	62.1	26.7
Amount transferred to Class H common stock in conjunction with the two-for-one			
stock split in the form of a 100% stock dividend	– (	6.6)	–
Balance at end of the year	2,614.0	6,235.2	6,764.6
Net Income Retained for Use in the Business:			
Balance at beginning of the year	28,970.5	25,771.7	23,888.7
Net income	4,224.3	4,856.3	3,550.9
Total	33,194.8	30,628.0	27,439.6
Cash dividends:			
Preferred stock, $5.00 series, $5.00 per share	7.7	7.7	7.7
Preferred stock, $3.75 series, $3.75 per share	3.0	3.0	3.0
Preference stock, E series, $0.96 per share in 1989, $0.68 in 1988, and $0.13 in 1987	9.4	6.7	1.3
Preference stock, H series, $1.44 per share in 1989, $0.88 in 1988, and $0.18 in 1987	14.1	8.6	1.7
$1-2/3 par value common stock, $3.00 per share in 1989 and $2.50 in 1988 and 1987	1,813.2	1,540.5	1,579.6
Class E common stock, $0.48 per share in 1989, $0.34 in 1988, and $0.26 in 1987			
(on a post-split basis)	45.6	34.8	27.4
Class H common stock, $0.72 per share in 1989, $0.44 in 1988, and $0.36 in 1987	71.1	56.2	47.2
Total cash dividends	1,964.1	1,657.5	1,667.9
Balance at end of the year	31,230.7	28,970.5	25,771.7
Accumulated Foreign Currency Translation and Other Adjustments:			
Balance at beginning of the year:			
Accumulated foreign currency translation adjustments	(459.9)(	231.7)(	482.8)
Net unrealized gains on marketable equity securities	160.9	151.3	160.8
Changes during the year:			
Accumulated foreign currency translation adjustments	104.4 (	228.2)	251.1
Net unrealized gains (losses) on marketable equity securities	78.1	9.6 (	9.5)
Balance at end of the year	(116.5)(	299.0)(	80.4)
Total Stockholders' Equity	$34,982.5	$35,671.7	$33,225.1

The equity of the Corporation and its subsidiaries in the accumulated net income or loss, since acquisition, of associates has been included in net income retained for use in the business.

At December 31, 1989, consolidated net income retained for use in the business attributable to $1-2/3 par value common, Class E common, and Class H common stocks was $30,020.6 million, $568.8 million, and $641.3 million, respectively.

Notes To
Financial Statements *(continued)*

NOTE 18. Profit Sharing Plans

In 1988, the profit sharing formula was changed to provide a payout when the Corporation's U.S. income before income taxes plus equity in U.S. earnings of finance subsidiaries exceeds a minimum annual return equal to 1.8% of U.S. sales and revenues. Specified percentages of profits, ranging from 7.5% to 16.0%, in excess of the minimum annual return equal to 1.8% through 6.9% of U.S. sales and revenues, less that portion of profit sharing allocable to nonparticipating employes, are distributed to eligible U.S. employes. The accrual for profit sharing was $22.1 million in 1989 and $114.1 million in 1988. GM's earnings in 1987 were not sufficient to generate a payment under the prior profit sharing formula.

NOTE 19. Segment Reporting

Industry Segments

While the major portion of the Corporation's operations is derived from the automotive products industry segment, GM also has financing and insurance operations and produces products and provides services in other industry segments. The automotive products segment consists of the design, manufacture, assembly, and sale of automobiles, trucks, and related parts and accessories.

The financing and insurance operations assist in the merchandising of General Motors' products as well as other products. GMAC and its subsidiaries, as well as certain other subsidiaries of GM, offer financial services and certain types of insurance to dealers and customers In addition, subsidiaries of GMAC are engaged in mortgage banking operations. The other products segment consists of military vehicles, radar and weapon control systems, guided missile systems, and defense satellites; the design, installation, and operation of business information and telecommunication systems; as well as the design, development, and manufacture of locomotives; turboshaft and turboprop engines for military and commercial aerospace usage; compressor, generator, and marine gas turbine engine applications; commercial satellites; and specialized automated production and test equipment. Because of the high degree of integration, substantial interdivisional and intersegment transfers of materials and services are made. Intersegment sales and revenues are made at negotiated selling prices.

Substantially all of the products in the automotive segment are marketed through retail dealers and through distributors and jobbers in the United States and Canada and through distributors and dealers overseas.

Information concerning operations by industry segment is displayed below and on the next page.

1989	Automotive Products	Financing & Insurance Operations	Other Products	Total
	(Dollars in Millions)			
Net Sales and Revenues:				
Outside	$99,106.1	$11,254.0	$12,851.7	$123,211.8
Intersegment	334.8	–	3,014.7	–
Total	$99,440.9	$11,254.0	$15,866.4	$123,211.8*
Operating Profit	$ 5,131.1	N/A**	$ 579.9	$ 5,711.0**
Identifiable Assets at Year-End	$64,598.0	$89,851.8	$16,782.2	$171,232.0
Depreciation and Amortization	$ 4,206.2	$ 1,583.5	$ 1,378.5	$ 7,168.2
Capital Expenditures	$ 6,287.6	$ 127.2	$ 1,090.3	$ 7,505.1
1988				
Net Sales and Revenues:				
Outside	$97,437.5	$10,664.9	$12,285.3	$120,387.7
Intersegment	339.6	3.0	2,866.6	–
Total	$97,777.1	$10,667.9	$15,151.9	$120,387.7*
Operating Profit	$ 5,614.5	N/A**	$ 175.7	$ 5,790.2**
Identifiable Assets at Year-End	$60,420.4	$84,444.8	$16,553.1	$161,418.3
Depreciation and Amortization	$ 4,050.6	$ 1,585.5	$ 1,444.9	$ 7,081.0
Capital Expenditures	$ 4,524.6	$ 127.4	$ 974.5	$ 5,626.5

Reference should be made to notes on page 43.

(continued)

Notes To
Financial Statements*(continued)*

NOTE 19. *(continued)*

1987	Automotive Products	Financing & Insurance Operations	Other Products	Total
	(Dollars in Millions)			
Net Sales and Revenues:				
Outside	$89,612.6	$10,920.8	$11,744.9	$112,278.3
Intersegment	278.0	7.3	2,870.7	–
Total	$89,890.6	$10,928.1	$14,615.6	$112,278.3*
Operating Profit	$ 3,379.9	N/A**	$ 420.2	$ 3,800.1**
Identifiable Assets at Year-End	$60,159.5	$84,713.0	$16,305.9	$161,178.4
Depreciation and Amortization	$ 4,695.3	$ 1,669.0	$ 1,462.6	$ 7,826.9
Capital Expenditures	$ 6,127.9	$ 111.3	$ 911.4	$ 7,150.6

*After elimination of intersegment transactions.
**Excludes Financing and Insurance Operations as they do not report Operating Profit.

A reconciliation of outside net sales and revenues to Total Net Sales and Revenues and of operating profit to Income before Income Taxes detailed in the Statement of Consolidated Income and a reconciliation of identifiable assets to Total Assets displayed in the Consolidated Balance Sheet follow:

(Dollars in Millions)	1989	1988	1987
Outside Net Sales and Revenues reported above	$123,211.8	$120,387.7	$112,278.3
Other Income	3,720.1	3,253.9	2,592.1
Total Net Sales and Revenues	$126,931.9	$123,641.6	$114,870.4
Total Operating Profit reported above	$ 5,711.0	$ 5,790.2	$ 3,800.1
Financing and Insurance Operations	1,551.7	1,802.8	2,386.6
Other Corporate Income and Expenses Less Intersegment Transactions	(864.4)	(858.1)	(1,778.2)
Income before Income Taxes	$ 6,398.3	$ 6,734.9	$ 4,408.5
Identifiable Assets	$171,232.0	$161,418.3	$161,178.4
Corporate Assets	5,445.2	6,512.5	4,231.1
Eliminations	(3,380.1)	(3,867.7)	(3,066.3)
Total Assets	$173,297.1	$164,063.1	$162,343.2

Geographic Segments

Net sales and revenues, net income, total and net assets, and average number of employes in the U.S. and in locations outside the U.S. are summarized below. Net income is after provisions for deferred income taxes applicable to that portion of the undistributed earnings not deemed to be indefinitely invested, less available tax credits and deductions, and appropriate consolidating adjustments. Interarea sales and revenues are made at negotiated selling prices.

1989	United States	Canada	Europe	Latin America	All Other	Total*
	(Dollars in Millions)					
Net Sales and Revenues:						
Outside (excluding GMAC)	$ 81,650.7	$ 6,903.5	$17,850.3	$3,507.2	$2,621.5	$112,533.2
GMAC and related operations	8,405.3	883.1	1,080.5	87.8	221.9	10,678.6
Other income	3,107.6	34.8	414.1	120.3	43.3	3,720.1
Subtotal outside	93,163.6	7,821.4	19,344.9	3,715.3	2,886.7	126,931.9
Interarea	10,185.1	9,825.3	395.1	1,293.2	128.5	–
Total	$103,348.7	$17,646.7	$19,740.0	$5,008.5	$3,015.2	$126,931.9
Net Income	$ 1,279.0	$ 288.5	$ 1,830.0	$ 488.4	$ 345.3	$ 4,224.3
Total Assets	$131,595.8	$13,187.4	$21,782.6	$4,589.3	$4,016.4	$173,297.1
Net Assets	$ 21,264.0	$ 3,025.7	$ 5,956.2	$3,352.9	$1,483.0	$ 34,982.5
Average Number of Employes (in thousands)	531	42	118	71	13	775

*After elimination of interarea transactions.

(continued)

Notes To
Financial Statements *(concluded)*

NOTE 19. *(concluded)*

1988	United States	Canada	Europe	Latin America	All Other	Total*
			(Dollars in Millions)			
Net Sales and Revenues:						
Outside (excluding GMAC)	$ 82,434.9	$ 6,534.8	$16,283.9	$2,433.4	$2,035.8	$109,722.8
GMAC and related operations	8,825.0	673.0	913.9	85.0	168.0	10,664.9
Other income	2,618.5	52.7	161.2	345.4	76.1	3,253.9
Subtotal outside	93,878.4	7,260.5	17,359.0	2,863.8	2,279.9	123,641.6
Interarea	9,392.2	9,195.9	415.3	1,407.6	43.4	–
Total	$103,270.6	$16,456.4	$17,774.3	$4,271.4	$2,323.3	$123,641.6
Net Income	$ 1,813.2	$ 387.2	$ 1,781.4	$ 539.6	$ 300.6	$ 4,856.3
Total Assets	$130,797.5	$11,054.7	$15,699.2	$4,278.9	$3,390.7	$164,063.1
Net Assets	$ 25,858.2	$ 2,849.0	$ 2,836.8	$2,929.8	$1,290.5	$ 35,671.7
Average Number of Employes (in thousands)	538	39	112	62	15	766

Certain amounts for 1988 have been reclassified to conform with 1989 classifications.

1987	United States	Canada	Europe	Latin America	All Other	Total*
Net Sales and Revenues:						
Outside (excluding GMAC)	$ 77,266.2	$ 5,791.3	$14,476.6	$1,904.0	$1,919.4	$101,357.5
GMAC and related operations	9,414.5	533.2	788.5	50.0	134.6	10,920.8
Other income	2,064.4	51.8	104.5	348.7	22.7	2,592.1
Subtotal outside	88,745.1	6,376.3	15,369.6	2,302.7	2,076.7	114,870.4
Interarea	8,731.3	6,978.9	305.5	958.5	166.1	–
Total	$ 97,476.4	$13,355.2	$15,675.1	$3,261.2	$2,242.8	$114,870.4
Net Income	$ 1,702.2	$ 42.9	$ 1,255.4	$ 445.0	$ 175.9	$ 3,550.9
Total Assets	$131,059.1	$ 9,838.4	$15,625.2	$3,612.7	$3,342.7	$162,343.2
Net Assets	$ 26,327.1	$ 2,463.6	$ 1,280.5	$2,462.2	$ 913.5	$ 33,225.1
Average Number of Employes (in thousands)	583	41	118	57	14	813

*After elimination of interarea transactions.

NOTE 20. Commitments and Contingent Liabilities

Minimum future commitments under operating leases having noncancellable lease terms in excess of one year, primarily for real property, aggregating $4,138.5 million, are payable $678.5 million in 1990, $507.2 million in 1991, $394.0 million in 1992, $307.9 million in 1993, $253.7 million in 1994, and $1,997.2 million in 1995 and thereafter. Certain of the leases contain escalation clauses and renewal or purchase options. Rental expenses under operating leases were $988.2 million in 1989, $879.6 million in 1988, and $913.6 million in 1987.

The Corporation and its subsidiaries are subject to potential liability under government regulations and various claims and legal actions which are pending or may be asserted against them. Some of the pending actions purport to be class actions. The aggregate ultimate liability of the Corporation and its subsidiaries under these government regulations, and under these claims and actions, was not determinable at December 31, 1989. In the opinion of management, such liability is not expected to have a material adverse effect on the Corporation's consolidated financial position.

Supplementary Information

Selected Quarterly Data

(Dollars in Millions)	1989 Quarters				1988 Quarters			
	1st	**2nd**	**3rd**	**4th**	**1st**	**2nd**	**3rd**	**4th**
Net sales and revenues	$33,238.5*	$33,536.3*	$28,793.1	$31,364.0	$29,811.1	$33,178.4	$28,221.3	$32,430.8
Income before income taxes	$ 2,443.1	$ 2,356.3	$ 763.3	$ 835.6	$ 1,191.9	$ 2,167.9	$ 1,070.1	$ 2,305.0
United States, foreign, and other income taxes	890.1	902.1	246.4	135.4	324.0	661.2	210.9	906.7
Income before cumulative effect of accounting change	1,553.0	1,454.2	516.9	700.2	867.9	1,506.7	859.2	1,398.3
Cumulative effect of accounting change	–	–	–	–	224.2	–	–	–
Net income	1,553.0	1,454.2	. 516.9	700.2	1,092.1	1,506.7	859.2	1,398.3
Dividends on preferred and preference stocks	8.6	8.5	8.6	8.5	6.5	6.5	6.5	6.5
Earnings on common stocks	$ 1,544.4	$ 1,445.7	$ 508.3	$ 691.7	$ 1,085.6	$ 1,500.2	$ 852.7	$ 1,391.8
Earnings attributable to common stocks:								
$1-2/3 par value before cumulative effect of accounting change	$ 1,443.5	$ 1,350.2	$ 432.1	$ 605.2	$ 749.1	$ 1,395.5	$ 755.1	$ 1,295.3
Cumulative effect of accounting change	–	–	–	–	218.1	–	–	–
Net earnings attributable to $1-2/3 par value	$ 1,443.5	$ 1,350.2	$ 432.1	$ 605.2	$ 967.2	$ 1,395.5	$ 755.1	$ 1,295.3
Class E	$ 40.6	$ 41.4	$ 43.2	$ 45.8	$ 36.8	$ 40.5	$ 40.4	$ 42.6
Class H before cumulative effect of accounting change	$ 60.3	$ 54.1	$ 33.0	$ 40.7	$ 75.5	$ 64.2	$ 57.2	$ 53.9
Cumulative effect of accounting change	–	–	–	–	6.1	–	–	–
Net earnings attributable to Class H	$ 60.3	$ 54.1	$ 33.0	$ 40.7	$ 81.6	$ 64.2	$ 57.2	$ 53.9

*First and second quarter amounts have been reclassified to conform with third quarter 1989 classifications.

The effective income tax rates for the 1989 quarters reflect the accrual of taxes on planned dividend remittances from foreign subsidiaries. In addition, the effective income tax rate for the 1989 fourth quarter reflects increased utilization of research and experimentation credits and favorable state and local tax returns as filed adjustments.

The effective income tax rates for the 1989 and 1988 quarters reflect the continuing amortization of investment tax credits earned in prior years and include the tax benefits related to the utilization of loss carryforwards at certain overseas operations. In addition, the effective income tax rate for the 1988 fourth quarter reflects a change in estimate related to taxes on foreign dividends.

Effective January 1, 1988, accounting procedures were changed to include in inventory certain manufacturing overhead costs previously charged directly to expense.

(continued)

Supplementary Information *(continued)*

Selected Quarterly Data *(concluded)*

(Dollars in Millions Except Per Share Amounts)	1989 Quarters				1988 Quarters			
	1st	2nd	3rd	4th	1st	2nd	3rd	4th
Average number of shares of common stocks outstanding (in millions):								
$1-2/3 par value	608.9	604.5	602.5	601.5	621.0	617.6	614.0	610.1
Class E[a]	98.9	94.8	93.1	91.4	100.8	103.1	102.8	100.4
Class H	114.8	90.0	89.5	88.9	129.5	127.7	127.4	127.2
Earnings per share attributable to common stocks:								
$1-2/3 par value before cumulative effect of accounting change	$2.37	$2.23	$0.72	$1.01	$1.21	$2.26	$1.23	$2.12
Cumulative effect of accounting change	–	–	–	–	0.35	–	–	–
Net earnings attributable to $1-2/3 par value	$2.37	$2.23	$0.72	$1.01	$1.56	$2.26	$1.23	$2.12
Class E[a]	$0.41	$0.44	$0.46	$0.50	$0.37	$0.39	$0.39	$0.42
Class H before cumulative effect of accounting change	$0.51	$0.60	$0.37	$0.46	$0.58	$0.50	$0.45	$0.43
Cumulative effect of accounting change	–	–	–	–	0.05	–	–	–
Net earnings attributable to Class H	$0.51	$0.60	$0.37	$0.46	$0.63	$0.50	$0.45	$0.43
Cash dividends per share of common stocks:								
$1-2/3 par value	$0.75	$0.75	$0.75	$0.75	$0.625	$0.625	$0.625	$0.625
Class E[a]	$0.12	$0.12	$0.12	$0.12	$0.085	$0.085	$0.085	$0.085
Class H	$0.18	$0.18	$0.18	$0.18	$0.11	$0.11	$0.11	$0.11
Common stock price range:								
$1-2/3 par value[b]:								
High	$47.31	$43.50	$50.50	$48.88	$36.94	$40.56	$40.25	$44.06
Low	$40.88	$39.13	$40.00	$40.63	$30.00	$34.94	$35.56	$36.81
Class E[a][c]:								
High	$23.38	$26.94	$27.94	$28.81	$21.94	$22.44	$21.50	$22.44
Low	$21.25	$22.13	$25.31	$26.06	$16.75	$18.25	$18.75	$19.63
Class H[d]:								
High	$28.50	$28.13	$32.13	$30.50	$40.63	$35.25	$30.88	$30.63
Low	$23.50	$25.75	$28.00	$24.13	$24.13	$26.63	$28.00	$25.13

(a) Adjusted to reflect the two-for-one stock split in the form of a 100% stock dividend declared February 5, 1990, payable March 10, 1990.

(b) The principal market is the New York Stock Exchange and prices are based on the Composite Tape. $1-2/3 par value common stock is also listed on the Midwest, Pacific, and Philadelphia stock exchanges. As of December 31, 1989, there were 953,450 holders of record of $1-2/3 par value common stock.

(c) The principal market is the New York Stock Exchange and prices are based on the Composite Tape. As of December 31, 1989, there were 445,708 holders of record of Class E common stock.

(d) The principal market is the New York Stock Exchange and prices are based on the Composite Tape. As of December 31, 1989, there were 523,665 holders of record of Class H common stock.

Supplementary Information *(continued)*

Selected Financial Data

(Dollars in Millions Except Per Share Amounts)	1989	1988	1987	1986	1985
Net sales and revenues	$126,931.9	$123,641.6	$114,870.4	$115,609.9	$106,655.8
Earnings attributable to $1-2/3 par value common stock	$ 3,831.0	$ 4,413.1	$ 3,178.9	$ 2,607.7	$ 3,883.6
Cash dividends on $1-2/3 par value	1,813.2	1,540.5	1,579.6	1,588.0	1,592.9
Dividend of Class H common shares	—	—	— (	0.5)	572.1
Net income retained in the year	$ 2,017.8	$ 2,872.6	$ 1,599.3	$ 1,020.2	$ 1,718.6
Earnings per share attributable to $1-2/3 par value common stock*	$6.33	$7.17	$5.03	$4.11	$6.14
Cash dividends per share of $1-2/3 par value*	3.00	2.50	2.50	2.50	2.50
Per share dividend of Class H common shares*	—	—	—	—	0.97
Net income per share retained in the year*	$3.33	$4.67	$2.53	$1.61	$2.67
Earnings attributable to Class E common stock	$ 171.0	$ 160.3	$ 139.1	$ 136.2	$ 103.8
Cash dividends on Class E	45.6	34.8	27.4	25.9	12.4
Net income retained in the year	$ 125.4	$ 125.5	$ 111.7	$ 110.3	$ 91.4
Earnings per share attributable to Class E common stock**	$1.81	$1.57	$1.33	$1.07	$0.79
Cash dividends per share of Class E**	0.48	0.34	0.26	0.20	0.10
Net income per share retained in the year**	$1.33	$1.23	$1.07	$0.87	$0.69
Earnings attributable to Class H common stock (issued in December 1985)	$ 188.1	$ 256.9	$ 219.2	$ 190.0	—
Cash dividends on Class H	71.1	56.2	47.2	38.4	—
Net income retained in the year	$ 117.0	$ 200.7	$ 172.0	$ 151.6	—
Earnings per share attributable to Class H common stock	$1.94	$2.01	$1.67***	$1.48***	—
Cash dividends per share of Class H	0.72	0.44	0.36***	0.30***	—
Net income per share retained in the year	$1.22	$1.57	$1.31***	$1.18***	—
Average number of shares of common stocks outstanding (in millions):					
$1-2/3 par value*	604.3	615.7	631.5	635.3	632.6
Class E**	94.5	101.8	105.2	127.5	133.1
Class H (issued in December 1985)	95.7	127.9	130.8***	127.8***	—
Cash dividends on capital stocks as a percent of net income	46.5%	34.1%	47.0%	56.5%	40.4%
Expenditures for real estate, plants, and equipment	$ 4,577.3	$ 3,432.1	$ 4,804.4	$ 8,159.5	$ 8,068.3****
Expenditures for special tools	$ 2,927.8	$ 2,194.4	$ 2,346.2	$ 3,625.3	$ 3,075.0
Cash and marketable securities	$ 10,213.3	$ 10,181.4	$ 7,819.3	$ 7,359.7	$ 7,924.9
Working capital (with GMAC on an equity basis)	$ 17,229.8	$ 17,728.9	$ 13,049.7	$ 3,920.3	$ 1,957.5
Total assets	$173,297.1	$164,063.1	$162,343.2	$150,157.1	$130,043.5
Long-term debt and capitalized leases (with GMAC on an equity basis)	$ 4,565.7	$ 4,535.7	$ 4,313.4	$ 4,325.3	$ 2,867.2

Effective January 1, 1988, accounting procedures were changed to include in inventory certain manufacturing overhead costs previously charged directly to expense. The effect of this change on 1988 earnings was a favorable adjustment of $218.1 million or $0.35 per share of $1-2/3 par value common stock and $6.1 million or $0.05 per share of Class H common stock. The revision in 1987 of estimated service lives of plants and equipment and special tools had the effect of reducing 1987 depreciation and amortization charges by $1,236.6 million or $1.28 per share of $1-2/3 par value common stock. The revision in 1987 by GMAC of rates of depreciation for automobiles on operating leases to retail customers had the effect of reducing 1987 depreciation charges by $424.5 million or $0.41 per share of $1-2/3 par value common stock. Financial data for years prior to 1986 have not been restated for the adoption effective January 1, 1986 of SFAS No. 87, Employers' Accounting for Pensions. The effect of adopting SFAS No. 87 was to increase net income for 1986 by $330.5 million or $0.48 per share of $1-2/3 par value common stock, $0.02 per share (post-split) of Class E common stock, and $0.17 per share of Class H common stock.

*Adjusted to reflect the two-for-one stock split in the form of a 100% stock dividend distributed on March 31, 1989.

**Adjusted to reflect the two-for-one stock split in the form of a 100% stock dividend declared February 5, 1990, payable March 10, 1990.

***Adjusted to reflect the two-for-one stock split in the form of a 100% stock dividend distributed on March 10, 1988.

****Includes $1,948.7 million of net property acquired in the Hughes acquisition.

(continued)

Supplementary Information *(concluded)*

Selected Financial Data *(concluded)*

(Dollars in Millions Except Per Share Amounts)	1984	1983	1982	1981	1980
Net sales and revenues	$93,144.8	$82,502.3	$67,747.7	$69,191.4	$62,698.0
Earnings (loss) attributable to $1-2/3 par value common stock	$ 4,498.3	$ 3,717.3	$ 949.8	$ 320.5	($ 775.4)
Cash dividends on $1-2/3 par value	1,510.0	879.3	737.3	717.6	861.2
Dividend of Class E common shares	586.7	–	–	–	–
Dividend of Class H common shares	–	–	–	–	–
Net income (loss) retained in the year	$ 2,401.6	$ 2,838.0	$ 212.5	($ 397.1)	($ 1,636.6)
Earnings (loss) per share attributable to $1-2/3 par value common stock*	$7.14	$5.92	$1.55	$0.53	($1.32)
Cash dividends per share of $1-2/3 par value*	2.38	1.40	1.20	1.20	1.48
Per share dividend of Class E common shares*	0.95	–	–	–	–
Per share dividend of Class H common shares	–	–	–	–	–
Net income (loss) per share retained in the year*	$3.81	$4.52	$0.35	($0.67)	($2.80)
Earnings attributable to Class E common stock (issued in 1984)	$ 5.7	–	–	–	–
Cash dividends on Class E	1.2	–	–	–	–
Net income retained in the year	$ 4.5	–	–	–	–
Earnings per share attributable to Class E common stock**	$0.08	–	–	–	–
Cash dividends per share of Class E**	0.0225	–	–	–	–
Net income per share retained in the year**	$0.0575	–	–	–	–
Earnings attributable to Class H common stock (issued in December 1985)	–	–	–	–	–
Cash dividends on Class H	–	–	–	–	–
Net income retained in the year	–	–	–	–	–
Earnings per share attributable to Class H common stock	–	–	–	–	–
Cash dividends per share of Class H	–	–	–	–	–
Net income per share retained in the year	–	–	–	–	–
Average number of shares of common stocks outstanding (in millions):					
$1-2/3 par value*	630.7	627.8	614.8	598.1	584.8
Class E (issued in 1984)**	72.6	–	–	–	–
Class H (issued in December 1985)	–	–	–	–	–
Cash dividends on capital stocks as a percent of net income	33.7%	23.9%	77.9%	219.1%	N.A.
Expenditures for real estate, plants, and equipment	$ 3,610.1	$ 1,932.2	$ 3,619.8	$ 6,568.5	$ 5,173.7
Expenditures for special tools	$ 2,452.1	$ 2,083.7	$ 2,601.1	$ 3,178.1	$ 2,600.0
Cash and marketable securities	$10,688.3	$ 8,237.4	$ 4,815.4	$ 3,038.2	$ 5,195.2
Working capital (with GMAC on an equity basis)	$ 6,276.7	$ 5,890.8	$ 1,658.1	$ 1,158.8	$ 3,212.1
Total assets	$98,414.9	$89,458.0	$81,197.3	$76,798.8	$64,499.5
Long-term debt and capitalized leases (with GMAC on an equity basis)	$ 2,772.9	$ 3,521.8	$ 4,745.1	$ 4,044.0	$ 2,058.3

Earnings and earnings per share attributable to common stocks in 1984 have been restated to reflect the Class E common stock amendment approved by the stockholders in December 1985. Data for years prior to 1983 have not been restated for the adoption of SFAS No. 52, Foreign Currency Translation. The effect of adopting SFAS No. 52 was to reduce net income for 1983 by about $422.5 million or $0.68 per share of $1-2/3 value common stock.

*Adjusted to reflect the two-for-one stock split in the form of a 100% stock dividend distributed on March 31, 1989.

**Adjusted to reflect the two-for-one stock splits in the form of 100% stock dividends distributed on June 10, 1985 and declared February 5, 1990, payable March 10, 1990.

■ APPENDIX B

■ Present Value and Future Value Tables

Table 1: FUTURE VALUE OF $1: $FV = (1 + i)^n$

n	1.5%	4.0%	4.5%	5.0%	5.5%	6.0%	7.0%
1	1.015000	1.040000	1.045000	1.050000	1.055000	1.060000	1.070000
2	1.030225	1.081600	1.092025	1.102500	1.113025	1.123600	1.144900
3	1.045678	1.124864	1.141166	1.157625	1.174241	1.191016	1.225043
4	1.061364	1.169859	1.192519	1.215506	1.238825	1.262477	1.310796
5	1.077284	1.216653	1.246182	1.276282	1.306960	1.338226	1.402552
6	1.093443	1.265319	1.302260	1.340096	1.378843	1.418519	1.500730
7	1.109845	1.315932	1.360862	1.407100	1.454679	1.503630	1.605781
8	1.126493	1.368569	1.422101	1.477455	1.534687	1.593848	1.718186
9	1.143390	1.423312	1.486095	1.551328	1.619094	1.689479	1.838459
10	1.160541	1.480244	1.552969	1.628895	1.708144	1.790848	1.967151
11	1.177949	1.539454	1.622853	1.710339	1.802092	1.898299	2.104852
12	1.195618	1.601032	1.695881	1.795856	1.901207	2.012196	2.252192
13	1.213552	1.665074	1.772196	1.885649	2.005774	2.132928	2.409845
14	1.231756	1.731676	1.851945	1.979932	2.116091	2.260904	2.578534
15	1.250232	1.800944	1.935282	2.078928	2.232476	2.396558	2.759032
16	1.268986	1.872981	2.022370	2.182875	2.355263	2.540352	2.952164
17	1.288020	1.947900	2.113377	2.292018	2.484802	2.692773	3.158815
18	1.307341	2.025817	2.208479	2.406619	2.621466	2.854339	3.379932
19	1.326951	2.106849	2.307860	2.526950	2.765647	3.025600	3.616528
20	1.346855	2.191123	2.411714	2.653298	2.917757	3.207135	3.869684
21	1.367058	2.278768	2.520241	2.785963	3.078234	3.399564	4.140562
22	1.387564	2.369919	2.633652	2.925261	3.247537	3.603537	4.430402
23	1.408377	2.464716	2.752166	3.071524	3.426152	3.819750	4.740530
24	1.429503	2.563304	2.876014	3.225100	3.614590	4.048935	5.072367
25	1.450945	2.665836	3.005434	3.386355	3.813392	4.291871	5.427433
26	1.472710	2.772470	3.140679	3.555673	4.023129	4.549383	5.807353
27	1.494800	2.883369	3.282010	3.733456	4.244401	4.822346	6.213868
28	1.517222	2.998703	3.429700	3.920129	4.477843	5.111687	6.648838
29	1.539981	3.118651	3.584036	4.116136	4.724124	5.418388	7.114257
30	1.563080	3.243398	3.745318	4.321942	4.983951	5.743491	7.612255

n	8.0%	9.0%	10.0%	12.0%	14.0%	16.0%	18.0%
1	1.080000	1.090000	1.100000	1.120000	1.140000	1.160000	1.180000
2	1.166400	1.188100	1.210000	1.254400	1.299600	1.345600	1.392400
3	1.259712	1.295029	1.331000	1.404928	1.481544	1.560896	1.643032
4	1.360489	1.411582	1.464100	1.573519	1.688960	1.810639	1.938778
5	1.469328	1.538624	1.610510	1.762342	1.925415	2.100342	2.287758
6	1.586874	1.677100	1.771561	1.973823	2.194973	2.436396	2.699554
7	1.713824	1.828039	1.948717	2.210681	2.502269	2.826220	3.185474
8	1.850930	1.992563	2.143589	2.475963	2.852586	3.278415	3.758859
9	1.999005	2.171893	2.357948	2.773079	3.251949	3.802961	4.435454
10	2.158925	2.367364	2.593742	3.105848	3.707221	4.411435	5.233836
11	2.331639	2.580426	2.853117	3.478550	4.226232	5.117265	6.175926
12	2.518170	2.812665	3.138428	3.895976	4.817905	5.936027	7.287593
13	2.719624	3.065805	3.452271	4.363493	5.492411	6.885791	8.599359
14	2.937194	3.341727	3.797498	4.887112	6.261349	7.987518	10.147244
15	3.172169	3.642482	4.177248	5.473566	7.137938	9.265521	11.973748
16	3.425943	3.970306	4.594973	6.130394	8.137249	10.748004	14.129023
17	3.700018	4.327633	5.054470	6.866041	9.276464	12.467685	16.672247
18	3.996019	4.717120	5.559917	7.689966	10.575169	14.462514	19.673251
19	4.315701	5.141661	6.115909	8.612762	12.055693	16.776517	23.214436
20	4.660957	5.604411	6.727500	9.646293	13.743490	19.460759	27.393035
21	5.033834	6.108808	7.400250	10.803848	15.667578	22.574481	32.323781
22	5.436540	6.658600	8.140275	12.100310	17.861039	26.186398	38.142061
23	5.871464	7.257874	8.954302	13.552347	20.361585	30.376222	45.007632
24	6.341181	7.911083	9.849733	15.178629	23.212207	35.236417	53.109006
25	6.848475	8.623081	10.834706	17.000064	26.461916	40.874244	62.668627
26	7.396353	9.399158	11.918177	19.040072	30.166584	47.414123	73.948980
27	7.988061	10.245082	13.109994	21.324881	34.389906	55.000382	87.259797
28	8.627106	11.167140	14.420994	23.883866	39.204493	63.800444	102.966560
29	9.317275	12.172182	15.863093	26.749930	44.693122	74.008515	121.500541
30	10.062657	13.267678	17.449402	29.959922	50.950159	85.849877	143.370638

Table 2: PRESENT VALUE OF \$1: $PV = \dfrac{1}{(1+i)^n}$

n	1.5%	4.0%	4.5%	5.0%	5.5%	6.0%	7.0%
1	0.985222	0.961538	0.956938	0.952381	0.947867	0.943396	0.934579
2	0.970662	0.924556	0.915730	0.907029	0.898452	0.889996	0.873439
3	0.956317	0.888996	0.876297	0.863838	0.851614	0.839619	0.816298
4	0.942184	0.854804	0.838561	0.822702	0.807217	0.792094	0.762895
5	0.928260	0.821927	0.802451	0.783526	0.765134	0.747258	0.712986
6	0.914542	0.790315	0.767896	0.746215	0.725246	0.704961	0.666342
7	0.901027	0.759918	0.734828	0.710681	0.687437	0.665057	0.622750
8	0.887711	0.730690	0.703185	0.676839	0.651599	0.627412	0.582009
9	0.874592	0.702587	0.672904	0.644609	0.617629	0.591898	0.543934
10	0.861667	0.675564	0.643928	0.613913	0.585431	0.558395	0.508349
11	0.848933	0.649581	0.616199	0.584679	0.554911	0.526788	0.475093
12	0.836387	0.624597	0.589664	0.556837	0.525982	0.496969	0.444012
13	0.824027	0.600574	0.564272	0.530321	0.498561	0.468839	0.414964
14	0.811849	0.577475	0.539973	0.505068	0.472569	0.442301	0.387817
15	0.799852	0.555265	0.516720	0.481017	0.447933	0.417265	0.362446
16	0.788031	0.533908	0.494469	0.458112	0.424581	0.393646	0.338735
17	0.776385	0.513373	0.473176	0.436297	0.402447	0.371364	0.316574
18	0.764912	0.493628	0.452800	0.415521	0.381466	0.350344	0.295864
19	0.753607	0.474642	0.433302	0.395734	0.361579	0.330513	0.276508
20	0.742470	0.456387	0.414643	0.376889	0.342729	0.311805	0.258419
21	0.731498	0.438834	0.396787	0.358942	0.324862	0.294155	0.241513
22	0.720688	0.421955	0.379701	0.341850	0.307926	0.277505	0.225713
23	0.710037	0.405726	0.363350	0.325571	0.291873	0.261797	0.210947
24	0.699544	0.390121	0.347703	0.310068	0.276657	0.246979	0.197147
25	0.689206	0.375117	0.332731	0.295303	0.262234	0.232999	0.184249
26	0.679021	0.360689	0.318402	0.281241	0.248563	0.219810	0.172195
27	0.668986	0.346817	0.304691	0.267848	0.235605	0.207368	0.160930
28	0.659099	0.333477	0.291571	0.255094	0.223322	0.195630	0.150402
29	0.649359	0.320651	0.279015	0.242946	0.211679	0.184557	0.140563
30	0.639762	0.308319	0.267000	0.231377	0.200644	0.174110	0.131367

n	8.0%	9.0%	10.0%	12.0%	14.0%	16.0%	18.0%
1	0.925926	0.917431	0.909091	0.892857	0.877193	0.862069	0.847458
2	0.857339	0.841680	0.826446	0.797194	0.769468	0.743163	0.718184
3	0.793832	0.772183	0.751315	0.711780	0.674972	0.640658	0.608631
4	0.735030	0.708425	0.683013	0.635518	0.592080	0.552291	0.515789
5	0.680583	0.649931	0.620921	0.567427	0.519369	0.476113	0.437109
6	0.630170	0.596267	0.564474	0.506631	0.455587	0.410442	0.370432
7	0.583490	0.547034	0.513158	0.452349	0.399637	0.353830	0.313925
8	0.540269	0.501866	0.466507	0.403883	0.350559	0.305025	0.266038
9	0.500249	0.460428	0.424098	0.360610	0.307508	0.262953	0.225456
10	0.463193	0.422411	0.385543	0.321973	0.269744	0.226684	0.191064
11	0.428883	0.387533	0.350494	0.287476	0.236617	0.195417	0.161919
12	0.397114	0.355535	0.318631	0.256675	0.207559	0.168463	0.137220
13	0.367698	0.326179	0.289664	0.229174	0.182069	0.145227	0.116288
14	0.340461	0.299246	0.263331	0.204620	0.159710	0.125195	0.098549
15	0.315242	0.274538	0.239392	0.182696	0.140096	0.107927	0.083516
16	0.291890	0.251870	0.217629	0.163122	0.122892	0.093041	0.070776
17	0.270269	0.231073	0.197845	0.145644	0.107800	0.080207	0.059980
18	0.250249	0.211994	0.179859	0.130040	0.094561	0.069144	0.050830
19	0.231712	0.194490	0.163508	0.116107	0.082948	0.059607	0.043077
20	0.214548	0.178431	0.148644	0.103667	0.072762	0.051385	0.036506
21	0.198656	0.163698	0.135131	0.092560	0.063826	0.044298	0.030937
22	0.183941	0.150182	0.122846	0.082643	0.055988	0.038188	0.026218
23	0.170315	0.137781	0.111678	0.073788	0.049112	0.032920	0.022218
24	0.157699	0.126405	0.101526	0.065882	0.043081	0.028380	0.018829
25	0.146018	0.115968	0.092296	0.058823	0.037790	0.024465	0.015957
26	0.135202	0.106393	0.083905	0.052521	0.033149	0.021091	0.013523
27	0.125187	0.097608	0.076278	0.046894	0.029078	0.018182	0.011460
28	0.115914	0.089548	0.069343	0.041869	0.025507	0.015674	0.009712
29	0.107328	0.082155	0.063039	0.037383	0.022375	0.013512	0.008230
30	0.099377	0.075371	0.057309	0.033378	0.019627	0.011648	0.006975

Table 3: FUTURE VALUE OF AN ORDINARY ANNUITY OF $1: $FV = \dfrac{(1 + i)^n - 1}{i}$

n	1.5%	4.0%	4.5%	5.0%	5.5%	6.0%	7.0%
1	1.000000	1.000000	1.000000	1.000000	1.000000	1.000000	1.000000
2	2.015000	2.040000	2.045000	2.050000	2.055000	2.060000	2.070000
3	3.045225	3.121600	3.137025	3.152500	3.168025	3.183600	3.214900
4	4.090903	4.246464	4.278191	4.310125	4.342266	4.374616	4.439943
5	5.152267	5.416323	5.470710	5.525631	5.581091	5.637093	5.750739
6	6.229551	6.632975	6.716892	6.801913	6.888051	6.975319	7.153291
7	7.322994	7.898294	8.019152	8.142008	8.266894	8.393838	8.654021
8	8.432839	9.214226	9.380014	9.549109	9.721573	9.897468	10.259803
9	9.559332	10.582795	10.802114	11.026564	11.256260	11.491316	11.977989
10	10.702722	12.006107	12.288209	12.577893	12.875354	13.180795	13.816448
11	11.863262	13.486351	13.841179	14.206787	14.583498	14.971643	15.783599
12	13.041211	15.025805	15.464032	15.917127	16.385591	16.869941	17.888451
13	14.236830	16.626838	17.159913	17.712983	18.286798	18.882138	20.140643
14	15.450382	18.291911	18.932109	19.598632	20.292572	21.015066	22.550488
15	16.682138	20.023588	20.784054	21.578564	22.408663	23.275970	25.129022
16	17.932370	21.824531	22.719337	23.657492	24.641140	25.672528	27.888054
17	19.201355	23.697512	24.741707	25.840366	26.996403	28.212880	30.840217
18	20.489376	25.645413	26.855084	28.132385	29.481205	30.905653	33.999033
19	21.796716	27.671229	29.063562	30.539004	32.102671	33.759992	37.378965
20	23.123667	29.778079	31.371423	33.065954	34.868318	36.785591	40.995492
21	24.470522	31.969202	33.783137	35.719252	37.786076	39.992727	44.865177
22	25.837580	34.247970	36.303378	38.505214	40.864310	43.392290	49.005739
23	27.225144	36.617889	38.937030	41.430475	44.111847	46.995828	53.436141
24	28.633521	39.082604	41.689196	44.501999	47.537998	50.815577	58.176671
25	30.063024	41.645908	44.565210	47.727099	51.152588	54.864512	63.249038
26	31.513969	44.311745	47.570645	51.113454	54.965981	59.156383	68.676470
27	32.986678	47.084214	50.711324	54.669126	58.989109	63.705766	74.483823
28	34.481479	49.967583	53.993333	58.402583	63.233510	68.528112	80.697691
29	35.998701	52.966286	57.423033	62.322712	67.711354	73.639798	87.346529
30	37.538681	56.084938	61.007070	66.438848	72.435478	79.058186	94.460786

n	8.0%	9.0%	10.0%	12.0%	14.0%	16.0%	18.0%
1	1.000000	1.000000	1.000000	1.000000	1.000000	1.000000	1.000000
2	2.080000	2.090000	2.100000	2.120000	2.140000	2.160000	2.180000
3	3.246400	3.278100	3.310000	3.374400	3.439600	3.505600	3.572400
4	4.506112	4.573129	4.641000	4.779328	4.921144	5.066496	5.215432
5	5.866601	5.984711	6.105100	6.352847	6.610104	6.877135	7.154210
6	7.335929	7.523335	7.715610	8.115189	8.535519	8.977477	9.441968
7	8.922803	9.200435	9.487171	10.089012	10.730491	11.413873	12.141522
8	10.636628	11.028474	11.435888	12.299693	13.232760	14.240093	15.326996
9	12.487558	13.021036	13.579477	14.775656	16.085347	17.518508	19.085855
10	14.486562	15.192930	15.937425	17.548735	19.337295	21.321469	23.521309
11	16.645487	17.560293	18.531167	20.654583	23.044516	25.732904	28.755144
12	18.977126	20.140720	21.384284	24.133133	27.270749	30.850169	34.931070
13	21.495297	22.953385	24.522712	28.029109	32.088654	36.786196	42.218663
14	24.214920	26.019189	27.974983	32.392602	37.581065	43.671987	50.818022
15	27.152114	29.360916	31.772482	37.279715	43.842414	51.659505	60.965266
16	30.324283	33.003399	35.949730	42.753280	50.980352	60.925026	72.939014
17	33.750226	36.973705	40.544703	48.883674	59.117601	71.673030	87.068036
18	37.450244	41.301338	45.599173	55.749715	68.394066	84.140715	103.740283
19	41.446263	46.018458	51.159090	63.439681	78.969235	98.603230	123.413534
20	45.761964	51.160120	57.274999	72.052442	91.024928	115.379747	146.627970
21	50.422921	56.764530	64.002499	81.698736	104.768418	134.840506	174.021005
22	55.456755	62.873338	71.402749	92.502584	120.435996	157.414987	206.344785
23	60.893296	69.531939	79.543024	104.602894	138.297035	183.601385	244.486847
24	66.764759	76.789813	88.497327	118.155241	158.658620	213.977607	289.494479
25	73.105940	84.700896	98.347059	133.333870	181.870827	249.214024	342.603486
26	79.954415	93.323977	109.181765	150.333934	208.332743	290.088267	405.272113
27	87.350768	102.723135	121.099942	169.374007	238.499327	337.502390	479.221093
28	95.338830	112.968217	134.209936	190.698887	272.889233	392.502773	566.480890
29	103.965936	124.135356	148.630930	214.582754	312.093725	456.303216	669.447450
30	113.283211	136.307539	164.494023	241.332684	356.786847	530.311731	790.947991

Table 4: PRESENT VALUE OF AN ORDINARY ANNUITY OF $1: $PV = \dfrac{1 - \dfrac{1}{(1+i)^n}}{i}$

n	1.5%	4.0%	4.5%	5.0%	5.5%	6.0%	7.0%
1	0.985222	0.961538	0.956938	0.952381	0.947867	0.943396	0.934579
2	1.955883	1.886095	1.872668	1.859410	1.846320	1.833393	1.808018
3	2.912200	2.775091	2.748964	2.723248	2.697933	2.673012	2.624316
4	3.854385	3.629895	3.587526	3.545951	3.505150	3.465106	3.387211
5	4.782645	4.451822	4.389977	4.329477	4.270284	4.212364	4.100197
6	5.697187	5.242137	5.157872	5.075692	4.995530	4.917324	4.766540
7	6.598214	6.002055	5.892701	5.786373	5.682967	5.582381	5.389289
8	7.485925	6.732745	6.595886	6.463213	6.334566	6.209794	5.971299
9	8.360517	7.435332	7.268790	7.107822	6.952195	6.801692	6.515232
10	9.222185	8.110896	7.912718	7.721735	7.537626	7.360087	7.023582
11	10.071118	8.760477	8.528917	8.306414	8.092536	7.886875	7.498674
12	10.907505	9.385074	9.118581	8.863252	8.618518	8.383844	7.942686
13	11.731532	9.985648	9.682852	9.393573	9.117079	8.852683	8.357651
14	12.543382	10.563123	10.222825	9.898641	9.589648	9.294984	8.745468
15	13.343233	11.118387	10.739546	10.379658	10.037581	9.712249	9.107914
16	14.131264	11.652296	11.234015	10.837770	10.462162	10.105895	9.446649
17	14.907649	12.165669	11.707191	11.274066	10.864609	10.477260	9.763223
18	15.672561	12.659297	12.159992	11.689587	11.246074	10.827603	10.059087
19	16.426168	13.133939	12.593294	12.085321	11.607654	11.158116	10.335595
20	17.168639	13.590326	13.007936	12.462210	11.950382	11.469921	10.594014
21	17.900137	14.029160	13.404724	12.821153	12.275244	11.764077	10.835527
22	18.620824	14.451115	13.784425	13.163003	12.583170	12.041582	11.061240
23	19.330861	14.856842	14.147775	13.488574	12.875042	12.303379	11.272187
24	20.030405	15.246963	14.495478	13.798642	13.151699	12.550358	11.469334
25	20.719611	15.622080	14.828209	14.093945	13.413933	12.783356	11.653583
26	21.398632	15.982769	15.146611	14.375185	13.662495	13.003166	11.825779
27	22.067617	16.329586	15.451303	14.643034	13.898100	13.210534	11.986709
28	22.726717	16.663063	15.742874	14.898127	14.121422	13.406164	12.137111
29	23.376076	16.983715	16.021889	15.141074	14.333101	13.590721	12.277674
30	24.015838	17.292033	16.288889	15.372451	14.533745	13.764831	12.409041

n	8.0%	9.0%	10.0%	12.0%	14.0%	16.0%	18.0%
1	0.925926	0.917431	0.909091	0.892857	0.877193	0.862069	0.847458
2	1.783265	1.759111	1.735537	1.690051	1.646661	1.605232	1.565642
3	2.577097	2.531295	2.486852	2.401831	2.321632	2.245890	2.174273
4	3.312127	3.239720	3.169865	3.037349	2.913712	2.798181	2.690062
5	3.992710	3.889651	3.790787	3.604776	3.433081	3.274294	3.127171
6	4.622880	4.485919	4.355261	4.111407	3.888668	3.684736	3.497603
7	5.206370	5.032953	4.868419	4.563757	4.288305	4.038565	3.811528
8	5.746639	5.534819	5.334926	4.967640	4.638864	4.343591	4.077566
9	6.246888	5.995247	5.759024	5.328250	4.946372	4.606544	4.303022
10	6.710081	6.417658	6.144567	5.650223	5.216116	4.833227	4.494086
11	7.138964	6.805191	6.495061	5.937699	5.452733	5.028644	4.656005
12	7.536078	7.160725	6.813692	6.194374	5.660292	5.197107	4.793225
13	7.903776	7.486904	7.103356	6.423548	5.842362	5.342334	4.909513
14	8.244237	7.786150	7.366687	6.628168	6.002072	5.467529	5.008062
15	8.559479	8.060688	7.606080	6.810864	6.142168	5.575456	5.091578
16	8.851369	8.312558	7.823709	6.973986	6.265060	5.668497	5.162354
17	9.121638	8.543631	8.021553	7.119630	6.372859	5.748704	5.222334
18	9.371887	8.755625	8.201412	7.249670	6.467420	5.817848	5.273164
19	9.603599	8.950115	8.364920	7.365777	6.550369	5.877455	5.316241
20	9.818147	9.128546	8.513564	7.469444	6.623131	5.928841	5.352746
21	10.016803	9.292244	8.648694	7.562003	6.686957	5.973139	5.383683
22	10.200744	9.442425	8.771540	7.644646	6.742944	6.011326	5.409901
23	10.371059	9.580207	8.883218	7.718434	6.792056	6.044247	5.432120
24	10.528758	9.706612	8.984744	7.784316	6.835137	6.072627	5.450949
25	10.674776	9.822580	9.077040	7.843139	6.872927	6.097092	5.466906
26	10.809978	9.928972	9.160945	7.895660	6.906077	6.118183	5.480429
27	10.935165	10.026580	9.237223	7.942554	6.935155	6.136364	5.491889
28	11.051078	10.116128	9.306567	7.984423	6.960662	6.152038	5.501601
29	11.158406	10.198283	9.369606	8.021806	6.983037	6.165550	5.509831
30	11.257783	10.273654	9.426914	8.055184	7.002664	6.177198	5.516806

■ INDEX

The letter *n* following a page number indicates a footnote.
A bold page number indicates that the term is defined on that page.